HarperCollins Concise World Atlas

Copyright © 2004 HarperCollins Publishers

No part of this publication may be used or reproduced in any manner
whatsoever without written permission except in the case of
brief quotations embodied in critical articles and reviews.
For information address HarperCollins Publishers Inc.,
10 East 53rd Street, New York, NY 10022.

HarperCollins books may be purchased for educational, business, or sales
promotional use. For information please write: Special Markets Department,
HarperCollins Publishers Inc., 10 East 53rd Street, New York, NY 10022.

First published as Collins World Atlas Concise Edition 2002 by
HarperCollins Publishers Ltd.

Maps © Collins Bartholomew Ltd 2004

Printed in Singapore by Imago

ISBN 0-06-052119-8

04 05 06 07 08 IM 10 9 8 7 6 5 4 3 2 1

HarperCollins CONCISE
WORLDATLAS

HarperResource
An Imprint of HarperCollinsPublishers

contents

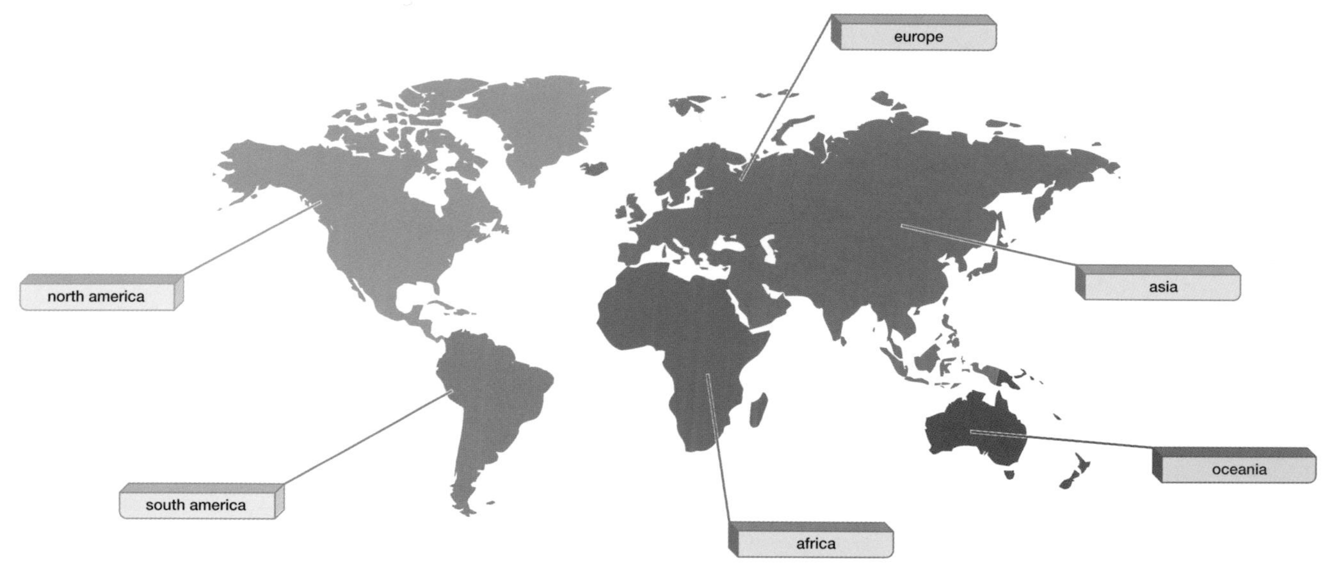

north america · europe · asia · south america · africa · oceania

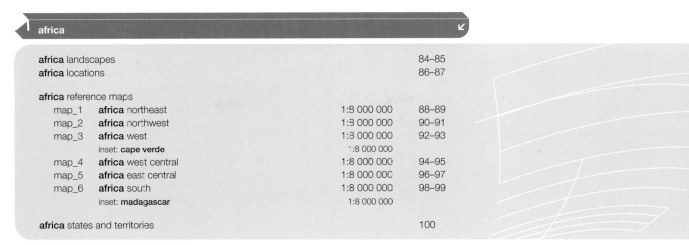

mapsymbols

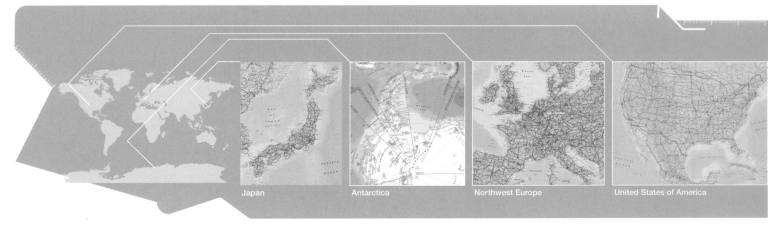

Japan Antarctica Northwest Europe United States of America

SETTLEMENTS

Population	National Capital	Administrative Capital	Other City or Town
over 5 million	**BEIJING** ✡	**Tianjin** ◉	**New York** ◉
1 million to 5 million	**KĀBUL** ✡	**Sydney** ◉	**Kaohsiung** ◉
500 000 to 1 million	BANGUI ✾	Trujillo ◎	Jeddah ◎
100 000 to 500 000	WELLINGTON ✿	Mansa ◎	Apucarana ⊙
50 000 to 100 000	PORT OF SPAIN ✿	Potenza ○	Arecibo ○
10 000 to 50 000	MALABO ✿	Chinhoyi ○	Ceres ○
1 000 to 10 000	VALLETTA ✿	Ati ○	Venta ○
under 1000		Chhukha ○	Gunnam ○

 Built-up area

BOUNDARIES

⸺⸺ International boundary

▪▫▪▫ Disputed international boundary or alignment unconfirmed

⸺⸺ Administrative boundary

••••• Ceasefire line

MISCELLANEOUS

---------- National park

·········· Reserve or Regional park

✽ Site of specific interest

▭▭▭ Wall

LAND AND SEA FEATURES

 Desert

⌄ Oasis

 Lava field

1234 △ Volcano height in metres

 Marsh

 Ice cap or Glacier

▱▱▱ Escarpment

Coral reef

)(1234 Pass height in metres

LAKES AND RIVERS

 Lake

Impermanent lake

 Salt lake or lagoon

 Impermanent salt lake

Dry salt lake or salt pan

 123 Lake height surface height above sea level, in metres

⸺⸺ River

------ Impermanent river or watercourse

‖ Waterfall

— Dam

∣ Barrage

RELIEF

Contour intervals and layer colours

Continents

metres
>6000 6000 5000 4000 3000 2000 1500 1000 500 200 100 0 <0
0 50 100 200 500 1000 2000 3000 4000 5000 6000 >6000

Oceans and Poles

metres
>6000 6000 5000 4000 3000 2000 1000 500 200 0 <0
0 200 2000 3000 4000 5000 6000 7000 >7000

1234 ▲ Summit height in metres   -123 Spot height height in metres   123 Ocean deep depth in metres

TRANSPORT

Motorway (tunnel; under construction)
Main road (tunnel; under construction)
Secondary road (tunnel; under construction)
Track
Main railway (tunnel; under construction)
Secondary railway (tunnel; under construction)
Other railway (tunnel; under construction)
Canal
✈ Main airport
✈ Regional airport

satellite imagery

The thematic pages in the atlas contain a wide variety of photographs and images. These are a mixture of 3-D perspective views, terrestrial and aerial photographs and satellite imagery. All are used to illustrate specific themes and to give an indication of the variety of imagery, and different means of visualizing the Earth, available today. The main types of imagery used in the atlas are described in the table below. The sensor for each satellite image is detailed on the acknowledgements page.

satellite/sensor name	launch dates	owner	aims and applications	web address	additional web address
Landsat 4, 5, 7	July 1972-April 1999	National Aeronautics and Space Administration (NASA), USA	The first satellite to be designed specifically for observing the Earth's surface. Originally set up to produce images of use for agriculture and geology. Today is of use for numerous environmental and scientific applications.	geo.arc.nasa.gov ls7pm3.gsfc.nasa.gov	asterweb.jpl.nasa.gov / earth.jsc.nasa.gov / earthnet.esrin.esa.it
SPOT 1, 2, 3, 4 (Satellite Pour l'Observation de la Terre)	February 1986-March 1998	Centre National d'Etudes Spatiales (CNES) and Spot Image, France	Particularly useful for monitoring land use, water resources research, coastal studies and cartography.	www.cnes.fr www.spotimage.fr	earthobservatory.nasa.gov / eol.jsc.nasa.gov / modis.gsfc.nasa.gov
Space Shuttle	Regular launches from 1981	NASA, USA	Each shuttle mission has separate aims. Astronauts take photographs with high specification hand held cameras. The Shuttle Radar Topography Mission (SRTM) in 2000 obtained the most complete near-global high-resolution database of the earth's topography.	science.ksc.nasa.gov/shuttle/countdown www.jpl.nasa.gov/srtm	seawifs.gsfc.nasa.gov / topex-www.jpl.nasa.gov / visibleearth.nasa.gov
IKONOS	September 1999	Space Imaging	First commercial high-resolution satellite. Useful for a variety of applications mainly Cartography, Defence, Urban Planning, Agriculture, Forestry and Insurance.	www.spaceimaging.com	rsi.ca / www.usgs.gov

SPOT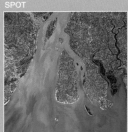
Landsat
Space Shuttle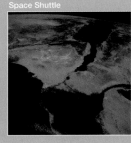
IKONOS

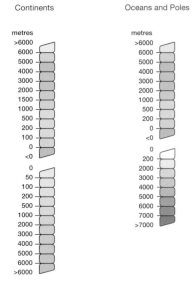

world

contents

Mount Everest, China/Nepal, highest mountain in the world at 8 848m.

Map labels

Queen Elizabeth Islands
Ellesmere Island
Parry Islands
Parry Channel
Banks Island
Victoria Island
Baffin Island
Baffin Bay
Greenland
Greenland Sea
Kap Morris Jesup
Jan Mayen
Iceland
Denmark Strait
Norwe
Faroe Is
Shetland
British Isles
Ireland
Great Britain

Beaufort Sea
Bering Strait
Arctic Circle
Brooks Range
Yukon
Mt McKinley
Aleutian Range 6194
Mt Logan 5959
Gulf of Alaska
Kodiak I.
Queen Charlotte Islands
Aleutian Islands
Vancouver Island

NORTH AMERICA
Rocky Mountains
Coast Ranges
Great Basin
Great Salt Lake
Columbia
Snake
Mackenzie Mts
Mackenzie
Peace
Great Bear Lake
Great Slave Lake
Reindeer Lake
Canadian Shield
L. Athabasca
Saskatchewan
L. Winnipeg
L. Nipigon
L. Superior
L. Michigan
L. Huron
L. Erie
L. Ontario
Great Plains
Missouri
Ohio
Appalachian Mountains
St Lawrence
Hudson Bay
Southampton
Foxe Basin
Pen. d'Ungava
C. Chidley
Labrador
Laurentian Plateau
Labrador Sea
Cape Farewell (Nunap Isua)
Reykjanes Ridge
Newfoundland
Nova Scotia
Sable I.
C. Cod
C. Hatteras
Bermuda
Sargasso Sea
Nares Deep

Guadalupe
Baja California
Sierra Madre Occidental
Rio Grande
Edwards Plateau
Coastal Plain
Gulf of Mexico
C. Falso
Bahía de Campeche
Yucatán
Sierra Madre del Sur
Sierra Madre Oriental
Cuba
Bahamas
West Indies
Greater Antilles
Hispaniola
Jamaica
Milwaukee Deep 8605
Caribbean Sea
Lesser Antilles
Barbados
Trinidad
Mid-Atlantic Ridge
Azores (Arquipélago dos Açores)
Madeira
Canary Islands (Islas Canarias)
Cabo de São Vicente
Iberian Peninsula
Balearic Islands
Cape Finisterre
Bay of Biscay
Haut Atlas
Atlas Mountains
Grand Erg Occidental
Erg Chech
Akchâr
Saha
Fouta Djallon
C. Vert
Cape Verde Islands (Ilhas do Cabo Verde)
Cape Verde Basin

ATLANTIC OCEAN
PACIFIC OCEAN

Hawaiian Islands
Hawaii
Tropic of Cancer
Northeast Pacific Basin
Islas Revillagigedo
Ile Clipperton
C. Mariato
Lago de Nicaragua
Cocos Ridge
I. de Malpelo
Galápagos Islands
Equator

Cord. Occidental
Cord. Oriental
Llanos
Orinoco
Guiana Highlands
Selvas
Japurá
Napo
Negro
Amazon/Amazonas
São Tomé
Annobón
C. Palmas
Gulf of Guinea
Bight of Benin

SOUTH AMERICA
Andes
Purus
Madeira
Tocantins
São Francisco
Brazilian Highlands
Mato Grosso
Fernando de Noronha
Ascension
St Helena
Brazil Basin
Ilha da Trindade
Ilhas Martin Vas
Mid-Atlantic Ridge
Angola Basin

Marquesas Islands
Polynesia
Society Islands
Tahiti
Tuamotu Islands
Niue
Cook Is
Rarotonga
Tropic of Capricorn
Tubuai Islands
Pitcairn Is
Easter Island
Isla Sala y Gómez
East Pacific Rise
San Félix
San Ambrosio
Juan Fernández Islands
Cerro Aconcagua 6959
Lake Titicaca
Altiplano
Peru-Chile Trench
Gran Chaco
Pilcomayo
Paraná
Paraguay
Uruguay
Pampas
Sierra do Mar
Lagoa dos Patos
Río de la Plata
Colorado
Bahía Blanca
Patagonia
Tristan da Cunha
Gough I.
Argentine Basin

Southwest Pacific Basin
Chile Rise
Isla de Chiloé
Pen. Valdés
C. Blanco
Tierra del Fuego
Falkland Islands
South Georgia
South Sandwich Islands
Cape Horn (Cabo de Hornos)
Drake Passage
Scotia Sea
South Orkney Is
South Shetland Is
Atlantic-I
Pacific-Antarctic Ridge
Southeast Pacific Basin
Peter I. Island
Antarctic Peninsula
Alexander Island
Palmer Land
Thurston I.
Ellsworth Land
Weddell Sea
Coats Land

Greenland, the world's largest island, located almost entirely within the Arctic Circle.

Elevation scale

metres
>6000
6000
5000
4000
3000
2000
1000
500
200
0
<0
0
200
1000
2000
3000
4000
5000
6000
7000
9000
>9000

Caspian Sea, Europe/Asia, the world's largest expanse of inland water.

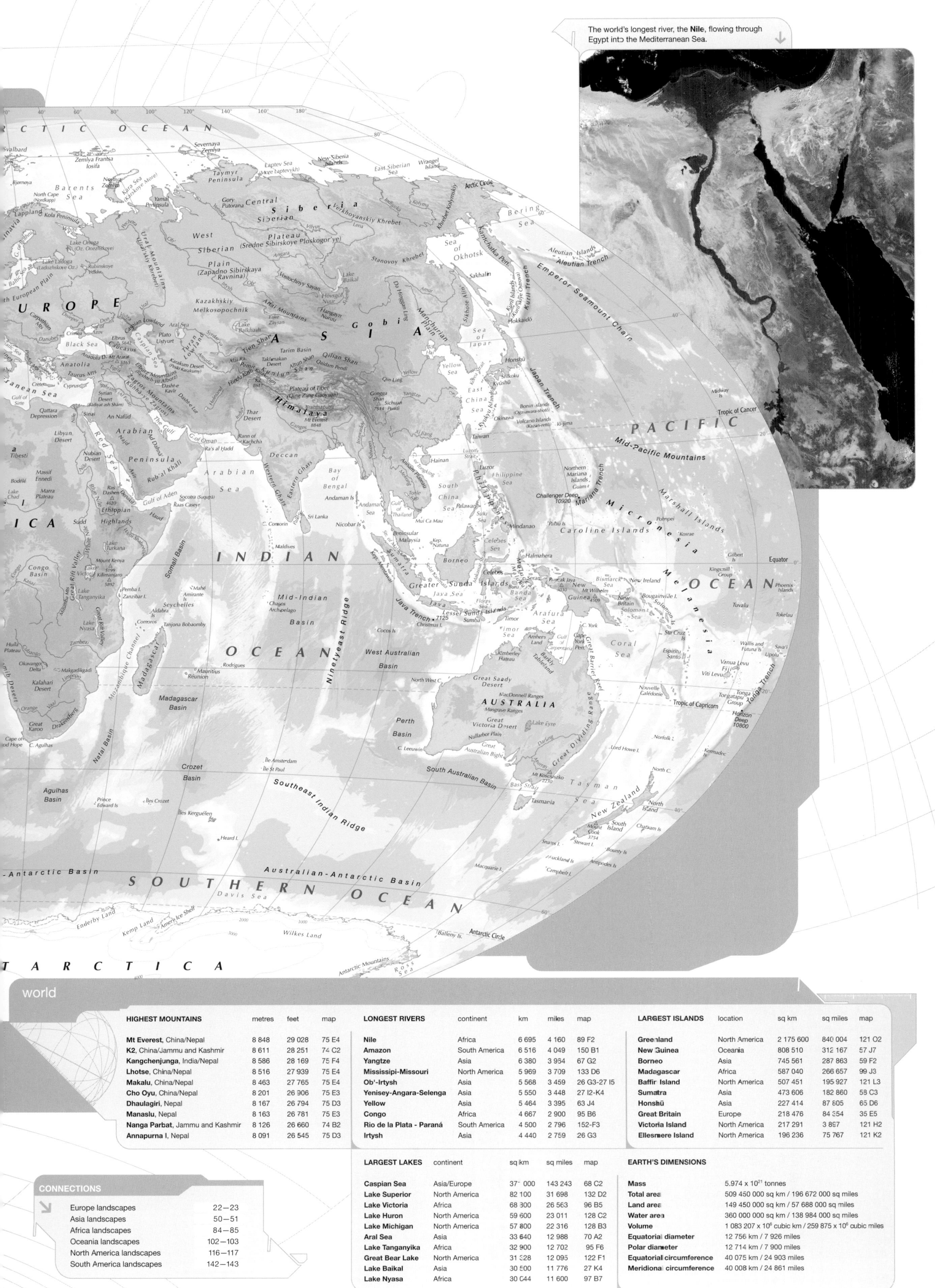

The world's longest river, the **Nile**, flowing through Egypt into the Mediterranean Sea.

world

HIGHEST MOUNTAINS	metres	feet	map
Mt Everest, China/Nepal	8 848	29 028	75 E4
K2, China/Jammu and Kashmir	8 611	28 251	74 C2
Kangchenjunga, India/Nepal	8 586	28 169	75 F4
Lhotse, China/Nepal	8 516	27 939	75 E4
Makalu, China/Nepal	8 463	27 765	75 E4
Cho Oyu, China/Nepal	8 201	26 906	75 E3
Dhaulagiri, Nepal	8 167	26 794	75 D3
Manaslu, Nepal	8 163	26 781	75 E3
Nanga Parbat, Jammu and Kashmir	8 126	26 660	74 B2
Annapurna I, Nepal	8 091	26 545	75 D3

LONGEST RIVERS	continent	km	miles	map
Nile	Africa	6 695	4 160	89 F2
Amazon	South America	6 516	4 049	150 B1
Yangtze	Asia	6 380	3 964	67 G2
Mississipi-Missouri	North America	5 969	3 709	133 D6
Ob'-Irtysh	Asia	5 568	3 459	26 G3-27 I5
Yenisey-Angara-Selenga	Asia	5 550	3 448	27 I2-K4
Yellow	Asia	5 464	3 395	63 J4
Congo	Africa	4 667	2 900	95 B6
Rio de la Plata - Paraná	South America	4 500	2 796	152-F3
Irtysh	Asia	4 440	2 759	26 G3

LARGEST ISLANDS	location	sq km	sq miles	map
Greenland	North America	2 175 600	840 004	121 O2
New Guinea	Oceania	808 510	312 167	57 J7
Borneo	Asia	745 561	287 863	59 F2
Madagascar	Africa	587 040	266 657	99 J3
Baffin Island	North America	507 451	195 927	121 L3
Sumatra	Asia	473 606	182 860	58 C3
Honshū	Asia	227 414	87 805	65 D6
Great Britain	Europe	218 476	84 354	35 E5
Victoria Island	North America	217 291	3 897	121 H2
Ellesmere Island	North America	196 236	75 767	121 K2

LARGEST LAKES	continent	sq km	sq miles	map
Caspian Sea	Asia/Europe	371 000	143 243	68 C2
Lake Superior	North America	82 100	31 698	132 D2
Lake Victoria	Africa	68 300	26 563	96 B5
Lake Huron	North America	59 600	23 011	128 C2
Lake Michigan	North America	57 800	22 316	128 B3
Aral Sea	Asia	33 640	12 988	70 A2
Lake Tanganyika	Africa	32 900	12 702	95 F6
Great Bear Lake	North America	31 328	12 095	122 F1
Lake Baikal	Asia	30 500	11 776	27 K4
Lake Nyasa	Africa	30 044	11 600	97 B7

EARTH'S DIMENSIONS	
Mass	5.974 x 10^{21} tonnes
Total area	509 450 000 sq km / 196 672 000 sq miles
Land area	149 450 000 sq km / 57 688 000 sq miles
Water area	360 000 000 sq km / 138 984 000 sq miles
Volume	1 083 207 x 10^6 cubic km / 259 875 x 10^6 cubic miles
Equatorial diameter	12 756 km / 7 926 miles
Polar diameter	12 714 km / 7 900 miles
Equatorial circumference	40 075 km / 24 903 miles
Meridional circumference	40 008 km / 24 861 miles

ARCTIC

Greenland
(Denmark)

Beaufort Sea

Jan Mayen
(Norway)

Victoria
Island

Baffin
Bay

Ellesmere Island

Point Hope

Bering Strait

Inuvik

Great Bear
Lake

Baffin Island

ICELAND

REYKJAVÍK

Faroe Islands
(Denmark)

Shetland
Islands

Yukon

U.S.A.

Whitehorse

Anchorage

Gulf
of Alaska

Iqaluit

NUUK

North
Sea

UNITED
KINGDOM

Edinburgh

DENMARK

NETH.

AMSTERDAM

Aleutian Islands

Great Slave
Lake

C A N A D A

Hudson
Bay

DUBLIN

REPUBLIC
OF IRELAND

LONDON

Belfast

THE HAGUE

BRUSSELS

Vancouver

Calgary

Edmonton

Lake
Winnipeg

Newfoundland

St John's

PARIS

FRANCE

Fraser

Seattle

Portland

Boise

Missouri

Lake
Superior

Winnipeg

Lake
Huron

Toronto

OTTAWA

Montreal

St Pierre and
Miquelon
(France)

PORTUGAL

MADRID

SPAIN

Barcelona

LISBON

Valencia

UNITED STATES

San Francisco

Milwaukee

Detroit

Lake
Michigan

Lake
Ontario

Cleveland

Lake Erie

Boston

New York

Azores
(Portugal)

RABAT

Madeira
(Portugal)

Casablanca

Chicago

OF AMERICA

Denver

St Louis

Indianapolis

Philadelphia

WASHINGTON D.C.

MOROCCO

ALGIER

ALGERIA

Los Angeles

Phoenix

El Paso

Dallas

Memphis

Atlanta

Bermuda
(U.K.)

LAÂYOUNE

Canary Islands
(Spain)

Tropic of Cancer

San Diego

San Antonio

Houston

New
Orleans

Jacksonville

Western
Sahara

Hawaiian Islands
(U.S.A.)

Monterrey

Gulf of
Mexico

Miami

NASSAU

THE BAHAMAS

MAURITANIA

MALI

Baja California

MEXICO

HAVANA

CUBA

NOUAKCHOTT

Guadalajara

MEXICO
CITY

Islas
Revillagigedo

DOMINICAN
REP.

HAITI

Puerto Rico
(U.S.A.)

BELIZE

ANTIGUA

SANTO
DOMINGO

CAPE VERDE

SENEGAL

DAKAR

PACIFIC

GUATEMALA

Kingston

JAMAICA

BELMOPAN

PRAIA

BANJUL

THE GAMBIA

BAMAKO

BURKINA

NIAMEY

GUATEMALA CITY

HONDURAS

TEGUCIGALPA

Caribbean

DOMINICA

Guadeloupe (France)

Martinique (France)

BISSAU

GUINEA-BISSAU

GUINEA

CONAKRY

OUAGADOUGOU

SAN SALVADOR

EL SALVADOR

NICARAGUA

Sea

ST VINCENT

ST LUCIA

BARBADOS

CÔTE

GHANA

Île Clipperton

MANAGUA

SAN JOSÉ

PANAMA CITY

GRENADA

Maracaibo

TRINIDAD
AND TOBAGO

Caracas

SIERRA LEONE

FREETOWN

MONROVIA

LIBERIA

YAMOUSSOUKRO

D'IVOIRE

Abidjan

ACCRA

Lago

EQUATO

GUI

OCEAN

COSTA RICA

PANAMA

Medellín

VENEZUELA

GEORGETOWN

GUYANA

PARAMARIBO

SUR.

CAYENNE

French Guiana

SÃO TOMÉ
AND PRÍNCIPE

Barranquilla

BOGOTÁ

COLOMBIA

Equator

Line Islands

INTERNATIONAL DATE LINE

Cali

QUITO

Galapagos
Islands
(Ecuador)

ECUADOR

Manaus

Belém

Amazon

Amazonas

Fortaleza

Fernando de Noronha
(Brazil)

Natal

Ascension
(U.K.)

KIRIBATI

Guayaquil

Trujillo

PERU

B R A Z I L

Teresina

Recife

ATLANTIC

LIMA

Salvador

St Helena
(U.K.)

Marquesas
Islands

LA PAZ

BOLIVIA

BRASÍLIA

American
Samoa

Tuamotu Islands

Arequipa

SUCRE

Santa Cruz

Goiânia

Belo Horizonte

Ilhas Martin Vaz
(Brazil)

Trindade
(Brazil)

Niue
(N.Z.)

Cook
Islands
(N.Z.)

Society
Islands

Tahiti

French

PARAGUAY

São Paulo

Rio de Janeiro

OCEAN

Rarotonga

Polynesia

Tubuai Islands

Tropic of Capricorn

ASUNCIÓN

Curitiba

Paraná

Porto Alegre

Pitcairn Is
(U.K.)

Easter Island
(Isla de Pascua)
(Chile)

Isla Sala y Gómez
(Chile)

URUGUAY

Córdoba

San Miguel
de Tucumán

MONTEVIDEO

Archipélago
Juan Fernández
(Chile)

Santiago

CHILE

ARGENTINA

BUENOS
AIRES

Mar del Plata

Tristan da Cunha
(U.K.)

Gough Island
(U.K.)

Falkland
Islands
(U.K.)

STANLEY

South Georgia and
South Sandwich Islands
(U.K.)

Bouv
(Norv

Punta
Arenas

Cape
Horn

South Orkney
Islands
(U.K.)

Weddell
Sea

ANTA

Washington D.C., leading international political centre
and capital city of the United States of America.

La Paz, the world's highest capital city, and joint
capital of Bolivia with Sucre.

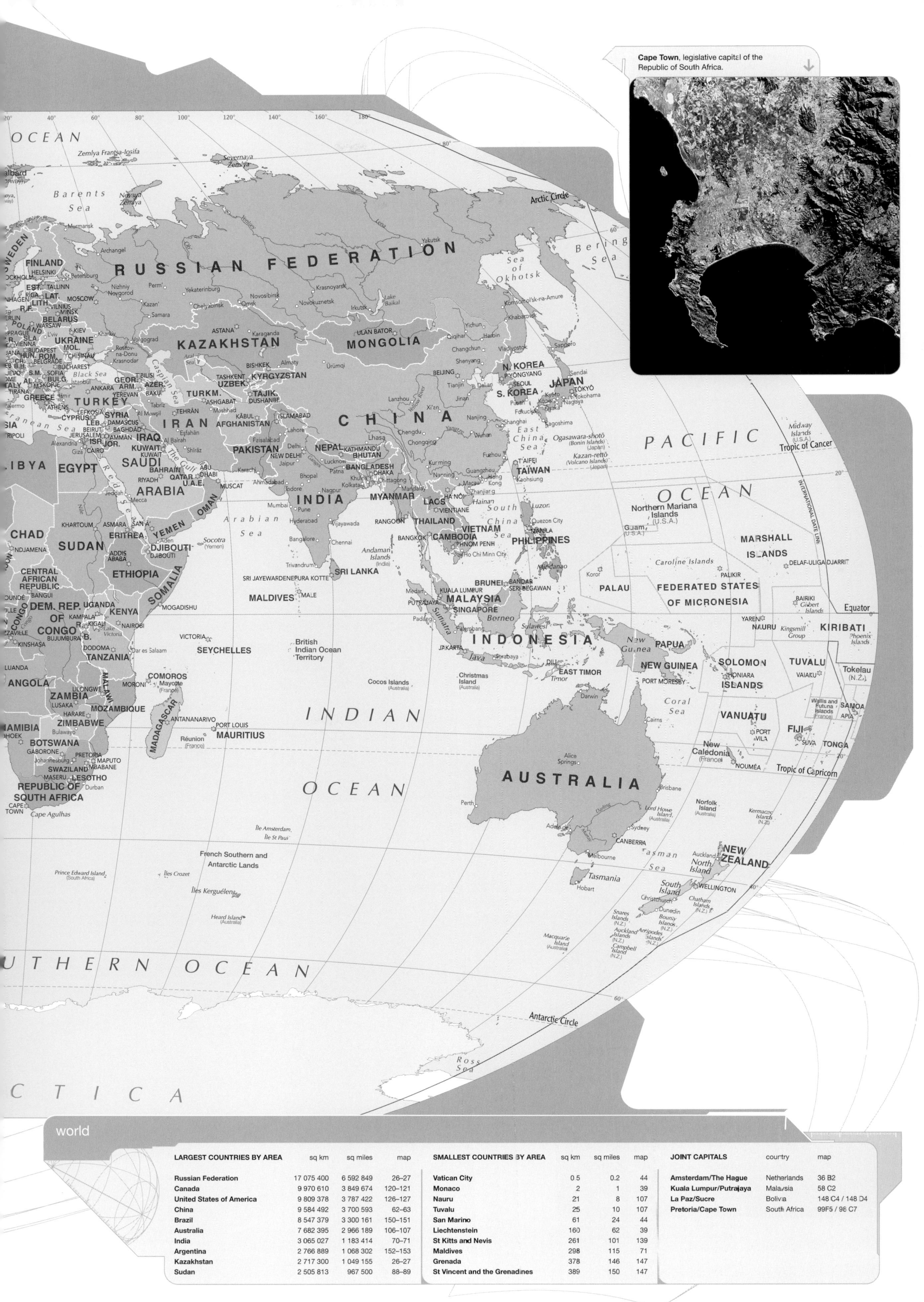

world

LARGEST COUNTRIES BY AREA	sq km	sq miles	map	SMALLEST COUNTRIES BY AREA	sq km	sq miles	map	JOINT CAPITALS	country	map
Russian Federation	17 075 400	6 592 849	26–27	Vatican City	0.5	0.2	44	Amsterdam/The Hague	Netherlands	36 B2
Canada	9 970 610	3 849 674	120–121	Monaco	2	1	39	Kuala Lumpur/Putrajaya	Malaysia	58 C2
United States of America	9 809 378	3 787 422	126–127	Nauru	21	8	107	La Paz/Sucre	Bolivia	148 C4 / 148 D4
China	9 584 492	3 700 593	62–63	Tuvalu	25	10	107	Pretoria/Cape Town	South Africa	99 F5 / 98 C7
Brazil	8 547 379	3 300 161	150–151	San Marino	61	24	44			
Australia	7 682 395	2 966 189	106–107	Liechtenstein	160	62	39			
India	3 065 027	1 183 414	70–71	St Kitts and Nevis	261	101	139			
Argentina	2 766 889	1 068 302	152–153	Maldives	298	115	71			
Kazakhstan	2 717 300	1 049 155	26–27	Grenada	378	146	147			
Sudan	2 505 813	967 500	88–89	St Vincent and the Grenadines	389	150	147			

Mount Etna

Kocaeli (İzmit)

Erzincan

Spitak

EURASIAN PLATE

Dushanbe

Ashgabat

Kangra

Manjil

Nepal/India

Khorāsan

Quetta

NW Iran

Gujarat

Hekla

Abruzzo

Messina

Ech Chélif

ARABIAN PLATE

AFRICAN PLATE

SOUTH AMERICAN PLATE

Nyiragongo

ANTARCTIC PLATE

San Andreas Fault, California, USA, one of the world's great seismic faults.

Unzen-dake

Liaoning

Hebei

Ningxia

Gansu

EURASIAN PLATE

Dushanbe

Qinghai

Kangra

Quetta

Sichuan

Nepal/India

Gujarat

Yunnan/Sichuan

PHILIPPINE PLATE

Mount Pinatubo

Mayon

INDO-AUSTRALIAN PLATE

Gunung Galunggung

Bali

ANTARCTIC PLATE

Klyuchevskaya Volcano, an active volcano on the Kamchatka Peninsula, eastern Russian Federation.

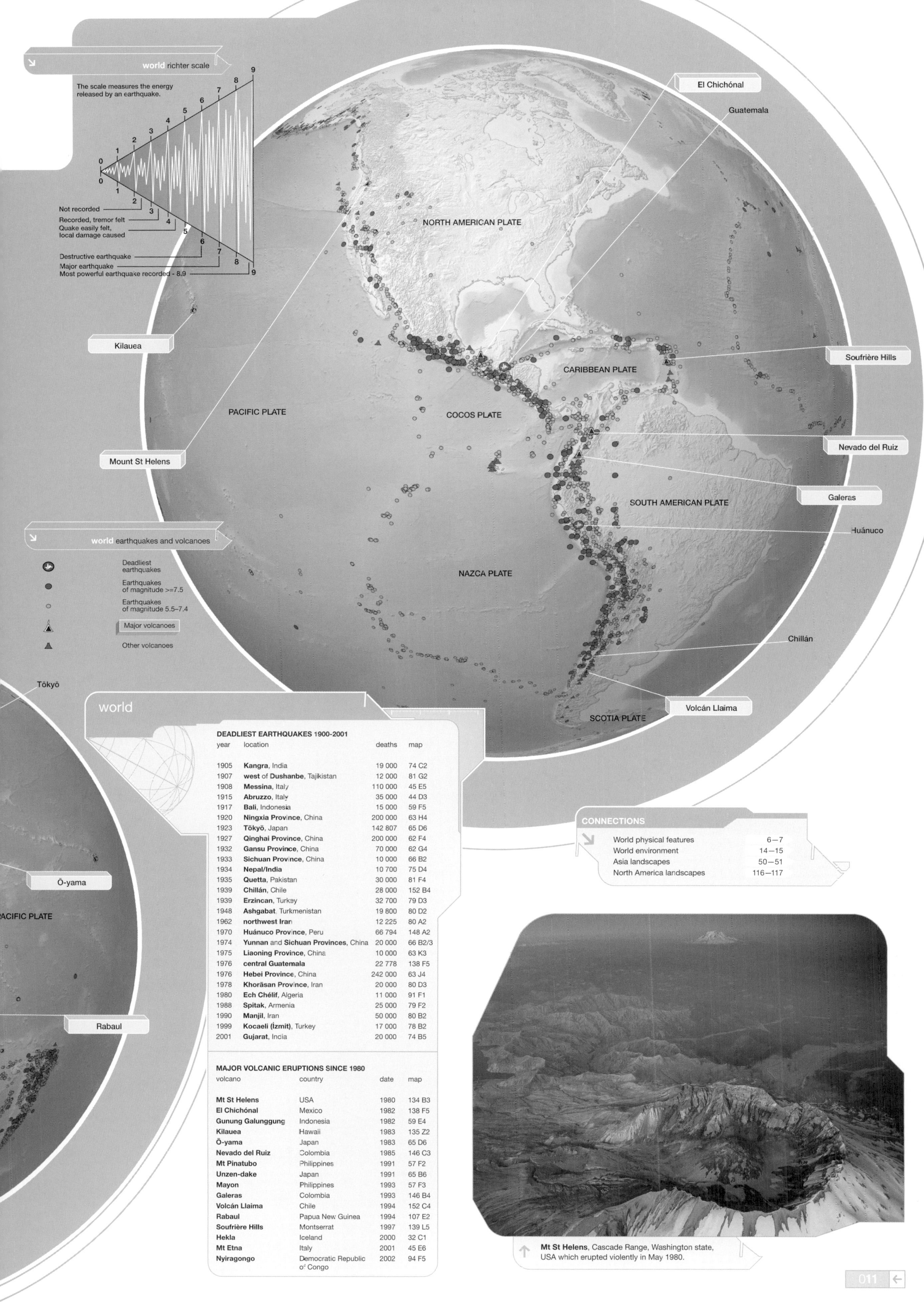

world richter scale

The scale measures the energy released by an earthquake.

9
8
7
6
5
4
3
2
1
0

Not recorded
Recorded, tremor felt
Quake easily felt, local damage caused
Destructive earthquake
Major earthquake
Most powerful earthquake recorded - 8.9

El Chichónal
Guatemala

NORTH AMERICAN PLATE

Kilauea

Mount St Helens

PACIFIC PLATE

COCOS PLATE

CARIBBEAN PLATE

Soufrière Hills

Nevado del Ruiz

Galeras

Huánuco

SOUTH AMERICAN PLATE

NAZCA PLATE

Chillán

Volcán Llaima

SCOTIA PLATE

world earthquakes and volcanoes

Deadliest earthquakes

Earthquakes of magnitude >=7.5

Earthquakes of magnitude 5.5–7.4

Major volcanoes

Other volcanoes

Tōkyō

Ō-yama

PACIFIC PLATE

Rabaul

DEADLIEST EARTHQUAKES 1900-2001

year	location	deaths	map
1905	**Kangra**, India	19 000	74 C2
1907	**west of Dushanbe**, Tajikistan	12 000	81 G2
1908	**Messina**, Italy	110 000	45 E5
1915	**Abruzzo**, Italy	35 000	44 D3
1917	**Bali**, Indonesia	15 000	59 F5
1920	**Ningxia Province**, China	200 000	63 H4
1923	**Tōkyō**, Japan	142 807	65 D6
1927	**Qinghai Province**, China	200 000	62 F4
1932	**Gansu Province**, China	70 000	62 G4
1933	**Sichuan Province**, China	10 000	66 B2
1934	**Nepal/India**	10 700	75 D4
1935	**Quetta**, Pakistan	30 000	81 F4
1939	**Chillán**, Chile	28 000	152 B4
1939	**Erzincan**, Turkey	32 700	79 D3
1948	**Ashgabat**, Turkmenistan	19 800	80 D2
1962	**northwest Iran**	12 225	80 A2
1970	**Huánuco Province**, Peru	66 794	148 A2
1974	**Yunnan and Sichuan Provinces**, China	20 000	66 B2/3
1975	**Liaoning Province**, China	10 000	63 K3
1976	**central Guatemala**	22 778	138 F5
1976	**Hebei Province**, China	242 000	63 J4
1978	**Khorāsan Province**, Iran	20 000	80 D3
1980	**Ech Chélif**, Algeria	11 000	91 F1
1988	**Spitak**, Armenia	25 000	79 F2
1990	**Manjil**, Iran	50 000	80 B2
1999	**Kocaeli (İzmit)**, Turkey	17 000	78 B2
2001	**Gujarat**, India	20 000	74 B5

MAJOR VOLCANIC ERUPTIONS SINCE 1980

volcano	country	date	map
Mt St Helens	USA	1980	134 B3
El Chichónal	Mexico	1982	138 F5
Gunung Galunggung	Indonesia	1982	59 E4
Kilauea	Hawaii	1983	135 Z2
Ō-yama	Japan	1983	65 D6
Nevado del Ruiz	Colombia	1985	146 C3
Mt Pinatubo	Philippines	1991	57 F2
Unzen-dake	Japan	1991	65 B6
Mayon	Philippines	1993	57 F3
Galeras	Colombia	1993	146 B4
Volcán Llaima	Chile	1994	152 C4
Rabaul	Papua New Guinea	1994	107 E2
Soufrière Hills	Montserrat	1997	139 L5
Hekla	Iceland	2000	32 C1
Mt Etna	Italy	2001	45 E6
Nyiragongo	Democratic Republic of Congo	2002	94 F5

CONNECTIONS

World physical features — 6–7
World environment — 14–15
Asia landscapes — 50–51
North America landscapes — 116–117

Mt St Helens, Cascade Range, Washington state, USA which erupted violently in May 1980.

CONNECTIONS

World physical features	6–7
World environment	14–15
Oceans features	156–157
Poles features	158–159

Computer generated image of **Hurricane Floyd** near the Florida coast, 1999, the deadliest US hurricane since 1972.

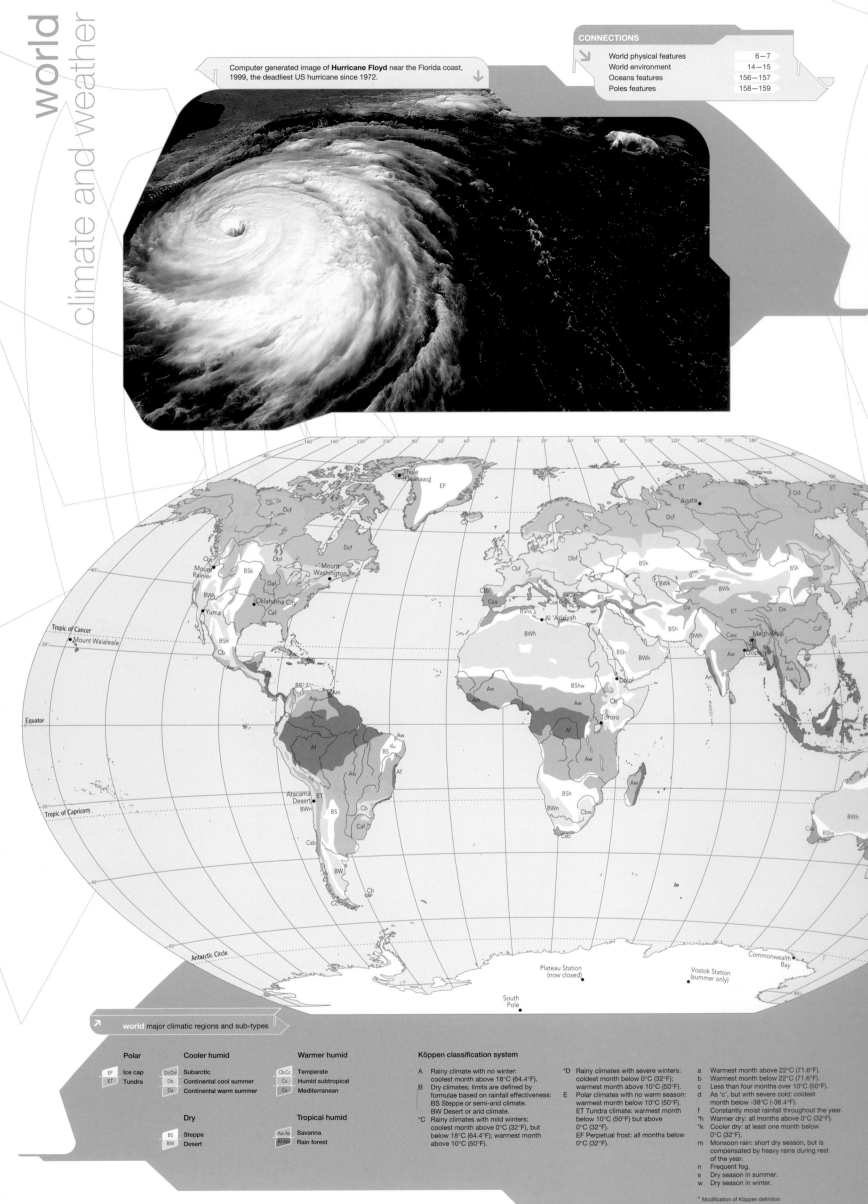

world major climatic regions and sub-types

Polar
- EF Ice cap
- ET Tundra

Cooler humid
- DcDd Subarctic
- Db Continental cool summer
- Da Continental warm summer

Dry
- BS Steppe
- BW Desert

Warmer humid
- CbCc Temperate
- Ca Humid subtropical
- Cs Mediterranean

Tropical humid
- AwAs Savanna
- AfAm Rain forest

Köppen classification system

A Rainy climate with no winter: coolest month above 18°C (64.4°F).
B Dry climates; limits are defined by formulae based on rainfall effectiveness:
BS Steppe or semi-arid climate.
BW Desert or arid climate.
*C Rainy climates with mild winters: coolest month above 0°C (32°F), but below 18°C (64.4°F); warmest month above 10°C (50°F).
*D Rainy climates with severe winters: coldest month below 0°C (32°F); warmest month above 10°C (50°F).
E Polar climates with no warm season: warmest month below 10°C (50°F).
ET Tundra climate: warmest month below 10°C (50°F) but above 0°C (32°F).
EF Perpetual frost: all months below 0°C (32°F).

a Warmest month above 22°C (71.6°F).
b Warmest month below 22°C (71.6°F).
c Less than four months over 10°C (50°F).
d As 'c', but with severe cold: coldest month below -38°C (-36.4°F).
f Constantly moist rainfall throughout the year.
*h Warmer dry: all months above 0°C (32°F).
*k Cooler dry: at least one month below 0°C (32°F).
m Monsoon rain: short dry season, but is compensated by heavy rains during rest of the year.
n Frequent fog.
s Dry season in summer.
w Dry season in winter.

* Modification of Köppen definition

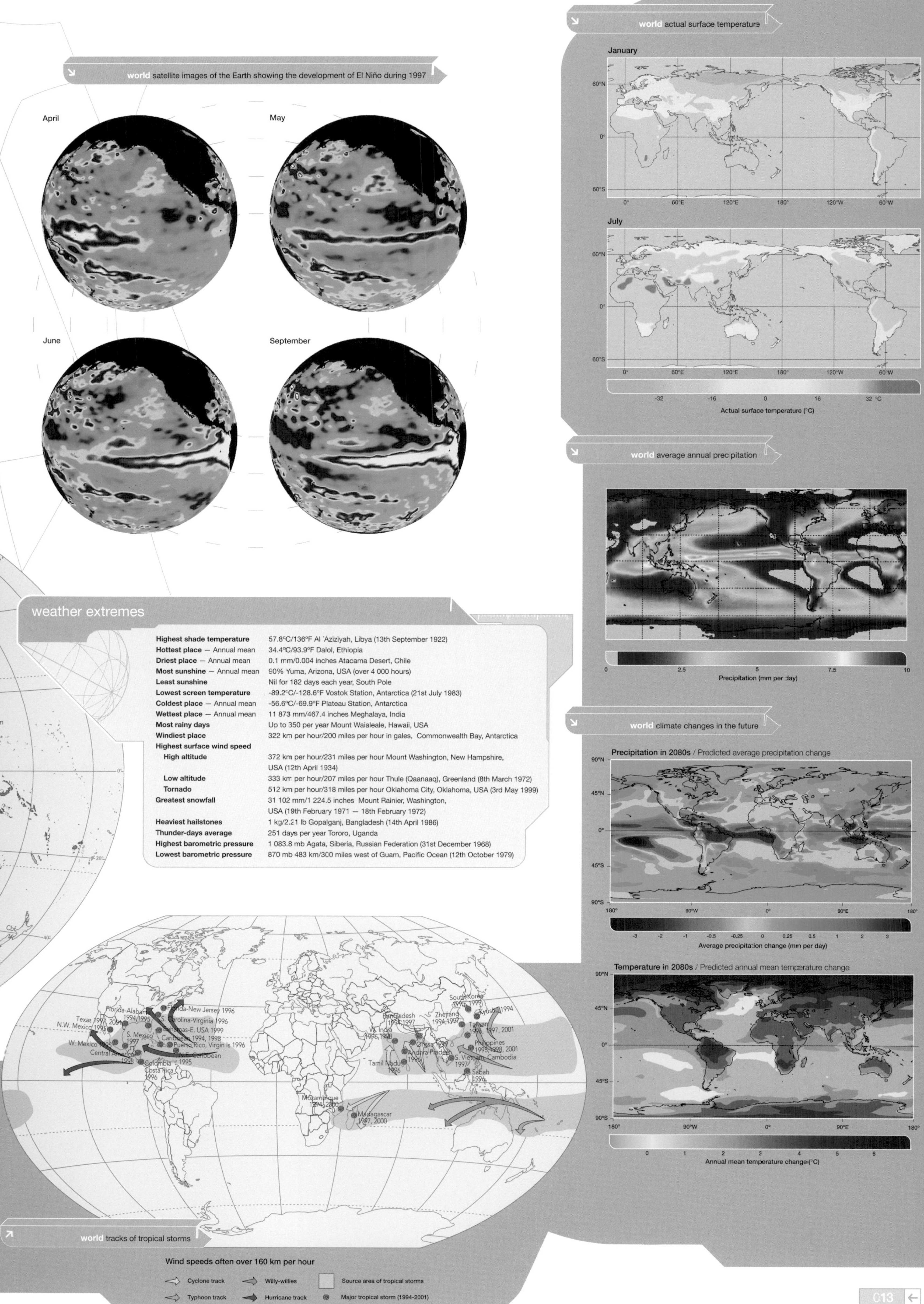

April

May

June

September

January

July

Actual surface temperature (°C)

Precipitation (mm per day)

Precipitation in 2080s / Predicted average precipitation change

Average precipitation change (mm per day)

Temperature in 2080s / Predicted annual mean temperature change

Annual mean temperature change (°C)

weather extremes

Highest shade temperature	57.8°C/136°F Al 'Azīzīyah, Libya (13th September 1922)
Hottest place — Annual mean	34.4°C/93.9°F Dalol, Ethiopia
Driest place — Annual mean	0.1 mm/0.004 inches Atacama Desert, Chile
Most sunshine — Annual mean	90% Yuma, Arizona, USA (over 4 000 hours)
Least sunshine	Nil for 182 days each year, South Pole
Lowest screen temperature	-89.2°C/-128.6°F Vostok Station, Antarctica (21st July 1983)
Coldest place — Annual mean	-56.6°C/-69.9°F Plateau Station, Antarctica
Wettest place — Annual mean	11 873 mm/467.4 inches Meghalaya, India
Most rainy days	Up to 350 per year Mount Waialeale, Hawaii, USA
Windiest place	322 km per hour/200 miles per hour in gales, Commonwealth Bay, Antarctica
Highest surface wind speed	
High altitude	372 km per hour/231 miles per hour Mount Washington, New Hampshire, USA (12th April 1934)
Low altitude	333 km per hour/207 miles per hour Thule (Qaanaaq), Greenland (8th March 1972)
Tornado	512 km per hour/318 miles per hour Oklahoma City, Oklahoma, USA (3rd May 1999)
Greatest snowfall	31 102 mm/1 224.5 inches Mount Rainier, Washington, USA (19th February 1971 — 18th February 1972)
Heaviest hailstones	1 kg/2.21 lb Gopalganj, Bangladesh (14th April 1986)
Thunder-days average	251 days per year Tororo, Uganda
Highest barometric pressure	1 083.8 mb Agata, Siberia, Russian Federation (31st December 1968)
Lowest barometric pressure	870 mb 483 km/300 miles west of Guam, Pacific Ocean (12th October 1979)

Wind speeds often over 160 km per hour

→ Cyclone track   ⇒ Willy-willies   □ Source area of tropical storms

→ Typhoon track   ➜ Hurricane track   ● Major tropical storm (1994-2001)

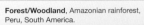
Forest/Woodland, Amazonian rainforest,
Peru, South America.

↑ **Urban**, La Paz, Bolivia.

↑ **Barren/Shrubland**, Death Valley,
California, USA.

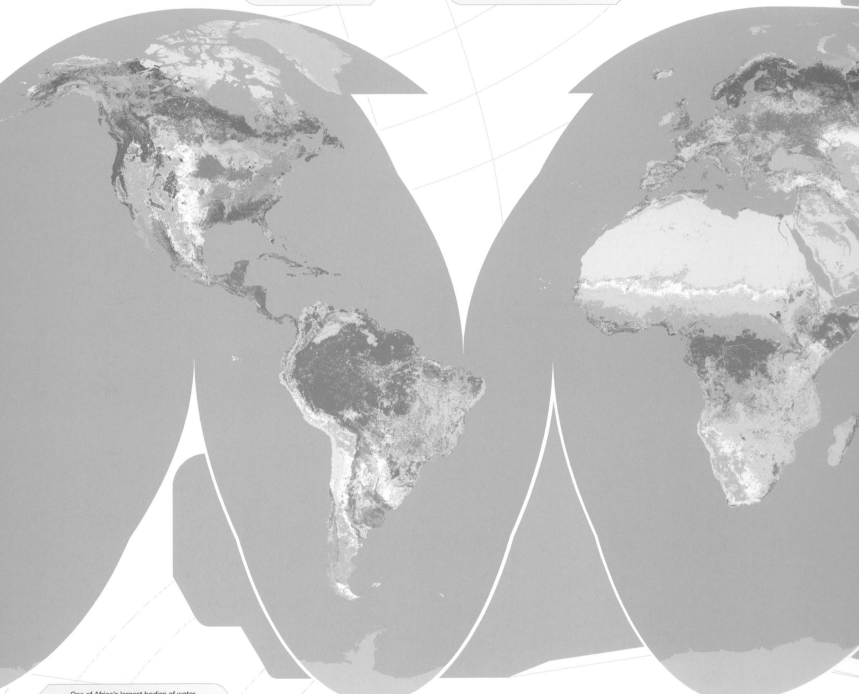

One of Africa's largest bodies of water,
Lake Chad, West Africa in 1973.

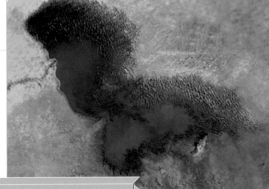

↗ **world** africa environmental changes

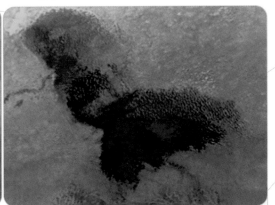
↑ **Lake Chad**, 1997, reduced in size as a result of massive
irrigation projects and an increasingly dry climate.

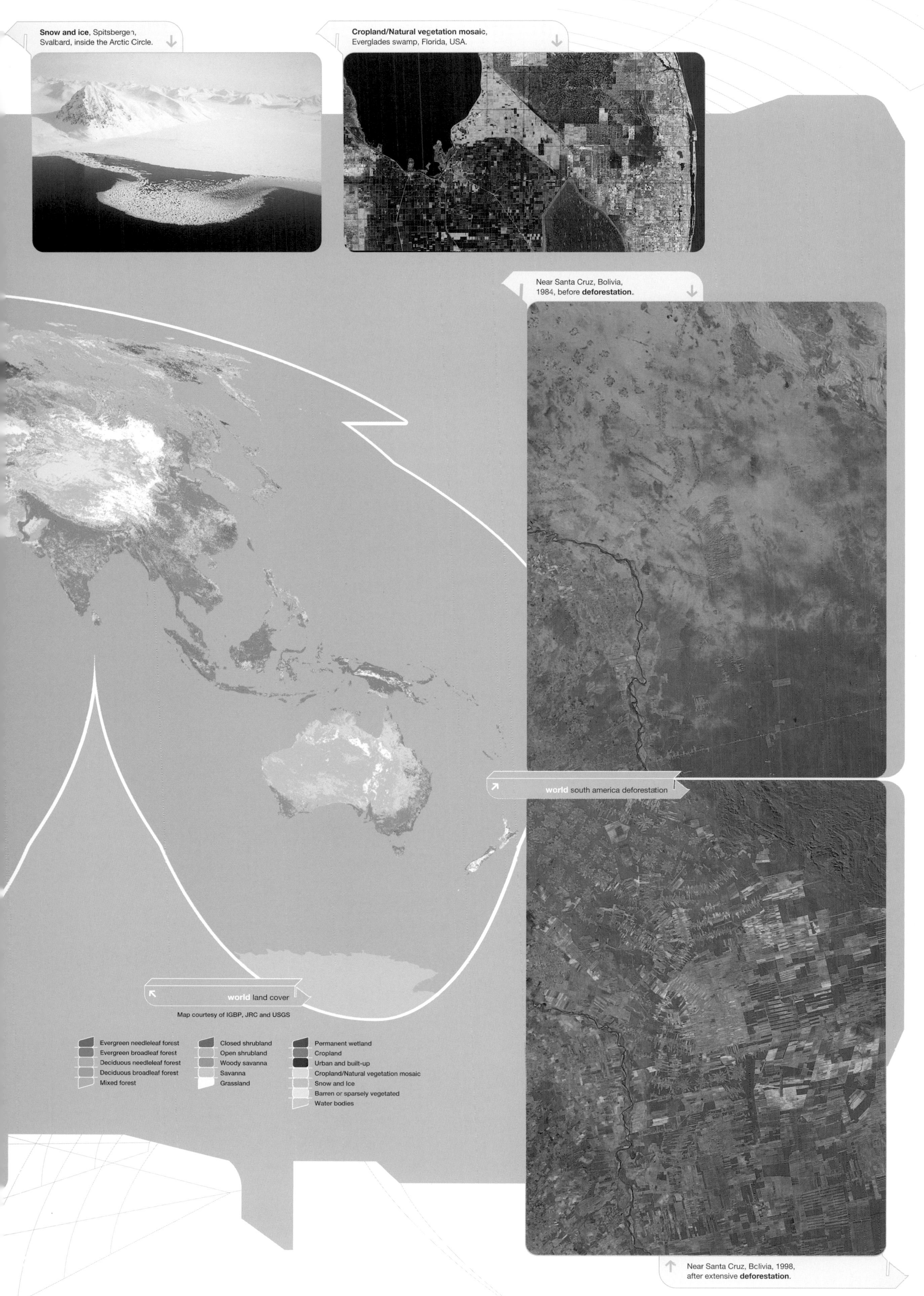

Snow and ice, Spitsbergen, Svalbard, inside the Arctic Circle. ↓

Cropland/Natural vegetation mosaic, Everglades swamp, Florida, USA.

Near Santa Cruz, Bolivia, 1984, before **deforestation**. ↓

↗ **world** south america deforestation

↖ **world** land cover

Map courtesy of IGBP, JRC and USGS

Evergreen needleleaf forest	Closed shrubland	Permanent wetland
Evergreen broadleaf forest	Open shrubland	Cropland
Deciduous needleleaf forest	Woody savanna	Urban and built-up
Deciduous broadleaf forest	Savanna	Cropland/Natural vegetation mosaic
Mixed forest	Grassland	Snow and Ice
		Barren or sparsely vegetated
		Water bodies

↑ Near Santa Cruz, Bolivia, 1998, after extensive **deforestation**.

world

TOP TEN COUNTRIES

country	rank	population
China	1	1 270 082 000
India	2	1 025 096 000
United States of America	3	285 926 000
Indonesia	4	214 840 000
Brazil	5	172 559 000
Pakistan	6	144 971 000
Russian Federation	7	144 664 000
Bangladesh	8	140 369 000
Japan	9	127 335 000
Nigeria	10	116 924 000

KEY POPULATION STATISTICS FOR MAJOR REGIONS

	population (millions) 2001	growth (per cent) 2000-2005	*infant mortality rate 1995-2000	**total fertility rate 1995-2000	life expectancy (years) 1995-2000
World	6 134	1.23	57	2.82	65.0
More developed regions	1 194	0.16	9	1.57	74.9
Less developed regions	4 940	1.48	63	3.10	63.0
Africa	813	2.33	87	5.27	51.4
Asia	3 721	1.26	57	2.70	65.8
Europe	726	-0.18	12	1.41	73.2
Latin America and the Caribbean	527	1.42	36	2.69	69.3
North America	317	0.88	7	2.00	76.7
Oceania	31	1.24	24	2.41	73.5

*Deaths of infants less than one year old per 1000 live births
**Estimate of number of children a woman will bear through her child-bearing years

CONNECTIONS

Village settlement in sparsely populated area of Côte d'Ivoire, West Africa.

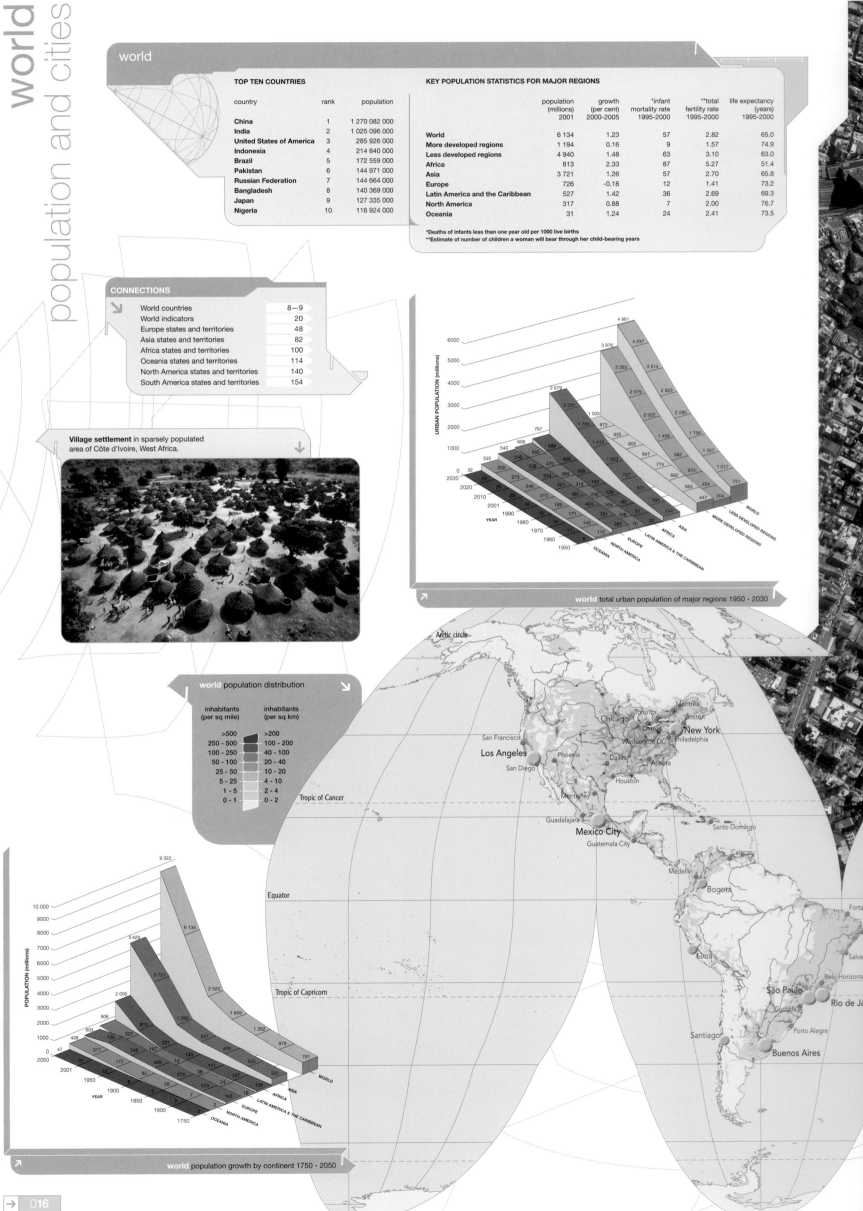

URBAN POPULATION (millions)

world total urban population of major regions 1950 - 2030

world population distribution

inhabitants (per sq mile)	inhabitants (per sq km)
>500	>200
250 - 500	100 - 200
100 - 250	40 - 100
50 - 100	20 - 40
25 - 50	10 - 20
5 - 25	4 - 10
1 - 5	2 - 4
0 - 1	0 - 2

POPULATION (millions)

world population growth by continent 1750 - 2050

Arctic circle

San Francisco
Los Angeles
San Diego
Phoenix
Dallas
Houston
Monterrey
Chicago
Detroit
Atlanta
Toronto
Montréal
Boston
New York
Washington DC
Philadelphia

Tropic of Cancer

Guadalajara
Mexico City
Guatemala City
Santo Domingo

Equator

Caracas
Medellín
Bogotá
Lima

Tropic of Capricorn

São Paulo
Curitiba
Rio de Ja
Porto Alegre
Santiago
Buenos Aires
Belo Horizonte
Fortale
Salva

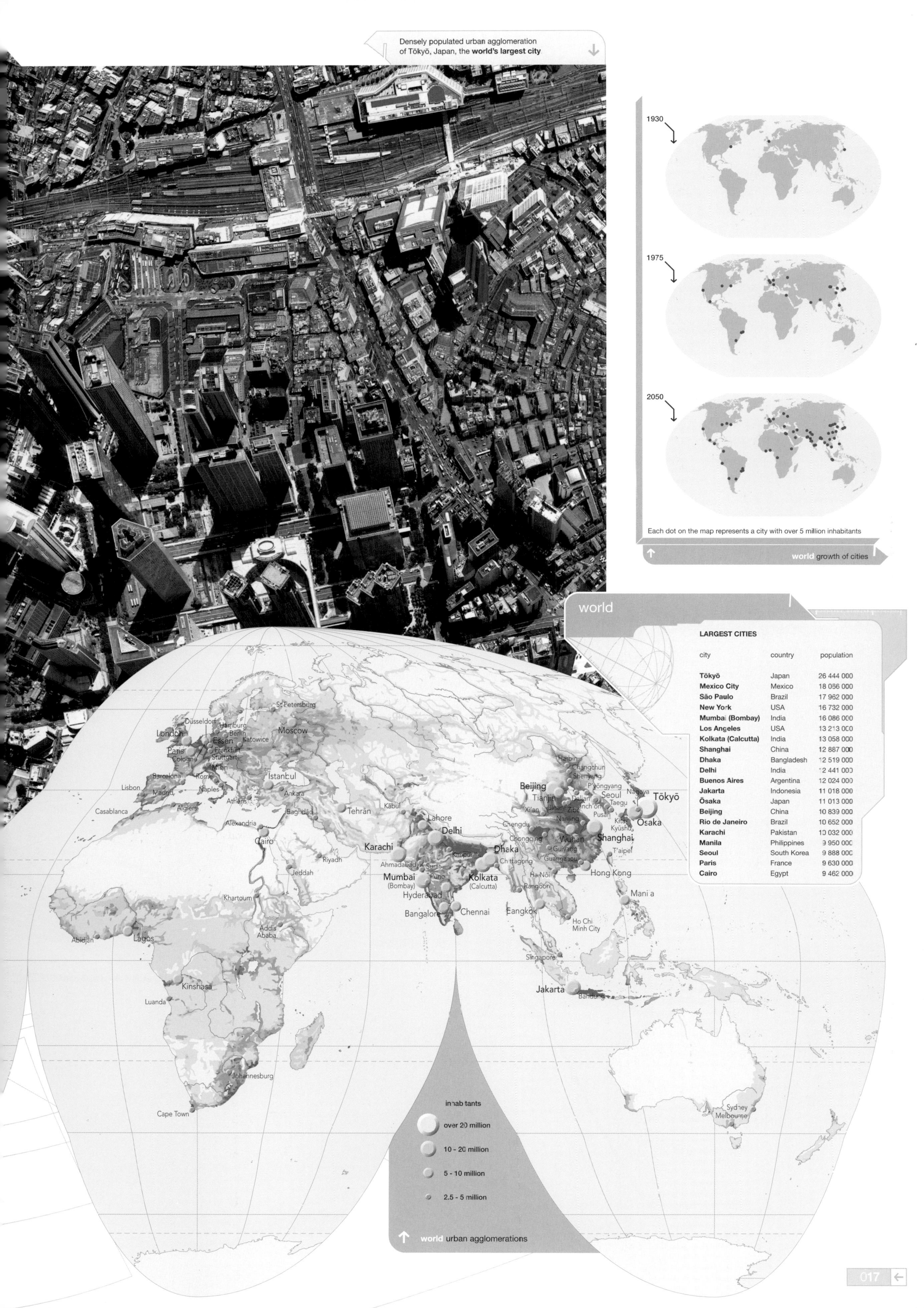

Densely populated urban agglomeration of Tōkyō, Japan, the **world's largest city**

1930

1975

2050

Each dot on the map represents a city with over 5 million inhabitants

world growth of cities

world

LARGEST CITIES

city	country	population
Tōkyō	Japan	26 444 000
Mexico City	Mexico	18 056 000
São Paulo	Brazil	17 962 000
New York	USA	16 732 000
Mumbai (Bombay)	India	16 086 000
Los Angeles	USA	13 213 000
Kolkata (Calcutta)	India	13 058 000
Shanghai	China	12 887 000
Dhaka	Bangladesh	12 519 000
Delhi	India	12 441 000
Buenos Aires	Argentina	12 024 000
Jakarta	Indonesia	11 018 000
Ōsaka	Japan	11 013 000
Beijing	China	10 839 000
Rio de Janeiro	Brazil	10 652 000
Karachi	Pakistan	10 032 000
Manila	Philippines	9 950 000
Seoul	South Korea	9 888 000
Paris	France	9 630 000
Cairo	Egypt	9 462 000

inhabitants

over 20 million

10 – 20 million

5 – 10 million

2.5 – 5 million

world urban agglomerations

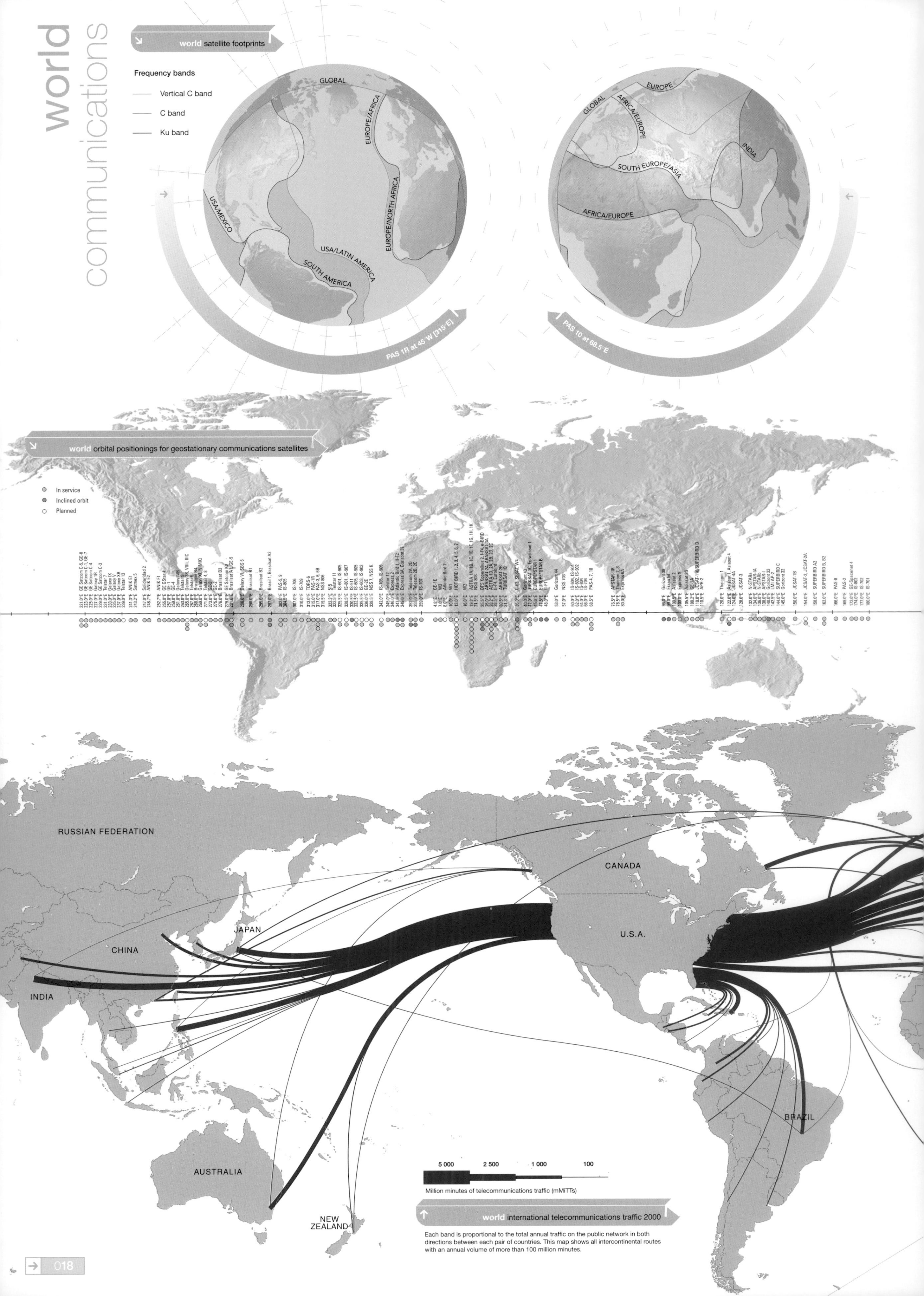

world communications

Frequency bands
— Vertical C band
— C band
— Ku band

GLOBAL
EUROPE/AFRICA
USA/MEXICO
USA/LATIN AMERICA
SOUTH AMERICA
EUROPE/NORTH AFRICA

PAS 1R at 45 W [315 E]

EUROPE
GLOBAL
AFRICA/EUROPE
INDIA
SOUTH EUROPE/ASIA
AFRICA/EUROPE

PAS 10 at 68.5 E

world orbital positionings for geostationary communications satellites

○ In service
● Inclined orbit
○ Planned

RUSSIAN FEDERATION
CANADA
JAPAN
CHINA
U.S.A.
INDIA
BRAZIL
AUSTRALIA
NEW ZEALAND

5 000   2 500   1 000   100

Million minutes of telecommunications traffic (mMiTTs)

world international telecommunications traffic 2000

Each band is proportional to the total annual traffic on the public network in both directions between each pair of countries. This map shows all intercontinental routes with an annual volume of more than 100 million minutes.

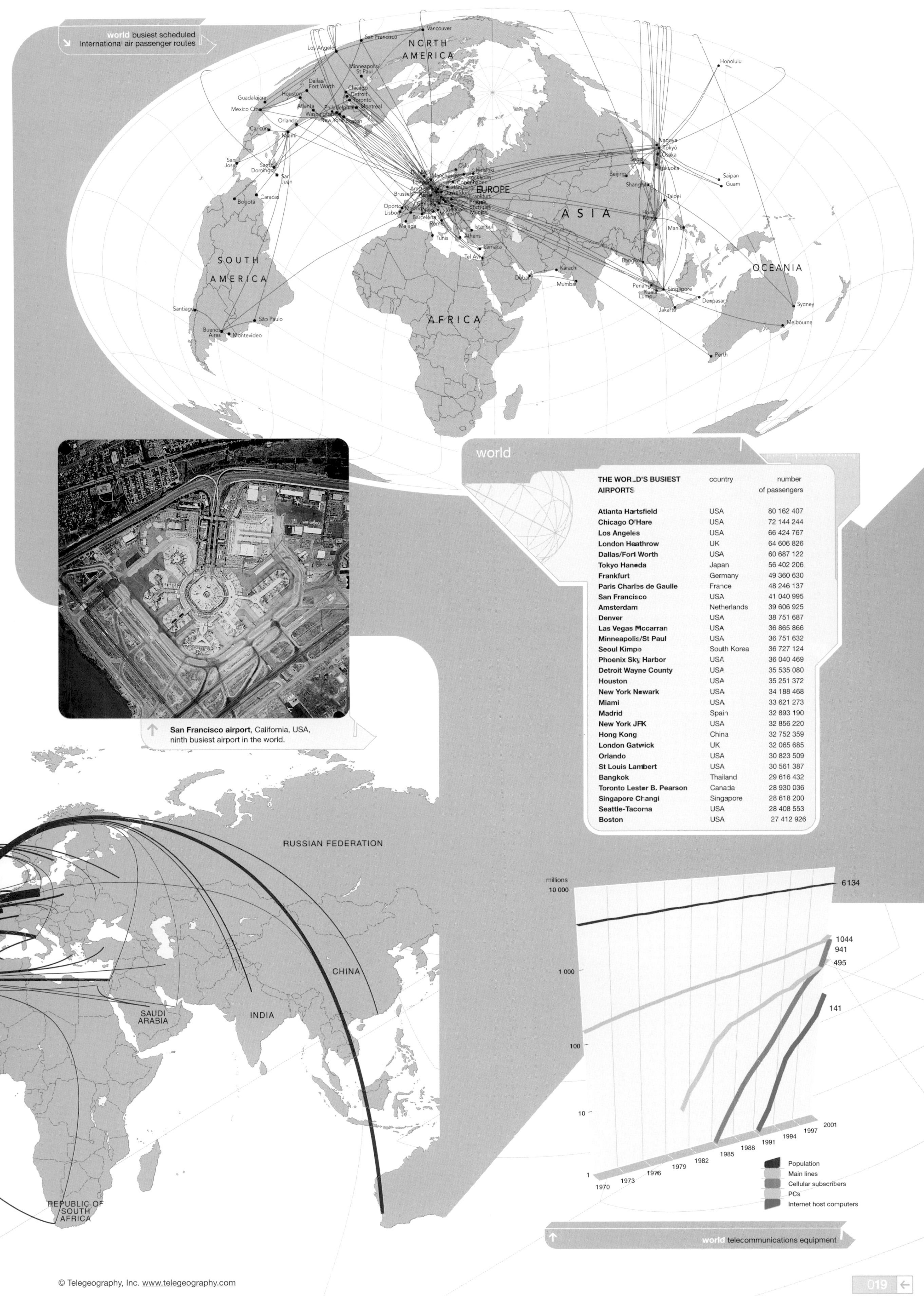

NORTH AMERICA

EUROPE

ASIA

OCEANIA

AFRICA

SOUTH AMERICA

Vancouver
San Francisco
Los Angeles
Minneapolis/St Paul
Dallas/Fort Worth
Guadalajara
Houston
Mexico City
Atlanta
Orlando
Cancún
Miami
San José
Santo Domingo
San Juan
Bogotá
Caracas

Honolulu
Nagoya
Tokyo
Osaka
Seoul
Fukuoka
Beijing
Shanghai
Saipan
Guam
Taipei
Hong Kong
Manila
Bangkok
Penang
Kuala Lumpur
Singapore
Jakarta
Denpasar
Sydney
Melbourne
Perth

Chicago
Detroit
Toronto
Montréal
Philadelphia
Washington
New York
Boston

Oslo
Helsinki
Stockholm
Copenhagen
Hamburg
Manchester
Amsterdam
Brussels
Frankfurt
Düsseldorf
Oporto
Lisbon
Barcelona
Madrid
Milan
Zürich
Rome
Málaga
Tunis
Athens
Istanbul
Tel Aviv
Larnaca
Dubai
Karachi
Mumbai

Santiago
São Paulo
Buenos Aires
Montevideo

world

San Francisco airport, California, USA, ninth busiest airport in the world.

THE WORLD'S BUSIEST AIRPORTS	country	number of passengers
Atlanta Hartsfield	USA	80 162 407
Chicago O'Hare	USA	72 144 244
Los Angeles	USA	66 424 767
London Heathrow	UK	64 606 826
Dallas/Fort Worth	USA	60 687 122
Tokyo Haneda	Japan	56 402 206
Frankfurt	Germany	49 360 630
Paris Charles de Gaulle	France	48 246 137
San Francisco	USA	41 040 995
Amsterdam	Netherlands	39 606 925
Denver	USA	38 751 687
Las Vegas Mccarran	USA	36 865 866
Minneapolis/St Paul	USA	36 751 632
Seoul Kimpo	South Korea	36 727 124
Phoenix Sky Harbor	USA	36 040 469
Detroit Wayne County	USA	35 535 080
Houston	USA	35 251 372
New York Newark	USA	34 188 468
Miami	USA	33 621 273
Madrid	Spain	32 893 190
New York JFK	USA	32 856 220
Hong Kong	China	32 752 359
London Gatwick	UK	32 065 685
Orlando	USA	30 823 509
St Louis Lambert	USA	30 561 387
Bangkok	Thailand	29 616 432
Toronto Lester B. Pearson	Canada	28 930 036
Singapore Changi	Singapore	28 618 200
Seattle-Tacoma	USA	28 408 553
Boston	USA	27 412 926

RUSSIAN FEDERATION

CHINA

SAUDI ARABIA

INDIA

REPUBLIC OF SOUTH AFRICA

millions
10 000

6134

1044
941
495

141

1 000

100

10

1

Population
Main lines
Cellular subscribers
PCs
Internet host computers

1970 1973 1976 1979 1982 1985 1988 1991 1994 1997 2001

world telecommunications equipment

Regional distribution of population (%)

14.9   30.6   7.8   8.5   4.9   22.4   10

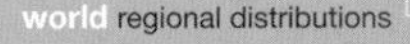

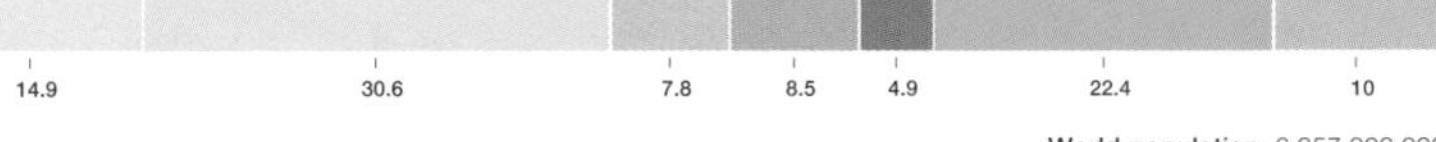

World population: 6 057 000 000

Regional distribution of land area (%)

24.2   12.2   18.1   15.3   8.2   3.9   18.1

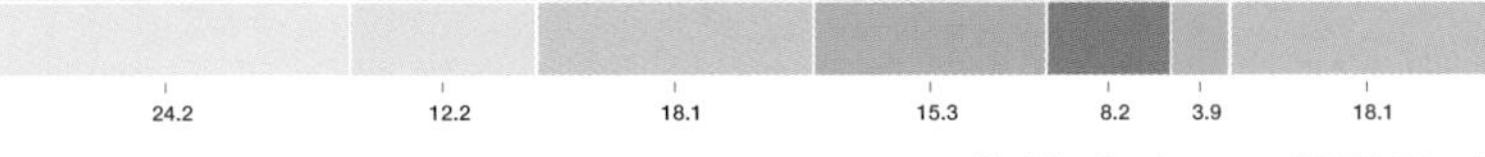

World land surface area: 133 806 000 sq km

Regional distribution of Gross National Income (%)

79.8   6.3   3.0   6.0   2.0   1.0
1.9

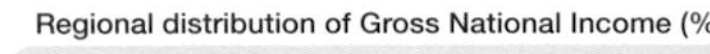

World Gross National Income: 31 315 000 million $

world regional distributions

- High-income economies
- East Asia and Pacific
- Europe and Central Asia
- Latin America and the Caribbean
- Middle East and North Africa
- South Asia
- Sub-Saharan Africa
- No data

world regions / as defined by the World Bank

HIGH-INCOME ECONOMIES

EUROPE AND CENTRAL ASIA

MIDDLE EAST AND NORTH AFRICA

SOUTH ASIA

EAST ASIA AND PACIFIC

SUB-SAHARAN AFRICA

LATIN AMERICA AND THE CARIBBEAN

HIGH-INCOME ECONOMIES

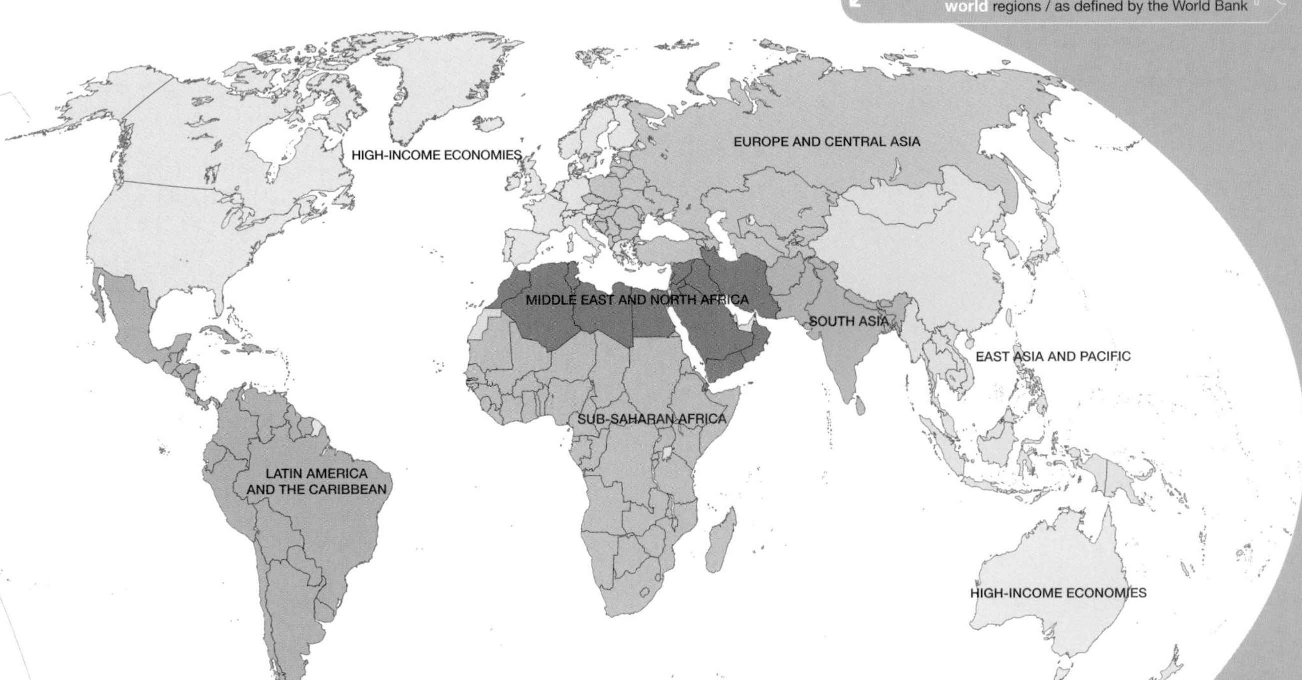

world indicators / by region

	World	High-income economies	East Asia and Pacific	Europe and Central Asia	Latin America and the Caribbean	Middle East and North Africa	South Asia	Sub-Saharan Africa
Population 2000 (millions)	6 057	903	1 855	474	516	295	1 355	659
Annual population growth (%)	1.31	0.68	0.95	0.07	1.53	1.90	1.92	2.43
Surface area (thousand sq km)	133 806	32 315	16 385	24 217	20 459	11 023	5 140	24 267
Gross National Income (million $)	31 315 000	24 994 000	1 962 000	953 000	1 895 000	618 000	595 000	310 000
Gross National Income per capita ($)	5 170	27 680	1 060	2 010	3 670	2 090	440	470
Life expectancy (years)	66	78	69	69	70	68	62	47
Infant mortality rate (per 1 000 live births)	54	6	35	20	29	43	73	91
Access to safe water (% of total population)	80	-	75	90	85	89	87	55
Adult illiteracy rate (% of population over 15 years)	-	-	14	3	12	35	45	39
Aid per capita (US $)	-	-	4.56	22.91	9.67	15.61	3.13	20.42

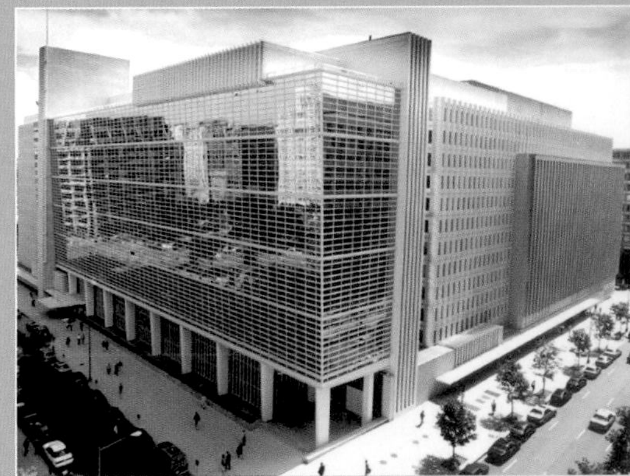

World Bank Headquarters, Washington DC

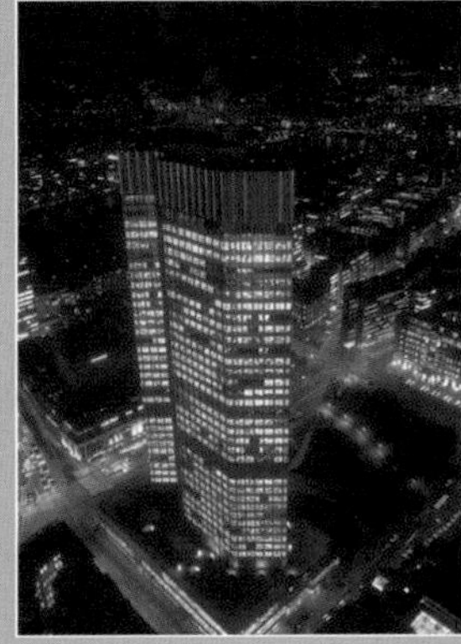

European Central Bank, Frankfurt

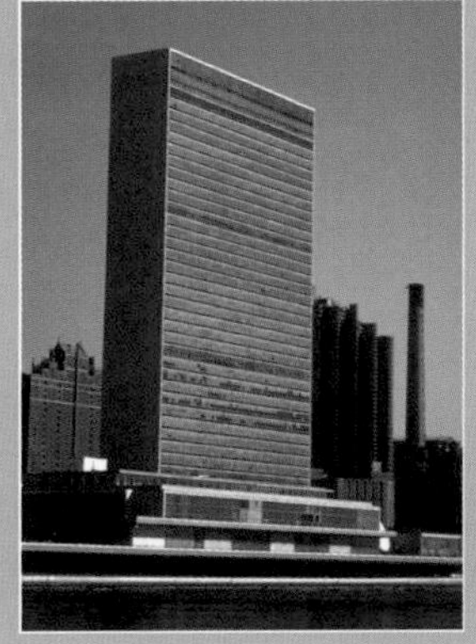

UN Headquarters, New York

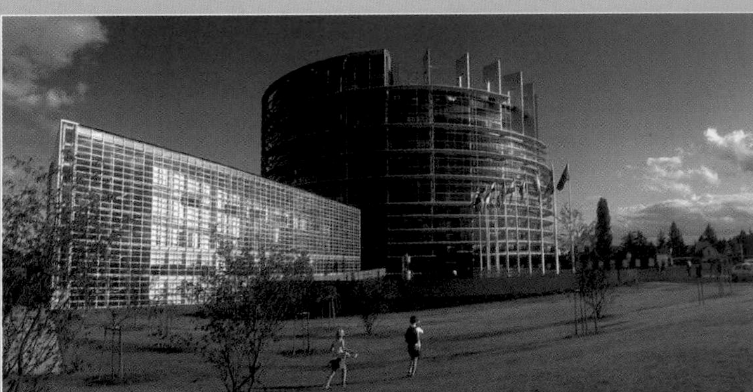

European Parliament, Strasbourg

europe

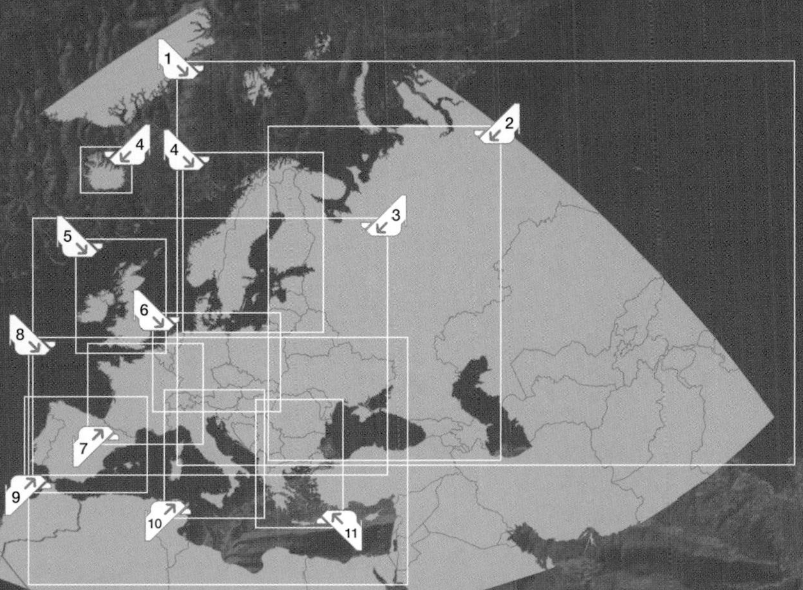

contents

europe landscapes

Atlantic Ocean
Cordillera Cantabrica
Great Britain
Bay of Biscay
Pyrenees
Massif Central
Corsica
Alps
Apennines
Adriatic Sea
Dinaric Alps
Lake Balaton
Carpathian Mountains
Balkan Mountains
Danube Delta
Black Sea
Crimea
Sea of Azov
Caucasus
Caspian Sea

europe cross section

Spitsbergen

Caucasus mountain range marking the boundary of Europe and Asia, contains Europe's highest peak, **Elbrus**.

Faroe Islands
Norwegian Sea
Scandinavia
Lappland
Gulf of Bothnia
Baltic Se
North Sea
Elbe River
Rhine River
Ireland
Great Britain
Seine River
English Channel
Alps
Loire River
Massif Central
Bay of Biscay
Pyrenees
Atlantic Ocean
Cordillera Cantabrica
Balearic Islands
Iberian Peninsula
Tagus River
Strait of Gibraltar

LARGEST ISLAND / Great Britain
218 476 sq km / 84 354 sq miles
Map reference 35 E4

CONNECTIONS

World physical features	6–7
World environment	14–15
Europe locations	24–25
Reference maps of Europe	26–47
Europe states and territories	48

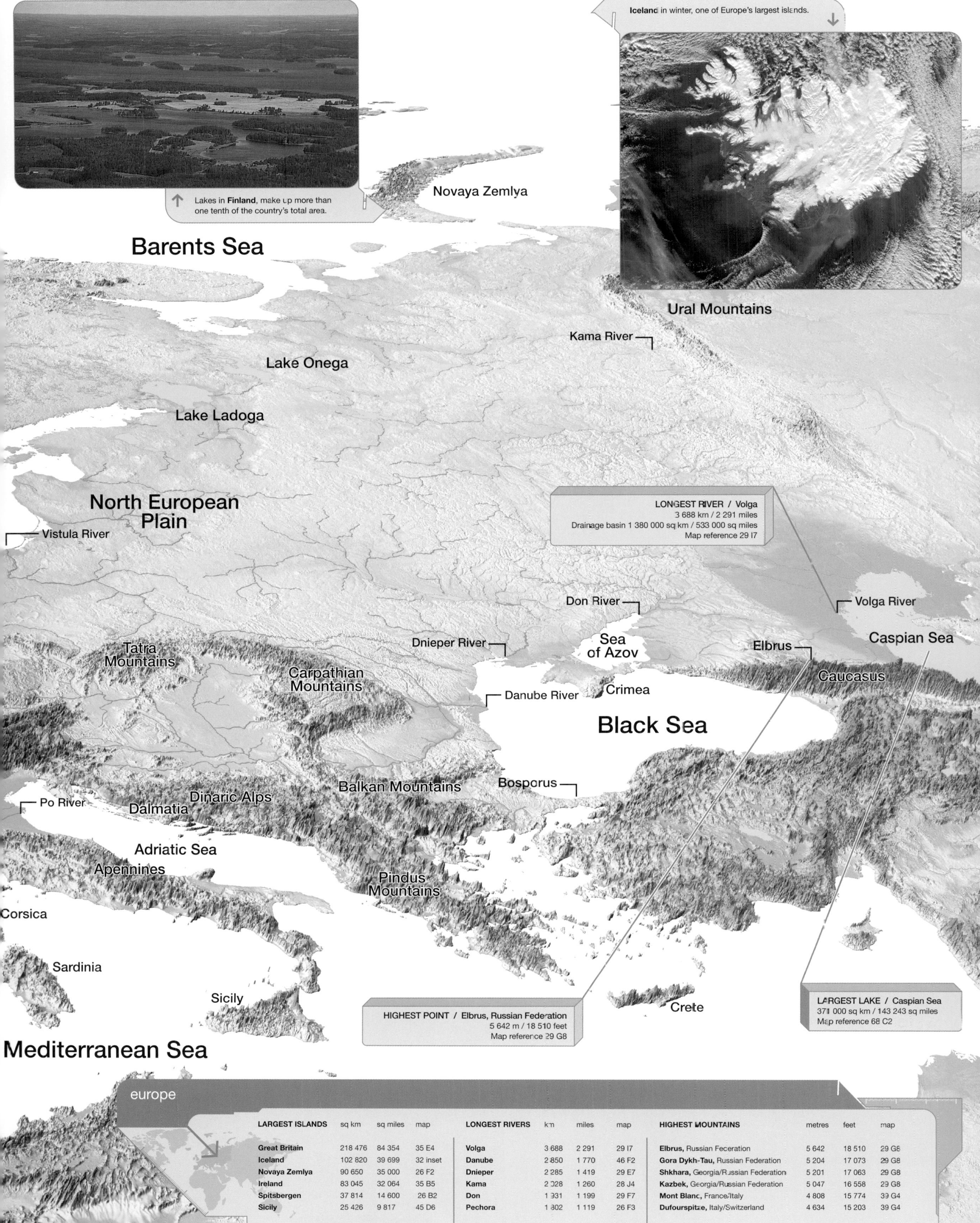

Lakes in **Finland**, make up more than one tenth of the country's total area.

Iceland in winter, one of Europe's largest islands.

Novaya Zemlya

Barents Sea

Ural Mountains

Kama River

Lake Onega

Lake Ladoga

North European Plain

Vistula River

LONGEST RIVER / Volga
3 688 km / 2 291 miles
Drainage basin 1 380 000 sq km / 533 000 sq miles
Map reference 29 I7

Don River

Volga River

Sea of Azov

Caspian Sea

Dnieper River

Elbrus

Tatra Mountains

Carpathian Mountains

Danube River

Crimea

Caucasus

Black Sea

Po River

Dalmatia

Dinaric Alps

Balkan Mountains

Bosporus

Adriatic Sea

Apennines

Pindus Mountains

Corsica

Sardinia

Sicily

Crete

LARGEST LAKE / Caspian Sea
371 000 sq km / 143 243 sq miles
Map reference 68 C2

HIGHEST POINT / Elbrus, Russian Federation
5 642 m / 18 510 feet
Map reference 29 G8

Mediterranean Sea

europe

LARGEST ISLANDS	sq km	sq miles	map
Great Britain	218 476	84 354	35 E4
Iceland	102 820	39 699	32 inset
Novaya Zemlya	90 650	35 000	26 F2
Ireland	83 045	32 064	35 B5
Spitsbergen	37 814	14 600	26 B2
Sicily	25 426	9 817	45 D6

LONGEST RIVERS	km	miles	map
Volga	3 688	2 291	29 I7
Danube	2 850	1 770	46 F2
Dnieper	2 285	1 419	29 E7
Kama	2 028	1 260	28 J4
Don	1 931	1 199	29 F7
Pechora	1 802	1 119	26 F3

HIGHEST MOUNTAINS	metres	feet	map
Elbrus, Russian Federation	5 642	18 510	29 G8
Gora Dykh-Tau, Russian Federation	5 204	17 073	29 G8
Shkhara, Georgia/Russian Federation	5 201	17 063	29 G8
Kazbek, Georgia/Russian Federation	5 047	16 558	29 G8
Mont Blanc, France/Italy	4 808	15 774	33 G4
Dufourspitze, Italy/Switzerland	4 634	15 203	39 G4

LARGEST LAKES	sq km	sq miles	map
Caspian Sea	371 000	143 243	68 C2
Lake Ladoga	18 390	7 100	28 D3
Lake Onega	9 600	3 706	28 E3
Vanern	5 585	2 156	33 D4
Rybinskoye Vodokhranilishche	5 180	2 000	28 F4

LAND AREA		map
Total land area	9 908 599 sq km / 3 825 731 sq miles	
Most northerly point	Ostrov Rudolfa, Russian Federation	26 F1
Most southerly point	Gavdos, Crete, Greece	47 D7
Most westerly point	Bjargtangar, Iceland	32 inset
Most easterly point	Mys Flissingskiy, Russian Federation	27 G2

europe
locations

Space Imaging

↑ Snow-capped mountains in the Swiss **Alps**.

↑ **Venice**, northeastern Italy, city of lagoons and islands connected by numerous canals and bridges.

CONNECTIONS

World countries	8–9
Europe landscapes	22–23
Reference maps of Europe	26–47
Europe states and territories	48
Atlantic Ocean	160–161
Arctic Ocean	166

↑ Rugged, mountainous landscape of southern Greece and the **Peloponnese Peninsula**.

ARCTIC OCEAN
Spitsbergen
Svalbard (Norway)
LONGYEARBYEN
Bjørnøya (Norway)
Jan Mayen (Norway)
Denmark Strait
North Cape
REYKJAVIK
ICELAND
Norwegian Sea
Faroe Islands (Denmark)
TÓRSHAVN
Shetland
Orkney
Outer Hebrides
ATLANTIC OCEAN
NORWAY
SWEDEN
FINLAND
Gulf of Bothnia
OSLO
STOCKHOLM
HELSINKI
TALLINN
ESTONIA
RIGA
LATVIA
LITHUANIA
VILNIUS
Baltic Sea
Skagerrak
Kattegat
Ålborg
DENMARK
COPENHAGEN
Odense
Bornholm
RUSSIAN FEDERATION
Kaliningrad
North Sea
Glasgow
Edinburgh
Belfast
REPUBLIC OF IRELAND
DUBLIN
UNITED KINGDOM
Liverpool
Leeds
Manchester
Birmingham
Cardiff
LONDON
NETHERLANDS
AMSTERDAM
THE HAGUE
Rotterdam
BRUSSELS
BELGIUM
Lille
Essen
Cologne
Bonn
Hamburg
Bremen
Hannover
BERLIN
Leipzig
GERMANY
Gdańsk
Bydgoszcz
Grodno
Białystok
Poznań
WARSAW
Brest
Łódź
POLAND
Wrocław
Katowice
Kraków
Lviv
English Channel
Channel Islands (U.K.)
Brest
Rennes
Nantes
PARIS
Orléans
LUXEMBOURG
Strasbourg
Stuttgart
PRAGUE
CZECH REPUBLIC
Brno
SLOVAKIA
Košice
FRANCE
Dijon
Munich
Salzburg
VIENNA
BRATISLAVA
Zurich
BERN
Innsbruck
LIECHTENSTEIN
SWITZERLAND
AUSTRIA
BUDAPEST
HUNGARY
Debrecen
Oradea
Szeged
Timişoara
ROMANIA
Bay of Biscay
Bordeaux
Geneva
Lyon
Milan
Venice
LJUBLJANA
SLOVENIA
ZAGREB
Trieste
CROATIA
BELGRADE
A Coruña
Oporto
Bilbao
ANDORRA
ANDORRA LA VELLA
Toulouse
Turin
Bologna
Nice
MONACO
Marseille
Florence
SAN MARINO
BOSNIA-HERZEGOVINA
SARAJEVO
SERBIA AND MONTENEGRO
Split
Adriatic Sea
Podgorica
SKOPJE
SOFIA
MACEDONIA
TIRANA
ALBANIA
PORTUGAL
Salamanca
MADRID
SPAIN
Zaragoza
Barcelona
LISBON
Tagus
Ebro
Corsica
VATICAN CITY
ROME
ITALY
Naples
Bari
Sardinia
Valencia
Minorca
Majorca
Ibiza
Balearic Islands
Seville
Córdoba
Cádiz
GIBRALTAR (U.K.)
Málaga
Cartagena
Ceuta (Spain)
Melilla (Spain)
Tyrrhenian Sea
Palermo
Sicily
Messina
Cosenza
Syracuse
Ionian Sea
Larisa
GREECE
ATHENS
VALLETTA
MALTA
Mediterranean Sea

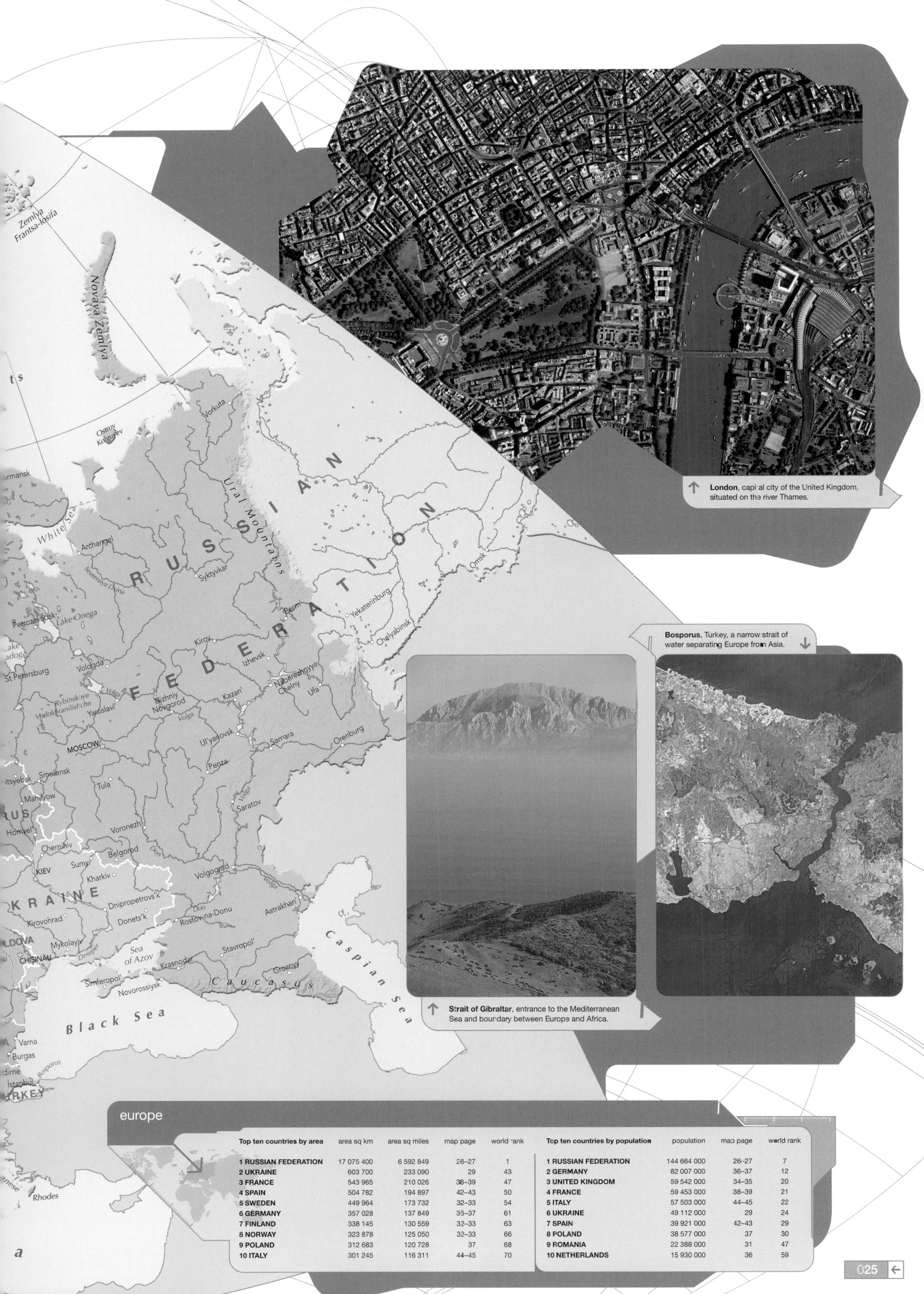

London, capital city of the United Kingdom, situated on the river Thames.

Bosporus, Turkey, a narrow strait of water separating Europe from Asia.

Strait of Gibraltar, entrance to the Mediterranean Sea and boundary between Europe and Africa.

europe

Top ten countries by area	area sq km	area sq miles	map page	world rank	Top ten countries by population	population	map page	world rank
1 RUSSIAN FEDERATION	17 075 400	6 592 849	26–27	1	1 RUSSIAN FEDERATION	144 664 000	26–27	7
2 UKRAINE	603 700	233 090	29	43	2 GERMANY	82 007 000	36–37	12
3 FRANCE	543 965	210 026	38–39	47	3 UNITED KINGDOM	59 542 000	34–35	20
4 SPAIN	504 782	194 897	42–43	50	4 FRANCE	59 453 000	38–39	21
5 SWEDEN	449 964	173 732	32–33	54	5 ITALY	57 503 000	44–45	22
6 GERMANY	357 028	137 849	36–37	61	6 UKRAINE	49 112 000	29	24
7 FINLAND	338 145	130 559	32–33	63	7 SPAIN	39 921 000	42–43	29
8 NORWAY	323 878	125 050	32–33	66	8 POLAND	38 577 000	37	30
9 POLAND	312 683	120 728	37	68	9 ROMANIA	22 388 000	31	47
10 ITALY	301 245	116 311	44–45	70	10 NETHERLANDS	15 930 000	36	59

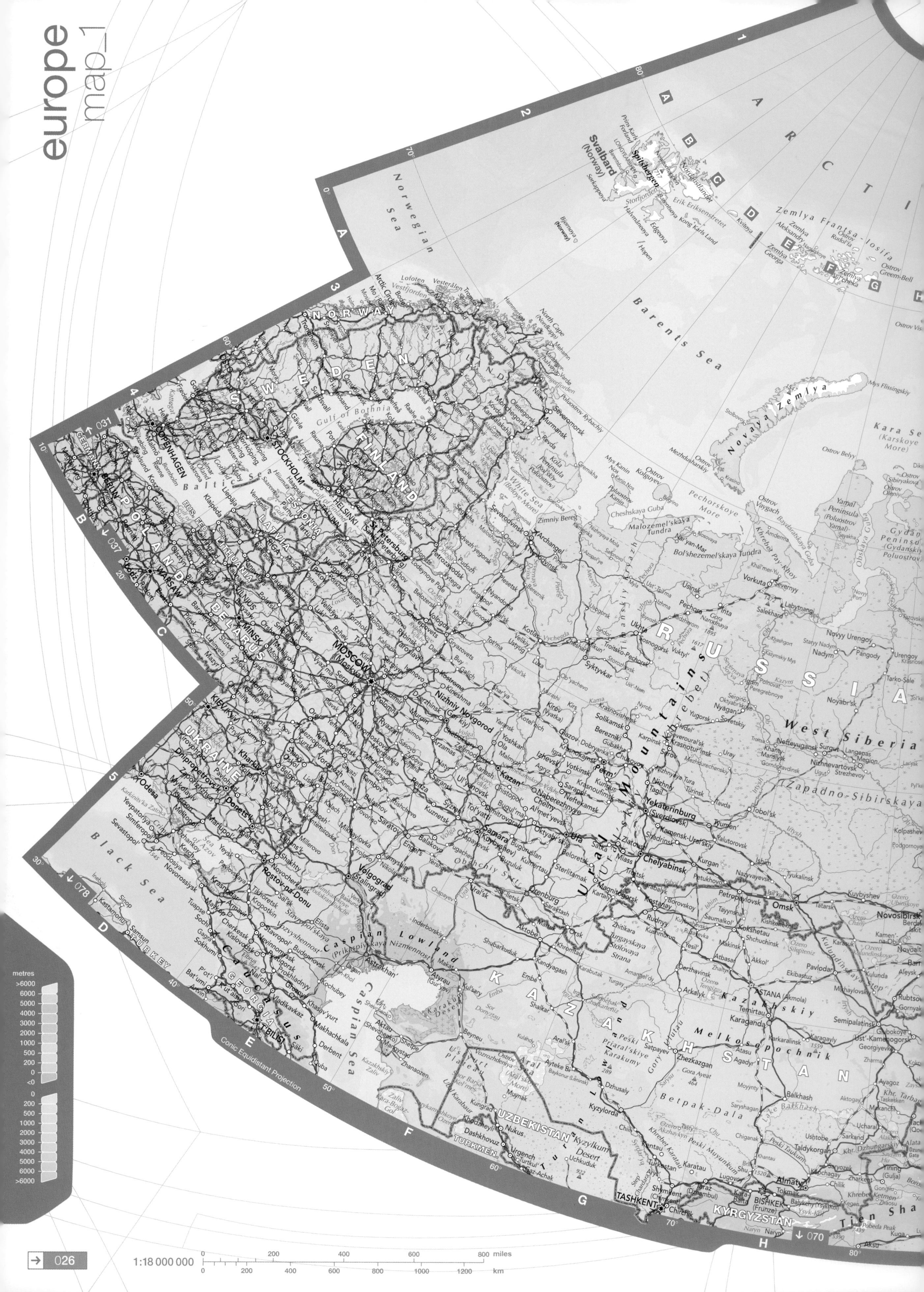
Norwegian Sea
Barents Sea
Svalbard (Norway)
Spitsbergen
Zemlya Frantsa-Iosifa
Novaya Zemlya
Kara Sea (Karskoye More)
Pechorskoye More
White Sea (Beloye More)
Baltic Sea
Gulf of Bothnia
Black Sea
Caspian Sea
Sea of Azov
Caspian Lowland (Prikaspiyskaya Nizmennost')
NORWAY
SWEDEN
FINLAND
ESTONIA
LATVIA
LITHUANIA
POLAND
BELARUS
UKRAINE
GERMANY
RUSSIA
KAZAKHSTAN
UZBEKISTAN
TURKMEN.
KYRGYZSTAN
GEORGIA
TURKEY
Caucasus
Ural Mountains
West Siberian
Kazakhskiy Melkosopochnik
Betpak-Dala
Kyzylkum Desert
Tien Shan
COPENHAGEN
STOCKHOLM
HELSINKI
RIGA
VILNIUS
MINSK
WARSAW
BERLIN
MOSCOW (Moskva)
St Petersburg
KIEV
TBILISI
ASTANA (Akmola)
TASHKENT
BISHKEK (Frunze)
Almaty
Murmansk
Archangel
Nizhniy Novgorod
Kazan'
Perm'
Yekaterinburg (Sverdlovsk)
Chelyabinsk
Omsk
Novosibirsk
Samara (Kuybyshev)
Volgograd (Stalingrad)
Rostov-na-Donu
Kharkiv
Dnipropetrovs'k
Donets'k
Odesa
Astrakhan'
Ufa
Orenburg
Karaganda
Conic Equidistant Projection
metres
>6000
6000
5000
4000
3000
2000
1000
500
200
0
<0
0
200
500
1000
2000
3000
4000
5000
6000
>6000
↑ 031
↓ 037
↓ 078
↓ 070
1:18 000 000
0 200 400 600 800 miles
0 200 400 600 800 1000 1200 km

↑ 120

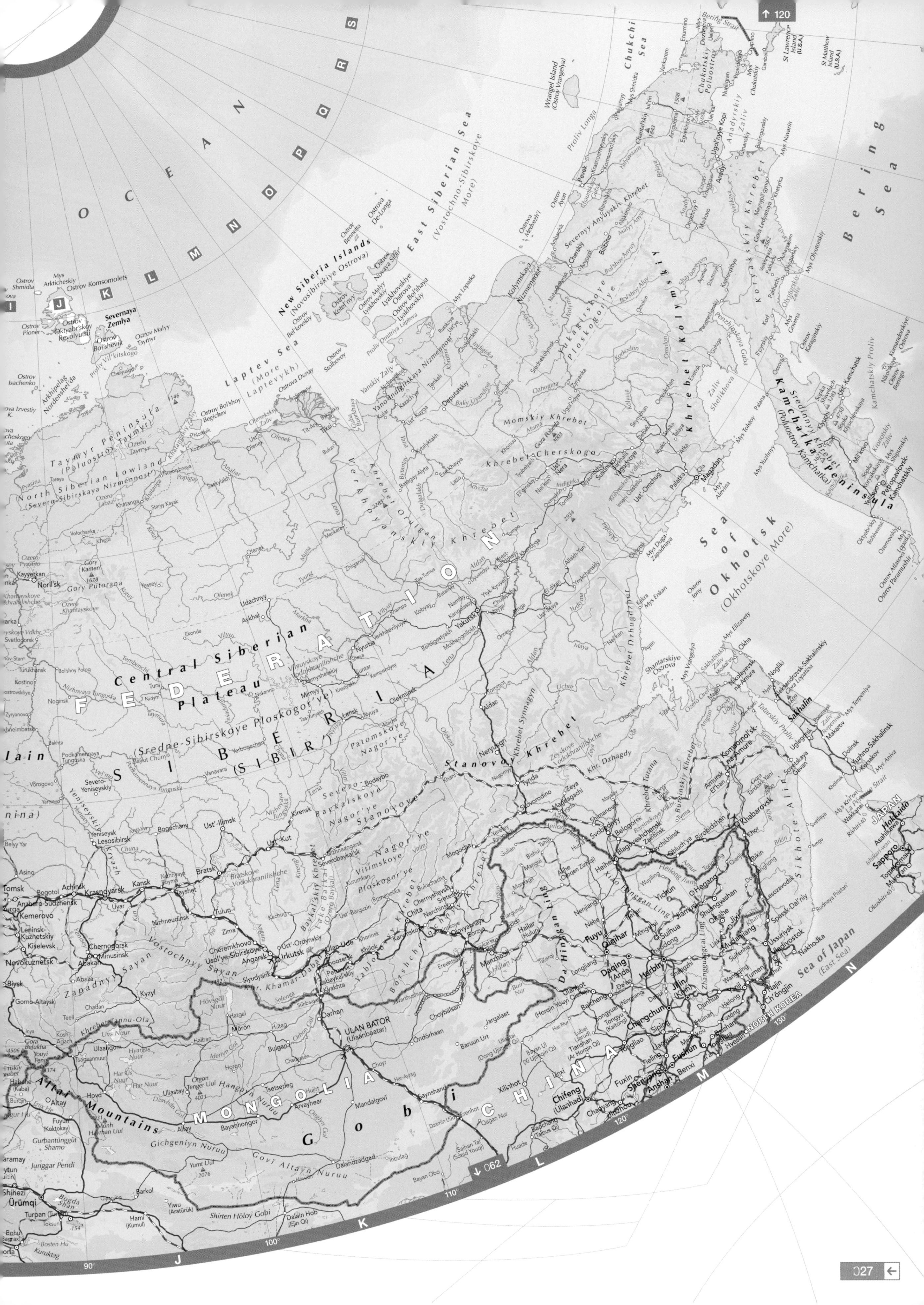
O C E A N
Chukchi Sea
Bering Strait
St Lawrence Island (U.S.A.)
St Matthew Island (U.S.A.)
Bering Sea
East Siberian Sea
(Vostochno-Sibirskoye More)
Wrangel Island (Ostrov Vrangelya)
New Siberia Islands
(Novosibirskiye Ostrova)
Laptev Sea
(More Laptevykh)
Severnaya Zemlya
Ostrov Komsomolets
Ostrov Bol'shevik
Taymyr Peninsula
(Poluostrov Taymyr)
North Siberian Lowland
(Severo-Sibirskaya Nizmennost')
Chukotskiy Poluostrov
Kolymskaya Nizmennost'
Yukagirskoye Ploskogor'ye
Khrebet Kolymskiy
Koryakskiy Khrebet
Kamchatka Peninsula
(Poluostrov Kamchatka)
Sredinnyy Khrebet
Momskiy Khrebet
Khrebet Cherskogo
Verkhoyanskiy Khrebet
Sea of Okhotsk
(Okhotskoye More)
Magadan
Petropavlovsk-Kamchatskiy
Sakhalin
Yuzhno-Sakhalinsk
Tatarskiy Proliv
Khrebet Dzhugdzhur
Stanovoy Khrebet
Yakutsk
Central Siberian Plateau
(Sredne-Sibirskoye Ploskogor'ye)
F E D E R A T I O N
S I B E R I A
(S I B I R')
Noril'sk
Gory Putorana
Patomskoye Nagor'ye
Severo-Baykal'skoye Nagor'ye
Stanovoye Nagor'ye
Vitimskoye Ploskogor'ye
Lake Baykal
Irkutsk
Bratsk
Krasnoyarsk
Tomsk
Kemerovo
Novokuznetsk
Biysk
Vostochnyy Sayan
Zapadnyy Sayan
Khrebet Tannu-Ola
Chita
Ulan-Ude
Khabarovsk
Vladivostok
Sea of Japan
(East Sea)
JAPAN
Hokkaido
Sapporo
Sikhote-Alin'
Da Hinggan Ling
Xiao Hinggan Ling
Harbin
Qiqihar
Jilin
Changchun
Shenyang
Anshan
Fushun
Chifeng
NORTH KOREA
C H I N A
M O N G O L I A
ULAN BATOR
(Ulaanbaatar)
Hangayn Nuruu
Altai Mountains
Gobi
Gov' Altayn Nuruu
Gichgeniyn Nuruu
Ürümqi
Junggar Pendi
Shirten Höloy Gobi
90°
100°
110°
120°
130°

↓ 062

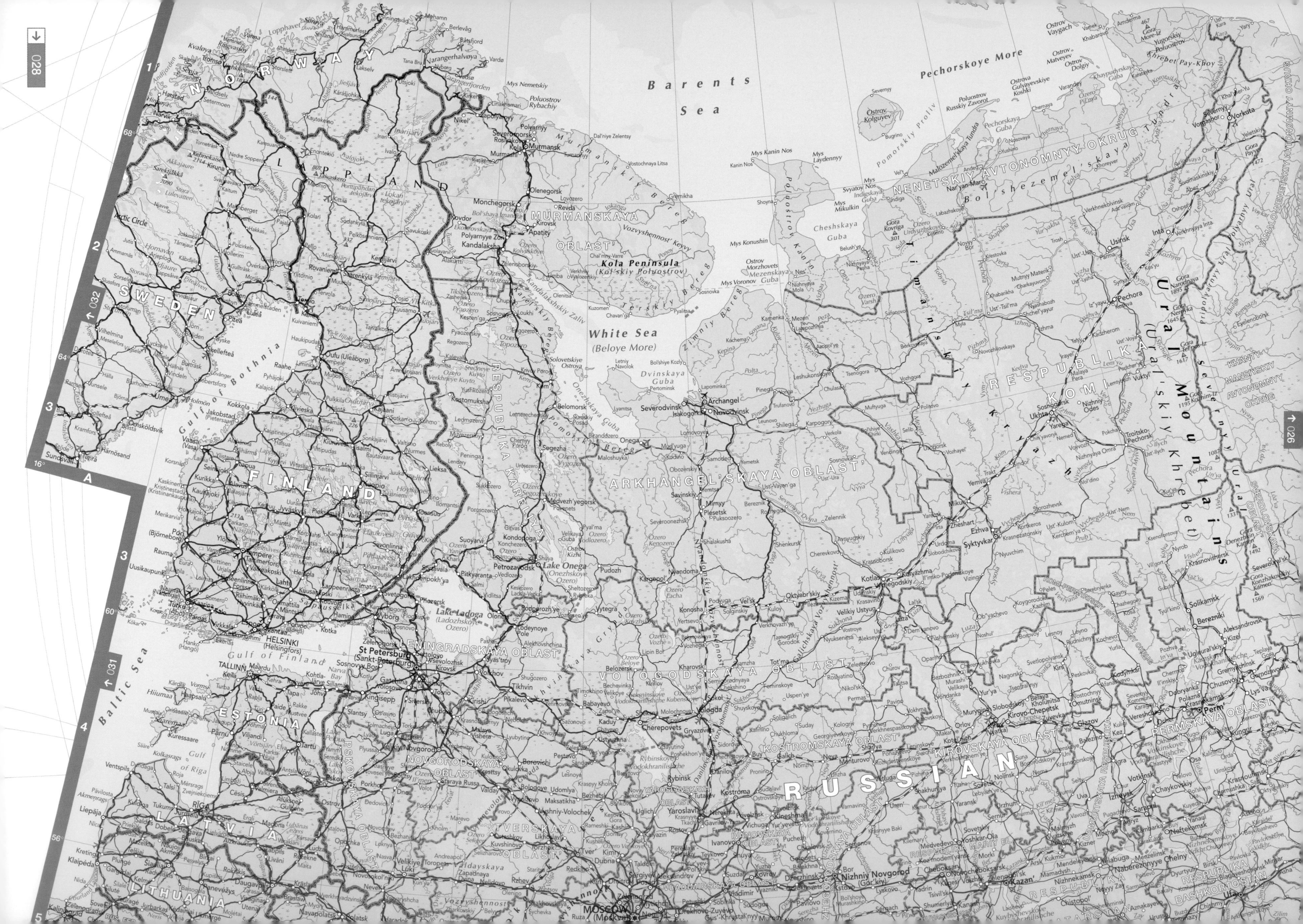

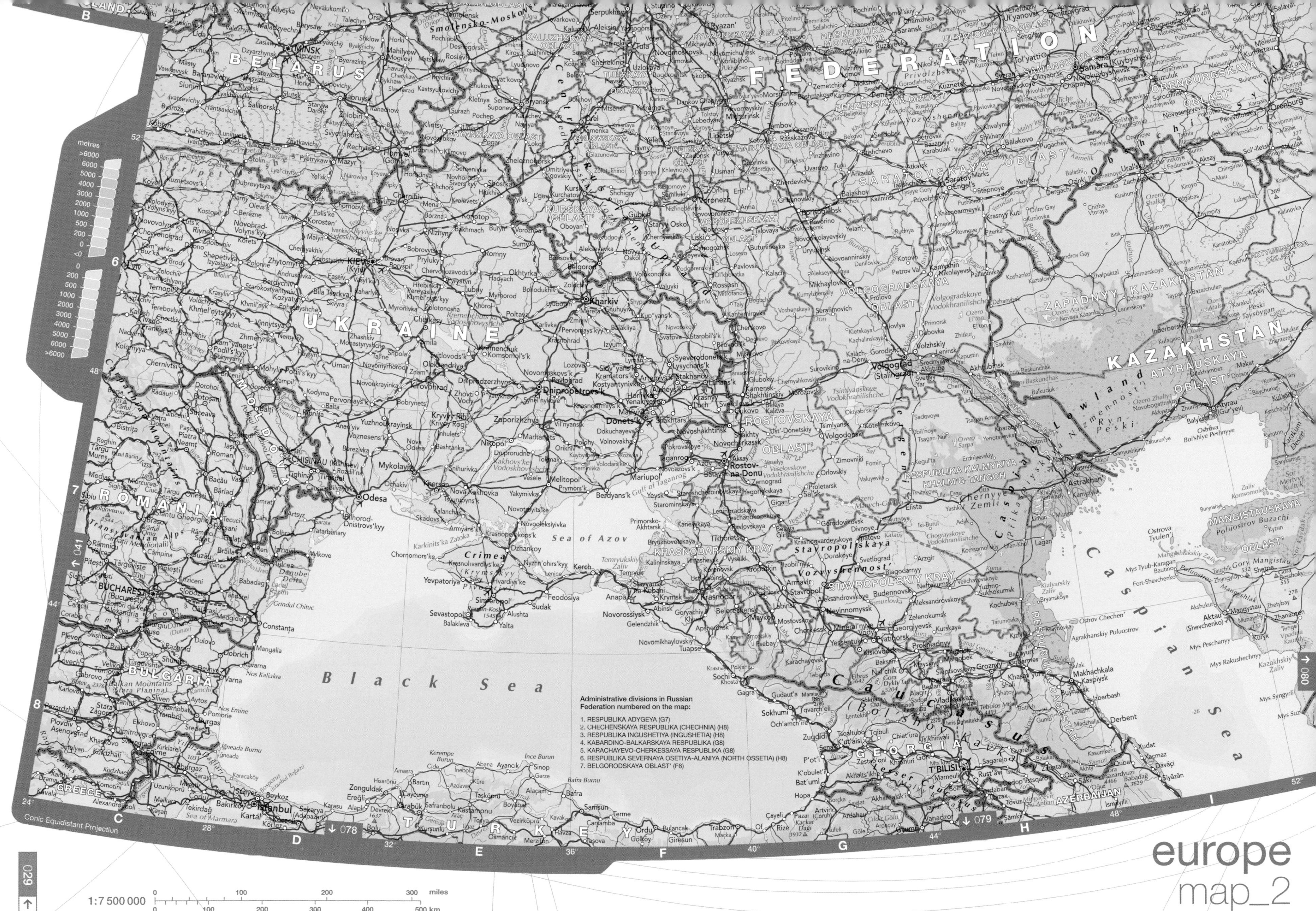

1:7 500 000

Conic Equidistant Projection

Administrative divisions in Russian Federation numbered on the map:

1. RESPUBLIKA ADYGEYA (G7)
2. CHECHENSKAYA RESPUBLIKA (CHECHNIA) (H8)
3. RESPUBLIKA INGUSHETIYA (INGUSHETIA) (H8)
4. KABARDINO-BALKARSKAYA RESPUBLIKA (G8)
5. KARACHAYEVO-CHERKESSKAYA RESPUBLIKA (G8)
6. RESPUBLIKA SEVERNAYA OSETIYA-ALANIYA (NORTH OSSETIA) (H8)
7. BELGORODSKAYA OBLAST' (F6)

Caspian Sea

Black Sea

Sea of Azov

RUSSIAN FEDERATION

KAZAKHSTAN

UKRAINE

BELARUS

ROMANIA

BULGARIA

MOLDOVA

TURKEY

GEORGIA

AZERBAIJAN

GREECE

Map labels

North Sea

ATLANTIC OCEAN

Bay of Biscay

Gulf of Gascony

Mar Cantábrico

Mediterranean Sea

Golfe du Lion

Golf de Sant Jordi

Costa Brava

English Channel (La Manche)

Strait of Dover (Pas de Calais)

Irish Sea

St George's Channel

Cardigan Bay

Bristol Channel

North Channel

The Minch

Moray Firth

Firth of Forth

Baie de Seine

Golfe de St-Malo

Donegal Bay

Galway Bay

Countries / Regions

UNITED KINGDOM

SCOTLAND

ENGLAND

WALES

NORTHERN IRELAND

REPUBLIC OF IRELAND

FRANCE

SPAIN

PORTUGAL

BELGIUM

NETHERLAND

LUXEMBOURG

ANDORRA

Grampian Mountains

Cordillera Cantábrica

Sierra de la Cabrera

Cities (selection)

DUBLIN, LONDON, PARIS, MADRID, AMSTERDAM, THE HAGUE ('s-Gravenhage), BRUSSELS (Bruxelles), LUXEMBOURG, ANDORRA LA VELLA

Aberdeen, Inverness, Fort William, Glasgow, Edinburgh, Dundee, St Andrews, Arbroath, Montrose, Perth, Fraserburgh, Peterhead, Elgin, Wick, Thurso, Helmsdale, Kirkwall, Lerwick

Newcastle upon Tyne, Sunderland, Durham, Middlesbrough, Whitby, Darlington, Berwick-upon-Tweed, Alnwick, Carlisle, Kendal, Lancaster, Preston, Blackpool, Liverpool, Manchester, Sheffield, Leeds, York, Kingston upon Hull, Grimsby, Lincoln, Derby, Nottingham, Leicester, Birmingham, Coventry, Worcester, Gloucester, Peterborough, Norwich, Great Yarmouth, Lowestoft, Ipswich, Cambridge, Bury St Edmunds, Colchester, Southend-on-Sea, Oxford, Reading, Luton, Milton Keynes, Swindon, Bristol, Bath, Cardiff, Swansea, Newport, Exeter, Plymouth, Torquay, Weymouth, Bournemouth, Southampton, Portsmouth, Brighton, Eastbourne, Hastings, Dover, Maidstone, Canterbury, Newquay, Truro, Penzance, Falmouth, Barnstaple, Taunton, Bridgwater, Shrewsbury, Aberystwyth, Carmarthen, Brecon, Barrow-in-Furness, Workington

Belfast, Londonderry, Ballymena, Bangor, Dundalk, Drogheda, Galway, Sligo, Ballina, Westport, Athlone, Mullingar, Naas, Dún Laoghaire, Wicklow, Carlow, Kilkenny, Wexford, Rosslare, Waterford, Cork, Kinsale, Skibbereen, Bantry, Killarney, Tralee, Limerick, Ennis

Cherbourg, Caen, Le Havre, Rouen, Dieppe, Amiens, Abbeville, Boulogne-sur-Mer, Calais, Lille, Charleroi, Namur, Reims, Châlons-en-Champagne, Troyes, Verdun, Nancy, Metz, Brest, Morlaix, St-Brieuc, St-Malo, Dinan, Rennes, Laval, Le Mans, Alençon, Angers, Nantes, St-Nazaire, La Roche-sur-Yon, La Rochelle, Niort, Poitiers, Tours, Orléans, Chartres, Versailles, Bourges, Châteauroux, Limoges, Angoulême, Périgueux, Bordeaux, Bergerac, Cahors, Agen, Montauban, Toulouse, Albi, Rodez, Aurillac, Clermont-Ferrand, St-Étienne, Lyon, Grenoble, Valence, Montélimar, Avignon, Nîmes, Montpellier, Béziers, Narbonne, Carcassonne, Perpignan, Marseille, Toulon, Aix-en-Provence, Tarbes, Lourdes, Pau, Bayonne, Dax, Mont-de-Marsan, Arcachon

A Coruña, Santiago de Compostela, Ferrol, Vigo, Pontevedra, Ourense, Lugo, Oviedo, Gijón, Avilés, Santander, Bilbao, San Sebastián (Donostia), Vitoria-Gasteiz, Pamplona, Logroño, Burgos, Valladolid, León, Palencia, Zamora, Salamanca, Ávila, Segovia, Soria, Zaragoza, Huesca, Lleida, Barcelona, Tarragona, Reus, Girona, Figueres, Manresa, Guadalajara, Alcalá de Henares, Cuenca, Teruel, Tortosa, Vinaròs

Oporto (Porto), Vila Nova de Gaia, Braga, Aveiro, Coimbra, Viseu, Guarda, Viana do Castelo, Póvoa de Varzim, Chaves, Bragança

Map margin / scale information

metres
>6000
6000
5000
4000
3000
2000
1000
500
200
0
200
1000
2000
3000
4000
5000
6000
>6000

Conic Equidistant Projection

1:7 500 000

0   100   200   300 miles

0   100   200   300   400   500 km

↓ 042

NORWAY

SWEDEN

DENMARK

FINLAND

ESTONIA

RUSSIAN FEDERATION

LATVIA

LITHUANIA

RUSSIAN FEDERATION

BELARUS

GERMANY

POLAND

UKRAINE

CZECH REPUBLIC

SLOVAKIA

MOLDOVA

AUSTRIA

HUNGARY

ROMANIA

SLOVENIA

CROATIA

BOSNIA-HERZEGOVINA

SERBIA AND MONTENEGRO

BULGARIA

ITALY

MACEDONIA

ALBANIA

GREECE

TURKEY

LIECHTENSTEIN

SWITZERLAND

Baltic Sea

Gulf of Bothnia

Gulf of Finland

Black Sea

Ligurian Sea

Aegean Sea

Carpathian Mountains

Balkan Mountains

Transylvanian Alps

Alps

OSLO
STOCKHOLM
HELSINKI
TALLINN
COPENHAGEN
VILNIUS
MINSK
WARSAW
BERLIN
KIEV
PRAGUE
VIENNA
BRATISLAVA
BUDAPEST
CHISINAU
LJUBLJANA
ZAGREB
BELGRADE
BUCHAREST
SARAJEVO
SOFIA
SKOPJE
TIRANA
ROME
VATICAN CITY
SAN MARINO

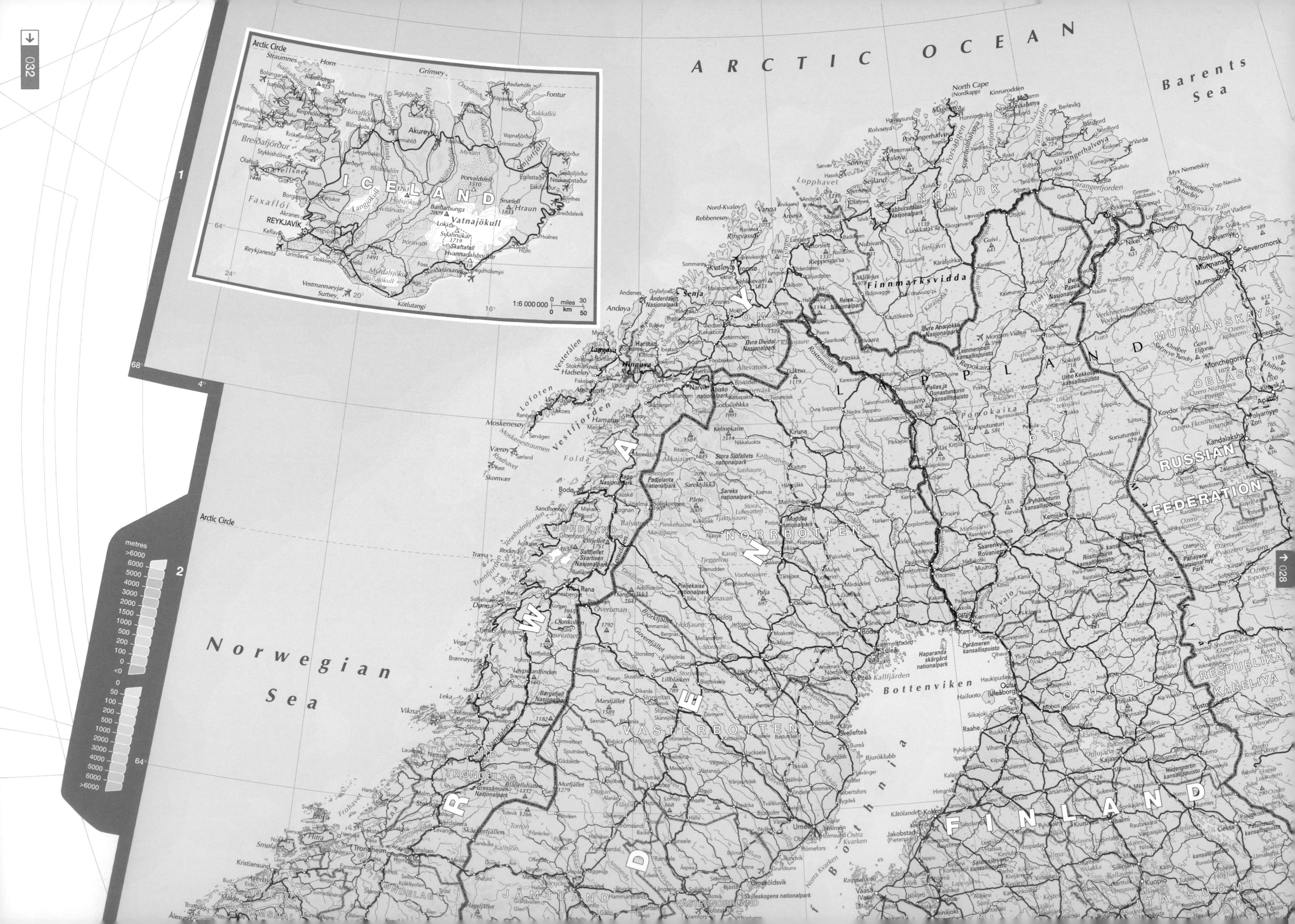

ARCTIC OCEAN
Barents Sea
Norwegian Sea
Bottenviken
NORWAY
SWEDEN
FINLAND
RUSSIAN FEDERATION
MURMANSKAYA OBLAST'
RESPUBLIKA KARELIYA
FINNMARK
TROMS
NORDLAND
NORRBOTTEN
VÄSTERBOTTEN
JÄMTLAND
LAPPI
OULU
Lappland
Finnmarksvidda
North Cape (Nordkapp)
Arctic Circle
Lofoten
Vesterålen
Vestfjorden
Narvik
Tromsø
Kiruna
Luleå
Oulu
Rovaniemi
Murmansk
Umeå
Trondheim
Bodø
Mo i Rana
ICELAND
REYKJAVÍK
Akureyri
Vatnajökull
Langjökull
Hofsjökull
Mýrdalsjökull
Faxaflói
Breiðafjörður
Grímsey
Surtsey
1:6 000 000
miles
km
metres
>6000
6000
5000
4000
3000
2000
1500
1000
500
200
100
0
<0
50
1
2
68°
64°
4°
16°
20°
24°

028
032

1:4 500 000
Conic Equidistant Projection

200 miles
km
0   50   100   150   200   250   300

→ 037

↓ 036

B   C   D   E   F   G

4   5

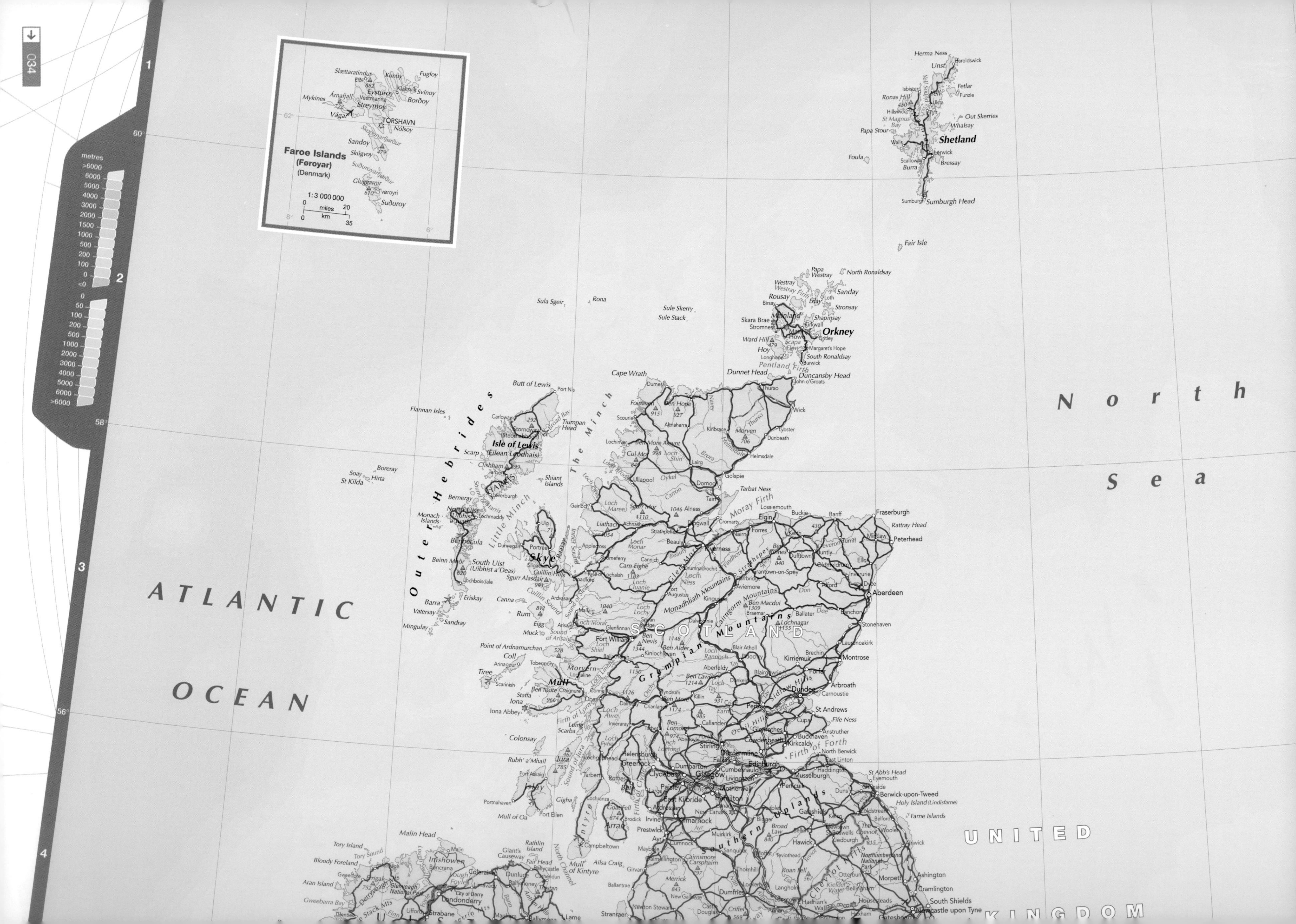

North Sea

Atlantic Ocean

United Kingdom

Scotland

Shetland

Herma Ness
Unst
Yell Sound
Ronas Hill
St Magnus Bay
Papa Stour
Foula
Fedlar
Fetlar
Out Skerries
Whalsay
Lerwick
Bressay
Burra
Scalloway
Sumburgh
Sumburgh Head

Fair Isle

Orkney
North Ronaldsay
Westray
Papa Westray
Sanday
Stronsay
Rousay
Shapinsay
Skara Brae
Stromness
Kirkwall
Hoy
South Ronaldsay
Burwick
Ward Hill
Longhope
St Margaret's Hope
Duncansby Head
Pentland Firth
Pentland Skerries

Cape Wrath
Dunnet Head
Thurso
Wick
Latheron
Dunbeath
Helmsdale

Naver
Kyle of Durness
Ben Hope
927
Altnaharra
Lairg
Brora
Golspie
Dornoch

Sule Skerry
Sule Stack

Rona

Sula Sgeir

Butt of Lewis
Port Nis
Isle of Lewis
Eilean Leòdhais
Stornoway
Carloway
Callanish
Scarp
Chladha

Flannan Isles

North Uist
Lochmaddy
Benbecula
South Uist
(Uibhist a Deas)
Barra
Vatersay
Mingulay
Sandray

St Kilda
Hirta
Soay
Boreray

Outer Hebrides

The Minch
Little Minch

Skye
Portree
Cuillin Hills
Rum
Eigg
Muck
Canna

Point of Ardnamurchan
Coll
Tiree
Mull
Iona
Staffa
Colonsay
Oban

Jura
Islay
Port Ellen

Sound of Jura

Mull of Kintyre
Campbeltown

Aberdeen
Fraserburgh
Peterhead
Rattray Head
Banff
Elgin
Lossiemouth
Buckie
Forres
Nairn
Inverness
Moray Firth

Grampian Mountains
Ben Macdui
1309
Cairn Gorm
Cairngorm Mountains
Ben Nevis
1344
Fort William
Ben Lawers
Pitlochry
Perth
Dundee
Arbroath
Montrose
Stonehaven
Brechin
St Andrews
Firth of Forth
Stirling
Falkirk
Glasgow
Edinburgh
Kilmarnock
Ayr
Merrick
843
Stranraer

Berwick-upon-Tweed
St Abb's Head
Holy Island (Lindisfarne)
Farne Islands
Cheviot Hills
The Cheviot
815
Morpeth
Newcastle upon Tyne
South Shields
Castle upon Tyne

North Channel
Rathlin Island
Fair Head
Giant's Causeway
Malin Head
Tory Island
Bloody Foreland
Aran Island

Faroe Islands
(Føroyar)
(Denmark)
1:3 000 000
0   20   35
miles
0   km
TÓRSHAVN
Streymoy
Eysturoy
Vágar
Sandoy
Suðuroy
Mykines
Nólsoy
Skúvoy
Stóra Dímun
Lítla Dímun
Borðoy
Viðoy
Svínoy
Fugloy
Kunoy
Kalsoy

metres
>6000
6000
5000
4000
3000
2000
1500
1000
500
200
0
<0
0
50
100
200
500
1000
2000
3000
4000
6000
>6000

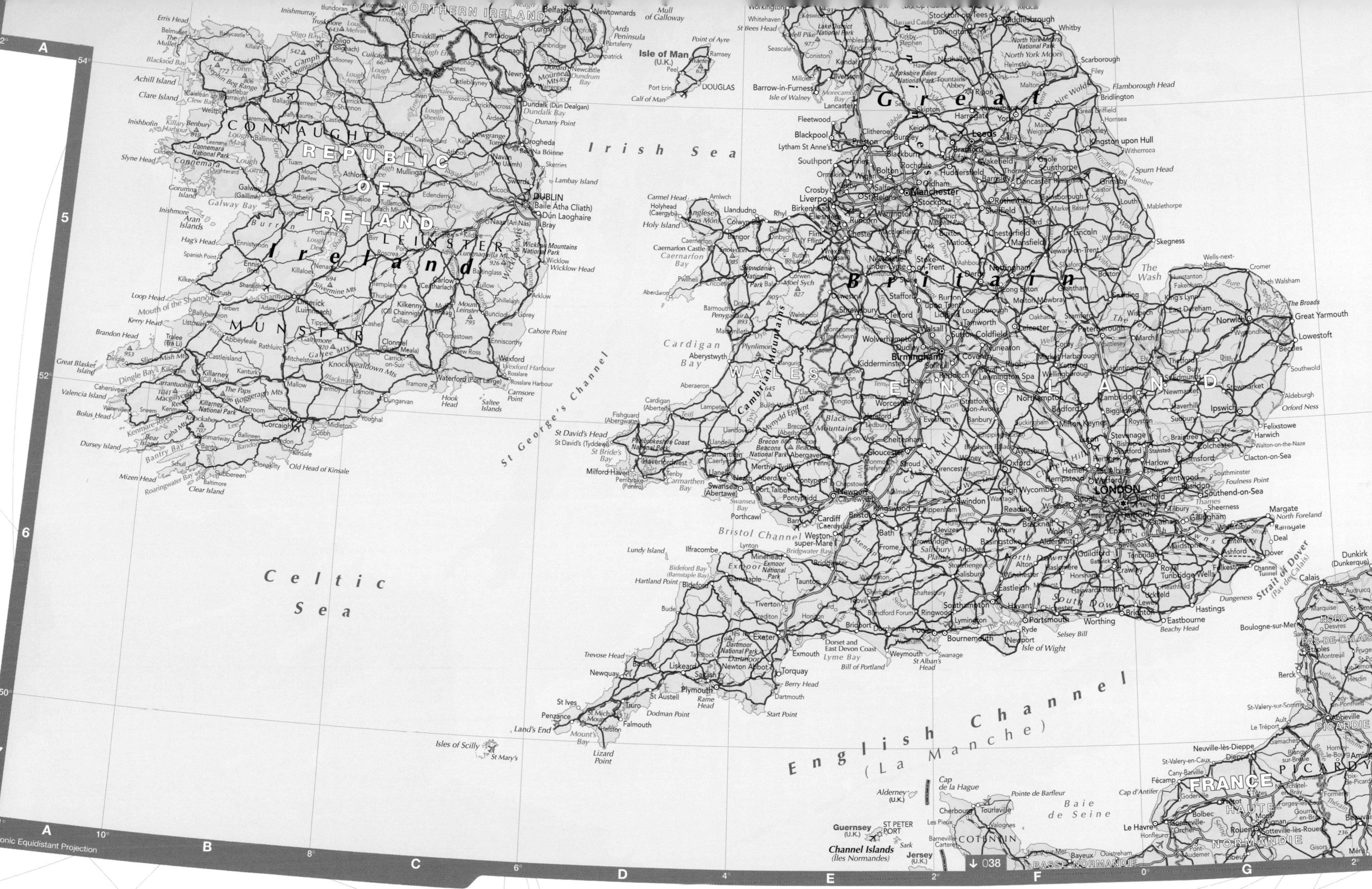

GREAT BRITAIN & IRELAND

NORTHERN IRELAND

REPUBLIC OF IRELAND

CONNAUGHT

LEINSTER

MUNSTER

Great Britain

ENGLAND

WALES

Cambrian Mountains

FRANCE

HAUTE-NORMANDIE

PICARDIE

NORD-PAS-DE-CALAIS

BASSE-NORMANDIE

COTENTIN

Isle of Man (U.K.)

DOUGLAS

DUBLIN (Baile Átha Cliath)

BELFAST

LONDON

Irish Sea

Celtic Sea

English Channel (La Manche)

Bristol Channel

St George's Channel

Cardigan Bay

Strait of Dover (Pas de Calais)

Baie de Seine

Channel Islands (Îles Normandes)

Guernsey (U.K.) ST PETER PORT

Jersey (U.K.) ST HELIER

Alderney (U.K.)

Sark

1:3 000 000

Conic Equidistant Projection

0   25   50   75   100   125 miles

0   25   50   75   100   150   175   200 km

→ 038

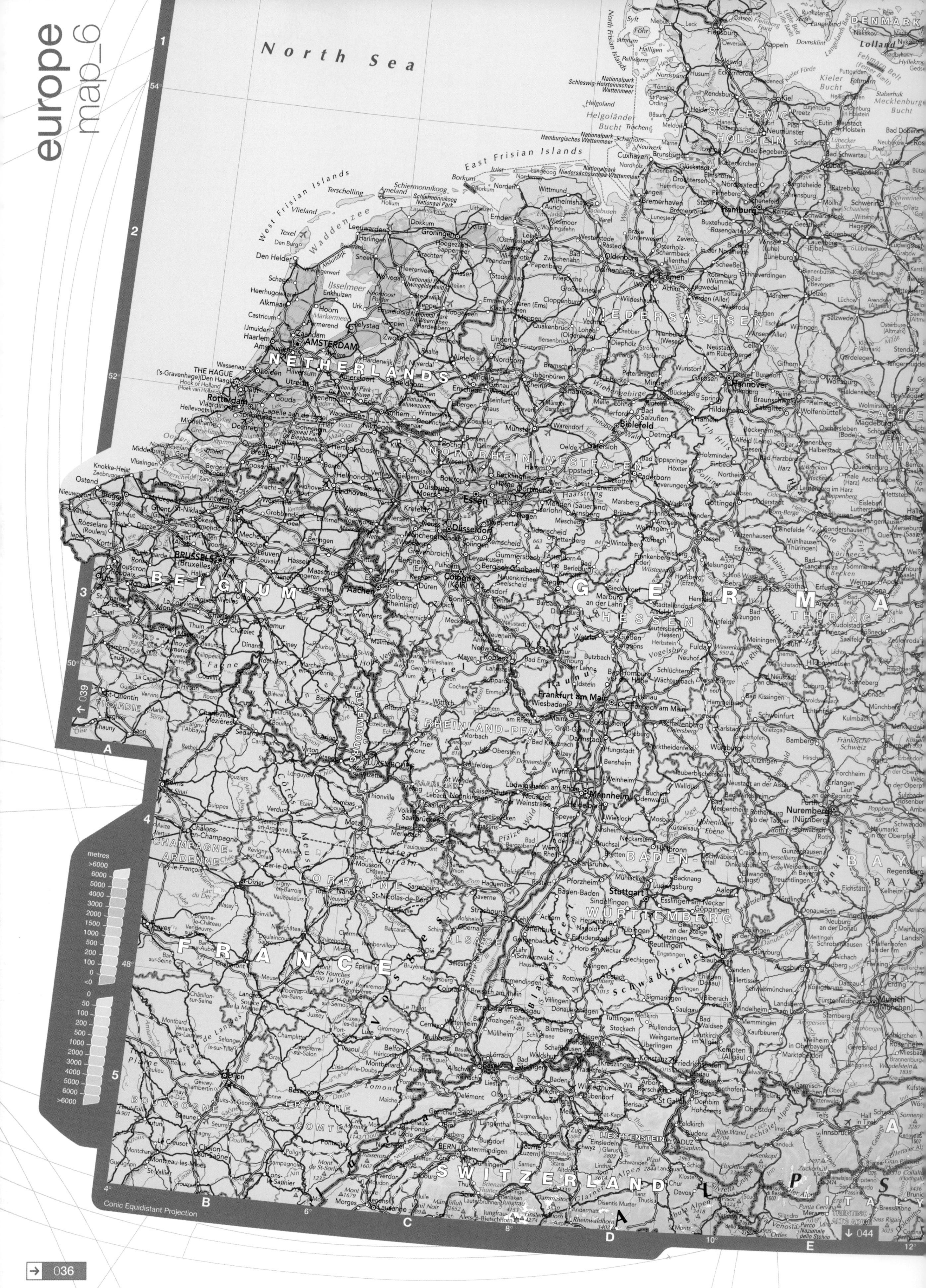
europe
map_6
North Sea
North Frisian Islands
East Frisian Islands
West Frisian Islands
Waddenzee
Helgoländer Bucht
Kieler Bucht
Mecklenburger Bucht
DENMARK
Lolland
Fehmarn
SCHLESWIG-HOLSTEIN
NIEDERSACHSEN
NORDRHEIN-WESTFALEN
HESSEN
THÜRINGEN
RHEINLAND-PFALZ
SAARLAND
BADEN-WÜRTTEMBERG
NETHERLANDS
BELGIUM
LUXEMBOURG
GERMANY
FRANCE
SWITZERLAND
LIECHTENSTEIN
ALPS
ITALY
AMSTERDAM
THE HAGUE
('s-Gravenhage)(Den Haag)
Rotterdam
Utrecht
BRUSSELS
(Bruxelles)
Antwerp
Ghent
Brugge
Ostend
Hamburg
Bremen
Hannover
Bielefeld
Düsseldorf
Essen
Dortmund
Duisburg
Cologne
(Köln)
Bonn
Aachen
Frankfurt am Main
Wiesbaden
Mainz
Mannheim
Heidelberg
Karlsruhe
Stuttgart
Nuremberg
(Nürnberg)
Munich
(München)
Augsburg
Kiel
Lübeck
Magdeburg
Kassel
Göttingen
Würzburg
Saarbrücken
Trier
Koblenz
Freiburg im Breisgau
Strasbourg
Metz
Nancy
Reims
Dijon
Besançon
Mulhouse
Basel
Zürich
BERN
Lausanne
Luzern
Innsbruck
CHAMPAGNE-ARDENNE
LORRAINE
ALSACE
BOURGOGNE
FRANCHE-COMTÉ
PICARDIE
NORD-PAS-DE-CALAIS
Vosges
Eifel
Taunus
Black Forest
Schwäbische Alb
Harz
Jura
metres
>6000
6000
5000
4000
3000
2000
1500
1000
500
200
100
0
<0
50
100
200
500
1000
2000
3000
4000
5000
6000
>6000
039
044
Conic Equidistant Projection
A
B
C
D
E
1
2
3
4
5
54°
52°
50°
48°
4°
6°
8°
10°
12°

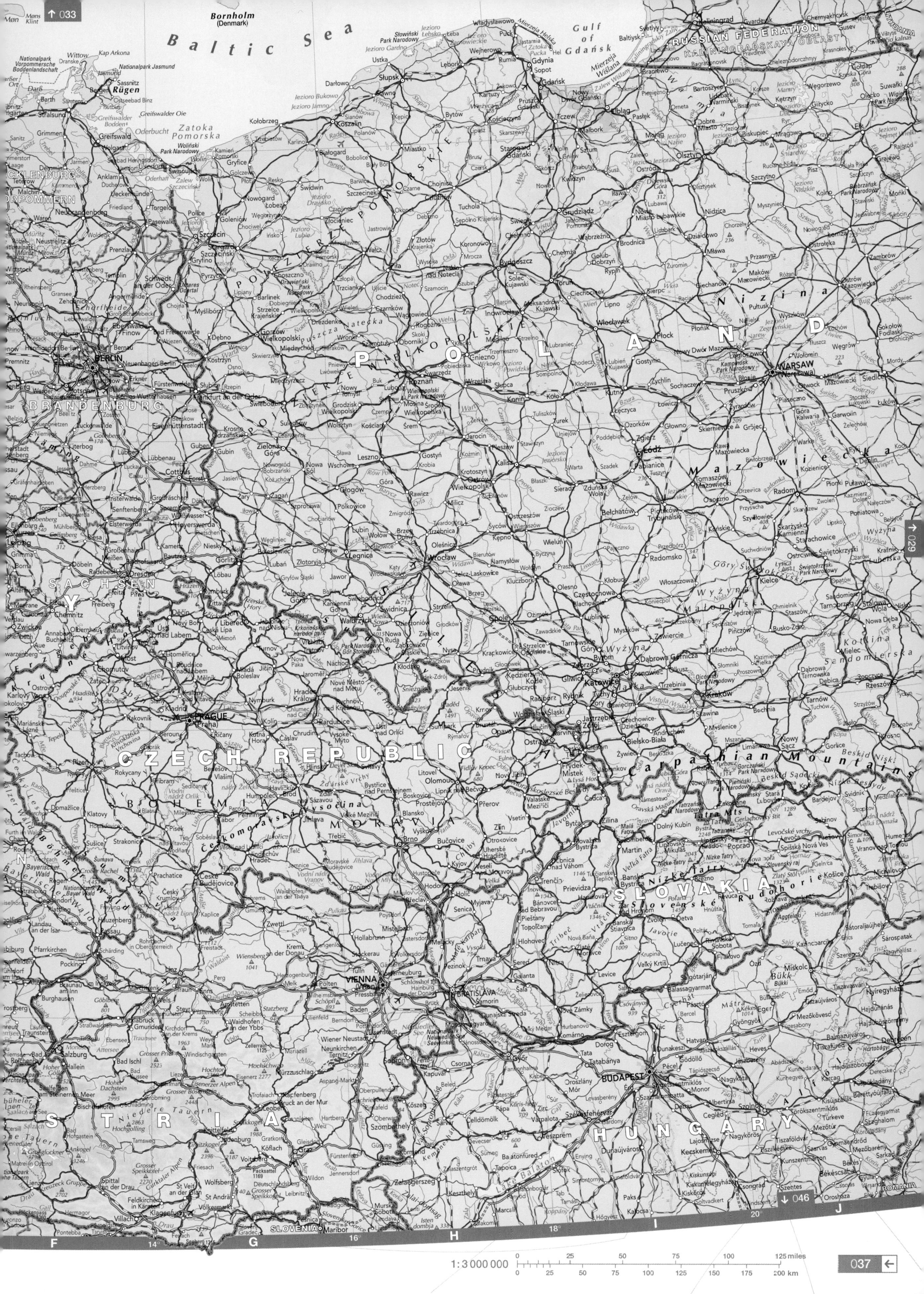

033
Bornholm (Denmark)
Baltic Sea
Gulf of Gdańsk
RUSSIAN FEDERATION
KALININGRADSKAYA OBLAST
LITHUANIA
Kaliningrad
Rügen
Zatoka Pomorska
MECKLENBURG-VORPOMMERN
BRANDENBURG
SACHSEN
Pojezierze Pomorskie
Pojezierze Wielkopolskie
POLAND
Nizina Mazowiecka
Gdańsk
Gdynia
Szczecin
Berlin
Poznań
Bydgoszcz
Toruń
Olsztyn
Białystok
Warsaw (Warszawa)
Łódź
Wrocław
Katowice
Kraków
Kielce
Radom
Dresden
Leipzig
Chemnitz
Prague (Praha)
CZECH REPUBLIC
BOHEMIA
MORAVIA
Brno
Ostrava
Olomouc
Sudety
Carpathian Mountains
Vysoké Tatry
Nízke Tatry
SLOVAKIA
Bratislava
Košice
Vienna (Wien)
Linz
Graz
Salzburg
AUSTRIA
Budapest
HUNGARY
Lake Balaton
Győr
Miskolc
SLOVENIA
Maribor
ROMANIA
029
046
F
G
H
I
J
14°
16°
18°
20°
1:3 000 000
0 25 50 75 100 125 miles
0 25 50 75 100 125 150 175 200 km

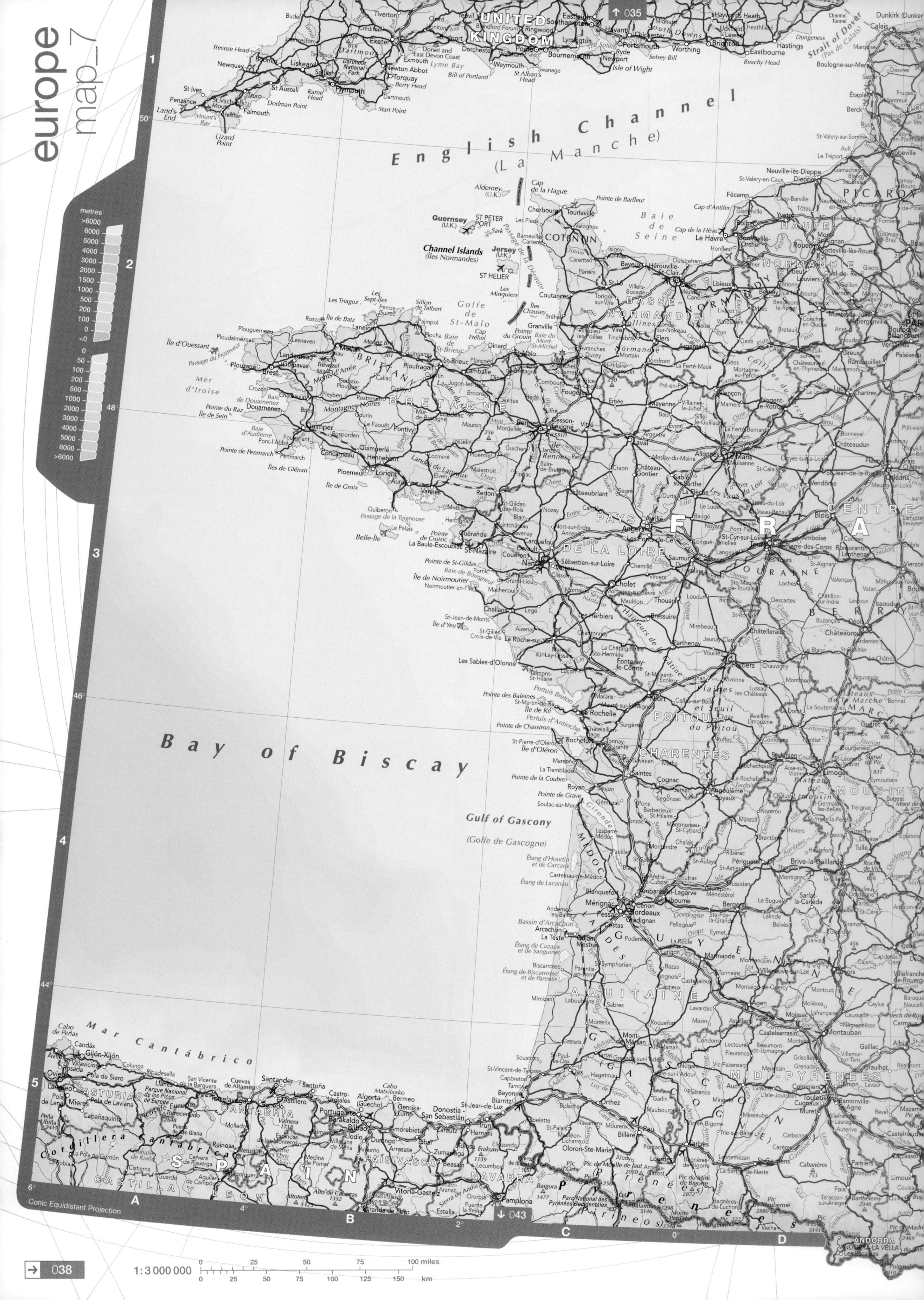
europe
map_7
metres
>6000
6000
5000
4000
3000
2000
1500
1000
500
200
100
0
<0
0
50
100
200
500
1000
2000
3000
4000
5000
6000
>6000
↑ 035
↓ 043
UNITED KINGDOM
English Channel
(La Manche)
Strait of Dover
(Pas de Calais)
Channel Islands
(Îles Normandes)
Guernsey (U.K.)
Jersey (U.K.)
Alderney (U.K.)
ST PETER PORT
ST HELIER
Golfe de St-Malo
Baie de Seine
COTENTIN
HAUTE-NORMANDIE
BASSE-NORMANDIE
PICARDY
BRITTANY
BRETAGNE
PAYS DE LA LOIRE
CENTRE
FRANCE
POITOU-CHARENTES
LIMOUSIN
AQUITAINE
MIDI-PYRÉNÉES
Bay of Biscay
Gulf of Gascony
(Golfe de Gascogne)
Mar Cantábrico
SPAIN
ASTURIAS
CANTABRIA
PAÍS VASCO
NAVARRA
CASTILLA Y LEÓN
Cordillera Cantábrica
Pyrénées
(Pirineos)
ANDORRA
ANDORRA LA VELLA
Plymouth
Southampton
Portsmouth
Brighton
Calais
Boulogne-sur-Mer
Cherbourg
Le Havre
Rouen
Caen
Brest
Quimper
Lorient
St-Brieuc
St-Malo
Rennes
Le Mans
Laval
Angers
Tours
Nantes
St-Nazaire
Cholet
La Rochelle
Poitiers
Limoges
Angoulême
Bordeaux
Bayonne
Pau
Toulouse
Montauban
Agen
Santander
Bilbao
Donostia-San Sebastián
Vitoria-Gasteiz
Pamplona
Oviedo
Gijón-Xixón
50°
48°
46°
44°
6°
4°
2°
0°
1
2
3
4
5
A
B
C
D
Conic Equidistant Projection
1:3 000 000
0
25
50
75
100 miles
0
25
50
75
100
125
150
km

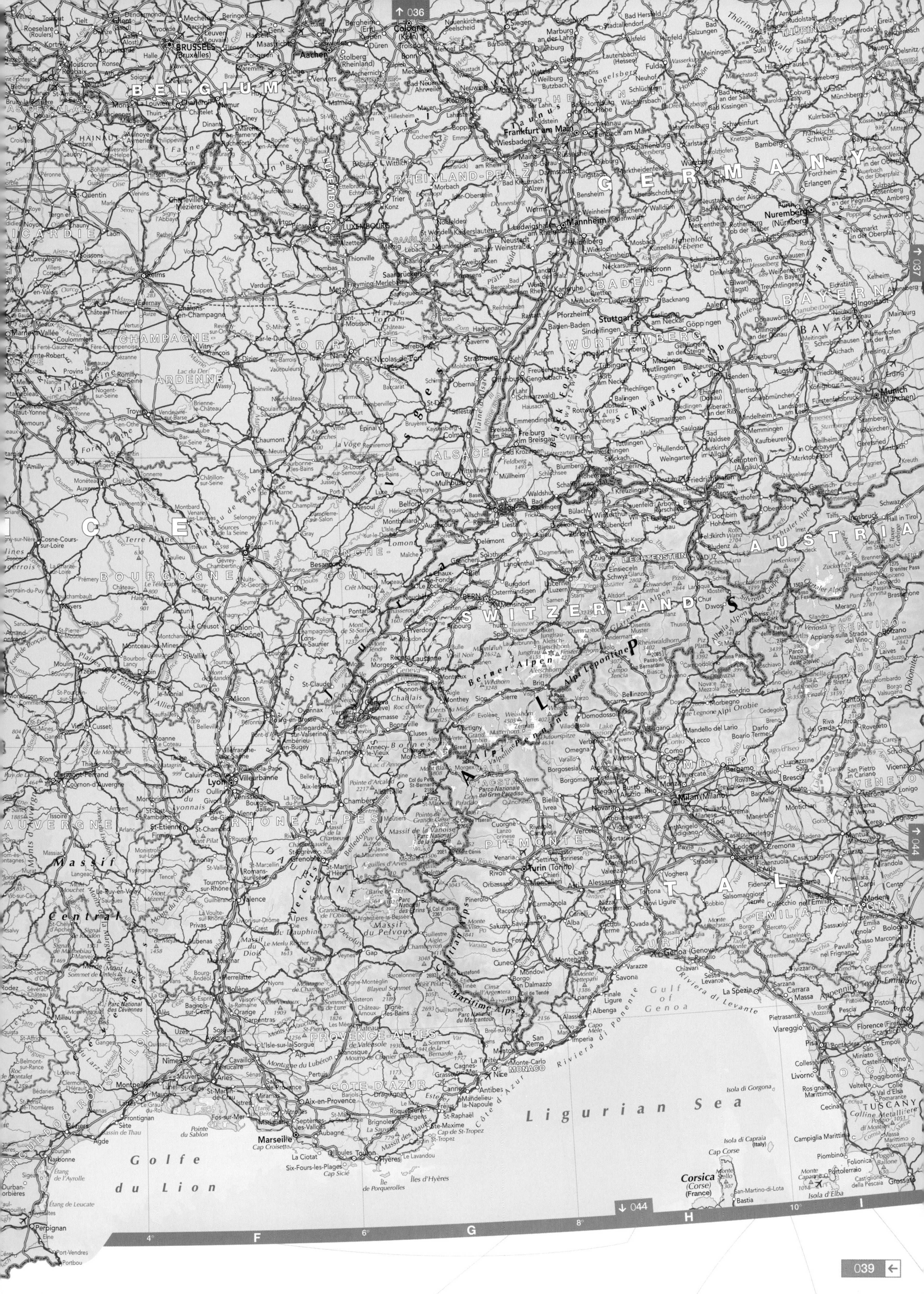

↑ 036
↑ 037
↑ 044
↓ 044
BELGIUM
GERMANY
LUXEMBOURG
SWITZERLAND
LIECHTENSTEIN
AUSTRIA
ITALY
MONACO
BAVARIA
BAYERN
BADEN-WÜRTTEMBERG
HESSEN
RHEINLAND-PFALZ
SAARLAND
THÜRINGEN
LORRAINE
ALSACE
CHAMPAGNE-ARDENNE
BOURGOGNE
FRANCHE-COMTÉ
RHÔNE-ALPES
AUVERGNE
PROVENCE-ALPES-CÔTE-D'AZUR
PIEMONTE
LOMBARDIA
LIGURIA
EMILIA-ROMAGNA
VENETO
TOSCANA
TUSCANY
TRENTINO-ALTO ADIGE
Massif Central
Vosges
Jura
ALPS
Berner Alpen
Alpi Lepontine
Maritime Alps
Cottian Alps
Black Forest
Schwäbische Alb
Ligurian Sea
Golfe du Lion
Gulf of Genoa
Lake Geneva
Corsica (Corse) (France)
Brussels (Bruxelles)
Frankfurt am Main
Stuttgart
Munich (München)
Nuremberg (Nürnberg)
Mannheim
Strasbourg
Lyon
Marseille
Turin (Torino)
Milan (Milano)
Genoa (Genova)
Geneva (Genève)
Bern
Zürich
Nice
4°
6°
8°
10°
F
G
H
I

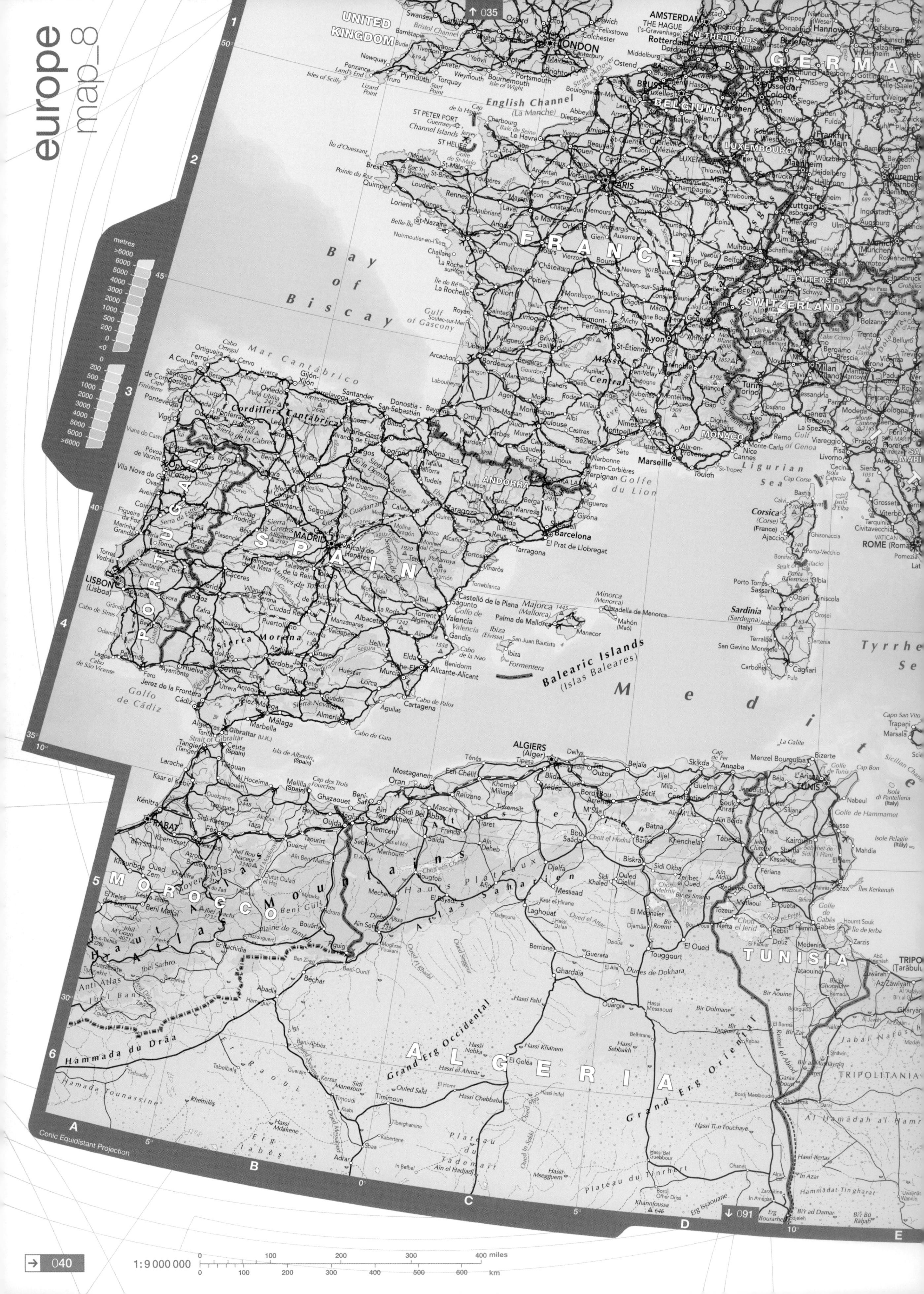
europe
map_8
↑ 035
↓ 091
→ 040
metres
>6000
6000
5000
4000
3000
2000
1000
500
200
0
<0
0
200
500
1000
2000
3000
4000
5000
6000
>6000
1:9 000 000
0 100 200 300 400 miles
0 100 200 300 400 500 600 km
Conic Equidistant Projection
UNITED KINGDOM
LONDON
AMSTERDAM
THE HAGUE ('s-Gravenhage)
NETHERLANDS
BRUSSELS (Bruxelles)
BELGIUM
LUXEMBOURG
GERMANY
English Channel (La Manche)
Channel Islands
FRANCE
PARIS
Bay of Biscay
Gulf of Gascony
Massif Central
Mar Cantábrico
Cordillera Cantábrica
SWITZERLAND
LIECHTENSTEIN
MONACO
ANDORRA
PORTUGAL
LISBON (Lisboa)
SPAIN
MADRID
Sierra Morena
Balearic Islands (Islas Baleares)
Majorca (Mallorca)
Minorca (Menorca)
Ibiza (Eivissa)
Golfe du Lion
Ligurian Sea
Corsica (Corse) (France)
Sardinia (Sardegna) (Italy)
ROME (Roma)
Tyrrhenian Sea
Mediterranean
Barcelona
Marseille
Valencia
Gibraltar (U.K.)
Strait of Gibraltar
Golfo de Cádiz
MOROCCO
RABAT
Haut Atlas
Anti Atlas
ALGIERS (Alger)
ALGERIA
Grand Erg Occidental
Grand Erg Oriental
Hammada du Drâa
Plateau du Tademaït
Plateau du Tinrhert
TUNIS
TUNISIA
TRIPOLITANIA
Al Hamādah al Hamrā'

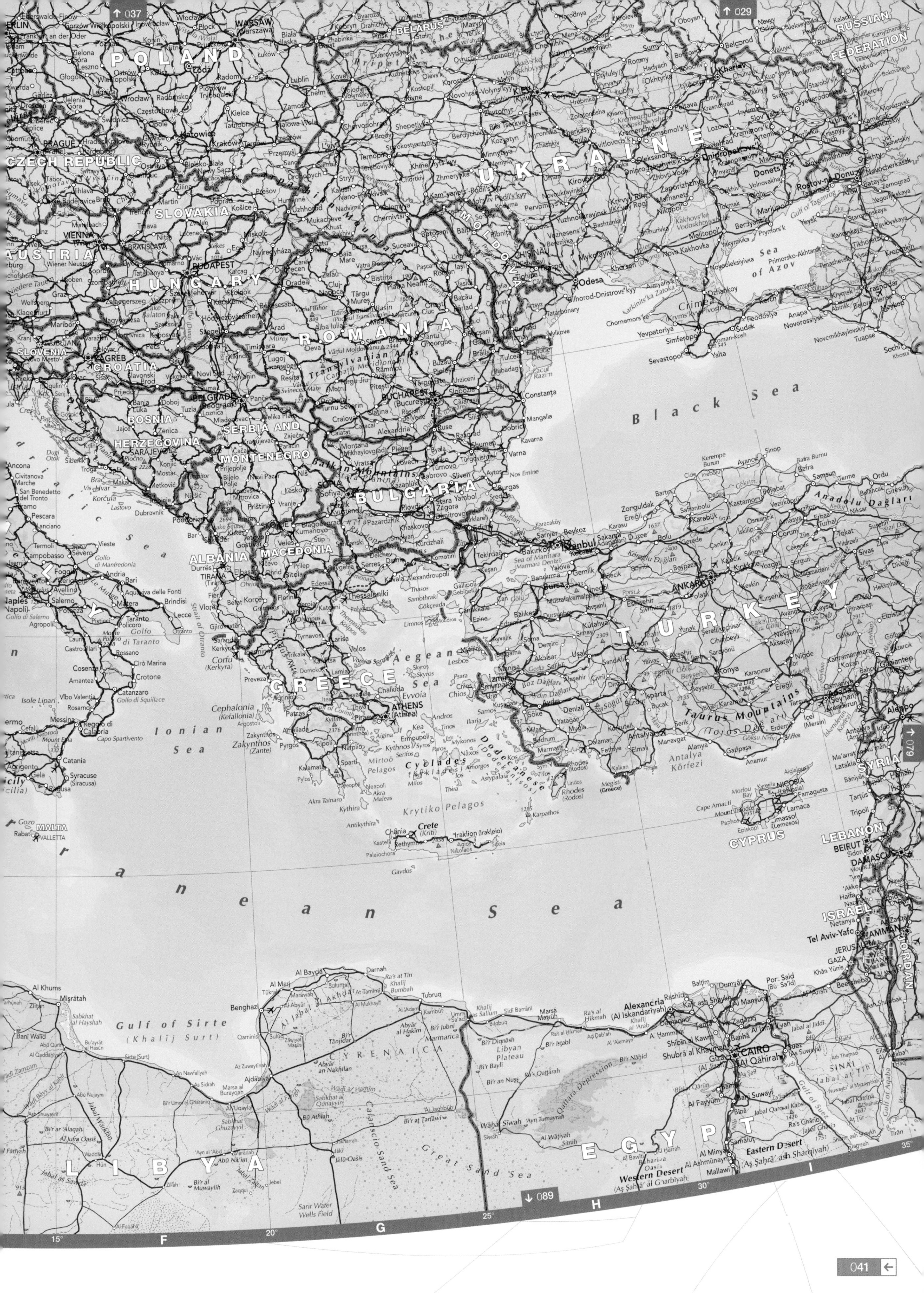

↑ 037
↑ 029
POLAND
WARSAW
BELARUS
RUSSIAN FEDERATION
UKRAINE
Kyiv
Kharkiv
Odesa
CZECH REPUBLIC
PRAGUE
SLOVAKIA
VIENNA
AUSTRIA
BRATISLAVA
BUDAPEST
HUNGARY
MOLDOVA
CHIŞINĂU
ROMANIA
Transylvanian Alps
BUCHAREST
Sea of Azov
Crimea
Black Sea
SLOVENIA
LJUBLJANA
ZAGREB
CROATIA
BOSNIA-HERZEGOVINA
SARAJEVO
BELGRADE (Beograd)
SERBIA AND MONTENEGRO
BULGARIA
SOFIA (Sofiya)
Balkan Mountains
SKOPJE
MACEDONIA
ALBANIA
TIRANA
ITALY
Istanbul
ANKARA
TURKEY
Anadolu Dağları
Taurus Mountains (Toros Dağları)
Sea of Marmara
GREECE
ATHENS (Athína)
Aegean Sea
Ionian Sea
Cyclades (Kykládes)
Dodecanese (Dodekanisos)
Krytiko Pelagos
Crete (Kriti)
Strait of Otranto
Golfo di Taranto
MALTA
VALLETTA
Mediterranean Sea
CYPRUS
NICOSIA
SYRIA
LEBANON
BEIRUT
DAMASCUS
ISRAEL
Tel Aviv-Yafo
JERUSALEM
AMMAN
JORDAN
GAZA
↑ 079
Gulf of Sirte (Khalīj Surt)
CYRENAICA
LIBYA
Benghazi
Libyan Plateau
Qattara Depression
Great Sand Sea
Calanscio Sand Sea
EGYPT
Alexandria (Al Iskandarīyah)
CAIRO (Al Qāhirah)
Western Desert (Aş Şahrā' al Gharbīyah)
Eastern Desert (Aş Şahrā' ash Sharqīyah)
SINAI
↓ 089
15°
20°
25°
30°
35°
F
G
H
I

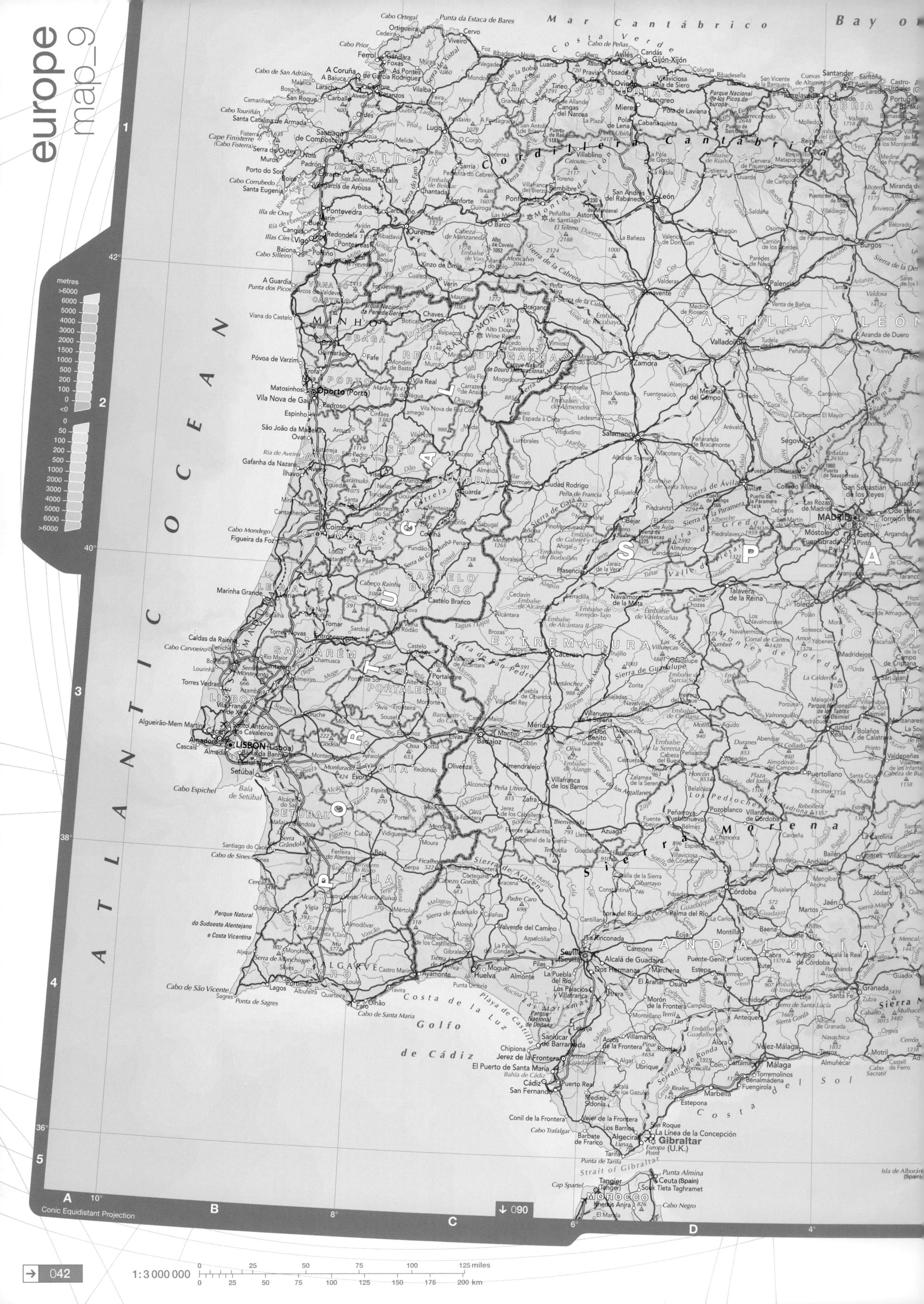
europe
map_9
Mar Cantábrico
Bay o
ATLANTIC OCEAN
PORTUGAL
SPAIN
Cordillera Cantábrica
GALICIA
ASTURIAS
CANTABRIA
CASTILLA Y LEÓN
EXTREMADURA
ANDALUCIA
MADRID
Sierra Morena
Sierra de Gredos
Montes de Toledo
Sierra de Aracena
Golfo de Cádiz
Costa de la Luz
Costa del Sol
Strait of Gibraltar
MOROCCO
Gibraltar (U.K.)
Ceuta (Spain)
MINHO
BRAGA
VIANA DO CASTELO
VILA REAL
BRAGANÇA
TRÁS-OS-MONTES
PORTO
AVEIRO
VISEU
GUARDA
COIMBRA
CASTELO BRANCO
LEIRIA
SANTARÉM
LISBOA
PORTALEGRE
ÉVORA
SETÚBAL
BEJA
ALGARVE
FARO
A Coruña
Santiago de Compostela
Oviedo
Gijón-Xijón
Santander
León
Burgos
Valladolid
Zamora
Salamanca
Segovia
Ávila
Toledo
Cáceres
Badajoz
Mérida
Ciudad Real
Córdoba
Jaén
Sevilla
Huelva
Cádiz
Jerez de la Frontera
Málaga
Granada
Porto
Oporto (Porto)
Coimbra
LISBON (Lisboa)
Setúbal
Évora
Faro
Cape Finisterre (Cabo Fisterra)
Cabo de São Vicente
Cabo Espichel
Cabo Trafalgar
Tarifa
Tangier (Tanger)
metres
>6000
6000
5000
4000
3000
2000
1500
1000
500
200
100
0
<0
0
50
100
200
500
1000
2000
3000
4000
5000
6000
>6000
1
2
3
4
5
A
B
C
D
10°
8°
6°
4°
42°
40°
38°
36°
Conic Equidistant Projection
↓ 090
1:3 000 000
0 25 50 75 100 125 miles
0 25 50 75 100 125 150 175 200 km

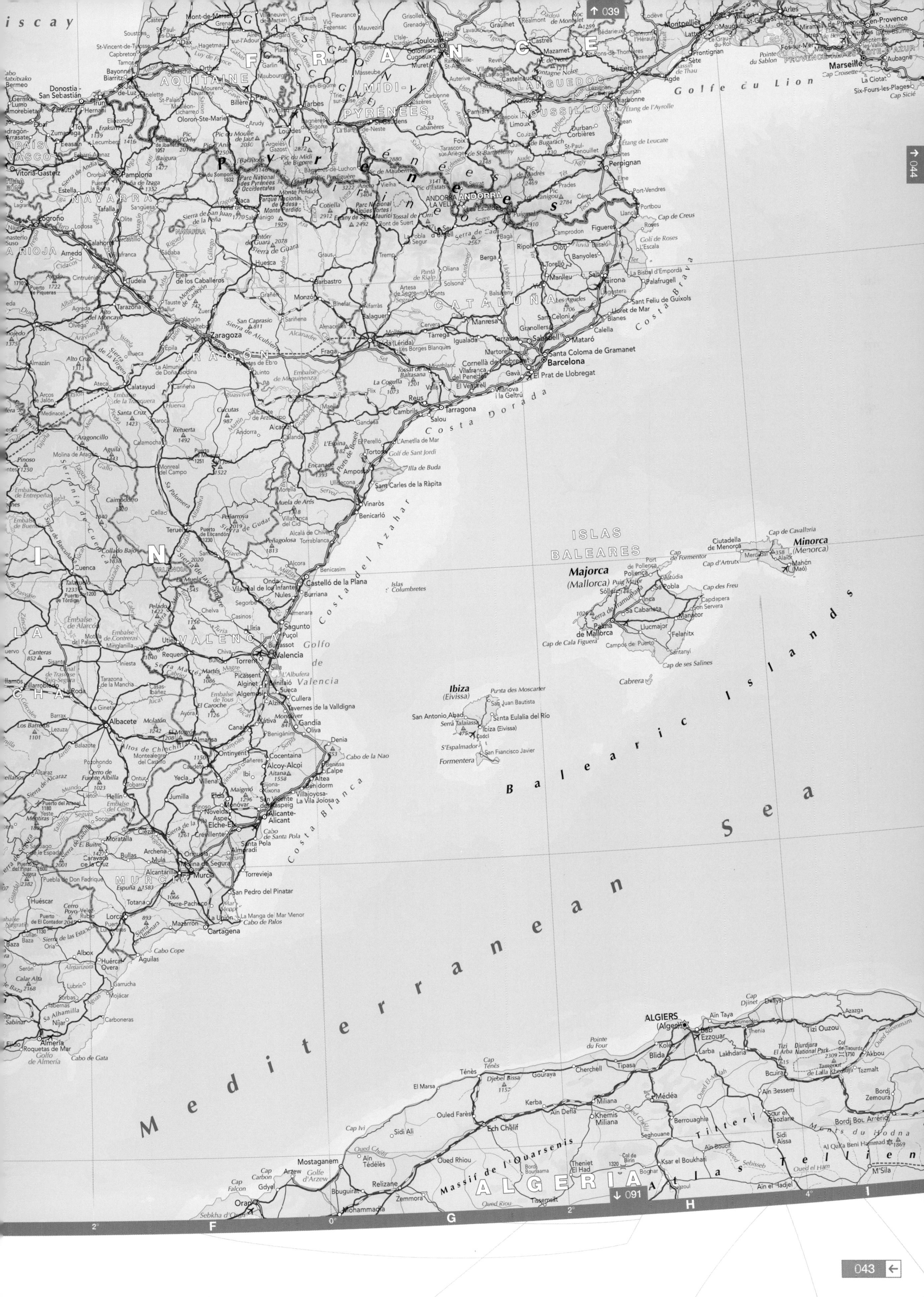

F R A N C E
AQUITAINE
MIDI-PYRÉNÉES
LANGUEDOC
ROUSSILLON
PROVENCE-ALPES-CÔTE-D'AZUR
Golfe du Lion
Montpellier
Marseille
Toulouse
Perpignan
Béziers
Narbonne
Carcassonne
Tarbes
Pau
Bayonne
Biarritz
Donostia - San Sebastián
Vitoria-Gasteiz
Pamplona
Logroño
NAVARRA
PAÍS VASCO
LA RIOJA
P y r é n é e s
P i r i n e o s
ANDORRA
ANDORRA LA VELLA
Zaragoza
ARAGÓN
Huesca
Lleida (Lérida)
CATALUÑA
Barcelona
Girona
Tarragona
Costa Brava
Costa Dorada
Teruel
Castelló de la Plana
Costa del Azahar
Valencia
VALENCIA
Golfo de Valencia
Cuenca
Albacete
Alicante-Alicant
Costa Blanca
Murcia
MURCIA
Cartagena
Almería
Golfo de Almería
ISLAS BALEARES
Majorca (Mallorca)
Palma de Mallorca
Minorca (Menorca)
Ibiza (Eivissa)
Formentera
Cabrera
Balearic Islands
Mediterranean Sea
ALGIERS (Alger)
Oran
Mostaganem
Tizi Ouzou
Blida
Médéa
Ech Chélif
ALGERIA
Atlas Tellien
Massif de l'Ouarsenis

↑ 039
↑ 044
↓ 091

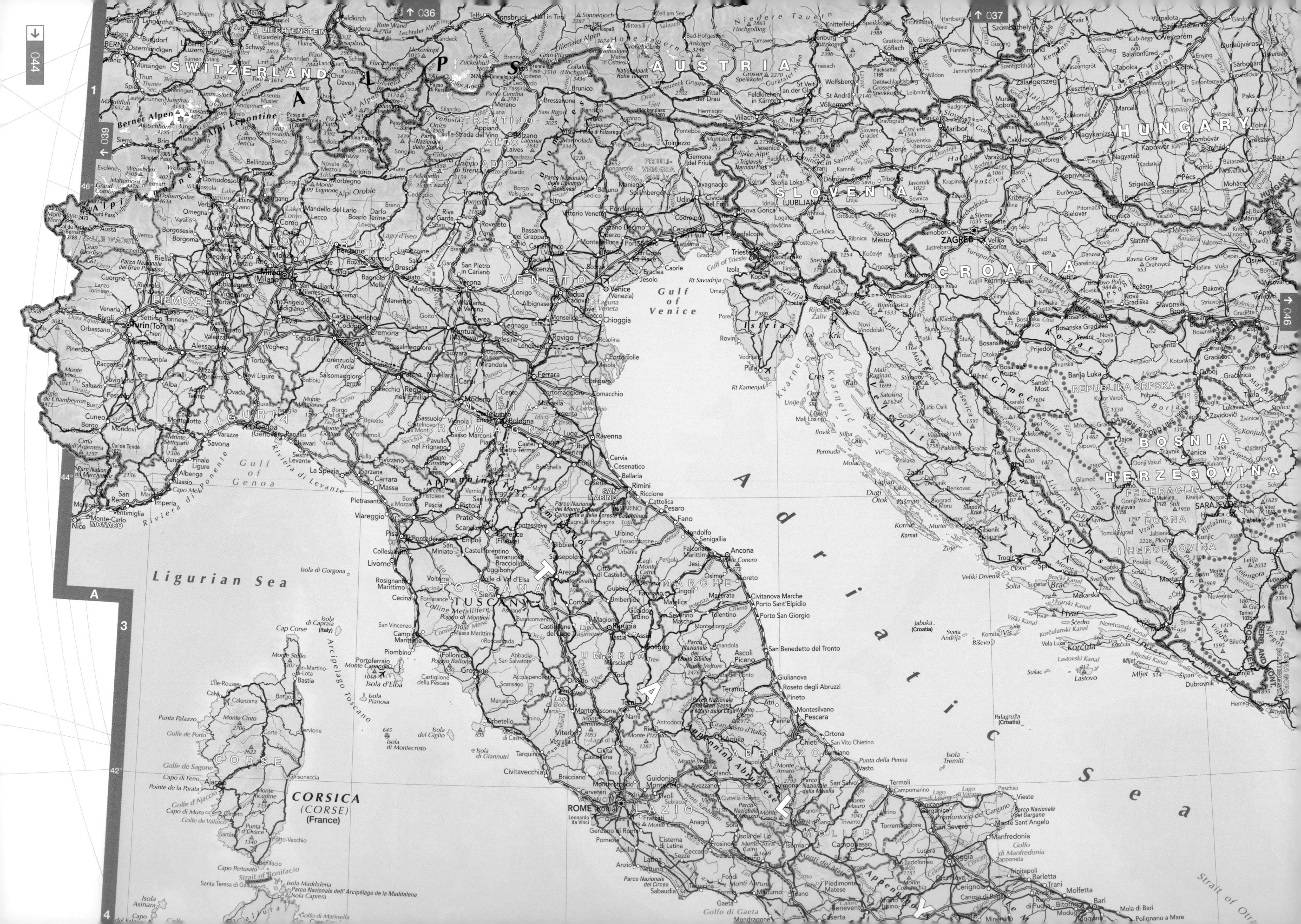

SWITZERLAND
LIECHTENSTEIN
AUSTRIA
A L P S
SLOVENIA
CROATIA
HUNGARY
BOSNIA-HERZEGOVINA
REPUBLIKA SRPSKA
FEDERACIJA BOSNA I HERCEGOVINA
I T A L Y
TRENTINO-ALTO ADIGE
FRIULI-VENEZIA GIULIA
LOMBARDIA
PIEMONTE
VENETO
LIGURIA
EMILIA-ROMAGNA
TOSCANA
TUSCANY
MARCHE
UMBRIA
ABRUZZO
LAZIO
MOLISE
CORSICA
(CORSE)
(France)
CORSE
Adriatic Sea
Ligurian Sea
Gulf of Venice
Gulf of Genoa
Gulf of Trieste
Riviera di Ponente
Riviera di Levante
Arcipelago Toscano
Strait of Bonifacio
Golfo di Gaeta
Appennino Tosco-Emiliano
Appennino Abruzzese
Alpi Lepontine
Alpi Orobie
Berner Alpen
Dolomiti
Velebit
Dinaric Alps
Kvarner
Istria
ROME
Milano (Milan)
Turin (Torino)
Genova (Genoa)
Venice (Venezia)
Bologna
Firenze (Florence)
Verona
Trieste
LJUBLJANA
ZAGREB
SARAJEVO
Ancona
Pescara
Perugia
Rijeka
Split
Dubrovnik
Bastia
Ajaccio
MONACO
SAN MARINO
Nice
Bern
Innsbruck
Graz
Pécs
Banja Luka
Bari
Foggia
Livorno
Pisa
La Spezia
Ravenna
Rimini
Pula
Zadar
Mostar
↑ 036
↑ 037
↑ 046
↓ 039
→ 044
A
1
3
4
46°
44°
42°

Tyrrhenian Sea

Ionian Sea

Mediterranean Sea

Golfo di Taranto

SARDINIA (SARDEGNA) (Italy)

SICILY (SICILIA)

CALABRIA

BASILICATA

Appennino Lucano

Isole Lipari

Sicilian Channel

MALTA

VALLETTA

TUNISIA

TUNIS

ALGERIA

Golfe de Tunis

Golfe de Hammamet

Isole Pelagie (Italy)

Isola di Lampedusa

Isola di Pantelleria (Italy)

Canal de la Galite

Palermo

Catania

Messina

Reggio di Calabria

Siracusa (Syracuse)

Taormina

Marsala

Trapani

Agrigento

Caltanissetta

Cagliari

Sassari

Oristano

Taranto

Brindisi

Salerno

Mount Etna

1:3 000 000

Conic Equidistant Projection

0   25   50   75   100   125 miles
0   25   50   75   100   125   150   175   200 km

metres
>6000
6000
5000
4000
3000
2000
1500
1000
500
200
100
0
<0

0
50
100
200
500
1000
2000
3000
4000
5000
6000
>6000

↑ 047
→ 091
↓ 091

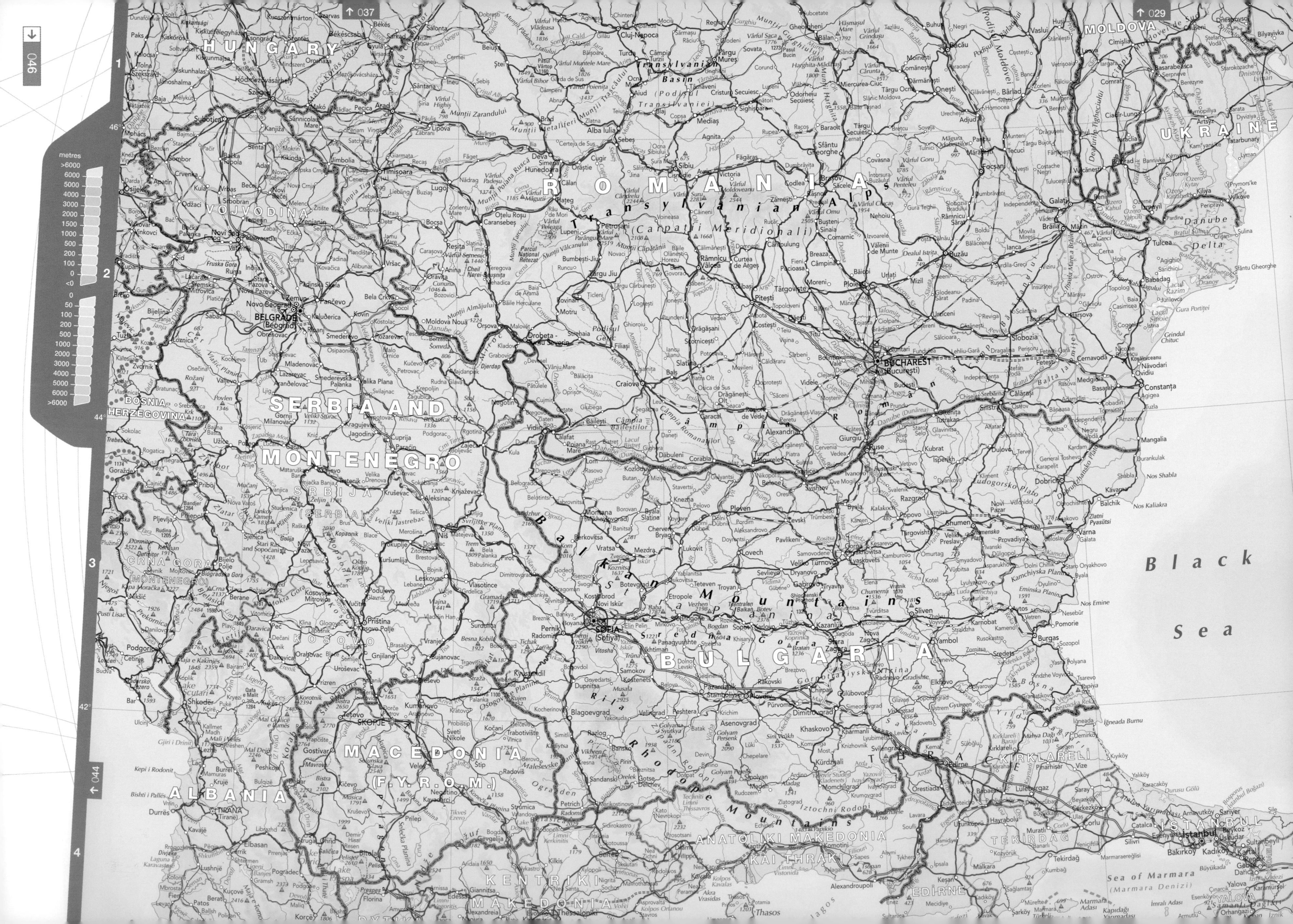

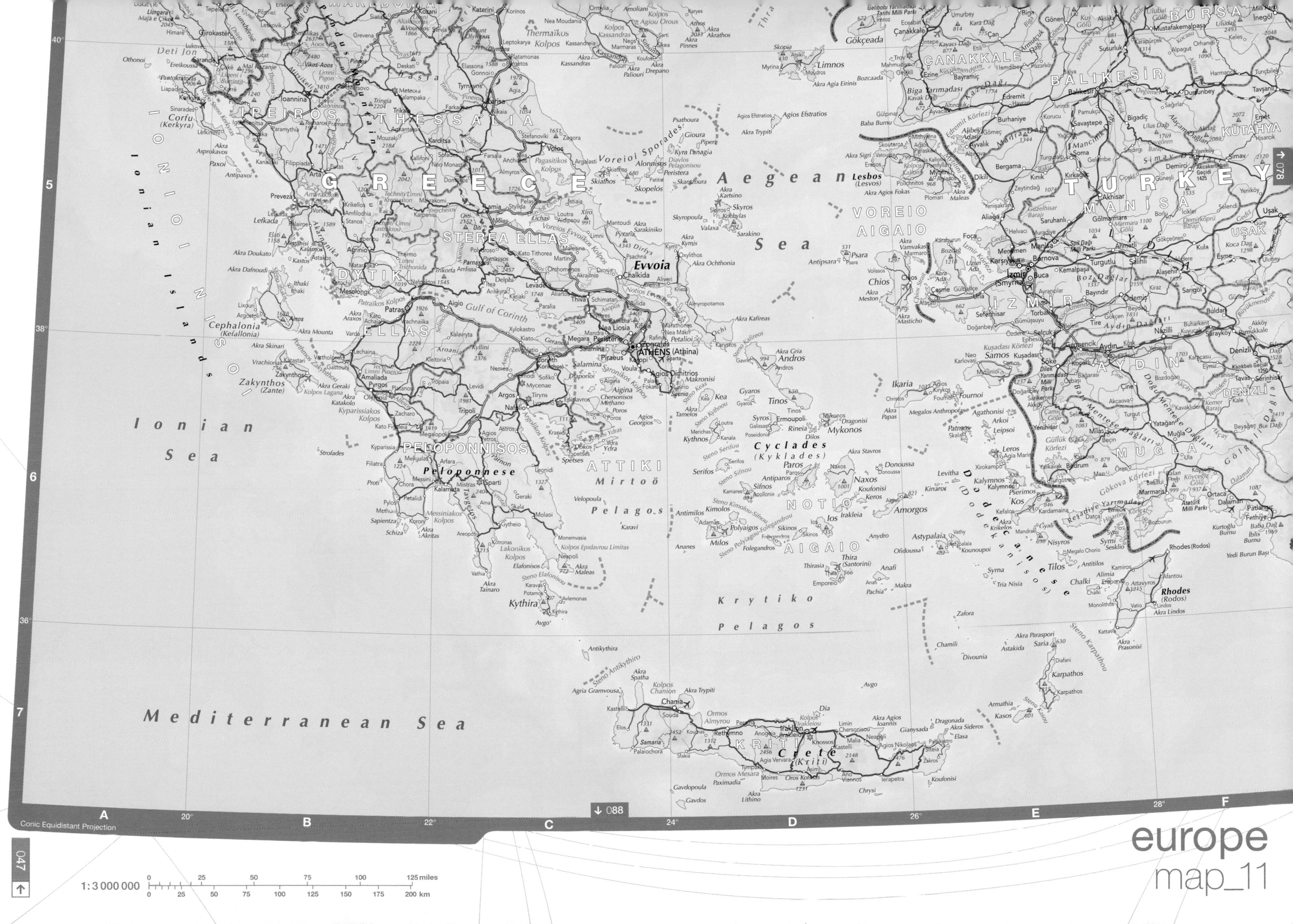

↑ 078

↓ 088

1:3 000 000

Conic Equidistant Projection

0   25   50   75   100   125 miles
0 25 50 75 100 125 150 175 200 km

T U R K E Y

BURSA
KÜTAHYA
MANISA
BALIKESİR
ÇANAKKALE
UŞAK
İZMİR
AYDIN
DENİZLİ
MUĞLA

Rhodes (Rodos)

Karpathos

Thrace

G R E E C E

THESSALIA
STEREA ELLAS
DYTIKI ELLAS
ATTIKI
PELOPONNISOS
HPEIROS
Pindus Mountains

ATHENS (Athina)
Piraeus
Chalkida
Evvoia

Voreioi Sporades

VOREIO AIGAIO

Lesbos (Lesvos)
Limnos
Chios
Samos
Ikaria

A e g e a n   S e a

Dodecanese (Dodekanisos)
Kos
Leros
Patmos

Cyclades (Kyklades)
Naxos
Paros
Andros
Tinos
Mykonos
Thira (Santorini)
Milos

NOTIO AIGAIO

Krytiko Pelagos

Mirtoö Pelagos

Kythira

I o n i a n   S e a

Cephalonia (Kefallonia)
Zakynthos (Zante)
Corfu (Kerkyra)

I o n i a n   I s l a n d s

K R I T I   Crete (Kriti)
Iraklion
Chania
Rethymno

M e d i t e r r a n e a n   S e a

Gulf of Corinth

A   B   C   D   E   F

5   6   7

40 38 36

20° 22° 24° 26° 28°

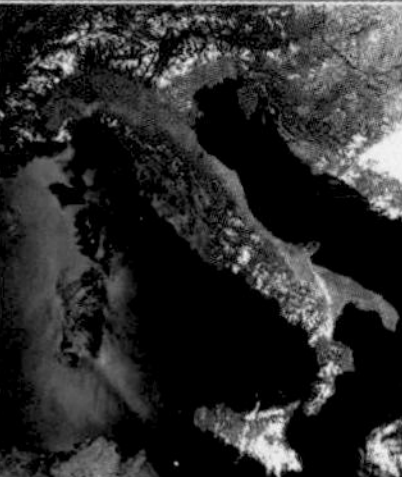

Italy

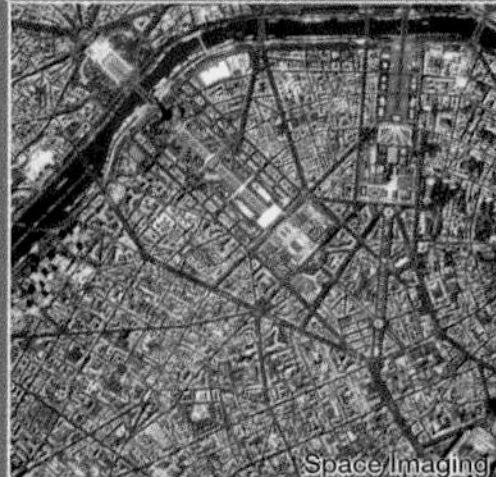

Paris, France

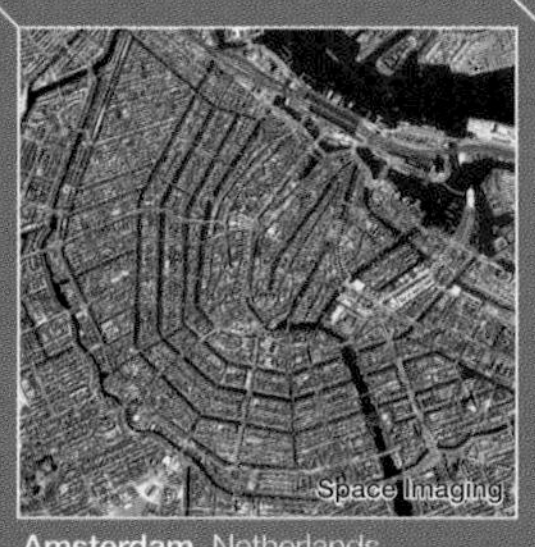

Amsterdam, Netherlands

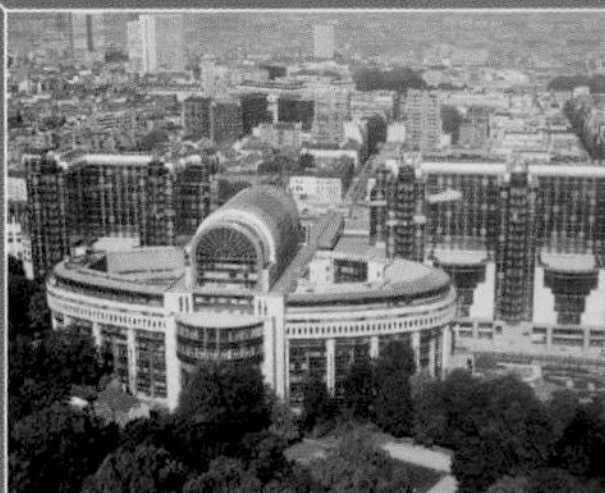

Brussels, Belgium

COUNTRIES		area sq km	area sq miles	population	capital	languages	religions	currency	map
ALBANIA		28 748	11 100	3 145 000	Tirana	Albanian, Greek	Sunni Muslim, Albanian Orthodox, Roman Catholic	Lek	46–47
ANDORRA		465	180	90 000	Andorra la Vella	Spanish, Catalan, French	Roman Catholic	Euro	43
AUSTRIA		83 855	32 377	8 075 000	Vienna	German, Croatian, Turkish	Roman Catholic, Protestant	Euro	36–37
BELARUS		207 600	80 155	10 147 000	Minsk	Belorussian, Russian	Belorussian Orthodox, Roman Catholic	Belarus rouble	31
BELGIUM		30 520	11 784	10 264 000	Brussels	Dutch (Flemish), French (Walloon), German	Roman Catholic, Protestant	Euro	36
BOSNIA-HERZEGOVINA		51 130	19 741	4 067 000	Sarajevo	Bosnian, Serbian, Croatian	Sunni Muslim, Serbian Orthodox, Roman Catholic, Protestant	Marka	44
BULGARIA		110 994	42 855	7 867 000	Sofia	Bulgarian, Turkish, Romany, Macedonian	Bulgarian Orthodox, Sunni Muslim	Lev	46
CROATIA		56 538	21 829	4 655 000	Zagreb	Croatian, Serbian	Roman Catholic, Serbian Orthodox, Sunni Muslim	Kuna	44
CZECH REPUBLIC		78 864	30 450	10 260 000	Prague	Czech, Moravian, Slovak	Roman Catholic, Protestant	Czech koruna	37
DENMARK		43 075	16 631	5 333 000	Copenhagen	Danish	Protestant	Danish krone	33
ESTONIA		45 200	17 452	1 377 000	Tallinn	Estonian, Russian	Protestant, Estonian and Russian Orthodox	Kroon	33
FINLAND		338 145	130 559	5 178 000	Helsinki	Finnish, Swedish	Protestant, Greek Orthodox	Euro	32–33
FRANCE		543 965	210 026	59 453 000	Paris	French, Arabic	Roman Catholic, Protestant, Sunni Muslim	Euro	38–39
GERMANY		357 028	137 849	82 007 000	Berlin	German, Turkish	Protestant, Roman Catholic	Euro	36–37
GREECE		131 957	50 949	10 623 000	Athens	Greek	Greek Orthodox, Sunni Muslim	Euro	46–47
HUNGARY		93 030	35 919	9 917 000	Budapest	Hungarian	Roman Catholic, Protestant	Forint	31
ICELAND		102 820	39 699	281 000	Reykjavik	Icelandic	Protestant	Icelandic króna	32
IRELAND, REPUBLIC OF		70 282	27 136	3 841 000	Dublin	English, Irish	Roman Catholic, Protestant	Euro	34–35
ITALY		301 245	116 311	57 503 000	Rome	Italian	Roman Catholic	Euro	44–45
LATVIA		63 700	24 595	2 406 000	Riga	Latvian, Russian	Protestant, Roman Catholic, Russian Orthodox	Lats	33
LIECHTENSTEIN		160	62	33 000	Vaduz	German	Roman Catholic, Protestant	Swiss franc	39
LITHUANIA		65 200	25 174	3 689 000	Vilnius	Lithuanian, Russian, Polish	Roman Catholic, Protestant, Russian Orthodox	Litas	33
LUXEMBOURG		2 586	998	442 000	Luxembourg	Letzeburgish, German, French	Roman Catholic	Euro	36
MACEDONIA (F.Y.R.O.M.)		25 713	9 928	2 044 000	Skopje	Macedonian, Albanian, Turkish	Macedonian Orthodox, Sunni Muslim	Macedonian denar	46
MALTA		316	122	392 000	Valletta	Maltese, English	Roman Catholic	Maltese lira	45
MOLDOVA		33 700	13 012	4 285 000	Chişinău	Romanian, Ukrainian, Gagauz, Russian	Romanian Orthodox, Russian Orthodox	Moldovan leu	29
MONACO		2	1	34 000	Monaco-Ville	French, Monegasque, Italian	Roman Catholic	Euro	39
NETHERLANDS		41 526	16 033	15 930 000	Amsterdam/The Hague	Dutch, Frisian	Roman Catholic, Protestant, Sunni Muslim	Euro	36
NORWAY		323 878	125 050	4 488 000	Oslo	Norwegian	Protestant, Roman Catholic	Norwegian krone	32–33
POLAND		312 683	120 728	38 577 000	Warsaw	Polish, German	Roman Catholic, Polish Orthodox	Zloty	37
PORTUGAL		88 940	34 340	10 033 000	Lisbon	Portuguese	Roman Catholic, Protestant	Euro	42
ROMANIA		237 500	91 699	22 388 000	Bucharest	Romanian, Hungarian	Romanian Orthodox, Protestant, Roman Catholic	Romanian leu	31
RUSSIAN FEDERATION		17 075 400	6 592 849	144 664 000	Moscow	Russian, Tatar, Ukrainian, local languages	Russian Orthodox, Sunni Muslim, Protestant	Russian rouble	26–27
SAN MARINO		61	24	27 000	San Marino	Italian	Roman Catholic	Euro	44
SERBIA AND MONTENEGRO		102 173	39 449	10 538 000	Belgrade	Serbian, Albanian, Hungarian	Serbian Orthodox, Montenegrin Orthodox, Sunni Muslim	Dinar, Euro	46
SLOVAKIA		49 035	18 933	5 403 000	Bratislava	Slovak, Hungarian, Czech	Roman Catholic, Protestant, Orthodox	Slovakian koruna	37
SLOVENIA		20 251	7 819	1 985 000	Ljubljana	Slovene, Croatian, Serbian	Roman Catholic, Protestant	Tolar	44
SPAIN		504 782	194 897	39 921 000	Madrid	Castilian, Catalan, Galician, Basque	Roman Catholic	Euro	42–43
SWEDEN		449 964	173 732	8 833 000	Stockholm	Swedish	Protestant, Roman Catholic	Swedish krona	32–33
SWITZERLAND		41 293	15 943	7 170 000	Bern	German, French, Italian, Romansch	Roman Catholic, Protestant	Swiss franc	39
UKRAINE		603 700	233 090	49 112 000	Kiev	Ukrainian, Russian	Ukrainian Orthodox, Ukrainian Catholic, Roman Catholic	Hryvnia	29
UNITED KINGDOM		244 082	94 241	59 542 000	London	English, Welsh, Gaelic	Protestant, Roman Catholic, Muslim	Pound sterling	34–35
VATICAN CITY		0.5	0.2	480	Vatican City	Italian	Roman Catholic	Euro	44

DEPENDENT TERRITORIES		territorial status	area sq km	area sq miles	population	capital	languages	religions	currency	map
Azores		Autonomous Region of Portugal	2 300	888	243 600	Ponta Delgada	Portuguese	Roman Catholic, Protestant	Euro	160
Faroe Islands		Self-governing Danish Territory	1 399	540	47 000	Tórshavn	Faroese, Danish	Protestant	Danish krone	34
Gibraltar		United Kingdom Overseas Territory	7	3	27 000	Gibraltar	English, Spanish	Roman Catholic, Protestant, Sunni Muslim	Gibraltar pound	42
Guernsey		United Kingdom Crown Dependency	78	30	64 555	St Peter Port	English, French	Protestant, Roman Catholic	Pound sterling	35
Isle of Man		United Kingdom Crown Dependency	572	221	76 000	Douglas	English	Protestant, Roman Catholic	Pound sterling	35
Jersey		United Kingdom Crown Dependency	116	45	89 136	St Helier	English, French	Protestant, Roman Catholic	Pound sterling	38

asia

contents

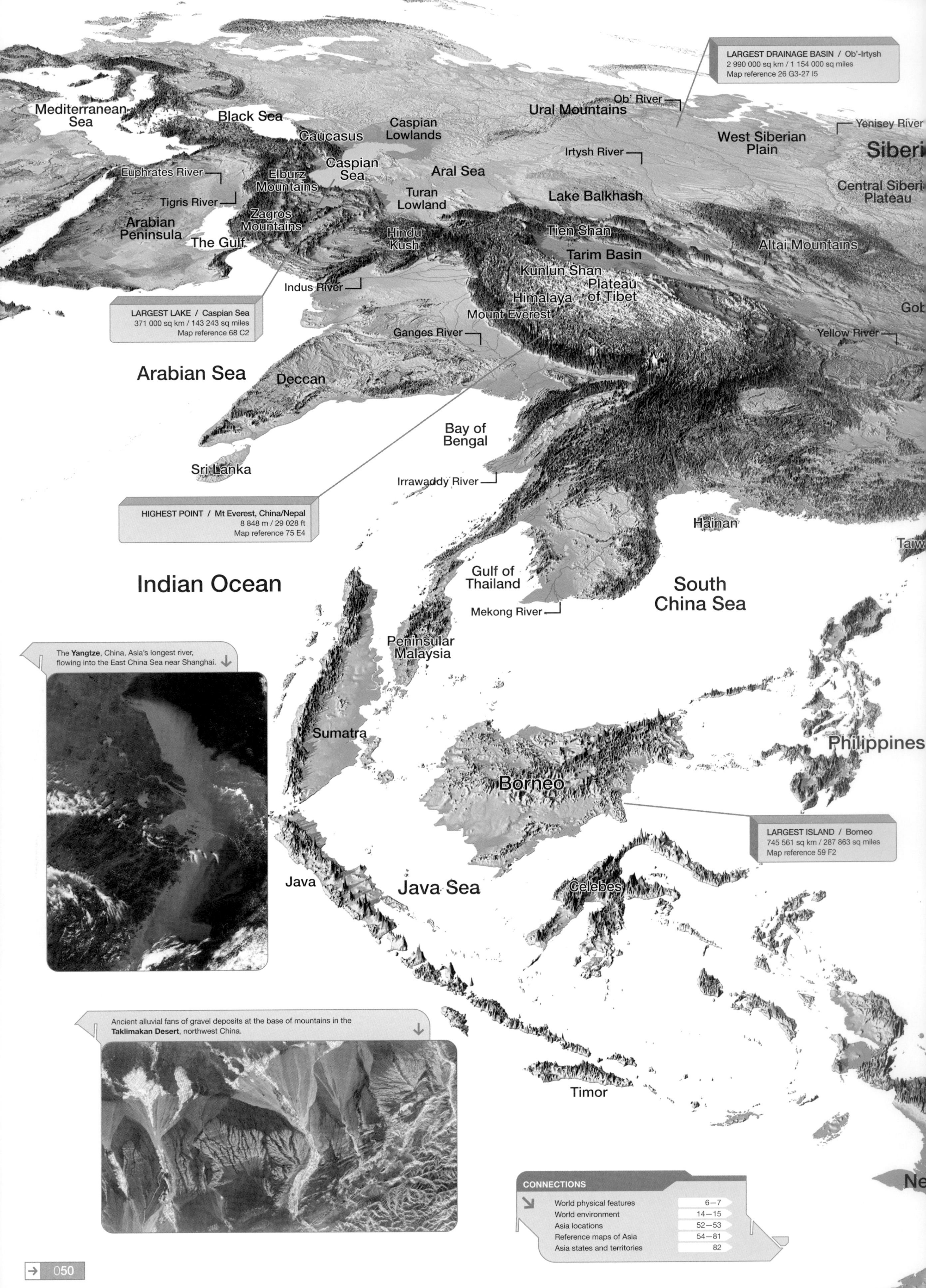

Mediterranean Sea

Black Sea

Caucasus

Caspian Lowlands

LARGEST DRAINAGE BASIN / Ob'-Irtysh
2 990 000 sq km / 1 154 000 sq miles
Map reference 26 G3-27 I5

Ural Mountains

Ob' River

West Siberian Plain

Siberi

Yenisey River

Irtysh River

Caspian Sea

Aral Sea

Euphrates River

Elburz Mountains

Turan Lowland

Lake Balkhash

Central Siberian Plateau

Tigris River

Zagros Mountains

Arabian Peninsula

The Gulf

Hindu Kush

Tien Shan

Altai Mountains

Tarim Basin

Kunlun Shan

Plateau of Tibet

Indus River

Himalaya

Mount Everest

Gob

LARGEST LAKE / Caspian Sea
371 000 sq km / 143 243 sq miles
Map reference 68 C2

Yellow River

Arabian Sea

Deccan

Ganges River

Sri Lanka

Bay of Bengal

Irrawaddy River

HIGHEST POINT / Mt Everest, China/Nepal
8 848 m / 29 028 ft
Map reference 75 E4

Hainan

Taiw

Indian Ocean

Gulf of Thailand

Mekong River

South China Sea

The **Yangtze**, China, Asia's longest river, flowing into the East China Sea near Shanghai.

Peninsular Malaysia

Sumatra

Philippines

Borneo

Java

Java Sea

Celebes

LARGEST ISLAND / Borneo
745 561 sq km / 287 863 sq miles
Map reference 59 F2

Timor

Ancient alluvial fans of gravel deposits at the base of mountains in the **Taklimakan Desert**, northwest China.

Ne

CONNECTIONS

Mediterranean Sea
Taurus Mountains
Black Sea
Cyprus
Caucasus
Elburz Mountains
Caspian Sea
Turan Lowland
Hindu Kush
Tien Shan
Kuniun Shan
Tarim Basin
Plateau of Tibet
Gobi
Qin Ling
Manchurian Plain
Bo Hai
Yellow Sea
Korea Strait
Sea of Japan
Honshū
Pacific Ocean

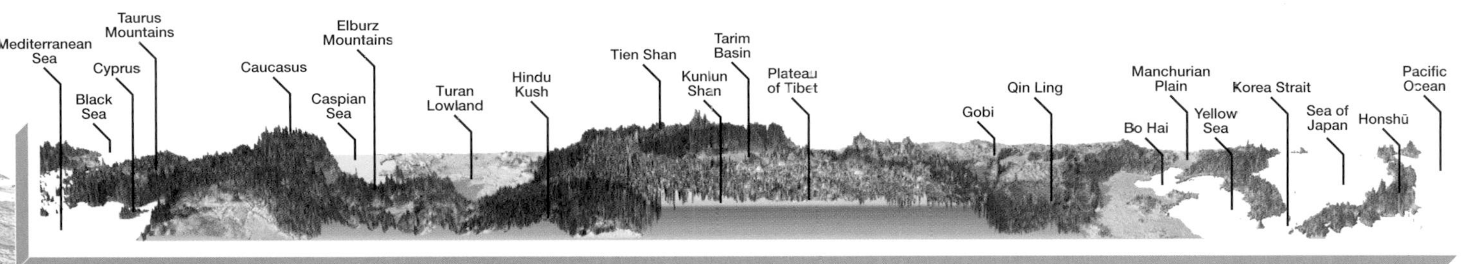

↑ asia cross section

Lena River

Arctic Ocean

Lake Baikal

Argun River

Heilong Jiang River

Sea of Okhotsk

Kamchatka Peninsula

Yangtze River

Yellow Sea

Sea of Japan

East China Sea

Honshū

Ryukyu Islands

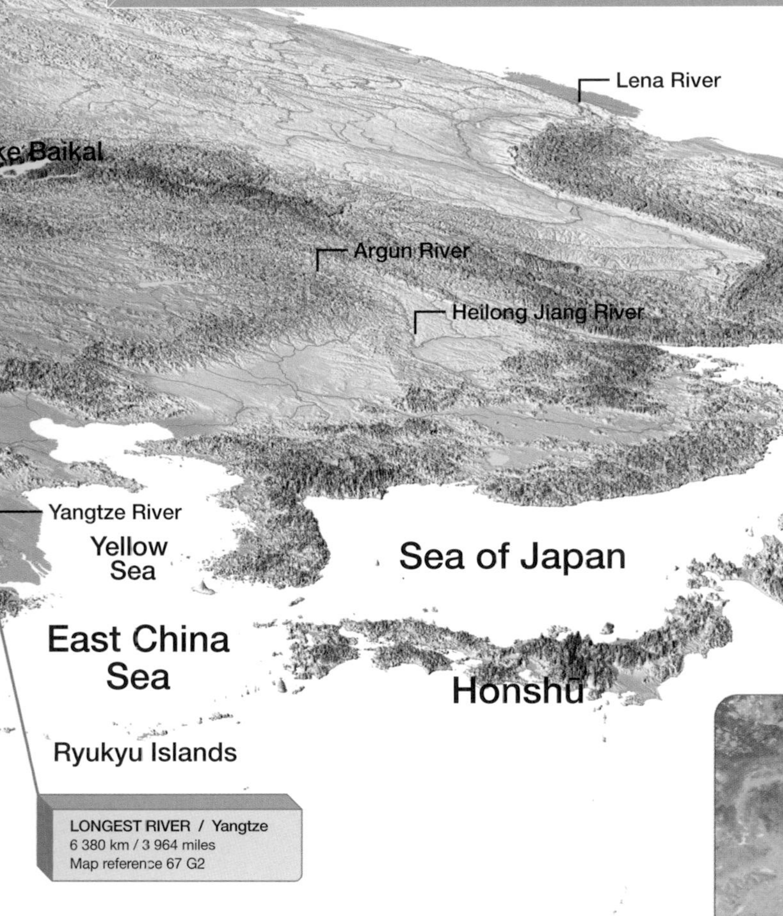

LONGEST RIVER / Yangtze
6 380 km / 3 964 miles
Map reference 67 G2

Pacific Ocean

Northern Mariana Islands

Palau

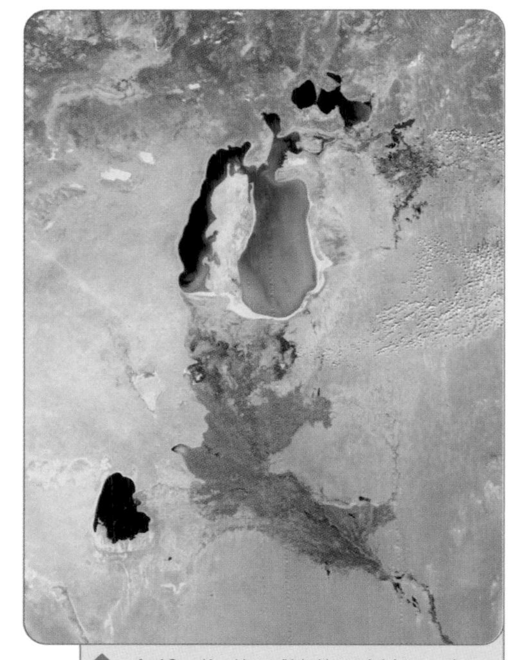

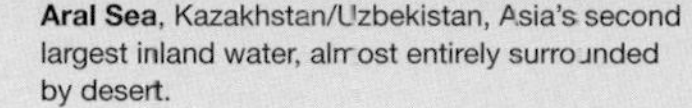

ice and snow covered peaks of volcanic mountains on the **Kamchatka Peninsula**, northeast Russian Federation. ↓

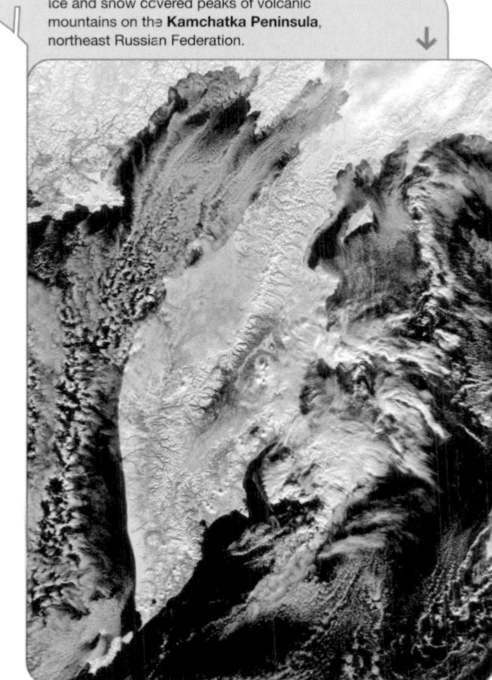

↑ **Aral Sea**, Kazakhstan/Uzbekistan, Asia's second largest inland water, almost entirely surrounded by desert.

uinea

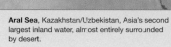

LARGEST ISLANDS	sq km	sq miles	map	LONGEST RIVERS	km	miles	map	HIGHEST MOUNTAINS	metres	feet	map
Borneo	745 561	287 863	59 F2	Yangtze	6 380	3 964	67 G2	Mt Everest, China/Nepal	8 848	29 028	75 E4
Sumatra	473 606	182 860	58 C3	Ob'-Irtysh	5 563	3 459	26 G3–27 I5	K2, China/Jammu and Kashmir	8 611	28 251	74 C2
Honshū	227 414	87 805	65 D6	Yenisey-Angara-Selenga	5 550	3 448	27 I2–K4	Kangchenjunga, India/Nepal	8 586	28 169	75 F4
Celebes	189 216	73 057	57 F6	Yellow	5 464	3 395	63 J4	Lhotse, China/Nepal	8 516	27 939	75 E4
Java	132 188	51 038	59 E4	Irtysh	4 440	2 759	26 G3	Makalu, China/Nepal	8 463	27 765	75 E4
Luzon	104 690	40 421	57 F2	Mekong	4 425	2 749	61 D3	Cho Oyu, China/Nepal	8 201	26 906	75 E3
Mindanao	94 630	36 537	57 F4	Heilong Jiang-Argun'	4 416	2 744	63 M2	Dhaulagiri, Nepal	8 167	26 794	75 D3
Hokkaidō	78 073	30 144	64 E4	Lena-Kirenga	4 400	2 734	27 M2–K4	Manaslu, Nepal	8 163	26 781	75 E3
Sakhalin	76 400	29 498	64 E2	Yenisey	4 090	2 541	27 I2	Nanga Parbat, Jammu and Kashmir	8 126	26 660	74 B2
Sri Lanka	65 610	25 332	72 D5	Ob'	3 701	2 300	26 H3	Annapurna I, Nepal	8 091	26 545	75 D3
Kyūshū	36 554	14 114	65 B6								
Taiwan	35 873	13 851	67 G4								

LARGEST LAKES	sq km	sq miles	map	LAND AREA		map
Caspian Sea	371 000	143 243	68 C2	Total land area	45 036 492 sq km / 17 388 686 sq miles	
Aral Sea	33 640	12 988	70 A2	Most northerly point	Mys Arkticheskiy, Russian Federation	27 J1
Lake Baikal	30 500	11 776	27 K4	Most southerly point	Pamana, Indonesia	57 F8
Lake Balkhash	17 400	6 718	70 D2	Most westerly point	Bozcaada, Turkey	106 A3
Ysyk-Kol	6 200	2 393	70 E3	Most easterly point	Mys Dezhneva, Russian Federation	27 T3

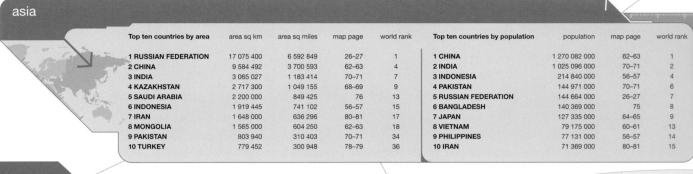

Top ten countries by area	area sq km	area sq miles	map page	world rank	Top ten countries by population	population	map page	world rank
1 RUSSIAN FEDERATION	17 075 400	6 592 849	26–27	1	1 CHINA	1 270 082 000	62–63	1
2 CHINA	9 584 492	3 700 593	62–63	4	2 INDIA	1 025 096 000	70–71	2
3 INDIA	3 065 027	1 183 414	70–71	7	3 INDONESIA	214 840 000	56–57	4
4 KAZAKHSTAN	2 717 300	1 049 155	68–69	9	4 PAKISTAN	144 971 000	70–71	6
5 SAUDI ARABIA	2 200 000	849 425	76	13	5 RUSSIAN FEDERATION	144 664 000	26–27	7
6 INDONESIA	1 919 445	741 102	56–57	15	6 BANGLADESH	140 369 000	75	8
7 IRAN	1 648 000	636 296	80–81	17	7 JAPAN	127 335 000	64–65	9
8 MONGOLIA	1 565 000	604 250	62–63	18	8 VIETNAM	79 175 000	60–61	13
9 PAKISTAN	803 940	310 403	70–71	34	9 PHILIPPINES	77 131 000	56–57	14
10 TURKEY	779 452	300 948	78–79	36	10 IRAN	71 369 000	80–81	15

Terraced agricultural land, **Bali**, Indonesia. ↓

ARM.   ARMENIA
AZ.   AZERBAIJAN
U.A.E.   UNITED ARAB EMIRATES

British Indian
Ocean Territory

↑ **Tōkyō**, administrative financial and
cultural centre, capital city of Japan.

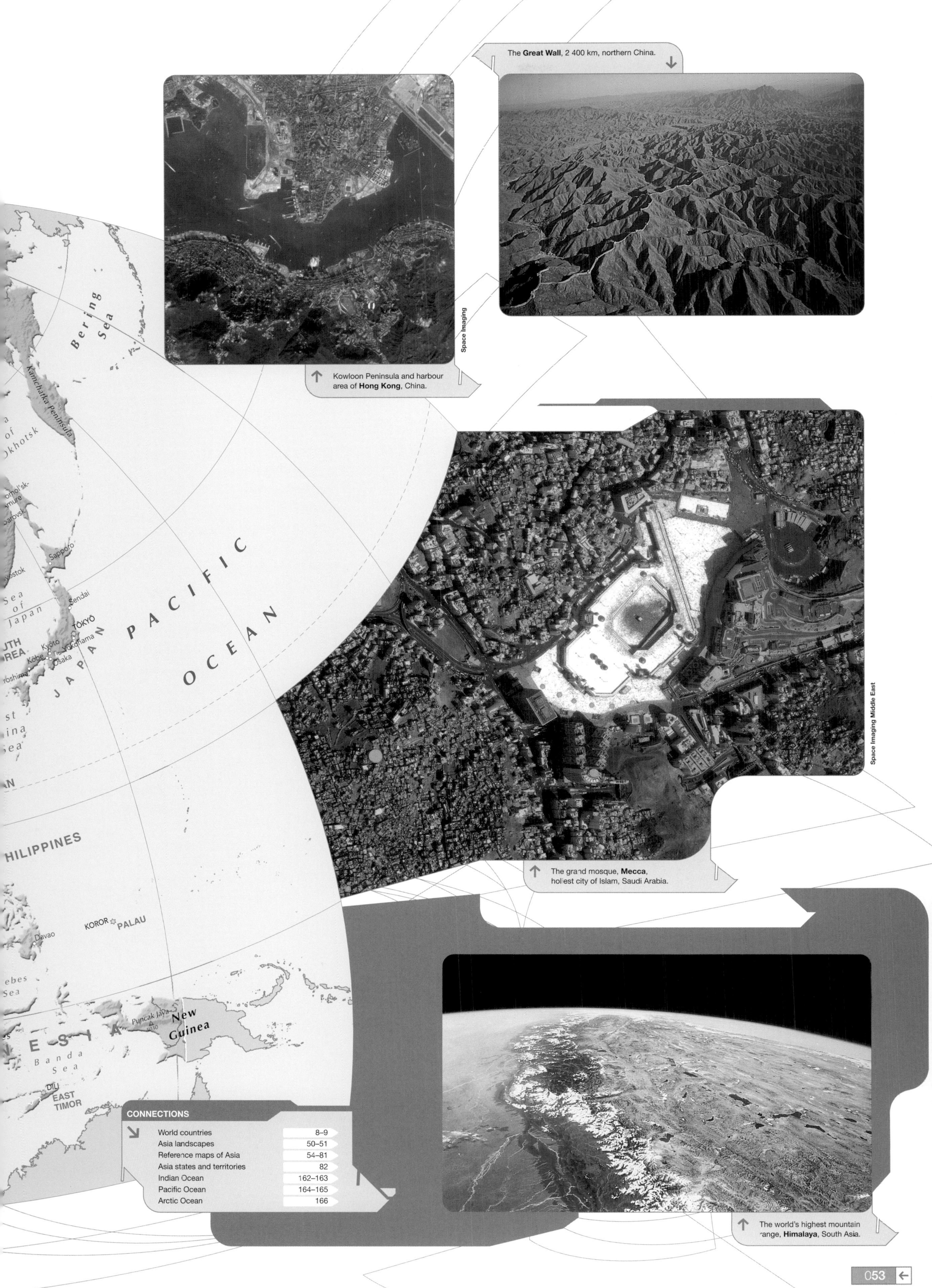

The **Great Wall**, 2 400 km, northern China.

Space Imaging

↑ Kowloon Peninsula and harbour area of **Hong Kong**, China.

Space Imaging Middle East

↑ The grand mosque, **Mecca**, holiest city of Islam, Saudi Arabia.

↑ The world's highest mountain range, **Himalaya**, South Asia.

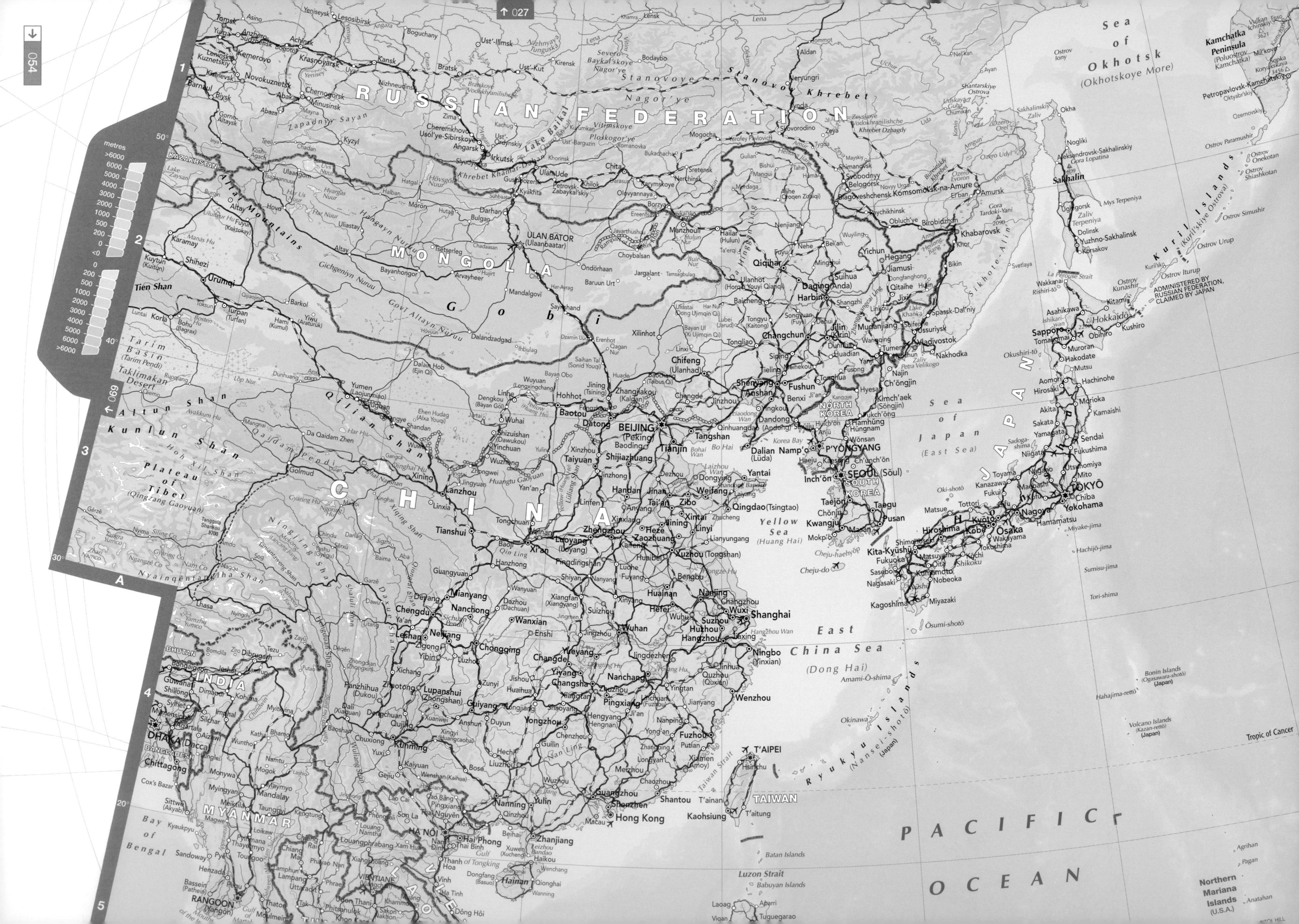

RUSSIAN FEDERATION
MONGOLIA
CHINA
JAPAN
NORTH KOREA
SOUTH KOREA
TAIWAN
INDIA
BHUTAN
BANGLADESH
MYANMAR
LAOS
VIETNAM
KAZAKHSTAN
Sea of Okhotsk (Okhotskoye More)
Sea of Japan (East Sea)
Yellow Sea (Huang Hai)
East China Sea (Dong Hai)
PACIFIC OCEAN
Bay of Bengal
Gobi
Plateau of Tibet (Qingzang Gaoyuan)
Tarim Basin (Tarim Pendi)
Taklimakan Desert
Kunlun Shan
Altun Shan
Tien Shan
Altai Mountains
Qilian Shan
Stanovoye Khrebet
Stanovoye Nagor'ye
Lake Baikal
Kamchatka Peninsula (Poluostrov Kamchatka)
Kuril Islands (Kuril'skiye Ostrova)
ADMINISTERED BY RUSSIAN FEDERATION, CLAIMED BY JAPAN
Ryukyu Islands (Nansei-shotō) (Japan)
Bonin Islands (Ogasawara-shotō) (Japan)
Volcano Islands (Kazan-rettō) (Japan)
Northern Mariana Islands (U.S.A.)
Tropic of Cancer
Luzon Strait
Taiwan Strait
Sakhalin
Hokkaidō
ULAN BATOR (Ulaanbaatar)
BEIJING (Peking)
P'YŎNGYANG
SEOUL (Sŏul)
TŌKYŌ
T'AIPEI
HA NÔI
VIENTIANE
DHAKA (Dacca)
RANGOON (Yangon)
Shanghai
Hong Kong
Tianjin
Harbin
Shenyang
Wuhan
Chongqing
Chengdu
Guangzhou
Xi'an
Lanzhou
Ürümqi
Lhasa
Kunming
Irkutsk
Khabarovsk
Vladivostok
Ōsaka
Sapporo
metres
>6000
6000
5000
4000
3000
2000
1000
500
200
0
<0
1
2
3
4
5
A
50°
40°
30°
20°

↑ 027
↑ 069

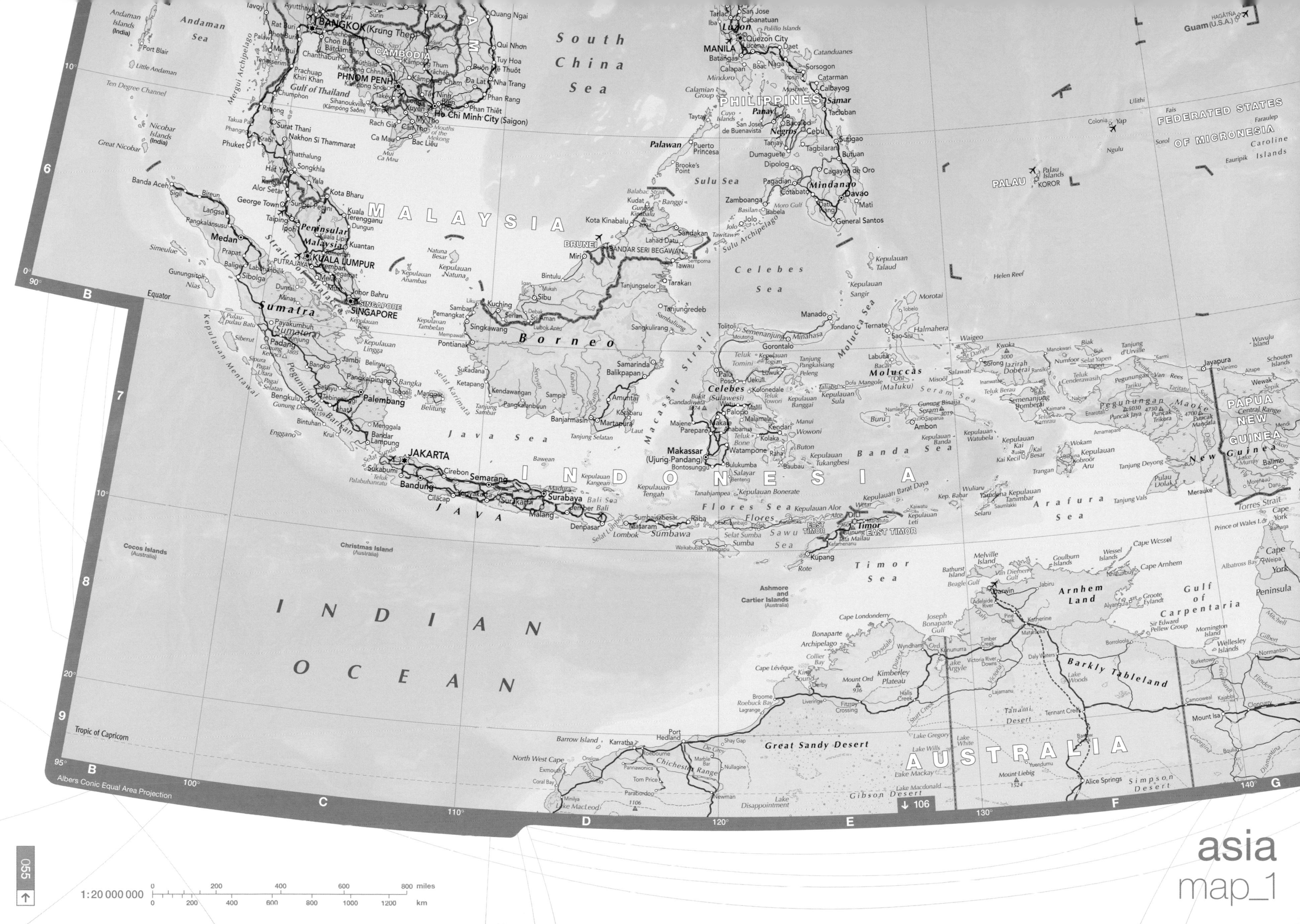
asia
map_1
South China Sea
INDIAN OCEAN
MALAYSIA
INDONESIA
AUSTRALIA
PHILIPPINES
CAMBODIA
BRUNEI
SINGAPORE
EAST TIMOR
PAPUA NEW GUINEA
PALAU
FEDERATED STATES OF MICRONESIA
BANGKOK (Krung Thep)
PHNOM PENH
KUALA LUMPUR
JAKARTA
MANILA
BANDAR SERI BEGAWAN
Ho Chi Minh City (Saigon)
Sumatra
Borneo
Celebes (Sulawesi)
Java
Moluccas (Maluku)
Java Sea
Celebes Sea
Sulu Sea
Banda Sea
Flores Sea
Timor Sea
Arafura Sea
Gulf of Carpentaria
Gulf of Thailand
Andaman Sea
Great Sandy Desert
Equator
Tropic of Capricorn
↓ 106
1:20 000 000
Albers Conic Equal Area Projection

C H I N A

YUNNAN
GUANGXI ZHUANGZU ZIZHIQU
GUANGDONG
FUJIAN

MYANMAR
LAOS
THAILAND
VIETNAM
CAMBODIA
INDO-CHINA

Tropic of Cancer

HA NỘI
Hai Phong
Gulf of Tongking
Hainan
Dongfang (Basuo)
Sanya

Hong Kong
Zhanjiang
Haikou
Guangzhou
Shenzhen
Shantou

Nanning
Yulin

VIENTIANE (Viangchan)
Louangphrabang
Vinh
Huế
Đà Nẵng
Quang Ngai
Qui Nhơn
Tuy Hoa
Nha Trang
Phan Rang
Phan Thiết

BANGKOK (Krung Thep)
Chiang Mai
Nakhon Ratchasima
Ubon Ratchathani

PHNOM PENH (Kâmpóng)
Hồ Chí Minh City (Saigon)

Paracel Islands (Xisha Qundao)
Macclesfield Bank
Scarborough Shoal

South China Sea

Gulf of Thailand

Spratly Islands

Andaman Sea

Palawan
Puerto Princesa

MALAYSIA
Kota Bharu
George Town
KUALA LUMPUR
PUTRAJAYA
Johor Bahru
SINGAPORE

BRUNEI
BANDAR SERI BEGAWAN
SABAH
Kota Kinabalu
SARAWAK
Kuching
B o r n e o
KALIMANTAN

Sumatra (Sumatera)
Medan
Padang
Palembang

Pontianak
Banjarmasin

Selat Karimata
Java Sea

INDIAN OCEAN

Bangka
Belitung

JAVA
JAKARTA
Bandung
Semarang
Surabaya
Yogyakarta
Bali
Denpasar
Lombok
Sumbawa

Bali Sea

Christmas Island (Australia)

Equator

Mercator Projection

metres
>6000
6000
5000
4000
3000
2000
1000
500
200
0
<0

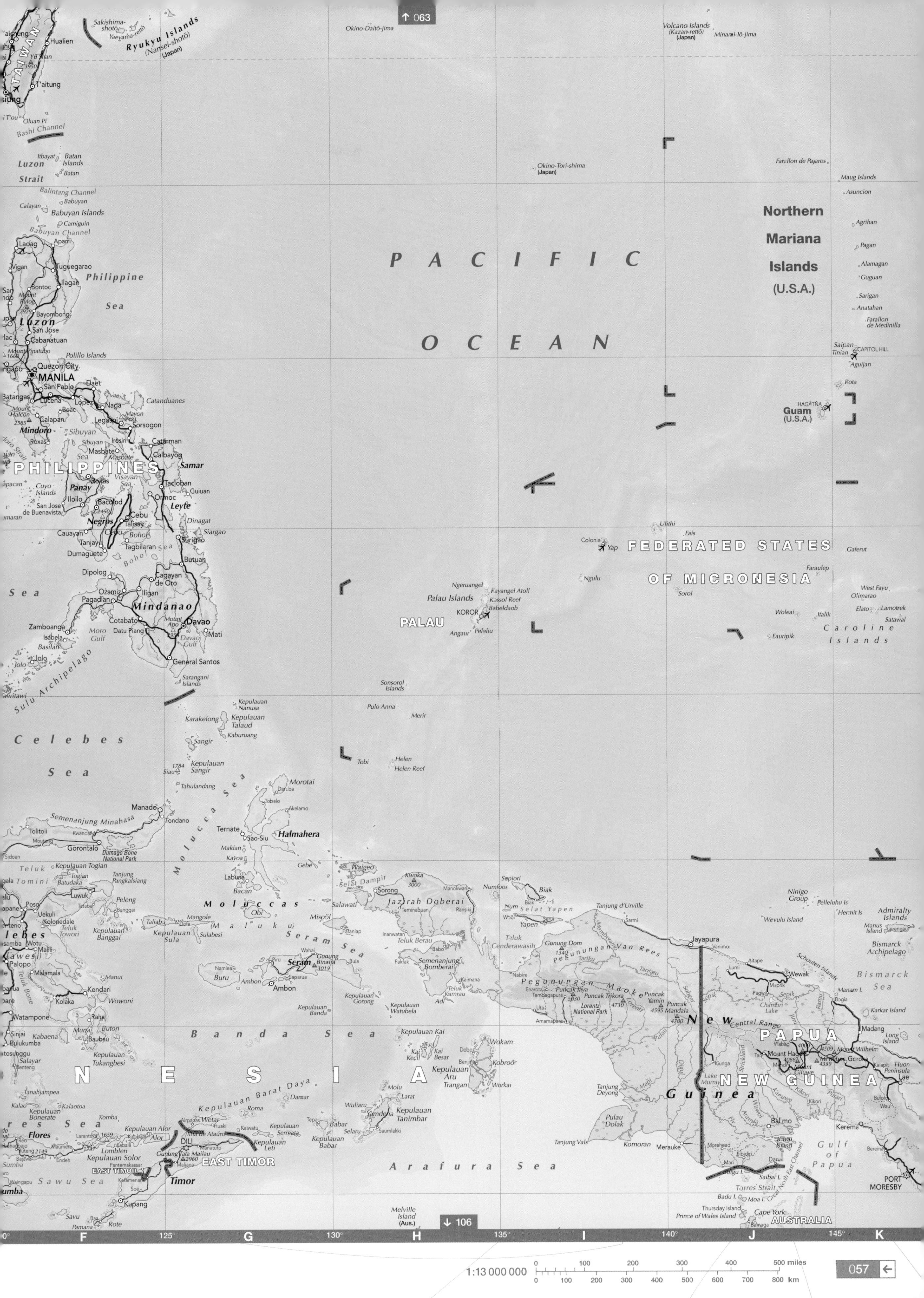

PACIFIC

OCEAN

TAIWAN

Sakishima-shotō

Yaeyama-rettō

Hualien

Ryukyu Islands

(Nansei-shotō)

(Japan)

Okino-Daitō-jima

Volcano Islands

(Kazan-rettō)

(Japan)

Minami-Iō-jima

T'aitung

Yu Yun

Oluan Pi

Bashi Channel

Itbayat

Batan
Islands

Batan

Maug Islands

Luzon
Strait

Okino-Tori-shima
(Japan)

Farallon de Pajaros

Asuncion

Balintang Channel
Babuyan

Northern

Agrihan

Calayan
Babuyan Islands
Camiguin
Babuyan Channel

Aparri

Mariana

Pagan

Laoag

Islands

Alamagan

Vigan

Tuguegarao
Ilagan

Philippine

(U.S.A.)

Guguan

San

Bontoc

Sea

Sarigan

Mount
Pulog

Bayombong

Anatahan

Luzon

San Jose

Farallon
de Medinilla

Mount Pinatubo

Cabanatuan

Saipan

CAPITOL HILL

Tac

Tinian

Quezon City

Aguijan

ngao

MANILA

San Pablo

Rota

Batangas

Lucena
Daet

Polillo Islands

Boac
Lopez
Naga

HAGÅTÑA

Calapan
Legaspi
Mayon
2421

Guam

Mount
Halcon
2585

Sorsogon

(U.S.A.)

Mindoro
Sibuyan

Catanduanes

Roxas
Irosin

Catarman

PHILIPPINES
Cuyo
Islands

Sibuyan
Sea

Masbate
Masbate

Calbayog

Samar

San Jose
de Buenavista

Iloilo

Panay

Roxas

Visayan Sea

Tacloban

Guiuan

Bacolod

Ormoc

Leyte

Cebu

Ulithi

Fais

Negros

Cebu
Talisay
Bohol

Dinagat

Gaferut

Cauayan

Siargao

Colonia

Sea

Tanjay

Bohol

Yap

FEDERATED STATES

Dumaguete

Tagbilaran

Bohol Sea

Surigao

Butuan

Dipolog

Cagayan
de Oro

Ngeruangel

Ngulu

OF MICRONESIA

Ozamiz

Iligan

Fayangel Atoll

Faraulep

West Fayu
O'limarao

Pagadian

Mindanao

Palau Islands

Kossol Reef

Sorol

Woleai

Ifalik

Elato
Lamotrek

Zamboanga
Cotabato

Mount
Apo
2954
Datu Piang

Davao

PALAU

KOROR

Babeldaob

Satawal

Eauripik

Caroline

Isabela
Basilan

*Moro
Gulf*

Davao
Gulf

Mati

Angaur
Peleliu

Islands

Jolo

General Santos

Sarangani
Islands

Sonsorol
Islands

NESIA

Sulu Archipelago

Pulo Anna

Merir

Celebes

Kepulauan
Nanusa

Sea

Karakelong

Kepulauan
Talaud

Tobi

Helen

Kaburuang

Helen Reef

Sangir
1784
Siau

Kepulauan
Sangir

Tahulandang

Morotai

Daruba

Molucca Sea

Tabelo
Akelamo

Manado

Semenanjung Minahasa

Tondano

Ternate
Makian

Sao-Siu

Halmahera

Tolitoli

Gorontalo

Kayoa

Dumaga Bone
National Park

Gebe

Waigeo

*Teluk
Tomini*

Kepulauan Togian

Tanjung
Pangkalsiang

Labuna

Bacan

Selat Dampir

Kwoka
3000

Sorong

Sepiori

Biak

Numfoor

Ninigo
Group

Pelelluhu Is

Luwuk

Peleng

Salawati

Jazirah Doberai

Manokwari

Num

Biak

Wevulu Island

Hermit Is

*Admiralty
Islands*

Manus
Island

Moluccas

Obi

Misool

Teminabuan

Ranski

Yapen

Selat Yapen

Sarmi

Aitape

Kepulauan
Sula

M a l u k u

Inanwatan

Wosi

Yapen

Jayapura

Lumi

Wewak

Kepulauan
Banggai

Mangole
Sulabesi

Taliab

Seram Sea

Teluk Berau

Babo

Fakfak

*Teluk
Cenderawasih*

Gunung Dom
3340

Peg unungan Van Rees

Tariku

Tarritatu

Mapik

*Bismarck
Sea*

lebes

Banggai

Namlea

Wahai

Gunung
Binaija
3019

Bula

Semenanjung
Bomberai

Kaimana

Nabire

Pegunungan Maok

Puncak
Jaya

Sepik

Pagei

Karkar Island

Uekuli

Seram

Piru

Saparua

Fakfak

Enarotali

Puncak
Trikora
4730

Yamin

Puncak
Mandala
4700

New

Chambri
Lake

Kolonedale

Buru

Ambon

Ambon

Adi

Central Range

Madang

Poso

PAPUA

Teluk
Towori

Kendari

Wowoni

Kepulauan
Gorong

Kepulauan
Watubela

Uta

Lorentz
National Park

Puncak
4595

Guinea

Mount Wilhelm
4509

Long
Island

Malamala

Kepulauan
Banda

Amamapare

NEW GUINEA

Palopo

Kolaka

Raha

Muna

Buton

Banda Sea

Kepulauan Kai

Wokam

Huon
Peninsula

Watampone

Sinjai

Kabaena

Baubau

Kai
Kecil

Kai
Besar

Dobo

Kobroor

Tanjung
Deyong

*Gulf
of
Papua*

Kereme

Bulukumba

Tukangbesi

Kepulauan
Aru

Lake
Murray

Kiunga

Balimo

Kalao
Kalaotoa

Komba

Kepulauan
Bonerate

Tanjung
Vals

Trangan

Workai

Mapi

Kikori

Wau

Salayar

Benteng

Kepulauan Barat Daya

Roma

Wetar

Molu

Larat

Wuliaru

Yamdena

Kepulauan
Tanimbar

Pulau
Dolak

Mari

Daru

AUSTRALIA

Tanahjampea

Damar

Kaliwatu

Tepa
Babar

Selaru

Komoran

Merauke

tres Sea

Kepulauan Alor

Alor

Kepulauan
Leti

Sermata

Kepulauan
Babar

Arafura Sea

Morehead

Saibai I.

PORT
MORESBY

Lomblen

DILI

Atauro

Gunung Tata Mailau
2960

Panterama

Badu I.

Moa I.

Flores

Kepulauan Solor

EAST TIMOR

Thursday Island

Prince of Wales Island

Sumba

Waingapu

Gunung Mutis
2149

EAST TIMOR

Timor

Maliana

Soe

Kupang

Sawu Sea

Savu

Rote

Melville
Island
(Aus.)

Cape York

P A C I F I C

O C E A N

N   E   S   I   A

*Teluk
Bone*

lebes

(*SULAWESI*)

Teluk

Mindanao

Moa I.

1:13 000 000

0   100   200   300   400   500 miles

0   100 200 300 400 500 600 700 800 km

0°   **F**   125°   **G**   130°   **H**   135°   **I**   140°   **J**   145°   **K**

THAILAND

MALAYSIA

SINGAPORE

SUMATERA UTARA

SUMATERA BARAT

JAMBI

SUMATERA SELATAN

BENGKULU

LAMPUNG

ACEH

KEDAH

PERAK

KELANTAN

TERENGGANU

PAHANG

SELANGOR

NEGERI SEMBILAN

JOHOR

MELAKA

Peninsular Malaysia

KUALA LUMPUR

PUTRAJAYA

RIAU

INDONESIA

INDIAN OCEAN

Equator

metres
>6000
6000
5000
4000
3000
2000
1000
500
200
0
<0
0
200
500
1000
2000
3000
4000
5000
6000
>6000

Singapore inset

MALAYSIA

SINGAPORE

Johor Bahru

WOODLANDS

SEMBAWANG

YISHUN

MANDAI

BUKIT PANJANG

CHOA CHU KANG

BUKIT BATOK

BUKIT TIMAH

JURONG

TUAS

CLEMENTI

QUEENSTOWN

TAMPINES

CHANGI

BEDOK

PASIR PANJANG

KATONG

GEYLANG

PAYA LEBAR

HOUGANG

PUNGGOL

SERANGOON

JALAN KAYU

SELETAR

Sentosa

Jurong Island

Strait of Singapore

Selat Johor

Selat Pandan

Selat Jurong

1 : 400 000

miles

km

103°40'   103°50'   104°00'

Mercator Projection

A 96°   B   100°   C 104°

↑ 056

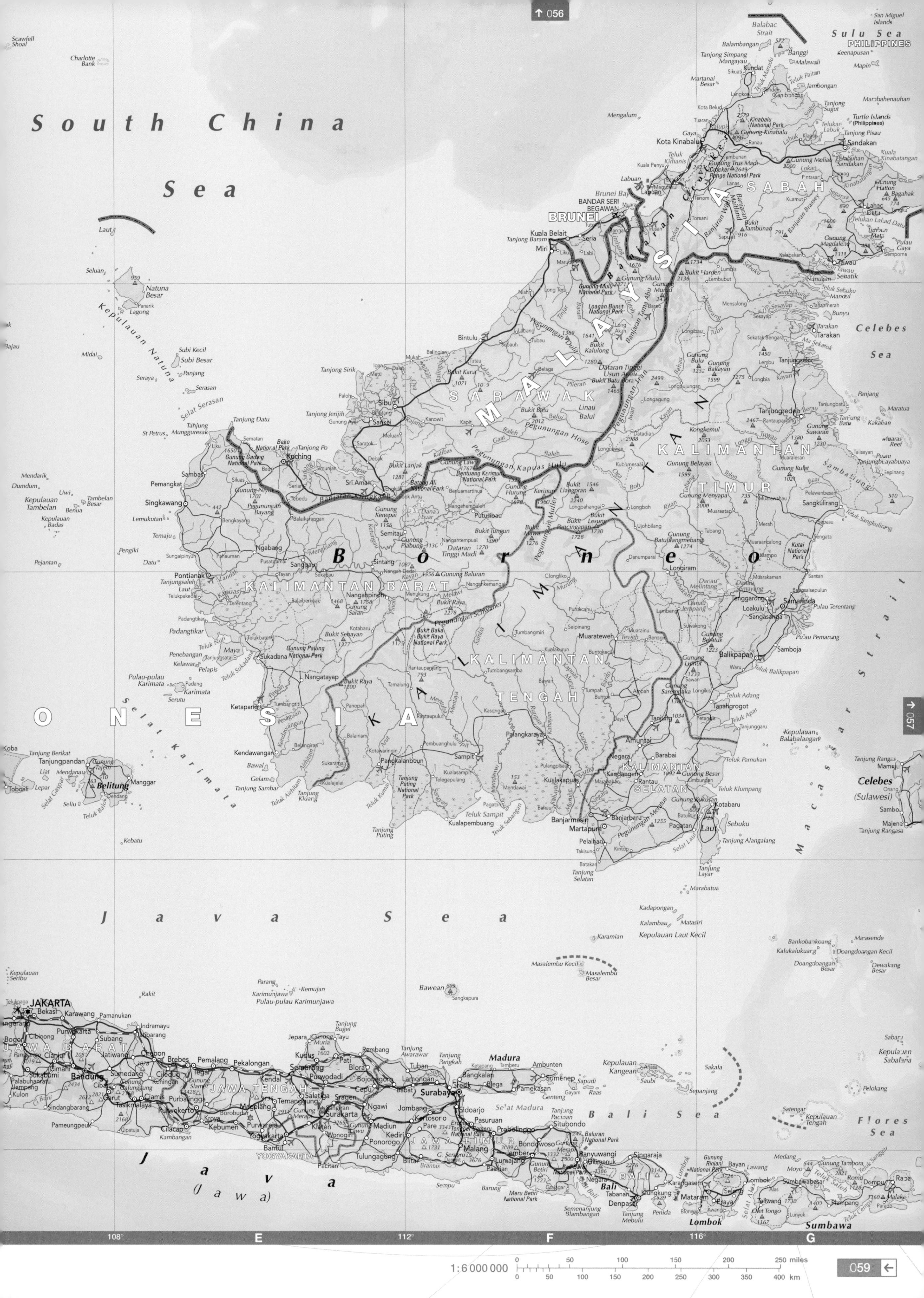
South China Sea
Scawfell Shoal
Charlotte Bank
Laut
Seluan
Natuna Besar
Kepulauan Natuna
Subi Kecil
Subi Besar
Midai
Panjang
Serasan
Selat Serasan
Tanjung Datu
St Petrus
Mendarik
Dumdum
Kepulauan Tambelan
Tambelan Besar
Kepulauan Badas
Pejantan
Sulu Sea
PHILIPPINES
Balabac Strait
Banggi
Kudat
Kota Kinabalu
Gunung Kinabalu
Sandakan
Turtle Islands (Philippines)
Labuan
BANDAR SERI BEGAWAN
BRUNEI
Kuala Belait
Miri
Tawau
SABAH
MALAYSIA
SARAWAK
Bintulu
Sibu
Kuching
Sri Aman
Singkawang
Pontianak
Celebes Sea
Tarakan
Tanjungredeb
KALIMANTAN TIMUR
Samarinda
Balikpapan
Borneo
KALIMANTAN BARAT
Sanggau
Sintang
Putusibau
KALIMANTAN TENGAH
Palangkaraya
Sampit
Pangkalanbuun
Ketapang
Kendawangan
Bukit Raya
Muaratewe
KALIMANTAN SELATAN
Banjarmasin
Kotabaru
Laut
Amuntai
Barabai
Makassar Strait
Kepulauan Balabalangan
Celebes (Sulawesi)
Selat Karimata
Belitung
Tanjungpandan
Manggar
INDONESIA
Java Sea
Kepulauan Laut Kecil
Masalembu Kecil
Masalembu Besar
Bawean
Pulau-pulau Karimunjawa
Kepulauan Seribu
JAKARTA
Bogor
Bandung
JAWA BARAT
Cirebon
Semarang
JAWA TENGAH
Yogyakarta
YOGYAKARTA
Surakarta
Surabaya
Madura
JAWA TIMUR
Malang
Banyuwangi
Bali Sea
Kepulauan Kangean
BALI
Denpasar
Singaraja
Lombok
Mataram
Sumbawa
Flores Sea
Java (Jawa)
108°
E
112°
F
116°
G
1:6 000 000
0 50 100 150 200 250 miles
0 50 100 150 200 250 300 350 400 km

057

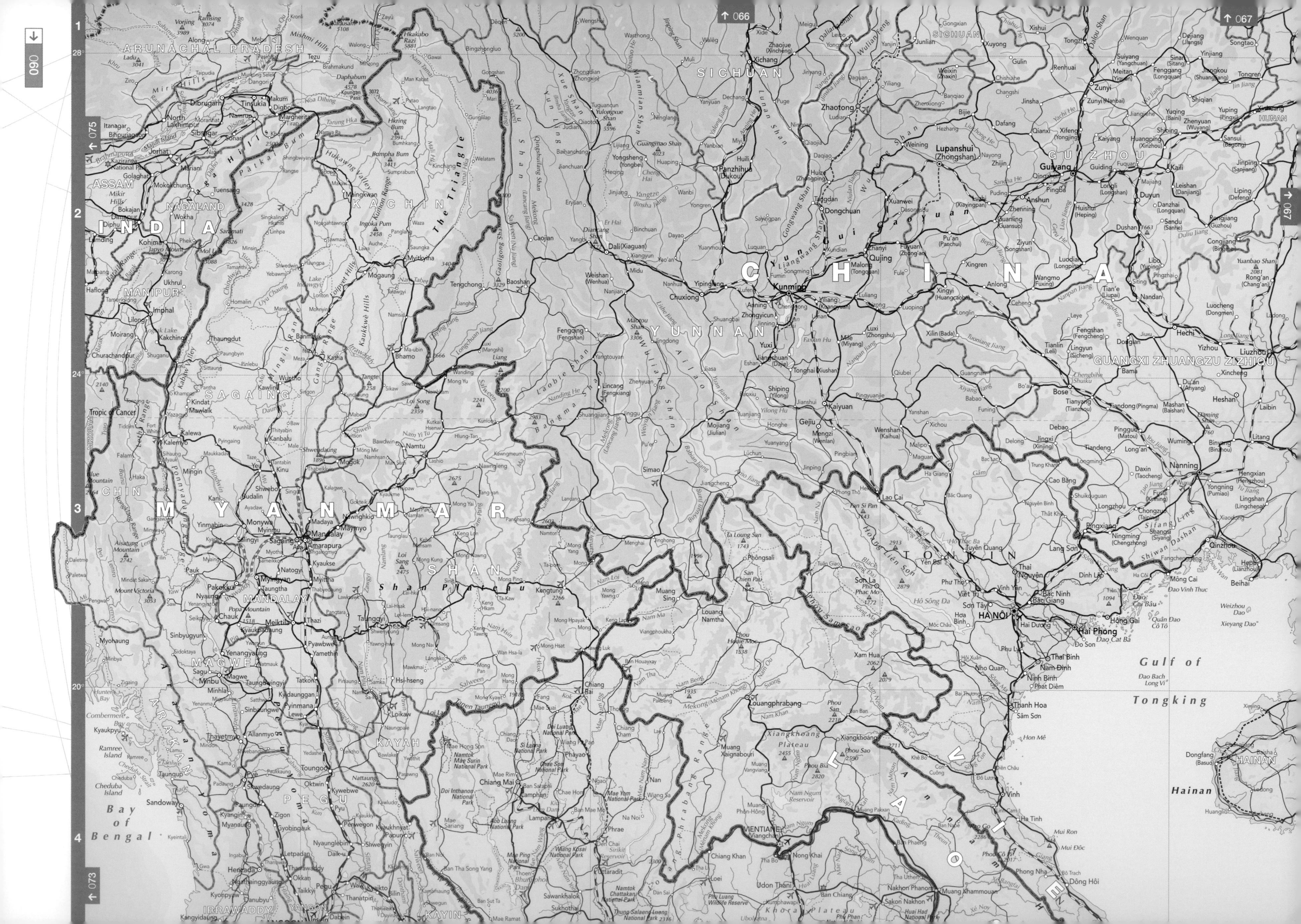

CHINA
MYANMAR
LAOS
VIETNAM
INDIA
YUNNAN
GUIZHOU
GUANGXI ZHUANGZU ZIZHIQU
SICHUAN
HUNAN
HAINAN
KACHIN
SHAN
SAGAING
MANDALAY
MAGWE
PEGU
ARAKAN
CHIN
KAYAH
KAYIN
IRRAWADDY
ARUNACHAL PRADESH
ASSAM
NAGALAND
MANIPUR
MIZORAM
TONKIN
Gulf of Tongking
Bay of Bengal
Hainan
HANOI
VIENTIANE
Kunming
Nanning
Guiyang
Mandalay
Hai Phong
Tropic of Cancer
↑ 066
↑ 067
→ 067
← 075
← 073

Major labels

Countries / Regions: INDO-CHINA, VIETNAM, CAMBODIA, THAILAND, LAOS, MALAYSIA, KEDAH, MON, COCHIN

Seas: South China Sea, Gulf of Thailand, Andaman Sea, Gulf of Martaban, Bight of Bangkok

Cities: PHNOM PENH, BANGKOK (Krung Thep), Ho Chi Minh City (Saigon), Đà Nẵng, Nha Trang, Cam Ranh, Phan Rang, Phan Thiết, Đà Lạt, Buôn Ma Thuột, Qui Nhơn, Quảng Ngãi, Kon Tum, Pleiku, Tây Ninh, Biên Hòa, Vũng Tàu, Long Xuyên, Rạch Giá, Cà Mau, Bạc Liêu, Sóc Trăng, Siĕmréab (Siem Reap), Bătdâmbâng, Kâmpóng Cham, Kâmpôt, Sihanoukville (Kâmpóng Saôm), Nakhon Ratchasima, Nonthaburi, Ayutthaya, Chanthaburi, Pattaya, Hua Hin, Prachuap Khiri Khan, Chumphon, Surat Thani, Nakhon Si Thammarat, Phatthalung, Songkhla, Hat Yai, Narathiwat, Yala, Kota Bharu, Alor Setar, Phuket, Krabi, Ranong, Trang, Satun, Mergui, Tavoy, Moulmein, Pegu

Ranges: Cardamom Range, Bilauktaung Range, TENASSERIM, Taungnyo Range

Islands: Andaman Islands (India), Ko Phuket, Ko Samui, Ko Phangan, Ko Tao, Ko Chang, Ko Kut, Phú Quốc (Đảo Phú Quốc), Mergui Archipelago, Great Coco Island, Little Coco Island, Preparis Island, Côn Sơn

Rivers / features: Mekong, Tônlé Sap, Mouths of the Mekong, Mouths of the Irrawaddy

Mercator Projection
1 : 6 000 000

↓ 058

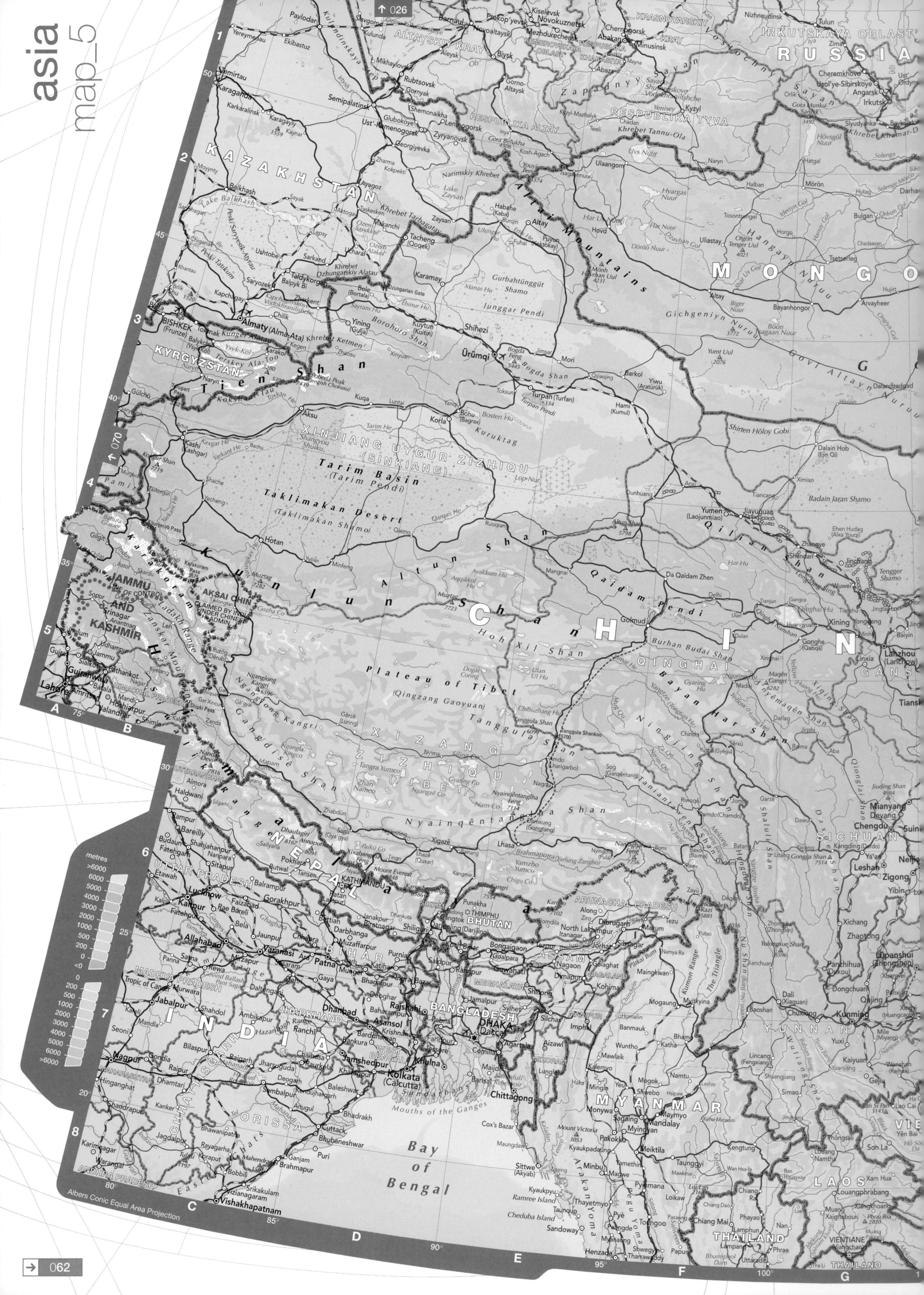
↑ 026
↑ 070
RUSSIA
KAZAKHSTAN
KYRGYZSTAN
MONGOLIA
CHINA
XINJIANG UYGUR ZIZHIQU (SINKIANG)
Tarim Basin (Tarim Pendi)
Taklimakan Desert (Taklimakan Shamo)
Tien Shan
Altai Mountains
Kunlun Shan
Altun Shan
Plateau of Tibet (Qingzang Gaoyuan)
XIZANG ZIZHIQU (TIBET)
QINGHAI
SICHUAN
YUNNAN
JAMMU AND KASHMIR
AKSAI CHIN CLAIMED BY INDIA UNDER CHINESE ADMIN
Karakoram
Himalaya
NEPAL
BHUTAN
BANGLADESH
INDIA
MYANMAR
LAOS
THAILAND
Bay of Bengal
Mouths of the Ganges
metres
>6000
6000
5000
4000
3000
2000
1000
500
200
0
<0
200
500
1000
2000
3000
4000
5000
6000
>6000
Albers Conic Equal Area Projection

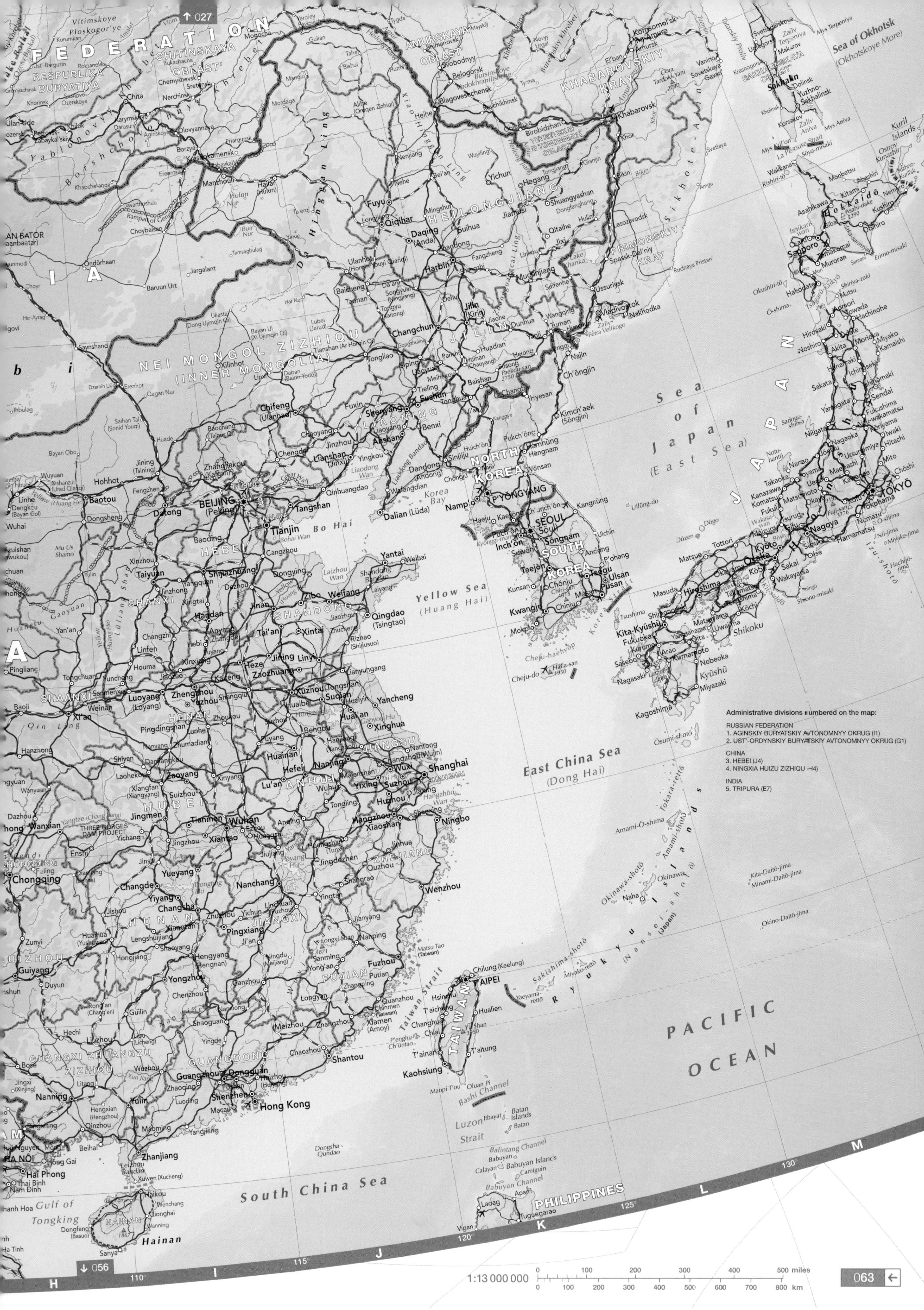

↑ 027
FEDERATION
CHITINSKAYA OBLAST'
RESPUBLIKA BURYATIYA
AMURSKAYA OBLAST'
KHABAROVSKIY KRAY
YEVREYSKAYA AVTONOMNAYA OBLAST'
PRIMORSKIY KRAY
SAKHALINSKAYA OBLAST'
Sea of Okhotsk
(Okhotskoye More)
Kuril Islands
Hokkaidō
Sapporo
Sakhalin
Khabarovsk
Komsomol'sk-na-Amure
Blagoveshchensk
Vladivostok
Nakhodka
Ussuriysk
Chita
ULAN BATOR
NEI MONGOL ZIZHIQU
(INNER MONGOLIA)
HEILONGJIANG
JILIN
LIAONING
Harbin
Qiqihar
Daqing
Changchun
Jilin (Kirin)
Shenyang
Fushun
Anshan
Dalian (Lüda)
Chifeng
NORTH KOREA
P'YONGYANG
SOUTH KOREA
SEOUL
Inch'ŏn
Taejŏn
Taegu
Pusan
Kwangju
Ulsan
Cheju-do
Korea Strait
Sea of Japan
(East Sea)
JAPAN
Honshū
Sendai
Niigata
TŌKYŌ
Yokohama
Nagoya
Kyōto
Ōsaka
Kōbe
Hiroshima
Kita-Kyūshū
Fukuoka
Nagasaki
Kumamoto
Kyūshū
Kagoshima
Shikoku
BEIJING (Peking)
TIANJIN
Tianjin
HEBEI
Bo Hai
Korea Bay
SHANXI
Taiyuan
Shijiazhuang
SHANDONG
Jinan
Qingdao (Tsingtao)
Yellow Sea
(Huang Hai)
HENAN
Zhengzhou
Luoyang (Loyang)
SHAANXI
Xi'an
JIANGSU
Nanjing
Shanghai
SHANGHAI
ANHUI
Hefei
Hangzhou
ZHEJIANG
Ningbo
Wenzhou
HUBEI
Wuhan
THREE GORGES DAM PROJECT
CHONGQING
Chongqing
HUNAN
Changsha
JIANGXI
Nanchang
FUJIAN
Fuzhou
Xiamen (Amoy)
East China Sea
(Dong Hai)
Ryukyu Islands
(Nansei-shotō)
(Japan)
Okinawa
Naha
TAIWAN
TAIPEI
Kaohsiung
Taiwan Strait
GUANGDONG
Guangzhou
Shenzhen
Hong Kong
Macau
Shantou
GUANGXI ZHUANGZU ZIZHIQU
Nanning
GUIZHOU
Guiyang
HAINAN
Hainan
Haikou
Gulf of Tongking
HA NOI
Hai Phong
South China Sea
Luzon Strait
Bashi Channel
Batan Islands
Babuyan Islands
PHILIPPINES
PACIFIC OCEAN
Administrative divisions numbered on the map:
RUSSIAN FEDERATION
1. AGINSKIY BURYATSKIY AVTONOMNYY OKRUG (I1)
2. UST'-ORDYNSKIY BURYATSKIY AVTONOMNYY OKRUG (G1)
CHINA
3. HEBEI (J4)
4. NINGXIA HUIZU ZIZHIQU (H4)
INDIA
5. TRIPURA (E7)
↓ 056
H I J K L M
110° 115° 120° 125° 130°
1:13 000 000
0 100 200 300 400 500 miles
0 100 200 300 400 500 600 700 800 km

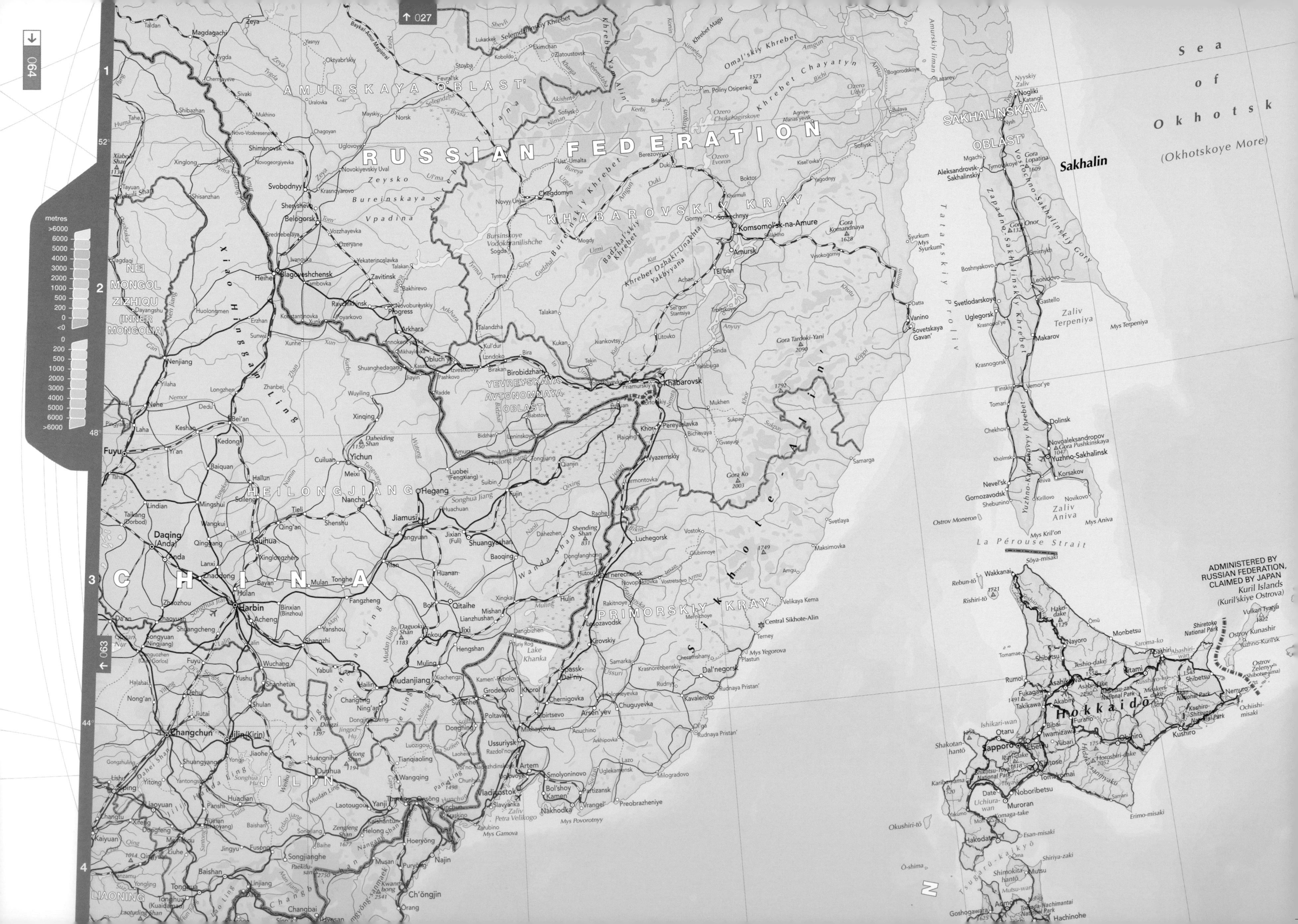
Sea of Okhotsk
(Okhotskoye More)
RUSSIAN FEDERATION
AMURSKAYA OBLAST'
KHABAROVSKIY KRAY
SAKHALINSKAYA OBLAST'
YEVREYSKAYA AVTONOMNAYA OBLAST'
PRIMORSKIY KRAY
CHINA
HEILONGJIANG
JILIN
LIAONING
NEI MONGOL ZIZHIQU (INNER MONGOLIA)
Sakhalin
Hokkaidō
Tatarskiy Proliv
La Pérouse Strait
Zaliv Terpeniya
Zaliv Aniva
Xiao Hinggan Ling
Sikhote-Alin'
ADMINISTERED BY RUSSIAN FEDERATION, CLAIMED BY JAPAN
Kuril Islands (Kuril'skiye Ostrova)
Khabarovsk
Komsomol'sk-na-Amure
Blagoveshchensk
Birobidzhan
Vladivostok
Nakhodka
Ussuriysk
Yuzhno-Sakhalinsk
Harbin
Changchun
Jilin (Kirin)
Daqing (Anda)
Qiqihar
Jiamusi
Mudanjiang
Sapporo
Hakodate
Asahikawa
Kushiro
Muroran
Wakkanai
Lake Khanka
metres
>6000
6000
5000
4000
3000
2000
1000
500
200
0
<0
0
200
500
1000
2000
3000
4000
5000
6000
>6000
027
063
064

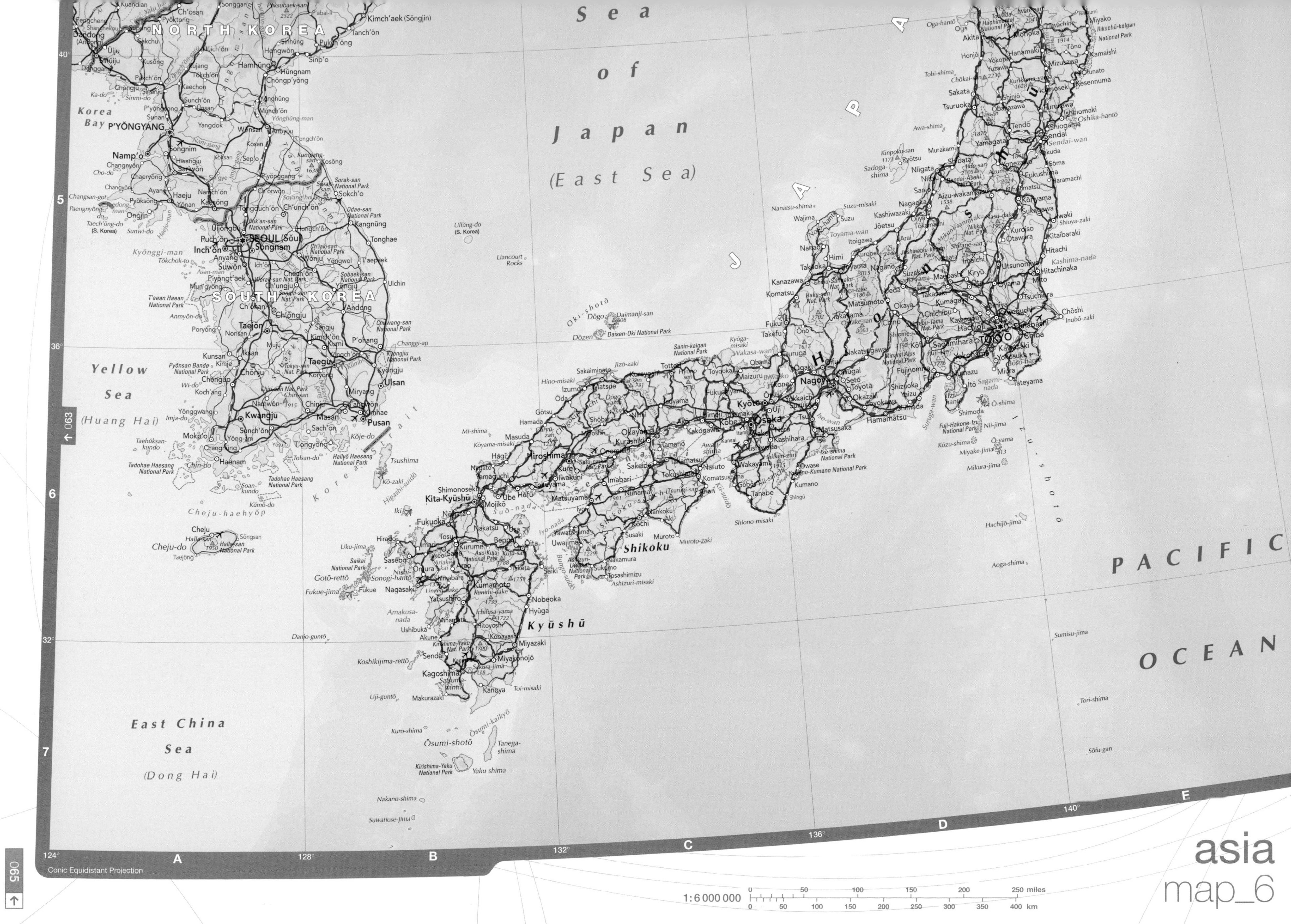

PACIFIC

OCEAN

E

Sea

of

Japan

(East Sea)

NORTH KOREA

SOUTH KOREA

SEOUL (SŎUL)

P'YŎNGYANG

Yellow
Sea

(Huang Hai)

Korea
Bay

East China
Sea

(Dong Hai)

Kyūshū

Shikoku

Pusan

Taegu

Kwangju

Hiroshima

Nagoya

Nagasaki

Kagoshima

Kita-Kyushu

Fukuoka

Shimonoseki

Ōsaka

Kyōto

Kōbe

Izu-shotō

Sumisu-jima

Tori-shima

Sōfu-gan

140°

136°

132°

128°

124°

40

36

32

5

6

7

A   B   C   D   E

1:6 000 000

Conic Equidistant Projection

0   50   100 150 200 250 miles

0   50 100 150 200 250 300 350 400 km

063

↑ 062
↑ 075

metres
>6000
6000
5000
4000
3000
2000
1000
500
200
0
<0
0
200
1000
2000
3000
4000
5000
6000
>6000

QINGHAI

GANSU

**XIZANG ZIZHIQU
(TIBET)**

SICHUAN

C H I N A

CHONGQING

GUIZHOU

INDIA

KACHIN

YUNNAN

M Y A N M A R

SHAN

KAYAH

PEGU

THAILAND

LAOS

VIETNAM

TONKIN

Tropic of Cancer

Mandalay
Maymyo
Amarapura
SAGAING
Kyaukse
Myitnge
Thabyedaung

Chengdu
Suining
Nanchong
Mianyang
Deyang
Neijiang
Zigong
Yibin
Leshan

Chongqing

Guiyang
Zunyi
Lupanshui
(Zhongshan)
Qujing

Kunming
Yuxi
Gejiu
Mengzi

Dali
Baoshan
Tengchong
Chuxiong
Simao
Pu'er

Chiang Mai
Chiang Rai

HÀ NỘI
Hải Phòng
Son La
Tuyên Quang
Yên Bái
Lang Son
Thái Nguyên
Bắc Ninh

Louang
Namtha
Luang Xiangkhoang
Xaignabouri

Gulf of Tonkin

Tropic of Cancer

↓ 061
↓ 060

Conic Equidistant Projection

→ 066

1   2   3   4   5

A   B   C

32°
28°
24°
20°

96°   100°   104°

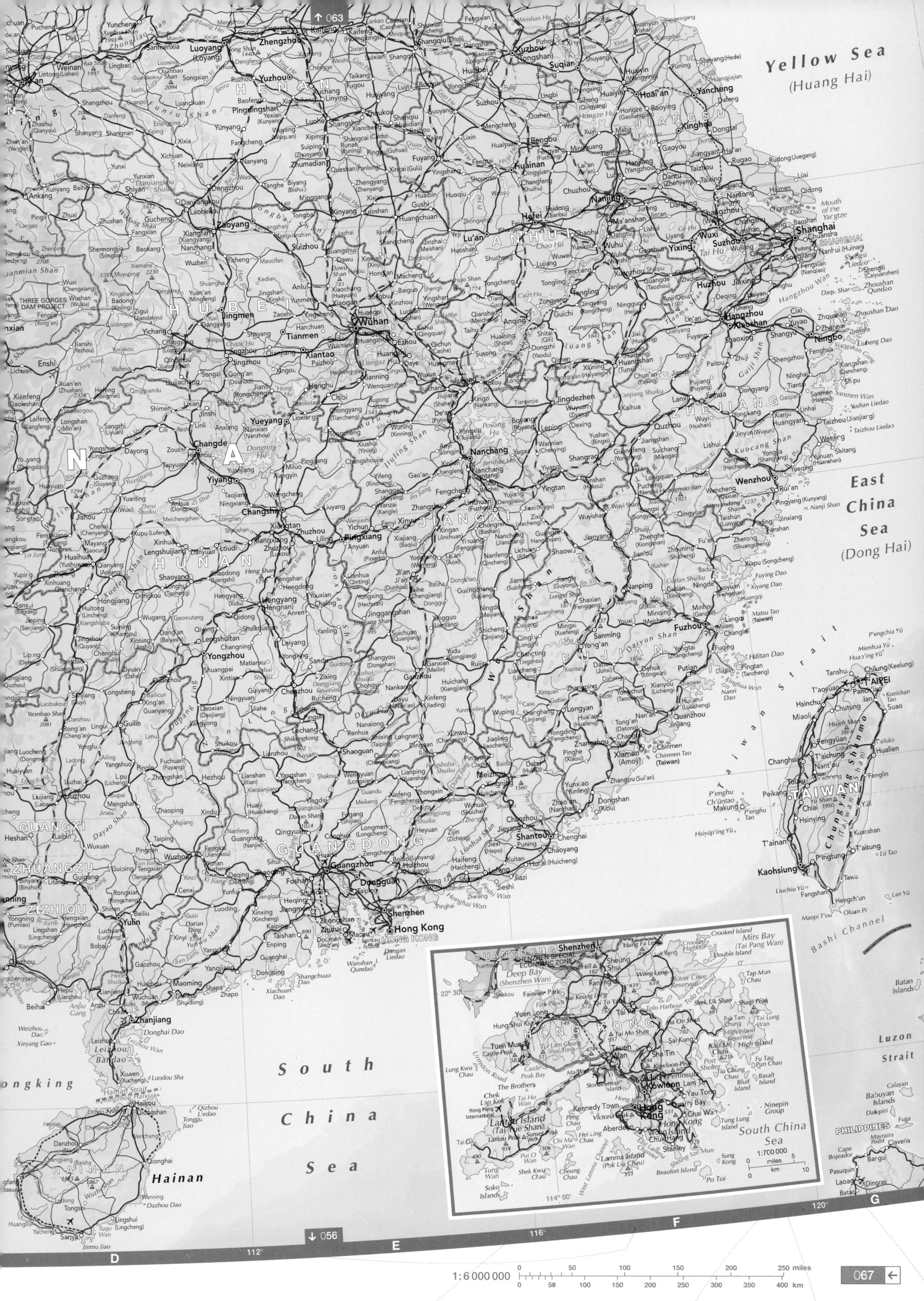

Yellow Sea
(Huang Hai)
East China Sea
(Dong Hai)
South China Sea
Taiwan Strait
Bashi Channel
Luzon Strait
HENAN
ANHUI
JIANGSU
HUBEI
HUNAN
JIANGXI
ZHEJIANG
FUJIAN
GUANGDONG
GUANGXI ZHUANGZU ZIZHIQU
TAIWAN
HAINAN
Hainan
SHANGHAI
HONG KONG
PHILIPPINES
Zhengzhou
Luoyang
Wuhan
Nanjing
Shanghai
Hangzhou
Hefei
Nanchang
Changsha
Fuzhou
Guangzhou
Shenzhen
Hong Kong
Macau
Xiamen
Shantou
Wenzhou
Ningbo
T'AIPEI
Kaohsiung
Haikou
Sanya
Zhanjiang
Guilin
Yichang
Jiujiang
Mouth of the Yangtze
THREE GORGES DAM PROJECT
1:700 000
1:6 000 000
miles
km

↑ 063
↓ 056

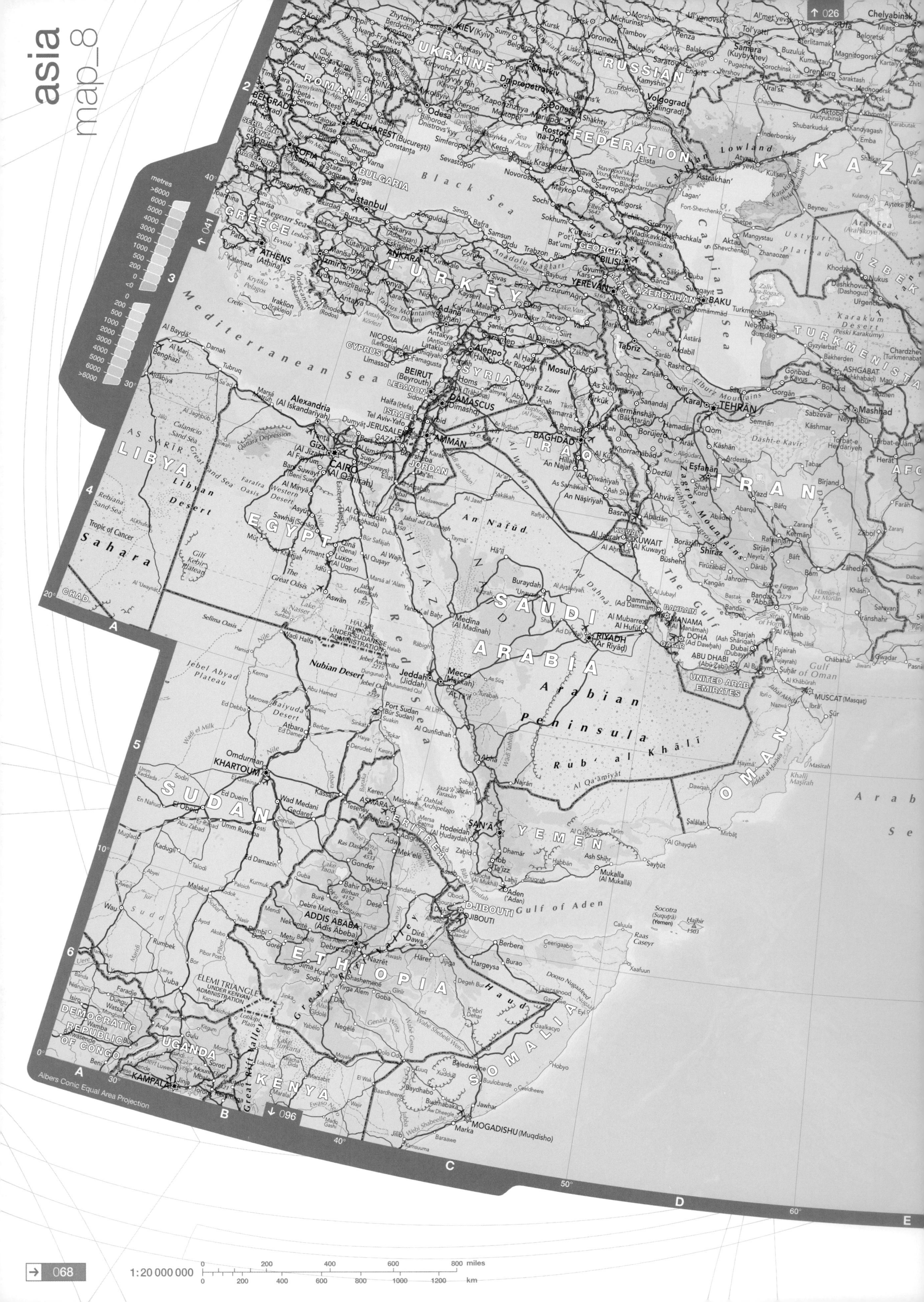

asia
map_8
↑ 026
↑ 041
↓ 096
→ 068
Albers Conic Equal Area Projection
1:20 000 000
0 200 400 600 800 miles
0 200 400 600 800 1000 1200 km
metres
>6000 6000 5000 4000 3000 2000 1000 500 200 0 <0
200 500 1000 2000 3000 4000 5000 6000 >6000
UKRAINE
RUSSIAN FEDERATION
ROMANIA
MOLDOVA
SERB. AND MONT.
MACEDONIA
BULGARIA
GREECE
TURKEY
GEORGIA
ARMENIA
AZERBAIJAN
KAZA
UZBEK
TURKMENISTAN
AFG
CYPRUS
SYRIA
LEBANON
ISRAEL
JORDAN
IRAQ
IRAN
KUWAIT
BAHRAIN
QATAR
UNITED ARAB EMIRATES
OMAN
SAUDI ARABIA
YEMEN
LIBYA
EGYPT
CHAD
SUDAN
ERITREA
DJIBOUTI
ETHIOPIA
SOMALIA
KENYA
UGANDA
DEMOCRATIC REPUBLIC OF CONGO
KIEV (Kyiv)
BUCHAREST (București)
BELGRADE (Beograd)
SOFIA (Sofiya)
SKOPJE
ATHENS (Athina)
Istanbul
ANKARA
NICOSIA (Lefkosia)
BEIRUT (Beyrouth)
DAMASCUS (Dimashq)
JERUSALEM
AMMAN
CAIRO (Al Qāhirah)
Alexandria (Al Iskandarīyah)
BAGHDAD
TBILISI
YEREVAN
BAKU
TEHRAN
KUWAIT (Al Kuwayt)
RIYADH (Ar Riyāḍ)
MANAMA (Al Manāmah)
DOHA (Ad Dawḩah)
ABU DHABI (Abū Ẓabī)
MUSCAT (Masqaṭ)
SAN'Ā
ASMARA
DJIBOUTI
ADDIS ABABA (Ādīs Ābeba)
KHARTOUM
KAMPALA
MOGADISHU (Muqdisho)
Black Sea
Mediterranean Sea
Caspian Sea
Red Sea
The Gulf
Gulf of Oman
Gulf of Aden
Arabian Sea
Arabian Peninsula
Rub' al Khālī
An Nafūd
Sahara
Libyan Desert
Nubian Desert
Tropic of Cancer

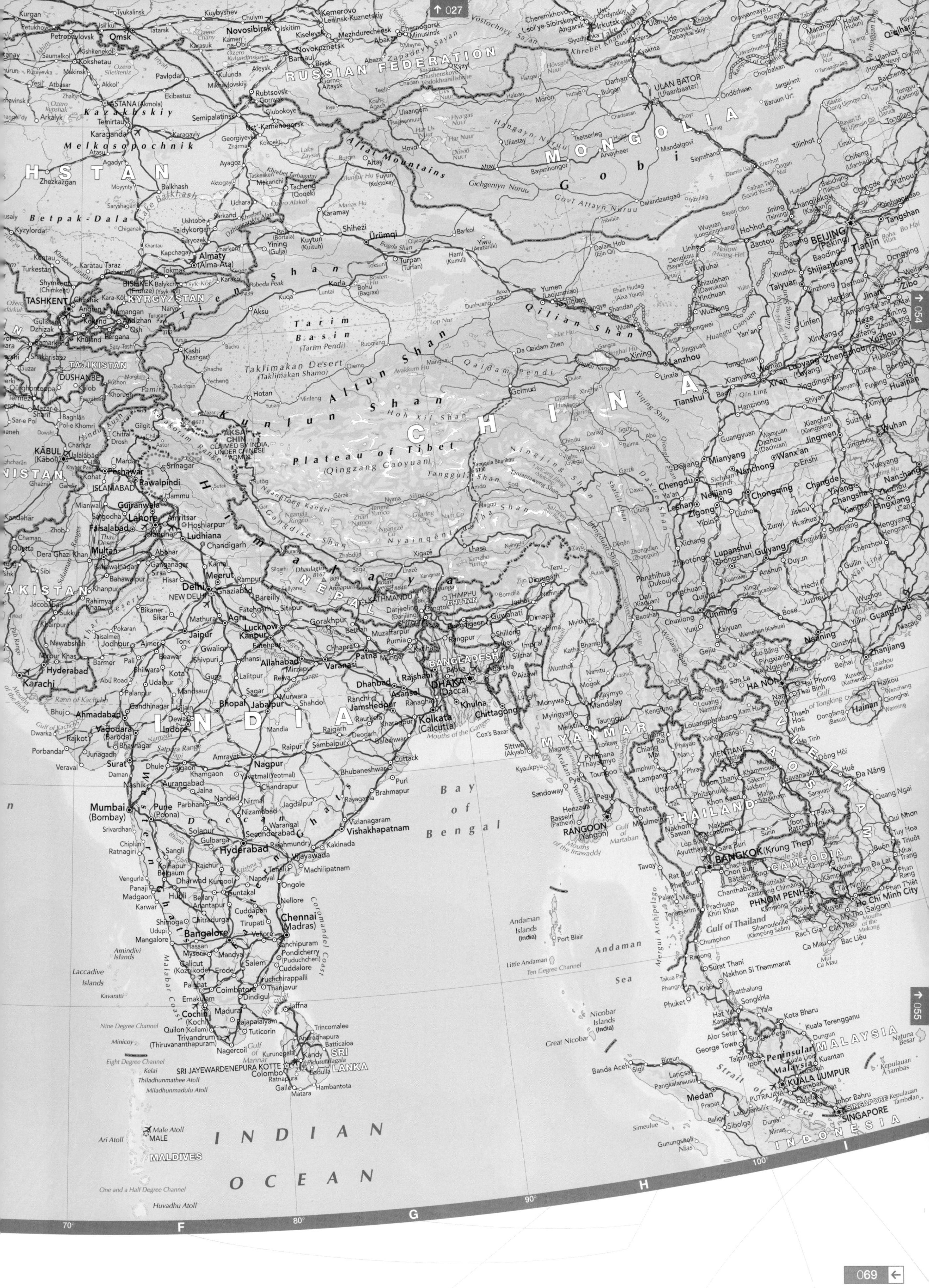

↑ 027
↑ 054
↑ 055
RUSSIAN FEDERATION
MONGOLIA
CHINA
INDIA
KAZAKHSTAN
KYRGYZSTAN
TAJIKISTAN
AFGHANISTAN
PAKISTAN
NEPAL
BHUTAN
BANGLADESH
MYANMAR
THAILAND
LAOS
VIETNAM
CAMBODIA
MALAYSIA
INDONESIA
SRI LANKA
MALDIVES
AKSAI CHIN
CLAIMED BY INDIA, UNDER CHINESE ADMIN.
ULAN BATOR (Ulaanbaatar)
BEIJING (Peking)
Tianjin
ASTANA (Akmola)
Almaty (Alma-Ata)
BISHKEK (Frunze)
TASHKENT
DUSHANBE
KĀBUL (Kābol)
ISLAMABAD
NEW DELHI
Delhi
KATHMANDU
THIMPHU
DHAKA (Dacca)
Kolkata (Calcutta)
Mumbai (Bombay)
Chennai (Madras)
Bangalore
Hyderabad
Karachi
Lahore
RANGOON (Yangon)
BANGKOK (Krung Thep)
PHNOM PENH
HA NOI
VIENTIANE
KUALA LUMPUR
SINGAPORE
SRI JAYEWARDENEPURA KOTTE
Colombo
MALE
Ürümqi
Lhasa
Chengdu
Chongqing
Kunming
Lanzhou
Xi'an
Wuhan
Novosibirsk
Omsk
Irkutsk
Ho Chi Minh City (Saigon)
Kazakhskiy Melkosopochnik
Betpak-Dala
Tien Shan
Altai Mountains
Gobi
Tarim Basin (Tarim Pendi)
Taklimakan Desert (Taklimakan Shamo)
Kunlun Shan
Altun Shan
Qilian Shan
Plateau of Tibet (Qingzang Gaoyuan)
Himalaya
Hindu Kush
Karakoram Range
Thar Desert
Deccan
Western Ghats
Eastern Ghats
Bay of Bengal
Andaman Sea
Gulf of Thailand
Gulf of Tongking
Strait of Malacca
Andaman Islands (India)
Nicobar Islands (India)
Laccadive Islands
INDIAN OCEAN
70°
80°
90°
100°
F
G
H
I

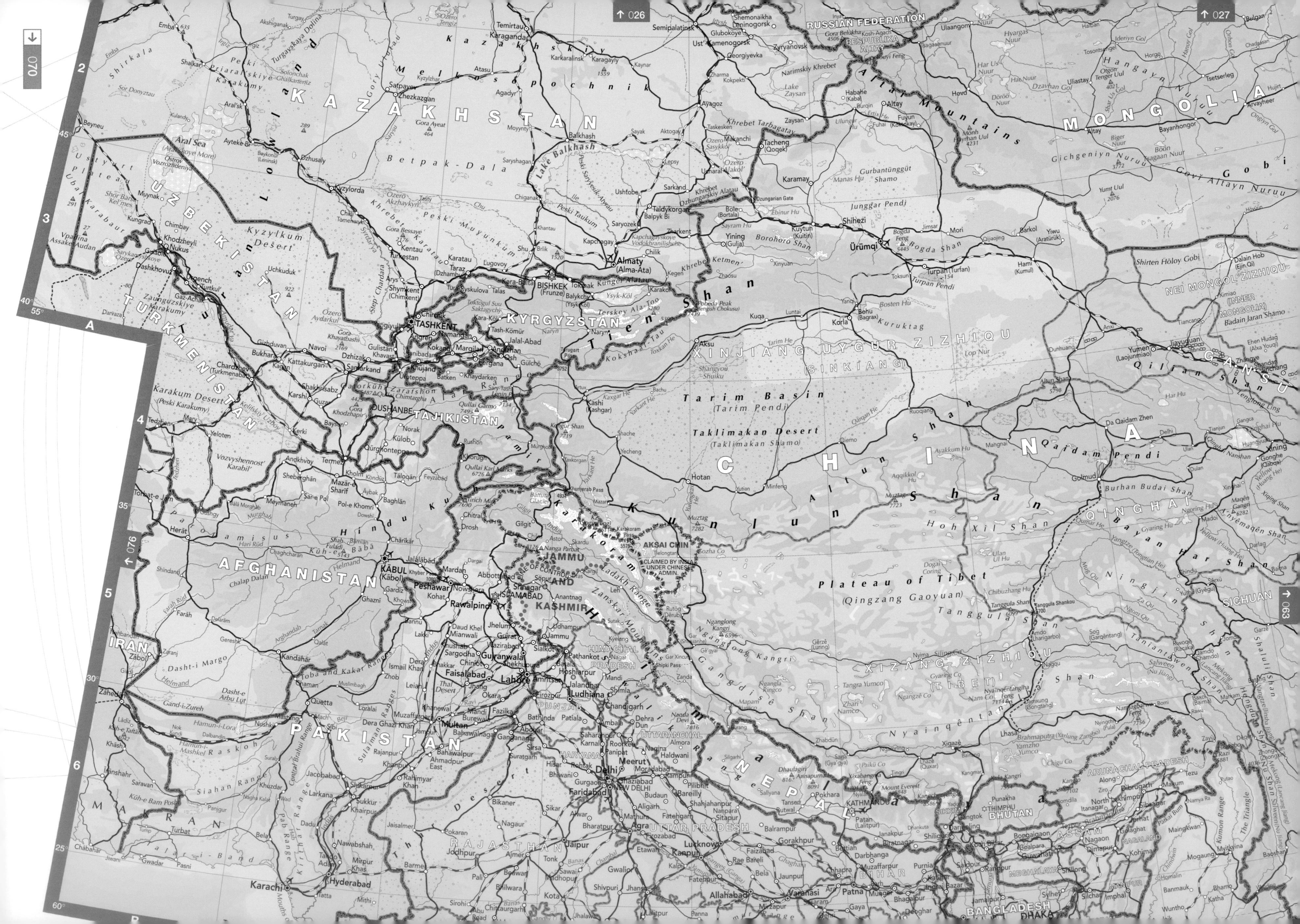

RUSSIAN FEDERATION
MONGOLIA
KAZAKHSTAN
UZBEKISTAN
TURKMENISTAN
KYRGYZSTAN
TAJIKISTAN
AFGHANISTAN
PAKISTAN
IRAN
NEPAL
BHUTAN
BANGLADESH
CHINA
XINJIANG UYGUR ZIZHIQU (SINKIANG)
XIZANG ZIZHIQU (TIBET)
QINGHAI
GANSU
SICHUAN
NEI MONGOL ZIZHIQU (INNER MONGOLIA)
JAMMU AND KASHMIR
AKSAI CHIN
CLAIMED BY INDIA UNDER CHINESE ADMIN.
LINE OF CONTROL
TASHKENT
BISHKEK (Frunze)
DUSHANBE
KABUL (Kābol)
ISLAMABAD
NEW DELHI
KATHMANDU
THIMPHU
DHAKA
Almaty (Alma-Ata)
Ürümqi
Lhasa
Karachi
Lahore
Delhi
Tarim Basin (Tarim Pendi)
Taklimakan Desert (Taklimakan Shamo)
Plateau of Tibet (Qingzang Gaoyuan)
Kunlun Shan
Tien Shan
Altun Shan
Hindu Kush
Karakoram Range
Aral Sea
Lake Balkhash
Kyzylkum Desert
Karakum Desert (Peski Karakumy)
Gobi
Altai Mountains
↓ 070
↑ 026
↑ 027
↑ 076
→ 063

INDIA

MYANMAR

Bay of Bengal

Arabian Sea

INDIAN OCEAN

Andaman Sea

ANDAMAN AND NICOBAR ISLANDS (India)

Andaman Islands

North Andaman
Middle Andaman
South Andaman
Port Blair
Little Andaman
Ten Degree Channel
Car Nicobar
Nicobar Islands
Great Nicobar

INDONESIA

Sumatra (Sumatera)
Banda Aceh
Sigli
Simeulue

SRI LANKA

Jaffna
Trincomalee
Batticaloa
Anuradhapura
Kandy
SRI JAYEWARDENEPURA KOTTE
Colombo
Moratuwa
Galle
Matara
Hambantota
Gulf of Mannar
Palk Strait

MALDIVES
MALE
Male Atoll
Ari Atoll
Addu Atoll

LAKSHADWEEP (India)
Laccadive Islands
Amindivi Islands
Minicoy
Nine Degree Channel
Eight Degree Channel

MAHARASHTRA
Mumbai (Bombay)
Pune (Poona)
Nagpur
Aurangabad
Nashik

KARNATAKA
Bangalore
Mysore
Mangalore
Belgaum
Hubli

ANDHRA PRADESH
Hyderabad
Secunderabad
Vijayawada
Vishakhapatnam
Nellore

TAMIL NADU
Chennai (Madras)
Madurai
Coimbatore
Salem
Tiruchchirappalli

KERALA
Cochin (Kochi)
Trivandrum (Thiruvananthapuram)
Calicut (Kozhikode)
Quilon (Kollam)
Alleppey (Alappuzha)

GOA
Panaji
Madgaon

ORISSA
Bhubaneshwar
Cuttack
Puri

CHHATTISGARH
Raipur
Bilaspur

MADHYA PRADESH
Bhopal
Jabalpur
Indore

GUJARAT
Ahmadabad
Vadodara (Baroda)
Surat
Rajkot

WEST BENGAL
Kolkata (Calcutta)

RANGOON (Yangon)

Chittagong
Khulna
Cox's Bazar

Deccan

Coromandel Coast
Malabar Coast

Cape Comorin

Administrative divisions in India numbered on the map:
1. DADRA AND NAGAR HAVELI (D7)
2. DAMAN AND DIU (D7)

metres
>6000
6000
5000
4000
3000
2000
1000
500
200
0
<0

0
200
500
1000
3000
4000
5000
6000
>6000

1:12 500 000

0   100   200   300   400   500 miles
0   100   200   300   400   500   600   700   800 km

Albers Conic Equal Area Projection

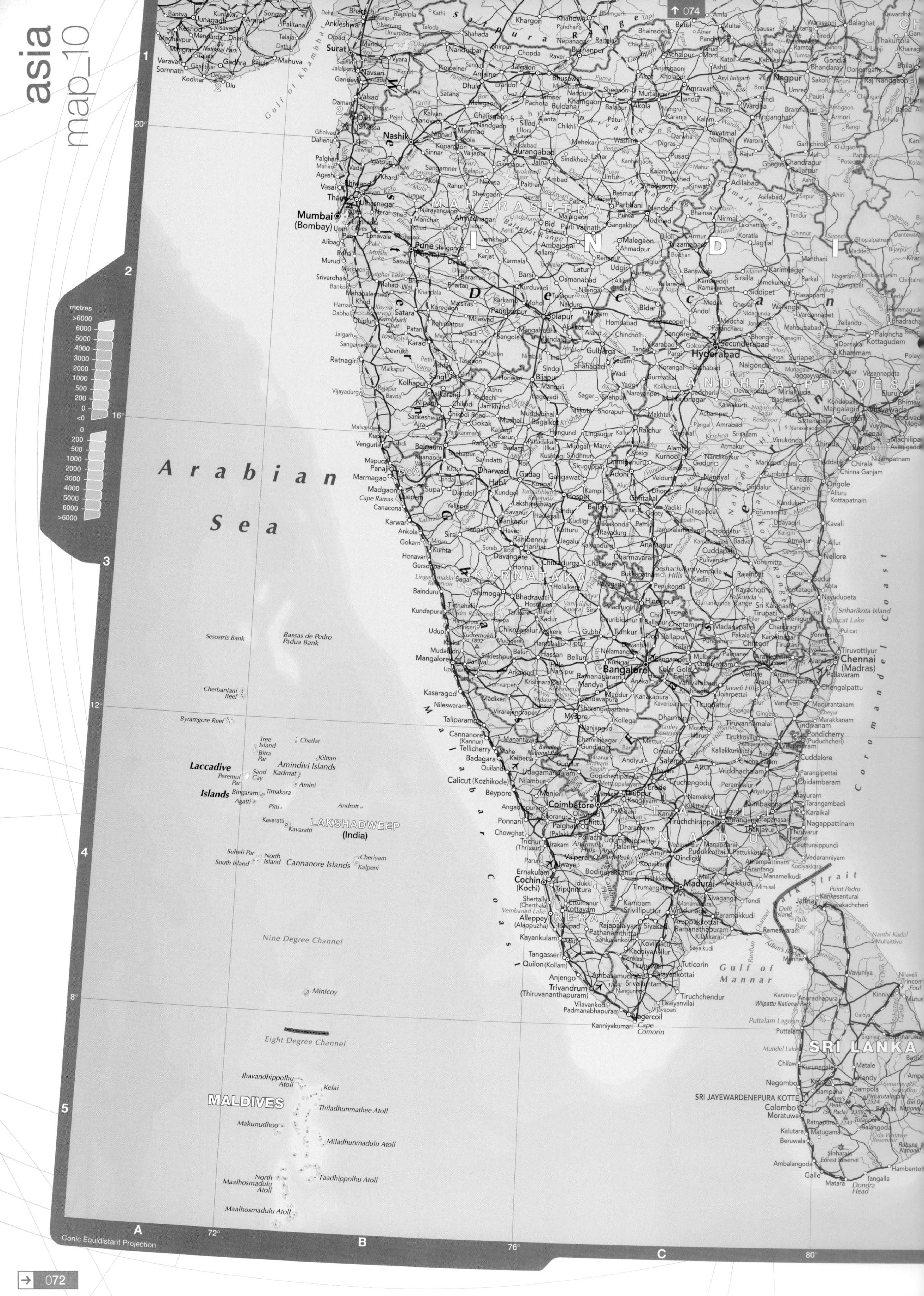
↑ 074
Arabian Sea
Gulf of Khambhat
Mumbai (Bombay)
Pune
Nashik
Surat
Aurangabad
Nagpur
Hyderabad
Secunderabad
Solapur
Kolhapur
Belgaum
Hubli
Dharwad
Bangalore
Mysore
Mangalore
Calicut (Kozhikode)
Cochin (Kochi)
Coimbatore
Madurai
Trivandrum (Thiruvananthapuram)
Chennai (Madras)
Pondicherry (Puducherri)
Nellore
Tirupati
Vijayawada
Guntur
Kurnool
Bellary
Davangere
Shimoga
Ratnagiri
Panaji
Madgaon
Karwar
Alleppey (Alappuzha)
Quilon (Kollam)
Tuticorin
Kanniyakumari
Cape Comorin
MAHARASHTRA
ANDHRA PRADESH
KARNATAKA
TAMIL NADU
KERALA
GOA
INDIA
Deccan
Western Ghats
Malabar Coast
Coromandel Coast
Satpura Range
Laccadive Islands
Amindivi Islands
Cannanore Islands
LAKSHADWEEP (India)
Nine Degree Channel
Minicoy
Eight Degree Channel
MALDIVES
Ihavandhippolhu Atoll
Thiladhunmathee Atoll
Miladhunmadulu Atoll
Faadhippolhu Atoll
North Maalhosmadulu Atoll
Maalhosmadulu Atoll
Makunudhoo
Kelai
Sesostris Bank
Bassas de Pedro Padua Bank
Cherbaniani Reef
Byramgore Reef
Gulf of Mannar
Palk Strait
SRI LANKA
SRI JAYEWARDENEPURA KOTTE
Colombo
Jaffna
Kandy
Negombo
Galle
Matara
metres
>6000
6000
5000
4000
3000
2000
1000
500
200
0
<0
0
200
500
1000
2000
3000
4000
5000
6000
>6000
20°
16°
12°
8°
72°
76°
80°
A
B
C
1
2
3
4
5
Conic Equidistant Projection

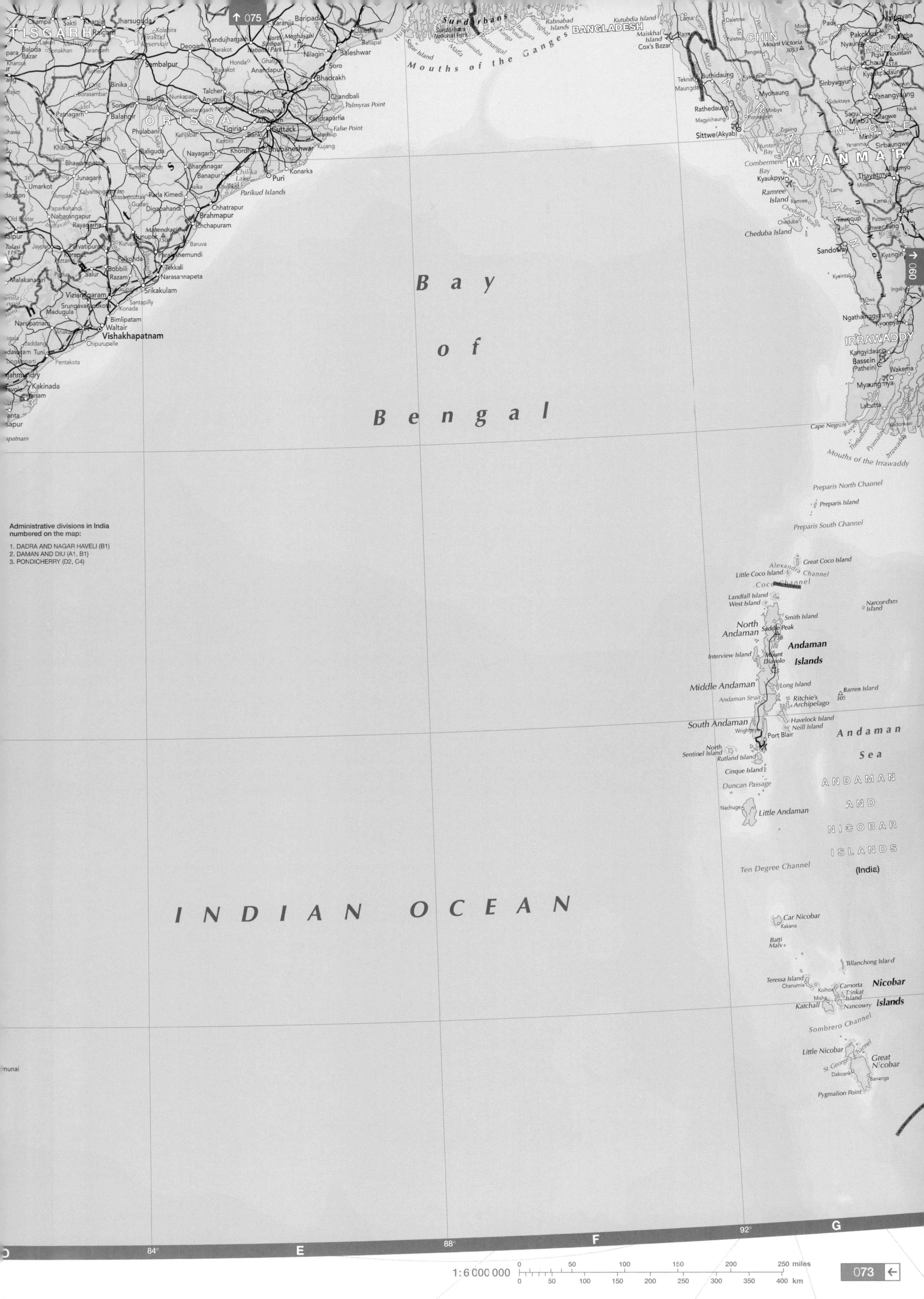

TISGARH

ORISSA

Vishakhapatnam

Mouths of the Ganges

BANGLADESH

Sundarbans
National Park

Bay

of

Bengal

Administrative divisions in India
numbered on the map:

1. DADRA AND NAGAR HAVELI (B1)
2. DAMAN AND DIU (A1, B1)
3. PONDICHERRY (D2, C4)

CHIN

MYANMAR

MAGWE

IRRAWADDY

Bassein
(Pathein)

PEGU

Cape Negrais

Mouths of the Irrawaddy

Preparis North Channel

Preparis Island

Preparis South Channel

Great Coco Island
Little Coco Island   Alexandra Channel
Coco Channel

Landfall Island
West Island   Narcondam
Island

Smith Island

**North
Andaman**   Saddle Peak   **Andaman**

Interview Island   Mount
Diavolo   **Islands**

Middle Andaman   Long Island

Andaman Strait   Ritchie's
Archipelago   Barren Island

South Andaman   Havelock Island
Wright   Neill Island   **A n d a m a n**

Port Blair   **S e a**

North
Sentinel Island   Rutland Island   ANDAMAN

Cinque Island

Duncan Passage   AND

Nachuge   NICOBAR

Little Andaman

ISLANDS

Ten Degree Channel

(India)

INDIAN OCEAN

Car Nicobar
Kakana

Batti
Malv

Tillanchong Island

Teressa Island
Chanumla   Katchal Camorta **Nicobar**
Koihao   Trinkat
Island   **Islands**
Katchall   Mishu
Nancowry

Sombrero Channel

Little Nicobar   St George's
Dakoan   **Great
Nicobar**
Bananga

Pygmalion Point

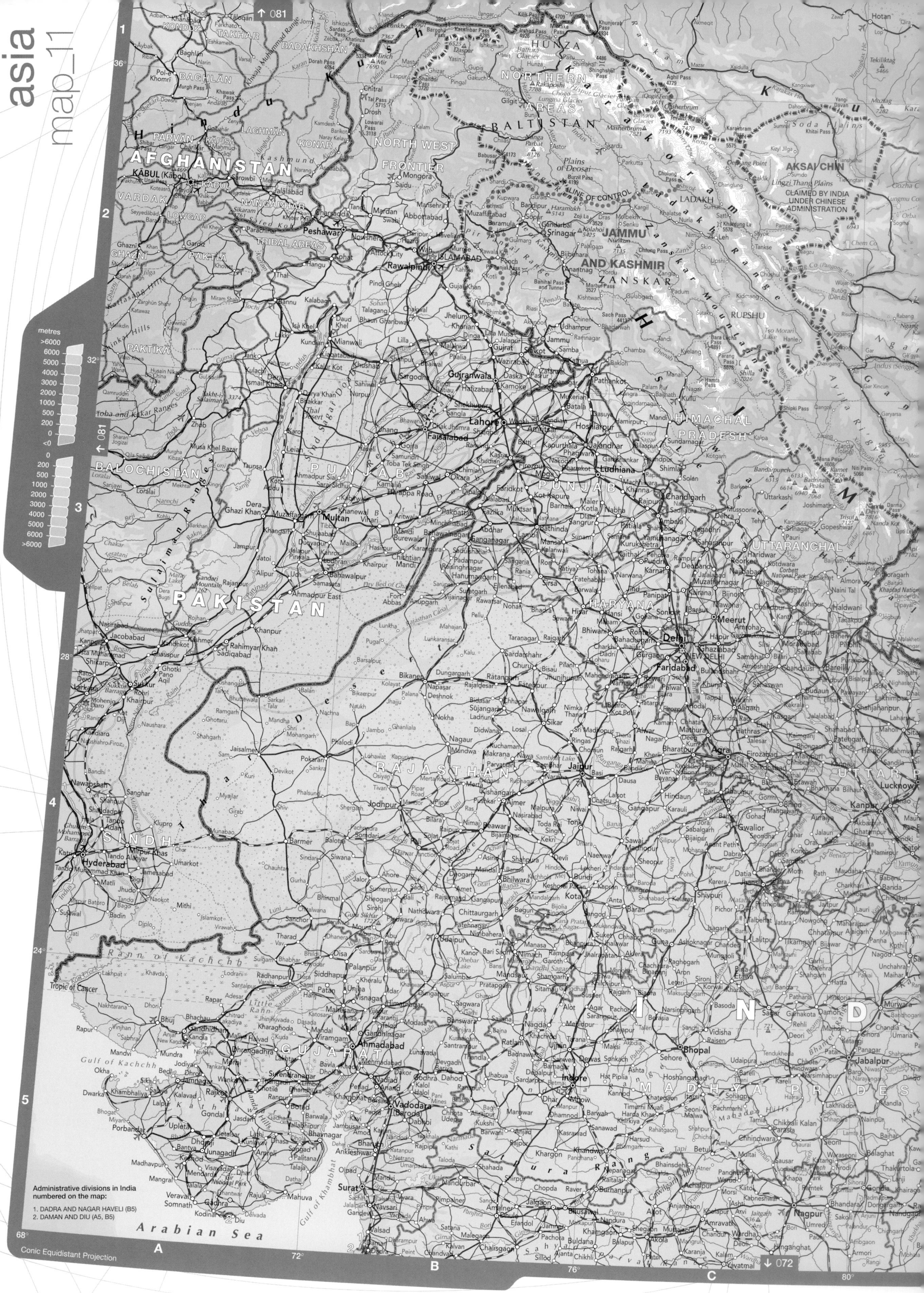
↑ 081
AFGHANISTAN
PAKISTAN
INDIA
NORTHERN AREAS
BALTISTAN
NORTH WEST FRONTIER
TRIBAL AREAS
JAMMU AND KASHMIR
LINE OF CONTROL
AKSAI CHIN
CLAIMED BY INDIA UNDER CHINESE ADMINISTRATION
BALOCHISTAN
PUNJAB
HIMACHAL PRADESH
UTTARANCHAL
HARYANA
RAJASTHAN
SINDH
GUJARAT
MADHYA PRADESH
UTTAR PRADESH
Thar Desert
Rann of Kachchh
Tropic of Cancer
Gulf of Kachchh
Gulf of Khambhat
Arabian Sea
metres
>6000
6000
5000
4000
3000
2000
1000
500
200
0
<0
0
200
500
1000
2000
3000
4000
5000
6000
>6000
↑ 081
Administrative divisions in India numbered on the map:
1. DADRA AND NAGAR HAVELI (B5)
2. DAMAN AND DIU (A5, B5)
Conic Equidistant Projection
A
B
C
68°
72°
76°
80°
↓ 072

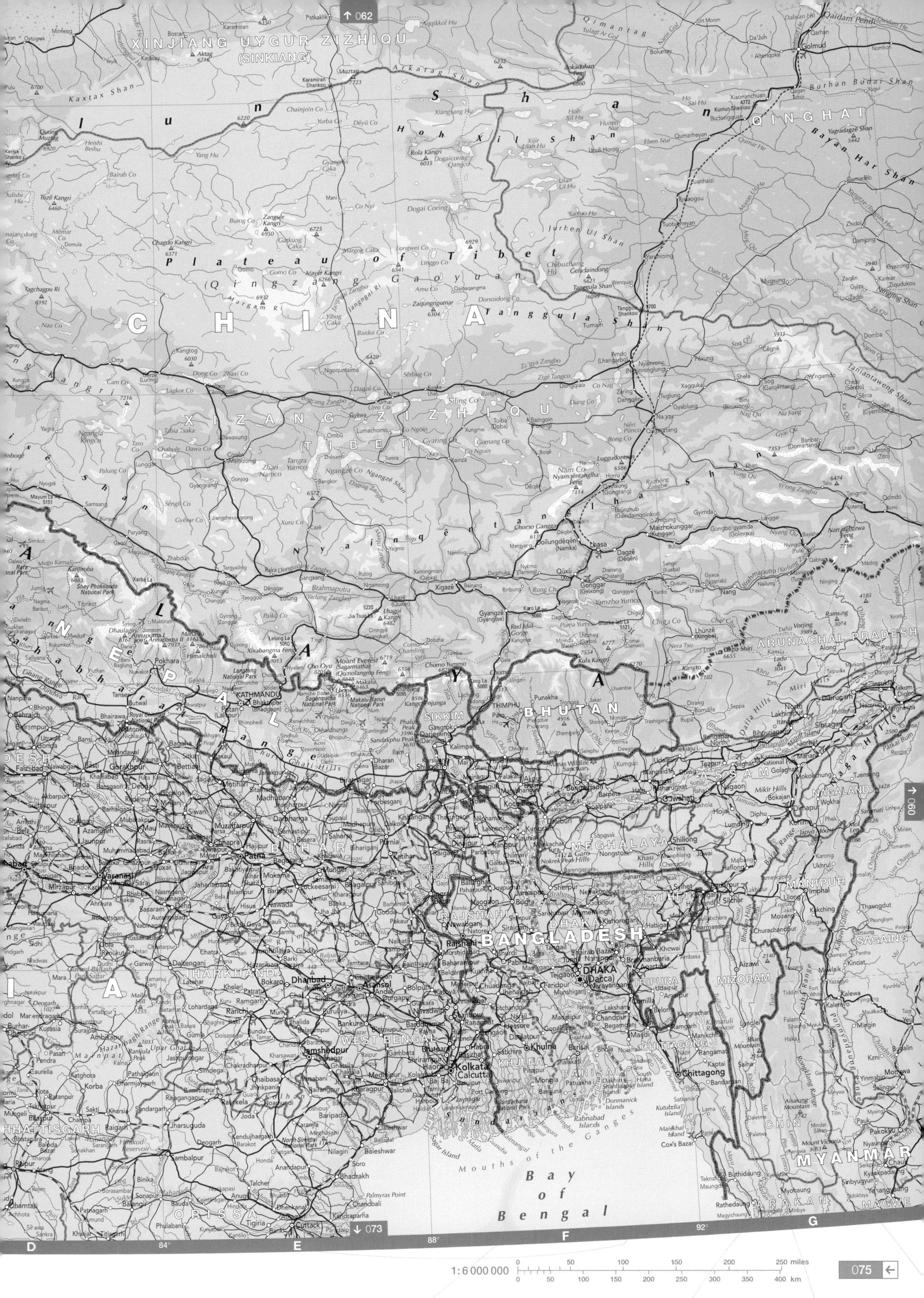

↑ 062
XINJIANG UYGUR ZIZHIQU
(SINKIANG)
Kunlun Shan
QINGHAI
Bayan Har Shan
Plateau of Tibet
(Qingzang Gaoyuan)
CHINA
Tanggula Shan
XIZANG ZIZHIQU
(TIBET)
Nyainqêntanglha Shan
NEPAL
HIMALAYA
BHUTAN
SIKKIM
ARUNACHAL PRADESH
ASSAM
NAGALAND
MEGHALAYA
MANIPUR
BIHAR
JHARKHAND
WEST BENGAL
BANGLADESH
RAJSHAHI
DHAKA
SYLHET
KHULNA
BARISAL
CHITTAGONG
TRIPURA
MIZORAM
CHIN
SAGAING
MYANMAR
MAGWE
ARAKAN
ORISSA
CHHATTISGARH
INDIA
KATHMANDU
THIMPHU
DHAKA (Dacca)
Kolkata (Calcutta)
Patna
Varanasi
Chittagong
Lhasa
Xigazê
Golmud
Mouths of the Ganges
Bay of Bengal
→ 060
↓ 073
D
E
F
G
84°
88°
92°
1:6 000 000
0 50 100 150 200 250 miles
0 50 100 150 200 250 300 350 400 km
075 ←

Black Sea

RUSSIAN FEDERATION

GEORGIA
T'BILISI

ARMENIA
YEREVAN

AZERBAIJAN
BAKU

KAZAKHSTAN

Aral Sea
(Aral'skoye More)

Ustyurt Plateau

UZBEKISTAN
Nukus

C a s p i a n   S e a

TURKMENISTAN
ASHGABAT
(Ashkhabad)

Turan Lowland

TURKEY

Aleppo (Halab)

CYPRUS

SYRIA
BEIRUT
(Beyrouth)
DAMASCUS
(Dimashq)

Mosul

Kirkūk

IRAQ
BAGHDĀD

TEHRĀN

I R A N

Eşfahān

Shīrāz

ISRAEL
Tel Aviv-Yafo
JERUSALEM

AMMAN
JORDAN

KUWAIT
KUWAIT
(Al Kuwayt)

BAHRAIN
MANAMA
(Al Manāmah)
QATAR
DOHA
(Ad Dawḥah)

Dubai (Dubayy)
ABU DHABI
(Abū Ẓabī)
UNITED ARAB EMIRATES

MUSCAT

O M A N

EGYPT

Tropic of Cancer

S A U D I   A R A B I A

A r a b i a n

Medina
(Al Madīnah)

RIYADH
(Ar Riyāḍ)

P e n i n s u l a

Mecca
(Makkah)
Jeddah
(Jiddah)

Red Sea

N u b i a n   D e s e r t

Port Sudan
(Bur Sūdān)

Gulf of Oman

R u b '   a l   K h ā l i

SUDAN

ERITREA
ASMARA

YEMEN
ṢAN'Ā'

Hodeidah
(Al Ḩudaydah)

Mukalla
(Al Mukallā)

A r a b i a n
S e a

Socotra
(Suquṭrā)
(Yemen)

ETHIOPIA
ADDIS ABABA
(Ādīs Ābeba)

Ethiopian
Highlands

DJIBOUTI
DJIBOUTI

Gulf of Aden

Aden ('Adan)

SOMALIA

metres
>6000
6000
5000
4000
3000
2000
1500
1000
500
200
100
0
<0
0
50
200
500
1000
2000
3000
4000
5000
6000
>6000

Albers Conic Equal Area Projection

1:13 000 000

0   100   200   300   400   500 miles

0   100   200   300   400   500   600   700   800 km

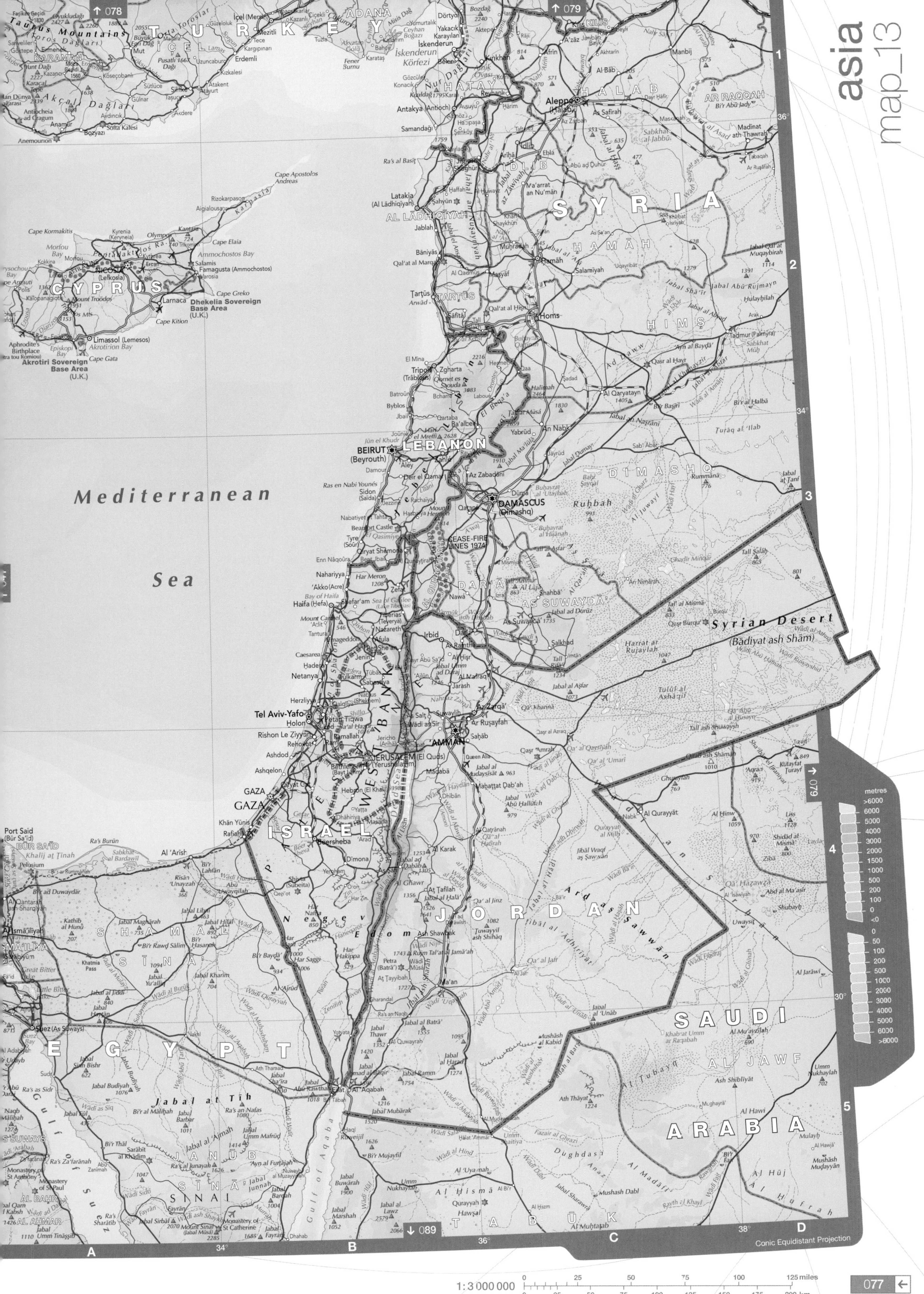

Conic Equidistant Projection

1:3 000 000

0 25 50 75 100 125 miles
0 25 50 75 100 125 150 175 200 km

metres
>6000
6000
4000
3000
2000
1500
1000
500
200
0
<0
50
100
200
500
1000
2000
3000
4000
5000
6000
>6000

↑ 029

Administrative divisions numbered on the map:

EGYPT
10. AD DAQAHLĪYAH (B5)
11. AL BUHAYRAH (B5)
12. AL GHARBĪYAH (B5)
13. AL ISKANDARĪYAH (B5)
14. AL QĀHIRAH (B5)
15. AS SUWAYS (C5)
16. BŪR SAʿĪD (C5)

17. DUMYĀṬ (B5)
18. ISMĀʿĪLĪYAH (C5)
19. KAFR ASH SHAYKH (B5)
20. MINŪFĪYA (B5)
21. QALYŪBĪYA (B5)
22. SHARQĪYAH (B5)

IRAN
23. CHAHĀR MAḤALL VA BAKHTĪARĪ (G4)
24. KOHKĪLŪYEH VA BŪYER AḤMADĪ (G5)

metres
>6000
6000
5000
4000
3000
2000
1000
500
200
0
0
200
1000
2000
3000
4000
5000
6000
>6000

Black Sea

Aegean Sea

Krytiko Pelagos

Mediterranean Sea

ROMANIA
BULGARIA
GREECE
TURKEY
CYPRUS
LEBANON
ISRAEL
JORDAN
LIBYA
EGYPT
UKRAINE

ANATOLIA
PISIDIA
Taurus Mountains
Balkan Mountains
Rhodope Mountains

BUCHAREST (Bucureşti)
İstanbul
Bursa
ANKARA
Konya
NICOSIA (Lefkosia)
BEIRUT (Beyrouth)
DAMASCUS
AMMĀN
JERUSALEM
CAIRO (Al Qāhirah)
Alexandria (Al Iskandarīyah)
Tel Aviv-Yafo
GAZA

Crete (Kriti)
Rhodes (Rodos)
Cyclades (Kyklades)
Evvoia
Lesbos (Lesvos)
Chios
Samos

Qattara Depression
Libyan Plateau
Great Sand Sea
SINAI
Gulf of Suez
Gulf of Aqaba

Conic Equidistant Projection

1:6 000 000

0 50 100 150 200 250 miles
0 50 100 150 200 250 300 350 400 km

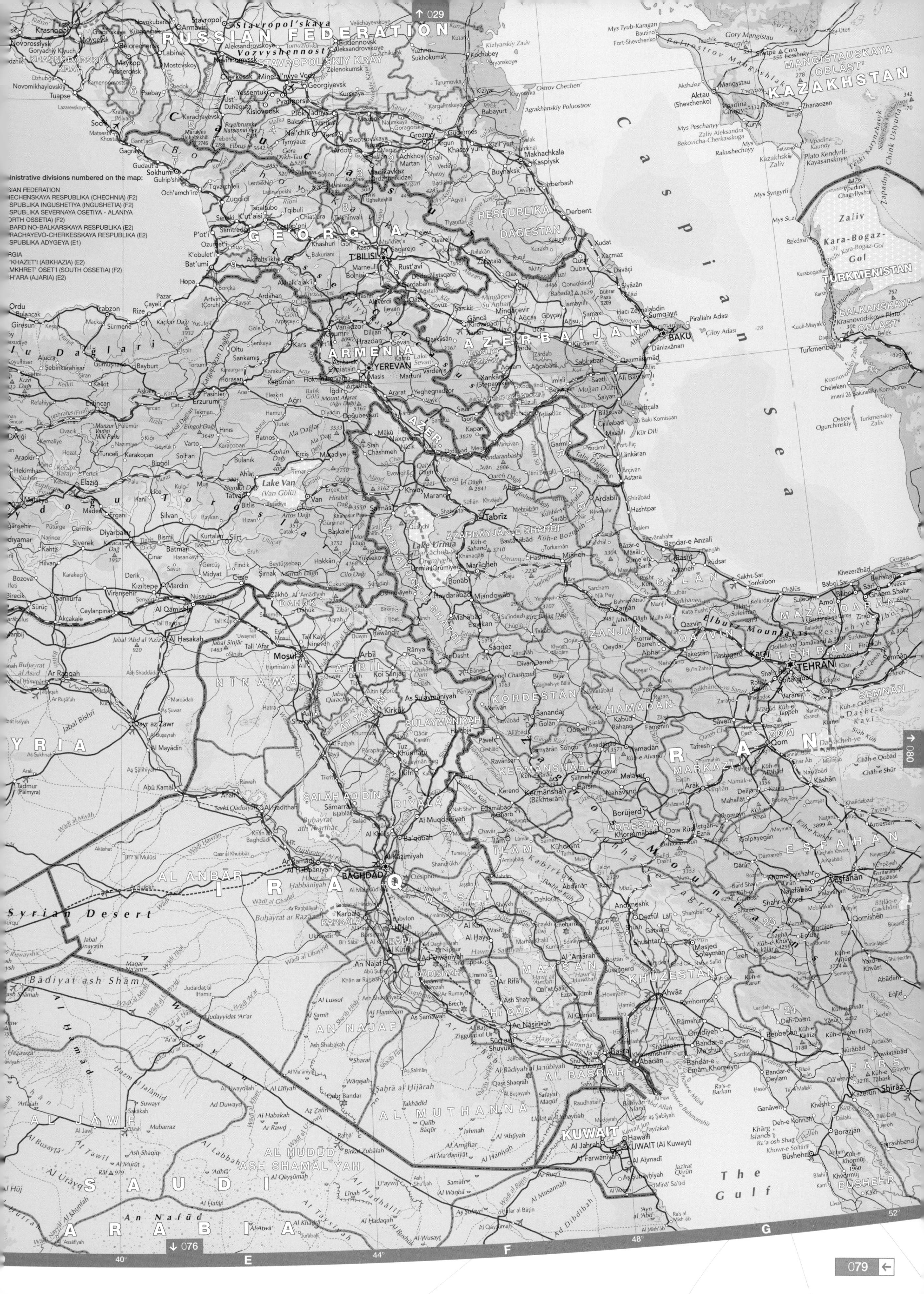

RUSSIAN FEDERATION
STAVROPOL'SKIY KRAY
KRASNODARSKIY KRAY
Caucasus
GEORGIA
ARMENIA
AZERBAIJAN
AZER.
KAZAKHSTAN
MANGISTAUSKAYA OBLAST'
TURKMENISTAN
BALKANSKAYA OBLAST'
RESPUBLIKA DAGESTAN
Caspian Sea
Zaliv Kara-Bogaz-Gol
IRAN
IRAQ
SYRIA
SAUDI ARABIA
KUWAIT
The Gulf
Syrian Desert
Lake Van
Lake Urmia
Elburz Mountains
Zagros Mountains
TEHRAN
BAGHDAD
T'BILISI
YEREVAN
BAKU
KUWAIT (Al Kuwayt)
ministrative divisions numbered on the map:
SIAN FEDERATION
HECHENSKAYA RESPUBLIKA (CHECHNIA) (F2)
SPUBLIKA INGUSHETIYA (INGUSHETIA) (F2)
SPUBLIKA SEVERNAYA OSETIYA - ALANIYA
ORTH OSSETIA) (F2)
BARDINO-BALKARSKAYA RESPUBLIKA (E2)
RACHAYEVO-CHERKESSKAYA RESPUBLIKA (E2)
SPUBLIKA ADYGEYA (E1)
RGIA
'KHAZET'I (ABKHAZIA) (E2)
MKHRET' OSET'I (SOUTH OSSETIA) (F2)
'H'ARA (AJARIA) (E2)

↑ 029
→ 080
↓ 076

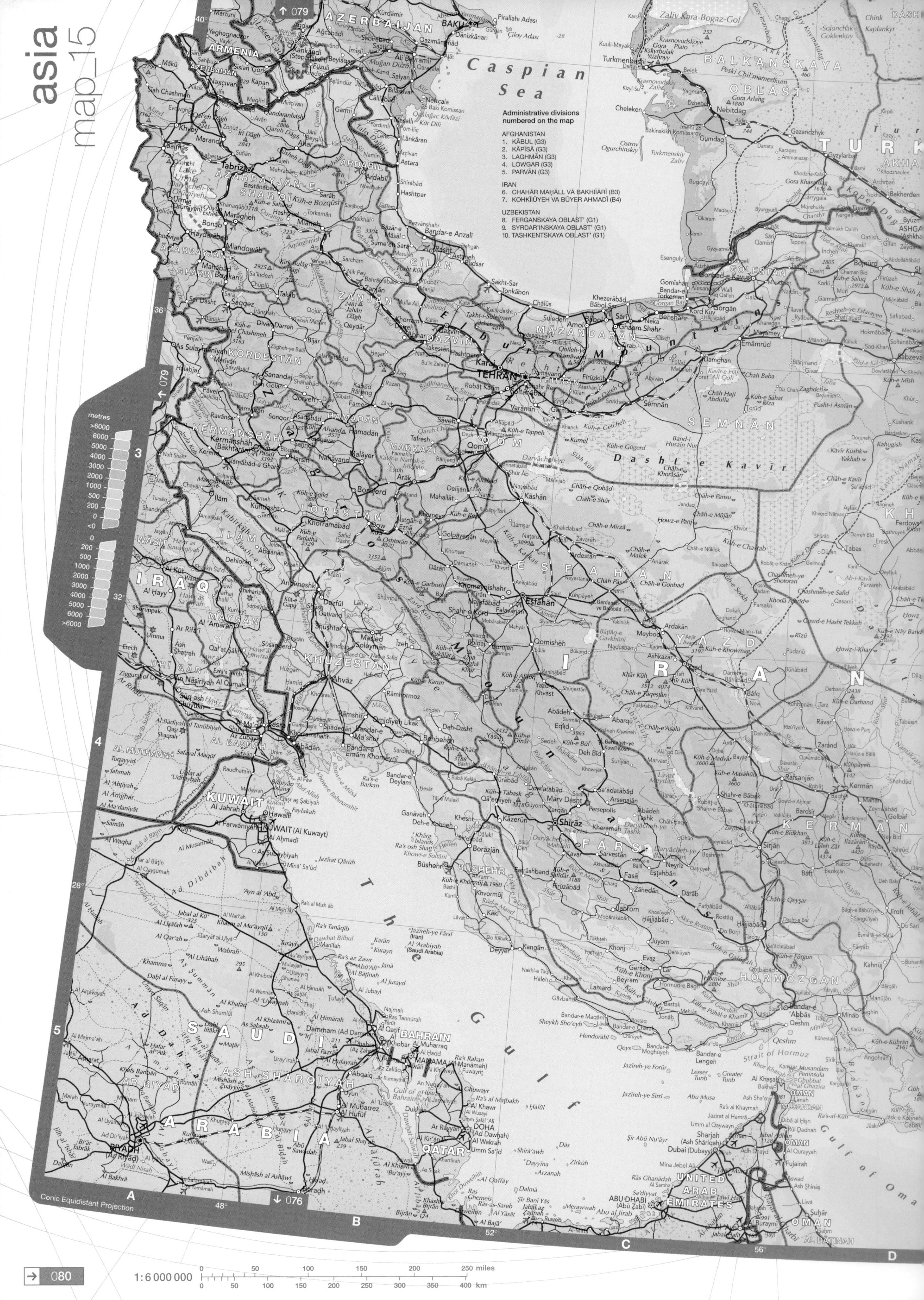
asia
map_15
Caspian Sea
Administrative divisions numbered on the map
AFGHANISTAN
1. KĀBUL (G3)
2. KĀPĪSĀ (G3)
3. LAGHMĀN (G3)
4. LOWGAR (G3)
5. PARVĀN (G3)
IRAN
6. CHAHĀR MAḨĀLL VĀ BAKHĪĀRĪ (B3)
7. KOHKĪLŪYEH VA BŪYER AHMADĪ (B4)
UZBEKISTAN
8. FERGANSKAYA OBLAST' (G1)
9. SYRDAR'INSKAYA OBLAST' (G1)
10. TASHKENTSKAYA OBLAST' (G1)
AZERBAIJAN
ARMENIA
I R A N
I R A Q
KUWAIT
BAHRAIN
QATAR
SAUDI ARABIA
UNITED ARAB EMIRATES
OMAN
TEHRAN
The Gulf
Gulf of Oman
Strait of Hormuz
Dasht-e Kavīr
Elburz Mountains
Zagros Mountains
metres
>6000
6000
5000
4000
3000
2000
1000
500
200
0
<0
0
200
500
1000
2000
3000
4000
5000
6000
>6000
↑ 079
↓ 076
Conic Equidistant Projection
A
B
C
D
3
4
5
40°
36°
32°
28°
48°
52°
56°
→ 080
1:6 000 000
0 50 100 150 200 250 miles
0 50 100 150 200 250 300 350 400 km

↑ 070

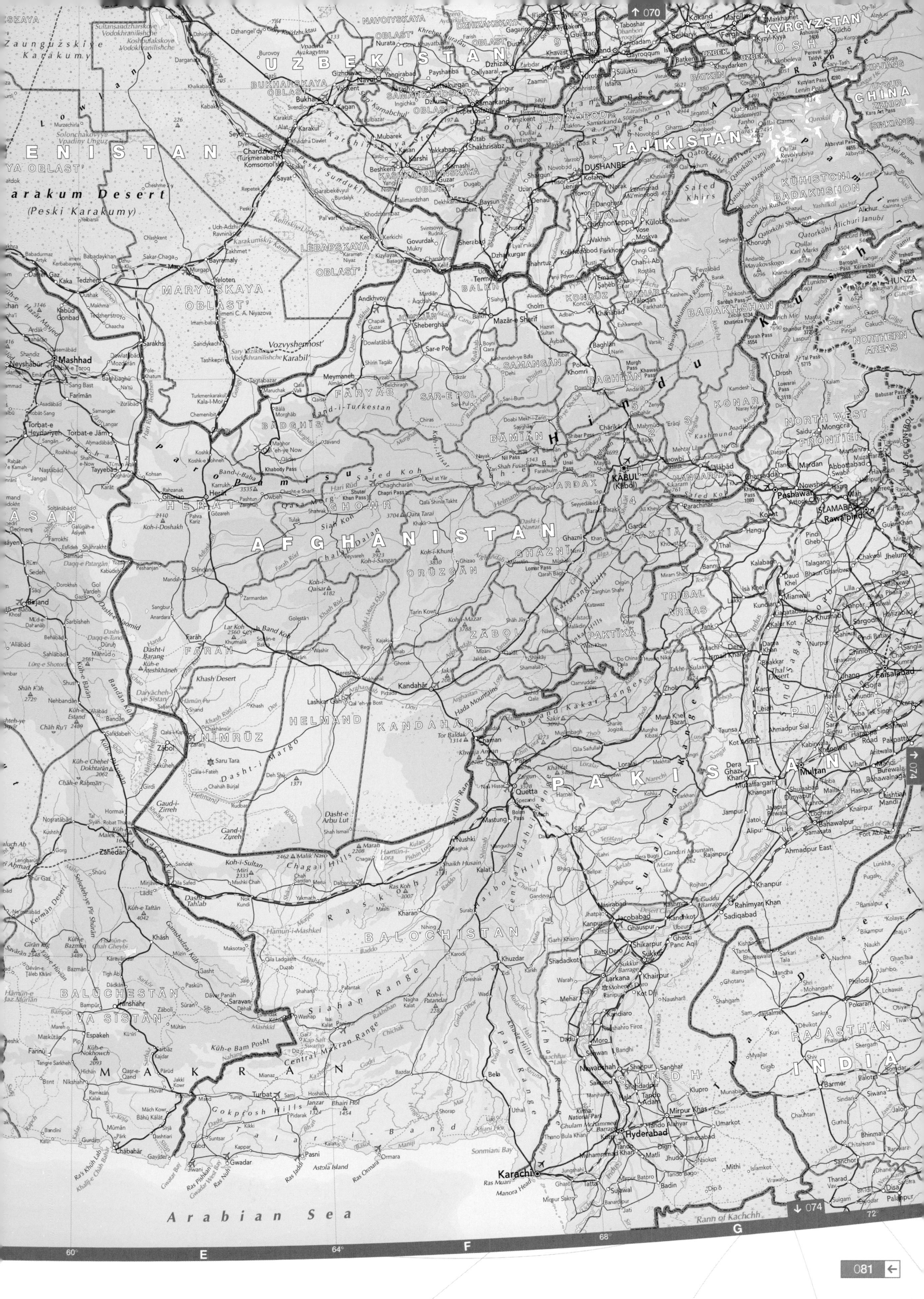
UZBEKISTAN
KYRGYZSTAN
TAJIKISTAN
AFGHANISTAN
PAKISTAN
INDIA
CHINA
XINJIANG UYGUR ZIZHIQU (SINKIANG)
Karakum Desert
(Peski Karakumy)
Zaunguzskiye Karakumy
NAVOIYSKAYA OBLAST'
DZHIZAKSKAYA OBLAST'
BUKHARSKAYA OBLAST'
SAMARKANDSKAYA OBLAST'
KASHKADAR'INSKAYA OBLAST'
SURKHANDAR'INSKAYA OBLAST'
LEBAPSKAYA OBLAST'
MARYYSKAYA OBLAST'
LENINOBOD
KHATLON
KŬHISTONI BADAKHSHON
OSH
BATKEN
NORTHERN AREAS
NORTH WEST FRONTIER
TRIBAL AREAS
PUNJAB
SINDH
BALOCHISTAN
RAJASTHAN
BALUCHESTĀN VA SĪSTĀN
MAKRAN
HERAT
FARAH
NĪMRŪZ
HELMAND
KANDAHAR
ZĀBOL
ORŪZGĀN
GHAZNĪ
PAKTĪKĀ
PAKTĪA
GHOWR
BĀDGHĪS
FĀRYĀB
JOWZJĀN
BALKH
SAMANGĀN
SAR-E POL
BĀMĪĀN
BAGHLĀN
KONDŪZ
TAKHĀR
BADAKHSHĀN
KONAR
NANGARHĀR
VARDAK
Paropamisus
Hindu Kush
Pamir
Safed Koh
Sulaiman Range
Central Brahui Range
Kirthar Range
Pab Range
Siahan Range
Central Makran Range
Chagai Hills
Toba and Kakar Ranges
Thar Desert
Thal Desert
Dasht-i Margo
Khash Desert
Kūh-e Bam Posht
Hamun-i-Mashkel
Rann of Kachchh
Arabian Sea
Tashkent
Samarkand
Bukhara
Karshi
Termez
DUSHANBE
Khŭjand
Fergana
Mazār-e Sharīf
Herāt
KABUL (Kabol)
Kandahār
Ghazni
Jalālābād
Peshawar
ISLAMABAD
Rawalpindi
Faisalabad
Multan
Quetta
Karachi
Hyderabad
Sukkur
Mashhad
Zāhedān
Chābahār
Gwadar
Mary
Chardzhev
LINE OF CONTROL
60°
64°
68°
72°
E
F
G

↑ 074
↓ 074

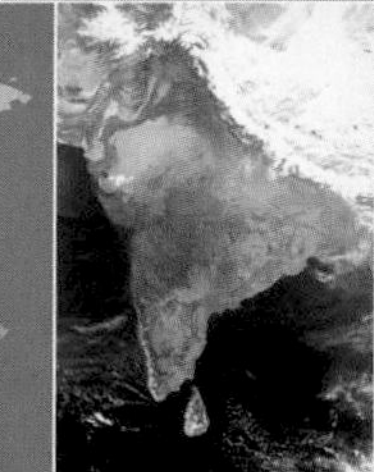
Indian subcontinent

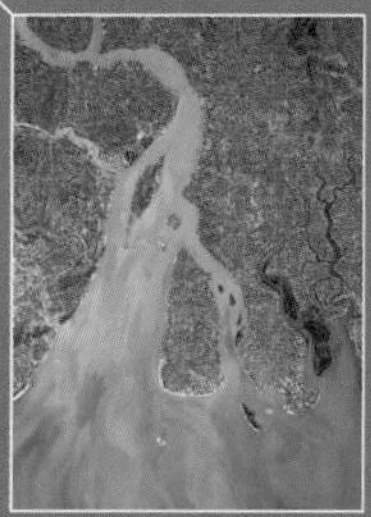
Ganges Delta, India

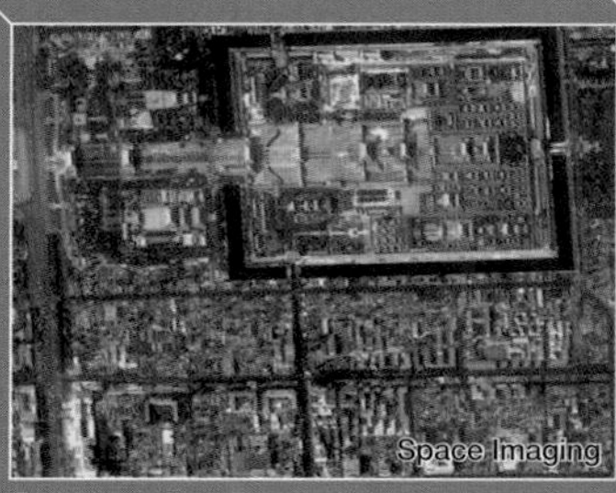
Forbidden City, Beijing, China

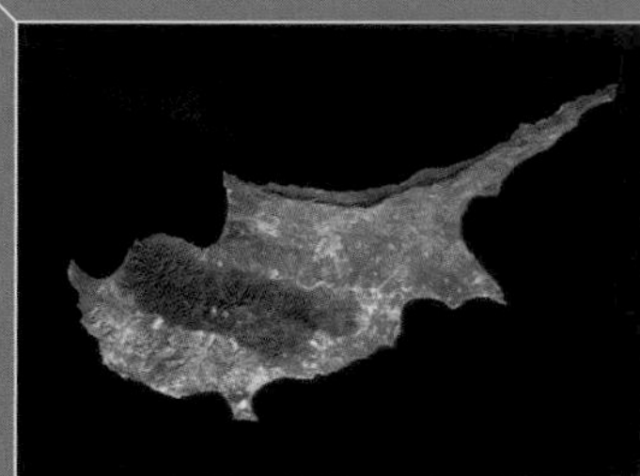
Space Imaging
Cyprus, eastern Mediterranean

COUNTRIES		area sq km	area sq miles	population	capital	languages	religions	currency	map
AFGHANISTAN		652 225	251 825	22 475 000	Kābul	Dari, Pushtu, Uzbek, Turkmen	Sunni Muslim, Shi'a Muslim	Afghani	81
ARMENIA		29 800	11 506	3 788 000	Yerevan	Armenian, Azeri	Armenian Orthodox	Dram	79
AZERBAIJAN		86 600	33 436	8 096 000	Baku	Azeri, Armenian, Russian, Lezgian	Shi'a Muslim, Sunni Muslim, Russian and Armenian Orthodox	Azerbaijani manat	79
BAHRAIN		691	267	652 000	Manama	Arabic, English	Shi'a Muslim, Sunni Muslim, Christian	Bahrain dinar	80
BANGLADESH		143 998	55 598	140 369 000	Dhaka	Bengali, English	Sunni Muslim, Hindu	Taka	75
BHUTAN		46 620	18 000	2 141 000	Thimphu	Dzongkha, Nepali, Assamese	Buddhist, Hindu	Ngultrum, Indian rupee	75
BRUNEI		5 765	2 226	335 000	Bandar Seri Begawan	Malay, English, Chinese	Sunni Muslim, Buddhist, Christian	Brunei dollar	59
CAMBODIA		181 000	69 884	13 441 000	Phnom Penh	Khmer, Vietnamese	Buddhist, Roman Catholic, Sunni Muslim	Riel	61
CHINA		9 584 492	3 700 593	1 270 082 000	Beijing	Mandarin, Wu, Cantonese, Hsiang, regional languages	Confucian, Taoist, Buddhist, Christian, Sunni Muslim	Yuan, HK dollar*, Macau pataca	62–63
CYPRUS		9 251	3 572	790 000	Nicosia	Greek, Turkish, English	Greek Orthodox, Sunni Muslim	Cyprus pound	77
EAST TIMOR		14 874	5 743	750 000	Dili	Portuguese, Tetun, English	Roman Catholic	United States dollar	108
GEORGIA		69 700	26 911	5 239 000	T'bilisi	Georgian, Russian, Armenian, Azeri, Ossetian, Abkhaz	Georgian Orthodox, Russian Orthodox, Sunni Muslim	Lari	79
INDIA		3 065 027	1 183 414	1 025 096 000	New Delhi	Hindi, English, many regional languages	Hindu, Sunni Muslim, Shi'a Muslim, Sikh, Christian	Indian rupee	70–71
INDONESIA		1 919 445	741 102	214 840 000	Jakarta	Indonesian, local languages	Sunni Muslim, Protestant, Roman Catholic, Hindu, Buddhist	Rupiah	56–57
IRAN		1 648 000	636 296	71 369 000	Tehrān	Farsi, Azeri, Kurdish, regional languages	Shi'a Muslim, Sunni Muslim	Iranian rial	80–81
IRAQ		438 317	169 235	23 584 000	Baghdād	Arabic, Kurdish, Turkmen	Shi'a Muslim, Sunni Muslim, Christian	Iraqi dinar	79
ISRAEL		20 770	8 019	6 172 000	Jerusalem	Hebrew, Arabic	Jewish, Sunni Muslim, Christian, Druze	Shekel	77
JAPAN		377 727	145 841	127 335 000	Tōkyō	Japanese	Shintoist, Buddhist, Christian	Yen	64–65
JORDAN		89 206	34 443	5 051 000	'Ammān	Arabic	Sunni Muslim, Christian	Jordanian dinar	77
KAZAKHSTAN		2 717 300	1 049 155	16 095 000	Astana	Kazakh, Russian, Ukrainian, German, Uzbek, Tatar	Sunni Muslim, Russian Orthodox, Protestant	Tenge	26
KUWAIT		17 818	6 880	1 971 000	Kuwait	Arabic	Sunni Muslim, Shi'a Muslim, Christian, Hindu	Kuwaiti dinar	79
KYRGYZSTAN		198 500	76 641	4 986 000	Bishkek	Kyrgyz, Russian, Uzbek	Sunni Muslim, Russian Orthodox	Kyrgyz som	70
LAOS		236 800	91 429	5 403 000	Vientiane	Lao, local languages	Buddhist, traditional beliefs	Kip	60–61
LEBANON		10 452	4 036	3 556 000	Beirut	Arabic, Armenian, French	Shi'a Muslim, Sunni Muslim, Christian	Lebanese pound	77
MALAYSIA		332 965	128 559	22 633 000	Kuala Lumpur, Putrajaya	Malay, English, Chinese, Tamil, local languages	Sunni Muslim, Buddhist, Hindu, Christian, traditional beliefs	Ringgit	58–59
MALDIVES		298	115	300 000	Male	Divehi (Maldivian)	Sunni Muslim	Rufiyaa	71
MONGOLIA		1 565 000	604 250	2 559 000	Ulan Bator	Khalka (Mongolian), Kazakh, local languages	Buddhist, Sunni Muslim	Tugrik (tögrög)	62–63
MYANMAR		676 577	261 228	48 364 000	Rangoon	Burmese, Shan, Karen, local languages	Buddhist, Christian, Sunni Muslim	Kyat	60–61
NEPAL		147 181	56 827	23 593 000	Kathmandu	Nepali, Maithili, Bhojpuri, English, local languages	Hindu, Buddhist, Sunni Muslim	Nepalese rupee	74–75
NORTH KOREA		120 538	46 540	22 428 000	P'yŏngyang	Korean	Traditional beliefs, Chondoist, Buddhist	North Korean won	64–65
OMAN		309 500	119 499	2 622 000	Muscat	Arabic, Baluchi, Indian languages	Ibadhi Muslim, Sunni Muslim	Omani riyal	76
PAKISTAN		803 940	310 403	144 971 000	Islamabad	Urdu, Punjabi, Sindhi, Pushtu, English	Sunni Muslim, Shi'a Muslim, Christian, Hindu	Pakistani rupee	70–71
PALAU		497	192	20 000	Koror	Palauan, English	Roman Catholic, Protestant, traditional beliefs	United States dollar	57
PHILIPPINES		300 000	115 831	77 131 000	Manila	English, Pilipino, Cebuano, local languages	Roman Catholic, Protestant, Sunni Muslim, Aglipayan	Philippine peso	56–57
QATAR		11 437	4 416	575 000	Doha	Arabic	Sunni Muslim	Qatari riyal	80
RUSSIAN FEDERATION		17 075 400	6 592 849	144 664 000	Moscow	Russian, Tatar, Ukrainian, local languages	Russian Orthodox, Sunni Muslim, Protestant	Russian rouble	26–27
SAUDI ARABIA		2 200 000	849 425	21 028 000	Riyadh	Arabic	Sunni Muslim, Shi'a Muslim	Saudi Arabian riyal	76
SINGAPORE		639	247	4 108 000	Singapore	Chinese, English, Malay, Tamil	Buddhist, Taoist, Sunni Muslim, Christian, Hindu	Singapore dollar	58
SOUTH KOREA		99 274	38 330	47 069 000	Seoul	Korean	Buddhist, Protestant, Roman Catholic	South Korean won	65
SRI LANKA		65 610	25 332	19 104 000	Sri Jayewardenepura Kotte	Sinhalese, Tamil, English	Buddhist, Hindu, Sunni Muslim, Roman Catholic	Sri Lankan rupee	72
SYRIA		185 180	71 498	16 610 000	Damascus	Arabic, Kurdish, Armenian	Sunni Muslim, Shi'a Muslim, Christian	Syrian pound	78–79
TAIWAN		36 179	13 969	22 300 000	T'aipei	Mandarin, Min, Hakka, local languages	Buddhist, Taoist, Confucian, Christian	Taiwan dollar	67
TAJIKISTAN		143 100	55 251	6 135 000	Dushanbe	Tajik, Uzbek, Russian	Sunni Muslim	Somoni	81
THAILAND		513 115	198 115	63 584 000	Bangkok	Thai, Lao, Chinese, Malay, Mon–Khmer languages	Buddhist, Sunni Muslim	Baht	60–61
TURKEY		779 452	300 948	67 632 000	Ankara	Turkish, Kurdish	Sunni Muslim, Shi'a Muslim	Turkish lira	78–79
TURKMENISTAN		488 100	188 456	4 835 000	Ashgabat	Turkmen, Uzbek, Russian	Sunni Muslim, Russian Orthodox	Turkmen manat	68
UNITED ARAB EMIRATES		83 600	32 278	2 654 000	Abu Dhabi	Arabic, English	Sunni Muslim, Shi'a Muslim	United Arab Emirates dirham	76
UZBEKISTAN		447 400	172 742	25 257 000	Tashkent	Uzbek, Russian, Tajik, Kazakh	Sunni Muslim, Russian Orthodox	Uzbek som	70
VIETNAM		329 565	127 246	79 175 000	Ha Nôi	Vietnamese, Thai, Khmer, Chinese, local languages	Buddhist, Taoist, Roman Catholic, Cao Dai, Hoa Hao	Dong	60–61
YEMEN		527 968	203 850	19 114 000	Şan'ā'	Arabic	Sunni Muslim, Shi'a Muslim	Yemeni rial	76

*Hong Kong dollar

DEPENDENT AND DISPUTED TERRITORIES		territorial status	area sq km	area sq miles	population	capital	languages	religions	currency	map
British Indian Ocean Territory		United Kingdom Overseas Territory	60	23	uninhabited					162
Christmas Island		Australian External Territory	135	52	2 135	The Settlement	English	Buddhist, Sunni Muslim, Protestant, Roman Catholic	Australian dollar	55
Cocos Islands (Keeling Islands)		Australian External Territory	14	5	637	West Island	English	Sunni Muslim, Christian	Australian dollar	55
French Southern and Antarctic Lands		French Overseas Territory	439 580	169 723	uninhabited					163
Gaza		Semi-autonomous region	363	140	3 311 000*	Gaza	Arabic	Sunni Muslim, Shi'a Muslim	Israeli shekel	77
Heard and McDonald Islands		Australian External Territory	412	159	uninhabited					163
Jammu and Kashmir		Disputed territory (India/Pakistan)	222 236	85 806	13 000 000					74
West Bank		Disputed territory	5 860	2 263			Arabic, Hebrew	Sunni Muslim, Jewish, Shi'a Muslim, Christian	Jordanian dinar, Israeli shekel	77

africa

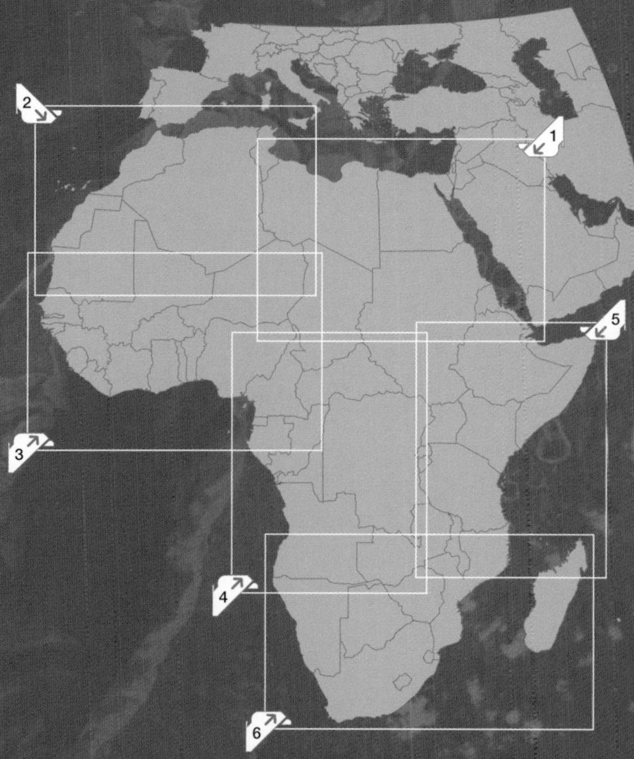

contents

		map coverage	scale

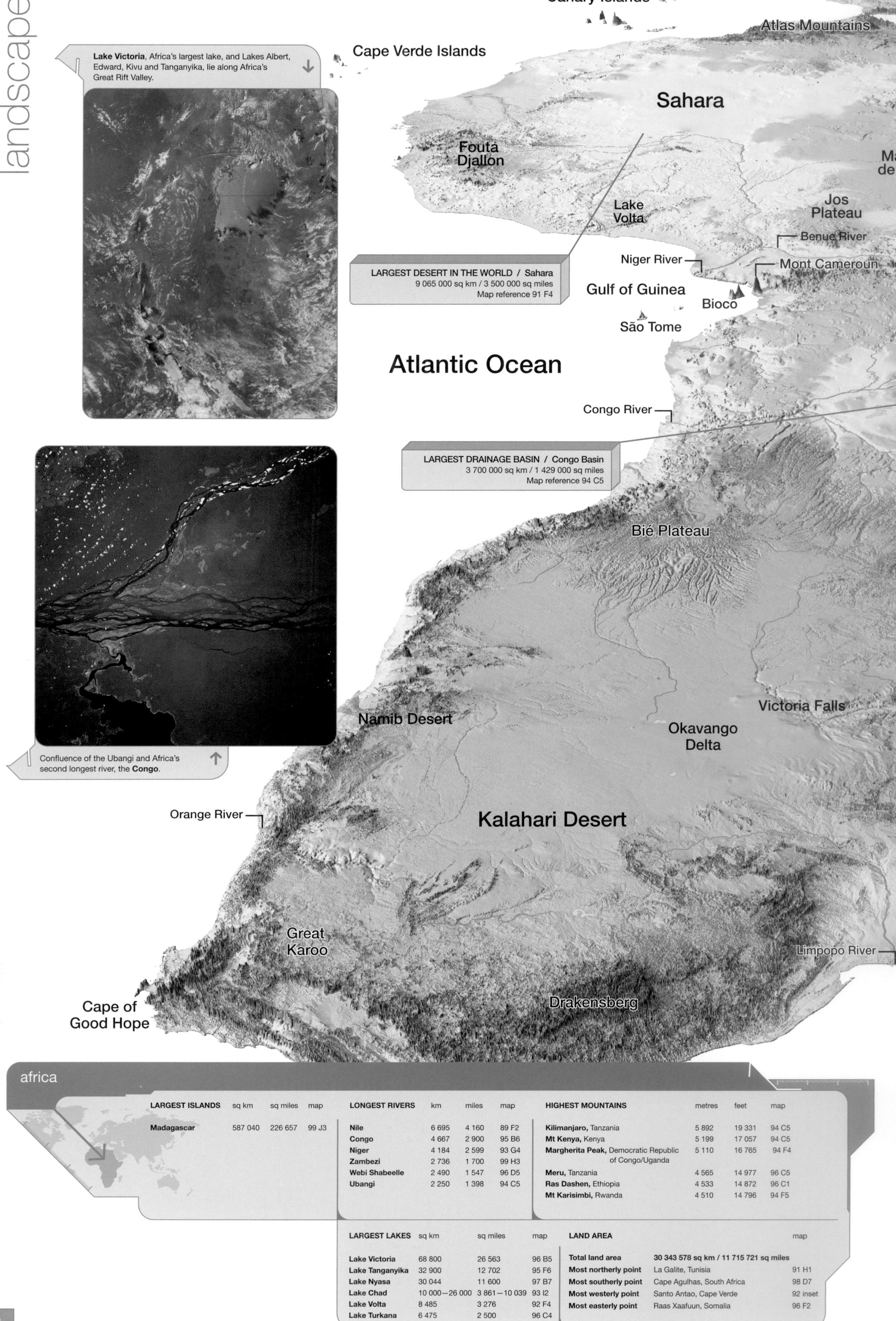

Canary Islands

Atlas Mountains

Cape Verde Islands

Sahara

Lake Victoria, Africa's largest lake, and Lakes Albert, Edward, Kivu and Tanganyika, lie along Africa's Great Rift Valley.

Fouta Djallon

Mass de l' A

Jos Plateau

Lake Volta

Benue River

Niger River

Mont Cameroun

LARGEST DESERT IN THE WORLD / Sahara
9 065 000 sq km / 3 500 000 sq miles
Map reference 91 F4

Gulf of Guinea

Bioco

São Tome

Atlantic Ocean

Congo River

LARGEST DRAINAGE BASIN / Congo Basin
3 700 000 sq km / 1 429 000 sq miles
Map reference 94 C5

Bié Plateau

Victoria Falls

Okavango Delta

Namib Desert

Confluence of the Ubangi and Africa's second longest river, the **Congo**.

Orange River

Kalahari Desert

Limpopo River

Great Karoo

Cape of Good Hope

Drakensberg

africa

LARGEST ISLANDS	sq km	sq miles	map
Madagascar	587 040	226 657	99 J3

LONGEST RIVERS	km	miles	map
Nile	6 695	4 160	89 F2
Congo	4 667	2 900	95 B6
Niger	4 184	2 599	93 G4
Zambezi	2 736	1 700	99 H3
Webi Shabeelle	2 490	1 547	96 D5
Ubangi	2 250	1 398	94 C5

HIGHEST MOUNTAINS	metres	feet	map
Kilimanjaro, Tanzania	5 892	19 331	94 C5
Mt Kenya, Kenya	5 199	17 057	94 C5
Margherita Peak, Democratic Republic of Congo/Uganda	5 110	16 765	94 F4
Meru, Tanzania	4 565	14 977	96 C5
Ras Dashen, Ethiopia	4 533	14 872	96 C1
Mt Karisimbi, Rwanda	4 510	14 796	94 F5

LARGEST LAKES	sq km	sq miles	map
Lake Victoria	68 800	26 563	96 B5
Lake Tanganyika	32 900	12 702	95 F6
Lake Nyasa	30 044	11 600	97 B7
Lake Chad	10 000—26 000	3 861—10 039	93 I2
Lake Volta	8 485	3 276	92 F4
Lake Turkana	6 475	2 500	96 C4

LAND AREA		map
Total land area	30 343 578 sq km / 11 715 721 sq miles	
Most northerly point	La Galite, Tunisia	91 H1
Most southerly point	Cape Agulhas, South Africa	98 D7
Most westerly point	Santo Antao, Cape Verde	92 inset
Most easterly point	Raas Xaafuun, Somalia	96 F2

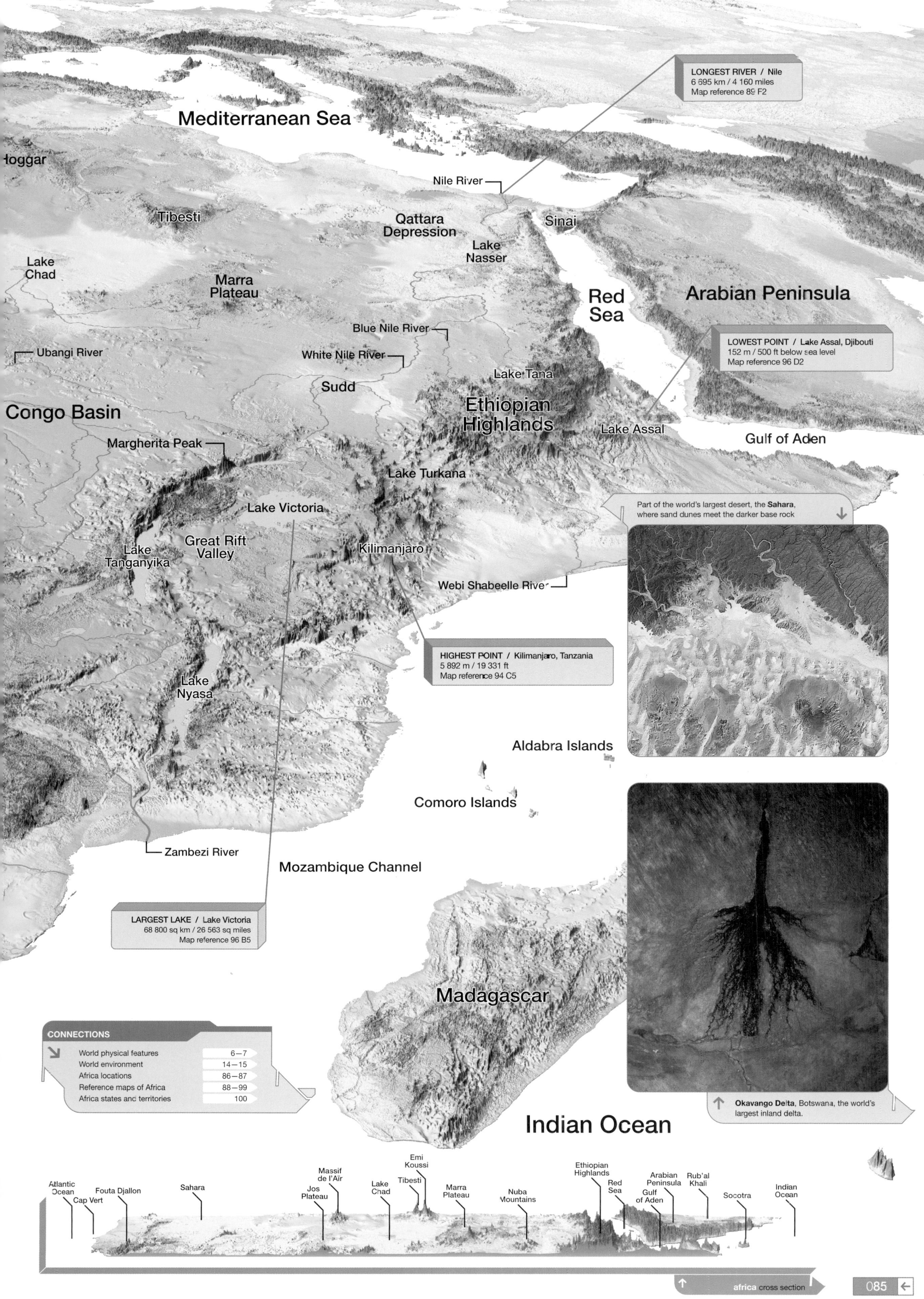

Mediterranean Sea

Hoggar

Tibesti

Lake
Chad

Marra
Plateau

Ubangi River

Congo Basin

Margherita Peak

Lake Victoria

Lake
Tanganyika

Great Rift
Valley

Lake
Nyasa

Zambezi River

Mozambique Channel

LONGEST RIVER / Nile
6 695 km / 4 160 miles
Map reference 89 F2

Nile River

Qattara
Depression

Lake
Nasser

Sinai

Blue Nile River

White Nile River

Sudd

Lake Tana

Ethiopian
Highlands

Lake Assal

Red
Sea

Arabian Peninsula

LOWEST POINT / Lake Assal, Djibouti
152 m / 500 ft below sea level
Map reference 96 D2

Gulf of Aden

Lake Turkana

Kilimanjaro

Webi Shabeelle River

Part of the world's largest desert, the **Sahara**,
where sand dunes meet the darker base rock

HIGHEST POINT / Kilimanjaro, Tanzania
5 892 m / 19 331 ft
Map reference 94 C5

Aldabra Islands

Comoro Islands

LARGEST LAKE / Lake Victoria
68 800 sq km / 26 563 sq miles
Map reference 96 B5

Madagascar

Okavango Delta, Botswana, the world's
largest inland delta.

Indian Ocean

Atlantic
Ocean

Cap Vert

Fouta Djallon

Sahara

Jos
Plateau

Massif
de l'Air

Lake Chad

Emi
Koussi

Tibesti

Marra
Plateau

Nuba
Mountains

Ethiopian
Highlands

Red
Sea

Gulf
of Aden

Arabian
Peninsula

Rub'al
Khali

Socotra

Indian
Ocean

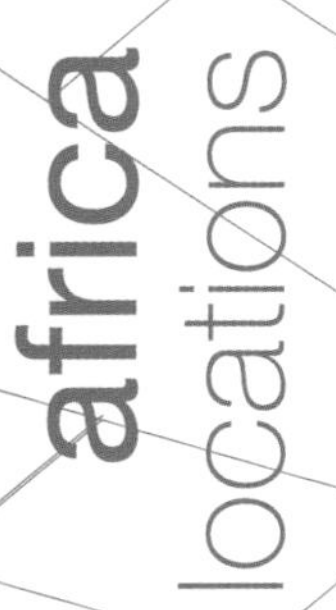

Namib Desert, arid region along the entire coast of Namibia, southwest Africa.

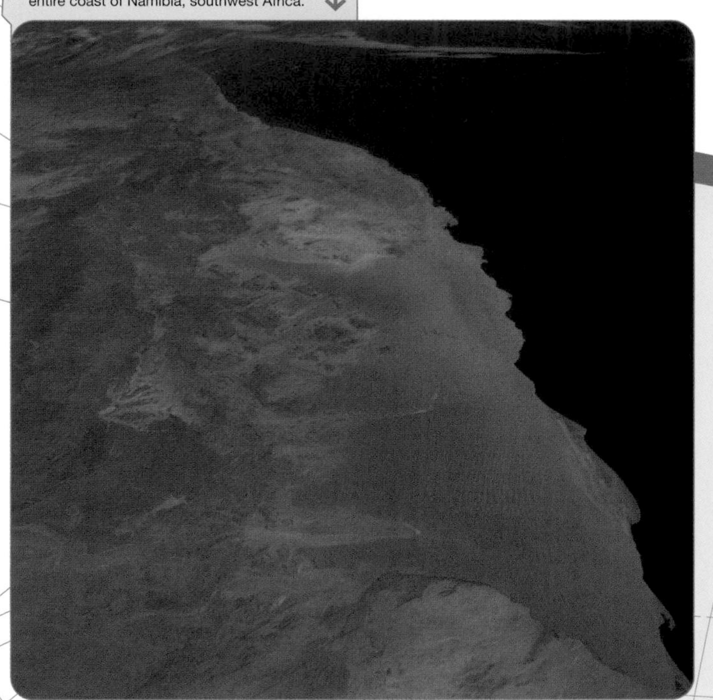

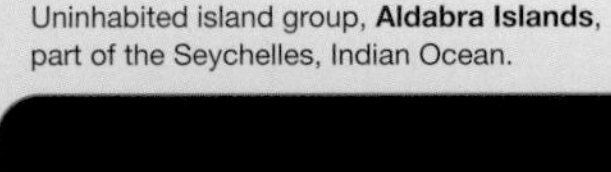

Uninhabited island group, Aldabra Islands, part of the Seychelles, Indian Ocean.

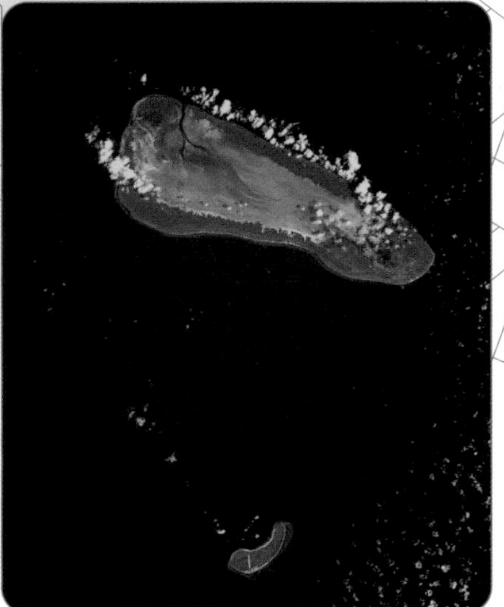

The Great Pyramids, on the west bank of the river Nile near Giza, Egypt.

Space Imaging

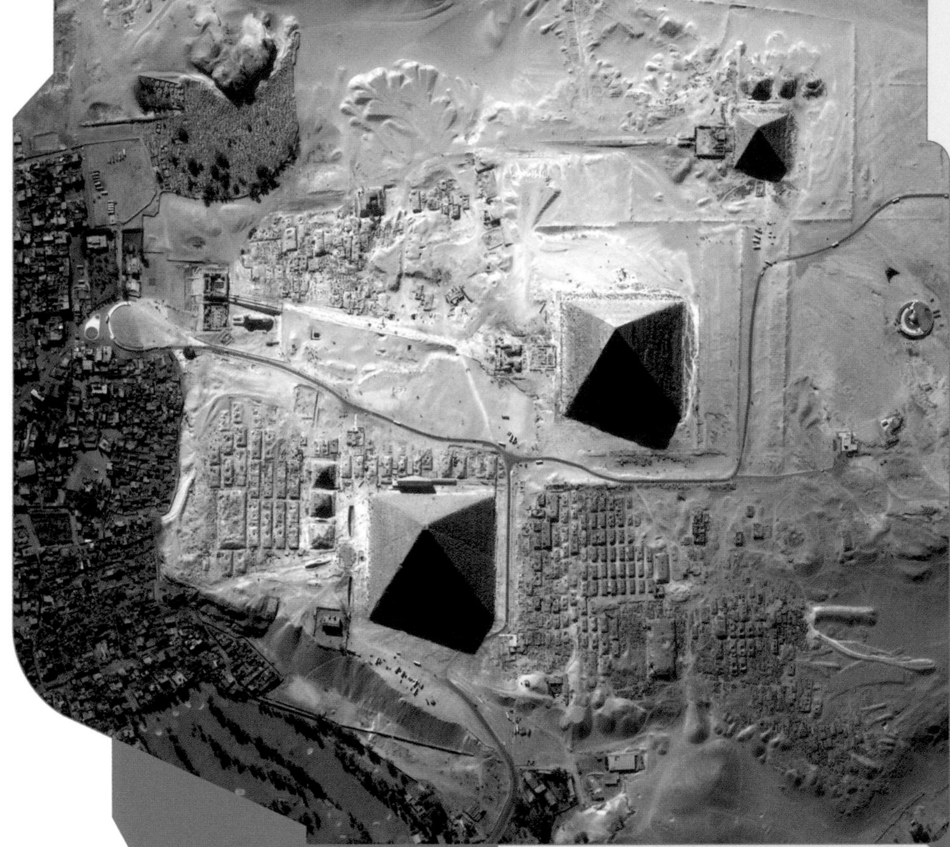

Top ten countries by area	area sq km	area sq miles	map page	world rank
1 SUDAN	2 505 813	967 500	88–89	10
2 ALGERIA	2 381 741	919 595	90–91	11
3 DEMOCRATIC REPUBLIC OF CONGO	2 345 410	905 568	94–95	12
4 LIBYA	1 759 540	679 362	88	16
5 CHAD	1 284 000	495 755	88	20
6 NIGER	1 267 000	489 191	93	21
7 ANGOLA	1 246 700	481 354	95	22
8 MALI	1 240 140	478 821	92–93	23
9 REPUBLIC OF SOUTH AFRICA	1 219 090	470 693	98–99	24
10 ETHIOPIA	1 133 880	437 794	96	26

Top ten countries by population	population	map page	world rank
1 NIGERIA	116 929 000	93	10
2 EGYPT	69 080 000	89	16
3 ETHIOPIA	64 459 000	96	18
4 DEMOCRATIC REPUBLIC OF CONGO	52 522 000	94–95	23
5 REPUBLIC OF SOUTH AFRICA	43 792 000	98–99	27
6 TANZANIA	35 965 000	96–97	32
7 SUDAN	31 809 000	88–89	33
8 KENYA	31 293 000	96	34
9 ALGERIA	30 841 000	90–91	36
10 MOROCCO	30 430 000	90–91	37

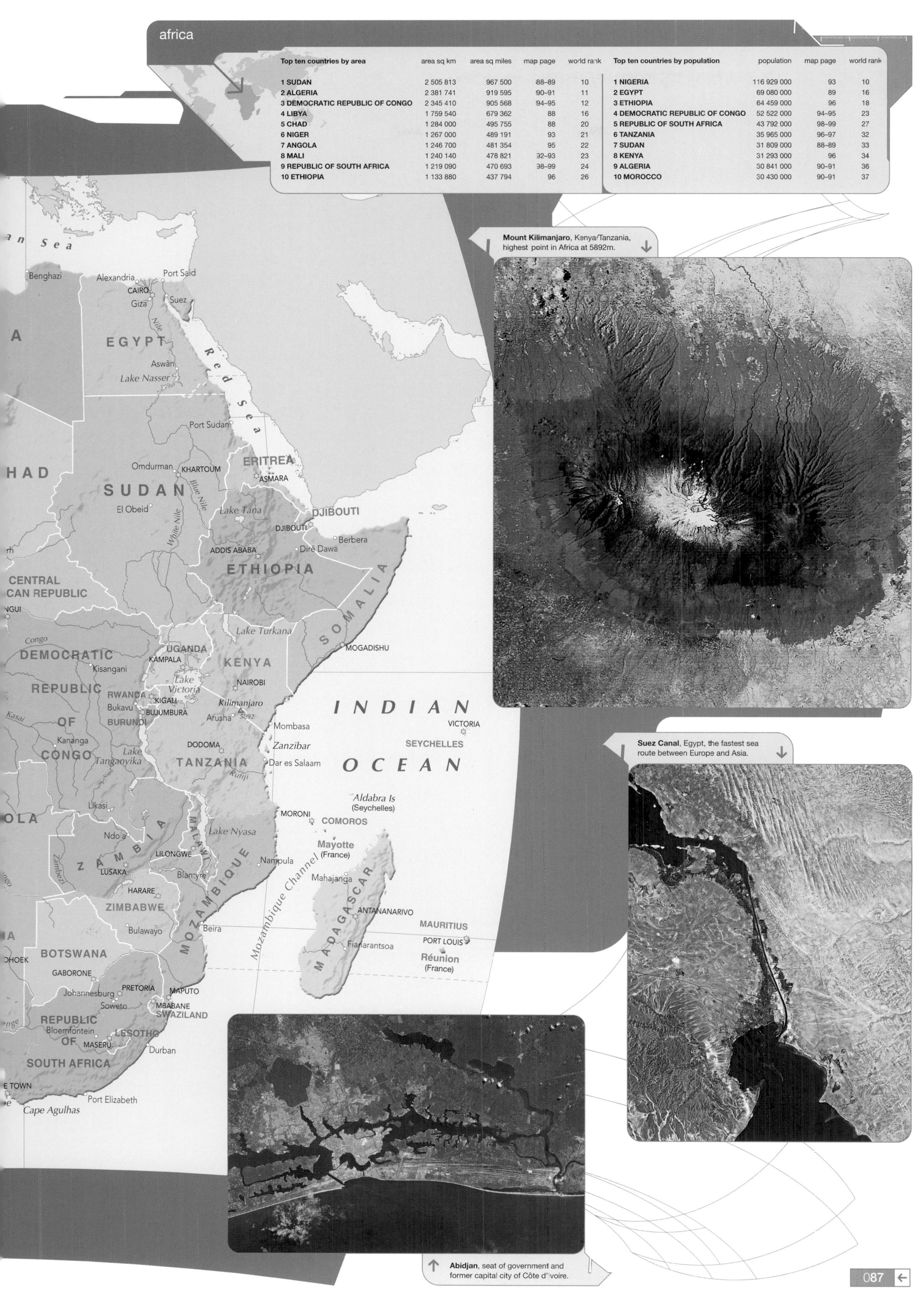

Mount Kilimanjaro, Kenya/Tanzania, highest point in Africa at 5892m.

Suez Canal, Egypt, the fastest sea route between Europe and Asia.

Abidjan, seat of government and former capital city of Côte d'Ivoire.

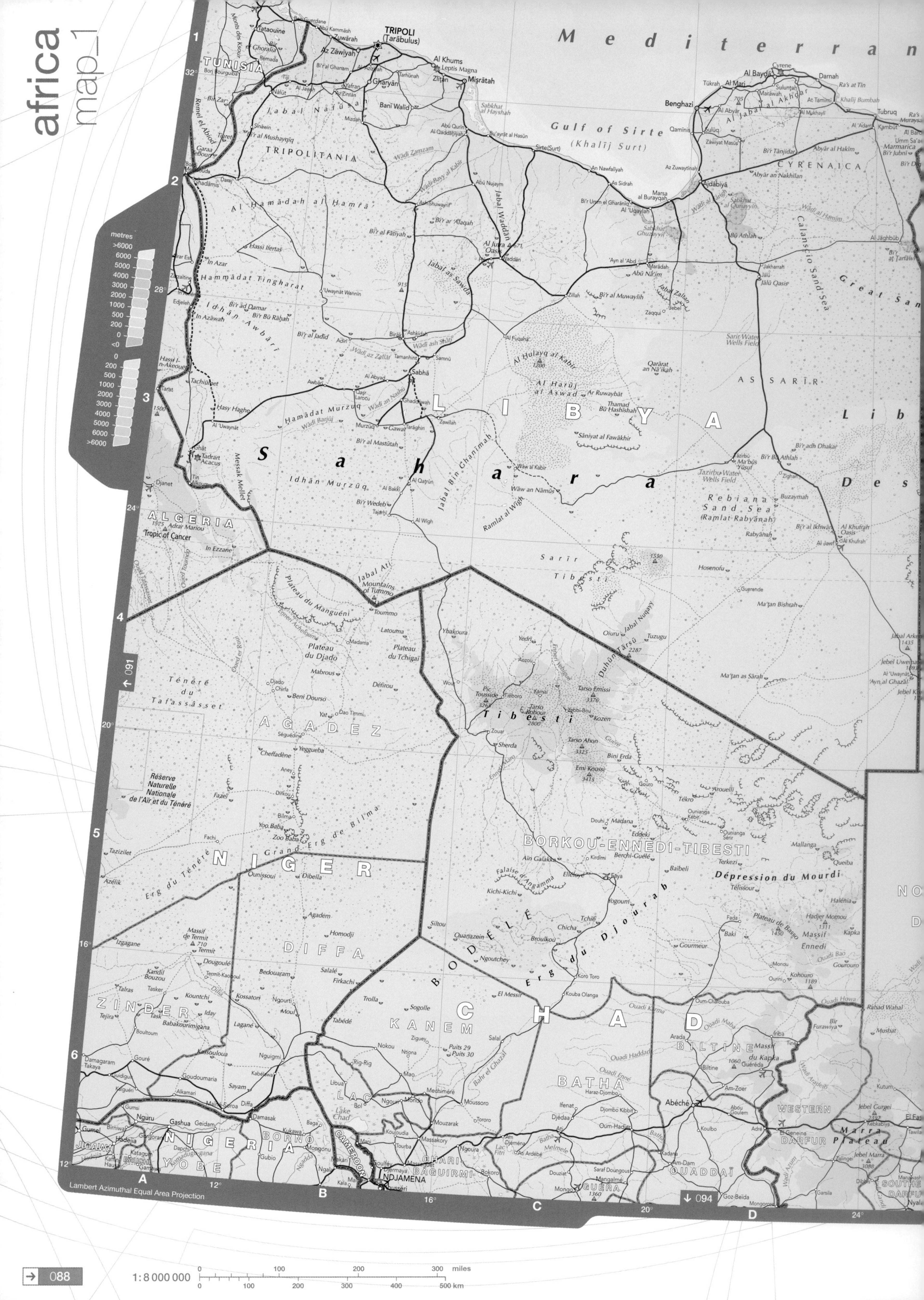

africa
map_1
Mediterranean
TRIPOLI
(Ṭarābulus)
TUNISIA
TRIPOLITANIA
Jabal Nafūsah
Gulf of Sirte
(Khalīj Surt)
Sirte(Surt)
Benghazi
Al Bayḑā
Darnah
Tubruq
Cyrene
Ajdābiyā
CYRENAICA
Al Jabal al Akhḑar
Miṣrātah
Al Khums
Leptis Magna
Zuwārah
Az Zāwiyah
Gharyān
Banī Walīd
Ghadāmis
Al Ḩamādah al Ḩamrā'
Hammādat Tingharat
Idhān Awbārī
Sabhā
Hamādat Murzuq
Murzuq
Ghāt
Tadrart Acacus
Idhān Murzūq
Jabal as Sawdā
Al Jufra Oasis
Al Harūj al Aswad
Al Hulayq al Kabīr
Calanscio Sand Sea
Great Sand Sea
Jālū Qasis
AS SARĪR
Rebiana Sand Sea
(Ramlat Rabyānah)
Al Khufrah Oasis
Sarīr Tibesti
Jabal Nuqay
L I B Y A
S a h a r a
Libyan Desert
ALGERIA
Tropic of Cancer
Jabal Ati
Mountains of Tummo
Plateau du Manguéni
Plateau du Djado
Plateau du Tchigaï
Ténéré du Tafassâsset
AGADEZ
Réserve Naturelle Nationale de l'Aïr et du Ténéré
Grand Erg de Bilma
Erg du Ténéré
Bilma
N I G E R
Tibesti
Pic Toussidé
3265
Emi Koussi
3415
Tarso Ahon
3325
BORKOU-ENNEDI-TIBESTI
Dépression du Mourdi
Faya
Massif Ennedi
Plateau de Basso
BODÉLÉ
Erg du Djourab
DIFFA
Massif de Termit
ZINDER
KANEM
LAC
C H A D
BATHA
BILTINE
Massif du Kapka
Abéché
OUADDAÏ
GUÉRA
CHARI-BAGUIRMI
NDJAMENA
CAMEROON
NIGERIA
BORNO
YOBE
JIGAWA
WESTERN DARFUR
Marra Plateau
Lambert Azimuthal Equal Area Projection
metres
>6000
6000
5000
4000
3000
2000
1000
500
200
0
<0
0
200
500
1000
2000
3000
4000
5000
6000
>6000
↑ 091
↓ 094
A
B
C
D
1
2
3
4
5
6
12°
16°
20°
24°
28°
32°
→ 088
1: 8 000 000
0 100 200 300 miles
0 100 200 300 400 500 km

↑ 077

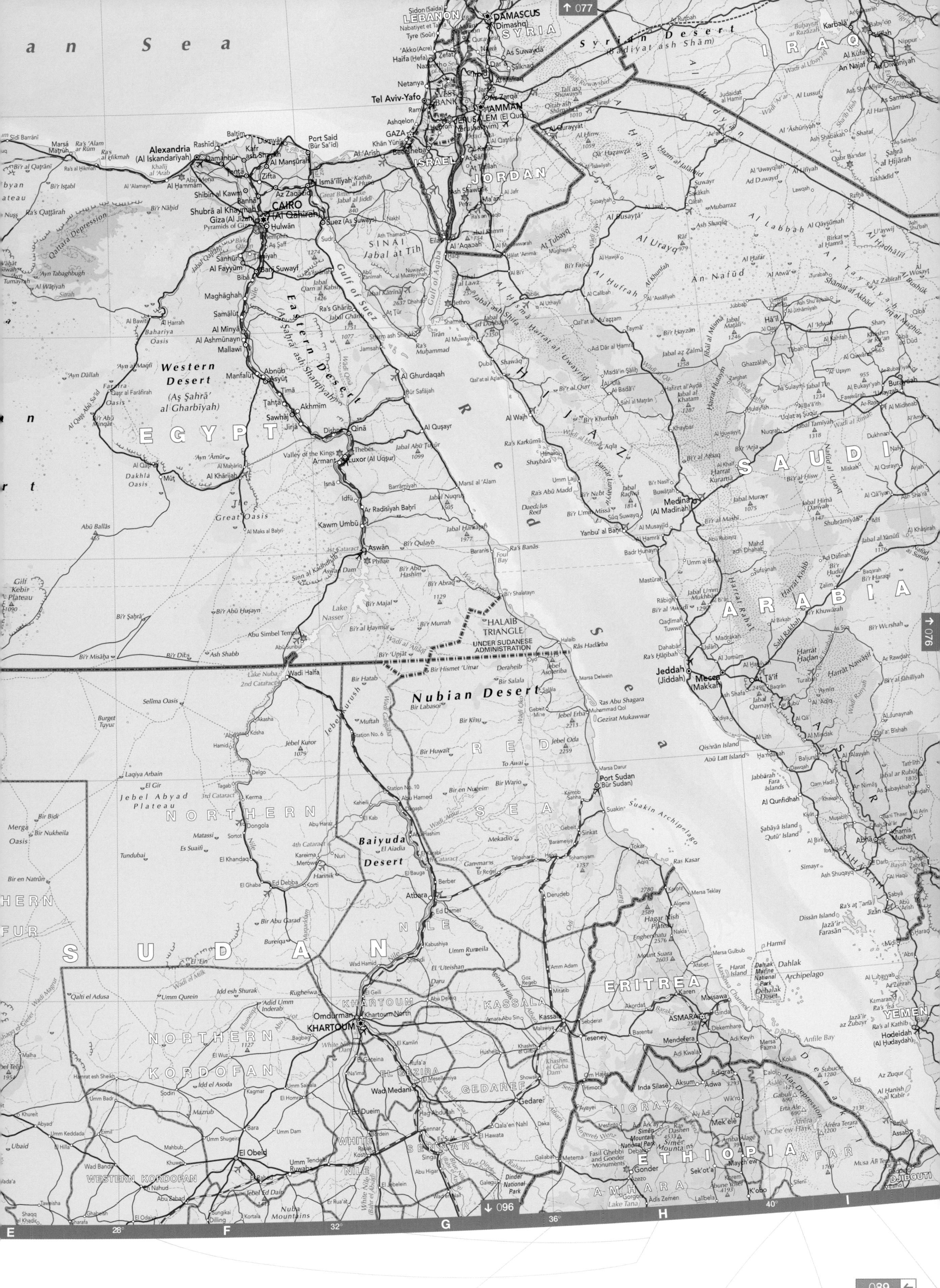

an Sea
LEBANON
DAMASCUS
(Dimashq)
SYRIA
Syrian Desert
(Badiyat ash Sham)
IRAQ
Karbala'
Al Kufah
An Najaf
Ad Diwaniyah
Tel Aviv-Yafo
WEST BANK
AMMAN
JERUSALEM (El Quds)
GAZA
ISRAEL
JORDAN
Alexandria
(Al Iskandariyah)
Port Said
(Bur Sa'id)
CAIRO
(Al Qahirah)
Giza (Al Jizah)
Qattara Depression
Suez (As Suways)
SINAI
Jabal at Tih
Gulf of Suez
Gulf of Aqaba
Eastern Desert
(Aş Şahra' ash Sharqiyah)
Western Desert
(Aş Şahra' al Gharbiyah)
EGYPT
Al Ghurdaqah
Luxor (Al Uqşur)
Valley of the Kings
Aswan
Aswan Dam
Lake Nasser
Abu Simbel Temple
HALAIB TRIANGLE
UNDER SUDANESE ADMINISTRATION
Wadi Halfa
Nubian Desert
Red Sea
Al Hamad
An Nafud
HIJAZ
SAUDI ARABIA
Medina
(Al Madinah)
Jeddah
(Jiddah)
Mecca
(Makkah)
At Ta'if
Abha
ASIR
Port Sudan
(Bur Sudan)
Suakin Archipelago
NORTHERN
Dongola
Baiyuda Desert
Atbara
NILE
SUDAN
KHARTOUM
Omdurman
Khartoum North
NORTHERN KORDOFAN
El Obeid
WESTERN KORDOFAN
WHITE NILE
SENNAR
EL GEZIRA
Wad Medani
GEDAREF
Gedaref
KASSALA
Kassala
ERITREA
ASMARA
Massawa
Dahlak Archipelago
TIGRAY
ETHIOPIA
AMHARA
AFAR
Gonder
Lake Tana
YEMEN
Hodeidah
(Al Hudaydah)
DJIBOUTI
Afar Depression
Nuba Mountains
Simen Mountains
E
28°
F
32°
G
36°
H
40°
I

↓ 096

→ 076

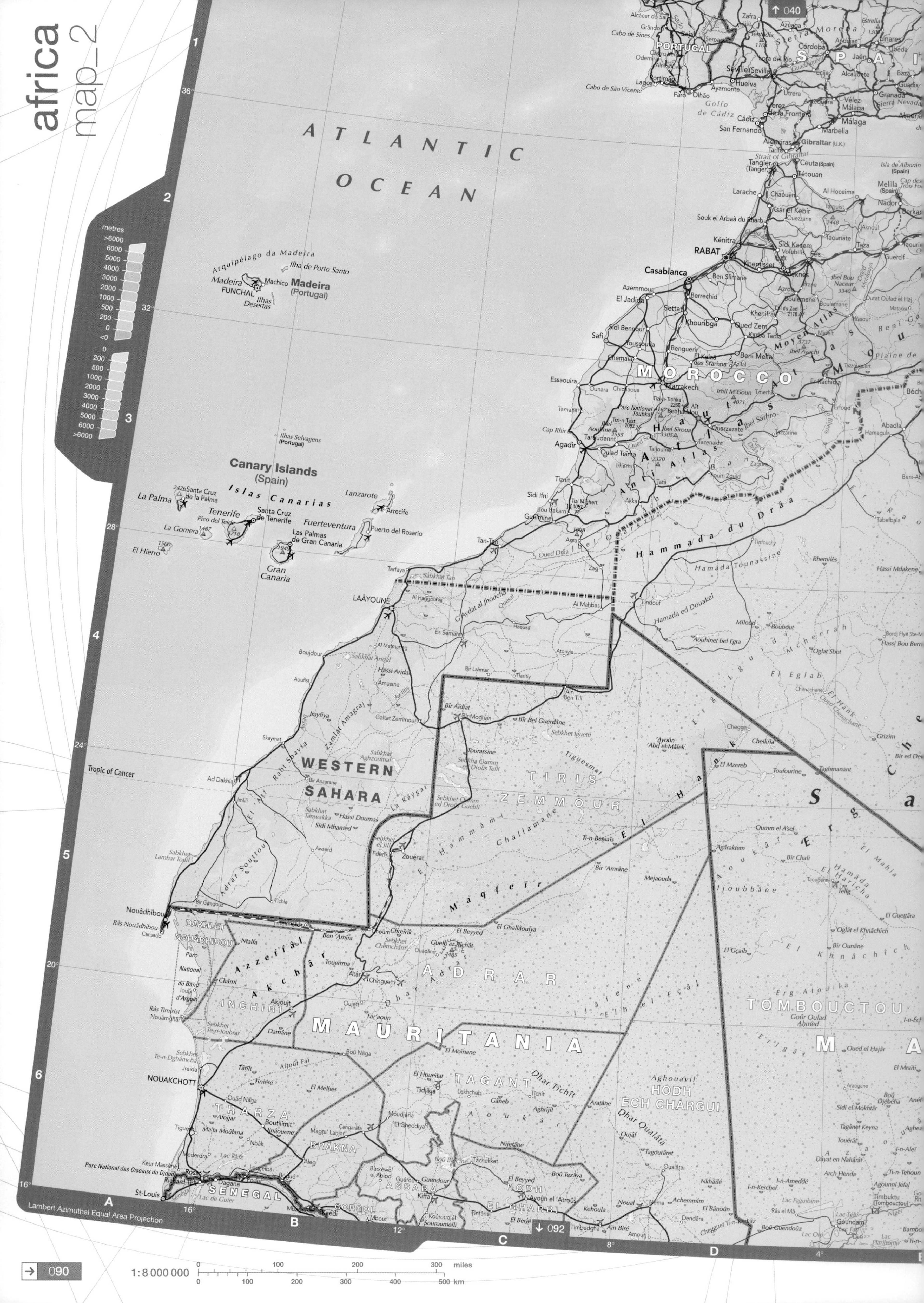
africa
map_2
↑ 040
↓ 092
→ 090
ATLANTIC
OCEAN
metres
>6000
6000
5000
4000
3000
2000
1000
500
200
0
<0
0
200
500
1000
2000
3000
4000
5000
6000
>6000
PORTUGAL
SPAIN
Lagos
Faro
Olhão
Huelva
Ayamonte
Seville (Sevilla)
Córdoba
Jaén
Écija
Utrera
Antequera
Granada
Vélez-Málaga
Málaga
Marbella
Jerez de la Frontera
Cádiz
San Fernando
Golfo de Cádiz
Algeciras
Gibraltar (U.K.)
Tarifa
Strait of Gibraltar
Tangier (Tanger)
Ceuta (Spain)
Tétouan
Isla de Alborán (Spain)
Melilla (Spain)
Nador
Al Hoceima
Chaouèn
Larache
Ksar el Kebir
Ouezzane
Souk el Arbaâ du Rharb
Kénitra
RABAT
Khemisset
Meknès
Fès
Taza
Taounate
Volubilis
Sidi Kacem
Casablanca
Ben Slimane
Azemmour
El Jadida
Berrechid
Settat
Khouribga
Oued Zem
Khenifra
Azrou
Boulemane
Ifrane
Jbel Bou Naceur 3340
Sidi Bennour
Safi
Youssoufia
Chemaia
Benguerir
El Kelaâ des Srarhna
Beni Mellal
Kasba Tadla
Moyen Atlas
Jbel Ayachi 3737
MOROCCO
Essaouira
Ounara
Chichaoua
Marrakech
Tizi-n-Tichka 2260
Irhil M'Goun 4071
Tinerhir
Er Rachidia
Erfoud
Parc National de Toubkal
Tizi-n-Test 2092
Jbel Toubkal
Aït Benhaddou
Jbel Siroua 3305
Ouarzazate
Jbel Sarhro
Haut Atlas
Tamanar
Cap Rhir
Agadir
Taroudannt
Oulad Teïma
Anti Atlas
Tazenakht
Taliouine
Irherm
Zagora
Foum Zguid
Tata
Tiznit
Sidi Ifni
Akka
Bou Izakarn
Tizi Mighert 1057
Guelmine
Tan-Tan
Assa
Zag
Oued Draa
Jbel Ouarkziz
Hammada du Drâa
Hamada Tounassine
Hamada ed Douakel
Tindouf
Abadla
Beni Abbès
Rhemilès
Hassi Mdakene
Tabelbala
Arquipélago da Madeira
Ilha de Porto Santo
Madeira
FUNCHAL
Machico
Madeira (Portugal)
Ilhas Desertas
Ilhas Selvagens (Portugal)
Canary Islands (Spain)
Islas Canarias
La Palma
Santa Cruz de la Palma
2426
Tenerife
Santa Cruz de Tenerife
Pico del Teide 3718
La Gomera
El Hierro
1500
Lanzarote
Arrecife
Fuerteventura
Puerto del Rosario
Las Palmas de Gran Canaria
Gran Canaria
1949
Tarfaya
Sabkhat Tah
LAÂYOUNE
Al Haggounia
Guelta Zemmur
Es Semara
Hagunia
Al Mahbas
Boujdour
Al Mamarang
Sabkhat Aridal
Hassi Aridal
Amasine
Aoufist
Bir Lahmar
Tifariti
Atonyia
Bir Aïdiat
Bir Mogrein
Bir Bel Guerdâne
Sebkhet Iguetti
Galtat Zemmour
Jrayfiya
Skaymat
Zemlat Amagraj
Sabkhat Aghzoumal
WESTERN SAHARA
Tropic of Cancer
Ad Dakhla
Bir Anzarane
Sabkhat Tanwakka
Hassi Doumas
Sidi Mhamed
La Rayyat
Imlili
Adrar Souttouf
Awserd
Tichla
Bir Gandouz
Sabkhet Lamhar Touil
Tourassine
Sebkha Oumm ed Droûs Telli
Sebkhet Oumm ed Droûs Guebli
TIRIS ZEMMOUR
Tiguesmat
Sebkhet el Jill
F'Derik
Zouérat
Ghallamane
El Hammâmi
Ti-n-Bessaïs
Bir 'Amrâne
Mejaouda
Maqteïr
El Hank
Erg Iguidi
Chegga
Cheikria
'Ayoûn 'Abd el Mâlek
Hamada
El Eglab
Mcherrah
Oglat Sbot
Bordj Flye Ste-Marie
Hassi Bou Bernous
Boubout
Miloud
Aouhinet bel Egra
Chenachane
Grizim
El Mzereb
Toufourine
Taghmanant
Oumm el A'sel
Agâraktem
Bir Chali
Aoukâr
Erg
Ijoubbâne
Taoudenni
Hamada el Haricha
Telig
El Mahia
El Guettâra
Oglât el Khnâchîch
Bir Ounâne
El Khnâchîch
Erg Atouila
El Gçaib
TOMBOUCTOU
Goûr Oulad Ahmed
Erg Chech
Nouâdhibou
Râs Nouâdhibou
Cansado
DAKHLET NOUÂDHIBOU
Parc National du Banc d'Arguin
Ntalfa
Azeffâl
Châmi
Akchâr
INCHIRI
Akjoujt
Ben 'Amira
Choûm
Chreirik
Sebkhet Chemchâm
Toueïrma
Atâr
Chinguetti
Ouadâne
Guelb er Richât
485
Ouâdâne
El Beyyed
El Ghallâouîya
ADRAR
Dhar Adrar
Oujeft
Far'aoun
Damâne
MAURITANIA
Râs Timirist
Nouâmghâr
Sebkhet Te-n-Ioubrar
Sebkhet Te-n-Dghâmcha
Jreïda
NOUAKCHOTT
Boû Nâga
Aftout Faï
Tâtilt
Tiniéré
El Melbes
El Moïnane
Ijâfene
El Beyyed
Oulad
TAGANT
El Houeïtat
Tidjikja
Lekhcheb
Dhar Tîchît
Ganeb
Aghrijît
Aratâne
Aghouavil
HODH ECH CHARGUI
Dhar Oualâta
Oujâf
Tagourâret
Oualâta
Ouâd Nâga
TRARZA
Afojjar
Boutilimit
Mâ'ta Moûlana
Tiguent
Nbâk
Mederdra
Lac R'kiz
Aleg
BRAKNA
Magta' Lahjar
Moudjéria
El Gheddiya
Cangarâfa
Aoukâr
Nijerâne
Keur Massene
Parc National des Oiseaux du Djoudj
Rosso
Richard Toll
Dagana
Podor
Bogué
Lac de Guier
St-Louis
SENEGAL
Kaédi
GORGOL
Mbout
Bârkéwol el Abiod
Guérou
Guendour
ASSABA
Kiffa
Kouroudjél
Souroumelli
Boû Blelne
Tâchekket
Tintâne
El Beyyed
HODH EL GHARBI
'Ayoûn el 'Atroûs
Boû Tezâya
Timbedgha
Aïn Biré
Kehoula
Noual
Néma
Achemmîm
Dendâra
Nkhâïlé
I-n-Kerchef
Lac Faguibine
El Bânoûn
I-n-Ameddé
Chegguet Ti-n-Kerkâz
Boû Guendoûz
Ras el Mâ
Lac Télé
Goundam
Lac Oro
Arch Henda
Timbuktu (Tombouctou)
Agounni Jefal
Ti-n-Tehoun
I-n-Alei
Dâyat en Nahârât
Touêrât
Tagânet Keyna
Sidi el Mokhtâr
Djoubha
Araouane
El Mraïti
Oued el Hajâr
Lambert Azimuthal Equal Area Projection
1:8 000 000
0
100
200
300
miles
0
100
200
300
400
500 km
A
B
C
D
1
2
3
4
5
6
36°
32°
28°
24°
20°
16°
16°
12°
8°
4°

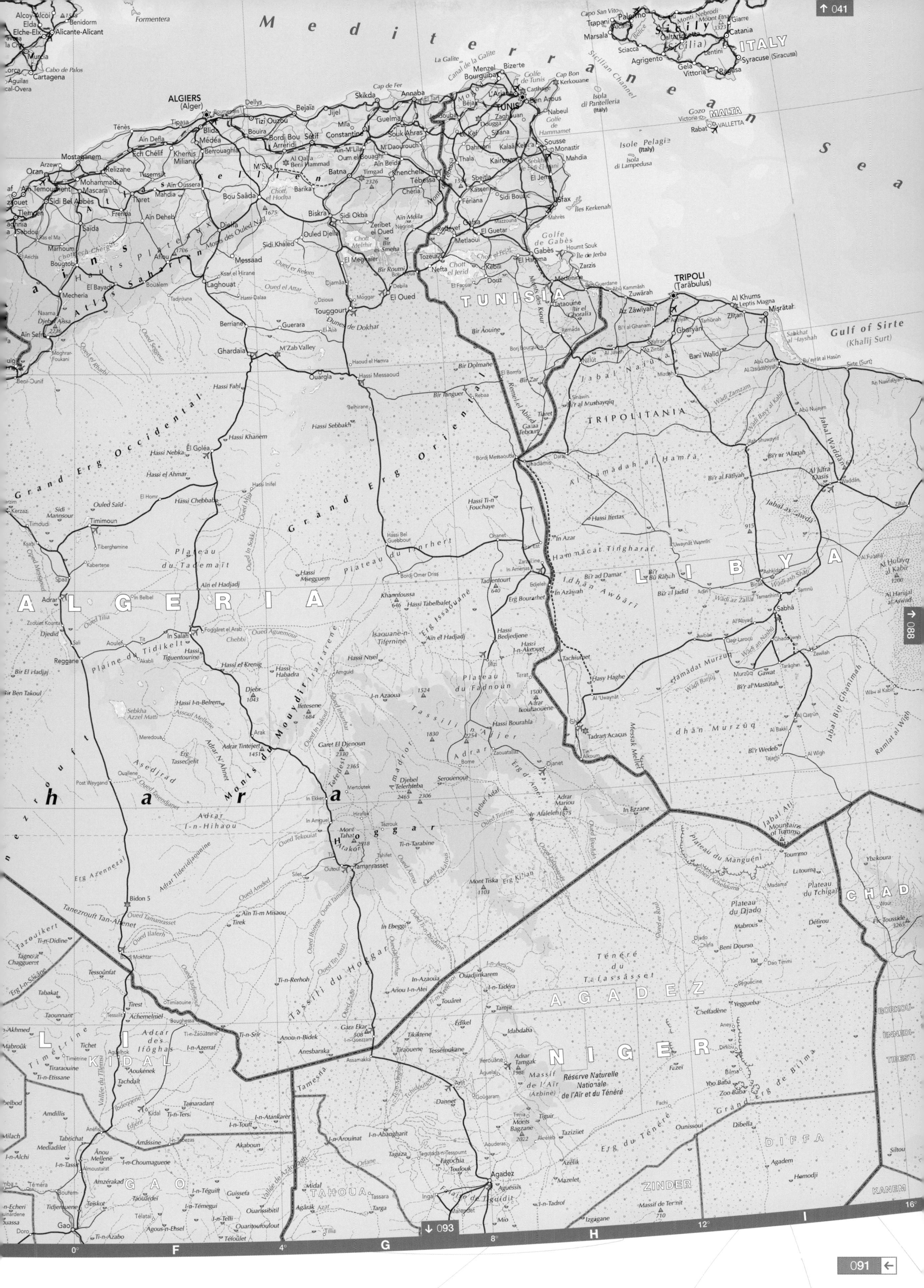

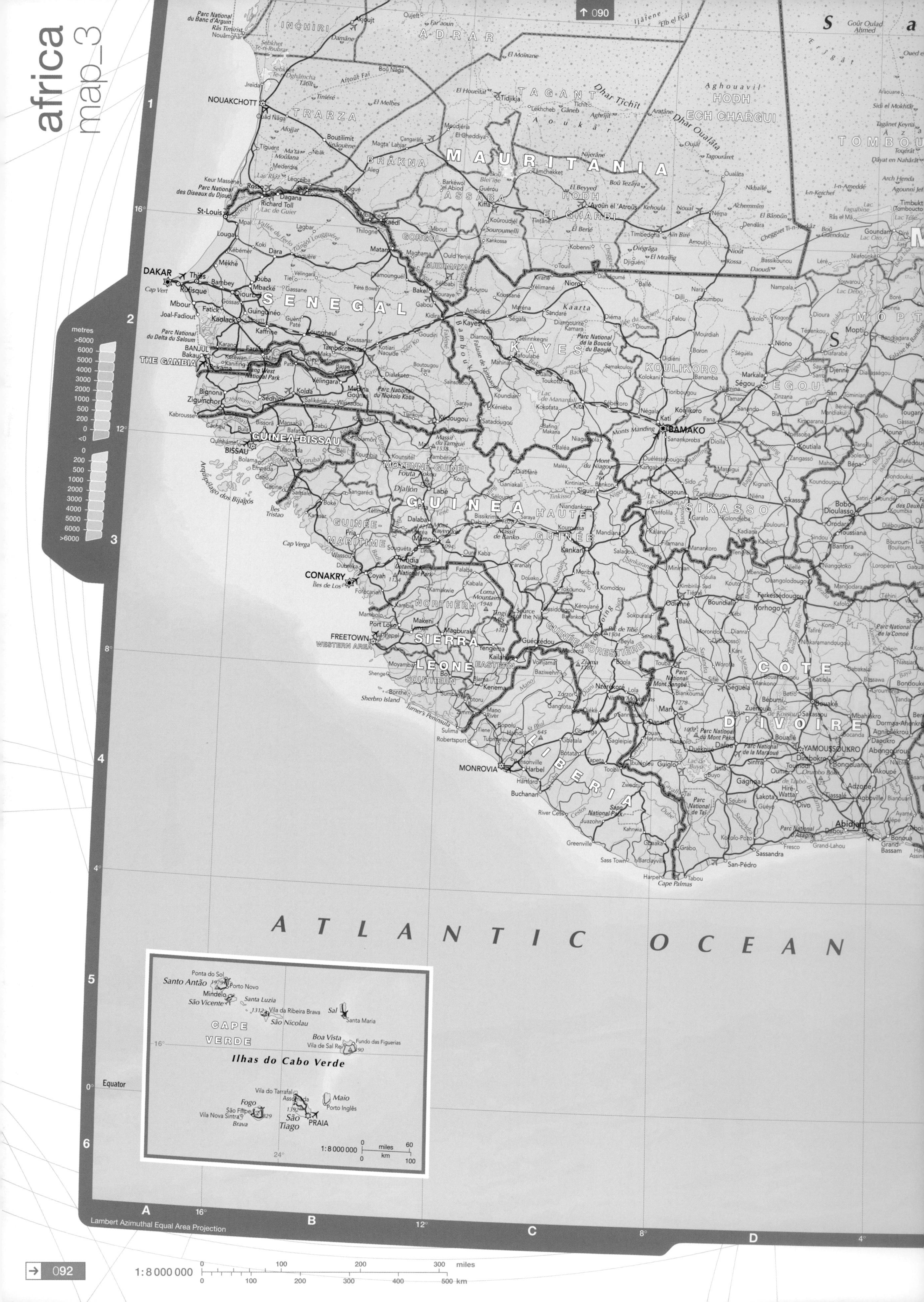

africa
map_3
↑ 090
1
2
3
4
5
6
A
B
C
D
16°
12°
8°
4°
0°
Equator
metres
>6000
6000
5000
4000
3000
2000
1000
500
200
0
<0
0
200
500
1000
2000
3000
4000
5000
6000
>6000
MAURITANIA
SENEGAL
THE GAMBIA
GUINEA-BISSAU
GUINEA
SIERRA
LEONE
LIBERIA
CÔTE D'IVOIRE
INCHIRI
ADRAR
TAGANT
TRARZA
BRAKNA
ASSABA
HODH EL GHARBI
HODH ECH CHARGUI
GORGOL
GUIDIMAKA
KAYES
KOULIKORO
SÉGOU
SIKASSO
TOMBOUCTOU
MOPTI
MOYENNE-GUINÉE
GUINÉE-MARITIME
HAUTE-GUINÉE
GUINÉE FORESTIÈRE
NORTHERN
EASTERN
SOUTHERN
WESTERN AREA
NOUAKCHOTT
DAKAR
BANJUL
BISSAU
CONAKRY
FREETOWN
MONROVIA
BAMAKO
YAMOUSSOUKRO
Abidjan
St-Louis
Thiès
Kaolack
Ziguinchor
Kayes
Kankan
Labé
Bouaké
Cap Vert
Cap Verga
Cape Palmas
Sherbro Island
Arquipélago dos Bijagós
ATLANTIC OCEAN
CAPE VERDE
Ilhas do Cabo Verde
Santo Antão
São Vicente
Mindelo
Porto Novo
Ponta do Sol
Santa Luzia
São Nicolau
Vila da Ribeira Brava
Sal
Santa Maria
Boa Vista
Vila de Sal Rei
Fundo das Figueiras
Maio
Porto Inglês
Fogo
São Filipe
Vila Nova Sintra
Brava
São Tiago
Assomada
Vila do Tarrafal
PRAIA
1:8 000 000
miles
km
0
60
100
Lambert Azimuthal Equal Area Projection
1:8 000 000
0
100
200
300
miles
0
100
200
300
400
500 km

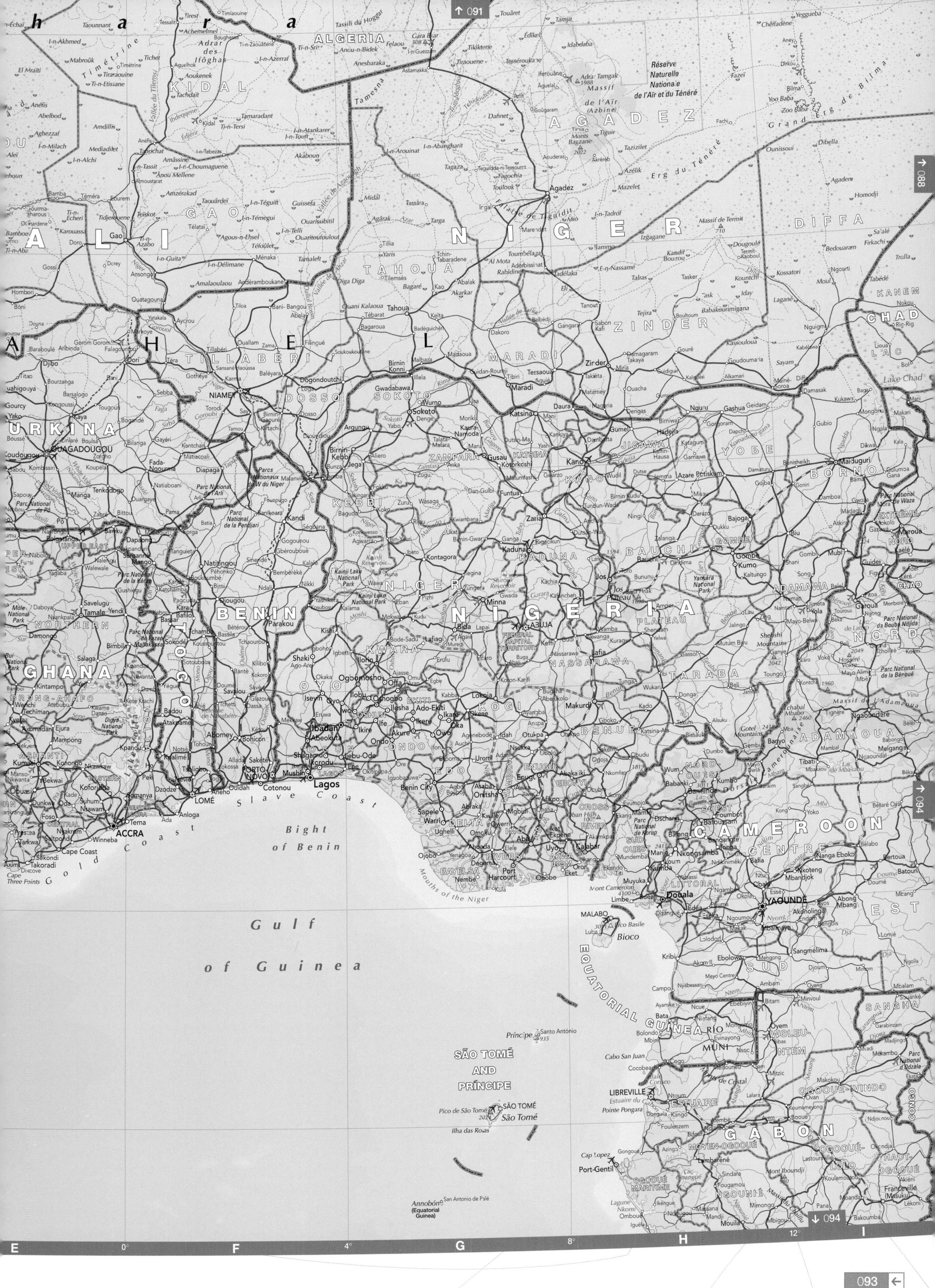

↑ 091
→ 088
→ 094
↓ 094
ALGERIA
NIGER
MALI
BURKINA
GHANA
TOGO
BENIN
NIGERIA
CHAD
CAMEROON
GABON
EQUATORIAL GUINEA
SÃO TOMÉ AND PRÍNCIPE
Gulf of Guinea
Bight of Benin
Slave Coast
Gold Coast
Mouths of the Niger
Lake Chad
Réserve Naturelle Nationale de l'Aïr et du Ténéré
Massif de l'Aïr (Azbine)
Grand Erg de Bilma
Erg du Ténéré
Adrar des Iforas
AGADEZ
TAHOUA
TILLABÉRI
DOSSO
MARADI
ZINDER
DIFFA
KIDAL
GAO
SAHEL
Agadez
Tahoua
NIAMEY
Maradi
Zinder
OUAGADOUGOU
Gao
Dori
Sokoto
Katsina
Kano
Kaduna
Zaria
Jos
ABUJA
Minna
Ilorin
Ogbomosho
Ibadan
Abeokuta
Lagos
PORTO NOVO
Cotonou
LOMÉ
ACCRA
Tema
Cape Coast
Sekondi
Takoradi
Kumasi
Tamale
Parakou
Benin City
Onitsha
Enugu
Port Harcourt
Calabar
Makurdi
Bauchi
Gombe
Maiduguri
Yola
Garoua
Douala
YAOUNDÉ
MALABO
Bioco
LIBREVILLE
Port-Gentil
Franceville
Lambaréné
SÃO TOMÉ
São Tomé
Príncipe
Annobón (Equatorial Guinea)
Mont Cameroun 4100
RÍO MUNI
E
F
G
H
I
0°
4°
8°
12°

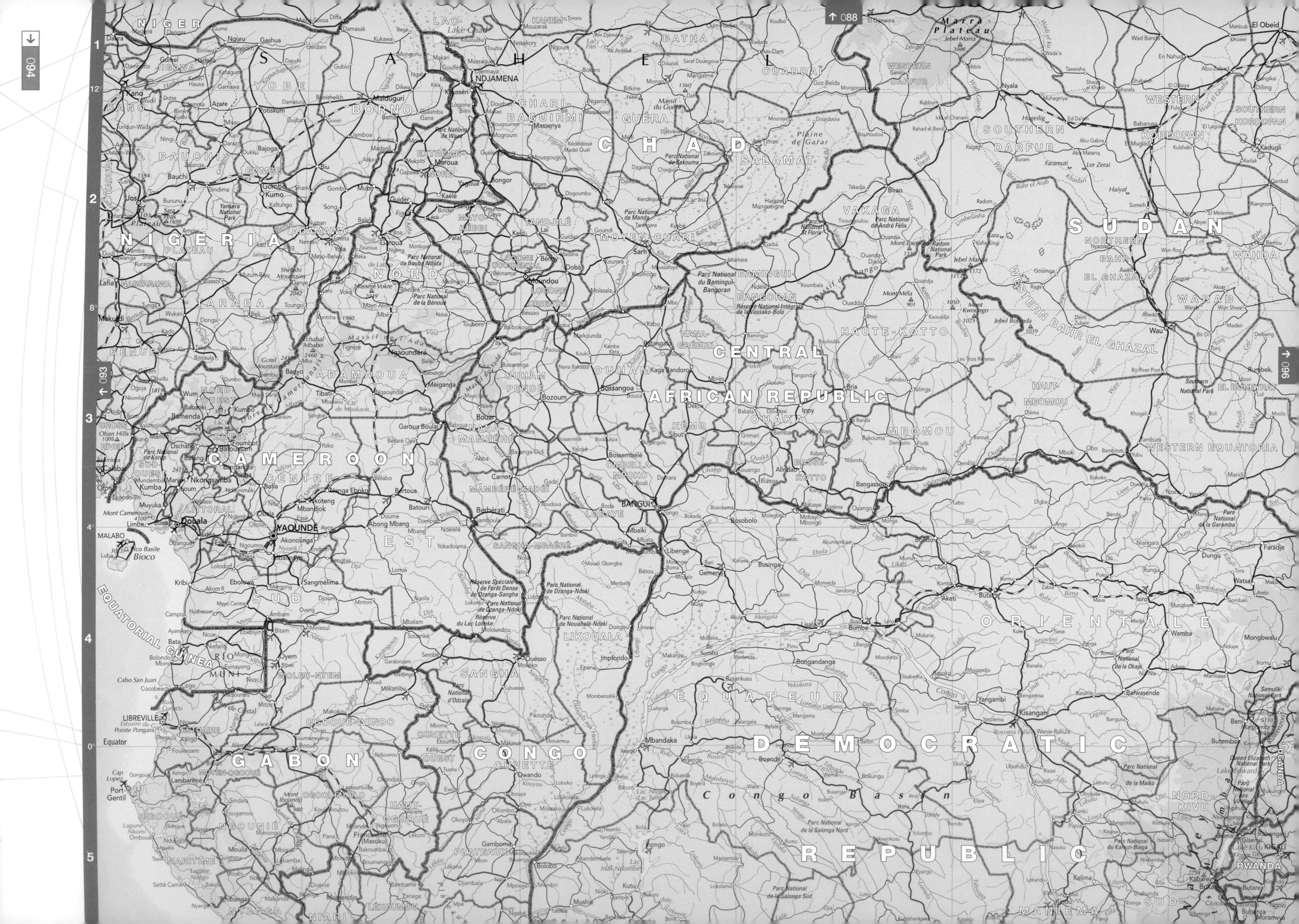
SUDAN
CHAD
NIGER
NIGERIA
CAMEROON
CENTRAL AFRICAN REPUBLIC
DEMOCRATIC REPUBLIC
CONGO
GABON
EQUATORIAL GUINEA
UGANDA
RWANDA
SAHEL
Congo Basin
NDJAMENA
BANGUI
YAOUNDÉ
LIBREVILLE
MALABO
↑ 088
→ 096
← 093

↑ 097

→ 098

ATLANTIC OCEAN

TANZANIA

Lake Tanganyika

CONGO
ORIENTAL
OCCIDENTAL
KASAI
BANDUNDU
KINSHASA
BRAZZAVILLE
KATANGA
ZAIRE

CABINDA (Angola)
Pointe-Noire
Boma

LUANDA

ANGOLA
LUNDA NORTE
LUNDA SUL
MALANJE
MOXICO
CUANZA NORTE
CUANZA SUL
BENGO
UIGE
BENGUELA
HUAMBO
BIÉ
HUILA
CUANDO CUBANGO
CUNENE
NAMIBE

Benguela
Lobito
Namibe
Sumbe

ZAMBIA
NORTH-WESTERN
WESTERN
COPPERBELT
CENTRAL
SOUTHERN
LUSAKA
Mongu
Solwezi
Lubumbashi
Likasi

ZIMBABWE

NAMIBIA
OVAMBOLAND
OKAVANGO
KUNENE
OSHIKOTO
OHANGWENA
OMUSATI

BOTSWANA
CAPRIVI STRIP

1:8 000 000

Lambert Azimuthal Equal Area Projection

metres
>6000
6000
5000
4000
3000
2000
1000
500
200
0
-0

0
200
500
1000
2000
3000
4000
5000
6000
>6000

miles
100 200 300
km
100 200 300 400 500

095 ←

096

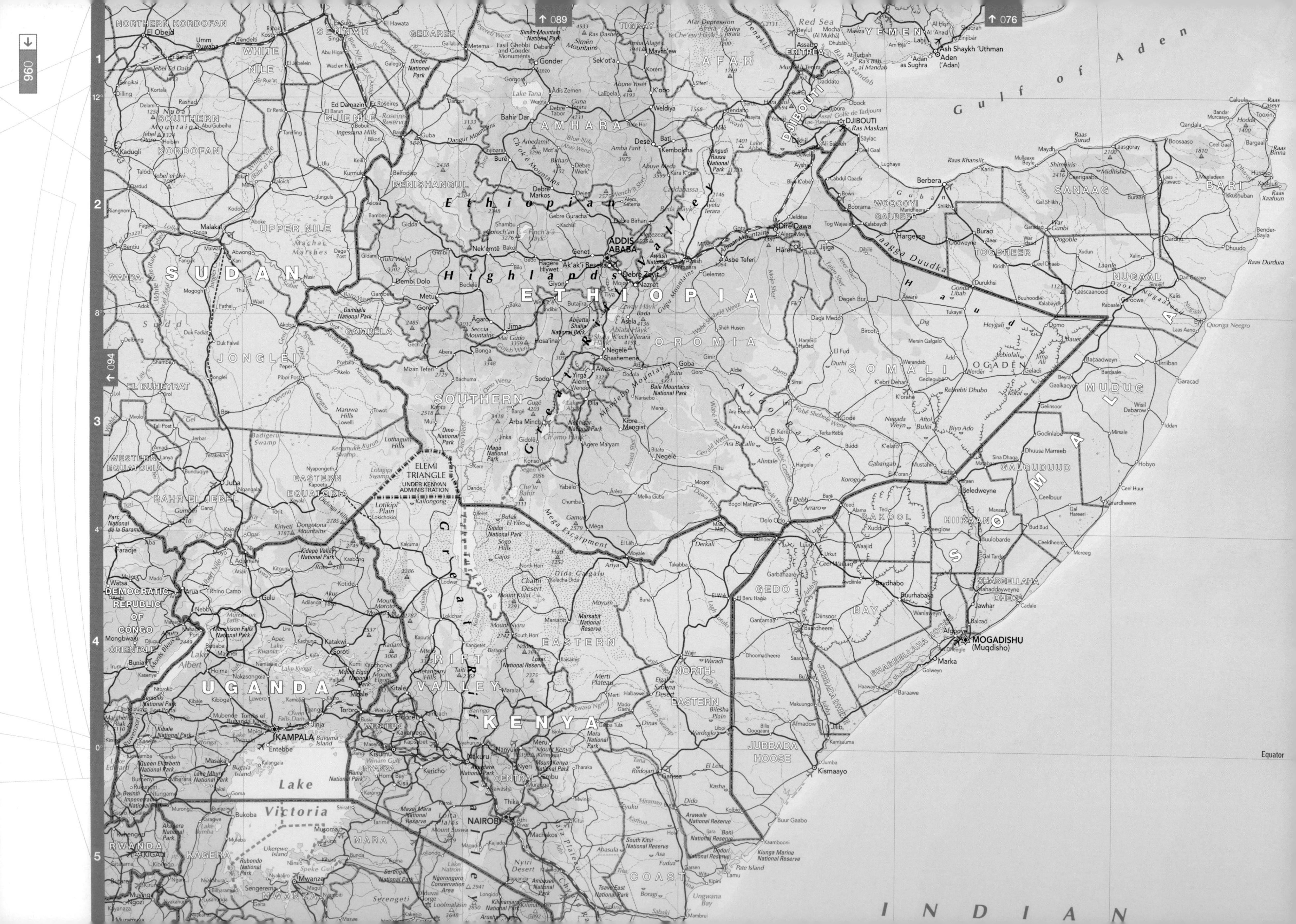

↑ 089
↑ 076
↑ 094
SUDAN
ETHIOPIA
SOMALIA
KENYA
UGANDA
YEMEN
ERITREA
DJIBOUTI
DEMOCRATIC REPUBLIC OF CONGO
RWANDA
Gulf of Aden
Red Sea
INDIAN
Lake Victoria
Equator
ADDIS ABABA
NAIROBI
MOGADISHU
(Muqdisho)
KAMPALA
DJIBOUTI
Ethiopian Highlands
Great Rift Valley
ELEMI TRIANGLE
UNDER KENYAN ADMINISTRATION
Haud
Ogaden
AFAR
AMHARA
TIGRAY
OROMIA
SOMALI
SOUTHERN
GAMBELA
BENISHANGUL
RIFT VALLEY
EASTERN
NORTH-EASTERN
CENTRAL
COAST
WESTERN
NYANZA
MUDUG
NUGAAL
BARI
SANAAG
TOGDHEER
WOQOOYI GALBEED
GALGUDUUD
HIIRAAN
BAKOOL
GEDO
BAY
JUBBADA HOOSE
JUBBADA DHEXE
SHABEELLAHA HOOSE
SHABEELLAHA DHEXE
UPPER NILE
JONGLEI
WHITE NILE
BLUE NILE
SENNAR
GEDAREF
NORTHERN KORDOFAN
SOUTHERN KORDOFAN
EL BUHEYRAT
WAHDA
WESTERN EQUATORIA
EASTERN EQUATORIA
BAHR EL JEBEL
ORIENTALE
MARA
KAGERA
MWANZA
Mega Escarpment
Great Rift Valley
Gonder
Bahir Dar
Dese
Dire Dawa
Harer
Jima
Nazret
Awasa
Hargeysa
Berbera
Kismaayo
Juba
Malakal
Marka
Jijiga
El Obeid
1
2
3
4
5
12°
8°
4°
0°

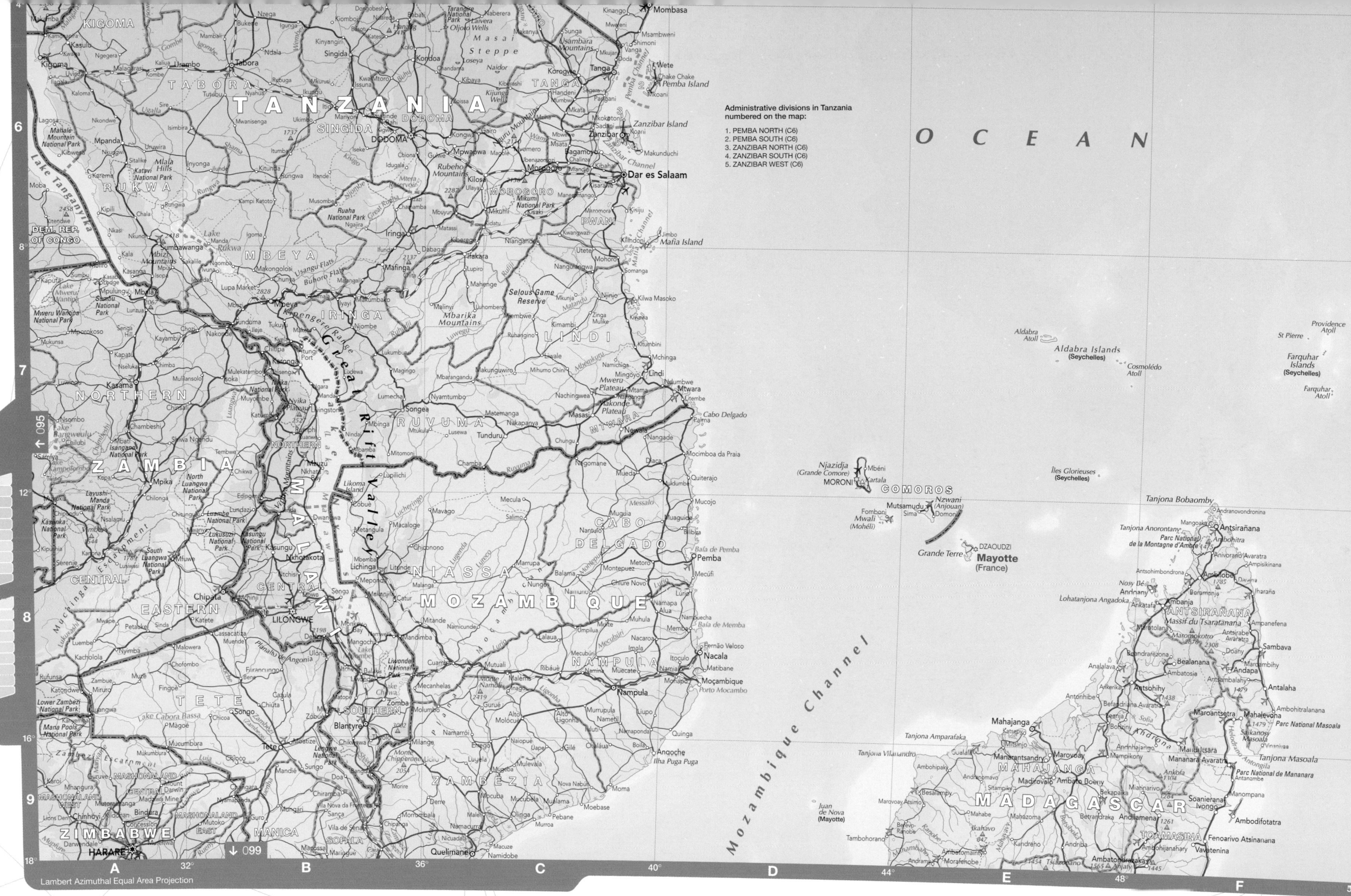

O C E A N

Providence
Atoll

St Pierre

Farquhar
Islands
(Seychelles)

Farquhar
Atoll

Cosmoledo
Atoll

Aldabra Islands
(Seychelles)

Aldabra
Atoll

Iles Glorieuses
(Seychelles)

DZAOUDZI
Mayotte
(France)

Grande Terre
Mutsamudu Anjouan
Fomboni Mwali
(Mohéli)

COMOROS

Njazidja
(Grande Comore)
MORONI Mbéni
Moutsamoudou

Administrative divisions in Tanzania
numbered on the map:

1. PEMBA NORTH (C6)
2. PEMBA SOUTH (C6)
3. ZANZIBAR NORTH (C6)
4. ZANZIBAR SOUTH (C6)
5. ZANZIBAR WEST (C6)

Mozambique Channel

MADAGASCAR

TANZANIA

MOZAMBIQUE

MALAWI

ZAMBIA

ZIMBABWE

HARARE

DODOMA

LILONGWE

Dar es Salaam

Great Rift Valley

Lake Tanganyika

Lake Malawi

1:8 000 000

Lambert Azimuthal Equal Area Projection

metres
>6000
6000
5000
4000
3000
2000
1000
500
200
0
200
500
1000
2000
3000
4000
6000
>6000

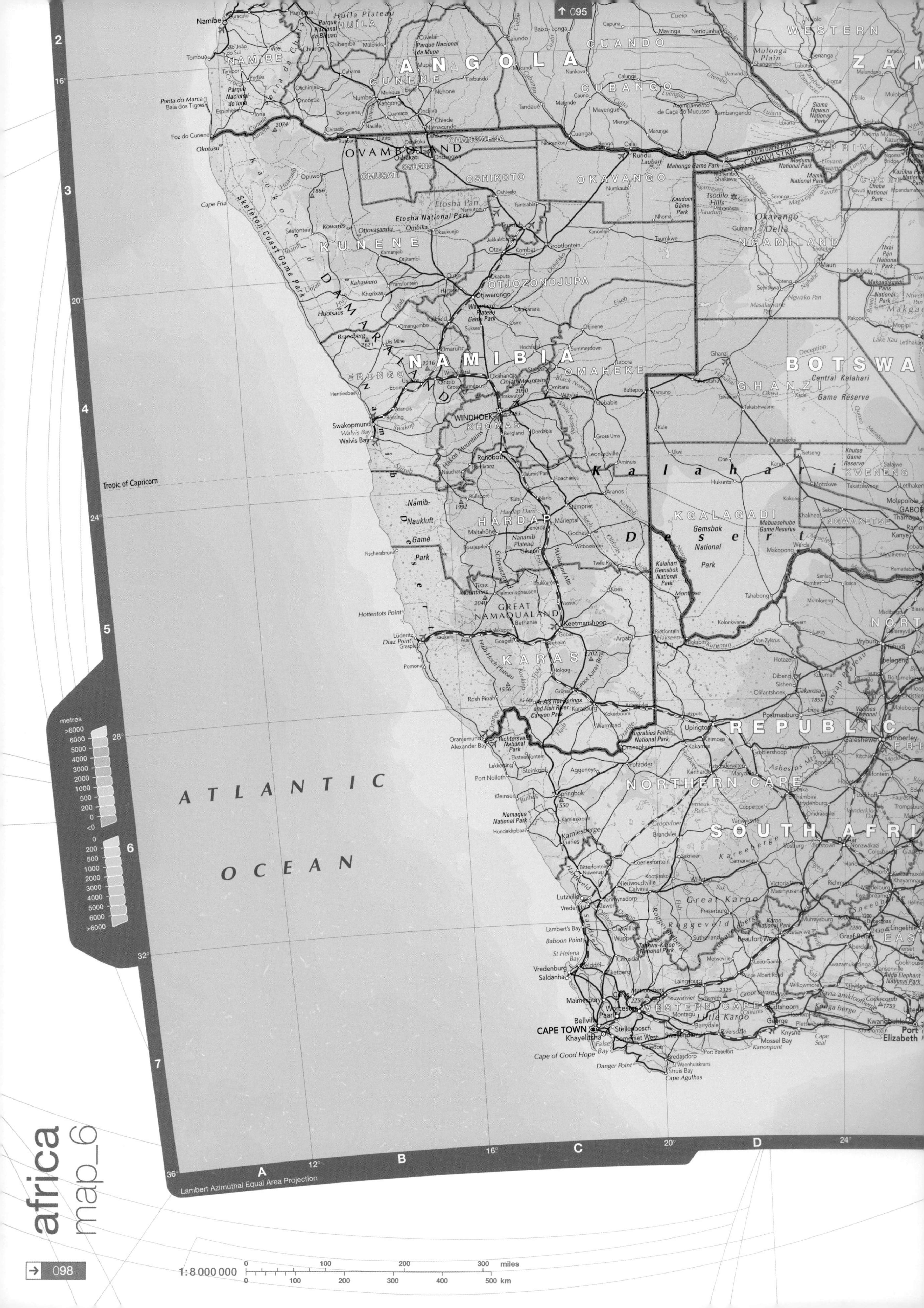

ATLANTIC

OCEAN

Tropic of Capricorn

ANGOLA

NAMIBIA

BOTSWANA

REPUBLIC

SOUTH AFRI

NORTHERN CAPE

WESTERN CAPE

CAPE TOWN

metres
>6000
6000
5000
4000
3000
2000
1000
500
200
0
<0
0
200
500
1000
2000
3000
4000
5000
6000
>6000

Lambert Azimuthal Equal Area Projection

1:8 000 000

0   100   200   300   miles
0 100 200 300 400 500 km

↑ 097

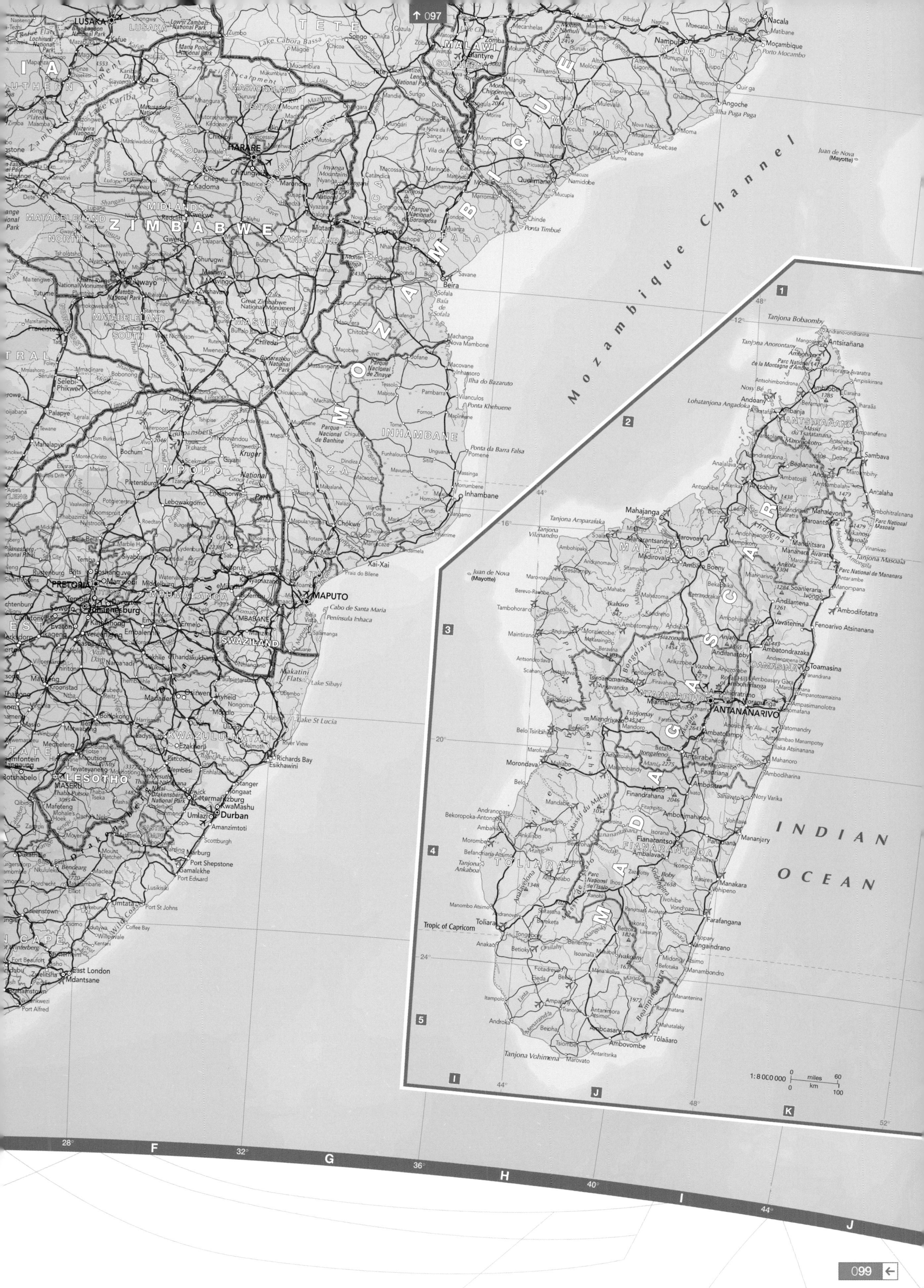

LUSAKA
TETE
MALAWI
Blantyre
Zomba
Nacala
Nampula
Moçambique
NAMPULA
Lake Cabora Bassa
Lake Kariba
HARARE
Chitungwiza
Kadoma
MASHONALAND CENTRAL
MASHONALAND EAST
MASHONALAND WEST
MIDLANDS
ZIMBABWE
MATABELELAND NORTH
MATABELELAND SOUTH
MANICALAND
MASVINGO
Bulawayo
Masvingo
Mutare
Great Zimbabwe National Monument
Quelimane
ZAMBEZIA
MOZAMBIQUE
SOFALA
Beira
Angoche
Mozambique Channel
Juan de Nova (Mayotte)
INHAMBANE
Inhambane
GAZA
Xai-Xai
MAPUTO
Maputo
LIMPOPO
Kruger National Park
Polokwane
PRETORIA
Johannesburg
Soweto
MPUMALANGA
MBABANE
SWAZILAND
Lake St Lucia
Richards Bay
KWAZULU-NATAL
LESOTHO
MASERU
Pietermaritzburg
Durban
Port Shepstone
Umtata
East London
Queenstown
Port Alfred
Tropic of Capricorn
MADAGASCAR
Antsiranana
ANTSIRANANA
Sambava
Antalaha
Mahajanga
MAHAJANGA
Toamasina
TOAMASINA
ANTANANARIVO
Antananarivo
Antsirabe
Morondava
Fianarantsoa
FIANARANTSOA
TOLIARA
Toliara
Manakara
Farafangana
Tôlañaro
Ambovombe
Tanjona Vohimena
Tanjona Bobaomby
INDIAN OCEAN
1:8 000 000
miles 60
km 100

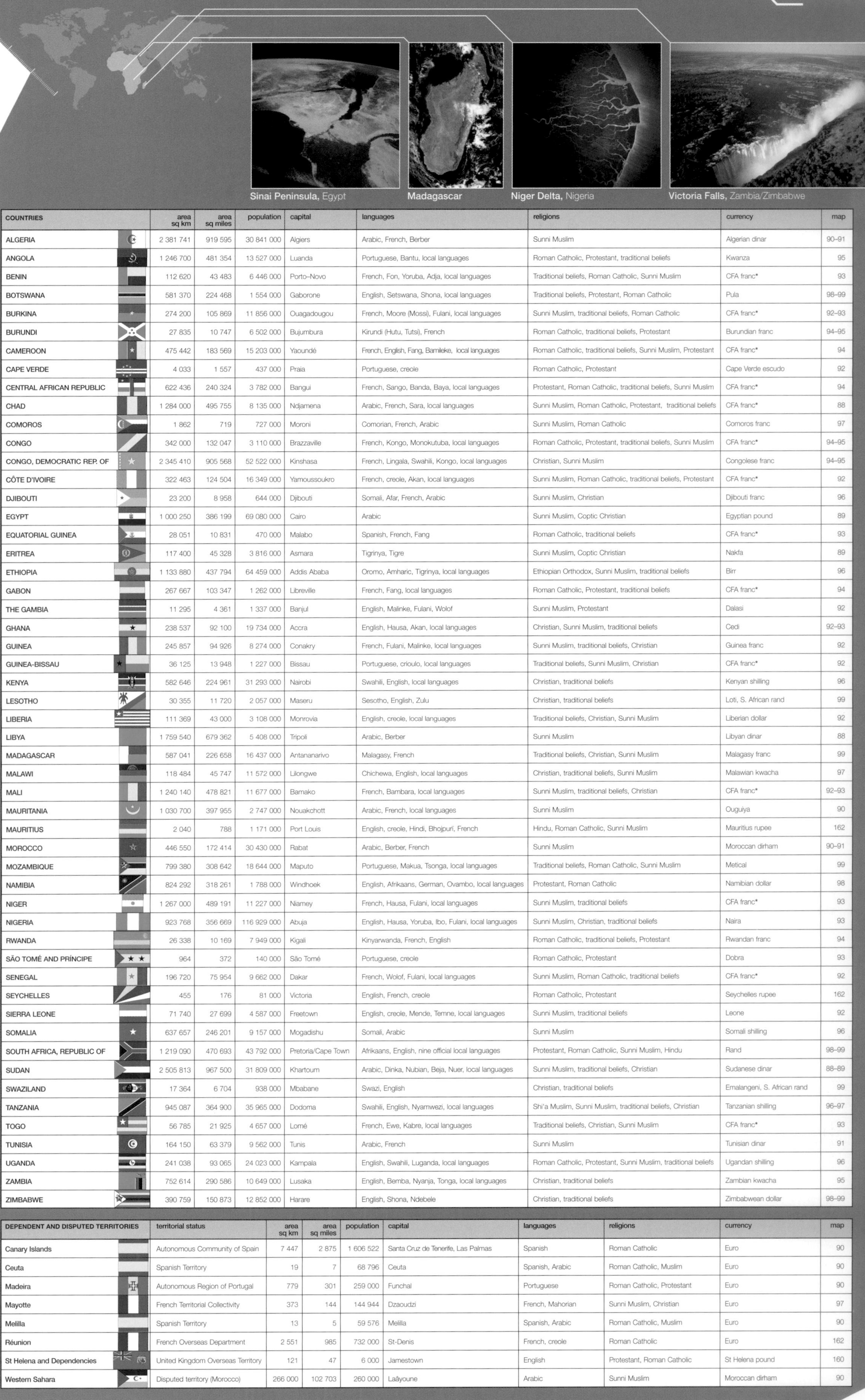

Sinai Peninsula, Egypt   **Madagascar**   **Niger Delta,** Nigeria   **Victoria Falls,** Zambia/Zimbabwe

COUNTRIES		area sq km	area sq miles	population	capital	languages	religions	currency	map
ALGERIA		2 381 741	919 595	30 841 000	Algiers	Arabic, French, Berber	Sunni Muslim	Algerian dinar	90–91
ANGOLA		1 246 700	481 354	13 527 000	Luanda	Portuguese, Bantu, local languages	Roman Catholic, Protestant, traditional beliefs	Kwanza	95
BENIN		112 620	43 483	6 446 000	Porto-Novo	French, Fon, Yoruba, Adja, local languages	Traditional beliefs, Roman Catholic, Sunni Muslim	CFA franc*	93
BOTSWANA		581 370	224 468	1 554 000	Gaborone	English, Setswana, Shona, local languages	Traditional beliefs, Protestant, Roman Catholic	Pula	98–99
BURKINA		274 200	105 869	11 856 000	Ouagadougou	French, Moore (Mossi), Fulani, local languages	Sunni Muslim, traditional beliefs, Roman Catholic	CFA franc*	92–93
BURUNDI		27 835	10 747	6 502 000	Bujumbura	Kirundi (Hutu, Tutsi), French	Roman Catholic, traditional beliefs, Protestant	Burundian franc	94–95
CAMEROON		475 442	183 569	15 203 000	Yaoundé	French, English, Fang, Bamileke, local languages	Roman Catholic, traditional beliefs, Sunni Muslim, Protestant	CFA franc*	94
CAPE VERDE		4 033	1 557	437 000	Praia	Portuguese, creole	Roman Catholic, Protestant	Cape Verde escudo	92
CENTRAL AFRICAN REPUBLIC		622 436	240 324	3 782 000	Bangui	French, Sango, Banda, Baya, local languages	Protestant, Roman Catholic, traditional beliefs, Sunni Muslim	CFA franc*	94
CHAD		1 284 000	495 755	8 135 000	Ndjamena	Arabic, French, Sara, local languages	Sunni Muslim, Roman Catholic, Protestant, traditional beliefs	CFA franc*	88
COMOROS		1 862	719	727 000	Moroni	Comorian, French, Arabic	Sunni Muslim, Roman Catholic	Comoros franc	97
CONGO		342 000	132 047	3 110 000	Brazzaville	French, Kongo, Monokutuba, local languages	Roman Catholic, Protestant, traditional beliefs, Sunni Muslim	CFA franc*	94–95
CONGO, DEMOCRATIC REP. OF		2 345 410	905 568	52 522 000	Kinshasa	French, Lingala, Swahili, Kongo, local languages	Christian, Sunni Muslim	Congolese franc	94–95
CÔTE D'IVOIRE		322 463	124 504	16 349 000	Yamoussoukro	French, creole, Akan, local languages	Sunni Muslim, Roman Catholic, traditional beliefs, Protestant	CFA franc*	92
DJIBOUTI		23 200	8 958	644 000	Djibouti	Somali, Afar, French, Arabic	Sunni Muslim, Christian	Djibouti franc	96
EGYPT		1 000 250	386 199	69 080 000	Cairo	Arabic	Sunni Muslim, Coptic Christian	Egyptian pound	89
EQUATORIAL GUINEA		28 051	10 831	470 000	Malabo	Spanish, French, Fang	Roman Catholic, traditional beliefs	CFA franc*	93
ERITREA		117 400	45 328	3 816 000	Asmara	Tigrinya, Tigre	Sunni Muslim, Coptic Christian	Nakfa	89
ETHIOPIA		1 133 880	437 794	64 459 000	Addis Ababa	Oromo, Amharic, Tigrinya, local languages	Ethiopian Orthodox, Sunni Muslim, traditional beliefs	Birr	96
GABON		267 667	103 347	1 262 000	Libreville	French, Fang, local languages	Roman Catholic, Protestant, traditional beliefs	CFA franc*	94
THE GAMBIA		11 295	4 361	1 337 000	Banjul	English, Malinke, Fulani, Wolof	Sunni Muslim, Protestant	Dalasi	92
GHANA		238 537	92 100	19 734 000	Accra	English, Hausa, Akan, local languages	Christian, Sunni Muslim, traditional beliefs	Cedi	92–93
GUINEA		245 857	94 926	8 274 000	Conakry	French, Fulani, Malinke, local languages	Sunni Muslim, traditional beliefs, Christian	Guinea franc	92
GUINEA-BISSAU		36 125	13 948	1 227 000	Bissau	Portuguese, crioulo, local languages	Traditional beliefs, Sunni Muslim, Christian	CFA franc*	92
KENYA		582 646	224 961	31 293 000	Nairobi	Swahili, English, local languages	Christian, traditional beliefs	Kenyan shilling	96
LESOTHO		30 355	11 720	2 057 000	Maseru	Sesotho, English, Zulu	Christian, traditional beliefs	Loti, S. African rand	99
LIBERIA		111 369	43 000	3 108 000	Monrovia	English, creole, local languages	Traditional beliefs, Christian, Sunni Muslim	Liberian dollar	92
LIBYA		1 759 540	679 362	5 408 000	Tripoli	Arabic, Berber	Sunni Muslim	Libyan dinar	88
MADAGASCAR		587 041	226 658	16 437 000	Antananarivo	Malagasy, French	Traditional beliefs, Christian, Sunni Muslim	Malagasy franc	99
MALAWI		118 484	45 747	11 572 000	Lilongwe	Chichewa, English, local languages	Christian, traditional beliefs, Sunni Muslim	Malawian kwacha	97
MALI		1 240 140	478 821	11 677 000	Bamako	French, Bambara, local languages	Sunni Muslim, traditional beliefs, Christian	CFA franc*	92–93
MAURITANIA		1 030 700	397 955	2 747 000	Nouakchott	Arabic, French, local languages	Sunni Muslim	Ouguiya	90
MAURITIUS		2 040	788	1 171 000	Port Louis	English, creole, Hindi, Bhojpuri, French	Hindu, Roman Catholic, Sunni Muslim	Mauritius rupee	162
MOROCCO		446 550	172 414	30 430 000	Rabat	Arabic, Berber, French	Sunni Muslim	Moroccan dirham	90–91
MOZAMBIQUE		799 380	308 642	18 644 000	Maputo	Portuguese, Makua, Tsonga, local languages	Traditional beliefs, Roman Catholic, Sunni Muslim	Metical	99
NAMIBIA		824 292	318 261	1 788 000	Windhoek	English, Afrikaans, German, Ovambo, local languages	Protestant, Roman Catholic	Namibian dollar	98
NIGER		1 267 000	489 191	11 227 000	Niamey	French, Hausa, Fulani, local languages	Sunni Muslim, traditional beliefs	CFA franc*	93
NIGERIA		923 768	356 669	116 929 000	Abuja	English, Hausa, Yoruba, Ibo, Fulani, local languages	Sunni Muslim, Christian, traditional beliefs	Naira	93
RWANDA		26 338	10 169	7 949 000	Kigali	Kinyarwanda, French, English	Roman Catholic, traditional beliefs, Protestant	Rwandan franc	94
SÃO TOMÉ AND PRÍNCIPE		964	372	140 000	São Tomé	Portuguese, creole	Roman Catholic, Protestant	Dobra	93
SENEGAL		196 720	75 954	9 662 000	Dakar	French, Wolof, Fulani, local languages	Sunni Muslim, Roman Catholic, traditional beliefs	CFA franc*	92
SEYCHELLES		455	176	81 000	Victoria	English, French, creole	Roman Catholic, Protestant	Seychelles rupee	162
SIERRA LEONE		71 740	27 699	4 587 000	Freetown	English, creole, Mende, Temne, local languages	Sunni Muslim, traditional beliefs	Leone	92
SOMALIA		637 657	246 201	9 157 000	Mogadishu	Somali, Arabic	Sunni Muslim	Somali shilling	96
SOUTH AFRICA, REPUBLIC OF		1 219 090	470 693	43 792 000	Pretoria/Cape Town	Afrikaans, English, nine official local languages	Protestant, Roman Catholic, Sunni Muslim, Hindu	Rand	98–99
SUDAN		2 505 813	967 500	31 809 000	Khartoum	Arabic, Dinka, Nubian, Beja, Nuer, local languages	Sunni Muslim, traditional beliefs, Christian	Sudanese dinar	88–89
SWAZILAND		17 364	6 704	938 000	Mbabane	Swazi, English	Christian, traditional beliefs	Emalangeni, S. African rand	99
TANZANIA		945 087	364 900	35 965 000	Dodoma	Swahili, English, Nyamwezi, local languages	Shi'a Muslim, Sunni Muslim, traditional beliefs, Christian	Tanzanian shilling	96–97
TOGO		56 785	21 925	4 657 000	Lomé	French, Ewe, Kabre, local languages	Traditional beliefs, Christian, Sunni Muslim	CFA franc*	93
TUNISIA		164 150	63 379	9 562 000	Tunis	Arabic, French	Sunni Muslim	Tunisian dinar	91
UGANDA		241 038	93 065	24 023 000	Kampala	English, Swahili, Luganda, local languages	Roman Catholic, Protestant, Sunni Muslim, traditional beliefs	Ugandan shilling	96
ZAMBIA		752 614	290 586	10 649 000	Lusaka	English, Bemba, Nyanja, Tonga, local languages	Christian, traditional beliefs	Zambian kwacha	95
ZIMBABWE		390 759	150 873	12 852 000	Harare	English, Shona, Ndebele	Christian, traditional beliefs	Zimbabwean dollar	98–99

DEPENDENT AND DISPUTED TERRITORIES		territorial status	area sq km	area sq miles	population	capital	languages	religions	currency	map
Canary Islands		Autonomous Community of Spain	7 447	2 875	1 606 522	Santa Cruz de Tenerife, Las Palmas	Spanish	Roman Catholic	Euro	90
Ceuta		Spanish Territory	19	7	68 796	Ceuta	Spanish, Arabic	Roman Catholic, Muslim	Euro	90
Madeira		Autonomous Region of Portugal	779	301	259 000	Funchal	Portuguese	Roman Catholic, Protestant	Euro	90
Mayotte		French Territorial Collectivity	373	144	144 944	Dzaoudzi	French, Mahorian	Sunni Muslim, Christian	Euro	97
Melilla		Spanish Territory	13	5	59 576	Melilla	Spanish, Arabic	Roman Catholic, Muslim	Euro	90
Réunion		French Overseas Department	2 551	985	732 000	St-Denis	French, creole	Roman Catholic	Euro	162
St Helena and Dependencies		United Kingdom Overseas Territory	121	47	6 000	Jamestown	English	Protestant, Roman Catholic	St Helena pound	160
Western Sahara		Disputed territory (Morocco)	266 000	102 703	260 000	Laâyoune	Arabic	Sunni Muslim	Moroccan dirham	90

oceania

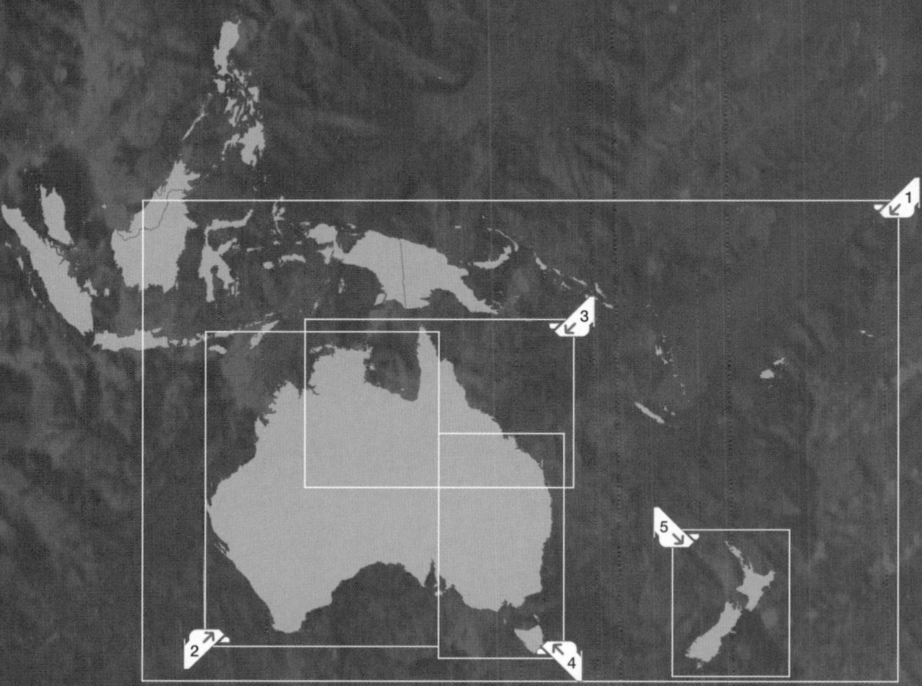

contents

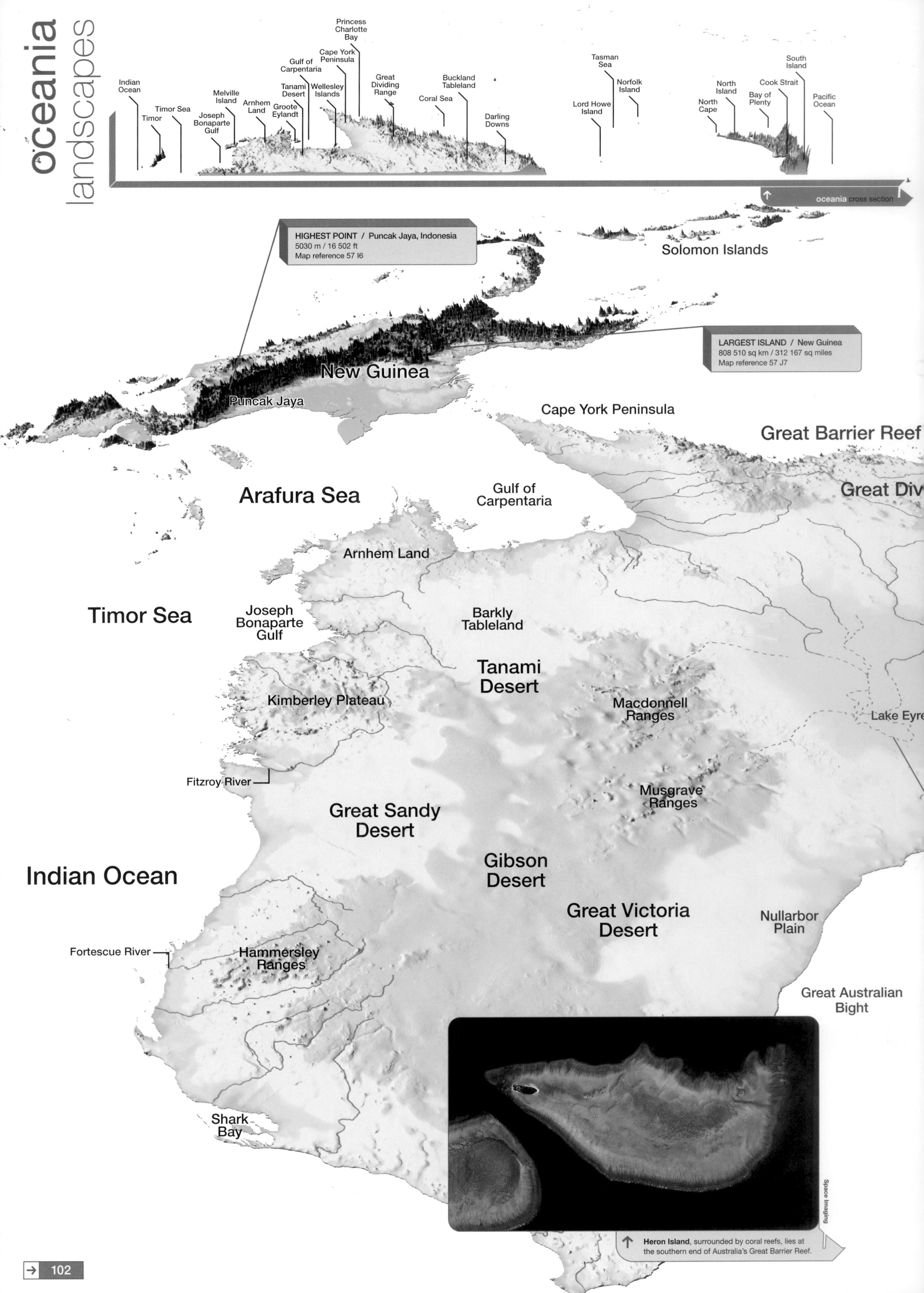

oceania cross section

Indian Ocean

Timor Sea

Joseph Bonaparte Gulf

Melville Island

Arnhem Land

Tanami Desert

Groote Eylandt

Wellesley Islands

Gulf of Carpentaria

Cape York Peninsula

Princess Charlotte Bay

Great Dividing Range

Coral Sea

Buckland Tableland

Darling Downs

Tasman Sea

Norfolk Island

Lord Howe Island

North Cape

North Island

Cook Strait

South Island

Bay of Plenty

Pacific Ocean

Timor

HIGHEST POINT / Puncak Jaya, Indonesia
5030 m / 16 502 ft
Map reference 57 I6

LARGEST ISLAND / New Guinea
808 510 sq km / 312 167 sq miles
Map reference 57 J7

New Guinea

Puncak Jaya

Solomon Islands

Cape York Peninsula

Great Barrier Reef

Arafura Sea

Gulf of Carpentaria

Great Div

Arnhem Land

Timor Sea

Joseph Bonaparte Gulf

Barkly Tableland

Tanami Desert

Macdonnell Ranges

Lake Eyre

Kimberley Plateau

Fitzroy River

Musgrave Ranges

Great Sandy Desert

Indian Ocean

Gibson Desert

Great Victoria Desert

Nullarbor Plain

Fortescue River

Hammersley Ranges

Great Australian Bight

Shark Bay

Space Imaging

Heron Island, surrounded by coral reefs, lies at the southern end of Australia's Great Barrier Reef.

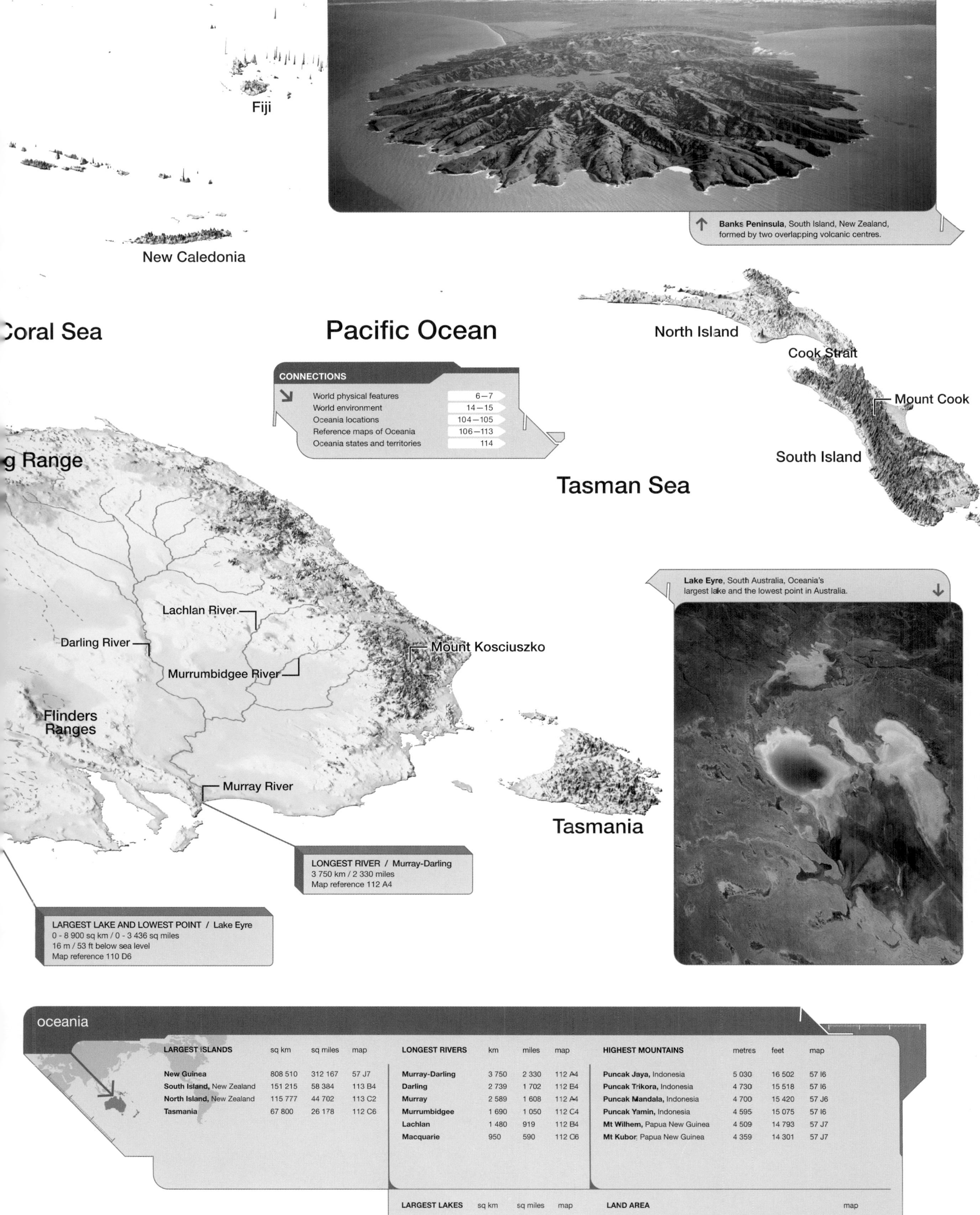

Fiji

New Caledonia

Coral Sea

Pacific Ocean

North Island

Cook Strait

Mount Cook

South Island

Tasman Sea

↑ **Banks Peninsula**, South Island, New Zealand, formed by two overlapping volcanic centres.

g Range

Lachlan River

Darling River

Murrumbidgee River

Mount Kosciuszko

Flinders Ranges

Murray River

Tasmania

Lake Eyre, South Australia, Oceania's largest lake and the lowest point in Australia. ↓

LONGEST RIVER / Murray-Darling
3 750 km / 2 330 miles
Map reference 112 A4

LARGEST LAKE AND LOWEST POINT / Lake Eyre
0 - 8 900 sq km / 0 - 3 436 sq miles
16 m / 53 ft below sea level
Map reference 110 D6

CONNECTIONS

World physical features	6 — 7
World environment	14 — 15
Oceania locations	104 — 105
Reference maps of Oceania	106 — 113
Oceania states and territories	114

oceania

LARGEST ISLANDS	sq km	sq miles	map
New Guinea	808 510	312 167	57 J7
South Island, New Zealand	151 215	58 384	113 B4
North Island, New Zealand	115 777	44 702	113 C2
Tasmania	67 800	26 178	112 C6

LONGEST RIVERS	km	miles	map
Murray-Darling	3 750	2 330	112 A4
Darling	2 739	1 702	112 E4
Murray	2 589	1 608	112 A4
Murrumbidgee	1 690	1 050	112 C4
Lachlan	1 480	919	112 B4
Macquarie	950	590	112 C6

HIGHEST MOUNTAINS	metres	feet	map
Puncak Jaya, Indonesia	5 030	16 502	57 I6
Puncak Trikora, Indonesia	4 730	15 518	57 I6
Puncak Mandala, Indonesia	4 700	15 420	57 J6
Puncak Yamin, Indonesia	4 595	15 075	57 I6
Mt Wilhem, Papua New Guinea	4 509	14 793	57 J7
Mt Kubor, Papua New Guinea	4 359	14 301	57 J7

LARGEST LAKES	sq km	sq miles	map
Lake Eyre	0-8 900	0-3 436	110 D6
Lake Torrens	0-5 780	0-2 232	112 A3

LAND AREA		map
Total land area	8 844 516 sq km / 3 414 887 sq miles (includes New Guinea and Pacific Island nations)	
Most northerly point	Eastern Island, North Pacific Ocean	164 G4
Most southerly point	Macquarie Island, South Pacific Ocean	164 E9
Most westerly point	Cape Inscription, Australia	109 A6
Most easterly point	Île Clipperton, North Pacific Ocean	165 K5

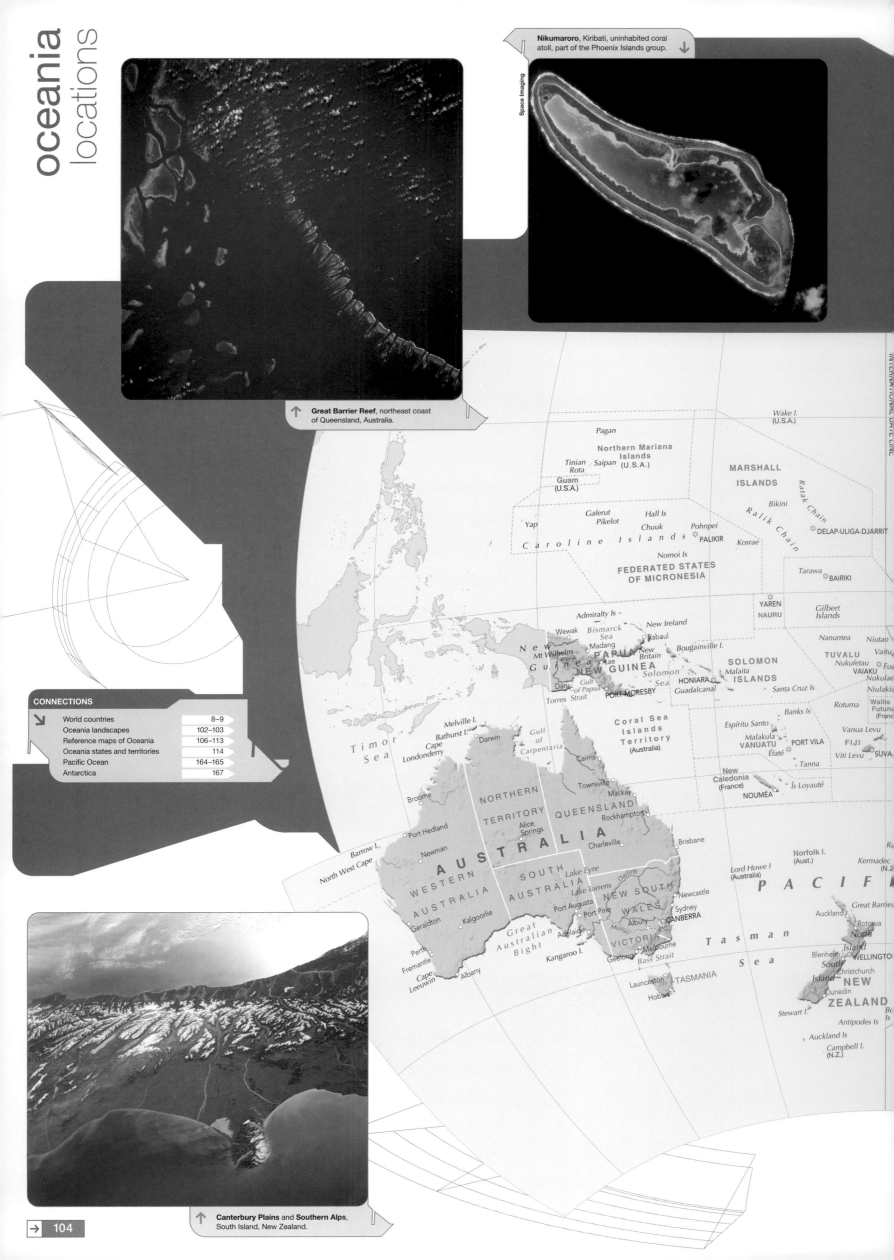

oceania locations

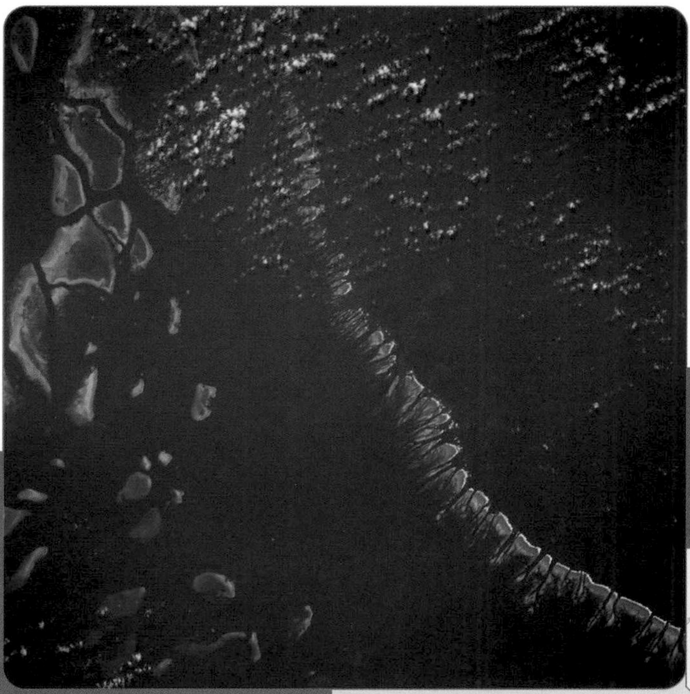

Great Barrier Reef, northeast coast of Queensland, Australia.

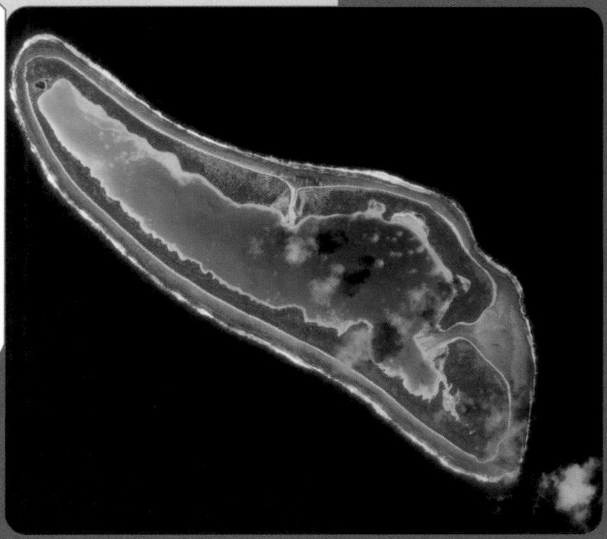

Space Imaging

Nikumaroro, Kiribati, uninhabited coral atoll, part of the Phoenix Islands group.

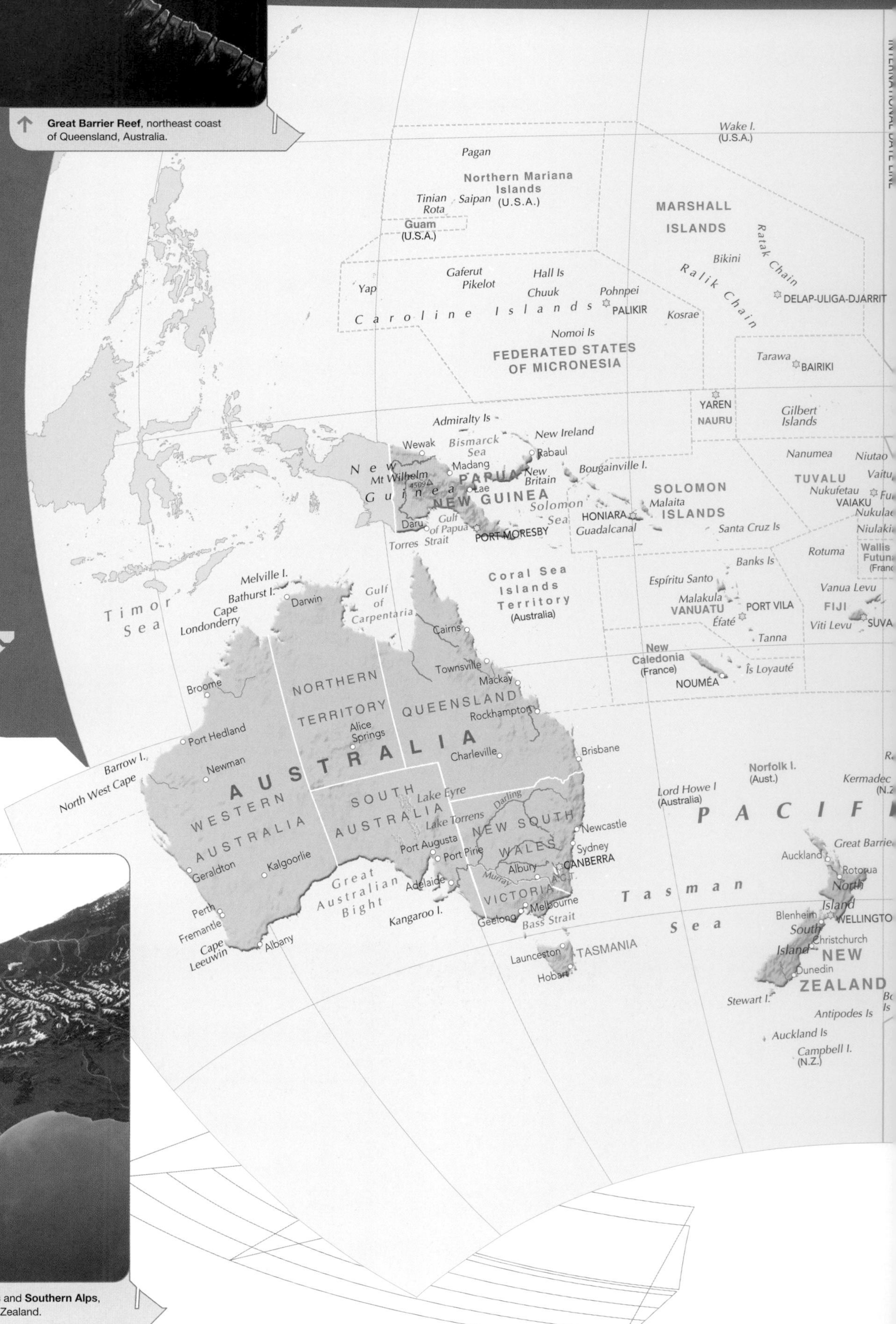

INTERNATIONAL DATE LINE
Wake I. (U.S.A.)
Pagan
Northern Mariana Islands (U.S.A.)
Tinian
Rota
Saipan
Guam (U.S.A.)
MARSHALL ISLANDS
Bikini
Ratak Chain
Ralik Chain
DELAP-ULIGA-DJARRIT
Yap
Gaferut
Pikelot
Hall Is
Chuuk
Pohnpei
PALIKIR
Kosrae
Caroline Islands
Nomoi Is
FEDERATED STATES OF MICRONESIA
Tarawa
BAIRIKI
YAREN
NAURU
Gilbert Islands
Admiralty Is
Wewak
Bismarck Sea
New Ireland
Rabaul
Madang
Mt Wilhelm
4509
New Guinea
PAPUA NEW GUINEA
New Britain
Lae
Bougainville I.
Solomon Sea
SOLOMON ISLANDS
Malaita
HONIARA
Guadalcanal
Daru
Gulf of Papua
PORT MORESBY
Torres Strait
Santa Cruz Is
Nanumea
Niutao
TUVALU
Nukufetau
VAIAKU
Rotuma
Coral Sea Islands Territory (Australia)
Espíritu Santo
Banks Is
Malakula
VANUATU
PORT VILA
Éfaté
Tanna
Vanua Levu
FIJI
Viti Levu
SUVA
New Caledonia (France)
NOUMÉA
Îs Loyauté
Melville I.
Bathurst I.
Darwin
Gulf of Carpentaria
Timor Sea
Cape Londonderry
Cairns
Townsville
Mackay
Rockhampton
Broome
NORTHERN TERRITORY
QUEENSLAND
Alice Springs
Port Hedland
Newman
AUSTRALIA
Charleville
Brisbane
Barrow I.
North West Cape
WESTERN AUSTRALIA
SOUTH AUSTRALIA
Lake Eyre
Lake Torrens
Darling
NEW SOUTH WALES
Newcastle
Sydney
CANBERRA
Port Augusta
Port Pirie
Albury
Murray
A.C.T.
Geraldton
Kalgoorlie
Great Australian Bight
Adelaide
VICTORIA
Melbourne
Geelong
Kangaroo I.
Bass Strait
Perth
Fremantle
Cape Leeuwin
Albany
Launceston
TASMANIA
Hobart
Norfolk I. (Aust.)
Lord Howe I (Australia)
Kermadec
PACIFIC
Tasman Sea
Auckland
Great Barrier
Rotorua
North Island
WELLINGTON
Blenheim
South Island
Christchurch
NEW ZEALAND
Dunedin
Stewart I.
Antipodes Is
Auckland Is
Campbell I. (N.Z.)

CONNECTIONS

World countries	8–9
Oceania landscapes	102–103
Reference maps of Oceania	106–113
Oceania states and territories	114
Pacific Ocean	164–165
Antarctica	167

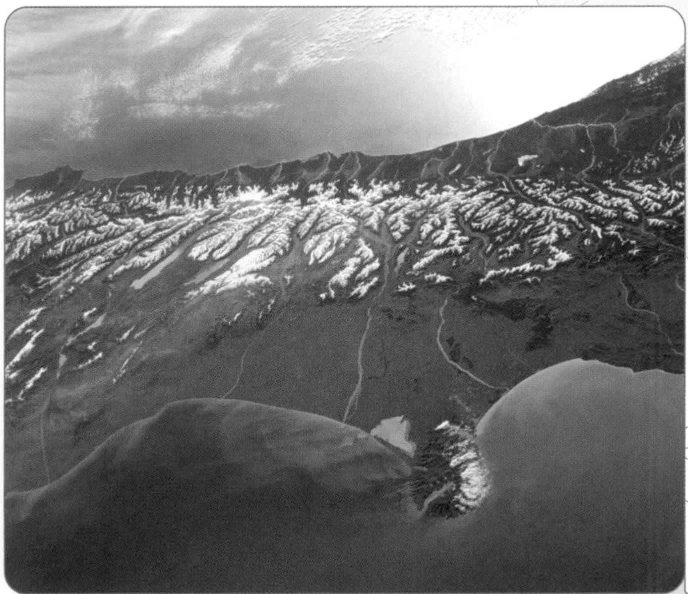

Canterbury Plains and **Southern Alps**, South Island, New Zealand.

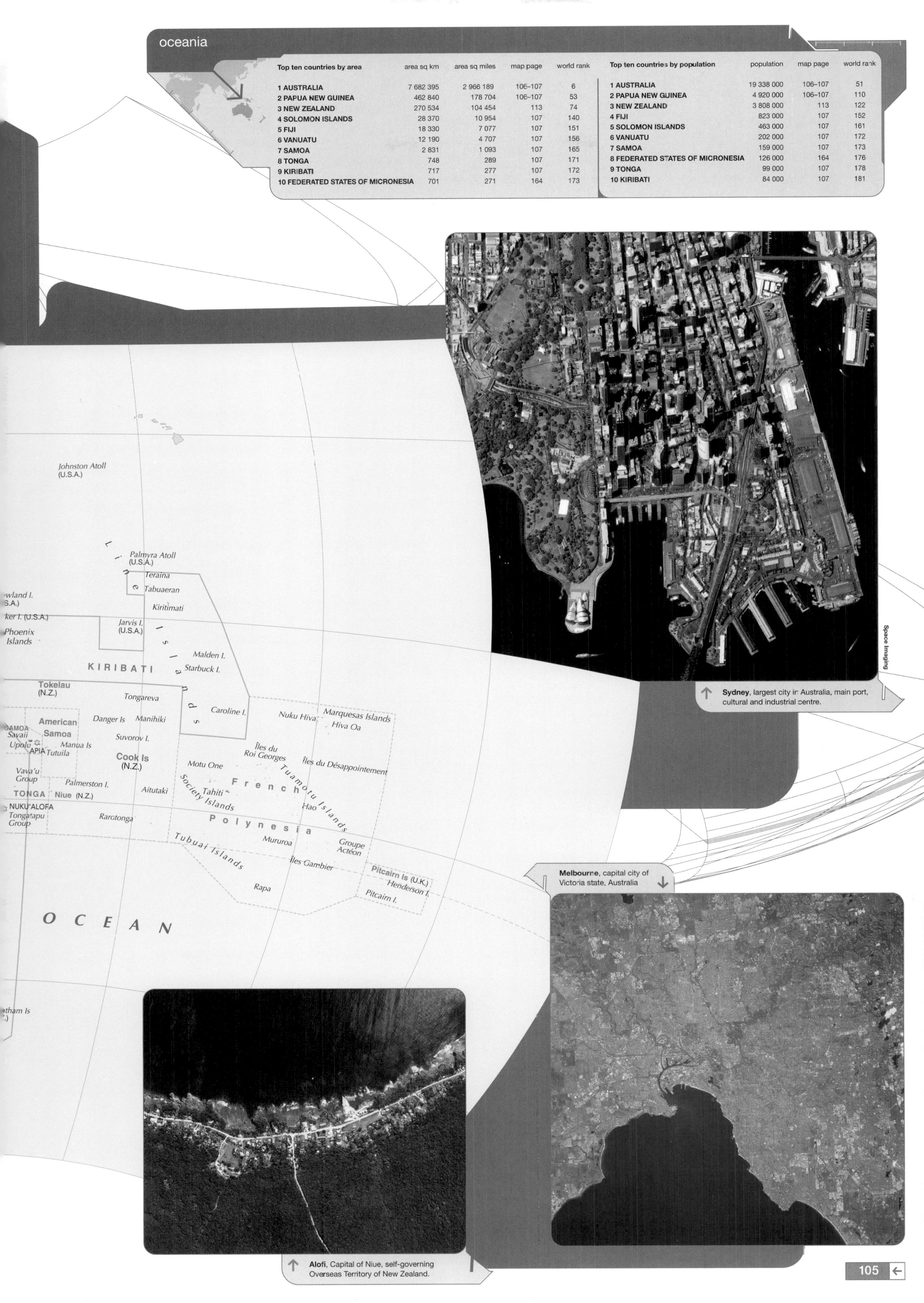

Top ten countries by area	area sq km	area sq miles	map page	world rank
1 AUSTRALIA	7 682 395	2 966 189	106–107	6
2 PAPUA NEW GUINEA	462 840	178 704	106–107	53
3 NEW ZEALAND	270 534	104 454	113	74
4 SOLOMON ISLANDS	28 370	10 954	107	140
5 FIJI	18 330	7 077	107	151
6 VANUATU	12 190	4 707	107	156
7 SAMOA	2 831	1 093	107	165
8 TONGA	748	289	107	171
9 KIRIBATI	717	277	107	172
10 FEDERATED STATES OF MICRONESIA	701	271	164	173

Top ten countries by population	population	map page	world rank
1 AUSTRALIA	19 338 000	106–107	51
2 PAPUA NEW GUINEA	4 920 000	106–107	110
3 NEW ZEALAND	3 808 000	113	122
4 FIJI	823 000	107	152
5 SOLOMON ISLANDS	463 000	107	161
6 VANUATU	202 000	107	172
7 SAMOA	159 000	107	173
8 FEDERATED STATES OF MICRONESIA	126 000	164	176
9 TONGA	99 000	107	178
10 KIRIBATI	84 000	107	181

Space Imaging

Sydney, largest city in Australia, main port, cultural and industrial centre.

Melbourne, capital city of Victoria state, Australia

Alofi, Capital of Niue, self-governing Overseas Territory of New Zealand.

105

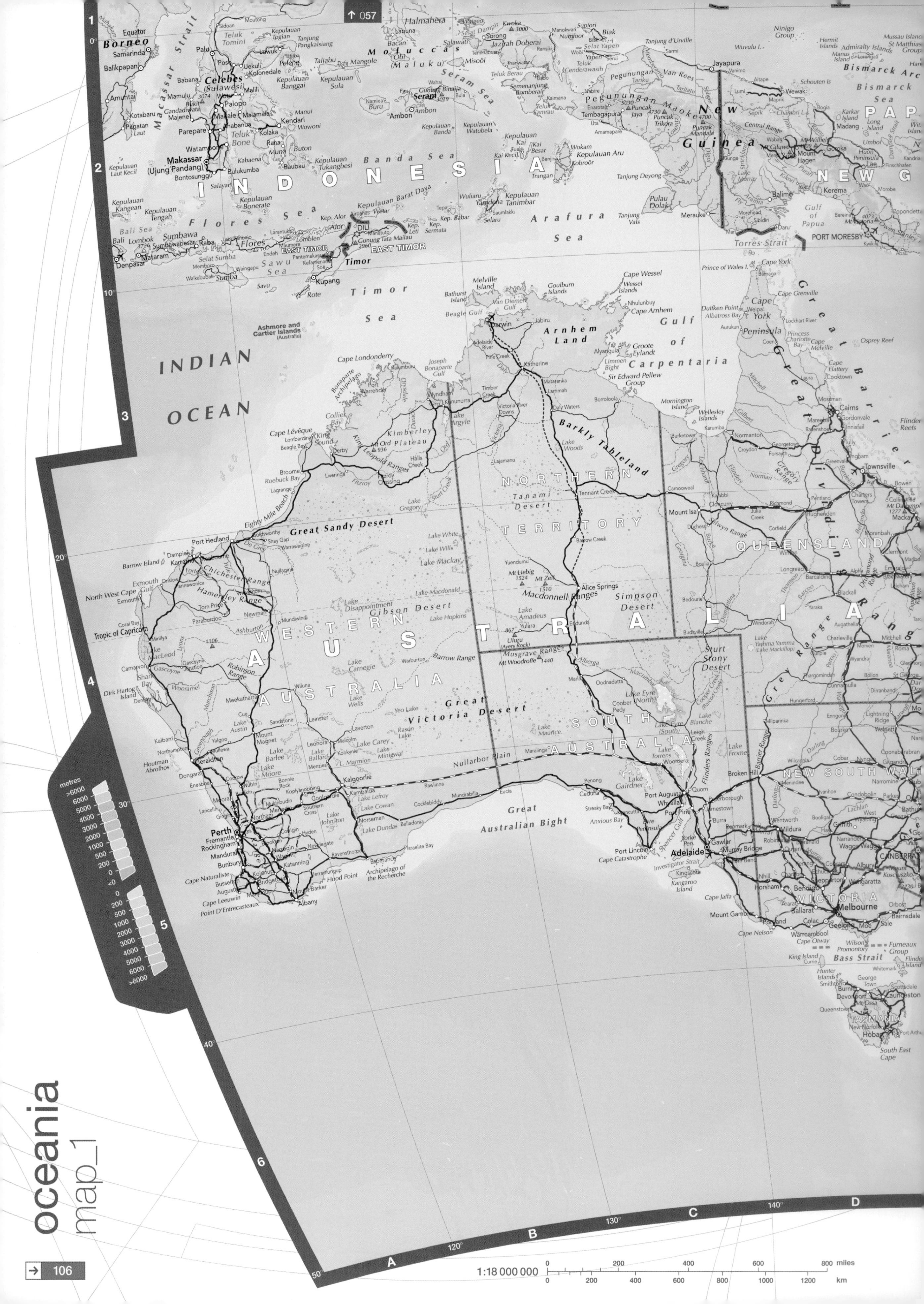

oceania
map_1

1:18 000 000

0   200   400   600   800 miles

0   200   400   600   800   1000   1200 km

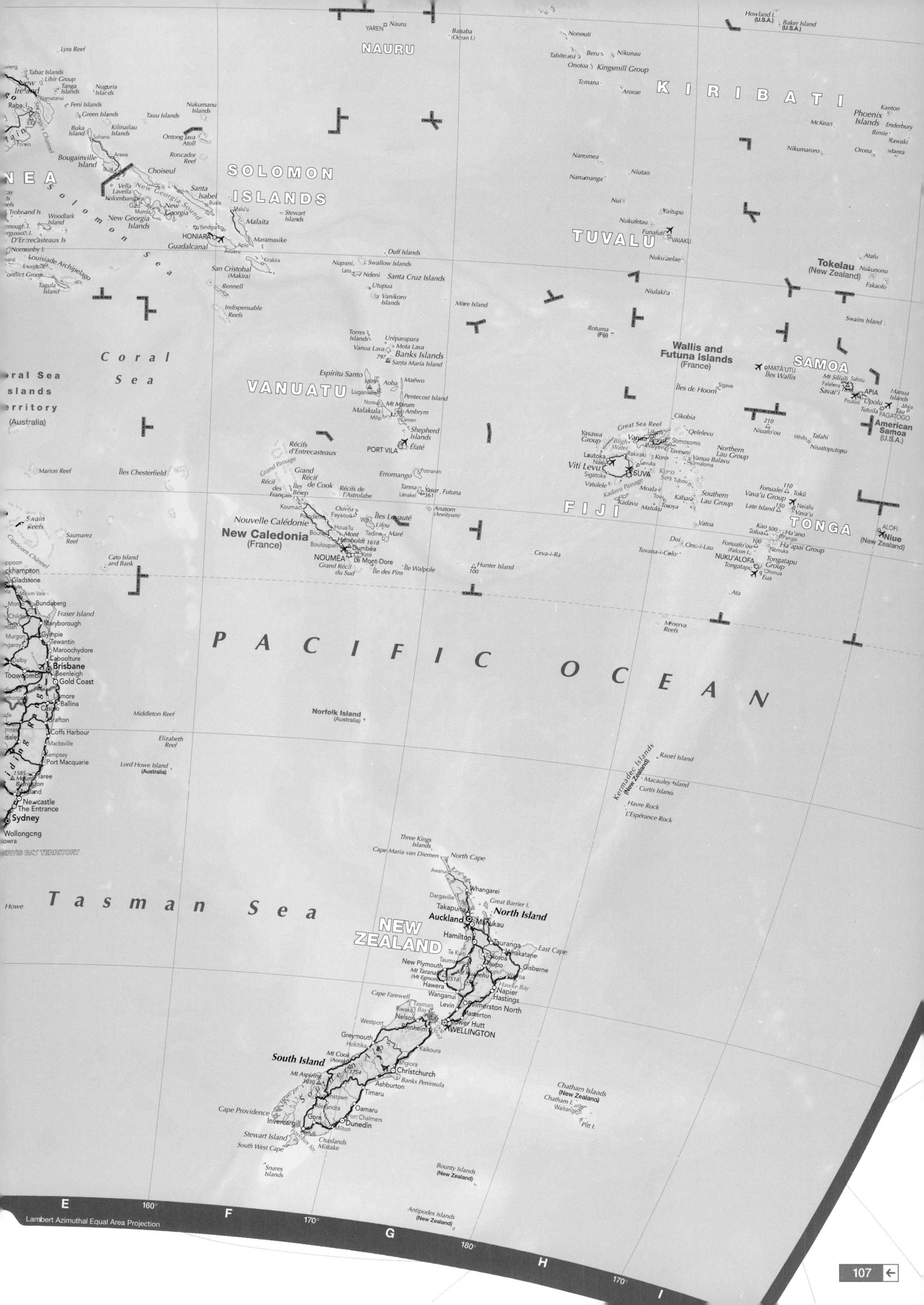

NAURU
YAREN
Nauru
Banaba (Ocean I.)
Howland I. (U.S.A.)
Baker Island (U.S.A.)
Lyra Reef
Tabar Islands
Lihir Group
Tanga Islands
Nuguria Islands
Feni Islands
Green Islands
Nukumanu Islands
Tauu Islands
Buka Island
Kilinailau Islands
Ontong Java Atoll
Roncador Reef
Bougainville Island
Choiseul
SOLOMON ISLANDS
Santa Isabel
Vella Lavella
Kolombangara
New Georgia Islands
New Georgia Sound
Malaita
Stewart Islands
HONIARA
Guadalcanal
Maramasike
Solomon Sea
Trobriand Is
Woodlark Island
D'Entrecasteaux Is
Louisiade Archipelago
Tagula Island
San Cristobal (Makira)
Rennell
Indispensable Reefs
Duff Islands
Nupani
Swallow Islands
Ndeni
Santa Cruz Islands
Utupua
Vanikoro Islands
Mitre Island
Nonouti
Beru
Nikunau
Tabiteuea
Onotoa
Kingsmill Group
Tamana
Arorae
KIRIBATI
Phoenix Islands
Kanton
Enderbury
McKean
Birnie
Rawaki
Nikumaroro
Orona
Manra
Nanumea
Niutao
Nanumanga
Nui
Vaitupu
Nukufetau
Funafuti
VAIAKU
TUVALU
Nukulaelae
Niulakita
Tokelau (New Zealand)
Atafu
Nukunonu
Fakaofo
Swains Island
Rotuma (Fiji)
Wallis and Futuna Islands (France)
MATĀ'UTU
Îles Wallis
Îles de Hoorn
Sigave
SAMOA
Savai'i
APIA
Upolu
Manua Islands
FAGATOGO
Tutuila
American Samoa (U.S.A.)
Niuafo'ou
Tafahi
Niuatoputapu
Coral Sea
Coral Sea Islands Territory (Australia)
Torres Islands
Uréparapara
Mota Lava
Vanua Lava
Banks Islands
Santa Maria Island
Espíritu Santo
Aoba
Maéwo
VANUATU
Luganville
Pentecost Island
Mt Marum
Malakula
Ambrym
Shepherd Islands
PORT VILA
Éfaté
Récifs d'Entrecasteaux
Marion Reef
Îles Chesterfield
Grand Passage
Grand Récif de Cook
Récif des Français
Îles Belep
Récifs de l'Astrolabe
Erromango
Tanna
Yasur
Futuna
Anatom (Aneityum)
Ouvéa
Îles Loyauté
Lifou
Maré
Nouvelle Calédonie
New Caledonia (France)
NOUMÉA
Le Mont-Dore
Grand Récif du Sud
Île des Pins
Île Walpole
Hunter Island
Ceva-i-Ra
Yasawa Group
Great Sea Reef
Vanua Levu
Cikobia
Qelelevu
Taveuni
Lautoka
Viti Levu
SUVA
Kadavu Passage
Kadavu
Northern Lau Group
Vanua Balavu
Koro Sea
Moala
Southern Lau Group
FIJI
Matuku
Totoya
Vatoa
Tuvana-i-Colo
Ono-i-Lau
Fonualei
Vava'u Group
Late Island
Neiafu
TONGA
Ha'apai Group
Tofua
Kao
NUKU'ALOFA
Tongatapu Group
'Eua
Ata
Niue (New Zealand)
ALOFI
Minerva Reefs
Swain Reefs
Saumarez Reef
Capricorn Channel
Cato Island and Bank
Rockhampton
Gladstone
Bundaberg
Fraser Island
Maryborough
Gympie
Maroochydore
Caboolture
Brisbane
Toowoomba
Beenleigh
Gold Coast
Lismore
Ballina
Grafton
Coffs Harbour
Macksville
Kempsey
Port Macquarie
Taree
Maitland
Newcastle
The Entrance
Sydney
Wollongong
Middleton Reef
Elizabeth Reef
Lord Howe Island (Australia)
PACIFIC OCEAN
Norfolk Island (Australia)
Kermadec Islands (New Zealand)
Raoul Island
Macauley Island
Curtis Island
Havre Rock
L'Espérance Rock
Tasman Sea
Three Kings Islands
Cape Maria van Diemen
North Cape
Whangarei
Dargaville
Great Barrier I.
North Island
Takapuna
Auckland
Manukau
Hamilton
NEW ZEALAND
Tauranga
Whakatane
East Cape
Rotorua
Taupo
Gisborne
New Plymouth
Mt Taranaki (Mt Egmont)
Hawera
Mt Ruapehu
Hawke Bay
Napier
Hastings
Wanganui
Palmerston North
Levin
Masterton
Cape Farewell
Tasman Bay
Nelson
Blenheim
Lower Hutt
WELLINGTON
Westport
Greymouth
Hokitika
Kaikoura
South Island
Mt Cook (Aoraki)
Christchurch
Banks Peninsula
Mt Aspiring
Ashburton
Timaru
Queenstown
Alexandra
Oamaru
Cape Providence
Invercargill
Gore
Port Chalmers
Dunedin
Milton
Stewart Island
Foveaux Str.
South West Cape
Chaslands Mistake
Snares Islands
Chatham Islands (New Zealand)
Chatham I.
Waitangi
Pitt I.
Bounty Islands (New Zealand)
Antipodes Islands (New Zealand)
E
F
G
H
I
160°
170°
180°
170°
Lambert Azimuthal Equal Area Projection

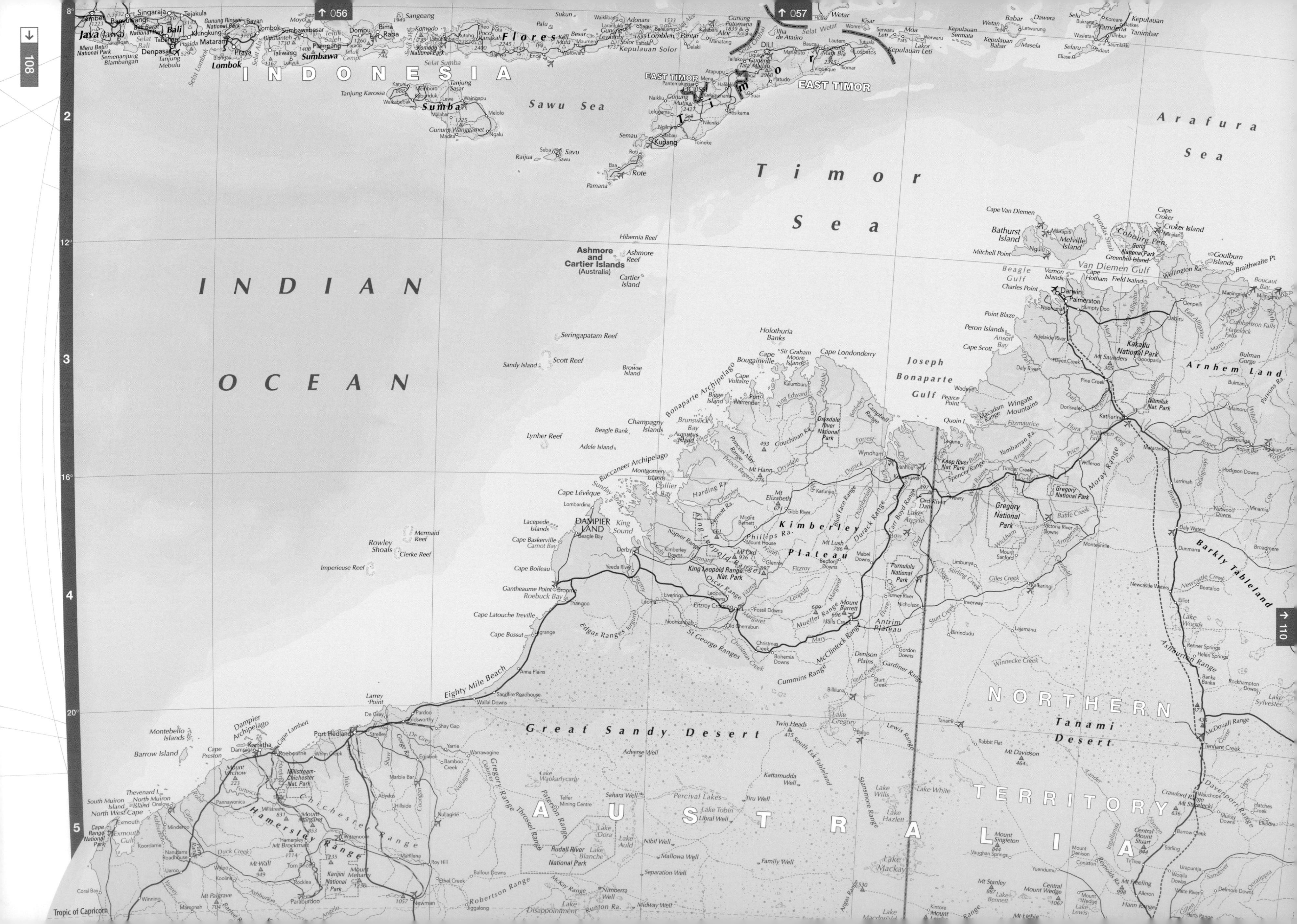

Arafura Sea

Timor Sea

Sawu Sea

INDIAN OCEAN

INDONESIA

Flores

Sumbawa

Lombok

Bali

Java

Sumba

EAST TIMOR

DILI

Kupang

Ashmore and
Cartier Islands
(Australia)

Ashmore
Reef

Cartier
Island

Hibernia Reef

Holothuria
Banks

Scott Reef

Seringapatam Reef

Sandy Island

Lynher Reef

Mermaid
Reef

Clerke Reef

Rowley
Shoals

Imperieuse Reef

Joseph
Bonaparte
Gulf

Van Diemen Gulf

Arnhem Land

Barkly Tableland

NORTHERN TERRITORY

AUSTRALIA

Tanami
Desert

Great Sandy Desert

Kimberley Plateau

Darwin

Palmerston

Kakadu
National Park

Gregory
National
Park

Bonaparte Archipelago

DAMPIER
LAND

King
Sound

Eighty Mile Beach

Gregory Range

Hamersley Range

Chichester Range

Karijini
National Park

Port Hedland

Dampier
Archipelago

Barrow Island

Montebello
Islands

North West Cape

Tropic of Capricorn

Cape
Van Diemen

Bathurst
Island

Melville
Island

Cape Croker

Coburg Pen.

Croker Island

Beagle
Gulf

Rudall River
National Park

King Leopold Ranges

Melville Island

8°

12°

16°

20°

2

3

4

5

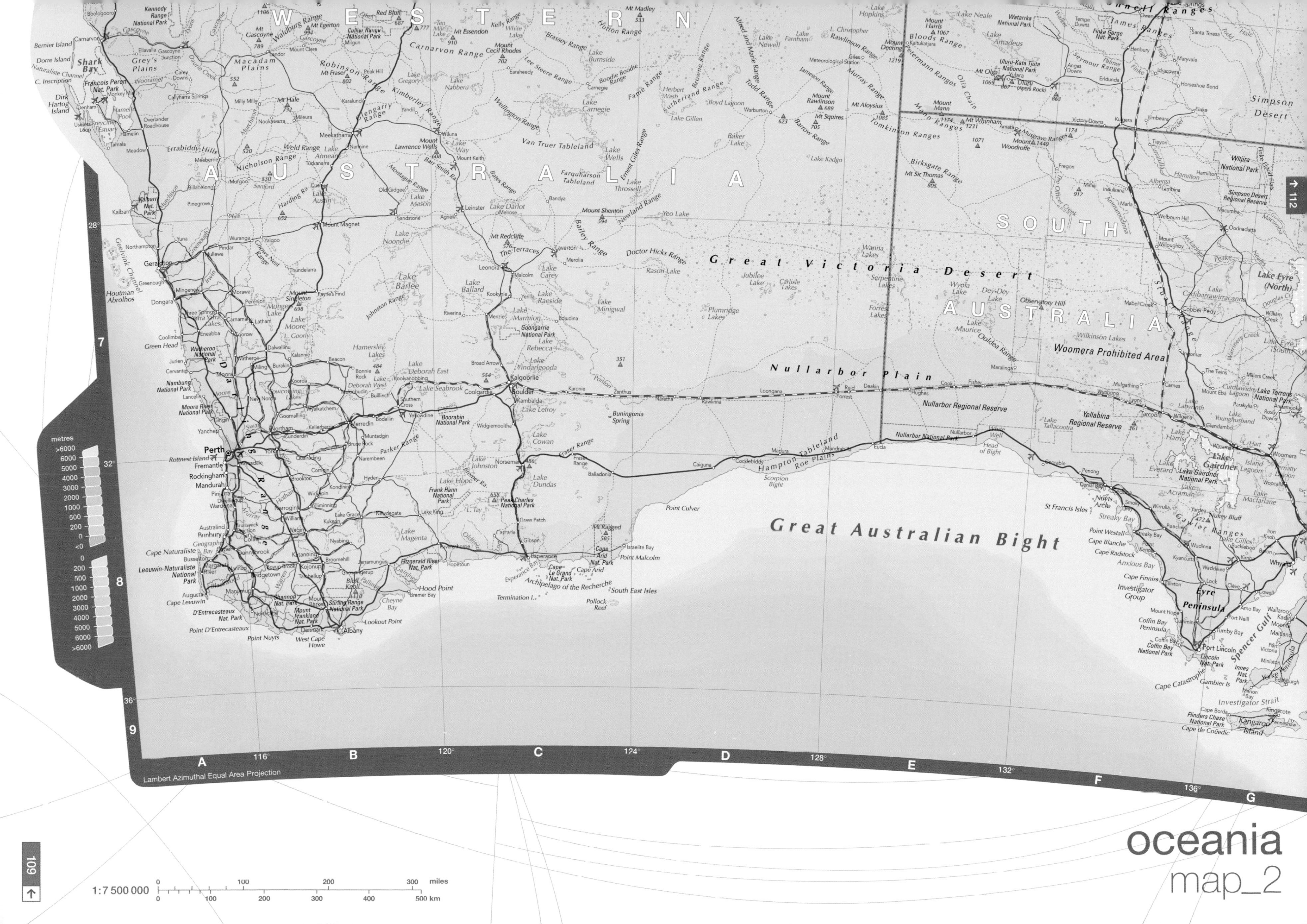

↑ 112

SOUTH

AUSTRALIA

WESTERN

AUSTRALIA

Great Victoria Desert

Nullarbor Plain

Nullarbor National Park

Nullarbor Regional Reserve

Woomera Prohibited Area

Yellabinna Regional Reserve

Great Australian Bight

Hampton Tableland

Lake Eyre (North)

Lake Eyre (South)

Lake Torrens

Lake Gairdner

Lake Everard

Lake Harris

Gawler Ranges

Eyre Peninsula

Spencer Gulf

Port Lincoln

Investigator Strait

Kangaroo Island

Flinders Chase National Park

Cape de Couedic

Simpson Desert

Simpson Desert Regional Reserve

James Ranges

Finke Gorge Nat. Park

Watarrka National Park

Uluru-Kata Tjuta National Park

Mt Olga

Ayers Rock (Uluru)

Petermann Ranges

Mann Ranges

Musgrave Ranges

Tomkinson Ranges

Birksgate Range

Mt Sir Thomas

Olia Chain

Rawlinson Range

Mount Rawlinson

Barrow Range

Alfred and Marie Range

Browne Range

Todd Range

Baker Lake

Lake Kadgo

Yeo Lake

Doctor Hicks Range

Raeson Lake

Ernest Giles Range

Van Truer Tableland

Bailey Range

Carnarvon Range

Robinson Ranges

Kimberley Range

Nicholson Range

Macadam Plains

Grey's Plains

Gascoyne Range

Kennedy Range National Park

Shark Bay

Dirk Hartog Island

Geelvink Channel

Houtman Abrolhos

Green Head

Namburg National Park

Moore River National Park

Rottnest Island

Perth

Fremantle

Rockingham

Mandurah

Bunbury

Geographe Bay

Cape Naturaliste

Leeuwin-Naturaliste National Park

Cape Leeuwin

Augusta

D'Entrecasteaux Nat. Park

Point D'Entrecasteaux

D a r l i n g   R a n g e

Stirling Range National Park

Mount Frankland Nat. Park

West Cape Howe

Albany

King George Sound

Fitzgerald River Nat. Park

Hood Point

Cheyne Bay

Bremer Bay

Point Culver

Point Malcolm

Israelite Bay

Cape Arid Nat. Park

Cape Le Grand Nat. Park

Esperance

Archipelago of the Recherche

Termination I.

South East Isles

Pollock Reef

Grass Patch

Cape Pasley

Cape Radstock

Cape Blanche

Point Wessall

Anxious Bay

Streaky Bay

St Francis Isles

Investigator Group

Coffin Bay

Coffin Bay Peninsula

Coffin Bay National Park

Lincoln Nat. Park

Kalgoorlie

Goongarrie National Park

Lake Carey

Lake Raeside

Lake Lefroy

Lake Cowan

Lake Dundas

Norseman

Widgiemooltha

Coolgardie

Kambalda

Boorabbin National Park

Frank Hann National Park

Peak Charles National Park

Lake Johnston

Lake Hope

Lake King

Lake Magenta

Fraser Range

Cable Range

Balladonia

Cocklebiddy

Madura

Mundrabilla

Eucla

Head of Bight

Yalata

Nullarbor

Forrest

Loongana

Rawlinna

Zanthus

Naretha

Cook

Watson

Ooldea

Tarcoola

Glendambo

Woomera

Pimba

Port Augusta

Whyalla

Cleve

Kimba

Wudinna

Ceduna

Penong

Fowlers Bay

Scorpion Bight

Lambert Azimuthal Equal Area Projection

1:7 500 000

metres
>6000
6000
5000
4000
3000
2000
1000
500
200
0
<0
200
500
1000
2000
3000
4000
5000
6000
>6000

A   B   C   D   E   F   G

9   8   7   28   32   36

116°   120°   124°   128°   132°   136°

0   100   200   300   400   500 km
0   100   200   300   miles

109 ←

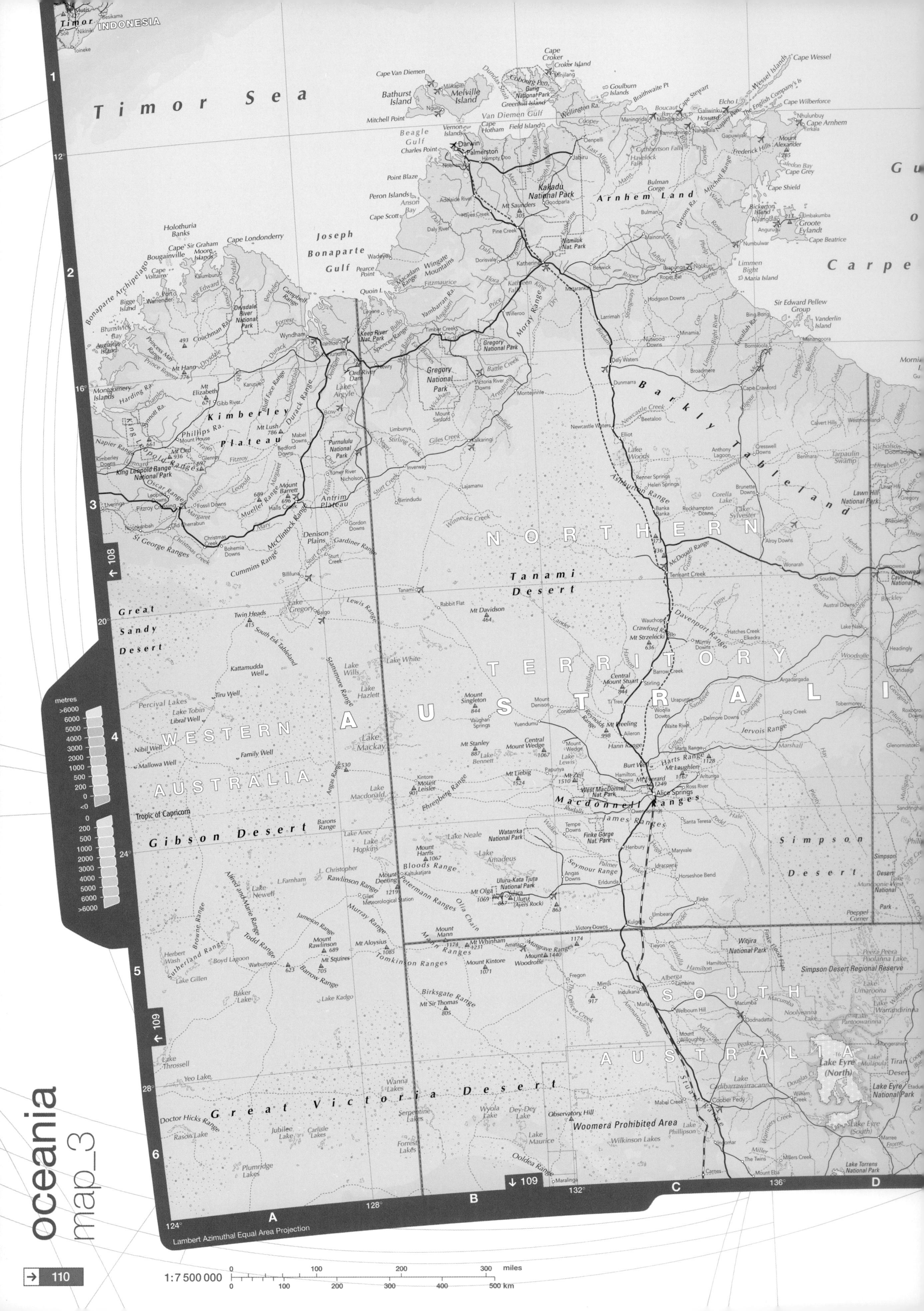

Timor Sea

INDONESIA

Timor

**Joseph
Bonaparte
Gulf**

Beagle
Gulf

Van Diemen Gulf

Kakadu
National Park

Arnhem Land

Gu

Carpe

**Kimberley
Plateau**

**Gregory
National
Park**

Barkly Tableland

**Great
Sandy
Desert**

N O R T H E R N

**Tanami
Desert**

W E S T E R N

A U S T R A L I

T E R R I T O R Y

A U S T R A L I A

Tropic of Capricorn

Gibson Desert

Macdonnell Ranges

Alice Springs

James Ranges

Simpson

Desert

Uluru-Kata Tjuta
National Park

Uluru
(Ayers Rock)

S O U T H

A U S T R A L I A

Lake Eyre
(North)

G r e a t   V i c t o r i a   D e s e r t

Woomera Prohibited Area

Simpson Desert Regional Reserve

Lake Eyre
National Park

Lake Eyre
(South)

metres
>6000
6000
5000
4000
3000
2000
1000
500
200
0
<0
0
200
500
1000
2000
3000
4000
5000
6000
>6000

A

128°

B

↓ 109

132°

C

136°

D

124°

Lambert Azimuthal Equal Area Projection

1:7 500 000

0   100   200   300   miles

0   100   200   300   400   500 km

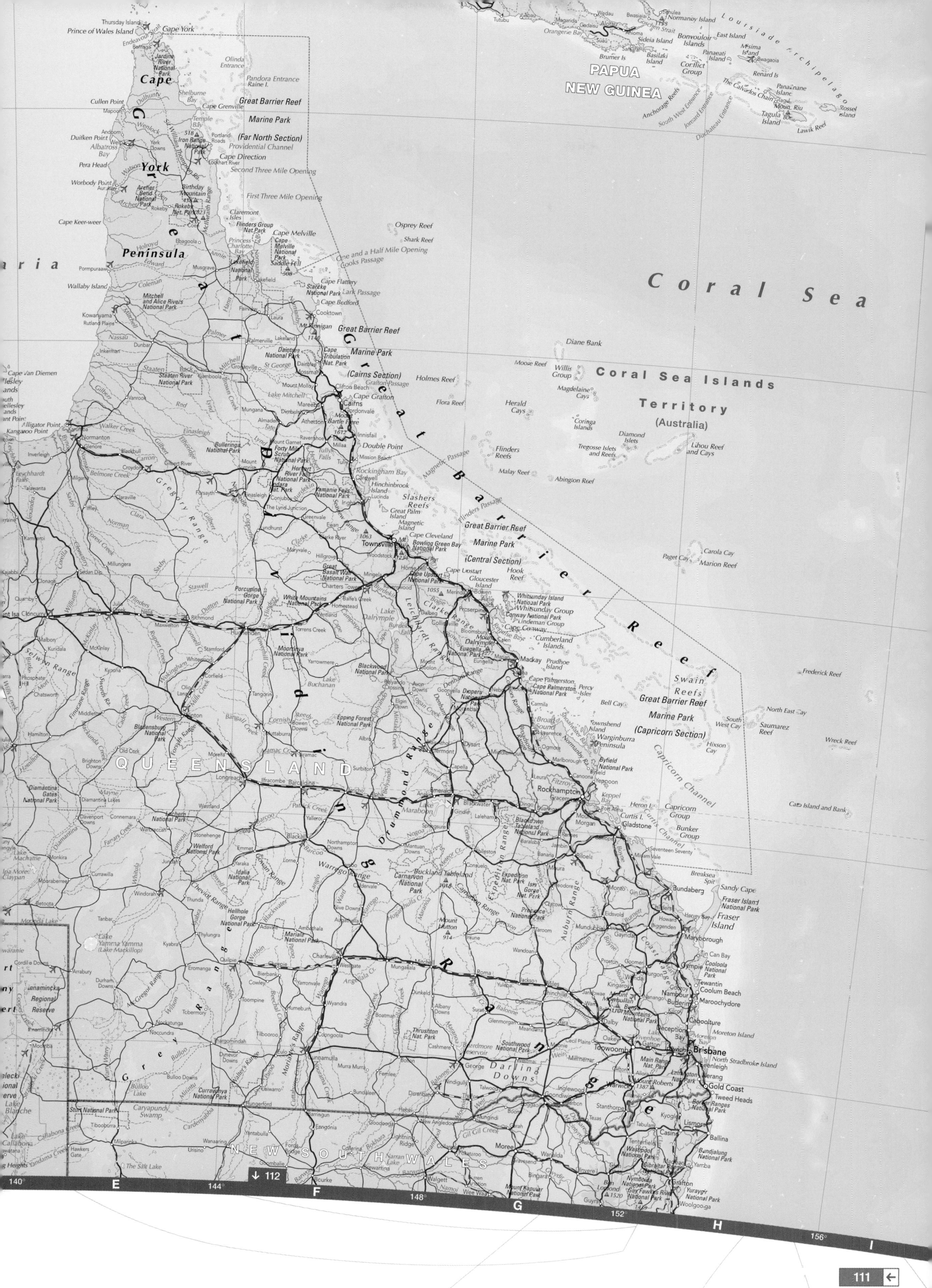

Coral Sea
Coral Sea Islands Territory
(Australia)
PAPUA NEW GUINEA
Louisiade Archipelago
QUEENSLAND
NEW SOUTH WALES
Great Barrier Reef
Great Barrier Reef Marine Park (Far North Section)
Great Barrier Reef Marine Park (Cairns Section)
Great Barrier Reef Marine Park (Central Section)
Great Barrier Reef Marine Park (Capricorn Section)
Great Dividing Range
Cape York Peninsula
Thursday Island
Prince of Wales Island
Cape York
Cape Grenville
Cape Direction
Cape Melville
Cape Flattery
Cape Bedford
Cooktown
Cairns
Cape Grafton
Townsville
Magnetic Island
Cape Cleveland
Bowen
Whitsunday Group
Mackay
Cumberland Islands
Rockhampton
Gladstone
Capricorn Channel
Bundaberg
Fraser Island
Maryborough
Gympie
Brisbane
Moreton Island
North Stradbroke Island
Gold Coast
Tweed Heads
Toowoomba
Warwick
Darling Downs
Lismore
Ballina
Grafton
Moree
Bourke
Walgett
Mount Isa
Cloncurry
Normanton
Kowanyama
Hughenden
Richmond
Charters Towers
Winton
Longreach
Barcaldine
Emerald
Blackall
Charleville
Roma
Cunnamulla
Quilpie
Mitchell
St George
Goondiwindi
Dalby
Kingaroy
Nambour
Maroochydore
Caboolture
Ipswich
Diane Bank
Willis Group
Magdelaine Cays
Herald Cays
Coringa Islands
Diamond Islets
Flinders Reefs
Holmes Reef
Flora Reef
Osprey Reef
Lihou Reef and Cays
Marion Reef
Frederick Reef
Saumarez Reef
Wreck Reef
Cato Island and Bank
Swain Reefs
Capricorn Group
Bunker Group
Sandy Cape
Breaksea Spit
Selwyn Range
Gregory Range
Grey Range
Warrego Range
Drummond Range
Expedition Range
Carnarvon National Park
Lake Yamma Yamma (Lake Mackillop)
Innamincka Regional Reserve
Sturt National Park
140°
E
144°
↓ 112
F
148°
G
152°
H
156°
I

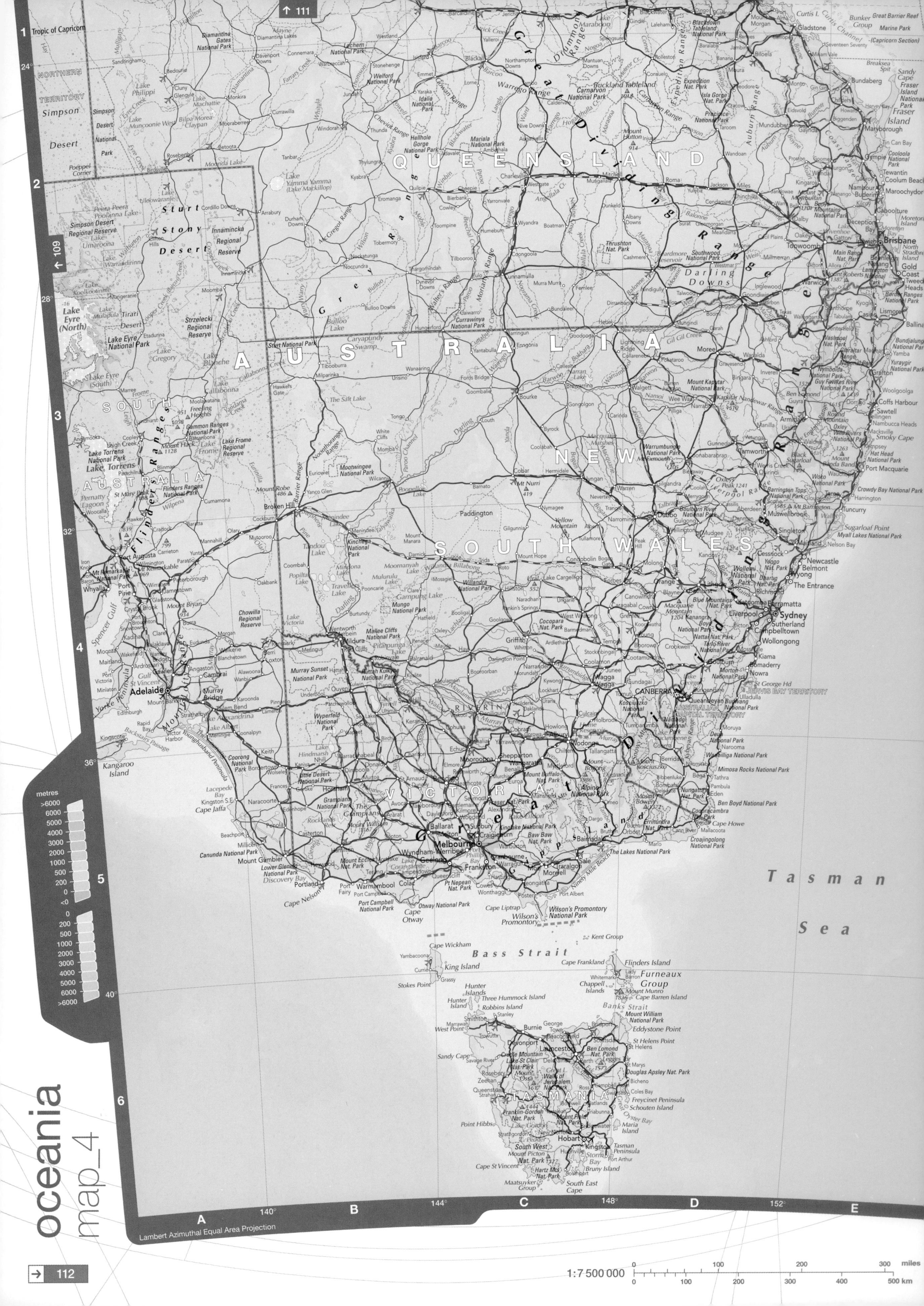

Tropic of Capricorn

24°

NORTHERN TERRITORY

Simpson

Desert

28°

Lake Eyre (North)

32°

SOUTH AUSTRALIA

AUSTRALIA

QUEENSLAND

Great Dividing Range

Brisbane

Gold Coast

Darling Downs

NEW

SOUTH WALES

Sydney

Wollongong

CANBERRA

AUSTRALIAN CAPITAL TERRITORY

VICTORIA

36°

Adelaide

Kangaroo Island

metres
>6000
6000
5000
4000
3000
2000
1000
500
200
0
<0
200
1000
2000
3000
4000
5000
6000
>6000

Melbourne

Great Dividing Range

Bass Strait

King Island

Furneaux Group

40°

Tasman

Sea

TASMANIA

Hobart

oceania
map_4

Lambert Azimuthal Equal Area Projection

1:7 500 000

A   140°   B   144°   C   148°   D   152°   E

0   100   200   300 miles
0   100   200   300   400   500 km

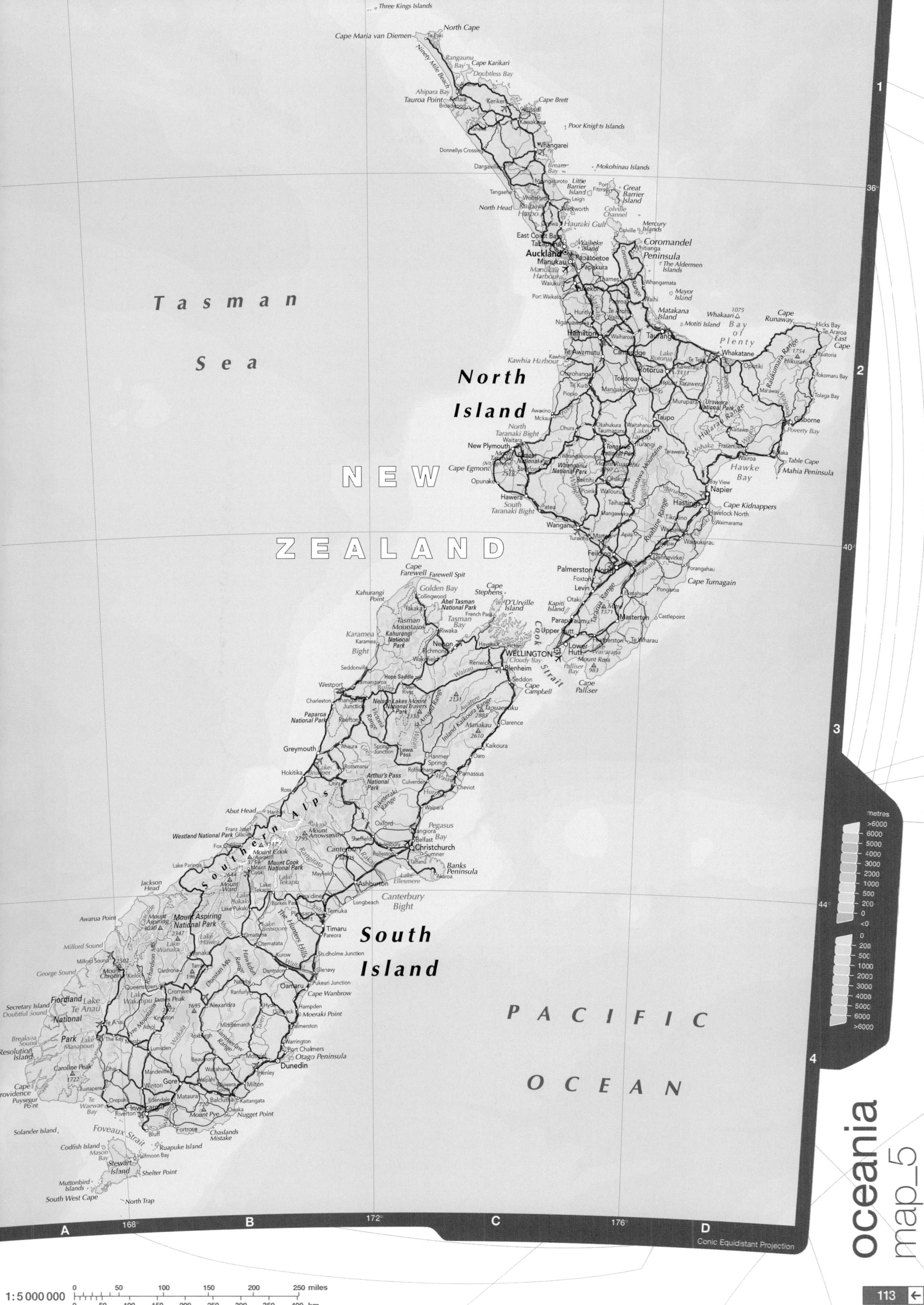

Three Kings Islands

North Cape
Cape Maria van Diemen   Te Paki
Rangaunu
Bay   Cape Karikari
Ninety Mile Beach   Doubtless Bay
Ahipara Bay   Kerikeri
Tauroa Point   Russell   Cape Brett
Broadwood   Kawakawa

Poor Knights Islands

Whangarei
Donnellys Crossing   Bream
Bay   Mokohinau Islands
Dargaville   Maungaturoto   Little
Barrier
Island   Port
Fitzroy   Great
Barrier
Island
Tangaehe   Warkworth   Colville
North Head   Leigh   Channel

T a s m a n   North Head
Wellsford   Mercury
Islands
Colville
Helensville   Hauraki Gulf   Whitianga   The Aldermen
Islands
S e a   East Coast Bays   Waiheke   Coromandel
Tatapuna   Island   Peninsula
Auckland   Papatoetoe
Manukau   Papakura   Whangamata
Manukau
Harbour   Thames   Mayor
Island
Waiuku   Pokeno   Whangamata
Por: Waikato   Coromandel   Whakaari △   1075   Cape
Runaway
Huntly   Te Aroha   Matakana   Hicks Bay
Ngaruawahia   Island   Motiti Island   Bay   Te Araroa
Whakatane   Waihi   of   East
Hamilton   Tauranga   Plenty   Cape
Kawhia Harbour   Waihou   Ruatoria
N o r t h   Te Awamutu   Cambridge   Te Teko   1754
Kawhia   Waiharoa   Rotorua   Opotiki   Hikurangi
Lake   Te Teko   Tokomaru Bay
I s l a n d   Otorohanga   Tokoroa   Rotorua   Kawerau
Te Kuiti   Mangakino   Waiotahi   Urewera   Tolaga Bay
Piopio   National Park   Ma'awai
Awakino   Ohura   Taupo   Gisborne
Mckau   Otahukura   Waitahanui   Poverty Bay

North   Taumarunui   Lake   Table Cape
Taranaki Bight   Taupo
N E W   Waitara   Turangi   Mahia Peninsula
New Plymouth   Whangamomona   Tongariro
National Park   Tarawera   Hawke
Mount Taranaki   Mount Ruapehu   Bay   Bay
Cape Egmont   (Mt Egmont)   Ohakune   Wairoa   Napier
2518   Raetihi   Ploinks   Waiouru   Bay View   Hastings
Opunake   Whanganui   Napier
National Park   Havelock North
Z E A L A N D   Hawera   Mangaweka   Hastings   Cape Kidnappers
South   Patea   Taihape   Waimarama
Taranaki Bight   Wanganui   Apiti   Waipukurau
Turakina   Feilding   Dannevirke   Porangahau
Marton   Palmerston North   Cape Turnagain
Cape   Foxton   Porangahau
Farewell   Farewell Spit   Levin   Pongaroa
Golden Bay   Cape   Otaki
Kahurangi   Collingwood   Stephens   D'Urville   Kapiti   Masterton
Point   Takaka   Island   Island   Paraparaumu   Castlepoint
Abel Tasman   French Pass   Upper Hutt
Tasman   National Park   Tasman   Te Wharau
Karamea   Mountains   Bay   Picton   Lower
Kahurangi   Riwaka   Havelock   Hutt   WELLINGTON
Karamea   National   Richmond   Blenheim   Cloudy Bay
Bight   Park   Nelson   Wairau   Mount Ross
Seddonville   Renwick   Palliser   983
Hope Saddle   Bay   Cape
Westport   Tapawera   Seddon   Palliser
Murchison   Cape
Charleston   Inangahua   Nelson Lakes   Campbell
Paparoa   Junction   2131
National Park   Reefton   National   Mount Travers
Park   2338   Awatere   Tapuaenuku
Inland Kaikoura Range   2885
Greymouth   Springs   Manakau
Junction   Lewis Pass   2610
Ahaura   Hanmer   Clarence
Hokitika   Springs   Kaikoura
Rotomanu   Reefton   Parnassus
Ross   Arthur's Pass   Culverden
National   Cheviot
Park   Waipara
Abut Head   Harihari   Oxford   Pegasus
Bay
Franz Josef   Sheffield   Rangiora
Westland National Park   Glacier   3117   Mount   Belfast   Banks
Fox Glacier   Arrowsmith   Christchurch   Peninsula
Mount Cook   2795   Sumner
Mount Cook   3754   Methven   Akaroa
Jackson   National Park   Mayfield
Head   2644   Lake   Canterbury
Mount   Tekapo   Plains
Ward   Ashburton
Lake   Lake
Pukaki   Temuka
Burkes Pass   Banks
Mount   Fairlie   Longbeach   Peninsula
Aspiring   Geraldine
3030   Mount Aspiring   Lake   Canterbury
National Park   2347   Tekapo   Timaru   Bight
Awarua Point   The Hunters Hills   Pareora
S o u t h   Studholme Junction
Milford Sound   Mount   Lake   Oamaru
Christina   Wanaka   Otematata
George Sound   Mount   Pukeuri Junction   Cape Wanbrow
Cardrona   Kurow   I s l a n d
Milford   Mount   Lake   Hampden
Sound   Aspiring   Hawea   Moeraki Point
Fiordland   Lake   2502   Cromwell   Alexandra   Middlemarch   Palmerston
Te Anau   Queenstown   1695   Hyde
Doubtful Sound   James Peak   Warrington
National   Kingston   Roxburgh   Port Chalmers
Park   Lake   Athol   Otago Peninsula
Breaksea   Manapouri   Dunedin
Sound   Lumsden   Beaumont   Milton
Resolution Island   Mandeville   Waihola
Cape   Caroline Peak   Gore   Mosgiel
Providence   1722   Clinton
Puysegur   Balclutha
Point   Edendale   Kaitangata
Te   Mataura   Owaka
Solander Island   Waewae   Invercargill   Mount Pye   Nugget Point
Bay   Riverton   Fortrose
Foveaux   Strait   Bluff   Chaslands
Codfish Island   Mistake
Mason   Ruapuke Island
Bay   Halfmoon Bay
Muttonbird   Stewart   Shelter Point
Islands   Island
South West Cape   North Trap

P A C I F I C

O C E A N

1:5 000 000   0   50   100   150   200   250 miles
0   50   100   150   200   250   300   350   400 km

Conic Equidistant Projection

metres
>6000
6000
5000
4000
3000
2000
1000
500
200
0
<0
0
200
500
1000
2000
3000
4000
5000
6000
>6000

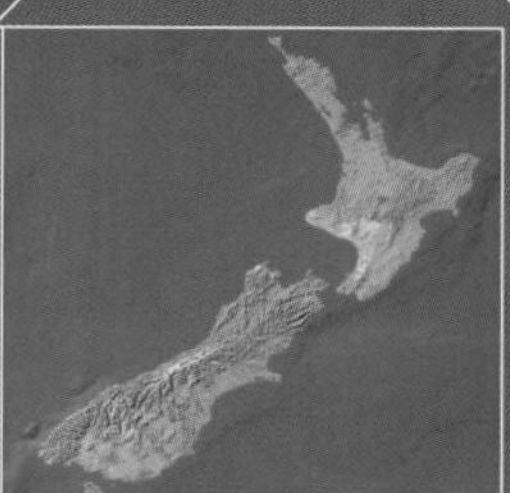

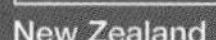

New Zealand

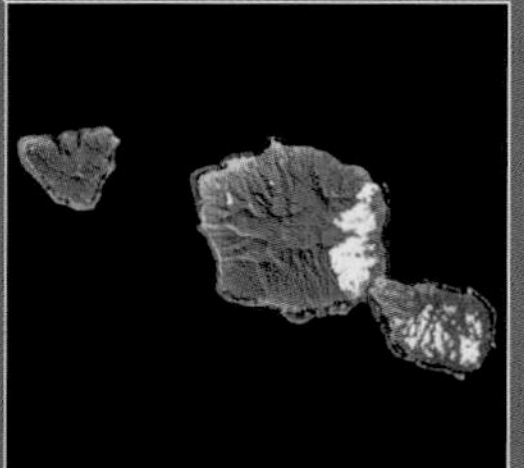

Tahiti and Moorea,
French Polynesia

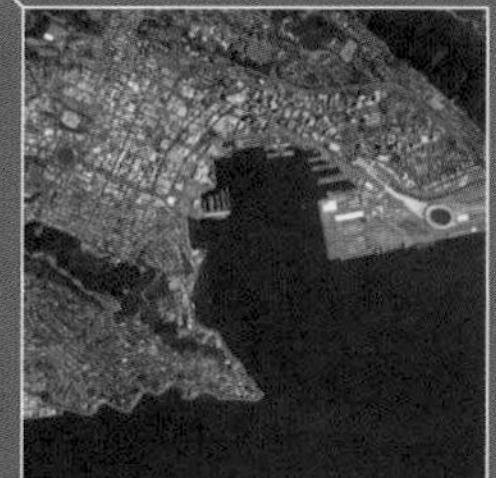

Wellington, New Zealand

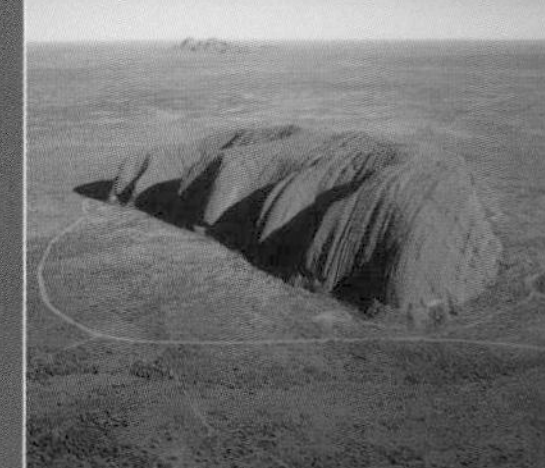

Uluru (Ayers Rock), Australia

COUNTRIES		area sq km	area sq miles	population	capital	languages	religions	currency	map
AUSTRALIA		7 682 395	2 966 189	19 338 000	Canberra	English, Italian, Greek	Protestant, Roman Catholic, Orthodox	Australian dollar	106–107
FIJI		18 330	7 077	823 000	Suva	English, Fijian, Hindi	Christian, Hindu, Sunni Muslim	Fiji dollar	107
KIRIBATI		717	277	84 000	Bairiki	Gilbertese, English	Roman Catholic, Protestant	Australian dollar	107
MARSHALL ISLANDS		181	70	52 000	Delap-Uliga-Djarrit	English, Marshallese	Protestant, Roman Catholic	United States dollar	164
MICRONESIA, FEDERATED STATES OF		701	271	126 000	Palikir	English, Chuukese, Pohnpeian, local languages	Roman Catholic, Protestant	United States dollar	164
NAURU		21	8	13 000	Yaren	Nauruan, English	Protestant, Roman Catholic	Australian dollar	107
NEW ZEALAND		270 534	104 454	3 808 000	Wellington	English, Maori	Protestant, Roman Catholic	New Zealand dollar	113
PAPUA NEW GUINEA		462 840	178 704	4 920 000	Port Moresby	English, Tok Pisin (creole), local languages	Protestant, Roman Catholic, traditional beliefs	Kina	106–107
SAMOA		2 831	1 093	159 000	Apia	Samoan, English	Protestant, Roman Catholic	Tala	107
SOLOMON ISLANDS		28 370	10 954	463 000	Honiara	English, creole, local languages	Protestant, Roman Catholic	Solomon Islands dollar	107
TONGA		748	289	99 000	Nuku'alofa	Tongan, English	Protestant, Roman Catholic	Pa'anga	107
TUVALU		25	10	10 000	Vaiaku	Tuvaluan, English	Protestant	Australian dollar	107
VANUATU		12 190	4 707	202 000	Port Vila	English, Bislama (creole), French	Protestant, Roman Catholic, traditional beliefs	Vatu	107

DEPENDENT TERRITORIES		territorial status	area sq km	area sq miles	population	capital	languages	religions	currency	map
American Samoa		United States Unincorporated Territory	197	76	70 000	Fagatoga	Samoan, English	Protestant, Roman Catholic	United States dollar	107
Ashmore and Cartier Islands		Australian External Territory	5	2	uninhabited					108
Baker Island		United States Unincorporated Territory	1	0.4	uninhabited					107
Clipperton, Île		French Overseas Territory	7	3	uninhabited					165
Cook Islands		Self-governing New Zealand Territory	293	113	20 000	Avarua	English, Maori	Protestant, Roman Catholic	New Zealand dollar	165
Coral Sea Islands Territory		Australian External Territory	22	8	uninhabited					107
French Polynesia		French Overseas Territory	3 265	1 261	237 000	Papeete	French, Tahitian, Polynesian languages	Protestant, Roman Catholic	CFP franc*	165
Guam		United States Unincorporated Territory	541	209	158 000	Hagåtña	Chamorro, English, Tapalog	Roman Catholic	United States dollar	57
Howland Island		United States Unincorporated Territory	2	1	uninhabited					107
Jarvis Island		United States Unincorporated Territory	5	2	uninhabited					165
Johnston Atoll		United States Unincorporated Territory	3	1	uninhabited					164
Kingman Reef		United States Unincorporated Territory	1	0.4	uninhabited					165
Midway Islands		United States Unincorporated Territory	6	2	uninhabited					164
New Caledonia		French Overseas Territory	19 058	7 358	220 000	Nouméa	French, local languages	Roman Catholic, Protestant, Sunni Muslim	CFP franc*	107
Niue		Self-governing New Zealand Territory	258	100	2 000	Alofi	English, Polynesian	Christian	New Zealand dollar	107
Norfolk Island		Australian External Territory	35	14	2 000	Kingston	English	Protestant, Roman Catholic	Australian Dollar	107
Northern Mariana Islands		United States Commonwealth	477	184	76 000	Capitol Hill	English, Chamorro, local languages	Roman Catholic	United States dollar	57
Palmyra Atoll		United States Unincorporated Territory	12	5	uninhabited					165
Pitcairn Islands		United Kingdom Overseas Territory	45	17	68	Adamstown	English	Protestant	New Zealand dollar	165
Tokelau		New Zealand Overseas Territory	10	4	1 000		English, Tokelauan	Christian	New Zealand dollar	107
Wake Island		United States Unincorporated Territory	7	3	uninhabited					164
Wallis and Futuna Islands		French Overseas Territory	274	106	15 000	Matā'utu	French, Wallisian, Futunian	Roman Catholic	CFP franc*	107

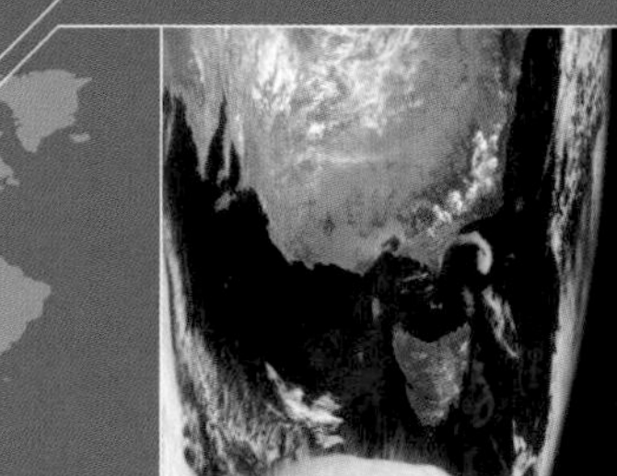

Tasmania, Australia

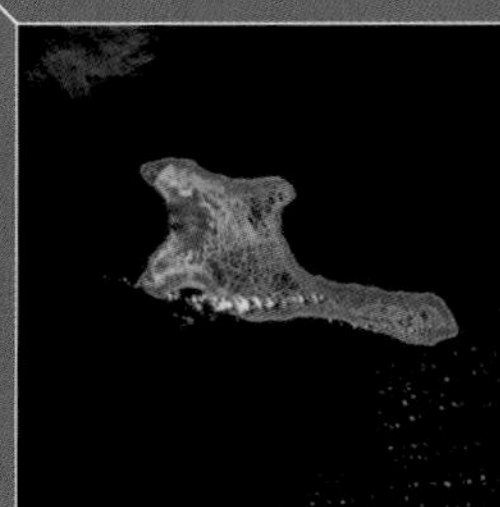

Kiritimati island, Kiribati

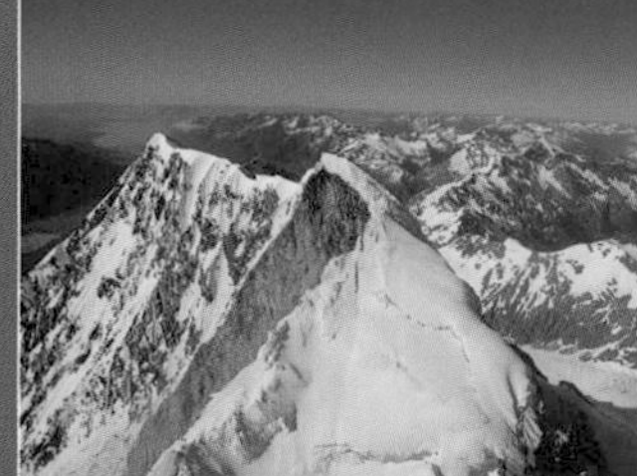

Mount Cook, New Zealand

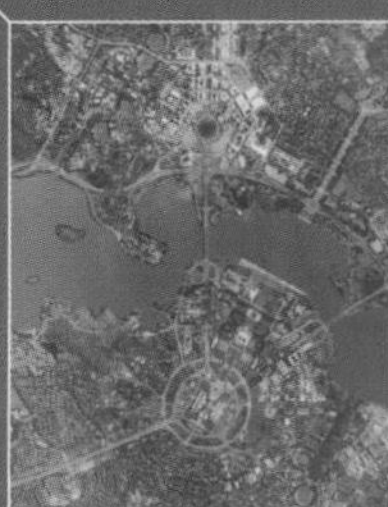

Canberra, Australia

northamerica

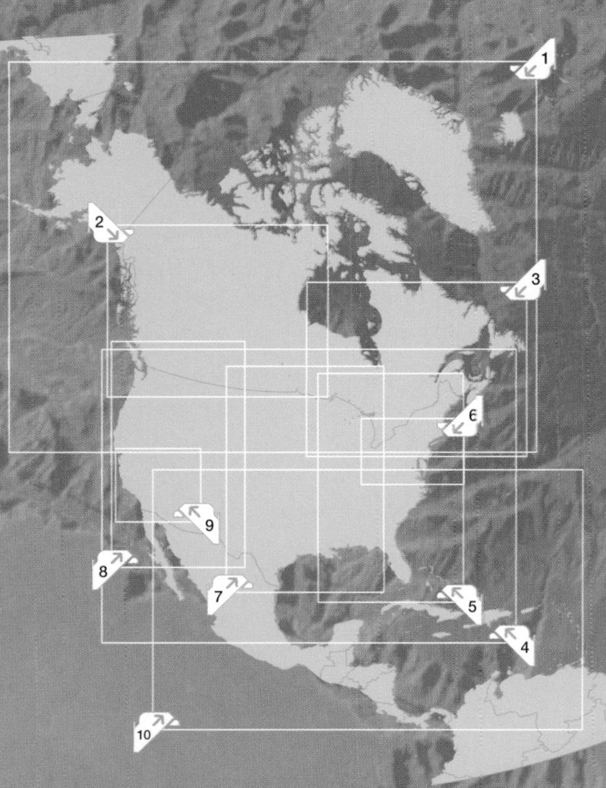

contents

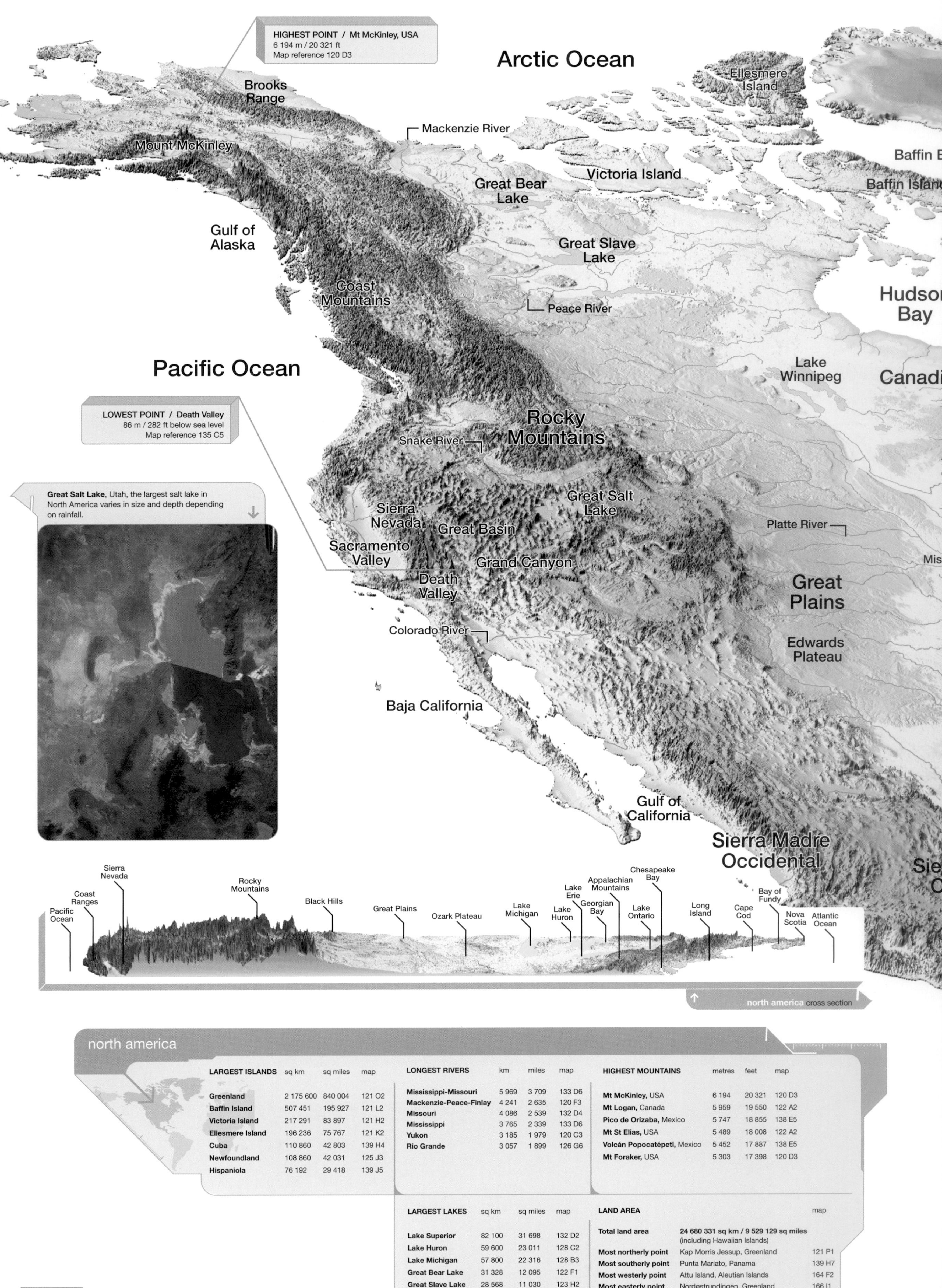

Arctic Ocean

Ellesmere Island

Baffin Bay

Baffin Island

Brooks Range

HIGHEST POINT / Mt McKinley, USA
6 194 m / 20 321 ft
Map reference 120 D3

Mount McKinley

Mackenzie River

Victoria Island

Great Bear Lake

Great Slave Lake

Gulf of Alaska

Peace River

Hudson Bay

Coast Mountains

Pacific Ocean

Lake Winnipeg

Canadia

LOWEST POINT / Death Valley
86 m / 282 ft below sea level
Map reference 135 C5

Great Salt Lake, Utah, the largest salt lake in North America varies in size and depth depending on rainfall.

Rocky Mountains

Snake River

Great Salt Lake

Platte River

Sierra Nevada

Great Basin

Sacramento Valley

Grand Canyon

Great Plains

Death Valley

Edwards Plateau

Colorado River

Miss

Baja California

Gulf of California

Sierra Madre Occidental

Sier O

Pacific Ocean — Coast Ranges — Sierra Nevada — Rocky Mountains — Black Hills — Great Plains — Ozark Plateau — Lake Michigan — Lake Huron — Lake Erie — Georgian Bay — Appalachian Mountains — Lake Ontario — Chesapeake Bay — Long Island — Cape Cod — Bay of Fundy — Nova Scotia — Atlantic Ocean

north america cross section

north america

LARGEST ISLANDS	sq km	sq miles	map
Greenland	2 175 600	840 004	121 O2
Baffin Island	507 451	195 927	121 L2
Victoria Island	217 291	83 897	121 H2
Ellesmere Island	196 236	75 767	121 K2
Cuba	110 860	42 803	139 H4
Newfoundland	108 860	42 031	125 J3
Hispaniola	76 192	29 418	139 J5

LONGEST RIVERS	km	miles	map
Mississippi-Missouri	5 969	3 709	133 D6
Mackenzie-Peace-Finlay	4 241	2 635	120 F3
Missouri	4 086	2 539	132 D4
Mississippi	3 765	2 339	133 D6
Yukon	3 185	1 979	120 C3
Rio Grande	3 057	1 899	126 G6

HIGHEST MOUNTAINS	metres	feet	map
Mt McKinley, USA	6 194	20 321	120 D3
Mt Logan, Canada	5 959	19 550	122 A2
Pico de Orizaba, Mexico	5 747	18 855	138 E5
Mt St Elias, USA	5 489	18 008	122 A2
Volcán Popocatépetl, Mexico	5 452	17 887	138 E5
Mt Foraker, USA	5 303	17 398	120 D3

LARGEST LAKES	sq km	sq miles	map
Lake Superior	82 100	31 698	132 D2
Lake Huron	59 600	23 011	128 C2
Lake Michigan	57 800	22 316	128 B3
Great Bear Lake	31 328	12 095	122 F1
Great Slave Lake	28 568	11 030	123 H2
Lake Erie	25 700	9 922	130 C2

LAND AREA		map
Total land area	24 680 331 sq km / 9 529 129 sq miles (including Hawaiian Islands)	
Most northerly point	Kap Morris Jessup, Greenland	121 P1
Most southerly point	Punta Mariato, Panama	139 H7
Most westerly point	Attu Island, Aleutian Islands	164 F2
Most easterly point	Nordøstrundingen, Greenland	166 I1

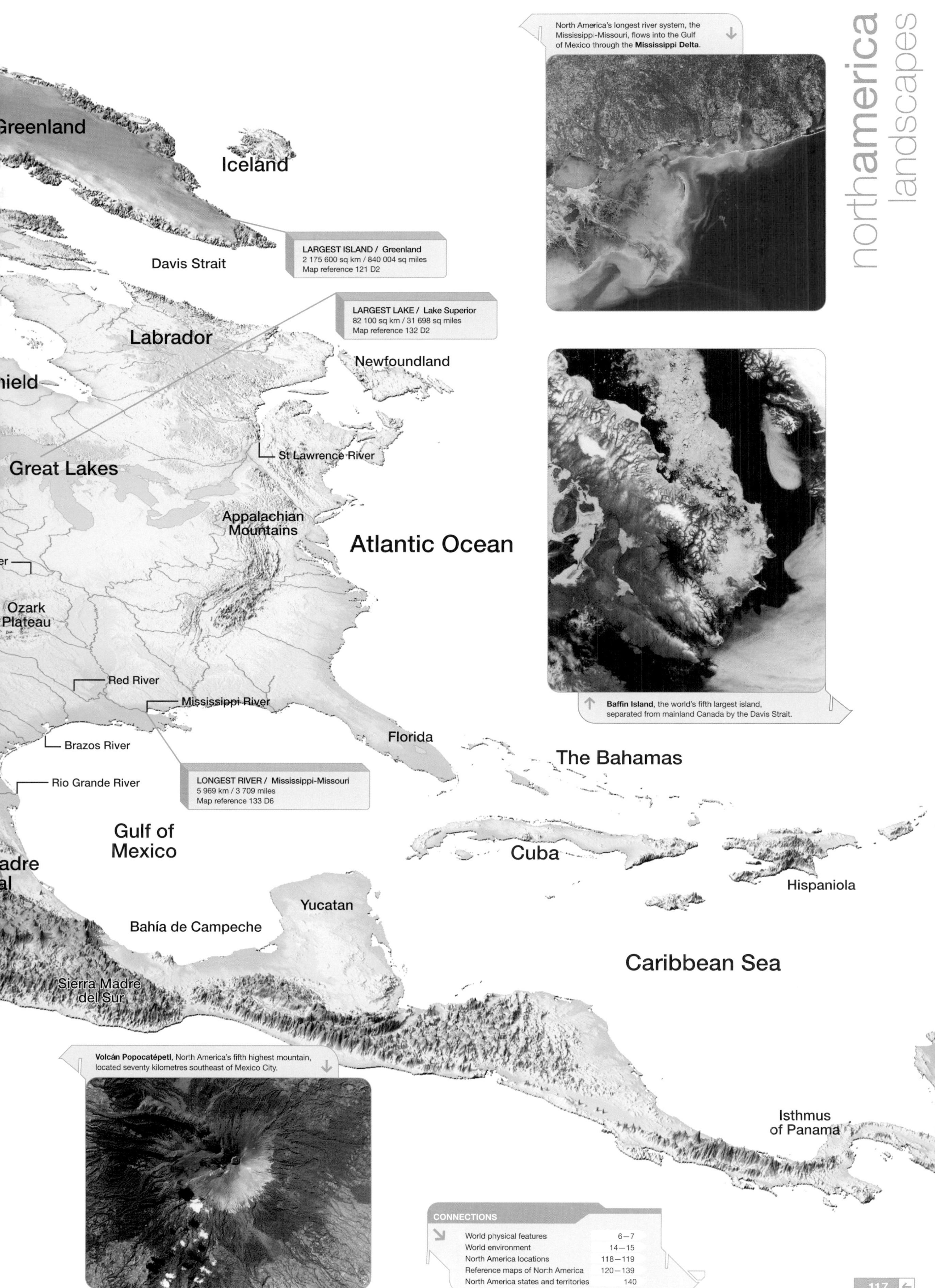

Greenland

Iceland

Davis Strait

Labrador

Newfoundland

Great Lakes

St Lawrence River

Appalachian Mountains

Atlantic Ocean

Ozark Plateau

Red River

Mississippi River

Brazos River

Florida

Rio Grande River

Gulf of Mexico

The Bahamas

Cuba

Hispaniola

Yucatan

Bahía de Campeche

Caribbean Sea

Sierra Madre del Sur

Isthmus of Panama

North America's longest river system, the Mississippi-Missouri, flows into the Gulf of Mexico through the **Mississippi Delta**.

Baffin Island, the world's fifth largest island, separated from mainland Canada by the Davis Strait.

Volcán Popocatépetl, North America's fifth highest mountain, located seventy kilometres southeast of Mexico City.

LARGEST ISLAND / Greenland
2 175 600 sq km / 840 004 sq miles
Map reference 121 D2

LARGEST LAKE / Lake Superior
82 100 sq km / 31 698 sq miles
Map reference 132 D2

LONGEST RIVER / Mississippi-Missouri
5 969 km / 3 709 miles
Map reference 133 D6

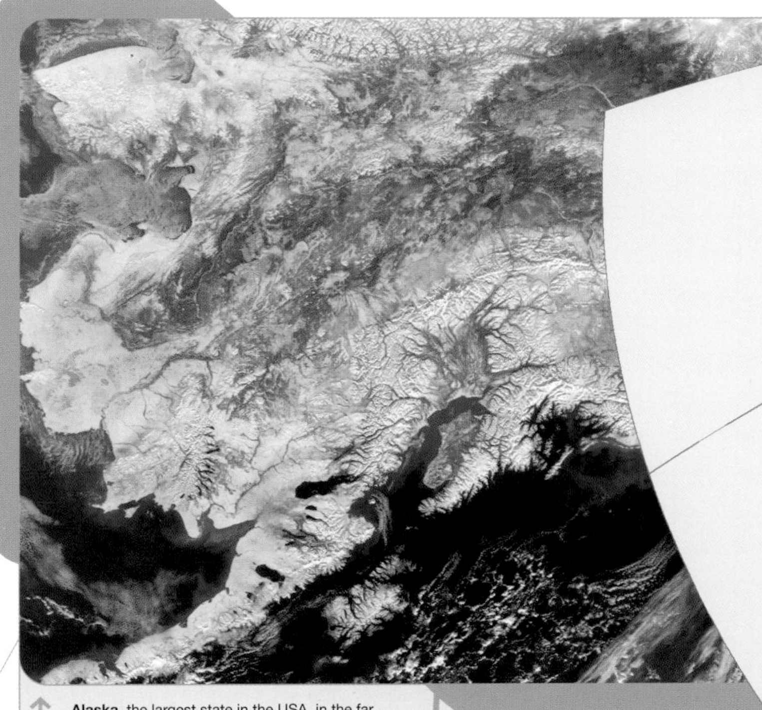

Alaska, the largest state in the USA, in the far northwest of North America.

Bering Sea

St Lawrence Island

Bering Strait

Point Hope

Barrow

Nome

Nunivak Island

Aleutian Islands

Bristol Bay

Yukon

Mount McKinley

Anchorage

Gulf of Alaska

Kodiak Island

Alexander Archipelago

Juneau

Fort Nelson

Prince Rupert

Whitehorse

TERRITORY

BRITISH

Prince George

COLUMBIA

Kamloops

Vancouver

Victoria

Olympia

Seattle

P A C I F I C

Portland

Salem

Columbia

WASHINGTON

OREGON

IDA

O C E A N

Twin Falls

HAWAII (U.S.A.)

Honolulu

Hawaiian Islands

Sacramento

San Francisco

Reno

Carson City

NEVADA

Salt Lak

The **Panama Canal**, Panama, linking the Pacific Ocean to the Atlantic Ocean.

Los Angeles

San Diego

Tijuana

CALIFORNIA

AR

Phe

Tuc

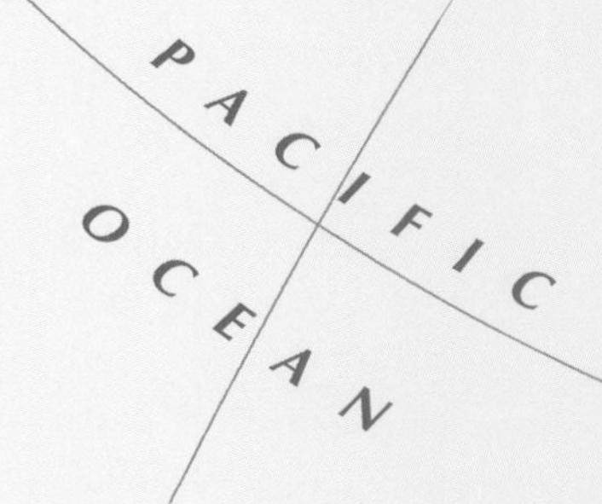

Guadalupe (Mex.)

Gulf of California

Baja California

La Pa

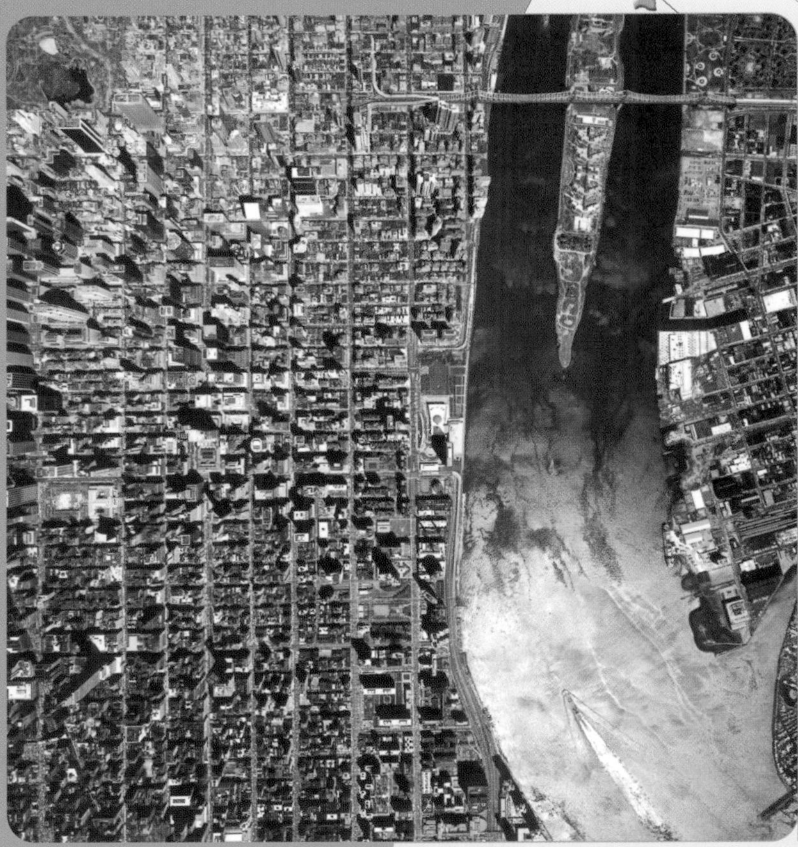

Los Angeles, USA, the world's eighth largest city, lying just south of the San Andreas Fault.

Islas Revillagigedo (Mex.)

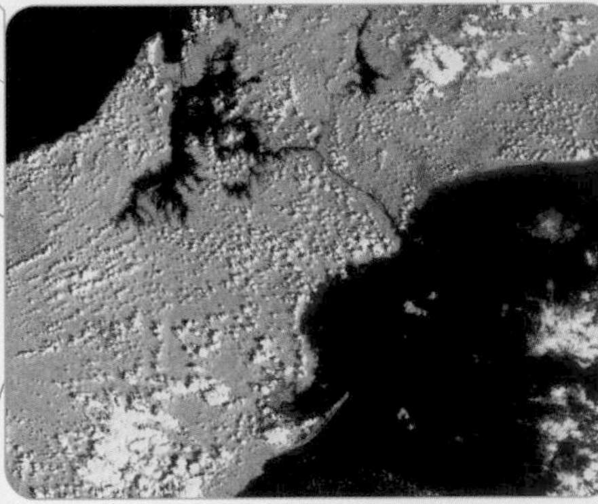

Manhattan and the East River in **New York**, USA, the sixth largest city in the world.

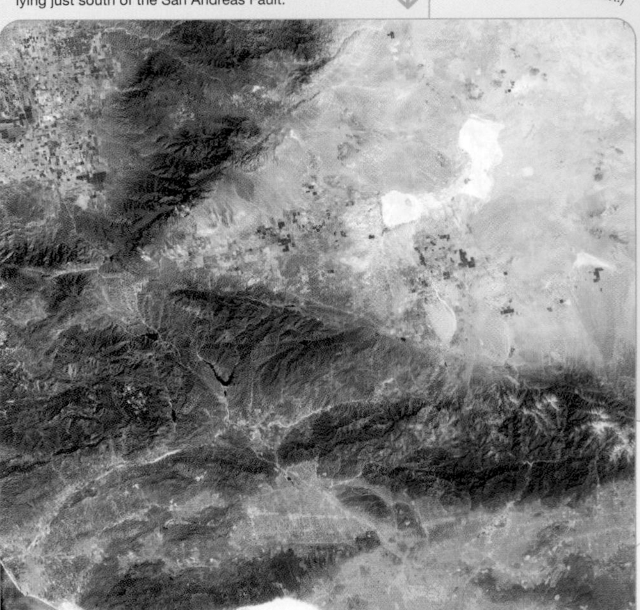

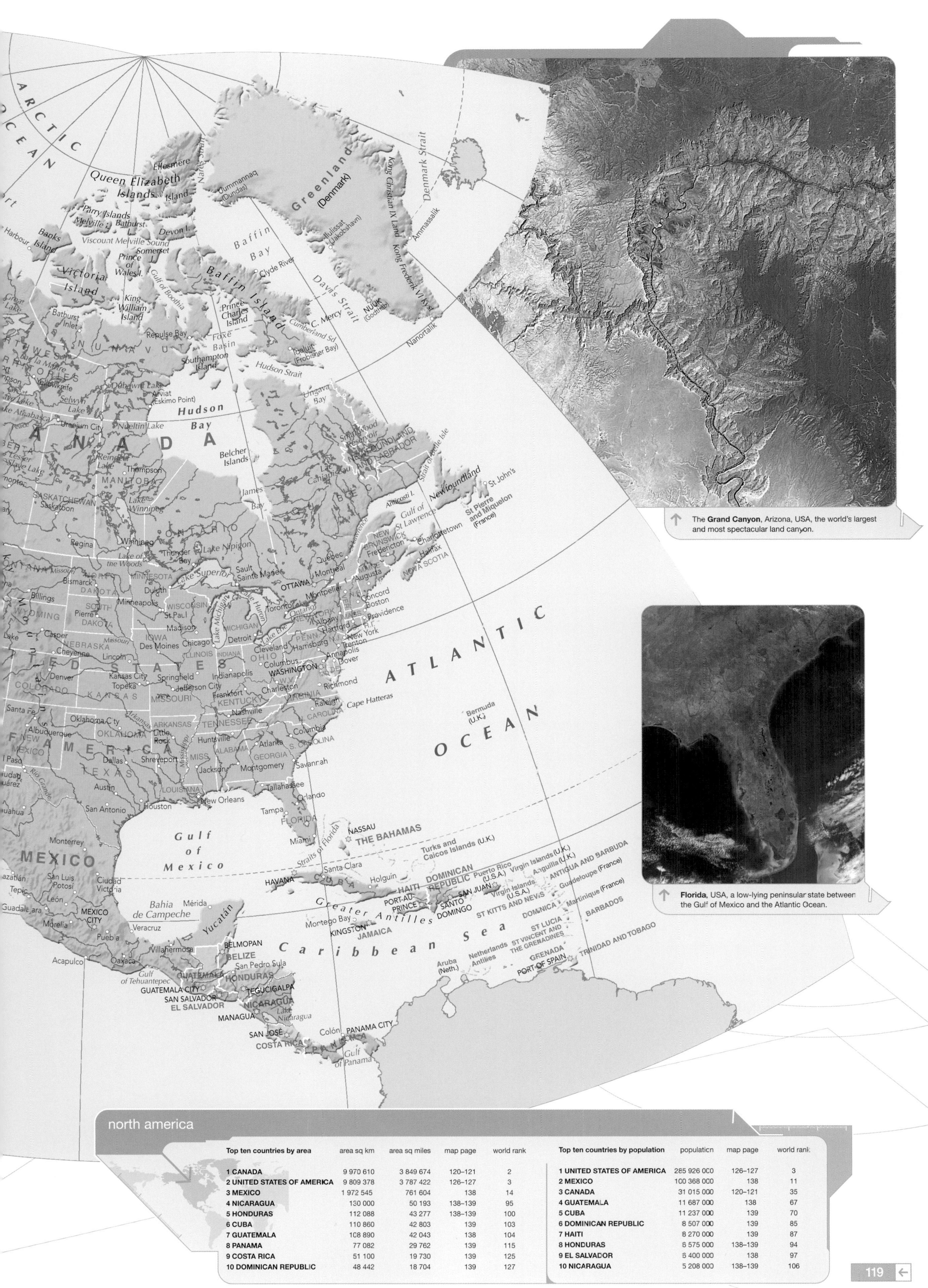

The **Grand Canyon**, Arizona, USA, the world's largest and most spectacular land canyon.

Florida, USA, a low-lying peninsular state between the Gulf of Mexico and the Atlantic Ocean.

Top ten countries by area	area sq km	area sq miles	map page	world rank
1 CANADA	9 970 610	3 849 674	120–121	2
2 UNITED STATES OF AMERICA	9 809 378	3 787 422	126–127	3
3 MEXICO	1 972 545	761 604	138	14
4 NICARAGUA	130 000	50 193	138–139	95
5 HONDURAS	112 088	43 277	138–139	100
6 CUBA	110 860	42 803	139	103
7 GUATEMALA	108 890	42 043	138	104
8 PANAMA	77 082	29 762	139	115
9 COSTA RICA	51 100	19 730	139	125
10 DOMINICAN REPUBLIC	48 442	18 704	139	127

Top ten countries by population	population	map page	world rank
1 UNITED STATES OF AMERICA	285 926 000	126–127	3
2 MEXICO	100 368 000	138	11
3 CANADA	31 015 000	120–121	35
4 GUATEMALA	11 687 000	138	67
5 CUBA	11 237 000	139	70
6 DOMINICAN REPUBLIC	8 507 000	139	85
7 HAITI	8 270 000	139	87
8 HONDURAS	6 575 000	138–139	94
9 EL SALVADOR	6 400 000	138	97
10 NICARAGUA	5 208 000	138–139	106

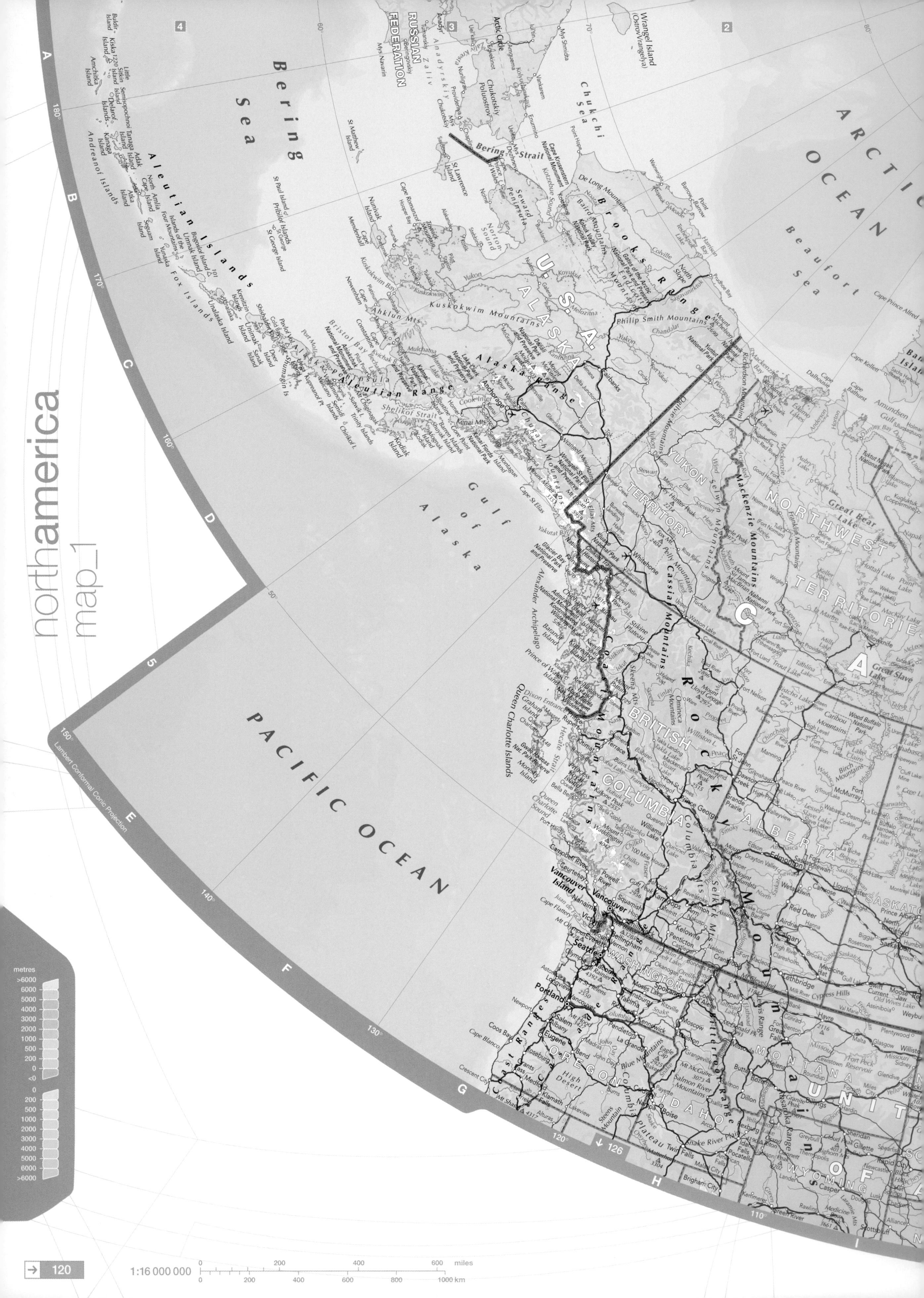

Lambert Conformal Conic Projection

Bering Sea

PACIFIC OCEAN

Gulf of Alaska

ARCTIC OCEAN

Beaufort Sea

Chukchi Sea

RUSSIAN FEDERATION

U.S.A.

ALASKA

Aleutian Islands

Andreanof Islands

Brooks Range

Alaska Range

Aleutian Range

Alaska Peninsula

YUKON TERRITORY

NORTHWEST TERRITORIES

BRITISH COLUMBIA

ALBERTA

SASKATCHEWAN

WASHINGTON

OREGON

IDAHO

MONTANA

WYOMING

UNITED STATES OF

Rocky Mountains

Coast Mountains

Vancouver Island

Bering Strait

Queen Charlotte Islands

Great Bear Lake

Great Slave Lake

Seattle

Portland

Vancouver

Anchorage

metres
>6000
6000
5000
4000
3000
2000
1000
500
200
0
<0
0
200
1000
2000
3000
4000
5000
6000
>6000

1:16 000 000

0   200   400   600   miles

0   200   400   600   800   1000 km

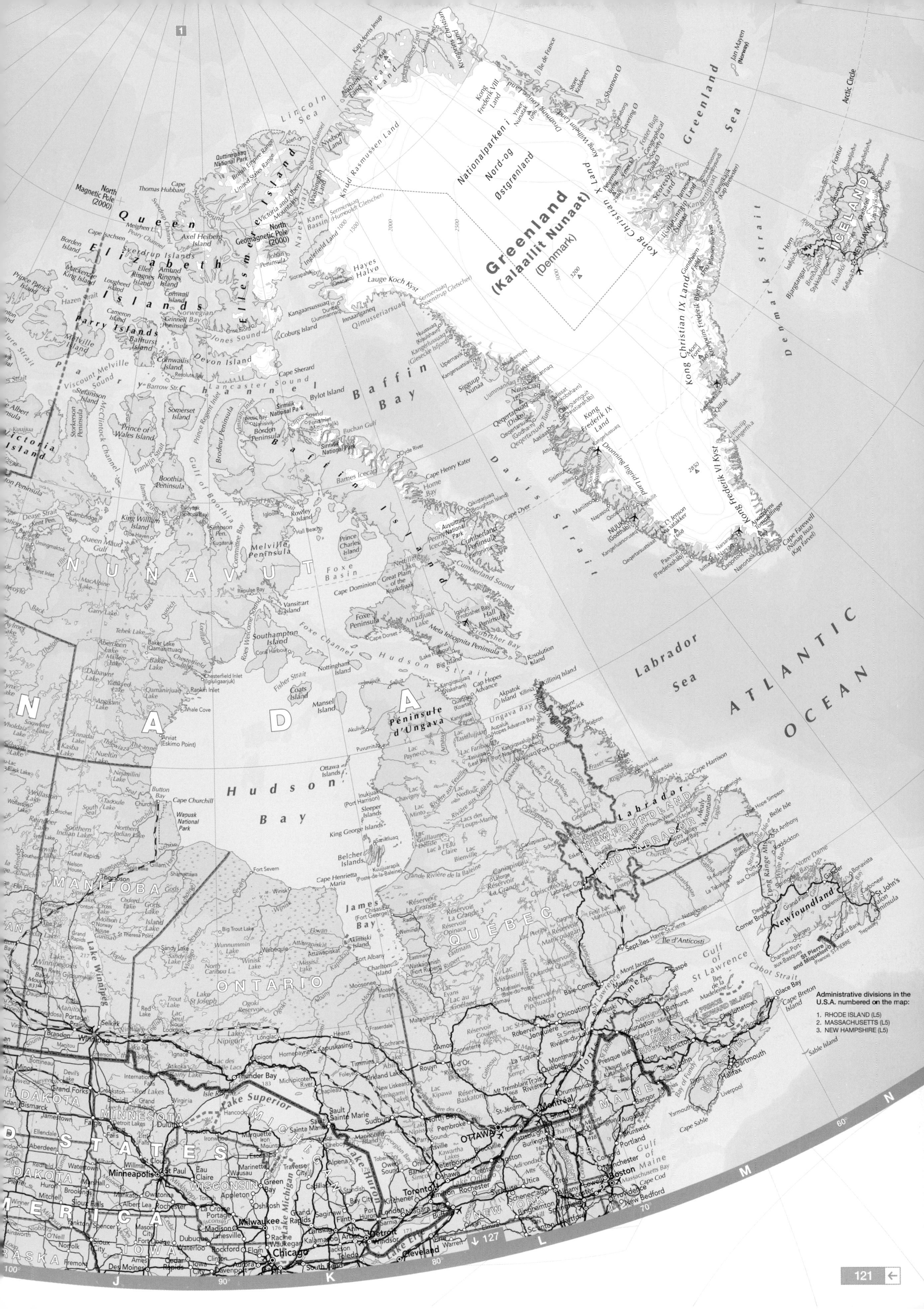

Administrative divisions in the
U.S.A. numbered on the map:

1. RHODE ISLAND (L5)
2. MASSACHUSETTS (L5)
3. NEW HAMPSHIRE (L5)

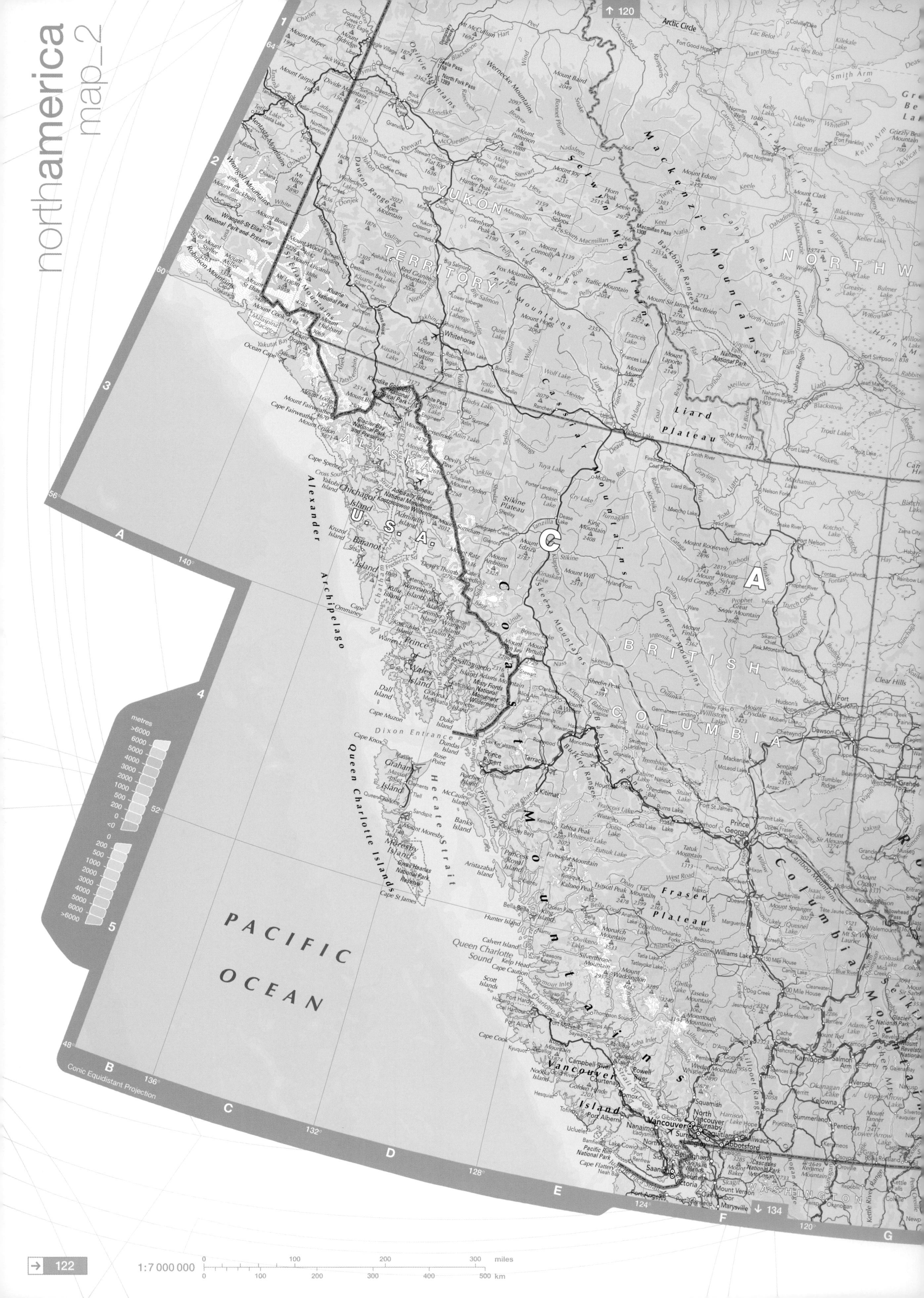

↑ 120
YUKON TERRITORY
NORTHW
BRITISH COLUMBIA
ALASKA
U.S.A.
CANADA
WASHINGTON
PACIFIC OCEAN
Selwyn Mountains
Mackenzie Mountains
Ogilvie Mountains
Wernecke Mountains
Cassiar Mountains
Coast Mountains
Skeena Mountains
Columbia Mountains
Selkirk Mountains
Liard Plateau
Fraser Plateau
Stikine Plateau
Alexander Archipelago
Queen Charlotte Islands
Hecate Strait
Dixon Entrance
Queen Charlotte Sound
Vancouver Island
Arctic Circle
Whitehorse
Dawson
Prince George
Prince Rupert
Vancouver
Victoria
Kamloops
Kelowna
Juneau
Fort Nelson
Dawson Creek
Fort St John
Kitimat
Terrace
Williams Lake
metres
>6000
6000
5000
4000
3000
2000
1000
500
200
0
<0
200
500
1000
2000
3000
4000
5000
6000
>6000
Conic Equidistant Projection
↓ 134
1:7 000 000
0
100
200
300
miles
0
100
200
300
400
500
km

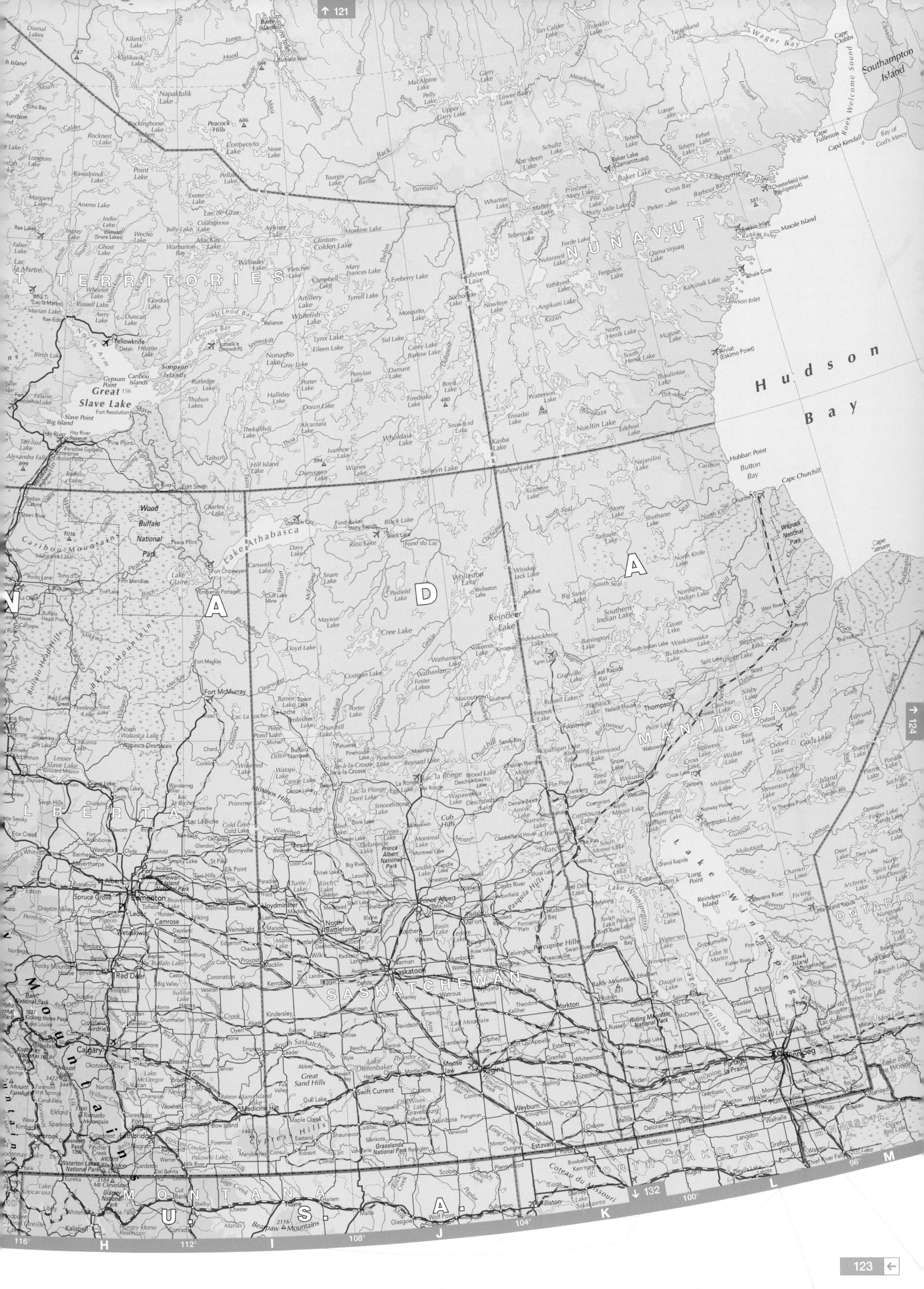

↑ 121
TERRITORIES
NUNAVUT
Hudson Bay
Southampton Island
Wager Bay
Great Slave Lake
Yellowknife
Baker Lake
Chesterfield Inlet
Rankin Inlet
Arviat (Eskimo Point)
Wood Buffalo National Park
Lake Athabasca
Fort Chipewyan
Fort Smith
Hay River
Wollaston Lake
Reindeer Lake
Churchill
Wapusk National Park
Cape Churchill
Southern Indian Lake
Thompson
MANITOBA
Lake Winnipeg
Lake Winnipegosis
Fort McMurray
ALBERTA
Edmonton
Red Deer
Calgary
Lethbridge
Medicine Hat
SASKATCHEWAN
Saskatoon
Prince Albert
North Battleford
Lloydminster
Regina
Moose Jaw
Swift Current
Yorkton
Weyburn
Estevan
Brandon
Winnipeg
Lake Manitoba
Riding Mountain National Park
Prince Albert National Park
Grasslands National Park
ONTARIO
MINNESOTA
NORTH DAKOTA
MONTANA
U.S.A.
CANADA
Rocky Mountains
↑ 124
↓ 132
116°
112°
108°
104°
100°
96°
H
I
J
K
L
M

↑ 121
↑ 123

H u d s o n   B a y

J a m e s   B a y

C A N A D A

MANITOBA
NUNAVUT
ONTARIO
MINNESOTA
WISCONSIN
MICHIGAN
ILLINOIS
INDIANA
OHIO
IOWA
PENNSYLVANIA
NEW YORK

U N I T E D   S T A T E S   O F   A M E R I C A

Lake Superior
Lake Michigan
Lake Huron
Lake Erie
Lake Ontario
Georgian Bay

Hudson Bay
Farmer Island
Ottawa Islands
Sleeper Islands
King George Islands
Baker's Dozen Islands
Belcher Islands
Flaherty Island
Long Island
Akimiski Island
North Twin Island
South Twin Island
Isle Royale
Isle Royale National Park
Manitoulin Island
Apostle Islands
Beaver Island

Thunder Bay
Sault Sainte Marie
Sault Sainte Marie
Marquette
Escanaba
Green Bay
Milwaukee
Chicago
Madison
Rockford
Detroit
Cleveland
Toronto
Mississauga
Hamilton
Buffalo
Rochester
Sudbury
North Bay
OTTAWA
Timmins
Kapuskasing
Cochrane
Moosonee

Lake of the Woods
Rainy Lake
Lake Nipigon
Lake Abitibi
Lake Nipissing
Lake Simcoe

metres
>6000
6000
5000
4000
3000
2000
1000
500
200
0
◁0
0
200
500
1000
2000
3000
4000
5000
6000
>6000

Conic Equidistant Projection

1:7 000 000

0   100   200   300   miles
0   100 200 300 400 500 km

→ 124
↑ 132
↓ 128

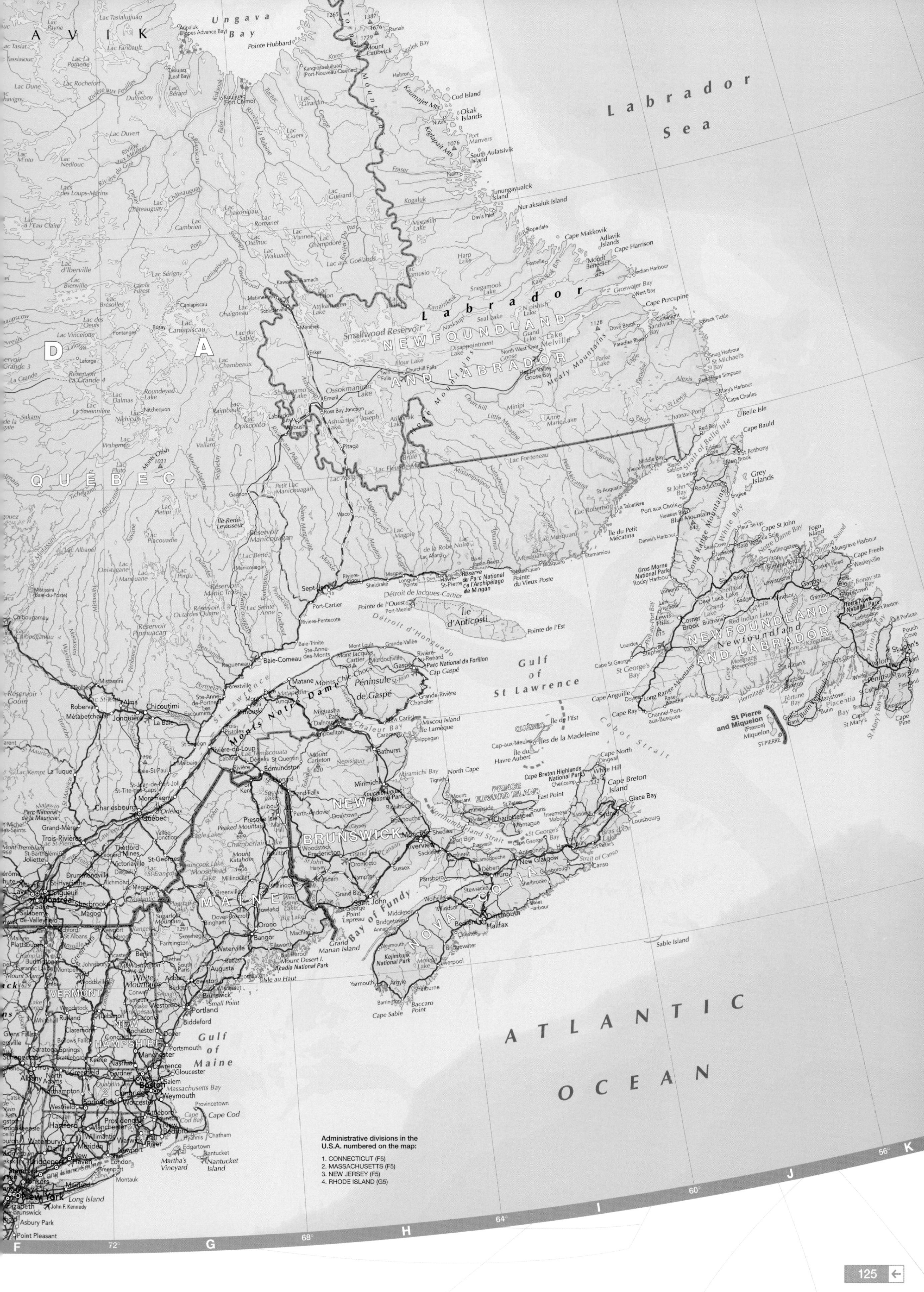

Administrative divisions in the
U.S.A. numbered on the map:

1. CONNECTICUT (F5)
2. MASSACHUSETTS (F5)
3. NEW JERSEY (F5)
4. RHODE ISLAND (G5)

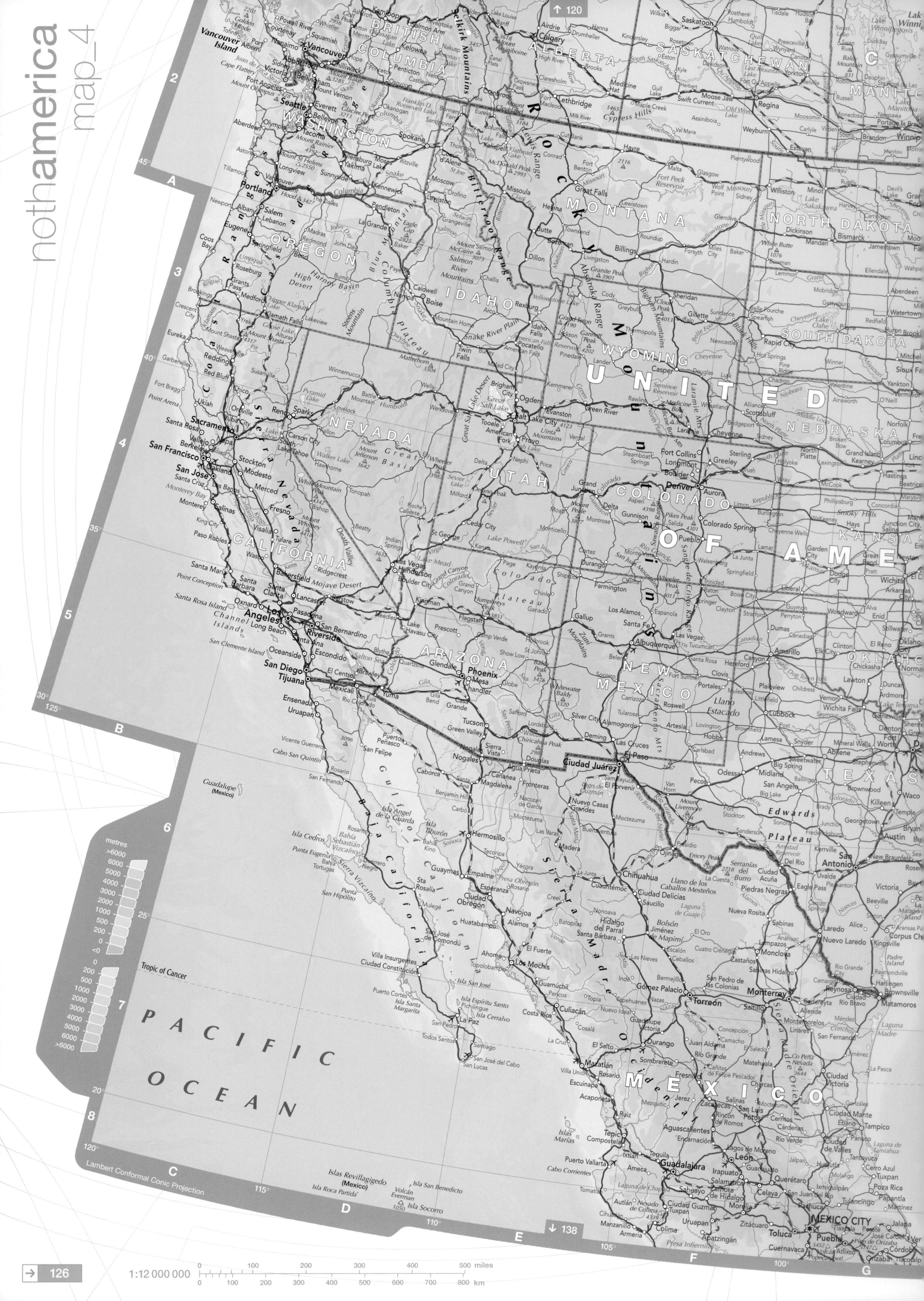
↑ 120
BRITISH COLUMBIA
ALBERTA
SASKATCHEWAN
WASHINGTON
OREGON
IDAHO
MONTANA
NORTH DAKOTA
SOUTH DAKOTA
WYOMING
NEBRASKA
NEVADA
UTAH
COLORADO
KANSAS
CALIFORNIA
ARIZONA
NEW MEXICO
OKLAHOMA
TEXAS
UNITED STATES OF AME
ROCKY MOUNTAINS
MEXICO
Sierra Madre Occidental
Sierra Madre Oriental
Baja California
Gulf of California
Great Basin
Colorado Plateau
Edwards Plateau
Llano Estacado
Mojave Desert
Sierra Nevada
Cascade Range
Coast Ranges
Vancouver Island
Vancouver
Seattle
Portland
Sacramento
San Francisco
San Jose
Los Angeles
San Diego
Tijuana
Las Vegas
Phoenix
Salt Lake City
Denver
Albuquerque
El Paso
Ciudad Juárez
Chihuahua
Monterrey
Guadalajara
MEXICO CITY
Tropic of Cancer
PACIFIC OCEAN
Islas Revillagigedo (Mexico)
Guadalupe (Mexico)
metres
>6000
6000
5000
4000
3000
2000
1000
500
200
0
<0
Lambert Conformal Conic Projection
↓ 138
1:12 000 000
0 100 200 300 400 500 miles
0 100 200 300 400 500 600 700 800 km

↑ 121

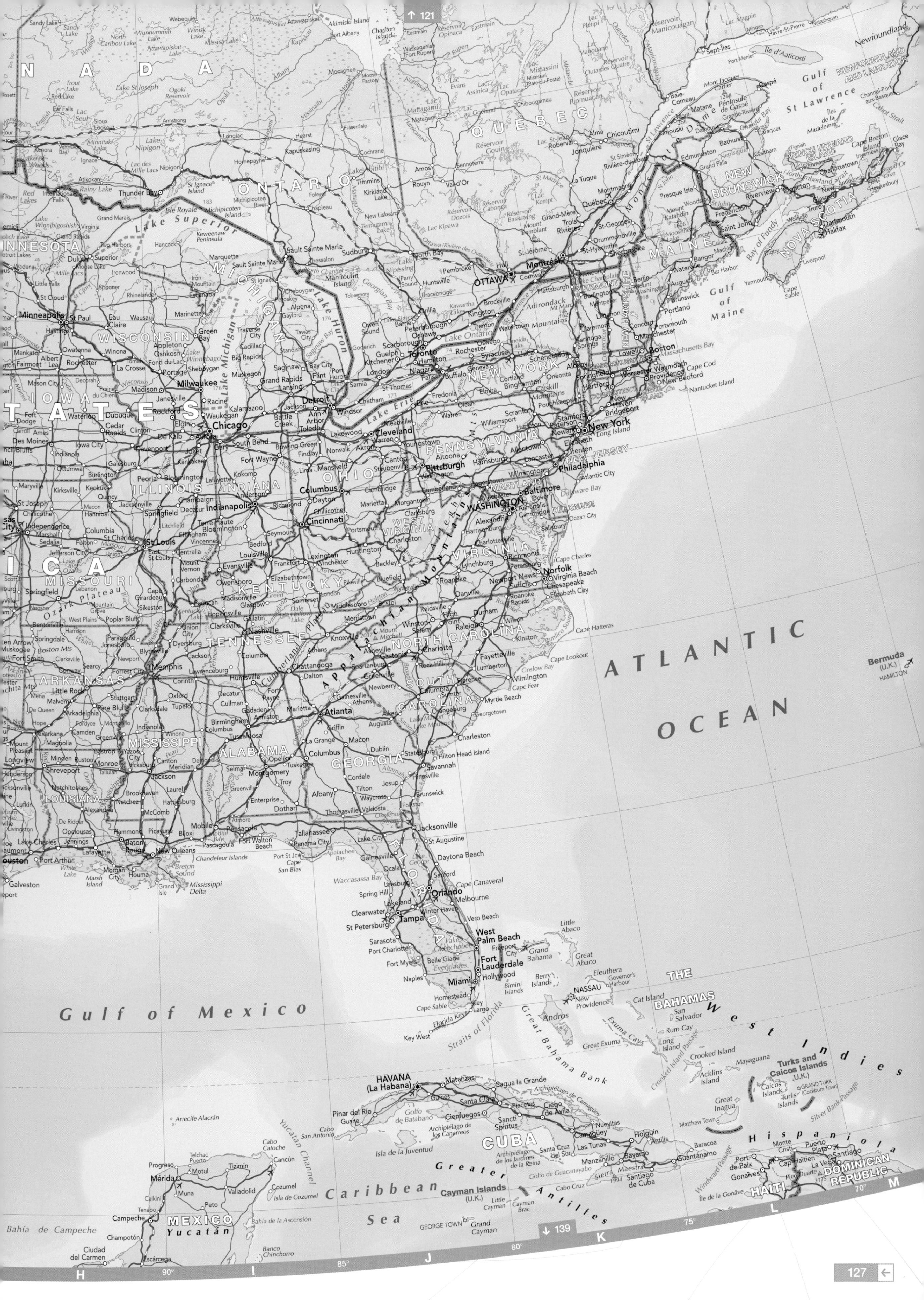

CANADA
QUEBEC
ONTARIO
NEW BRUNSWICK
NOVA SCOTIA
PRINCE EDWARD ISLAND
NEWFOUNDLAND AND LABRADOR
Newfoundland
Gulf of St Lawrence
Lake Superior
Lake Michigan
Lake Huron
Lake Erie
Lake Ontario
UNITED STATES OF AMERICA
MINNESOTA
WISCONSIN
MICHIGAN
IOWA
ILLINOIS
INDIANA
OHIO
PENNSYLVANIA
NEW YORK
VERMONT
NEW HAMPSHIRE
MAINE
MASSACHUSETTS
CONNECTICUT
RHODE ISLAND
NEW JERSEY
MARYLAND
DELAWARE
WEST VIRGINIA
VIRGINIA
KENTUCKY
MISSOURI
TENNESSEE
NORTH CAROLINA
SOUTH CAROLINA
ARKANSAS
MISSISSIPPI
ALABAMA
GEORGIA
LOUISIANA
FLORIDA
Appalachian Mountains
Gulf of Maine
ATLANTIC OCEAN
Cape Hatteras
Bermuda (U.K.)
HAMILTON
OTTAWA
Montréal
Toronto
Québec
Halifax
Chicago
Detroit
Cleveland
Pittsburgh
Philadelphia
New York
Boston
Baltimore
WASHINGTON
Norfolk
Cincinnati
Indianapolis
St Louis
Milwaukee
Minneapolis
Nashville
Memphis
Atlanta
Charlotte
Jacksonville
New Orleans
Orlando
Tampa
Miami
Gulf of Mexico
Straits of Florida
THE BAHAMAS
NASSAU
West Indies
Turks and Caicos Islands (U.K.)
CUBA
HAVANA (La Habana)
Greater Antilles
Hispaniola
HAITI
DOMINICAN REPUBLIC
Cayman Islands (U.K.)
GEORGE TOWN
Caribbean Sea
MEXICO
Yucatán
Bahía de Campeche
Yucatan Channel
H
I
J
K
L
M
90°
85°
80°
75°
70°

↓ 139

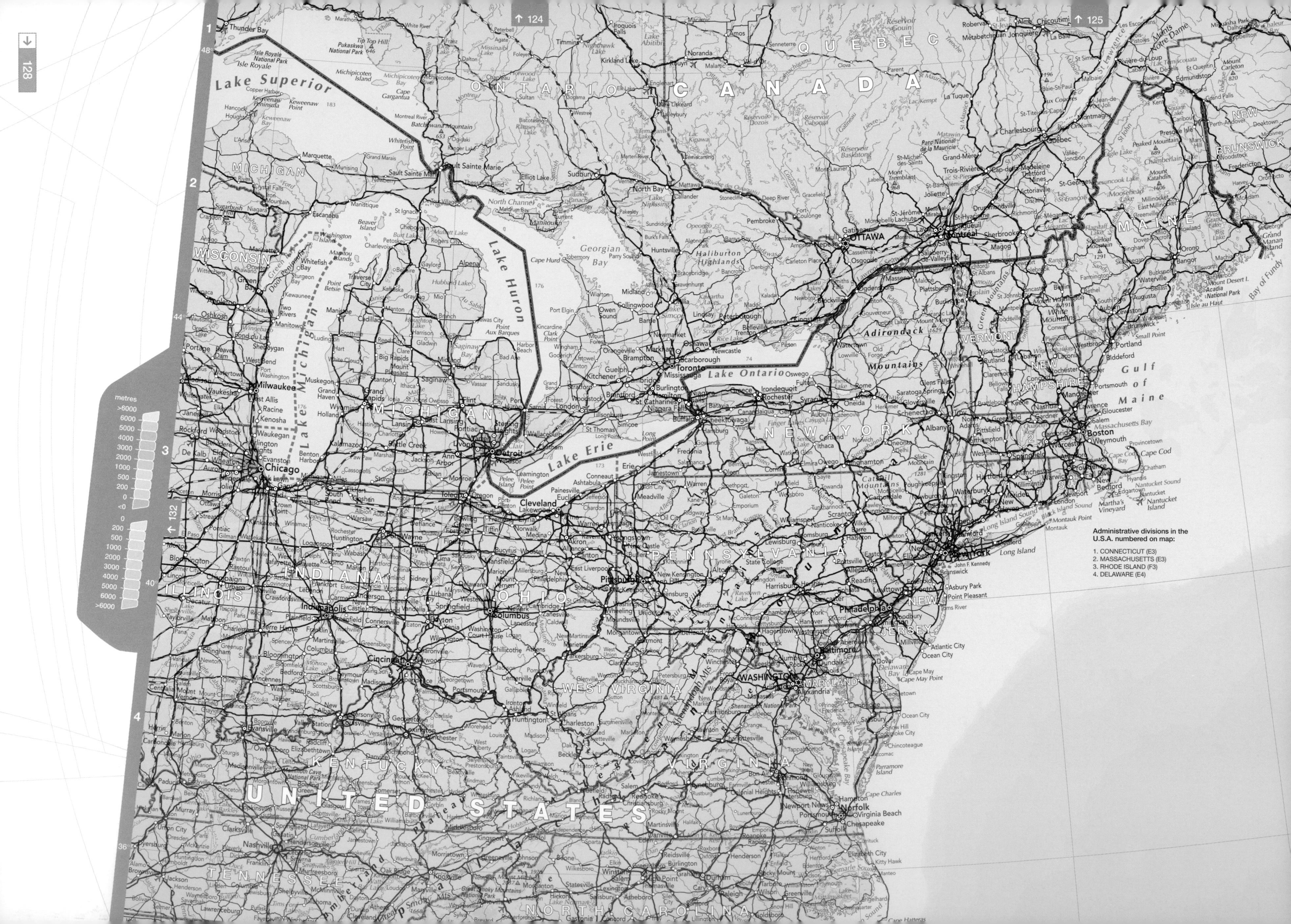

Administrative divisions in the
U.S.A. numbered on map:

1. CONNECTICUT (E3)
2. MASSACHUSETTS (E3)
3. RHODE ISLAND (F3)
4. DELAWARE (E4)

metres
>6000
6000
5000
4000
3000
2000
1000
500
200
<0
0
200
500
1000
2000
3000
4000
5000
6000
>6000

A T L A N T I C

O C E A N

THE BAHAMAS

Little Abaco

Great Abaco

Marsh Harbour

Cooper's Town

Little Bahama Bank

West End

Grand Bahama

Freeport

Bimini Islands

Berry Islands

New Providence

NASSAU

Adelaide

Andros Town

Nicholl's Town

Andros

Great Bahama Bank

Tongue of the Ocean

Spanish Wells

Dunmore Town

Eleuthera

Governor's Harbour

Rock Sound

James Cistern

Arthur's Town

Cat Island

Little San Salvador

San Salvador

Cockburn Town

Rum Cay

Stella Maris

Long Island

Deadman's Cay

Clarence Town

Crooked Island

Acklins Island

Samana Cay

Exuma Cays

George Town

Great Exuma

Rollewille

Exuma Sound

Wemys Bight

Great Bahama Bank

Anguilla Cays

Cay Sal

Dog Rocks

Nicholas Channel

Double Headed Shot Cays

Straits of Florida

G u l f   o f   M e x i c o

Gulf Coastal Plain

Mississippi Delta

Chandeleur Islands

Breton Sound

Apalachee Bay

S O U T H   A M E R I C A

SOUTH CAROLINA

GEORGIA

ALABAMA

FLORIDA

Wilmington

Cape Fear

Myrtle Beach

Charleston

Hilton Head Island

Savannah

Brunswick

Jacksonville

Jacksonville Beach

St Augustine

Ormond Beach

Daytona Beach

New Smyrna Beach

Cape Canaveral

Merritt Island

Melbourne

Palm Bay

Vero Beach

Sebastian

Fort Pierce

St Lucie City

Stuart

Hobe Sound

West Palm Beach

Delray Beach

Boca Raton

Fort Lauderdale

Hollywood

Miami Beach

Miami

Biscayne Bay

Biscayne National Park

Key Largo

Orlando

Kissimmee

Winter Haven

Tampa

St Petersburg

Clearwater

Bradenton

Sarasota

Venice

Englewood

Cape Coral

Fort Myers

Naples

Everglades

Everglades National Park

Homestead

Cape Sable

Florida Bay

Marathon

Key West

Marquesas Keys

Dry Tortugas

Pine Islands

Ten Thousand Islands

CUBA

HAVANA (La Habana)

Cardenas

Matanzas

Atlanta

Birmingham

Montgomery

Columbus

Albany

Tallahassee

Panama City

Pensacola

Mobile

Gulf Shores

Tropic of Cancer

1 : 6 500 000

Lambert Conformal Conic Projection

0   50   100   150   200   250   300   miles

0   50   100   150   200   250   300   350   400   450   500   km

↓ 139

133

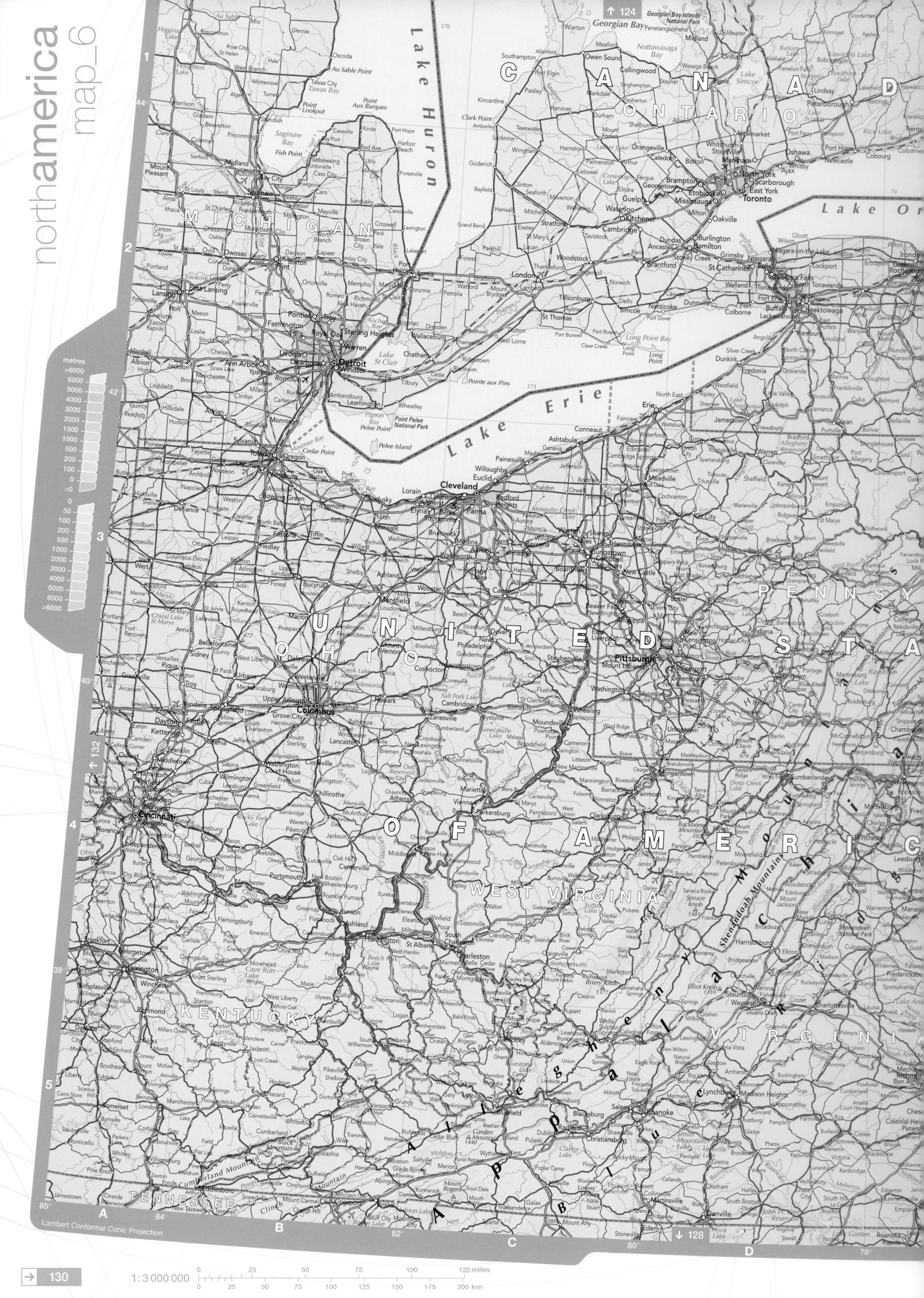

↑ 125

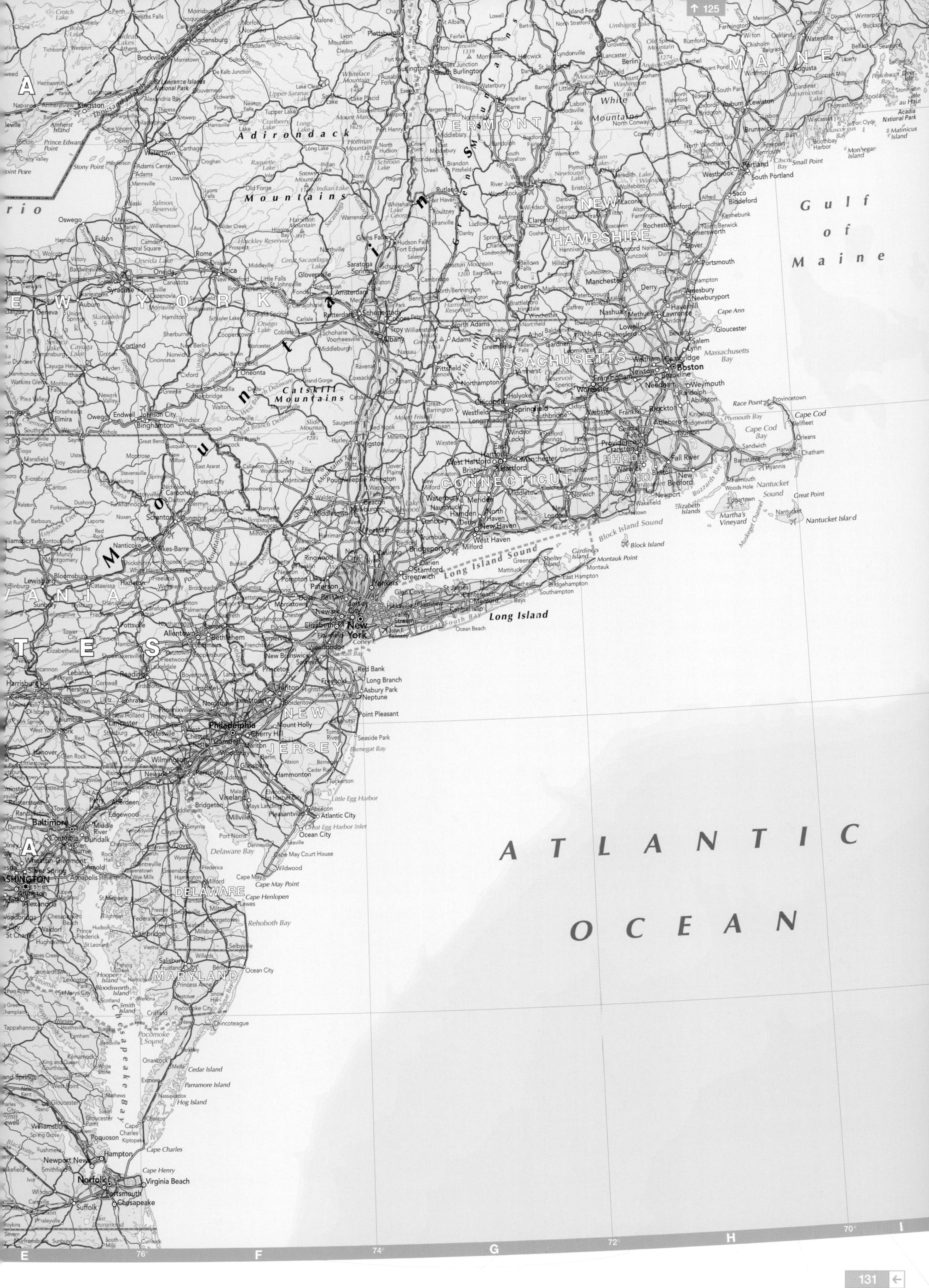
MAINE
VERMONT
NEW HAMPSHIRE
MASSACHUSETTS
RHODE ISLAND
CONNECTICUT
NEW YORK
NEW JERSEY
DELAWARE
MARYLAND
Adirondack Mountains
Catskill Mountains
White Mountains
Green Mountains
Gulf of Maine
Massachusetts Bay
Cape Cod Bay
Cape Cod
Nantucket Sound
Nantucket Island
Martha's Vineyard
Block Island Sound
Block Island
Long Island Sound
Long Island
Montauk Point
Delaware Bay
Chesapeake Bay
Cape May
Cape Henlopen
Cape Charles
Cape Henry
Boston
Providence
Hartford
Albany
New York
Philadelphia
Baltimore
Wilmington
Norfolk
Atlantic City
ATLANTIC OCEAN
E
76°
F
74°
G
72°
H
70°

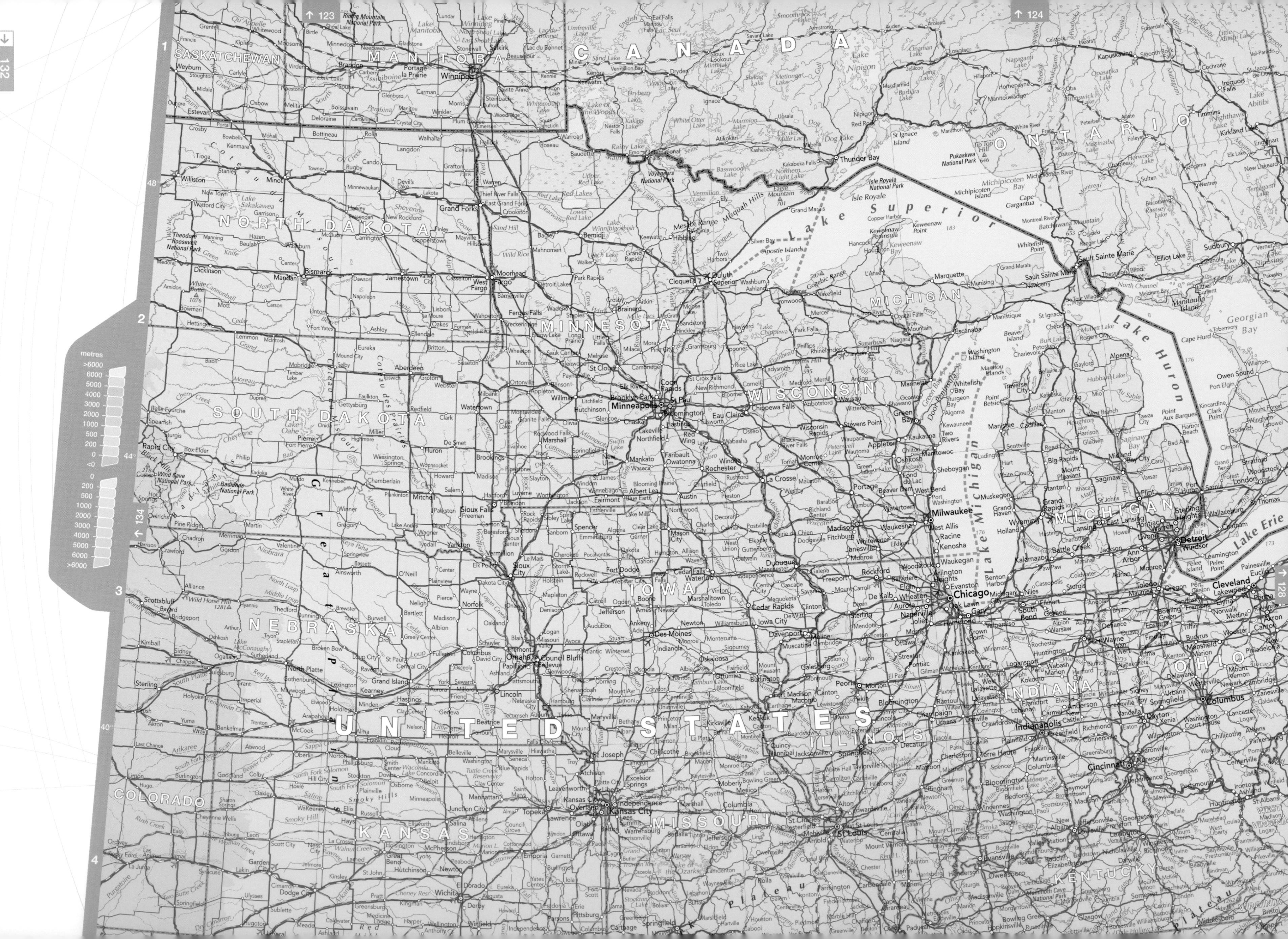

↑ 129

→ 138

↓ 135

↓ 135

Gulf of Mexico

MEXICO

COAHUILA

NUEVO LEÓN

TAMAULIPAS

Sierra Madre Oriental

TEXAS

NEW MEXICO

OKLAHOMA

ARKANSAS

LOUISIANA

MISSISSIPPI

ALABAMA

GEORGIA

FLORIDA

TENNESSEE

UNITED STATES OF AMERICA

Edwards Plateau

Stockton Plateau

Llano Estacado

Ouachita Mountains

Mississippi Delta

Chandeleur Islands

Laguna Madre

1:6 500 000

Lambert Conformal Conic Projection

miles
0   50   100   150   200   250   300

0   50   100   150   200   250   300   350   400   450   500 km

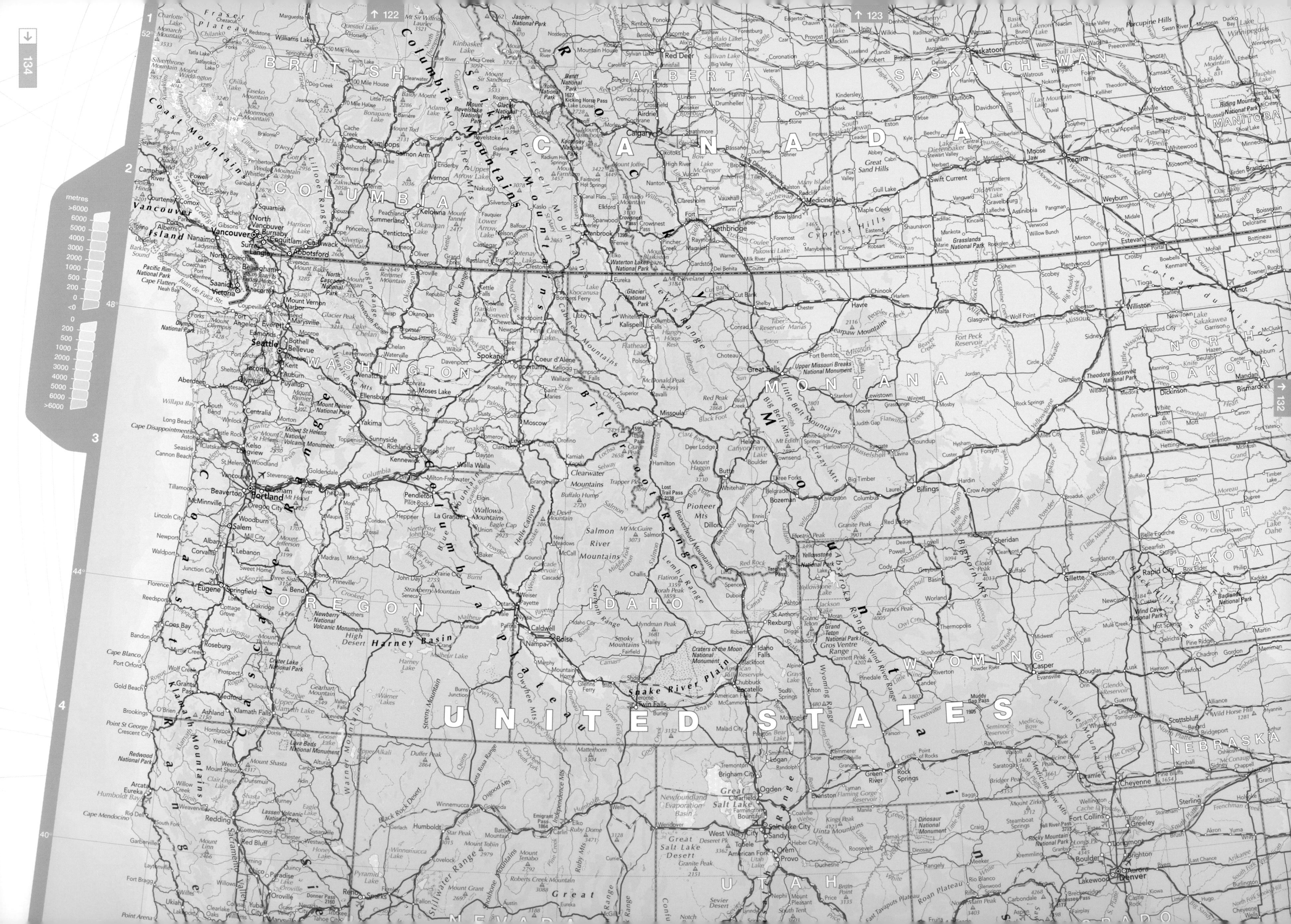

PACIFIC OCEAN

U N I T E D   S T A T E S   O F   A M E R I C A

CALIFORNIA

NEVADA

ARIZONA

NEW MEXICO

TEXAS

M E X I C O

CHIHUAHUA

SONORA

BAJA CALIFORNIA

BAJA CALIFORNIA SUR

COAHUILA

Gulf of California

Baja California

HAWAII (U.S.A.)

Hawaii

Oahu

Maui

Kauai

Molokai

Lanai

Kahoolawe

Niihau

Honolulu

Hilo

1:6 500 000

Lambert Conformal Conic Projection

San Francisco

Los Angeles

San Diego

Las Vegas

Phoenix

Tucson

Albuquerque

Santa Fe

El Paso

Ciudad Juárez

Chihuahua

Hermosillo

Tijuana

Sacramento

Fresno

↑ 133

↓ 138

1:6 500 000

miles

km

0   50   100   150   200   250   300   miles

0   100   200   300   400   500 km

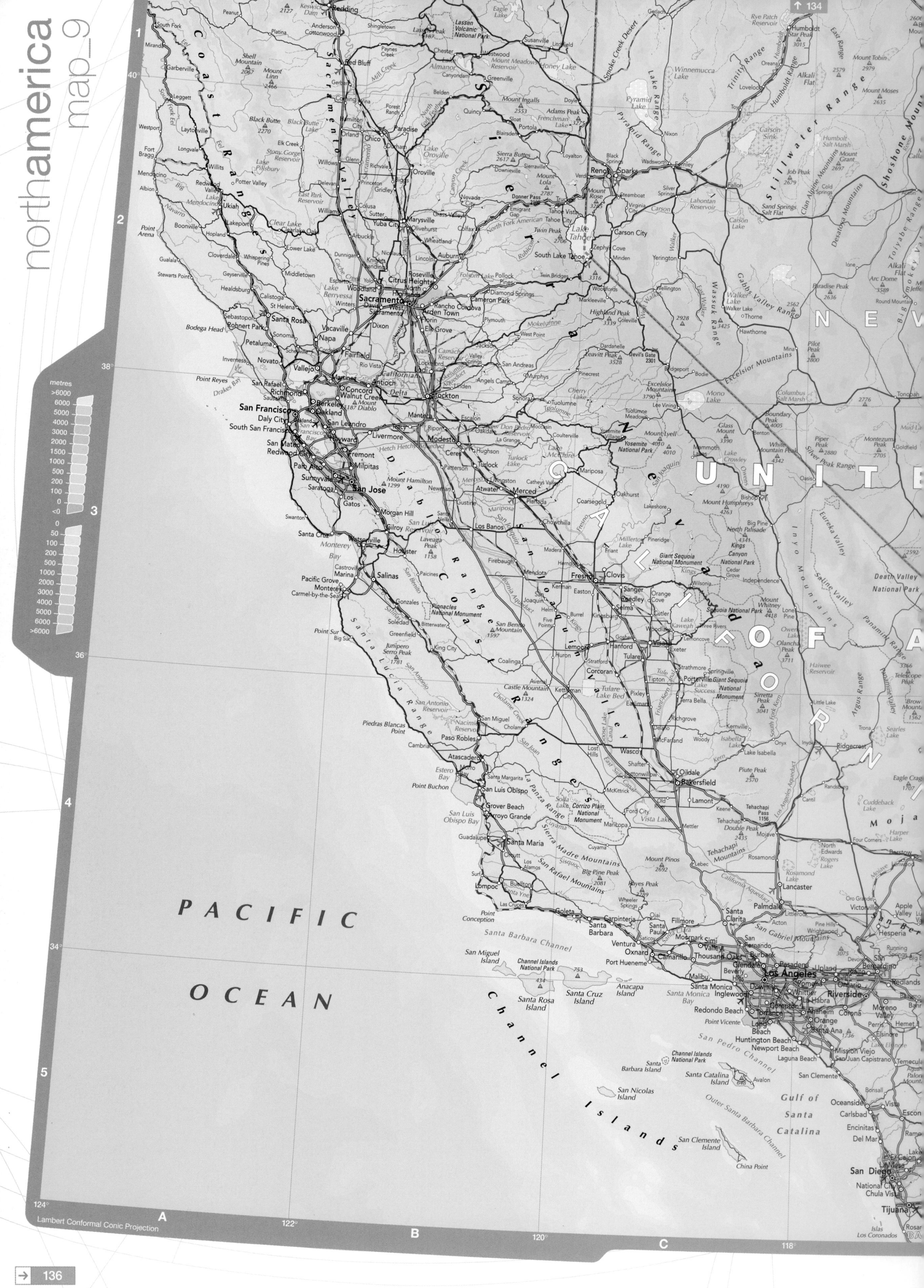
northamerica
map_9
↑ 134
metres
>6000
6000
5000
4000
3000
2000
1500
1000
500
200
100
0
<0
0
50
100
200
500
1000
2000
3000
4000
5000
6000
>6000
PACIFIC
OCEAN
UNITED
NEV
CALIFORNIA
Coast Ranges
Sacramento Valley
Sierra Nevada
Diablo Range
San Joaquin Valley
Santa Lucia Range
Coast Ranges
Channel Islands
Mojave
San Francisco
Oakland
San Jose
Sacramento
Stockton
Modesto
Fresno
Bakersfield
Reno
Carson City
Los Angeles
San Diego
Tijuana
Santa Barbara
San Luis Obispo
Monterey Bay
Santa Barbara Channel
San Pedro Channel
Gulf of Santa Catalina
Lake Tahoe
Yosemite National Park
Sequoia National Park
Death Valley National Park
Lambert Conformal Conic Projection
124°
122°
120°
118°
40°
38°
36°
34°
A
B
C
1
2
3
4
5

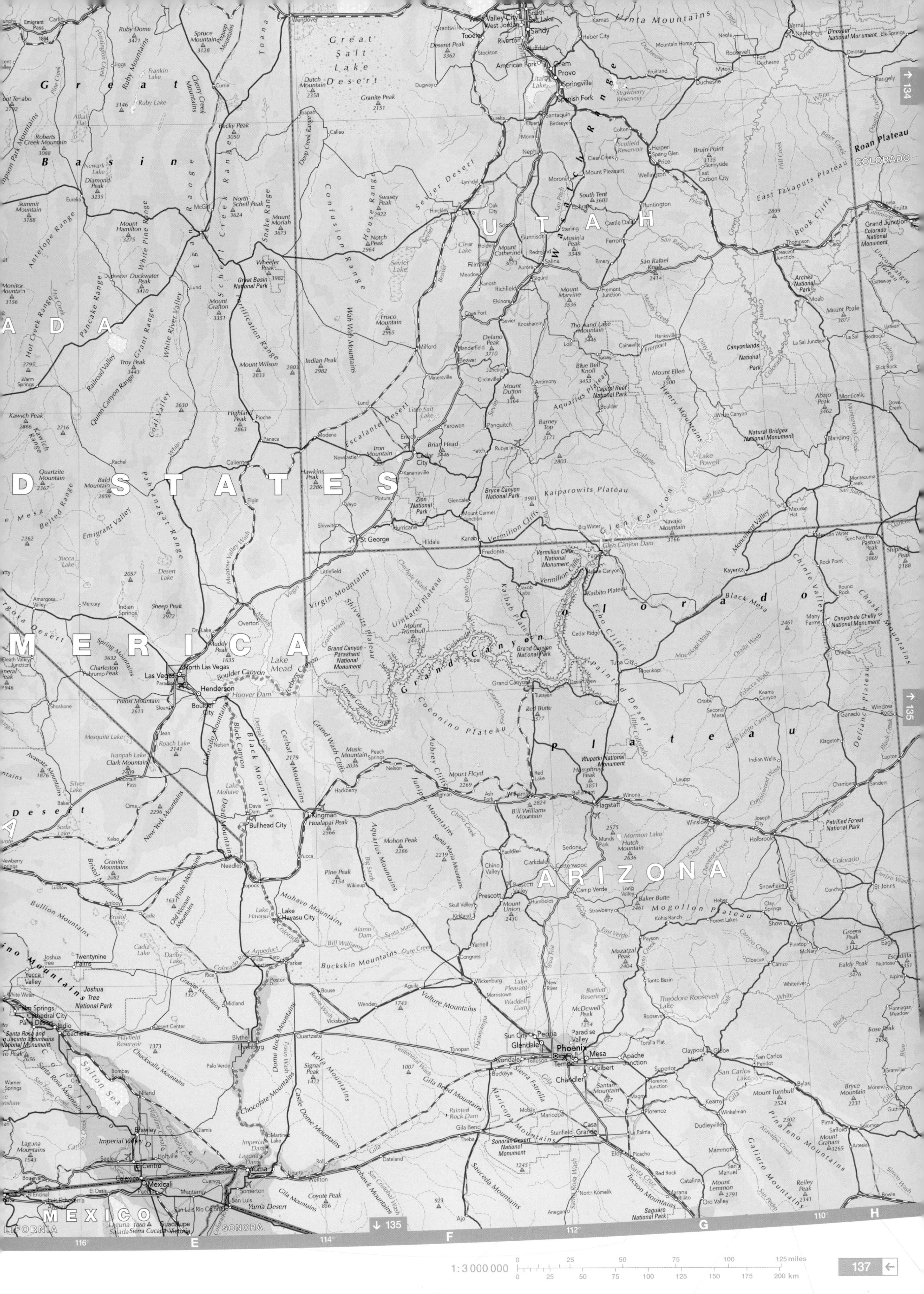Great Salt Lake Desert
Great Basin
UTAH
ARIZONA
COLORADO
UNITED STATES OF AMERICA
MEXICO
SONORA
Colorado Plateau
Uinta Mountains
Wasatch Range
Salt Lake City
West Valley City
West Jordan
Sandy
Tooele
Riverton
American Fork
Orem
Provo
Springville
Spanish Fork
Utah Lake
Sevier Desert
Escalante Desert
Confusion Range
House Range
Wah Wah Mountains
Snake Range
Schell Creek Range
Egan Range
White Pine Range
Ruby Mountains
Ruby Dome
Toana
Deep Creek Range
Great Basin National Park
Wheeler Peak
3982
Cedar City
St George
Zion National Park
Bryce Canyon National Park
Capitol Reef National Park
Canyonlands National Park
Arches National Park
Natural Bridges National Monument
Kaiparowits Plateau
Glen Canyon
Glen Canyon Dam
Lake Powell
Henry Mountains
Aquarius Plateau
Roan Plateau
East Tavaputs Plateau
Book Cliffs
Grand Junction
Colorado National Monument
Uncompahgre Plateau
Moab
Dinosaur National Monument
Vermilion Cliffs
Vermilion Cliffs National Monument
Kaibab Plateau
Grand Canyon
Grand Canyon National Park
Grand Canyon - Parashant National Monument
Coconino Plateau
Painted Desert
Black Mesa
Monument Valley
Chinle Valley
Chuska Mountains
Canyon de Chelly National Monument
Petrified Forest National Park
Flagstaff
Humphreys Peak
3851
Wupatki National Monument
Tuba City
Page
Kayenta
Winslow
Holbrook
Mogollon Plateau
Prescott
Sedona
Lake Mead
Hoover Dam
Las Vegas
North Las Vegas
Henderson
Boulder City
Black Mountains
Lake Mohave
Bullhead City
Kingman
Needles
Lake Havasu City
Mohave Mountains
Buckskin Mountains
Parker
Blythe
Kofa Mountains
Castle Dome Mountains
Chocolate Mountains
Yuma
Yuma Desert
Gila Bend Mountains
Sonoran Desert National Monument
Maricopa Mountains
Sierra Estrella
Phoenix
Glendale
Mesa
Tempe
Chandler
Gilbert
Casa Grande
Apache Junction
Theodore Roosevelt Lake
Globe
San Carlos Lake
Pinaleno Mountains
Galiuro Mountains
Tucson Mountains
Saguaro National Park
Salton Sea
Imperial Valley
Brawley
El Centro
Calexico
Mexicali
Palm Springs
Cathedral City
Palm Desert
Indio
Coachella
Joshua Tree National Park
Twentynine Palms
Santa Rosa and San Jacinto Mountains National Monument
Chuckwalla Mountains
Bullion Mountains
Old Woman Mountains
New York Mountains
Clark Mountain
Spring Mountains
Charleston Peak
3632
Pahranagat Range
Quinn Canyon Range
Grant Range
Pancake Range
Antelope Range
Hot Creek Range
Kawich Range
Belted Range
Emigrant Valley
Amargosa Desert
Death Valley Junction
Virgin Mountains
Shivwits Plateau
Uinkaret Plateau
Hualapai Peak
Cerbat Mountains
Aquarius Mountains
Juniper Mountains
Bill Williams Mountain
Vulture Mountains
Wickenburg
Dome Rock Mountains
Sauceda Mountains
Mohawk Mountains
Gila Mountains
116°
114°
112°
110°
E
F
G
H
↓ 135
↑ 134
↑ 135
1:3 000 000
0 25 50 75 100 125 miles
0 25 50 75 100 125 150 175 200 km

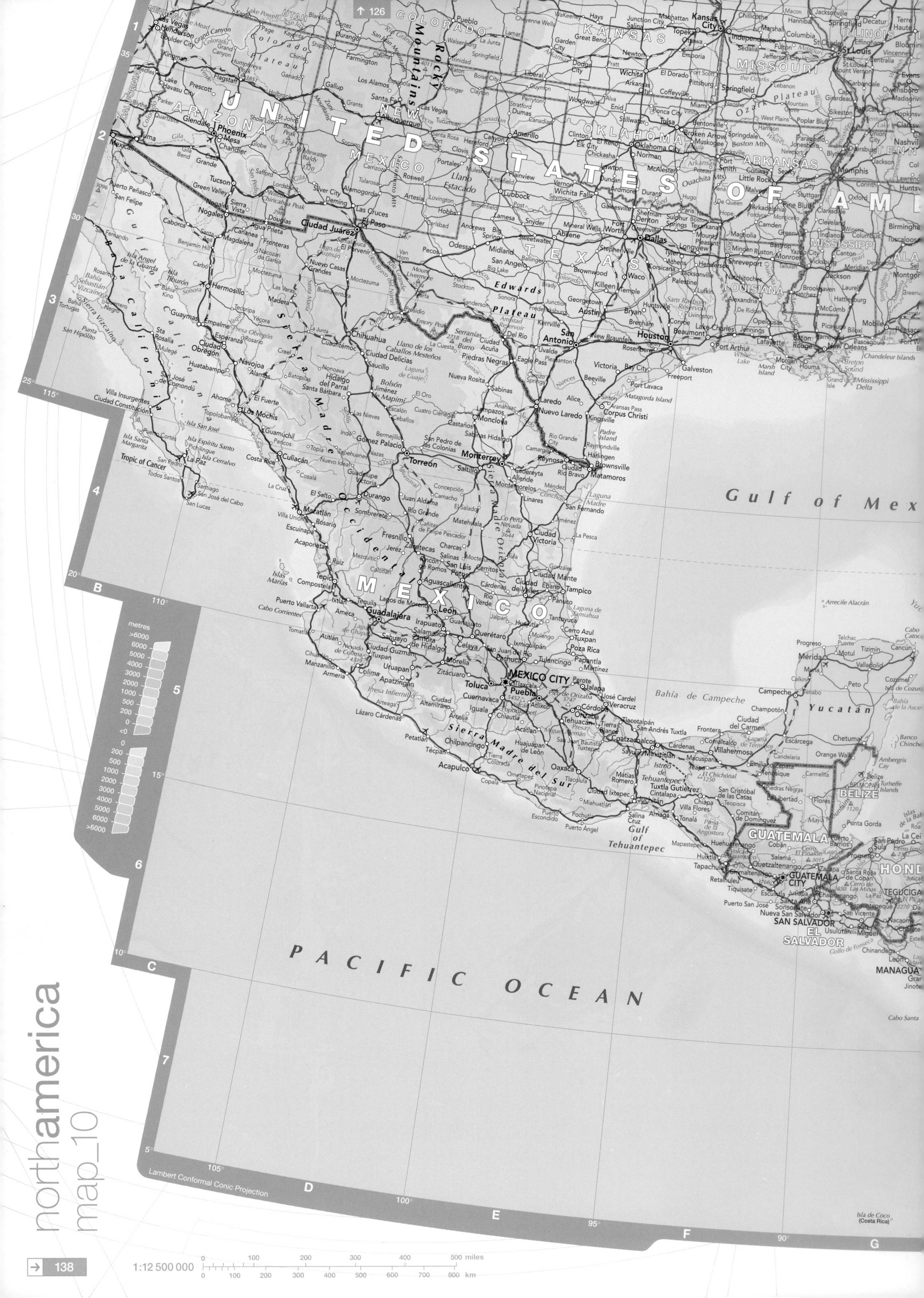

UTAH

COLORADO

KANSAS

MISSOURI

ILLINOIS

U N I T E D   S T A T E S   O F   A M E

ARIZONA

NEW
MEXICO

OKLAHOMA

ARKANSAS

TENN.

MISSISSIPPI

ALA.

LOUISIANA

T E X A S

M E X I C O

Rocky Mountains

Colorado Plateau

Sierra Madre Occidental

Sierra Madre Oriental

Baja California

Gulf of California

Gulf of Mexico

Bahía de Campeche

Yucatán

Sierra Madre del Sur

P A C I F I C   O C E A N

Gulf of Tehuantepec

GUATEMALA

BELIZE

EL SALVADOR

HOND

Tropic of Cancer

Las Vegas
Henderson
Boulder City
Kingman
Phoenix
Mesa
Chandler
Tucson
Nogales
Mexicali
Yuma
Hermosillo
Guaymas
Ciudad Obregón
Los Mochis
Culiacán
La Paz
Mazatlán
Tepic
Guadalajara
León
MEXICO CITY
Puebla
Acapulco
Chihuahua
Ciudad Juárez
El Paso
Monterrey
Torreón
Saltillo
Durango
Dallas
Houston
San Antonio
Austin
Laredo
Nuevo Laredo
Matamoros
Reynosa
Tampico
Veracruz
Oaxaca
GUATEMALA CITY
SAN SALVADOR

northamerica
map_10

metres
>6000
6000
5000
4000
3000
2000
1000
500
200
0
<0
0
200
500
1000
2000
3000
4000
5000
6000
>6000

1:12 500 000

Lambert Conformal Conic Projection

0   100   200   300   400   500 miles

0   100   200   300   400   500   600   700   800 km

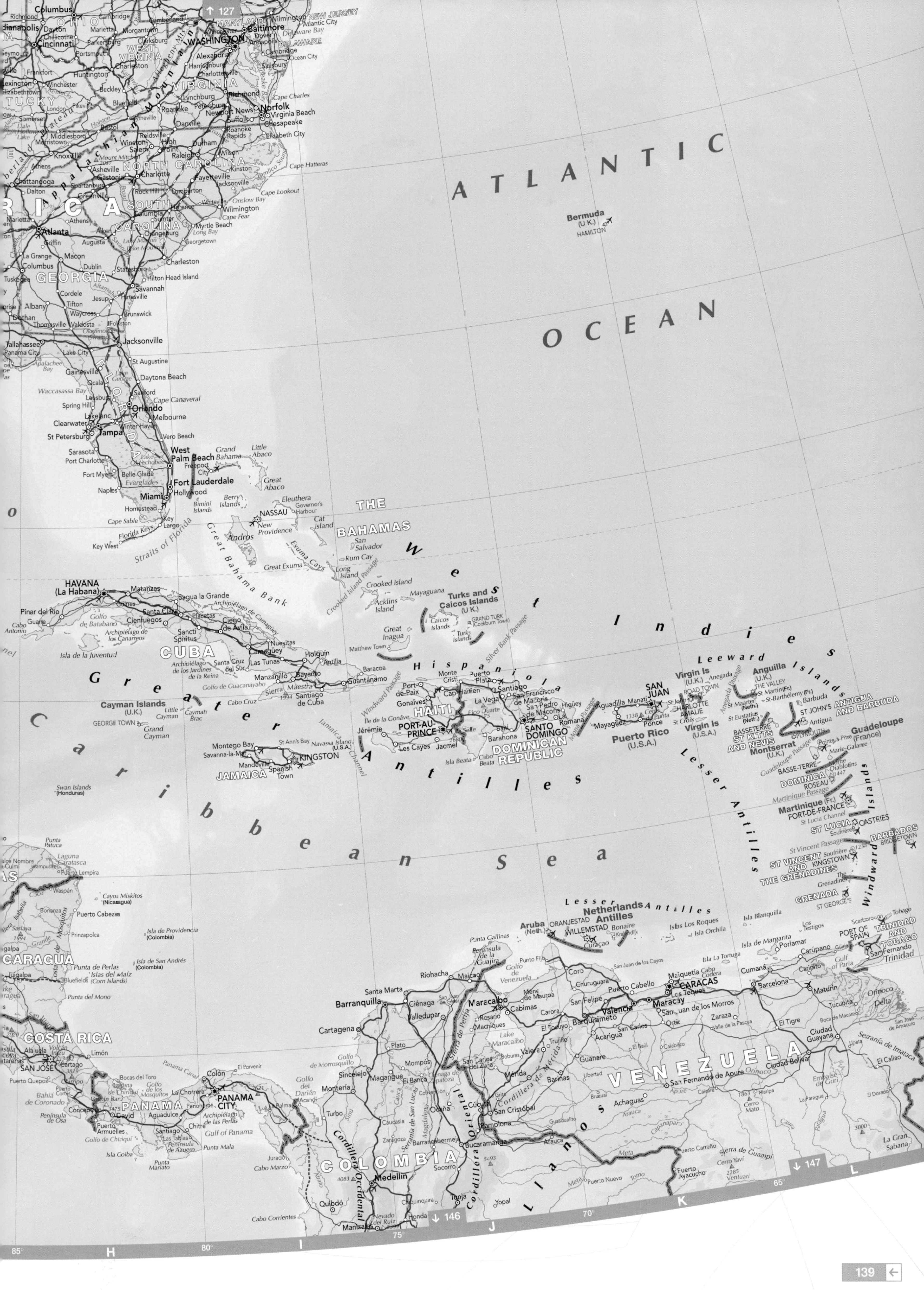
↑ 127
ATLANTIC
OCEAN
Bermuda
(U.K.)
HAMILTON
Columbus
OHIO
Cincinnati
WEST VIRGINIA
Charleston
VIRGINIA
MARYLAND
WASHINGTON
Baltimore
NEW JERSEY
DELAWARE
Atlantic City
Delaware Bay
Alexandria
Richmond
Norfolk
Newport News
Virginia Beach
Chesapeake
Cape Charles
Lynchburg
Roanoke
Danville
Durham
Raleigh
NORTH CAROLINA
Charlotte
Winston-Salem
Cape Hatteras
Cape Lookout
Wilmington
Cape Fear
Onslow Bay
SOUTH CAROLINA
Columbia
Myrtle Beach
Long Bay
Georgetown
Charleston
Hilton Head Island
Savannah
Atlanta
Augusta
Macon
Columbus
GEORGIA
Brunswick
Albany
Valdosta
Tallahassee
Jacksonville
St Augustine
Daytona Beach
Gainesville
Ocala
Orlando
Cape Canaveral
Melbourne
Tampa
Clearwater
St Petersburg
Lakeland
Vero Beach
Sarasota
Port Charlotte
Fort Myers
Naples
West Palm Beach
Fort Lauderdale
Hollywood
Miami
Homestead
Key Largo
Florida Keys
Key West
Cape Sable
Straits of Florida
Grand Bahama
Freeport City
Little Abaco
Great Abaco
Eleuthera
Bimini Islands
Berry Islands
NASSAU
New Providence
Andros
Cat Island
THE BAHAMAS
San Salvador
Rum Cay
Exuma Cays
Great Exuma
Long Island
Great Bahama Bank
Crooked Island
Crooked Island Passage
Acklins Island
Mayaguana
Turks and Caicos Islands
(U.K.)
GRAND TURK
(Cockburn Town)
Great Inagua
Matthew Town
Silver Bank Passage
HAVANA
(La Habana)
Matanzas
Pinar del Rio
Cabo Antonio
Golfo de Batabanó
Cienfuegos
Santa Clara
Sagua la Grande
Sancti Spíritus
Ciego de Ávila
Camagüey
Nuevitas
Las Tunas
Holguín
CUBA
Isla de la Juventud
Manzanillo
Bayamo
Santiago de Cuba
Guantánamo
Baracoa
Sierra Maestra
Golfo de Guacanayabo
Cayman Islands
(U.K.)
GEORGE TOWN
Grand Cayman
Little Cayman
Cayman Brac
Greater Antilles
Caribbean Sea
West Indies
Hispaniola
Windward Passage
HAITI
PORT-AU-PRINCE
Cap-Haïtien
Gonaïves
Jérémie
Les Cayes
Jacmel
DOMINICAN REPUBLIC
SANTO DOMINGO
Santiago
La Vega
San Pedro de Macorís
La Romana
Higüey
Barahona
Isla Beata
Cabo Beata
Mona Passage
JAMAICA
KINGSTON
Montego Bay
Spanish Town
Mandeville
Jamaica Channel
Navassa Island
(U.S.A.)
Puerto Rico
(U.S.A.)
SAN JUAN
Ponce
Mayagüez
Virgin Is
(U.K.)
ROAD TOWN
CHARLOTTE AMALIE
Virgin Is
(U.S.A.)
Anegada
Anegada Passage
Anguilla
(U.K.)
THE VALLEY
Leeward Islands
St Martin (Fr.)
St Maarten (Neth.)
St-Barthélemy (Fr.)
Barbuda
ST JOHN'S
ANTIGUA AND BARBUDA
Antigua
BASSETERRE
ST KITTS AND NEVIS
Montserrat
(U.K.)
Guadeloupe
(France)
BASSE-TERRE
Guadeloupe Passage
DOMINICA
ROSEAU
Dominica Passage
Martinique (Fr.)
FORT-DE-FRANCE
Martinique Passage
St Lucia Channel
ST LUCIA
CASTRIES
St Vincent Passage
BARBADOS
BRIDGETOWN
ST VINCENT AND THE GRENADINES
KINGSTOWN
Grenadines
GRENADA
ST GEORGE'S
Lesser Antilles
Windward Islands
Tobago
TRINIDAD AND TOBAGO
PORT OF SPAIN
Trinidad
Lesser Antilles
Netherlands Antilles
Aruba
(Neth.)
ORANJESTAD
WILLEMSTAD
Curaçao
Bonaire
Isla Blanquilla
Los Roques
Isla La Orchila
Isla de Margarita
Los Testigos
Isla La Tortuga
Swan Islands
(Honduras)
Punta Patuca
Cayos Miskitos
(Nicaragua)
Puerto Cabezas
Isla de Providencia
(Colombia)
Isla de San Andrés
(Colombia)
Punta de Perlas
Islas del Maíz
(Corn Islands)
Bluefields
CARAGUA
COSTA RICA
SAN JOSÉ
Limón
Puerto Quepos
Península de Osa
PANAMA
PANAMA CITY
Colón
Gulf of Panama
Golfo de Chiriquí
David
Isla Coiba
Punta Mariato
Golfo del Darién
Golfo de Morrosquillo
COLOMBIA
Barranquilla
Santa Marta
Cartagena
Riohacha
Valledupar
Sincelejo
Montería
Medellín
Bucaramanga
Cúcuta
Quibdó
Cabo Corrientes
Cordillera Occidental
Cordillera Oriental
Península de la Guajira
Golfo de Venezuela
Maracaibo
Lake Maracaibo
Coro
Punto Fijo
VENEZUELA
CARACAS
Valencia
Maracay
Barquisimeto
Puerto Cabello
Barcelona
Cumaná
Maturín
Ciudad Bolívar
Ciudad Guayana
San Fernando de Apure
Mérida
San Cristóbal
Barinas
Llanos
Orinoco
Puerto Ayacucho
Gulf of Paria
↓ 146
↓ 147
85°
80°
75°
70°
65°
H
I
J
K
L

Cuba, Caribbean Sea

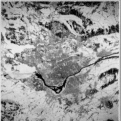
Montreal, Canada

The Pentagon, Washington DC, USA

Mexicali, Mexico/USA border

COUNTRIES		area sq km	area sq miles	population	capital	languages	religions	currency	map
ANTIGUA AND BARBUDA		442	171	65 000	St John's	English, creole	Protestant, Roman Catholic	East Caribbean dollar	139
THE BAHAMAS		13 939	5 382	308 000	Nassau	English, creole	Protestant, Roman Catholic	Bahamian dollar	139
BARBADOS		430	166	268 000	Bridgetown	English, creole	Protestant, Roman Catholic	Barbados dollar	139
BELIZE		22 965	8 867	231 000	Belmopan	English, Spanish, Mayan, creole	Roman Catholic, Protestant	Belize dollar	138
CANADA		9 970 610	3 849 674	31 015 000	Ottawa	English, French	Roman Catholic, Protestant, Eastern Orthodox, Jewish	Canadian dollar	120–121
COSTA RICA		51 100	19 730	4 112 000	San José	Spanish	Roman Catholic, Protestant	Costa Rican colón	139
CUBA		110 860	42 803	11 237 000	Havana	Spanish	Roman Catholic, Protestant	Cuban peso	139
DOMINICA		750	290	71 000	Roseau	English, creole	Roman Catholic, Protestant	East Caribbean dollar	139
DOMINICAN REPUBLIC		48 442	18 704	8 507 000	Santo Domingo	Spanish, creole	Roman Catholic, Protestant	Dominican peso	139
EL SALVADOR		21 041	8 124	6 400 000	San Salvador	Spanish	Roman Catholic, Protestant	El Salvador colón, United States dollar	138
GRENADA		378	146	94 000	St George's	English, creole	Roman Catholic, Protestant	East Caribbean dollar	139
GUATEMALA		108 890	42 043	11 687 000	Guatemala City	Spanish, Mayan languages	Roman Catholic, Protestant	Quetzal, United States dollar	138
HAITI		27 750	10 714	8 270 000	Port-au-Prince	French, creole	Roman Catholic, Protestant, Voodoo	Gourde	139
HONDURAS		112 088	43 277	6 575 000	Tegucigalpa	Spanish, Amerindian languages	Roman Catholic, Protestant	Lempira	138–139
JAMAICA		10 991	4 244	2 598 000	Kingston	English, creole	Protestant, Roman Catholic	Jamaican dollar	139
MEXICO		1 972 545	761 604	100 368 000	Mexico City	Spanish, Amerindian languages	Roman Catholic, Protestant	Mexican peso	138
NICARAGUA		130 000	50 193	5 208 000	Managua	Spanish, Amerindian languages	Roman Catholic, Protestant	Córdoba	138–139
PANAMA		77 082	29 762	2 899 000	Panama City	Spanish, English, Amerindian languages	Roman Catholic, Protestant, Sunni Muslim	Balboa	139
ST KITTS AND NEVIS		261	101	38 000	Basseterre	English, creole	Protestant, Roman Catholic	East Caribbean dollar	139
ST LUCIA		616	238	149 000	Castries	English, creole	Roman Catholic, Protestant	East Caribbean dollar	139
ST VINCENT AND THE GRENADINES		389	150	114 000	Kingstown	English, creole	Protestant, Roman Catholic	East Caribbean dollar	139
TRINIDAD AND TOBAGO		5 130	1 981	1 300 000	Port of Spain	English, creole, Hindi	Roman Catholic, Hindu, Protestant, Sunni Muslim	Trinidad and Tobago dollar	147
UNITED STATES OF AMERICA		9 809 378	3 787 422	285 926 000	Washington DC	English, Spanish	Protestant, Roman Catholic, Sunni Muslim, Jewish	United States dollar	126–127

DEPENDENT TERRITORIES		territorial status	area sq km	area sq miles	population	capital	languages	religions	currency	map
Anguilla		United Kingdom Overseas Territory	155	60	12 000	The Valley	English	Protestant, Roman Catholic	East Caribbean dollar	139
Aruba		Self-governing Netherlands Territory	193	75	104 000	Oranjestad	Papiamento, Dutch, English	Roman Catholic, Protestant	Arubian florin	146
Bermuda		United Kingdom Overseas Territory	54	21	63 000	Hamilton	English	Protestant, Roman Catholic	Bermuda dollar	139
Cayman Islands		United Kingdom Overseas Territory	259	100	40 000	George Town	English	Protestant, Roman Catholic	Cayman Islands dollar	139
Greenland		Self-governing Danish Territory	2 175 600	840 004	56 000	Nuuk (Godthåb)	Greenlandic, Danish	Protestant	Danish krone	121
Guadeloupe		French Overseas Department	1 780	687	431 000	Basse-Terre	French, creole	Roman Catholic	Euro	139
Martinique		French Overseas Department	1 079	417	386 000	Fort-de-France	French, creole	Roman Catholic, traditional beliefs	Euro	139
Montserrat		United Kingdom Overseas Territory	100	39	3 000	Plymouth	English	Protestant, Roman Catholic	East Caribbean dollar	139
Navassa Island		United States Unincorporated Territory	5	2	uninhabited					139
Netherlands Antilles		Self-governing Netherlands Territory	800	309	217 000	Willemstad	Dutch, Papiamento, English	Roman Catholic, Protestant	Netherlands guilder	146
Puerto Rico		United States Commonwealth	9 104	3 515	3 952 000	San Juan	Spanish, English	Roman Catholic, Protestant	United States dollar	139
St Pierre and Miquelon		French Territorial Collectivity	242	93	7 000	St-Pierre	French	Roman Catholic	Euro	125
Turks and Caicos Islands		United Kingdom Overseas Territory	430	166	17 000	Grand Turk	English	Protestant	United States dollar	139
Virgin Islands (U.K.)		United Kingdom Overseas Territory	153	59	24 000	Road Town	English	Protestant, Roman Catholic	United States dollar	139
Virgin Islands (U.S.A.)		United States Unincorporated Territory	352	136	122 000	Charlotte Amalie	English, Spanish	Protestant, Roman Catholic	United States dollar	139

southamerica

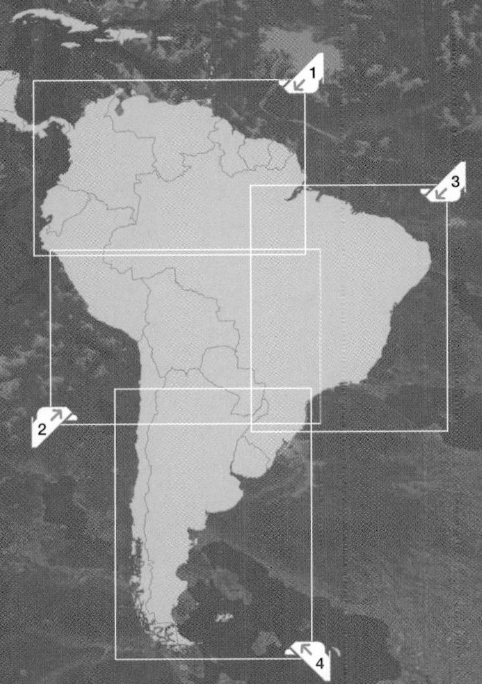

contents

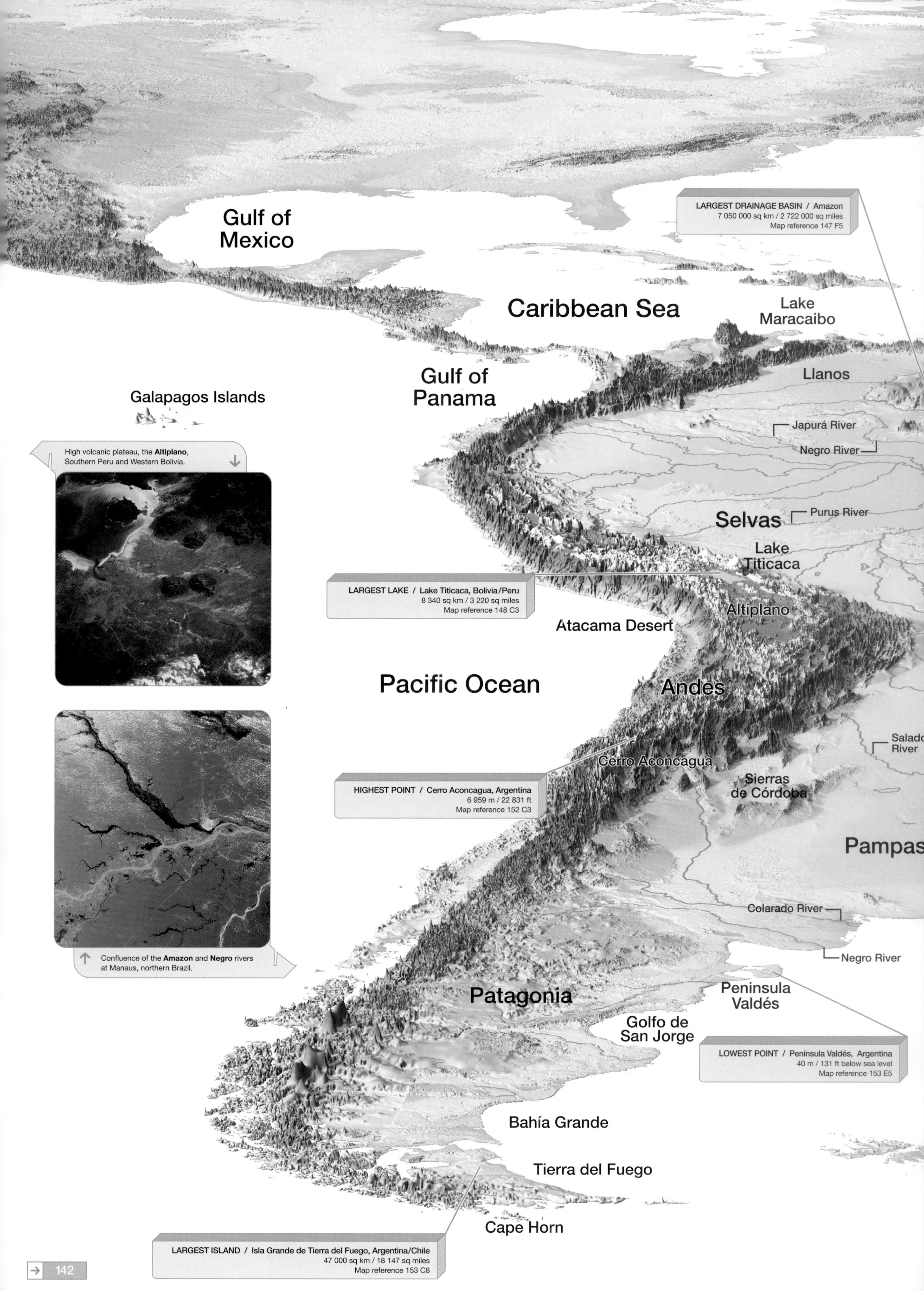

Gulf of
Mexico

Caribbean Sea

Lake
Maracaibo

LARGEST DRAINAGE BASIN / Amazon
7 050 000 sq km / 2 722 000 sq miles
Map reference 147 F5

Gulf of
Panama

Llanos

Galapagos Islands

Japurá River

Negro River

High volcanic plateau, the **Altiplano**,
Southern Peru and Western Bolivia. ↓

Selvas

Purus River

Lake
Titicaca

LARGEST LAKE / Lake Titicaca, Bolivia/Peru
8 340 sq km / 3 220 sq miles
Map reference 148 C3

Altiplano

Atacama Desert

Pacific Ocean

Andes

Salado
River

Cerro Aconcagua

Sierras
de Córdoba

HIGHEST POINT / Cerro Aconcagua, Argentina
6 959 m / 22 831 ft
Map reference 152 C3

Pampas

↑ Confluence of the **Amazon** and **Negro** rivers
at Manaus, northern Brazil.

Colarado River

Negro River

Patagonia

Peninsula
Valdés

Golfo de
San Jorge

LOWEST POINT / Península Valdés, Argentina
40 m / 131 ft below sea level
Map reference 153 E5

Bahía Grande

Tierra del Fuego

Cape Horn

LARGEST ISLAND / Isla Grande de Tierra del Fuego, Argentina/Chile
47 000 sq km / 18 147 sq miles
Map reference 153 C8

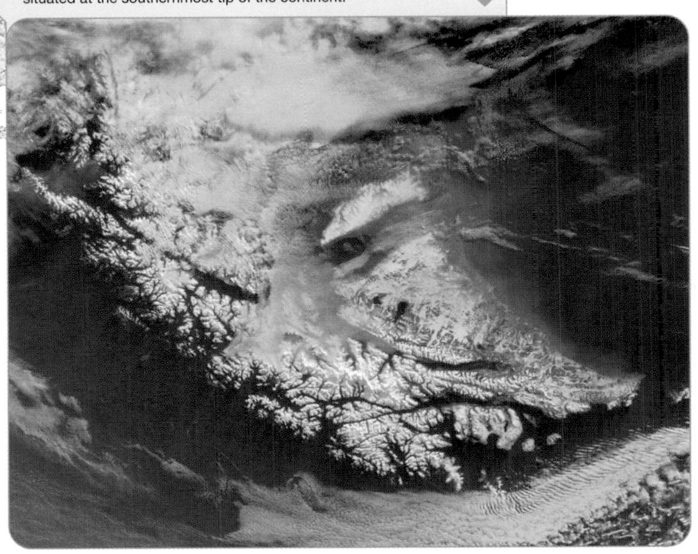

Isla Grande de Terra del Fuego, South America's largest island, situated at the southernmost tip of the continent.

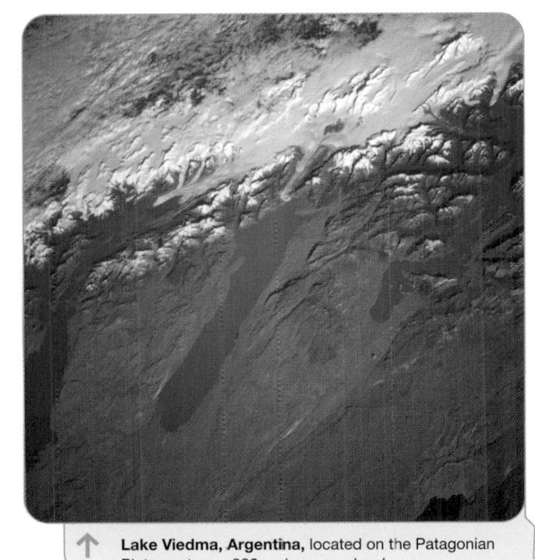

↑ **Lake Viedma, Argentina,** located on the Patagonian Plateau at over 300m above sea level.

Orinoco River

Orinoco River Delta

Angel Falls

Guiana Highlands

Mouths of the Amazon

Amazon Basin

Amazon River

LONGEST RIVER / Amazon
6 516 km / 4 049 miles
Map reference 150 B1

Tocantins River

Madeira River

Sao Francisco River

Mato Grosso

Pantanal

Brazilian Highlands

Gran Chaco

CONNECTIONS

Paraná River

Río de la Plata

Atlantic Ocean

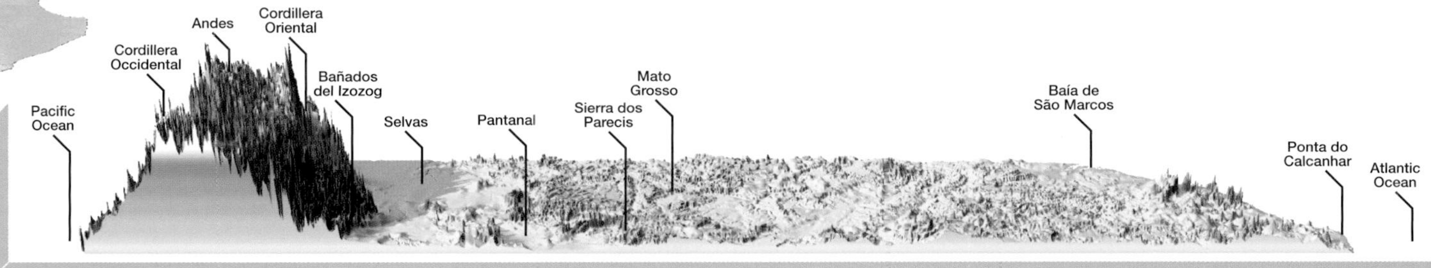

Pacific Ocean — Cordillera Occidental — Andes — Cordillera Oriental — Bañados del Izozog — Selvas — Pantanal — Sierra dos Parecis — Mato Grosso — Baía de São Marcos — Ponta do Calcanhar — Atlantic Ocean

↑ **south america** cross section

south america

LARGEST ISLANDS	sq km	sq miles	map
Isla Grande de Tierra del Fuego	47 000	18 147	153 C8
Isla de Chiloe	8 394	3 240	153 B5
East Falkland	6 760	2 610	153 F7
West Falkland	5 413	2 090	153 E7

LONGEST RIVERS	km	miles	map
Amazon	6 516	4 049	150 B1
Río de la Plata-Paraná	4 500	2 796	152 F3
Purus	3 218	1 999	147 F5
Madeira	3 200	1 988	147 G5
Sao Francisco	2 900	1 802	150 E4
Tocantins	2 750	1 708	150 B2

HIGHEST MOUNTAINS	metres	feet	map
Cerro Aconcagua, Argentina	6 959	22 831	152 C3
Nevado Ojos del Salado, Argentina/Chile	6 908	22 664	152 C1
Cerro Bonete, Argentina	6 872	22 546	152 C1
Cerro Pissis, Argentina	6 858	22 500	152 C1
Cerro Tupungato, Argentina/Chile	6 800	22 211	152 C3
Cerro Meredario, Argentina	6 770	22 211	152 B3

LARGEST LAKES	sq km	sq miles	map
Lake Titicaca	8 340	3 220	148 C3

LAND AREA		map
Total land area	17 815 420 sq km / 6 878 572 sq miles	
Most northerly point	Punta Gallinas, Colombia	146 D1
Most southerly point	Cape Horn, Chile	153 D8
Most westerly point	Galapagos Islands, Ecuador	160 H6
Most easterly point	Ilhas Martin Vas, Atlantic Ocean	161 M7

Parallel ranges of South America's longest mountain system, the **Andes**.

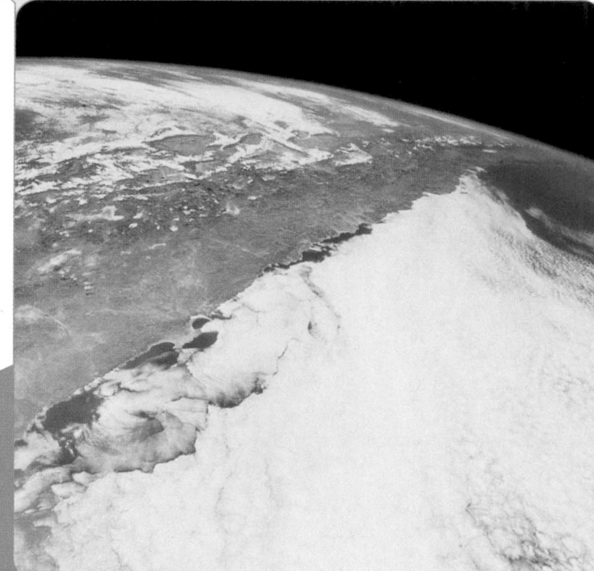

Galapagos Islands, Ecuador, a group of volcanic islands lying on the equator in the eastern Pacific Ocean.

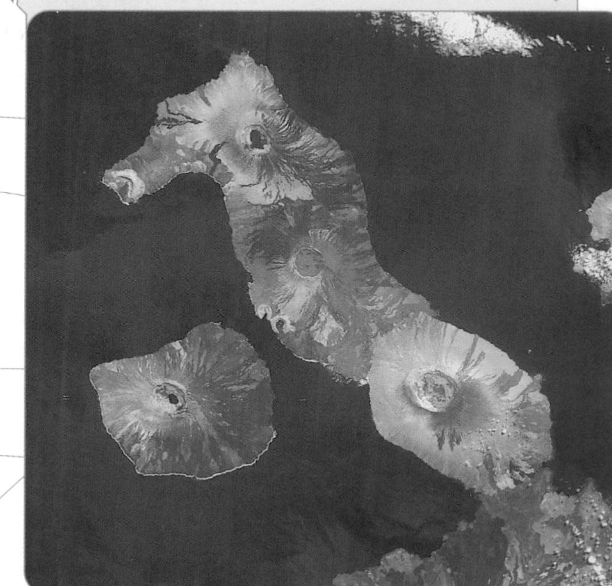

Isla de Coco

Galapagos Islands (Ecuador)

P A C

O

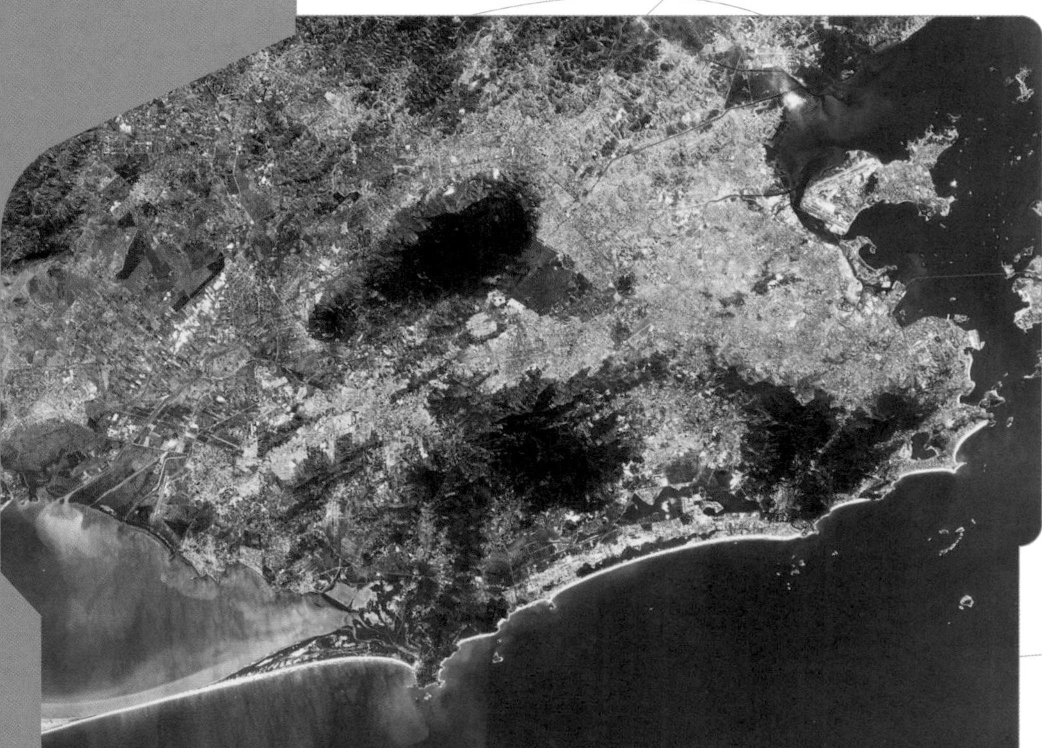

↑ **Rio de Janeiro**, southeast Brazil, third largest city in South America.

south america

Top ten countries by area	area sq km	area sq miles	map page	world rank	Top ten countries by population	population	map page	world rank
1 BRAZIL	8 547 379	3 300 161	150–151	5	1 BRAZIL	172 559 000	150–151	5
2 ARGENTINA	2 766 889	1 068 302	152–153	8	2 COLOMBIA	42 803 000	146	28
3 PERU	1 285 216	496 225	148	19	3 ARGENTINA	37 488 000	152–153	31
4 COLOMBIA	1 141 748	440 831	146	25	4 PERU	26 093 000	148	38
5 BOLIVIA	1 098 581	424 164	148–149	27	5 VENEZUELA	24 632 000	146–147	40
6 VENEZUELA	912 050	352 144	146–147	32	6 CHILE	15 402 000	152–153	60
7 CHILE	756 945	292 258	152–153	37	7 ECUADOR	12 880 000	146	64
8 PARAGUAY	406 752	157 048	149	58	8 BOLIVIA	8 516 000	148–149	84
9 ECUADOR	272 045	105 037	146	73	9 PARAGUAY	5 636 000	149	100
10 GUYANA	214 969	83 000	147	82	10 URUGUAY	3 361 000	152	127

Massive deforestation in the **Amazonian rainforest**, Rondônia, Brazil.

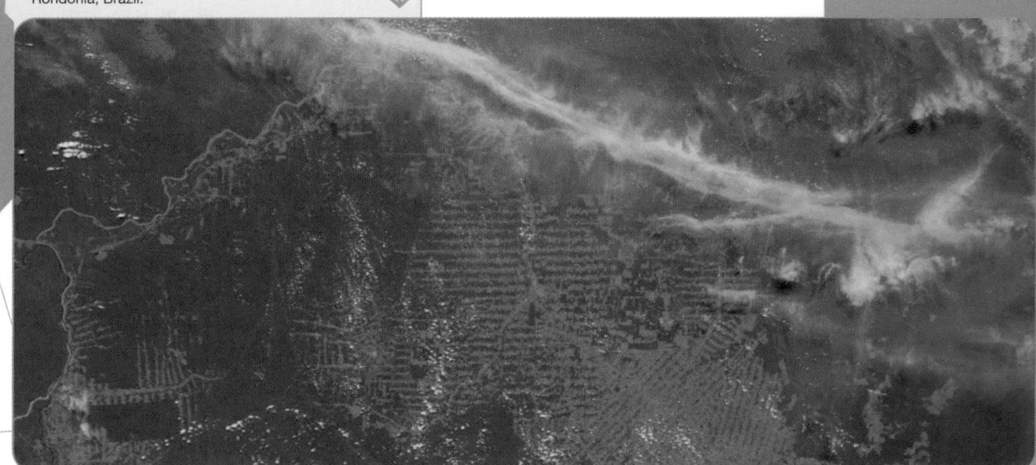

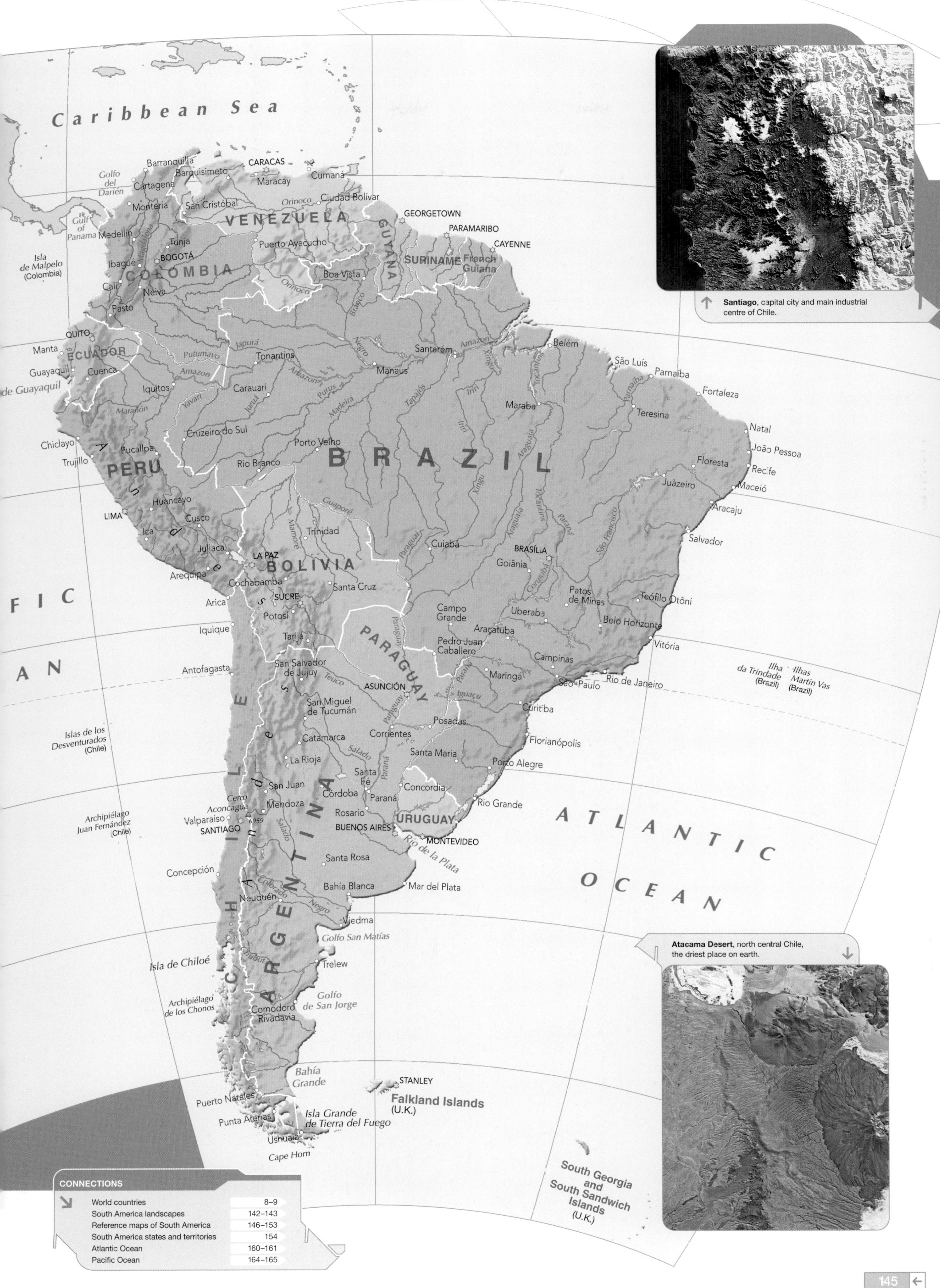

Caribbean Sea

Golfo del Darién
Barranquilla
Cartagena
Monteria
CARACAS
Barquisimeto
Maracay
Cumaná
Isla de Malpelo (Colombia)
Gulf of Panama
Medellín
San Cristóbal
VENEZUELA
Orinoco
Ciudad Bolívar
GEORGETOWN
PARAMARIBO
CAYENNE
Tunja
BOGOTÁ
Puerto Ayacucho
GUYANA
SURINAME
French Guiana
Ibagué
COLOMBIA
Cali
Neiva
Boa Vista
Orinoco
Branco
Pasto
QUITO
ECUADOR
Putumayo
Japurá
Tonantins
Santarém
Amazon
Belém
São Luís
Parnaíba
Fortaleza
Manta
Guayaquil
de Guayaquil
Cuenca
Amazon
Manaus
Teresina
Iquitos
Marañón
Yavari
Carauari
Purus
Iça
Maraba
Natal
João Pessoa
Chiclayo
Trujillo
PERU
Cruzeiro do Sul
Juruá
Madeira
Porto Velho
Rio Branco
B R A Z I L
Tapajós
Xingu
Tocantins
Araguaia
Parnaíba
Floresta
Recife
Maceió
Juàzeiro
São Francisco
Aracaju
Huancayo
LIMA
Cusco
Ica
Juliaca
Trinidad
Guaporé
Mamoré
BRASÍLIA
Goiânia
Salvador
Arequipa
LA PAZ
BOLIVIA
Cochabamba
SUCRE
Santa Cruz
Patos de Minas
Teófilo Otôni
Arica
Potosí
Paraguay
Campo Grande
Uberaba
Belo Horizonte
Iquique
Tarija
Pedro Juan Caballero
Araçatuba
Campinas
Vitória
Antofagasta
San Salvador de Jujuy
Teuco
PARAGUAY
Maringá
São Paulo
Rio de Janeiro
Ilha da Trindade (Brazil)
Ilhas Martin Vas (Brazil)
Islas de los Desventurados (Chile)
San Miguel de Tucumán
ASUNCIÓN
Paraná
Curitiba
Catamarca
Corrientes
Posadas
Iguaçu
Florianópolis
La Rioja
Salado
Paraná
Santa Maria
Porto Alegre
Archipiélago Juan Fernández (Chile)
San Juan
Santa Fé
Córdoba
Paraná
Concordia
Rio Grande
Cerro Aconcagua 6959
Mendoza
Rosario
URUGUAY
Valparaíso
Salado
A R G E N T I N A
BUENOS AIRES
MONTEVIDEO
SANTIAGO
Santa Rosa
Rio de la Plata
Concepción
Colorado
Bahía Blanca
Mar del Plata
Neuquén
Negro
Viedma
Golfo San Matías
Isla de Chiloé
Trelew
Archipiélago de los Chonos
Golfo de San Jorge
Comodoro Rivadavia
Bahía Grande
STANLEY
Falkland Islands (U.K.)
Puerto Natales
Punta Arenas
Isla Grande de Tierra del Fuego
Ushuaia
Cape Horn
South Georgia and South Sandwich Islands (U.K.)

A T L A N T I C   O C E A N

Santiago, capital city and main industrial centre of Chile.

Atacama Desert, north central Chile, the driest place on earth.

Administrative divisions
numbered on the map:

COLOMBIA
1. BOGOTÁ (C3)
2. QUINDÍO (C3)
3. RISARALDA (C3)

ECUADOR
4. BOLÍVAR (B5)
5. CHIMBORAZO (B5)
6. TUNGURAHUA (B5)
7. ZAMORA-CHINCHIPE (B5)

metres
>6000
6000
5000
4000
3000
2000
1000
500
200
<0
0
200
500
1000
2000
3000
4000
5000
6000
>6000

PACIFIC

OCEAN

C a r i b b e a n   S e a

Lesser   Antilles

PANAMA

Gulf of Panama

COLOMBIA

ECUADOR

PERU

VENEZUELA

↓ 148

Lambert Azimuthal Equal Area Projection

1 : 8 250 000

0   50   100   150   200   250   300 miles

0   100   200   300   400   500 km

St Vincent KINGSTOWN Speightstown Six Cross Roads
Bequia ST VINCENT BRIDGETOWN BARBADOS
Mustique AND THE Port of Spain
The Canouan GRENADINES
Grenadines Hillsborough Carriacou
GRENADA Ronde
ST GEORGE'S Grenville

Isla Blanquilla

Isla Los Testigos Plymouth Charlotteville Tobago
de Margarita Scarborough
NUEVA ESPARTA La Asunción
Juangriego Porlamar PORT
Isla OF SPAIN Trinidad TRINIDAD
Península de Paria AND
Río Caribe Güiria Chaguanas TOBAGO
SUCRE Carúpano Gulf Sangre Grande
Cumaná of Paria San Juan Claro
Barcelona Guanta Bonasse San Fernando
Aragua de Caripe Pedernales
Barcelona Caripito Isla Mariusa
MONAGAS Mariusa Punta Araguapiche
Maturín Orinoco
ANZOÁTEGUI Delta
El Tigre DELTA AMACURO isla Corocoro
Santa María Waini Point
de Ipire Barrancas Morawhanna
Ciudad Guayana Mabaruma
Puerto Ordaz San José
de Amacuro Port Kaituma
Ciudad El Pao Matthews
Bolívar Ridge Baramanni
Ciudad 792 Serranía de Imataca La Horqueta
Piar Arakaka Koriabo
BOLÍVAR Bochinche Anna Regina
Cuyuni Spring Garden
El Callao Tumeremo Vreed-en-Hoop GEORGETOWN
Cerro Mito Kamaria Paradise
1863 Serranía Turagua El Dorado Arimu Mine Bartica Fort Wellington
1839 P.N. Canaima Kamarang Peters Mine New Amsterdam
La Paragua Callejito Rockstone Mara
Hato la Vergareña Kamakusa Linden Nickerie
Angel Falls Imbaimadai Convertón PARAMARIBO Nieuw
Cerro Venamo Ituni Amsterdam
Cerro Guaiquinima 2100 Mahdia Kwakwani Lelydorp Wanhatti
1672 Parque King Takama Onverwacht Pointe Isère
Nacional George VI Washabo Brownsweg Albina Organabo
Auyan Canaima 2040 Falls Apoera St-Laurent- Iracoubo
Tepui Avanganna Kangaruma Moengo du-Maroni Kourou
3000 2810 Kaieteur Apatou Tonate
La Gran Falls Bakhuis CAYENNE
Sabana Mount Gebergte Professor Roura
Aparurén Roraima Stuwmeer van Blommestein St Élie Kaw
Uacauyén Saverétik Meer Délices Pointe Béhague
Serra del Santa Elena Kurupukari Pokigron Grand Santi Cabo Orange
Zamuro Merume Normandia Apoteri Tafelberg Belizon
1240 Annai 1026 Cottica Régina
Cerro Curutú Serra Merari Juliana Top Wilhelmina Ouanary
1800 Peraitepuy Limão Yupukarri 1230 Gebergte St Georges
Castisiña Pirara Kumaka 558 Oiapoque
Kanuku Mountains Dadanawa Saül Cabo Cassiporé
Parque Nacional Lethem Shea Eilerts de Haan Gebergte P.N. de Cabo Orange
Parima-Tapirapecó Boa Esperança 882 Pontoetoe Clévelandia
São Bento Isherton Cronoque Oranje Gebergte Ouanary
Serra do Apiaú Boa Vista Biloku Kapiting 690 Oscar
Serra Parima Conceição Kuyuwini Talima Mitaraca
Serra Curupira 1450 Asoenangka 635 Oiapoque
RORAIMA Caracaraí 734 Yaripo Serra Lombarda
Sierra de Unturán Vista Alegre Merimum AMAPÁ
Serra Tutu-Tului Serra Malaripo Amapá
São José Barauaná Novo Novo
do Anauá Serra Mapireme Aporema
P.N. Iarauarune Maloca Serra do Navio
Pico Catrimani Porto Grande
da Neblina Parque Nacional Ferreira Gomes
do Rio Branco Boiaçu Mouths
Tapurucuará O Tapera Trombetas Macapá of the
União do Maruá Cuminá Porto Santana Amazon
Tupanaóca Mazagão Ilha
Carvoeiro Monte Dourado Queimada
Barcelos Moura Porteira Afuá Chaves
Tucandera Represa Cachoeira Breves
de Balbina das Capoeiras Santa Maria Gurupá
Carvoeiro Brás Porto de Moz
Nova Paraíso Oriximiná Óbidos Alenquer Prainha Melgaço
Balbina Juruti Monte Alegre Breves
AMAZONAS Santo Antônio Feijó Nhamundá Juriti Velho Santarém Porto do
Conceição Silves Barreirinha Alter do Chão Aveiro
Manaus Urucará Parintins Belterra Vitória Belo
Manacapuru Itacoatiara Óbidos Boa Vista do Monte
Careiro Autazes Aveiro Altamira
BRAZIL Novo Olinda Brasília Legal Tucuruí
do Norte Itaituba
Coari Careiro do Castanho Vila Braga P.N.
Codajás Borba Amazônia São Lu's
Anamã Diamantina Cantagalo
Anori São Paga Conta Porto Alegre
Pedro Bacabal
Novo Vista Alegre Sem Tripa Lontra
Aripuanã Terra Preta Altamira Porto
Tambaqui São Lus Nova Forte Veneza Porto do Barka
Francisco Tucuruapé
Vencedor Capoeira São Mariano
Novo Aripuanã Jacareacanga Araras Barbacena
Manicoré Araras
Constância Cachoeira Nazaré
dos Baetas da Chacorão
Democracia Cachoeira Jaí PARÁ São Sebastião
Canutama das Capoeiras São Félix
Samaúma Barra de São Manuel
Lábrea Pirapetinga Conceição Xingara

VENEZUELA GUYANA SURINAME French Guiana

Guiana Highlands Pakaraima Mountains Serra Tumucumaque

BRAZIL PARÁ AMAPÁ

Ilha de Marajó

PACIFIC

OCEAN

PERU

LORETO
SAN MARTÍN
AMAZONAS
LA LIBERTAD
ANCASH
HUANUCO
UCAYALI
PASCO
JUNÍN
LIMA
HUANCAVELICA
ICA
AYACUCHO
APURIMAC
CUSCO
AREQUIPA
PUNO
MOQUEGUA
TACNA
TARAPACÁ
ANTOFAGASTA
ATACAMA
POTOSÍ
ORURO
LA PAZ
BENI
BOLIVIA
JUJUY
CATAMARCA
TUCUMÁN

ACRE
AMAZONAS
PANDO
MADRE DE DIOS
RONDÔNIA

CHILE
Desierto de Atacama
Cordillera de la Costa

LIMA
Callao
La Paz
SUCRE
Cochabamba
Oruro
Potosí

Tropic of Capricorn

metres
>6000
6000
5000
4000
3000
2000
1000
500
200
0
<0
0
200
500
1000
2000
3000
4000
5000
6000
>6000

southamerica
map_2

Lambert Azimuthal Equal Area Projection

80°   A   76°   B   72°   C   68°   D

1
8°
2
12°
3
16°
4
20°
5
24°
6

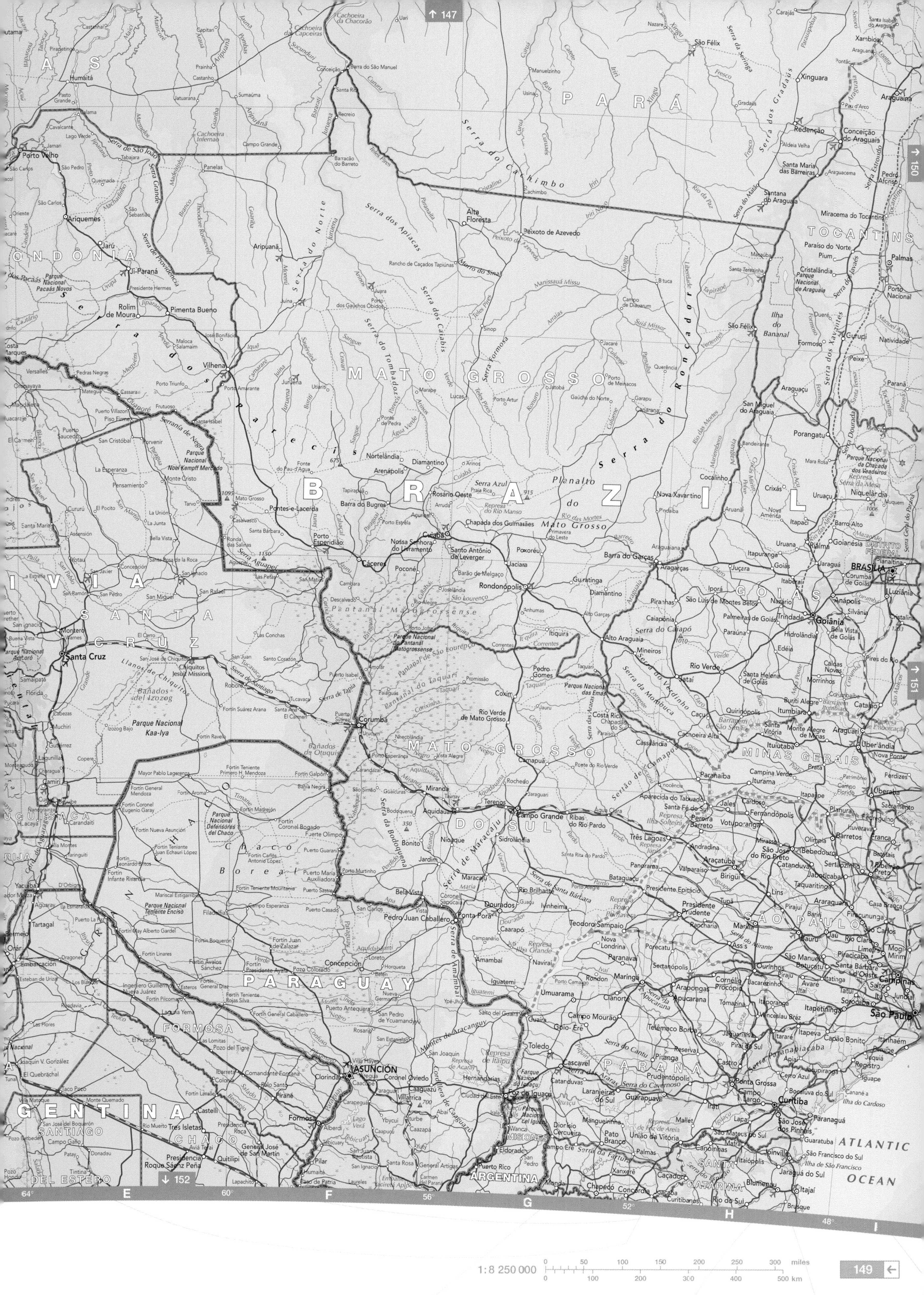

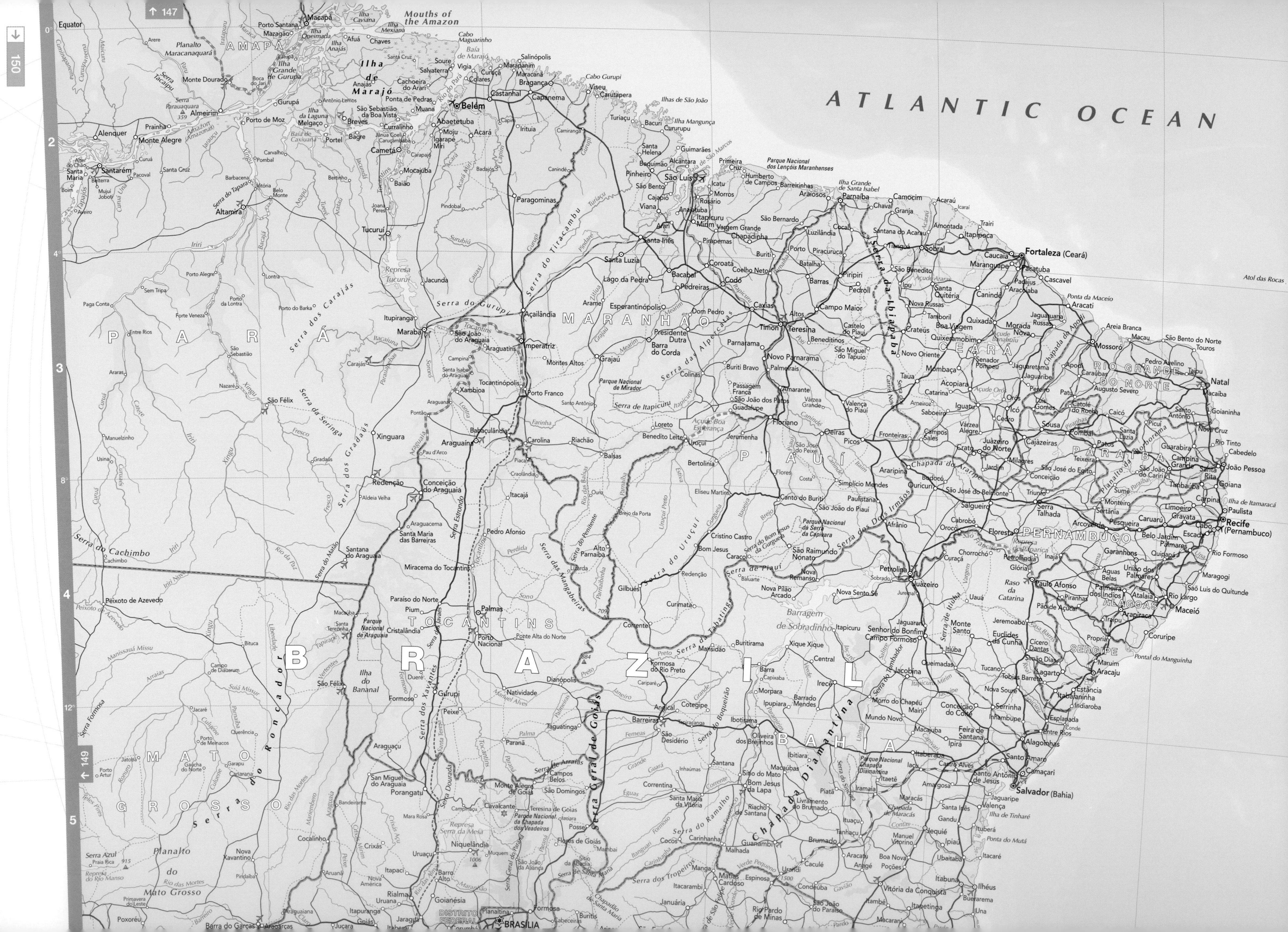

ATLANTIC OCEAN
B R A Z I L
MARANHÃO
PIAUÍ
CEARÁ
RIO GRANDE DO NORTE
PARAÍBA
PERNAMBUCO
ALAGOAS
SERGIPE
BAHIA
TOCANTINS
PARÁ
AMAPÁ
MATO GROSSO
DISTRITO FEDERAL
BRASÍLIA
Fortaleza (Ceará)
Recife (Pernambuco)
Salvador (Bahia)
Natal
João Pessoa
Maceió
Aracaju
Teresina
São Luís
Belém
Macapá
Palmas
Mouths of the Amazon
Ilha de Marajó
Equator
Serra da Ibiapaba
Chapada Diamantina
Serra Geral de Goiás
Serra do Roncador
Atol das Rocas

↑ 147
↑ 149

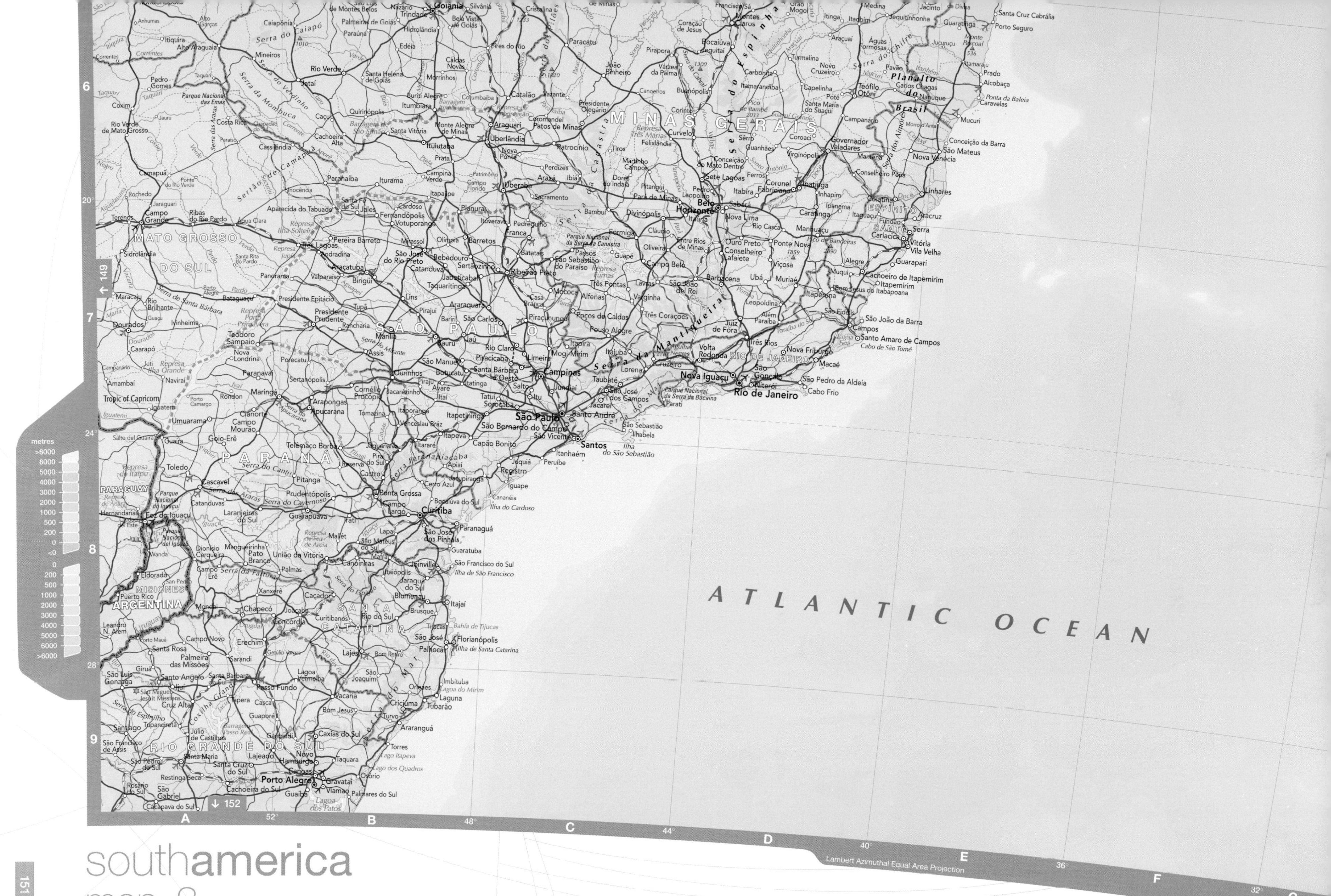

southamerica

map_3

Lambert Azimuthal Equal Area Projection

1:8 250 000

ATLANTIC OCEAN

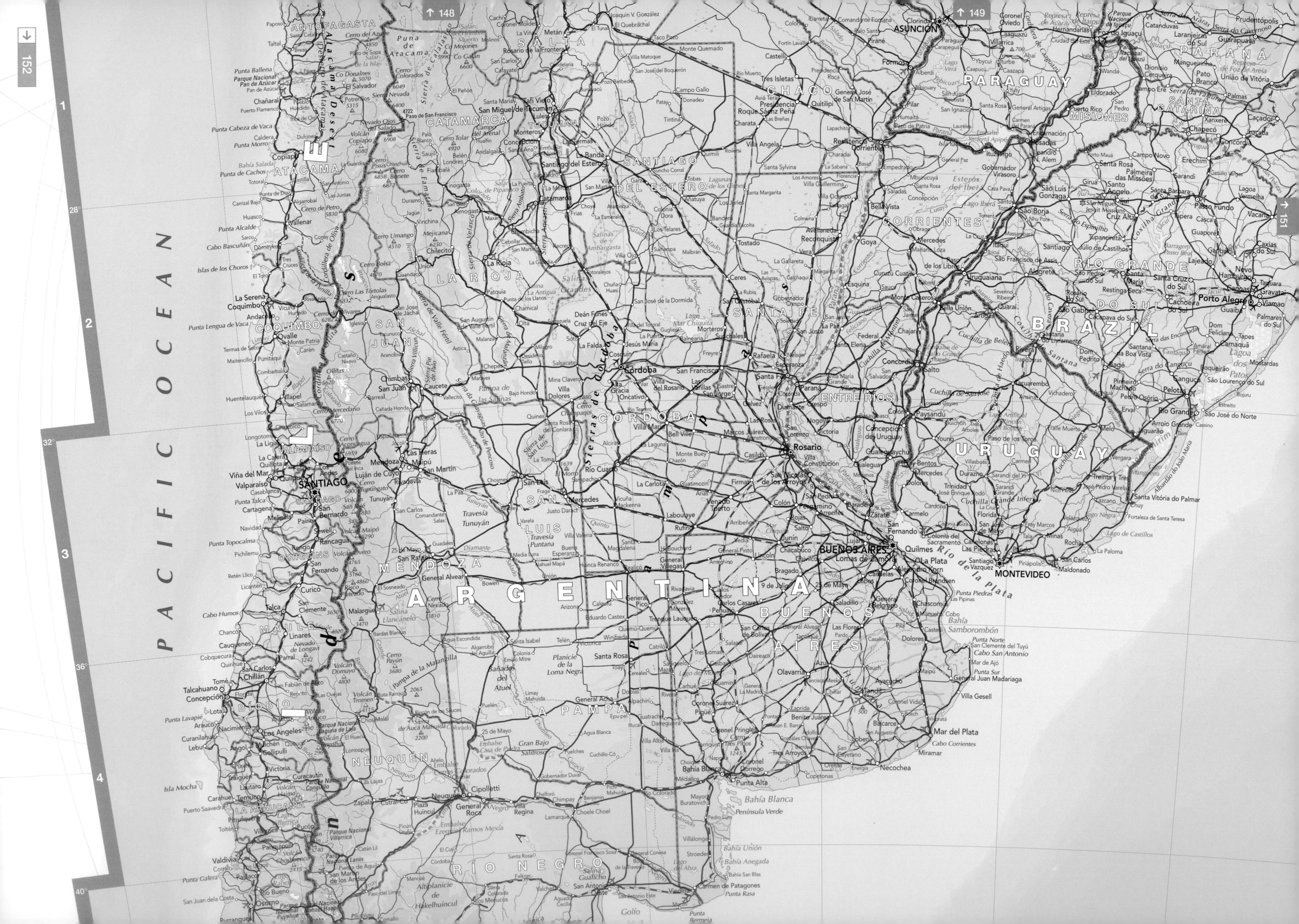

ATLANTIC

OCEAN

Falkland Islands
(U.K.)

West
Falkland

East
Falkland

Cape
Dolphin

Pebble
Island

Port
Stephens

Cape
Meredith

Volunteer Point
Cape Pembroke
STANLEY
Choiseul Sound

Weddell Island

Beauchene Island

South Georgia (U.K.) inset:
South Georgia
(U.K.)
North
Cape
Willis
Islands
Cape
Alexandra
Cumberland Bay
King Edward Point
Mount Paget
2934
Cape Vahsel
Cape
Disappointment

1:8 250 000
miles 0 60 100
km

ATLANTICA
CHILENA
MAGALLANES

CHUBUT

Golfo
de
San Jorge

SANTA
CRUZ

Comodoro
Rivadavia

Trelew
Rawson
Puerto Madryn

Punta Norte
Punta Delgada
Golfo
Nuevo
Golfo
San José
Península
Valdés

Cabo Raso
Cabo San José
Bahía
Camarones
Cabo Dos Bahías

Cabo Tres Puntas
Cabo Blanco

Punta Medanosa

Golfo San Jorge

Puerto Deseado

Puerto
Santa Cruz
Río
Gallegos
Cabo Buen Tiempo
Punta Loyola
Cabo Vírgenes
Punta Dungeness

San Julián

Río Grande

Isla
Grande
de
Tierra
del Fuego

TIERRA DEL
FUEGO

Punta
Arenas

Puerto Natales

Isla
de los Estados
Estrecho de Le Maire

Cabo San Diego
Isla Nueva
Isla Lennox
Islas Wollaston
Cabo de Hornos
Cape Horn (Cabo de Hornos)
Parque Nacional de Hornos

Strait of Magellan
Estrecho de Magallanes

Isla Navarino

AISÉN

Archipiélago
de los Chonos

Isla Wellington

Isla Madre
de Dios
Isla Duque
de York
Isla Santa Inés
Isla Desolación

Península de Taitao
Golfo
de
Penas

Canal Moraleda

Chiloé
Puerto Montt
Ancud

Cabo Quilán
Isla Guafo

Cape Horn (Cabo de Hornos)

metres
>6000
6000
5000
4000
3000
2000
1000
500
200
0
<0

miles 0 50 100 150 200 250 300
0 100 200 300 400 500 km

153

1:8 250 000
Lambert Azimuthal Equal Area Projection

Falkland Islands,
South Atlantic Ocean

Lake Titcaca, Bolivia/Peru

Amazon rainforest,
Ecuador

Buenos Aires, Argentina

COUNTRIES		area sq km	area sq miles	population	capital	languages	religions	currency	map
ARGENTINA		2 766 889	1 068 302	37 488 000	Buenos Aires	Spanish, Italian, Amerindian languages	Roman Catholic, Protestant	Argentinian peso	152–153
BOLIVIA		1 098 581	424 164	8 516 000	La Paz/Sucre	Spanish, Quechua, Aymara	Roman Catholic, Protestant, Baha'i	Boliviano	148–149
BRAZIL		8 547 379	3 300 161	172 559 000	Brasília	Portuguese	Roman Catholic, Protestant	Real	150–151
CHILE		756 945	292 258	15 402 000	Santiago	Spanish, Amerindian languages	Roman Catholic, Protestant	Chilean peso	152–153
COLOMBIA		1 141 748	440 831	42 803 000	Bogotá	Spanish, Amerindian languages	Roman Catholic, Protestant	Colombian peso	146
ECUADOR		272 045	105 037	12 880 000	Quito	Spanish, Quechua, other Amerindian languages	Roman Catholic	US dollar	146
GUYANA		214 969	83 000	763 000	Georgetown	English, creole, Amerindian languages	Protestant, Hindu, Roman Catholic, Sunni Muslim	Guyana dollar	147
PARAGUAY		406 752	157 048	5 636 000	Asunción	Spanish, Guaraní	Roman Catholic, Protestant	Guaraní	149
PERU		1 285 216	496 225	26 093 000	Lima	Spanish, Quechua, Aymara	Roman Catholic, Protestant	Sol	148
SURINAME		163 820	63 251	419 000	Paramaribo	Dutch, Surinamese, English, Hindi	Hindu, Roman Catholic, Protestant, Sunni Muslim	Suriname guilder	147
URUGUAY		176 215	68 037	3 361 000	Montevideo	Spanish	Roman Catholic, Protestant, Jewish	Uruguayan peso	152
VENEZUELA		912 050	352 144	24 632 000	Caracas	Spanish, Amerindian languages	Roman Catholic, Protestant	Bolívar	146–147

DEPENDENT TERRITORIES		territorial status	area sq km	area sq miles	population	capital	languages	religions	currency	map
Falkland Islands		United Kingdom Overseas Territory	12 170	4 699	2 000	Stanley	English	Protestant, Roman Catholic	Falkland Islands pound	153
French Guiana		French Overseas Department	90 000	34 749	170 000	Cayenne	French, creole	Roman Catholic	Euro	147
South Georgia and South Sandwich Islands		United Kingdom Overseas Territory	4 066	1 570	uninhabited					161

Orinoco River,
Colombia/Venezuela

Angel Falls, Venezuela

Machupicchu, Peru

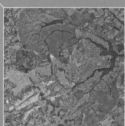
Brasília, Brazil

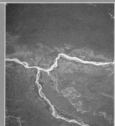

oceansandpoles

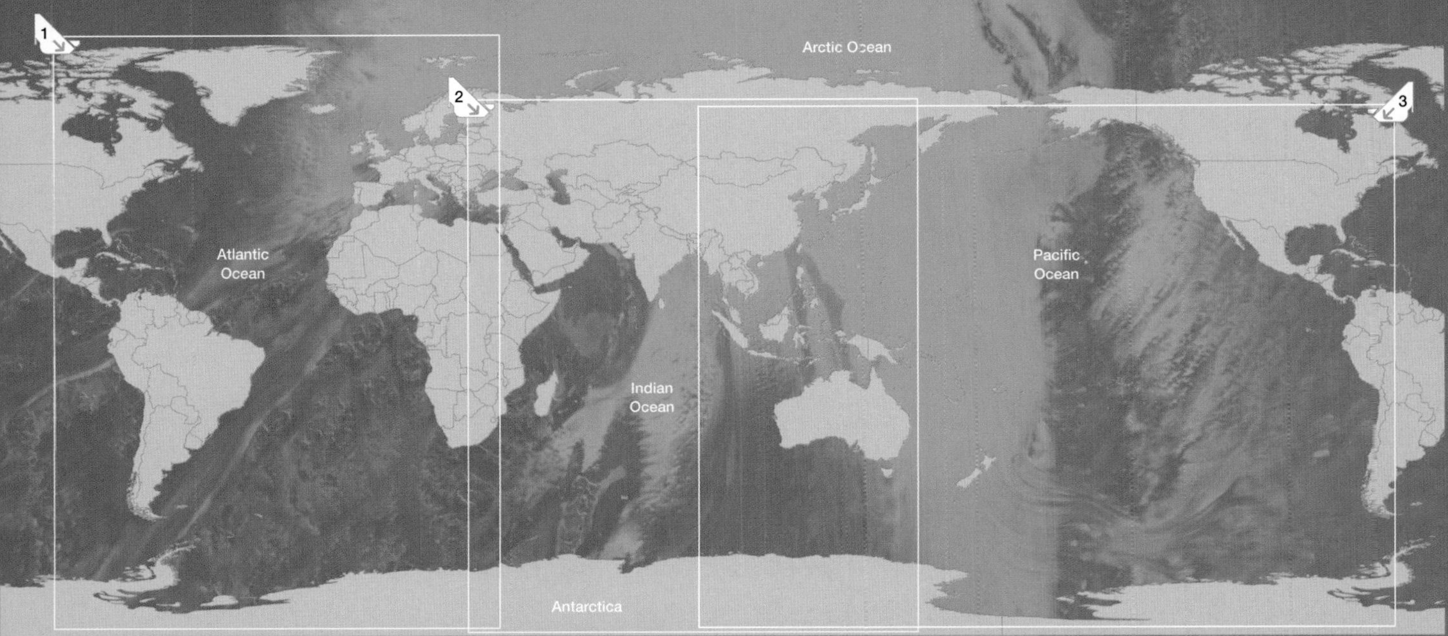

Arctic Ocean

Atlantic
Ocean

Pacific
Ocean

Indian
Ocean

Antarctica

contents

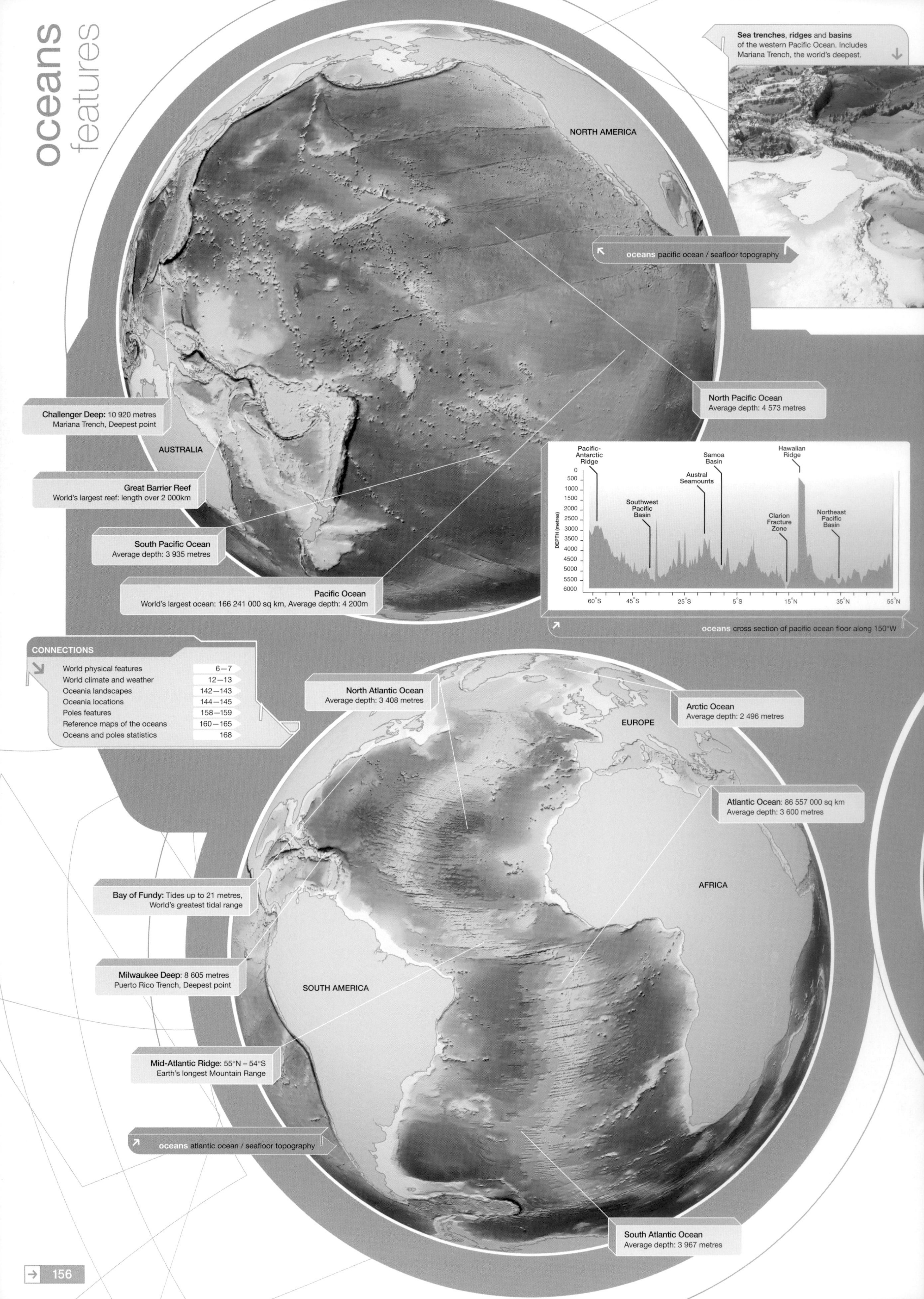

Sea trenches, ridges and basins of the western Pacific Ocean. Includes Mariana Trench, the world's deepest.

oceans pacific ocean / seafloor topography

NORTH AMERICA

North Pacific Ocean
Average depth: 4 573 metres

Challenger Deep: 10 920 metres
Mariana Trench, Deepest point

AUSTRALIA

Great Barrier Reef
World's largest reef: length over 2 000km

South Pacific Ocean
Average depth: 3 935 metres

Pacific Ocean
World's largest ocean: 166 241 000 sq km, Average depth: 4 200m

Pacific-Antarctic Ridge

Samoa Basin

Hawaiian Ridge

Austral Seamounts

Southwest Pacific Basin

Clarion Fracture Zone

Northeast Pacific Basin

DEPTH (metres)
0
500
1000
1500
2000
2500
3000
3500
4000
4500
5000
5500
6000

60°S   45°S   25°S   5°S   15°N   35°N   55°N

oceans cross section of pacific ocean floor along 150°W

North Atlantic Ocean
Average depth: 3 408 metres

Arctic Ocean
Average depth: 2 496 metres

EUROPE

Atlantic Ocean: 86 557 000 sq km
Average depth: 3 600 metres

Bay of Fundy: Tides up to 21 metres,
World's greatest tidal range

AFRICA

Milwaukee Deep: 8 605 metres
Puerto Rico Trench, Deepest point

SOUTH AMERICA

Mid-Atlantic Ridge: 55°N – 54°S
Earth's longest Mountain Range

oceans atlantic ocean / seafloor topography

South Atlantic Ocean
Average depth: 3 967 metres

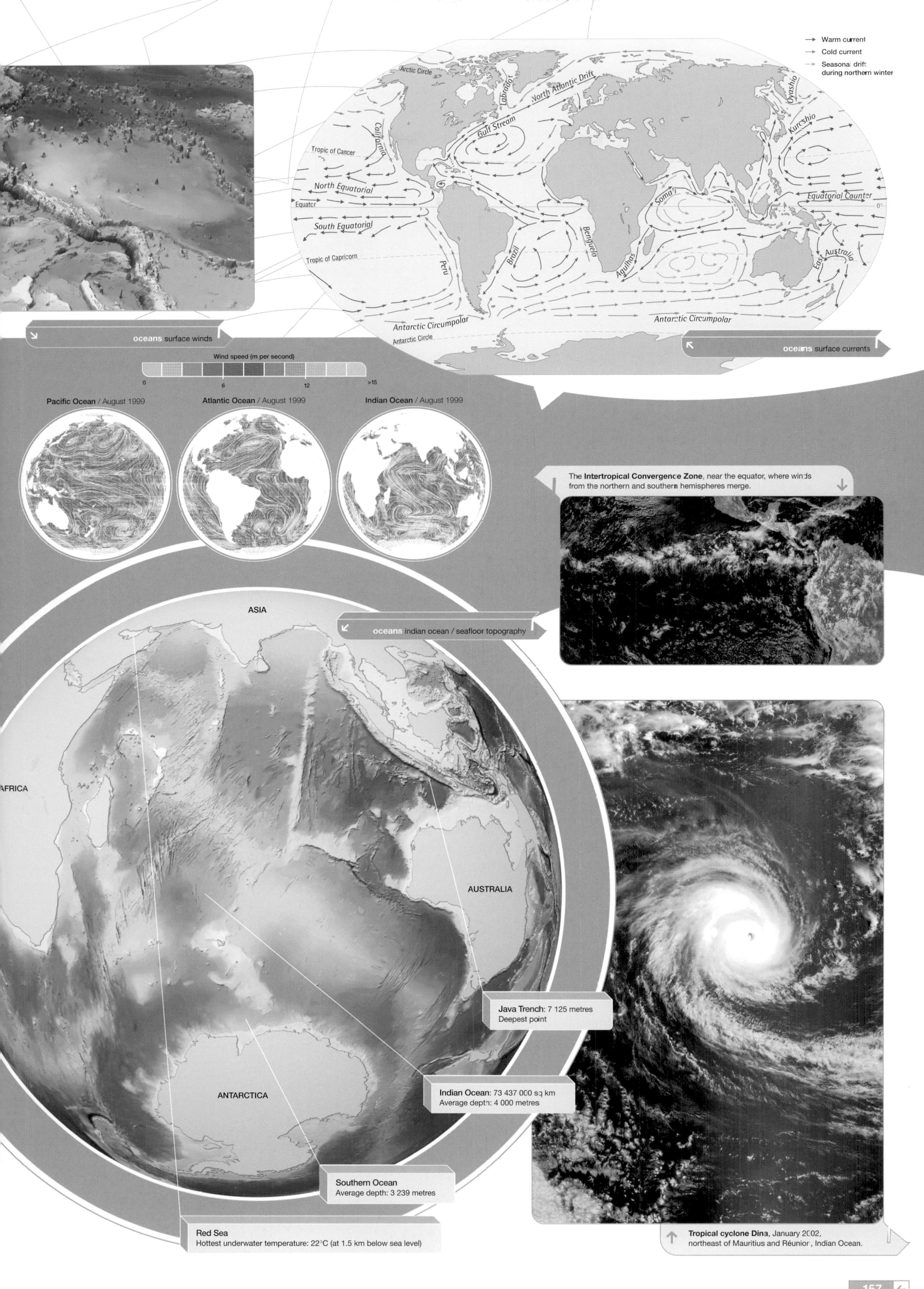

Warm current
Cold current
Seasonal drift:
during northern winter

Arctic Circle
Labrador
North Atlantic Drift
Oyashio
California
Gulf Stream
Kuroshio
Tropic of Cancer
North Equatorial
Equator
Somali
Equatorial Counter
South Equatorial
0°
Tropic of Capricorn
Peru
Brazil
Benguela
Agulhas
East Australia

Antarctic Circumpolar
Antarctic Circumpolar
Antarctic Circle

Wind speed (m per second)

0   6   12   >15

Pacific Ocean / August 1999   Atlantic Ocean / August 1999   Indian Ocean / August 1999

The **Intertropical Convergence Zone**, near the equator, where winds
from the northern and southern hemispheres merge.

ASIA

AFRICA

AUSTRALIA

Java Trench: 7 125 metres
Deepest point

Indian Ocean: 73 437 000 sq km
Average depth: 4 000 metres

ANTARCTICA

Southern Ocean
Average depth: 3 239 metres

Red Sea
Hottest underwater temperature: 22°C (at 1.5 km below sea level)

Tropical cyclone Dina, January 2002,
northeast of Mauritius and Réunion, Indian Ocean.

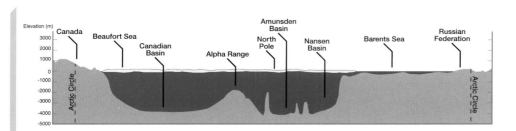

Elevation (m)

Canada | Beaufort Sea | Canadian Basin | Alpha Range | North Pole | Amunsden Basin | Nansen Basin | Barents Sea | Russian Federation

Arctic Circle — Arctic Circle

↑ **poles** cross section of Arctic Ocean from northwest Canada to northwest Russia

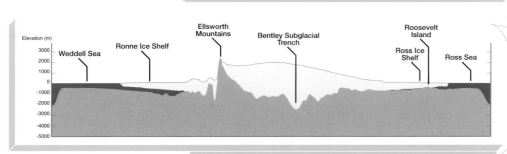

Elevation (m)

Weddell Sea | Ronne Ice Shelf | Ellsworth Mountains | Bentley Subglacial Trench | Roosevelt Island | Ross Ice Shelf | Ross Sea

↑ **poles** cross section of West Antarctica from Ronne Ice Shelf to Ross Ice Shelf

Antarctica, frozen continent lying around the South Pole. ↓

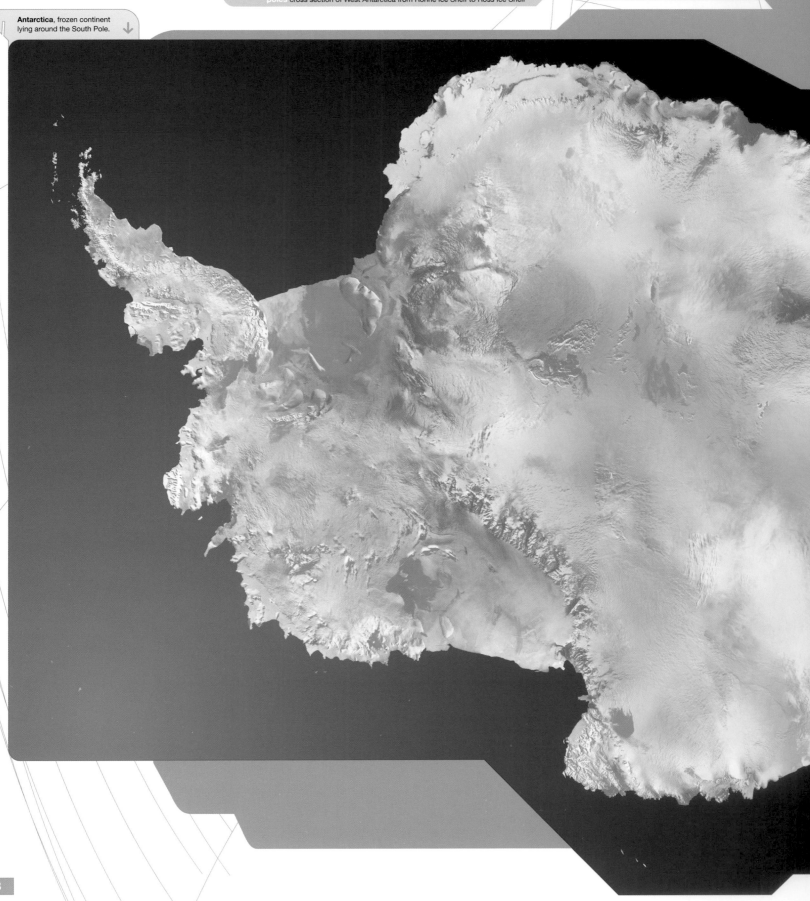

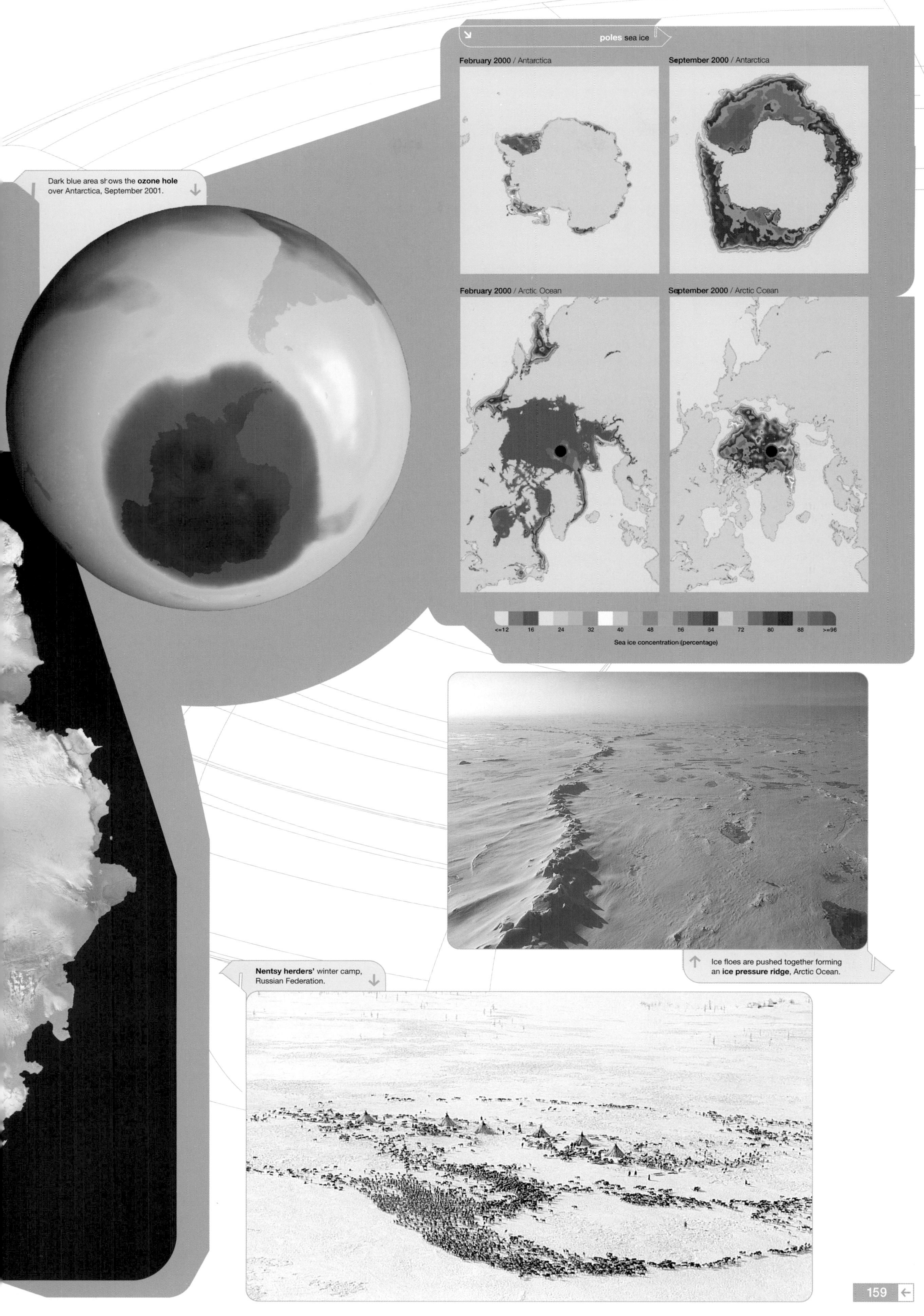

Dark blue area shows the **ozone hole** over Antarctica, September 2001.

February 2000 / Antarctica

September 2000 / Antarctica

February 2000 / Arctic Ocean

September 2000 / Arctic Ocean

<=12   16   24   32   40   48   56   64   72   80   88   >=96

Sea ice concentration (percentage)

Ice floes are pushed together forming an **ice pressure ridge**, Arctic Ocean.

Nentsy herders' winter camp, Russian Federation.

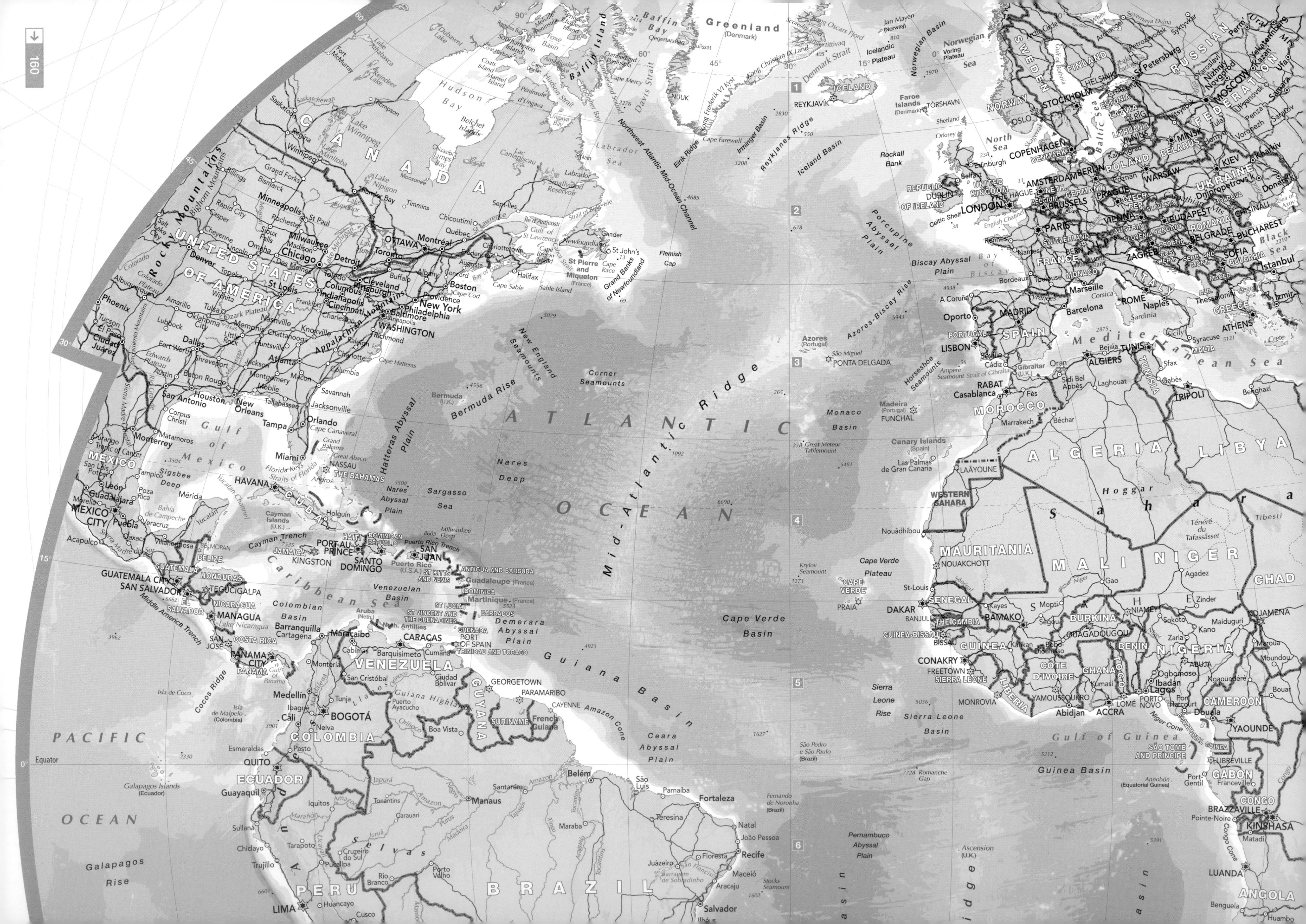

ATLANTIC
OCEAN
PACIFIC
OCEAN
Mid-Atlantic Ridge
CANADA
UNITED STATES OF AMERICA
MEXICO
BRAZIL
PERU
COLOMBIA
VENEZUELA
ECUADOR
GUYANA
SURINAME
Greenland (Denmark)
ICELAND
Hudson Bay
Labrador Sea
Baffin Island
Gulf of Mexico
Caribbean Sea
Sargasso Sea
Guiana Basin
Cape Verde Basin
Gulf of Guinea
Guinea Basin
Norwegian Basin
Iceland Basin
Irminger Basin
Reykjanes Ridge
Porcupine Abyssal Plain
Biscay Abyssal Plain
Azores-Biscay Rise
Hatteras Abyssal Plain
Nares Abyssal Plain
Bermuda Rise
New England Seamounts
Corner Seamounts
Northwest Atlantic Mid-Ocean Channel
Ceara Abyssal Plain
Demerara Abyssal Plain
Pernambuco Abyssal Plain
Sierra Leone Basin
Galapagos Rise
Cocos Ridge
Middle America Trench
Rocky Mountains
UNITED KINGDOM
REPUBLIC OF IRELAND
FRANCE
SPAIN
PORTUGAL
ITALY
GERMANY
POLAND
SWEDEN
NORWAY
FINLAND
RUSSIAN FEDERATION
UKRAINE
BELARUS
ROMANIA
GREECE
MOROCCO
ALGERIA
LIBYA
TUNISIA
MAURITANIA
MALI
NIGER
CHAD
NIGERIA
SENEGAL
GUINEA
SIERRA LEONE
LIBERIA
CÔTE D'IVOIRE
GHANA
BURKINA
CAMEROON
GABON
CONGO
ANGOLA
WESTERN SAHARA
LONDON
PARIS
MADRID
LISBON
ROME
BERLIN
MOSCOW
WASHINGTON
New York
OTTAWA
MEXICO CITY
HAVANA
CARACAS
BOGOTÁ
QUITO
LIMA
DAKAR
ALGIERS
RABAT
Equator

→ 160

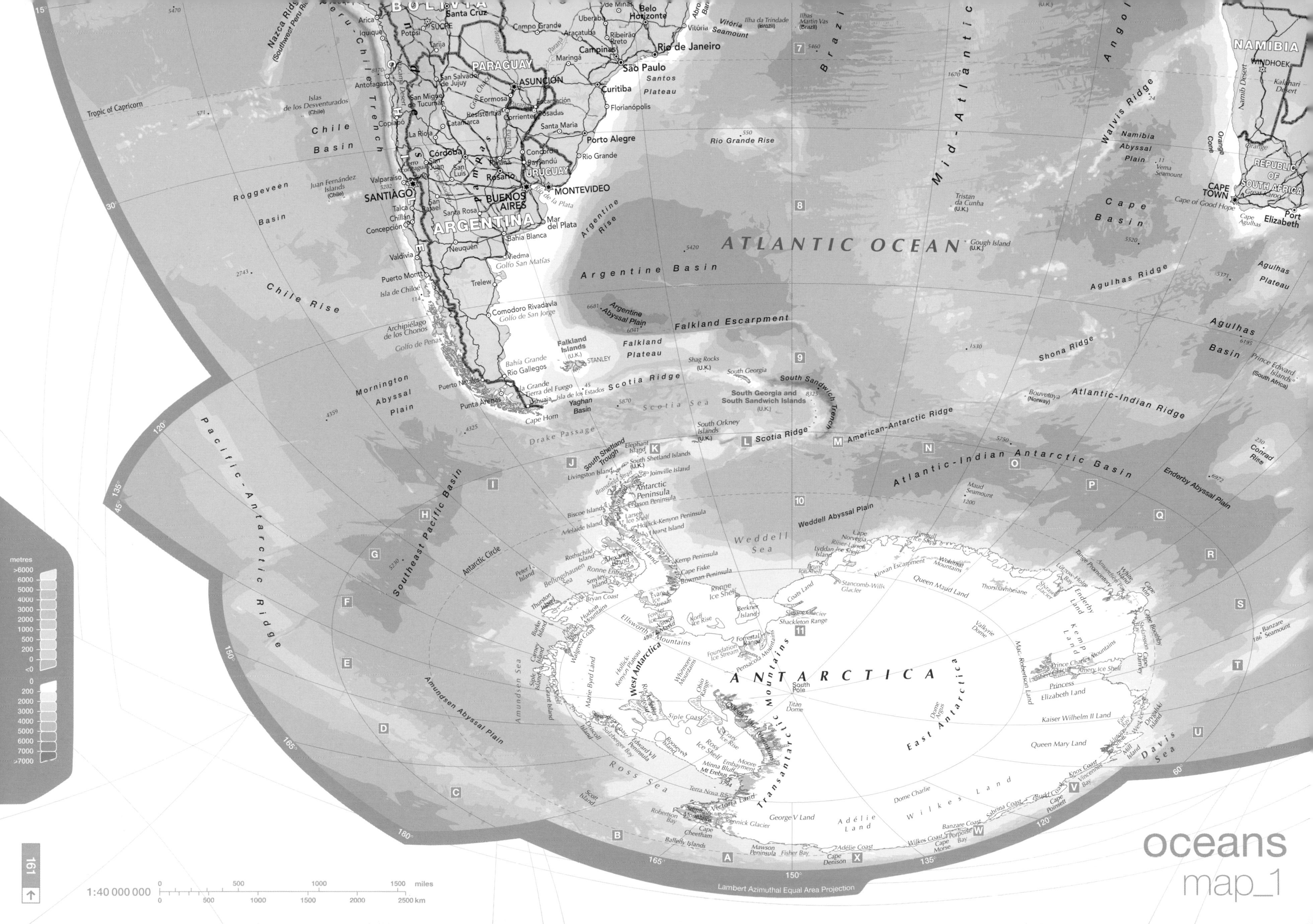

oceans
map_1
ATLANTIC OCEAN
ANTARCTICA
West Antarctica
East Antarctica
Transantarctic Mountains
BOLIVIA
PARAGUAY
URUGUAY
ARGENTINA
NAMIBIA
REPUBLIC OF SOUTH AFRICA
SANTIAGO
BUENOS AIRES
MONTEVIDEO
ASUNCIÓN
CAPE TOWN
WINDHOEK
Rio de Janeiro
São Paulo
Porto Alegre
Curitiba
Florianópolis
Belo Horizonte
Santa Cruz
Córdoba
Rosario
Mar del Plata
Bahía Blanca
Valparaíso
Concepción
Puerto Montt
Punta Arenas
Cape Horn
Port Elizabeth
Cape of Good Hope
Falkland Islands (U.K.)
STANLEY
South Georgia
South Georgia and South Sandwich Islands (U.K.)
South Orkney Islands (U.K.)
South Shetland Islands (U.K.)
Tristan da Cunha (U.K.)
Gough Island (U.K.)
Bouvetøya (Norway)
Prince Edward Islands (South Africa)
Juan Fernández Islands (Chile)
Islas de los Desventurados (Chile)
Argentine Basin
Argentine Abyssal Plain
Argentine Rise
Falkland Escarpment
Falkland Plateau
Scotia Ridge
Scotia Sea
South Sandwich Trench
American-Antarctic Ridge
Atlantic-Indian Ridge
Atlantic-Indian Antarctic Basin
Weddell Abyssal Plain
Weddell Sea
Drake Passage
Yaghan Basin
South Shetland Trough
Mid-Atlantic Ridge
Rio Grande Rise
Walvis Ridge
Namibia Abyssal Plain
Cape Basin
Agulhas Ridge
Agulhas Plateau
Agulhas Basin
Shona Ridge
Conrad Rise
Enderby Abyssal Plain
Maud Seamount
Chile Basin
Chile Rise
Peru-Chile Trench
Nazca Ridge
Roggeveen Basin
Mornington Abyssal Plain
Southeast Pacific Basin
Pacific-Antarctic Ridge
Amundsen Abyssal Plain
Amundsen Sea
Ross Sea
Davis Sea
Antarctic Circle
Tropic of Capricorn
Antarctic Peninsula
Palmer Land
Ellsworth Land
Marie Byrd Land
Queen Maud Land
Enderby Land
Kemp Land
Mac. Robertson Land
Princess Elizabeth Land
Kaiser Wilhelm II Land
Queen Mary Land
Wilkes Land
Adélie Land
George V Land
Victoria Land
Ronne Ice Shelf
Ross Ice Shelf
Amery Ice Shelf
South Pole
Vinson Massif 4897
Mt Erebus 3794
metres
>6000
6000
5000
4000
3000
2000
1000
500
200
0
<0
0
200
2000
3000
4000
5000
6000
7000
>7000
1:40 000 000
0 500 1000 1500 miles
0 500 1000 1500 2000 2500 km
Lambert Azimuthal Equal Area Projection

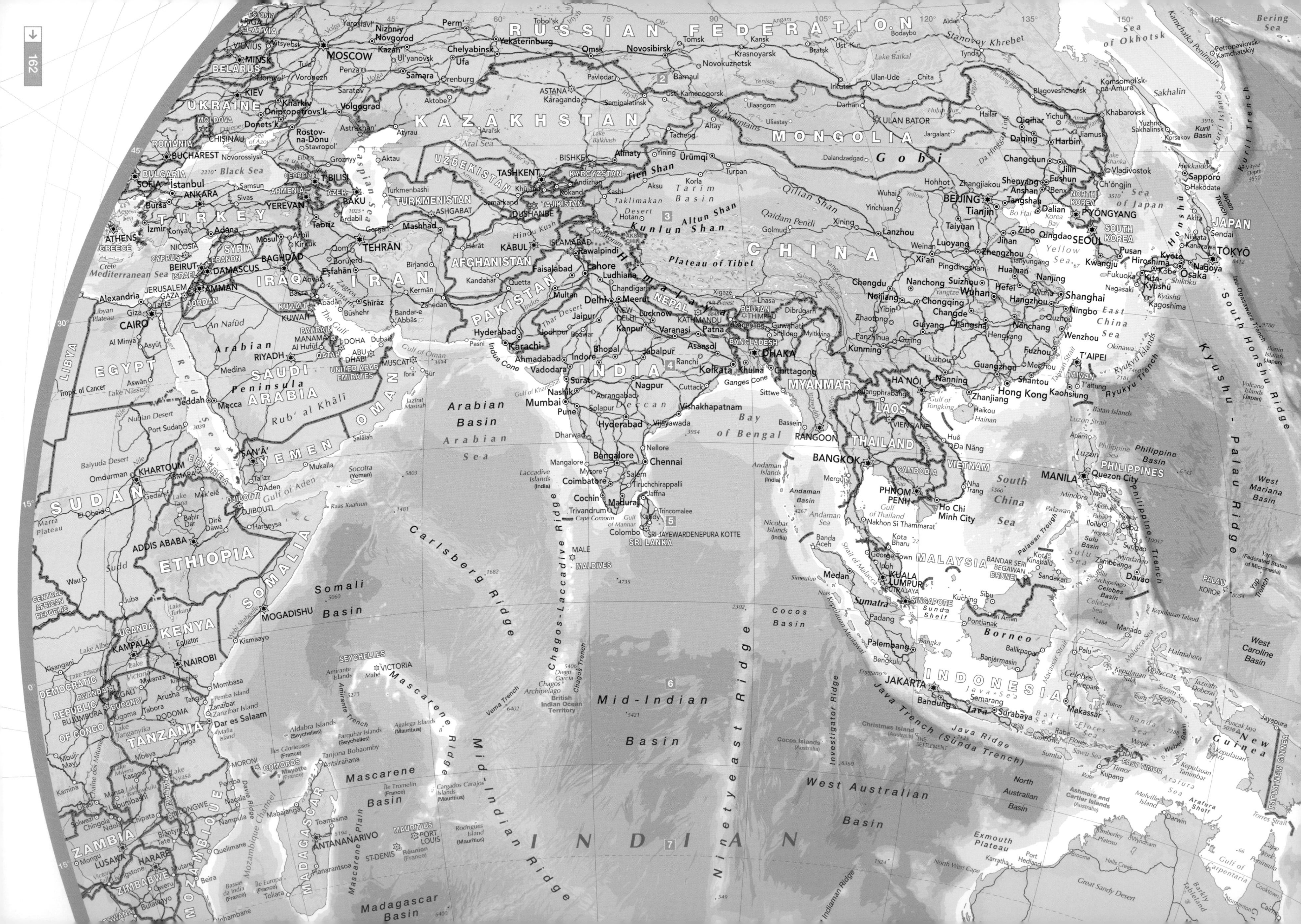
RUSSIAN FEDERATION
KAZAKHSTAN
MONGOLIA
CHINA
INDIA
PAKISTAN
AFGHANISTAN
IRAN
IRAQ
SAUDI ARABIA
OMAN
YEMEN
EGYPT
SUDAN
ETHIOPIA
SOMALIA
KENYA
TANZANIA
ZAMBIA
ZIMBABWE
MOZAMBIQUE
MADAGASCAR
TURKEY
UKRAINE
BELARUS
ROMANIA
BULGARIA
GREECE
SYRIA
JORDAN
UZBEKISTAN
TURKMENISTAN
KYRGYZSTAN
TAJIKISTAN
NEPAL
BHUTAN
BANGLADESH
MYANMAR
THAILAND
LAOS
VIETNAM
CAMBODIA
MALAYSIA
INDONESIA
PHILIPPINES
JAPAN
NORTH KOREA
SOUTH KOREA
TAIWAN
SRI LANKA
MALDIVES
SEYCHELLES
MAURITIUS
COMOROS
MOSCOW
BEIJING
TŌKYŌ
SEOUL
P'YONGYANG
Shanghai
Hong Kong
MANILA
BANGKOK
HA NOI
JAKARTA
SINGAPORE
KUALA LUMPUR
NEW DELHI
Mumbai
Kolkata
DHAKA
KĀBUL
ISLAMABAD
TEHRĀN
BAGHDAD
RIYADH
CAIRO
KHARTOUM
ADDIS ABABA
NAIROBI
MOGADISHU
Dar es Salaam
ANTANANARIVO
ULAN BATOR
ASTANA
TASHKENT
ANKARA
Gobi
Plateau of Tibet
Caspian Sea
Black Sea
Mediterranean Sea
Red Sea
Arabian Sea
Bay of Bengal
South China Sea
East China Sea
Sea of Japan
Sea of Okhotsk
Bering Sea
INDIAN
Arabian Basin
Somali Basin
Mascarene Basin
Mid-Indian Basin
West Australian Basin
North Australian Basin
Cocos Basin
Carlsberg Ridge
Mid-Indian Ridge
Ninetyeast Ridge
Chagos-Laccadive Ridge
Java Trench (Sunda Trench)
Kyushu - Palau Ridge
South Honshu Ridge
Kuril Trench
Philippine Trench
Mozambique Channel
162

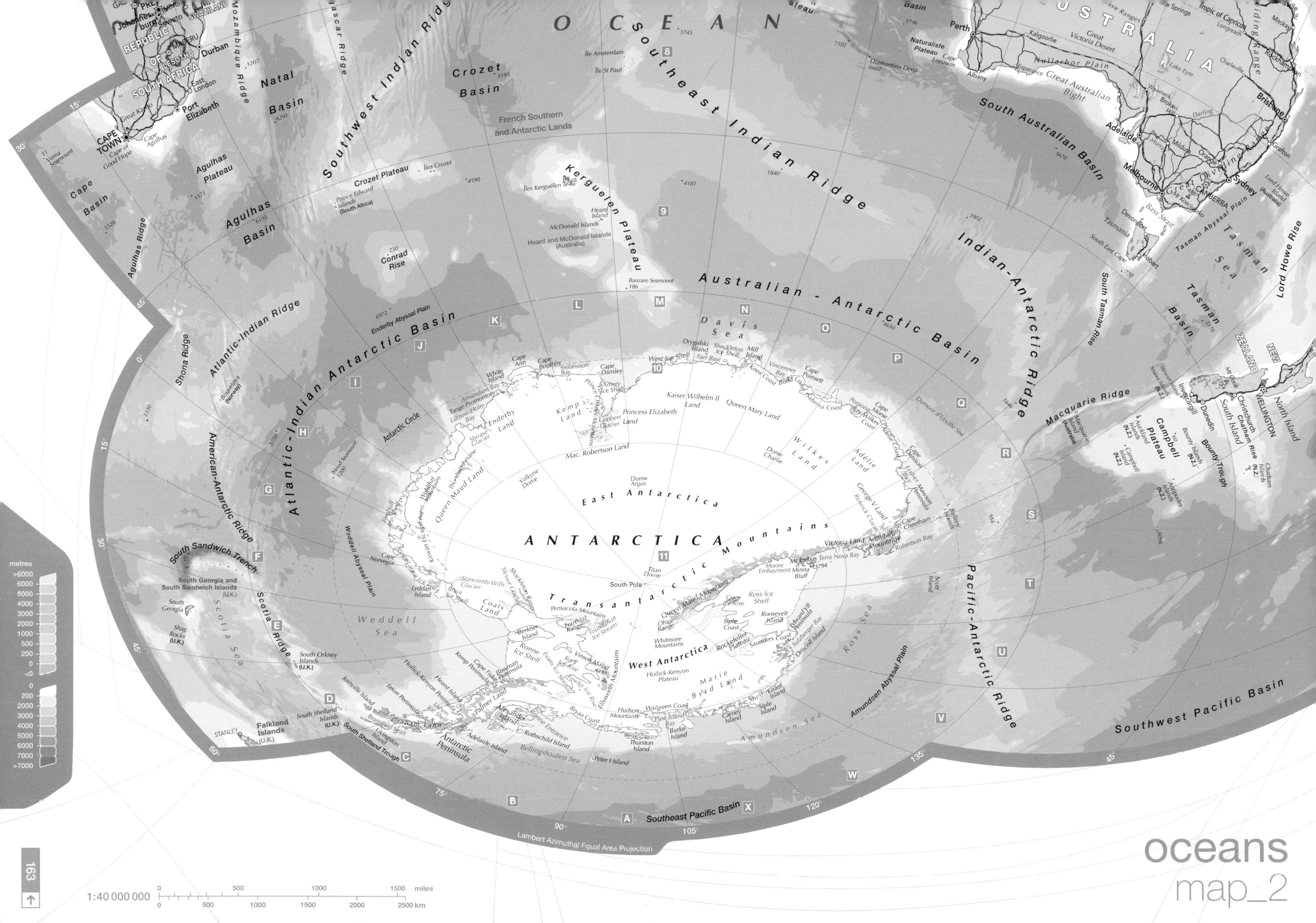

OCEAN
Southeast Indian Ridge
Southwest Indian Ridge
Crozet Basin
Natal Basin
Mozambique Ridge
Agulhas Plateau
Agulhas Basin
Cape Basin
Agulhas Ridge
Crozet Plateau
Conrad Rise
French Southern and Antarctic Lands
Kerguelen Plateau
Heard and McDonald Islands (Australia)
South Australian Basin
Indian-Antarctic Ridge
Australian - Antarctic Basin
Atlantic-Indian Antarctic Basin
Enderby Abyssal Plain
Atlantic-Indian Ridge
Shona Ridge
American-Antarctic Ridge
South Sandwich Trench
Scotia Ridge
Scotia Sea
Weddell Sea
Weddell Abyssal Plain
Davis Sea
ANTARCTICA
East Antarctica
West Antarctica
Transantarctic Mountains
South Pole
Ross Sea
Amundsen Sea
Bellingshausen Sea
Antarctic Peninsula
Pacific-Antarctic Ridge
Amundsen Abyssal Plain
Southwest Pacific Basin
Southeast Pacific Basin
Macquarie Ridge
Campbell Plateau
Bounty Trough
Tasman Basin
Tasman Sea
Lord Howe Rise
South Tasman Rise
NEW ZEALAND
AUSTRALIA
REPUBLIC OF SOUTH AFRICA
CAPE TOWN
Durban
Perth
Adelaide
Melbourne
Sydney
Brisbane
Hobart
WELLINGTON
Lambert Azimuthal Equal Area Projection
metres
1:40 000 000
miles
km

oceans map_2

MONGOLIA
ULAN BATOR

Sea of Okhotsk
Kamchatka Peninsula
Bering Sea
Aleutian Basin

CHINA
BEIJING
Gobi

Shenyang
Changchun
Harbin
Jilin

NORTH KOREA
PYONGYANG
SEOUL
SOUTH KOREA

Sea of Japan
JAPAN
TOKYO
Osaka
Kyoto
Honshū
Kyūshū

Kuril Islands
Kuril Trench
Emperor Seamount Chain
Emperor Trough

Northwest Pacific Basin

NEPAL
BHUTAN
INDIA
BANGLADESH
Kolkata
Hyderabad
Bay of Bengal
Visakhapatnam

MYANMAR
RANGOON
THAILAND
BANGKOK
LAOS
VIENTIANE
CAMBODIA
PHNOM PENH
VIETNAM
HANOI
Ho Chi Minh City

East China Sea
Shanghai
Hong Kong
Kaohsiung
T'AIPEI
TAIWAN

Ryukyu Islands
Ryukyu Trench

Mapmakers Seamounts
Mid - Pacific Mountains
Midway Islands
Hawaii

South China Sea
PHILIPPINES
MANILA
Quezon City
Cebu
Davao

Philippine Sea
Philippine Trench

West Mariana Basin
Mariana Trench
Challenger Deep 10920
East Mariana Basin
Magellan Seamounts

PALAU
KOROR

Caroline Islands
FEDERATED STATES OF MICRONESIA
East Caroline Basin
West Caroline Basin

MARSHALL ISLANDS
Kwajalein

MICRONESIA

Central Pacific Basin

KIRIBATI

MALAYSIA
KUALA LUMPUR
SINGAPORE
Sumatra
Borneo
Sulawesi
Celebes Sea
Sunda Shelf

Cocos Basin
Equator

NAURU
YAREN
Melanesian Basin
Gilbert Islands
BAIRIKI

INDONESIA
JAKARTA
Java Sea
Makassar
Surabaya
Bandung
Bali Sea
Flores Sea
Banda Sea
Arafura Sea
EAST TIMOR
DILI

New Guinea
PAPUA NEW GUINEA
PORT MORESBY
Bismarck Sea
Solomon Sea
SOLOMON ISLANDS
HONIARA

TUVALU
FUNAFUTI

Wallis and Futuna (France)
SAMOA

Java Trench (Sunda Trench)
Investigator Ridge

Ashmore and Cartier Islands (Australia)
Darwin
North Australian Basin

Coral Sea Basin
VANUATU
PORT VILA
NEW CALEDONIA (France)
NOUMEA
FIJI
SUVA
TONGA

Coral Sea

West Australian Basin
INDIAN OCEAN

AUSTRALIA
Great Sandy Desert
Great Victoria Desert
Alice Springs
Perth
Adelaide
CANBERRA
Sydney
Brisbane
Melbourne
Tasmania
Hobart

Great Australian Bight
South Australian Basin

Lord Howe Rise
Norfolk Island Ridge
South Fiji Basin
New Caledonia Trough
Tasman Sea
Tasman Basin

NEW ZEALAND
WELLINGTON
Auckland
North Island
South Island
Christchurch
Chatham Rise
Dunedin
Campbell Plateau
Bounty Trough

Southeast Indian Ridge
Australian - Antarctic Basin
Indian - Antarctic Ridge

1 : 45 000 000

metres
>6000 6000 5000 4000 3000 2000 1000 500 0 <0 0 200 2000 3000 4000 5000 6000 7000 >7000

Lambert Azimuthal Equal Area Projection

0 400 800 1200 miles
0 400 800 1200 1600 2000 km

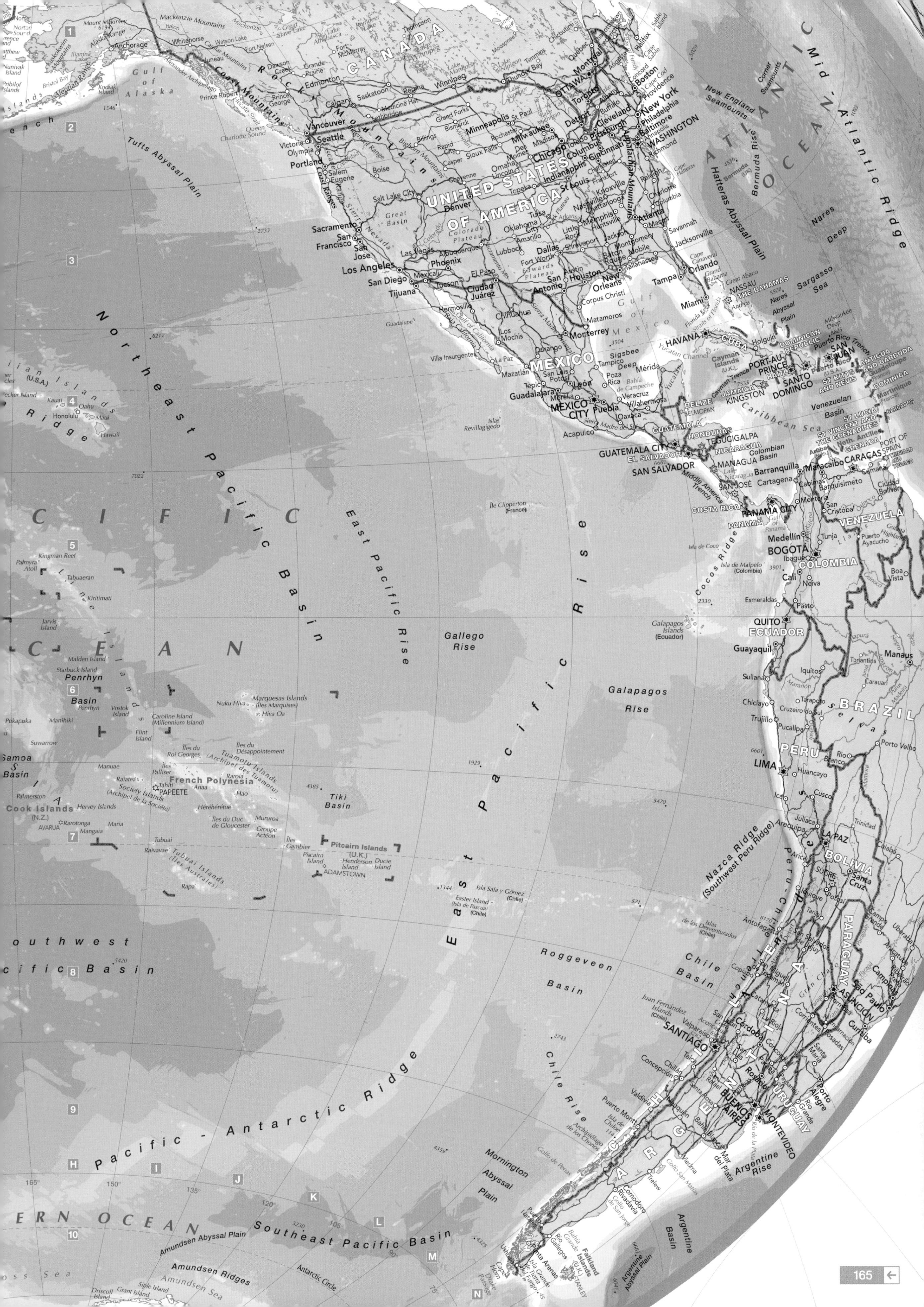
CANADA
UNITED STATES OF AMERICA
MEXICO
ATLANTIC OCEAN
Mid-Atlantic Ridge
Gulf of Alaska
Rocky Mountains
Coast Mountains
Mount McKinley
Anchorage
Vancouver
Seattle
Portland
Sacramento
San Francisco
San Jose
Los Angeles
San Diego
Tijuana
Phoenix
Denver
Salt Lake City
Edmonton
Calgary
Winnipeg
Minneapolis
Chicago
Detroit
Toronto
Montreal
OTTAWA
Boston
New York
Philadelphia
WASHINGTON
Atlanta
Dallas
Houston
San Antonio
New Orleans
Miami
Orlando
Tampa
Gulf of Mexico
Monterrey
MEXICO CITY
Guadalajara
Puebla
HAVANA
CUBA
NASSAU
THE BAHAMAS
Sargasso Sea
Hatteras Abyssal Plain
Bermuda Rise
New England Seamounts
Nares Deep
Caribbean Sea
KINGSTON
PORT-AU-PRINCE
SANTO DOMINGO
SAN JUAN
GUATEMALA CITY
SAN SALVADOR
TEGUCIGALPA
MANAGUA
SAN JOSÉ
PANAMA CITY
CARACAS
VENEZUELA
BOGOTÁ
COLOMBIA
QUITO
ECUADOR
Guayaquil
LIMA
PERU
LA PAZ
BOLIVIA
SUCRE
PARAGUAY
ASUNCIÓN
BRAZIL
São Paulo
SANTIAGO
BUENOS AIRES
MONTEVIDEO
URUGUAY
ARGENTINA
Falkland Islands
Argentine Basin
Argentine Rise
Northeast Pacific Basin
East Pacific Rise
Gallego Rise
Galapagos Rise
Galapagos Islands (Ecuador)
Cocos Ridge
Middle America Trench
Peru-Chile Trench
Nazca Ridge (Southwest Peru Ridge)
Chile Basin
Chile Rise
Roggeveen Basin
Easter Island (Isla de Pascua) (Chile)
Pitcairn Islands (U.K.)
ADAMSTOWN
Tiki Basin
French Polynesia
PAPEETE
Tahiti
Marquesas Islands
Tuamotu Islands
Cook Islands
Penrhyn Basin
Hawaiian Islands
Honolulu
Kingman Reef
Southwest Pacific Basin
Pacific - Antarctic Ridge
Southeast Pacific Basin
Mornington Abyssal Plain
Amundsen Abyssal Plain
Amundsen Ridges
Amundsen Sea
Antarctic Circle
SOUTHERN OCEAN

ARCTIC OCEAN

ATLANTIC OCEAN

PACIFIC OCEAN

CANADA

U.S.A

RUSSIAN FEDERATION

GREENLAND (Kalaallit Nunaat) (Denmark)

ICELAND

NORWAY

SWEDEN

FINLAND

DENMARK

POLAND

GERMANY

UNITED KINGDOM

BELARUS

ESTONIA

LATVIA

LITHUANIA

KAZAKHSTAN

North Pole

North Magnetic Pole (2000)

North Geomagnetic Pole (2000)

Arctic Circle

Seas and water bodies: Beaufort Sea, Chukchi Sea, East Siberian Sea, Laptev Sea, Kara Sea, Barents Sea, White Sea, Greenland Sea, Norwegian Sea, Baffin Bay, Davis Strait, Labrador Sea, Hudson Strait, Denmark Strait, Irminger Basin, Iceland Basin, Norwegian Basin, Greenland Basin, Gulf of Alaska, Bering Sea, Bristol Bay, North Sea, Baltic Sea, Gulf of Bothnia, Gulf of Finland

Ocean floor features: Canada Basin, Canadian Abyssal Plain, Northwind Ridge, Chukchi Plateau, Chukchi Abyssal Plain, Mendeleyev Ridge, Alpha Ridge, Makarov Basin, Lomonosov Ridge, Amundsen Basin, Arctic Mid-Ocean Ridge, Nansen Basin, Yermak Plateau, Voronin Trough, Central Kara Rise, Aleutian Trench, Faroe-Iceland Ridge, Voring Plateau, Icelandic Plateau, Jan Mayen Fracture Zone, Greenland Fracture Zone, Boreas Abyssal Plain

Scale: 1:26 000 000

0 200 400 600 800 1000 miles

0 200 400 600 800 1000 1200 1400 1600 km

Polar Stereographic Projection

Legend — metres:
>6000
6000
5000
4000
3000
2000
1000
500
200
0
<0
200
2000
3000
4000
5000
6000
7000
>7000

ATLANTIC OCEAN

Research stations numbered on the map:

1. Comandante Ferraz (Brazil) A2
2. Arctowski (Poland) A2
3. Jubany (Argentina) A2
4. King Sejong (Korea) A2
5. Artigas (Uruguay) A2
6. Presidente Eduardo Frei (Chile) A2
7. Bellingshausen (Rus. Fed.) A2
8. Great Wall (China) A2
9. Capitán Arturo Prat (Chile) A2
10. General Bernardo O'Higgins (Chile) A2
11. Scott Base (N.Z.) H1
12. McMurdo (U.S.A.) H1
13. Escudero (Chile) A2

SOUTHERN OCEAN

QUEEN MAUD LAND (Norway)

East Antarctica

West Antarctica

Transantarctic Mountains

Polar Plateau

South Pole
Amundsen-Scott (U.S.A.)

South Geomagnetic Pole (2000)

Vostok (Rus. Fed.)

South Magnetic Pole (2000)

ROSS DEPENDENCY (New Zealand)

AUSTRALIAN ANTARCTIC TERRITORY

ADÉLIE LAND (France)

PACIFIC OCEAN

INDIAN OCEAN

Weddell Sea

Ross Sea

Ronne Ice Shelf

Ross Ice Shelf

Filchner Ice Shelf

Wilkes Land

Queen Maud Land

Enderby Land

Davis Sea

ARGENTINE CLAIM

BRITISH ANTARCTIC TERRITORY

CHILEAN CLAIM

Drake Passage

Scotia Sea

Scotia Ridge

American-Antarctic Ridge

Atlantic-Indian-Antarctic Basin

Australian-Antarctic Basin

Atlantic Ocean

Indian-Antarctic Ridge

Macquarie Ridge

Antarctic Peninsula

Bellingshausen Sea

Amundsen Sea

Antarctic Circle

Polar Stereographic Projection

Boundaries on the map represent the status of territorial claims at the time the Antarctic Treaty was implemented in 1959. Under the treaty, such claims are held in abeyance in the interest of international co-operation for scientific purposes.

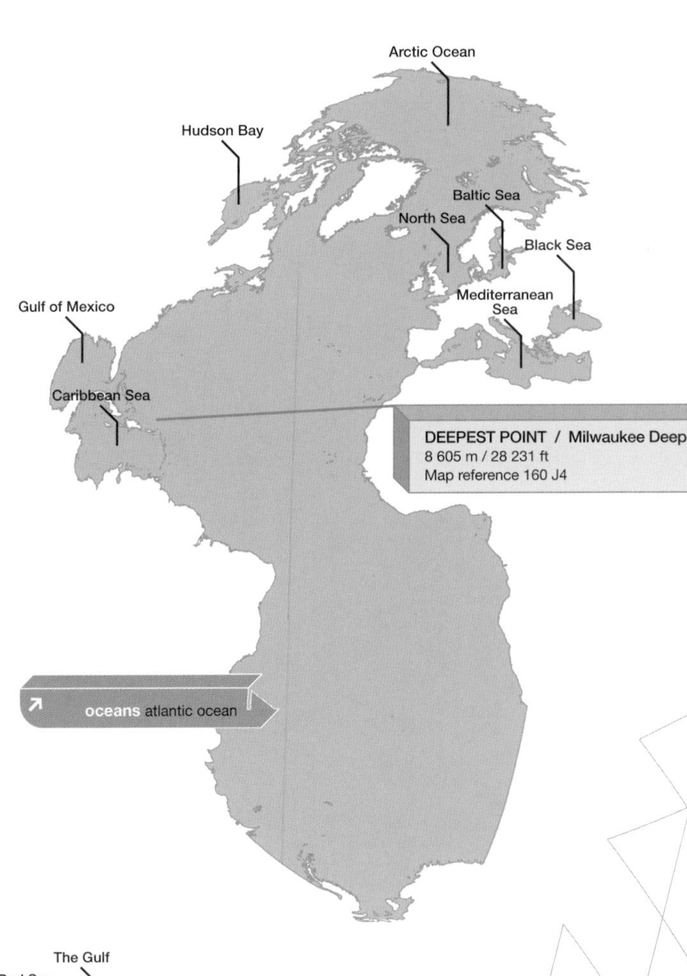

Arctic Ocean

Hudson Bay

Baltic Sea

North Sea

Black Sea

Mediterranean Sea

Gulf of Mexico

Caribbean Sea

DEEPEST POINT / Milwaukee Deep
8 605 m / 28 231 ft
Map reference 160 J4

↗ oceans atlantic ocean

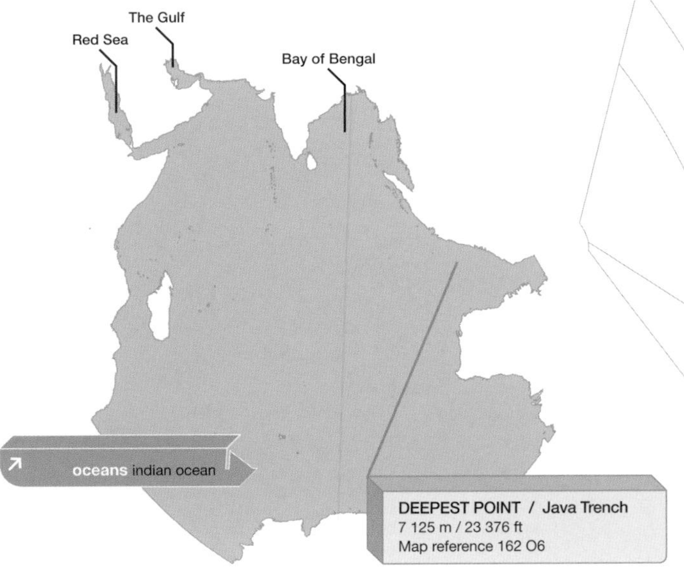

The Gulf

Red Sea

Bay of Bengal

↗ oceans indian ocean

DEEPEST POINT / Java Trench
7 125 m / 23 376 ft
Map reference 162 O6

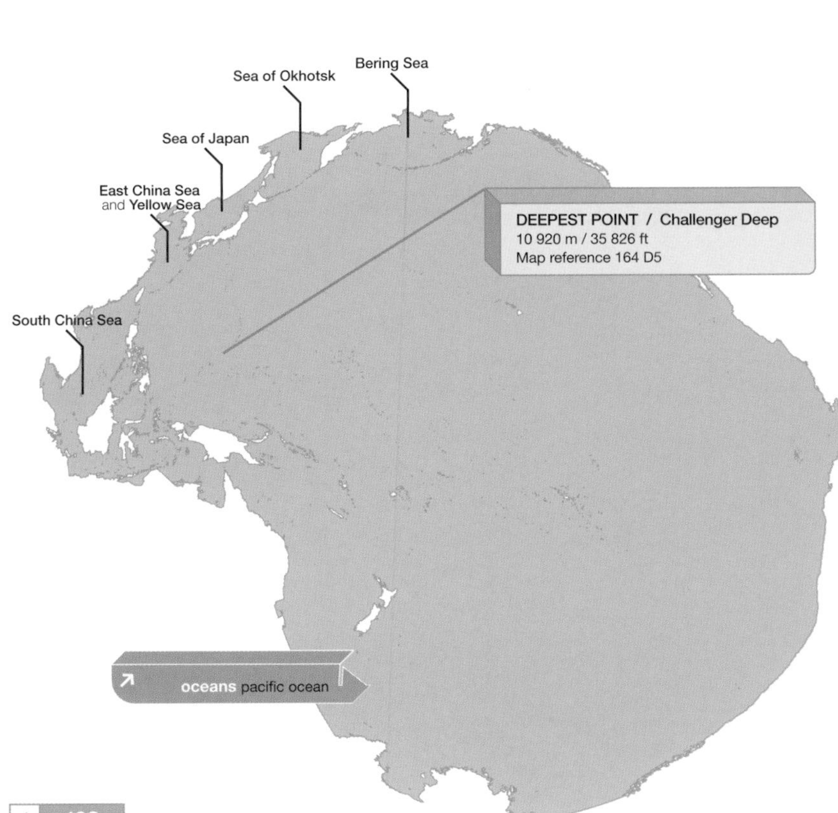

Sea of Okhotsk

Bering Sea

Sea of Japan

East China Sea and Yellow Sea

DEEPEST POINT / Challenger Deep
10 920 m / 35 826 ft
Map reference 164 D5

South China Sea

↗ oceans pacific ocean

ANTARCTICA		
HIGHEST MOUNTAINS	metres	feet
Vinson Massif	4 897	16 066
Mt Tyree	4 852	15 918
Mt Kirkpatrick	4 528	14 855
Mt Markham	4 351	14 275
Mt Jackson	4 190	13 747
Mt Sidley	4 181	13 717
AREA	sq km	sq miles
Total land area (excluding ice shelves)	12 093 000	4 669 292
Ice shelves	1 559 000	601 954
Exposed rock	49 000	18 920
HEIGHTS	metres	feet
Lowest bedrock elevation (Bentley Subglacial Trench)	-2 496	-8 189
Maximum ice thickness (Astrolabe Subglacial Basin)	4 776	15 669
Mean ice thickness (including ice shelves)	1 859	6 099
VOLUME	cubic km	cubic miles
Ice sheet (including ice shelves)	25 400 000	10 160 000
CLIMATE	°C	°F
Lowest screen temperature (Vostok Station, 21st July 1983)	-89.2	-128.6
Coldest place – Annual mean (Plateau Station)	-56.6	-69.9

ATLANTIC OCEAN	area sq km	area sq miles	maximum depth metres	feet
Atlantic Ocean	86 557 000	33 420 000	8 605	28 231
Arctic Ocean	9 485 000	3 662 000	5 450	17 880
Caribbean Sea	2 512 000	970 000	7 680	25 196
Mediterranean Sea	2 510 000	969 000	5 121	16 800
Gulf of Mexico	1 544 000	596 000	3 504	11 495
Hudson Bay	1 233 000	476 000	259	849
North Sea	575 000	222 000	661	2 168
Black Sea	508 000	196 000	2 245	7 365
Baltic Sea	382 000	147 000	460	1 509
INDIAN OCEAN	area sq km	area sq miles	maximum depth metres	feet
Indian Ocean	73 427 000	28 350 000	7 125	23 376
Bay of Benga	2 172 000	839 000	4 500	14 763
Red Sea	453 000	175 000	3 040	9 973
The Gulf	238 000	92 000	73	239
PACIFIC OCEAN	area sq km	area sq miles	maximum depth metres	feet
Pacific Ocean	166 241 000	64 186 000	10 920	35 826
South China Sea	2 590 000	1 000 000	5 514	18 090
Bering Sea	2 261 000	873 000	4 150	13 615
Sea of Okhotsk (Okhotskoye More)	1 392 000	537 000	3 363	11 033
East China Sea (Dong Hai) and Yellow Sea (Huang Hai)	1 202 000	464 000	2 717	8 913
Sea of Japan (East Sea)	1 013 000	391 000	3 743	12 280

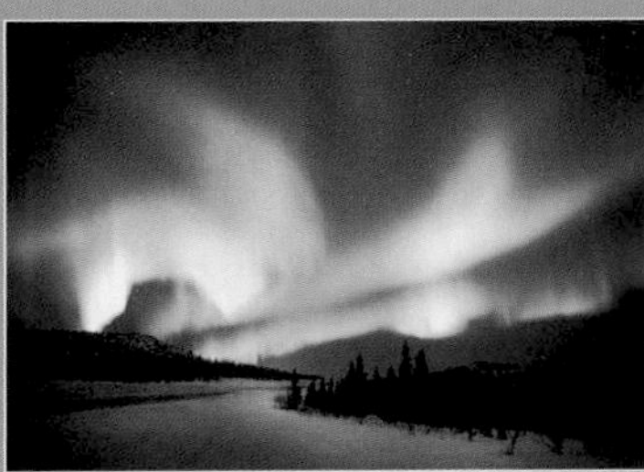

Aurora borealis (northern lights), Alaska, USA

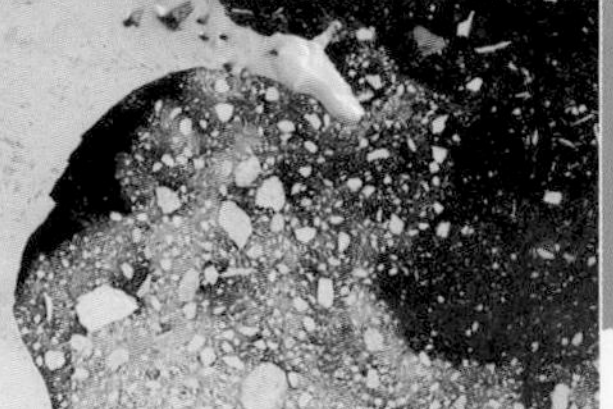

Vortex cloud patterns, Isla Socorro, Pacific Ocean

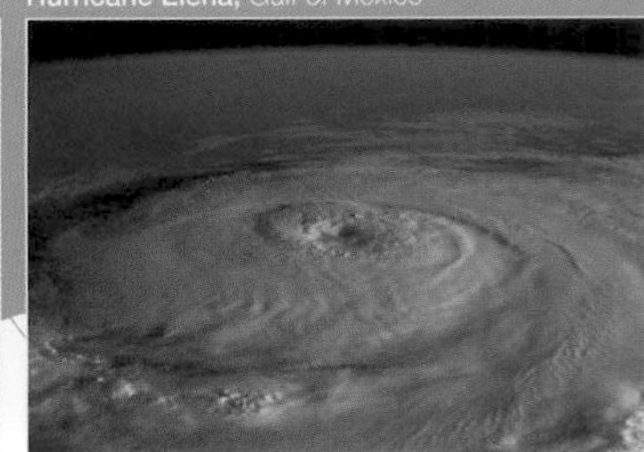

Larsen Ice Shelf, Antarctica

Hurricane Elena, Gulf of Mexico

introduction to the index

The index includes all names shown on the reference maps in the atlas. Each entry includes the country or geographical area in which the feature is located, a page number and an alphanumeric reference. Additional entry details and aspects of the index are explained below.

Name forms
The names policy in this atlas is generally to use local name forms which are officially recognized by the governments of the countries concerned. Rules established by the Permanent Committee on Geographical Names for British Official Use (PCGN) are applied to the conversion of non-roman alphabet names, for example in the Russian Federation, into the roman alphabet used in English.

However, English conventional name forms are used for the most well-known places for which such a form is in common use. In these cases, the local form is included in brackets on the map and appears as a cross-reference in the index. Other alternative names, such as well-known historical names or those in other languages, may also be included in brackets on the map and as cross-references in the index. All country names and those for international physical features appear in their English forms. Names appear in full in the index, although they may appear in abbreviated form on the maps.

Referencing
Names are referenced by page number and by grid reference. The grid reference relates to the alphanumeric values which appear in the margin of each map. These reflect the graticule on the map – the letter relates to longitude divisions, the number to latitude divisions.

Names are generally referenced to the largest scale map page on which they appear. For large geographical features, including countries, the reference is to the largest scale map on which the feature appears in its entirety, or on which the majority of it appears.

Rivers are referenced to their lowest downstream point – either their mouth or their confluence with another river. The river name will generally be positioned as close to this point as possible.

Alternative names
Alternative names appear as cross-references and refer the user to the index entry for the form of the name used on the map.

For rivers with multiple names - for example those which flow through several countries - all alternative name forms are included within the main index entries, with details of the countries in which each form applies.

Administrative qualifiers
Administrative divisions are included in entries to differentiate duplicate names - entries of exactly the same name and feature type within the one country - where these division names are shown on the maps. In such cases, duplicate names are alphabetized in the order of the administrative division names.

Additional qualifiers are included for names within selected geographical areas, to indicate more clearly their location.

Descriptors
Entries, other than those for towns and cities, include a descriptor indicating the type of geographical feature. Descriptors are not included where the type of feature is implicit in the name itself, unless there is a town or city of exactly the same name.

Insets
Where relevant, the index clearly indicates [inset] if a feature appears on an inset map.

Alphabetical order
The Icelandic characters Þ and þ are transliterated and alphabetized as 'Th' and 'th'. The German character ß is alphabetized as 'ss'. Names beginning with Mac or Mc are alphabetized exactly as they appear. The terms Saint, Sainte, etc. are abbreviated to St, Ste, etc, but alphabetized as if in the full form.

Numerical entries
Entries beginning with numerals appear at the beginning of the index, in numerical order. Elsewhere, numerals are alphabetized before 'a'.

Permuted terms
Names beginning with generic geographical terms are permuted - the descriptive term is placed after, and the index alphabetized by, the main part of the name. For example, Mount Everest is indexed as Everest, Mount; Lake Superior as Superior, Lake. This policy is applied to all languages. Permuting has not been applied to names of towns, cities or administrative divisions beginning with such geographical terms. These remain in their full form, for example, Lake Isabella, USA.

Gazetteer entries and connections
Selected entries have been extended to include gazetteer-style information. Important geographical facts which relate specifically to the entry are included within the entry in coloured type.

Entries for features which also appear on, or which have a topical link to, the thematic pages of the atlas include a reference to those pages.

abbreviations

admin. dist.	administrative district	IA	Iowa	plat.	plateau
admin. div.	administrative division	ID	Idaho	P.N.G.	Papua New Guinea
admin. reg.	administrative region	IL	Illinois	Port.	Portugal
Afgh.	Afghanistan	imp. l.	impermanent lake	pref.	prefecture
AK	Alaska	IN	Indiana	prov.	province
AL	Alabama	Indon.	Indonesia	pt	point
Alg.	Algeria	Kazakh.	Kazakhstan	Qld	Queensland
AR	Arkansas	KS	Kansas	Que.	Québec
Arg.	Argentina	KY	Kentucky	r.	river
aut. comm.	autonomous community	Kyrg.	Kyrgyzstan	reg	region
aut. div.	autonomous division	l.	lake	res.	reserve
aut. reg.	autonomous region	LA	Louisiana	resr	reservoir
aut. rep.	autonomous republic	lag.	lagoon	RI	Rhode Island
AZ	Arizona	Lith.	Lithuania	Rus. Fed.	Russian Federation
Azer.	Azerbaijan	Lux.	Luxembourg	S.	South, Southern
b.	bay	MA	Massachusetts	S.A.	South Australia
Bangl.	Bangladesh	Madag.	Madagascar	salt l.	salt lake
B.C.	British Columbia	Man.	Manitoba	Sask.	Saskatchewan
Bol.	Bolivia	MD	Maryland	SC	South Carolina
Bos.-Herz.	Bosnia-Herzegovina	ME	Maine	SD	South Dakota
Bulg.	Bulgaria	Mex.	Mexico	sea chan.	sea channel
c.	cape	MI	Michigan	Serb. and Mont.	Serbia and Montenegro
CA	California	MN	Minnesota	Sing.	Singapore
Cent. Afr. Rep.	Central African Republic	MO	Missouri	Switz.	Switzerland
CO	Colorado	Moz.	Mozambique	Tajik.	Tajikistan
Col.	Colombia	MS	Mississippi	Tanz.	Tanzania
CT	Connecticut	MT	Montana	Tas.	Tasmania
Czech Rep.	Czech Republic	mt.	mountain	terr.	territory
DC	District of Columbia	mts	mountains	Thai.	Thailand
DE	Delaware	N.	North, Northern	TN	Tennessee
Dem. Rep. Congo	Democratic Republic of Congo	nat. park	national park	Trin. and Tob.	Trinidad and Tobago
depr.	depression	N.B.	New Brunswick	Turkm.	Turkmenistan
dept	department	NC	North Carolina	TX	Texas
des.	desert	ND	North Dakota	U.A.E.	United Arab Emirates
Dom. Rep.	Dominican Republic	NE	Nebraska	U.K.	United Kingdom
E.	East, Eastern	Neth.	Netherlands	Ukr.	Ukraine
Equat. Guinea	Equatorial Guinea	NH	New Hampshire	U.S.A.	United States of America
esc	escarpment	NJ	New Jersey	UT	Utah
est.	estuary	NM	New Mexico	Uzbek.	Uzbekistan
Eth.	Ethiopia	N.S.	Nova Scotia	VA	Virginia
Fin.	Finland	N.S.W.	New South Wales	Venez.	Venezuela
FL	Florida	N.T.	Northern Territory	Vic.	Victoria
for.	forest	NV	Nevada	vol.	volcano
Fr. Guiana	French Guiana	N.W.T.	Northwest Territories	vol. crater	volcanic crater
F.Y.R.O.M.	Former Yugoslav Republic of Macedonia	NY	New York	VT	Vermont
g.	gulf	N.Z.	New Zealand	W.	West, Western
GA	Georgia	OH	Ohio	WA	Washington
Guat.	Guatemala	OK	Oklahoma	W.A.	Western Australia
HI	Hawaii	OR	Oregon	WI	Wisconsin
H.K.	Hong Kong	PA	Pennsylvania	WV	West Virginia
Hond.	Honduras	P.E.I.	Prince Edward Island	WY	Wyoming
i.	island	pen.	peninsula	Y.T.	Yukon Territory

↓ 1

1st Cataract *rapids* Egypt 89 G3
2nd Cataract *rapids* Sudan 89 F4
3rd Cataract *rapids* Sudan 89 F5
5th Cataract *rapids* Sudan 89 G5
4th Cataract *rapids* Sudan 89 G5
9 de Julio Arg. 152 E3
25 de Mayo *Buenos Aires* Arg. 152 E3
25 de Mayo *La Pampa* Arg. 152 D4
25 de Mayo *Mendoza* Arg. 152 C3
26 Bakı Komissarı Azer. 79 G3
70 Mile House Canada 122 F5
100 Mile House Canada 122 F5
150 Mile House Canada 122 F4

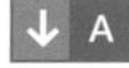

Aabenraa Denmark *see* Åbenrå
Aachen Germany 36 C3
Aalborg Denmark *see* Ålborg
Aalen Germany 36 E4
Aalesund Norway *see* Ålesund
Aaley Lebanon *see* 'Aley
Aalst Belgium 39 F1
Aanaar Fin. *see* Inari
Äänekoski Fin. 32 G3
Aarau Switz. 39 H3
Aarberg Switz. 39 G3
Aarhus Denmark *see* Århus
Aarlen Belgium *see* Arlon
Aarschot Belgium 39 F1
Aasiaat Greenland 121 N3
Aath Belgium *see* Ath
Aavasaksa Fin. 32 F2
Aba China 66 B1
Aba Dem. Rep. Congo 96 A4
Aba Nigeria 93 G4
Abā ad Dūd Saudi Arabia 89 J3
Abā al Afan *oasis* Saudi Arabia 76 E6
Abacaxis *r.* Brazil 147 G6
Abadan Iran *see* Ābādān
Ābādān Iran 80 B4
Ābādeh Iran 80 C4
Ābādeh Ţashk Iran 80 C4
Abadla Alg. 90 E3
Abádszalók Hungary 37 J5
Abaetetuba Brazil 150 B2
Abagnar Qi China *see* Xilinhot
Abaí Para. 149 G6
Abaiang *atoll* Kiribati 164 F5
A Baiuca Spain 42 B1
Abaji Nigeria 93 G3
Abajo Peak U.S.A. 137 H3
Abakaliki Nigeria 93 H4
Abakan Rus. Fed. 62 E1
Abala Congo 94 B5
Abala Niger 93 F2
Abalak Niger 93 G2
Abana Turkey 78 C2
Abancay Peru 148 B3
Abanga *r.* Gabon 94 A5
Abarqū Iran 80 C4
Abarshahr Iran *see* Neyshābūr
Abashiri Japan 64 F3
Abashiri-wan *b.* Japan 64 F3
Abasula *waterhole* Kenya 96 C5
Abau P.N.G. 106 D3
Abaya, Lake Eth. 96 C3
Ābaya Hāyk' Eth. *see* Abaya, Lake
Ābay Wenz *r.* Eth./Sudan 76 B7 *see* Blue Nile
Abaza Rus. Fed. 62 E1
Abba Cent. Afr. Rep. 94 B3
Abbadia San Salvatore Italy 44 C3
Abbāsābād Iran 80 D3
Abbasanta *Sardinia* Italy 45 B4
Abbatis Villa France *see* Abbeville
Abbe, Lake Djibouti/Eth. 96 D2
Abbeville France 38 D1
Abbeville *GA* U.S.A. 129 C6
Abbeville *LA* U.S.A. 133 C6
Abbeville *SC* U.S.A. 129 C5
Abbey Canada 123 I5
Abbeyfeale Rep. of Ireland 35 B5
Abbiategrasso Italy 44 B2
Abborrträsk Sweden 32 E2
Abbot Ice Shelf Antarctica 167 K2
Abbotsford Canada 134 B2
Abbotsford U.S.A. 132 D2
Abbott *NM* U.S.A. 135 F5
Abbott *VA* U.S.A. 130 C5
Abbott *WV* U.S.A. 130 C4
Abbottabad Pak. 81 H3
'Abd al 'Azīz, Jabal *hill* Syria 79 E3
'Abd al Kūrī *i.* Yemen 76 E7
'Abd Allah, Khawr *sea chan.* Iraq/Kuwait 79 G5
Abd al Ma'asīr *well* Saudi Arabia 77 D4
Ābdānān Iran 80 A3
Abdollāhābād Iran 80 D2
Abdulino Rus. Fed. 29 J5
Abéché Chad 88 D6
Abejukolo Nigeria 93 G4
Abelbod *well* Mali 93 E1
Abellinum Italy *see* Avellino
Abel Tasman National Park N.Z. 113 C3
Abengourou Côte d'Ivoire 92 E4
Abenójar Spain 42 D3
Åbenrå Denmark 33 C5
Abensberg Germany 36 E4
Abeokuta Nigeria 93 F4
Abera Eth. 96 B3
Aberaeron U.K. 35 D5
Abercorn Zambia *see* Mbala
Aberdare U.K. 35 E6
Aberdare National Park Kenya 96 C5
Aberdaron U.K. 35 D5
Aberdaugleddau U.K. *see* Milford Haven
Aberdeen Australia 112 D4
Aberdeen *Hong Kong* China 67 [inset]
Aberdeen S. Africa 98 E7
Aberdeen U.K. 34 E3
Aberdeen *MD* U.S.A. 131 E4
Aberdeen *MS* U.S.A. 129 A5
Aberdeen *SD* U.S.A. 132 B2
Aberdeen *WA* U.S.A. 134 B3
Aberdeen Lake Canada 123 L1
Aberfeldy U.K. 34 E3
Aberfoyle U.K. 34 D3
Abergavenny U.K. 35 E6
Abergwaun U.K. *see* Fishguard
Aberhonddu U.K. *see* Brecon
Abermaw U.K. *see* Barmouth
Abertawe U.K. *see* Swansea
Aberteifi U.K. *see* Cardigan
Aberystwyth U.K. 35 D5
Abeshr Chad *see* Abéché
Abez' Rus. Fed. 28 L2
Abhā Saudi Arabia 89 I5
Abhar Iran 80 B2
Abhar Rūd *r.* Iran 80 B3
Abia *state* Nigeria 93 G4
Abiad, Bahr el *r.* Sudan/Uganda 96 B2 *see* White Nile
Ābiata Hāyk' *l.* Eth. 96 C3
Ab-i-Bazuft *r.* Iran 80 B4
Abibe, Serranía de *mts* Col. 146 B2

▶Abidjan Côte d'Ivoire 92 D4
Former capital of Côte d'Ivoire. 4th most populous city in Africa.
africa 86–87
world 16–17

Ab-i-Istada *l.* Afgh. 81 G3
Abijatta-Shalla National Park Eth. 96 C3
Ab-i-Kavīr *salt flat* Iran 80 D3
Abilene *KS* U.S.A. 132 B4
Abilene *TX* U.S.A. 133 B5
Abingdon U.S.A. 130 B5
Abington U.S.A. 131 H2
Abington Reef Australia 111 G3
Abinsk Rus. Fed. 29 F7
Ab-i-Panja *r.* Afgh./Tajik. *see* Pyandzh
Ab-i-Safed *r.* Afgh. 81 F2
Abiseo, Parque Nacional *nat. park* Peru 148 A1
Abisko nationalpark *nat. park* Sweden 32 E1
Abitibi *r.* Canada 124 D3
Abitibi, Lake Canada 124 D3
Āb Naft *r.* Iraq 79 F4
Abnūb Egypt 89 F3
Åbo Fin. *see* Turku
Abohar India 74 B3
Aboisso Côte d'Ivoire 92 E4
Aboke Sudan 96 B2
Abomey Benin 93 F4
Abongabong, Gunung *mt.* Indon. 58 B1
Abong Mbang Cameroon 93 I5
Abou Déia Chad 94 C2
Abou Goulem Chad 88 D6
Abqaiq Saudi Arabia 76 D4
Abra, Lago del *l.* Arg. 152 E5
Abraka Nigeria 93 G4
Abra Pampa Arg. 148 D5
'Abri Sudan 89 F4
Abrolhos Bank *sea feature* S. Atlantic Ocean 161 L7
Abrud Romania 46 C1
Abruzzi *admin. reg.* Italy *see* Abruzzo
Abruzzo *admin. reg.* Italy 44 D3
Abruzzo, Parco Nazionale d' *nat. park* Italy 44 D4
'Abs Yemen 89 I5
Absalom, Mount Antarctica 167 B1
Absaroka Range *mts* U.S.A. 134 E3
Absecon U.S.A. 131 F4
Abşeron Yarımadası *pen.* Azer. 79 G2
Abţar, Jabal al *hills* Syria 77 C2
Abū aḍ Ḍuhūr Syria 77 C2
Abū al Ḥusayn, Qā' *imp. l.* Jordan 77 D3
Abū 'Alī *i.* Saudi Arabia 80 B5
Abu al Jirab *i.* U.A.E. 80 C5
Abū 'Āmūd, Wādī *watercourse* Jordan 77 C4
Abū 'Arīsh Saudi Arabia 89 I5
Abū Ballāş *hill* Egypt 89 E3
Abu Deleiq Sudan 89 G6

▶Abu Dhabi U.A.E. 80 C5
Capital of the United Arab Emirates.

Abu Gabra Sudan 94 E2
Abu Gubeiha Sudan 96 A2
Abū Ḥafnah, Wādī *watercourse* Jordan 77 D3
Abū Ḥallūfah, Jabal *hill* Jordan 77 C4
Abu Hamed Sudan 89 G5
Abu Haraz Sudan 89 G5
Abu Hashim Sudan 89 G5
Abu Higar Sudan 89 G6

▶Abuja Nigeria 93 G3
Capital of Nigeria.

Abū Kamāl Syria 79 E4
Abū Kammāsh Libya 88 A1
Abu La'ot *watercourse* Sudan 89 F6
Abū Latt Island Saudi Arabia 89 I5
Abū Madd, Ra's *hd* Saudi Arabia 89 H3
Abu Matariq Sudan 94 E2
Abu Mena *tourist site* Egypt 78 B5
Abu Mena *tourist site* Egypt 89 F2
Abumombazi Dem. Rep. Congo 94 D4
Abu Musa *i.* The Gulf 80 C5
Abū Mūsá, Jazīreh-ye *i.* The Gulf *see* Abu Musa
Abunã *r.* Bol. 148 D2
Abunã Brazil 148 D2
Abunai Brazil 146 E5
Abū Nā'im *well* Libya 88 C2
Abune Yosēf *mt.* Eth. 96 C2
Abu Zabad Sudan 89 F6
Abū Nujaym Libya 88 B2
Abū Qīr, Khalīj *b.* Egypt 78 B5
Abū Qurīn Libya 88 B2
Abū Rawthah, Jabal *mt.* Egypt 77 B5
Aburo *mt.* Dem. Rep. Congo 96 A4
Abu Road India 74 B4
Abū Rubayq Saudi Arabia 89 H4
Abū Rujmayn, Jabal *mts* Syria 77 D2
Abū Sawādah *well* Saudi Arabia 80 B5
Abu Shagara, Ras *pt* Sudan 89 H4
Abu Simbel Temple *tourist site* Egypt 89 F4
Abū Şukhayr Iraq 79 F5
Abū Şunbul Egypt 89 F4
Abu Tabaq *well* Sudan 76 A5
Abū Ţarfā', Wādī *watercourse* Egypt 77 A5
Abut Head N.Z. 113 B3
Abū Ţuyūr, Jabal *mt.* Egypt 89 G3
Abū 'Uwayqīlah *well* Egypt 77 B4
Abuye Meda *mt.* Eth. 96 C2
Abu Zabad Sudan 89 F6
Abū Ẓabī U.A.E. *see* Abu Dhabi
Abū Ẓanīmah Egypt 89 G2
Abwong Sudan 96 B2
Åby Sweden 33 E4
Abyad Sudan 89 E6
Abyaḍ, Jabal al *mts* Syria 77 C2
Abyār al Hakīm *well* Libya 88 D2
Abyār an Nakhīlah *well* Libya 88 D2
Abydos Australia 108 B5
Abyei Sudan 94 F2
Abyssinia *country* Africa *see* Ethiopia
Acacias Col. 146 C4
Acadia *prov.* Canada *see* Nova Scotia
Acadia National Park U.S.A. 131 I1
Açailândia Brazil 150 C3
Acamarachi *mt.* Chile *see* Pili, Cerro
Acampamento de Caça do Mucusso Angola 95 D9
Acandí Col. 146 B2
Acaponeta Mex. 126 E7
Acapulco Mex. 138 E5
Acapulco de Juárez Mex. *see* Acapulco
Acará Brazil 150 B2
Acará *r.* Brazil 150 B2
Acará Mirí *r.* Brazil 150 B2
Acaraú Brazil 150 D2
Acaraú *r.* Brazil 150 D2
Acaray, Represa de *resr* Para. 149 G6
Acarí Peru 148 B3
Acarí *r.* Peru 148 B3
Acari, Serra *hills* Brazil/Guyana 147 G4
Acarigua Venez. 146 D2
Acatlan Mex. 138 E5
Accho Israel *see* 'Akko
Accomac U.S.A. 131 F5
Accomack U.S.A. *see* Accomac

▶Accra Ghana 93 E4
Capital of Ghana.

Aceguá Brazil 152 G2
Aceh *admin. dist.* Indon. 58 B1
Achacachi Bol. 148 C4
Achaguas Venez. 146 D3
Achalpur India 74 C5
Achampet India 72 C2
Achan Rus. Fed. 64 D2
Achanta India 73 D2
Achayvayam Rus. Fed. 27 R3
Acheh *admin. dist.* Indon. *see* Aceh
Achemelmel *well* Mali 91 F5
Achemmīm *well* Mauritania 92 D1
Acheng China 64 A3
Achern Germany 36 D4
Achhota India 72 D1
Achikulak Rus. Fed. 79 F1
Achill Island Rep. of Ireland 35 A5
Achim Germany 36 D2
Achin *admin. dist.* Indon. *see* Aceh
Achinsk Rus. Fed. 27 J4
Achit Rus. Fed. 28 K4
Achkhoy-Martan Rus. Fed. 79 F2
Achnasheen U.K. 34 D3
Aci Castello *Sicily* Italy 45 E6
Acıgöl *l.* Turkey 78 B3
Acıpayam Turkey 78 B3
Acireale *Sicily* Italy 45 E6
Ackerman U.S.A. 129 A5
Acklins Island Bahamas 127 L7
Acobamba Peru 148 B2
Acomayo *Cusco* Peru 148 C3
Acomayo *Huánuco* Peru 148 A2

▶Aconcagua, Cerro *mt.* Arg. 152 C3
Highest mountain in South America.
southamerica 142–143

Acopiara Brazil 150 E3
Acora Peru 148 C3
A Coruña Spain 42 B1
Acostambo Peru 148 B3
Acquapendente Italy 44 C3
Acqui Terme Italy 44 B2
Acragas *Sicily* Italy *see* Agrigento
Acraman, Lake *salt flat* Australia 109 F8
Acre *r.* Brazil 148 D2
Acre *state* Brazil 148 C2
Acre Israel *see* 'Akko
Acri Italy 45 F5
Actéon, Groupe *is* Fr. Polynesia 165 I7
Acton Canada 130 C2
Acton U.S.A. 136 C4
Açuã *r.* Brazil 149 D1
Acunum Acusio France *see* Montélimar
Açurizal Brazil 149 F3
Ada Ghana 93 F4
Ada *OH* U.S.A. 130 B3
Ada *OK* U.S.A. 133 B5
Ada Serb. and Mont. 46 B2
Ādaba Eth. 96 C3
Adabazar Turkey *see* Sakarya
Adaf, Djebel *mts* Alg. 91 H5
Adaja *r.* Spain 42 D2
Adak U.S.A. 120 B4
Adak Island U.S.A. 120 B4
Adalia Turkey *see* Antalya
Adam Oman 76 F5
Adam, Mount Falkland Is 153 F7
Adamaoua *prov.* Cameroon 93 I4
Adamas Greece 47 D6
Adamawa *state* Nigeria 93 H3
Adamclisi Romania 46 E2
Adamello *mt.* Italy 44 C1
Adams *MA* U.S.A. 131 G2
Adams *NY* U.S.A. 131 E2
Adam's Bridge *sea feature* India/Sri Lanka 72 C4
Adams Center U.S.A. 131 E2
Adams Lake Canada 122 G5
Adams Mountain U.S.A. 122 D4
Adam's Peak Sri Lanka 72 D5
Adams Peak U.S.A. 136 B2

▶Adamstown Pitcairn Is 165 J7
Capital of the Pitcairn Islands.

'Adan Yemen *see* Aden
Adana Turkey 78 C3
Adana *prov.* Turkey 77 B1
Adana Yemen *see* Aden
'Adan as Sughra Yemen 96 E1
Adang, Teluk *b.* Indon. 59 G3
Adani Nigeria 93 G4
Adapazari Turkey *see* Sakarya
Adare Rep. of Ireland 35 B5
Adare, Cape Antarctica 167 H2
Adaut Indon. 108 E2
Adavale Australia 111 F5
Adban Afgh. 81 G2
Adda *r.* Italy 44 B2
Aḍ Ḍab'ah Egypt 41 H5
Ad Dabbah Sudan *see* Ed Debba
Ad Dafīnah Saudi Arabia 89 I4
Ad Daghghārah Iraq 79 F4
Ad Dahnā' *des.* Saudi Arabia 76 D5
Ad Dakhla W. Sahara 90 B5
Ad Damir Sudan *see* Ed Damer
Ad Dammām Saudi Arabia *see* Dammam
Addanki India 72 C3
Ad Daqahlīyah *governorate* Egypt 78 B5
Ad Dār al Ḥamrā' Saudi Arabia 89 H3
Ad Darb Saudi Arabia 89 I5
Addatigala India 73 D2
Ad Dawḥah Qatar *see* Doha
Ad Dawr *plain* Syria 77 C2
Ad Dibdibah *plain* Saudi Arabia 80 A5
Ad Dir'īyah Saudi Arabia 76 D5

▶Addis Ababa Eth. 96 C2
Capital of Ethiopia.

Addison U.S.A. 131 E2
Ad Dīwānīyah Iraq 79 F5
Ad Dīwānīyah *governorate* Iraq *see* Al Qādisīyah
Addo Elephant National Park S. Africa 98 E7
Addoo Atoll Maldives *see* Addu Atoll
Addu Atoll Maldives 71 D12
Ad Duwayd *well* Saudi Arabia 89 I2
Ad Duwaym Sudan *see* Ed Dueim
Adel U.S.A. 132 C3

▶Adelaide Australia 112 A4
State capital of South Australia.

Adelaide Bahamas 129 D7
Adelaide Island Antarctica 167 L2
Adelaide River Australia 110 B2
Adelebsen Germany 36 D3
Adele Island Australia 108 C3
Adélie Coast Antarctica 167 G2
Adélie Land *reg.* Antarctica 167 G2
Aden Yemen 76 C7
Aden, Gulf of Somalia/Yemen 96 E2
Aderbissinat Niger 93 G2
Aderno *Sicily* Italy *see* Adrano
Adesar India 74 A5
Adhámas Greece *see* Adamas
Adhan, Jabal *mt.* U.A.E. 80 D5
Adh Dhayd U.A.E. 80 C5
'Adhfā' *well* Saudi Arabia 79 E5
'Ādhirīyāt, Jibāl al *mts* Jordan 77 C4
Adi *i.* Indon. 57 H6
Ādī Ārk'ay Eth. 89 H6
Adícora Venez. 146 D2
'Adid Umm Inderab *well* Sudan 89 F6
Adige *r.* Italy 44 D2
Ādīgrat Eth. 89 H6
Adıgüzel Barajı *resr* Turkey 78 B3
Adi Keyih Eritrea 89 H6
Adi Kwala Eritrea 89 H6
Adilabad India 72 C2
Adilanga Uganda 96 B4
Adin U.S.A. 134 B4
Adīrī Libya 88 B3
Adirondack Mountains U.S.A. 131 F1
Ādīs Alem Eth. 68 B6
Ādīs Zemen Eth. 96 C1
Adi Ugri Eritrea *see* Mendefera
Adıyaman Turkey 79 D3
Adjud Romania 46 E1
Adjumani Uganda 96 A4
Adlavik Islands Canada 125 J2
Admiralty Inlet Canada 121 K2
Admiralty Island U.S.A. 120 F4
Admiralty Island National Monument - Kootznoowoo Wilderness *nat. park* U.S.A. 120 F4
Admiralty Islands P.N.G. 57 K6
Admiralty Mountains Antarctica 164 F10
Ādo Eth. 96 E3
Ado-Ekiti Nigeria 93 G4
Adok Sudan 96 A2
Adolfo Gonzáles Chaves Arg. 152 E4
Adolfsström Sweden 32 E2
Adonara *i.* Indon. 108 C2
Adoni India 72 C3
Adour *r.* France 38 C5
Adra India 75 E5
Adra Spain 42 E4
Adra *r.* Spain 42 E4
Adramyttium Turkey *see* Edremit
Adramyttium, Gulf of Turkey *see* Edremit Körfezi
Adrano *Sicily* Italy 45 E6
Adrar Alg. 91 E4
Adrar *mts* Alg. 91 G4
Adrar *hills* Mali *see* Ifôghas, Adrar des
Adrar *admin. reg.* Mauritania 90 C5
Adraskand *r.* Afgh. 81 E3
Adré Chad 88 D6
Adrian *MI* U.S.A. 130 A3
Adrian *TX* U.S.A. 133 A5
Adrianople Turkey *see* Edirne
Adrianopolis Turkey *see* Edirne
Adriatic Sea Europe 44 D2
Adua Eth. *see* Ādwa
Adunara *i.* Indon. *see* Adonara
Adur India 72 C4
Adusa Dem. Rep. Congo 94 F4
Adutiškis Lith. 33 G5
Aduwa Eth. *see* Ādwa
Adverse Well Australia 108 C5
Ādwa Eth. 89 H6
Adwufia Ghana 92 E4
Adycha *r.* Rus. Fed. 27 N3
Adygeysk Rus. Fed. 79 D1
Adyk Rus. Fed. 29 H7
Adzhiyan Turkm. 80 C2
Adzopé Côte d'Ivoire 92 E4
Adz'va *r.* Rus. Fed. 28 L2
Adz'vavom Rus. Fed. 28 K2
Aegean Sea Greece/Turkey 47 D5
Aegina *i.* Greece *see* Aigina
Aegviidu Estonia 33 G4
Aegyptus *country* Africa *see* Egypt
Aela Jordan *see* Al 'Aqabah
Aelana Jordan *see* Al 'Aqabah
Aelia Capitolina Israel/West Bank *see* Jerusalem
Aenus Turkey *see* Enez
Ærø *i.* Denmark 36 E1
Aesernia Italy *see* Isernia
A Estrada Spain 42 B1
Afabet Eritrea 89 H5
Afal *watercourse* Saudi Arabia *see* 'Ifāl, Wādī
Afanas'yevo Rus. Fed. 28 J4
Afándou Greece *see* Afantou
Afantou Greece 47 F6
Afar *admin. reg.* Eth. 96 D1
Afar Depression Eritrea/Eth. 89 I6
Affreville Alg. *see* Khemis Miliana
Afghānestān *country* Asia *see* Afghanistan
▶Afghanistan *country* Asia 81 F3
asia 52–53, 82
Afgooye Somalia 96 E4
'Afīf Saudi Arabia 89 I4
Afikpo Nigeria 93 G4
Afium Karahissar Turkey *see* Afyon
Åfjord Norway 32 C3
Aflou Alg. 91 F2
Afmadow Somalia 96 D4
Afognak Island U.S.A. 120 D4
Afojjar *well* Mauritania 92 B1
A Fonsagrada Spain 42 C1
Afragola Italy 45 E4
Afrânio Brazil 150 D4
Āfrēra Terara *vol.* Eth. 96 D1
Āfrēra YeChe'ew Hāyk' *l.* Eth. 96 D1
Africa Nova *country* Africa *see* Tunisia
'Afrīn Syria 77 C1
'Afrīn, Nahr *r.* Syria/Turkey 77 C1
Afşin Turkey 78 D3
Afsluitdijk *barrage* Neth. 36 B2
Aftol *well* Eth. 96 E3
Afton U.S.A. 134 E4
Aftoût Faï *depr.* Mauritania 92 B1
Afuá Brazil 150 B2
'Afula Israel 77 B3
Afyon Turkey 78 B3
Afyonkarahisar Turkey *see* Afyon
Aga-Buryat Autonomous Okrug *admin. div.* Rus. Fed. *see* Aginskiy Buryatskiy Avtonomnyy Okrug
Agadem *well* Niger 93 I1
Agadès Niger *see* Agadez
Agadez Niger 93 G1
Agadez *dept* Niger 93 H1
Agadir Morocco 90 C3
Agadyr' Kazakh. 70 D2
Agaie Nigeria 93 G3
Agalega Islands Mauritius 162 K6
Agana Guam *see* Hagåtña
Agar India 74 C5
Agârak *well* Niger 93 G1
Agâraktem *well* Mali 90 D5
Āgaro Eth. 96 C3
Agartala India 75 F5
Agashi India 72 B2
Agate Canada 124 D3
Agathe France *see* Agde
Agathonisi *i.* Greece 47 E6
Agatti *i.* India 72 B4
Agbor Bojiboji Nigeria 93 G4
Agboville Côte d'Ivoire 92 D4
Ağcabädi Azer. 79 F2
Ağdam Azer. 79 F3
Ağdaş Azer. 79 F2
Agdash Azer. *see* Ağdaş
Agde France 39 E5
Agdzhabedi Azer. *see* Ağcabädi
Agedabia Libya *see* Ajdābiyā
Agen France 38 D4
Agenebode Nigeria 93 G4
Āgere Maryam Eth. 96 C3
Aggeneys S. Africa 98 C6
Aggershus *county* Norway *see* Akershus
Aggteleki *nat. park* Hungary 37 J4
Aghezzaf *well* Mali 93 E1
Aghil Pass China/Jammu and Kashmir 74 C1
Aghireşu Romania 46 C1
Aghouâvil *des.* Mauritania 92 D1
Aghrījīt *well* Mauritania 92 C1
Aghzoumal, Sabkhat *salt pan* W. Sahara 90 B4
Agia Greece 47 C5
Agia Eirinis, Akra *pt* Greece 47 D5
Agia Marina Greece 47 E6
Agiasos Greece 47 E5
Agia Vervara Greece 47 D7
Agigea Romania 46 F2
Agighiol Romania 46 F2
Agiguan *i.* N. Mariana Is *see* Aguijan
Ağın Turkey 79 D3
Aginskiy Buryatskiy Avtonomnyy Okrug *admin. div.* Rus. Fed. 63 I1
Aginskoye Rus. Fed. 63 I1
Aginum France *see* Agen
Agios Dimitrios Greece 47 C6
Agios Efstratios Greece 47 D5
Agios Efstratios *i.* Greece 47 D5
Agios Fokas, Akra *pt* Greece 47 E5
Agios Georgios *i.* Greece 47 C6
Agios Ioannis, Akra *pt* Greece 47 D7
Agios Kirykos Greece 47 E6
Agios Nikolaos Greece 47 D7
Agios Paraskevi Greece 47 E5
Agios Petros Greece 47 C6
Agiou Orous, Kolpos *b.* Greece 47 C4
Agirwat Hills Sudan 89 G5
Agly *r.* France 39 E5
Agnantero Greece 47 B5
Agnew Australia 109 C7
Agnibilékrou Côte d'Ivoire 92 E4
Agnita Romania 46 D2
Agniye-Afanas'yevsk Rus. Fed. 64 D2
Agno *r.* Italy 44 C2
Agnone Italy 44 E4
Ago-Are Nigeria 93 F3
Agounni Jefal *well* Mali 92 E1
Agous-n-Ehsel *well* Mali 93 F1
Agout *r.* France 38 D5
Agra India 74 C4
Agrakhanskiy Poluostrov *pen.* Rus. Fed. 79 F2
Agram Croatia *see* Zagreb
Agreda Spain 43 F2
Agri *r.* Italy 45 F4
Ağrı Turkey 79 E3
Agria Gramvousa *i.* Greece 47 C7
Ağrı Dağı *mt.* Turkey *see* Ararat, Mount
Agrigan *i.* N. Mariana Is *see* Agrihan
Agrigento *Sicily* Italy 45 D6
Agrigentum *Sicily* Italy *see* Agrigento
Agrihan *i.* N. Mariana Is 57 K2
Agrinio Greece 47 B5
Agropoli Italy 45 E4
Agryz Rus. Fed. 28 J4
Ågskaret Norway 32 D2
Ağstafa Azer. 79 F2
Ağsu Azer. 79 G2
Agua Blanca Arg. 152 D4
Agua Clara Bol. 148 D3
Água Clara Brazil 149 G5
Aguaclara Col. 146 C3
Aguadilla Puerto Rico 139 K5
Aguado Cecilio Arg. 152 D5
Aguadulce Panama 139 H7
Agua Escondida Arg. 152 C4
Agua Fria *r.* U.S.A. 137 F5
Aguanaval *r.* Mex. 126 F7
Aguanga U.S.A. 136 D5
Aguanus *r.* Canada 125 I3
Aguapeí Brazil 149 F4
Aguapeí *r.* Brazil 149 H5
Aguapeí, Serra *hills* Brazil 149 F4
Agua Prieta Mex. 135 E7
Aguaragüe, Cordillera de *mts* Bol. 149 E5
Aguaray Arg. 149 E5
A Guardia Spain 42 B2
Aguaro-Guariquito, Parque Nacional *nat. park* Venez. 146 E2
Aguas *r.* Spain 43 F4
Águas Belas Brazil 150 E4
Aguascalientes Mex. 126 F7
Águas Formosas Brazil 151 D6
Aguasvivas *r.* Spain 43 F2
Água Verde *r.* Brazil 149 F3
Agudo Spain 42 D3
Águeda Port. 42 B2
Águeda *r.* Port./Spain 42 C2
Aguelal Niger 93 H1
Aguelhok Mali 93 F1
Aguemour, Oued *watercourse* Alg. 91 F4
Aguessis *well* Niger 91 H6
Aguié Niger 93 G2
Aguijan *i.* N. Mariana Is 57 K3
Aguila *mt.* Spain 43 F2
Aguila U.S.A. 135 D6
Aguilar de Campóo Spain 42 D1
Águilas Spain 43 F4

▶Agulhas, Cape S. Africa 98 D7
Most southerly point of Africa.

Agulhas Basin *sea feature* Indian Ocean 163 I9
Agulhas Negras *mt.* Brazil 151 C7
Agulhas Plateau *sea feature* Indian Ocean 163 I8
Agulhas Ridge *sea feature* S. Atlantic Ocean 161 O8
Aguntum Italy *see* San Candido
Ağva Turkey 78 B2
Agvali Rus. Fed. 79 F2
Agwarra Nigeria 93 G3
Agwei *r.* Sudan 96 B3
Ahaggar *plat.* Alg. *see* Hoggar
Ahar Iran 80 A2
Ahaura N.Z. 113 B3
Ahaus Germany 36 C2
Ahigal Spain 42 C2
Ahillo *mt.* Spain 42 D4
Ahioma P.N.G. 111 G1
Ahipara Bay N.Z. 113 C1
Ahiri India 72 D2
Ahklun Mountains U.S.A. 120 C4
Ahlat Turkey 79 E3
Ahmadabad India 74 B5
Aḥmadābād Iran 81 E3
Aḥmad al Bāqir, Jabal *mt.* Jordan 77 B5
Ahmadnagar India 72 B2
Ahmadpur India 72 C2
Ahmadpur East Pak. 81 G4
Ahmadpur Sial Pak. 81 G4
Ahmar Mountains Eth. 96 D2
Ahmedabad India *see* Ahmadabad
Ahmednagar India *see* Ahmadnagar
Ahmetli Turkey 47 E5
Ahoada Nigeria 93 G4
Ahome Mex. 126 E6
Ahore India 74 B4
Ahram Iran 80 B4
Ahraura India 75 D4
Ahrensburg Germany 36 E2
Ahtme Estonia 33 G4
Āhū Iran 80 B4
Ahun France 38 E3
Ahuriri *r.* N.Z. 113 B4
Ahvāz Iran 80 B4
Ahvenanmaa *is* Fin. *see* Åland Islands
Ahwa India 72 B1
Aḥwar Yemen 76 D7
Ahwāz Iran *see* Ahvāz
Ai *r.* China 65 A4
Ai-Ais Namibia 98 C5
Ai-Ais Hot Springs and Fish River Canyon Park *nature res.* Namibia 98 C5
Aichach Germany 36 E4
Aidin Turkm. 80 C2
Aigialı Greece 47 D6
Aigialousa Cyprus 77 B2
Aigina Greece 47 C6
Aigina *i.* Greece 47 C6
Aiginio Greece 46 C4
Aigio Greece 47 C5
Aigle Switz. 39 G3
Aigle de Chambeyron *mt.* France 39 G4
Aigoual, Mont *mt.* France 39 E4
Aiguá Uruguay 152 G3
Aigües Tortes i Estany de St Maurici, Parque Nacional d' *nat. park* Spain 43 G1
Aiguille de Scolette *mt.* France/Italy 39 G4
Aiguilles d'Arves *mts* France 39 G4
Aiguille Verte *mt.* France 39 G4
Aigurande France 38 D3
Aihua China *see* Yunxian
Aihui China *see* Heihe
Aija Peru 148 A2
Aijal India *see* Aizawl
Aiken U.S.A. 129 C5
Ailao Shan *mts* China 66 B3
Aileron Australia 110 C4
Ailigandi Panama 146 B2
Ailing China 67 D3
Ailinglapalap *atoll* Marshall Is 164 F6
Ailsa Craig *i.* U.K. 34 D4
Aimogasta Arg. 152 D2
Aimorés, Serra dos *hills* Brazil 151 D6
Ain *r.* France 39 F4
Ainaži Latvia 33 G4
Aïn Beïda Alg. 91 G2
Aïn Beni Mathar Morocco 90 E2
'Aïn Ben Tili Mauritania 90 C4
Aïn Bessem Alg. 43 H4
Aïn Biré *well* Mauritania 92 C1
Aïn Boucif Alg. 43 H5
Aïn Defla Alg. 91 F1
Aïn Deheb Alg. 91 F2
Aïn Draham Tunisia 45 B6
Aïn el Hadjadj *well* Alg. 91 F3
'Aïn el Hadjadj *well* Alg. 91 G4
Aïn el Hadjel Alg. 43 H5
Aïn Galakka *spring* Chad 88 C5
Aïn Mdila *well* Alg. 91 G2
Aïn-M'Lila Alg. 91 G1
Ainos *nat. park* Greece 47 B5
Aïn Oussera Alg. 91 F2
Aïn Salah Alg. *see* In Salah
Aïn Sefra Alg. 91 E2
Ainsworth U.S.A. 132 B3
Aintab Turkey *see* Gaziantep
Aïn Taya Alg. 43 H4
Aïn Tédélès Alg. 43 G5
Aïn Temouchent Alg. 91 E2
Aïn Ti-m Misaou *well* Alg. 91 F5
Aipe Col. 146 C4
Aiquile Bol. 148 D4
Air *i.* Indon. 59 D2
Airão Brazil 147 F5
Airbangis Indon. 58 B2
Airdrie Canada 134 D2
Aire *r.* France 39 F2
Aire-sur-l'Adour France 38 C5
Airhitam *r.* Indon. 59 E3
Airhitam, Teluk *b.* Indon. 59 E3
Airlie Beach Australia 111 G4
Airolo Switz. 39 H3
Airpanas Indon. 57 G7
Air Ronge Canada 123 J4
Aisatung Mountain Myanmar 60 A3
Aisch *r.* Germany 36 E4
Aisén *admin. reg.* Chile 153 B6
Aishihik Canada 122 B2
Aishihik Lake Canada 122 B2
Aisími Greece *see* Aisymi
Aisne *r.* France 39 E2
Aïssa, Djebel *mt.* Alg. 91 E2
Aisymi Greece 46 D4
Aitana *mt.* Spain 43 F3
Aitape P.N.G. 57 J6
Aït Benhaddou *tourist site* Morocco 90 D3
Aitkin U.S.A. 132 C2
Aiud Romania 46 C1
Aivadzh Tajik. 81 G2
Aiviekste *r.* Latvia 33 G4
Aix France *see* Aix-en-Provence
Aix *r.* France 39 F4
Aix-en-Othe France 39 E2
Aix-en-Provence France 39 F5
Aixe-sur-Vienne France 38 D4
Aix-la-Chapelle Germany *see* Aachen
Aix-les-Bains France 39 F4
Āiy Ādī Eth. 89 H6
Aiyiáli Greece *see* Aigiali
Aíyina *i.* Greece *see* Aigina
Aiyínion Greece *see* Aiginio
Aíyion Greece *see* Aigio
Aizawl India 75 G5
Aizenay France 38 C3
Aizkraukle Latvia 33 G4
Aizpute Latvia 33 F4
Aizu-wakamatsu Japan 65 D5
Ajaccio *Corsica* France 31 G5
Ajaccio, Golfe d' *b. Corsica* France 44 B4
Ajaigarh India 74 D4
Ajajú *r.* Col. 146 C4
Ajanta India 72 B1
Ajanta Range *hills* India *see* Sahyadriparvat Range
Ajasse Nigeria 93 G3
Ajax Canada 130 D2
Ajayameru India *see* Ajmer
Ajban U.A.E. 80 C5
Ajdābiyā Libya 88 D2
Ajdovščina Slovenia 44 D2
a-Jiddét *des.* Oman *see* Ḥarāsīs, Jiddat al
Ajka Hungary 37 H5
'Ajlūn Jordan 77 B3
'Ajmah, Jabal al *mts* Egypt 77 B5
Ajman U.A.E. 80 C5
Ajmer India 74 B4
Ajmer-Merwara India *see* Ajmer
Ajo U.S.A. 137 F5
Ajra India 72 B2
Akabira Japan 64 E4
Akabli Alg. 91 F4
Akaboun *well* Mali 93 F1
Akademii Nauk, Khrebet *mt.* Tajik. *see* Akademiyai Fanho, Qatorkŭhi
Akademiyai Fanho, Qatorkŭhi *mt.* Tajik. 81 G2
Akagera National Park Rwanda 96 A5
Āk'ak'ī Beseka Eth. 96 C2
Akalkot India 72 C2
Akama, Akra *c.* Cyprus *see* Arnauti, Cape
Akamagaseki Japan *see* Shimonoseki
Akamkpa Nigeria 93 H4
Akan National Park Japan 64 F4
Akarkar *well* Niger 93 G2
Akarnanika *mts* Greece 47 B5
Akaroa N.Z. 113 C3

Akasha Sudan 89 F4
'Akāshat Iraq 79 D4
Äkäsjokisuu Fin. 32 F2
Akbarābād Iran 80 C4
Akbarpur Uttar Pradesh India 74 D4
Akbarpur Uttar Pradesh India 75 D4
Akbaytal Tajik. 81 H2
Akbaytal Pass Tajik. 81 H2
Akbou Alg. 43 I4
Akbulak Rus. Fed. 29 J6
Akçadağ Turkey 79 D3
Akçakale Turkey 79 D3
Akçakertikbeli Geçidi pass Turkey 47 F5
Akçakoca Turkey 78 B2
Akçali Dağlari mt. Turkey 78 C3
Akçalı Dağları mts Turkey 77 A1
Akçaova Turkey 47 E6
Akçay r. Turkey 47 F6
Akchâr reg. Mauritania 90 B6
Akdağ mt. Turkey 47 F5
Akdağlar mts Turkey 78 B3
Akdağmadeni Turkey 78 C3
Akdere Turkey 77 A1
Akelamo Indon. 57 G5
Akelo Sudan 96 B3
Åkersberga Sweden 33 E4
Akershus county Norway 33 C3
Åkerstrømmen Norway 33 C3
Aketi Dem. Rep. Congo 94 D4
Akgyr Erezi hills Turkm. see Akkyr, Gory
Akhalk'alak'i Georgia 79 E2
Akhal Oblast admin. div. Turkm. see Akhal'skaya Oblast'
Akhal'skaya Oblast' admin. div. Turkm. 81 D2
Akhalts'ikhe Georgia 79 E2
Akhḍar, Al Jabal al mts Libya 88 D2
Akhḍar, Jabal mts Oman 76 F5
Akheloy Bulg. 46 E3
Akhisar Turkey 78 A3
Akhmīm Egypt 89 F3
Akhnoor Jammu and Kashmir 74 B2
Akhsu Azer. see Ağsu
Akhta Armenia see Hrazdan
Akhtarīn Syria 77 C1
Akhtubinsk Rus. Fed. 29 H6
Akhty Rus. Fed. 79 F2
Akhtyrka Ukr. see Okhtyrka
Aki Japan 65 C6
Akiéni Gabon 94 B5
Akimiski Island Canada 124 D2
Akıncılar Turkey see Selçuk
Akishma r. Rus. Fed. 64 C1
Akita Japan 65 E5
Akjoujt Mauritania 92 B1
Akka Morocco 90 C3
Akkajaure l. Sweden 32 E2
Akkerman Ukr. see Bilhorod-Dnistrovs'kyy
'Akko Israel 77 B3
Akkol' Kazakh. 26 H4
Akkol' Atyrauskaya Oblast' Kazakh. 29 I7
Akköy Aydın Turkey 78 A3
Akköy Denizli Turkey 47 F6
Akkul' Kazakh. see Akkol'
Akkuş Turkey 78 D2
Akkyr, Gory hills Turkm. 80 C1
Akkystau Kazakh. 29 I7
Aklavik Canada 120 F3
Aklera India 74 C4
Ak-Mechet Kazakh. see Kyzylorda
Akmenrags pt Latvia 33 F4
Akmeqit China 74 C1
Akmola Kazakh. see Astana
Akmolinsk Kazakh. see Astana
Akniste Latvia 33 G4
Aknoul Morocco 90 E2
Akō Japan 65 C6
Akobo Sudan 96 B3
Akobo Wenz r. Eth./Sudan 96 B3
Akodia India 74 C5
Akola Maharashtra India 72 B2
Akola Maharashtra India 72 C1
Akom II Cameroon 93 H5
Akonolinga Cameroon 93 I5
Akop Sudan 94 F2
Akordat Eritrea 89 H6
Akören Turkey 78 C3
Akot India 74 C5
Akouménaye Fr. Guiana 147 H4
Akoupé Côte d'Ivoire 92 E4
Akpatok Island Canada 121 M3
Akraifnio Greece 47 C5
Akranes Iceland 32 [inset]
Akrathos, Akra pt Greece 47 D4
Akrérèb Niger 93 H1
Akritas, Akra pt Greece 47 B6
Akron CO U.S.A. 132 A3
Akron OH U.S.A. 130 C3
Akrotirion Bay Cyprus 77 A2
Akrotirion, Kolpos b. Cyprus see Akrotirion Bay
Akrotiri Sovereign Base Area military base Cyprus 77 A2

▶Aksai Chin terr. Asia 74 C2
Disputed territory (China/India).

Aksakal Turkey 47 F4
Aksakovo Bulg. 46 E3
Aksaray Turkey 78 C3
Aksay Kazakh. 29 J6
Aksay Rus. Fed. 29 F7
Akşehir Turkey 78 B3
Akşehir Gölü l. Turkey 78 B3
Akseki Turkey 78 B3
Aksenovo Rus. Fed. 29 J5
Aks-e Rostam r. Iran 80 C4
Akshiganak Kazakh. 70 B2
Akshukur Kazakh. 79 G2
Aksu China 70 F3
Aksu Kazakh. 29 J6
Aksu r. Tajik. see Oksu
Aksu r. Turkey 78 B3
Āksum Eth. 89 H6
Aktag mt. China 75 E1
Aktash Uzbek. 81 F2
Aktau Kazakh. 79 G2
Aktepe Turkey 77 C1
Aktobe Kazakh. 26 F4
Aktogay Kazakh. 70 E2
Aktsyabrski Belarus 29 D5
Aktyubinsk Kazakh. see Aktobe
Aktyubinskaya Oblast' admin. div. Kazakh. 29 K6
Aktyubinsk Oblast admin. div. Kazakh. see Aktyubinskaya Oblast'
Akujärvi Fin. 32 G1
Akula Dem. Rep. Congo 94 D4
Akulivik Canada 121 L3
Akumadan Ghana 93 E4
Akune Japan 65 B6
Akur mt. Uganda 96 B4
Akure Nigeria 93 G4
Akureyri Iceland 32 [inset]
Akwa Ibom state Nigeria 93 G4
Akwanga Nigeria 93 H3
Akyab Myanmar see Sittwe
Akyatan Gölü salt l. Turkey 77 B1
Akzhaykyn, Ozero salt l. Kazakh. 70 C3
Ål Norway 33 C3
Ala Italy 44 C2
'Alā, Jabal al hills Syria 77 C2
Alabama r. U.S.A. 129 B6
Alabama state U.S.A. 129 B5
Alabaster U.S.A. 129 B5
Al 'Abṭīyah well Iraq 79 F5
Al Abyaḍ Libya 88 B3
Al Abyār Libya 88 D1
Alaca Turkey 78 C2
Alacahan Turkey 79 D3
Alaçam Turkey 78 C2
Alaçam Dağları mts Turkey 47 F5
Alacant Spain see Alicante-Alicant
Alaçatı Turkey 47 E5
Alacrán, Arrecife reef Mex. 127 I7
Al Adabīyah Egypt 77 A5
Aladag mt. Bulg. 46 D4
Aladağ Turkey 78 C3
Ala Dag mt. Turkey 79 E3
Ala Dağlar mts Turkey 79 E3
Ala Dağları mts Turkey 78 C3
Al 'Adam Libya 88 D2
Alaejos Spain 42 D2
Alagapuram India 72 C4
Alagir Rus. Fed. 29 H8
Alagoas state Brazil 150 E4
Alagoinhas Brazil 150 E5
Alagón Spain 43 F2
Alagón r. Spain 42 C3
Alahanpanjang Indon. 58 C3
Alahärmä Fin. 32 F3
Al Aḥmadī Kuwait 79 G5
Alaid, Ostrov i. Rus. Fed. see Atlasova, Ostrov
Alaior Spain 43 I3
Alai Range mts Asia 70 D4
Alaivān Iran 80 C3
Al Ajām Saudi Arabia 80 B5
Alajärvi Fin. 32 F3
Al 'Ajrūd Egypt 77 A4
Al 'Ajrūd well Egypt 77 B4
Alajuela Costa Rica 139 H6
Alakanuk U.S.A. 120 C3
Alaknanda r. India 74 C3
Alakol', Ozero salt l. Kazakh. 70 F2
Ala Kul salt l. Kazakh. see Alakol', Ozero
Alakurtti Rus. Fed. 32 H2
Al 'Alamayn Egypt 89 F2
Alalaú r. Brazil 147 F5
Al 'Alayyah Saudi Arabia 89 I5
Alama Somalia 96 D3
Al 'Amādīyah Iraq 79 E3
Alamagan i. N. Mariana Is 57 K2
Alamaguan i. N. Mariana Is see Alamagan
Al'Amār Saudi Arabia 89 J3
Al 'Amārah Iraq 79 F5
'Alam ar Rūm, Ra's pt Egypt 89 E2
'Alāmarvdasht watercourse Iran 80 C4
Al Amghar waterhole Iraq 79 F5
Al 'Āmirīyah Egypt 78 B5
Alamito Creek r. U.S.A. 135 F7
Alamo U.S.A. 128 A5
Alamo Dam U.S.A. 137 F4
Alamogordo U.S.A. 135 F6
Alamo Heights U.S.A. 133 B6
Alamos Mex. 135 E8
Alamos r. Mex. 126 F6
Alamos, Sierra mts Mex. 135 E8
Alamosa U.S.A. 135 F5
Alamosa Creek r. U.S.A. 135 F6
Alampur India 72 C3
Al 'Anad Yemen 96 E1
Alanäs Sweden 32 D2
Al Anbār governorate Iraq 79 E4
Aland India 72 C2
Aland r. Iran 80 A2
Åland is Fin. see Åland Islands
Åland Islands Fin. 33 E3
Ålands Hav sea chan. Fin./Sweden 33 E4
Alandur India 72 D3
Alangalang, Tanjung pt Indon. 59 G3
Alang Besar i. Indon. 58 C2
Alange, Embalse de resr Spain 42 C3
Alanggantang i. Indon. 58 D3
Alanya Turkey 78 C3
'Alā' od Dīn Iran 80 C4
Alapaha r. U.S.A. 129 C6
Alapli Turkey 29 D8
Alappuzha India see Alleppey
Al 'Aqabah Jordan 78 C5
Al 'Aqīq Saudi Arabia 89 I4
Al 'Arabīyah as Sa'ūdīyah country Asia see Saudi Arabia
Alarcón, Embalse de resr Spain 43 E3
Al Arīn Saudi Arabia 89 I5
Al 'Arīsh Egypt 89 G2
Al Arṭāwīyah Saudi Arabia 76 D4
Alas Indon. 59 G5
Alas, Selat sea chan. Indon. 59 G5
Alaşehir Turkey 78 B3
Alashiya country Asia see Cyprus
Al Ashmūnayn Egypt 89 F3
Al 'Āshūrīyah well Iraq 89 I2
▶Alaska state U.S.A. 120 D3
northamerica 118–119
Alaska, Gulf of U.S.A. 120 E4
Alaska Highway Canada/U.S.A. 122 A2
Alaska Peninsula U.S.A. 120 C4
Alaska Range mts U.S.A. 120 E3
Al 'Assāfīyah Saudi Arabia 89 H2
Alassio Italy 44 B2
Ălăt Azer. 79 G3
Alat Uzbek. 81 E2
Alataw Shankou pass China/Kazakh. see Dzungarian Gate
Al Atwā' well Saudi Arabia 89 I2
Alatyr' Rus. Fed. 29 H5
Alatyr' r. Rus. Fed. 29 H5
Alausí Ecuador 146 B5
Alaverdi Armenia 79 F2
Ala-Vuokki Fin. 32 H2
Alavus Fin. 32 F3
Alawoona Australia 112 B4
Alaykel' Kyrg. see Alaykuu
Alaykuu Kyrg. 81 H1
Alay Kyrka Toosu mts Asia see Alai Range
Al 'Ayn U.A.E. 80 C5
Alayskiy Khrebet mts Asia see Alai Range
Alazani r. Azer./Georgia 79 F2
Alazeya r. Rus. Fed. 27 P2
Al 'Azīzīyah Iraq 79 F4

▶Al 'Azīzīyah Libya 88 B1
Highest recorded shade temperature in the world.
world 12–13

Alba Italy 44 B2
Al Ba'ā'ith Saudi Arabia 89 I3
Al Bāb Syria 77 C1
Albacete Spain 43 F3
Al Badā'i' Saudi Arabia 89 H3
Alba de Tormes Spain 42 D2
Al Bādiyah al Janūbīyah hill Iraq 79 F5
Ålbæk Denmark 33 C4
Al Baḥr al Aḥmar governorate Egypt 77 A5
Al Baḥrayn country Asia see Bahrain
Alba Iulia Romania 46 C1
Al Bajā' well U.A.E. 80 B5
Al Bakhrā well Saudi Arabia 80 A5
Al Bakkī Libya 88 B3
Albalate de Arzobispo Spain 43 F2
Albanel, Lac l. Canada 125 F3
▶Albania country Europe 46 A4
europe 24–25, 48
Albany Australia 109 B8
Albany r. Canada 124 D2
Albany GA U.S.A. 129 B6
Albany MO U.S.A. 132 C3

▶Albany NY U.S.A. 131 G2
State capital of New York.

Albany OH U.S.A. 130 B4
Albany OR U.S.A. 134 B3
Albany TX U.S.A. 133 B5
Albany Downs Australia 111 G5
Albardão do João Maria coastal area Brazil 152 G3
Al Bardī Libya 88 E2
Al Baṣrah governorate Iraq 79 F5
Al Baṭḥa' marsh Iraq 79 F5
Al Bāṭinah admin. reg. Oman 80 D5
Al Bāṭinah i. Saudi Arabia 80 B5
Albatross Bay Australia 111 E2
Al Bawītī Egypt 89 F2
Al Bayḍā' Libya 88 D1
Al Bayḍā' Yemen 76 D7
Albemarle U.S.A. 128 C5
Albemarle Sound sea chan. U.S.A. 128 D5
Albenga Italy 44 B2
Alberche r. Spain 42 D3
Alberdi Para. 149 F6
Alberga watercourse Australia 110 C5
Albert Australia 112 C4
Albert France 39 E2
Albert, Lake Australia 112 A4
Albert, Lake Dem. Rep. Congo/Uganda 96 A4
Albert, Parc National nat. park Dem. Rep. Congo see Virunga, Parc National des
Alberta prov. Canada 123 H4
Albertirsa Hungary 37 I5
Albert Kanaal canal Belgium 36 B3
Albert Lea U.S.A. 132 C3
Albert Nile r. Sudan/Uganda 96 B4
Alberto de Agostini, Parque Nacional nat. park Chile 153 C8
Albertville Dem. Rep. Congo see Kalémié
Albertville France 39 G4
Albertville U.S.A. 129 B5
Albi France 38 E5
Albia U.S.A. 132 C3
Al Bi'ār Saudi Arabia 89 H4
Al Biḍah des. Saudi Arabia 80 B5
Albignasego Italy 44 C2
Albina Suriname 147 H3
Albion CA U.S.A. 136 A2
Albion IN U.S.A. 128 B3
Albion MI U.S.A. 130 A2
Albion NE U.S.A. 132 B3
Albion NY U.S.A. 130 D2
Albion PA U.S.A. 130 C3
Al Bi'r Saudi Arabia 89 H2
Al Birk Saudi Arabia 89 I5
Al Birkah Saudi Arabia 89 I4
Alborán, Isla de i. Spain 42 E5
Ålborg Denmark 33 C4
Ålborg Bugt b. Denmark 33 C4
Alborz, Reshteh-ye mts Iran see Elburz Mountains
Albota Romania 46 D2
Albox Spain 43 E4
Albro Australia 111 F4
Albstadt Germany 36 D4
Al Budayyi Bahrain 80 B5
Albufeira Port. 42 B4
Al Buḥayrah governorate Egypt 78 B5
Al Bukayrīyah Saudi Arabia 89 I3
Albula Alpen mts Switz. 39 H3
Albuquerque U.S.A. 135 F6
Al Buraymī Oman 76 F5
Albury Australia 112 C5
Al Buşayrah Syria 79 E4
Al Busayṭā' plain Saudi Arabia 89 H2
Al Buşayyah Iraq 79 F5
Al Bushūk well Saudi Arabia 89 J2
Al Buwī well Oman 76 F6
Alca Peru 148 B3
Alcácer do Sal Port. 42 B3
Alcáçovas r. Port. 42 B3
Alcalá de Chivert Spain 43 G2
Alcalá de Guadaira Spain 42 D4
Alcalá de Henares Spain 42 E2
Alcalá de los Gazules Spain 42 D4
Alcalá la Real Spain 42 E4
Alcalde, Punta pt Chile 152 C2
Alcamo Sicily Italy 45 D6
Alcanadre r. Spain 43 G2
Alcañiz Spain 43 F2
Alcântara Brazil 150 C2
Alcántara Spain 42 C3
Alcántara, Embalse de resr Spain 42 C3
Alcántara II, Embalse de resr Spain 42 C3
Alcantara Lake Canada 123 I2
Alcantarilla Spain 43 F4
Alcaraz Spain 43 E3
Alcaraz, Sierra de mts Spain 43 E3
Alcaria Ruiva hill Port. 42 C4
Alcarrache r. Port./Spain 42 C3
Alcaudete Spain 42 D4
Alcázar de San Juan Spain 42 E3
Alcazarquivir Morocco see Ksar el Kebir
Alchevs'k Ukr. 29 F6
Alcira Arg. 152 D3
Alcira Spain see Alzira
Alcobaça Brazil 151 E6
Alconchel Spain 42 C3
Alcora Spain 43 G2
Alcorneo r. Port./Spain 42 C3
Alcoy-Alcoi Spain 43 F3
Alcubierre, Sierra de mts Spain 43 F2
Alcúdia Spain 43 H3
Aldabra Atoll Seychelles 97 E7
▶Aldabra Islands is Seychelles 97 E7
africa 86–87
Aldama Mex. 135 F7
Aldan Rus. Fed. 27 M4
Aldan r. Rus. Fed. 27 M3
Aldeburgh U.K. 35 G5
Aldeia Velha Brazil 150 B4
Aldeia Viçosa Angola 95 B7
Alder Creek U.S.A. 131 F2
Alderney i. Channel Is 38 B2
Aldershot U.K. 35 F6
Alderson U.S.A. 130 C5
Aldie Eth. 96 D3
Aleg Mauritania 92 B1
Alegre Brazil 151 D7
Alegrete Brazil 152 G2
Alegros Mountain U.S.A. 135 E6
Alejandro Korn Arg. 152 F3
Alekhovshchina Rus. Fed. 28 E3
Aleksandra Bekovicha-Cherkassogo, Zaliv b. Kazakh. 79 G2
Aleksandriya Ukr. see Oleksandriya
Aleksandropol Armenia see Gyumri
Aleksandrov Rus. Fed. 28 F4
Aleksandrov Gay Rus. Fed. 29 I6
Aleksandrovka Rus. Fed. 29 J5
Aleksandrovo Bulg. 46 D3
Aleksandrovsk Rus. Fed. 28 K4
Aleksandrovsk Ukr. see Zaporizhzhya
Aleksandrovskiy Rus. Fed. see Aleksandrovsk
Aleksandrovskoye Stavropol'skiy Kray Rus. Fed. 29 G7
Aleksandrovskoye Stavropol'skiy Kray Rus. Fed. 29 H7
Aleksandrovsk-Sakhalinskiy Rus. Fed. 64 E2
Aleksandrów Kujawski Poland 37 I2
Aleksandry, Zemlya i. Rus. Fed. 26 E1
Alekseyevka Kazakh. see Akkol'
Alekseyevka Belgorodskaya Oblast' Rus. Fed. 29 F6
Alekseyevka Belgorodskaya Ob'ast' Rus. Fed. 29 F6
Alekseyevskaya Rus. Fed. 29 G6
Aleksin Rus. Fed. 29 F5
Aleksinac Serb. and Mont. 46 B3
Alèmbé Gabon 94 A5
'Alem Ketema Eth. 96 C2
'Alem Maya Eth. 96 D2
Além Paraíba Brazil 151 D7
Ålen Norway 32 C3
Alençon France 38 D2
Alenquer Brazil 147 H5
Alenuihaha Channel U.S.A. 135 [inset] Z1
Alep Syria see Aleppo
Alépé Côte d'Ivoire 92 E4
Aleppo Syria 78 D3
Aler r. India 72 C2
Alert Canada 121 M1
Alerta Peru 148 C2
Alès France 39 F4
Aleşd Romania 31 J4
Aleshki Ukr. see Tsyurupyns'k
Aleşkirt Turkey see Eleşkirt
Alessandria Italy 44 B2
Alessio Albania see Lezhë
Ålesund Norway 32 B3
Aletschhorn mt. Switz. 39 G3
Aleutian Basin sea feature Bering Sea 164 F2
Aleutian Islands U.S.A. 120 B4
Aleutian Range mts U.S.A. 120 D4
Aleutian Trench sea feature N. Pacific Ocean 164 G2
Alevina, Mys c. Rus. Fed. 27 P4
Alevişik Turkey see Samandağı
Alexander, Mount Australia 110 D2
Alexander Archipelago is U.S.A. 120 F4
Alexander Bay S. Africa 98 C6
Alexander City U.S.A. 129 B5
Alexander Island Antarctica 167 L2
Alexandra Australia 112 C5
Alexandra r. Australia 111 D3
Alexandra N.Z. 113 B4
Alexandra, Cape S. Georgia 153 [inset]
Alexandra Channel India 73 G3
Alexandra Falls Canada 123 G2
Alexandra Land i. Rus. Fed. see Aleksandry, Zemlya
Alexandreia Greece 46 C4
Alexandretta Turkey see İskenderun
Alexandria Afgh. see Ghaznī

▶Alexandria Egypt 89 F2
5th most populous city in Africa.
world 16–17

Alexandria Romania 46 D3
Alexandria Turkm. see Mary
Alexandria KY U.S.A. 130 A4
Alexandria LA U.S.A. 133 C6
Alexandria VA U.S.A. 131 E4
Alexandria Arachoton Afgh. see Kandahār
Alexandria Areion Afgh. see Herāt
Alexandria Bay U.S.A. 131 F1
Alexandria Prophthasia Afgh. see Farāh
Alexandrina, Lake Australia 112 A4
Alexandroupoli Greece 46 D4
Alexis r. Canada 125 J2
'Āley Lebanon 77 B3
Aleyak Iran 80 D2
Aleysk Rus. Fed. 26 I4
Alfambra r. Spain 43 F2
Alfaro Spain 43 F1
Alfarràs Spain 43 G2
Al Farūq reg. Saudi Arabia 80 B5
Al Farwānīyah Kuwait 76 D4
Al Farwānīyah Kuwait 79 F5
Al Fas Morocco see Fès
Al Fashn Egypt 78 B5
Alfatar Bulg. 46 E3
Al Fatḥah Iraq 79 E4
Al Fāw Iraq 79 G5
Al Fayyūm Egypt 89 F2
Al Fayyūm governorate Egypt 78 B5
Alfeios r. Greece 47 B6
Alfeld (Leine) Germany 36 D3
Alfenas Brazil 151 C7
Alfios r. Greece see Alfeios
Alföld plain Hungary 37 J5
Alford U.K. 34 E3
Alfred U.S.A. 131 H2
Alfred and Marie Range hills Australia 109 D6
Alfta Sweden 33 E3
Al Fujayrah U.A.E. see Fujairah
Al Fuqahā' Libya 88 C3
Al Furāt r. Iraq/Syria 76 C3 see Euphrates
Algabas Kazakh. 29 J6
Algar Spain 42 D4
Ålgård Norway 33 B4
Algarrobal Chile 152 C2
Algarrobo del Aguilla Arg. 152 D4
Algarve reg. Port. 42 B4
Algeciras Spain 42 D4
Algemesí Spain 43 F3
Algena Eritrea 89 H5
Alger Alg. see Algiers
Alger U.S.A. 130 A1

▶Algeria country Africa 91 F4
2nd largest country in Africa.
africa 86–87, 100

Al Gharbīyah governorate Egypt 78 B5
Al Ghawr plain Jordan/West Bank 77 B4
Al Ghayḍah Yemen 76 E6
Alghero Sardinia Italy 45 B4
Al Ghurdaqah Egypt 89 G3
Al Ghuwayr well Qatar 80 B5
Al Ghwaybiyah Saudi Arabia 76 D4

▶Algiers Alg. 91 F1
Capital of Algeria.

Alginet Spain 43 F3
Algodón r. Peru 146 D5
Algodor r. Spain 42 E3
Algoma U.S.A. 132 E2
Algona U.S.A. 132 C3
Algonac U.S.A. 130 B2
Algonquin Park Canada 124 E4
Algorta (Guecho) Spain 42 E1
Algsjö Sweden 32 E2
Alguerao-Moz. see Hacufera
Algueirão-Mem Martins Port. 42 B3
Al Habakah well Saudi Arabia 79 E5
Al Ḥabbānīyah Iraq 79 E4
Al Ḥadaqah well Saudi Arabia 79 F5
Al Ḥadd Bahrain 80 B5
Al Ḥadhālīl plat. Saudi Arabia 89 I2
Al Ḥadīthah Iraq 79 E4
Al Ḥafar well Saudi Arabia 89 I2
Al Ḥaffah Syria 77 C2
Al Haggounia W. Sahara 90 B4
Al Ḥā'ir Saudi Arabia 80 A5
Al Ḥajar al Gharbī mts Oman 76 F5
Al Ḥajar ash Sharqī mts Oman 76 F5
Alhama r. Spain 43 F1
Al Ḥamād plain Asia 76 B3
Al Ḥamādah al Ḥamrā' plat. Libya 88 A2
Alhama de Granada Spain 42 E4
Alhama de Murcia Spain 91 E1
Alhamilla, Sierra hills Spain 43 E4
Al Ḥammām Egypt 89 F2
Al Ḥammām well Iraq 79 E5
Al Ḥamrā' Saudi Arabia 89 H4
Al Ḥanish al Kabīr i. Yemen 89 I6
Al Ḥaniyah esc. Iraq 79 F5
Al Ḥaqū Saudi Arabia 89 I5
Al Ḥarrah Egypt 89 F2
Al Ḥarūj al Aswad hills Libya 88 C3
Al Ḥasakah Syria 79 E3
Al Ḥāshimīyah Iraq 79 F4
Al Ḥatīfah plain Saudi Arabia 80 A5
Al Ḥawī salt pan Saudi Arabia 77 D5
Al Ḥawīyah Saudi Arabia 89 I4
Al Ḥawjā' Saudi Arabia 89 H2
Al Ḥayy Iraq 79 F4
Al Ḥazm Saudi Arabia 77 C5
Al Ḥazm al-Jawf Yemen 76 C6
Al Ḥibāk des. Saudi Arabia 76 E6
Al Ḥillah governorate Iraq see Bābil
Al Ḥillah Saudi Arabia 76 D5
Al Ḥimārah well Saudi Arabia 80 B5
Al Hindīyah Iraq 79 F4
Al Ḥinnāh Saudi Arabia 80 B5
Al Ḥinw mt. Saudi Arabia 89 H2
Al Ḥismā plain Saudi Arabia 77 B5
Al Ḥiṣn Jordan 77 B3
Al Ḥiṣn Yemen 96 E1
Al Hoceima Morocco 90 E2
Al Ḥudaydah Yemen see Hodeidah
Al Ḥudūd ash Shamālīyah prov. Saudi Arabia 79 E5
Al Ḥufayrah well Saudi Arabia 80 B5
Al Ḥufrah reg. Saudi Arabia 89 H2
Al Hufūf Saudi Arabia 76 D4
Al Ḥūj hills Saudi Arabia 77 D5
Al Ḥulayq al Kabīr hills Libya 88 C3
Al Ḥunayy Saudi Arabia 80 B5
Al Ḥuwayyiṭ Saudi Arabia 89 I3
Al Ḥuwayẓ Syria 77 C2
Ali China 74 C2
'Alīābād Hormozgan Iran 80 C4
'Alīābād Khorāsan Iran 81 D3
'Alīābād Khorāsan Iran 81 E4
'Alīābād Kordestān Iran 80 A3
'Alīābād Qom Iran 80 B3
Alīābād, Kūh-e mt. Iran 80 B3
Aliağa Turkey 78 A3
Aliakmonas r. Greece 47 C4
Aliakmonas, Limni l. Greece 47 B4
Aliartos Greece 47 C5
Alibag India 72 B2
Äli Bayramlı Azer. 79 G3
Alibey Adası i. Turkey 47 E5
Alibunar Serb. and Mont. 46 B2
Alicante-Alicant Spain 43 F3
Alice U.S.A. 133 B7
Alice, Punta pt Italy 45 F5
Alice Arm Canada 122 D4
Alice Springs Australia 110 C4
Alice Town Bahamas 129 D7
Aliceville U.S.A. 129 A5
Alichur Tajik. 81 H2
Alichur r. Tajik. 81 H2
Alichuri Janubi, Qatorkŭhi mts Tajik. 81 H2
Alicudi, Isola i. Isole Lipari Italy 45 E5
Al 'Idwah well Saudi Arabia 89 I3
Aliero Nigeria 93 G2
Alife Italy 44 E4
Aligarh India 74 C4
Alīgūdarz Iran 80 B3
Alihe China 63 K1
Alījūq, Kūh-e mt. Iran 80 B4
'Alī Kheyl Afgh. 81 G3
Al Ikhwān is Yemen 76 E7
Alima r. Congo 94 C5
Al Imārāt al 'Arabīyah al Muttaḥidah country Asia see United Arab Emirates
Alimia i. Greece 47 E6
Alindao Cent. Afr. Rep. 94 D3
Alinghar r. Afgh. 81 G3
Alingsås Sweden 33 D4
Alintale well Eth. 96 D3
Aliova r. Turkey 78 B3
Alipur Pak. 81 G4
Alipur Duar India 75 F4
Aliquippa U.S.A. 130 C3
Alirajpur India 74 B5
Ali Sabieh Djibouti 96 D2
Al 'Isāwīyah Saudi Arabia 89 H2
Al Iskandarīyah Egypt see Alexandria
Al Iskandarīyah governorate Egypt 78 B5
Aliskerovo Rus. Fed. 27 Q3
Al Ismā'īlīyah Egypt 89 G2
Aliste r. Spain 42 C2
Aliveri Greece 47 D5
Alix Canada 123 H4
Aliyaha r. Ukr. 46 F2
Al Jafr Jordan 78 D5
Al Jāfūrah des. Saudi Arabia 76 E4
Al Jaghbūb Libya 88 E2
Al Jahrah Kuwait 79 F5
Al Jamalīyah Qatar 80 B5
Al Jarāwī well Saudi Arabia 77 D4
Al Jawf Libya 88 D3
Al Jawf Saudi Arabia 89 H2
Al Jawf prov. Saudi Arabia 77 D5
Al Jawlān hills Syria see Golan
Al Jawsh Libya 88 A1
Al Jaza'ir Alg. see Algiers
Alj Beyk Iran 80 C2
Aljezur Port. 42 B4
Al Jiṭhāmīyah Saudi Arabia 89 I3
Al Jīzah Egypt see Giza
Al Jīzah governorate Egypt 78 B5
Al Jubayl Saudi Arabia 76 D4
Al Jubayl hills Saudi Arabia 80 A5
Al Jubaylah Saudi Arabia 80 A5
Aljucén r. Spain 42 C3
Al Jufra Oasis Libya 88 B2
Al Jumūm Saudi Arabia 89 H4
Al Junaynah Saudi Arabia 89 I4
Al Jurayd i. Saudi Arabia 80 B5
Al Juwayf depr. Syria 77 C3
Al Kahfah Saudi Arabia 89 I3
Alkali Flat salt flat NV U.S.A. 136 C1
Alkali Flat salt flat NV U.S.A. 136 E1
Alkaliya r. Ukr. 46 G2
Alkamari Niger 93 H2
Al Karak Jordan 78 C5
Al Kāẓimīyah Iraq 79 F4
Al Khābūrah Oman 76 F5
Al Khaḍrā' well Saudi Arabia 79 E5
Al Khafaq well Saudi Arabia 80 A5
Al Khalf Saudi Arabia 89 I3
Al Khalīl West Bank see Hebron
Al Khāliṣ Iraq 79 F4
Al Khārijah Egypt 89 F3
Al Kharrārah Qatar 80 B5
Al Khaṣab Oman 76 F4
Al Khasfah well Oman 76 E6
Al Khāṣirah Saudi Arabia 89 I4
Al-Khatam reg. U.A.E. 80 C5
Al Khawr Qatar 80 B5
Al Khīṣah well Saudi Arabia 80 B5
Al Khiẓāmī well Saudi Arabia 80 B5
Al Khobar Saudi Arabia 80 B5
Al Khubrah Saudi Arabia 80 B5
Al Khufrah Libya 88 D3
Al Khufrah Oasis Libya 88 D3
Al Khums Libya 88 B1
Al Khunfah sand area Saudi Arabia 89 H2
Al Khunn Saudi Arabia 76 D5
Al Khuwayr Qatar 80 B5
Al Kifl Iraq 79 F4
Al Kir'ānah Qatar 80 B5
Alkmaar Neth. 36 B2
Al Kūfah Iraq 79 F4
Al Kumayt Iraq 79 F4
Al Kūt Iraq 79 F4
Al Kuwayt country Asia see Kuwait
Al Kuwayt Kuwait see Kuwait
Al Labbah plain Saudi Arabia 89 I2
Al Ladhiqīyah Syria see Latakia
Al Lādhiqīyah governorate Syria 77 B2
Allagadda India 72 C3
Allahabad India 75 D4
Al Lajā lava field Syria 77 C3
Allakh-Yun' Rus. Fed. 27 N3
Allanmyo Myanmar 60 A4
'Allāqī, Wādī al watercourse Egypt 89 G4
Allariz Spain 42 C1
Alldays S. Africa 99 F4
Allegheny r. U.S.A. 130 D3
Allegheny Mountains U.S.A. 130 B5
Allegheny Reservoir U.S.A. 130 D3
Allen, Lough l. Rep. of Ireland 35 B4
Allen, Mount U.S.A. 122 A2
Allendale U.S.A. 129 C5
Allende Coahuila Mex. 133 A6
Allende Nuevo León Mex. 126 F6
Allenford Canada 130 C1
Allenstein Poland see Olsztyn
Allensville U.S.A. 130 B4
Allentown U.S.A. 131 F3
Alleppey India 72 C4
Aller r. Germany 36 D2
Alliance NE U.S.A. 134 G4
Alliance OH U.S.A. 130 C3
Al Lībīyah country Africa see Libya
Allier r. France 39 E3
Al Liffiyah well Iraq 79 E5
Alligator Point Australia 111 E3
Al Lihābah well Saudi Arabia 80 A5
Allikhe India 72 C2
Allinge-Sandvig Denmark 33 D5
Al Liṣāfah well Saudi Arabia 80 A5
Al Lisān pen. Jordan 77 B4
Allison U.S.A. 132 C3
Alliston Canada 130 D1
Al Līth Saudi Arabia 89 I4
Al Liwā' oasis U.A.E. 76 E5
Allonnes Pays de la Loire France 38 D3
Allora Australia 111 H6
Allschwil Switz. 39 G3
Al Luḥayyah Yemen 89 I6
Allur India 72 D3
Alluru Kottapatnam India 72 D3
Al Lussuf well Iraq 79 E5
Alma Canada 125 G3
Alma KS U.S.A. 132 B4
Alma MI U.S.A. 130 A2
Alma NE U.S.A. 132 B3
Al Ma'āniyah Iraq 79 E5
Alma-Ata Kazakh. see Almaty
Almacelles Spain 43 G2
Almada Port. 42 B3
Al Madāfi' plat. Saudi Arabia 77 C5
Al Ma'danīyāt well Iraq 79 F5
Almaden Australia 111 F3
Almadén Spain 42 D3
Al Madīnah Saudi Arabia see Medina
Al Mafraq Jordan 78 D4
Al Maghāriq Egypt 89 F3
Al Mahbas W. Sahara 90 C4
Al Maḥmūdīyah Iraq 79 F4
Al Mahwīt Yemen 76 C6
Al Majma'ah Saudi Arabia 76 D4
Almăjului, Munții mts Romania 46 C2
Al Maks al Baḥrī Egypt 89 F3
Al Malsūnīyah reg. Saudi Arabia 80 B5
Al Manāmah Bahrain see Manama
Almanor, Lake U.S.A. 136 B1
Almansa Spain 43 F3
Al Manṣūrah Egypt 89 F2
Almanzor mt. Spain 42 D2
Almanzora r. Spain 43 F4
Al Ma'qil Iraq 79 F5
Almār Afgh. 81 F3
Almar r. Spain 42 D2
Al Mariyyah U.A.E. 76 E5
Al Marj Libya 88 D1
Almas, Rio das r. Brazil 150 B5
Al Matmarfag W. Sahara 90 B4

▶Almaty Kazakh. 70 E3
Former capital of Kazakhstan.

Al Mayādīn Syria 79 E4
Almazán Spain 43 E2
Almeida Port. 42 C2
Almeirim Brazil 147 H5
Almeirim Port. 42 B3
Almelo Neth. 36 C2
Almenara Brazil 151 D6
Almenara Spain 43 F3
Almenara, Sierra de hills Spain 43 F4
Almendra, Embalse de resr Spain 42 C2
Almendralejo Spain 42 C3
Almere Neth. 36 B2
Almería Spain 43 E4
Almería, Golfo de b. Spain 43 E4
Al'metievsk Rus. Fed. see Al'met'yevsk
Al'met'yevsk Rus. Fed. 28 J5
Älmhult Sweden 33 D4
Al Miḍhnab Saudi Arabia 89 J3
Al Miḥrāḍ reg. Saudi Arabia 76 E5
Almina, Punta pt Spain 42 D5
Al Mindak Saudi Arabia 89 I4
Al Minyā Egypt 89 F2
Al Minyā governorate Egypt 78 B5
Al-Mirfa U.A.E. 80 C5
Almirós Greece see Almyros
Al Mish'āb Saudi Arabia 76 D4
Al Mismīyah Syria 77 C3
Almodôvar Port. 42 B4
Almodóvar del Campo Spain 42 D3
Almont U.S.A. 130 B2
Almonte Spain 42 C4
Almonte r. Spain 42 C3
Almora India 73 C3
Almoradí Spain 43 F3
Almorox Spain 42 D2
Al Mota well Niger 93 G2
Almoustarat Mali 93 F1
Al Mu'ayzilah hill Saudi Arabia 77 D5
Al Mubarrez Saudi Arabia 76 D4
Al Mudairib Oman 76 F5
Al Mudawwarah Jordan 78 D5
Al Muharraq Bahrain 80 B5
Al Muḥtaṭab depr. Saudi Arabia 77 C5
Al Mukallā Yemen see Mukalla
Al Mukhā Yemen see Mocha
Al Mukhaylī Libya 88 D1
Almuñécar Spain 42 E4
Al Muqdādīyah Iraq 79 F4
Al Mūrītānīyah country Africa see Mauritania
Al Murūt well Saudi Arabia 79 D5
Al Musannāh ridge Saudi Arabia 80 A4
Al Musayjīd Saudi Arabia 89 H3
Al Muthannā governorate Iraq 79 F5
Al Muwayliḥ Saudi Arabia 89 G3

173

Bañados de Otuquis marsh Bol. 149 F4
Banalia Dem. Rep. Congo 94 E4
Banamba Mali 92 D2
Banan China 66 C2
Banana Australia 111 G5
Bananal, Ilha do i. Brazil 150 B4
Bananga India 73 G5
Banankoro Guinea 92 C3
Banapur India 73 E2
Banarlı Turkey 46 E4
Banas r. India 74 C4
Banâs, Ra's pt Egypt 89 G4
Banaz Turkey 78 B3
Ban Ban Laos 60 C4
Banbar China 75 G3
Banbridge U.K. 35 C4
Ban Bua Yai Thai. 61 C5
Banbury U.K. 35 F5
Banca Romania 46 E1
Banc d'Arguin, Parc National du nat. park Mauritania 90 A5
Ban Chiang tourist site Thai. 60 C4
Banchory U.K. 34 E3
Bancroft Canada 124 E4
Bancroft Zambia see Chililabombwe
Band Iran 80 D3
Banda Dem. Rep. Congo 94 E3
Banda Madhya Pradesh India 74 C4
Banda Uttar Pradesh India 74 D4
Banda, Kepulauan is Indon. 57 G6
Banda Aceh Indon. 58 A1
Banda Banda, Mount Australia 112 E3
Bandahara, Gunung mt. Indon. 58 B2
Bandai-Asahi National Park Japan 65 D5
Bandama r. Côte d'Ivoire 92 D4
Bandama Blanc r. Côte d'Ivoire 92 D3
Bandān Iran 81 E4
Bandān Kūh mts Iran 81 E4
Bandar India see Machilipatnam
Bandar Abbas Iran see Bandar-e 'Abbās
Bandaragung Indon. 58 D4
Bandarban Bangl. 75 G5
Bandar-e 'Abbās Iran 80 D5
Bandar-e Anzalī Iran 80 B2
Bandar-e Chārak Iran 80 C5
Bandar-e Deylam Iran 80 B4
Bandar-e Emām Khomeynī Iran 80 B4
Bandar-e Lengeh Iran 80 C5
Bandar-e Maqām Iran 80 C5
Bandar-e Ma'shur Iran 80 B4
Bandar-e Moghūyeh Iran 80 C5
Bandar-e Pahlavī Iran see Bandar-e Anzalī
Bandar-e Shāh Iran see Bandar-e Torkeman
Bandar-e Shāhpūr Iran see Bandar-e Emām Khomeynī
Bandar-e Torkeman Iran 80 C2
Bandar Lampung Indon. 58 D4
Bandar Murcaayo Somalia 96 F2
Bandarpunch mt. India 74 C3
▶Bandar Seri Begawan Brunei 59 F1
Capital of Brunei.
Banda Sea Indon. 57 H7
Bandeirante Brazil 150 B5
Bandeiras, Pico de mt. Brazil 151 D7
Bandera Arg. 152 E2
Bandera U.S.A. 133 B6
Banderas Mex. 135 F7
Bandhi Pak. 81 G5
Bandhogarh India 74 D5
Bandi r. India 74 B4
Bandia r. India 72 D2
Bandiagara Mali 92 E2
Bandiagara, Falaise de esc. Mali 92 E2
Band-i-Amir r. Afgh. 81 F2
Band-i-Baba mts Afgh. 81 E3
Band-i-Husain Nun mts Iran 80 C3
Bandikui India 74 C4
Bandinī Iran 81 D5
Bandipur Jammu and Kashmir 74 B2
Bandipur National Park India 72 C4
Bandırma Turkey 78 A2
Band-i-Turkestan mts Afgh. 81 E3
Bandjarmasin Indon. see Banjarmasin
Bandjer pass Serb. and Mont. 46 A3
Bandon Rep. of Ireland 35 B6
Bandon r. Rep. of Ireland 35 B6
Ban Don Thai. see Surat Thani
Bandon U.S.A. 134 A4
Ban Don, Ao b. Thai. 61 B6
Band Qir Iran 80 B4
Bandula Moz. 99 G3
Bandundu Dem. Rep. Congo 94 C5
Bandundu prov. Dem. Rep. Congo 95 C6
Bandung Indon. 59 D4
Bandya Australia 109 C7
Băneasa Romania 46 E2
Băneasa Romania 46 E2
Bāneh Iran 80 A3
Banera India 74 B4
Bañeres Spain 43 F3
Banff Canada 134 D2
Banff U.K. 34 E3
Banff National Park Canada 123 G5
Banfora Burkina 92 D3
Bang Cent. Afr. Rep. 94 B3
Banga Dem. Rep. Congo 95 D6
Bangall Creek watercourse Australia 111 F4
Bangalore India 72 C3
Banganapalle India 72 C3
Banganga r. India 74 C4
Bangangté Cameroon 93 H4
Bangaon India 75 F5
Bangar Brunei 59 F1
Bangara r. Bangl. 75 F5
Bangarapet India 72 C3
Bangassou Cent. Afr. Rep. 94 D3
Bangdag Co salt l. China 75 D2
Bangfai, Xé r. Laos 60 D4
Banggai Indon. 57 F6
Banggai, Kepulauan is Indon. 57 F6
Banggi i. Sabah Malaysia 59 G1
Banghāzī Libya see Benghazi
Banghiang, Xé r. Laos 61 D4
Bangka i. Indon. 58 D3
Bangka, Selat sea chan. Indon. 58 D3
Bangkalan Indon. 59 F4
Bangkaru i. Indon. 58 B2
Bangkinang Indon. 58 C2
Bangko Indon. 58 C3
Bangkog Co salt l. China 75 F3
▶Bangkok Thai. 61 C5
Capital of Thailand.
Bangkok, Bight of b. Thai. 61 C5
Bangkor China 75 E3
Bangla state India see West Bengal
▶Bangladesh country Asia 75 F5
8th most populous country in the world.
asia 52–53, 82
world 16–17
Bang Lang Reservoir Thai. 58 C1
Bangma Shan mts China 66 A4
Bang Mun Nak Thai. 61 C4
Bångnäs Sweden 32 D2
Bangolo Côte d'Ivoire 92 D4
Bangong Co salt l. China/Jammu and Kashmir 74 C2
Bangor Gwynedd, Wales U.K. 35 D5
Bangor Northern Ireland U.K. 35 D4
Bangor ME U.S.A. 127 M3
Bangor PA U.S.A. 131 F3
Bangriposi India 75 E5
Bangsalsepulun Indon. 59 G3
Bang Saphan Yai Thai. 61 B6
Bangu Dem. Rep. Congo 95 D7
▶Bangui Cent. Afr. Rep. 94 C3
Capital of Central African Republic.
Bangui Phil. 67 G5
Bangula Malawi 97 B9
Bangunpurba Indon. 58 B2
Banguru Dem. Rep. Congo 94 E4
Bangweulu, Lake Zambia 95 F7
Banhā Egypt 89 F2
Banhine, Parque Nacional de nat. park Moz. 99 G4
Ban Houayxay Laos 60 C3
Ban Houei Sai Laos see Ban Houayxay
Bani Burkina 93 E2
Bani Cent. Afr. Rep. 94 D3
Baní Dom. Rep. 139 J5
Bani r. Mali 92 D2
Bani, Jbel ridge Morocco 90 C3
Bania Cent. Afr. Rep. 94 C3
Bani-Bangou Niger 93 F2
Banifing r. Mali 92 D2
Banifing r. Mali 92 D2
Banihal Pass and Tunnel Jammu and Kashmir 74 B2
Banikoara Benin 93 F3
Banī Mazār Egypt 78 B5
Banister r. U.S.A. 130 D5
Banī Suwayf Egypt 89 F2
Banī Suwayf governorate Egypt 78 B5
Banī Thawr Saudi Arabia 89 I5
Banitsa Bulg. 46 C3
Banī Walīd Libya 88 B2
Bāniyās Syria 78 C4
Banja Luka Bos.-Herz. 44 F2
Banjar India 74 C3
Banjarbaru Indon. 59 F3
Banjarmasin Indon. 59 F3
Banjes, Liqeni i resr Albania 46 B4
▶Banjul Gambia 92 A2
Capital of The Gambia.
Banka India 75 E4
Banka Banka Australia 110 C3
Bankapur India 72 B3
Ban Khao Yoi Thai. 61 B5
Banki India 73 E1
Bankim Cameroon 93 H4
Banko, Massif de mt. Guinea 92 C3
Bankobankoang i. Indon. 59 G4
Bankol India 72 B2
Bankon Guinea 92 C3
Banks Island B.C. Canada 122 D4
Banks Island N.W.T. Canada 120 G2
Banks Islands Vanuatu 107 F3
▶Banks Peninsula N.Z. 113 C3
oceania 102–103
Banks Strait Australia 112 D6
Bankura India 75 E5
Bankya Bulg. 46 C3
Bankya Bulg. 46 C3
Ban Lamduan Thai. 61 C5
Banloc Romania 46 B2
Ban Mae Mo Thai. 60 B4
Banmauk Myanmar 60 A2
Bann r. U.K. 35 C4
Ban Napè Laos 60 D4
Ban Na San Thai. 61 B6
Bannerman Town Bahamas 129 D7
Banning U.S.A. 136 D5
Banningville Dem. Rep. Congo see Bandundu
Bannivka Ukr. 46 F2
Ban Noi Myanmar 60 B4
Bannu Pak. 81 G3
Bañolas Spain see Banyoles
Baños Ecuador 146 B5
Baños de Puritama Chile 148 C5
Bánovce nad Bebravou Slovakia 37 I4
Banow Afgh. see Andarāb
Ban Phaeng Thai. 60 D4
Ban Phai Thai. 61 C4
Ban Phon Laos 61 D5
Banphot Phisai Thai. 61 B5
Ban Pong Thai. 61 B5
Banqiao China 66 C3
Ban Saraphi Thai. 60 B4
Ban Sawi Thai. 61 B6
Bansgaon India 75 D4
Bansi Rajasthan India 74 B4
Bansi Uttar Pradesh India 74 C4
Bansi Uttar Pradesh India 75 D4
Banská Bystrica Slovakia 37 I4
Banská Štiavnica Slovakia 37 I4
Bansko Bulg. 46 C4
Bansloi r. India 75 E4
Ban Sut Ta Thai. 60 B4
Banswada India 72 C2
Banswara India 74 B5
Bantè Benin 93 F3
Ban Tha Kham Thai. 61 B6
Ban Tha Song Yang Thai. 60 B4
Banthat mts Cambodia see Cardamom Range
Ban Tha Tako Thai. 61 C5
Ban Tha Tum Thai. 61 C5
Ban Thung Luang Thai. 61 B5
Bantry Rep. of Ireland 35 B6
Bantry Bay Rep. of Ireland 35 B6
Bantul Indon. 59 E4
Bantva India 74 A5
Bantval India 72 B3
Banyak, Pulau-pulau is Indon. 58 B2
Banyo Cameroon 93 H4
Banyoles Spain 43 H1
Banyuwangi Indon. 59 F5
Banzare Coast Antarctica 167 G2
Banzare Seamount sea feature Indian Ocean 163 M9
Banzart Tunisia see Bizerte
Banzyville Dem. Rep. Congo see Mobayi-Mbongo
Bao, Embalse de resr Spain see Vao, Embalse de
Bao, Ouadi watercourse Chad 88 D5
Baochang China 63 J3
Baocheng China 66 C1
Baoding China 63 J4
Baofeng China 67 E1
Baoji Shaanxi China 66 C1
Baoji Shaanxi China 66 C1
Baokang China 67 D2
Bao Lôc Vietnam 61 D6
Baoqing China 64 C3
Baoro Cent. Afr. Rep. 94 B3
Baoshan Shanghai China 67 G2
Baoshan Yunnan China 66 A3
Baotou China 63 I3
Baoulé r. Mali 92 C2
Baoulé r. Mali 92 D2
Baoxing China 66 B2
Baoxiu China 66 B4
Baoying China 67 F1
Baoyou China see Ledong
Bap India 74 B4
Bapatla India 72 D3
Bapaume France 39 E1
Bapu China see Meigu
Baqarah Saudi Arabia 89 I4
Baqiu China see Xiajiang
Baqrān Saudi Arabia 89 I4
Ba'qūbah Iraq 79 F4
Bar Serb. and Mont. 46 A3
Bara Nigeria 93 H3
Bara Sudan 89 F6
Bara well Sudan 94 E2
Baraawe Somalia 96 E4
Barabai Indon. 59 F3
Bara Banki India 74 D4
Barabhum India 75 E5
Baraboo U.S.A. 132 D3
Barabouié Burkina 93 E2
Baracaldo Spain see Barakaldo
Baracoa Cuba 127 L7
Baradā, Nahr r. Syria 77 C3
Baradero Arg. 152 F3
Bărăganului, Câmpia plain Romania 46 E2
Baragoi Kenya 96 C4
Baragua, Sierra de mts Venez. 146 D2
Barahona Dom. Rep. 139 J5
Barail Range mts India 75 G4
Bara Issa r. Mali 92 E1
Barak Afgh. 81 G2
Barak r. India 75 G4
Baraka watercourse Eritrea/Sudan 89 H5
Barakaldo Spain 42 E1
Barakī Barak Afgh. 81 G3
Barakot India 75 E5
Baralaba Australia 111 G5
Bara Lacha Pass India 74 C2
Baram r. Sarawak Malaysia 59 F1
Baram, Tanjong pt Sarawak Malaysia 59 F1
Baramanni Guyana 147 G3
Baramati India 72 B2
Barameiya Sudan 89 H5
Baramula Jammu and Kashmir 74 B2
Baran India 74 C4
Baran r. Pak. 81 G5
Bārān, Kūh-e mts Iran 81 E3
Baranavichy Belarus 29 C5
Barang, Dasht-i des. Afgh. 81 E3
Baranikha Rus. Fed. 27 Q3
Baranīs Egypt 89 G4
Baranof Island U.S.A. 120 F4
Baranovichi Belarus see Baranavichy
Baranowicze Belarus see Baranavichy
Barão de Melgaço Brazil 149 G4
Baraolt Romania 46 D1
Baraqueville France 38 E4
Bararati r. Brazil 149 F1
Barat Daya, Kepulauan is Indon. 57 G7
Baratta Australia 112 A4
Barauaná, Serra mts Brazil 147 F4
Baraut India 74 C3
Barbacena Minas Gerais Brazil 151 D7
Barbacena Pará Brazil 147 H5
▶Barbados country West Indies 147 G1
northamerica 118–119, 140
Barbar, Jabal mt. Egypt 77 A5
Barbara Lake Canada 124 C3
Barbastro Spain 43 G1
Barbate de Franco Spain 42 D4
Bārbele Latvia 33 G4
Barbezieux-St-Hilaire France 38 C4
Barbigha India 75 E4
Barbosa Col. 146 C3
Barbour Bay Canada 123 M2
Barbours U.S.A. 131 E3
Barbourville U.S.A. 130 B5
Barbuda i. Antigua and Barbuda 139 L5
Barcaldine Australia 111 F4
Barce Libya see Al Marj
Barcellona Pozzo di Gotto Sicily Italy 45 E5
Barcelona Spain 43 H2
Barcelona Venez. 147 E2
Barcelonnette France 39 G4
Barcelos Brazil 147 F5
Barcin Poland 37 H2
Barcino Spain see Barcelona
Barclayville Liberia 92 C4
Barcoo watercourse Australia 111 E5
Barcoo Creek watercourse Australia see Cooper Creek
Barcoo National Park Australia see Welford National Park
Barcs Hungary 44 F2
Bärdä Azer. 79 F2
Bardaale Somalia 96 E3
Bárðarbunga mt. Iceland 32 [inset]
Bardas Blancas Arg. 152 C3
Bardaskan Iran 80 D3
Bardawīl, Sabkhat al lag. Egypt 77 A4
Barddhaman India 75 E5
Bardejov Slovakia 37 J4
Bardera Somalia see Baardheere
Bard Shah Iran 80 B3
Bardsīr Iran 80 D4
Bardstown U.S.A. 128 B4
Barduli Italy see Barletta
Bardwell U.S.A. 128 A4
Barē Eth. 96 D3
Bareilly India 74 C3
Bareli India 74 C5
Barengapara India 75 F4
Barentsburg Svalbard 26 B2
Barents Island Svalbard see Barentsøya
Barentsøya i. Svalbard 26 C2
Barents Sea Arctic Ocean 26 D2
Barentu Eritrea 89 H6
Bareo Sarawak Malaysia 59 F2
Barfleur, Pointe de pt France 38 C2
Barga China 75 D3
Bargaal Somalia 96 F2
Bārgāh Iran 80 D5
Bargē Eth. 96 C3
Bargi India 74 C5
Bargırı Turkey see Muradiye
Bargteheide Germany 36 E2
Barguna Bangl. 75 F5
Barguir India 72 C4
Barhaj India 75 D4
Barhalganj India 75 D4
Bar Harbor U.S.A. 128 F2
Barharwa India 75 E4
Bari Dem. Rep. Congo 94 C4
Bari India 74 C4
Bari Italy 44 F4
Bari admin. reg. Somalia 96 F2
Bari Doab lowland Pak. 74 B3
Barika Alg. 91 G2
Barikot Afgh. 74 A2
Barikot Nepal 75 D3
Barima r. Guyana 147 G2
Barinas Venez. 146 D2
Barinas state Venez. 146 D2
Baringa Dem. Rep. Congo 94 D4
Baringo, Lake Kenya 96 C4
Baripada India 75 E5
Bariri Brazil 149 H5
Bari Sadri India 74 B4
Barisal Bangl. 75 F5
Barisal admin. div. Bangl. 75 F5
Barisan, Pegunungan mts Indon. 58 C3
Barito r. Indon. 59 F3
Baritu, Parque Nacional nat. park Arg. 149 D5
Barium Italy see Bari
Barjols France 39 G5
Barjūj, Wādī watercourse Libya 88 B3
Barkam China 66 B2
Barkan, Ra's-e pt Iran 80 B4
Barkava Latvia 33 G4
Barkerville Canada 122 F4
Barkéwol el Abiod Mauritania 92 B1
Barkhan Pak. 81 G4
Barki Saraiya India 75 E4
Barkley, Lake U.S.A. 128 B4
Barkley Sound inlet Canada 134 A2
Barkly East S. Africa 99 E6
Barkly Tableland reg. Australia 110 C3
Barkol China 70 H3
Barkot India 74 C3
Bârlad Romania 46 E1
Bârladului, Podişul plat. Romania 46 E1
Bar-le-Duc France 39 F2
Barlee, Lake salt flat Australia 109 B7
Barlee Range hills Australia 108 A5
Barletta Italy 44 F4
Barlinek Poland 37 G2
Barlow Canada 122 B2
Barlow Lake Canada 123 K2
Barmedman Australia 112 C4
Barmen-Elberfeld Germany see Wuppertal
Barmer India 74 A4
Barm Fīrūz, Kūh-e mt. Iran 79 G5
Barmouth U.K. 35 D5
Barnagar India 74 B5
Barnala India 74 B3
Barnard Castle U.K. 35 F4
Barnato Australia 112 C3
Barnaul Rus. Fed. 62 C1
Barnegat U.S.A. 131 F4
Barnegat Bay U.S.A. 131 F4
Barnesboro U.S.A. 130 D3
Barnes Icecap Canada 121 L2
Barnesville GA U.S.A. 129 C5
Barnesville MN U.S.A. 132 B2
Barnet U.S.A. 131 G1
Barneville-Carteret France 38 C2
Barney Top mt. U.S.A. 137 G3
Barnhart U.S.A. 133 A6
Barnsley U.K. 35 F5
Barnstable U.S.A. 131 H3
Barnstaple U.K. 35 D6
Barnstaple Bay U.K. see Bideford Bay
Barnwell U.S.A. 129 C5
Baro Nigeria 93 G3
Baroda Gujarat India see Vadodara
Baroda Madhya Pradesh India 74 C4
Baroghil Pass Afgh. 81 H2
Barong China 66 A2
Barons Range hills Australia 108 D6
Baroua Cent. Afr. Rep. 94 E3
Baro Wenz r. Eth. 96 B2
Barpeta India 75 F4
Bar Pla Soi Thai. see Chon Buri
Barqah, Jabal mt. Egypt 77 B5
Barques, Point Aux U.S.A. 130 B1
Barquisimeto Venez. 146 D2
Barra Brazil 150 D4
Barra i. U.K. 34 C3
Barracão do Barreto Brazil 149 F2
Barrackville U.S.A. 130 C4
Barra do Bugres Brazil 149 F3
Barra do Corda Brazil 150 C3
Barra do Cuanza Angola 95 B7
Barra do Garças Brazil 149 G3
Barrado Mendes Brazil 150 D4
Barra do São Manuel Brazil 149 F1
Barra Falsa, Ponta da pt Moz. 99 G4
Barraigh i. U.K. see Barra
Barrāmīyah Egypt 89 G3
Barranca Peru 148 A2
Barranca Venez. 146 C2
Barrancabermeja Col. 146 C3
Barrancas r. Arg. 152 C4
Barrancas Barinas Venez. 146 D2
Barrancas Monagas Venez. 147 F2
Barranco de Loba Col. 146 C2
Barranquilla Atlántico Col. 146 C2
Barranquilla Guaviare Col. 146 C4
Barranquita Peru 146 B6
Barras Brazil 150 D3
Barrax Spain 43 E3
Barre U.S.A. 131 G1
Barreal Arg. 152 C2
Barre des Ecrins mt. France 39 G4
Barreiras Brazil 150 C5
Barreirinha Brazil 147 G5
Barreirinhas Brazil 150 D2
Barreiro r. Brazil 149 G3
Barren Island India 73 G3
Barren Islands U.S.A. 120 D4
Barretos Brazil 149 H5
Barrett, Mount Australia 108 D4
Barrhead Canada 123 H4
Barrie Canada 130 D1
Barrier Bay Antarctica 167 E2
Barrière Canada 122 F5
Barrier Range hills Australia 112 B3
Barrington Canada 125 H5
Barrington, Mount Australia 112 D4
Barrington Lake Canada 123 K3
Barrington Tops National Park Australia 112 D4
Barringun Australia 112 C3
Barro Alto Brazil 149 H3
Barrow Arg. 152 E4
Barrow r. Rep. of Ireland 35 C5
Barrow U.S.A. 120 D1
Barrow, Point U.S.A. 120 D2
Barrow Creek Australia 110 C4
Barrow-in-Furness U.K. 35 E4
Barrow Island Australia 108 A5
Barrow Range hills Australia 110 A5
Barrow Strait Canada 121 J2
Barr Smith Range hills Australia 109 C6
Barry U.K. 35 E6
Barrydale S. Africa 98 D7
Barry Islands Canada 123 I1
Barry Mountains Australia 112 C5
Barrys Bay Canada 124 E4
Barryville U.S.A. 131 F3
Barsalogo Burkina 93 E2
Barshi India see Barsi
Barsi India 72 B2
Barstow U.S.A. 136 D4
Barsur India 72 D2
Bar-sur-Aube France 39 F2
Bar-sur-Seine France 39 F2
Bārta r. Latvia 33 F4
Bartang r. Tajik. 81 G2
Barth Germany 37 F1
Bartica Guyana 147 G3
Bartın Turkey 78 C2
Bartle Frere, Mount Australia 111 F3
Bartlesville U.S.A. 133 B4
Bartlett U.S.A. 132 B3
Bartlett Lake Canada 123 G2
Bartlett Reservoir U.S.A. 137 G5
Barton U.S.A. 131 G1
Bartoszyce Poland 37 J1
Bartow U.S.A. 129 C7
Barú, Volcán vol. Panama 139 H7
Baruipur India 75 F5
Barumun r. Indon. 58 C2
Barung i. Indon. 59 F5
Barus Indon. 58 B2
Baruun Urt Mongolia 63 I2
Baruva India 73 E2
Barwa India 75 E5
Barwah India 74 C5
Barwala Gujarat India 74 A5
Barwala Haryana India 74 B3
Barwani India 74 B5
Barwa Sagar India 74 C4
Barwice Poland 37 H2
Barwon r. Australia 111 F6
Barycz r. Poland 37 H3
Barygaza India see Bharuch
Barysaw Belarus 29 D5
Barysh Rus. Fed. 29 H5
Bāsa'īdū Iran 80 C5
Basaga Turkm. 81 F2
Basail Arg. 152 F1
Basăk, Tônlé r. Cambodia 61 D6
Basalt Island Hong Kong China 67 [inset]
Basanga Dem. Rep. Congo 95 E6
Basankusu Dem. Rep. Congo 94 C4
Basantpur India 75 E4
Basarabeasca Moldova 46 F1
Basarabi Romania 46 F2
Basargechar Armenia see Vardenis
Basavilbaso Arg. 152 F3
Bas-Congo prov. Dem. Rep. Congo 95 B6
Bascuñán, Cabo c. Chile 152 C2
Bascuñana, Sierra de mts Spain 43 E2
Basel Switz. 39 G3
Basel-Mulhouse airport France 39 G3
Basentello r. Italy 45 F4
Basento r. Italy 45 F4
Bashākerd, Kūhhā-ye mts Iran 80 D5
Bashan China see Chongren
Bashanta Rus. Fed. see Gorodovikovsk
Bashaw Canada 123 H4
Bashgul r. Afgh. 81 G3
Bāshī Iran 80 B4
Bashi Channel Taiwan 67 G4
Bashimuke Dem. Rep. Congo 95 E6
Bashkiria aut. rep. Rus. Fed. see Bashkortostan, Respublika
Bashkirskaya A.S.S.R. aut. rep. Rus. Fed. see Bashkortostan, Respublika
Bashkortostan, Respublika aut. rep. Rus. Fed. 28 K5
Bashmakovo Rus. Fed. 29 G5
Bāsht Iran 80 B4
Bashtanka Ukr. 29 E7
Basi India 74 C4
Basia India 75 E5
Basilaki Island P.N.G. 111 G1
Basilan i. Phil. 57 F4
Basildon U.K. 35 G6
Basile, Pico mt. Equat. Guinea 93 H5
Basilicata admin. reg. Italy 45 E4
Basin U.S.A. 134 E3
Basingstoke U.K. 35 F6
Basin Lake Canada 123 J4
Bāsīra r. Iraq 79 F4
Basirhat India 75 F5
Basīţ, Ra's al pt Syria 77 B2
Başkale Turkey 79 F3
Baskatong, Réservoir Canada 124 F4
Baskerville, Cape Australia 108 C4
Başkomutan Milli Parkı nat. park Turkey 78 B3
Baskunchak, Ozero l. Rus. Fed. 29 H6
Basle Switz. see Basel
Basmat India 72 C2
Baso i. Indon. 58 C3
Basoda India 74 C5
Basoko Dem. Rep. Congo 94 D4
Basongo Dem. Rep. Congo 95 D6
Basotu Tanz. 97 B6
Basque Country aut. comm. Spain see País Vasco
Basra Iraq 79 F5
Bassano Canada 123 H5
Bassano del Grappa Italy 44 C2
Bassar Togo 93 F3
Bassas da India reef Indian Ocean 162 J7
Bassas de Pedro Padua Bank sea feature India 72 B3
Bassawa Côte d'Ivoire 92 D3
Bassein Myanmar 60 A4
Bassein r. Myanmar 61 A4
Basse-Kotto pref. Cent. Afr. Rep. 94 D3
Basse-Normandie admin. reg. France 38 C2
Basse Santa Su Gambia 92 B2
▶Basse-Terre Guadeloupe 139 L5
Capital of Guadeloupe.
▶Basseterre St Kitts and Nevis 139 L5
Capital of St Kitts and Nevis.
Bassett NE U.S.A. 132 B3
Bassett VA U.S.A. 130 D5
Bassikounou Mauritania 92 D2
Bassila Benin 93 F3
Basso, Plateau de Chad 88 D5
Bass Strait Australia 112 C5
Basswood Lake Canada 124 B3
Båstad Sweden 33 D4
Bastak Iran 80 C5
Bastānābād Iran 80 A2
Basti India 75 D4
Bastia Corsica France 39 H5
Bastia Italy 44 D3
Bastian U.S.A. 130 C5
Bastogne Belgium 39 F1
Bastrop LA U.S.A. 127 H5
Bastrop TX U.S.A. 133 B6
Bastuträsk Sweden 32 F2
Basu, Tanjung pt Indon. 58 C3
Basul r. Pak. 81 F5
Basuo China see Dongfang
Basutoland country Africa see Lesotho
Bas-Zaïre prov. Dem. Rep. Congo see Bas-Congo
Bat mt. Croatia 44 F3
Bata Equat. Guinea 93 H5
Batabanó, Golfo de b. Cuba 127 J7
Batac Phil. 67 G5
Batagay-Alyta Rus. Fed. 27 N3
Bataguaçu Brazil 149 G5
Batak Bulg. 46 D4
Batakan Indon. 59 F4
Batala India 74 B3
Batalha Brazil 150 D3
Batalha Port. 42 B3
Batam i. Indon. 58 D2
Batama Dem. Rep. Congo 94 E4
Batamay Rus. Fed. 27 M3
Batan i. Phil. 57 F1
Batang China 66 A2
Batangafo Cent. Afr. Rep. 94 C3
Batang Ali National Park Sarawak Malaysia 59 F2
Batangas Phil. 57 F3
Batanghari r. Indon. 58 D3
Batangtoru Indon. 58 B2
Batan Islands Phil. 57 F1
Bátaszék Hungary 46 A1
Batatais Brazil 149 I5
Batavia Indon. see Jakarta
Batavia NY U.S.A. 130 D2
Batavia OH U.S.A. 130 A4
Bataysk Rus. Fed. 29 F7
Batchawana Mountain Canada 124 C4
Bătdâmbâng Cambodia 61 C5
Bateemeucica, Gunung mt. Indon. 58 A1
Batéké, Plateaux Congo 94 B5
Båteng Norway 32 G1
Batesburg U.S.A. 129 C5
Bates Range hills Australia 109 C6
Batesville AR U.S.A. 133 D5
Batesville MS U.S.A. 133 D5
Batetskiy Rus. Fed. 28 D4
Bath Canada 131 E1
Bath U.K. 35 E6
Bath ME U.S.A. 131 I2
Bath NY U.S.A. 131 E2
Bath PA U.S.A. 131 F3
Batha pref. Chad 88 C6
Batha watercourse Chad 88 C6
Bathinda India 74 B3
Bathurst Australia 112 D4
Bathurst Canada 125 H4
Bathurst Gambia see Banjul
Bathurst, Cape Canada 120 G2
Bathurst Inlet Canada 123 I1
Bathurst Inlet inlet Canada 123 I1
Bathurst Island Australia 110 B1
Bathurst Island Canada 121 J2
Batī Eth. 96 D2
Batia Benin 93 F3
Batié Burkina 92 E3
Batı Menteşe Dağları mts Turkey 47 E6
Bāţin, Wādī al watercourse Asia 79 F5
Batı Toroslar mts Turkey 78 B3
Batken Kyrg. 70 D4
Batken admin. div. Kyrg. 81 G2
Batkes Indon. 108 E1
Bāţlāq-e Gavkhūnī marsh Iran 80 C3
Batman Turkey 79 E3
Batna Alg. 91 G2
Batok, Bukit Sing. 58 [inset]
▶Baton Rouge U.S.A. 127 H5
State capital of Louisiana.
Batopilas Mex. 135 F8
Batote Jammu and Kashmir 74 B2
Batouri Cameroon 93 I4
Batrā' tourist site Jordan see Petra
Batrā', Jabal al mt. Jordan 77 B5
Ba Tri Vietnam 61 D6
Batroûn Lebanon 77 B2
Båtsfjord Norway 32 H1
Battambang Cambodia see Bătdâmbâng
Batti India 74 B3
Batticaloa Sri Lanka 72 D5
Batti Malv i. India 73 G4
Battipaglia Italy 45 E4
Battle r. Canada 123 I4
Battle Creek r. Australia 110 B2
Battle Creek U.S.A. 132 E3
Battleford Canada 123 I4
Battle Mountain U.S.A. 136 D1
Battura Glacier Jammu and Kashmir 74 B1
Batu mt. Eth. 96 C3
Batu, Bukit mt. Sarawak Malaysia 59 F2
Batu, Pulau-pulau is Indon. 58 B3
Batu, Tanjung pt Indon. 59 G2
Batubetumbang Indon. 58 D3
Batu Bora, Bukit mt. Sarawak Malaysia 59 F2
Batudaka i. Indon. 57 F6
Batu Gajah Malaysia 58 C1
Batulanteh mt. Indon. 108 B2
Batulicin Indon. 59 G3
Batulilangmebang, Gunung mt. Indon. 59 F2
Batum Georgia see Bat'umi
Bat'umi Georgia 79 E2
Batumonga Indon. 58 C3
Batu Pahat Malaysia 58 C2
Baturaja Indon. 58 D4
Batys Qazaqstan Oblysy admin. div. Kazakh. see Zapadnyy Kazakhstan
Batz, Île de i. France 38 A2
Bau r. Brazil 149 G1
Bau Sarawak Malaysia 59 E2
Baubau Indon. 57 F7
Baucau East Timor 108 D2
Bauchi Nigeria 93 H3
Bauchi state Nigeria 93 H3
Bauda India 73 E1
Baudette U.S.A. 132 C1
Baudo, Serrania de mts Col. 146 B3
Baudouinville Dem. Rep. Congo see Moba
Bauet well Eth. 96 E3
Baugé France 38 C3
Baukau East Timor see Baucau
Bauld, Cape Canada 125 K3
Baunei Sardinia Italy 45 B4
Bauru Brazil 149 H5
Bauska Latvia 33 G4
Bautino Kazakh. 79 G1
Bautzen Germany 37 G3
Bavaria land Germany see Bayern
Bavda India 72 B2
Båven l. Sweden 33 E4
Baviaanskloofberge mts S. Africa 98 D7
Bavispe Mex. 135 E7
Bavispe r. Mex. 135 E7
Bavla India 74 B5
Bavly Rus. Fed. 28 J5
Baw Myanmar 60 A3
Bawal India 74 C3
Bawal i. Indon. 59 E3
Bawan Indon. 59 F3
Baw Baw National Park Australia 112 C5
Bawdwin Myanmar 60 B3
Bawean i. Indon. 59 F4
Bawku Ghana 93 E3
Bawlake Myanmar 60 B4
Bawolung China 66 B2
Baxian China see Banan
Baxley U.S.A. 129 C6
Baxoi China 66 A2
Bay admin. reg. Somalia 96 D4
Baya r. Côte d'Ivoire 92 E4
Bayad Alg. 45 B7
Bayamo Cuba 127 K7
Bayan China 64 A3
Bayan Indon. 59 G5
Bayana India 74 C4
Bayang, Pegunungan mts Indon. 59 E2
Bayanga-Didi Cent. Afr. Rep. 94 B3
Bayan Gol China see Dengkou
Bayan Har Shan mts China 70 H4
Bayan Har Shankou pass China 66 A1
Bayanhongor Mongolia 62 G2
Bayano, Lago l. Panama 146 B2
Bayan Obo China 63 H3
Bayan Ul China 63 J3
Bayard NE U.S.A. 132 A3
Bayard WV U.S.A. 130 D4
Bayat Turkey 78 B3
Bayāz Iran 80 C4
Bay Bulls Canada 125 K4
Bayburt Turkey 79 E2
Baychunas Kazakh. 29 J7
Bay City MI U.S.A. 130 B2
Bay City TX U.S.A. 133 B6
Baydaratskaya Guba Rus. Fed. 26 G3
Baydhabo Somalia 96 D4
Bayelsa state Nigeria 93 G4
Bayerischer Wald mts Germany 37 F4
Bayerischer Wald nat. park Germany 37 F4
Bayern land Germany 36 E4
Bayer Wald, Nationalpark nat. park Germany 37 F4
Bayeux France 38 C2
Bayfield Canada 130 C2
Bayındır Turkey 78 A3
Bay Islands Hond. see La Bahía, Islas de
Bayizhen China 75 G3
Bayjī Iraq 79 E4
Baykal, Ozero l. Rus. Fed. see Baikal, Lake

Baykal-Amur Magistral Rus. Fed. **64** B1
Baykal Range *mts* Rus. Fed. *see* **Baykal'skiy Khrebet**
Baykal'sk Rus. Fed. **62** G1
Baykal'skiy Khrebet *mts* Rus. Fed. **63** H1
Baykan Turkey **79** E3
Baykibashevo Rus. Fed. **28** K5
Baykit Rus. Fed. **27** J3
Baykonur Kazakh. **70** B2
Baykonyr Kazakh. *see* **Baykonur**
Bay Minette U.S.A. **129** B6
Bayombong Phil. **57** F2
Bayona Spain *see* **Baiona**
Bayonne France **38** C5
Bayóvar Peru **146** A6
Bay Port U.S.A. **130** B2
Bayqongyr Kazakh. *see* **Baykonur**
Bayramaly Turkm. **81** E2
Bayramiç Turkey **78** A3
Bayreuth Germany **36** E4
Bayrūt Lebanon *see* **Beirut**
Baysh *watercourse* Saudi Arabia **89** I5
Bayshonas Kazakh. *see* **Baychunas**
Bay Springs U.S.A. **129** A6
Baysun Uzbek. **81** F2
Bayt Lahm West Bank *see* **Bethlehem**
Baytown U.S.A. **133** C6
Bayunglincir Indon. **58** C3
Bay View N.Z. **113** D2
Bayy al Kabīr, Wādī *watercourse* Libya **88** B2
Baza Spain **43** E4
Baza, Sierra de *mts* Spain **43** E4
Bazarchulan Kazakh. **29** I6
Bazardyuzi, Gora *mt.* Azer./Rus. Fed. **79** F2
Bāzār-e Māsāl Iran **80** B2
Bazarnyy Karabulak Rus. Fed. **29** H5
Bazarshulan Kazakh. *see* **Bazarchulan**
Bazartobe Kazakh. **29** I6
Bazaruto, Ilha do *i.* Moz. **99** G4
Bazas France **38** C4
Bazdar Pak. **81** F5
Bazhong China **66** C2
Baziwehn Liberia **92** C3
Bazmān Iran **81** E5
Bazmān, Kūh-e *mt.* Iran **81** E4
Bcharre Lebanon **77** C2
Be *r.* Vietnam **61** D6
Bé, Nossi *i.* Madag. *see* **Bé, Nosy**
Bé, Nosy *i.* Madag. **99** [inset] K2
Beach City U.S.A. **130** C3
Beachport Australia **112** B5
Beachy Head U.K. **35** G6
Beacon Australia **109** B7
Beacon U.S.A. **131** G3
Beaconsfield Australia **112** C6
Beagle, Canal *sea chan.* Arg. **153** C8
Beagle Bank *reef* Australia **108** C3
Beagle Bay Australia **108** C4
Beagle Gulf Australia **110** B2
Bealanana Madag. **99** [inset] K2
Béal an Átha Rep. of Ireland *see* **Ballina**
Béal Átha na Sluaighe Rep. of Ireland *see* **Ballinasloe**
Beampingaratra *mts* Madag. **99** [inset] J5
Beandrarezona Madag. **99** [inset] K2
Bear *r.* U.S.A. **134** D4
Bearalváhki Norway *see* **Berlevåg**
Bear Creek Canada **122** B1
Beardmore Glacier Antarctica **167** H1
Beardmore Reservoir Australia **111** G5
Beardstown U.S.A. **132** D3
Bear Island Arctic Ocean *see* **Bjørnøya**
Bear Island Canada **124** D2
Bear Island Rep. of Ireland **35** B6
Bear Lake Canada **123** L4
Bear Lake U.S.A. **134** E4
Bearma *r.* India **74** C4
Bearpaw Mountains U.S.A. **134** E2
Bearskin Lake Canada **124** B2
Beas *r.* India **74** B3
Beasain Spain **43** E1
Beata, Cabo *c.* Dom. Rep. **139** J5
Beata, Isla *i.* Dom. Rep. **139** J5
Beatrice U.S.A. **132** B3
Beatrice Zimbabwe **99** F3
Beatrice, Cape Australia **110** D2
Beatton *r.* Canada **122** F3
Beatty U.S.A. **137** D3
Beattyville Canada **124** E3
Beattyville U.S.A. **130** B5
Beaucaire France **39** F5
Beauchene Island Falkland Is **153** F8
Beaufort *Sabah* Malaysia **59** F1
Beaufort *NC* U.S.A. **129** D5
Beaufort *SC* U.S.A. **129** C5
Beaufort Castle *tourist site* Lebanon **77** B3
Beaufort Island *Hong Kong* China **67** [inset]
Beaufort Sea Canada/U.S.A. **120** G2
Beaufort West S. Africa **98** D7
Beaulieu-sur-Dordogne France **38** D4
Beauly U.K. **34** D3
Beauly *r.* U.K. **34** D3
Beaumont Belgium **39** F1
Beaumont N.Z. **113** B4
Beaumont *CA* U.S.A. **136** D5
Beaumont *MS* U.S.A. **129** A6
Beaumont *TX* U.S.A. **133** C6
Beaumont-de-Lomagne France **38** D5
Beaumont-le-Roger France **38** D2
Beaune France **39** F3
Beauraing Belgium **39** F1
Beauséjour Canada **123** L5
Beauvais France **38** E2
Beauval Canada **123** J4
Beaver *r. Alta/Sask.* Canada **123** J4
Beaver *r. Ont.* Canada **124** C2
Beaver *r. Y.T.* Canada **122** C2
Beaver *r. Y.T.* Canada **122** E3
Beaver U.S.A. **137** F2
Beaver *r. OK* U.S.A. **133** A4
Beaver *r. UT* U.S.A. **137** F2
Beaver Creek Canada **122** A2
Beaver Creek *r. MT* U.S.A. **134** F2
Beaver Creek *r. ND* U.S.A. **132** A2
Beaver Creek *r. NE* U.S.A. **132** B3
Beaver Dam *KY* U.S.A. **128** B4
Beaver Dam *WI* U.S.A. **132** D3
Beaver Falls U.S.A. **130** C3
Beaverhead *r.* U.S.A. **134** D3
Beaverhead Mountains U.S.A. **134** D3
Beaverhill Lake Canada **123** H4
Beaver Hill Lake Canada **123** M4
Beaver Island U.S.A. **132** E2
Beaverlodge Canada **122** G4
Beaver Run Reservoir U.S.A. **130** D3
Beaverton *MI* U.S.A. **130** A2
Beaverton *OR* U.S.A. **134** B3
Beawar India **74** B4
Beazley Arg. **152** D3
Bebedouro Brazil **149** H5
Bebra Germany **36** D3
Bêca China **66** A2
Beccles U.K. **35** G5
Bečej Serb. and Mont. **46** B2
Becerreá Spain **42** C1
Becerrero *hill* Spain **42** D4
Béchar Alg. **90** E3
Becharof Lake U.S.A. **120** D4
Bechevinka Rus. Fed. **28** F4
Bechuanaland *country* Africa *see* **Botswana**
Beçin Turkey **47** E6
Beckley U.S.A. **130** C5
Becky Peak U.S.A. **137** E2
Bečva *r.* Czech Rep. **37** H4
Beda Hāyk' *l.* Eth. **96** D2
Bédarieux France **39** E5
Bedeau Alg. *see* **Ras el Ma**
Bedelē Eth. **96** C2
Bedford Canada **125** I4
Bedford U.K. **35** F5
Bedford *IN* U.S.A. **128** B4
Bedford *NY* U.S.A. **131** G3
Bedford *PA* U.S.A. **130** D3
Bedford *VA* U.S.A. **130** D5
Bedford, Cape Australia **111** F2
Bedford Downs Australia **108** D4
Bedford Heights U.S.A. **130** C3
Bedi India **74** A5
Bedinggong Indon. **58** D3
Bednja *r.* Croatia **44** F1
Bednodem'yanovsk Rus. Fed. **29** G5
Bedok Sing. **58** [inset]
Bedok, Sungai *r.* Sing. **58** [inset]
Bedok Jetty Sing. **58** [inset]
Bedok Reservoir Sing. **58** [inset]
Bedouaram *well* Niger **93** I2
Bedourie Australia **111** D5
Bedrock U.S.A. **137** H2
Beechal Creek *watercourse* Australia **111** F5
Beech Fork Lake U.S.A. **130** B4
Beechy Canada **123** J5
Beelitz Germany **37** F2
Beenleigh Australia **111** H5
Beer Somalia **96** E2
Beersheba Israel **77** B4
Beer Sheva *watercourse* Israel **77** B4
Beeskow Germany **37** G2
Beetaloo Australia **110** C3
Beethoven Peninsula Antarctica **167** L2
Beeville U.S.A. **133** B6
Befale Dem. Rep. Congo **94** D4
Befandriana Atsimo Madag. **99** [inset] I4
Befandriana Avaratra Madag. **99** [inset] K2
Befori Dem. Rep. Congo **94** D4
Befotaka Madag. **99** [inset] J4
Bega Australia **112** D5
Bega *r.* Romania **46** B2
Begamganj Bangl. **75** F5
Begari *r.* Pak. **81** G4
Begicheva, Ostrov *i.* Rus. Fed. *see* **Bol'shoy Begichev, Ostrov**
Begun India **74** B4
Begusarai India **75** E4
Behābād Iran **81** D3
Béhague, Pointe *pt* Fr. Guiana **147** I3
Behbehān Iran **80** B4
Beheira *governorate* Egypt *see* **Al Buḩayrah**
Behm Canal *sea chan.* U.S.A. **122** D4
Behrendt Mountains Antarctica **167** L2
Behshahr Iran **80** C2
Behsūd Afgh. **81** F3
Bei'an China **64** A2
Beiba China **66** C1
Beibei China **66** C2
Beichuan China **66** C2
Beida Libya *see* **Al Bayḍā'**
Beigang Taiwan *see* **Peikang**
Beihai China **67** D4
Bei Jiang *r.* China **67** E4

▶**Beijing** China **63** J4
Capital of China.
asia 82
world 16–17

Beijing *municipality* China **63** J3
Beilen Neth. **36** C2
Beiliu China **67** D4
Béinamar Chad **94** B2
Beinn Mhòr *hill* U.K. **34** C3
Beinn na Faoghlia *i.* U.K. *see* **Benbecula**
Beira Moz. **99** G3
Beira *prov.* Moz. *see* **Sofala**
Beiru *r.* China **67** E1

▶**Beirut** Lebanon **77** B3
Capital of Lebanon.

Beiseker Canada **123** H5
Beitbridge Zimbabwe **99** F4
Beiuş Romania **46** C1
Beja Port. **42** C3
Beja *admin. dist.* Port. **42** B4
Béja Tunisia **91** H1
Bejaïa Alg. **91** G1
Béjar Spain **42** D2
Bejestān Iran **80** D3
Beji *r.* Pak. **81** G4
Béka *Est* Cameroon **93** I4
Béka *Nord* Cameroon **93** I3
Bekapaika Madag. **99** [inset] J3
Bekasi Indon. **59** D4
Bekdash Turkm. **79** H2
Beke Dem. Rep. Congo **95** E7
Békés Hungary **37** J5
Békéscsaba Hungary **37** J5
Beketovskaya Rus. Fed. **28** F3
Bekily Madag. **99** [inset] J5
Bekopaka Madag. **99** [inset] J3
Bekoropoka-Antongo Madag. **99** [inset] I4
Bekovo Rus. Fed. **29** G5
Bekwai Ghana **93** E4
Bekyem Ghana **93** E4
Bela *Bihar* India **75** E4
Bela *Uttar Pradesh* India **75** D4
Bela Pak. **81** F5
Belab *r.* Pak. **81** G4
Bela-Bela S. Africa **99** F5
Bélabo Cameroon **93** I4
Bela Crkva Serb. and Mont. **46** B2
Belaga *Sarawak* Malaysia **59** F2
Bel Air U.S.A. **131** E4
Belalcázar Spain **42** D3
Belangiran Indon. **59** E3
Bela Palanka Serb. and Mont. **46** C3
Belapur India **72** B2
▶**Belarus** *country* Europe **31** K2
europe 24–25, 48
Belasica *mts* Bulg./Macedonia **46** C4
Belasitsa *mts* Bulg./Macedonia *see* **Belasica**
Belau *country* N. Pacific Ocean *see* **Palau**
Bela Vista *Amazonas* Brazil **146** E4
Bela Vista *Mato Grosso do Sul* Brazil **149** F5
Bela Vista Moz. **99** G5
Bela Vista de Goiás Brazil **149** H4
Belawan Indon. **58** B2
Belaya *mt.* Eth. **76** B7
Belaya *r.* Rus. Fed. **27** R3
Belaya Glina Rus. Fed. **29** G7
Belaya Kalitva Rus. Fed. **29** G6
Belaya Kholunitsa Rus. Fed. **28** I4
Belayan *r.* Indon. **59** G3
Belayan, Gunung *mt.* Indon. **59** F2
Belaya Tserkva Ukr. *see* **Bila Tserkva**
Belbédji Niger **93** G2
Bełchatów Poland **37** I3
Belcher U.S.A. **130** B5
Belcher Islands Canada **124** E1
Belchiragh Afgh. **81** F3
Beldanga India **75** F5
Belden U.S.A. **136** B1
Beldibi Turkey **47** F6
Beleapani *reef* India *see* **Cherbaniani Reef**
Belebey Rus. Fed. **29** J5
Beled Hungary **37** H5
Beledweyne Somalia **96** E3
Belek Turkm. **80** C2
Bélèl Cameroon **93** I4
Belel Nigeria **93** I3
Belém Brazil **150** B2
Belén Arg. **152** D1
Belén Para. **149** F5
Belen Turkey **78** D3
Belen U.S.A. **135** F6
Belén, Cuchilla de *hills* Uruguay **152** F2
Belene Bulg. **46** D3
Bélep, Îles *is* New Caledonia **107** F3
Belesar, Embalse de *resr* Spain **42** C1
Belev Rus. Fed. **29** F5
Belevi Turkey **47** E5
Belfast N.Z. **113** C3

▶**Belfast** U.K. **35** D4
Capital of Northern Ireland.

Belfast U.S.A. **131** I1
Bēlfodiyo Eth. **96** B2
Belford U.K. **34** F4
Belfort France **39** G3
Belgaum India **72** B3
Belgian Congo *country* Africa *see* **Congo, Democratic Republic of**
België *country* Europe *see* **Belgium**
Belgique *country* Europe *see* **Belgium**
▶**Belgium** *country* Europe **36** B3
europe 24–25, 48
Belgorod Rus. Fed. **29** F6
Belgorod-Dnestrovskyy Ukr. *see* **Bilhorod-Dnistrovs'kyy**
Belgorod Oblast *admin. div.* Rus. Fed. *see* **Belgorodskaya Oblast'**
Belgorodskaya Oblast' *admin. div.* Rus. Fed. **29** F6
Belgrade *ME* U.S.A. **131** I1
Belgrade *MT* U.S.A. **134** E3

▶**Belgrade** Serb. and Mont. **46** B2
Capital of Serbia and Montenegro.

Belgrano II *research station* Antarctica **167** A1
Belhirane Alg. **91** G3
Béli Guinea-Bissau **92** B3
Beli Nigeria **93** H4
Belice *r. Sicily* Italy **45** D6
Beliliou *i.* Palau *see* **Peleliu**
Beli Lom *r.* Bulg. **46** E3
Beli Manastir Croatia **44** G2
Belington U.S.A. **130** D4
Belingwe Zimbabwe *see* **Mberengwa**
Belinskiy Rus. Fed. **29** G5
Belinț Romania **46** B2
Belinyu Indon. **58** D3
Beli Timok *r.* Serb. and Mont. **46** C2
Belitung *i.* Indon. **59** E3
Belize Angola **95** B6

▶**Belize** Belize **138** G5
Former capital of Belize.

▶**Belize** *country* Central America **138** G5
northamerica 118–119, 140
Bélizon Fr. Guiana **147** H3
Beljak Austria *see* **Villach**
Beljanica *mt.* Serb. and Mont. **46** B2
Bel'kovskiy, Ostrov *i.* Rus. Fed. **27** N2
Bell Australia **111** G5
Bell *r.* Australia **112** D4
Bell *r.* Canada **124** E3
Bella Bella Canada **122** D4
Bellac France **38** D3
Bella Coola Canada **122** E4
Bella Coola *r.* Canada **122** E4
Bellaire *MI* U.S.A. **128** B2
Bellaire *TX* U.S.A. **133** C6
Bellaria Italy **44** D2
Bellary India **72** C3
Bella Unión Uruguay **152** F2
Bella Vista *Corrientes* Arg. **152** F2
Bella Vista *Santa Cruz* Arg. **153** C7
Bella Vista Bol. **149** E3
Bella Vista Para. **149** F5
Bellavista Peru **146** C5
Bell Cay *reef* Australia **111** G4
Belle U.S.A. **130** C4
Belledonne *mts* France **39** F4
Bellefontaine U.S.A. **130** B3
Belle Fourche U.S.A. **134** G3
Belle Fourche *r.* U.S.A. **134** G3
Bellegarde-sur-Valserine France **39** F3
Belle Glade U.S.A. **129** C7
Belle-Île *i.* France **38** B3
Belle Isle *i.* Canada **125** K3
Belle Isle, Strait of Canada **125** J3
Bellemont U.S.A. **137** G4
Belleville Canada **131** E1
Belleville France **39** F3
Belleville U.S.A. **132** B4
Bellevue *NE* U.S.A. **132** C3
Bellevue *OH* U.S.A. **130** B3
Bellevue *WA* U.S.A. **134** B3
Belley France **39** F4
Bellin Canada *see* **Kangirsuk**
Bellingen Australia **112** E3
Bellingham U.K. **34** E4
Bellingham U.S.A. **134** B2
Bellingshausen *research station* Antarctica **167** A2
Bellingshausen Sea Antarctica **167** L2
Bellinzona Switz. **39** H3
Bello Col. **146** C3
Bellows Falls U.S.A. **131** G2
Bellpat Pak. **81** G4
Belluno Italy **44** D1
Belluru India **72** C3
Bell Ville Arg. **152** E3
Bellville S. Africa **98** C7
Bellville U.S.A. **130** B3
Bellwood U.S.A. **130** D3
Belly *r.* Canada **123** H5
Bélmez Spain **42** D3
Belmont Australia **112** D4
Belmont U.S.A. **130** D2
Belmonte Brazil **151** E5
Belmonte Port. **42** C2
Belmont-sur-Rance France **39** E5

▶**Belmopan** Belize **138** G5
Capital of Belize.

Belmore Creek *r.* Australia **111** E3
Belmullet Rep. of Ireland **35** B4
Belo Madag. **99** [inset] J4
Belo More *sea* Rus. Fed. *see* **White Sea**
Belogorsk Rus. Fed. **64** B2
Belogradchik Bulg. **46** C3
Beloha Madag. **99** [inset] J5
Belo Horizonte Brazil **151** D6
Beloit U.S.A. **132** D3
Belo Jardim Brazil **150** E4
Belo Monte *Pará* Brazil **147** I5
Belo Monte *Piauí* Brazil *see* **Batalha**
Belomorsk Rus. Fed. **28** E2
Belonia India **75** F5
Belorado Spain **42** E1
Belorechensk Rus. Fed. **29** F7
Belorechenskaya Rus. Fed. *see* **Belorechensk**
Belören *Adıyaman* Turkey **78** D3
Belören Turkey **78** C3
Beloretsk Rus. Fed. **26** F4
Belorussia *country* Europe *see* **Belarus**
Belorusskaya S.S.R. *country* Europe *see* **Belarus**
Beloslav Bulg. **46** E3
Belostok Poland *see* **Białystok**
Belot, Lac *l.* Canada **122** E1
Belotintsi Bulg. **46** C3
Belo Tsiribihina Madag. **99** [inset] J3
Belovo Bulg. **46** D3
Beloye, Ozero *l.* Rus. Fed. **28** F3
Beloye More *sea* Rus. Fed. *see* **White Sea**
Belozersk Rus. Fed. **28** F3
Belpre U.S.A. **130** C4
Belted Range *mts* U.S.A. **137** D3
Belterra Brazil **147** H5
Belton *MO* U.S.A. **132** C4
Belton *TX* U.S.A. **133** B6
Bel'ts' Moldova *see* **Bălţi**
Bel'tsy Moldova *see* **Bălţi**
Belukha, Gora *mt.* Kazakh./Rus. Fed. **70** G2
Belur India **72** B3
Belush'ye Rus. Fed. **28** H2
Belva U.S.A. **130** C4
Belvès France **38** D4
Belvidere *IL* U.S.A. **132** D3
Belvidere *NJ* U.S.A. **131** F3
Belyando *r.* Australia **111** F4
Belyando Crossing Australia **111** F4
Belyayevka Ukr. *see* **Bilyayivka**
Belyy Rus. Fed. **28** E5
Belyy, Ostrov *i.* Rus. Fed. **26** H2
Belyy Yar Rus. Fed. **27** I4
Belzig Germany **37** F2
Belzoni U.S.A. **133** D5
Bełżyce Poland **37** K3
Bemaraha, Plateau du Madag. **99** [inset] J3
Bembe Angola **95** B6
Bembèrèkè Benin **93** F3
Bembibre Spain **42** C1
Bemidji U.S.A. **132** C2
Bëna Burkina **92** D2
Bena Dibele Dem. Rep. Congo **95** D6
Benagin Indon. **59** F3
Ben Alder *mt.* U.K. **34** D3
Benalla Australia **112** C5
Benalmádena Spain **42** D4
Ben 'Amîra *well* Mauritania **90** B5
Benares India *see* **Varanasi**
Ben Arous Tunisia **91** H1
Benavente Spain **42** D1
Benavides Bol. **148** D3
Benbecula *i.* U.K. **34** C3
Ben Boyd National Park Australia **112** D5
Benbury *hill* Rep. of Ireland **35** B5
Bend U.S.A. **134** B3
Bendearg *mt.* S. Africa **99** E6
Bendela Dem. Rep. Congo **94** C5
Bender Moldova *see* **Tighina**
Bender-Bayla Somalia **96** F2
Bendery Moldova *see* **Tighina**
Bendigo Australia **112** C5
Bēne Latvia **33** F4
Bene Moz. **97** B8
Benedict, Mount Canada **125** J2
Beneditinos Brazil **150** D3
Benedito Leite Brazil **150** C3
Bénéna Mali **92** D2
Benenitra Madag. **99** [inset] J4
Benešov Czech Rep. **37** G4
Benevento Italy **44** E4
Beneventum Italy *see* **Benevento**
Beng, Nam *r.* Laos **60** C4
Bengal, Bay of *sea* Indian Ocean **73** F2
Bengamisa Dem. Rep. Congo **94** E4
Bengbis Cameroon **93** I5
Bengbu China **67** F1
Benghazi Libya **88** D1
Benghisa Point Malta **45** E7
Bengkalis Indon. **58** C2
Bengkalis *i.* Indon. **58** C2
Bengkayang Indon. **59** E2
Bengkulu Indon. **58** C3
Bengkulu *prov.* Indon. **58** C3
Bengo Angola **95** C9
Bengo *prov.* Angola **95** B7
Bengtsfors Sweden **33** D4
Benguela Angola **95** B8
Benguela *prov.* Angola **95** B8
Ben Guerdane Tunisia **91** H2
Benguerir Morocco **90** D2
Benha Egypt *see* **Banhā**
Ben Hope *hill* U.K. **34** D2
Beni *dept* Bol. **148** D3
Beni *r.* Bol. **148** D2
Beni Dem. Rep. Congo **94** F4
Beni Nepal **75** D3
Beni-Abbès Alg. **90** E3
Benicarló Spain **43** G2
Benicasim Spain **43** G2
Benidorm Spain **43** F3
Beni Dourso *well* Niger **88** B4
Benifaió Spain **43** F3
Benifayo Spain *see* **Benifaió**
Benigánim Spain **43** F3
Beni Guil *reg.* Morocco **90** E2
Beni Mellal Morocco **90** D2
▶**Benin** *country* Africa **93** F3
africa 86–87, 100
Benin *r.* Nigeria **93** G4
Benin, Bight of *g.* Africa **93** F4
Benin City Nigeria **93** G4
Beni-Ounif Alg. **91** E3
Beni-Saf Alg. **91** E2
Benishangul *admin. reg.* Eth. **96** B2
Benisheikh Nigeria **93** I3
Benissa Spain **43** G3
Beni Suef Egypt *see* **Banī Suwayf**
Beni Suef *governorate* Egypt *see* **Banī Suwayf**
Benithora *r.* India **72** C2
Benito *r.* Equat. Guinea *see* **Mbini**
Benito Juárez Arg. **152** F4
Benjamin U.S.A. **133** B5
Benjamin, Isla *i.* Chile **153** B6
Benjamin Hill Mex. **135** E7
Benjamin Zorrillo Arg. **152** D4
Benjina Indon. **57** H7
Benkelman U.S.A. **132** A3
Benkovac Croatia **44** E2
Ben Lawers *mt.* U.K. **34** D3
Ben Lomond *mt.* Australia **112** D3
Ben Lomond *hill* U.K. **34** D3
Ben Lomond National Park Australia **112** C6
Ben Macdui *mt.* U.K. **34** E3
Ben Mahidi Alg. **45** A6
Benmara Australia **110** D3
Ben More *hill* U.K. **34** C3
Ben More *mt.* U.K. **34** D3
Benmore, Lake N.Z. **113** B4
Ben More Assynt *hill* U.K. **34** D2
Bennett Canada **122** C3
Bennett, Lake *salt flat* Australia **110** B4
Bennetta, Ostrov *i.* Rus. Fed. **27** O2
Bennett Island Rus. Fed. *see* **Bennetta, Ostrov**
Bennettsville U.S.A. **129** D5
Ben Nevis *mt.* U.K. **34** D3
Bennington *NH* U.S.A. **131** H2
Bennington *VT* U.S.A. **131** G2
Bénoué *r.* Cameroon **93** I3
Bénoy Chad **94** C2
Ben Rinnes *hill* U.K. **34** E3
Bensheim Germany **36** D4
Ben Slimane Morocco **90** D2
Benson *AZ* U.S.A. **135** E7
Benson *MN* U.S.A. **132** C2
Bensonville Liberia **92** C4
Bens Run U.S.A. **130** C4
Bent Iran **81** D5
Benta Seberang Malaysia **58** C1
Benteng Indon. **57** F7
Bentiaba Angola **95** B8
Bentinck Island Myanmar **61** B6
Bentiu Sudan **94** F2
Bent Jbail Lebanon **77** B3
Bentley Canada **123** H4
Bentleyville U.S.A. **130** C3
Benton *AR* U.S.A. **133** C5
Benton *CA* U.S.A. **136** C3
Benton *IL* U.S.A. **128** A4
Benton *KY* U.S.A. **128** A4
Benton *MO* U.S.A. **132** D4
Bentong Malaysia *see* **Bentung**
Benton Harbor U.S.A. **132** E3
Bentonville U.S.A. **133** C4
Bên Tre Vietnam **61** D6
Bentuang Karimun National Park Indon. **59** F2
Bentung Malaysia **58** C2
Benua *i.* Indon. **59** D2
Benuamartinus Indon. **59** F2
Benue *r.* Nigeria **93** G4
Benue *state* Nigeria **93** H4
Benum, Gunung *mt.* Malaysia **58** C2
Benwa Zambia **95** E7
Benwood U.S.A. **130** C3
Benxi China **63** K3
Ben Zireg Alg. **90** E3
Beograd Serb. and Mont. *see* **Belgrade**
Beohari India **75** D4
Béoumi Côte d'Ivoire **92** D4
Bepagut, Gunung *mt.* Indon. **58** C4
Bepian Jiang *r.* China **66** C3
Beppu Japan **65** B6
Bequia *i.* St Vincent **147** F1
Bequimão Brazil **150** C2
Bera Bangl. **75** F4
Berach *r.* India **74** B4
Beramanja Madag. **99** [inset] K2
Berane Serb. and Mont. **46** A3
Bérard, Lac *l.* Canada **125** G1
Berasia India **74** C5
Berastagi Indon. **58** B2
Berat Albania **46** A4
Beratus, Gunung *mt.* Indon. **59** G3
Berau *r.* Indon. **59** G2
Berau, Teluk *b.* Indon. **57** H6
Beravina Madag. **99** [inset] J3
Berbak National Park Indon. **58** D3
Berber Sudan **89** G5
Berbera Somalia **96** E2
Berbérati Cent. Afr. Rep. **94** B3
Bercel Hungary **37** I5
Berceto Italy **44** B2
Berchi-Guélé *well* Chad **88** C5
Berchtesgaden, Nationalpark *nat. park* Germany **37** F5
Berck France **38** D1
Berdichev Ukr. *see* **Berdychiv**
Berdigestyakh Rus. Fed. **27** M3
Berdsk Rus. Fed. **26** I4
Berdyans'k Ukr. **29** F7
Berdychiv Ukr. **29** D6
Berea *KY* U.S.A. **130** A5
Berea *OH* U.S.A. **130** C3
Beregovo Ukr. *see* **Berehove**
Berehove Ukr. **31** J3
Bereina P.N.G. **57** K7
Bereketa Madag. **99** [inset] J4
Berekum Ghana **92** E4
Berenguela Bol. **148** C4
Berenice Libya *see* **Benghazi**
Berens *r.* Canada **123** L4
Berens River Canada **123** L4
Berenty Madag. **99** [inset] J4
Beresford U.S.A. **132** B3
Berești Romania **46** E1
Berettyó *r.* Hungary **37** J5
Berettyóújfalu Hungary **37** J5
Berevo Madag. **99** [inset] J3
Berevo-Ranobe Madag. **99** [inset] J3
Bereza Belarus *see* **Byaroza**
Berezino Belarus *see* **Byerazino**
Berezivka Ukr. **29** D7
Berezne Ukr. **29** C6
Bereznik Rus. Fed. **28** G3
Berezniki Rus. Fed. **28** K4
Berezovka Rus. Fed. **28** K4
Berezovka Ukr. *see* **Berezivka**
Berezovyy Rus. Fed. **64** C2
Berezyne Ukr. **46** F1
Berga Spain **43** G1
Bergama Turkey **78** A3
Bergamo Italy **44** B2
Bergantes *r.* Spain **43** F2
Bergby Sweden **33** E3
Bergen *Mecklenburg-Vorpommern* Germany **37** F1
Bergen *Niedersachsen* Germany **36** D2
Bergen Norway **33** B3
Bergen U.S.A. **130** E2
Bergen op Zoom Neth. **36** B3
Bergerac France **38** D4
Bergheim (Erft) Germany **36** C3
Bergisch Gladbach Germany **36** C3
Bergland Namibia **98** C4
Bergnäs Sweden **32** F2
Bergnäsviken Sweden **32** E2
Bergomum Italy *see* **Bergamo**
Bergsjö Sweden **33** E3
Berhala, Selat *sea chan.* Indon. **58** C3
Berhampur India *see* **Baharampur**
Berheci *r.* Romania **46** E1
Berikat, Tanjung *pt* Indon. **59** D3
Beringa, Ostrov *i.* Rus. Fed. **27** Q4
Beringen Belgium **39** F1
Beringovskiy Rus. Fed. **27** R3
Bering Sea N. Pacific Ocean **164** F2
Bering Strait Rus. Fed./U.S.A. **120** C3
Berja Spain **42** E4
Berkåk Norway **32** C3
Berkane Morocco **90** E2
Berkel *r.* Neth. **36** C2
Berkeley *r.* Australia **108** D3
Berkeley U.S.A. **136** A3
Berkeley Springs U.S.A. **130** D4
Berkner Island Antarctica **167** A1
Berkovitsa Bulg. **46** C3
Berkshire Hills U.S.A. **131** G2
Berlevåg Norway **32** H1

▶**Berlin** Germany **37** F2
Capital of Germany.

Berlin *MD* U.S.A. **131** F4
Berlin *NH* U.S.A. **131** H1
Berlin *NJ* U.S.A. **131** F4
Berlin *OH* U.S.A. **130** C3
Berlin *PA* U.S.A. **130** D4
Berlişte Romania **46** B2
Berme Turkm. **80** D2
Bermeja, Punta *pt* Arg. **152** E5
Bermejillo Mex. **126** F6
Bermejo *r.* Arg. **152** E3
Bermejo *r.* Arg./Bol. **149** F6
Bermejo Bol. **149** D5
Bermeo Spain **43** E1

▶**Bermuda** *terr.* N. Atlantic Ocean **127** N5
United Kingdom Overseas Territory.
northamerica 118–119, 140

Bermuda Rise *sea feature* N. Atlantic Ocean **160** J4

▶**Bern** Switz. **39** G3
Capital of Switzerland.

Bernalda Italy **45** F4
Bernardo O'Higgins, Parque Nacional *nat. park* Chile **153** B7
Bernau Germany **37** F2
Bernau am Chiemsee Germany **37** F5
Bernay France **38** D2
Bernburg (Saale) Germany **36** E3
Berndorf Austria **37** H5
Berne Switz. *see* **Bern**
Berne U.S.A. **130** A3
Berner Alpen *mts* Switz. **39** G3
Berneray *i.* U.K. **34** C3
Bernese Alps *mts* Switz. *see* **Berner Alpen**
Bernesga *r.* Spain **42** D1
Bernier Island Australia **109** A6
Bernina Pass Switz. **39** I3
Berninches *mt.* Spain **43** E2
Bernstadt U.S.A. **130** A5
Beroea Greece *see* **Veroia**
Beroea Syria *see* **Aleppo**
Beroroha Madag. **99** [inset] J4
Beroun Czech Rep. **37** G4
Berounka *r.* Czech Rep. **37** G4
Berovina Madag. *see* **Beravina**
Berovo Macedonia **46** C4
Berre, Étang de *lag.* France **39** F5
Berrechid Morocco **90** D2
Berri Australia **112** B4
Berriane Alg. **91** F2
Berridale Australia **112** D5
Berrouaghia Alg. **91** F1
Berry *reg.* France **38** D3
Berry Creek *r.* Canada **123** I5
Berryessa, Lake U.S.A. **136** A2
Berry Head U.K. **35** E6
Berry Islands Bahamas **129** D7
Berryville U.S.A. **130** E4
Bersenbrück Germany **36** C2
Berté, Lac *l.* Canada **125** G3
Bertinho Brazil **150** B2
Bertolinia Brazil **150** D3
Bertoua Cameroon **93** I4
Beru *atoll* Kiribati **107** G2
Beruri Brazil **147** F5
Beruwala Sri Lanka **72** C5
Berwick-upon-Tweed U.K. **34** E4
Berytus Lebanon *see* **Beirut**
Berzasca Romania **46** B2
Bērzaune Latvia **33** G4
Bès *r.* France **39** E4
Besalampy Madag. **99** [inset] J3
Besalú Spain **43** H1
Besançon France **39** G3
Besar *i.* Indon. **108** C2
Besar, Gunung *mt.* Indon. **59** F3
Besbre *r.* France **39** E3
Beshariq Uzbek. *see* **Besharyk**
Besharyk Uzbek. **81** G1
Beshkent Uzbek. **81** F2
Besheh Iran **80** C4
Besikama Indon. **108** D2
Beşiri Turkey **79** E3
Beskid Niski *hills* Poland **37** J4
Beskid Sądecki *mts* Poland **37** J4
Beskra Alg. *see* **Biskra**
Beslan Rus. Fed. **29** H8
Besna Kobila *mt.* Serb. and Mont. **46** C3
Besnard Lake Canada **123** J4
Besni Turkey **79** D3
Besor *watercourse* Israel **77** B4
Beşparmak Dağları *mts* Cyprus *see* **Pentadaktylos Range**
Béssao Chad **94** B3
Bessarabka Moldova *see* **Basarabeasca**
Bessaye, Gora *mt.* Kazakh. **70** C3
Bessemer U.S.A. **132** D2
Besshoky, Gora *hill* Kazakh. **79** H1
Bessines-sur-Gartempe France **38** D3
Bessonovka Rus. Fed. **29** H5
Bessou, Mont de *hill* France **38** E4
Beswick Australia **110** C2
Betafo Madag. **99** [inset] J3
Betanzos Bol. **148** D4
Betanzos Spain **42** B1
Bétaré Oya Cameroon **93** I4
Bete Hor Eth. **96** C2
Bétérou Benin **93** F3
Betet *i.* Indon. **58** D3
Beth, Oued *r.* Morocco **90** D2
Bethanie Namibia **98** C5
Bethany U.S.A. **132** C3
Bethari Nepal **75** D4
Bethel *AK* U.S.A. **120** C3
Bethel *ME* U.S.A. **131** H1
Bethel *OH* U.S.A. **130** A4
Bethesda *MD* U.S.A. **131** E4
Bethesda *OH* U.S.A. **130** C3
Bethlehem S. Africa **99** F6
Bethlehem U.S.A. **131** F3
Bethlehem West Bank **77** B4
Béthune France **39** E1
Betioky Madag. **99** [inset] J4
Betiri, Gunung *mt.* Indon. **59** F5
Bet Lehem West Bank *see* **Bethlehem**
Betma India **74** B5
Betong Thai. **61** C7
Betoota Australia **111** E5
Bétou Congo **94** C4
Betpak-Dala *plain* Kazakh. **70** D2
Betrandraka Madag. **99** [inset] J3
Betroka Madag. **99** [inset] J4
Bet She'an Israel **77** B3
Betsiamites *r.* Canada **125** G3
Betsiboka *r.* Madag. **99** [inset] J2
Betsie, Point U.S.A. **128** B2
Bettiah India **75** E4
Betul India **74** C5
Betwa *r.* India **74** C4
Betws-y-coed U.K. **35** E5
Béu Angola **95** B6
Beulah U.S.A. **132** A2
Beuthen Poland *see* **Bytom**
Beuvron *r.* France **38** D3
Beverley U.K. **35** F5
Beverly *MA* U.S.A. **131** H2
Beverly *OH* U.S.A. **130** C4
Beverly Hills U.S.A. **136** C4
Beverungen Germany **36** D3
Beyağaç Turkey **47** F6
Beyazköy Turkey **46** E4
Beyce Turkey *see* **Orhaneli**
Beydağ Turkey **47** F5
Bey Dağları *mts* Turkey **78** B3
Beykoz Turkey **78** B2
Beyla Guinea **92** C3
Beylagan Azer. *see* **Beyläqan**
Beyläqan Azer. **79** F3
Beylul Eritrea **89** I6
Beyneu Kazakh. **70** A2
Beypazarı Turkey **78** B2
Beypınarı Turkey **79** D3
Beypore India **72** B4
Beyra Somalia **96** E3
Beyram Iran **80** C5
Beyrouth Lebanon *see* **Beirut**
Beyşehir Turkey **78** B3
Beyşehir Gölü *l.* Turkey **78** B3
Beytüşşebap Turkey **79** E3
Bezameh Iran **80** D3
Bezbozhnik Rus. Fed. **28** I4

Bezdan Serb. and Mont. 46 A2
Bezenjān Iran 80 D4
Bezhanitsy Rus. Fed. 31 L1
Bezhetsk Rus. Fed. 31 N1
Béziers France 39 E5
Bezmein Turkm. see Byuzmeyin
Bezwada India see Vijayawada
Bhabhar India 74 A4
Bhabra India 74 B5
Bhabua India 75 D4
Bhachau India 74 A5
Bhadar r. India 74 A5
Bhadarwah Jammu and Kashmir 74 B2
Bhadgaon Nepal see Bhaktapur
Bhadohi India 75 D4
Bhadra India 74 B3
Bhadrachalam India 72 D2
Bhadrachalam Road Station India see Kottagudem
Bhadrakh India 75 E5
Bhadra Reservoir India 72 B3
Bhadravati India 72 B3
Bhag Pak. 81 F4
Bhagalpur India 75 E4
Bhagirathi r. India 75 F5
Bhainsa India 72 C2
Bhainsdehi India 74 C5
Bhairab Bazar Bangl. 75 F4
Bhairawa Nepal 75 D4
Bhairawaha Nepal see Bhairawa
Bhairi Hol mt. Pak. 81 F5
Bhakkar Pak. 81 G4
Bhaktapur Nepal 75 E4
Bhalki India 72 C2
Bhalwal Pak. 81 H3
Bhamgarh India 74 C5
Bhamo Myanmar 60 B2
Bhandara India 74 C5
Bhander India 74 C4
Bhanjanagar India 73 E2
Bhanpura India 74 B4
Bhanrer Range hills India 74 C5
Bharat country Asia see India
Bharatpur India 74 C4
Bharatpur Nepal 75 E4
Bhareli r. India 75 G4
Bhari r. Pak. 81 E5
Bharthana India 74 C4
Bharuch India 74 B5
Bhatapara India 75 D5
Bhatarsaigh i. U.K. see Vatersay
Bhatghar Lake India 72 B2
Bhatinda India see Bathinda
Bhatnair India see Hanumangarh
Bhatpara India 75 F5
Bhaun Gharibwal Pak. 81 H3
Bhavani India 72 C4
Bhavani r. India 72 C4
Bhavani Sagar l. India 72 C4
Bhavnagar India 74 B5
Bhawana Pak. 81 H4
Bhawanipatna India 73 D2
Bhearnaraigh, Eilean i. U.K. see Berneray
Bheemavaram India see Bhimavaram
Bhera Pak. 81 H3
Bheri r. Nepal 75 D3
Bhilai India 75 D5
Bhildi India 74 B4
Bhilwara India 74 B4
Bhima r. India 72 C2
Bhimavaram India 72 D2
Bhimbar Pak. 74 B2
Bhimnagar India 75 E4
Bhimphedi Nepal 75 E4
Bhind India 74 C4
Bhinga India 75 D4
Bhinmal India 74 B4
Bhiwandi India 72 B2
Bhiwani India 74 C3
Bhogat India 74 A5
Bhojpur Nepal 75 E4
Bhola Bangl. 75 F5
Bhongaon India 74 C4
Bhongir India 72 C2
Bhongweni S. Africa 99 F6
Bhopal India 74 C5
Bhopalpatnam India 72 D2
Bhor India 72 B2
Bhrigukaccha India see Bharuch
Bhuban India 73 E1
Bhubaneshwar India 73 E1
Bhubaneswar India see Bhubaneshwar
Bhuban Hills India 75 G4
Bhuj India 74 A5
Bhumiphol Dam Thai. 60 B4
Bhusawal India 74 B5
▶Bhutan country Asia 75 F4
asia 52–53, 82
Bhuttewala India 74 A4
Biá r. Brazil 146 E5
Bia, Monts mts Dem. Rep. Congo 95 E7
Bia, Phou mt. Laos 60 C4
Bīabān mts Iran 80 D5
Biafra, Bight of g. Africa see Benin, Bight of
Biak Indon. 57 I6
Biak i. Indon. 57 I6
Biała r. Poland 37 J3
Biała Piska Poland 37 K2
Biała Podlaska Poland 31 J2
Białobrzegi Poland 37 J3
Białogard Poland 37 G2
Biały Bór Poland 37 H2
Białystok Poland 31 J2
Bianco Italy 45 F5
Bianga Cent. Afr. Rep. 94 D3
Biankouma Côte d'Ivoire 92 D4
Bianouan Côte d'Ivoire 92 E4
Biaora India 74 C5
Bīārjmand Iran 80 C2
Biarritz France 38 C5
Bi'ār Tabrāk well Saudi Arabia 80 A5
Biasca Switz. 39 H3
Bibā Egypt 89 F2
Bibai Japan 64 E4
Bibala Angola 95 B8
Bibas Gabon 94 A4
Bibbenluke Australia 112 D5
Bibbiena Italy 44 C3
Biberach an der Riß Germany 36 D4
Bibiani Ghana 93 E4
Bibiyana r. Bangl. 75 F4
Biblos Lebanon see Jbail
Bicheng China see Bishan
Bicheno Australia 112 D6
Bichevaya Rus. Fed. 64 C3
Bichi r. Rus. Fed. 64 D1
Bickerton Island Australia 110 D2
Bicuari, Parque Nacional do nat. park Angola 95 B8
Bid India 72 B2
Bida Nigeria 93 G3
Bidache France 38 C5
Bidar India 72 C2
Bidasar India 74 B4
Biddeford U.S.A. 131 H2
Bideford U.K. 35 D6
Bideford Bay U.K. 35 D6
Bidjovagge Norway 32 F1
Bidkhan, Kūh-e mt. Iran 80 D4
Bidokht Iran 81 D3
Bidon 5 tourist site Alg. 91 F5
Bidzhan Rus. Fed. 64 B3
Bidzhan r. Rus. Fed. 64 C3
Bié Angola see Kuito
Bié prov. Angola 95 C8
Biebrza r. Poland 37 K2
Biebrzański Park Narodowy nat. park Poland 37 K2
Biedenkopf Germany 36 D3
Biel Switz. 39 G3
Bielefeld Germany 36 D2
Bielitz Poland see Bielsko-Biała
Biella Italy 44 B2
Bielsko-Biała Poland 37 I4
Bienenbüttel Germany 36 E2
Biên Hoa Vietnam 61 D6
Bienne r. France 39 F3
Bienne Switz. see Biel
Bienvenida hill Spain 42 C3
Bienville, Lac l. Canada 125 F2
Bierbank Australia 111 F5
Bierutów Poland 37 H3
Biesiesvlei S. Africa 98 E5
Bièvre Belgium 39 F2
Biferno r. Italy 44 E4
Bifoun Gabon 94 A5
Bifröst Iceland 32 [inset]
Big r. U.S.A. 136 A2
Biga Turkey 78 A2
Biga r. Turkey 47 E4
Bigadiç Turkey 78 B3
Biga Yarımadası pen. Turkey 47 E5
Big Bear Lake U.S.A. 136 D4
Big Belt Mountains U.S.A. 134 E3
Big Bend National Park U.S.A. 133 A6
Big Black r. U.S.A. 133 D5
Big Blue r. U.S.A. 132 B4
Big Canyon watercourse U.S.A. 133 A6
Biger Nuur salt l. Mongolia 70 I2
Big Fork r. U.S.A. 132 C1
Biggar Canada 134 F1
Biggar U.K. 34 E4
Biggar, Lac l. Canada 124 F3
Bigge Island Australia 108 D3
Biggenden Australia 111 H5
Bigger, Mount Canada 122 B3
Biggleswade U.K. 35 F5
Biggs U.S.A. 136 B2
Big Hole r. U.S.A. 134 D3
Bighorn r. U.S.A. 134 F3
Bighorn Mountains U.S.A. 134 F3
Big Island i. Nunavut Canada 121 L3
Big Island i. N.W.T. Canada 123 G2
Big Island U.S.A. 130 D5
Big Kalzas Lake Canada 122 C2
Big Lake U.S.A. 133 A6
Big Lake l. U.S.A. 128 G2
Big Muddy Creek r. U.S.A. 134 F2
Bignona Senegal 92 A2
Bigobo Dem. Rep. Congo 95 E6
Big Otter r. U.S.A. 130 D5
Big Pine U.S.A. 136 C3
Big Pine Peak U.S.A. 136 C4
Big Rapids U.S.A. 132 E3
Big River Canada 123 J4
Big Salmon Canada 122 C2
Big Salmon r. Canada 122 C2
Big Sand Lake Canada 123 L3
Big Sandy watercourse U.S.A. 137 F4
Big Sandy Creek r. U.S.A. 134 G5
Big Sioux r. U.S.A. 132 B3
Big Smokey Valley U.S.A. 136 D2
Big Spring U.S.A. 133 A5
Big Stone Canada 123 I5
Big Sur U.S.A. 136 B3
Big Timber U.S.A. 134 E3
Big Trout Lake Canada 124 B2
Big Trout Lake l. Canada 124 B2
Big Valley Canada 123 H4
Big Water U.S.A. 137 G3
Bihać Bos.-Herz. 44 E2
Bihar state India 75 E4
Bihariganj India 75 E4
Bihar Sharif India 75 E4
Bihor, Vârful mt. Romania 46 C1
Bihpuriagaon India 75 G4
Bijagós, Arquipélago dos is Guinea-Bissau 92 A3
Bijainagar India 74 B4
Bijaipur India 74 C4
Bijapur India 72 B2
Bījār Iran 80 A3
Bijarpur India 72 D2
Bijawar India 74 C4
Bijbehara Jammu and Kashmir 74 B2
Bijeljina Bos.-Herz. 46 A2
Bijelolasica mt. Croatia 44 E2
Bijelo Polje Serb. and Mont. 46 A3
Bijie China 66 C3
Bijni India 75 F4
Bijnor India 74 C3
Bijolia India 74 B4
Bijrān well Saudi Arabia 80 B5
Bijrān, Khashm hill Saudi Arabia 76 E5
Bikampur India 74 B4
Bikaner India 74 B3
Bikin Rus. Fed. 64 C3
Bikin r. Rus. Fed. 64 C3
Bikini atoll Marshall Is 164 F5
Bikori Sudan 96 B2
Bikoro Dem. Rep. Congo 94 C5
Bikou China 66 C1
Bikramganj India 75 E4
Bilanga Burkina 93 E2
Bilara India 74 B4
Bilari India 74 C3
Bilaspur Chhattisgarh India 75 D5
Bilaspur Himachal Pradesh India 74 C3
Biläsuvar Azer. 79 G3
Bila Tserkva Ukr. 29 D6
Bilauktaung Range mts Myanmar/Thai. 61 B5
Bilbao Spain 42 E1
Bilbays Egypt 78 B5
Bilbo Spain see Bilbao
Bíldudalur Iceland 32 [inset]
Bileća Bos.-Herz. 44 G3
Bilecik Turkey 78 B2
Bilesha Plain Kenya 96 D4
Biłgoraj Poland 31 J3
Bilharamulo Tanz. 96 A5
Bilhaur India 74 D4
Bilhorod-Dnistrovs'kyy Ukr. 29 D7
Bili Chad 94 C2
Bili r. Dem. Rep. Congo 94 D3
Bilibino Rus. Fed. 27 Q3
Bilibiza Moz. 97 D8
Bilin Myanmar 60 B4
Bilisht Albania 46 B4
Bilis Qooqaani Somalia 96 D4
Bill U.S.A. 134 F4
Billabalong Australia 109 A6
Billabong Creek r. Australia see Moulamein Creek
Billère France 38 C5
Billiluna Australia 108 D4
Billings U.S.A. 134 E3
Billiton i. Indon. see Belitung
Bill of Portland hd U.K. 35 E6
Billund airport Denmark 33 C5
Bill Williams r. U.S.A. 137 E4
Bill Williams Mountain U.S.A. 137 F4
Bilma Niger 93 I1
Bīlo Eth. 96 C2
Biloela Australia 111 G5
Bilohir"ya Ukr. 29 C6
Biloku Guyana 147 G4
Biloli India 72 C2
Bilovods'k Ukr. 29 F6
Biloxi U.S.A. 129 A6
Bilpa Morea Claypan salt flat Australia 111 D5
Biltine Chad 88 D6
Biltine pref. Chad 88 D6
Bilugyun Island Myanmar 61 B4
Bilyayivka Ukr. 29 D7
Bima r. Dem. Rep. Congo 94 E4
Bima Indon. 108 B2
Bimbe Angola 95 B7
Bimbila Ghana 93 F3
Bimini Islands Bahamas 129 D7
Bimlipatam India 73 D2
Bina-Etawa India 74 C4
Binaija, Gunung mt. Indon. 57 G6
Bīnālūd, Kūh-e mts Iran 81 D2
Binatang Sarawak Malaysia 59 E2
Binboğa Dağı mt. Turkey 78 D3
Binchuan China 66 B3
Binder Chad 94 B2
Bindki India 74 D4
Bindu Dem. Rep. Congo 95 C6
Bindura Zimbabwe 99 F3
Binefar Spain 43 G2
Binga Zimbabwe 99 E3
Binga, Monte mt. Moz. 99 G3
Bingara Australia 112 D3
Bingaram i. India 72 B4
Bing Bong Australia 110 D2
Bingen am Rhein Germany 36 C4
Bingham U.S.A. 128 F2
Binghamton U.S.A. 131 F2
Bin Ghanīmah, Jabal hills Libya 88 B3
Bingmei China see Congjiang
Bingöl Turkey 79 E3
Bingol Dağı mt. Turkey 79 E3
Bingxi China see Yushan
Bingzhongluo China 66 A2
Binh Sơn Vietnam 61 E5
Bini Erda well Chad 88 C4
Binika India 75 D5
Binjai Indon. 58 B2
Binna, Raas pt Somalia 96 F2
Binnaway Australia 112 D3
Binpur India 75 E5
Bintan i. Indon. 58 D2
Bintang, Bukit mts Malaysia 58 C1
Bintuhan Indon. 58 C4
Bintulu Sarawak Malaysia 59 F2
Binxian Heilong. China 64 A3
Binxian Shaanxi China 66 D1
Binyang China 67 D4
Bin-Yauri Nigeria 93 G3
Binzhou Guangxi China see Binyang
Binzhou Heilong. China see Binxian
Biobío admin. reg. Chile 152 B4
Biobío r. Chile 152 B4
Bioco i. Equat. Guinea 93 H5
Biograd na Moru Croatia 44 E3
Biogradska Gora nat. park Serb. and Mont. 46 A3
Bioko i. Equat. Guinea see Bioco
Bir India see Bid
Bira Rus. Fed. 64 C2
Bira r. Rus. Fed. 64 C2
Bi'r Abraq well Egypt 89 G4
Bi'r Abū Daraj well Egypt 77 A5
Bir Abu Garad well Sudan 89 F5
Bi'r Abū Hashīm well Egypt 89 G4
Bi'r Abū Ḥuṣayn well Egypt 89 F4
Bi'r Abū Jady oasis Syria 77 D1
Bi'r Abū Minqār well Egypt 89 E3
Bi'r ad Damar well Libya 88 A3
Bi'r ad Duwaydār well Egypt 77 A4
Bi'r adh Dhakar well Libya 88 D3
Bîr Aïdiat well Mauritania 90 C4
Birāk Libya 88 B3
Birakan Rus. Fed. 64 B2
Bi'r al Aṭbaq well Saudi Arabia 89 H3
Bi'r al 'Awādī well Saudi Arabia 89 H4
Bi'r al Fātīyah well Libya 88 B2
Bi'r al Ghanam Libya 88 B1
Bi'r al Ḥalbā well Syria 77 D2
Bi'r al Ḥaymūr well Egypt 89 G4
Bi'r al Ḥisw well Saudi Arabia 89 I3
Bi'r al Ikhwān well Libya 88 D3
Bi'r al Jadīd well Libya 88 B3
Bi'r al Jāhilīyah well Saudi Arabia 89 I4
Bi'r al Khamsah well Egypt 78 A5
Bi'r al Māliḥah well Egypt 77 A5
Bi'r al Mashī well Saudi Arabia 89 H3
Bi'r al Mastūtah well Libya 88 B3
Bi'r al Mushayqiq well Libya 88 A2
Bi'r al Muwaylih well Libya 88 C2
Bi'r al Qaṭrānī well Egypt 89 E2
Bi'r al Qurr well Saudi Arabia 89 H3
Bir 'Amrâne well Mauritania 90 C5
Birandozero Rus. Fed. 28 F3
Bi'r an Nuṣṣ well Egypt 89 E2
Bir Anzarane W. Sahara 90 B5
Birao Cent. Afr. Rep. 94 D2
Bir Aouine well Tunisia 91 H2
Bi'r ar 'Alaqah well Libya 88 B2
Bi'r 'Arja well Saudi Arabia 89 I3
Bi'r ar Rābiyah well Egypt 78 A5
Bi'r ar Rummānah Egypt 77 A4
Biratnagar Nepal 75 E4
Bi'r aṭ Ṭarfāwī well Libya 88 E2
Bi'r 'Azīz well Saudi Arabia 76 E5
Bi'r Baṣīrī well Syria 77 C2
Bi'r Bayḍā' well Egypt 77 B4
Bi'r Baylī well Egypt 88 E2
Bir Bel Guerdâne well Mauritania 90 C4
Bir Ben Takoul well Alg. 91 E4
Bir Bidi well Sudan 89 E5
Bi'r Bū Athlah well Libya 88 D3
Bi'r Bū Raḥah well Libya 88 A3
Birch r. Canada 123 H3
Bir Chali well Mali 90 D5
Birch Hills Canada 123 J4
Birchip Australia 112 B4
Birch Lake N.W.T. Canada 123 G2
Birch Lake Sask. Canada 123 I4
Birch Mountains Canada 123 H3
Birch River Canada 123 K4
Birch River U.S.A. 130 C4
Bircot Eth. 96 D3
Bir Di Sudan 94 F3
Bi'r Dibs well Egypt 89 F4
Bi'r Diqnāsh well Egypt 88 E2
Bird Island N. Mariana Is see Farallon de Medinilla
Bir Dolmane well Alg. 91 H3
Birdsboro U.S.A. 131 F3
Birdseye U.S.A. 137 G2
Birdsville Australia 111 D5
Birdum r. Australia 110 C2
Birecik Turkey 79 D3
Bir ed Deheb well Alg. 90 E4
Bir el Ghoralia well Tunisia 91 H2
Bir El Hadjaj well Alg. 91 E4
Birendranagar Nepal see Surkhet
Bir en Natrûn well Sudan 89 E5
Bir en Nugeim well Sudan 89 G5
Bir es Smeha well Alg. 91 G2
Bireun Indon. 58 B1
Bi'r Fāḍil well Saudi Arabia 76 D5
Bi'r Fajr well Saudi Arabia 89 H2
Bir Furawiya well Sudan 88 D6
Bir Gandouz W. Sahara 90 A5
Birhan mt. Eth. 96 C2
Bi'r Haraqī well Saudi Arabia 89 I4
Bi'r Ḥasanah well Egypt 77 A4
Bir Hatab well Sudan 89 G4
Bi'r Ḥayzān well Saudi Arabia 89 H3
Bir Hismet 'Umar well Sudan 89 G4
Bi'r Ḥudūf well Saudi Arabia 89 I3
Bir Huwait well Sudan 89 G4
Bi'r Ibn Hirmās Saudi Arabia see Al Bi'r
Birigüi Brazil 149 H5
Birin, Col de pass Alg. 43 H5
Birini Cent. Afr. Rep. 94 D3
Bi'r Iṣṭabl well Egypt 89 E2
Bīrjand Iran 81 D3
Bi'r Jubnī well Libya 88 E2
Birkat al Ḥamrā well Saudi Arabia 89 I2
Birkat Zubālah waterhole Saudi Arabia 79 E5
Birkeland Norway 33 C4
Birkenhead U.K. 35 E5
Bi'r Khurbah hills Saudi Arabia 76 C6
Bi'r Khurbah well Saudi Arabia 89 H3
Bi'r Khuwārah well Saudi Arabia 89 I4
Bir Kiau well Sudan 89 G4
Bīrkim Iraq 79 F3
Birkirkara Malta 45 E7
Birksgate Range hills Australia 110 B5
Bir Labasoi well Sudan 89 G4
Bîrlad Romania see Bârlad
Bi'r Lahfān well Egypt 77 A4
Bir Lahmar W. Sahara 90 C4
Birlik Kazakh. see Brlik
Bi'r Majal well Egypt 89 G4
Birmingham U.K. 35 F5
Birmingham U.S.A. 129 B5
Bîr Mogreïn Mauritania 90 C4
Bi'r Mujayfil well Saudi Arabia 77 B5
Bi'r Murrah well Egypt 89 G4
Bi'r Nabt well Saudi Arabia 89 H3
Bi'r Nāḥid oasis Egypt 89 F2
Bi'r Nasīf Saudi Arabia 89 H3
Birni Benin 93 F3
Birnie i. Kiribati 107 H2
Birnin-Gaouré Niger 93 F2
Birnin-Gwari Nigeria 93 G3
Birnin-Kebbi Nigeria 93 G2
Birnin Konni Niger 93 G2
Birnin Kudu Nigeria 93 H3
Birniwa Nigeria 93 H2
Bir Nukheila well Sudan 89 E5
Birobidzhan Rus. Fed. 64 C2
Bir Ounâne well Mali 90 E5
Birpur India 75 E4
Bi'r Qaṣīr as Sirr well Egypt 78 A5
Bi'r Qulayb well Egypt 89 G3
Birr Rep. of Ireland 35 C5
Bi'r Rawḍ Sālim well Egypt 77 A4
Birrindudu Australia 110 B3
Bir Roumi well Alg. 91 G2
Bi'r Sābil Iraq 79 E4
Bi'r Ṣaḥrā' well Egypt 89 F4
Bir Salala well Sudan 89 G4
Birsay U.K. 34 E2
Bi'r Shalatayn Egypt 89 G4
Birsk Rus. Fed. 28 J5
Bi'r Tābah Egypt 77 B5
Bir Tanguer well Alg. 91 H3
Bi'r Tānjidar well Libya 88 D2
Bi'r Thāl well Egypt 77 A5
Birthday Mountain Australia 111 E2
Birtle Canada 123 K5
Biru China 75 G3
Bi'r Udayb well Egypt 77 A5
Biruintsa Moldova see Ştefan Vodă
Bi'r Umm el Gharāniq Libya 88 C2
Bi'r Umm Missā well Saudi Arabia 89 H3
Bi'r 'Unjāt well Egypt 89 G4
Birur India 72 B3
Biruxiong China see Biru
Bir Wario well Sudan 89 G5
Bi'r Wedeb well Libya 88 B3
Bi'r Wurshah well Saudi Arabia 89 I4
Biržai Lith. 33 G4
Bir Zar well Tunisia 91 H3
Bisalpur India 74 C3
Bisau India 74 B3
Biscarrosse France 38 C4
Biscarrosse et de Parentis, Étang de l. France 38 C4
Biscay, Bay of sea France/Spain 30 C4
Biscay Abyssal Plain sea feature N. Atlantic Ocean 160 N3
Biscayne Bay U.S.A. 129 C7
Biscayne National Park U.S.A. 129 C7
Bischofshofen Austria 37 F5
Bischofswerda Germany 37 G3
Biscoe Islands Antarctica 167 L2
Biscotasing Canada 124 D4
Bisert' r. Rus. Fed. 28 K4
Biševo i. Croatia 44 E3
Bishan China 66 C2
Bishbek Kyrg. see Bishkek

▶Bishkek Kyrg. 62 A3
Capital of Kyrgyzstan.

Bishnupur India 75 E5
Bisho S. Africa 99 E7
Bishop U.S.A. 136 C3
Bishop Auckland U.K. 35 F4
Bishop's Stortford U.K. 35 G6
Bishopville U.S.A. 129 C5
Bishrī, Jabal hills Syria 79 D4
Bishti i Pallës pt Albania 46 A4
Bishui Heilong. China 63 K1
Bishui Henan China see Biyang
Bisinaca Col. 146 D3
Biskra Alg. 91 G2
Biskupiec Poland 37 J2

▶Bismarck U.S.A. 134 G3
State capital of North Dakota.

Bismarck Archipelago is P.N.G. 57 K6
Bismarck Sea P.N.G. 57 K6
Bismil Turkey 79 E3
Bison U.S.A. 132 A2
Bīsotūn Iran 80 A3
Bispgården Sweden 32 E3
Bissa, Djebel mt. Alg. 43 G4
Bissamcuttak India 73 D2

▶Bissau Guinea-Bissau 92 B3
Capital of Guinea-Bissau.

Bissaula Nigeria 93 H4
Bissett Canada 123 M5
Bissikrima Guinea 92 C3
Bissorã Guinea-Bissau 92 B2
Bistcho Lake Canada 122 G3
Bistra mt. Macedonia 46 B4
Bistra r. Romania 46 C2
Bistra mt. Serb. and Mont. 46 B3
Bistreţ Romania 46 C3
Bistreţ, Lacul l. Romania 46 C3
Bistriţa Romania 31 K4
Bistriţa r. Romania 46 E1
Bistriţsa r. Bulg. 46 C4
Biswan India 74 D4
Bisztynek Poland 37 J1
Bitam Gabon 94 A4
Bitata Eth. 96 C3
Bitburg Germany 36 C4
Bitche France 39 G2
Bitik Kazakh. 29 I6
Bitkine Chad 94 C2
Bitlis Turkey 79 E3
Bitola Macedonia 46 B4
Bitolj Macedonia see Bitola
Bitonto Italy 44 F4
Bitrān, Jabal hill Saudi Arabia 76 D5
Bitra Par reef India 72 B4
Bitter Creek r. UT U.S.A. 137 H2
Bitter Creek r. WY U.S.A. 134 E4
Bitterfontein S. Africa 98 C6
Bitterroot r. U.S.A. 134 D3
Bitterroot Range mts U.S.A. 134 D3
Bitterwater U.S.A. 136 B3
Bittou Burkina 93 E3
Bituca Brazil 150 A4
Biu Nigeria 93 I3
Biula Angola 95 D7
Biwa-ko l. Japan 65 C6
Biyang China 67 E1
Bīye K'obē Eth. 96 D2
Biyo Ado well Eth. 96 E3
Biysk Rus. Fed. 62 D1
Bizerta Tunisia see Bizerte
Bizerte Tunisia 91 H1
Bīzhanābād Iran 80 D5

▶Bjargtangar hd Iceland 32 [inset]
Most westerly point of Europe.

Bjarkøy Norway 32 E1
Bjästa Sweden 32 E3
Bjelasica mts Serb. and Mont. 46 A3
Bjelašnica mts Bos.-Herz. 44 G3
Bjelovar Croatia 44 F2
Bjerkvik Norway 32 E1
Bjøllånes Norway 32 D2
Bjøneroa Norway 33 C3
Björbo Sweden 33 D3
Bjørkelangen Norway 33 C4
Björkfjället mts Sweden 32 E2
Björkliden Sweden 32 E1
Björklinge Sweden 33 E3
Björksele Sweden 32 E2
Bjorli Norway 33 C3
Björna Sweden 32 E3
Bjørnafjorden b. Norway 33 B3
Björneborg Fin. see Pori
Bjørnfjell Norway 32 E1

▶Bjørnøya i. Arctic Ocean 26 B2
Part of Norway.

Bjørnstad Norway 32 H1
Bjurholm Sweden 32 E3
Bjuröklubb pt Sweden 32 F2
Bjursås Sweden 33 D3
Bla Mali 92 D2
Blace Kosovo, Srbija Serb. and Mont. 46 B3
Blace Srbija Serb. and Mont. 46 B3
Blachownia Poland 37 I3
Black r. Canada 123 L5
Black r. AR U.S.A. 127 H4
Black r. AR U.S.A. 133 D5
Black r. AZ U.S.A. 137 G5
Black r. MI U.S.A. 130 B2
Black r. WI U.S.A. 132 D2
Blackall Australia 111 F5
Blackbear r. Canada 124 B2
Blackbull Australia 111 E3
Blackburn U.K. 35 E5
Blackburn, Mount U.S.A. 122 A2
Black Butte mt. U.S.A. 136 A2
Black Butte Lake U.S.A. 136 A2
Black Canyon gorge U.S.A. 137 E4
Black Canyon of the Gunnison National Park U.S.A. 135 F5
Black Creek watercourse U.S.A. 137 H4
Blackdown Tableland National Park Australia 111 G4
Blackfoot U.S.A. 134 D4
Black Foot r. U.S.A. 134 D3
Black Forest mts Germany 36 D5
Black Hills SD U.S.A. 126 F3
Black Hills SD U.S.A. 134 F3
Black Island Canada 123 L5
Black Lake Canada 123 J3
Black Lake l. Canada 123 J3
Black Mesa ridge U.S.A. 137 G3
Black Mountain U.S.A. 130 B5
Black Mountains hills U.K. 35 E6
Black Mountains U.S.A. 137 E4
Black Nossob watercourse Namibia 98 C4
Black Pagoda India see Konarka
Blackpool U.K. 35 E5
Black River U.S.A. 131 F1
Black River r. Vietnam 60 D3
Black River Falls U.S.A. 132 D2
Black Rock hill Jordan see 'Unāb, Jabal al
Black Rock Desert U.S.A. 134 C4
Blacksburg U.S.A. 130 C5
Black Sea Asia/Europe 29 F8
Blackshear U.S.A. 129 C6
Blacksod Bay Rep. of Ireland 35 A4
Black Springs U.S.A. 136 C2
Blackstone r. N.W.T. Canada 122 F2
Blackstone r. Y.T. Canada 122 B1
Blackstone U.S.A. 130 D5
Black Sugarloaf mt. Australia 112 D3
Black Tickle Canada 125 K2
Black Volta r. Africa 92 E3
also known as Mouhoun
Blackwater Australia 111 G4
Blackwater watercourse Australia 111 F5
Blackwater r. Canada 122 E2
Blackwater r. Rep. of Ireland 35 C5
Blackwater r. U.S.A. 131 E5
Blackwater watercourse U.S.A. 133 A5
Blackwater Lake Canada 122 F2
Blackwood r. Australia 109 A8
Blackwood National Park Australia 111 F4
Bladensburg National Park Australia 111 E4
Blåfjellshatten mt. Norway 32 D2
Blagodarnyy Rus. Fed. 29 G7
Blagoevgrad Bulg. 46 C3
Blagoveshchensk Amurskaya Oblast' Rus. Fed. 64 A2
Blagoveshchensk Rus. Fed. 28 K5
Blaikiston, Mount Canada 123 H5
Blain France 38 C3
Blaine U.S.A. 130 E3
Blaine Lake Canada 123 J4
Blair U.S.A. 132 B3
Blair Athol Australia 111 F4
Blair Atholl U.K. 34 E3
Blairgowrie U.K. 34 E3
Blairs U.S.A. 130 D5
Blairsden U.S.A. 136 B2
Blairsville U.S.A. 128 C5
Blaj Romania 46 C1
Blakang Mati, Pulau i. Sing. see Sentosa
Blakely U.S.A. 129 B6
Blakeslee U.S.A. 131 F3
Blama Sierra Leone 92 C4
Blambangan, Semenanjung pen. Indon. 59 F5

▶Blanc, Mont mt. France/Italy 39 G4
5th highest mountain in Europe.
europe 22–23

Blanca, Bahía b. Arg. 152 E4
Blanca, Cordillera mts Peru 148 A2
Blanca, Sierra mt. U.S.A. 135 F6
Blanca Peak U.S.A. 135 F5
Blanche, Cape Australia 109 F8
Blanche, Lake salt flat S.A. Australia 111 D6
Blanche, Lake salt flat W.A. Australia 108 C5
Blanchester U.S.A. 130 B4
Blanchetown Australia 112 A4
Blanco r. Arg. 152 C2
Blanco r. Bol. 149 D3
Blanco r. Peru 146 C6
Blanco r. Spain 42 D4
Blanco, Cape U.S.A. 134 A4
Blanc-Sablon Canada 125 J3
Bland r. Australia 112 C4
Bland U.S.A. 130 C5
Blanda r. Iceland 32 [inset]
Blandford Forum U.K. 35 E6
Blanding U.S.A. 137 H3
Blanes Spain 43 H2
Blangkejeren Indon. 58 B2
Blangpidie Indon. 58 B2
Blangy-sur-Bresle France 38 D2
Blanice r. Czech Rep. 37 G4
Blanquefort France 38 C4
Blanquilla, Isla i. Venez. 147 E2
Blansko Czech Rep. 37 H4
Blantyre Malawi 97 B8
Blarney Rep. of Ireland 35 B6
Blåsjø l. Norway 33 B4
Blaskavlen mt. Norway 33 B3
Błaszki Poland 37 I3
Blatná Czech Rep. 37 F4
Blattniksele Sweden 32 E2
Blaubeuren Germany 36 D4
Blåvands Huk pt Denmark 33 C5
Blavet r. France 38 B3
Blaye France 38 C4
Blayeul Sommet mt. France 39 G4
Blayney Australia 112 D4
Blaze, Point Australia 110 B2
Blega Indon. 59 F4
Blekinge county Sweden 33 D4
Blenheim Canada 130 C2
Blenheim N.Z. 113 C3
Blenheim Palace tourist site U.K. 35 F6
Bletoppen mt. Norway 33 C4
Bleus, Monts mts Dem. Rep. Congo 96 A4
Blida Alg. 91 F1
Bligh Water b. Fiji 107 G3
Blind River Canada 124 D4
Blinman Australia 112 A3
Bliss U.S.A. 134 D4
Blissfield MI U.S.A. 130 B3
Blissfield OH U.S.A. 130 C3
Blitar Indon. 59 F5
Block Island U.S.A. 131 H3
Block Island Sound sea chan. U.S.A. 131 H3
Bloemfontein S. Africa 99 E6
Bloemhof Dam S. Africa 98 E5
Blois France 38 D3
Blöndulón l. Iceland 32 [inset]
Blönduós Iceland 32 [inset]
Blongas Indon. 59 G5
Błonie Poland 37 J2
Bloods Range mts Australia 110 B5
Bloodsworth Island U.S.A. 131 E4
Bloodvein r. Canada 123 L5
Bloody Foreland pt Rep. of Ireland 34 B4
Bloomer U.S.A. 132 D2
Bloomfield IA U.S.A. 132 C3
Bloomfield IN U.S.A. 128 B4
Bloomfield NM U.S.A. 135 F5
Blooming Prairie U.S.A. 132 C3
Bloomington IL U.S.A. 132 D3
Bloomington IN U.S.A. 128 B4
Bloomington MN U.S.A. 132 C2
Bloomsburg U.S.A. 131 E3
Bloomsbury Australia 111 G4
Blora Indon. 59 E4
Blossburg U.S.A. 131 E3
Blosseville Kyst coastal area Greenland 121 Q3
Blountstown U.S.A. 129 B6
Bludenz Austria 36 D5
Blue r. U.S.A. 133 C5
Blue watercourse U.S.A. 137 H5
Blue Bell Knoll mt. U.S.A. 137 G2
Blue Earth U.S.A. 132 C3
Blue Earth r. U.S.A. 132 C2
Bluefield U.S.A. 130 C5
Bluefields Nicaragua 139 H6
Blue Knob hill U.S.A. 130 D3
Blue Lagoon National Park Zambia 95 E8
Blue Mountain Canada 125 J3
Blue Mountain India 75 G5
Blue Mountains Australia 112 D4
Blue Mountains U.S.A. 134 C3
Blue Mountains National Park Australia 112 D4
Blue Nile r. Eth./Sudan 89 G6
also known as Ābay Wenz (Ethiopia), Azraq, Bahr el (Sudan)
Blue Nile state Sudan 96 B2
Bluenose Lake Canada 120 H3
Blue Rapids U.S.A. 132 B4
Blue Ridge GA U.S.A. 128 B5
Blue Ridge VA U.S.A. 130 D5
Blue Ridge mts U.S.A. 130 C5
Blue River Canada 122 G4
Blue Stack Mountains hills Rep. of Ireland 34 B4
Bluestone Lake U.S.A. 130 C5
Bluff N.Z. 113 B4
Bluff City U.S.A. 130 B5
Bluffdale U.S.A. 137 G1
Bluff Face Range hills Australia 108 D4
Bluff Island Hong Kong China 67 [inset]
Bluff Knoll mt. Australia 109 B8
Bluffton IN U.S.A. 128 B3
Bluffton OH U.S.A. 130 B3
Blumberg Germany 36 D5
Blumenau Brazil 151 B8
Blyth r. Australia 110 C2
Blythe U.S.A. 137 E5
Blytheville U.S.A. 127 I4
Bø Norway 33 C4
Bo Sierra Leone 92 C4
Boac Phil. 57 F3
Boa Esperança Brazil 147 F4
Boa Esperança, Açude resr Brazil 150 D3
Boa Hora Brazil 148 D2
Bo'ai China 66 C4
Boal Spain 42 C1
Boali Cent. Afr. Rep. 94 C3
Boa Nova Brazil 150 D5
Boardman U.S.A. 130 C3
Boatman Australia 111 F5
Boa Viagem Brazil 150 E3
Boa Vista Amazonas Brazil 146 C6
Boa Vista Amazonas Brazil 147 E5
Boa Vista Pará Brazil 147 H5
Boa Vista Roraima Brazil 147 F4
Boa Vista i. Cape Verde 92 [inset]
Bobai China 67 D4
Bobaomby, Tanjona c. Madag. 99 [inset] K1
Bobbili India 73 D2
Bobbio Italy 44 B2
Bobcayegon Canada 130 D1
Bobigny France 39 E2
Bobo-Dioulasso Burkina 92 D3
Bobolice Poland 37 H2
Bobonong Botswana 99 F4
Boborás Spain 42 B1
Bobotov Kuk mt. Serb. and Mont. see Durmitor
Bobovdol Bulg. 46 C3
Bóbr r. Poland 37 G3
Bobriki Rus. Fed. see Novomoskovsk
Bobrinets Ukr. see Bobrynets'
Bobrov Rus. Fed. 29 G6
Bobrovitsa Ukr. see Bobrovytsya

Bobrovytsya Ukr. 29 D6
Bobruysk Belarus see Babruysk
Bobrynets' Ukr. 29 E6
Bobs Lake Canada 131 E1
Bobso China 66 B1
Bobuk Sudan 96 B2
Bobures Venez. 146 D2
Boby mt. Madag. 99 [inset] J4
Boca de la Travesía Arg. 152 D5
Boca del Pao Venez. 147 E2
Boca de Macareo Venez. 147 F2
Boca de Uracoa Venez. 147 F2
Boca do Acre Brazil 148 D2
Boca do Curuquetê Brazil 148 D2
Boca do Jari Brazil 147 I5
Boca do Moaco Brazil 148 C1
Bocaiúva Brazil 151 D6
Bocaiúva do Sul Brazil 151 B8
Boca Mavaca Venez. 147 E4
Bocanda Côte d'Ivoire 92 D4
Bocaranga Cent. Afr. Rep. 94 B3
Boca Raton U.S.A. 129 C7
Bocas del Toro Panama 139 H7
Bochinche Venez. 147 F3
Bochnia Poland 37 J4
Bocholt Germany 36 C3
Bochum Germany 36 C3
Bochum S. Africa 99 F4
Bockenem Germany 36 E2
Bocoio Angola 95 B8
Bocşa Romania 46 B2
Boda Cent. Afr. Rep. 94 C3
Böda Sweden 33 E4
Bodallin Australia 109 B7
Bodaybo Rus. Fed. 27 L4
Bode r. Germany 36 E3
Bodega Head U.S.A. 136 A2
Bodélé reg. Chad 88 C5
Boden Sweden 32 F2
Bodensee l. Germany/Switz. see Constance, Lake
Bode-Sadu Nigeria 93 G3
Bodhan India 72 C2
Bodh Gaya India 75 E4
Bodie U.S.A. 136 C2
Bodinayakkanur India 72 C4
Bodión r. Spain 42 C3
Bodmin U.K. 35 D6
Bodø Norway 32 D2
Bodocó Brazil 150 E3
Bodoquena Brazil 149 F5
Bodoquena, Serra da hills Brazil 149 F5
Bodoukpa Cent. Afr. Rep. 94 C3
Bodrog r. Hungary 37 J4
Bodrum Turkey 78 A3
Bodsjö Sweden 32 D3
Bódva r. Hungary 37 J4
Bodva r. Slovakia 37 J4
Boechout Belgium 36 B3
Boedo r. Spain 42 D1
Boende Dem. Rep. Congo 94 D5
Boerne U.S.A. 133 B6
Boeuf r. U.S.A. 133 D6
Boftsa Norway 32 H1
Bogale Myanmar 61 A4
Bogale r. Myanmar 61 A5
Bogalusa U.S.A. 133 D6
Bogan r. Australia 112 C3
Bogandé Burkina 93 E2
Bogan Gate Australia 112 C4
Bogangolo Cent. Afr. Rep. 94 C3
Boğazlıyan Turkey 78 C3
Bogbonga Dem. Rep. Congo 94 C4
Bogcang Zangbo r. China 75 E3
Bogda Feng mt. China 70 G3
Bogdan mt. Bulg. 46 D3
Bogdanci Macedonia 46 C4
Bogda Shan mts China 70 G3
Bogen Norway 32 E1
Boggabilla Australia 111 G6
Boggeragh Mountains hills Rep. of Ireland 35 B5
Boghar Alg. 43 H5
Boghari Alg. see Ksar el Boukhari
Bogia P.N.G. 57 J6
Bogie r. Australia 111 F4
Bogodukhov Ukr. see Bohodukhiv
Bogol Manya Eth. 96 D3
Bogong, Mount Australia 112 C5
Bogor Indon. 59 D4
Bogoroditsk Rus. Fed. 29 F5
Bogorodskoye Khabarovskiy Kray Rus. Fed. 64 E1
Bogorodskoye Kirovskaya Oblast' Rus. Fed. 28 I4
Bogoslof Island U.S.A. 120 C4
▶Bogotá Col. 146 C3
Capital of Colombia and 5th most populous city in South America.
world 16–17
Bogotol Rus. Fed. 27 I4
Bogoyavlenskoye Rus. Fed. see Pervomayskiy
Bogra Bangl. 75 F4
Boguchany Rus. Fed. 27 J4
Boguchar Rus. Fed. 29 G6
Bogué Mauritania 92 B1
Boh r. Indon. 59 F2
Bo Hai g. China 63 J4
Bohain-en-Vermandois France 39 E2
Bohai Wan b. China 63 J4
Bohemia reg. Czech Rep. 37 G3
Bohemia Downs Australia 108 D4
Bohemian Forest mts Germany see Böhmer Wald
Bohicon Benin 93 F4
Bohlokong S. Africa 99 F6
Böhmen reg. Czech Rep. see Bohemia
Böhmer Wald mts Germany 37 F4
Bohodukhiv Ukr. 29 E6
Bohol i. Phil. 57 F4
Bohol Sea Phil. 57 F4
Bohu China 70 G3
Boiaçu Brazil 147 F5
Boigu Island Australia 57 J7
Boila Moz. 99 H3
Boileau, Cape Australia 108 C4
Boim Brazil 147 H5
Boinu r. Myanmar 60 A3
Boiro Spain 42 B1
Bois r. Brazil 149 H4
Bois, Lac des l. Canada 122 E1
Bois de Sioux r. U.S.A. 132 B2
▶Boise U.S.A. 134 C4
State capital of Idaho.
Boise r. U.S.A. 134 C4
Boise City U.S.A. 135 G5
Boissevain Canada 123 K5
Boite r. Italy 44 D1
Boitumelong S. Africa 98 E5
Boizenburg Germany 36 E2
Bojano Italy 44 E4
Bojeador, Cape Phil. 67 G5
Bojnik Serb. and Mont. 46 B3
Bojnūrd Iran 80 D2
Bojonegoro Indon. 59 E4
Bojuru Brazil 152 H3
Bokada Dem. Rep. Congo 94 C3
Bokadaban Feng mt. China 75 F1
Bokajan India 75 G4
Bokaro India 75 E5
Bokatola Dem. Rep. Congo 94 C5
Boké Guinea 92 B3
Bokhara r. Australia 112 C3
Boknafjorden sea chan. Norway 33 B4
Boko Congo 95 B6
Boko Dem. Rep. Congo 95 C6
Bokoko Dem. Rep. Congo 94 E3
Bokolo Gabon 94 A5
Bokoro Chad 88 C6
Bokoro Dem. Rep. Congo 94 C5
Bokote Dem. Rep. Congo 94 D5
Bokovskaya Rus. Fed. 29 G6
Bokpyin Myanmar 61 B6
Bokspits S. Africa 98 D5
Boktor Rus. Fed. 64 D2
Bokungu Dem. Rep. Congo 94 D5
Bokurdak Turkm. see Bakhardok
Bokwankusu Dem. Rep. Congo 94 D5
Bol Chad 88 B6
Bola, Bahr watercourse Chad 94 C2
Bolaiti Dem. Rep. Congo 94 E5
Bolama Guinea-Bissau 92 B3
Bolan r. Pak. 81 F4
Bolanda, Jebel mt. Sudan 94 E3
Bolaños de Calatrava Spain 42 E3
Bolan Pass Pak. 81 F4
Bolbec France 38 D2
Boldajī Iran 80 B4
Boldu Romania 46 E2
Bole China 70 F3
Bole Ghana 93 E3
Boleko Dem. Rep. Congo 94 C5
Bolesławiec Poland 37 G3
Bolgar Rus. Fed. 28 I5
Bolgatanga Ghana 93 E3
Bolgrad Ukr. see Bolhrad
Bolhrad Ukr. 29 D7
Boli China 64 B3
Boli Sudan 94 F3
Bolia Dem. Rep. Congo 94 C5
Boliden Sweden 32 F2
Bolintin-Vale Romania 46 D2
Bolívar Antioquia Col. 146 B3
Bolívar Cauca Col. 146 B4
Bolívar dept Col. 146 C2
Bolívar prov. Ecuador 146 B5
Bolívar Peru 148 A1
Bolivar MO U.S.A. 132 C4
Bolivar NY U.S.A. 130 D2
Bolivar TN U.S.A. 128 A5
Bolívar state Venez. 147 F3
▶Bolivia country S. America 148 D4
5th largest country in South America.
southamerica 144–145, 154
world 14–15
Boljevac Serb. and Mont. 46 B3
Bolkhov Rus. Fed. 29 F5
Bolków Poland 37 H3
Bollène France 39 F4
Bollnäs Sweden 33 E3
Bollon Australia 111 F6
Bollstabruk Sweden 32 E3
Bolmen l. Sweden 33 D4
Bolnisi Georgia 79 F2
Bolobo Dem. Rep. Congo 94 C5
Bologna Italy 44 C2
Bolognesi Peru 148 B2
Bologoye Rus. Fed. 28 E4
Bolomba Dem. Rep. Congo 94 C4
Bolombo r. Dem. Rep. Congo 94 D4
Bolon' Rus. Fed. see Achan
Bolondo Equat. Guinea 93 H5
Bolovens, Phouphieng plat. Laos 61 D5
Bolozo Congo 94 B4
Bolpur India 75 E5
Bolsa, Cerro mt. Arg. 152 C2
Bolsena, Lago di l. Italy 44 C3
Bol'shakovo Rus. Fed. 33 F5
Bol'shaya Chernigovka Rus. Fed. 29 I5
Bol'shaya Glushitsa Rus. Fed. 29 I5
Bol'shaya Imandra, Ozero l. Rus. Fed. 28 E2
Bol'shaya Kokshaga r. Rus. Fed. 28 H4
Bol'shaya Rogovaya r. Rus. Fed. 28 L2
Bol'shaya Synya r. Rus. Fed. 28 K2
Bol'shaya Usa Rus. Fed. 28 J4
Bol'sheretsk Rus. Fed. 27 P4
Bol'shevik, Ostrov i. Rus. Fed. 27 K2
Bol'shezemel'skaya Tundra lowland Rus. Fed. 28 J2
Bol'shiye Chirki Rus. Fed. 28 H3
Bol'shiye Kozly Rus. Fed. 28 F2
Bol'shiye Peshnyye, Ostrova is Kazakh. 29 I7
Bol'shoy Aluy r. Rus. Fed. 27 P3
Bol'shoy Anyuy r. Rus. Fed. 27 Q3
Bol'shoy Begichev, Ostrov i. Rus. Fed. 27 L2
Bol'shoy Berezovyy, Ostrov i. Rus. Fed. 33 H3
Bol'shoye Murashkino Rus. Fed. 28 H5
Bol'shoy Irgiz r. Rus. Fed. 29 H6
Bol'shoy Kamen' Rus. Fed. 64 C4
Bol'shoy Kavkaz mts Asia/Europe see Caucasus
Bol'shoy Lyakhovskiy, Ostrov i. Rus. Fed. 27 O2
Bol'shoy Porog Rus. Fed. 27 J3
Bol'shoy Tokmak Kyrg. see Tokmak
Bol'shoy Tokmak Ukr. see Tokmak
Bol'shoy Uzen' r. Kazakh./Rus. Fed. 29 I6
Bol'shoy Zelenchuk r. Rus. Fed. 79 E1
Bolsward Neth. 36 B2
Bolton Canada 130 D2
Bolton U.K. 35 E5
Bolu Turkey 78 B2
Bolungarvík Iceland 32 [inset]
Boluntay China 75 G1
Boluo China 67 E4
Bolus Head Rep. of Ireland 35 A6
Bolvadin Turkey 78 B3
Bolyarovo Bulg. 46 E3
Bolzano Italy 44 C1
Boma Dem. Rep. Congo 95 B6
Bomaderry Australia 112 D4
Bomai China 66 A2
Bombala Australia 112 D5
Bombarral Port. 42 B3
Bombay India see Mumbai
Bombay Beach U.S.A. 137 E5
Bomberai, Semenanjung pen. Indon. 57 H6
Bomberai Peninsula Indon. see Bomberai, Semenanjung
Bombo r. Dem. Rep. Congo 95 B5
Bom Comércio Brazil 148 D2
Bomdila India 75 G4
Bomi China 62 F6
Bomili Dem. Rep. Congo 94 E4
Bom Jardim Brazil 148 D2
Bom Jesus Piauí Brazil 150 C4
Bom Jesus Rio Grande do Sul Brazil 151 B9
Bom Jesus da Gurgueia, Serra do hills Brazil 150 D4
Bom Jesus da Lapa Brazil 150 D5
Bom Jesus do Itabapoana Brazil 151 D7
Bømlo i. Norway 33 B4
Bomokandi r. Dem. Rep. Congo 94 E4
Bom Retiro Brazil 151 B8
Bon, Cap c. Tunisia 91 H1
Bona Alg. see Annaba
Bona, Mount U.S.A. 122 A2
Bonāb Iran 80 A2
Bon Air U.S.A. 130 E5
Bonaire i. Neth. Antilles 146 D1
Bonandolok Indon. 58 B2
Bonanza Nicaragua 139 H6
Bonaparte Archipelago is Australia 110 A2
Bonaparte Lake Canada 134 B2
Bonasse Trin. and Tob. 147 F2
Bonavista Canada 121 N5
Bonavista Bay Canada 125 K3
Bondo Équateur Dem. Rep. Congo 94 D5
Bondo Orientale Dem. Rep. Congo 94 D4
Bondoukou Côte d'Ivoire 92 E3
Bondoukui Burkina 92 E3
Bondowoso Indon. 59 F4
Bondyuzhskiy Rus. Fed. see Mendeleyevsk
Bône Alg. see Annaba
Bone, Teluk b. Indon. 57 F7
Bonerate, Kepulauan is Indon. 57 F7
▶Bonete, Cerro mt. Arg. 152 C1
3rd highest mountain in South America.
Bonfinópolis de Minas Brazil 151 C6
Bonga Eth. 96 C3
Bongaigaon India 75 F4
Bongandanga Dem. Rep. Congo 94 D4
Bongani S. Africa 98 D6
Bongba China 75 D2
Bong Co l. China 75 F3
Bongo, Massif des mts Cent. Afr. Rep. 94 D2
Bongo, Serra do mts Angola 95 B7
Bongolava mts Madag. 99 [inset] J3
Bongor Chad 94 B2
Bongouanou Côte d'Ivoire 92 D4
Bông Son Vietnam 61 E5
Bönhamn Sweden 32 E3
Boni Mali 93 E2
Bonifacio Corsica France 31 G5
Bonifacio, Bocche di strait France/Italy see Bonifacio, Strait of
Bonifacio, Bouches de strait France/Italy see Bonifacio, Strait of
Bonifacio, Strait of France/Italy 44 B4
Boni National Reserve nature res. Kenya 96 D5
▶Bonin Islands N. Pacific Ocean 54 G4
Part of Japan.
Bonito Brazil 149 F5
▶Bonn Germany 36 C3
Former capital of Germany.
Bonna Germany see Bonn
Bonnat France 38 D3
Bonners Ferry U.S.A. 134 C2
Bonnet, Lac du resr Canada 123 M5
Bonnet Plume r. Canada 122 C1
Bonneval France 38 D2
Bonneville France 39 G3
Bonnie Rock Australia 109 B7
Bonnyville Canada 123 I4
Bonom Mhai mt. Vietnam 61 D6
Bononia Italy see Bologna
Bonorva Sardinia Italy 45 B4
Bonoua Côte d'Ivoire 92 E4
Bonsall U.S.A. 136 D5
Bonthe Sierra Leone 92 B4
Bontoc Phil. 57 F2
Bontosunggu Indon. 57 E7
Bontrug S. Africa 98 E7
Bonvouloir Islands P.N.G. 111 G1
Bonyhád Hungary 44 G1
Boo Sweden 33 E4
Boodie Boodie Range hills Australia 109 C6
Book Cliffs ridge U.S.A. 137 H2
Booker U.S.A. 133 A4
Boola Guinea 92 C3
Booligal Australia 112 C4
Boologooro Australia 109 A6
Boomi Australia 112 D3
Boone IA U.S.A. 132 C3
Boone NC U.S.A. 128 C4
Boone Lake U.S.A. 130 B5
Boones Mill U.S.A. 130 D5
Booneville AR U.S.A. 133 C5
Booneville KY U.S.A. 130 B5
Booneville MS U.S.A. 128 A5
Boonsboro U.S.A. 130 E4
Böön Tsagaan Nuur salt l. Mongolia 70 I2
Boonville CA U.S.A. 136 A2
Boonville IN U.S.A. 128 B4
Boonville MO U.S.A. 132 C4
Boopi r. Bol. 148 D3
Boorabin National Park Australia 109 C7
Booroma Somalia 96 D2
Booroorban Australia 112 C4
Boorowa Australia 112 D4
Boosaaso Somalia 96 F2
Boothbay Harbor U.S.A. 131 I2
Boothby, Cape Antarctica 167 D2
Boothia, Gulf of Canada 121 K3
Boothia Peninsula Canada 121 J2
Booué Gabon 94 A5
Bopolu Liberia 92 C4
Boppard Germany 36 C3
Boqê China 75 F3
Boqueirão Brazil 152 G2
Boqueirão, Serra do hills Brazil 150 C5
Bor Rus. Fed. 28 H4
Bor Sudan 96 A3
Bor Turkey 78 C3
Bor Serb. and Mont. 46 C2
Boragi waterhole Kenya 96 C5
Borah Peak U.S.A. 134 D3
Boraraigh i. U.K. see Boreray
Borås Sweden 33 D4
Borasambar India 73 D1
Borāzjān Iran 80 B4
Borba Brazil 147 G6
Borba Port. 42 C3
Borbollón, Embalse del resr Spain 42 C2
Borborema, Planalto da plat. Brazil 150 E3
Borcea, Braţul watercourse Romania 46 E2
Borchalo Georgia see Marneuli
Borchgrevink Coast Antarctica 167 H2
Borçka Turkey 79 E2
Bor Dağı mt. Turkey 47 F6
Bordeaux France 38 C4
Bordein Sudan 89 G6
Borden Canada 125 I4
Borden Island Canada 121 H2
Borden Peninsula Canada 121 K2
Bordentown U.S.A. 131 F3
Border Ranges National Park Australia 112 E3
Bordertown Australia 112 B5
Borðeyri Iceland 32 [inset]
Bordj Bou Arréridj Alg. 91 G1
Bordj Bounaama Alg. 43 G5
Bordj Flye Ste-Marie Alg. 90 E4
Bordj Messaouda Alg. 91 H3
Bordj Mokhtar Alg. 91 F5
Bordj Omar Driss Alg. see Bordj Omer Driss
Bordj Omer Driss Alg. 91 G3
Borðoy i. Faroe Is 34 [inset]
Boré Mali 92 E2
Boreas Abyssal Plain sea feature Arctic Ocean 166 H1
Borensberg Sweden 33 D4
Boreray i. U.K. 34 B3
Borgå Fin. see Porvoo
Borgarfjörður Iceland 32 [inset]
Borgarnes Iceland 32 [inset]
Børgefjell Nasjonalpark nat. park Norway 32 D2
Borger U.S.A. 133 A5
Borgholm Sweden 33 E4
Borgo Corsica France 44 B3
Borgo a Mozzano Italy 44 C3
Borgomanero Italy 44 B2
Borgo San Dalmazzo Italy 44 A2
Borgo San Lorenzo Italy 44 C3
Borgosesia Italy 44 B2
Borgo Val di Taro Italy 44 B2
Borgo Valsugana Italy 44 C1
Borgsjåbrotet mt. Norway 33 C3
Bori India 72 C1
Bori r. India 74 B5
Borino Bulg. 46 D4
Borisoglebsk Rus. Fed. 29 G6
Borisov Belarus see Barysaw
Borisovka Rus. Fed. 29 F6
Borispol' Ukr. see Boryspil'
Bo River Post Sudan 94 E3
Boriziny Madag. 99 [inset] J2
Borja mts Bos.-Herz. 44 F2
Borja Peru 146 B6
Borjas Blancas Spain see Les Borges Blanques
Borj Bourguiba Tunisia 91 H2
Borken Germany 36 C3
Borkenes Norway 32 E1
Borkou-Ennedi-Tibesti pref. Chad 88 C5
Borkovskaya Rus. Fed. 28 I2
Borkum Germany 36 C2
Borkum i. Germany 36 C2
Borlänge Sweden 33 D3
Borlaug Norway 33 B3
Borlu Turkey 78 B3
Borna Germany 37 F3
Born-Berge hill Germany 36 E3
Borne Alg. 91 G4
▶Borneo i. Asia 59 F2
Largest island in Asia and 3rd in the world.
asia 50–51
world 6–7
Bornes mts France 39 G4
Bornholm i. Denmark 33 D5
Bornholmsgattet strait Denmark/Sweden 33 D5
Borno state Nigeria 93 I3
Bornova Turkey 78 A3
Borobudur tourist site Indon. 59 E4
Borodino Rus. Fed. 166 F2
Borodinskoye Rus. Fed. 33 H3
Borohoro Shan mts China 70 F3
Boromo Burkina 92 E3
Boron Mali 92 D2
Borovan Bulg. 46 C3
Borovichi Rus. Fed. 28 E4
Borovo Selo Croatia 44 G2
Borovoy Rus. Fed. 28 I4
Borovskoy Kazakh. 26 G4
Borroloola Australia 110 D3
Børsa Norway 32 C3
Borşa Romania 31 K4
Borsad India 74 B5
Børselv Norway 32 G1
Borshchiv Ukr. 29 C6
Borshchovochnyy Khrebet mts Rus. Fed. 63 H2
Borsippa tourist site Iraq 79 F4
Bortala China see Bole
Bort-les-Orgues France 39 E4
Borūjen Iran 80 B4
Borūjerd Iran 80 B3
Borushtitsa Bulg. 46 D3
Boryspil' Ukr. 31 L3
Borzna Ukr. 29 E6
Borzya Rus. Fed. 27 L4
Bosa Sardinia Italy 45 B4
Bosanska Dubica Bos.-Herz. 44 F2
Bosanska Gradiška Bos.-Herz. 44 F2
Bosanska Kostajnica Bos.-Herz. 44 F2
Bosanska Krupa Bos.-Herz. 44 F2
Bosanski Brod Bos.-Herz. 44 G2
Bosanski Novi Bos.-Herz. 44 F2
Bosanski Petrovac Bos.-Herz. 44 F2
Bosanski Šamac Bos.-Herz. 44 G2
Boscawen U.S.A. 131 H2
Boscawen Island Tonga see Niuatoputopu
Bosch Arg. 152 F4
Bose China 66 C4
Boshnyakovo Rus. Fed. 64 E2
Boshruyeh Iran 80 D3
Bosilegrad Serb. and Mont. 46 C3
Bosiljgrad Serb. and Mont. see Bosilegrad
Boskovice Czech Rep. 37 H4
Bosna r. Bos.-Herz. 44 G2
Bosna hills Bulg. 46 E3
Bosna i Hercegovina country Europe see Bosnia-Herzegovina
Bosna Saray Bos.-Herz. see Sarajevo
▶Bosnia-Herzegovina country Europe 44 F2
europe 24–25, 48
Boso Dem. Rep. Congo 94 D4
Bosobolo Dem. Rep. Congo 94 C3
Bōsō-hantō pen. Japan 65 E6
Bososama Dem. Rep. Congo 94 D3
▶Bosporus strait Turkey 46 F4
europe 24–25
Bosque Spain 42 B1
Bossaga Turkm. see Basaga
Bossangoa Cent. Afr. Rep. 94 C3
Bossembélé Cent. Afr. Rep. 94 C3
Bossemptélé Cent. Afr. Rep. see Bossentélé
Bossentélé Cent. Afr. Rep. 94 C3
Bossier City U.S.A. 133 C5
Bossiesvlei Namibia 98 C5
Bossut, Cape Australia 108 C4
Bostan China 75 E1
Bostān Iran 80 A4
Bosten Hu l. China 70 G3
Boston U.K. 35 F5
▶Boston U.S.A. 131 H2
State capital of Massachusetts.
Boston Mountains U.S.A. 133 C5
Bosut r. Croatia 44 G2
Boswell U.S.A. 130 D3
Botad India 74 A5
Botata Liberia 92 C4
Boteå Sweden 32 E3
Boteti r. Botswana 98 E4
Botev mt. Bulg. 46 D3
Botevgrad Bulg. 46 C3
Bothell U.S.A. 134 B3
Bothnia, Gulf of Fin./Sweden 32 E3
Bothwell Australia 112 C6
Bothwell Canada 130 C2
Boticas Port. 42 C2
Botin mt. Bos.-Herz. 44 G3
Botlikh Rus. Fed. 79 F2
Botoşani Romania 31 K4
Bô Trach Vietnam 60 D4
Botro Côte d'Ivoire 92 D4
Botshabelo S. Africa 99 E6
Botsmark Sweden 32 F2
▶Botswana country Africa 98 D4
africa 86–87, 100
Bottenviken g. Fin./Sweden 32 F2
Bottineau U.S.A. 134 G2
Bottrop Germany 36 C3
Botucatu Brazil 149 H5
Bouaflé Côte d'Ivoire 92 D4
Bouaké Côte d'Ivoire 92 D4
Boualem Alg. 91 F2
Bouandougou Côte d'Ivoire 92 D3
Bouanga Congo 94 C5
Bouar Cent. Afr. Rep. 94 B3
Bou Arada Tunisia 45 B6
Bouârfa Morocco 91 E2
Bou Aroua Alg. 91 G2
Bouba Ndjida, Parc National de nat. park Cameroon 93 I3
Boû Bleï'ine well Mauritania 92 C1
Boubout well Alg. 90 D4
Bouca Cent. Afr. Rep. 94 C3
Boucaut Bay Australia 110 C2
Bouctouche Canada 125 H4
Boû Djébéha well Mali 93 E1
Boudoua Cent. Afr. Rep. 94 C3
Bouenza admin. reg. Congo 95 B6
Bouenza r. Congo 94 B6
Bougainville, Cape Australia 108 D3
Bougainville Island P.N.G. 107 E2
Boughessa Mali 93 F1
Bougie Alg. see Bejaïa
Bougoumen Chad 94 B2
Bougouni Mali 92 D3
Bougtob Alg. 91 F2
Boû Guendoûz well Mali 92 D1
Bougzoul Alg. 43 H5
Bouillon Belgium 39 F2
Bouira Alg. 91 F1
Bou Izakarn Morocco 90 C3
Boujdour W. Sahara 90 B4
Boukoumbé Benin 93 F3
Boulder Australia 109 C7
Boulder CO U.S.A. 134 F4
Boulder MT U.S.A. 134 D3
Boulder UT U.S.A. 137 G3
Boulder Canyon gorge U.S.A. 137 E3
Boulder City U.S.A. 137 E4
Boulemane Morocco 90 D2
Boulemane Morocco 90 D2
Boulevard U.S.A. 137 D5
Boulhaut Morocco see Ben Slimane
Boulia Australia 111 D4
Boulogne France see Boulogne-sur-Mer
Boulogne r. France 38 C3
Boulogne-Billancourt France 38 E2
Boulogne-sur-Mer France 38 D1
Boulou r. Cent. Afr. Rep. 94 E3
Boulouba Cent. Afr. Rep. 94 D3
Bouloupari New Caledonia 107 F4
Boulsa Burkina 93 E2
Boultoum Niger 93 H2
Boumango Gabon 94 B5
Boumba r. Cameroon 94 B4
Boumbé I r. Cent. Afr. Rep. 94 B3
Boumerdes Alg. 91 F1
Bouna Côte d'Ivoire 92 E3
Bou Naceur, Jbel mt. Morocco 90 E2
Boû Nâga Mauritania 92 B1
Boundary U.S.A. 122 A1
Boundary Peak U.S.A. 136 C3
Boundiali Côte d'Ivoire 92 D3
Boung r. Vietnam 61 E4
Boungou r. Cent. Afr. Rep. 94 D3
Bountiful U.S.A. 134 E4
Bounty Islands N.Z. 107 G6
Bounty Trough sea feature S. Pacific Ocean 164 F9
Bourail New Caledonia 107 F4
Bourbince r. France 39 F3
Bourbon-Lancy France 39 E3
Bourbonne-les-Bains France 39 F3
Bourem Mali 93 E1
Bouressa Mali see Boughessa
Bourganeuf France 38 D4
Bourg-en-Bresse France 39 F3
Bourges France 38 E3
Bourgneuf, Baie de b. France 38 B3
Bourgogne admin. reg. France 39 F3
Bourgoin-Jallieu France 39 F4
Bourg-St-Andéol France 39 F4
Bourg-St-Maurice France 39 G4
Bourke Australia 111 F6
Bournemouth U.K. 35 F6
Bouroum-Bouroum Burkina 92 E3
Bourtoutou Chad 94 D2
Bourzanga Burkina 93 E2
Bou Saâda Alg. 91 G2
Bou Salem Tunisia 45 B6
Bouse U.S.A. 137 E5
Bouse Wash watercourse U.S.A. 137 E4
Boussé Burkina 93 E2
Bousso Chad 94 C2
Boû Tezâya well Mauritania 92 C1
Boutilimit Mauritania 92 B1
Boutougou Fara Senegal 92 B2
▶Bouvetøya terr. S. Atlantic Ocean 161 O9
Dependency of Norway.
Boven Kapuas Mountains Indon./Malaysia see Kapuas Hulu, Pegunungan
Bow r. Australia 108 E4
Bow r. Alta Canada 123 I5
Bow r. Alta Canada 134 E2
Bowa China see Muli
Bowbells U.S.A. 132 A1
Bowden U.S.A. 130 D4
Bowen Arg. 152 D3
Bowen Australia 111 G4
Bowen r. Australia 111 F4
Bowen, Mount Australia 112 D5
Bowen Downs Australia 111 F4
Bowers Ridge sea feature Bering Sea 164 F2
Bowie AZ U.S.A. 137 H5
Bowie TX U.S.A. 133 B5
Bow Island Canada 123 I5
Bowkan Iran 80 A2
Bowling Green KY U.S.A. 128 B4
Bowling Green MO U.S.A. 132 D4
Bowling Green OH U.S.A. 130 B3
Bowling Green VA U.S.A. 131 E4
Bowling Green Bay National Park Australia 111 F3
Bowman U.S.A. 134 G3
Bowman Island Antarctica 167 F2
Bowman Peninsula Antarctica 167 L2
Bown Somalia 96 D2
Bowo Sichuan China see Bomai
Bowo Xizang China see Bomi
Bowser Lake Canada 122 D3
Box Elder U.S.A. 132 A2
Box Elder r. U.S.A. 134 G3
Boxholm Sweden 33 D4
Boxtel Neth. 36 B3
Boyabat Turkey 78 C2
Boyacá dept Col. 146 C3
Boyalık Turkey see Çiçekdağı
Boyana tourist site Bulg. 46 C3
Boyang China 67 F2
Boyd Lagoon salt flat Australia 109 D6
Boyd Lake Canada 123 K2
Boydton U.S.A. 130 D5
Boyer r. U.S.A. 132 C3
Boyera Dem. Rep. Congo 94 C5
Boyertown U.S.A. 131 F3
Boykins U.S.A. 131 E5
Boyle Canada 123 H4
Boyle Rep. of Ireland 35 B5
Boyne r. Qld Australia 111 G4
Boyne r. Qld Australia 111 G5
Boyne r. Rep. of Ireland 35 C5
Boyni Qara Afgh. 81 F2
Boyo Cent. Afr. Rep. 94 D3
Boyoma, Chutes waterfall Dem. Rep. Congo see Boyoma Falls
Boyoma Falls Dem. Rep. Congo 94 E4
Boysun Uzbek. see Baysun
Boyuibe Bol. 149 E5
Boyup Brook Australia 109 B8
Bozashy Tübegi pen. Kazakh. see Buzachi, Poluostrov
Bozburun Turkey 78 B3
▶Bozcaada i. Turkey 78 A3
Most westerly point of Asia.
Bozdağ mt. Turkey 47 E5
Bozdağ mt. Turkey 77 C1
Boz Dağları mts Turkey 78 A3
Bozdoğan Turkey 78 B3
Bozeman U.S.A. 134 E3
Bozen Italy see Bolzano
Bozhou China 67 E1
Bozkır Turkey 78 C3
Bozouls France 39 E4
Bozoum Cent. Afr. Rep. 94 C3
Bozova Turkey 79 D3
Bozovici Romania 46 C2
Bozqūsh, Kūh-e mts Iran 80 A2
Bozüyük Turkey 78 B3
Bozyazı Turkey 77 A1
Bra Italy 44 A2
Brač i. Croatia 44 F3
Bracara Port. see Braga
Bracciano Italy 44 D3
Bracciano, Lago di l. Italy 44 D3
Bracebridge Canada 124 E4
Bräcke Sweden 32 D3
Brackettville U.S.A. 133 A6
Brački Kanal sea chan. Croatia 44 F3
Bracknell U.K. 35 F6
Brad Romania 46 C1
Bradano r. Italy 45 F4
Bradenton U.S.A. 129 C7
Bradford U.K. 35 F5
Bradford PA U.S.A. 130 D3
Bradford VT U.S.A. 131 G2
Bradshaw U.S.A. 130 C5
Brady U.S.A. 133 B6
Braemar U.K. 34 E3
Braga Port. 42 B2
Braga admin. dist. Port. 42 B2
Bragado Arg. 152 E3
Bragança Brazil 150 C2
Bragança Port. 42 C2
Bragança admin. dist. Port. 42 C2
Brahmakund India 60 E2
Brahmanbaria Bangl. 75 F5
Brahmani r. India 73 E1
Brahmapur India 73 E2
Brahmaputra r. China/India 75 F4
also known as Dihang (India) or Yarlung Zangbo (China)
Brăila Romania 46 E2
Brăilei, Insula Mare a i. Romania 46 E2
Braine France 39 E2
Brainerd U.S.A. 132 C2
Braintree U.K. 35 G6
Braithwaite Point Australia 110 C1
Braives Belgium 39 F1
Brake (Unterweser) Germany 36 D2
Brâkna admin. reg. Mauritania 92 B1
Brakwater Namibia 98 C4
Bralorne Canada 122 F5
Bramhapuri India 72 C1
Bramming Denmark 33 C5
Brampton Canada 130 D2
Brampton U.K. 34 E4
Bramsche Germany 36 D2
Bramsöfjärden l. Sweden 33 E3
Brancaleone Italy 45 F6
Branch Canada 125 K4
Branco r. Mato Grosso Brazil 149 E2
Branco r. Roraima Brazil 147 F5
Brandberg mt. Namibia 98 B4
Brändbo Sweden 33 E3
Brandbu Norway 33 C3
Brande Denmark 33 C5
Brandenburg Germany 37 F2
Brandenburg land Germany 37 F2
Brandenburg U.S.A. 128 B4
Brändö Fin. 33 F3
Brandon Canada 134 H2
Brandon MS U.S.A. 133 D5
Brandon SD U.S.A. 132 B3
Brandon VT U.S.A. 131 G2
Brandon Head Rep. of Ireland 35 A5
Brandonville U.S.A. 130 D4
Brandvlei S. Africa 98 D6
Brandvoll Norway 32 E1
Brani, Pulau i. Sing. 58 [inset]
Braniewo Poland 37 I1
Brännberg Sweden 32 F2
Brannenburg Germany 36 F5
Bransfield Strait Antarctica 167 L2
Brantas r. Indon. 59 F4
Brantford Canada 130 C2
Brantôme France 38 D4
Brás Brazil 147 G5
Brasaljce Serb. and Mont. 46 B3
Bras d'Or Lake Canada 125 I4
Brasil country S. America see Brazil
Brasil, Planalto do plat. Brazil 151 D6
Brasileia Brazil 148 C2
▶Brasília Brazil 149 I3
Capital of Brazil.
southamerica 154
Brasília de Minas Brazil 151 C6
Brasília Legal Brazil 147 H5
Braslav Belarus see Braslaw
Braslaw Belarus 31 K2
Braşov Romania 46 D2
Brassey, Banjaran mts Sabah Malaysia 59 G1
Brassey Range hills Australia 109 C6
Bratan mt. Bulg. 46 D3
▶Bratislava Slovakia 37 H4
Capital of Slovakia.
Bratsk Rus. Fed. 27 K4
Bratskoye Vodokhranilishche resr Rus. Fed. 27 K4
Brattleboro U.S.A. 131 G2
Brattmon Sweden 33 D3
Brattvåg Norway 32 B3
Bratunac Bos.-Herz. 46 A2
Braunau am Inn Austria 37 F4
Braunschweig Germany 36 E2
Brava i. Cape Verde 92 [inset]
Brave U.S.A. 130 C4
Bråviken inlet Sweden 33 E4
Bravo, Cerro mt. Bol. 148 D4
Bravo del Norte, Río r. Mex. 133 B7
Bravo del Norte, Río r. Mex./U.S.A. see Rio Grande
Brawley U.S.A. 137 E5
Bray Rep. of Ireland 35 C5
Braye r. France 38 D3
Bray-sur-Seine France 39 E2
Brazeau r. Canada 123 H4

▶Brazil country S. America 150 B4
Largest country in South America and 5th in the world. Most populous country in South America and 5th in the world.
southamerica 144–145, 154
world 8–9, 14–15, 16–17
Brazil Basin sea feature S. Atlantic Ocean 160 M7
Brazos r. U.S.A. 133 C6
▶Brazzaville Congo 95 B6
Capital of Congo.
Brčko Bos.-Herz. 44 G2
Brda r. Poland 37 I2
Brdy hills Czech Rep. 37 F4
Bré Rep. of Ireland see Bray
Breaksea Sound inlet N.Z. 113 A4
Breaksea Spit Australia 111 H5
Bream Bay N.Z. 113 C1
Breas Chile 152 C1
Breaza Romania 46 D2
Brebes Indon. 59 E4
Brechin U.K. 34 E3
Brecht Belgium 36 B3
Breckenridge CO U.S.A. 134 F5
Breckenridge MN U.S.A. 132 B2
Breckenridge TX U.S.A. 133 B5
Brecknock, Península pen. Chile 153 B8
Břeclav Czech Rep. 37 H4
Brecon U.K. 35 E6
Brecon Beacons reg. U.K. 35 E6
Brecon Beacons National Park U.K. 35 E6
Breda Neth. 36 B3
Bredasdorp S. Africa 98 D7
Bredviken Sweden 32 D2
Bregalnica r. Macedonia 46 B4
Bregenz Austria 36 D5
Bregovo Bulg. 46 C2
Bréhal France 38 C2
Breiðafjörður b. Iceland 32 [inset]
Breiðdalsvík Iceland 32 [inset]
Breil-sur-Roya France 39 G5
Breisach am Rhein Germany 36 C4
Breivikeidet Norway 32 E1
Brejo r. Brazil 150 D4
Brejo da Porta Brazil 150 C4
Brekstad Norway 32 C3
Bremen Germany 36 D2
Bremen GA U.S.A. 129 B5
Bremen OH U.S.A. 130 B4
Bremer Bay Australia 109 B8
Bremerhaven Germany 36 D2
Bremer Range hills Australia 109 C8
Bremersdorp Swaziland see Manzini
Bremervörde Germany 36 D2
Breń r. Poland 37 J3
Brenham U.S.A. 133 B6
Brenna Norway 32 D2
Brennero Italy 44 C1
Brennero, Passo di pass Austria/Italy see Brenner Pass
Brennerpaß pass Austria/Italy see Brenner Pass
Brenner Pass Austria/Italy 36 E5
Breno Italy 44 C2
Brenta r. Italy 44 D2
Brenta, Gruppo di mts Italy 44 C1
Brentwood U.K. 35 G6
Brenzone Italy 44 C2
Brescia Italy 44 C2
Breslau Poland see Wrocław
Bresle r. France 38 D1
Brésolles, Lac l. Canada 125 G2
Bressanone Italy 44 C1
Bressay i. U.K. 34 F1
Bressuire France 38 C3
Brest Belarus 31 J2
Brest France 38 A2
Brest-Litovsk Belarus see Brest
Brestovac Serb. and Mont. 46 B3
Bretagne admin. reg. France 38 B2
Brețcu Romania 46 E1
Breteuil Haute-Normandie France 38 D2
Breteuil Picardie France 38 E2
Breton Canada 123 H4
Breton Sound b. U.S.A. 129 A6
Brett, Cape N.Z. 113 C1
Bretten Germany 36 D4
Breu r. Brazil/Peru 148 B2
Breueh, Pulau i. Indon. 58 A1
Brevard U.S.A. 128 C5
Breves Brazil 150 B2
Brewarrina Australia 112 C3
Brewster NE U.S.A. 132 B3
Brewster OH U.S.A. 130 C3
Brewster WA U.S.A. 134 C2
Brewster, Kap c. Greenland see Kangikajik
Brewton U.S.A. 129 B6
Breytovo Rus. Fed. 28 F4
Brezhnev Rus. Fed. see Naberezhnyye Chelny
Brežice Slovenia 44 E2
Breznik Bulg. 46 C3
Breznitsa Bulg. 46 C4
Brezno Slovakia 37 I4
Brezovo Bulg. 46 D3
Brezovo Polje hill Croatia 44 F2
Bria Cent. Afr. Rep. 94 D3
Briakan Rus. Fed. 64 C1
Briançon France 39 G4
Brian Head mt. U.S.A. 137 F3
Briare France 39 E3
Briceni Moldova 29 C6
Brichany Moldova see Briceni
Bridgehampton U.S.A. 131 G3
Bridgeport AL U.S.A. 133 E5
Bridgeport CA U.S.A. 136 C2
Bridgeport CT U.S.A. 131 G3
Bridgeport MI U.S.A. 130 B2
Bridgeport NE U.S.A. 134 G4
Bridgeport TX U.S.A. 133 B5
Bridger Peak U.S.A. 134 F4
Bridgeton U.S.A. 131 F4
Bridgetown Australia 109 B8
▶Bridgetown Barbados 147 G1
Capital of Barbados.
Bridgetown Canada 125 H4
Bridgeville U.S.A. 131 F4
Bridgewater Australia 112 C6
Bridgewater Canada 125 H4
Bridgewater MA U.S.A. 131 H3
Bridgewater NY U.S.A. 131 F2
Bridgewater VA U.S.A. 130 D4
Bridgton U.S.A. 131 H1
Bridgwater U.K. 35 E6
Bridgwater Bay U.K. 35 E6
Bridlington U.K. 35 F4
Bridport Australia 112 C6
Bridport U.K. 35 E6
Brie reg. France 39 E2
Briec France 38 B2
Brie-Comte-Robert France 39 E2
Brieg Poland see Brzeg
Brienne-le-Château France 39 F2
Brienzer See l. Switz. 39 G3
Briery Knob mt. U.S.A. 130 C4
Brig Switz. 39 G3
Brigham City U.S.A. 134 D4
Brighton Canada 130 E1
Brighton U.K. 35 F6
Brighton CO U.S.A. 134 F5
Brighton MI U.S.A. 130 B2
Brighton NY U.S.A. 130 E2
Brighton WV U.S.A. 130 B4
Brighton Downs Australia 111 E4
Brignoles France 39 G5
Brikama Gambia 92 A2
Brilon Germany 36 D3
Brimnes Iceland 32 [inset]
Brindisi Italy 45 F4
Brinkley U.S.A. 133 D5
Brionne France 38 D2
Brioude France 39 E4
Brisay Canada 125 G2
▶Brisbane Australia 111 H5
State capital of Queensland and 3rd most populous city in Oceania.
Brisighella Italy 44 C2
Bristol U.K. 35 E6
Bristol CT U.S.A. 131 G3
Bristol FL U.S.A. 129 B6
Bristol NH U.S.A. 131 H2
Bristol RI U.S.A. 131 H3
Bristol TN U.S.A. 130 B5
Bristol VT U.S.A. 131 G1
Bristol Bay U.S.A. 120 C4
Bristol Channel est. U.K. 35 D6
Bristol Lake U.S.A. 137 E4
Bristol Mountains U.S.A. 137 D4
Britannia Island New Caledonia see Maré
British Antarctic Territory Antarctica 167 L2
British Columbia prov. Canada 122 F5
British Empire Range mts Canada 121 K1
British Guiana country S. America see Guyana
British Honduras country Central America see Belize
▶British Indian Ocean Territory terr. Indian Ocean 162 L6
United Kingdom Overseas Territory.
asia 52–53, 82
British Solomon Islands country S. Pacific Ocean see Solomon Islands
Brito Godins Angola see Kiwaba N'zogi
Brits S. Africa 99 E5
Britstown S. Africa 98 D6
Brittany admin. reg. France see Bretagne
Brittany reg. France 38 B2
Britton U.S.A. 132 B2
Brive-la-Gaillarde France 38 D4
Briviesca Spain 42 E1
Brixia Italy see Brescia
Brlik Kazakh. 70 D3
Brno Czech Rep. 37 H4
Broach India see Bharuch
Broad r. U.S.A. 129 C5
Broad Arrow Australia 109 C7
Broadback r. Canada 124 E3
Broad Bay U.K. 34 C2
Broadford U.K. 34 D3
Broad Law hill U.K. 34 E4
Broadmere Australia 110 C3
Broad Sound sea chan. Australia 111 G4
Broadsound Range hills Australia 111 G4
Broadus U.S.A. 134 F3
Broadway U.S.A. 130 D4
Broadwood N.Z. 113 C1
Broby Sweden 33 D4
Brocēni Latvia 33 F4
Brochet Canada 123 K3
Brocken mt. Germany 36 E3
Brockman, Mount Australia 108 B5
Brockport NY U.S.A. 130 E2
Brockport PA U.S.A. 130 D3
Brockton U.S.A. 131 H2
Brockville Canada 131 F1
Brockway U.S.A. 130 D3
Brod Macedonia 46 B4
Broderick Falls Kenya see Webuye
Brodeur Peninsula Canada 121 K2
Brodhead U.S.A. 130 A5
Brodheadsville U.S.A. 131 F3
Brodick U.K. 34 D4
Brodnica Poland 37 I2
Brody Ukr. 29 C6
Brok r. Poland 37 J2
Broken Arrow U.S.A. 133 C4
Broken Bow NE U.S.A. 132 B3
Broken Bow OK U.S.A. 133 C5
Broken Bow Reservoir U.S.A. 133 C5
Brokenhead r. Canada 123 L5
Broken Hill Australia 112 B3
Broken Hill Zambia see Kabwe
Broken Plateau sea feature Indian Ocean 163 N8
Brokopondo Suriname 147 H3
Brokopondo Stuwmeer resr Suriname see Professor van Blommestein Meer
Bromberg Poland see Bydgoszcz
Bromo Tengger Semeru National Park Indon. 59 F4
Brønderslev Denmark 33 C4
Brong-Ahafo admin. reg. Ghana 93 E4
Brønnøysund Norway 32 D2
Bronson U.S.A. 129 C6
Bronte Sicily Italy 45 E6
Brooke's Point Phil. 56 E4
Brookfield U.S.A. 132 C4
Brookhaven U.S.A. 127 H5
Brookings OR U.S.A. 134 A4
Brookings SD U.S.A. 132 B2
Brookline U.S.A. 131 H2
Brooklyn U.S.A. 130 A2
Brooklyn Park U.S.A. 132 C2
Brookneal U.S.A. 130 D5
Brooks Canada 134 E2
Brooks U.S.A. 131 I1
Brooks Brook Canada 122 C2
Brooks Range mts U.S.A. 120 E3
Brooksville FL U.S.A. 129 C6
Brooksville KY U.S.A. 130 A4
Brookton Australia 109 B8
Brookville U.S.A. 130 D3
Broom, Loch inlet U.K. 34 D3
Broome Australia 108 C4
Broomehill Australia 109 B8
Broons France 38 B2
Brora r. U.K. 34 E2
Brøstadbotn Norway 32 E1
Brosville U.S.A. 130 D5
Brothers U.S.A. 134 B4
Brou France 38 D2
Broughton Island Canada see Qikiqtarjuaq
Broulkou well Chad 88 C5
Brovary Ukr. 29 D6
Brown City U.S.A. 130 B2
Brown Creek r. Australia 111 E3
Browne Range hills Australia 109 D6
Brownfield U.S.A. 133 A5
Brown Mountain U.S.A. 136 D4
Brownstown U.S.A. 128 B4
Brownsville PA U.S.A. 130 D3
Brownsville TN U.S.A. 128 A5
Brownsville TX U.S.A. 133 B7
Brownsweg Suriname 147 H3
Brownwood U.S.A. 133 B6
Browse Island Australia 108 C3
Brozas Spain 42 C3
Bruay-la-Bussière France 39 E1
Bruce U.S.A. 129 A5
Bruce Rock Australia 109 B7
Bruchsal Germany 36 D4
Bruck an der Leitha Austria 37 H4
Bruck an der Mur Austria 37 G5
Bruges Belgium see Brugge
Brugge Belgium 36 A3
Bruin KY U.S.A. 130 B4
Bruin PA U.S.A. 130 D3
Bruin Point mt. U.S.A. 137 G2
Bruint India 66 A2
Brukkaros Namibia 98 C5
Brûlé Canada 122 G4
Brûlé, Lac l. Canada 125 I2
Brumado Brazil 150 D5
Brumer Islands P.N.G. 111 G1
Brú Na Bóinne tourist site Rep. of Ireland 35 C5
Brundisium Italy see Brindisi
Bruneau r. U.S.A. 134 D4
▶Brunei country Asia 59 F1
asia 52–53, 82
Brunei Brunei see Bandar Seri Begawan
Brunei Bay Malaysia 59 F1
Brunette Downs Australia 110 C3
Brunflo Sweden 32 D3
Brunico Italy 44 C1
Brünn Czech Rep. see Brno
Brunna Sweden 33 E4
Brunner, Lake N.Z. 113 B3
Bruno Canada 134 F1
Brunsbüttel Germany 36 D2
Brunswick Germany see Braunschweig
Brunswick GA U.S.A. 129 C6
Brunswick ME U.S.A. 131 I2
Brunswick OH U.S.A. 130 C3
Brunswick, Península de pen. Chile 153 C8
Brunswick Bay Australia 108 D3
Brunswick Junction Australia 109 A8
Brunswick Lake Canada 124 D3
Bruntál Czech Rep. 37 H4
Brunt Ice Shelf Antarctica 167 B2
Bruny Island Australia 112 C6
Brus Serb. and Mont. 46 B3
Brusa Turkey see Bursa
Brush U.S.A. 134 G4
Brusque Brazil 151 B8
Brussel Belgium see Brussels
▶Brussels Belgium 39 F1
Capital of Belgium.
europe 48
Brusy Poland 37 H2
Bruthen Australia 112 C5
Bruxelles Belgium see Brussels
Bruyères France 39 G2
Bruzual Venez. 146 D2
Bryan OH U.S.A. 130 A3
Bryan TX U.S.A. 133 B6
Bryan, Mount Australia 112 A4
Bryan Coast Antarctica 167 L2
Bryansk Rus. Fed. 29 E5
Bryanskaya Oblast' admin. div. Rus. Fed. 29 E5
Bryansk Oblast admin. div. Rus. Fed. see Bryanskaya Oblast'
Bryanskoye Rus. Fed. 79 F1
Bryant Pond U.S.A. 131 H1
Bryce Canyon National Park U.S.A. 137 F3
Bryce Mountains U.S.A. 137 H5
Bryne Norway 33 B4
Bryukhovetskaya Rus. Fed. 29 F7
Brzava r. Serb. and Mont. 46 B2
Brzeg Poland 37 H3
Brzeg Dolny Poland 37 H3
Brześć nad Bugiem Belarus see Brest
Brzozów Poland 37 K4
Bua Angola 95 B6
Bu'aale Somalia 96 D4
Buala Solomon Is 107 E2
Buandougou Côte d'Ivoire see Bouandougou
Buatan Indon. 58 C2
Bū Athlah well Libya 88 D2
Bu'ayj well Saudi Arabia 80 B5
Bu'ayrāt al Hasūn Libya 88 B2
Bubanza Burundi 94 F5
Bubi r. Zimbabwe 99 F4
Būbīyān Island Kuwait 79 G5
Buca Turkey 47 E5
Bucak Turkey 78 B3
Bucaramanga Col. 146 C3
Buccaneer Archipelago is Australia 108 C4
Buchan Australia 112 D5
Buchanan Liberia 92 C4
Buchanan U.S.A. 130 D5
Buchanan, Lake salt flat Australia 111 F4
Buchan Gulf Canada 121 L2
Buchans Canada 125 J3
▶Bucharest Romania 46 E2
Capital of Romania.
Buchen (Odenwald) Germany 36 D4
Bucholz in der Nordheide Germany 36 D2
Buchon, Point U.S.A. 136 B4
Bucin, Pasul pass Romania 46 D1
Bückeburg Germany 36 D2
Buckeye U.S.A. 137 F5
Buckhannon U.S.A. 130 C4
Buckhannon r. U.S.A. 130 D4
Buckhaven U.K. 34 E3
Buckhorn Lake Canada 130 D1
Buckie U.K. 34 E3
Buckingham U.K. 35 F5
Buckingham PA U.S.A. 131 F3
Buckingham VA U.S.A. 130 D5
Buckland U.S.A. 120 C3
Buckland Tableland reg. Australia 111 G5
Buckleboo Australia 109 G8
Buckle Island Antarctica 167 H2
Buckley watercourse Australia 110 D4
Buckley Bay Antarctica 167 G2
Buckskin Mountains U.S.A. 137 F4
Bucksport U.S.A. 131 I1
Bučovice Czech Rep. 37 H4
București Romania see Bucharest
Bucyrus U.S.A. 130 B3
Bud Norway 32 B3
Buda, Illa de i. Spain 43 G2
Buda-Kashalyova Belarus 31 L2
Budalin Myanmar 60 A3
▶Budapest Hungary 37 I5
Capital of Hungary.
Budaun India 74 C3
Bud Bud Somalia 96 E3
Budd Coast Antarctica 167 F2
Buddi Eth. 96 D3
Buddusò Sardinia Italy 45 B4
Bude U.K. 35 D6
Budennovsk Rus. Fed. 29 H7
Buderim Australia 111 H5
Budești Romania 46 E2
Budīyah, Jabal hills Egypt 77 A5
Budogoshch' Rus. Fed. 28 E4
Budongquan China 75 G2
Budoni Sardinia Italy 45 B4
Būdszentmihály Hungary see Tiszavasvári
Budva Serb. and Mont. 46 A3
Budwang National Park Australia 112 D4
Budweis Czech Rep. see České Budějovice
Buea Cameroon 93 H4
Buëch r. France 39 G4
Buellton U.S.A. 136 B4
Buena Esperanza Arg. 152 D3
Buenaventura Col. 146 B4
Buenaventura Mex. 135 F7
Buena Vista Bol. 149 E4
Buena Vista i. N. Mariana Is see Tinian
Buena Vista CO U.S.A. 134 F5
Buena Vista VA U.S.A. 130 D5
Buendia, Embalse de resr Spain 43 E2
Buenga r. Angola 95 B6
Buengas Angola 95 B6
Buenópolis Brazil 151 C6
▶Buenos Aires Arg. 152 F3
Capital of Argentina. 2nd most populous city in South America.
southamerica 154
world 16–17
Buenos Aires prov. Arg. 152 E4
Buenos Aires Amazonas Col. 146 D5
Buenos Aires Guaviare Col. 146 C4
Buenos Aires, Lago l. Arg./Chile 153 B6
Buen Pasto Arg. 153 C6
Buen Tiempo, Cabo c. Arg. 153 C7
Buerarema Brazil 150 E5
Buesaco Col. 146 B4
Bueu Spain 42 B1
Buey, Cabeza de mt. Spain 42 E3
Búfalo Mex. 135 F8
Buffalo r. Canada 123 H2
Buffalo MO U.S.A. 132 C4
Buffalo NY U.S.A. 130 D2
Buffalo OK U.S.A. 132 B4
Buffalo SD U.S.A. 134 G3
Buffalo TX U.S.A. 133 B6
Buffalo WY U.S.A. 134 F3
Buffalo r. U.S.A. 128 B5
Buffalo Head Hills Canada 123 G3
Buffalo Head Prairie Canada 123 G3
Buffalo Hump mt. U.S.A. 134 D3
Buffalo Lake Alta Canada 134 D1
Buffalo Lake N.W.T. Canada 123 H2
Buffalo Narrows Canada 123 I4
Buffalo Range Zimbabwe 99 F4
Buffels watercourse S. Africa 98 C6
Buffels Drift S. Africa 99 E4
Buford U.S.A. 129 B5
Buftea Romania 46 D2
Bug r. Poland 37 K3
Buga Col. 146 B4
Buga Nigeria 93 G3
Bugala Island Uganda 96 B5
Bugana Nigeria 93 G4
Bugarach, Pic de mt. France 38 E5
Bugdayli Turkm. 80 C2
Bugeat France 38 D4
Bugel, Tanjung pt Indon. 59 E4
Bugojno Bos.-Herz. 44 F2
Bugrino Rus. Fed. 28 I1
Bugsuk i. Phil. 56 E4
Bugul'ma Rus. Fed. 28 J5
Bügür China see Luntai
Buguruslan Rus. Fed. 29 J5
Būhābād Iran 80 C4
Buharkent Turkey 47 F6
Buhera Zimbabwe 99 F3
Buhoro Flats plain Tanz. 97 B7
Buhu r. Tanz. 97 B6
Buhuși Romania 46 E1
Buick Canada 122 F3
Builth Wells U.K. 35 E5
Buin P.N.G. 107 E2
Bui National Park Ghana 93 E3
Buinsk Rus. Fed. 28 I5
Bu'in Zahrā Iran 80 B3
Buir Nur l. Mongolia 63 J2
Buitepos Namibia 98 C4
Bujalance Spain 42 D4
Bujanovac Serb. and Mont. 46 B3
Bujoru Romania 46 D3
▶Bujumbura Burundi 94 F5
Capital of Burundi.
Buk Poland 37 H2
Bukachacha Rus. Fed. 63 J1
Buka Island P.N.G. 107 E2
Bukama Dem. Rep. Congo 95 E7
Būkand Iran 80 C4
Bukavu Dem. Rep. Congo 94 F5
Bukedi Dem. Rep. Congo 95 C6
Bukene Tanz. 97 B6
Bukeya Dem. Rep. Congo 95 E7
Bukhara Uzbek. 81 F2
Bukhara Oblast admin. div. Uzbek. see Bukharskaya Oblast'
Bukharskaya Oblast' admin. div. Uzbek. 81 E1
Bukhoro Uzbek. see Bukhara
Bukhoro Wiloyati admin. div. Uzbek. see Bukharskaya Oblast'
Bukima Tanz. 96 B5
Bukit Baka Bukit Raya National Park Indon. 59 F3
Bukit Timah Sing. 58 [inset]
Bukit Timah hill Sing. 58 [inset]
Bukittinggi Indon. 58 C3
Bükk mts Hungary 37 J4
Bukkapatnam India 72 C3
Bükki nat. park Hungary 37 J4
Bükkzsérc Hungary 37 J5
Bukoba Tanz. 96 A5
Bukowo, Jezioro lag. Poland 37 H1
Bukrane Indon. 108 E1
Bükreș Romania see Bucharest
Buku, Tanjung pt Indon. 58 D3
Bukum, Pulau i. Sing. 58 [inset]
Būl, Kūh-e mt. Iran 80 C4
Bula Guinea-Bissau 92 B2
Bula Indon. 57 H6
Bülach Switz. 39 H3
Bulancak Turkey 79 D2
Bulandshahr India 74 C3
Bulanık Turkey 79 E3
Bulanovo Rus. Fed. 29 J5
Bulava Rus. Fed. 64 E2
Bulawayo Zimbabwe 99 F4
Buldan Turkey 78 B3
Buldana India 72 C1
Buldibuyo Peru 148 A2
Buldir Island U.S.A. 120 A4
Bulei well Eth. 96 E3
Bulembu Swaziland 99 F5
Bulgan Mongolia 62 G2
Bulgar Rus. Fed. see Bolgar
▶Bulgaria country Europe 46 D3
europe 24–25, 48
Bŭlgariya country Europe see Bulgaria
Bulkley Ranges mts Canada 122 D4
Bullaque r. Spain 42 D3
Bullas Spain 43 F3
Bulle Switz. 39 G3
Bullen r. Canada 123 K1
Buller r. N.Z. 113 B3
Bulleringa National Park Australia 111 E3
Bullfinch Australia 109 B7
Bullhead City U.S.A. 137 E4
Bullion Mountains U.S.A. 137 D4
Bullo r. Australia 110 B2
Bulloo watercourse Australia 111 E6
Bulloo Downs Australia 111 E6
Bulloo Lake salt flat Australia 111 E6
Bull Shoals Lake U.S.A. 133 C4
Büllsport Namibia 98 C5
Bulman Australia 110 C2
Bulman Gorge Australia 110 C2
Bulmer Lake Canada 122 F2
Buloh, Pulau i. Sing. 58 [inset]
Bulolo P.N.G. 57 K7
Bulqizë Albania 46 B4
Bulu, Gunung mt. Indon. 59 G2
Buluk well Kenya 96 C3
Bulukumba Indon. 57 F7
Bulun Rus. Fed. 27 M2
Bulungu Bandundu Dem. Rep. Congo 95 C6
Bulungu Kasai Occidental Dem. Rep. Congo 95 D6
Bulungur Uzbek. 81 F2
Bumba Bandundu Dem. Rep. Congo 95 C6
Bumba Équateur Dem. Rep. Congo 94 D4
Bumbah, Khalīj b. Libya 88 D1
Bumbești-Jiu Romania 46 C2
Bumhkang Myanmar 60 B2
Bumpha Bum mt. Myanmar 60 B2
Buna Dem. Rep. Congo 94 C5
Buna Kenya 96 C4
Bunazi Tanz. 96 A5
Bunbury Australia 109 A8
Bunclody Rep. of Ireland 35 C5
Buncrana Rep. of Ireland 34 C4
Bunda Tanz. 96 B5
Bundaberg Australia 111 H5
Bundaleer Australia 111 F6
Bundi India 74 B4
Bundibugyo Uganda 96 A4
Bundjalung National Park Australia 112 E3
Bundoran Rep. of Ireland 35 B4
Bundu India 75 E5
Bunduqiya Sudan 96 A3
Bunë r. Albania/Serb. and Mont. 46 A4
Bunga r. Nigeria 93 H2
Bungalaut, Selat sea chan. Indon. 58 B3
Bung Boraphet l. Thai. 61 C5
Bungendore Australia 112 D4
Bunger Hills Antarctica 167 F2
Bungil Creek r. Australia 111 G5
Bungle Bungle National Park Australia see Purnululu National Park
Bungo Angola 95 B6
Bungo-suidō sea chan. Japan 65 C6
Bunguran, Kepulauan is Indon. see Natuna, Kepulauan
Bunguran, Pulau i. Indon. see Natuna Besar
Bunia Dem. Rep. Congo 96 A4
Buningonia well Australia 109 C7
Bunji Jammu and Kashmir 74 B2
Bunker Group atolls Australia 111 H4
Bunkie U.S.A. 133 D6
Bunkris Sweden 33 D3
Bunnell U.S.A. 129 C6
Buñol Spain 43 F3
Bunsuru watercourse Nigeria 93 G2
Buntok Indon. 59 F3
Buntokecil Indon. 59 F3
Bununu Nigeria 93 H3
Bunya Mountains National Park Australia 111 G5
Bünyan Turkey 78 C3
Bunyu i. Indon. 59 G2
Bunza Nigeria 93 G2
Buonconvento Italy 44 C3
Buôn Mê Thuột Vietnam 61 E5
Buorkhaya, Guba b. Rus. Fed. 27 N2
Bup r. China 75 E3
Buqayq Saudi Arabia see Abqaiq
Buqbuq Egypt 89 E2
Bura Kenya 96 C5
Buraan Somalia 96 F2
Burakin Australia 109 B7
Buram Sudan 94 E2
Burang China 62 C5
Burannoye Rus. Fed. 29 J6
Burao Somalia 96 E2
Buraydah Saudi Arabia 89 I3
Burayevo Rus. Fed. 28 J5
Burbach Germany 36 D3
Burbank U.S.A. 136 C4
Burcher Australia 112 C4
Burdalyk Turkm. 81 F2
Burdekin r. Australia 111 F3
Burdekin Falls Australia 111 F4
Burdigala France see Bordeaux
Burdur Turkey 78 B3
Burdwan India see Barddhaman
Burē Eth. 96 C2
Bure r. U.K. 35 G5
Bureå Sweden 32 F2
Bureinskiy Khrebet mts Rus. Fed. 64 C2
Bureiqa well Sudan 89 F5
Bureya r. Rus. Fed. 64 B2
Bureya Rus. Fed. see Novobureyskiy
Bureya Range mts Rus. Fed. see Bureinskiy Khrebet
Burgas Bulg. 46 E3
Burgaw U.S.A. 129 D5
Burg bei Magdeburg Germany 36 E2
Burgdorf Germany 36 E2
Burgdorf Switz. 39 G3
Burgeo Canada 125 J4
Burgersdorp S. Africa 99 E6
Burgersfort S. Africa 99 F5
Burgess U.S.A. 131 E5
Burget Tuyur waterhole Sudan 89 E4
Burghausen Germany 37 F4
Burgin U.S.A. 130 A5
Burgos Mex. 133 B7
Burgos Spain 42 E1
Burgsvik Sweden 33 E4
Burhabalanga r. India 75 E5
Burhan Budai Shan mts China 70 H4
Burhaniye Turkey 47 E5
Burhanpur India 74 C5
Burhar-Dhanpuri India 75 D5
Burhi Gandak r. India 75 E4
Buriat-Mongol Republic aut. rep. Rus. Fed. see Buryatiya, Respublika
Burin Canada 125 K4
Burin Peninsula Canada 125 K4
Buriram Thai. 61 C5
Buriti Brazil 150 D2
Buriti r. Brazil 149 F3
Buriti Alegre Brazil 149 H4
Buriti Bravo Brazil 150 D3
Buritirama Brazil 150 D4
Buritis Brazil 150 C5
Burjassot Spain 43 F3
Burkburnett U.S.A. 133 B5
Burke watercourse Australia 111 D4
Burke Island Antarctica 167 K2
Burkes Pass N.Z. 113 B4
Burkesville U.S.A. 128 B4
Burketown Australia 111 D3
Burkeville U.S.A. 130 D5
Burkhala Rus. Fed. 27 O3
▶Burkina country Africa 93 E2
africa 86–87, 100
Burkina Faso country Africa see Burkina
Burk's Falls Canada 124 E4
Burley U.S.A. 134 D4
Burlin Kazakh. 29 J6
Burlington Canada 130 D2
Burlington CO U.S.A. 134 G5
Burlington IA U.S.A. 132 D3
Burlington KS U.S.A. 132 C4
Burlington NC U.S.A. 128 D4
Burlington VT U.S.A. 131 G1
Burly Rus. Fed. 28 K5
Burma country Asia see Myanmar
Burnaby Canada 122 F5
Burnet U.S.A. 133 B6
Burnett r. Australia 111 H5
Burney U.S.A. 134 B4
Burney, Monte vol. Chile 153 B8
Burnham U.S.A. 131 I1
Burnie Australia 112 C6
Burning Springs U.S.A. 130 B5
Burnley U.K. 35 E5
Burns U.S.A. 134 C4
Burnside r. Canada 123 I1
Burnside U.S.A. 130 A5
Burnside, Lake salt flat Australia 109 C6
Burns Junction U.S.A. 134 C4
Burns Lake Canada 122 E4
Burnsville U.S.A. 130 C4
Burnt r. U.S.A. 134 C3
Burnt Lake Canada see Brûlé, Lac
Burntwood r. Canada 123 L4
Burntwood Lake Canada 123 K4
Burog Co l. China 75 E2
Burovoy Uzbek. 81 E1
Burqin China 70 G2
Burqu' Jordan 77 D3
Burra Australia 112 A4
Burra i. U.K. 34 F1
Burrel Albania 46 B4
Burrel U.S.A. 136 C3
Burren reg. Rep. of Ireland 35 B5
Burren Junction Australia 112 D3
Burriana Spain 43 F3
Burro, Serranías del mts Mex. 126 F6
Burr Oak Reservoir U.S.A. 130 B4
Burruyacú Arg. 152 D1
Bursa Turkey 78 B2
Bursa prov. Turkey 47 F4
Būr Safājah Egypt 89 G3
Būr Sa'īd Egypt see Port Said
Būr Sa'īd governorate Egypt 77 A4
Burshinskoye Vodokhranilishche resr Rus. Fed. 64 B2
Būr Sudan Sudan see Port Sudan
Burt Lake U.S.A. 132 E2
Burtnieku ezers l. Latvia 33 G4
Burton U.S.A. 130 B2
Burton, Lac l. Canada 124 E2
Burton upon Trent U.K. 35 F5
Burträsk Sweden 32 F2
Burtundy Australia 112 B4
Burt Well Australia 110 C4
Buru i. Indon. 57 G6
Burūk, Wādī al watercourse Egypt 77 A4
Burullus, Lake lag. Egypt 78 B5
Burultokay China see Fuhai
Burūn, Ra's pt Egypt 77 A4
▶Burundi country Africa 95 F5
africa 86–87, 100
Burunniy Rus. Fed. see Tsagan Aman
Bururi Burundi 95 F5
Burwash Landing Canada 122 B2
Burwell U.S.A. 132 B3
Burwick U.K. 34 E2
Buryatia aut. rep. Rus. Fed. see Buryatiya, Respublika
Buryatiya, Respublika aut. rep. Rus. Fed. 63 I1
Buryatskaya Mongolskaya A.S.S.R. aut. rep. Rus. Fed. see Buryatiya, Respublika
Buryn' Ukr. 29 E6
Burynshyk Kazakh. 29 I7
Bury St Edmunds U.K. 35 G5
Burzil Pass Jammu and Kashmir 74 B2
Busalla Italy 44 B2
Busan S. Korea see Pusan
Busanga Dem. Rep. Congo 94 D5
Busca Italy 44 A2
Buseire Syria see Al Buşayrah
Būshehr Iran 80 B4
Būshehr prov. Iran 80 B4
Bushenyi Uganda 96 A5
Bushire Iran see Būshehr
Bushkill U.S.A. 131 F3
Busia Kenya 96 B4
Busing, Pulau i. Sing. 58 [inset]
Businga Dem. Rep. Congo 94 D4
Busira r. Dem. Rep. Congo 94 C5
Buskerud county Norway 33 C3
Busko-Zdrój Poland 37 J3
Busselton Australia 109 A8
Bușteni Romania 46 D2
Bustillos, Lago l. Mex. 135 F7
Busto Arsizio Italy 44 B2
Büsum Germany 36 D1
Busu Modanda Dem. Rep. Congo 94 C4
Buta Dem. Rep. Congo 94 E4
Butajīra Eth. 96 C2
Butan Bulg. 46 C3
Butang Group is Thai. 61 B7
Buta Ranquil Arg. 152 C4
Butare Rwanda 94 F5
Butaritari atoll Kiribati 164 F6
Bute i. U.K. 34 D4
Butembo Dem. Rep. Congo 94 F4
Butha Buthe Lesotho 99 F6
Buthidaung Myanmar 73 G1
Butiaba Uganda 96 A4
Butler AL U.S.A. 129 A5
Butler GA U.S.A. 129 B5
Butler IN U.S.A. 130 A3
Butler KY U.S.A. 130 A4
Butler MO U.S.A. 132 C4
Butler PA U.S.A. 130 D3
Buton i. Indon. 57 F6
Butrintit, Liqeni i l. Albania 47 B5
Buttahatchee r. U.S.A. 129 A5
Butte U.S.A. 134 D3
Butterworth Malaysia 58 C1
Buttes, Sierra mt. U.S.A. 136 B2
Butt of Lewis hd U.K. 34 C2
Button Bay Canada 123 M3
Buttonwillow U.S.A. 136 C4
Butuan Phil. 57 G4
Buturlinovka Rus. Fed. 29 G6
Butwal Nepal 75 D4
Butzbach Germany 36 D3
Bützow Germany 36 E2
Buuhoodle Somalia 96 E3
Buulobarde Somalia 96 E4
Buur Gaabo Somalia 96 D5
Buurhabaka Somalia 96 E4
Buvuma Island Uganda 96 B4
Buwārah, Jabal mt. Saudi Arabia 77 B5
Buwāṭah Saudi Arabia 89 H3
Buxar India 75 E4
Buxtehude Germany 36 D2
Buxton U.K. 35 F5
Buy Rus. Fed. 28 G4
Buy r. Rus. Fed. 28 J4
Buynaksk Rus. Fed. 79 F2
Buyo Côte d'Ivoire 92 D4
Buyo, Lac de l. Côte d'Ivoire 92 D4
Buyuan Jiang r. China 66 B4
Büyükada i. Turkey 46 F4
Büyük Egri Dağ mt. Turkey 77 A1
Büyükkarıştıran Turkey 46 E4

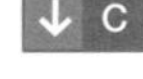

Chaacha Turkm. 81 E2
Chābahār Iran 81 E5
Chablais mts France 39 G3
Chablis France 39 E3
Chabre ridge France 39 F4
Chabrol i. New Caledonia see Lifou
Chabyêr Caka salt l. China 75 E3
Chaca Chile 148 C4
Chacabuco Arg. 152 E3
Chacarilla Bol. 148 C4
Chachapoyas Peru 146 B6
Chachaura-Binaganj India 74 C4
Chäche Turkm. see Chaacha
Chachoengsao Thai. 61 C5
Chaco prov. Arg. 152 E1
Chaco Boreal reg. Para. 149 F5
Chaco Culture National Historical Park nat. park U.S.A. 135 F5
Chacorão, Cachoeira da waterfall Brazil 147 G6
Chacra de Piros Peru 148 B2

▶Chad country Africa 88 C6
5th largest country in Africa.
africa 86–87, 100

▶Chad, Lake Africa 88 B6
4th largest lake in Africa.
africa 84–85
world 14–15

Chadaasan Mongolia 62 G2
Chadan Rus. Fed. 27 J4
Chadileo r. Arg. 152 D4
Chadron U.S.A. 134 G4
Chadyr-Lunga Moldova see Ciadîr-Lunga
Chae Hom Thai. 60 B4
Chaeryŏng N. Korea 65 A5
Chae Son National Park Thai. 60 B4
Chaffee U.S.A. 132 D4
Chaffers, Isla i. Chile 153 B6
Chafurray Col. 146 C4
Chagai Pak. 81 F4
Chagai Hills Afgh./Pak. 81 E4
Chagdo Kangri reg. China 75 E2
Chaghā Khūr mt. Iran 80 B4
Chaghcharān Afgh. 81 F3
Chagny France 39 F3
Chagos Archipelago is Indian Ocean 162 L6
Chagos-Laccadive Ridge sea feature Indian Ocean 162 L6
Chagos Trench sea feature Indian Ocean 162 L6
Chagoyan Rus. Fed. 64 B1
Chagres, Parque Nacional nat. park Panama 146 B2
Chaguanas Trin. and Tob. 147 F2
Chaguaramas Venez. 146 E2
Chagyl Turkm. 80 C1
Chagyllyshor, Vpadina depr. Turkm. 79 H2
Chaha r. Ukr. 46 F2
Chahah Burjal Afgh. 81 E4
Chaharbagh Afgh. 81 G3
Chahār Maḩāll va Bakhtīārī prov. Iran 80 B3
Chah Baba well Iran 80 C3
Chāh Bahār, Khalīj-e b. Iran 81 E5
Chāh-e 'Asalū well Iran 80 C4
Chāh-e Bābā well Iran 81 D3
Chāh-e Gonbad well Iran 80 C3
Chāh-e Kavīr well Iran 80 D3
Chāh-e Khorāsān well Iran 80 C3
Chāh-e Malek well Iran 80 C3
Chāh-e Mīrzā well Iran 80 C3
Chāh-e Mūjān well Iran 80 C3
Chāh-e Nūklok Iran 80 C3
Chāh-e Pansu well Iran 80 C3
Chāh-e Qeyşar well Iran 80 C4
Chāh-e Qobād well Iran 80 C3
Chāh-e Raḩmān well Iran 81 D4
Chāh-e Shūr well Iran 80 C3
Chāh-e Tāqestān well Iran 80 C4
Chāh-e Tūnī well Iran 80 D3
Chāh Haji Abdulla well Iran 80 C3
Chāh Ḩaqq Iran 80 C4
Chah-i-Ab Afgh. 81 G2
Chāh Pās well Iran 80 C3
Chāh Ru'ī well Iran 81 D4
Chah Sandan Pak. 81 E4
Chai r. China 64 A4
Chaibasa India 75 E5
Chaigneau, Lac l. Canada 125 H2
Chaillu, Massif du mts Gabon 94 A5
Chainat Thai. 61 C5
Chainjoin Co l. China 75 E2
Chaitén Chile 153 B5
Chai Wan Hong Kong China 67 [inset]
Chaiya Thai. 61 B6
Chaiyaphum Thai. 61 C5
Chajarí Arg. 152 F2
Chakai India 75 E4
Chakar r. Pak. 81 G4
Chake Chake Tanz. 97 C6
Chakhānsūr Afgh. 81 E4
Chakia India 75 D4
Chak Jhumra Pak. 81 H4
Chakradharpur India 75 E5
Chakulia India 75 E5
Chakwal Pak. 81 H3
Chala Peru 148 B3
Chala Tanz. 97 A6
Chalais France 38 D4
Chalap Dalan mts Afgh. 81 F3
Chalatenango El Salvador 138 G6
Chaláua Moz. 99 H3
Chalaxung China 66 A1
Chalbi Desert Kenya 96 C4
Chalcedon Turkey see Kadıköy
Chaleur Bay inlet Canada 125 H3
Chaleurs, Baie de inlet Canada see Chaleur Bay
Chalía r. Arg. 153 C7
Chaling China 67 E3
Chalinze Tanz. 97 C6
Chalisgaon India 72 B1
Chalkar, Ozero salt l. Kazakh. see Shalkar, Ozero
Chalki Greece 47 E6
Chalki i. Greece 47 E6
Chalkida Greece 47 C5
Challakere India 72 C3
Challans France 38 C3
Challapata Bol. 148 D4

▶Challenger Deep sea feature N. Pacific Ocean 164 D5
Deepest point in the world (Mariana Trench).
oceans 156–157, 168

Challis U.S.A. 134 D3
Chalmette U.S.A. 133 D6
Chal'mny-Varre Rus. Fed. 28 F2
Châlons-en-Champagne France 39 F2
Châlons-sur-Marne France see Châlons-en-Champagne
Chalon-sur-Saône France 39 F3
Chalt Jammu and Kashmir 74 B1
Châlus France 38 D4
Chālūs Iran 80 B2
Cham Germany 37 F4
Chama U.S.A. 135 F5
Chama r. U.S.A. 135 F5
Chamamba Tanz. 97 B6
Chaman Pak. 81 F4
Chaman Bid Iran 80 D2
Chamao, Khao mt. Thai. 61 C5
Chamba India 74 C2
Chamba Tanz. 97 C7
Chambal r. India 74 C4
Chambeaux, Lac l. Canada 125 G2
Chamberlain r. Australia 108 D4
Chamberlain Canada 123 J5
Chamberlain U.S.A. 132 B3
Chamberlain Lake U.S.A. 128 F2
Chambers U.S.A. 137 H4
Chambersburg U.S.A. 130 E4
Chambéry France 39 F4
Chambeshi Zambia 97 A7
Chambeshi r. Zambia 97 A8
Chambi, Jebel mt. Tunisia 40 D4
Chambira r. Peru 146 C6
Chambri Lake P.N.G. 57 J6
Chamdo China see Qamdo
Chamechaude mt. France 39 F4
Châmi well Mauritania 90 B5
Chamical Arg. 152 D2
Chamili i. Greece 47 E7
Ch'amo Hāyk' l. Eth. 96 C3
Chamoli India see Gopeshwar
Chamonix-Mont-Blanc France 39 G4
Chamouse, Montagne de mt. France 39 F4
Champa India 75 D5
Champagne-Ardenne admin. reg. France 39 F2
Champagnole France 39 F3
Champagny Islands Australia 108 D3
Champaign U.S.A. 132 D3
Champaquí, Cerro mt. Arg. 152 D2
Champara mt. Peru 148 A2
Champasak Laos 61 D5
Champdoré, Lac l. Canada 125 H2
Champion Canada 123 H5
Champlain NY U.S.A. 128 E2
Champlain VA U.S.A. 131 E4
Champlain, Lake Canada/U.S.A. 128 E2
Champlitte France 39 F3
Champotón Mex. 127 H8
Chamrajnagar India 72 C4
Cham Siyāh Iran 80 B4
Chamusca Port. 42 B3
Chamzinka Rus. Fed. 29 H5
Chan, Ko i. Thai. 61 B6
Chana Thai. 61 C7
Chanak Turkey see Çanakkale
Chañar Arg. 152 C4
Chañaral Chile 152 C1
Chanārān Iran 81 D2
Chança r. Port./Spain see Chanza
Chanco Chile 152 B3
Chanda India see Chandrapur
Chandalar r. U.S.A. 120 E3
Chandama Tanz. 97 C6
Chandausi India 74 C3
Chandbali India 73 E1
Chandeleur Islands U.S.A. 129 A6
Chanderi India 74 C4
Chandia India 74 D5
Chandigarh India 74 C3
Chandil India 75 E5
Chandler Canada 125 H3
Chandler U.S.A. 137 G5
Chandless r. Brazil 148 C2
Chandpur Bangl. 75 F5
Chandpur India 74 C3
Chandragiri India 72 C3
Chandrapur India 72 C2
Chandur India 72 C1
Chandvad India 72 B1
Chandyr r. Turkm. 80 C2
Chang, Ko i. Thai. 61 C5
Chang'an China see Rong'an
Changane r. Moz. 99 G5
Changara Moz. 99 G3
Changbai China 64 B4
Changbai Shan mts China/N. Korea 64 A4
Changchow Fujian China see Zhangzhou
Changchow Jiangsu China see Changzhou
Changchun China 64 A4
Changde China 67 D2
Changfeng China 67 F1
Changge China 67 E1
Changgi-ap pt S. Korea 65 B5
Changgo China 75 E3
Chang Hu l. China 67 E2
Changhua Taiwan 67 G3
Changhua Jiang r. China 67 D5
Changhŭng S. Korea 65 A6
Changi Sing. 58 [inset]
Changjiang China 67 D5
Chang Jiang r. China 67 G2 see Yangtze
Changjin-gang r. N. Korea 65 A4
Changkiang China see Zhanjiang
Changle China 67 F3
Changleng China see Xinjian
Changlung Jammu and Kashmir 74 C2
Changning Hunan China 67 E3
Changning Jiangxi China see Xunwu
Changnyŏn N. Korea 65 A5
Ch'ang-pai Shan mts China/N. Korea see Changbai Shan
Changpu China see Suining
Changsan-got pt N. Korea 65 A5
Changsha China 67 E2
Changshi China 66 C3
Changshou China 66 C2
Changshoujie China 67 E2
Changshu China 67 G2
Changtai China 67 F3
Changteh China see Changde
Changting Fujian China 67 F3
Changting Heilong. China 64 B3
Changtu China 64 A4
Ch'angwŏn S. Korea 65 B6
Changxing China 67 F2
Changyang China 67 D2
Changyŏn N. Korea 65 A5
Changzhi China 63 I4
Changzhou China 67 F2
Chañi, Nevado de mt. Arg. 148 D6
Chania Greece 47 D7
Chanion, Kolpos b. Greece 47 C7
Channel Islands English Chan. 38 B2
Channel Islands U.S.A. 136 C5
Channel Islands National Park U.S.A. 136 C4
Channel-Port-aux-Basques Canada 125 J4
Channel Rock i. Bahamas 129 D8
Channel Tunnel France/U.K. 38 D1
Chantada Spain 42 C1
Chantal'skiy mt. Rus. Fed. 27 R3
Chanthaburi Thai. 61 C5
Chantilly France 39 E2
Chantonnay France 38 C3
Chanumla India 73 G4
Chany, Ozero salt l. Rus. Fed. 26 H4
Chanza r. Port./Spain 42 C4
Chao Peru 148 A2
Chaohu China 67 F2
Chao Hu l. China 67 F2
Chao Phraya r. Thai. 61 C5
Chaouèn Morocco 90 D2
Chaoyang Guangdong China 67 F4
Chaoyang Heilong. China see Jiayin
Chaoyang Jilin China see Huinan
Chaoyang Liaoning China 63 K3
Chaozhou China 67 F4
Chapada Diamantina, Parque Nacional nat. park Brazil 150 D5
Chapada dos Guimarães Brazil 149 G3
Chapada dos Veadeiros, Parque Nacional da nat. park Brazil 150 C5
Chapadão do Sul Brazil 151 A6
Chapadinha Brazil 150 D2
Chapais Canada 125 F3
Chapak Guzar Afgh. 81 F2
Chapala, Laguna de l. Mex. 126 F7
Chapare r. Bol. 148 D3
Chāparra Peru 148 B3
Chaparral Col. 146 C4
Chapayev Kazakh. 26 F4
Chapayevsk Rus. Fed. 29 I5
Chapecó Brazil 151 A8
Chapecó r. Brazil 151 A8
Chapleau Canada 124 D4
Chaplin Canada 123 J5
Chaplino Rus. Fed. 27 S3
Chaplygin Rus. Fed. 29 F5
Chapmanville U.S.A. 130 B5
Chappell U.S.A. 132 A3
Chappell Islands Australia 112 C6
Chapra India see Chhapra
Chapri Pass Afgh. 81 F3
Charadai Arg. 152 F1
Charagua Bol. 149 E4
Charana Bol. 148 C4
Charapita Col. 146 C5
Charata Arg. 152 E1
Charcas Mex. 138 D4
Char Chu r. China 75 G3
Charcot Island Antarctica 167 L2
Chard Canada 123 I4
Chard U.K. 35 E6
Chardara, Step' plain Kazakh. 70 C3
Chardon U.S.A. 130 C3
Chardzhev Turkm. 81 E2
Chardzhou Turkm. see Chardzhev
Chardzhouskaya Oblast' admin. div. Turkm. see Lebapskaya Oblast'
Charente r. France 38 C4
Charg Iran 80 C4
Chari r. Cameroon/Chad 94 B1
Chari-Baguirmi pref. Chad 94 C2
Chārīkār Afgh. 81 G3
Charikot Nepal 75 E4
Chariton U.S.A. 132 C3
Chariton r. U.S.A. 132 C4
Chärjew Turkm. see Chardzhev
Charkayuvom Rus. Fed. 28 J2
Charkhari India 74 C4
Charkhi Dadri India 74 C3
Charkhlik China see Ruoqiang
Charleroi Belgium 39 F1
Charles, Cape U.S.A. 131 F5
Charlesbourg Canada 125 G4
Charles City IA U.S.A. 132 C3
Charles City VA U.S.A. 131 E5
Charles de Gaulle airport France 39 E2
Charles Lake Canada 123 I3
Charles Point Australia 110 B2
Charleston N.Z. 113 B3
Charleston IL U.S.A. 128 A4
Charleston SC U.S.A. 129 D5

▶Charleston WV U.S.A. 130 C4
State capital of West Virginia.

Charleston Peak U.S.A. 137 E3
Charlestown NH U.S.A. 131 G2
Charlestown RI U.S.A. 131 H3
Charles Town U.S.A. 130 E4
Charleville Australia 111 F5
Charleville Rep. of Ireland see Rathluirc
Charleville-Mézières France 39 F2
Charlevoix U.S.A. 132 E2
Charley r. U.S.A. 122 A1
Charlie Lake Canada 122 F3
Charlotte MI U.S.A. 130 A2
Charlotte NC U.S.A. 128 C5

▶Charlotte Amalie Virgin Is (U.S.A.) 139 L5
Capital of the U.S. Virgin Islands.

Charlotte Bank sea feature S. China Sea 59 D1
Charlotte Lake Canada 122 E4
Charlottesville U.S.A. 130 D4

▶Charlottetown Canada 125 I4
Provincial capital of Prince Edward Island.

Charlotteville Trin. and Tob. 147 F2
Charlton Australia 112 B5
Charlton Island Canada 124 E2
Charmes France 39 G2
Charnley r. Australia 108 D4
Charron Lake Canada 123 M4
Charsadda Pak. 81 G3
Charshanga Turkm. 81 F2
Charters U.S.A. 130 B4
Charters Towers Australia 111 F4
Chartres France 38 D2
Chas India 75 E5
Chās mt. Port. 42 B2
Chaschuil Arg. 152 C1
Chascomús Arg. 152 F3
Chase Canada 122 G5
Chase City U.S.A. 130 D5
Chashkent Turkm. 81 E2
Chashmeh-ye Safid spring Iran 80 D3
Chashmeh-ye Shotoran well Iran 80 C3
Chashniki Belarus 29 D5
Chasia reg. Greece 47 B5
Chasico Arg. 153 D5
Chaska U.S.A. 132 C2
Chaslands Mistake c. N.Z. 113 B4
Chasŏng N. Korea 64 A4
Chassezac r. France 39 F4
Chassiron, Pointe de pt France 38 C3
Chastab, Kūh-e mts Iran 80 C3
Chastyye Rus. Fed. 28 J4
Chasuta Peru 146 B6
Chāt Iran 80 C2
Chatang China see Zhanang
Château-Arnoux France 39 F4
Châteaubriant France 38 C3
Château-Chinon France 39 E3
Château-du-Loir France 38 D3
Châteaudun France 38 D2
Château-Gontier France 38 C3
Châteauguay r. Canada 125 G1
Châteauguay, Lac l. Canada 125 G1
Châteaulin France 38 A2
Châteauneuf-en-Thymerais France 38 D2
Châteauneuf-sur-Loire France 38 E3
Chateau Pond l. Canada 125 J2
Châteaurenault France 38 D3
Châteauroux France 38 D3
Château-Salins France 39 G2
Château-Thierry France 39 E2
Châtelaillon-Plage France 38 C3
Châtelet Belgium 39 F1
Châtellerault France 38 D3
Châtenois France 39 F2
Chatfield U.S.A. 132 C3
Chatham Canada 130 B2
Chatham U.K. 35 G6
Chatham MA U.S.A. 131 I3
Chatham NY U.S.A. 131 G2
Chatham VA U.S.A. 130 D5
Chatham, Isla i. Chile 153 B7
Chatham Island Samoa see Savai'i
Chatham Island S. Pacific Ocean 107 H6
Chatham Islands S. Pacific Ocean 107 H6
Chatham Rise sea feature S. Pacific Ocean 164 G8
Chatham Sound sea chan. Canada 122 D4
Chatham Strait U.S.A. 122 C3
Châtillon-sur-Indre France 38 D3
Châtillon-sur-Seine France 39 F3
Chatom U.S.A. 129 A6
Chatra India 75 E4
Chatra Nepal 75 E4
Chatsu India 74 B4
Chatsworth Australia 111 E4
Chatsworth U.S.A. 129 B5
Chatsworth Zimbabwe 99 F3
Chattagam Bangl. see Chittagong
Chattahoochee U.S.A. 129 B6
Chattahoochee r. U.S.A. 129 B6
Chattanooga U.S.A. 128 B5
Chatturat Thai. 61 C5
Châu Đôc Vietnam 61 D6
Chauffailles France 39 F3
Chauhtan India 74 A4
Chauk Myanmar 60 A3
Chauka r. India 74 D4
Chaukhamba mts India see Badrinath Peaks
Chaumont France 39 F2
Chauncey U.S.A. 130 B4
Chaungwabyin Myanmar 61 B5
Chaunskaya Guba b. Rus. Fed. 27 Q3
Chauny France 39 E2
Chau Phu Vietnam see Châu Đôc
Chaurai India 74 C5
Chausey, Îles is France 38 C2
Chausy Belarus see Chavusy
Chautauqua, Lake U.S.A. 130 D2
Chauvigny France 38 D3
Chauvin Canada 123 I4
Chavakachcheri Sri Lanka 72 D4
Chaval Brazil 150 D2
Chavan'ga Rus. Fed. 28 F2
Chavār Iran 80 A3
Chaves Brazil 150 B2
Chaves Port. 42 C2
Chaves Valdivia Peru 146 B6
Chavigny, Lac l. Canada 125 F1
Chavusy Belarus 29 D5
Chawal r. Pak. 81 F4
Chây r. Vietnam 60 D3
Chayanta r. Bol. 148 D4
Chayatyn, Khrebet ridge Rus. Fed. 64 D1
Chayevo Rus. Fed. 28 F4
Chaykovskiy Rus. Fed. 28 J4
Chazhegovo Rus. Fed. 28 J3
Chazón Arg. 152 E3
Chazy U.S.A. 131 G1
Cheat r. U.S.A. 130 D4
Cheb Czech Rep. 37 F3
Chebbi salt l. Alg. 91 F4
Cheboksary Rus. Fed. 28 H4
Cheboygan U.S.A. 132 E2
Chechen', Ostrov i. Rus. Fed. 79 F2
Ch'ech'eng Taiwan 67 G4
Checheniya aut. rep. Rus. Fed. see Chechenskaya Respublika
Chechenskaya Respublika aut. rep. Rus. Fed. 79 F2
Chechnia aut. rep. Rus. Fed. see Chechenskaya Respublika
Chechnya aut. rep. Rus. Fed. see Chechenskaya Respublika
Chech'ŏn S. Korea 65 B5
Checotah U.S.A. 133 C5
Chedabucto Bay Canada 125 I4
Cheduba Myanmar 60 A4
Cheduba Island Myanmar 60 A4
Cheduba Strait Myanmar 60 A4
Chée r. France 39 F2
Cheektowaga U.S.A. 130 D2
Cheepash r. Canada 124 D3
Cheepie Australia 111 F5
Cheetham, Cape Antarctica 167 H2
Cheffadène well Niger 93 I1
Chefoo China see Yantai
Chefornak U.S.A. 120 C3
Chegdomyn Rus. Fed. 64 C2
Chegga Mauritania 90 D4
Cheggué watercourse Mauritania 92 C1
Chegguet Ti-n-Kerkâz des. Mauritania 92 D1
Chegutu Zimbabwe 99 F3
Chehalis r. U.S.A. 134 B3
Cheharīz tourist site Iraq 79 F4
Chehel Chashmeh, Kūh-e hill Iran 80 A3
Chehel Dokhtarān, Kūh-e mt. Iran 81 E4
Chehell'āyeh Iran 80 D4
Chekria well Alg. 90 D4
Cheile Nerei-Beuşniţa nat. park Romania 46 B2
Cheju S. Korea 65 A6
Cheju-do i. S. Korea 65 A6
Cheju-haehyŏp sea chan. S. Korea 65 A6
Chek Chue Hong Kong China see Stanley
Chekhov Rus. Fed. 64 E3
Chekiang prov. China see Zhejiang
Chek Lap Kok i. Hong Kong China 67 [inset]
Chekshino Rus. Fed. 28 G4
Chela, Serra da mts Angola 95 B9
Chelan U.S.A. 134 B3
Chelan, Lake U.S.A. 134 B2
Cheleken Turkm. 80 C2
Chelforó Arg. 152 D4
Chélif, Oued r. Alg. 43 G4
Chelm Poland 31 J3
Chelmer r. U.K. 35 G6
Chelmno Poland 37 I2
Chelmsford U.K. 35 G6
Chelmsford U.S.A. 131 H2
Chełmża Poland 37 I2
Chelsea U.S.A. 130 A2
Cheltenham U.K. 35 E6
Chelva Spain 43 F3
Chelyabinsk Rus. Fed. 26 G4
Chelyan U.S.A. 130 C4
Chelyuskin Rus. Fed. 27 K2
Chemaïa Morocco 90 C2
Chembe Zambia 95 F7
Chemchâm, Sebkhet salt flat Mauritania 90 B5
Chem Co l. China 74 C2
Chemenibit Turkm. 81 E3
Chemillé France 38 C3
Chemmis Egypt see Akhmīm
Chemnitz Germany 37 F3
Chemulpo S. Korea see Inch'ŏn
Chemult U.S.A. 134 B4
Chemung r. U.S.A. 131 E3
Chenab r. India/Pak. 74 A3
Chenachane, Oued watercourse Alg. 90 E4
Chendir r. Turkm. see Chandyr
Cheney U.S.A. 134 C3
Cheney Reservoir U.S.A. 132 B4
Chengalpattu India 72 D3
Chengam India 72 C3
Chengbihe Shuiku resr China 66 C3
Chengbu China 67 D3
Chengchow China see Zhengzhou
Chengde China 63 J3
Chengdu China 66 C2
Chenggong China 66 B3
Chenghai China 67 F4
Cheng Hai l. China 66 B3
Chengjiang China see Taihe
Chengkou China 67 D2
Chengmai China 67 D5
Chengshou China see Yingshan
Chengtu China see Chengdu
Chengxian China see Fuquan
Chengxiang Chongqing China see Wuxi
Chengxiang Jiangxi China see Quannan
Chengxiang Sichuan China see Mianning
Chengzhong China see Ningming
Chennai India 72 D3
Chenstokhov Poland see Częstochowa
Chenting, Tanjong pt Sing. 58 [inset]
Chenxi China 67 D3
Chenyang China see Chenxi
Chenying China see Wannian
Chenzhou China 67 E3
Cheom Ksan Cambodia see Choâm Khsant
Chepelare Bulg. 46 D4
Chepén Peru 148 A1
Chepes Arg. 152 D2
Chepstow U.K. 35 E6
Cheptsa r. Rus. Fed. 28 I4
Cher r. France 39 D3
Chera state India see Kerala
Cherangany Hills Kenya 96 B4
Cheraw U.S.A. 129 D5
Cherbaniani Reef India 72 A3
Cherbourg France 38 C2
Cherchell Alg. 43 H4
Cherchen China see Qiemo
Cherdakly Rus. Fed. 29 I5
Chère r. France 38 C3
Chereapani reef India see Byramgore Reef
Cherekha r. Rus. Fed. 33 H4
Cheremkhovo Rus. Fed. 62 G1
Cheremshany Rus. Fed. 64 C3
Cheremukhovka Rus. Fed. 28 I4
Cherepovets Rus. Fed. 28 F4
Cherevkovo Rus. Fed. 28 H3
Chergui, Chott ech imp. l. Alg. 91 E2
Chéria Alg. 91 G2
Cherial India 72 C2
Cheriton U.S.A. 131 F5
Cheriyam i. India 72 B4
Cherkassy Ukr. see Cherkasy
Cherkasy Ukr. 29 E6
Cherkessk Rus. Fed. 29 G7
Cherla India 72 D2
Chermenze Angola 95 D8
Chermoz Rus. Fed. 28 K4
Chernaya Rus. Fed. 28 K1
Chernaya r. Rus. Fed. 28 K1
Chernevo Rus. Fed. 33 H4
Chernigov Ukr. see Chernihiv
Chernigovka Rus. Fed. 64 C3
Chernihiv Ukr. 29 D6
Cherni Lom r. Bulg. 46 D3
Cherninivka Ukr. 29 F7
Cherni Vrŭkh mt. Bulg. 46 C3
Chernivtsi Ukr. 29 C6
Chernobyl' Ukr. see Chornobyl'
Chernogorsk Rus. Fed. 62 E1
Chernoostrovskoye Rus. Fed. 27 I3
Chernovtsy Ukr. see Chernivtsi
Chernoye More sea Asia/Europe see Black Sea
Chernushka Rus. Fed. 28 K4
Chernyakhiv Ukr. 29 D6
Chernyakhovsk Rus. Fed. 37 J1
Chernyanka Rus. Fed. 29 F6
Chernyayeve Rus. Fed. 64 A1
Chernyshevsk Rus. Fed. 63 J1
Chernyshevskiy Rus. Fed. 27 L3
Chernyshkovskiy Rus. Fed. 29 G6
Chernyye Zemli reg. Rus. Fed. 29 H7
Chernyy Irtysh r. China/Kazakh. see Ertix He
Chernyy Otrog Rus. Fed. 29 J6
Chernyy Porog Rus. Fed. 28 E3
Chernyy Rynok Rus. Fed. see Kochubey
Chernyy Yar Rus. Fed. 29 H6
Cherokee IA U.S.A. 132 C3
Cherokee OK U.S.A. 133 B4
Cherokees, Lake o' the U.S.A. 133 C4

▶Cherrapunji India 75 F4
Highest recorded annual rainfall in the world.
world 12–13

Cherry Creek r. U.S.A. 132 A2
Cherry Creek Mountains U.S.A. 137 E1
Cherry Hill U.S.A. 131 F4
Cherry Lake U.S.A. 136 C2
Cherry Valley Canada 131 E2
Cherskiy Rus. Fed. 27 Q3
Cherskogo, Khrebet mts Rus. Fed. 27 O3
Chersonisos Methano pen. Greece 47 C6
Cherthala India see Shertally
Chertkov Ukr. see Chortkiv
Chertkovo Rus. Fed. 29 G6
Cherven Bryag Bulg. 46 D3
Chervonoarmeyskoye Ukr. see Vil'nyans'k
Chervonoarmiys'k Ukr. see Krasnoarmiys'k
Chervonograd Ukr. see Chervonohrad
Chervonohrad Ukr. 29 C6
Chervonozavods'ke Ukr. 29 E6
Chervyen' Belarus 29 D5
Cherykaw Belarus 31 L2
Chesaning U.S.A. 130 A2
Chesapeake U.S.A. 131 E5
Chesapeake Bay U.S.A. 131 E4
Chesapeake Beach U.S.A. 131 E4
Cheshme Vtoroy Turkm. 81 E2
Cheshskaya Guba b. Rus. Fed. 28 H2
Chesht-e Sharīf Afgh. 81 E3
Chesnokovka Rus. Fed. see Novoaltaysk
Chester Canada 125 H4
Chester U.K. 35 E5
Chester CA U.S.A. 136 B1
Chester IL U.S.A. 132 D4
Chester MT U.S.A. 134 E2
Chester NJ U.S.A. 131 F3
Chester OH U.S.A. 130 C4
Chester PA U.S.A. 131 F4
Chester SC U.S.A. 129 C5
Chester VA U.S.A. 130 E5
Chester r. U.S.A. 131 E4
Chesterfield U.K. 35 F5
Chesterfield U.S.A. 132 D4
Chesterfield, Îles is New Caledonia 107 E3
Chesterfield Inlet Canada 123 N2
Chesterfield Inlet inlet Canada 123 M2
Chestertown U.S.A. 131 E4
Chestnut Ridge U.S.A. 130 D3
Chesuncook Lake U.S.A. 128 F2
Chéticamp Canada 125 I4
Chetlat i. India 72 B4
Chetopa U.S.A. 132 C4
Chetumal Mex. 138 G5
Chetwynd Canada 122 F4
Cheung Chau Hong Kong China 67 [inset]
Chevelon Creek r. U.S.A. 137 G4
Cheviot N.Z. 113 C3
Cheviot Hills U.K. 34 E4
Cheviot Range hills Australia 111 E5
Chevreulx r. Canada 125 F2
Che'w Bahir salt l. Eth. 96 C3
Chewelah U.S.A. 134 C2
Cheyenne OK U.S.A. 133 B5

▶Cheyenne WY U.S.A. 134 F4
State capital of Wyoming.

Cheyenne r. U.S.A. 134 G3
Cheyenne Wells U.S.A. 134 G5
Cheyne Bay Australia 109 B8
Cheyur India 72 D3
Cheyyar r. India 72 C3
Chezacut Canada 122 E4
Chhabra India 74 C4
Chhapar India 74 B4
Chhapra India 75 E4
Chhata India 74 C4
Chhatak Bangl. 75 F4
Chhatarpur Jharkhand India 75 E4
Chhatarpur Madhya Pradesh India 74 C4
Chhatrapur India 73 E2
Chhattisgarh state India 75 D5
Chhay Arêng, Stœng r. Cambodia 61 C6
Chhibramau India 74 C4
Chhindwara India 74 C5
Chhlong, Prêk r. Cambodia 61 D5
Chhota Chhindwara India 74 C5
Chhota Udepur India 74 B5
Chhuk Cambodia see Phumĭ Chhuk
Chhukha Bhutan 75 F4
Chiai Taiwan 67 G4
Ch'iak-san National Park S. Korea 65 B5
Chiang Dao Thai. 60 B4
Chiange Angola 95 B8
Chiang Kham Thai. 60 C4
Chiang Khan Thai. 60 C4
Chiang Mai Thai. 60 B4
Chiang Rai Thai. 60 B4
Chiani r. Italy 44 D3
Chiapa Mex. 138 F5
Chiat'ura Georgia 79 E2
Chiautla Mex. 138 E5
Chiavari Italy 44 B2
Chiavenno Italy 44 B1
Chiba Japan 65 E6
Chibemba Angola 95 B8
Chibi China 67 E2
Chibia Angola 95 B8
Chibizovka Rus. Fed. see Zherdevka
Chiboma Moz. 99 G4
Chibougamau Canada 125 F3
Chibougamau, Lac l. Canada 125 F3
Chibu-Sangaku National Park Japan 65 D5
Chibuto Moz. 99 G5
Chibuzhang Hu l. China 70 H5
Chicacole India see Srikakulam

▶Chicago U.S.A. 132 E3
4th most populous city in North America.
world 16–17

Chicala Angola 95 C7
Chicapa r. Angola 95 D6
Chic-Chocs, Monts mts Canada 125 H3
Chicha well Chad 88 C5
Chichagof Island U.S.A. 120 F4
Chichak r. Pak. 81 F5
Chichaoua Morocco 90 C3
Chichas, Cordillera de mts Bol. 148 D5
Chicheng China see Pengxi
Chichester U.K. 35 F6
Chichester Range mts Australia 108 B5
Chichgarh India 72 D1
Chichibu Japan 65 D6
Chichibu-Tama National Park Japan 65 D6
Chichiriviche Venez. 146 D2
Chicholi India 74 C5
Chickahominy r. U.S.A. 131 E5
Chickasawhay r. U.S.A. 129 A6
Chickasha U.S.A. 133 B5
Chiclayo Peru 146 B6
Chico r. Chubut Arg. 153 C5
Chico r. Chubut Arg. 153 D6
Chico r. Santa Cruz Arg. 153 C7
Chico U.S.A. 136 B2
Chicoa Moz. 99 G2
Chicobea i. Fiji see Cikobia
Chicomo Moz. 99 G5
Chiconono Moz. 97 B8
Chicopee U.S.A. 131 G2
Chicoutimi Canada 125 G3
Chicoutimi r. Canada 125 G3
Chicualacuala Moz. 99 F4
Chicuma Angola 95 B8
Chidambaram India 72 C4
Chido China 75 G3
Chiede Angola 95 C9
Chiefland U.S.A. 129 C6
Chiemsee l. Germany 37 F5
Chiengi Zambia 95 F7
Chiengmai Thai. see Chiang Mai
Chienti r. Italy 44 D3
Chieo Lan Reservoir Thai. 61 B6
Chieri Italy 44 A2
Chiers r. France 39 F2
Chiese r. Italy 44 C2
Chieti Italy 44 E3
Chifeng China 63 J3
Chifre, Serra do mts Brazil 151 D6
Chiganak Kazakh. 70 D2
Chiginagak, Mount vol. U.S.A. 120 D4
Chignik U.S.A. 120 D4
Chigorodó Col. 146 B3
Chigu China 75 F3
Chigubo Moz. 99 G4
Chigu Co l. China 70 H6
Chihli, Gulf of China see Bo Hai
Chihuahua Mex. 135 F7
Chihuahua state Mex. 133 A7
Chiili Kazakh. 70 C3
Chikalda India 74 C5
Chikan China 67 D4
Chikaskia r. U.S.A. 132 B4
Chik Ballapur India 72 C3
Chikhali Kalan Parasia India 74 C5
Chikhli India 72 C1
Chikmagalur India 72 B3
Chikodi India 72 B2
Chikodi Road India 72 B2
Chikwa Zambia 97 B7
Chikwawa Malawi 97 B9
Chila Angola 95 B8
Chilanko r. Canada 122 F4
Chilanko Forks Canada 122 E4
Chilas Jammu and Kashmir 74 B2
Chilaw Sri Lanka 72 C5
Chilcaya Chile 148 C4
Chilcotin r. Canada 122 F5
Childers Australia 111 H5
Childress U.S.A. 133 A5
▶Chile country S. America 152 B6
southamerica 144–145, 154
Chile Basin sea feature S. Pacific Ocean 165 M8
Chile Chico Chile 153 C6
Chilecito Arg. 152 D2
Chilengue, Serra do mts Angola 95 B8
Chile Rise sea feature S. Pacific Ocean 165 M8
Chilete Peru 148 A1
Chilia-Nouă Ukr. see Kiliya
Chilik Kazakh. 70 E3
Chilika Lake India 73 E2
Chililabombwe Zambia 95 E8

Dārestān Iran 80 C4
Darfo Boario Terme Italy 44 C2
Dargai Pak. 81 G3
Darganata Turkm. 81 E1
Dargaville N.Z. 113 C1
Dargo Australia 112 C5
Darhan Mongolia 62 H2
Darıca Turkey 46 F4
Darien CT U.S.A. 131 G3
Darien GA U.S.A. 129 C6
Darién, Golfo del g. Col. 146 B2
Darién, Parque Nacional de nat. park Panama 146 B3
Darién, Serranía del mts Panama 146 B2
Dar'inskoye Kazakh. 29 I6
Darjeeling India 75 F4
Darjiling India see Darjeeling
Dārkhovīn Iran 80 B4
Darlag China 66 A1
▶Darling r. Australia 112 B4
2nd longest river in Oceania. Part of the longest (Murray-Darling).
oceania 102–103
Darling Downs hills Australia 111 G5
Darling Range hills Australia 109 A8
Darlington U.K. 35 F4
Darlington U.S.A. 129 D5
Darlington Point Australia 112 C4
Darlot, Lake salt flat Australia 109 C6
Darłowo Poland 37 H1
Dărmănești Romania 46 E1
Darma Pass China/India 74 D3
Darmstadt Germany 36 D4
Darna r. India 72 B2
Darnah Libya 88 D1
Darnick Australia 112 B4
Darnley, Cape Antarctica 167 E2
Darnley Bay Canada 120 G3
Daroca Spain 43 F2
Daroot-Korgan Kyrg. 81 H2
Darovskoy Rus. Fed. 28 H4
Dar Pahn Iran 80 D5
Darregueira Arg. 152 E4
Darreh Bīd Iran 80 D3
Darreh Gaz Iran 81 D2
Darreh Gozaru r. Iran see Gīzeh Rūd
Darreh-ye Bāhābād Iran 80 C4
Darreh-ye Shekārī r. Afgh. 81 G3
Darro watercourse Eth. 96 D3
Darsa i. Yemen 76 E7
Darsi India 72 C3
Darß pen. Germany 37 F1
Darßer Ort c. Germany 37 F1
Darta Turkm. 81 E1
Dartford U.K. 35 G6
Dartmoor hills U.K. 35 D6
Dartmoor National Park U.K. 35 E6
Dartmouth Canada 125 I4
Dartmouth U.K. 35 E6
Dartmouth Reservoir Australia 112 C5
Daru P.N.G. 57 J7
Daru waterhole Sudan 89 G5
Daruba Indon. 57 G5
Daruvar Croatia 44 F2
Darvaza Turkm. 81 D1
Darvoz, Qatorkŭhi mts Tajik. 81 G2
Darwendale Zimbabwe 99 F3
Darwha India 72 C1
▶Darwin Australia 110 B2
Capital of Northern Territory.
Darwin Falkland Is 153 F7
Darwin, Canal sea chan. Chile 153 B6
Darwin, Monte mt. Chile 153 C8
Darya Khan Pak. 81 G4
Dar"yoi Amu r. Asia see Amudar'ya
Dar"yoi Sir r. Asia see Syrdar'ya
Dārzīn Iran 80 D4
Dās i. U.A.E. 80 C5
Dasada India 74 A5
Dashhowuz Turkm. see Dashkhovuz
Dashkesan Azer. see Daşkäsän
Dashkhovuz Turkm. 76 F1
Dashkhovuz Oblast admin. div. Turkm. see Dashkhovuzskaya Oblast'
Dashkhovuzskaya Oblast' admin. div. Turkm. 80 D1
Dashköpri Turkm. see Tashkepri
Dashoguz Turkm. see Dashkhovuz
Dasht Iran 80 D2
Dasht r. Pak. 81 E5
Dasht-e Bar Iran 80 D4
Dasht-e Palang r. Iran 80 C4
Dashtiari Iran 81 E5
Daska Pak. 74 B2
Daşkäsän Azer. 79 F2
Dasongshu China 66 C3
Daspar mt. Pak. 81 H2
Dassa Benin 93 F4
Da Suifen He r. China 64 B4
Dasuya India 74 B3
Datadian Indon. 59 F2
Datça Turkey 78 A3
Date Japan 64 E4
Date Creek watercourse U.S.A. 137 F4
Dateland U.S.A. 137 F5
Datha India 74 B5
Datia India 74 C4
Datian China 67 F3
Datian Ding mt. China 67 D4
Datong Fujian China see Tong'an
Datong Shanxi China 63 I3
Datta Rus. Fed. 64 E2
Datu i. Indon. 59 E2
Datu, Tanjung c. Indon./Malaysia 59 E2
Datu Piang Phil. 57 F4
Daudkandi Bangl. 75 F5
Daud Khel Pak. 81 G3
Daudnagar India 75 E4
Daudzeva Latvia 33 G4
Daugai Lith. 33 G5
Daugava r. Latvia 33 G4
Daugavpils Latvia 33 G5
Daulatabad Iran see Malāyer
Daulatpur Bangl. 75 F5
Daule Ecuador 146 B5
Daun Germany 36 C3
Daund India 72 B2
Daung Kyun i. Myanmar 61 B5
Daungyu r. Myanmar 60 A3
Dauphin Canada 134 G2
Dauphiné reg. France 39 F4
Dauphiné, Alpes du mts France 39 F4
Dauphin Lake Canada 123 L5
Daura Nigeria 93 H2
Daurie Creek r. Australia 109 A6
Dausa India 74 C4
Dâu Tiếng, Hồ resr Vietnam 61 D6
Däväçi Azer. 79 G2
Davangere India 72 B3
Davao Phil. 57 G4
Davao Gulf Phil. 57 G4
Dāvarān Iran 80 D4
Dāvar Panāh Iran 81 E5
Davenport IA U.S.A. 132 D3
Davenport WA U.S.A. 134 C3
Davenport Downs Australia 111 E5
Davenport Range hills Australia 110 C4
Daveyton S. Africa 99 F5
David Panama 139 H7
David City U.S.A. 132 B3
Davidson Canada 134 F2
Davidson, Mount Australia 110 B4
Davie Ridge sea feature Indian Ocean 162 J6
Davis research station Antarctica 167 E2
Davis i. Myanmar see Than Kyun
Davis CA U.S.A. 136 B2
Davis WV U.S.A. 130 D4
Davis, Mount U.S.A. 130 D4
Davis Bay Antarctica 167 G2
Davis Dam U.S.A. 137 E4
Davis Inlet Canada 125 I2
Davison U.S.A. 130 B2
Davis Sea Antarctica 167 F2
Davis Strait Canada/Greenland 121 N3
Davlekanovo Rus. Fed. 28 J5
Davos Switz. 39 H3
Davy U.S.A. 130 C5
Davy Lake Canada 123 I3
Dawa Co l. China 75 E3
Dawa Wenz r. Eth. 96 D3
Dawaxung China 75 E3
Dawê China 66 B2
Dawei Myanmar see Tavoy
Dawei b. Myanmar see Tavoy
Dawera i. Indon. 108 E1
Dawhat Bilbul b. Saudi Arabia 80 B5
Dawna Range mts Myanmar/Thai. 60 B4
Dawqah Oman 76 E6
Dawqah Saudi Arabia 89 I5
Dawson r. Australia 111 G4
Dawson Canada 122 B1
Dawson GA U.S.A. 129 B6
Dawson ND U.S.A. 132 B2
Dawson, Isla i. Chile 153 C8
Dawson Creek Canada 122 F4
Dawson Inlet Canada 123 M2
Dawson Range mts Canada 122 A2
Dawsons Landing Canada 122 E5
Dawu Hubei China 67 E2
Dawu Qinghai China see Maqên
Dawu Sichuan China 66 B2
Dawu Taiwan see Tawu
Dawukou China see Shizuishan
Dawu Shan hill China 67 E2
Dax France 38 C5
Daxian China see Dazhou
Daxiang Ling mts China 66 B2
Daxin China 66 C4
Daxing Yunnan China see Ninglang
Daxing Yunnan China see Lüchun
Daxue China see Wencheng
Daxue Shan mts China 66 B2
Dayan China see Lijiang
Dayangshu China 64 A2
Dayao China 66 B3
Dayao Shan mts China 67 D4
Ḑayat en Nahārāt well Mali 92 E1
Daye China 67 E2
Daying Jiang r. China 66 A3
Dayishan China see Guanyun
Daylesford Australia 112 C5
Dayong China 67 D2
Dayr Abū Sa'īd Jordan 77 B3
Dayr az Zawr Syria 79 E4
Dayr Ḥāfir Syria 77 C1
Daysland Canada 123 H4
Dayton OH U.S.A. 130 A4
Dayton TN U.S.A. 128 B5
Dayton TX U.S.A. 133 C6
Dayton WA U.S.A. 134 C3
Daytona Beach U.S.A. 129 C6
Dayu China 67 E3
Dayu Indon. 59 F3
Dayu Ling mts China 67 E3
Da Yunhe canal China 67 F1
Dayyīna i. U.A.E. 80 C5
Dazhe China see Pingyuan
Dazhongji China see Dafeng
Dazhou China 66 C2
Dazhou Dao i. China 67 D5
Dazhu China 66 C2
Dazu China 66 C2
Dazu Rock Carvings tourist site China 66 C2
De Aar S. Africa 98 E6
Deadman's Cay Bahamas 129 E8
Dead Mountains U.S.A. 137 E4
▶Dead Sea salt l. Asia 76 B3
Lowest point in the world and in Asia.
Deakin Australia 109 E7
Deal U.K. 35 G6
Dean r. Canada 122 E4
De'an China 67 E2
Deán Funes Arg. 152 D2
Deanuvuotna inlet Norway see Tanafjorden
Dearborn U.S.A. 130 B2
Dease r. B.C. Canada 122 D3
Dease r. N.W.T. Canada 123 G1
Dease Arm b. Canada 122 F1
Dease Lake Canada 122 D3
Dease Lake l. Canada 122 D3
Dease Strait Canada 121 I3
Death Valley U.S.A. 136 D3
▶Death Valley depr. U.S.A. 136 D3
Lowest point in the Americas.
northamerica 116–117
world 14–15
Death Valley Junction U.S.A. 137 D3
Death Valley National Park U.S.A. 136 D3
Deaver U.S.A. 134 E3
Debak Sarawak Malaysia 59 E2
Debao China 66 C4
Debar Macedonia 46 B4
Debark Eth. 96 C1
Debden Canada 123 J4
Debert Canada 125 I4
Debesy Rus. Fed. 28 J4
Dębica Poland 37 J3
De Biesbosch, Nationaal Park nat. park Neth. 36 B3
Debila Alg. 91 G2
Debin Rus. Fed. 27 P3
Dęblin Poland 37 J3
Dębno Poland 37 G2
Débo, Lac l. Mali 92 D2
Deborah East, Lake salt flat Australia 109 B7
Deborah West, Lake salt flat Australia 109 B7
Debre Birhan Eth. 96 C2
Debrecen Hungary 37 J5
Debre Markos Eth. 96 C2
Debre Tabor Eth. 96 C2
Debre Werk' Eth. 96 C2
Debre Zeyit Eth. 96 C2
Debrzno Poland 37 G2
Deçan Serb. and Mont. see Dečani
Dečani Serb. and Mont. 46 B3
Decatur AL U.S.A. 133 E5
Decatur GA U.S.A. 129 B5
Decatur IL U.S.A. 128 A4
Decatur IN U.S.A. 130 A3
Decatur TX U.S.A. 133 B5
Decazeville France 38 E4
▶Deccan plat. India 72 C2
Plateau making up most of southern and central India.
Deception watercourse Botswana 98 E4
Deception Bay Australia 111 H5
Dechang China 66 B3
Decheng China see Deqing
Děčín Czech Rep. 37 G3
Decize France 39 E3
Decorah U.S.A. 132 D3
Dedegöl Dağları mts Turkey 78 B3
Dedop'listsqaro Georgia 79 F2
Dédougou Burkina 92 E2
Dedovichi Rus. Fed. 28 D4
Dedu China 64 A2
Dedza Malawi 97 B8
Dee r. England/Wales U.K. 35 E5
Dee r. Scotland U.K. 34 E3
Deeg India 74 C4
Deep Bay Hong Kong China 67 [inset]
Deep Creek Lake U.S.A. 130 D4
Deep Creek Range mts U.S.A. 137 F2
Deep River Canada 124 E4
Deep River U.S.A. 131 G3
Deering, Mount Australia 109 E6
Deer Island AK U.S.A. 120 C4
Deer Island ME U.S.A. 131 I1
Deer Lake Nfld. and Lab. Canada 125 J3
Deer Lake Ont. Canada 123 M4
Deer Lake l. Canada 123 M4
Deer Lodge U.S.A. 134 D3
Deer Park U.S.A. 134 C3
Deesa India see Disa
Defeng China see Liping
Defensores del Chaco, Parque Nacional nat. park Para. 149 E5
Defiance U.S.A. 130 A3
Defiance Plateau U.S.A. 137 H4
Défirou well Niger 88 B4
De Funiak Springs U.S.A. 129 B6
Degana India 74 B4
Degano r. Italy 44 D1
Degebe r. Port. 42 C3
Degeh Bur Eth. 96 D2
Dégelis Canada 125 G4
Degema Nigeria 93 G4
Degerfors Sweden 33 D4
Deggendorf Germany 37 F4
Degh r. Pak. 81 H4
Değirmencik r. Turkey 47 F5
Değirmenlik Cyprus see Kythrea
De Grey Australia 108 B5
De Grey r. Australia 108 B5
Degtevo Rus. Fed. 29 G6
Dehaj Iran 80 C4
Dehak Iran 81 E5
Dehalak Deset i. Eritrea 89 I6
Deh Bakrī Iran 80 D4
Deh Barez Iran see Fāryāb
Deh Bīd Iran 80 C4
Deh-Dasht Iran 80 B4
Dehdez Iran 80 B4
Dehej India 74 B5
Deh-e Khalīfeh Iran 80 B4
Deh-e Kohneh Iran 80 B4
Dehgāh Iran 80 B2
Deh Golān Iran 80 A3
Dehi Afgh. 81 F3
Deh Khvājeh Iran 80 C4
Dehkūyeh Iran 80 C5
Dehlorān Iran 80 A3
De Hoge Veluwe, Nationaal Park nat. park Neth. 36 B2
Dehqonobod Uzbek. see Dekhkanabad
Dehra Dun India 74 C3
Dehri India 75 E4
Deh Shū Afgh. 81 E4
Dehua China 67 F3
Dehui China 64 A3
Deim Zubeir Sudan 94 E3
Deinze Belgium 39 E1
Deir el Qamar Lebanon 77 B3
Deir-ez-Zor Syria see Dayr az Zawr
Dej Romania 31 J4
Dejë, Mal mt. Albania 46 B4
Dejen Eth. 96 C2
Deji China see Rinbung
Dejiang China 66 D2
Deka Drum Zimbabwe 99 E3
De Kalb IL U.S.A. 132 D3
De Kalb TX U.S.A. 133 C5
De Kalb Junction U.S.A. 131 F1
De-Kastri Rus. Fed. 27 O4
Dekemhare Eritrea 89 H6
Dekese Dem. Rep. Congo 94 D5
Dekhkanabad Uzbek. 81 F2
Dékoa Cent. Afr. Rep. 94 C3
Delaki Indon. 108 D2
Delami Sudan 96 A2
De Land U.S.A. 129 C6
Delano U.S.A. 136 C4
Delano Peak U.S.A. 137 F2
▶Delap-Uliga-Djarrit Marshall Is 164 F5
Capital of the Marshall Islands, on Majuro atoll.
Delārām Afgh. 81 E3
Delareyville S. Africa 98 E5
Delarof Islands U.S.A. 120 B4
Delaronde Lake Canada 123 J4
Delaware U.S.A. 130 B3
Delaware r. KS U.S.A. 132 C4
Delaware r. NJ/PA U.S.A. 131 F4
Delaware state U.S.A. 131 F4
Delaware, East Branch r. U.S.A. 131 F3
Delaware, West Branch r. U.S.A. 131 F3
Delaware Bay U.S.A. 131 F4
Delaware City U.S.A. 131 F4
Delay r. Canada 125 G1
Delbarton U.S.A. 130 B5
Delbeng Sudan 94 F3
Del Bonita Canada 123 H5
Delčevo Macedonia 46 C4
Delegate Australia 112 D5
Delémont Switz. 39 G3
Delevan U.S.A. 136 A2
Delft Neth. 36 B2
Delft Island Sri Lanka 72 C4
Delfzijl Neth. 36 C2
Delgado, Cabo c. Moz. 97 D7
Delgo Sudan 89 F4
Delhi Canada 130 C2
Delhi China 70 I4
▶Delhi India 74 C3
world 16–17
Delhi LA U.S.A. 133 D5
Delhi NY U.S.A. 131 F2
Deli i. Indon. 58 D4
Deli r. Turkey 79 E3
Delice r. Turkey 78 C2
Délices Fr. Guiana 147 H3
Delījān Iran 80 B3
Déline Canada 122 F1
Delingha China see Delhi
Delisle Canada 123 J5
Delitzsch Germany 37 F3
Dellys Alg. 91 F1
Del Mar U.S.A. 136 D5
Delmenhorst Germany 36 D2
Delmont U.S.A. 130 D3
Delmore Downs Australia 110 C4
Delnice Croatia 44 E2
Delong China 66 C4
De-Longa, Ostrova is Rus. Fed. 27 P2
De Long Islands Rus. Fed. see De-Longa, Ostrova
De Long Mountains U.S.A. 120 C3
De Long Strait Rus. Fed. see Longa, Proliv
Deloraine Australia 112 C6
Deloraine Canada 123 K5
Delphi tourist site Greece 47 C5
Delphi U.S.A. 128 B3
Delphos U.S.A. 130 A3
Delray Beach U.S.A. 129 C7
Del Rio Mex. 135 E7
Del Rio U.S.A. 133 A6
Delsbo Sweden 33 E3
Delta state Nigeria 93 G4
Delta CO U.S.A. 135 E5
Delta OH U.S.A. 130 A3
Delta UT U.S.A. 137 F2
Delta Amacuro state Venez. 147 F2
Delta du Saloum, Parc National du nat. park Senegal 92 A2
Delta Junction U.S.A. 120 E3
Delvada India 72 A1
Delvinë Albania 47 B5
Dema r. Rus. Fed. 29 J5
Demavend mt. Iran see Damāvand, Qolleh-ye
Demba Dem. Rep. Congo 95 D6
Dembia Cent. Afr. Rep. 94 E3
Dembī Dolo Eth. 96 B2
Demerara Guyana see Georgetown
Demerara Abyssal Plain sea feature S. Atlantic Ocean 160 K5
Demidov Rus. Fed. 31 L2
Deming U.S.A. 135 F6
Demini r. Brazil 147 F5
Demini, Serras do mts Brazil 147 F4
Demirci Turkey 78 B3
Demir Hisar Macedonia 46 B4
Demirköprü Barajı resr Turkey 78 B3
Demirköy Turkey 46 E4
Demirler r. Turkey 47 F5
Demmin Germany 37 F2
Democracia Brazil 147 F6
Demopolis U.S.A. 129 B5
Dempo, Gunung vol. Indon. 58 C4
Dempster Highway Canada 122 B1
Dêmqog Jammu and Kashmir 74 C2
Dem'yanovo Rus. Fed. 28 H3
Denakil reg. Eritrea/Eth. 89 I6
Denali National Park and Preserve U.S.A. 120 D3
Denare Beach Canada 123 K4
Denau Uzbek. 81 F2
Denbigh Canada 124 E4
Denbigh U.K. 35 E5
Den Bosch Neth. see 's-Hertogenbosch
Den Burg Neth. 36 B2
Den Chai Thai. 60 C4
Dendang Indon. 59 D3
Dendâra Mauritania 92 D1
Dendermonde Belgium 39 F1
Dendi mt. Eth. 76 B8
Đeneral Janković Serb. and Mont. 46 B3
Denezhkin Kamen', Gora mt. Rus. Fed. 28 K3
Dengas Niger 93 H2
Denge Nigeria 93 G2
Dengfeng China 67 E1
Dênggar China 75 E3
Dengjiabu China see Yujiang
Dêngka China see Têwo
Dêngkagoin China see Têwo
Dengkou China 63 H3
Dêngqên China 75 G3
Dengta China 67 E4
Denguiro Cent. Afr. Rep. 94 D3
Dengxian China see Dengzhou
Dengzhou China 67 E1
Den Haag Neth. see The Hague
Denham Australia 109 A6
Denham r. Australia 108 E3
Denham Range mts Australia 111 G4
Den Helder Neth. 36 B2
Denholm Canada 123 I4
Denia Spain 43 G3
Denial Bay Australia 109 F8
Deniliquin Australia 112 C4
Denison IA U.S.A. 132 C3
Denison TX U.S.A. 133 B5
Denison, Cape Antarctica 167 G2
Denison Plains Australia 108 E4
Denizli Turkey 78 C3
Denizli prov. Turkey 47 F6
Denman Australia 112 D4
Denman Glacier Antarctica 167 F2
Denmark Australia 109 B8
▶Denmark country Europe 33 C5
europe 24–25, 48
Denmark Strait Greenland/Iceland 121 C3
Dennison U.S.A. 130 C3
Dennisville U.S.A. 131 F4
Denow Uzbek. see Denau
Denpasar Indon. 59 F5
Denton MD U.S.A. 131 F4
Denton TX U.S.A. 133 E5
D'Entrecasteaux, Point Australia 109 A8
D'Entrecasteaux, Récifs reef New Caledonia 107 F3
D'Entrecasteaux Islands P.N.G. 107 E2
D'Entrecasteaux National Park Australia 109 A8
Dents du Midi mt. Switz. 39 G3
▶Denver U.S.A. 134 F5
State capital of Colorado.
Denys r. Canada 124 E2
Deoband India 74 C3
Deobhog India 73 D2
Deogarh Orissa India 75 E5
Deogarh Rajasthan India 74 B4
Deogarh mt. India 75 D5
Deoghar India 75 E4
Deoli India 72 C1
Deori India 74 C5
Deoria India 75 D4
Deosai, Plains of Jammu and Kashmir 74 B2
Depalpur India 74 B5
De Pas, Rivière r. Canada 125 H2
Depew U.S.A. 130 D2
Deposit U.S.A. 131 F2
Depsang Point hill Aksai Chin 74 C2
Deputatskiy Rus. Fed. 27 N3
Dêqên Xizang China 75 F3
Dêqên Xizang China 75 F3
Dêqên Xizang China see Dagzê
Dêqên Yunnan China 66 A2
Deqing Guangdong China 67 D4
Deqing Zhejiang China 67 G2
De Queen U.S.A. 133 C5
De Quincy U.S.A. 133 C6
Der, Lac du l. France 39 F2
Dera Bugti Pak. 81 G4
Dera Ghazi Khan Pak. 81 G4
Deraheib reg. Sudan 89 G4
Dera Ismail Khan Pak. 81 G4
Derbent Rus. Fed. 29 I8
Derbent Uzbek. 81 F2
Derbesiye Turkey see Şenyurt
Derby Australia 108 C4
Derby U.K. 35 F5
Derby CT U.S.A. 131 G3
Derby KS U.S.A. 132 B4
Derecske Hungary 37 J5
Derg, Lough l. Rep. of Ireland 35 B5
Dergachi Rus. Fed. 29 I6
De Ridder U.S.A. 133 C6
Derik Turkey 79 E3
Derinkuyu Turkey 78 C3
Derkali well Kenya 96 D4
Derna Libya see Darnah
Dêrong China 66 A2
Derre Moz. 99 H3
Derry U.K. see Londonderry
Derry U.S.A. 131 H2
Derryveagh Mountains hills Rep. of Ireland 34 B4
Dêrub China see Rutög
Derudeb Sudan 89 H5
Derventa Bos.-Herz. 44 F2
Derwent r. Derbyshire, England U.K. 35 F5
Derwent r. England U.K. 35 F5
Derweze Turkm. see Darvaza
Derzhavino Rus. Fed. 29 J5
Derzhavinsk Kazakh. 26 G4
Derzhavinskiy Kazakh. see Derzhavinsk
Desaguadero r. Arg. 152 D3
Desaguadero r. Bol. 148 C4
Désappointement, Îles du is Fr. Polynesia 165 I6
Desatoya Mountains U.S.A. 136 D2
Descalvado Brazil 149 F4
Descartes France 38 D3
Deschambault Lake Canada 123 K4
Deschambault Lake l. Canada 123 K4
Desē Eth. 96 C2
Deseada Chile 148 C5
Deseado Arg. 153 D6
Deseado r. Arg. 153 D6
Desemboque Mex. 135 D7
Deseret Peak U.S.A. 137 F1
Desertas, Ilhas is Madeira 90 A2
Desert Canal Pak. 81 G4
Desert Center U.S.A. 137 E5
Desert Lake U.S.A. 137 E3
Desert View U.S.A. 137 G3
Deshler U.S.A. 130 B3
Deshnok India 74 B4
Desierto de Tello Arg. 152 D2
Desierto de Sechura des. Peru 146 A6
Deskati Greece 47 B5
De Smet U.S.A. 132 B2
▶Des Moines IA U.S.A. 132 C3
State capital of Iowa.
Des Moines NM U.S.A. 132 A4
Des Moines r. U.S.A. 132 D3
Desna r. Rus. Fed./Ukr. 29 D6
Desnățui r. Romania 46 C3
Desnogorsk Rus. Fed. 31 M2
Desnudo, Cerro mt. Arg. 153 C6
Desolación, Isla i. Chile 153 B8
Despotovac Serb. and Mont. 46 B2
Dessau Germany 37 F3
Dessye Eth. see Desē
Destruction Bay Canada 122 B2
Desvres France 38 D1
Deta Romania 46 B2
Detah Canada 123 H2
Dete Zimbabwe 99 E3
Deti Jon b. Albania/Greece 47 A4
Đetinja r. Serb. and Mont. 46 B3
Detmold Germany 36 D3
De Tour Village U.S.A. 132 F2
Detrital Wash watercourse U.S.A. 137 E3
Detroit U.S.A. 130 B2
Detroit Lakes U.S.A. 132 C2
Dett Zimbabwe see Dete
Detva Slovakia 37 I4
Deua National Park Australia 112 D4
Deurne Neth. 36 B3
Deutschland country Europe see Germany
Deutschlandsberg Austria 37 G5
Deva Romania 46 C2
Deva U.K. see Chester
Devana U.K. see Aberdeen
Devanhalli India 72 C3
Devarkonda India 72 C2
Deve Bair pass Macedonia see Velbŭzhdki Prokhod
Devecser Hungary 37 H5
Develi Turkey 78 C3
Deveron r. U.K. 34 E3
Devesel Romania 46 C2
Devét Skal hill Czech Rep. 37 H4
Devgadh Bariya India 74 B5
Devghar India see Deoghar
Devikot India 74 A4
Devils r. U.S.A. 133 A6
Devil's Gate pass U.S.A. 136 C2
Devil's Lake U.S.A. 132 B1
Devils Lake l. U.S.A. 133 A6
Devil's Paw mt. U.S.A. 120 F4
Devil's Point Bahamas 129 E7
Devil's Thumb mt. Canada/U.S.A. 122 C3
Devin Bulg. 46 D4
Devine U.S.A. 133 B6
Devizes U.K. 35 F6
Devli India 74 B4
Devnya Bulg. 46 E3
Devoll r. Albania 46 A4
Dévoluy mts France 39 F4
Devon Island Canada 121 J2
Devonport Australia 112 C6
Devore U.S.A. 136 D4
Devrek Turkey 78 B2
Devrez r. Turkey 78 C2
Devrukh India 72 B2
Dewa, Tanjung pt Indon. 58 A2
Dewakang Besar i. Indon. 59 G4
Dewanganj Bangl. 75 F4
Dewangiri Bhutan 75 F4
Dewas India 74 C5
De Weerribben, Nationaal Park nat. park Neth. 36 C2
Dewelē Eth. 96 D2
De Witt AR U.S.A. 133 D5
De Witt IA U.S.A. 132 D3
Dexing China 67 F2
Dexter MO U.S.A. 132 D4
Dexter NM U.S.A. 135 F6
Dexter NY U.S.A. 131 E1
Deyang China 66 C2
Dey-Dey Lake salt flat Australia 110 B6
Deyhuk Iran 80 D3
Deynau Turkm. see Dyanev
Deyong, Tanjung pt Indon. 57 I7
Dēyū Co l. China 75 E2
Deyyer Iran 80 B5
Dez r. Iran 80 B4
Dezadeash Canada 122 B2
Dezfūl Iran 80 B3
▶Dezhneva, Mys c. Rus. Fed. 120 C3
Most easterly point of Asia.
Dezhou Shandong China 63 J4
Dezhou Sichuan China see Dechang
Dezh Shāhpūr Iran see Marīvān
Dhading Nepal 75 E4
Dhahab Egypt 89 G2
Dhahab, Wādī adh r. Syria 77 B3
Dhāhiriya West Bank 77 B4
Dhahran Saudi Arabia 80 B5
▶Dhaka Bangl. 75 F5
Capital of Bangladesh and 5th most populous city in Asia.
world 16–17
Dhaka admin. div. Bangl. 75 F5
Dhaleswari r. Bangl. 75 F5
Dhaleswari r. India 75 G4
Dhalgaon India 72 B2
Dhamār Yemen 76 C7
Dhamnod India 74 B5
Dhamtari India 72 D1
Dhanbad India 75 E5
Dhandhuka India 74 B5
Dhanera India 74 B4
Dhangarhi Nepal 74 D3
Dhang Range mts Nepal 75 D3
Dhankuta Nepal 75 E4
Dhar India 74 B5
Dhar Adrar hills Mauritania 90 B6
Dharampur India 72 B1
Dharan Bazar Nepal 75 E4
Dharapuram India 72 C4
Dhari India 74 A5
Dharmanagar India 75 G4
Dharmapuri India 72 C3
Dharmavaram India 72 C3
Dharmjaygarh India 75 D5
Dharmkot India 74 B3
Dharoor watercourse Somalia 96 F2
Dhar Oualâta hills Mauritania 92 D1
Dhar Tichit hills Mauritania 92 C1
Dharug National Park Australia 112 D4
Dharur India 72 C2
Dharwad India 72 B3
Dharwar India see Dharwad
Dhasa India 74 A5
Dhasan r. India 74 C4
▶Dhaulagiri mt. Nepal 75 D3
7th highest mountain in the world and in Asia.
asia 50–51
world 6–7
Dhaulpur India 74 C4
Dhaurahra India 74 D4
Dhawlagiri mt. Nepal see Dhaulagiri
Dhebar Lake India 74 B4
Dhekelia Sovereign Base Area military base Cyprus 77 A2
Dhekiajuli India 75 G4
Dhenkanal India 73 E1
Dheskáti Greece see Deskati
Dhiafánion Greece see Diafani
Dhibān Jordan 77 B4
Dhidhimótikhon Greece see Didymoteicho
Dhing India 75 G4
Dhī Qār governorate Iraq 79 F5
Dhirwāh, Wādī adh watercourse Jordan 77 C4
Dhodhekánisos is Greece see Dodecanese
Dhokós i. Greece see Dokos
Dhola India 74 A5
Dholka India 74 B5
Dhomokós Greece see Domokos
Dhone India 72 C3
Dhoomadheere Somalia 96 D4
Dhoraji India 74 A5
Dhori India 74 A5
Dhragonádha i. Greece see Dragonada
Dhragónisos i. Greece see Dragonisi
Dhrangadhra India 74 A5
Dhrol India 74 A5
Dhrosiá Greece see Drosia
Dhubāb Yemen 96 D1
Dhubri India see Dhuburi
Dhuburi India 75 F4
Dhule India 72 B1
Dhulia India see Dhule
Dhulian India 75 E4
Dhunche Nepal 75 E4
Dhuudo Somalia 96 F2
Dhuusa Marreeb Somalia 96 E3
Dhytikí Ellás admin. reg. Greece see Dytiki Ellas
Dhytikí Makedhonía admin. reg. Greece see Dytiki Makedonia
Dia i. Greece 47 D7
Diablo, Mount U.S.A. 136 B3
Diablo Range mts U.S.A. 136 B3
Diaca Moz. 97 C7
Diafani Greece 47 E7
Diafarabé Mali 92 D2
Diaka r. Mali 92 D2
Dialakoto Senegal 92 B2
Diallassagou Mali 92 E2
Diamante Arg. 152 E3
Diamante r. Arg. 152 D3
Diamante Italy 45 E5
Diamantina watercourse Australia 111 D5
Diamantina Brazil 147 F6
Diamantina, Chapada plat. Brazil 150 D5
Diamantina Deep sea feature Indian Ocean 163 N8
Diamantina Gates National Park Australia 111 E4
Diamantina Lakes Australia 111 E4
Diamantino Mato Grosso Brazil 149 F3
Diamantino Mato Grosso Brazil 151 A6
Diamond Harbour India 75 F5
Diamond Islets Australia 111 G3
Diamond Peak U.S.A. 137 E2
Diamond Springs U.S.A. 136 B2
Diamondville U.S.A. 134 E4
Diamou Mali 92 C2
Diamounguél Senegal 92 B2
Dianbai China 67 D4
Dianbu China see Feidong
Diancang Shan mt. China 66 B3
Dian Chi l. China 66 B3
Diandioumé Mali 92 C2
Diane Bank sea feature Australia 111 G2
Diangounté Kamara Mali 92 C2
Diani r. Guinea 92 C4
Dianjiang China 66 C2
Diano Marina Italy 44 B3
Dianópolis Brazil 150 C4
Dianra Côte d'Ivoire 92 D3
Diapaga Burkina 93 F2
Diaporioi i. Greece 47 C6
Diarizos r. Cyprus 77 A2
Diatifèrè Guinea 92 C3
Diavolo, Mount India 73 G3
Diaz Point Namibia 98 B5
Dibā al Ḥiṣn U.A.E. 80 D5
Dibang r. India see Dingba Qu
Dibaya Dem. Rep. Congo 95 D6
Dibbis Sudan 88 E6
Dibella well Niger 93 I1
Dibeng S. Africa 98 D5
Dibilē Eth. 96 D2
Dibrugarh India 75 G4
Dibulla Col. 146 C2
Dickens U.S.A. 133 A5
Dickinson U.S.A. 134 G3
Dickson U.S.A. 128 B4
Dicle r. Turkey 79 E3 see Tigris
Dida Galgalu reg. Kenya 96 C4
Didiéni Mali 92 C2
Didinga Hills Sudan 96 B3
Dido waterhole Kenya 96 D5
Didsbury Canada 134 D2
Didwana India 74 B4
Didymoteicho Greece 46 E4
Didžiasalis Lith. 33 G5
Die France 39 F4

Diébougou Burkina **92** E3
Dieburg Germany **36** D4
Diedenhofen France *see* **Thionville**
Diefenbaker, Lake Canada **123** I5
Diège *r.* France **38** E4
Diego de Almagro, Isla *i.* Chile **153** B7
Diégo Suarez Madag. *see* **Antsirañana**
Diégrâga *well* Mauritania **92** C2
Diéké Guinea **92** C4
Diekirch Lux. **39** G2
Diéma Mali **92** C2
Diên Châu Vietnam **60** D4
Diepholz Germany **36** D2
Dieppe France **38** D2
Dierks U.S.A. **133** C5
Di'er Songhua Jiang *r.* China **64** A3
Dietikon Switz. **39** H3
Diffa Niger **93** I2
Diffa *dept* Niger **93** I1
Dig *well* Eth. **96** E3
Diga Diga *well* Niger **93** F2
Digapahandi India **73** E2
Digba Dem. Rep. Congo **94** E3
Digboi India **75** G4
Digby Canada **127** M3
Digerbergen *hill* Sweden **33** D3
Digerberget *hill* Sweden **33** D3
Diggi India **74** B4
Diglur India **72** C2
Digne-les-Bains France **39** G4
Digoin France **39** E3
Digras India **72** C1
Digri Pak. **81** G5
Digul *r.* Indon. **57** I7
Digya National Park Ghana **93** E4
Dihang *r.* India **75** G3 *see* **Brahmaputra**
Diinsoor Somalia **96** D4
Dijlah, Nahr *r.* Iraq/Syria **79** F4 *see* **Tigris**
Dijon France **39** F3
Dik Chad **94** C2
Dikanäs Sweden **32** E2
Diken India **74** B4
Dikhil Djibouti **96** D2
Dikho *r.* India **75** G4
Dikili Turkey **47** E5
Diksal India **72** B2
Dikson Rus. Fed. **26** I2
Dikwa Nigeria **93** I2
Dīla Eth. **96** C3
Dilaram Iran **80** D4
Dilek Yarımadası Milli Parkı *nat. park* Turkey **47** E6
Dili Dem. Rep. Congo **94** E4

▶**Dili** East Timor **57** G7
Capital of East Timor.

Dilia *watercourse* Niger **93** I2
Dilijan Armenia **79** F2
Di Linh Vietnam **61** E6
Dilizhan Armenia *see* **Dilijan**
Dillenburg Germany **36** D3
Dilley U.S.A. **133** B6
Dilli Mali **92** D2
Dilling Sudan **89** F6
Dillingen an der Donau Germany **36** E4
Dillingham U.S.A. **120** D4
Dillon *r.* Canada **123** I4
Dillon *MT* U.S.A. **134** D3
Dillon *SC* U.S.A. **129** D5
Dillsburg U.S.A. **131** E3
Dillwyn U.S.A. **130** D5
Dilolo Dem. Rep. Congo **95** D7
Dilos *i.* Greece **47** D6
Diltāwa Iraq **79** F4
Dimapur India **75** G4
Dimashq Syria *see* **Damascus**
Dimashq *governorate* Syria **77** C3
Dimbelenge Dem. Rep. Congo **95** D6
Dimbokro Côte d'Ivoire **92** D4
Dimboola Australia **112** B5
Dimbulah Australia **111** F3
Dimitrovgrad Bulg. **46** D3
Dimitrovgrad Rus. Fed. **29** I5
Dimitrovgrad Serb. and Mont. **46** C3
Dimitrovo Bulg. *see* **Pernik**
Dimmitt U.S.A. **133** A5
Dimona Israel **77** B4
Dinagat *i.* Phil. **57** G3
Dinajpur Bangl. **75** F4
Dinan France **38** B2
Dinanagar India **74** B2
Dinangourou Mali **93** E2
Dinant Belgium **39** F1
Dinapur India **75** E4
Dinar Turkey **78** B3
Dīnār, Kūh-e *mt.* Iran **80** B4
Dinara *mt.* Bos.-Herz. **44** F2
Dinara Planina *mts* Bos.-Herz./Croatia *see* **Dinaric Alps**
Dinard France **38** B2
Dinaric Alps *mts* Bos.-Herz./Croatia **44** F2
Dinas *well* Kenya **96** C4
Dinbych U.K. *see* **Denbigh**
Dinbych-y-Pysgod U.K. *see* **Tenby**
Dinder *r.* Sudan **89** G6
Dinder National Park Sudan **89** G6
Dindigul India **72** C4
Dindima Nigeria **93** H3
Dindiza Moz. **99** G4
Dindori India **74** D5
Dinga Dem. Rep. Congo **95** C6
Dinga Pak. **81** H3
Dingba Qu *r.* India **75** G4
Dingbujie China **67** E2
Dingla Nepal **75** E4
Dingle Rep. of Ireland **35** A5
Dingle Bay Rep. of Ireland **35** A5
Dingnan China **67** E3
Dingo Australia **111** G4
Dingolfing Germany **37** F4
Dingping China *see* **Linshui**
Dingras Phil. **67** G5
Dingwall Canada **125** I4
Dingwall U.K. **34** D3
Dingyuan China **67** F1
Dinhata India **75** F4
Dinh Lâp Vietnam **60** D3
Dinkel *r.* Neth. **36** C2
Dinkelsbühl Germany **36** E4
Dinngyê China **75** E3
Dinokwe Botswana **99** E4
Dinosaur U.S.A. **137** H1
Dinosaur National Monument *nat. park* U.S.A. **137** H1
Dintiteladas Indon. **58** D4
Dinwiddie U.S.A. **130** E5
Dioïla Mali **92** D2
Diois, Massif du *mts* France **39** F4
Dion *r.* Guinea **92** C3
Dionísio Cerqueira Brazil **151** A8
Dioscurias Georgia *see* **Sokhumi**
Diospolis Magna *tourist site* Egypt *see* **Thebes**
Dioumara Mali **92** C2
Dioundiou Niger **93** F2
Dioura Mali **92** D2
Diourbel Senegal **92** A2
Dipalpur Pak. **74** B3
Dipayal Nepal **74** D3
Diphu India **75** G4
Dipkarpaz Cyprus *see* **Rizokarpason**
Diplo Pak. **81** G5
Dipolog Phil. **57** F4
Dipperu National Park Australia **111** G4
Dipu China *see* **Anji**
Dir Pak. **81** G3
Dīrah U.A.E. **80** C5
Dirang India **75** G4
Diré Mali **92** E1
Direction, Cape Australia **111** E2
Dirē Dawa Eth. **96** D2
Dirfys *mts* Greece **47** C5
Dirhami Estonia **33** F4
Dirico Angola **95** D9
Dirillo *r. Sicily* Italy **45** E6
Dirk Hartog Island Australia **109** A6
Dirkou Niger **93** I1
Dirranbandi Australia **111** G6
Ḑirs Saudi Arabia **89** I5
Dirschau Poland *see* **Tczew**
Dirty Devil *r.* U.S.A. **137** G3
Disa India **74** B4
Disang *r.* India **75** G4
Disappointment, Cape S. Georgia **153** [inset]
Disappointment, Cape U.S.A. **134** A3
Disappointment, Lake *salt flat* Australia **108** C5
Disappointment Lake Canada **125** I2
Discovery Bay Australia **112** B5
Disentis Muster Switz. **39** H3
Disgrazia, Monte *mt.* Italy **44** B1
Dishnā Egypt **89** G3
Disko *i.* Greenland *see* **Qeqertarsuaq**
Disko Bugt *b.* Greenland *see* **Qeqertarsuup Tunua**
Dismal Lakes Canada **123** G1
Dispur India **75** F4
Disputanta U.S.A. **131** E5
Disraëli Canada **125** G4
Diss U.K. **35** G5
Dissān Island Saudi Arabia **89** I5
Distrito Federal *admin. dist.* Brazil **149** I3
Distrito Federal *admin. dist.* Venez. **146** E2
Dittaino *r. Sicily* Italy **45** E6
Diu India **72** A1
Dīvān Darreh Iran **80** A3
Divehi *country* Indian Ocean *see* **Maldives**
Divénié Congo **94** B5
Dives *r.* France **38** C2
Divichi Azer. *see* **Däväçi**
Divide Mountain U.S.A. **122** A2
Divinópolis Brazil **151** C7
Divisor, Sierra de *mts* Peru *see* **Ultraoriental, Cordillera**
Divjaka *nat. park* Albania **46** A4
Divnoye Rus. Fed. **29** G7
Divo Côte d'Ivoire **92** D4
Divor *r.* Port. **42** B3
Divounia *i.* Greece **47** E7
Divriği Turkey **79** D3
Divuma Dem. Rep. Congo **95** D7
Diwaniyah Iraq *see* **Ad Dīwānīyah**
Dixcove Ghana **93** E4
Dixmont U.S.A. **131** I1
Dixon *CA* U.S.A. **136** B2
Dixon *IL* U.S.A. **132** D3
Dixon Entrance *sea chan.* Canada/U.S.A. **120** F4
Dixonville Canada **123** G3
Diyadin Turkey **79** E3
Diyālá *governorate* Iraq **79** F4
Diyālá, Nahr *r.* Iraq **79** F4
Diyarbakır Turkey **79** E3
Diyodar India **74** A4
Diz Pak. **81** E5
Dizak Iran *see* **Dāvar Panāh**
Dizangué Cameroon **93** H5
Diz Chah Iran **80** C3
Dize Turkey *see* **Yüksekova**
Dizney U.S.A. **130** B5
Dja *r.* Cameroon **93** I5
Djado Niger **88** B4
Djado, Plateau du Niger **88** B4
Djakarta Indon. *see* **Jakarta**
Djakovica Serb. and Mont. *see* **Đakovica**
Djamâa Alg. **91** G2
Djamba Dem. Rep. Congo **95** D7
Djambala Congo **94** B5
Djampie Dem. Rep. Congo **94** C5
Djampiel Cameroon **94** B3
Djanet Alg. **91** H4
Djebr *mt.* Alg. **91** F4
Djébrène Chad **94** C2
Djédaa Chad **88** C6
Djedid *well* Alg. **91** E4
Djelfa Alg. **91** F2
Djéma Cent. Afr. Rep. **94** E3
Djèmber Chad **94** C2
Djeneral Jankovič Serb. and Mont. *see* **Đeneral Janković**
Djenné Mali **92** D2
Djerdap *nat. park* Serb. and Mont. **46** C2
Djermaya Chad **88** B6
Djia Dem. Rep. Congo **94** D5
Djibo Burkina **93** E2
Djiborosso Côte d'Ivoire **92** D3
▶**Djibouti** *country* Africa **96** D2
africa 86–87, 100

▶**Djibouti** Djibouti **96** D2
Capital of Djibouti.

Djidjelli Alg. *see* **Jijel**
Djiguéni Mauritania **92** C2
Djolu Dem. Rep. Congo **94** D4
Djombo Kibbit Chad **88** C6
Djoua *r.* Congo/Gabon **94** B4
Djoubissi Cent. Afr. Rep. **94** D3
Djougou Benin **93** F3
Djoum Cameroon **93** I5
Djugu Dem. Rep. Congo **96** A4
Djuma Dem. Rep. Congo **95** C6
Djúpivogur Iceland **121** R3
Djurås Sweden **33** D3
Djurdjura National Park Alg. **43** I4
Djurö nationalpark *nat. park* Sweden **33** D4
Dlairi India **74** B3
Dmitriya Lapteva, Proliv *sea chan.* Rus. Fed. **27** O2
Dmitriyev-L'govskiy Rus. Fed. **29** E5
Dmitriyevsk Ukr. *see* **Makiyivka**
Dmitrov Rus. Fed. **28** F4
Dmytriyevs'k Ukr. *see* **Makiyivka**
Dnepr *r.* Rus. Fed. **29** D5 *see* **Dnieper**
Dneprodzerzhinsk Ukr. *see* **Dniprodzerzhyns'k**
Dnepropetrovsk Ukr. *see* **Dnipropetrovs'k**
Dneprorudnoye Ukr. *see* **Dniprorudne**
Dnestrovsc Moldova **46** F1

▶**Dnieper** *r.* Europe **29** D6
3rd longest river in Europe.
Also spelt Dnepr (Rus. Fed.) or Dnipro (Ukraine) or Dnyapro (Belarus).
europe 22–23

Dniester *r.* Moldova **31** L4
Dniester *r.* Ukr. **29** C6
also spelt Dnister (Ukraine) or Nistru (Moldova)
Dnipro *r.* Ukr. **29** D6 *see* **Dnieper**
Dniprodzerzhyns'k Ukr. **29** E6
Dnipropetrovs'k Ukr. **29** E6
Dniprorudne Ukr. **29** E7
Dnister *r.* Ukr. **29** C6 *see* **Dniester**
Dnistrov'ky Lyman *l.* Ukr. **46** G1
Dno Rus. Fed. **28** D4
Dnyapro *r.* Belarus **29** D6 *see* **Dnieper**
Doa Moz. **99** G3
Doabi Mekh-i-Zarin Afgh. **81** F3
Doaktown Canada **125** H4
Doangdoangan Besar *i.* Indon. **59** G4
Doangdoangan Kecil *i.* Indon. **59** G4
Doany Madag. **99** [inset] K2
Doba Chad **94** C2
Doba China *see* **Toiba**
Dobbs, Cape Canada **123** O1
Dobele Latvia **33** F4
Döbeln Germany **37** F3
Doberai, Jazirah *pen.* Indon. **57** H6
Doberai Peninsula Indon. *see* **Doberai, Jazirah**
Döbern Germany **37** G3
Dobiegniew Poland **37** G2
Doblas Arg. **152** D4
Dobo Indon. **57** H7
Doboj Bos.-Herz. **44** G2
Do Borji Iran **80** C4
Dobre Miasto Poland **37** J2
Dobreşti Romania **46** C1
Dobrich Bulg. **46** E3
Dobrinka Rus. Fed. **29** G5
Dobroteşti Romania **46** D2
Dobroye Rus. Fed. **29** F5
Dobruchi Rus. Fed. **33** G4
Dobrudzhansko Plato *plat.* Bulg. **46** E3
Dobrush Belarus **29** D5
Dobryanka Rus. Fed. **28** K4
Dobskie, Jezioro *l.* Poland **37** J1
Dobzha China **75** F3
Doce *r.* Brazil **151** E6
Do China Qala Afgh. **81** G4
Doctor Hicks Range *hills* Australia **109** D7
Doctor Petru Groza Romania *see* **Ştei**
Doda Tanz. **97** C6
Dod Ballapur India **72** C3
Dodecanese *is* Greece **47** E7
Dodekanisos *is* Greece *see* **Dodecanese**
Dodge City U.S.A. **132** A4
Dodgeville U.S.A. **132** D3
Dodman Point U.K. **35** D6
Dodola Eth. **96** C3

▶**Dodoma** Tanz. **97** B6
Capital of Tanzania.

Dodoma *admin. reg.* Tanz. **97** B6
Dodori National Reserve *nature res.* Kenya **96** D5
Doetinchem Neth. **36** C3
Dofa Indon. **57** G6
Doftana *r.* Romania **46** D2
Dog *r.* Canada **124** B3
Dogai Coring *salt l.* China **70** G5
Dogaicoring Qangco *salt l.* China **75** F2
Doğanbey *Aydın* Turkey **47** E6
Doğanbey *İzmir* Turkey **47** E5
Doğanşehir Turkey **79** D3
Dog Creek Canada **122** F5
Doghārūn Iran **81** E3
Dog Lake *Ont.* Canada **124** C3
Dog Lake *Ont.* Canada **132** D1
Dōgo *i.* Japan **65** C5
Dogoble *well* Somalia **96** E3
Dogondoutchi Niger **93** G2
Dogoumbo Chad **94** C2
Dōgo-yama *mt.* Japan **65** C6
Dog Rocks *is* Bahamas **129** D7
Doğubeyazıt Turkey **79** F3
Doğu Menteşe Dağları *mts* Turkey **78** B3

▶**Doha** Qatar **80** B5
Capital of Qatar.

Dohad India *see* **Dahod**
Dohazari Bangl. **75** G5
Doi *i.* Fiji **107** H4
Doi Inthanon National Park Thai. **60** B4
Doi Luang National Park Thai. **60** B4
Doilungdêqên China **75** F3
Doïranis, Limni *l.* Greece/Macedonia *see* **Dojran, Lake**
Doire U.K. *see* **Londonderry**
Doisanagar India **75** E5
Dois Irmãos, Serra dos *hills* Brazil **150** D4
Dojran, Lake Greece/Macedonia **46** C4
Dojransko Ezero *l.* Greece/Macedonia *see* **Dojran, Lake**
Doka Sudan **89** G6
Dokali Iran **80** C3
Dokhara, Dunes de *des.* Alg. **91** G2
Dokkum Neth. **36** B2
Dokos *i.* Greece **47** C6
Dokri Pak. **81** G5
Dokshukino Rus. Fed. *see* **Nartkala**
Dokshytsy Belarus **33** G5
Doksy Czech Rep. **37** G3
Dokuchayevs'k Ukr. **29** F7
Dolak, Pulau *i.* Indon. **57** I7
Dolavón Arg. **153** D5
Dolbeau Canada **125** F3
Dol-de-Bretagne France **38** C2
Dole France **39** F3
Dolgellau U.K. **35** E5
Dolgiy, Ostrov *i.* Rus. Fed. **28** K1
Dolgoye Rus. Fed. **29** F5
Dolinsk Rus. Fed. **64** E3
Dolisie Congo *see* **Loubomo**
Doljevac Serb. and Mont. **46** B3
Dolleman Island Antarctica **167** L2
Dolni Chiflik Bulg. **46** E3
Dolni Dŭbnik Bulg. **46** D3
Dolno Kamartsi Bulg. **46** C3
Dolno Levski Bulg. **46** D3
Dolný Kubín Slovakia **37** I4
Dolomites *mts* Italy **44** D1
Dolomiti *mts* Italy *see* **Dolomites**
Dolomiti Bellunesi, Parco Nazionale delle *nat. park* Italy **44** C1
Dolomitiche, Alpi *mts* Italy *see* **Dolomites**
Dolo Odo Eth. **96** D3
Dolores Arg. **152** F4
Dolores Uruguay **152** F3
Dolores *r.* U.S.A. **137** H2
Dolphin, Cape Falkland Is **153** F7
Dolphin and Union Strait Canada **120** H3
Đô Lương Vietnam **60** D4
Dolyna Ukr. **31** J3
Dom, Gunung *mt.* Indon. **57** I6
Domaniç Turkey **78** B3
Domartang China *see* **Banbar**
Domažlice Czech Rep. **37** F4
Domba China **75** G2
Dombås Norway **33** C3
Dombe Moz. **99** G3
Dombe Grande Angola **95** B8
Dombóvár Hungary **44** G1
Dombrau Poland *see* **Dąbrowa Górnicza**
Dombrovitsa Ukr. *see* **Dubrovytsya**
Dombrowa Poland *see* **Dąbrowa Górnicza**
Domda China *see* **Qingshuihe**
Dome Argus *ice feature* Antarctica **167** E1
Dome Charlie *ice feature* Antarctica **167** F2
Dome Circe *ice feature* Antarctica *see* **Dome Charlie**
Domel Island Myanmar *see* **Letsok-aw Kyun**
Dome Rock Mountains U.S.A. **137** E5
Domeyko Chile **152** C2
Dom Feliciano Brazil **152** G2
Domfront France **38** C2
▶**Dominica** *country* West Indies **139** L5
northamerica 118–119, 140
Dominicana, República *country* West Indies *see* **Dominican Republic**
▶**Dominican Republic** *country* West Indies **139** J5
northamerica 118–119, 140
Dominion, Cape Canada **121** L3
Domiongo Dem. Rep. Congo **95** D6
Domka Bhutan **75** F4
Domneşti Romania **46** D2
Domneşti Romania **46** D2
Domo Eth. **96** E3
Domodossola Italy **44** B1
Domokos Greece **47** C5
Domoni Comoros **97** E8
Dom Pedrito Brazil **152** G2
Dom Pedro Brazil **150** C3
Dompu Indon. **59** G5
Domula China **75** D2
Domuyo, Volcán *vol.* Arg. **152** C4
Domžale Slovenia **44** E1
Don *r.* India **72** C2

▶**Don** *r.* Rus. Fed. **29** F7
5th longest river in Europe.
europe 22–23

Don *r.* U.K. **34** E3
Don, Xé *r.* Laos **61** D5
Donadeu Arg. **152** E1
Donald Australia **112** B5
Donaldsonville U.S.A. **133** D6
Donalnes, Cerro *mt.* Chile **152** C1
Donalsonville U.S.A. **129** B6
Doñana, Parque Nacional de *nat. park* Spain **42** C4
Donau *r.* Austria/Germany **36** G4 *see* **Danube**
Donaueschingen Germany **36** D5
Donauwörth Germany **36** E4
Don Benito Spain **42** D3
Doncaster U.K. **35** F5
Dondo Angola **95** B7
Dondo Moz. **99** G3
Dondra Head Sri Lanka **72** D5
Donegal Rep. of Ireland **35** B4
Donegal Bay Rep. of Ireland **35** B4
Donets'k Ukr. **29** F7
Dønfoss Norway **33** C3
Donga *r.* Cameroon/Nigeria **93** H3
Donga Nigeria **93** H4
Dong'an China **67** D3
Dongara Australia **109** A7
Dongargarh India **74** D5
Dongbo China *see* **Mêdog**
Dongchuan *Yunnan* China **66** B3
Dongchuan *Yunnan* China *see* **Yao'an**
Dongco China **75** E2
Dong Co *l.* China **75** E2
Dongfang China **67** D5
Dongfanghong China **64** C3
Dongfeng China **64** A4
Donggala Indon. **57** E6
Donggang China **65** A5
Donggou China *see* **Donggang**
Dongguan China **67** E3
Dongguan China **67** E4
Đông Ha Vietnam **60** D4
Donghai China **67** F1
Dong Hai *sea* N. Pacific Ocean *see* **East China Sea**
Donghai Dao *i.* China **67** D4
Dong He *r.* China **66** C2
Đông Hới Vietnam **60** D4
Dong Jiang *r.* China **67** E4
Dongjiang Reservoir China **67** E2
Dongjingcheng China **64** B3
Dongkait, Tanjung *pt* Indon. **59** G3
Dongkou China **67** D3
Donglan China **66** C3
Dongmen China *see* **Luocheng**
Dongning China **64** B3
Dongo Angola **95** B8
Dongo Italy **44** B1
Dongobesh Tanz. **97** B6
Dongola Sudan **89** F5
Dongotona Mountains Sudan **96** B3
Dongou Congo **94** C4
Dong Phraya Fai *mts* Thai. **61** C4
Dong Phraya Yen *esc.* Thai. **61** C5
Dongping *Guangdong* China **67** E4
Dongping *Hunan* China *see* **Anhua**
Dongpo China *see* **Meishan**
Dongqiao China **75** F3
Dongshan *Fujian* China **67** F4
Dongshan *Jiangsu* China *see* **Jiangning**
Dongshan *Jiangxi* China *see* **Shangyou**
Dongshao China **67** E3
Dongsha Qundao *is* China **63** J7
Dongsheng China **63** I4
Dongshuan China *see* **Tangdan**
Dongtai China **67** G1
Dongtai *r.* China **67** G1
Dongting Hu *l.* China **67** E2
Dongtou China **67** G3
Donguena Angola **95** B9
Dongula Gabon **94** A4
Dong Ujimqin Qi China *see* **Uliastai**
Dongxiang China **67** F2
Dongxiang China *see* **Xuanhan**
Dongyang China **67** G2
Dongying China **63** J4
Dongzhi China **67** F2
Doniphan U.S.A. **133** D4
Donjek *r.* Canada **122** A2
Donji Miholjac Croatia **44** G2
Donji Vakuf Bos.-Herz. **44** F2
Donji Zemunik Croatia **44** E2
Donmanick Islands Bangl. **75** F5
Dønna *i.* Norway **32** D2
Donnelly Canada **123** G4
Donnellys Crossing N.Z. **113** C1
Donner Pass U.S.A. **136** B2
Donnersberg *hill* Germany **36** C4
Donnybrook Australia **109** A8
Donostia - San Sebastián Spain **43** F1
Donoussa Greece **47** D6
Donoussa *i.* Greece **47** D6
Donskoye Rus. Fed. **29** G7
Donthami *r.* Myanmar **60** B4
Doomadgee Australia **110** D3
Door Peninsula U.S.A. **128** B2
Dooxo Nugaaleed *valley* Somalia **96** F2
Do Qu *r.* China **66** B2
Dor *watercourse* Afgh. **81** E4
Dora, Lake *salt flat* Australia **108** C5
Do Rāh Iran **80** B5
Dorah Pass Pak. **81** G2
Doramarkog China **66** A1
Doran Lake Canada **123** I2
Dora Riparia *r.* Italy **44** A2
D'Orbigny Bol. **149** E5
Dorbod China *see* **Taikang**
Đorče Petrov Macedonia **46** B3
Dorchester U.K. **35** E6
Dordabis Namibia **98** C4
Dordogne *r.* France **39** C4
Dordrecht Neth. **36** B3
Dordrecht S. Africa **99** E6
Doré Lake Canada **123** J4
Doré Lake *l.* Canada **123** J4
Dores do Indaiá Brazil **151** C6
Dorey Mali **93** E2
Dorgali *Sardinia* Italy **45** B4
Dori *r.* Afgh. **81** F4
Dori Burkina **93** E2
Doring *r.* S. Africa **98** C6
Dorisvale Australia **110** B2
Dormaa-Ahenkro Ghana **92** E4
Dormans France **39** E2
Dornakal India **72** D2
Dornbirn Austria **36** D5
Dornoch U.K. **34** D3
Doro Mali **93** E1
Dorog Hungary **37** I5
Dorohoi Romania **31** K4
Dorokhsh Iran **81** D3
Döröö Nuur *salt l.* Mongolia **62** E2
Dorostol Bulg. *see* **Silistra**
Dorotea Sweden **32** E2
Dorowa Zimbabwe **99** F3
Dorpat Estonia *see* **Tartu**
Dorre Island Australia **109** A6
Dorrigo Australia **112** E3
Dorris U.S.A. **134** B4
Dorsale Camerounaise *slope* Cameroon/Nigeria **93** H4
Dorset and East Devon Coast *tourist site* U.K. **35** E6
Dorsoidong Co *l.* China **75** F2
Dortmund Germany **36** C3
Dorton U.S.A. **130** B5
Dörtyol Turkey **78** D3
Doruma Dem. Rep. Congo **94** E3
Dorūneh Iran **80** D3
Dorylaeum Turkey *see* **Eskişehir**
Do Sārī Iran **80** D4
Dos Bahías, Cabo *c.* Arg. **153** D6
Doshakh, Koh-i- *mt.* Afgh. **81** E3
Dos Hermanas Spain **42** D4
Đo Son Vietnam **60** D3
Dospat Bulg. **46** D4
Dos Pozos Arg. **153** D5
Dosse *r.* Germany **37** F2
Dosso Niger **93** F2
Dosso *dept* Niger **93** F2
Dossor Kazakh. **29** J7
Dothan U.S.A. **129** B6
Douai France **39** E1
Douako Guinea **92** C3
Douala Cameroon **93** H4
Douarnenez France **38** A2
Douarnenez, Baie de *b.* France **38** A2
Double Headed Shot Cays *is* Bahamas **129** C8
Double Island *Hong Kong* China **67** [inset]
Double Mountain Fork *r.* U.S.A. **133** A5
Double Peak U.S.A. **136** C4
Double Point Australia **111** F3
Double Springs U.S.A. **129** B5
Doubs *r.* France/Switz. **39** F3
Doubtful Sound *inlet* N.Z. **113** A4
Doubtless Bay N.Z. **113** C1
Doué-la Fontaine France **38** C3
Douentza Mali **92** E2
Dougga *tourist site* Tunisia **91** H1

▶**Douglas** Isle of Man **35** D4
Capital of the Isle of Man.

Douglas S. Africa **98** D6
Douglas *AZ* U.S.A. **135** E7
Douglas *GA* U.S.A. **129** C6
Douglas *WY* U.S.A. **134** F4
Douglas Apsley National Park Australia **112** D6
Douglas Channel Canada **122** D4
Douglas Creek *watercourse* Australia **110** D6
Douglas Creek *r.* U.S.A. **137** H1
Douglas Reef *i.* Japan *see* **Okino-Tori-shima**
Dougoulé *well* Niger **93** H2
Douhi Chad **88** C5
Douhudi China *see* **Gong'an**
Doukato, Akra *pt* Greece **47** B5
Doulaincourt-Saucourt France **39** F2
Douliu Taiwan *see* **Touliu**
Doullens France **38** E1
Doumè Benin **93** F3
Doumé Cameroon **93** I4
Doumé *r.* Cameroon **93** I4
Doumen China **67** E4
Douna Mali **93** E2
Doupovské Hory *mts* Czech Rep. **37** F3
Dourada, Serra *mts* Brazil **150** B5
Dourados Brazil **151** A7
Dourados *r.* Brazil **151** A7
Dourbali Chad **94** B2
Dourdou *r.* France **39** E4
Dourdoura Chad **94** D2
Douro *r.* Port. **42** C2
also known as Duero (Spain)
Douro Internacional, Parque Natural do *nature res.* Port. **42** C2
Doushi China *see* **Gong'an**
Doushui Shuiku *resr* China **67** E3
Douve *r.* France **38** C2
Douz Tunisia **91** H2
Douze *r.* France **38** C5
Douziat Chad **88** C6
Dove *r.* U.K. **35** F5
Dove Brook Canada **125** J2
Dove Creek U.S.A. **137** H3
Dover U.K. **35** G6

▶**Dover** *DE* U.S.A. **131** F4
State capital of Delaware.

Dover *NH* U.S.A. **131** H2
Dover *NJ* U.S.A. **131** F3
Dover *OH* U.S.A. **130** C3
Dover, Strait of France/U.K. **38** D1
Dover-Foxcroft U.S.A. **128** F2
Dover Plains U.S.A. **131** G3
Dovey *r.* U.K. *see* **Dyfi**
Dovnsklint *cliff* Denmark **36** E1
Dovrefjell *mts* Norway **33** C3
Dovrefjell Nasjonalpark *nat. park* Norway **33** C3
Dow, Lake Botswana *see* **Xau, Lake**
Dowa Malawi **97** B8
Dowghā'ī Iran **81** D2
Dowi, Tanjung *pt* Indon. **58** B2
Dowlatābād Afgh. **81** F2
Dowlatābād *Fārs* Iran **80** B4
Dowlatābād *Khorāsan* Iran **80** D2
Dowlatābād *Khorāsan* Iran **81** E2
Dowl at Yār Afgh. **81** F3
Downey U.S.A. **136** C5
Downham Market U.K. **35** G5
Downieville U.S.A. **136** B2
Downpatrick U.K. **35** D4
Downs U.S.A. **132** B4
Downsville U.S.A. **131** F2
Dow Rūd Iran **80** B3
Dow Sar Iran **80** B3
Dowshī Afgh. **81** G3
Doyle U.S.A. **136** B1
Doyles Canada **125** J4
Doyrentsi Bulg. **46** D3
Dozdān *r.* Iran **80** D5
Dōzen *is* Japan **65** C5
Dozois, Réservoir Canada **124** E4
Drâa, Oued *watercourse* Morocco **90** C3
Drachten Neth. **36** C2
Dragalina Romania **46** E2
Dragan *l.* Sweden **32** D2
Drăgăneşti-Olt Romania **46** D2
Drăgăneşti-Vlaşca Romania **46** D2
Drăgăşani Romania **46** D2
Dragoman Bulg. **46** C3
Dragonada *i.* Greece **47** E7
Dragones Arg. **149** E5
Dragonisi *i.* Greece **47** D6
Dragon's Mouths *strait* Trin. and Tob./Venez. **147** F2
Dragør Denmark **33** D5
Dragsfjärd Fin. **33** F3
Draguignan France **39** G5
Drăguşeni Romania **46** E2
Drahichyn Belarus **29** C5
Drakensberg *mts* Lesotho/S. Africa **99** F6
Drakensberg *mts* S. Africa **99** F5
Drake Passage S. Atlantic Ocean **161** J9
Drakes Bay U.S.A. **136** A3
Drakulya *r.* Ukr. **46** F2
Drama Greece **46** D4
Drammen Norway **33** C4
Drang, Prêk *r.* Cambodia **61** D5
Drangedal Norway **33** C4
Drangme Chhu *r.* Bhutan **75** F4
Dranov, Lacul *l.* Romania **46** F2
Dranske Germany **37** F1
Draper, Mount U.S.A. **122** B3
Drapsaca Afgh. *see* **Kondūz**
Dras Jammu and Kashmir **74** B2
Drau *r.* Austria **37** G5
Drava *r.* Europe **31** I4
Dráva *r.* Hungary **44** G2
Dravinja *r.* Slovenia **44** E1
Dravograd Slovenia **44** E1
Drawa *r.* Poland **37** G2
Drawieński Park Narodowy *nat. park* Poland **37** G2
Drawno Poland **37** G2
Drawsko, Jezioro *l.* Poland **37** H2
Drayton Valley Canada **123** H4
Drebber Germany **36** D2
Dreistelzberge *hill* Germany **36** D3
Drenovets Bulg. **46** C3
Drepano, Akra *pt* Greece **47** C5
Dresden Canada **130** B2
Dresden Germany **37** F3
Dresden U.S.A. **128** A4
Dreux France **38** D2
Drevsjø Norway **33** D3
Drewryville U.S.A. **131** E5
Drezdenko Poland **37** G2
Driftwood U.S.A. **130** D3
Driggs U.S.A. **134** E4
Drin *r.* Albania **46** A3
Drina *r.* Bos.-Herz./Serb. and Mont. **44** G2
Drincea *r.* Romania **46** C2
Drini i Zi *r.* Albania **46** B3
Drinit, Gjiri i *b.* Albania **46** A4
Drino *r.* Albania **47** B4
Driscoll Island Antarctica **167** J1
Drissa Belarus *see* **Vyerkhnyadzvinsk**
Drniš Croatia **44** F3
Drobeta - Turnu Severin Romania **46** C2
Drochtersen Germany **36** D2
Drogheda Rep. of Ireland **35** C5
Drogichin Belarus *see* **Drahichyn**
Drogobych Ukr. *see* **Drohobych**
Drohiczyn Poland **37** K2
Drohobych Ukr. **31** J3
Droichead Átha Rep. of Ireland *see* **Drogheda**
Droitwich U.K. **35** E5
Dronne *r.* France **38** C4
Dronning Ingrid Land *reg.* Greenland **121** O3
Dronning Louise Land *reg.* Greenland **121** Q2
Dropt *r.* France **38** C4
Drosh Pak. **81** G3
Drosia Greece **47** C5
Drowning *r.* Canada **124** C3
Druk-Yul *country* Asia *see* **Bhutan**
Drumheller Canada **134** D2
Drummond, Lake U.S.A. **131** E5
Drummond Island Kiribati *see* **McKean**
Drummond Range *hills* Australia **111** F5
Drummondville Canada **125** F4
Drummore U.K. **35** D4
Drumnadrochit U.K. **34** D3
Druskieniki Lith. *see* **Druskininkai**
Druskininkai Lith. **31** K2
Druya Belarus **33** G5
Druzhina Rus. Fed. **27** O3
Drwęca *r.* Poland **37** I2
Dry *r.* Australia **110** C2
Dryanovo Bulg. **46** D3
Dryazhno Rus. Fed. **33** H4
Dryberry Lake Canada **132** C1
Dry Cimarron *r.* U.S.A. **132** A4
Dryden Canada **124** A3
Dryden U.S.A. **131** E2
Dry Fork *r.* U.S.A. **134** F4
Drygalski Ice Tongue Antarctica **167** H1
Drygalski Island Antarctica **167** F2
Dry Lake U.S.A. **137** E3
Dry Ridge U.S.A. **130** A4
Drysdale *r.* Australia **110** A2
Drysdale River National Park Australia **108** D3
Dry Tortugas *is* U.S.A. **129** C7
Drzewica Poland **37** J3
Dschang Cameroon **93** H4
Dua *r.* Dem. Rep. Congo **94** D4
Dūāb *r.* Iran **80** B3
Du'an China **66** D4
Duaringa Australia **111** G4
Duarte, Pico *mt.* Dom. Rep. **127** L8
Ḑubā Saudi Arabia **89** G3
Dubai U.A.E. **80** C5
Dubawnt *r.* Canada **123** L2
Dubawnt Lake Canada **123** K2
Dubayy U.A.E. *see* **Dubai**
Dubbagh, Jabal ad *mt.* Saudi Arabia **89** G3
Dubbo Australia **112** D4
Dube *r.* Liberia **92** D4
Dübendorf Switz. **39** H3

▶**Dublin** Rep. of Ireland **35** C5
Capital of the Republic of Ireland.

Dublin *GA* U.S.A. **129** C5
Dublin *VA* U.S.A. **130** C5
Dubna Rus. Fed. **28** F4
Dubnica nad Váhom Slovakia **37** I4
Dubno Ukr. **29** C6
Dubois U.S.A. **134** D3
Du Bois U.S.A. **130** D3
Dubovka Rus. Fed. **29** H6
Dübrar Pass Azer. **79** G2
Dubréka Guinea **92** B3
Dubris U.K. *see* **Dover**
Dubrovnik Croatia **44** G3
Dubrovytsya Ukr. **29** C6
Dubuque U.S.A. **132** D3
Duc de Gloucester, Îles du *is* Fr. Polynesia **165** I7
Ducey France **38** C2
Duchateau Entrance *sea chan.* P.N.G. **111** H1
Ducherow Germany **37** F2
Duchesne U.S.A. **137** G1

Duchesne r. U.S.A. 137 H1
Duchess Australia 111 D4
Duchess Canada 123 I5
Ducie Island Pitcairn Is 165 J7
Duck r. U.S.A. 128 B4
Duck Bay Canada 134 G1
Duck Creek r. Australia 108 B5
Duckwater U.S.A. 137 E2
Duckwater Peak U.S.A. 137 E2
Đuc Trong Vietnam 61 E6
Duda r. Col. 146 C4
Duderstadt Germany 36 E3
Dudhi India 75 D4
Dudinka Rus. Fed. 27 I3
Dudley U.K. 35 E5
Dudleyville U.S.A. 137 G5
Dudna r. India 72 C2
Duékoué Côte d'Ivoire 92 D4
Duen, Bukit vol. Indon. 58 C3
Dueré Brazil 150 B4
Duerna r. Spain 42 D1
Duero r. Spain 43 D2
also known as Douro (Portugal)
Duffer Peak U.S.A. 134 C4
Duffield U.S.A. 130 B5
Duff Islands Solomon Is 107 F2
Duffreboy, Lac l. Canada 125 G1
Dufftown U.K. 34 E3
Dufourspitze mt. Italy/Switz. 44 A2
Dufrost Canada 123 L5
Dugab Uzbek. 81 F2
Duga Resa Croatia 44 E2
Duga-Zapadnaya, Mys c. Rus. Fed. 27 O4
Dughdash mts Saudi Arabia 77 C5
Dughoba Uzbek. see Dugab
Dugi Otok i. Croatia 44 E2
Dugo Selo Croatia 44 F2
Düğüncübaşı Turkey 46 E4
Dugway U.S.A. 137 F1
Du He r. China 67 D1
Duhūn Tārsū mts Chad/Libya 88 C4
Duida-Marahuaca, Parque Nacional nat. park Venez. 147 E4
Duifken Point Australia 111 E2
Duisburg Germany 36 C3
Duitama Col. 146 C3
Dujiangyan China 66 B2
Dukān Dam Iraq 79 F4
Dukat mt. Serb. and Mont. 46 C3
Dukathole S. Africa 99 E6
Dukat i Ri Albania 47 A4
Duke Island U.S.A. 122 D4
Duke of Clarence atoll Tokelau see Nukunonu
Duke of York atoll Tokelau see Atafu
Duk Fadiat Sudan 96 A3
Duk Faiwil Sudan 96 A3
Dukhān Qatar 80 B5
Dukhnah Saudi Arabia 89 I3
Duki Rus. Fed. 64 C2
Duki r. Rus. Fed. 64 C2
Dukku Nigeria 93 H3
Dukou China see Panzhihua
Dūkštas Lith. 33 G5
Dulan China 70 I4
Dulawan Phil. see Datu Piang
Dulce r. Arg. 152 E2
Dulce r. Spain 43 E2
Dulce U.S.A. 135 F5
Dulce Nombre de Culmí Hond. 139 G5
Dulcinea Chile 152 C1
Dulgalakh r. Rus. Fed. 27 N3
Dŭlgopol Bulg. 46 E3
Dulhunty r. Australia 111 E1
Dulishi Hu salt l. China 75 D2
Dulit, Pegunungan mts Sarawak Malaysia 59 F2
Duliu Jiang r. China 66 D3
Dullabchara India 75 G4
Dülmen Germany 36 C3
Dulovo Bulg. 46 E3
Duluth U.S.A. 132 C2
Dūmā Syria 77 C3
Dumago Bone National Park Indon. 57 F5
Dumaguete Phil. 57 F4
Dumai Indon. 58 C2
Dumaran i. Phil. 57 F3
Dumaresq r. Australia 112 D3
Dumas AR U.S.A. 133 D5
Dumas TX U.S.A. 133 A5
Dumayr Syria 78 D4
Dumayr, Jabal mts Syria 77 C3
Dumbarton U.K. 34 D4
Dumbéa New Caledonia 107 F4
Dumbo Cameroon 93 H4
Dumbrăveni Romania 46 E2
Dumbrăviţa Romania 46 D2
Dumdum i. Indon. 59 D2
Dumfries U.K. 34 E4
Dumka India 75 E4
Dummagudem India 72 D2
Dummerstorf Germany 37 F2
Dumoine r. Canada 124 E4
Dumont d'Urville research station Antarctica 167 G2
Dumont d'Urville Sea Antarctica 167 G2
Dumraon India 75 E4
Dumyāṭ Egypt 89 F2
Dumyāṭ governorate Egypt 78 B5
Duna r. Hungary 37 G4 see Danube
Dünaburg Latvia see Daugavpils
Dunaföldvár Hungary 37 I5
Dunaj r. Slovakia 37 G4 see Danube
Dunajec r. Poland 37 J3
Dunajská Streda Slovakia 37 H5
Dunakeszi Hungary 37 I5
Dunany Point Rep. of Ireland 35 C5
Dunărea r. Romania 46 B2 see Danube
Dunaújváros Hungary 37 I5
Dunav r. Bulg./Croatia/Serb. and Mont. 46 B2 see Danube
Dunavtsi Bulg. 46 C3
Dunay r. Ukr. 46 B2 see Danube
Dunay, Ostrova is Rus. Fed. 27 M2
Dunback N.Z. 113 B4
Dunbar Australia 111 E3
Dunbar U.S.A. 130 D4
Dunbeath U.K. 34 E2
Duncan AZ U.S.A. 135 E6
Duncan OK U.S.A. 133 B5
Duncan, Cape Canada 124 D2
Duncan Lake Canada 123 H2
Duncannon U.S.A. 131 E3
Duncan Passage India 73 G4
Duncansby Head U.K. 34 E2
Dundaga Latvia 33 F4
Dundalk Rep. of Ireland 35 C4
Dundalk U.S.A. 131 E4
Dundalk Bay Rep. of Ireland 35 C5
Dundas Canada 130 D2
Dundas Greenland 121 M2
Dundas, Lake salt flat Australia 109 C8
Dundas Island Canada 122 D4
Dundas Strait Australia 110 B1
Dún Dealgan Rep. of Ireland see Dundalk
Dundee S. Africa 99 F6
Dundee U.K. 34 E3
Dundee U.S.A. 131 E2
Dundrum Bay U.K. 35 D4
Dundwa Range mts India/Nepal 75 D4
Dune, Lac l. Canada 125 F1
Dunedin N.Z. 113 B4
Dunfermline U.K. 34 E3
Dungannon U.K. 35 C4
Dún Garbhán Rep. of Ireland see Dungarvan
Dungargarh India 74 B3
Dungarpur India 74 B5
Dungarvan Rep. of Ireland 35 C5
Dung Co l. China 75 F3
Dungeness hd U.K. 35 G6
Dungeness, Punta pt Arg. 153 C8
Dungu Dem. Rep. Congo 94 F4
Dungun Malaysia 58 C1
Dungunab Sudan 68 B4
Dunhou China see Ji'an
Dunhua China 64 B4
Dunhuang China 70 H3
Dunkeld Australia 111 G5
Dunkeld U.K. 34 E3
Dunkirk France 38 E1
Dunkirk U.S.A. 130 D2
Dunkwa Ghana 93 E4
Dún Laoghaire Rep. of Ireland 35 C5
Dunlap U.S.A. 128 B5
Dunluce tourist site U.K. 34 C4
Dunmanway Rep. of Ireland 35 B6
Dunmarra Australia 110 C3
Dunmore PA U.S.A. 131 F3
Dunmore WV U.S.A. 130 D4
Dunmore Town Bahamas 129 D7
Dunn U.S.A. 128 D5
Dunnet Head U.K. 34 E2
Dunnigan U.S.A. 136 B2
Dunning U.S.A. 132 A3
Dunnville Canada 130 D2
Dunolly Australia 112 B5
Duns U.K. 34 E4
Dunsmuir U.S.A. 134 B4
Dunstan Mountains N.Z. 113 B4
Duntroon N.Z. 113 B4
Dunvegan U.K. 34 C3
Dunvegan Lake Canada 123 J2
Dunyapur Pak. 81 G4
Duobukur r. China 64 A2
Dupang Ling mts China 67 D3
Duperré Alg. see Aïn Defla
Dupnitsa Bulg. 46 C3
Dupree U.S.A. 132 A2
Duque de Bragança Angola see Calandula
Duque de York, Isla i. Chile 153 B7
Dura r. Eth. 96 C2
Durack r. Australia 110 A2
Durack Range hills Australia 108 D4
Dura Europos Syria see Aş Şālihīyah
Durağan Turkey 78 C2
Durance r. France 39 F5
Durand U.S.A. 130 B2
Duranes hill Spain 42 D3
Durango Mex. 126 F7
Durango state Mex. 133 A7
Durango Spain 43 E1
Durango U.S.A. 135 F5
Durankulak Bulg. 46 F3
Durant MS U.S.A. 133 D5
Durant OK U.S.A. 133 B5
Duratón r. Spain 42 D2
Durazno Arg. 152 C2
Durazno Uruguay 152 F3
Durazzo Albania see Durrës
Durban S. Africa 99 F6
Durban-Corbières France 39 E5
Durbin U.S.A. 130 D4
Durbuy Belgium 39 F1
Dúrcal Spain 42 E4
Đurđevac Croatia 44 F1
Durdura, Raas pt Somalia 96 F2
Düren Germany 36 C3
Düren Iran 80 D3
Duren, Kūh-e mt. Iran 80 D3
Durg India 75 D5
Durgapur Bangl. 75 F4
Durgapur India 75 E5
Durham Canada 130 C1
Durham U.K. 35 F4
Durham CA U.S.A. 136 B2
Durham NC U.S.A. 128 D5
Durham NH U.S.A. 131 H2
Durham Downs Australia 111 E5
Durhi well Eth. 96 D3
Duri Indon. 58 C2
Durlas Rep. of Ireland see Thurles
Durleşti Moldova 29 D7
Durmitor mt. Serb. and Mont. 46 A3
Durmitor nat. park Serb. and Mont. 46 A3
Durness U.K. 34 D2
Durocortorum France see Reims
Durostorum Bulg. see Silistra
Durovernum U.K. see Canterbury
Durrës Albania 46 A4
Dursey Island Rep. of Ireland 35 A6
Dursunbey Turkey 78 B3
Durtal France 38 C3
Duru r. Dem. Rep. Congo 94 F4
Dūruḩ Iran 81 E3
Durukhsi Somalia 96 E2
Durusu Gölü l. Turkey 46 F4
Durūz, Jabal ad mt. Syria 77 C3
D'Urville, Tanjung pt Indon. 57 I6
D'Urville Island N.Z. 113 C3
Durzab Afgh. 81 F3
Dushak Turkm. 81 D2
Dushan China 66 C3

▶Dushanbe Tajik. 81 G2
Capital of Tajikistan.

Dushore U.S.A. 131 E3
Düsseldorf Germany 36 C3
Dusti Tajik. 81 G2
Dustlik Uzbek. 81 G1
Dusty U.S.A. 134 C3
Dutch East Indies country Asia see Indonesia
Dutch Guiana country S. America see Suriname
Dutch Mountain U.S.A. 137 F1
Dutch West Indies terr. West Indies see Netherlands Antilles
Dutsan-Wai Nigeria 93 H3
Dutse Nigeria 93 H3
Dutsin-Ma Nigeria 93 G2
Dutton r. Australia 111 E4
Dutton Canada 130 C2
Dutton, Mount U.S.A. 137 F2
Duval Canada 134 F2
Duved Sweden 32 D3
Duvert, Lac l. Canada 125 G1
Duvno Bos.-Herz. see Tomislavgrad
Duweihin well Saudi Arabia 80 B5
Duweihin, Khor b. Saudi Arabia/U.A.E. 80 B5
Duwin Iraq 79 F3
Duyinzeik Myanmar 60 B4
Duyun China 66 C3
Duzab Pak. 81 E5
Düzce Turkey 78 B2
Duzdab Iran see Zāhedān
Dve Mogili Bulg. 46 D3
Dvinsk Latvia see Daugavpils
Dvinskaya Guba g. Rus. Fed. 28 F2
Dvor Croatia 44 F2
Dwangwa Malawi 97 B8
Dwarka India 74 A5
Dwarsberg S. Africa 99 E5
Dwellingup Australia 109 B8
Dwingelderveld, Nationaal Park nat. park Neth. 36 C2
Dyanev Turkm. 81 E2
Dyankovo Bulg. 46 E3
Dyat'kovo Rus. Fed. 29 E5
Dyce U.K. 34 E3
Dyer, Cape Canada 121 M3
Dyersburg U.S.A. 128 A4
Dyfi r. U.K. 35 E5
Dyje r. Austria/Czech Rep. 37 H4

▶Dykh-Tau, Gora mt. Rus. Fed. 29 G8
2nd highest mountain in Europe.
europe 22–23

Dylewska Góra hill Poland 37 I2
Dynevor Downs Australia 111 F6
Dyrrhachium Albania see Durrës
Dysart Australia 111 G4
Dytiki Ellas admin. reg. Greece 47 B5
Dytiki Makedonia admin. reg. Greece 47 B4
Dyuendyu Rus. Fed. 27 N3
Dyulino Bulg. 46 E3
Dyurtyuli Rus. Fed. 28 J5
Dyviziya Ukr. 46 F2
Dzamīn Üüd Mongolia 63 I3
Dzanga-Ndoki, Parc National de nat. park Cameroon 94 B4

▶Dzaoudzi Mayotte 97 E8
Capital of Mayotte.

Dzaudzhikau Rus. Fed. see Vladikavkaz
Dzavhan Gol r. Mongolia 70 H2
Džbán mts Czech Rep. 37 F3
Dzerzhinsk Belarus see Dzyarzhynsk
Dzerzhinsk Rus. Fed. 28 G4
Dzhagdy, Khrebet mts Rus. Fed. 27 M4
Dzhaki-Unakhta Yakbyyana, Khrebet mts Rus. Fed. 64 C2
Dzhalalabad Azer. see Cälilabad
Dzhalal-Abad Kyrg. see Jalal-Abad
Dzhaltyr Kazakh. see Zhaltyr
Dzhambeyty Kazakh. see Zhympity
Dzhambul Kazakh. see Taraz
Dzhangala Kazakh. 29 I6
Dzhangel'dy Uzbek. 81 E1
Dzhankel'dy Uzbek. see Dzhangel'dy
Dzhankoy Ukr. 29 E7
Dzhanybek Kazakh. 29 H6
Dzharkent Kazakh. see Zharkent
Dzharkurgan Uzbek. 81 F2
Dzhebel Turkm. 80 C2
Dzhelondi Tajik. see Dzhilandy
Dzhetygara Kazakh. see Zhitikara
Dzhezkazgan Kazakh. see Zhezkazgan
Dzhigirbent Turkm. 81 E1
Dzhilandy Tajik. 81 H2
Dzhingil'dy Uzbek. see Dzhangel'dy
Dzhirgatal' Tajik. see Jirgatol
Dzhizak Uzbek. 81 F1
Dzhizak Oblast admin. div. Uzbek. see Dzhizakskaya Oblast'
Dzhizakskaya Oblast' admin. div. Uzbek. 81 F1
Dzhokhar Ghala Rus. Fed. see Groznyy
Dzhubga Rus. Fed. 79 D1
Dzhu-Dzhu-Klu Turkm. 81 E2
Dzhugdzhur, Khrebet mts Rus. Fed. 27 N4
Dzhul'fa Azer. see Culfa
Dzhuma Uzbek. 81 F2
Dzhungarskiy Alatau, Khrebet mts China/Kazakh. 70 E3
Dzhusaly Kazakh. 70 B2
Działdowo Poland 37 J2
Dzierżoniów Poland 37 H3
Dzioua Alg. 91 G2
Dzodze Ghana 93 F4
Dzungarian Basin China see Junggar Pendi
Dzungarian Gate pass China/Kazakh. 70 F2
Dzuunmod Mongolia 63 H2
Dzyarzhynsk Belarus 29 C5

E

Eabamet Lake Canada 124 C3
Eads U.S.A. 132 A4
Eagar U.S.A. 137 H4
Eagle r. Canada 125 J2
Eagle U.S.A. 122 A1
Eagle Cap mt. U.S.A. 134 C3
Eagle Crags mt. U.S.A. 136 D4
Eagle Creek r. Canada 123 J4
Eagle Lake CA U.S.A. 136 B1
Eagle Lake ME U.S.A. 128 F2
Eagle Mountain U.S.A. 132 D2
Eagle Pass U.S.A. 133 A6
Eagle Peak U.S.A. 135 F7
Eagle Plain Canada 120 F3
Eagle Rock U.S.A. 130 D5
Eaglesham Canada 122 G4
Eagle Village U.S.A. 122 A1
Eap i. Micronesia see Yap
Earaheedy Australia 109 C6
Ear Falls Canada 124 A3
Earlimart U.S.A. 136 C4
Earn r. U.K. 34 E3
Earp U.S.A. 137 E4
Earth U.S.A. 133 A5
East Alligator r. Australia 110 C2
East Antarctica reg. Antarctica 167 F1
East Ararat U.S.A. 131 F3
East Aurora U.S.A. 130 D2
East Baines r. Australia 110 B2
East Bay inlet U.S.A. 129 B6
East Bengal country Asia see Bangladesh
Eastbourne U.K. 35 G6
East Brady U.S.A. 130 D3
East Branch U.S.A. 131 F3
East Cape N.Z. 113 D2
East Cape Rus. Fed. see Dezhneva, Mys
East Carbon City U.S.A. 137 G2
East Caroline Basin sea feature N. Pacific Ocean 164 D5
East China Sea N. Pacific Ocean 63 L5
East Coast Bays N.Z. 113 C2
East Dereham U.K. 35 G5
Eastend Canada 123 I5

▶Easter Island S. Pacific Ocean 165 K7
Part of Chile.

Eastern admin. reg. Ghana 93 E4
Eastern prov. Kenya 96 C5
Eastern prov. Sierra Leone 92 C3
Eastern prov. Zambia 97 A8
Eastern Cape prov. S. Africa 99 E6
Eastern Desert Egypt 89 G3
Eastern Equatoria state Sudan 96 B3
Eastern Ghats mts India 72 C4

▶Eastern Island U.S.A. 164 G4
Most northerly point of Oceania.

Eastern Nara canal Pak. 81 G5
Eastern Samoa terr. S. Pacific Ocean see American Samoa
Eastern Sayan Mountains Rus. Fed. see Vostochnyy Sayan
Eastern Taurus plat. Turkey see Güneydoğu Toroslar
Eastern Transvaal prov. S. Africa see Mpumalanga
Easterville Canada 123 L4
East Falkland i. Falkland Is 153 F8
East Frisian Islands Germany 36 C2
East Grand Forks U.S.A. 132 B2
East Hampton U.S.A. 131 G3
East Hartford U.S.A. 131 G3
East Indiaman Ridge sea feature Indian Ocean 162 N7
East Island P.N.G. 111 H1
East Jamaica U.S.A. 131 G2
East Kilbride U.K. 34 D4
East Lamma Channel Hong Kong China 67 [inset]
Eastland U.S.A. 133 B5
East Lansing U.S.A. 130 A2
Eastleigh U.K. 35 F6
East Linton U.K. 34 E4
East Liverpool U.S.A. 130 C3
East London S. Africa 99 E7
Eastmain Canada 124 E2
Eastmain r. Canada 125 E2
East Mariana Basin sea feature N. Pacific Ocean 164 E5
East Middlebury U.S.A. 131 G2
East Millinocket U.S.A. 128 F2
East Naples U.S.A. 129 C7
Easton CA U.S.A. 136 C3
Easton MD U.S.A. 131 E4
Easton PA U.S.A. 131 F3
East Pacific Rise sea feature N. Pacific Ocean 165 K4
East Pakistan country Asia see Bangladesh
East Park Reservoir U.S.A. 136 A2
East Point Canada 125 I4
East Range mts U.S.A. 136 D1
East Retford U.K. see Retford
East Ridge U.S.A. 128 B5
East St Louis U.S.A. 127 H4
East Sea N. Pacific Ocean see Japan, Sea of
East Shoal Lake Canada 123 L5
East Siberian Sea Rus. Fed. 27 O2
East Side Canal r. U.S.A. 136 C4
East Tavaputs Plateau U.S.A. 137 H2
▶East Timor country Asia 108 D2
asia 52–53, 82
East Tons r. India 75 E4
East Verde r. U.S.A. 137 G4
East Walker r. U.S.A. 136 C2
East York Canada 130 D2
Eaton CO U.S.A. 134 F4
Eaton OH U.S.A. 130 A4
Eatonia Canada 123 I5
Eaton Rapids U.S.A. 130 A2
Eatonton U.S.A. 129 C5
Eau Claire U.S.A. 132 D2
Eauripik atoll Micronesia 57 J4
Eauripik Rise - New Guinea Rise sea feature N. Pacific Ocean 164 D5
Eaurypyg atoll Micronesia see Eauripik
Eauze France 38 D5
Ebagoola Australia 111 E2
Eban Nigeria 93 G3
Ebano Mex. 126 G7
Ebebiyin Equat. Guinea 93 H5
Ebeltoft Denmark 33 C4
Ebenerde Namibia 98 C5
Ebensburg U.S.A. 130 D3
Ebensee Austria 37 F5
Eberswalde-Finow Germany 37 F2
Ebetsu Japan 64 E4
Ebian China 66 B2
Ebi Nor salt l. China see Ebinur Hu
Ebinur Hu salt l. China 70 F3
Ebla tourist site Syria 77 C2
Ebnat-Kappel Switz. 39 H3
Ebola r. Dem. Rep. Congo 94 D4
Ebolowa Cameroon 93 H5
Ebony Namibia 98 B4
Ebonyi state Nigeria 93 H4
Ebre r. Spain see Ebro
Ebro r. Spain 43 G2
Ebro, Embalse del resr Spain 42 E1
Eburacum U.K. see York
Ebusus i. Spain see Ibiza
Ecbatana Iran see Hamadān
Eccles U.S.A. 130 C5
Eceabat Turkey 47 E4
Echarri-Aranaz Spain 43 E1
Ech Chélif Alg. 91 F1
Ech Chertia, Sebkhet salt pan Tunisia 45 C7
Echeng China see Ezhou
Echinos Greece 46 D4
Echmiadzin Armenia see Ejmiatsin
Echo Bay N.W.T. Canada 120 H3
Echo Bay N.W.T. Canada 123 G1
Echo Cliffs esc. U.S.A. 137 G3
Echoing r. Canada 123 M4
Echternach Lux. 39 G2
Echuca Australia 112 C5
Écija Spain 42 D4
Ečka Serb. and Mont. 46 B2
Eckernförde Germany 36 D1
Eckerö Fin. 33 E3
Eckman U.S.A. 130 C5
Eclipse Sound sea chan. Canada 121 K2
Écrins, Parc National des nat. park France 39 G4
▶Ecuador country S. America 146 B5
southamerica 144–145, 154
Ed Eritrea 89 I6
Ed Sweden 33 C4
Eday i. U.K. 34 E2
Ed Da'ein Sudan 94 E2
Ed Dair, Jebel mt. Sudan 89 F6
Ed Damazin Sudan 96 B2
Ed Damer Sudan 89 G5
Ed Debba Sudan 89 F5
Eddeki well Chad 88 C5
Eddies Cove Canada 125 J3
Ed Dueim Sudan 89 G6
Eddystone Point Australia 112 D6
Eddyville U.S.A. 128 A4
Ede Neth. 36 B2
Edéa Cameroon 93 H5
Edehon Lake Canada 123 L2
Edéia Brazil 149 H4
Eden Australia 112 D5
Eden r. U.K. 34 E4
Eden NC U.S.A. 130 D5
Eden TX U.S.A. 133 B6
Edenburg S. Africa 98 E6
Edencale N.Z. 113 B4
Edenderry Rep. of Ireland 35 C5
Edenhope Australia 112 B5
Edenton U.S.A. 128 D4
Eder r. Germany 36 D3
Edessa Greece 46 C4
Edessa Turkey see Şanlıurfa
Edevik Sweden 32 D3
Edfu Egypt see Idfū
Edgar Ranges hills Australia 108 C4
Edgartown U.S.A. 131 H3
Edgecumbe Island Solomon Is see Utupua
Edgefield U.S.A. 129 C5
Edge Island Svalbard see Edgeøya
Edgeøya i. Svalbard 26 C2
Edgerton Canada 123 I4
Edgerton U.S.A. 130 E5
Edgewood U.S.A. 131 E4
Édhessa Greece see Edessa
Édîkel well Niger 93 G1
Edina U.S.A. 132 C3
Edinboro U.S.A. 130 C3
Edinburg TX U.S.A. 133 B7
Edinburg VA U.S.A. 130 D4

▶Edinburgh U.K. 34 E4
Capital of Scotland.

Edincik Turkey 47 E4
Edingeni Malawi 97 B8
Edirne Turkey 78 A2
Edirne prov. Turkey 46 E4
Edisto r. U.S.A. 129 C5
Edith, Mount U.S.A. 134 E3
Edithburgh Australia 112 A4
Edjeleh Libya 88 A3
Édjérir watercourse Mali 93 F1
Edjudina Australia 109 C7
Edmond U.S.A. 133 B5
Edmonds U.S.A. 134 B3

▶Edmonton Canada 123 H4
Provincial capital of Alberta.

Edmund Lake Canada 123 M4
Edmundston Canada 125 G4
Edna U.S.A. 133 B6
Edo Japan see Tōkyō
Edo state Nigeria 93 G4
Edolo Italy 44 C1
Edom reg. Israel/Jordan 77 B4
Edremit Turkey 78 A3
Edremit Körfezi b. Turkey 78 A3
Edsbro Sweden 33 E4
Edsbyn Sweden 33 D3
Edsele Sweden 32 E3
Edson Canada 123 G4
Eduardo Castex Arg. 152 D3
Eduni, Mount Canada 122 D1
Edward r. Australia 111 E2
Edward, Lake Dem. Rep. Congo/Uganda 94 F5
Edward, Mount Antarctica 167 L1
Edwardesabad Pak. see Bannu
Edwards U.S.A. 131 F1
Edwards Plateau U.S.A. 133 A6
Edwardsville U.S.A. 132 D4
Edward VII Peninsula Antarctica 167 I1
Edziza, Mount Canada 122 D3
Edzo Canada see Rae-Edzo
Eel r. U.S.A. 136 A1
Eel, South Fork r. U.S.A. 136 A1
Eesti country Europe see Estonia
Éfaté i. Vanuatu 107 F3
Efes tourist site Turkey see Ephesus
Effingham U.S.A. 128 A4
Efsus Turkey see Afşin
Ega r. Spain 43 F1
Egadi, Isole is Sicily Italy 45 C5
Egadi Islands Sicily Italy see Egadi, Isole
Egan Range mts U.S.A. 137 E2
Egbe Nigeria 93 G3
Egedesminde Greenland see Aasiaat
Eger r. Germany 36 F3
Eger Hungary 37 J5
Egersund Norway 33 B4
Egerton, Mount Australia 109 B6
Eggenfelden Germany 37 F4
Egg Harbor City U.S.A. 131 F4
Egg Lake Canada 123 J4
Egilsstaðir Iceland 32 [inset]
Eğin Turkey see Kemaliye
Eginbah Australia 108 B5
Eğirdir Turkey 78 B3
Eğirdir Gölü l. Turkey 78 B3
Égletons France 38 E4
Eglinton Island Canada 121 H2
Eglisau Switz. 39 H3
Egmont, Cape N.Z. 113 C2
Egmont, Mount vol. N.Z. see Taranaki, Mount
Egmont National Park N.Z. 113 C2
Egua Col. 146 E3
Éguas r. Brazil 150 C5
Egvekinot Rus. Fed. 27 S3

▶Egypt country Africa 89 F2
2nd most populous country in Africa.
africa 86–87, 100

Ehcel well Mali see Agous-n-Ehsel
Ehen Hudag China 70 J4
Ehingen (Donau) Germany 36 D4
Ehrenberg U.S.A. 137 E5
Ehrenberg Range hills Australia 110 B4
Eibar Spain 43 E1
Eibergen Neth. 36 C2
Eichstätt Germany 36 E4
Eide Norway 32 B3
Eider r. Germany 36 D1
Eidfjord Norway 33 B3
Eiði Faroe Is 34 [inset]
Eidsvåg Norway 32 C3
Eidsvold Australia 111 G5
Eidsvoll Norway 33 C3
Eifel hills Germany 36 C3
Eigg i. U.K. 34 C3
Eight Degree Channel India/Maldives 72 B5
Eights Coast Antarctica 167 K2
Eighty Mile Beach Australia 108 C4
Eilat Israel 77 B5
Eildon, Lake Australia 112 C5
Eileen Lake Canada 123 J2
Eilenburg Germany 37 F3
Eilerts de Haan Gebergte mts Suriname 147 G4
Einasleigh Australia 111 F3
Einasleigh r. Australia 111 E3
Einbeck Germany 36 D3
Eindhoven Neth. 36 B3
Einsiedeln Switz. 39 H3
Éire country Europe see Ireland, Republic of
Eirik Ridge sea feature N. Atlantic Ocean 160 L2
Eiriosgaigh i. U.K. see Eriskay
Eiru r. Brazil 146 D6
Eirunepé Brazil 146 D6
Eisberg hill Germany 36 D3
Eiseb watercourse Namibia 98 D3
Eisenach Germany 36 E3
Eisenerz Austria 37 G5
Eisenerzer Alpen mts Austria 37 G5
Eisenhüttenstadt Germany 37 G2
Eisenstadt Austria 37 H5
Eišiškės Lith. 33 G5
Eisleben Lutherstadt Germany 36 E3
Eitape P.N.G. see Aitape
Eivissa Spain see Ibiza
Eivissa i. Spain see Ibiza
Ejea de los Caballeros Spain 43 F1
Ejeda Madag. 99 [inset] J5
Ejin Qi China see Dalain Hob
Ej Jill, Sebkhet salt flat Mauritania 90 B5
Ejmiadzin Armenia see Ejmiatsin
Ejmiatsin Armenia 79 F2
Ejura Ghana 93 E4
Ekalaka U.S.A. 134 F3
Ekang Nigeria 93 H4
Ékata Gabon 94 B4
Ekenäs Fin. 33 F4
Ekenäs Sweden 33 D4
Ekenäs skärgårds Nationalpark nat. park Fin. 33 F4
Ekerem Turkm. see Okarem
Eket Nigeria 93 G4
Eketahuna N.Z. 113 C3
Ekhinos Greece see Echinos
Ekhmîm Egypt see Akhmīm
Ekibastuz Kazakh. 26 H4
Ekimchan Rus. Fed. 64 C1
Ekiti state Nigeria 93 G4
Ekoli Dem. Rep. Congo 94 E5
Ekonda Rus. Fed. 27 K3
Ekondo Titi Cameroon 93 H4
Ekostrovskaya Imandra, Ozero l. Rus. Fed. 32 I2
Ekouamou Congo 94 C4
Ekpoma Nigeria 93 G4
Eksere Turkey see Gündoğmuş
Ekshärad Sweden 33 D3
Eksjö Sweden 33 D4
Ekstenfontein S. Africa 98 C6
Ekström Ice Shelf Antarctica 167 B2
Ekträsk Sweden 32 E2
Ekwan r. Canada 124 D2
El Aaiún W. Sahara see Laâyoune
Elafonisos i. Greece 47 C6
Elafonisou, Steno sea chan. Greece 47 C6
Elaia, Cape Cyprus 77 B2
El Aladia well Sudan 89 G5
El 'Alamein Egypt see Al 'Alamayn
El Alamo Mex. 135 C7
El Alia Alg. 91 G2
El Alia Tunisia 45 B6
El Alto Peru 146 A6
Elands r. S. Africa 99 F5
El Aouinet Alg. 45 A7
El Arahal Spain 42 D4
El Araïche Morocco see Larache
El Aricha Alg. 91 E2
Elasa i. Greece 47 E7
El Ashmûnein Egypt see Al Ashmūnayn
El Asnam Alg. see Ech Chélif
Elassona Greece 47 C5
El Astillero Spain 42 E1
El 'Atf reg. W. Sahara 90 B5
Eleti mt. Greece 47 B5
Elato atoll Micronesia 57 K4
Elazığ Turkey 79 D3
Elba, Isola d' i. Italy 44 C3
El Bahret el Ahmar governorate Egypt see Al Baḩr al Aḩmar
El'ban Rus. Fed. 64 D2
El Banco Col. 146 C2
El Bânoûn well Mauritania 92 D1
El Barco de Ávila Spain 42 D2
El Barco de Valdeorras Spain see O Barco
El Barreal salt l. Mex. 135 F7
El Baun Sudan 96 B2
Elbasan Albania 46 B4
Elbaşı Turkey 78 C3
El Bauga Sudan 89 G5
El Baúl Venez. 146 D2
El Bayadh Alg. 91 F1
Elbe r. Germany 37 D2
also known as Labe (Czech Republic)
'Elb el Fçâl des. Mauritania 92 C1
El Beqa'a valley Lebanon 77 C2
El Berié well Mauritania 92 C1
Elberta U.S.A. 137 G2
Elberton U.S.A. 129 C5
El Beru Hagia Somalia 96 D4
Elbeuf France 38 D2
Elbeyli Turkey 77 C1
El Beyyed well Mauritania 90 C5
El Beyyed well Mauritania 92 C1
Elbing Poland see Elbląg
Elbistan Turkey 78 D3
Elbląg Poland 37 I1
Elbląski, Kanał canal Poland 37 I1
El Bolsón Arg. 153 C5
El Borma Tunisia 91 H3
El Boulaïda Alg. see Blida
Elbow Lake U.S.A. 132 B2

▶Elbrus mt. Rus. Fed. 29 G8
Highest mountain in Europe.
europe 22–23

El Buheyrat state Sudan 94 F3
El Buitre mt. Spain 43 F3
El Burgo de Osma Spain 42 E2
Elburz Mountains Iran 80 B2
El Cain Arg. 153 C5
El Cajon U.S.A. 136 D5
El Callao Venez. 147 F3
El Campo U.S.A. 133 B6
El Canton Venez. 146 D3
El Capulin r. Mex. 133 A7
El Carmelo Venez. 146 D2
El Carmen Beni Bol. 149 E3
El Carmen Santa Cruz Bol. 149 F4
El Carmen Ecuador 146 B5
El Caroche mt. Spain 43 F3
El Centro U.S.A. 137 E5
El Cerro Bol. 149 E4
El Chaparro Venez. 147 E2
Elche-Elx Spain 43 F3
El Chichonal vol. Mex. 138 F5
El Chilicote Mex. 135 F7
Elcho Island Australia 110 C1
El Coca Ecuador see Puerto Francisco de Orellana
El Cocuy, Parque Nacional nat. park Col. 146 C3
El Collado hill Spain 42 D3
El Contador, Puerto de pass Spain 43 E4
El Cuy Arg. 152 C4
Elda Spain 43 F3
Elde r. Germany 36 E2
El Debb well Eth. 96 D3
El Desemboque Mex. 135 D7
El Diamante Mex. 133 A6
El Difícil Col. 146 C2
El'dikan Rus. Fed. 27 N3
El Diviso Col. 146 B4
El Djezair Alg. see Algiers
El Doctor Mex. 135 D7
Eldon U.S.A. 132 C4
Eldorado Arg. 152 G1
El Dorado Col. 146 D4
El Dorado AR U.S.A. 133 C5
El Dorado KS U.S.A. 132 B4
Eldorado U.S.A. 133 A6
El Dorado Venez. 147 F3
Eldorado Mountains U.S.A. 137 E4
Eldoret Kenya 96 B4
Eldridge, Mount U.S.A. 122 A1
Elea, Cape Cyprus see Elaia, Cape
Eleanor U.S.A. 130 C4
Electric Peak U.S.A. 134 E3
El Eglab plat. Alg. 90 D4
El 'Ein well Sudan 89 F5
Eleja Latvia 33 F4
El Ejido Spain 43 E4
Elek Hungary 37 J5
Elek r. Rus. Fed. see Ilek
Elektrėnai Lith. 33 G5
Elele Nigeria 93 G4

▶Elemi Triangle terr. Africa 96 B3
Disputed territory (Ethiopia/Kenya/Sudan) administered by Kenya.

Elena Bulg. 46 D3
El Encanto Col. 146 C5
El Encinal Mex. 137 D5
Elephanta Caves tourist site India 72 B2
Elephant Butte Reservoir U.S.A. 135 F6
Elephant Island Antarctica 167 A2
Eleşkirt Turkey 79 E3
Eleuthera i. Bahamas 129 D7

Eleven Point r. U.S.A. 133 D4
El Fahs Tunisia 45 B6
El Faiyûm Egypt see Al Fayyūm
El Faiyûm governorate Egypt see Al Fayyūm
El Faouar Tunisia 91 H2
El Fasher Sudan 88 E6
El Ferrol Spain see Ferrol
El Ferrol del Caudillo Spain see Ferrol
El Fud Eth. 96 D3
El Fuerte Mex. 126 E6
El Fula Sudan 94 F2
Elgå Norway 33 C3
Elgal waterhole Kenya 96 C4
El Gçaïb well Mali 90 D5
El Geili Sudan 89 G6
El Geneina Sudan 88 D6
El Geteina Sudan 89 G6
El Gezira state Sudan 89 G6
El Ghaba Sudan 89 F5
El Ghalla, Wadi watercourse Sudan 94 E2
El Ghallâouîya well Mauritania 90 C5
El Gheddiya Mauritania 92 C1
El Ghor plain Jordan/West Bank see Al Ghawr
Elgin U.K. 34 E3
Elgin IL U.S.A. 132 D3
Elgin NV U.S.A. 137 E3
Elgin OR U.S.A. 134 C3
Elgin TX U.S.A. 133 B6
Elgin Down Australia 111 F4
El'ginskiy Rus. Fed. 27 O3
El Gir well Sudan 89 F5
El Giza Egypt see Giza
El Giza governorate Egypt see Al Jīzah
El Goléa Alg. 91 F3
El Golfo de Santa Clara Mex. 135 D7
Elgon, Mount Uganda 96 B4
Elgoras, Gora hill Rus. Fed. 32 H1
El Guante Mex. 135 F7
El Guetar Tunisia 91 H2
El Gueṭṭâra well Mali 90 E5
El Hamma Tunisia 91 H2
El Ḥammâmi reg. Mauritania 90 C5
El Hank reg. Alg. 90 D4
El Ḥank esc. Mali/Mauritania 90 C5
El Haouaria Tunisia 45 C6
El Hawata Sudan 89 G6
El Hierro i. Canary Is 90 A4
El Hilla Sudan 89 E6
El Homr Alg. 91 F3
El Homra Sudan 89 F6
El Houeïtat well Mauritania 92 C1
El Huecu Arg. 152 C4
Eli well Niger 93 H2
Eliase Indon. 108 E2
Elias Garcia Angola 95 D7
Elichpur India see Achalpur
Elila Dem. Rep. Congo 94 E5
Elila r. Dem. Rep. Congo 94 E5
Elim U.S.A. 120 C3
Elimberrum France see Auch
Elin Pelin Bulg. 46 C3
Eliozondo Spain 43 F1
Elipa Dem. Rep. Congo 94 E5
Élisabetha Dem. Rep. Congo 94 D4
Élisabethville Dem. Rep. Congo see Lubumbashi
Eliseu Martins Brazil 150 D4
El Iskandarîya Egypt see Alexandria
El Iskandarîya governorate Egypt see Al Iskanarīyah
Elista Rus. Fed. 29 H7
Elizabeth U.S.A. 131 F3
Elizabeth, Mount Australia 108 D4
Elizabeth City U.S.A. 128 D4
Elizabeth Creek r. Australia 110 D3
Elizabeth Islands U.S.A. 131 H3
Elizabeth Reef Australia 107 E4
Elizabethtown KY U.S.A. 128 B4
Elizabethtown NC U.S.A. 129 D5
Elizabethtown NY U.S.A. 131 G1
Elizabethville U.S.A. 131 E3
Elizavety, Mys c. Rus. Fed. 27 O4
El Jadida Morocco 90 C2
El Jebelein Sudan 89 G6
El Jem Tunisia 91 H2
Elk r. Canada 123 H5
Ełk Poland 37 K2
Ełk r. Poland 37 K2
Elk r. MD U.S.A. 131 F4
Elk r. TN U.S.A. 128 B5
El Kaa Lebanon see Qaa
El Kab Sudan 89 G5
Elkader U.S.A. 132 D3
El Kala Alg. 45 B6
El Kamlin Sudan 89 G6
El Karabi Sudan 89 G5
Elk City U.S.A. 133 B5
Elk Creek U.S.A. 136 A2
Elkedra Australia 110 C4
El Kelaâ des Srarhna Morocco 90 D2
Ēl Kerē Eth. 96 D3
Elkford Canada 123 H5
Elk Grove U.S.A. 136 B2
El Khalil West Bank see Hebron
El Khandaq Sudan 89 F5
El Khârga Egypt see Al Khārijah
Elkhart IN U.S.A. 132 E3
Elkhart KS U.S.A. 132 A4
El Khartûm Sudan see Khartoum
El Khenachich esc. Mali see El Khnâchîch
El Khnâchîch esc. Mali 90 D5
Elkhorn U.S.A. 132 D3
Elkhorn r. U.S.A. 132 B3
Elkhovo Bulg. 46 E3
Elki Turkey see Beytüşşebap
Elkin U.S.A. 128 C4
Elkins U.S.A. 130 D4
Elk Island National Park Canada 123 H4
Elk Lake Canada 124 D4
Elkland U.S.A. 131 E3
Elko Canada 123 H5
Elko U.S.A. 134 D4
Ēl K'oran Eth. 96 E3
Elk Point Canada 123 I4
Elk Point U.S.A. 132 B3
Elk River U.S.A. 132 C2
El Ksaib Ounane well Mali see El Gçaïb
El Ksour Tunisia 45 B7
Elk Springs U.S.A. 137 H1
Elkton MD U.S.A. 131 F4
Elkton VA U.S.A. 130 D4
Elkview U.S.A. 130 C4
El Lagowa Sudan 94 F2
Ellas country Europe see Greece
Ellavalla Australia 109 A6
Ellaville U.S.A. 129 B5
Ellef Ringnes Island Canada 121 I2
Ēl Lēh Eth. 96 C4
El Leiń well Kenya 96 D5
Elléloyé well Chad 88 C5
Ellen, Mount U.S.A. 137 G2
Ellenabad India 74 B3
Ellenboro U.S.A. 130 C4
Ellendale DE U.S.A. 131 F4
Ellendale ND U.S.A. 132 B2
Ellensburg U.S.A. 134 B3
Ellenville U.S.A. 131 F3
Ellesmere, Lake N.Z. 113 C3
▶Ellesmere Island Canada 121 K2
4th largest island in North America and 10th in the world.
northamerica 116–117
world 6–7
Ellesmere Port U.K. 35 E5
Ellice r. Canada 123 K1
Ellice Island atoll Tuvalu see Funafuti
Ellice Islands country S. Pacific Ocean see Tuvalu
Ellicottville U.S.A. 130 D2
Elliot Australia 110 C3
Elliot S. Africa 99 E6
Elliot, Mount Australia 111 F3
Elliot Knob mt. U.S.A. 130 D4
Elliot Lake Canada 124 D4
Ellis U.S.A. 132 B4
Ellisras S. Africa 99 E4
Elliston Australia 109 F8
Elliston U.S.A. 130 C5
Ellon U.K. 34 E3
Ellora Caves tourist site India 72 B1
Ellsworth KS U.S.A. 132 B4
Ellsworth ME U.S.A. 128 F2
Ellsworth WI U.S.A. 132 C2
Ellsworth Mountains Antarctica 167 L1
Ellwangen (Jagst) Germany 36 E4
El Mahia reg. Mali 90 E5
El Maitén Arg. 153 C5
Elmalı Turkey 78 B3
El Malpais National Monument nat. park U.S.A. 135 F6
El Mango Venez. 146 E4
El Manṣûra Egypt see Al Manṣūrah
El Manteco Venez. 147 F3
El Manzla Morocco 42 D5
El Marsa Alg. 43 G4
El Marsa Tunisia 45 C6
El Medo Eth. 96 D3
El Meghaïer Alg. 91 G2
El Melemm Sudan 94 F2
El Melhes well Mauritania 92 B1
El Mesellemiya Sudan 89 G6
El Messir well Chad 88 C6
El Miamo Venez. 147 F3
El Mina Lebanon 77 B2
El Minya governorate Egypt see Al Minyā
Elmira Canada 130 C2
Elmira U.S.A. 131 E2
El Moïnane well Mauritania 92 C1
Elmore Australia 112 C5
El Morro mt. Arg. 152 D3
El Mraïfig well Mauritania 92 C2
El Mraïti well Mali 93 E1
Elmshorn Germany 36 D2
El Muglad Sudan 94 E2
El Mugrón mt. Spain 43 F3
El Mzereb well Mali 90 D4
Elne France 39 E5
El Oasis Mex. 137 E5
El Obeid Sudan 89 F6
El Odaiya Sudan 89 F6
El Oro prov. Ecuador 146 B5
El Oro Mex. 126 F6
Elos Greece 47 C7
El Oued Alg. 91 G2
Eloy U.S.A. 137 G5
El Palmar Venez. 147 F3
El Pao Bolívar Venez. 147 F2
El Pao Cojedes Venez. 146 D2
El Paso IL U.S.A. 132 D3
El Paso KS U.S.A. see Derby
El Paso TX U.S.A. 135 F7
El Peñón Arg. 152 D1
El Perelló Spain 43 G2
Elphinstone i. Myanmar see Thayawthadangyi Kyun
El Picacho mt. Hond. 138 G6
El Pinalón, Cerro mt. Guat. 138 G5
El Pino, Sierra mts Mex. 133 A6
El Pintado Arg. 149 E6
El Pluma Arg. 153 C6
El Pocito Bol. 149 E3
El Porvenir Col. 146 D3
El Porvenir Mex. 135 F7
El Porvenir Panama 146 B2
El Prat de Llobregat Spain 43 H2
El Puerto de Santa María Spain 42 C4
El Qâhira Egypt see Cairo
El Qâhira governorate Egypt see Al Qāhirah
El Qasimiye r. Lebanon 77 B3
El Quds Israel/West Bank see Jerusalem
El Quebrachal Arg. 152 D1
El Real Panama 146 B2
El Reno U.S.A. 133 B5
El Rey, Parque Nacional nat. park Arg. 149 D6
El Rosario watercourse Mex. 135 D7
Elrose Canada 123 I5
Elsa Canada 122 C2
Elsa r. Italy 44 C3
El Sahuaro Mex. 135 D7
El Salado Arg. 153 D7
El Salado Mex. 126 F7
El Salto Mex. 126 E7
▶El Salvador country Central America 138 G6
northamerica 118–119, 140
El Salvador Chile 152 C1
Elsen Nur l. China 75 G2
El Serrat Andorra 43 G1
Elsinore Denmark see Helsingør
Elsinore CA U.S.A. 136 D5
Elsinore UT U.S.A. 137 F2
Elsinore Lake U.S.A. 136 D5
El Sosneado Arg. 152 C3
Elsterwerda Germany 37 F3
El Sueco Mex. 135 F7
El Suweis Egypt see Suez
El Suweis governorate Egypt see Al Suways
El Tama, Parque Nacional nat. park Venez. 146 C3
El Tarf Alg. 91 H1
El Teleno mt. Spain 42 C1
El Tigre Venez. 147 E2
El Tocuyo Venez. 146 D2
El'ton Rus. Fed. 29 H6
El'ton, Ozero l. Rus. Fed. 29 H6
El Toro Chile 152 C2
El Totumo Venez. 146 C2
El Tunal Arg. 152 D1
El Tuparro, Parque Nacional nat. park Col. 146 D3
El Turbio Chile 153 B7
El Uqṣur Egypt see Luxor
Eluru India 72 D2
El 'Uteishan well Sudan 89 G5
Elva Estonia 28 C4
Elvas Port. 42 C3
Elven France 38 B3
El Vendrell Spain 43 G2
Elvenes Norway 32 H1
Elverum Norway 33 C3
El Viejo mt. Col. 146 C3
Elvire r. Australia 108 E4
Elvo r. Italy 44 B2
El Wak Kenya 96 D4
Elwood IN U.S.A. 132 E3
Elwood NE U.S.A. 132 B3
Elwood NJ U.S.A. 131 F4
El Wuz Sudan 89 F6
Ely U.K. 35 G5
Ely MN U.S.A. 132 D2
Ely NV U.S.A. 137 E2
El Yagual Venez. 146 D3
El Yibo well Kenya 96 C3
Elyria U.S.A. 130 B3
Elysburg U.S.A. 131 E3
El Zagâzig Egypt see Az Zaqāzīq
Emām Qolī Iran 81 D2
Emāmrūd Iran 80 C2
Emām Ṣaḥeb Afgh. 81 G2
Emām Taqī Iran 81 D2
Emas, Parque Nacional das nat. park Brazil 149 G4
Emba Kazakh. 70 A2
Emba r. Kazakh. 70 A2
Embalenhle S. Africa 99 F5
Embarcación Arg. 149 D5
Embarras Portage Canada 123 I3
Embi Kazakh. see Emba
Embira r. Brazil see Envira
Émbonas Greece see Emponas
Emborcação, Represa de resr Brazil 149 I4
Emborion Greece see Emporeio
Embu Kenya 96 C5
Embundo Angola 95 C9
Emden Germany 36 C2
Emecik Turkey 47 E6
Emei China see Emeishan
Emeishan China 66 B2
Emei Shan mt. China 66 B2
Emerald Australia 111 G4
Emeril Canada 125 H2
Emerita Augusta Spain see Mérida
Emerson Canada 123 L5
Emerson U.S.A. 130 B4
Emery U.S.A. 137 G2
Emesa Syria see Homs
Emet Turkey 78 B3
Emigrant Gap U.S.A. 136 B2
Emigrant Pass U.S.A. 137 D1
Emigrant Valley U.S.A. 137 E3
eMijindini S. Africa 99 F5
Emi Koussi mt. Chad 88 C5
Emile r. Canada 123 G2
Emiliano Zapata Mex. 138 F5
Emilia-Romagna admin. reg. Italy 44 C2
Emine, Nos pt Bulg. 46 E3
Eminska Planina hills Bulg. 46 E3
Emirdağ Turkey 78 B3
Emir Dağı mt. Turkey 78 B3
Emlenton U.S.A. 130 D3
Emmaboda Sweden 33 D4
Emmahaven Indon. see Telukbayur
Emmaste Estonia 33 F4
Emmaus U.S.A. 131 F3
Emmeloord Neth. 36 B2
Emmelshausen Germany 36 C3
Emmen Neth. 36 C2
Emmen Switz. 39 H3
Emmendingen Germany 36 C4
Emmerich Germany 36 C3
Emmet Australia 111 F5
Emmetsburg U.S.A. 132 C3
Emmiganuru India 72 C3
Emmitsburg U.S.A. 131 E4
Emo Canada 124 A3
Emőd Hungary 37 J5
Emona Slovenia see Ljubljana
Emory U.S.A. 133 C5
Emory Peak U.S.A. 133 A6
Empada Guinea-Bissau 92 B3
Empalme Mex. 135 E8
Empedrado Arg. 152 F1
Emperor Seamount Chain sea feature N. Pacific Ocean 164 F2
Emperor Trough sea feature N. Pacific Ocean 164 F2
Empexa, Salar de salt flat Bol. 148 C5
Empoli Italy 44 C3
Emponas Greece 47 E6
Emporeio Greece 47 D6
Emporia KS U.S.A. 132 B4
Emporia VA U.S.A. 130 E5
Emporium U.S.A. 130 D3
Empress Canada 123 I5
Empress Mine Zimbabwe 99 F3
Empty Quarter des. Saudi Arabia see Rub' al Khālī
'Emrānī Iran 81 D3
Ems r. Germany 36 C2
Ems-Jade-Kanal canal Germany 36 C2
Emumägi hill Estonia 33 G4
Emzinoni S. Africa 99 F5
Enafors Sweden 32 D3
Enamuna Brazil 147 F3
Enarotali Indon. 57 I6
Encanadé mt. Spain 43 G2
Encantadas, Serra das hills Brazil 152 G2
Encarnación Mex. 126 F7
Encarnación Para. 152 G1
Enchi Ghana 92 E4
Encinas mt. Spain 42 E3
Encinitas U.S.A. 136 D5
Encino U.S.A. 135 F6
Encón Arg. 152 D3
Encontrados Venez. 146 C2
Encs Hungary 37 J4
Endau Malaysia 58 C2
Endau r. Malaysia 58 C2
Endeavour Strait Australia 111 E1
Endeh Indon. 57 F7
Enderbury i. Kiribati 107 H2
Enderby Canada 122 G5
Enderby Abyssal Plain sea feature Indian Ocean 163 J9
Enderby Land reg. Antarctica 167 D2
Endicott Mountains U.S.A. 120 D3
Endimari r. Brazil 148 D2
Endom Cameroon 93 I5
Endwell U.S.A. 131 E2
Ene r. Peru 148 B2
Eneabba Australia 109 A7
Enemutu Brazil 147 G3
Energía Arg. 152 F4
Enewetak atoll Marshall Is 164 F6
Enez Turkey 78 A2
Enfidaville Tunisia 45 C6
Enfield U.S.A. 128 D4
Engan Norway 32 C3
Engaños, Rio de los r. Col. see Yari
Engelhard U.S.A. 128 E5
Engel's Rus. Fed. 29 H6
Engerdal Norway 33 C3
Enggano i. Indon. 58 C4
Enghershatu mt. Eritrea 89 H5
Engineer Canada 122 C3
Engkilili Sarawak Malaysia 59 E2
England admin. div. U.K. 35 F5
Englee Canada 125 K3
Englehart Canada 124 E4
Englewood FL U.S.A. 129 C7
Englewood OH U.S.A. 130 A4
English r. Canada 123 M5
English U.S.A. 128 B4
English Bazar India see Ingraj Bazar
English Channel France/U.K. 30 D3
English Coast Antarctica 167 L2
Engozero Rus. Fed. 28 E2
Engstingen Germany 36 D4
Engures ezers l. Latvia 33 F4
Enguri r. Georgia 79 E2
Enhlalakahle S. Africa 99 F6
Enid U.S.A. 133 B4
Enipefs r. Greece 47 C5
eNjesuthi mt. Lesotho 99 F6
Enkan, Mys pt Rus. Fed. 27 O4
Enkeldoorn Zimbabwe see Chivhu
Enkhuizen Neth. 36 B2
Enköping Sweden 33 E4
Enle China see Zhenyuan
Enna Sicily Italy 45 E6
Ennadai Lake Canada 123 K2
En Nahud Sudan 89 F6
E-n-Nassamé well Niger 93 H2
Enné, Ouadi watercourse Chad 88 C6
Ennedi, Massif mts Chad 88 D5
Enneri Achelouma watercourse Niger 91 I5
Enneri Maro watercourse Chad 88 C5
Enneri Yebigué watercourse Chad 88 C4
Enngonia Australia 111 F6
Ennis Rep. of Ireland 35 B5
Ennis MT U.S.A. 134 E3
Ennis TX U.S.A. 133 B5
Enniscorthy Rep. of Ireland 35 C5
Enniskillen U.K. 35 C4
Ennistymon Rep. of Ireland 35 B5
Enn Nâqoûra Lebanon 77 B3
Enns Austria 37 G4
Enns r. Austria 37 G4
Eno Fin. 32 H3
Enoch U.S.A. 137 F3
Enonkoski Fin. 33 H3
Enontekiö Fin. 32 F1
Enoree r. U.S.A. 129 C5
Enping China 67 E4
Enschede Neth. 36 C2
Ensenada Mex. 135 C7
Ensenada de Utria nat. park Col. 146 B3
Enshi China 67 D2
Ensley U.S.A. 129 B6
Entebbe Uganda 96 B4
Enterprise Canada 123 G2
Enterprise U.S.A. 129 B6
Entrance Canada 122 G4
Entrepeñas, Embalse de resr Spain 43 E2
Entre Rios prov. Arg. 152 F3
Entre Rios Bahia Brazil 150 E4
Entre Rios Pará Brazil 147 H6
Entre Rios Moz. see Malema
Entre Rios de Minas Brazil 151 C7
Entroncamento Port. 42 B3
Entuba Zimbabwe 99 E3
Enugu Nigeria 93 G4
Enugu state Nigeria 93 G4
Enurmino Rus. Fed. 27 S3
Envigado Col. 146 C3
Envira Brazil 148 C1
Envira r. Brazil 148 C1
Enying Hungary 37 I5
Eo r. Spain 42 C1
Eochaill Rep. of Ireland see Youghal
Eooa i. Tonga see Eua
Epe Nigeria 93 F4
Epéna Congo 94 C4
Épernay France 39 E2
Ephesus tourist site Turkey 47 E6
Ephraim U.S.A. 137 G2
Ephrata PA U.S.A. 131 E3
Ephrata WA U.S.A. 134 C3
Epidamnus Albania see Durrës
Epidavros tourist site Greece 47 C6
Epidavrou Limiras, Kolpos b. Greece 47 C6
Épila Spain 43 F2
Épinal France 39 G2
Epirus admin. reg. Greece see Ipeiros
Episkopi Cyprus 77 A2
Episkopi Bay Cyprus 77 A2
Episkopis, Kolpos b. Cyprus see Episkopi Bay
Epping U.K. 35 G6
Epping U.S.A. 131 H2
Epping Forest National Park Australia 111 F4
Eppynt, Mynydd hills U.K. 35 E5
Epsom U.K. 35 F6
Epte r. France 38 D2
Epu-pel Arg. 152 D4
Epuyén Arg. 153 C5
Eqlīd Iran 80 C4
Équateur prov. Dem. Rep. Congo 94 D4
▶Equatorial Guinea country Africa 93 H5
africa 86–87, 100
Equeipa Venez. 147 F3
Era r. Italy 44 C3
Eraclea Italy 44 D2
Erakurri mt. Spain 43 F1
Erandol India 72 B1
Erawan National Park Thai. 61 B5
Erba, Jebel mt. Sudan 89 H4
Erbaa Turkey 78 D2
Erbendorf Germany 36 F4
Erbeskopf hill Germany 36 C4
Ercan airport Cyprus 77 A2
Erçek Turkey 79 E3
Erciş Turkey 79 E3
Erciyes Dağı mt. Turkey 78 C3
Érd Hungary 37 I5
Erdaobaihe China see Baihe
Erdaogou China 75 G2
Erdao Jiang r. China 64 A4
Erdek Turkey 78 A2
Erdemli Turkey 78 C3
Erding Germany 36 E4
Erdniyevskiy Rus. Fed. 29 H7
Erdre r. France 38 C3
Eré Peru 146 C5
Erebato r. Venez. 147 E3
Erebus, Mount vol. Antarctica 167 H1
Erech tourist site Iraq 79 F5
Erechim Brazil 151 A8
Ereentsav Mongolia 63 J2
Ereğli Turkey 78 C3
Ereğli Turkey 78 B2
Erego Moz. see Errego
Erei, Monti mts Sicily Italy 45 E6
Ereikoussa i. Greece 47 A5
Erementaū Kazakh. see Yereymentau
Erenhot China 63 I3
Erenik r. Serb. and Mont. 46 B3
Eresk Iran 80 D3
Eresma r. Spain 42 D2
Eresos Greece 47 D5
Eretria Greece 47 C5
Erevan Armenia see Yerevan
Erfoud Morocco 90 D3
Erfurt Germany 36 E3
Ergani Turkey 79 D3
Erg Atouila des. Mali 90 D5
Erg Azennezal des. Alg. 91 E5
Erg Bourarhet des. Alg. 91 H4
'Erg Chech des. Alg./Mali 90 D5
Erg d' Amer des. Alg. 91 H4
Erg du Djourab des. Chad 88 C6
Erg du Ténéré des. Niger 93 H1
Ergene r. Turkey 78 A2
Erg labès des. Alg. 90 E4
Erg Iguidi des. Alg./Mauritania 90 D4
'Erg I-n-Sâkâne des. Mali 91 E5
Erg Issaouane des. Alg. 91 G4
Erg Kilian des. Alg. 91 H5
Ērgļi Latvia 33 G4
Erg Tassedjefit des. Alg. 91 F4
Erguig r. Chad 94 B2
Ergun He r. China/Rus. Fed. see Argun'
Er Hai l. China 66 B3
Eria r. Spain 42 D1
Erie KS U.S.A. 132 C4
Erie PA U.S.A. 130 C2
Erie, Lake Canada/U.S.A. 130 C2
'Erîgât des. Mali 92 D1
Erik Eriksenstretet sea chan. Svalbard 26 C2
Erikoussa i. Greece see Ereikoussa
Eriksdale Canada 123 L5
Erimo-misaki c. Japan 64 E4
Eriskay i. U.K. 34 C3
Erithraí Greece see Erythres
Erithropótamos r. Greece see Erydropotamos
▶Eritrea country Africa 89 H6
africa 86–87, 100
Erkech-Tam Kyrg. 81 H2
Erkner Germany 37 F2
Erlangen Germany 36 E4
Erlangping China 67 D1
Erldunda Australia 110 C5
Erlong Shan mt. China 64 B4
Ermelo S. Africa 99 F5
Ermenek Turkey 78 C3
Ermenek r. Turkey 77 A1
Ermil Sudan 89 E6
Ermont Egypt see Armant
Ermoupoli Greece 47 D6
Ernakulam India 72 C4
Erne r. Rep. of Ireland/U.K. 35 B4
Ernée France 38 C2
Ernest Giles Range hills Australia 109 C6
Ernest Sound sea chan. U.S.A. 122 C4
Erode India 72 C4
Eromanga Australia 111 E5
Erongo admin. reg. Namibia 98 B4
Erqu China see Zhouzhi
Errabiddy Hills Australia 109 A6
Er Rachidia Morocco 90 D3
Er Rahad Sudan 89 F6
Erramala Hills India 72 C3
Er Raoui des. Alg. 90 E3
Errego Moz. 99 H3
Er Renk Sudan 96 B2
Errigal hill Rep. of Ireland 34 B4
Errinundra National Park Australia 112 D5
Erris Head Rep. of Ireland 35 A4
Er Rogel Sudan 89 G5
Erromango i. Vanuatu 107 F3
Erronan i. Vanuatu see Futuna
Er Roseires Sudan 96 B2
Er Rua'at Sudan 89 G6
Ersekë Albania 47 B4
Erta Ale vol. Eth. 89 I6
Ertil' Rus. Fed. 29 G6
Ertis r. Kazakh./Rus. Fed. see Irtysh
Ertix He r. China/Kazakh. 70 G2
Erufu Nigeria 93 G3
Eruh Turkey 79 E3
Eruwa Nigeria 93 F4
Erval Brazil 152 G3
Erve r. France 38 C3
Erwitte Germany 36 D3
Erydropotamos r. Greece 46 E4
Erythres Greece 47 C5
Eryuan China 66 A3
Erzen r. Albania 46 A4
Erzerum Turkey see Erzurum
Erzgebirge mts Czech Rep./Germany 37 F3
Erzhan China 64 A2
Erzincan Turkey 79 D3
Erzurum Turkey 79 E3
Esa-ala P.N.G. 107 E2
Esan-misaki pt Japan 64 E4
Esbjerg Denmark 33 C5
Esbo Fin. see Espoo
Escada Brazil 150 F4
Escalante r. U.S.A. 137 G3
Escalante Desert U.S.A. 137 F3
Escalón Mex. 126 F6
Escalon U.S.A. 136 B3
Escambia r. U.S.A. 129 B6
Escanaba U.S.A. 132 E2
Escandón, Puerto de pass Spain 43 F2
Escárcega Mex. 127 H8
Escaut r. Belgium 39 E1
Esche Germany 36 C2
Esch-sur-Alzette Lux. 39 F2
Eschwege Germany 36 E3
Eschweiler Germany 36 C3
Escoma Bol. 148 C3
Escondido r. Mex. 133 A6
Escondido U.S.A. 136 D5
Escudilla mt. U.S.A. 137 H5
Escuinapa Mex. 126 E7
Escuintla Guat. 138 F6
Escusa mt. Spain 42 D2
Eséka Cameroon 93 H5
Ese-Khayya Rus. Fed. 27 N3
Eşen Turkey 78 B3
Esence Turkey 47 F4
Esenguly Turkm. 80 C2
Esenköy Turkey 46 F4
Esenyurt Turkey 46 F4
Ésera r. Spain 43 G1
Eşfahān Iran 80 B3
Eşfahān prov. Iran 80 C3
Esfandak Iran 81 E5
Esfarayen, Reshteh-ye mts Iran 80 D2
Esfideh Iran 81 D3
Esgueva r. Spain 42 D2
Eshan China 66 B3
Eshkamesh Afgh. 81 G2
Eshowe S. Africa 99 F6
Esikhawini S. Africa 99 G6
Esil Kazakh. see Yesil'
Esil r. Kazakh./Rus. Fed. see Ishim
Esino r. Italy 44 D3
Esk r. Australia 112 C6
Esk r. U.K. 34 E4
Esker Canada 125 H2
Eskifjörður Iceland 32 [inset]
Eski Gediz Turkey 78 B3
Eskilstuna Sweden 33 E4
Eskimo Lakes Canada 120 F3
Eskimo Point Canada see Arviat
Eski Mosul Iraq 79 E3
Eskipazar Turkey 78 C2
Eskişehir Turkey 78 B3
Esla r. Spain 42 C2
Esla, Embalse de resr Spain see Ricobayo, Embalse de
Eslāmābād-e Gharb Iran 80 A3
Esler Dağı mt. Turkey 47 F6
Eslöv Sweden 33 D5
Esmā'īlī-ye Soflá Iran 80 D4
Eşme Turkey 78 B3
Esmeralda, Isla i. Chile 153 B7
Esmeraldas Ecuador 146 B4
Esmeraldas prov. Ecuador 146 B4
Esmont U.S.A. 130 D5
Espakeh Iran 81 E5
Espalha r. Brazil see São Francisco
Espalion France 39 E4
Espalmador, Isla i. Spain see S'Espalmador
España country Europe see Spain
Espanola Canada 124 D4
Espanola U.S.A. 135 F5
Esparto U.S.A. 136 A2
Espelette France 38 C5
Esperance Australia 109 C8
Esperance Bay Australia 109 C8
Esperantinópolis Brazil 150 C3
Esperanza research station Antarctica 167 A2
Esperanza Santa Cruz Arg. 153 C7
Esperanza Santa Fé Arg. 152 E2
Esperanza Mex. 135 E8
Esperanza Peru 148 C2
Espichel, Cabo c. Port. 42 B3
Espiel Spain 42 D3
Espigão, Serra do mts Brazil 151 B8
Espinazo Mex. 133 A7
Espinhaço, Serra do mts Brazil 151 D6
Espinheira Angola 95 B9
Espinheira hill Port. 42 C3
Espinho Port. 42 B2
Espinilho, Serra do hills Brazil 151 A9
Espino Venez. 147 E2
Espinosa Brazil 150 D5
Espinosa de los Monteros Spain 42 E1
Espírito Santo Brazil see Vila Velha
Espírito Santo state Brazil 151 D6
Espíritu Bol. 148 D4
Espíritu Santo i. Vanuatu 107 F3
Espíritu Santo, Isla i. Mex. 138 B4
Esplanada Brazil 150 E4
Espoo Fin. 33 G3
Espuña mt. Spain 43 F4
Espungabera Moz. 99 G4
Esqueda Mex. 135 E7
Esquel Arg. 153 C5
Esquina Arg. 152 F2
Esrange Sweden 32 F2
Essaouira Morocco 90 C3
Essé Cameroon 93 H4
Es Semara W. Sahara 90 C4
▶Essen Germany 36 C3
5th most populous city in Europe.
world 16–17
Essendon, Mount Australia 109 C6
Essex Canada 130 B2
Essex CA U.S.A. 137 E4
Essex NY U.S.A. 131 G1
Essex Junction U.S.A. 131 G1
Esslingen am Neckar Germany 36 D4
Esso Rus. Fed. 27 P4
Essonne r. France 38 E2
Essu Estonia 33 G4
Es Suaifi well Sudan 89 F5
Es Suki Sudan 89 G6
Est prov. Cameroon 93 I4
Estaca de Bares, Punta da pt Spain 42 C1
Eşṭahbān Iran 80 C4
Estância Brazil 150 E4
Estancia U.S.A. 135 F6
Estancia Camerón Chile 153 C8
Estancia Carmen Arg. 153 C8
Estand, Kūh-e mt. Iran 81 E4
Estarreja Port. 42 B2
Estats, Pic d' mt. France/Spain 43 G1
Estcourt S. Africa 99 F6
Este Italy 44 C2
Esteban de Urizar Arg. 149 D5
Estelí Nicaragua 138 G6
Estella Spain 43 E1
Estena r. Spain 42 D3
Estepa Spain 42 D4
Estepona Spain 42 D4
Esterel reg. France 39 G5
Esterhazy Canada 123 K5
Estero Bay U.S.A. 136 B4
Esteros Para. 149 E5
Estes Park U.S.A. 134 F4
Estevan Canada 134 G2
Estherville U.S.A. 132 C3
Estill U.S.A. 129 C5
Estiva r. Brazil 150 C3
Eston Canada 134 E2
▶Estonia country Europe 33 G4
europe 24–25, 48
Estonskaya S.S.R. country Europe see Estonia
Estreito Brazil 152 H2
Estrela, Serra da mts Port. 42 C2
Estrella mt. Spain 43 E3
Estrella, Punta pt Mex. 135 D7
Estrella, Sierra mts U.S.A. 137 F5
Estremadura reg. Port. 42 B3
Estremoz Port. 42 C3
Estrondo, Serra hills Brazil 150 B4
Etuaire prov. Gabon 94 A4
Estūh Iran 80 B3
Esztergom Hungary 37 I5
Etadunna Australia 110 D6
Etah India 74 C4
Étain France 39 F2
Etamamiou Canada 125 J3
Étampes France 38 E2
Étaples France 38 D1
Etawah Rajasthan India 74 C4
Etawah Uttar Pradesh India 74 C4
Etelä-Suomi prov. Fin. 33 G3
eThandakukhanya S. Africa 99 F5
Ethel watercourse Australia 109 B6
Ethelbert Canada 123 K5
Ethel Creek Australia 108 C5
E'Thembini S. Africa 98 D6
Etheridge r. Australia 111 E3
▶Ethiopia country Africa 96 C2
3rd most populous country in Africa.
africa 86–87, 100
Ethiopian Highlands mts Eth. 96 C2
Etili Turkey 47 E5
Etimesğut Turkey 78 C3
Etna r. Norway 33 C3
Etna, Mount vol. Sicily Italy 45 E6
Etobicoke Canada 130 D2
Etolin Island U.S.A. 122 C3
Etorofu-tō i. Rus. Fed. see Iturup, Ostrov
Etosha National Park Namibia 98 B3
Etosha Pan salt pan Namibia 98 C3
Etoumbi Congo 94 B4
Etowah r. U.S.A. 133 E5
Etropole Bulg. 46 D3
Ettelbruck Lux. 39 G2
Ettumanur India 72 C4
Etxarri-Aranatz Spain see Echarri-Aranaz
Etzicom Coulee r. Canada 123 I5
Eua i. Tonga 107 H4
Eubank U.S.A. 130 A5
Euboea i. Greece see Evvoia
Eucla Australia 109 E7
Euclid U.S.A. 130 C3
Euclides da Cunha Brazil 150 E4
Eucumbene, Lake Australia 112 D5
Eudora U.S.A. 133 D5
Eudunda Australia 112 A4
Eufaula AL U.S.A. 129 B6
Eufaula OK U.S.A. 133 C5
Eufaula Lake resr U.S.A. 133 C5
Eugene U.S.A. 134 B3
Eugenia, Punta pt Mex. 135 D8
Eulo Australia 111 F6
Eungella Australia 111 G4
Eungella National Park Australia 111 G4
Eunice LA U.S.A. 133 C6
Eunice NM U.S.A. 133 A5
▶Euphrates r. Asia 76 C3
Longest river in western Asia.
Also known as Al Furāt (Iraq/Syria) or Fırat (Turkey).
Eupora U.S.A. 129 A5
Eura Fin. 33 F3
Eure r. France 38 D2
Eureka CA U.S.A. 134 A4
Eureka IL U.S.A. 124 B5
Eureka KS U.S.A. 132 B4
Eureka MT U.S.A. 134 D2
Eureka NV U.S.A. 137 E2
Eureka OH U.S.A. 130 B4
Eureka SD U.S.A. 132 B2
Eureka UT U.S.A. 137 F2

Eureka Springs U.S.A. 133 C4
Eureka Valley U.S.A. 136 D3
Eurinilla watercourse Australia 112 B3
Euriowie Australia 112 B3
Euroa Australia 112 C5
Europa, Île i. Indian Ocean 162 J7
Europa, Picos de mts Spain 42 D1
Europa, Punta de pt Gibraltar see Europa Point
Europa Point Gibraltar 42 D4
Eustis U.S.A. 129 C6
Eutaw U.S.A. 129 B5
Eutin Germany 36 E1
Eutsuk Lake Canada 122 E4
Evale Angola 95 B9
Evans, Lac l. Canada 124 E3
Evansburg Canada 123 H4
Evans City U.S.A. 130 C3
Evans Ice Stream Antarctica 167 L1
Evanston IL U.S.A. 132 E3
Evanston WY U.S.A. 134 E4
Evansville IN U.S.A. 128 B4
Evansville WY U.S.A. 134 F4
Eva Perón Arg. see La Plata
Eva Perón prov. Arg. see La Pampa
Evaton S. Africa 99 E5
Evaz Iran 80 C5
Evening Shade U.S.A. 133 D4
Evensk Rus. Fed. 27 P3
Everard, Lake salt flat Australia 109 F7
Everard, Mount Australia 110 C4
Everek Turkey see Develi

▶Everest, Mount China/Nepal 75 E4
Highest mountain in the world and in Asia.
asia 50–51
world 6–7

Everett PA U.S.A. 130 D3
Everett WA U.S.A. 134 B3
▶Everglades swamp U.S.A. 129 C7
world 14–15
Everglades National Park U.S.A. 129 C7
Evergreen U.S.A. 129 B6
Everman, Volcán vol. Mex. 126 D8
Everson U.S.A. 134 B2
Evertsberg Sweden 33 D3
Evesham U.K. 35 F5
Évian-les-Bains France 39 G3
Evijärvi Fin. 32 F3
Evinayong Equat. Guinea 93 H5
Evington U.S.A. 130 D5
Evinos r. Greece 47 B5
Evje Norway 33 B4
Evolène Switz. 39 G3
Évora Port. 42 C3
Évora admin. dist. Port. 42 C3
Evoron, Ozero l. Rus. Fed. 64 D2
Evosmo Greece 46 C4
Evowghlī Iran 80 A2
Évreux France 38 D2
Évron France 38 C2
Evros r. Greece/Turkey 46 E4
Evrotas r. Greece 47 C6
Évry France 39 E2
Evvoia i. Greece 47 D5
Ewan Australia 111 F3
Ewaso Ngiro r. Kenya 96 D4
Ewe, Loch b. U.K. 34 D3
Ewo Congo 94 B5
Excelsior Mountain U.S.A. 136 C2
Excelsior Mountains U.S.A. 136 C2
Excelsior Springs U.S.A. 132 C4
Exe r. U.K. 35 E6
Executive Committee Range mts Antarctica 167 J1
Exeter Canada 130 C2
Exeter U.K. 35 E6
Exeter CA U.S.A. 136 C3
Exeter NH U.S.A. 131 H2
Exeter Lake Canada 123 I1
Exmoor hills U.K. 35 E6
Exmoor National Park U.K. 35 E6
Exmore U.S.A. 131 F5
Exmouth Australia 108 A5
Exmouth U.K. 35 E6
Exmouth, Mount Australia 112 D3
Exmouth Gulf Australia 108 A5
Exmouth Plateau sea feature Indian Ocean 162 O7
Expedition National Park Australia 111 G5
Expedition Range mts Australia 111 G5
Exploits r. Canada 125 K3
Exton U.S.A. 131 F3
Extremadura aut. comm. Spain 42 E3
Extrême-Nord prov. Cameroon 93 I3
Exuma Cays is Bahamas 129 D7
Exuma Sound sea chan. Bahamas 129 E7
Eya r. Rus. Fed. 29 F7
Eyangu Dem. Rep. Congo 94 D5
Eyasi, Lake salt l. Tanz. 96 B5
Eyawadi r. Myanmar see Irrawaddy
Eyeberry Lake Canada 123 J2
Eyelenoborsk Rus. Fed. 28 L2
Eyemouth U.K. 34 E4
Eyjafjallajökull ice cap Iceland 32 [inset]
Eyjafjörður inlet Iceland 32 [inset]
Eyl Somalia 96 F3
Eylau Rus. Fed. see Bagrationovsk
Eymet France 38 D4
Eymir Turkey 47 F5
Eymoutiers France 38 D4
Eyre r. France 38 C4
Eyre (South), Lake salt flat Australia 110 D6

▶Eyre, Lake salt flat Australia 110 D6
Largest lake in Oceania and lowest point.
oceania 102–103

Eyre Creek watercourse Australia 110 D5
Eyre Mountains N.Z. 113 B4
Eyre Peninsula Australia 109 F8
Eyrieux r. France 39 F4
Eysturoy i. Faroe Is 34 [inset]
Eyuku waterhole Kenya 96 C5
Eyumojok Cameroon 93 H4
Eyvānakī Iran 80 C3
Ezakheni S. Africa 99 F6
Ezel U.S.A. 130 B5
Ezequiel Ramos Mexía, Embalse resr Arg. 152 C4
Ezernieki Latvia 33 G4
Ezhou China 67 E2
Ezhva Rus. Fed. 28 I3
Ezine Turkey 78 A3
Ezinepazar Turkey 78 D2
Ezo i. Japan see Hokkaidō
Ezousa r. Cyprus 77 A2
Ezra's Tomb tourist site Iraq 79 F5

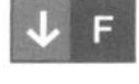

Faadhippolhu Atoll Maldives 72 B5
Fabens U.S.A. 135 F7
Faber, Mount Sing. 58 [inset]
Faber Lake Canada 123 G2
Fåborg Denmark 33 C5
Fabriano Italy 44 D3
Facatativá Col. 146 C3
Fachi Niger 93 H1
Factoryville U.S.A. 131 F3
Fada Chad 88 D5
Fada-Ngourma Burkina 93 F2
Fadnoun, Plateau du Alg. 91 H4
Faenza Italy 44 C2
Færingehavn Greenland see Kangerluarsoruseq
Færoerne terr. N. Atlantic Ocean see Faroe Islands
Faeroes terr. N. Atlantic Ocean see Faroe Islands
Fafa r. Cent. Afr. Rep. 94 C3
Fafanlap Indon. 57 H6
Fafe Port. 42 B2
Fafen Shet' watercourse Eth. 96 E3
Faga watercourse Burkina 93 F2
Făgăraş Romania 46 D2

▶Fagatogo American Samoa 107 H3
Capital of American Samoa.

Fagersta Sweden 33 D4
Făget Romania 46 C2
Fagnano, Lago l. Arg./Chile 153 C8
Fagne reg. Belgium 39 F1
Fagochia well Niger 93 G1
Faguibine, Lac l. Mali 92 D1
Fagurhólsmýri Iceland 32 [inset]
Fagwir Sudan 96 A2
Fahliān, Rūdkhāneh-ye watercourse Iran 80 B4
Fahraj Iran 80 C4
Fā'id Egypt 77 A4
Fairbanks U.S.A. 120 E3
Fairborn U.S.A. 130 A4
Fairbury U.S.A. 132 B3
Fairfax U.S.A. 131 G1
Fairfield CA U.S.A. 136 A2
Fairfield IA U.S.A. 132 D3
Fairfield ID U.S.A. 134 D4
Fairfield IL U.S.A. 128 A4
Fairfield OH U.S.A. 130 A4
Fairfield TX U.S.A. 133 B6
Fairgrove U.S.A. 130 B2
Fair Haven U.S.A. 131 G2
Fair Head U.K. 34 C4
Fair Hill U.S.A. 131 F4
Fair Isle i. U.K. 34 F2
Fairlee U.S.A. 131 G2
Fairmont MN U.S.A. 132 C3
Fairmont WV U.S.A. 130 C4
Fairmont Hot Springs Canada 123 H5
Fairplay U.S.A. 134 F5
Fairplay, Mount U.S.A. 122 A2
Fairview Australia 111 F2
Fairview Canada 122 G3
Fairview KY U.S.A. 130 B4
Fairview OK U.S.A. 133 B4
Fairview PA U.S.A. 130 C2
Fairview Park Hong Kong China 67 [inset]
Fairweather, Cape U.S.A. 122 B3
Fairweather, Mount Canada/U.S.A. 120 F4
Fais i. Micronesia 57 J4
Faisalabad Pak. 81 H4
Faizabad Afgh. see Feyzābād
Faizabad India 75 D4
Fajr, Wādī watercourse Saudi Arabia 89 H2
Fakaofo atoll Tokelau 164 G6
Fakenham U.K. 35 G5
Fakfak Indon. 57 H6
Fakhrabad Iran 80 C4
Fakiragram India 75 F4
Fakiyska Reka r. Bulg. 46 E3
Fakse Denmark 33 D5
Fakse Bugt b. Denmark 33 D5
Falaba Sierra Leone 92 C3
Falagountou Burkina 93 F2
Falaise France 38 C2
Falaise Lake Canada 123 G2
Falakata India 75 F4
Falam Myanmar 60 A3
Falavarjan Iran 80 B3
Falcarragh Rep. of Ireland 34 B4
Fălciu Romania 46 F1
Falcón state Venez. 146 D2
Falconara Marittima Italy 44 D3
Falcone, Capo del c. Sardinia Italy 44 B4
Falcon Island Tonga see Fonuafo'ou
Falcon Lake Canada 123 M5
Falcon Lake l. Mex./U.S.A. 133 B7
Falelima Samoa 107 H3
Falémé r. Mali/Senegal 92 B2
Falerii Italy see Civita Castellana
Falfurrias U.S.A. 133 B7
Falher Canada 123 G4
Falkenberg Germany 37 F3
Falkenberg Sweden 33 D4
Falkensee Germany 37 F2
Falkirk U.K. 34 E4
Falkland Escarpment sea feature S. Atlantic Ocean 161 K9

▶Falkland Islands terr. S. Atlantic Ocean 153 F7
United Kingdom Overseas Territory.
southamerica 144–145, 154

Falkland Plateau sea feature S. Atlantic Ocean 161 K9
Falkland Sound sea chan. Falkland Is 153 E8
Falkner Arg. 152 D5
Falköping Sweden 33 D4
Fall r. U.S.A. 132 C4
Fallieres Coast Antarctica 167 L2
Fallon U.S.A. 136 C2
Fall River U.S.A. 131 H3
Fall River Pass U.S.A. 134 F4
Falls City U.S.A. 132 C3
Falls Creek U.S.A. 130 D3
Falmouth U.K. 35 D6
Falmouth KY U.S.A. 130 A4
Falmouth MA U.S.A. 131 H3
Falmouth VA U.S.A. 130 E4
Falou Mali 92 D2
False r. Canada 125 G1
False Bay S. Africa 98 C7
False Point India 73 E1
Falso Cabo de Hornos c. Chile 153 C8
Falster i. Denmark 33 C5
Fălticeni Romania 31 K4
Falun Sweden 33 D3
Falzarego, Passo di pass Italy 44 D1
Famagusta Cyprus 77 A2
Famagusta Bay Cyprus see Ammochostos Bay
Famatina, Sierra de mts Arg. 152 C2
Famenin Iran 80 B3
Fame Range hills Australia 109 C6
Family Well Australia 108 D5
Fana Mali 92 D2
Fanandrana Madag. 99 [inset] K3
Fanchang China 67 F2
Fandriana Madag. 99 [inset] J4
Fang Thai. 60 B4
Fangak Sudan 96 A2
Fangcheng Guangxi China see Fangchenggang
Fangcheng Henan China 67 E1
Fangchenggang China 67 D4
Fangdou Shan mts China 67 D2
Fangshan Taiwan 67 G4
Fangxian China 67 D1
Fangzheng China 64 B3
Fani i Vogël r. Albania 46 A4
Fankuai China 66 D2
Fankuaidian China see Fankuai
Fanling Hong Kong China 67 [inset]
Fannem Norway 32 C3
Fannūj Iran 81 D5
Fanø i. Denmark 33 C5
Fano Italy 44 D3
Fanoualie i. Tonga see Fonualei
Fanshan China 67 G3
Fan Si Pan mt. Vietnam 60 C3
Fanum Fortunae Italy see Fano
Farab Turkm. see Farap
Faradje Dem. Rep. Congo 94 F4
Faradofay Madag. see Tôlañaro
Farafangana Madag. 99 [inset] J4
Farafenni Gambia 92 B2
Farāfirah, Wāḥāt al Egypt see Farafra Oasis
Farafra Oasis Egypt 89 F3
Farāgheh Iran 80 C4
Farāh Afgh. 81 E3
Farāh prov. Afgh. 81 E3
Farahābād Iran see Khezerābād
Farah Rūd watercourse Afgh. 81 E4
Farakhulm Afgh. 81 G3
Farallon de Medinilla i. N. Mariana Is 57 K2
Farallon de Pajaros vol. N. Mariana Is 57 J1
Farallones de Cali, Parque Nacional nat. park Col. 146 B4
Faramuti I. Sudan 94 E2
Faranah Guinea 92 C3
Faraoani Romania 46 E1
Far'aoun well Mauritania 92 B1
Farap Turkm. 81 E2
Farasān, Jazā'ir is Saudi Arabia 89 I5
Faratsiho Madag. 99 [inset] J3
Faraulep atoll Micronesia 57 J4
Fardes r. Spain 42 E4
Farewell, Cape Greenland 121 O3
Farewell, Cape N.Z. 113 C3
Farewell Spit N.Z. 113 C3
Färgelanda Sweden 33 D4
Farghona Uzbek. see Fergana
Farghona Wiloyati admin. div. Uzbek. see Ferganskaya Oblast'
Fargo U.S.A. 132 B2
Faribault U.S.A. 132 C2
Faribault, Lac l. Canada 125 G1
Faridabad India 74 C3
Faridkot India 74 B3
Faridpur Bangl. 75 F5
Faridpur India 74 C3
Färig Iran 81 D2
Fārigh, Wādī al watercourse Libya 88 C2
Färila Sweden 33 D3
Farīmān Iran 81 D3
Farinha r. Brazil 150 C3
Farish Uzbek. 81 F1
Färjestaden Sweden 33 E4
Farkadhon Greece 47 C5
Farkhar Afgh. see Farkhato
Farkhato Afgh. 81 G2
Farkhor Tajik. 81 G2
Farmahin Iran 80 B3
Farmer City U.S.A. 132 D3
Farmer Island Canada 124 D1
Farmerville U.S.A. 133 C5
Farmington ME U.S.A. 131 H1
Farmington MO U.S.A. 132 D4
Farmington NH U.S.A. 131 H2
Farmington NM U.S.A. 135 E5
Farmington UT U.S.A. 134 E4
Farmington Hills U.S.A. 130 B2
Far Mountain Canada 122 E4
Farmville U.S.A. 130 D5
Farne Islands U.K. 34 F4
Farnham U.S.A. 131 E5
Farnham, Lake salt flat Australia 109 D6
Farnham, Mount Canada 123 G5
Far North Section Australia see Great Barrier Reef Marine Park (Far North Section)
Faro Brazil 147 G5
Faro r. Cameroon 93 I3
Faro Canada 122 C2
Faro Port. 42 C4
Faro admin. dist. Port. 42 B4
Fårö i. Sweden 33 E4
Faro, Serra do mts Spain 42 C1
Faroe-Iceland Ridge sea feature Arctic Ocean 166 I2

▶Faroe Islands terr. N. Atlantic Ocean 34 [inset]
Self-governing Danish Territory.
europe 24–25, 48

Fårösund Sweden 33 E4
Farquar Atoll i. Seychelles 97 F7
Farquhar Islands Seychelles 97 F7
Farquharson Tableland hills Australia 109 C6
Farrandsville U.S.A. 130 E3
Farrars Creek watercourse Australia 111 E5
Farrāshband Iran 80 C4
Farr Bay Antarctica 167 F2
Farrokhī Iran 81 D3
Farrukhabad India see Fatehgarh
Fārs prov. Iran 80 C4
Farsakh Iran 80 C3
Farsala Greece 47 C5
Farson U.S.A. 134 E4
Farsund Norway 33 B4
Fărtăneşti Romania 46 E2
Fartura, Serra da mts Brazil 151 A8
Farvel, Kap c. Greenland see Farewell, Cape
Farwell U.S.A. 133 A5
Fāryāb prov. Afgh. 81 F2
Fāryāb Hormozgan Iran 80 D5
Fāryāb Kermān Iran 80 D4
Fasā Iran 80 C4
Fasano Italy 45 F4
Faşikan Geçidi pass Turkey 77 A1
Fasil Ghebbi and Gonder Monuments tourist site Eth. 96 C1
Fastiv Ukr. 29 D6
Fastov Ukr. see Fastiv
Fatehabad India 74 B3
Fatehgarh Madhya Pradesh India 74 C4
Fatehgarh Uttar Pradesh India 74 C4
Fatehnagar India 74 B4
Fatehpur Rajasthan India 74 B4
Fatehpur Uttar Pradesh India 74 D4
Fatehpur Sikri India 74 C4
Fatḥābād Iran 80 C4
Fathai Sudan 96 A2
Fati, Lac l. Mali 92 E1
Fatick Senegal 92 A2
Fattoilep atoll Micronesia see Faraulep
Fatuma Dem. Rep. Congo 95 F6
Faulkton U.S.A. 132 B2
Faulquemont France 39 G2
Fauquier Canada 122 G5
Fauresmith S. Africa 98 E6
Fauske Norway 32 D2
Favalto, Monte mt. Italy 44 D3
Favignana Sicily Italy 45 D6
Favignana, Isola i. Sicily Italy 45 D6
Fawcett Canada 123 H4
Fawn r. Canada 124 B2
Fawwārah Saudi Arabia 89 I3
Faxaflói b. Iceland 32 [inset]
Faxälven r. Sweden 32 E3
Faxian Hu l. China 66 B3
Faya Chad 88 C5
Fayaoué New Caledonia 107 F4
Fayette MO U.S.A. 132 C4
Fayette MS U.S.A. 133 D6
Fayette OH U.S.A. 130 A3
Fayetteville AR U.S.A. 133 C4
Fayetteville NC U.S.A. 128 D5
Fayetteville NY U.S.A. 131 E2
Fayetteville PA U.S.A. 130 E4
Fayetteville TN U.S.A. 128 B5
Fayetteville WV U.S.A. 130 C4
Faylakah i. Kuwait 79 G5
Fayrān well Egypt 77 A5
Fayrān, Wādī watercourse Egypt 77 A5
Fayranī, Jabal mt. Egypt 77 B5
Fazair al Ghrazi watercourse Saudi Arabia 77 C5
Fazao Malfakassa, Parc National de nat. park Togo 93 F3
Fazeī well Niger 93 H1
Fazilka India 74 B3
Fazrān, Jabal hill Saudi Arabia 76 D4
Fdérik Mauritania 90 B5
Fead Group is P.N.G. see Nuguria Islands
Feale r. Rep. of Ireland 35 B5
Fear, Cape U.S.A. 129 D5
Feather r. U.S.A. 136 B2
Feather, North Fork r. U.S.A. 136 B2
Featherston N.Z. 113 C3
Fécamp France 38 D2
Federacija Bosna i Hercegovina aut. div. Bos.-Herz. 44 G2
Federal Arg. 152 F2
Federal Capital Territory admin. div. Nigeria 93 G3
Federal District admin. dist. Brazil see Distrito Federal
Federal District admin. dist. Venez. see Distrito Federal
Federalsburg U.S.A. 131 F4
Federated Malay States country Asia see Malaysia
Federation of Bosnia and Herzegovina aut. div. Bos.-Herz. see Federacija Bosna i Hercegovina
Fedorov Kazakh. see Fedorovka
Fedorovka Kazakh. 29 I6
Fehet Lake Canada 123 M1
Fehmarn i. Germany 36 E1
Fehmarn Belt strait Denmark/Germany 33 C5
Feia, Lagoa lag. Brazil 151 D7
Feidong China 67 F2
Feijó Brazil 148 C2
Feilding N.Z. 113 C3
Feio r. Brazil see Aguapeí
Feira Zambia see Luangwa
Feira de Santana Brazil 150 E5
Feira do Monte Spain 42 C1
Feixi China 67 F2
Fejaj, Chott el salt l. Tunisia 91 H2
Fejø i. Denmark 36 E1
Feke Turkey 78 C3
Felanitx Spain 43 H3
Felaou well Alg. 93 G1
Feldberg mt. Germany 39 G3
Feldkirch Austria 36 D5
Feldkirchen in Kärnten Austria 37 G5
Feliciano r. Arg. 152 F2
Felicity U.S.A. 130 A4
Felidhu Atoll Maldives 71 D11
Felixlândia Brazil 151 C6
Felixstowe U.K. 35 G6
Felletin France 38 E4
Fellowsville U.S.A. 130 D4
Felsberg Germany 36 D3
Felsina Italy see Bologna
Feltre Italy 44 C1
Femeas r. Brazil 150 C5
Femer Bælt strait Denmark/Germany see Fehmarn Belt
Femminamorta, Monte mt. Italy 45 F5
Femundsmarka Nasjonalpark nat. park Norway 33 D3
Fenelon Falls Canada 130 D1
Fener Burnu hd Turkey 77 B1
Fénérive Madag. see Fenoarivo Atsinanana
Fengari mt. Greece 46 D4
Fengcheng Fujian China see Yongding
Fengcheng Guangdong China see Xinfeng
Fengcheng Guangxi China see Fengshan
Fengcheng Jiangxi China 67 E2
Fengcheng Liaoning China 65 A4
Fengdu China 66 C2
Fenggang Fujian China see Shaxian
Fenggang Guizhou China 66 C3
Fenggang Jiangxi China see Yihuang
Fenggeling China 66 C1
Fenghua China 67 G2
Fenghuang China 67 D3
Fengjiaba China see Wangcang
Fengjie China 67 D2
Fengkai China 67 D4
Fenglin Taiwan 67 G4
Fengqing China 66 A3
Fengshan Fujian China see Luoyuan
Fengshan Guangxi China 66 C3
Fengshan Hubei China see Luotian
Fengshan Yunnan China see Fengqing
Fengshuba Shuiku resr China 67 E3
Fengtai China 67 F1
Fengxian Jiangsu China 67 F1
Fengxian Shaanxi China 66 C1
Fengxian Shanghai China 67 G2
Fengxiang Heilong. China see Luobei
Fengxiang Yunnan China see Lincang
Fengyang China 67 F1
Fengyi Guizhou China see Zheng'an
Fengyi Sichuan China see Maoxian
Fengyüan Taiwan 67 G3
Fengzhen China 63 I3
Feni Bangl. 75 F5
Feni Islands P.N.G. 107 E2
Fenny r. Bangl./India 75 F5
Feno, Capo di c. Corsica France 44 B4
Fenoarivo Atsinanana Madag. 99 [inset] K3
Fenoarivo Be Madag. 99 [inset] J3
Fenton U.S.A. 130 B2
Fenwick U.S.A. 130 C4
Fenyi China 67 E3
Feodosiya Ukr. 78 C1
Fer, Cap de c. Alg. 91 G1
Férai Greece see Feres
Ferdows Iran 80 D3
Fère-Champenoise France 39 E2
Feres Greece 46 E4
Ferfer Somalia 96 E3
Fergana Uzbek. 81 G1
Fergana Oblast admin. div. Uzbek. see Ferganskaya Oblast'
Ferganskaya Oblast' admin. div. Uzbek. 81 G1
Fergus Canada 130 C2
Fergus Falls U.S.A. 132 B2
Ferguson Lake Canada 123 L2
Fergusson r. Australia 110 B2
Fergusson Island P.N.G. 107 E2
Fériana Tunisia 91 H2
Ferjukot Iceland 32 [inset]
Ferkessédougou Côte d'Ivoire 92 D3
Ferlach Austria 37 G5
Ferlo, Vallée du watercourse Senegal 92 B2
Fermont Canada 125 H2
Fermoselle Spain 42 C2
Fermoy Rep. of Ireland 35 B5
Fernandina Beach U.S.A. 129 C6
Fernando de Magallanes, Parque Nacional nat. park Chile 153 B8
Fernando de Noronha i. Brazil 161 L6
Fernandópolis Brazil 149 H5
Fernando Póo i. Equat. Guinea see Bioco
Fernão Veloso Moz. 97 D8
Fernie Canada 134 D2
Fernlee Australia 111 F6
Fernley U.S.A. 136 C2
Ferns Rep. of Ireland 35 C5
Ferozepore India see Firozpur
Ferrara Italy 44 C2
Ferrato, Capo c. Sardinia Italy 45 B5
Ferreira do Alentejo Port. 42 B3
Ferreira-Gomes Brazil 147 I4
Ferrellsburg U.S.A. 130 B4
Ferreñafe Peru 146 B6
Ferriday U.S.A. 133 D6
Ferrol Spain 42 B1
Ferron U.S.A. 137 G2
Ferros Brazil 151 D6
Ferrum U.S.A. 130 C5
Ferryland Canada 125 K4
Ferryville Tunisia see Menzel Bourguiba
Fertő-tavi nat. park Hungary 37 H5
Fès Morocco 90 D2
Feshi Dem. Rep. Congo 95 C6
Fessenden U.S.A. 132 B2
Fété Bowé Senegal 92 B2
Feteşti Romania 46 E2
Feteşti-Gară Romania 46 E2
Fethiye Turkey see Yazıhan
Fethiye Muğla Turkey 78 B3
Fetisovo Kazakh. 79 H2
Fetlar i. U.K. 34 F1
Feuilles, Rivière aux r. Canada 125 G1
Feurs France 39 F4
Fevral'sk Rus. Fed. 64 B1
Fevzipaşa Turkey 78 D3
Feyzābād Afgh. 81 G2
Fez Morocco see Fès
Fiambalá Arg. 152 D1
Fian Ghana 93 E3
Fianarantsoa Madag. 99 [inset] J4
Fianarantsoa prov. Madag. 99 [inset] J4
Fianga Chad 94 B2
Ficalho hill Port. 42 C4
Fiche Eth. 76 B8
Fidenza Italy 44 C2
Fidjeland Norway 33 B4
Fidlův Kopec hill Czech Rep. 37 H4
Field U.S.A. 130 B5
Field Island Australia 110 C2
Fieni Romania 46 D2
Fier Albania 46 A4
Fierzes, Liqeni i resr Albania 46 B3
Fife Ness pt U.K. 34 E3
Fifth Cataract rapids Sudan see 5th Cataract
Fifth Meridian Canada 123 H3
Figari, Capo c. Sardinia Italy 44 B4
Figeac France 38 E4
Figueira r. Port. 42 B3
Figueira da Foz Port. 42 B2
Figueras Spain see Figueres
Figueres Spain 43 H1
Figuig Morocco 91 E2
Figuil Cameroon 93 I3

▶Fiji country S. Pacific Ocean 107 G3
4th most populous and 5th largest country in Oceania.
oceania 104–105, 114

Fik' Eth. 96 D2
Filabusi Zimbabwe 99 F4
Filadelfia Italy 45 F5
Filadelfia Para. 149 E5
Fil'akovo Slovakia 37 I4
Filamana Mali 92 D3
Filchner Ice Shelf Antarctica 167 A1
Filey U.K. 35 F4
Filiaşi Romania 46 C2
Filiates Greece 47 B5
Filiatra Greece 47 B6
Filibe Bulg. see Plovdiv
Filicudi, Isola i. Isole Lipari Italy 45 E5
Filingué Niger 93 F2
Filiouri r. Greece 46 D4
Filipinas country Asia see Philippines
Filippiada Greece 47 B5
Filippoi tourist site Greece 46 D4
Filipstad Sweden 33 D4
Fillan Norway 32 C3
Fillmore CA U.S.A. 136 C4
Fillmore UT U.S.A. 137 F2
Filtu Eth. 96 D3
Fimbull Ice Shelf Antarctica 167 C2
Finale Ligure Italy 44 B2
Fincastle U.S.A. 130 D5
Finch'a'ā Hāyk' l. Eth. 96 C2
Findhorn r. U.K. 34 E3
Fındık Turkey 79 E3
Findlay U.S.A. 130 B3
Fine U.S.A. 131 F1
Finger Lake Canada 123 M4
Finger Lakes U.S.A. 131 E2
Fingoè Moz. 97 A8
Finiels, Sommet de mt. France 39 E4
Finike Turkey 78 B3
Finike Körfezi b. Turkey 78 B3
Finisterre Spain see Fisterra
Finisterre, Cabo c. Spain see Finisterre, Cape
Finisterre, Cape Spain 42 B1
Finke Australia 110 C5
Finke watercourse Australia 110 C5
Finke Flood Flats lowland Australia 110 C5
Finke Gorge National Park Australia 110 C5
▶Finland country Europe 32 G3
europe 24–25, 48
Finland, Gulf of Europe 33 F4
Finlay r. Canada 122 E3
Finlay, Mount Canada 122 E3
Finlay Forks Canada 122 F4
Finley Australia 112 C4
Finley U.S.A. 132 B2
Finn r. Rep. of Ireland 34 C4
Finne ridge Germany 36 E3
Finnigan, Mount Australia 111 F2
Finniss, Cape Australia 109 F8
Finnmark county Norway 32 G1
Finnmarksvidda reg. Norway 32 F1
Finnskog Norway 33 D3
Finnsnes Norway 32 E1
Finschhafen P.N.G. 106 D2
Finspång Sweden 33 D4
Finsteraarhorn mt. Switz. 39 H3
Finsterwalde Germany 37 F3
Finucane Range hills Australia 111 E4
Fiora r. Italy 44 C3
Fiordland National Park N.Z. 113 A4
Fiorenzuola d'Arda Italy 44 B2
Firat r. Turkey 76 B2 see Euphrates
Firavahana Madag. 99 [inset] J3
Firebaugh U.S.A. 136 E3
Firedrake Lake Canada 123 J2
Firenze Italy see Florence
Fireside Canada 122 E3
Firesteel Creek r. U.S.A. 132 B3
Firiña Venez. 147 E3
Firk, Sha'īb watercourse Iraq 79 F5
Firkachi well Niger 93 I2
Firmat Arg. 152 E3
Firminy France 39 F4
Firovo Rus. Fed. 31 M1
Firozabad India 74 C4
Firozpur Haryana India 74 C4
Firozpur Punjab India 74 B3
First Cataract rapids Egypt see 1st Cataract
First Three Mile Opening sea chan. Australia 111 F2
Fīrūzābād Iran 80 C4
Fīrūzeh Iran 80 D2
Fīrūzkūh Iran 80 C3
Fischersbrunn Namibia 98 B5
Fish watercourse Namibia 98 C6
Fish r. S. Africa 98 D6
Fisher Australia 109 E7
Fisher Bay Antarctica 167 G2
Fisher Glacier Antarctica 167 E2
Fisher River Canada 123 L5
Fisher Strait Canada 121 K3
Fishersville U.S.A. 130 D4
Fishguard U.K. 35 D6
Fishing Creek U.S.A. 131 E4
Fishing Lake Canada 123 M4
Fish Lake Canada 122 F2
Fish Point U.S.A. 130 B2
Fishponds Hong Kong China 67 [inset]
Fiskå Norway 33 B3
Fiske, Cape Antarctica 167 L2
Fiskebøl Norway 32 D1
Fiskenæsset Greenland see Qeqertarsuatsiaat
Fismes France 39 E2
Fisterra Spain 42 B1
Fisterra, Cabo Spain see Finisterre, Cape
Fitampito Madag. 99 [inset] J4
Fitchburg MA U.S.A. 131 H2
Fitchburg WI U.S.A. 132 D3
Fitchville U.S.A. 130 B3
Fitjar Norway 33 B4
Fitri, Lac l. Chad 88 C6
Fitzcarrald Peru 148 B2
Fitzgerald River National Park Australia 109 B8
Fitz Hugh Sound sea chan. Canada 122 D5
Fitzmaurice r. Australia 110 B2
Fitz Roy Arg. 153 D6
Fitzroy r. Qld Australia 111 G4
Fitzroy r. W.A. Australia 110 A3
Fitzroy Crossing Australia 110 A3
Fiume Croatia see Rijeka
Five Points U.S.A. 136 B3
Fivizzano Italy 44 C2
Fizi Dem. Rep. Congo 95 F6
Fizuli Azer. see Füzuli
Fjällsjönäs Sweden 32 E2
Fjellbu Norway 32 E1
Fjerritslev Denmark 33 C4
Flå Norway 33 C3
Flaga Iceland 32 [inset]
Flagstaff U.S.A. 137 G4
Flagstaff Lake U.S.A. 128 F2
Flaherty Island Canada 124 E1
Flåm Norway 33 B3
Flambeau r. U.S.A. 132 D2
Flamborough Head U.K. 35 F4
Fläming hills Germany 37 F2
Flaming Gorge Reservoir U.S.A. 134 E4
Flannagan Lake U.S.A. 130 B5
Flannan Isles U.K. 34 C2
Flåsjön l. Sweden 32 D2
Flat r. Canada 122 E2
Flathead r. U.S.A. 126 D2
Flathead Lake U.S.A. 134 D3
Flatiron mt. U.S.A. 134 D3
Flat Island S. China Sea 56 E3
Flat Lick U.S.A. 130 B5
Flattery, Cape Australia 111 F2
Flattery, Cape U.S.A. 134 A2
Flat Top mt. Canada 122 B2
Flatwillow Creek r. U.S.A. 134 F3
Flatwoods KY U.S.A. 130 B4
Flatwoods WV U.S.A. 130 C4
Fleetwood U.K. 35 E5
Fleetwood U.S.A. 131 F3
Flekkefjord Norway 33 B4
Flemingsburg U.S.A. 130 B4
Flemington U.S.A. 131 F3
Flemish Cap sea feature N. Atlantic Ocean 160 L2
Flen Sweden 33 E4
Flensborg Fjord inlet Denmark/Germany 33 C5
Flensburg Germany 36 D1
Flensburger Förde inlet Denmark/Germany see Flensborg Fjord
Flers France 38 C2
Flesherton Canada 130 C1
Fletcher Lake Canada 123 I2
Fletcher Peninsula Antarctica 167 L2
Fleurance France 38 D5
Fleur de Lys Canada 125 J3
Fleur-de-May, Lac l. Canada 125 H3
Fleury-les-Aubrais France 38 D3
Flinders r. Australia 111 E3
Flinders Chase National Park Australia 109 G8
Flinders Group National Park Australia 111 F2
Flinders Island Australia 112 D5
Flinders Passage Australia 111 G3
Flinders Ranges mts Australia 112 A4
Flinders Ranges National Park Australia 112 A3
Flinders Reefs Australia 111 G3
Flin Flon Canada 123 K4
Flint U.K. 35 E5
Flint U.S.A. 130 B2
Flint r. GA U.S.A. 129 B6
Flint r. MI U.S.A. 130 B2
Flint Island Kiribati 165 H6
Flintstone U.S.A. 130 D4
Flisa Norway 33 D3
Flisa r. Norway 33 D3

▶Flissingskiy, Mys c. Rus. Fed. 26 G2
Most easterly point of Europe.

Flix Spain 43 G2
Flöha Germany 37 F3
Flood Range mts Antarctica 167 J1
Flora r. Australia 110 B2
Florac France 39 E4
Florala U.S.A. 129 B6
Flora Reef Australia 111 F3
Floraville Australia 111 D3
Flor de Punga Peru 146 C6
Florence Italy 44 C3
Florence AL U.S.A. 128 B5
Florence AZ U.S.A. 137 G5
Florence KY U.S.A. 130 A4
Florence OR U.S.A. 134 A4
Florence SC U.S.A. 129 D5
Florence Junction U.S.A. 137 G5
Florencia Arg. 152 F2
Florencia Col. 146 C4
Florentia Italy see Florence

Florentino Ameghino Arg. 153 D5
Florentino Ameghino, Embalse resr Arg. 153 D5
Flores Brazil 150 D3
Flores Guat. 138 G5
Flores i. Indon. 57 F7
Florescência Brazil 148 C2
Flores de Goiás Brazil 150 C5
Flores Sea Indon. 57 E7
Floresta Brazil 150 E4
Floresville U.S.A. 133 B6
Floriano Brazil 150 D3
Floriano Peixoto Brazil 148 D2
Florianópolis Brazil 151 B8
Florida Bol. 149 E4
Florida Chile 152 B4
Florida Uruguay 152 F3
▶Florida state U.S.A. 129 C6
northamerica 118–119
Florida, Straits of Bahamas/U.S.A. 129 C8
Florida Bay U.S.A. 129 C7
Florida Keys is U.S.A. 129 C7
Florida Negra Arg. 153 D7
Floridia Sicily Italy 45 E6
Florin U.S.A. 136 B2
Florina Greece 46 B4
Florø Norway 33 B3
Flour Lake Canada 125 H2
Floyd U.S.A. 130 C5
Floyd, Mount U.S.A. 137 F4
Floydada U.S.A. 133 A5
Fluchthorn mt. Austria/Switz. 39 I3
Flums Switz. 39 H3
Flushing Neth. see Vlissingen
Flushing U.S.A. 130 C3
Fluvià r. Spain 43 H1
Fly r. P.N.G. 57 J7
Flying Fish, Cape Antarctica 167 K2
Foam Lake Canada 123 K5
Foča Bos.-Herz. 44 G3
Foça Turkey 78 A3
Focşani Romania 46 E2
Fodé Cent. Afr. Rep. 94 D3
Foelsche r. Australia 110 D2
Fogang China 67 E4
Fogelsville U.S.A. 131 F3
Foggâret el Arab Alg. 91 F4
Foggia Italy 44 E4
Foglia r. Italy 44 D3
Föglö Fin. 33 F3
Fogo i. Cape Verde 92 [inset]
Fogo Island Canada 125 K3
Föhr i. Germany 36 D1
Foinaven hill U.K. 34 D2
Foix France 38 D5
Fokku Nigeria 93 G3
Folarskarnuten mt. Norway 33 B3
Folda sea chan. Norway 32 D2
Foldereid Norway 32 D2
Folegandros Greece 47 D6
Folegandros i. Greece 47 D6
Foley Botswana 99 E4
Foley U.S.A. 129 B6
Foleyet Canada 124 D3
Foligno Italy 44 D3
Folkestone U.K. 35 G6
Folkston U.S.A. 129 C6
Folldal Norway 33 C3
Föllinge Sweden 32 D3
Follonica Italy 44 C3
Folsom U.S.A. 130 C4
Folsom Lake U.S.A. 136 B2
Fomboni Comoros 97 D8
Fomin Rus. Fed. 29 G7
Fominskoye Rus. Fed. 28 G4
Fonda U.S.A. 131 F2
Fond-du-Lac Canada 123 J3
Fond du Lac r. Canada 123 J3
Fond du Lac U.S.A. 132 D3
Fonde U.S.A. 130 B5
Fondevila Spain 42 B2
Fondi Italy 44 D4
Fon Going ridge Guinea 92 C3
Fonni Sardinia Italy 45 B4
Fonsagrada Spain see A Fonsagrada
Fonseca, Golfo do b. Central America 138 G6
Fontainebleau France 39 E2
Fontanges Canada 125 G2
Fontas Canada 122 F3
Fontas r. Canada 122 F3
Fonte Boa Brazil 147 E5
Fonte do Pau-d'Agua Brazil 149 F3
Fontenay-le-Comte France 38 C3
Fonteneau, Lac l. Canada 125 I3
Fontur pt Iceland 32 [inset]
Fonuafo'ou i. Tonga 107 H4
Fonuafu'u i. Tonga see Fonuafo'ou
Fonualei i. Tonga 107 H3
Fonyód Hungary 37 H5
Foochow China see Fuzhou
Foping China 66 D1
Foraker, Mount U.S.A. 120 D3
Forat Iran 80 C3
Foraulep atoll Micronesia see Faraulep
Forbes Australia 112 D4
Forbesganj India 75 E4
Forchheim Germany 36 E4
Ford r. U.S.A. 132 E2
Ford City CA U.S.A. 136 C4
Ford City PA U.S.A. 130 D3
Førde Norway 33 B3
Forde Lake Canada 123 L2
Ford Range mts Antarctica 167 J1
Fords Bridge Australia 112 C3
Fordyce U.S.A. 133 C5
Forécariah Guinea 92 B3
Forel, Mont mt. Greenland 121 P3
Foremost Canada 123 I5
Foresight Mountain Canada 122 E4
Forest Canada 130 C2
Forest MS U.S.A. 133 D5
Forest OH U.S.A. 130 B3
Forest VA U.S.A. 130 D5
Forestburg Canada 123 H4
Forest City U.S.A. 131 F3
Forest Creek r. Australia 111 E3
Forest Lakes U.S.A. 137 G4
Forest Park U.S.A. 129 B5
Forest Ranch U.S.A. 136 B2
Forestville Canada 125 G3
Forestville U.S.A. 130 B2
Forêt Dense de Dzanga-Sangha, Réserve Spéciale de res. Cameroon 94 B4
Forêt des Deux Balé nat. park Burkina 92 E3
Forfar U.K. 34 E3
Forges-les-Eaux France 38 D2
Forillon, Parc National de nat. park Canada 125 H3
Forish Uzbek. see Farish
Forks U.S.A. 134 A3
Forksville U.S.A. 131 E3
Fork Union U.S.A. 130 D5
Forlì Italy 44 D2
Forman U.S.A. 132 B2
Formentera i. Spain 43 G3
Formentor, Cap de c. Spain 43 H3
Formerie France 38 D2
Former Yugoslav Republic of Macedonia country Europe see Macedonia
Formia Italy 44 D4
Formiga Brazil 151 C7
Formosa Arg. 152 F1
Formosa prov. Arg. 149 F6
Formosa country Asia see Taiwan
Formosa Brazil 150 C5
Formosa, Serra hills Brazil 149 G3
Formosa do Rio Preto Brazil 150 C4
Formosa Strait China/Taiwan see Taiwan Strait
Formoso Brazil 150 B4
Formoso r. Bahia Brazil 150 C5
Formoso r. Tocantins Brazil 150 B4
Fornos Moz. 99 G4
Forolshogna mt. Norway 32 C3
Forres U.K. 34 E3
Forrest Australia 109 E7
Forrest r. Australia 108 E3
Forrestal Range mts Antarctica 167 A1
Forrest City U.S.A. 127 H4
Forrest Lakes salt flat Australia 109 E7
Forsand Norway 33 B4
Forsayth Australia 111 E3
Forsbakken Norway 32 E1
Forssa Fin. 33 F3
Forst Germany 37 G3
Forsyth GA U.S.A. 129 C5
Forsyth MO U.S.A. 133 C4
Forsyth MT U.S.A. 134 F3
Forsyth Range hills Australia 111 E4
Fort Abbas Pak. 81 H4
Fort Albany Canada 124 D2
Fortaleza Pando Bol. 148 D2
Fortaleza Pando Bol. 148 D3
Fortaleza Brazil 150 E2
Fortaleza de Santa Teresa Uruguay 152 G3
Fort Archambault Chad see Sarh
Fort Ashby U.S.A. 130 D4
Fort Assiniboine Canada 123 H4
Fort Augustus U.K. 34 D3
Fort Babine Canada 122 E4
Fort Beaufort S. Africa 99 E7
Fort Benton U.S.A. 134 E3
Fort Brabant Canada see Tuktoyaktuk
Fort Bragg U.S.A. 136 A2
Fort Carillon U.S.A. see Ticonderoga
Fort Carnot Madag. see Ikongo
Fort Charlet Alg. see Djanet
Fort Chimo Canada see Kuujjuaq
Fort Chipewyan Canada 123 I3
Fort Collins U.S.A. 134 F4
Fort-Coulonge Canada 124 E4
Fort Crampel Cent. Afr. Rep. see Kaga Bandoro
Fort-Dauphin Madag. see Tôlañaro
Fort Davis U.S.A. 133 A6
▶Fort-de-France Martinique 139 L6
Capital of Martinique.
Fort de Kock Indon. see Bukittinggi
Fort de Polignac Alg. see Illizi
Fort Deposit U.S.A. 129 B5
Fort Dodge U.S.A. 132 C3
Fort Duchesne U.S.A. 137 H1
Forte, Monte hill Sardinia Italy 45 B4
Fort Edward U.S.A. 131 G2
Forte Nordeste Angola 95 D6
Fort Erie Canada 130 D2
Fortescue r. Australia 108 B5
Forte Veneza Brazil 147 H6
Fort Flatters Alg. see Bordj Omer Driss
Fort Foureau Cameroon see Kousséri
Fort Franklin Canada see Déline
Fort Gardel Alg. see Zaouatallaz
Fort Garland U.S.A. 135 F5
Fort Gay U.S.A. 130 B4
Fort George Canada see Chisasibi
Fort Good Hope Canada 122 D1
Fort Gouraud Mauritania see Fdérik
Forth r. U.K. 34 E3
Forth, Firth of est. U.K. 34 E3
Fort Hall Kenya see Muranga
Fort Hertz Myanmar see Putao
Fortification Range mts U.S.A. 137 E2
Fortín Aroma Para. 149 E5
Fortín Ávalos Sánchez Para. 149 E5
Fortín Boquerón Para. 149 F5
Fortín Carlos Antonio López Para. 149 F5
Fortín Coronel Bogado Para. 149 F5
Fortín Coronel Eugenio Garay Para. 149 E5
Fortín Galpón Para. 149 F4
Fortín General Caballero Para. 149 F6
Fortín General Diaz Para. 149 E5
Fortín General Mendoza Para. 149 E5
Fortín Infante Rivarola Para. 149 E5
Fortín Juan de Zalazar Para. 149 F5
Fortín Lavalle Arg. 152 E1
Fortín Leonardo Britos Para. 149 E5
Fortín Linares Para. 149 E5
Fortín Madrejón Para. 149 F5
Fortín May Alberto Gardel Para. 149 E5
Fortín Nueva Asunción Para. 149 E5
Fortín Pilcomayo Arg. 149 E5
Fortín Presidente Ayala Para. 149 F5
Fortín Ravelo Bol. 149 E4
Fortín Suárez Arana Bol. 149 E4
Fortín Teniente Juan Echauri López Para. 149 E5
Fortín Teniente Mountania Para. 149 F5
Fortín Teniente Primero H. Mendoza Para. 149 F4
Fortín Teniente Rojas Silva Para. 149 E6
Fort Jameson Zambia see Chipata
Fort Johnston Malawi see Mangochi
Fort Kent U.S.A. 128 F2
Fort Lamy Chad see Ndjamena
Fort Laperrine Alg. see Tamanrasset
Fort Lauderdale U.S.A. 129 C7
Fort Liard Canada 122 F2
Fort Mackay Canada 123 I3
Fort Macleod Canada 134 D2
Fort Madison U.S.A. 124 B5
Fort Manning Malawi see Mchinji
Fort McMurray Canada 123 I3
Fort McPherson Canada 120 F3
Fort Myers U.S.A. 129 C7
Fort Nelson Canada 122 F3
Fort Nelson r. Canada 122 F3
Fort Norman Canada see Tulita
Fort Orange U.S.A. see Albany
Fortore r. Italy 44 E4
Fort Payne U.S.A. 133 E5
Fort Peck Reservoir U.S.A. 134 F3
Fort Pierce U.S.A. 129 C7
Fort Pierre U.S.A. 132 A2
Fort Portal Uganda 96 A4
Fort Providence Canada 123 G2
Fort Qu'Appelle Canada 134 G2
Fort Randall U.S.A. see Cold Bay
Fort Recovery U.S.A. 130 A3
Fort Resolution Canada 123 H2
Fortrose N.Z. 113 B4
Fort Rosebery Zambia see Mansa
Fort Rousset Congo see Owando
Fort Rupert Canada see Waskaganish
Fort St James Canada 122 E4
Fort St John Canada 122 F3
Fort Sandeman Pak. see Zhob
Fort Saskatchewan Canada 123 H4
Fort Scott U.S.A. 132 C4
Fort Severn Canada 124 C1
Fort-Shevchenko Kazakh. 79 G1
Fort Simpson Canada 122 F2
Fort Smith Canada 123 H2
Fort Smith U.S.A. 133 C5
Fort Stockton U.S.A. 133 A6
Fort Sumner U.S.A. 135 F6
Fort Trinquet Mauritania see Bîr Mogreïn
Fortune Bay Canada 125 K4
Fort Valley U.S.A. 129 C5
Fort Vermilion Canada 123 G3
Fort Victoria Zimbabwe see Masvingo
Fort Walton U.S.A. see Fort Walton Beach
Fort Walton Beach U.S.A. 129 B6
Fort Ware Canada see Ware
Fort Wayne U.S.A. 132 E3
Fort Wellington Guyana 147 G3
Fort White Myanmar 60 A3
Fort William U.K. 34 D3
Fort Worth U.S.A. 133 B5
Fort Yates U.S.A. 132 A2
Fortymile r. Canada/U.S.A. 122 A1
Forty Mile Scrub National Park Australia 111 F3
Fort Yukon U.S.A. 120 E3
Forum Iulii France see Fréjus
Forūr, Jazīreh-ye i. Iran 80 C5
Forvik Norway 32 D2
Foshan China 67 E4
Foskvallen Sweden 33 D3
Fosna pen. Norway 32 C3
Foso Ghana 93 E4
Foss Iceland 32 [inset]
Fossano Italy 44 A2
Fosshóll Iceland 32 [inset]
Fossil U.S.A. 134 B3
Fossil Downs Australia 108 D4
Fossombrone Italy 44 D3
Fos-sur-Mer France 39 F5
Foster Australia 112 C5
Foster Bugt b. Greenland 121 Q2
Foster Lakes Canada 123 J3
Fostoria U.S.A. 130 B3
Fotadrevo Madag. 99 [inset] J5
Fotuna i. Vanuatu see Futuna
Fouesnant France 38 A3
Fougamou Gabon 94 A5
Fougères France 38 C2
Foula i. U.K. 34 E1
Foulamôri Guinea 92 B2
Foul Bay Egypt 89 G4
Foulenzem Gabon 94 A5
Foulness Point U.K. 35 G6
Foul Point Sri Lanka 72 D4
Foumbot Cameroon 93 H4
Foum Zguid Morocco 90 D3
Foundation Ice Stream glacier Antarctica 167 L1
Founougo Benin 93 F3
Fountains Abbey tourist site U.K. 35 F4
Four, Pointe de pt Alg. 43 H4
Fourchambault France 39 E3
Fourches, Mont des hill France 39 F2
Four Corners U.S.A. 136 D4
Four Mountains, Islands of the U.S.A. 120 C4
Fournoi Greece 47 E6
Fournoi i. Greece 47 E6
Fouta Djallon reg. Guinea 92 B3
Foveaux Strait N.Z. 113 A4
Fowler CO U.S.A. 135 F5
Fowler IN U.S.A. 128 B3
Fowler MI U.S.A. 130 A2
Fowler Ice Rise Antarctica 167 L1
Fowlerville U.S.A. 130 A2
Fox r. U.S.A. 132 D3
Foxas Spain 42 B1
Fox Creek Canada 123 G4
Foxe Basin g. Canada 121 L3
Foxe Channel Canada 121 K3
Foxen l. Sweden 33 C4
Foxe Peninsula Canada 121 L3
Fox Glacier N.Z. 113 B3
Fox Islands U.S.A. 120 C4
Fox Lake Canada 123 H3
Fox Mountain Canada 122 C2
Foxton N.Z. 113 C3
Fox Valley Canada 123 I5
Foyle r. Rep. of Ireland/U.K. 34 C4
Foyle, Lough b. Rep. of Ireland/U.K. 34 C4
Foz Spain 42 C1
Foz de Areia, Represa de resr Brazil 151 B8
Foz de Gregório Brazil 146 D6
Foz do Copeá Brazil 147 F5
Foz do Cunene Angola 95 A9
Foz do Iguaçu Brazil 151 A8
Foz do Jutaí Brazil 146 E5
Foz do Mamoriá Brazil 146 E5
Foz do Riosinho Brazil 148 C1
Frackville U.S.A. 131 E3
Fraga Arg. 152 D3
Fraga Spain 43 G2
Fraile Muerto Uruguay 152 G3
Frakes, Mount Antarctica 167 K1
Framingham U.S.A. 131 H2
Framnes Mountains Antarctica 167 E2
Franca Brazil 149 I5
Français, Récif des reef New Caledonia 107 F3
Francavilla Fontana Italy 45 F4
▶France country Europe 38 E3
3rd largest and 4th most populous country in Europe.
europe 24–25, 48
France, Île de i. Greenland 121 R2
Frances Australia 112 B5
Frances r. Canada 122 D2
Frances Lake Canada 122 D2
Frances Lake l. Canada 122 D2
Franceville Gabon 94 B5
Franche-Comté admin. reg. France 39 G3
Francis Canada 123 K5
Francis atoll Kiribati see Beru
Francisco de Orellana Ecuador see Puerto Francisco de Orellana
Francisco de Orellana Peru 146 C5
Francisco I. Madero Mex. 133 A7
Francisco Meeks Arg. 152 F4
Francisco Sá Brazil 151 D6
Francisco Zarco Mex. 135 C6
Francistown Botswana 99 E4
Francofonte Sicily Italy 45 E6
François Lake Canada 122 E4
Francois Peron National Park Australia 109 A6
Francs Peak U.S.A. 134 E4
Frankenberg (Eder) Germany 36 D3
Frankenmuth U.S.A. 130 B2
Frankford Canada 130 E1
Frankfort IN U.S.A. 132 E3
▶Frankfort KY U.S.A. 130 A4
State capital of Kentucky.
Frankfort OH U.S.A. 130 B4
Frankfurt am Main Germany 36 D3
Frankfurt an der Oder Germany 37 G2
Frank Hann National Park Australia 109 C8
Frankin Lake U.S.A. 137 E1
Fränkische Alb hills Germany 36 E4
Fränkische Schweiz reg. Germany 36 E4
Frankland, Cape Australia 112 C5
Franklin GA U.S.A. 133 E5
Franklin IN U.S.A. 128 B4
Franklin LA U.S.A. 133 D6
Franklin MA U.S.A. 131 H2
Franklin NC U.S.A. 128 C5
Franklin NE U.S.A. 132 B3
Franklin NH U.S.A. 131 H2
Franklin NJ U.S.A. 131 F3
Franklin OH U.S.A. 130 A4
Franklin PA U.S.A. 130 D3
Franklin TN U.S.A. 128 B5
Franklin TX U.S.A. 133 B6
Franklin VA U.S.A. 131 E5
Franklin WV U.S.A. 130 D4
Franklin D. Roosevelt Lake U.S.A. 126 C2
Franklin Furnace U.S.A. 130 B4
Franklin-Gordon National Park Australia 112 C6
Franklin Island Antarctica 167 H1
Franklin Lake Canada 123 M1
Franklin Mountains Canada 122 F2
Franklin Strait Canada 121 J2
Franklinton U.S.A. 133 D6
Franklinville U.S.A. 130 D2
Frankrike Sweden 32 D3
Fransfontein Namibia 98 B4
Fränsta Sweden 33 E3
Frantsa-Iosifa, Zemlya is Rus. Fed. 26 F2
Franz Canada 124 C3
Franz Josef Glacier N.Z. 113 B3
Franz Josef Land is Rus. Fed. see Frantsa-Iosifa, Zemlya
Frascati Italy 44 D4
Fraser r. B.C. Canada 134 B2
Fraser r. Nfld. and Lab. Canada 125 I1
Fraser, Mount Australia 109 B6
Fraserburg S. Africa 98 D6
Fraserburgh U.K. 34 E3
Fraserdale Canada 124 D3
Fraser Island Australia 111 H5
Fraser Island National Park Australia 111 H5
Fraser Lake Canada 122 E4
Fraser National Park Australia 112 C5
Fraser Plateau Canada 122 E4
Fraser Range Australia 109 C8
Fraser Range hills Australia 109 C8
Frasertown N.Z. 113 D2
Frătești Romania 46 D3
Frauenfeld Switz. 39 H3
Fray Bentos Uruguay 152 F3
Fray Marcos Uruguay 152 G3
Frederica U.S.A. 131 F4
Fredericia Denmark 33 C5
Frederick MD U.S.A. 130 E4
Frederick OK U.S.A. 133 B5
Frederick Hills Australia 110 C2
Frederick Reef Australia 111 H4
Fredericksburg TX U.S.A. 133 B6
Fredericksburg VA U.S.A. 130 E4
Frederick Sound sea chan. U.S.A. 122 C3
Fredericktown MO U.S.A. 132 D4
Fredericktown OH U.S.A. 130 B3
▶Fredericton Canada 125 H4
Provincial capital of New Brunswick.
Fredericton airport Canada 128 G2
Frederikshåb Greenland see Paamiut
Frederikshavn Denmark 33 C4
Frederiksværk Denmark 33 D5
Fredonia AZ U.S.A. 137 F3
Fredonia KS U.S.A. 132 C4
Fredonia NY U.S.A. 130 D2
Fredrika Sweden 32 E2
Fredriksberg Sweden 33 D3
Fredrikshamn Fin. see Hamina
Fredrikstad Norway 33 C4
Freehold U.S.A. 131 F3
Freeland U.S.A. 131 F3
Freeling, Mount Australia 110 C4
Freeling Heights hill Australia 111 D6
Freels, Cape Canada 125 K3
Freeman U.S.A. 132 B3
Freeport IL U.S.A. 132 D3
Freeport ME U.S.A. 131 H2
Freeport PA U.S.A. 130 D3
Freeport TX U.S.A. 133 C6
Freeport City Bahamas 129 D7
Freer U.S.A. 133 B7
Free State prov. S. Africa 99 E6
▶Freetown Sierra Leone 92 B3
Capital of Sierra Leone.
Freewood Acres U.S.A. 131 F3
Fregenal de la Sierra Spain 42 C3
Fregon Australia 110 C5
Fréhel, Cap c. France 38 B2
Freiberg Germany 37 F3
Freiburg Switz. see Fribourg
Freiburg im Breisgau Germany 36 C4
Freising Germany 36 E4
Freistadt Austria 37 G4
Freital Germany 37 F3
Freixo de Espada à Cinta Port. 42 C2
Fréjus France 39 G5
Frekhaug Norway 33 B3
Fremantle Australia 109 A8
Fremont CA U.S.A. 136 B3
Fremont NE U.S.A. 132 B3
Fremont OH U.S.A. 130 B3
Fremont r. U.S.A. 137 G2
Fremont Junction U.S.A. 137 G2
Frenchburg U.S.A. 130 B5
French Congo country Africa see Congo
French Creek r. U.S.A. 130 D3
▶French Guiana terr. S. America 147 H4
French Overseas Department.
southamerica 144–145, 154
French Guinea country Africa see Guinea
Frenchman r. U.S.A. 134 F2
Frenchman Creek r. U.S.A. 132 A3
Frenchman Lake U.S.A. 136 B2
French Pass N.Z. 113 C3
▶French Polynesia terr. S. Pacific Ocean 165 I7
French Overseas Territory.
oceania 104–105, 114
French Somaliland country Africa see Djibouti
▶French Southern and Antarctic Lands terr. Indian Ocean 163 L8
French Overseas Territory.
asia 52–53, 82
French Sudan country Africa see Mali
French Territory of the Afars and Issas country Africa see Djibouti
Frenchtown U.S.A. 131 F3
Frenda Alg. 91 F2
Fresco r. Brazil 147 I6
Fresco Côte d'Ivoire 92 D4
Fresnillo Mex. 126 F7
Fresno U.S.A. 136 C3
Fresno r. U.S.A. 136 B3
Fressel, Lac l. Canada 125 F2
Freu, Cap des c. Spain 43 H3
Freudenstadt Germany 36 D4
Frew watercourse Australia 110 C4
Frewsburg U.S.A. 130 D2
Freycinet Estuary inlet Australia 109 A6
Freycinet Peninsula Australia 112 D6
Freyming-Merlebach France 39 G2
Freyre Arg. 152 E2
Freyung Germany 37 F4
Fria Guinea 92 B3
Fria, Cape Namibia 98 B3
Friant U.S.A. 136 C3
Friant-Kern Canal U.S.A. 136 C4
Frias Arg. 152 D2
Fribourg Switz. 39 G3
Frick Switz. 39 H3
Friday Harbor U.S.A. 134 B2
Friedberg Germany 36 E4
Friedens U.S.A. 130 D3
Friedland Germany 37 F2
Friedland Rus. Fed. see Pravdinsk
Friedrichshafen Germany 36 D5
Friend U.S.A. 132 B3
Friendly Islands country S. Pacific Ocean see Tonga
Friesach Austria 37 G5
Friesack Germany 37 F2
Friesoythe Germany 36 C2
Frio r. TX U.S.A. 133 B6
Frio r. TX U.S.A. 133 B6
Frio watercourse U.S.A. 133 A5
Friol Spain 42 C1
Frisco Mountain U.S.A. 137 F2
Frissell, Mount U.S.A. 131 G2
Friuli - Venezia Giulia admin. reg. Italy 44 D1
Frobisher Bay Canada see Iqaluit
Frobisher Bay b. Canada 121 M3
Frobisher Lake Canada 123 I3
Frohavet b. Norway 32 C3
Frohburg Germany 37 F3
Frohnleiten Austria 37 G5
Frolovo Rus. Fed. 29 G6
Frome watercourse Australia 110 D6
Frome U.K. 35 E6
Frome, Lake salt flat Australia 112 A3
Fromveur, Passage du strait France 38 A2
Fronteira Port. 42 C3
Fronteiras Brazil 150 D3
Frontera Coahuila Mex. 133 A7
Frontera Mex. 138 F5
Fronteras Mex. 135 E7
Frontignan France 39 E5
Front Royal U.S.A. 130 D4
Frosinone Italy 44 D4
Frostburg U.S.A. 130 D4
Frøya i. Norway 32 C3
Føroyar terr. N. Atlantic Ocean see Faroe Islands
Fruges France 38 E1
Fruita U.S.A. 137 H2
Fruitland MD U.S.A. 131 F4
Fruitland UT U.S.A. 137 G1
Frunze Kyrg. 81 G1
Frunze Kyrg. see Bishkek
Frunzenskoye Kyrg. see Frunze
Frusino Italy see Frosinone
Fruska Gora nat. park Serb. and Mont. 46 A2
Frutuoso Brazil 149 E3
Frýdek-Místek Czech Rep. 37 I4
Fryeburg U.S.A. 131 H1
Fu'an China 67 F3
Fucheng China see Fengyang
Fuchuan China 67 D3
Fuchun Jiang r. China 67 G2
Fude China 67 F3
Fuding China 67 G3
Fudua waterhole Kenya 96 C5
Fuengirola Spain 42 D4
Fuenlabrada Spain 42 E2
Fuente Albilla, Cerro de mt. Spain 43 F3
Fuente de Cantos Spain 42 C3
Fuente Obejuna Spain 42 D3
Fuentesaúco Spain 42 D2
Fuentes de Ebro Spain 43 F2
Fuerte Olimpo Para. 149 F5
Fuerteventura i. Canary Is 90 B3
Fuga i. Phil. 67 G5
Fugloy i. Faroe Is 34 [inset]
Fuglstad Norway 32 D2
Fugou China 67 E1
Fuhai China 70 G2
Fujairah U.A.E. 80 D5
Fujeira U.A.E. see Fujairah
Fuji China see Luxian
Fuji Japan 65 D6
Fujian prov. China 67 F3
Fu Jiang r. China 66 C2
Fuji-Hakone-Izu National Park Japan 65 D6
Fujin China 64 B3
Fujinomiya Japan 65 D6
Fuji-san vol. Japan 65 D6
Fukagawa Japan 64 E4
Fûkah Egypt 78 A5
Fukien prov. China see Fujian
Fukuchiyama Japan 65 C6
Fukue Japan 65 B6
Fukue-jima i. Japan 65 B6
Fukui Japan 65 D5
Fukuoka Japan 65 B6
Fukushima Japan 65 E5
Fûl, Jabal hill Egypt 77 A5
Fulacunda Guinea-Bissau 92 B3
Fülād Maialleh Iran 80 C2
Fulchhari Bangl. 75 F4
Fulda Germany 36 D3
Fulda r. Germany 36 D3
Fule China 66 C3
Fuli China see Jixian
Fuliji China 67 F1
Fulin China see Hanyuan
Fuling China 66 C2
Fulitun China see Jixian
Fullerton U.S.A. 132 B3
Fullerton, Cape Canada 123 N2
Fulnek Czech Rep. 37 H4
Fulton KY U.S.A. 128 A4
Fulton MO U.S.A. 132 D4
Fulton MS U.S.A. 129 A5
Fulton NY U.S.A. 131 E2
Fulunäs Sweden 33 D3
Fumay France 39 F2
Fumel France 38 D4
Fumin China 66 B3
Funabashi Japan 65 D6
Funafuti atoll Tuvalu 107 G2
Funan China see Fusui
Funäsdalen Sweden 33 D3
▶Funchal Madeira 90 A2
Capital of Madeira.
Fundación Col. 146 C2
Fundão Brazil 151 D6
Fundão Port. 42 C2
Fundi Italy see Fondi
Fundición Mex. 135 E8
Fundo das Figuerias Cape Verde 92 [inset]
Fundulea Romania 46 E2
Fundy, Bay of g. Canada 125 H4
Fünen i. Denmark see Fyn
Funeral Peak U.S.A. 137 D3
Fünfkirchen Hungary see Pécs
Funhalouro Moz. 99 G4
Funing Jiangsu China 67 F1
Funing Yunnan China 66 C4
Funiu Shan mts China 67 D1
Funsi Ghana 93 E3
Funtua Nigeria 93 G3
Funzie U.K. 34 F1
Fuqing China 67 F3
Fuquan China 66 C3
Furancungo Moz. 97 B8
Furano Japan 64 E4
Fūrgun, Kūh-e mt. Iran 80 D5
Furmanov Rus. Fed. 28 G4
Furmanovo Kazakh. see Zhalpaktal
Furnas, Represa resr Brazil 151 C7
Furneaux Group is Australia 112 D6
Furnes Belgium see Veurne
Fürstenau Germany 36 C2
Fürstenberg Germany 37 F2
Fürstenfeld Austria 37 H5
Fürstenfeldbruck Germany 36 E4
Fürstenwalde Germany 37 G2
Fürth Germany 36 E4
Furth im Wald Germany 37 F4
Furudal Sweden 33 D3
Furukawa Japan 65 E5
Fury and Hecla Strait Canada 121 K3
Fusagasugá Col. 146 C3
Fusan S. Korea see Pusan
Fushun Liaoning China 63 K3
Fushun Sichuan China 66 C2
Fusong China 64 A4
Fusui China 66 C4
Fu Tau Pun Chau i. Hong Kong China 67 [inset]
Futog Serb. and Mont. 46 A2
Futuna i. Vanuatu 107 G3
Futuna Islands is Wallis and Futuna Is see Hoorn, Îles de
Futun Xi r. China 67 F3
Fuwayriṭ Qatar 80 B5
Fuxian China see Wafangdian
Fuxin China 63 K3
Fuxing China see Wangmo
Fuxinzhen China see Fuxin
Fuyang Anhui China 67 E1
Fuyang Guangxi China see Fuchuan
Fuyang Zhejiang China 67 F2
Fuying Dao i. China 67 G3
Fuyu Heilong. China 63 K2
Fuyu Jilin China see Songyuan
Fuyu Jilin China 64 A3
Fuyuan Heilong. China 64 C2
Fuyuan Yunnan China 66 C3
Fuyun China 70 G2
Füzesabony Hungary 37 J5
Füzesgyarmat Hungary 37 J5
Fuzhou Fujian China 67 F3
Fuzhou Jiangxi China see Linchuan
Füzuli Azer. 79 F3
Fwamba Dem. Rep. Congo 95 D6
Fyn county Denmark 33 C5
Fyn i. Denmark 33 C5
Fyne, Loch inlet U.K. 34 D4
Fyresvatn l. Norway 33 C4
F.Y.R.O.M. (Former Yugoslav Republic of Macedonia) country Europe see Macedonia

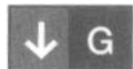
Gaâfour Tunisia 45 B6
Gaalkacyo Somalia 96 E3
Gaat r. Sarawak Malaysia 59 F2
Gabakly Turkm. see Kabakly
Gabangab well Eth. 96 E3
Gabas r. France 38 C5
Gabbs Valley Range mts U.S.A. 136 C2
Gabd Pak. 81 E5
Gabela Angola 95 B7
Gaberones Botswana see Gaborone
Gabès Tunisia 91 H2
Gabès, Golfe de g. Tunisia 91 H2
Gabès, Gulf of Tunisia see Gabès, Golfe de
Gabgaba, Wadi watercourse Sudan 89 G4
▶Gabon country Africa 94 A5
africa 86–87,100
Gabon, Estuaire du est. Gabon 94 A4
▶Gaborone Botswana 98 E5
Capital of Botswana.
Gabou Senegal 92 B2
Gabriel y Galán, Embalse de resr Spain 42 C2
Gābrīk Iran 80 D5
Gābrīk watercourse Iran 80 D5
Gabrovnitsa Bulg. 46 C3
Gabrovo Bulg. 46 D3
Gabú Guinea-Bissau 92 B2
Gabuli vol. Eth. 89 I6
Gacé France 38 D2
Gacko Bos.-Herz. 44 G3
Gadag India 72 B3
Gadaisu P.N.G. 111 G1
Gäddede Sweden 32 D2
Gadê China 66 A1
Gades Spain see Cádiz
Gadhada India 74 A5
Gadhra India 72 A1
Gadsden U.S.A. 129 B5
Gadwal India 72 C2
Gadyach Ukr. see Hadyach
Gadyn Turkm. 81 E2
Gadzi Cent. Afr. Rep. 94 C3
Gæi'dnuvuop'pi Norway 32 F1
Găeşti Romania 46 D2
Gaeta Italy 44 D4
Gaeta, Golfo di g. Italy 44 D4
Gafanha da Nazaré Port. 42 B2
Gaferut i. Micronesia 57 K4
Gafsa Tunisia 91 H2
Gagal Chad 94 B2
Gagarin Rus. Fed. 28 E5
Gagarin Uzbek. 81 G1
Gagere watercourse Nigeria 93 G2
Gagliano del Capo Italy 45 G5
Gagnoa Côte d'Ivoire 92 D4
Gagnon Canada 125 G3
Gago Coutinho Angola see Lumbala N'guimbo
Gagra Georgia 79 E2
Gaiab watercourse Namibia 98 C6
Gaibandha Bangl. 75 F4
Gail r. Austria 37 F5
Gaillac France 38 D5
Gaillimh Rep. of Ireland see Galway
Gaillon France 38 D2
Gaindainqoinkor China see Lhünzhub
Gaindaingoinkor China see Lhünzhub
Gainesboro U.S.A. 133 E4
Gainesville FL U.S.A. 129 C6
Gainesville GA U.S.A. 133 F5
Gainesville MO U.S.A. 133 C4
Gainesville TX U.S.A. 133 B5
Gainsborough U.K. 35 F5
Gairdner r. Australia 109 B8
Gairdner, Lake salt flat Australia 109 F7
Gairloch U.K. 34 D3
Gairo Tanz. 97 C6
Gaja r. Hungary 37 I5
Gajah Hutan, Bukit hill Malaysia 58 C1
Gaji r. Nigeria 93 H3
Gajol India 75 F4
Gajos well Kenya 96 C4

Gakarosa mt. S. Africa 98 D5
Gakem Nigeria 93 H4
Gakuch Jammu and Kashmir 74 B1
Gala China 75 F3
Galán, Cerro mt. Arg. 152 D1
Galana r. Kenya 96 D5
Galand Iran 80 C2
Galangue Angola 95 C8
Galanta Slovakia 37 H4
Galápagos, Islas see Galapagos Islands

▶Galapagos Islands Pacific Ocean 165 L6
Part of Ecuador. Most westerly point of South America.
southamerica 144–145

Galapagos Rise sea feature Pacific Ocean 165 L6
Galashiels U.K. 34 E4
Galata Bulg. 46 E3
Galați Romania 46 F2
Galatista Greece 47 C4
Galatone Italy 45 G4
Galax U.S.A. 130 C5
Galaymor Turkm. see Kala-I-Mor
Galdhøpiggen mt. Norway 33 C3
Galeana Mex. 135 F7
Galegu Sudan 89 G6
Galena AK U.S.A. 120 D3
Galena IL U.S.A. 132 D3
Galena MD U.S.A. 131 F4
Galena MO U.S.A. 133 C4
Galena Bay Canada 122 G5
Galera, Punta pt Chile 152 B5
Galera, Punta pt Ecuador 146 A4
Galeras vol. Col. 146 B4
Galesburg U.S.A. 132 D3
Galeshewe S. Africa 98 E6
Galeton U.S.A. 130 E3
Galga r. Hungary 37 I5
Galguduud admin. reg. Somalia 96 E3
Gal Hareeri Somalia 96 E3
Galich Rus. Fed. 28 G4
Galichskaya Vozvyshennost' hills Rus. Fed. 28 G4
Galicia aut. comm. Spain 42 C1
Galičica nat. park Macedonia 46 B4
Galilee, Sea of l. Israel 77 B3
Galissas Greece 47 D6
Galiuro Mountains U.S.A. 137 G5
Galiwinku Australia 110 C2
Gallabat Sudan 89 H6
Gallatin MO U.S.A. 132 C4
Gallatin TN U.S.A. 128 B4
Gallatin r. U.S.A. 134 E3
Galle Sri Lanka 72 D5
Gállego r. Spain 43 F2
Gallego Rise sea feature Pacific Ocean 165 K6
Gallegos r. Arg. 153 C7
Gallegos, Cabo c. Chile 153 B6
Gallia country Europe see France

▶Gallinas, Punta pt Col. 146 D1
Most northerly point of South America.

Gallipoli Italy 45 G4
Gallipoli Turkey 78 A2
Gallipolis U.S.A. 130 B4
Gällivare Sweden 32 F2
Gallo r. Spain 43 E2
Gällö Sweden 32 D3
Gallo, Capo c. Sicily Italy 45 D5
Gallup KY U.S.A. 130 B4
Gallup NM U.S.A. 135 E6
Gallur Spain 43 F2
Gallura reg. Sardinia Italy 44 B4
Gallyaaral Uzbek. 81 F1
Galma watercourse Nigeria 93 G3
Galoya Sri Lanka 72 D4
Gal Oya National Park Sri Lanka 72 D5
Gal Shiikh Somalia 96 E2
Galt U.S.A. 136 B2
Gal Tardo Somalia 96 E4
Galtat Zemmour W. Sahara 90 B4
Galtee Mountains hills Rep. of Ireland 35 B5
Galtymore hill Rep. of Ireland 35 B5
Galūgāh, Kūh-e mts Iran 80 C4
Galūgāh-e Āsīyeh Iran 81 D3
Galunggung, Gunung vol. Indon. 59 E4
Galveston U.S.A. 133 C6
Galveston Bay U.S.A. 133 C6
Galvez Arg. 152 E3
Galwa Nepal 75 D3
Galway Rep. of Ireland 35 B5
Galway Bay Rep. of Ireland 35 B5
Găm r. Vietnam 60 D3
Gamaches France 38 D2
Gamalakhe S. Africa 99 F6
Gámas Fin. see Kaamanen
Gamawa Nigeria 93 H2
Gamba China 75 F3
Gambēla Eth. 96 B2
Gambēla admin. reg. Eth. 96 B3
Gambēla National Park Eth. 96 B3
Gambell U.S.A. 27 S3
Gambia r. Gambia 92 A2
▶Gambia, The country Africa 92 A2
africa 86–87, 100
Gambie r. Senegal 92 B2
Gambier, Îles is Fr. Polynesia 165 J7
Gambier Islands Australia 109 G8
Gambo Canada 125 K3
Gamboma Congo 94 B5
Gamboola Australia 111 E3
Gamboula Cent. Afr. Rep. 94 B3
Gamda China see Zamtang
Gamlakarleby Fin. see Kokkola
Gamleby Sweden 33 E4
Gammams well Sudan 89 G5
Gammelstaden Sweden 32 F2
Gammon Ranges National Park Australia 112 A3
Gamova, Mys pt Rus. Fed. 64 B4
Gampaha Sri Lanka 72 D5
Gampola Sri Lanka 72 D5
Gamshadzai Kūh mts Iran 81 E4
Gamtog China 66 A2
Gamud mt. Eth. 96 C3
Gan r. China 64 A2
Gana China see Gengda
Ganado U.S.A. 137 H4
Gananoque Canada 131 E1
Ganāveh Iran 80 B4
Gäncä Azer. 79 F2
Gand Belgium see Ghent
Ganda Angola 95 B8
Gandadiwata, Bukit mt. Indon. 56 E6
Gandai India 74 D5
Gandajika Dem. Rep. Congo 95 D6
Gándara Spain 42 B1
Gandarbal Jammu and Kashmir 74 B2
Gandari Mountain Pak. 81 G4
Gandava Pak. 81 F4
Gander Canada 125 K3
Gander r. Nfld. and Lab. Canada 121 N5
Gander r. Nfld. and Lab. Canada 125 K3
Gandesa Spain 43 G2
Gandevi India 72 B1
Gandhidham India 74 A5
Gandhinagar India 74 B5
Gandhi Sagar resr India 74 B4
Gandi, Wadi watercourse Sudan 94 E2
Gandía Spain 43 F3
Gand-i-Zureh plain Afgh. 81 E4
Gandomān Iran 80 B4
Gandu Brazil 150 E5
Gandvik Norway 32 H1
Gandzha Azer. see Gäncä
Gâneb well Mauritania 92 C1
Ganga r. Bangl./India see Ganges
Ganga Nigeria 93 G3
Ganga r. Sri Lanka 72 D5
Gangakher India 72 C2
Gangán Arg. 153 C5
Gangán, Pampa de plain Arg. 153 C5
Ganganagar India 74 B3
Gangapur Maharashtra India 72 B2
Gangapur Rajasthan India 74 B4
Gangapur Rajasthan India 74 C4
Gangara Niger 93 H2
Gangavali r. India 72 B3
Gangaw Myanmar 60 A3
Gangawati India 72 C3
Gangaw Range mts Myanmar 60 B3
Gangca China 70 J4
Gangdhar India 74 B5
Gangdisê Shan mts China 70 F5
Ganges r. Bangl./India 74 F5
Ganges France 39 E5
▶Ganges, Mouths of the Bangl./India 75 F5
asia 82
Ganges Cone sea feature Indian Ocean 162 M4
Gangi Sicily Italy 45 E6
Ganglota Liberia 92 C4
Gangra Turkey see Çankırı
Gangtok India 75 F4
Gangu China 66 C1
Ganiakali Guinea 92 C3
Ganjam India 71 G8
Gan Jiang r. China 67 F2
Ganluo China 66 B2
Gannat France 39 E3
Gannett Peak U.S.A. 134 E4
Gänserndorf Austria 37 H4
Ganshui China 66 C2
Gansu prov. China 70 I3
Gantamaa Somalia 96 D4
Gantheaume Point Australia 108 C4
Gant'iadi Georgia 79 E2
Ganting China see Huxian
Gantsevichi Belarus see Hantsavichy
Ganxian China 67 E3
Ganye Nigeria 93 I3
Ganyushkino Kazakh. 29 I7
Ganzhe China see Minhou
Ganzhou China 67 E3
Ganzi Sudan 96 A3
Gao Mali 93 E1
Gao admin. reg. Mali 93 F1
Gao'an China 67 E2
Gaocheng China see Litang
Gaochun China 67 F2
Gaocun China see Mayang
Gaohebu China 67 F2
Gaojian China 67 G2
Gaoleshan China see Xianfeng
Gaoliangjian China see Hongze
Gaoligong Shan mts China 66 A3
Gaoling China 67 D1
Gaomutang China 67 D3
Gaotangling China see Wangcheng
Gaoua Burkina 92 E3
Gaoxiong Taiwan see Kaohsiung
Gaoyou China 67 F1
Gaoyou Hu l. China 67 F1
Gaozhou China 67 D4
Gap France 39 G4
Gapuwiyak Australia 110 C2
Gaqoi China 75 D3
Gar China 70 F5
Gar Pak. 81 E5
Gar' r. Rus. Fed. 64 B1
Garaa Tebourt well Tunisia 91 H3
Garabekevyul Turkm. 81 F2
Garabil Belentligi hills Turkm. see Karabil', Vozvyshennost'
Garabinzam Congo 94 B4
Garabogazköl Aylagy b. Turkm. see Kara-Bogaz-Gol, Zaliv
Garabogazköl Bogazy sea chan. Turkm. see Kara-Bogaz-Gol, Proliv
Garacad Somalia 96 F3
Garadag Somalia 96 E2
Gara Ekar hill Alg. 91 G6
Garagoa Col. 146 C3
Garagum des. Kazakh. see Karakum Desert
Garagum des. Turkm. see Karakum Desert
Garah Australia 112 D3
Garalo Mali 92 D3
Garamätnyyaz Turkm. see Karamet-Niyaz
Garamba r. Dem. Rep. Congo 94 F4
Garanhuns Brazil 150 E4
Garapu Brazil 150 A5
Garar, Plaine de plain Chad 94 D2
Garba Cent. Afr. Rep. 94 D3
Garbahaarey Somalia 96 D4
Garba Tula Kenya 96 C4
Garberville U.S.A. 136 A1
Garbo China see Lhozhag
Garbosh, Kūh-e mt. Iran 80 B3
Garbsen Germany 36 D2
Garcia Sola, Embalse de resr Spain 42 D3
Gard r. France 39 F5
Garda Italy 44 C2
Garda, Lake Italy 44 C2
Gardabani Georgia 79 F2
Gârda de Sus Romania 46 C1
Gardelegen Germany 36 E2
Garden City U.S.A. 132 A4
Garden Hill Canada 123 M4
Garden Mountain U.S.A. 130 C5
Gardermoen airport Norway 33 C3
Gardinas Belarus see Hrodna
Gardiner U.S.A. 131 I1
Gardiner Range hills Australia 110 B3
Gardiners Island U.S.A. 131 G3
Gardīz Afgh. 81 G3
Gardner atoll Micronesia see Faraulep
Gardner U.S.A. 131 H2
Gardner Inlet Antarctica 167 L1
Gardner Island Kiribati see Nikumaroro
Gardner Pinnacles is U.S.A. 165 G4
Gardno, Jezioro lag. Poland 37 H1
Gárdony Hungary 37 I5
Gardsjönås Sweden 32 E2
Gardslösa Sweden 33 E4
Gáregasnjárga Fin. see Karigasniemi
Gares Spain see Puente la Reina
Garešnica Croatia 44 F2
Garet El Djenoun mt. Alg. 91 G4
Gare Tigre Fr. Guiana 147 H3
Garfield U.S.A. 135 F5
Gargáligas r. Spain 42 D3
Gargano, Parco Nazionale del nat. park Italy 44 E4
Gargantua, Cape Canada 124 C4
Gargunsa China see Gar
Gargždai Lith. 33 F5
Garhakota India 74 C5
Garhbeta India 75 E5
Garhchiroli India 72 D1
Garhi India 74 B5
Garhi Khairo Pak. 81 F4
Garhi Malehra India 74 C4
Garhmuktesar India 74 C3
Garhshankar India 74 C3
Garibaldi Brazil 151 B9
Garibaldi Canada 134 B2
Gariep Dam resr S. Africa 98 E6
Garies S. Africa 98 C6
Garissa Kenya 96 C5
Garkalne Latvia 33 G4
Garkung Caka l. China 75 E2
Garland U.S.A. 133 B5
Garliava Lith. 33 F5
Gârliciu Romania 46 F2
Garlin France 38 C5
Garm Tajik. see Gharm
Garmab Afgh. 81 F3
Garmdasht Iran 80 B4
Garmeh Iran 80 D2
Garmī Iran 80 B2
Garmisch-Partenkirchen Germany 36 E5
Garmo, Qullai mt. Tajik. 81 G2
Garmsar Iran 80 C3
Garner U.S.A. 132 C3
Garnett U.S.A. 132 C4
Garnpung Lake imp. l. Australia 112 B4
Garo Hills India 75 F4
Garonne r. France 38 C4
Garoowe Somalia 96 F2
Garoth India 74 B4
Garou, Lac l. Mali 93 E1
Garoua Cameroon 93 I3
Garoua Boulai Cameroon 94 B3
Garqêntang China see Sog
Garrison KY U.S.A. 130 B4
Garrison ND U.S.A. 132 A2
Garrucha Spain 43 F4
Garrygala Turkm. 80 D2
Garry Lake Canada 123 K1
Garsen Kenya 96 D5
Garshy Turkm. see Karshi
Garsila Sudan 88 D6
Gartar China see Qianning
Gartempe r. France 38 D3
Gartog China see Markam
Gartok China see Garyarsa
Garut Indon. 59 D4
Garwa India 75 D4
Garwolin Poland 37 J3
Gar Xincun China 70 F5
Gary IN U.S.A. 132 E3
Gary WV U.S.A. 130 C5
Garyarsa China 74 D3
Garyi China 66 A2
Garyū-zan mt. Japan 65 C6
Garza Arg. 152 E2
Gar Zangbo r. China 74 C2
Garzê China 66 A2
Garzón Col. 146 C4
Gasan-Kuli Turkm. see Esenguly
Gascogne reg. France see Gascony
Gascogne, Golfe de g. France/Spain see Gascony, Gulf of
Gascony reg. France 38 C5
Gascony, Gulf of France/Spain 38 B5
Gascoyne r. Australia 109 A6
Gascoyne, Mount Australia 109 B6
Gascoyne Junction Australia 109 A5
Gascuña, Golfo de g. France/Spain see Gascony, Gulf of
Gasherbrum mt. Jammu and Kashmir 74 C2
Gasht Iran 81 E5
Gashua Nigeria 93 H2
Gaspar, Selat sea chan. Indon. 59 D3
Gaspé Canada 125 H3
Gaspé, Cap c. Canada 125 H3
Gaspé, Péninsule de pen. Canada 125 H3
Gassan Burkina 92 E2
Gassan vol. Japan 65 E5
Gassane Senegal 92 B2
Gassaway U.S.A. 130 C4
Gassol Nigeria 93 H3
Gasteiz Spain see Vitoria-Gasteiz
Gastello Rus. Fed. 64 E2
Gaston, Lake U.S.A. 130 E5
Gastonia U.S.A. 128 C5
Gastouni Greece 47 B6
Gastre Arg. 153 C5
Gata, Cabo de c. Spain 43 E4
Gata, Cape Cyprus 77 A2
Gata, Sierra de mts Spain 42 C2
Gataga r. Canada 122 E3
Gătaia Romania 46 B2
Gatas, Akra c. Cyprus see Gata, Cape
Gatchina Rus. Fed. 28 D4
Gateshead U.K. 34 F4
Gates of the Arctic National Park and Preserve U.S.A. 120 D3
Gatesville U.S.A. 133 B6
Gateway U.S.A. 137 H2
Gatico Chile 148 C5
Gatineau Canada 124 F4
Gatineau r. Canada 124 F4
Gatong China see Jomda
Gatooma Zimbabwe see Kadoma
Gatton Australia 111 H5
Gatvand Iran 80 B3
Gatwick airport U.K. 35 F6
Gaúcha do Norte Brazil 150 A5
Gaud-i-Zirreh depr. Afgh. 81 E4
Gauer Lake Canada 123 L3
Gauhati India see Guwahati
Gauja r. Latvia 33 G4
Gaujas nacionālais parks nat. park Latvia 33 G4
Gaul country Europe see France
Gaula r. Norway 32 C3
Gauley Bridge U.S.A. 130 C4
Gaupne Norway 33 B3
Gaurdak Turkm. see Govurdak
Gaurella India 75 D5
Gauribidanur India 72 C3
Gaurnadi Bangl. 75 F5
Gauteng prov. S. Africa 99 F5
Gavà Spain 43 H2
Gavarr Armenia see Kamo
Gavāter Iran 81 E5
Gāvbandī Iran 80 C5
Gāvbūs, Kūh-e mts Iran 80 C5
Gavdopoula i. Greece 47 D7

▶Gavdos i. Greece 47 D7
Most southerly point of Europe.

Gave r. France 38 C5
Gāveh Rūd r. Iran 80 A3
Gavião r. Brazil 150 D5
Gavião Port. 42 C3
Gävle Sweden 33 E3
Gävleborg county Sweden 33 D3
Gävlebukten b. Sweden 33 E3
Gavrilov-Yam Rus. Fed. 28 F4
Gavrio Greece 47 D6
Gawai Myanmar 60 B2
Gawan India 75 E4
Gawat well Libya 88 B3
Gawilgarh Hills India 74 C5
Gawler Australia 112 A4
Gawler Ranges hills Australia 109 F8
Gäwür watercourse Turkm. see Gyaur
Gaya r. China 64 B4
Gaya India 75 E4
Gaya i. Sabah Malaysia 59 G1
Gaya Niger 93 F3
Gaya, Pulau i. Sabah Malaysia 59 G1
Gayam Indon. 59 F4
G'Aydat al Jhoucha ridge W. Sahara 90 C4
Gayéri Burkina 93 F2
Gaylord U.S.A. 132 E2
Gayndah Australia 111 G5
Gayny Rus. Fed. 28 J3
Gaysin Ukr. see Haysyn
Gayutino Rus. Fed. 28 F4
Gaz Iran 80 D5

▶Gaza terr. Asia 77 B4
Semi-autonomous region.
asia 82

▶Gaza Gaza 77 B4
Capital of Gaza.

Gaza prov. Moz. 99 G4
Gaz-Achak Turkm. 76 G1
Gazandzhyk Turkm. 80 C2
Gazawa Cameroon 93 I3
Gaziantep Turkey 78 D3
Gazik Iran 81 E3
Gazimağusa Cyprus see Famagusta
Gazipaşa Turkey 78 C3
Gazli Uzbek. 81 E1
Gazojak Turkm. see Gaz-Achak
Gbaaka Liberia 92 D4
Gbarnga Liberia 92 C4
Gbatala Liberia 92 C4
Gbérouboué Benin 93 F3
Gboko Nigeria 93 H4
Gbwado Dem. Rep. Congo 94 D4
Gdańsk Poland 37 I1
Gdańsk, Gulf of Poland/Rus. Fed. 37 I1
Gdańska, Zatoka g. Poland/Rus. Fed. see Gdańsk, Gulf of
Gdingen Poland see Gdynia
Gdov Rus. Fed. 28 C4
Gdyel Alg. 43 F5
Gdynia Poland 37 I1
Gearhart Mountain U.S.A. 134 B4
Gebe i. Indon. 57 G5
Gebeit Sudan 89 H5
Gebeit Mine Sudan 89 H4
Gebre Guracha Eth. 96 C2
Gebze Turkey 46 F4
Gech'a Eth. 96 B3
Gecheng China see Chengkou
Gedaref Sudan 89 G6
Gedaref state Sudan 89 G6
Gediz r. Turkey 78 A3
Gedlegubē Eth. 96 E3
Gēdo Eth. 96 C2
Gedo admin. reg. Somalia 96 D4
Gedong, Tanjong pt Sing. 58 [inset]
Gedser Denmark 33 C5
Geel Belgium 36 B3
Geelong Australia 112 C5
Geelvink Channel Australia 109 A7
Geesthacht Germany 36 E2
Gēgē r. Lith. 33 F5
Gê'gyai China 70 F5
Ge Hu l. China 67 F2
Geidam Nigeria 93 H2
Geiersberg hill Germany 36 D4
Geikie r. Canada 123 K3
Geilo Norway 33 C3
Geiselhöring Germany 37 F4
Geislingen an der Steige Germany 36 D4
Geita Tanz. 96 B5
Gejiu China 66 B4
Gel r. Sudan 96 A3
Gel watercourse Sudan 94 F2
Gela Sicily Italy 45 E6
Gela r. Sicily Italy 45 E6
Gela, Golfo di g. Sicily Italy 45 E6
Geladaindong mt. China 75 F2
Geladī Eth. 96 E3
Gelam i. Indon. 59 E3
Geldern Germany 36 C3
Gelembe Turkey 47 E5
Gelemso Eth. 96 D2
Gelendzhik Rus. Fed. 29 F7
Gelephu Bhutan 75 F4
Gelibolu Turkey see Gallipoli
Gelibolu Yarımadası pen. Turkey 47 E4
Gelibolu Yarımadası Tarihi Milli Parkı nat. park Turkey 47 E4
Gelidonya Burnu pt Turkey see Yardımcı Burnu
Gelincik Dağı mt. Turkey 78 B3
Gelinsoor Somalia 96 E3
Gelmord Iran 80 D3
Gelnica Slovakia 37 J4
Gemas Malaysia 58 C2
Gembu Nigeria 93 H4
Gemena Dem. Rep. Congo 94 C4
Gemerek Turkey 78 D3
Gemlik Turkey 78 B2
Gemlik Körfezi b. Turkey 46 F4
Gemlufall Iceland 32 [inset]
Gemona del Friuli Italy 44 D1
Gémozac France 38 C4
Gemsbok National Park Botswana 98 D5
Genal r. Spain 42 D4
Genalē Wenz r. Eth. 96 D3
General Acha Arg. 152 D4
General Alvear Buenos Aires Arg. 152 E4
General Alvear Mendoza Arg. 152 D3
General Artigas Para. 149 F6
General Belgrano Arg. 152 F3
General Bernardo O'Higgins research station Antarctica 167 A2

▶General Carrera, Lago l. Arg./Chile 153 B6
Deepest lake in South America.

General Conesa Arg. 152 D5
General Freire Angola see Muxaluando
General José de San Martín Arg. 152 F1
General Juan Madariaga Arg. 152 F4
General Lagos Chile 148 C4
General La Madrid Arg. 152 E4
General Machado Angola see Camacupa
General Martín Miguel de Güemes Arg. 148 D6
General Paz Arg. 152 F1
General Pico Arg. 152 E3
General Pinto Arg. 152 E3
General Roca Arg. 152 D4
General Santos Phil. 57 G4
General Terán Mex. 133 B7
General Toshevo Bulg. 46 F3
General Trías Mex. 135 F7
General Villegas Arg. 152 E3
Genesee U.S.A. 130 E3
Genesee r. U.S.A. 130 E2
Geneseo U.S.A. 130 E2
Genet Eth. 96 C2
Geneva Switz. 39 G3
Geneva AL U.S.A. 129 B6
Geneva NE U.S.A. 132 B3
Geneva NY U.S.A. 131 E2
Geneva OH U.S.A. 130 C3
Geneva, Lake France/Switz. 39 G3
Genève Switz. see Geneva
Genf Switz. see Geneva
Gengda China 66 B1
Gengenbach Germany 36 D4
Genglou China 67 E4
Geni r. Sudan 96 B3
Genil r. Spain 42 D4
Genk Belgium 39 F1
Gennargentu, Monti del mts Sardinia Italy 45 B5
Genoa Australia 112 D5
Genoa Italy 44 B2
Genoa, Gulf of Italy 44 B2
Genova Italy see Genoa
Genteng Indon. 59 D4
Genteng i. Indon. 59 F4
Genthin Germany 36 F2
Genua Italy see Genoa
Genzano di Roma Italy 44 D4
Geoagiu r. Romania 46 C1
Geographe Bay Australia 109 A8
Geographical Society Ø i. Greenland 121 Q2
Georga, Zemlya i. Rus. Fed. 26 E1
George r. Canada 125 H1
George S. Africa 98 D7
George, Lake Australia 112 D4
George, Lake FL U.S.A. 129 C6
George, Lake NY U.S.A. 131 G2
George Land i. Rus. Fed. see Georga, Zemlya
Georges Mills U.S.A. 131 G2
George Sound inlet N.Z. 113 A4
Georgetown Australia 111 E3
George Town Australia 112 C6
George Town Bahamas 129 E8
Georgetown Canada 130 D2

▶George Town Cayman Is 139 H5
Capital of the Cayman Islands.

Georgetown Gambia 92 B2

▶Georgetown Guyana 147 G3
Capital of Guyana.

George Town Malaysia 58 C1
Georgetown DE U.S.A. 131 F4
Georgetown GA U.S.A. 129 B6
Georgetown KY U.S.A. 130 A4
Georgetown OH U.S.A. 130 B4
Georgetown SC U.S.A. 129 D5
Georgetown TX U.S.A. 133 B6
George VI Sound sea chan. Antarctica 167 L2
George V Land reg. Antarctica 167 H2
George West U.S.A. 133 B6
▶Georgia country Asia 79 E2
asia 52–53, 82
Georgia state U.S.A. 129 C5
Georgia, Strait of Canada 122 E5
Georgian Bay Canada 130 C1
Georgian Bay Islands National Park Canada 130 D1
Georgi Dimitrov, Yazovir resr Bulg. see Koprinka, Yazovir
Georgina watercourse Australia 110 D5
Georgi Traykov Bulg. see Dolni Chiflik
Georgiu-Dezh Rus. Fed. see Liski
Georgiyevka Kazakh. 70 F2
Georgiyevsk Rus. Fed. 29 G7
Georgiyevskoye Rus. Fed. 28 H4
Gera Germany 36 F3
Gerakarou Greece 46 C4
Geraki Greece 47 C6
Geraki, Akra pt Greece 47 B6
Geral de Goiás, Serra hills Brazil 150 C4
Geraldine N.Z. 113 B4
Geral do Paraná, Serra hills Brazil 149 I3
Geraldton Australia 109 A7
Geraneia mts Greece 47 C6
Gerar watercourse Israel 77 B4
Gerāsh Iran 80 C5
Gerber U.S.A. 136 A1
Gercüş Turkey 79 E3
Gerdauen Rus. Fed. see Zheleznodorozhnyy
Gerede Turkey 78 C2
Gerede r. Turkey 78 C2
Gereshk Afgh. 81 F4
Geretsried Germany 36 E5
Gergovie tourist site France 39 E4
Gerik Malaysia 58 C1
Gerimenj Iran 81 D3
Gerlach U.S.A. 136 C1
Gerlachovský štít mt. Slovakia 37 J4
Gerlospaß pass Austria 36 F5
Germania country Europe see Germany
Germanicea Turkey see Kahramanmaraş
Germansen Landing Canada 122 E4
German South-West Africa country Africa see Namibia
Germantown U.S.A. 133 D5

▶Germany country Europe 36 E3
2nd most populous country in Europe.
europe 24–25, 48

Germencik Turkey 47 E6
Gernika-Lumo Spain 43 E1
Gerolstein Germany 36 C3
Gerolzhofen Germany 36 E4
Gerona Spain see Girona
Gerrit Denys is P.N.G. see Lihir Group
Gers r. France 38 D4
Gersoppa India 72 B3
Géryville Alg. see El Bayadh
Gêrzê China 70 F5
Gerze Turkey 78 C2
Geschriebenstein hill Austria 37 H5
Gesoriacum France see Boulogne-sur-Mer
Gessler Arg. 152 E2
Geta Fin. 33 E3
Getafe Spain 42 E2
Getcheh, Kūh-e hills Iran 80 C3
Gete r. Belgium 39 F1
Getic, Podișul plat. Romania 46 C2
Gettysburg PA U.S.A. 131 E4
Gettysburg SD U.S.A. 132 B2
Gettysburg National Military Park nat. park U.S.A. 131 E4
Getu He r. China 66 C3
Getúlio Vargas Brazil 151 A8
Getz Ice Shelf Antarctica 167 J2
Geumapang r. Indon. 58 B2
Geureudong, Gunung vol. Indon. 58 B1
Gevān-e Ţāleb Khānī Iran 81 D5
Gevaş Turkey 79 E3
Gevgelija Macedonia 46 C4
Gevrai India 72 B2
Gevrey-Chambertin France 39 F3
Gex France 39 G3
Gey Iran see Nīkshahr
Geyikli Turkey 47 E5
Geylang Sing. 58 [inset]
Geylang r. Sing. 58 [inset]
Geyserville U.S.A. 136 A2
Ghaap Plateau S. Africa 98 D5
Ghabeish Sudan 89 E6
Ghadaf, Wādī al watercourse Iraq 79 E4
Ghadaf, Wādī al watercourse Jordan 77 C4
Ghadamés Libya see Ghadāmis
Ghadāmis Libya 88 A2
Ghaddūwah Libya 88 B3
Ghaem Shahr Iran 80 C2
Ghaggar, Dry Bed of watercourse Pak. 81 H4
Ghaghara r. India 75 E4
Ghaghra India 75 E5
Ghalkarteniz, Solonchak salt marsh Kazakh. 70 B2
Ghallamane reg. Mauritania 90 C5
Ghallaorol Uzbek. see Gallyaaral
▶Ghana country Africa 93 E3
africa 86–87, 100
Ghanādah, Rās pt U.A.E. 80 C5
Ghanliala India 74 B4
Ghantwar India 72 A1
Ghanwā Saudi Arabia 80 B5
Ghanzi Botswana 98 D4
Ghanzi admin. dist. Botswana 98 D4
Ghap'an Armenia see Kapan
Gharandal Jordan 77 B4
Gharbīya governorate Egypt see Al Gharbīyah
Ghardaïa Alg. 91 F2
Ghardimaou Tunisia 45 B6
Ghar el Melh Tunisia 45 C6
Ghārib, Jabal mt. Egypt 89 G2
Gharm Tajik. 81 G2
Gharo Pak. 81 F5
Gharyān Libya 88 B1
Gharz, Wādī al watercourse Syria 77 C3
Ghāt Libya 88 A3
Ghatampur India 74 D4
Ghatgan India 75 E5
Ghatol India 74 B5
Ghatsila India 75 E5
Ghauspur Pak. 81 G4
Ghawdex i. Malta see Gozo
Ghazal, Bahr el watercourse Chad 88 C6
Ghazal, Bahr el r. Sudan 96 A2
Ghazaouet Alg. 91 E2
Ghaziabad India 74 C3
Ghazipur India 75 D4
Ghazira, Ghubbat al inlet Oman 80 D5
Ghazna Afgh. see Ghaznī
Ghaznī Afgh. 81 G3
Ghaznī prov. Afgh. 81 F3
Ghazni r. Afgh. 81 F3
Ghazzālah Saudi Arabia 89 I3
Ghemeis, Ras pt U.A.E. 80 B5
Ghent Belgium 39 E1
Ghent U.S.A. 130 C5
Gheorghe Gheorghiu-Dej Romania see Onești
Gheorgheni Romania 46 D1
Ghijduwon Uzbek. see Gizhduvan
Ghīnah, Wādī al watercourse Saudi Arabia 77 D4
Ghioroiu Romania 46 C2
Ghisonaccia Corsica France 31 G5
Ghizao Afgh. 81 F3
Ghizar Jammu and Kashmir 74 B1
Ghod India 72 B2
Ghod r. India 72 B2
Gholvad India 72 B1
Ghorak Afgh. 81 F3
Ghorband r. Afgh. 81 G3
Ghost Lake Canada 123 H2
Ghotaru India 74 A4
Ghotki Pak. 81 G5
Ghowr prov. Afgh. 81 F3
Ghuari r. India 75 E4
Ghudamis Libya see Ghadāmis
Ghugus India 72 C2
Ghulam Mohammed Barrage Pak. 81 G5
Ghurayfah hill Saudi Arabia 77 C4
Ghūrī Iran 80 C4
Ghurian Afgh. 81 E3
Ghuzayyil, Sabkhat salt marsh Libya 88 C2
Ghuzor Uzbek. see Guzar
Gia Đinh Vietnam 61 D6
Giaginskaya Rus. Fed. 79 E1
Gialias r. Cyprus 77 A2
Giang r. Vietnam 60 D4
Gia Nghia Vietnam 61 D5
Giannitsa Greece 46 C4
Giannutri, Isola di i. Italy 44 C3
Giant's Causeway lava field U.K. 34 C4
Giant Sequoia National Monument nat. park U.S.A. 136 C3
Gianysada i. Greece 47 E7
Giarmata Romania 46 B2
Giarre Sicily Italy 45 E6
Gibarrayo hill Spain 42 D4
Gibb r. Australia 108 D3
Gibb River Australia 108 D4
Gibeon Namibia 98 C5
Gibraleón Spain 42 C4

▶Gibraltar Europe 42 D4
United Kingdom Overseas Territory.
europe 24–25, 48

▶Gibraltar, Strait of Morocco/Spain 42 C5
europe 24–25
Gibraltar Range National Park Australia 112 E3
Gibson Australia 109 C8
Gibson Desert Australia 110 A5
Gibsons Canada 122 F5
Gichgeniyn Nuruu mts Mongolia 62 E2
Gīdamī Eth. 96 B2
Gidda Eth. 96 B2
Giddalur India 72 C3
Gīddī, Gebel el hill Egypt see Jiddī, Jabal al
Giddings U.S.A. 133 B6
Giddi Pass hill Egypt see Jiddī, Jabal al
Gideälven r. Sweden 32 E3
Gīdolē Eth. 96 C3
Gien France 39 E3
Giesecke Isfjord inlet Greenland see Kangerlussuaq
Gießen Germany 36 D3
Gīfan Iran 80 D2
Gifhorn Germany 36 E2
Gift Lake Canada 123 H4
Gifu Japan 65 D6
Gigant Rus. Fed. 29 G7
Gigante Col. 146 C4
Gigha i. U.K. 34 D4
Gighera Romania 46 C3
Giglio, Isola del i. Italy 44 C3
Gijón-Xijón Spain 42 D1
Gila r. U.S.A. 137 E5
Gila Bend U.S.A. 137 F5
Gila Bend Mountains U.S.A. 137 F5
Gila Mountains U.S.A. 137 E5
Gīlān prov. Iran 80 B2
Gilău Romania 46 C1
Gīlāzi Azer. 79 G2
Gilbert r. Australia 111 E3
Gilbert AZ U.S.A. 137 G5
Gilbert WV U.S.A. 130 C5
Gilbert Islands Kiribati 164 F5
Gilbert Islands country Pacific Ocean see Kiribati
Gilbert Ridge sea feature Pacific Ocean 164 F5
Gilbert River Australia 111 E3
Gilbués Brazil 150 C4
Gilé Moz. 99 H3
Giles Creek r. Australia 110 B3
Giles Meteorological Station Australia 109 E6
Gilf Kebir Plateau Egypt see Jilf al Kabīr, Haḑabat al
Gilgandra Australia 112 D3
Gil Gil Creek r. Australia 112 D3
Gilgit Jammu and Kashmir 74 B2

Gilgit r. Jammu and Kashmir 74 B2
Gilgunnia Australia 112 C4
Gilimanuk Indon. 59 F5
Gılındire Turkey see Aydıncık
Gillam Canada 123 M3
Gillen watercourse Australia 110 C4
Gillen, Lake salt flat Australia 109 D6
Gilles, Lake salt flat Australia 109 G8
Gillett U.S.A. 131 E3
Gillette U.S.A. 134 F3
Gilliat Australia 111 E4
Gillingham U.K. 35 G6
Gilman U.S.A. 132 E3
Gilmer U.S.A. 133 C5
Gilort r. Romania 46 C2
Gilroy U.S.A. 136 B3
Giluwe, Mount P.N.G. 57 J7
Gīmbī Eth. 96 B2
Gimo Sweden 33 E3
Gimont France 38 D5
Ginda Eritrea 89 H6
Gindie Australia 111 G4
Ginebra, Laguna l. Bol. 148 D3
Gingee India 72 C3
Gin Gin Australia 111 G5
Gingin Australia 109 A7
Gīnīr Eth. 96 D3
Ginzo de Limia Spain see Xinzo de Limia
Gioia, Golfo di b. Italy 45 E5
Gioia del Colle Italy 45 F4
Gioura i. Greece 47 D5
Gipouloux r. Canada 124 F2
Gippsland reg. Australia 112 C5
Girab India 74 A4
Girān Rig mt. Iran 81 D4
Girard U.S.A. 130 C3
Girardin, Lac l. Canada 125 H1
Girdar Dhor r. Pak. 81 F5
Girdi Iran 81 E4
Giresun Turkey 79 D2
Girgenti Sicily Italy see Agrigento
Giri r. Dem. Rep. Congo 94 C4
Giridih India 75 E4
Girna r. India 74 B5
Gir National Park India 74 A5
Girne Cyprus see Kyrenia
Giromagny France 39 G3
Girón Ecuador 146 B5
Giron Sweden see Kiruna
Girona Spain 43 H2
Gironde est. France 38 C4
Girou r. France 38 D5
Giruá Brazil 151 A9
Girvan U.K. 34 D4
Girvas Rus. Fed. 28 E3
Gisborne N.Z. 113 D2
Gisenyi Rwanda 94 F5
Gislaved Sweden 33 D4
Gisors France 38 D2
Gissar Tajik. see Hisor
Gissar Range mts Tajik./Uzbek. 81 F2
Gissarskiy Khrebet mts Tajik./Uzbek. see Gissar Range
Gitarama Rwanda 94 F5
Gitega Burundi 94 F5
Giuba r. Somalia see Jubba
Giubega Romania 46 C2
Giulianova Italy 44 D3
Giurgiu Romania 46 D3
Givar Iran 80 D2
Give Denmark 33 C5
Givors France 39 F4
Giyani S. Africa 99 F4
Giyon Eth. 96 C2
Giza Egypt 89 F2
▶Giza Pyramids tourist site Egypt 89 F2 africa 86–87
Gīzeh Rūd r. Iran 80 A3
Gizhduvan Uzbek. 81 F1
Gizhiga Rus. Fed. 27 Q3
Gizo Solomon Is 107 E2
Giżycko Poland 37 J1
Gjalicë e Lumës, Mal mt. Albania 46 B3
Gjerde Norway 33 B3
Gjirokastër Albania 47 B4
Gjoa Haven Canada 121 J3
Gjögur Iceland 32 [inset]
Gjøra Norway 32 C3
Gjøvik Norway 33 C3
Gjuhëzës, Kepi i pt Albania 47 A4
Glace Bay Canada 125 J4
Glacier Bay U.S.A. 122 C3
Glacier Bay National Park and Preserve U.S.A. 120 F4
Glacier National Park Canada 122 G5
Glacier National Park U.S.A. 134 D2
Glacier Peak vol. U.S.A. 134 B2
Glade Spring U.S.A. 130 C5
Gladstone Qld Australia 111 G4
Gladstone S.A. Australia 112 A4
Gladstone Canada 123 L5
Gladstone U.S.A. 130 D5
Gladwin U.S.A. 130 A2
Gladys U.S.A. 130 D5
Gladys Lake Canada 122 C3
Glamis U.S.A. 137 E5
Glamoč Bos.-Herz. 44 F2
Glan r. Austria 37 G5
Glan r. Germany 36 C4
Glan l. Sweden 33 D4
Glarner Alpen mts Switz. 39 H3
Glarus Switz. 39 H3
Glasfjorden l. Sweden 33 D4
Glasgow U.K. 34 D4
Glasgow KY U.S.A. 128 B4
Glasgow MT U.S.A. 134 F2
Glasgow VA U.S.A. 130 D5
Glaslyn Canada 123 I4
Glassboro U.S.A. 131 F4
Glass Mountain U.S.A. 136 C3
Glauchau Germany 37 F3
Glavacioc r. Romania 46 D2
Glavan Bulg. 46 E3
Glăvăneşti Romania 46 E1
Glavinitsa Bulg. 46 E3
Glavnik Serb. and Mont. 46 B3
Glazoué Benin 93 F4
Glazov Rus. Fed. 28 J4
Glazunovka Rus. Fed. 29 F5
Gleichen Canada 123 H5
Gleisdorf Austria 37 G5
Gleiwitz Poland see Gliwice
Glen Sweden 32 D3
Glen U.S.A. 131 H1
Glen Allen U.S.A. 130 E5
Glénan, Îles de is France 38 B3
Glenavy N.Z. 113 B4
Glenboro Canada 123 L5
Glen Burnie U.S.A. 131 E4
Glen Canyon gorge U.S.A. 137 G3
Glen Canyon Dam U.S.A. 137 G3
Glencoe KY U.S.A. 130 A4
Glencoe MN U.S.A. 132 C2
Glen Cove U.S.A. 131 G3
Glendale AZ U.S.A. 137 F5
Glendale CA U.S.A. 136 C4
Glendale UT U.S.A. 137 F3
Glendale Lake U.S.A. 130 D3
Glendambo Australia 109 F7
Glendive U.S.A. 134 F3
Glendon Canada 123 I4
Glendo Reservoir U.S.A. 134 F4
Glenelg r. Australia 112 B5
Glenfinnan U.K. 34 D3
Glengarry Range hills Australia 109 B6
Glengyle Australia 111 D5
Glen Innes Australia 111 G6
Glenlyon Peak Canada 122 C2
Glen More valley U.K. 34 D3
Glenmorgan Australia 111 G5
Glenn U.S.A. 136 A2
Glennallen U.S.A. 120 E3
Glennie U.S.A. 130 B1
Glenns U.S.A. 131 E5
Glenns Ferry U.S.A. 134 D4
Glenora Canada 122 D3
Glenore Australia 111 E3
Glenormiston Australia 110 D4
Glen Rock U.S.A. 131 E4
Glen Rogers U.S.A. 130 C5
Glen Rose U.S.A. 133 B5
Glenrothes U.K. 34 E3
Glenroy Australia 108 D4
Glens Falls U.S.A. 131 G2
Glenties Rep. of Ireland 34 B4
Glenveagh National Park Rep. of Ireland 34 C4
Glenville U.S.A. 130 C4
Glen Wilton U.S.A. 130 D5
Glenwood AR U.S.A. 133 C5
Glenwood IA U.S.A. 132 C3
Glenwood MN U.S.A. 132 C2
Glenwood WV U.S.A. 130 B4
Glenwood Springs U.S.A. 134 F5
Glevum U.K. see Gloucester
Glina r. Bos.-Herz./Croatia 44 F2
Glina Croatia 44 F2
Glittertinden mt. Norway 33 C3
Gliwice Poland 37 I3
Globe U.S.A. 137 G5
Glodeanu-Sărat Romania 46 E2
Glodeni Romania 46 D1
Glogau Poland see Głogów
Gloggnitz Austria 37 G5
Glogovac Serb. and Mont. 46 B3
Głogów Poland 37 H3
Głogówek Poland 37 H3
Glomfjord Norway 32 D2
Glomma r. Norway 33 C4
Glommersträsk Sweden 32 E2
Glória Brazil 150 E4
Glorieuses, Îles is Indian Ocean 97 E7
Glorioso Islands Indian Ocean see Glorieuses, Îles
Gloucester Australia 112 D3
Gloucester U.K. 35 E6
Gloucester MA U.S.A. 131 H2
Gloucester VA U.S.A. 131 E5
Gloucester Island Australia 111 G4
Gloucester Point U.S.A. 131 E5
Gloversville U.S.A. 131 F2
Glovertown Canada 125 K3
Glöwen Germany 36 F2
Głowno Poland 37 I3
Głubczyce Poland 37 H3
Glubinnoye Rus. Fed. 64 C3
Glubokiy Rus. Fed. 29 G6
Glubokoye Belarus see Hlybokaye
Glubokoye Kazakh. 70 F1
Glücksburg (Ostsee) Germany 36 D1
Glückstadt Germany 36 D2
Gluggarnir hill Faroe Is 34 [inset]
Glukhov Ukr. see Hlukhiv
Gmünd Austria 37 G4
Gmunden Austria 37 F5
Gnadenhutten U.S.A. 130 C3
Gnarp Sweden 33 E3
Gnesen Poland see Gniezno
Gniew Poland 37 I2
Gniezno Poland 37 H2
Gnisvärd Sweden 33 E4
Gnjilane Serb. and Mont. 46 B3
Gnowangerup Australia 109 B8
Gnows Nest Range hills Australia 109 B7
Goa state India 72 B3
Goageb Namibia 98 C5
Goalpara India 75 F4
Goaso Ghana 93 E4
Goat Fell hill U.K. 34 D4
Goba Eth. 96 D3
Gobabis Namibia 98 C4
Gobannium U.K. see Abergavenny
Gobas Namibia 98 C5
Gobernador Crespo Arg. 152 E2
Gobernador Duval Arg. 152 D4
Gobernador Gregores Arg. 153 C7
Gobernador Mayer Arg. 153 C7
Gobernador Virasoro Arg. 152 F2
Gobi des. China/Mongolia 70 K3
Gobi Desert China/Mongolia see Gobi
Göblberg hill Austria 37 F4
Gobō Japan 65 C6
Goch Germany 36 C3
Gochas Namibia 98 C5
Go Công Vietnam 61 D6
Godagari Bangl. 75 F4
Godavari r. India 72 D2
Godavari, Mouths of the India 69 G5
Godbout r. Canada 125 H3
Godda India 75 E4
Godē Eth. 96 D3
Godeal hill Port. 42 B3
Godech Bulg. 46 C3
Goderich Canada 130 C2
Goderville France 38 D2
Godhavn Greenland see Qeqertarsuaq
Godhra India 74 B5
Godinlabe Somalia 96 E3
Gödöllő Hungary 37 I5
Gods r. Canada 123 M3
Gods Lake Canada 123 M4
God's Mercy, Bay of Canada 123 O2
Godthåb Greenland see Nuuk
Godučohkka mt. Sweden 32 E1
Godwin-Austen, Mount China/Jammu and Kashmir see K2
Goedgegun Swaziland see Nhlangano
Goéland, Lac au l. Canada 127 K2
Goélands, Lac aux l. Canada 125 I2
Goes Neth. 36 A3
Goffstown U.S.A. 131 H2
Gogama Canada 124 D4
Gogebic Range hills U.S.A. 132 D2
Gogland, Ostrov i. Rus. Fed. 33 G3
Gogounou Benin 93 F3
Gogra India see Ghaghra
Gogra r. India see Ghaghara
Gogrial Sudan 94 F2
Gogunda India 74 B4
Gohad India 74 C4
Gohana India 74 C3
Goharganj India 74 C5
Goiana Brazil 150 F3
Goianésia Brazil 149 H3
Goiânia Brazil 149 H4
Goianinha Brazil 150 F3
Goiás Brazil 149 H3
Goiás state Brazil 149 H4
Goincang China 66 B1
Goio-Erê Brazil 151 A8
Goito Italy 44 C2
Gojeb Wenz r. Eth. 96 C3
Gojra Pak. 81 H4
Gokak India 72 B2
Gokarn India 72 B3
Gökçeada i. Turkey 78 A2
Gökçedağ Turkey 78 B3
Gökçen Turkey 47 E5
Gökçeören Turkey 47 F5
Gökdere r. Turkey 77 A1
Gökirmak r. Turkey 78 C2
Goklenkuy, Solonchak salt l. Turkm. 80 D1
Gökova Turkey see Ula
Gökova Körfezi b. Turkey 78 A3
Gokprosh Hills Pak. 81 E5
Göksun Turkey 78 D3
Göksu Nehri r. Turkey 78 C3
Gokteik Myanmar 60 B3
Göktepe Turkey 77 A1
Gokwe Zimbabwe 99 F3
Gol Norway 33 C3
Gola India 74 D3
Golaghat India 75 G4
Golakganj India 75 F4
Golan hills Syria 77 B3
Golbāf Iran 80 D4
Golbahār Afgh. 81 G3
Gölbaşı Turkey 78 D3
Golconda India 72 C2
Golconda U.S.A. 134 C4
Gölçük Turkey see Etili
Gölcük Turkey 78 B2
Gölcük r. Turkey 47 F5
Golczewo Poland 37 G2
Gold U.S.A. 130 E3
Gołdap Poland 37 K1
Gołdapa r. Poland 37 J1
Gold Beach U.S.A. 134 A4
Goldberg Germany 36 F2
Gold Coast country Africa see Ghana
Gold Coast Australia 111 H6
Gold Coast coastal area Ghana 93 E4
Golden Canada 134 C2
Golden Bay N.Z. 113 C3
Goldendale U.S.A. 134 B3
Golden Hinde mt. Canada 134 A2
Golden Meadow U.S.A. 133 D6
Golden Valley Zimbabwe 99 F3
Goldfield U.S.A. 136 D3
Gold River Canada 122 E5
Goldsboro U.S.A. 128 D5
Goldsworthy Australia 108 B5
Goldthwaite U.S.A. 133 B6
Goldvein U.S.A. 130 E4
Göle Turkey 79 E2
Goleniów Poland 37 G2
Golestān Afgh. 81 E3
Golestān prov. Iran 80 C2
Goleta U.S.A. 136 C4
Golfo di Orosei Gennargentu e Asinara, Parco Nazionale del nat. park Sardinia Italy 45 B4
Gölgeli Dağları mts Turkey 78 B3
Goliad U.S.A. 133 B6
Golija nat. park Serb. and Mont. 46 B3
Golija Planina mts Serb. and Mont. 46 B3
Golingka China see Gongbo'gyamda
Gölköy Turkey 79 D2
Gölmarmara Turkey 47 E5
Golmberg hill Germany 37 F2
Golmud China 70 H4
Golmud He r. China 75 G1
Golodnaya Step' plain Uzbek. 81 F1
Golpāyegān Iran 80 B3
Golspie U.K. 34 E3
Golub-Dobrzyń Poland 37 I2
Golungo Alto Angola 95 B7
Gol Vardeh Iran 81 E3
Golweyn Somalia 96 E4
Golyama Syutkya mt. Bulg. 46 D4
Golyam Perelik mt. Bulg. 46 D4
Golyam Persenk mt. Bulg. 46 D4
Goma Dem. Rep. Congo 94 F5
Goma Uganda 96 A5
Gomang Co salt l. China 75 F3
Gomati r. India 74 D4
Gombak, Bukit hill Sing. 58 [inset]
Gombari Dem. Rep. Congo 94 F4
Gombe Nigeria 93 H3
Gombe state Nigeria 93 H3
Gombe r. Tanz. 97 A6
Gombi Nigeria 93 I3
Gombroon Iran see Bandar-e 'Abbās
Gömeç Turkey 47 E5
Gomel' Belarus see Homyel'
Gómez Palacio Mex. 126 F6
Gomīshān Iran 80 C2
Gomo China 75 E2
Gomo Co salt l. China 75 E2
Gonabad Iran see Jüymand
Gonaïves Haiti 127 L8
Gonarezhou National Park Zimbabwe 99 F4
Gonbad-e Kavus Iran 80 C2
Gonda India 75 D4
Gondal India 74 A5
Gonda Libah well Eth. 96 E2
Gondar Col. 146 C5
Gondar Eth. see Gonder
Gonder Eth. 96 C1
Gondey Chad 94 C2
Gondia India 74 D5
Gönen Turkey 78 A2
Gönen r. Turkey 47 E4
Gonfreville-l'Orcher France 38 D2
Gong'an China 67 E2
Gongbalou China see Gamba
Gongbo'gyamda China 75 G3
Gonggar China 75 F3
Gongga Shan mt. China 66 B2
Gonghe China 70 J4
Gongjiang China see Yudu
Gongliu China 26 I5
Gongola r. Nigeria 93 I3
Gongolgon Australia 112 C3
Gongoué Gabon 94 A5
Gongquan China see Gongxian
Gongshan China 66 A3
Gongtang China see Damxung
Gongwang Shan mts China 66 B3
Gongxian Henan China see Gongyi
Gongxian Sichuan China 66 C2
Gongyi China 67 E1
Gongzhuling China 64 A4
Goniądz Poland 37 K2
Goniri Nigeria 93 I3
Gonjo China 66 A2
Gonjog China 75 E3
Gonnesa Sardinia Italy 45 B5
Gonnoi Greece 47 C5
Gonzáles Mex. 126 G7
Gonzales CA U.S.A. 136 B3
Gonzales TX U.S.A. 133 B6
González Moreno Arg. 152 E3
Gonzalo Vásquez Panama 146 B2
Goochland U.S.A. 130 E5
Goodenough, Cape Antarctica 167 G2
Goodenough Island P.N.G. 107 E2
Gooderham Canada 130 D1
Good Hope, Cape of S. Africa 98 C7
Goodland U.S.A. 132 A4
Goodooga Australia 112 C3
Goodparla Australia 110 C2
Goodspeed Nunataks nunataks Antarctica 167 E2
Goodwood r. Canada 125 G2
Goole U.K. 35 F5
Goolgowi Australia 112 C4
Goomalling Australia 109 B7
Goombalie Australia 112 C3
Goomeri Australia 111 H5
Goonda Moz. 99 G3
Goondiwindi Australia 111 G6
Goongarrie National Park Australia 109 C7
Goonyella Australia 111 F4
Goorly, Lake salt flat Australia 109 B7
Goose r. Canada 125 I2
Goose r. U.S.A. 132 B2
Goose Bay Canada see Happy Valley - Goose Bay
Goose Creek U.S.A. 129 C5
Goose Creek r. U.S.A. 134 D4
Goose Green Falkland Is 153 F7
Goose Lake U.S.A. 134 B4
Goose Lake Canal r. U.S.A. 136 C4
Gooty India 72 C3
Gopalganj Bangl. 75 F5
Gopalganj India 75 E4
Gopeshwar India 74 C3
Gopichettipalayam India 72 C4
Gopiganj India 75 D4
Göppingen Germany 36 D4
Góra Poland 37 H3
Goradiz Azer. see Horadiz
Goragorskiy Rus. Fed. 79 F2
Góra Kalwaria Poland 37 J3
Gorakhpur India 75 D4
Goražde Bos.-Herz. 46 A3
Gorczański Park Narodowy nat. park Poland 37 J4
Gorda, Sierra mts Spain 42 D4
Gördalen Sweden 33 D3
Gördes Turkey 78 B3
Gordon r. Canada 123 O1
Gordon U.S.A. 132 A3
Gordon, Lake Australia 112 C6
Gordon Downs Australia 108 E4
Gordon Lake Canada 123 H2
Gordonsville U.S.A. 130 D4
Gordonvale Australia 111 F3
Goré Chad 94 C3
Gorē Eth. 96 B2
Gore N.Z. 113 B4
Gore U.S.A. 130 D4
Gore Point U.S.A. 120 D4
Gorey Rep. of Ireland 35 C5
Gorg Iran 81 D4
Gorgān Iran 80 C2
Gorgan Bay Iran 80 C2
Gorge Range hills Australia 108 B5
Gorgol admin. reg. Mauritania 92 B1
Gorgona, Isola di i. Italy 44 B3
Gorgora Eth. 96 C1
Gorgoram Nigeria 93 H2
Gorham U.S.A. 131 H1
Gori Georgia 79 F2
Gorinchem Neth. 36 B3
Goris Armenia 79 F3
Goritsy Rus. Fed. 28 F4
Gorizia Italy 44 D2
Gorkhā Nepal 75 E4
Gorki Belarus see Horki
Gor'kiy Rus. Fed. see Nizhniy Novgorod
Gor'kovskaya Oblast' admin. div. Rus. Fed. see Nizhegorodskaya Oblast'
Gor'kovskoye Vodokhranilishche resr Rus. Fed. 28 G4
Gorlice Poland 37 J4
Görlitz Germany 37 G3
Gorlovka Ukr. see Horlivka
Gormi India 74 C4
Gorna Dzhumaya Bulg. see Blagoevgrad
Gorna Oryakhovitsa Bulg. 46 D3
Gorni Dŭbnik Bulg. 46 D3
Gornja Radgona Slovenia 44 E1
Gornji Matejevac Serb. and Mont. 46 B3
Gornji Milanovac Serb. and Mont. 46 B2
Gornji Vakuf Bos.-Herz. 44 F3
Gorno-Altaysk Rus. Fed. 62 D1
Gorno-Altayskaya Avtonomnaya Oblast' aut. rep. Rus. Fed. see Altay, Respublika
Gorno-Badakhshan aut. rep. Tajik. see Kŭhistoni Badakhshon
Gornopravdinsk Rus. Fed. 26 G3
Gornotrakiyska Nizina lowland Bulg. 46 D3
Gornozavodsk Permskaya Oblast' Rus. Fed. 28 K4
Gornozavodsk Sakhalinskaya Oblast' Rus. Fed. 64 E3
Gornyak Rus. Fed. 26 I4
Gornyy Rus. Fed. 64 E2
Gornyy Altay aut. rep. Rus. Fed. see Altay, Respublika
Gornyy Badakhshan aut. rep. Tajik. see Kŭhistoni Badakhshon
Goro Eth. 96 D3
Goro i. Fiji see Koro
Goroch'an mt. Eth. 96 C2
Gorodets Rus. Fed. 28 G4
Gorodishche Penzenskaya Oblast' Rus. Fed. 29 H5
Gorodishche Volgogradskaya Oblast' Rus. Fed. 29 H6
Gorodok Belarus see Haradok
Gorodok Ukr. see Horodok
Gorodovikovsk Rus. Fed. 29 G7
Goroka P.N.G. 57 K7
Goroke Australia 112 B5
Gorokhovets Rus. Fed. 28 G4
Gorom Gorom Burkina 93 E2
Gorong, Kepulauan is Indon. 57 H6
Gorongosa Moz. 99 G3
Gorongosa mt. Moz. 99 G3
Gorongosa, Parque Nacional de nat. park Moz. 99 G3
Gorontalo Indon. 57 F5
Goroubi watercourse Niger 93 F2
Gorouol r. Burkina/Niger 93 F2
Gorshechnoye Rus. Fed. 29 F6
Gór Stołowych, Park Narodowy nat. park Poland 37 H3
Goru, Vârful mt. Romania 46 E2
Gorumna Island Rep. of Ireland 35 B5
Goryachiy Klyuch Rus. Fed. 29 F7
Gorzów Wielkopolski Poland 37 G2
Gosainthan mt. China see Xixabangma Feng
Goschen Strait P.N.G. 111 G1
Goshen CA U.S.A. 136 C3
Goshen IN U.S.A. 132 E3
Goshen NH U.S.A. 131 G2
Goshen VA U.S.A. 130 D5
Goshogawara Japan 64 E4
Goslar Germany 36 E3
Gospić Croatia 44 E2
Gossas Senegal 92 A2
Gosse watercourse Australia 110 C3
Gossi Mali 93 E2
Gossinga Sudan 94 E2
Gostivar Macedonia 46 B4
Gostyń Poland 37 H3
Gostynin Poland 37 I2
Gosu China 66 A1
Gota Eth. 96 D2
Götaälven r. Sweden 33 C4
Göteborg Sweden see Gothenburg
Gotel Mountains Cameroon/Nigeria 93 H4
Götene Sweden 33 D4
Gotenhafen Poland see Gdynia
Gotha Germany 36 E3
Gothem Sweden 33 E4
Gothenburg Sweden 33 C4
Gothenburg U.S.A. 132 A3
Gothèye Niger 93 F2
Gotland i. Sweden 33 E4
Gotō-rettō is Japan 65 B6
Gotse Delchev Bulg. 46 C4
Gotska Sandön Sweden 33 E4
Gotska Sandön i. Sweden 33 E4
Gōtsu Japan 65 C6
Gottero, Monte mt. Italy 44 B2
Göttingen Germany 36 D3
Gottne Sweden 32 E3
Gott Peak Canada 134 B2
Gottwaldov Czech Rep. see Zlín
Gotval'd Ukr. see Zmiyiv
Gouako Cent. Afr. Rep. 94 D3
Gouda Neth. 36 B2
Goudiri Senegal 92 B2
Goudoumaria Niger 93 H2
Goûgaram Niger 93 G1
▶Gough Island S. Atlantic Ocean 161 N8 Dependency of St Helena.
Gouin, Réservoir Canada 125 F3
Goulburn Australia 112 D4
Goulburn Islands Australia 110 C1
Goulburn River National Park Australia 112 D4
Gould Coast Antarctica 167 J1
Goulféy Cameroon 88 B6
Goulia Côte d'Ivoire 92 D3
Goulou atoll Micronesia see Ngulu
Goumbou Mali 92 D2
Gouna Cameroon 93 I3
Goundam Mali 92 E1
Goundi Chad 94 C2
Gounou-Gaya Chad 94 B2
Gouraya Alg. 43 G4
Gouraye Mauritania 92 B2
Gourcy Burkina 93 E2
Gourdon France 38 D4
Gouré Niger 93 H2
Gourin France 38 B2
Gouripur Bangl. 75 F4
Gourma-Rharous Mali 93 E1
Gourmeur well Chad 88 D5
Gournay-en-Bray France 38 D2
Gouro Chad 88 C5
Goûr Oulad Ahmed reg. Mali 90 D5
Gourouro well Chad 88 D5
Gouveia Port. 42 C2
Gouverneur U.S.A. 131 F1
Gove, Barragem do resr Angola 95 B8
Govedartsi Bulg. 46 C3
Govena, Mys hd Rus. Fed. 27 Q4
Governador Valadares Brazil 151 D6
Governor's Harbour Bahamas 129 D7
Govĭ Altayn Nuruu mts Mongolia 62 F3
Govind Ballash Pant Sagar resr India 75 D4
Govindgarh India 75 D4
Govind Sagar resr India 74 C3
Govurdak Turkm. 81 F2
Gowanda U.S.A. 130 D2
Gowan Range hills Australia 111 F5
Gowd-e Ahmar Iran 80 C4
Gowdeh, Rūd-e watercourse Iran 80 C5
Gowd-e Hasht Tekkeh waterhole Iran 80 D3
Gowmal Kalay Afgh. 81 G3
Gowurdak Turkm. see Govurdak
Goya Arg. 152 F2
Göyçay Azer. 79 F2
Goyder r. Australia 110 C2
Goyder watercourse Australia 110 C5
Goymatdag hills Turkm. see Koymatdag, Gory
Göynük Turkey 79 E3
Göynük Turkey 78 B2
Gözareh Afgh. 81 E3
Goz-Beïda Chad 88 D6
Gözcüler Turkey 77 B1
Gozha Co salt l. China 70 F5
Gozo i. Malta 45 E6
Goz Regeb Sudan 89 G5
Graaf-Reinet S. Africa 98 E7
Grabia r. Poland 37 I3
Grabo Côte d'Ivoire 92 D4
Grabovica Serb. and Mont. 46 C2
Grabow Germany 36 E2
Grabowa r. Poland 37 H1
Gračac Croatia 44 E2
Gračanica Bos.-Herz. 44 G2
Gracefield Canada 124 E4
Gracemere Australia 111 G4
Grachevka Rus. Fed. 29 J5
Gradačac Bos.-Herz. 44 G2
Gradaús Brazil 150 B3
Gradaús, Serra dos hills Brazil 150 B4
Gradets Bulg. 46 E3
Gradignan France 38 C4
Gradishte hill Bulg. 46 E3
Gradiška Bos.-Herz. see Bosanska Gradiška
Gradište Croatia 44 G2
Grădiştea Romania 46 E2
Grado Italy 44 D2
Grado Spain 42 C1
Grady U.S.A. 133 A5
Gräfenhainichen Germany 37 F3
Gräftåvallen Sweden 32 D3
Grafton Australia 111 H6
Grafton ND U.S.A. 132 B1
Grafton WV U.S.A. 130 C4
Grafton, Cape Australia 111 F3
Grafton, Mount U.S.A. 137 E2
Grafton Passage Australia 111 F3
Graham NC U.S.A. 128 D4
Graham TX U.S.A. 133 B5
Graham, Mount U.S.A. 137 H5
Graham Bell Island Rus. Fed. see Greem-Bell, Ostrov
Graham Island Canada 122 C4
Graham Land reg. Antarctica 167 L2
Grahamstown S. Africa 99 E7
Grajagan Indon. 59 F5
Grajaú Brazil 150 C3
Grajaú r. Brazil 150 C2
Grajewo Poland 37 K2
Gram Denmark 33 C5
Gramada mt. Serb. and Mont. 46 C3
Gramat France 38 D4
Gramatikovo Bulg. 46 E3
Grammichele Sicily Italy 45 E6
Grammos mt. Greece 47 B4
Gramoz, Mal mt. Albania/Greece 47 B4
Grampian U.S.A. 130 D3
Grampian Mountains U.K. 34 D3
Grampians, The mts Australia 112 B5
Grampians National Park Australia 112 B5
Gramsh Albania 46 B4
Gran Hungary see Esztergom
Granada Col. 146 C4
Granada Nicaragua 138 G6
Granada Spain 42 E4
Gran Altiplanicie Central plain Arg. 153 C7
Gran Baja San Julián valley Arg. 153 C7
Gran Bajo depr. Arg. 153 D6
Gran Bajo Salitroso salt flat Arg. 152 D4
Granby U.S.A. 134 F4
Gran Canaria i. Canary Is 90 B4
Gran Chaco reg. Arg./Para. 149 E6
Grand r. MO U.S.A. 132 E3
Grand r. SD U.S.A. 132 A2
Grandas de Salime Spain 42 C1
Grand Atlas mts Morocco see Haut Atlas
Grand Bahama i. Bahamas 129 D7
Grand Bank Canada 125 K4
Grand Banks of Newfoundland sea feature N. Atlantic Ocean 160 K3
Grand-Bassam Côte d'Ivoire 92 E4
Grand Bay Canada 125 H4
Grand Bend Canada 130 C2
Grand Canal China see Da Yunhe
Grand Canal Rep. of Ireland 35 C5
Grand Canary i. Canary Is see Gran Canaria
Grand Canyon U.S.A. 137 F3
▶Grand Canyon gorge U.S.A. 137 F3 northamerica 118–119
Grand Canyon National Park U.S.A. 137 F3
Grand Canyon - Parashant National Monument nat. park U.S.A. 137 F3
Grand Cayman i. Cayman Is 127 J8
Grand Combin mt. Switz. 39 G4
Grande r. Arg. 152 C4
Grande r. Santa Cruz Bol. 149 E4
Grande r. Santa Cruz Bol. 149 E4
Grande r. Bahia Brazil 150 D4
Grande r. São Paulo Brazil 151 B7
Grande r. Nicaragua 139 H6
Grande r. Peru 148 B3
Grande, Bahía b. Arg. 153 C7
Grande, Ciénaga lag. Col. 146 C2
Grande, Serra hills Brazil 149 E2
Grande, Serra mt. Brazil 147 F4
Grande Cache Canada 122 G4
Grande Comore i. Comoros see Njazidja
Grande Leyre r. France 38 C4
Grande Prairie Canada 122 G4
Grand Erg de Bilma des. Niger 93 I1
Grand Erg Occidental des. Alg. 91 E3
Grand Erg Oriental des. Alg. 91 G3
Grande-Rivière Canada 125 H3
Grande Ronde r. U.S.A. 134 C3
Grandes, Salinas salt marsh Arg. 148 D5
Grande Terre i. Mayotte 97 E8
Grande Tête de l'Obiou mt. France 39 F4
Grande-Vallée Canada 125 H3
Grand Falls N.B. Canada 125 H4
Grand Falls Nfld. and Lab. Canada 121 N5
Grand Forks Canada 122 G5
Grand Forks U.S.A. 132 B2
Grand Gorge U.S.A. 131 F2
Grand Haven U.S.A. 132 E3
Grandin, Lac l. Canada 122 G1
Grand Island U.S.A. 132 B3
Grand Isle U.S.A. 127 H6
Grand Junction U.S.A. 137 H2
Grand-Lahou Côte d'Ivoire 92 D4
Grand Lake N.B. Canada 125 H4
Grand Lake Nfld. and Lab. Canada 125 I2
Grand Lake Nfld. and Lab. Canada 125 J3
Grand Lake U.S.A. 133 C6
Grand Lake St Marys U.S.A. 130 A3
Grand Manan Island Canada 125 H4
Grand Marais MI U.S.A. 132 E2
Grand Marais MN U.S.A. 132 D2
Grand-Mère Canada 125 F4
Grândola Port. 42 B3
Grândola, Serra de mts Port. 42 B3
Grand Passage New Caledonia 107 F3
Grand Rapids Canada 123 L4
Grand Rapids MI U.S.A. 132 E3
Grand Rapids MN U.S.A. 132 C2
Grand Récif de Cook reef New Caledonia 107 F3
Grand Récif du Sud reef New Caledonia 107 F4
Grand St Bernard, Col du pass Italy/Switz. see Great St Bernard Pass
Grand Santi Fr. Guiana 147 H3
Grand Teton mt. U.S.A. 134 E4
Grand Teton National Park U.S.A. 134 E4
▶Grand Turk Turks and Caicos Is 127 L7 Capital of the Turks and Caicos Islands.
Grand Wash watercourse U.S.A. 137 E3
Grand Wash Cliffs mts U.S.A. 137 E4
Grañén Spain 43 F2
Granger U.S.A. 134 E4
Grängesberg Sweden 33 D3
Grangeville U.S.A. 134 C3
Granhult Sweden 32 F2
Granisle Canada 122 E4
Granite Falls U.S.A. 132 C2
Granite Mountains CA U.S.A. 137 E4
Granite Mountains CA U.S.A. 137 E5
Granite Peak MT U.S.A. 134 E3
Granite Peak UT U.S.A. 137 F1
Granitola, Capo c. Sicily Italy 45 D6
Granja Brazil 150 D2
Gran Laguna Salada l. Arg. 153 D6
Gran Morelos Mex. 135 F7
Granollers Spain 43 H2
Gran Pajonal plain Peru 148 B2
Gran Paradiso mt. Italy 44 A2
Gran Paradiso, Parco Nazionale del nat. park Italy 44 A2
Gran Pilastro mt. Austria/Italy 36 E5
Gran San Bernardo, Colle del pass Italy/Switz. see Great St Bernard Pass
Gran Sasso d'Italia mts Italy 44 D3
Gran Sasso e Monti della Laga, Parco Nazionale del nat. park Italy 44 D3
Gransee Germany 37 F2
Grant U.S.A. 132 A3
Grant, Mount U.S.A. 136 D2
Grantham U.K. 35 F5
Grant Island Antarctica 167 J2
Grantown-on-Spey U.K. 34 E3
Grant Range mts U.S.A. 137 E2
Grants U.S.A. 135 F6
Grantsburg U.S.A. 132 C2
Grants Pass U.S.A. 134 B4
Grantsville U.S.A. 137 F1
Granville Canada 122 B2
Granville France 38 C2
Granville AZ U.S.A. 137 H5
Granville NY U.S.A. 131 G2
Granville Lake Canada 123 K3
Granvin Norway 33 B3
Grão Mogol Brazil 151 D6
Gras, Lac de l. Canada 123 I1
Graskop S. Africa 99 F5
Gräsö i. Sweden 33 E3
Grasplatz Namibia 98 B5
Grass r. Canada 123 L3
Grasse France 39 G5
Grass Lake U.S.A. 130 A2
Grasslands National Park Canada 123 J5
Grass Patch Australia 109 C8
Grassrange U.S.A. 134 E3
Grass Valley U.S.A. 136 B2
Grassy Australia 112 C6
Grästorp Sweden 33 D4
Gratkorn Austria 37 G5
Graudenz Poland see Grudziądz
Graulhet France 38 D5
Graus Spain 43 G1
Gravata Brazil 150 F4
Gravataí Brazil 151 B9
Grave, Pointe de pt France 38 C4
Gravelbourg Canada 123 J5
Gravenhurst Canada 124 E4
Grave Peak U.S.A. 134 D3

Gravesend Australia 112 D3
Gravina in Puglia Italy 45 F4
Gravina Island U.S.A. 122 D4
Gray France 39 F3
Gray KY U.S.A. 130 A5
Gray ME U.S.A. 131 H2
Gray Lake Canada 123 I2
Grayling r. Canada 122 E3
Grayling U.S.A. 132 E2
Grays Lake U.S.A. 134 E4
Grayville U.S.A. 128 B4
Graz Austria 37 G5
Grdelica Serb. and Mont. 46 C3
Greasy Lake Canada 122 F2
Great Abaco i. Bahamas 129 D7
Great Australian Bight g. Australia 109 E8
Great Bahama Bank sea feature Bahamas 129 D7
Great Barrier Island N.Z. 113 C2
▶Great Barrier Reef Australia 111 F1
oceania 104–105
oceans 156–157
Great Barrier Reef Marine Park (Cairns Section) Australia 111 F3
Great Barrier Reef Marine Park (Capricorn Section) Australia 111 G4
Great Barrier Reef Marine Park (Central Section) Australia 111 G3
Great Barrier Reef Marine Park (Far North Section) Australia 111 F2
Great Barrington U.S.A. 131 G2
Great Basalt Wall National Park Australia 111 F3
Great Basin U.S.A. 137 D2
Great Basin National Park U.S.A. 137 E2
Great Bear r. Canada 122 E1

▶Great Bear Lake Canada 122 G1
4th largest lake in North America and 8th in the world.
northamerica 116–117
world 6–7

Great Belt sea chan. Denmark 33 C5
Great Bend KS U.S.A. 132 B4
Great Bend PA U.S.A. 131 F3
Great Bitter Lake Egypt 89 G2
Great Blasket Island Rep. of Ireland 35 A5

▶Great Britain i. U.K. 35 E4
Largest island in Europe and 8th in the world.
europe 22–23
world 6–7

Great Coco Island Cocos Is 61 A5
Great Dividing Range mts Australia 111 F5
Great Driffield U.K. 35 F4
Great Eastern Erg des. Alg. see Grand Erg Oriental
Great Egg Harbor Inlet U.S.A. 131 F4
Greater Antilles is Caribbean Sea 127 J7
Greater Khingan Mountains China see Da Hinggan Ling
Greater Tunb i. The Gulf 80 C5
Great Exuma i. Bahamas 129 E8
Great Falls U.S.A. 134 E3
Great Fish r. S. Africa 99 E7
Great Gandak r. India 75 E4
Great Inagua i. Bahamas 127 L7
Great Karoo plat. S. Africa 98 D7
Great Kei r. S. Africa 99 F7
Great Lake Australia 112 C6

▶Great Lakes Canada/U.S.A. 124
Consist of Lakes Erie, Huron, Michigan, Ontario and Superior.

Great Meteor Tablemount sea feature N. Atlantic Ocean 160 M4
Great Miami r. U.S.A. 130 A4
Great Namaqualand reg. Namibia 98 C5
Great Nicobar i. India 73 G5
Great North East Channel Australia/P.N.G. 57 J7
Great Oasis, The Egypt 89 F3
Great Ouse r. U.K. 35 G5
Great Oyster Bay Australia 112 D6
Great Palm Island Australia 111 F3
Great Plain of the Koukdjuak Canada 121 L3
Great Plains U.S.A. 132 A3
Great Point U.S.A. 131 H3
Great Rift Valley Africa 96 B5
Great Ruaha r. Tanz. 97 C6
Great Sacandaga Lake U.S.A. 131 F2
Great St Bernard Pass Italy/Switz. 39 G4
▶Great Salt Lake UT U.S.A. 134 D4
northamerica 116–117
Great Salt Lake Desert U.S.A. 137 F1
Great Sand Dunes National Park U.S.A. 135 F5
Great Sand Hills Canada 123 I5
Great Sand Sea des. Egypt/Libya 88 E2
Great Sandy Desert Australia 110 A4
Great Sandy Island Australia see Fraser Island
Great Sea Reef Fiji 107 G3

▶Great Slave Lake Canada 123 H2
Deepest and 5th largest lake in North America.
northamerica 116–117

Great Smoky Mountains U.S.A. 128 B5
Great Smoky Mountains National Park U.S.A. 128 C5
Great Snow Mountain Canada 122 E3
Great South Bay U.S.A. 131 G3
Great Victoria Desert Australia 110 B6
Great Wall research station Antarctica 167 A2
▶Great Wall tourist site China 63 J3
asia 52–53
Great Western Erg des. Alg. see Grand Erg Occidental
Great West Torres Islands Myanmar 61 B6
Great Yarmouth U.K. 35 G5
Great Zab r. Iraq see Zāb al Kabīr, Nahr az
Great Zimbabwe National Monument tourist site Zimbabwe 99 F4
Grebbestad Sweden 33 C4
Grebenkovskiy Ukr. see Hrebinka
Grebyonka Ukr. see Hrebinka
Greci, Vârful hill Romania 46 F2
Greco, Cape Cyprus see Greko, Cape
Greco, Monte mt. Italy 44 D4
Gredos, Sierra de mts Spain 42 D2
Greec Chile 153 C8
▶Greece country Europe 47 B5
europe 24–25, 48
Greece U.S.A. 130 E2
Greeley U.S.A. 134 F4
Greely Center U.S.A. 132 B3
Greem-Bell, Ostrov i. Rus. Fed. 26 G1
Green r. Canada 127 M2
Green r. KY U.S.A. 128 B4
Green r. ND U.S.A. 132 A2
Green r. WY U.S.A. 137 H2
Green Bay U.S.A. 132 D2
Green Bay b. U.S.A. 132 E2
Greencastle U.S.A. 130 E4
Green Cove Springs U.S.A. 129 C6
Greendale IN U.S.A. 130 A4
Greendale KY U.S.A. 130 A4
Greene U.S.A. 131 F2
Greeneville U.S.A. 128 C4
Greenfield CA U.S.A. 136 B3
Greenfield IN U.S.A. 128 B4
Greenfield MA U.S.A. 131 G2
Greenfield MO U.S.A. 132 C4
Greenfield OH U.S.A. 130 B4
Green Head Australia 109 A7
Greenhill Island Australia 110 C1
Green Island Taiwan see Lü Tao
Green Islands P.N.G. 107 E2
Green Lake Canada 123 J4
Green Lake U.S.A. 132 D3

▶Greenland terr. N. America 121 O2
Self-governing Danish Territory. Largest island in the world and in North America.
northamerica 116–117, 118–119, 140
world 6–7

Greenland Fracture Zone sea feature Arctic Ocean 166 I1
Greenland Sea Greenland/Svalbard 166 I1
Green Mountains U.S.A. 131 G1
Greenock U.K. 34 D4
Greenough Australia 109 A7
Greenough r. Australia 109 A7
Greenport U.S.A. 131 G3
Green River U.S.A. 134 E4
Greensboro AL U.S.A. 129 B5
Greensboro MD U.S.A. 131 F4
Greensboro NC U.S.A. 128 D4
Greensburg IN U.S.A. 128 B4
Greensburg KS U.S.A. 132 B4
Greensburg KY U.S.A. 128 B4
Greensburg LA U.S.A. 133 D6
Greensburg PA U.S.A. 130 D3
Greens Peak U.S.A. 137 H4
Greenup IL U.S.A. 128 A4
Greenup KY U.S.A. 130 B4
Greenvale Australia 111 F3
Green Valley U.S.A. 135 E7
Greenville Canada 122 D4
Greenville Liberia 92 C4
Greenville AL U.S.A. 129 B6
Greenville CA U.S.A. 136 B1
Greenville ME U.S.A. 128 F2
Greenville MI U.S.A. 132 D4
Greenville MS U.S.A. 127 H5
Greenville NC U.S.A. 128 D5
Greenville OH U.S.A. 130 A3
Greenville PA U.S.A. 130 C3
Greenville SC U.S.A. 129 C5
Greenville TX U.S.A. 133 B5
Greenwich CT U.S.A. 131 G3
Greenwich OH U.S.A. 130 B3
Greenwood AR U.S.A. 133 C5
Greenwood MS U.S.A. 133 D5
Greenwood SC U.S.A. 129 C5
Greer U.S.A. 128 C5
Gregório r. Brazil 148 C1
Gregory r. Australia 110 D3
Gregory MI U.S.A. 130 A2
Gregory SD U.S.A. 132 B3
Gregory, Lake salt flat S.A. Australia 110 D6
Gregory, Lake salt flat W.A. Australia 109 B6
Gregory, Lake salt flat W.A. Australia 110 A4
Gregory Downs Australia 110 D3
Gregory National Park Australia 110 B3
Gregory Range hills Qld Australia 111 E3
Gregory Range hills W.A. Australia 108 C5
Greifswald Germany 37 F1
Greifswalder Bodden b. Germany 37 F1
Greifswalder Oie i. Germany 37 F1
Greiz Germany 36 F3
Greko, Cape Cyprus 77 B2
Gremikha Rus. Fed. 28 F1
Gremyachinsk Permskaya Oblast' Rus. Fed. 28 K4
Gremyachinsk Respublika Buryatiya Rus. Fed. 63 H1
Grenå Denmark 33 C4
Grenada U.S.A. 133 D5
▶Grenada country West Indies 147 F1
northamerica 118–119, 140
Grenade France 38 D5
Grenade-sur-l'Adour France 38 C5
Grenchen Switz. 39 G3
Grenen spit Denmark 33 C4
Grenfell Australia 112 D4
Grenfell Canada 123 K5
Grenoble France 39 F4
Grense-Jakobselv Norway 32 H1
Grenville Grenada 147 F1
Grenville, Cape Australia 111 E1
Grenville Island Fiji see Rotuma
Greshak Pak. 81 F5
Gresham U.S.A. 134 B3
Gresik Indon. 59 F4
Gressåmoen Nasjonalpark nat. park Norway 32 D2
Gretna LA U.S.A. 133 D6
Gretna VA U.S.A. 130 D5
Grevelingen sea chan. Neth. 36 A3
Greven Germany 36 C2
Grevena Greece 47 B4
Grevenbroich Germany 36 C3
Grevenmacher Lux. 39 G2
Grevesmühlen Germany 36 E2
Grey r. Canada 125 J4
Grey r. N.Z. 113 B3
Grey, Cape Australia 110 D2
Greybull U.S.A. 134 E3
Greybull r. U.S.A. 134 E3
Grey Hunter Peak Canada 122 C2
Grey Islands Canada 125 K3
Greylock, Mount U.S.A. 131 G2
Greymouth N.Z. 113 B3
Grey Range hills Australia 111 E6
Grey's Plains Australia 109 A6
Greystone Zimbabwe 99 F4
Greytown S. Africa 99 F6
Gria, Akra pt Greece 47 D6
Gribanovskiy Rus. Fed. 29 G6
Gribingui r. Cent. Afr. Rep. 94 C2
Gridley U.S.A. 136 B2
Griffin U.S.A. 129 B5
Griffith Australia 112 C4
Griffithsville U.S.A. 130 C4
Grigan i. N. Mariana Is see Agrihan
Grignols France 38 C4
Grik Malaysia see Gerik
Grimari Cent. Afr. Rep. 94 D3
Grimma Germany 37 F3
Grimmen Germany 37 F1
Grimsby Canada 130 D2
Grimsby U.K. 35 F5
Grímsey i. Iceland 32 [inset]
Grimshaw Canada 123 G3
Grímsstaðir Iceland 32 [inset]
Grimstad Norway 33 C4
Grindavík Iceland 32 [inset]
Grindsted Denmark 33 C5
Grindul Chituc spit Romania 46 F2
Grindușu, Vârful mt. Romania 46 E1
Grinnell Peninsula Canada 121 J2
Griquatown S. Africa 98 D6
Grise Fiord Canada 121 K2
Grishino Ukr. see Krasnoarmiys'k
Grisik Indon. 58 C3
Grisolles France 38 D5
Grisslehamn Sweden 33 E3
Gritley U.K. 34 E2
Grizim well Alg. 90 E4
Grizzly Bear Mountain Canada 122 F1
Grmeč mts Bos.-Herz. 44 F2
Grobbendonk Belgium 36 B3
Grobiņa Latvia 33 F4
Groblersdal S. Africa 99 F5
Groblershoop S. Africa 98 D6
Gröbming Austria 37 F5
Grodekovo Rus. Fed. 64 B3
Grodków Poland 37 H3
Grodno Belarus see Hrodna
Grodzisk Wielkopolski Poland 37 H2
Gröf Iceland 32 [inset]
Groganville Australia 111 F3
Groix, Île de i. France 38 B3
Grójec Poland 37 J3
Grombalia Tunisia 45 C6
Gronau (Westfalen) Germany 36 C2
Grong Norway 32 D2
Groningen Neth. 36 C2
Groningen Suriname 147 H3
Grønland terr. N. America see Greenland
Groote Eylandt i. Australia 110 D2
Grootfontein Namibia 98 C3
Groot Karas Berg plat. Namibia 98 C5
Groot Letaba r. S. Africa 99 F4
Groot Swartberge mts S. Africa 98 D7
Grootvloer salt pan S. Africa 98 D6
Groot Winterberg mt. S. Africa 99 E7
Gros Morne National Park Canada 125 J3
Grosne r. France 39 F3
Gross Barmen Namibia 98 C4
Großenhain Germany 37 F3
Großenkneten Germany 36 D2
Großer Arber mt. Germany 37 F4
Grösser Bösenstein mt. Austria 37 G5
Grosser Priel mt. Austria 37 G5
Großer Rachel mt. Germany 37 F4
Grosser Speikkofel mt. Austria 37 F5
Grosser Speikkogel mt. Austria 37 G5
Grosseto Italy 44 C3
Groß-Gerau Germany 36 D4
Großglockner mt. Austria 37 F5
Großräschen Germany 37 G3
Groß Schönebeck Germany 37 F2
Gross Ums Namibia 98 C4
Großvenediger mt. Austria 37 F5
Grosuplje Slovenia 44 E2
Gros Ventre Range mts U.S.A. 134 E4
Groswater Bay Canada 125 J2
Groton NY U.S.A. 131 E2
Groton SD U.S.A. 132 B2
Grottoes U.S.A. 130 D4
Grouard Mission Canada 123 G4
Grouin, Pointe du pt France 38 C2
Groumania Côte d'Ivoire 92 E4
Grove U.S.A. 133 C4
Grove City OH U.S.A. 130 B4
Grove City PA U.S.A. 130 C3
Grove Hill U.S.A. 129 B6
Grövelsjön Sweden 33 D3
Grove Mountains Antarctica 167 E2
Grover Beach U.S.A. 136 B4
Groveton NH U.S.A. 131 H1
Groveton TX U.S.A. 133 C6
Grovfjord Norway 32 E1
Groznyy Rus. Fed. 29 H8
Grubišno Polje Croatia 44 F2
Grudovo Bulg. see Sredets
Grudziądz Poland 37 I2
Grums Sweden 33 D4
Grünau Namibia 98 C5
Grünberg Poland see Zielona Góra
Grundforsen Sweden 33 D3
Grundsuna Sweden 32 E3
Grundy U.S.A. 130 B5
Gruver U.S.A. 133 A4
Gruzinskaya S.S.R. country Asia see Georgia
Gryazi Rus. Fed. 29 F5
Gryazovets Rus. Fed. 28 G4
Grybów Poland 37 J4
Gryfice Poland 37 G2
Gryfino Poland 37 G2
Gryfów Śląski Poland 37 G3
Gryllefjord Norway 32 E1
Grytviken S. Georgia 153 [inset]
Gua India 75 E5
Guà r. Italy 44 C2
Guacanayabo, Golfo de b. Cuba 127 K7
Guacharía r. Col. 146 D3
Guaçu Brazil 151 A7
Guadaira r. Spain 42 C4
Guadajira r. Spain 42 C3
Guadajoz r. Spain 42 D4
Guadalajara Mex. 126 F7
Guadalajara Spain 42 E2
Guadalaviar r. Spain 43 F2
Guadalcacín, Embalse de resr Spain 42 D4
Guadalcanal i. Solomon Is 107 F2
Guadalcanal Spain 42 D3
Guadalén r. Spain 42 E3
Guadales Arg. 152 D3
Guadalhorce, Embalse de resr Spain 42 D4
Guadalimar r. Spain 42 E4
Guadalmez r. Spain 42 D3
Guadalope r. Spain 43 F2
Guadalquivir r. Spain 42 C4
Guadalupe Brazil 150 D3
Guadalupe Mex. 133 A7
Guadalupe i. Mex. 126 C6
Guadalupe watercourse Mex. 135 C6
Guadalupe Peru 148 A1
Guadalupe Spain 42 D3
Guadalupe U.S.A. 136 B4
Guadalupe r. TX U.S.A. 133 B6
Guadalupe r. TX U.S.A. 133 B6
Guadalupe, Sierra de mts Spain 42 D3
Guadalupe Mountains National Park U.S.A. 135 F7
Guadalupe Victoria Baja California Mex. 137 E5
Guadalupe Victoria Mex. 126 F7
Guadamez r. Spain 42 D3
Guadarrama r. Spain 42 D3
Guadarrama Venez. 146 D2
Guadarrama, Puerto de pass Spain 42 D2
Guadarrama, Sierra de mts Spain 42 D2
Guadazaón r. Spain 43 F3

▶Guadeloupe terr. West Indies 139 L5
French Overseas Department.
northamerica 118–119, 140

Guadeloupe Passage Caribbean Sea 139 L5
Guadiana r. Port./Spain 42 C4
Guadiana Menor r. Spain 42 E4
Guadiaro r. Spain 42 D4
Guadiato r. Spain 42 D4
Guadiela r. Spain 43 E2
Guadiervas r. Spain 42 D2
Guadix Spain 42 E4
Guafo, Isla i. Chile 153 B5
Guaíba Brazil 151 B9
Guaicuras Brazil 149 F5
Guaillabamba r. Ecuador 146 B4
Guaina Venez. 147 F3
Guainía dept Col. 146 D4
Guainía r. Col./Venez. 146 E4
Guaiquinima, Cerro mt. Venez. 147 F3
Guaíra Brazil 151 A8
Guajará Mirim Brazil 148 D2
Guaje, Laguna de l. Mex. 133 A6
Guaje, Llano de plain Mex. 133 A7
Guajira dept Col. 146 C2
Gualala U.S.A. 136 A2
Gualaquiza Ecuador 146 B5
Gualdo Tadino Italy 44 D3
Gualeguay Arg. 152 F3
Gualeguay r. Arg. 152 F3
Gualeguaychu Arg. 152 F3
Gualicho, Salina salt flat Arg. 152 D5
Gualjaina Arg. 153 C5
Guallatiri vol. Chile 148 C4

▶Guam terr. N. Pacific Ocean 57 J3
United States Unincorporated Territory.
oceania 104–105, 114

Guamini Arg. 152 E4
Guampí, Sierra de mts Venez. 147 E3
Guamúchil Mex. 126 E6
Guan r. China 67 F1
Guanabara Brazil 148 C2
Guanajay Cuba 129 C8
Guanajuato Mex. 126 F7
Guanambi Brazil 150 D5
Guanare Venez. 146 E2
Guanare Viejo r. Venez. 146 E2
Guanarito Venez. 146 D2
Guanarito r. Venez. 146 D2
Guanay Bol. 148 C3
Guandacol Arg. 152 C2
Guandaokou China 67 D1
Guandu China 67 E3
Guane Cuba 127 J7
Guang'an China 66 C2
Guangchang China 67 F3
Guangde China 67 F2
Guangdong prov. China 67 E4
Guangfeng China 67 F2
Guanghai China 67 E4
Guanghan China 66 C2
Guanghua China see Laohekou
Guangmao Shan mt. China 66 B3
Guangming China see Xide
Guangming Ding mt. China 67 F2
Guangnan China 66 C3
Guangning China 67 E4
Guangshui China 67 E2
Guangxi aut. reg. China see Guangxi Zhuangzu Zizhiqu
Guangxi Zhuangzu Zizhiqu aut. reg. China 67 C4
Guangyuan China 66 C1
Guangze China 67 F3
Guangzhou China 67 E4
Guanhães Brazil 151 D6
Guanling China 66 C3
Guanmian Shan mts China 67 D2
Guanpo China 67 D1
Guansuo China see Guanling
Guanta Venez. 147 E2
Guantánamo Cuba 127 K7
Guanxian China see Dujiangyan
Guanyang China 67 D3
Guanyinqiao China 66 B2
Guanyun China 67 F1
Guapay r. Bol. see Grande
Guapé Brazil 151 C7
Guaporé r. Bol./Brazil 149 D2
Guaporé Brazil 151 B9
Guaporé state Brazil see Rondônia
Guaqui Bol. 148 C4
Guará r. Brazil 150 C5
Guara, Sierra de mts Spain 43 F1
Guarabira Brazil 150 F3
Guaranda Ecuador 146 B5
Guarapari Brazil 151 D7
Guarapuava Brazil 151 B8
Guaratinga Brazil 151 E6
Guaratuba Brazil 151 B8
Guarayos Bol. 148 C3
Guarda Port. 42 C2
Guarda admin. dist. Port. 42 C2
Guardafui, Cape Somalia see Caseyr, Raas
Guardal r. Spain 43 E4
Guardatinajas Venez. 146 E2
Guardia Escolta Arg. 152 E2
Guardo Spain 42 D1
Guardunha, Serra de mts Port. 42 C3
Guareña Spain 42 C3
Guariba r. Brazil 149 E1
Guárico state Venez. 146 E2
Guarrojo r. Col. 146 D3
Guasdualito Venez. 146 D3
Guasuba r. India 75 F5

▶Guatemala country Central America 138 F5
4th most populous country in Central and North America.
northamerica 118–119, 140

▶Guatemala City Guat. 138 F6
Capital of Guatemala.

Guatimozín Arg. 152 E3
Guatrache Arg. 152 E4
Guatrochi Arg. 153 D5
Guaviare dept Col. 146 D4
Guaviare r. Col. 146 E3
Guayabal Col. 146 D3
Guayaguas, Sierra de mts Arg. 152 D2
Guayapo, Serranía mts Venez. 146 E3
Guayaquil Ecuador 146 A5
Guayaquil, Golfo de g. Ecuador 146 A5
Guayaramerín Bol. 148 D2
Guayas prov. Ecuador 146 A5
Guayatayoc, Lago de imp. l. Arg. 148 D5
Guaymas Mex. 135 E8
Guayquiraró r. Arg. 152 F2
Guba Eth. 96 B2
Gubakha Rus. Fed. 26 F4
Guban plain Somalia 96 E2
Gubbi India 72 C3
Gubbio Italy 44 D3
Gubdor Rus. Fed. 28 K3
Guben Germany 37 G3
Gübene Bulg. 46 D3
Gubin Poland 37 G3
Gubio Nigeria 93 I2
Gubkin Rus. Fed. 29 F6
Gucheng China 67 D1
Gudalur India 72 C4
Gudar, Sierra de mts Spain 43 F2
Gudari India 73 D2
Gudaut'a Georgia 79 E2
Gudbrandsdalen valley Norway 33 C3
Guddu Barrage Pak. 81 G4
Gudermes Rus. Fed. 79 F2
Gudi Nigeria 93 H3
Gudivada India 72 D2
Gudiyattam India 72 C3
Gudri r. Pak. 81 E5
Güdül Turkey 78 C2
Gudur Andhra Pradesh India 72 C3
Gudur Andhra Pradesh India 72 C3
Gudvangen Norway 33 B3
Gudzhal r. Rus. Fed. 64 C2
Guè, Rivière du r. Canada 125 G1
Guéckédou Guinea 92 C3
Guelb er Richât hill Mauritania 90 C5
Guélengdeng Chad 94 B2
Guelma Alg. 91 G1
Guelmine Morocco 90 C3
Guelph Canada 130 C2
Guendour well Mauritania 90 C6
Guènt Paté Senegal 92 B2
Guer France 38 B3
Guéra pref. Chad 94 C2
Guéra, Massif du mts Chad 94 C2
Guérande France 38 B3
Guerara Alg. 91 G2
Guérard, Lac l. Canada 125 H1
Guercif Morocco 90 E2
Guéré watercourse Chad 88 C5
Guéréda Chad 88 D6
Guerende Libya 88 D4
Guéret France 38 D3
Guernica Spain see Gernika-Lumo

▶Guernsey terr. Channel Is 35 E7
United Kingdom Crown Dependency.
europe 24–25, 48

Guernsey U.S.A. 134 F4
Guérou Mauritania 92 C1
Guerrero Mex. 133 A6
Guerrero Negro Mex. 135 D8
Guers, Lac l. Canada 125 H1
Guerzim Alg. 91 E3
Gueugnon France 39 F3
Guéyo Côte d'Ivoire 92 D4
Gufu China see Xingshan
Gugē mt. Eth. 96 C3
Gügerd, Küh-e mts Iran 80 C3
Guglieri Arg. 152 E2
Guguan i. N. Mariana Is 57 K2
Gugu Mountains Eth. 96 C2
Guhakolak, Tanjung pt Indon. 58 D4
Guhe China 67 F2
Güh Küh mt. Iran 80 D5
Guhuai China see Pingyu
Guiana Basin sea feature N. Atlantic Ocean 160 K5
Guiana Highlands mts S. America 147 E3
Guichen France 38 C3
Guichi China 67 F2
Guichón Uruguay 152 F3
Guidan-Roumji Niger 93 G2
Guidari Chad 94 C2
Guider Cameroon 93 I3
Guidiguir Niger 93 H2
Guidimaka admin. reg. Mauritania 92 B2
Guiding China 66 C3
Guidong China 67 E3
Guidonia-Montecelio Italy 44 D4
Guier, Lac de l. Senegal 92 B1
Guietsou Gabon 94 A5
Guigang China 67 D4
Guiglo Côte d'Ivoire 92 D4
Gui Jiang r. China 67 D4
Guiji Shan mts China 67 G2
Guijuelo Spain 42 D2
Guildford U.K. 35 F6
Guilherand France 39 F4
Guilherme Capelo Angola see Cacongo
Guilin China 67 D3
Guillaume-Delisle, Lac l. Canada 121 L4
Guillaumes France 39 G4
Guillestre France 39 G4
Guimarães Brazil 150 C2
Guimarães Port. 42 B2
▶Guinea country Africa 92 C3
africa 86–87, 100
Guinea, Gulf of Africa 93 G5
Guinea Basin sea feature N. Atlantic Ocean 160 N5
▶Guinea-Bissau country Africa 92 B2
africa 86–87, 100
Guinea-Conakry country Africa see Guinea
Guinea Ecuatorial country Africa see Equatorial Guinea
Guiné-Bissau country Africa see Guinea-Bissau
Guinée country Africa see Guinea
Guinée-Forestière admin. reg. Guinea 92 C3
Guinée-Maritime admin. reg. Guinea 92 B3
Güines Cuba 129 C8
Guines France 38 D1
Guingamp France 38 B2
Guinguinéo Senegal 92 B2
Guipavas France 38 A2
Guiping China 67 D4
Guiratinga Brazil 151 A6
Güiria Venez. 147 F2
Guise France 39 E2
Guissefa well Mali 93 F1
Guitiriz Spain 42 C1
Guiuan Phil. 57 G3
Guivi hill Fin. 32 G1
Guixi China see Dianjiang
Guiyang Guizhou China 66 C3
Guiyang Hunan China 67 E3
Guizhou prov. China 66 C3
Guizi China 67 D4
Gujan-Mestras France 38 C4
Gujarat state India 74 B5
Gujar Khan Pak. 81 H3
Guja Nigeria 93 I3
Gujerat state India see Gujarat
Gujranwala Pak. 74 B2
Gujrat Pak. 74 B2
Gukou China 67 F3
Gukovo Rus. Fed. 29 F6
Gulabgarh Jammu and Kashmir 74 C2
Gulabie Uzbek. 70 A3
Gulbahçe Turkey 47 E5
Gulbarga India 72 C2
Gulbene Latvia 33 G4
Gul'cha Kyrg. see Gülchö
Gülchö Kyrg. 70 C3
Gülek Turkey 78 C3
Gülek Boğazı pass Turkey 78 C3
Gulfport U.S.A. 129 A6
Gulf Shores U.S.A. 129 B6
Gulgong Australia 112 D4
Gulian China 63 K1
Gulin China 66 C3
Gulistan Pak. 81 F4
Gulistan Uzbek. 81 G1
Guliston Uzbek. see Gulistan
Gulja China see Yining
Gul Kach Pak. 81 G4
Gull r. Canada 124 B3
Gullbrå Norway 33 B3
Gullkrona fjärd b. Fin. 33 F4
Gull Lake Canada 134 E2
Gullspång Sweden 33 D4
Gullträsk Sweden 32 F2
Güllük Turkey 47 E6
Güllük Körfezi b. Turkey 78 A3
Gulmarg Jammu and Kashmir 74 B2
Gülnar Turkey 78 C3
Gülpınar Turkey 47 E5
Gulrip'shi Georgia 79 E2
Gülşehir Turkey 78 C3
Gulu China see Xincai
Gulu Uganda 96 B4
Gülübovo Bulg. 46 D3
Gulumba Gana Nigeria 93 I3
Gulwe Tanz. 97 C6
Gulyantsi Bulg. 46 D3
Gulyayevskiye Koshki, Ostrova is Rus. Fed. 28 J1
Gumal r. Pak. 81 G4
Gumare Botswana 98 D3
Gumbinnen Rus. Fed. see Gusev
Gumbiri mt. Sudan 96 A3
Gumdag Turkm. 80 C2
Gumel Nigeria 93 H2
Gümgüm Turkey see Varto
Gumla India 75 E5
Gummersbach Germany 36 C3
Gumpang r. Indon. 58 B1
Gumsi Nigeria 93 H2
Gümüşhane Turkey 79 D2
Gümüşsuyu Turkey 47 E5
Guna India 74 C4
Gunan China see Qijiang
Guna Terara mt. Eth. 96 C2
Gund r. Tajik. 81 G2
Gundagai Australia 112 D4
Gundji Dem. Rep. Congo 94 D4
Gundlakamma r. India 72 D3
Gundlupet India 72 C4
Gündoğmuş Turkey 78 C3
Güneşli Turkey 47 F5
Güney Turkey 47 F5
Güneydoğu Toroslar plat. Turkey 107 D3
Gunglilap Myanmar 60 B2
Gungu Dem. Rep. Congo 95 C6
Gungue Angola 95 B8
Gunib Rus. Fed. 79 F2
Gunisao r. Canada 123 L4
Gunja Croatia 44 G2
Gunnarn Sweden 32 E2
Gunnbjørn Fjeld nunatak Greenland 121 Q3
Gunnedah Australia 112 D3
Gunnison CO U.S.A. 135 F5
Gunnison UT U.S.A. 137 G2
Gunnison r. U.S.A. 137 H2
Gunong Ayer Sarawak Malaysia see Gunung Ayer
Güns Hungary see Kőszeg
Gunt r. Tajik. see Gund
Guntakal India 72 C3
Guntur India 72 D2
Gununa Australia 110 D3
Gunung Ayer Sarawak Malaysia 59 E2
Gunung Gading National Park Sarawak Malaysia 59 E2
Gunung Leuser National Park Indon. 58 B2
Gunung Mulu National Park Sarawak Malaysia 59 F1
Gunung Palung National Park Indon. 59 E3
Gunung Rinjani National Park Indon. 59 G5
Gunungsitoli Indon. 58 B2
Gunungtua Indon. 58 B2
Gunupur India 73 D2
Günyüzü Turkey 78 B3
Gunza Angola see Porto Amboim
Günzburg Germany 36 E4
Gunzenhausen Germany 36 E4
Guo He r. China 67 E1
Guo He r. China 67 F1
Guoluezhen China see Lingbao
Guoyang China 67 F1
Guozhen China see Baoji
Gupis Jammu and Kashmir 74 B1
Gurais Jammu and Kashmir 74 B2
Gura Portiței sea chan. Romania 46 F2
Gurara r. Nigeria 93 G3
Gura Teghii Romania 46 E2
Gurba r. Dem. Rep. Congo 94 E4
Gurbantünggüt Shamo des. China 70 G3
Gurdim Iran 81 E5
Gurdon U.S.A. 133 C5
Güre Turkey 78 B3
Gurgān Azer. 80 B1
Gurgan Iran see Gorgān
Gurgaon India 74 C3
Gurgei, Jebel mt. Sudan 88 E6
Gurghiu r. Romania 46 D1
Gurghiului, Munții mts Romania 46 D1
Gurgueia r. Brazil 150 D3
Gurha India 74 A4
Guri, Embalse de resr Venez. 147 F3
Gurig National Park Australia 110 C1
Gurktaler Alpen mts Austria 37 F5
Gurmatkal India 72 C2
Guro Moz. 99 G3
Gürpınar Turkey 79 E3
Gurramkonda India 72 C3
Gürsu Turkey 47 F4
Gurué Moz. 99 H2
Gürün Turkey 78 D3
Gurupá Brazil 147 I5
Gurupa, Ilha Grande de i. Brazil 147 I5
Gurupi Brazil 150 B4
Gurupi r. Brazil 150 C2
Gurupi, Cabo c. Brazil 150 C2
Gurupi, Serra do hills Brazil 150 B3
Guru Sikhar mt. India 74 B4
Guruve Zimbabwe 99 F3
Guruwe Zimbabwe see Guruve
Gur'yev Kazakh. see Atyrau
Gur'yevsk Rus. Fed. 28 F5
Gur'yevskaya Oblast' admin. div. Kazakh. see Atyrauskaya Oblast'
Gusau Nigeria 93 G2
Gusev Rus. Fed. 37 K1
Gushgy Turkm. 81 E3
Gushgy r. Turkm. 81 E2
Gushi China 67 E1
Gushiegu Ghana 93 E3
Gusinoozersk Rus. Fed. 27 K4
Guskara India 75 E5
Gus'-Khrustal'nyy Rus. Fed. 28 G5
Guspini Sardinia Italy 45 B5
Güssing Austria 37 H5
Gustavo Sotelo Mex. 135 D7
Gustavus U.S.A. 122 C3
Gustine U.S.A. 136 B3
Güstrow Germany 37 F2
Gütersloh Germany 36 D3
Guthrie AZ U.S.A. 137 H5
Guthrie KY U.S.A. 128 B4
Guthrie OK U.S.A. 133 B5
Guthrie TX U.S.A. 133 A5
Gutian Fujian China 67 F3
Gutian Fujian China 67 F3
Gutian Shuiku resr China 67 F3
Gutiérrez Bol. 149 E4
Guttenberg U.S.A. 132 D3
Gutu Zimbabwe 99 F3
Guvertfjället mts Sweden 32 E2
Guwahati India 75 F4
Guwēr Iraq 79 E3
Guwlumayak Turkm. see Kuuli-Mayak
▶Guyana country S. America 147 G3
southamerica 144–145, 154
Guyane Française terr. S. America see French Guiana
Guyang China see Guzhang
Guyenne reg. France 38 C4
Guy Fawkes River National Park Australia 112 E3
Guyi China see Sanjiang
Guymon U.S.A. 133 A4
Güyom Iran 80 C4
Guyong China see Jiangle
Guyra Australia 112 D3
Guysborough Canada 125 I4

Hauts Plateaux Alg. 91 E2
Haut-Zaïre prov. Dem. Rep. Congo see Orientale
Hauvo Fin. see Nagu
Hauzenberg Germany 37 F4

▶Havana Cuba 129 C8
Capital of Cuba.

Havana U.S.A. 132 D3
Havant U.K. 35 F6
Havasu, Lake U.S.A. 137 E4
Havel r. Germany 37 E2
Haveli Pak. 81 H4
Havelian Pak. 81 H3
Havelock Canada 130 E1
Havelock N.Z. 113 C3
Havelock Swaziland see Bulembu
Havelock U.S.A. 129 D5
Havelock Falls Australia 110 C2
Havelock Island India 73 G4
Havelock North N.Z. 113 D2
Haverfordwest U.K. 35 D6
Haverhill U.K. 35 G5
Haverhill U.S.A. 131 H2
Haveri India 72 B3
Haverö Sweden 33 D3
Havlíčkův Brod Czech Rep. 37 G4
Havøysund Norway 32 G1
Havran Turkey 47 E5
Havre U.S.A. 134 E2
Havre Aubert, Île du i. Canada 125 I4
Havre de Grace U.S.A. 131 E4
Havre Rock i. N.Z. 107 H5
Havre-St-Pierre Canada 125 I3
Havsa Turkey 46 E4
Havza Turkey 78 C2
Hawaii i. U.S.A. 135 [inset] Z1
Hawaii state U.S.A. 135 [inset] Z2
Hawaiian Islands N. Pacific Ocean 165 G4
Hawaiian Ridge sea feature N. Pacific Ocean 165 G4
Hawaii Volcanoes National Park U.S.A. 135 [inset] Z2
Ḩawallī Kuwait 79 G5
Ḩawar i. The Gulf see Ḩuwār
Hawea, Lake N.Z. 113 B4
Hawera N.Z. 113 C2
Hawes U.K. 35 E4
Hawesville U.S.A. 128 B4
Hawick U.K. 34 E4
Ḩawīzah, Hawr al imp. l. Iraq 79 F5
Hawkdun Range mts N.Z. 113 B4
Hawke Bay N.Z. 113 D2
Hawker Australia 112 A3
Hawkers Gate Australia 112 B3
Hawkes Bay Canada 125 J3
Hawkins Peak U.S.A. 137 F3
Hawlēr Iraq see Arbīl
Hawley U.S.A. 131 F3
Hawng Luk Myanmar 60 B3
Ḩawrān, Wādī watercourse Iraq 79 E4
Ḩawşal hills Saudi Arabia 77 B5
Hawthorne U.S.A. 136 C2
Hay Australia 112 C4
Hay watercourse Australia 110 D5
Hay r. Canada 123 H2
Hayachine-san mt. Japan 65 E5
Haydān, Wādī al r. Jordan 77 B4
Haydarābad Iran 80 A2
Hayes r. Canada 123 M3
Hayes Creek Australia 110 B2
Hayes Halvø pen. Greenland 121 M2
Hayf Yemen 76 E7
Hayfield Reservoir U.S.A. 137 E5
Hayl Oman 80 D5
Hayl, Wādī watercourse Syria 77 C3
Haymā' Oman 76 F6
Haymana Turkey 78 C3
Haymarket U.S.A. 130 E4
Hayotboshi Toghi mt. Uzbek. see Khayatbashi, Gora
Hayrabolu Turkey 78 A2
Hay River Canada 123 H2
Hay River Reserve Canada 123 H2
Hays U.S.A. 132 B4
Hayshah, Sabkhat al salt pan Libya 88 B2
Haysi U.S.A. 130 B5
Haysyn Ukr. 29 D6
Ḩayţān, Jabal hill Egypt 77 A4
Hayward CA U.S.A. 136 A3
Hayward WI U.S.A. 132 D2
Haywards Heath U.K. 35 F6
Hazard U.S.A. 130 B5
Hazaribag India 75 E5
Hazaribagh Range mts India 75 D5
Hazār Masjed, Kūh-e mts Iran 81 D2
Hazebrouck France 39 E1
Hazelton Canada 122 E4
Hazen U.S.A. 132 A2
Hazen Strait Canada 121 H2
Hazlehurst GA U.S.A. 129 C6
Hazlehurst MS U.S.A. 133 D6
Hazleton U.S.A. 131 F3
Hazlett, Lake salt flat Australia 108 E5
Hazrat Sultan Afgh. 81 F2
Hazro Pak. 81 H3
H. Bouchard Arg. 152 E3
Headingly Australia 110 D4
Head of Bight b. Australia 109 E7
Healdsburg U.S.A. 136 A2

▶Heard and McDonald Islands terr. Indian Ocean 163 L9
Australian External Territory.
asia 82

Heard Island Indian Ocean 163 L9
Hearne U.S.A. 133 B6
Hearne Lake Canada 123 H2
Hearst Canada 124 D3
Hearst Island Antarctica 167 L2
Heart r. U.S.A. 132 A2
Heath r. Bol./Peru 148 C3
Heathcote Australia 112 C5
Heathfield U.K. 35 G6
Heathrow airport U.K. 35 F6
Heathsville U.S.A. 131 E5
Heavener U.S.A. 133 C5
Hebbronville U.S.A. 133 B7
Hebei prov. China 63 J4
Hebel Australia 111 F6
Heber U.S.A. 137 G4
Heber City U.S.A. 137 G1
Heber Springs U.S.A. 133 C5
Hebi China 63 I4
Hebron Canada 125 I1
Hebron U.S.A. 132 B3
Hebron West Bank 77 B4
Hebros r. Greece/Turkey see Evros
Heby Sweden 33 E4
Hecate Strait Canada 122 D4
Hecheng Jiangxi China see Zixi
Hecheng Zhejiang China see Qingtian
Hechi China 66 D3
Hechingen Germany 36 D4
Hechuan Chongqing China 66 C2
Hechuan Jiangxi China see Yongxing
Hedberg Sweden 32 E2
Hede China see Sheyang
Hédé France 38 C2
Hede Sweden 33 D3
Hedemora Sweden 33 D3
Hedenäset Sweden 32 F2
Hede Shuiku resr China 67 D4
Hedesunda Sweden 33 E3
He Devil Mountain U.S.A. 134 C3
Hedmark county Norway 33 C3
Heerenveen Neth. 36 B2
Heerhugowaard Neth. 36 B2
Heerlen Neth. 36 B3
Ḩefa Israel see Haifa
Hefei China 67 F2
Hefeng China 67 D2
Heflin U.S.A. 129 B5
Hegang China 64 B3
Heiban Sudan 96 A2
Heidan r. Jordan see Haydān, Wādī al
Heide Germany 36 D1
Heidelberg Germany 36 D4
Heihe China 64 A2
Heilbronn Germany 36 D4
Heiligenbeil Rus. Fed. see Mamonovo
Heiligenhafen Germany 36 E1
Hei Ling Chau i. Hong Kong China 67 [inset]
Heilongjiang prov. China 64 B3
Heilong Jiang r. China 64 B3
also known as Amur (Rus. Fed.)
Heilungkiang prov. China see Heilongjiang
Heinävesi Fin. 32 H3
Heinola Fin. 33 G3
Heinz Bay Myanmar 61 B5
Heinze Islands Myanmar 61 B5
Heishi Beihu l. China 75 D2
Heishui China 66 B1
Heisker Islands U.K. see Monach Islands
Hejaz reg. Saudi Arabia see Hijaz
Hejiang China 66 C2
He Jiang r. China 67 D4
Hekimhan Turkey 79 D3
Hekla vol. Iceland 32 [inset]
Hekou Hubei China 67 E2
Hekou Jiangxi China see Yanshan
Hekou Sichuan China see Yajiang
Hekou Yunnan China 66 B4
Hel Poland 37 I1
Helagsfjället mt. Sweden 32 D3
Helem India 75 G4
Helen i. Palau 57 H5
Helena AR U.S.A. 133 D5

▶Helena MT U.S.A. 134 D3
State capital of Montana.

Helena OH U.S.A. 130 B3
Helen Reef Palau 57 H5
Helensburgh U.K. 34 D3
Helen Springs Australia 110 C3
Helenwood U.S.A. 130 A5
Helgoland i. Germany 36 C1
Helgoländer Bucht b. Germany 36 D1
Helgoland i. Germany see Helgoland
Heligoland Bight b. Germany see Helgoländer Bucht
Helixi China see Ningguo
Hella Iceland 32 [inset]
Hellas country Europe see Greece
Helleh r. Iran 80 B4
Hellespont strait Turkey see Dardanelles
Hellevoetsluis Neth. 36 B3
Hellhole Gorge National Park Australia 111 F5
Helligskogen Norway 32 F1
Hellín Spain 43 F3
Hells Canyon gorge U.S.A. 134 C3
Hell-Ville Madag. see Andoany
Helm U.S.A. 136 B3
Helmand prov. Afgh. 81 E4
Helmand r. Afgh. 81 E4
Helmantica Spain see Salamanca
Helme r. Germany 36 E3
Helmeringhausen Namibia 98 C5
Helmond Neth. 36 B3
Helmsdale U.K. 34 E2
Helmsdale r. U.K. 34 E2
Helmsley U.K. 35 F4
Helmstedt Germany 36 E2
Helodrano Antongila b. Madag. 99 [inset] K2
Helong China 64 B4
Helper U.S.A. 137 G2
Helsingborg Sweden 33 D4
Helsingfors Fin. see Helsinki
Helsingør Denmark 33 D4

▶Helsinki Fin. 33 G3
Capital of Finland.

Helston U.K. 35 D6
Heltermaa Estonia 33 F4
Helvacı Turkey 47 E5
Helvetic Republic country Europe see Switzerland
Helvetinjärven kansallispuisto nat. park Fin. 33 F3
Helwān Egypt see Ḩulwān
Hemel Hempstead U.K. 35 F6
Hemet U.S.A. 136 D5
Hemmoor Germany 36 D2
Hemnesberget Norway 32 D2
Hemphill U.S.A. 133 C6
Hempstead U.S.A. 133 B6
Hemse Sweden 33 E4
Hemsedal Norway 33 C3
Hemsedal valley Norway 33 C3
Henan China 66 B1
Henan prov. China 67 E1
Henares r. Spain 42 E2
Henashi-zaki pt Japan 64 D4
Henbury Australia 110 C5
Hendawashi Tanz. 97 B5
Henderson KY U.S.A. 128 B4
Henderson NC U.S.A. 128 D4
Henderson NV U.S.A. 137 E3
Henderson NY U.S.A. 131 E2
Henderson TN U.S.A. 128 A5
Henderson TX U.S.A. 133 C5
Henderson Island Pitcairn Is 165 J7
Hendersonville U.S.A. 128 B4
Hendorābī i. Iran 80 C5
Hengch'un Taiwan 67 G4
Hengdong China 67 E3
Hengduan Shan mts China 66 A2
Hengelo Neth. 36 C2
Hengnan China see Hengyang
Hengshan Heilong. China 64 B3
Hengshan Hunan China 67 E3
Heng Shan mt. China 67 E3
Hengshui China see Chongyi
Hengxian China 67 D4
Hengyang Hunan China 67 E3
Hengyang Hunan China 67 E3
Hengzhou China see Hengxian
Henley N.Z. 113 B4
Henlopen, Cape U.S.A. 131 F4
Hennebont France 38 B3
Hennef (Sieg) Germany 36 C3
Hennessey U.S.A. 133 B4
Hennigsdorf Berlin Germany 37 F2
Henniker U.S.A. 131 H2
Henrietta U.S.A. 133 B5
Henrietta Maria, Cape Canada 124 D2
Henrique de Carvalho Angola see Saurimo
Henry, Cape U.S.A. 131 E5
Henryetta U.S.A. 133 C5
Henry Ice Rise Antarctica 167 L1
Henry Kater, Cape Canada 121 M3
Henry Mountains U.S.A. 137 G2
Hensall Canada 130 C2
Henshaw, Lake U.S.A. 137 D5
Hentiesbaai Namibia 98 B4
Henzada Myanmar 60 A4
Heping Guizhou China see Huishui
Heping Guizhou China see Yanhe
Hepo China see Jiexi
Heppner U.S.A. 134 C3
Hepu China 67 D4
Heqing Guangdong China 67 E4
Heqing Yunnan China 66 B3
Heraclea Turkey see Ereğli
Heraclea Pontica Turkey see Ereğli
Heraklion Greece see Iraklion
Herald Cays atolls Australia 111 G3
Herāt Afgh. 81 E3
Herāt prov. Afgh. 81 E3
Hérault r. France 39 E5
Herbert r. Australia 111 F3
Herbert watercourse Australia 110 D3
Herbert Canada 134 F2
Herbert Downs Australia 110 D4
Herbert River Falls National Park Australia 111 F3
Herbert Wash salt flat Australia 109 D6
Herbignac France 38 B3
Herbstein Germany 36 D3
Herceg-Novi Serb. and Mont. 44 G3
Hercules Dome ice feature Antarctica 167 K1
Hereford U.K. 35 E5
Hereford U.S.A. 133 A5
Héréhérétué atoll Fr. Polynesia 165 I7
Herford Germany 36 D2
Héricourt France 39 G3
Herington U.S.A. 132 B4
Herisau Switz. 39 H3
Herkimer U.S.A. 131 F2
Hermagor Austria 37 F5
Herma Ness hd U.K. 34 F1
Hermann U.S.A. 132 D4
Hermel Lebanon 77 C2
Hermidale Australia 112 C3
Hermitage MO U.S.A. 132 C4
Hermitage PA U.S.A. 130 C3
Hermitage Bay Canada 125 J4
Hermite, Islas is Chile 153 D8
Hermit Islands P.N.G. 57 K6
Hermon, Mount Lebanon/Syria 77 B3
Hermonthis Egypt see Armant
Hermopolis Magna Egypt see Al Ashmūnayn
Hermosillo Mex. 135 E7
Hernád r. Hungary 37 J5
also spelt Hornád (Slovakia)
Hernandarias Para. 149 G6
Hernando U.S.A. 133 D5
Hernani Spain 43 F1
Herndon CA U.S.A. 136 C3
Herndon WV U.S.A. 130 C5
Herne Germany 36 C3
Herning Denmark 33 C4
Heroica Nogales Mex. see Nogales
▶Heron Island i. Australia 111 G4
oceania 102–103
Hérouville-St-Clair France 38 C2
Herowābād Iran see Khalkhāl
Herrenberg Germany 36 D4
Herrera del Duque Spain 42 D3
Herrin U.S.A. 128 A4
Herrljunga Sweden 33 D4
Hervik Sweden 33 E4
Hers r. France 38 D5
Hershey U.S.A. 131 E3
Hertford U.K. 35 F6
Hertford U.S.A. 128 D4
Hervey Bay Australia 111 H5
Hervey Islands Cook Is 165 H7
Herzberg Germany 37 F3
Herzliyya Israel 77 B3
Herzogenburg Austria 37 G4
Ḩeşār Iran 80 B4
Ḩeşār Iran 80 B3
Hesdin France 38 E1
Heshan China 67 D4
Heshengqiao China 67 E2
Hesperia U.S.A. 136 D4
Hesquiat Canada 122 E5
Hess r. Canada 122 C2
Hesse land Germany see Hessen
Hesselberg hill Germany 36 E4
Hessen land Germany 36 D3
Hestvika Norway 32 C3
Het r. Laos 60 D3
Hetch Hetchy Aqueduct canal U.S.A. 136 A3
Hettinger U.S.A. 132 A2
Hettstedt Germany 36 E3
Heung Kong Tsai Hong Kong China see Aberdeen
Heves Hungary 37 J5
Ḩevron West Bank see Hebron
Hewlett U.S.A. 130 E5
Hexenkopf mt. Austria 36 E5
Hexham U.K. 34 E4
Heydebreck Poland see Kędzierzyn-Koźle
Heygali well Eth. 96 E3
Heyuan China 67 E4
Heywood Australia 112 B5
Heze China 63 J4
Hezhang China 66 C3
Hezhou China 67 D3
Hezuozhen China 66 B1
Hialeah U.S.A. 129 C7
Hiawatha U.S.A. 132 C4
Hibbing U.S.A. 132 C2
Hibbs, Point U.S.A. 112 C6
Hibernia Reef Australia 108 C3
Hichān Iran 81 E5
Hickman U.S.A. 128 A4
Hickory U.S.A. 128 C5
Hicks Bay N.Z. 113 D2
Hicksville NY U.S.A. 131 G3
Hicksville OH U.S.A. 130 A3
Hico U.S.A. 133 B5
Hidaka-sanmyaku mts Japan 64 E4
Hidalgo Mex. 133 B7
Hidalgo del Parral Mex. 126 E6
Hidasnémeti Hungary 37 J4
Hidrolândia Brazil 149 H4
Hierosolyma Israel/West Bank see Jerusalem
Higashi-suidō sea chan. Japan 65 B6
Higgins Bay U.S.A. 131 F2
Higgins Lake U.S.A. 130 A1
High Atlas mts Morocco see Haut Atlas
High Desert U.S.A. 134 B4
High Island i. Hong Kong China 67 [inset]
High Island U.S.A. 133 C6
High Island Reservoir Hong Kong China 67 [inset]
Highland U.S.A. 131 G3
Highland Peak CA U.S.A. 136 C2
Highland Peak NV U.S.A. 137 E3
Highland Springs U.S.A. 131 E5
High Level Canada 123 G3
High Level Canal India 73 E1
Highline Canal U.S.A. 137 E5
Highmore U.S.A. 132 B2
High Point U.S.A. 128 D5
High Prairie Canada 123 G4
High River Canada 134 D2
Highrock Lake Canada 123 K4
High Springs U.S.A. 129 C6
High Tatras mts Poland/Slovakia see Tatra Mountains
Hightstown U.S.A. 131 F3
High Wycombe U.K. 35 F6
Higüey Dom. Rep. 139 K5
Hihifo Tonga 107 H3
Hiidenportin kansallispuisto nat. park Fin. 32 H3
Hiiraan Somalia 96 E3
Hiiraan admin. reg. Somalia 96 E3
Hiiumaa i. Estonia 33 F4
Ḩijānah, Buḩayrat al imp. l. Syria 77 C3
Hijaz reg. Saudi Arabia 89 H3
Ḩikmah, Ra's al pt Egypt 89 E2
Hikone Japan 65 D6
Hikurangi mt. N.Z. 113 D2
Hilāl, Jabal hill Egypt 77 A4
Hilaricos Chile 148 C5
Hilary Coast Antarctica 167 H1
Hildale U.S.A. 137 F3
Hildburghausen Germany 36 E3
Hildesheim Germany 36 D2
Hili Bangl. 75 F4
Hillah Iraq 79 F4
Hill City U.S.A. 132 B4
Hill Creek r. U.S.A. 137 H2
Hillerød Denmark 33 D5
Hillerstorp Sweden 33 D4
Hillesheim Germany 36 C3
Hillgrove Australia 111 F3
Hill Island Lake Canada 123 I2
Hillsboro IL U.S.A. 132 D4
Hillsboro ND U.S.A. 132 B2
Hillsboro NH U.S.A. 131 H2
Hillsboro OH U.S.A. 130 B4
Hillsboro TX U.S.A. 133 B5
Hillsborough Grenada 147 F1
Hillsborough, Cape Australia 111 G4
Hillsdale MI U.S.A. 130 A3
Hillsdale NY U.S.A. 131 G2
Hillside Australia 108 B5
Hillsport Canada 124 C3
Hillston Australia 112 C4
Hillsville U.S.A. 130 C5
Hillswick U.K. 34 F1
Hilo U.S.A. 135 [inset] Z2
Hilton Australia 111 D4
Hilton U.S.A. 130 E2
Hilton Head Island U.S.A. 129 C5
Hilvan Turkey 79 D3
Hilversum Neth. 36 B2
Himachal Pradesh state India 74 C3
Ḩimā Darīyah, Jabal mt. Saudi Arabia 89 I3
▶Himalaya mts Asia 74 C2
asia 52–53
world 6–7
Himalchul mt. Nepal 75 E3
Himanka Fin. 32 F2
Himarë Albania 47 A4
Himatnagar India 74 B5
Himeji Japan 65 C6
Himi Japan 65 D5
Himora Eth. 89 H6
Ḩimş Syria see Homs
Ḩimş governorate Syria 77 D2
Ḩimş, Baḩrat resr Syria see Qaţţīnah, Buḩayrat
Hinako i. Indon. 58 B2
Hinchinbrook Island Australia 111 F3
Hinckley MN U.S.A. 132 C2
Hinckley UT U.S.A. 137 F2
Hinckley Reservoir U.S.A. 131 F2
Hind, Wādī al watercourse Saudi Arabia 77 B5
Hinda Congo 95 B6
Hindaun India 74 C4
Hindelang Germany 36 E5
Hindenburg Poland see Zabrze
Hindman U.S.A. 130 B5
Hindmarsh, Lake dry lake Australia 112 B5
Hindola India 73 E1
Hindoli India 74 B4
Hindoria India 74 C5
Hindri r. India 72 C3
Hindu Kush mts Afgh./Pak. 81 F3
Hindupur India 72 C3
Hines Creek Canada 122 G3
Hinesville U.S.A. 129 C6
Hinganghat India 72 C1
Hingol r. Pak. 81 F5
Hingol r. Pak. see Girdar Dhor
Hınıs Turkey 79 E3
Hinnøya i. Norway 32 D1
Hinojedo mt. Spain 43 E2
Hino-misaki pt Japan 65 C6
Hinsdale U.S.A. 131 G2
Hinterzarten Germany 36 D5
Hinthada Myanmar see Henzada
Hinton KY U.S.A. 130 A4
Hinton WV U.S.A. 130 C5
Hiort i. U.K. see Hirta
Hipólito Mex. 133 A7
Hipponium Italy see Vibo Valentia
Hippo Regius Alg. see Annaba
Hippo Zarytus Tunisia see Bizerte
Hirabit Dağ mt. Turkey 79 F3
Hirado Japan 65 B6
Hirafok Alg. 91 G5
Hirakud Reservoir India 75 D5
Hiraman watercourse Kenya 96 C5
Hiré-Watta Côte d'Ivoire 92 D4
Hiriyur India 72 C3
Hirosaki Japan 64 E4
Hiroshima Japan 65 C6
Hirschaid Germany 36 E4
Hirschberg Germany 36 E3
Hirschberg Poland see Jelenia Góra
Hirsingue France 39 G3
Hirson France 39 F2
Hîrşova Romania see Hârşova
Hirta i. U.K. 34 B3
Hirtshals Denmark 33 C4
Hisar India 74 B3
Hisar, Koh-i- mts Afgh. 81 F3
Hisarcık Turkey 47 F5
Hisarköy Turkey see Domaniç
Hisarönü Turkey 78 C2
Hisarönü Körfezi b. Turkey 47 E6
Ḩisb, Sha'īb watercourse Iraq 79 F5
Hisor Tajik. 81 G2
Hisor Tizmasi mts Tajik./Uzbek. see Gissar Range
Hispalis Spain see Seville
Hispania country Europe see Spain

▶Hispaniola i. Caribbean Sea 127 L7
Consists of the Dominican Republic and Haiti.

Hispur Glacier Jammu and Kashmir 74 B1
Hissar India see Hisar
Hisua India 75 E4
Hīt Iraq 79 E4
Hitachi Japan 65 E5
Hitachinaka Japan 65 E5
Hitoyoshi Japan 65 B6
Hitra i. Norway 32 C3
Hiva Oa i. Fr. Polynesia 165 I6
Hixon Canada 122 F4
Hixson Cay reef Australia 111 H4
Hiyon watercourse Israel 77 B4
Hizan Turkey 79 E3
Hjallerup Denmark 33 C4
Hjälmaren l. Sweden 33 D4
Hjelle Norway 33 B3
Hjelmeland Norway 33 B4
Hjerkinn Norway 33 C3
Hjo Sweden 33 D4
Hjørring Denmark 33 C4
Hjuvik Sweden 33 C4
Hka, Nam r. Myanmar 60 B3
Hkakabo Razi mt. Myanmar 60 B1
Hkok r. Myanmar 60 B3
Hkring Bum mt. Myanmar 60 B2
Hlabisa S. Africa 99 F6
Hlaing r. Myanmar 60 B4
Hlako Kangri mt. China see Lhagoi Kangri
Hlinsko Czech Rep. 37 G4
Hlohlowane S. Africa 99 E6
Hlohovec Slovakia 37 H4
Hlotse Lesotho 99 F6
Hlučín Czech Rep. 37 I4
Hlukhiv Ukr. 29 E6
Hlung-Tan Myanmar 60 B3
Hlybokaye Belarus 31 K2
Hnilec r. Slovakia 37 J4
Hnúšťa Slovakia 37 I4
Ho Ghana 93 F4
Hoa Binh Vietnam 60 D3
Hoachanas Namibia 98 C4
Hoang Liên Son mts Vietnam 60 C3
Hoang Sa is S. China Sea see Paracel Islands
Hoanib watercourse Namibia 98 B3
Hoarusib watercourse Namibia 98 B3

▶Hobart Australia 112 C6
State capital of Tasmania.

Hobart U.S.A. 133 B5
Hobbs U.S.A. 135 G6
Hobbs Coast Antarctica 167 J1
Hobe Sound U.S.A. 129 C7
Hobot Xar Qi China see Xin Bulag
Hobro Denmark 33 C4
Hoburg Sweden 33 E4
Hoburgen pt Sweden 33 E4
Hobyo Somalia 96 F3
Hochfeiler mt. Austria/Italy see Gran Pilastro
Hochfeld Namibia 98 C4
Hochgall mt. Austria/Italy see Collalto
Hochgolling mt. Austria 37 F5
Hochharz nat. park Germany 36 E3
Hô Chi Minh Vietnam see Ho Chi Minh City
Ho Chi Minh City Vietnam 61 D6
Hochschwab mt. Austria 37 G5
Hochtor mt. Austria 37 G5
Hocking r. U.S.A. 130 C4
Hodal India 74 C4
Hodda mt. Somalia 96 F2
Hodeidah Yemen 76 C7
Hodgesville U.S.A. 130 C4
Hodgson Downs Australia 110 C2
Hodh Ech Chargui admin. reg. Mauritania 92 D1
Hodh El Gharbi admin. reg. Mauritania 92 C1
Hódmezővásárhely Hungary 46 B1
Hodmo watercourse Somalia 96 E2
Hodna, Chott el salt l. Alg. 91 G2
Hodonín Czech Rep. 37 H4
Hoek van Holland Neth. see Hook of Holland
Hoeryŏng N. Korea 64 B4
Hof Germany 36 E3
Hoffman Mountain U.S.A. 131 G2
Hofmeyr S. Africa 98 E6
Höfn Iceland 32 [inset]
Hofors Sweden 33 E3
Hofsjökull ice cap Iceland 32 [inset]
Hōfu Japan 65 B6
Hofuf Saudi Arabia see Al Hufūf
Höganäs Sweden 33 D4
Hoganthulla Creek r. Australia 111 F5
Hogg, Mount Canada 122 C2
Hoggar plat. Alg. 91 G5
Hog Island U.S.A. 131 F5
Högsby Sweden 33 E4
Høgste Breakulen mt. Norway 33 B3
Hőgyész Hungary 37 I5
Hoh r. U.S.A. 134 A3
Hohenems Austria 36 D5
Hohenloher Ebene plain Germany 36 D4
Hohensalza Poland see Inowrocław
Hoher Dachstein mt. Austria 37 F5
Hoher Göll mt. Austria/Germany 37 F5
Hohe Rhön mts Germany 36 D3
Hohe Tauern mts Austria 37 F5
Hohe Tauern, Nationalpark nat. park Austria 37 F5
Hohe Venn moorland Belgium 39 G1
Hohhot China 63 I3
Hoh Xil Hu salt l. China 75 F2
Hoh Xil Shan mts China 70 G4
Hôi An Vietnam 61 E5
Hoima Uganda 96 A4
Hoisington U.S.A. 132 B4
Hôi Xuân Vietnam 60 D3
Hojagala Turkm. see Khodzha-Kala
Hojai India 75 G4
Hojambaz Turkm. see Khodzhambaz
Hökensås hills Sweden 33 D4
Hokitika N.Z. 113 B3
Hokkaidō i. Japan 64 E4
Hokksund Norway 33 C4
Hokmābād Iran 80 D2
Hoktemberyan Armenia 79 F2
Hol Buskerud Norway 33 C3
Hol Nordland Norway 32 E1
Hola Kenya 96 C5
Holalkere India 72 C3
Holanda Bol. 148 D3
Holbæk Denmark 33 C5
Holberg Canada 122 D5
Holbrook Australia 112 C4
Holbrook U.S.A. 137 G4
Holden Canada 123 H4
Holden U.S.A. 137 F2
Holdenville U.S.A. 133 B5
Holdich Arg. 153 C6
Holdrege U.S.A. 132 B3
Hole Narsipur India 72 C3
Holgate U.S.A. 130 A3
Holguín Cuba 127 K7
Holíč Slovakia 37 H4
Hollabrunn Austria 37 H4
Holland country Europe see Netherlands
Holland MI U.S.A. 132 E3
Holland NY U.S.A. 130 D2
Hollandale U.S.A. 133 D5
Hollandia Indon. see Jayapura
Hollands Diep est. Neth. 36 B3
Hollick-Kenyon Peninsula Antarctica 167 L2
Hollick-Kenyon Plateau Antarctica 167 K1
Hollis U.S.A. 133 B5
Hollister U.S.A. 136 B3
Hollola Fin. 33 G3
Hollum Neth. 36 B2
Holly U.S.A. 130 B2
Holly Springs U.S.A. 128 A5
Hollywood U.S.A. 129 C7
Holm Norway 32 D2
Holman Canada 120 H2
Holmes Reef Australia 111 F3
Holmgard Rus. Fed. see Velikiy Novgorod
Holmön i. Sweden 32 F3
Holmsund Sweden 32 F3
Holmudden pt Sweden 33 E4
Holod r. Romania 46 C1
Ḩolon Israel 77 B3
Holoog Namibia 98 C5
Holothuria Banks reef Australia 108 C3
Holroyd r. Australia 111 E2
Holstebro Denmark 33 C4
Holstein U.S.A. 132 C3
Holsteinsborg Greenland see Sisimiut
Holston r. U.S.A. 130 B5
Holston Lake U.S.A. 130 C5
Holt U.S.A. 130 A2
Holton U.S.A. 132 C4
Holtville U.S.A. 137 E5
Holtwood U.S.A. 131 E4
Holyhead U.K. 35 D5
Holy Island England U.K. 34 F4
Holy Island Wales U.K. 35 D5
Holyoke CO U.S.A. 134 G4
Holyoke MA U.S.A. 131 G2
Holy See Europe see Vatican City
Holzkirchen Germany 36 E5
Holzminden Germany 36 D3
Homa Bay Kenya 96 B5
Homalin Myanmar 60 A2
Homathko r. Canada 122 E5
Homāyūnshahr Iran see Khomeynīshahr
Homberg (Efze) Germany 36 D3
Hombori Mali 93 E2
Hombre Muerto, Salar del salt flat Arg. 152 D1
Home Bay Canada 121 M3
Home Hill Australia 111 F3
Homer AK U.S.A. 120 D4
Homer LA U.S.A. 133 C5
Homer MI U.S.A. 130 A2
Homer City U.S.A. 130 D3
Homerville U.S.A. 129 C6
Homestead Australia 111 F4
Homestead U.S.A. 129 C7
Homewood U.S.A. 129 B5
Hommelvik Norway 32 C3
Homnabad India 72 C2
Homocea Romania 46 E1
Homodji well Niger 93 I1
Homoine Moz. 99 G4
Homs Libya see Al Khums
Homs Syria 78 D4
Homyel' Belarus 29 D5
Honaker U.S.A. 130 C5
Honan prov. China see Henan
Honavar India 72 B3
Hon Bai Canh i. Vietnam 61 D6
Hon Chông Vietnam 61 D6
Hon Chuôi i. Vietnam 61 D6
Honda Col. 146 C3
Honda India 75 E5
Hondeklipbaai S. Africa 98 C6
Hondo NM U.S.A. 135 F6
Hondo TX U.S.A. 133 B6

▶Honduras country Central America 138 G6
5th largest country in Central and North America.
northamerica 118–119, 140

Hønefoss Norway 33 C3
Honesdale U.S.A. 131 F3
Honey Brook U.S.A. 131 F3
Honey Lake U.S.A. 136 B1
Honfleur France 38 D2
Hong'an China 67 E2
Hongch'ŏn S. Korea 65 A5
Hông Gai Vietnam 60 D3
Honghai Wan b. China 67 E4
Honghe China 66 B4
Hong He r. China 67 E1
Honghu China 67 E2
Hong Hu l. China 67 E2
Hongjiang Hunan China 67 D3
Hongjiang Sichuan China see Wangcang
▶Hong Kong Hong Kong China 67 [inset]
asia 52–53, 82
world 16–17
Hong Kong special admin. reg. China 67 [inset]
Hong Kong Harbour sea chan. Hong Kong China 67 [inset]
Hong Kong Island Hong Kong China 67 [inset]
Hông Ngư Vietnam 61 D6
Hongqiao China see Qidong
Hongqizhen China see Tongshi
Hongshan China 66 A2
Hongshui He r. China 66 D4
Honguedo, Détroit d' sea chan. Canada 125 H3
Hongwŏn N. Korea 65 A4
Hongyuan China 66 B1
Hongze China 67 F1
Hongze Hu l. China 67 F1

▶Honiara Solomon Is 107 E2
Capital of the Solomon Islands.

Honiton U.K. 35 E6
Honjō Japan 65 E5
Honkajoki Fin. 33 F3
Hon Khoai i. Vietnam 61 D6
Hon Mê i. Vietnam 60 D4
Hon Minh Hoa i. Vietnam 61 D6
Honnali India 72 B3
Honningsvåg Norway 32 G1
Honokaa U.S.A. 135 [inset] Z1

▶Honolulu U.S.A. 135 [inset] Z1
State capital of Hawaii.

Hon Rai i. Vietnam 61 D6

▶Honshū i. Japan 65 C6
3rd largest island in Asia and 7th in the world.
asia 50–51
world 6–7

Honwad India 72 B2
Hood r. Canada 123 I1
Hood, Mount vol. U.S.A. 134 B3
Hood Point Australia 109 B8
Hood River U.S.A. 134 B3
Hoogeveen Neth. 36 C2
Hoogezand-Sappemeer Neth. 36 C2
Hooghly r. mouth India see Hugli
Hooker U.S.A. 132 A4
Hook Head Rep. of Ireland 35 C5
Hook of Holland Neth. 36 B3
Hook Reef Australia 111 G3
Hoonah U.S.A. 122 C3
Hooper Bay U.S.A. 120 C3
Hooper Island U.S.A. 131 E4
Hoopstad S. Africa 98 E5
Hoorn Neth. 36 B2
Hoorn, Îles de is Wallis and Futuna Is 107 H3
Hoorn Islands Wallis and Futuna Is see Hoorn, Îles de
Hoover Dam U.S.A. 137 E3
Hoover Memorial Reservoir U.S.A. 130 B3
Hóp lag. Iceland 32 [inset]
Hopa Turkey 79 E2
Hope Canada 134 B2
Hope U.S.A. 133 C5
Hope, Lake salt flat Australia 109 C8
Hope, Point U.S.A. 166 B2
Hopedale Canada 125 I2
Hopei prov. China see Hebei

Ilgaz Dağları *mts* Turkey **78** C2
Ilgın Turkey **78** B3
Ilhabela Brazil **151** C7
Ilha Grande Brazil **147** E5
Ilha Grande, Represa *resr* Brazil **151** A7
Ilha Solteira, Represa *resr* Brazil **149** H5
Ílhavo Port. **42** B2
Ilhéus Brazil **150** E5
Ili Kazakh. *see* **Kapchagay**
Ilia Romania **46** C2
Iliamna Lake U.S.A. **120** D4
İliç Turkey **79** D3
Il'ich Kazakh. **81** G1
Il'ichevsk Azer. *see* **Şärur**
Ilici Spain *see* **Elche-Elx**
Iligan Phil. **57** F4
Ilimananngip Nunaa *i.* Greenland **121** Q2
Ilimpeya *r.* Rus. Fed. **27** K3
Il'inskiy *Permskaya Oblast'* Rus. Fed. **28** J4
Il'inskiy *Sakhalinskaya Oblast'* Rus. Fed. **64** E3
Il'insko-Podomskoye Rus. Fed. **28** H3
Iliomar East Timor **108** D2
Ilion U.S.A. **131** F2
Ilirska Bistrica Slovenia **44** E2
Ilium *tourist site* Turkey *see* **Troy**
Iliysk Kazakh. *see* **Kapchagay**
Ilkal India **72** C3
Ill *r.* France **39** G2
Illapel Chile **152** C2
Illapel *r.* Chile **152** C2
Ille *r.* France **38** C2
Illela Nigeria **93** G2
Iller *r.* Germany **36** D4
Illertissen Germany **36** E4
Illescas Spain **42** E2
Illimani, Nevado de *mt.* Bol. **148** D4
Illinois *r.* U.S.A. **132** D4
Illinois *state* U.S.A. **132** D4
Illizi Alg. **91** H4
Illueca Spain **43** F2
Ilm *r.* Germany **36** E3
Il'men', Ozero *l.* Rus. Fed. **28** D4
Ilmenau Germany **36** E3
Ilo Peru **148** C4
Ilobu Nigeria **93** G4
Iloilo Phil. **57** F3
Ilomantsi Fin. **28** D3
Ilorin Nigeria **93** G3
Ilova *r.* Croatia **44** F2
Ilovatka Rus. Fed. **29** H6
Ilovik *i.* Croatia **44** E2
Ilovlya Rus. Fed. **29** G6
Ilovlya *r.* Rus. Fed. **29** G6
Iłowa Poland **37** G3
Il'pyrskiy Rus. Fed. **27** Q3
Il'pyrskoye Rus. Fed. *see* **Il'pyrskiy**
Ilūkste Latvia **33** G5
Ilulissat Greenland **121** N3
Ilunde Tanz. **97** B6
Ilva *i.* Italy *see* **Elba, Isola d'**
Ilych *r.* Rus. Fed. **28** K3
Iłżanka *r.* Poland **37** J3
Imabari Japan **65** C6
Imaichi Japan **65** D5
Imala Moz. **97** C8
Imām al Ḩamzah Iraq **79** F5
Imam-baba Turkm. **81** E2
İmamoğlu Turkey **78** C3
Iman Rus. Fed. *see* **Dal'nerechensk**
Iman *r.* Rus. Fed. **64** C3
Imari Japan **65** B6
Imata Peru **148** C3
Imataca, Serranía de *mts* Venez. **147** F3
Imatra Fin. **33** H3
Imbabura *prov.* Ecuador **146** B4
Imbaimadai Guyana **147** F3
Imbituba Brazil **151** B9
imeni 26 Bakinskikh Komissarov Azer. *see* **26 Bakı Komissarı**
imeni 26 Bakinskikh Komissarov Turkm. **80** C2
imeni C. A. Niyazova Turkm. **81** E2
imeni Chapayevka Turkm. *see* **imeni C. A. Niyazova**
imeni Gastello Rus. Fed. **27** O3
imeni Kalinina Tajik. **81** H2
imeni Kerbabayeva Turkm. **81** E2
imeni Petra Stuchki Latvia *see* **Aizkraukle**
imeni Poliny Osipenko Rus. Fed. **64** D1
Imeri, Serra *mts* Brazil **147** E4
Imese Dem. Rep. Congo **94** C4
Īmī Eth. **96** D3
Imishli Azer. *see* **İmişli**
İmişli Azer. **79** G3
Imit Jammu and Kashmir **74** B1
Imja-do *i.* S. Korea **65** A6
Imjin-gang *r.* N. Korea/S. Korea **65** A5
Imlay City U.S.A. **130** B2
Imlili W. Sahara **90** B5
Immokalee U.S.A. **129** C7
Imo *state* Nigeria **93** G4
Imola Italy **44** C2
Imotski Croatia **44** F3
Imperatriz Brazil **150** C3
Imperia Italy **44** B3
Imperial U.S.A. **132** A3
Imperial Dam U.S.A. **137** E5
Imperial Valley *plain* U.S.A. **137** E5
Imperieuse Reef Australia **108** B4
Impfondo Congo **94** C4
Imphal India **75** G4
İmralı Adası *i.* Turkey **46** F4
İmroz Turkey **78** A2
İmroz *i.* Turkey *see* **Gökçeada**
imrun Turkey *see* **Pütürge**
Imst Austria **36** E5
Imtān Syria **77** C3
Imuris Mex. **135** E7
In *r.* Rus. Fed. **64** C2
I-n-Abangharit *well* Niger **93** G1
In Afaleleh *well* Alg. **91** H5
Inago Moz. **99** H2
Inahuaya Peru **148** B1
Inajá Brazil **150** E4
Inajá, Serra do *hills* Brazil **149** H2
I-n-Akhmed *well* Mali **93** E1
I-n-Alchi *well* Mali **93** E1
I-n-Aleï *well* Mali **93** E1
Inambari Peru **148** C3
Inambari *r.* Peru **148** C3
I-n-Ameddé *well* Mali **92** D1
In Aménas Alg. **91** H3
In Amguel Alg. **91** G5
Inangahua Junction N.Z. **113** B3
Inanwatan Indon. **57** H6
Iñapari Peru **148** C2
Inari Fin. **32** G1
Inarijärvi *l.* Fin. **32** G1
Inarijoki *r.* Fin./Norway **32** G1
I-n-Arouinat *well* Niger **93** G1
I-n-Atankarer *well* Mali **93** F1
Inauini *r.* Brazil **148** D2
I-n-Azaoua *well* Alg. **91** G4
In-Azaoua *well* Alg. **91** G5
I-n-Azaoua *watercourse* Niger **91** G5
In Azar *well* Libya **88** A2
In Azāwah *well* Libya **88** A3
I-n-Azerraf *well* Mali **93** F1
In Belbel Alg. **91** F4
Inca Spain **43** H3
İnca de Oro Chile **152** C1
İnce Burun *pt* Turkey **78** C2
Incheh Iran **80** D2
Inchiri *admin. reg.* Mauritania **90** B5
Inch'ŏn S. Korea **65** A5
Inchope Moz. **99** G3
I-n-Choumaguene *well* Mali **93** F1
Incirli Turkey *see* **Karasu**
Incomati *r.* Moz. **99** G5
Incudine, Monte *mt. Corsica* France **44** B4
Indalsälven *r.* Sweden **32** E3
Indalsto Norway **33** B3
Indargarh *Madhya Pradesh* India **74** C4
Indargarh *Rajasthan* India **74** C4
Inda Silasē Eth. **89** H6
Indawgyi, Lake Myanmar **60** B2
Indé Mex. **126** E6
I-n-Délimane *well* Mali **93** F2
Independence *CA* U.S.A. **136** C3
Independence *IA* U.S.A. **132** D3
Independence *KS* U.S.A. **132** C4
Independence *KY* U.S.A. **130** A4
Independence *MO* U.S.A. **132** C4
Independence *VA* U.S.A. **130** C5
Independence Fjord *inlet* Greenland **121** Q1
Independence Mountains U.S.A. **134** C4
Independencia Bol. **148** D4
Independenţa Romania **46** E2
Independenţa Romania **46** E2
Independenţa Romania **46** F3
Inder, Ozero *salt l.* Kazakh. **29** I6
Inderborskiy Kazakh. **26** F5
Indi India **72** C2

▶**India** *country* Asia **71** E7
2nd most populous country in the world and in Asia. 3rd largest country in Asia and 7th in the world.
asia 52–53, 82
world 8–9, 16–17

Indiana U.S.A. **130** D3
Indiana *state* U.S.A. **132** E3
Indian-Antarctic Ridge *sea feature* Indian Ocean **163** O9

▶**Indianapolis** U.S.A. **128** B4
State capital of Indiana.

Indian Cabins Canada **123** G3
Indian Desert India/Pak. *see* **Thar Desert**
Indian Fields U.S.A. **130** B5
Indian Harbour Canada **125** J2
Indian Lake U.S.A. **131** F2
Indian Lake *l. NY* U.S.A. **131** F2
Indian Lake *l. OH* U.S.A. **130** B3
Indian Lake *l. PA* U.S.A. **130** D3

▶**Indian Ocean** **162** L7
3rd largest ocean in the world.
oceans 156–157, 168

Indianola *IA* U.S.A. **132** C3
Indianola *MS* U.S.A. **127** H5
Indian Peak U.S.A. **137** F2
Indian Springs U.S.A. **137** E3
Indian Wells U.S.A. **137** G4
Indiaroba Brazil **150** E4
Indibir Eth. **96** C2
Indiga Rus. Fed. **28** I2
Indigirka *r.* Rus. Fed. **27** O2
Indigskaya Guba *b.* Rus. Fed. **28** I2
Indija Serb. and Mont. **46** B2
Indin Lake Canada **123** H1
Indio U.S.A. **137** D5
Indispensable Reefs Solomon Is **107** F3
Indo-China *reg.* Asia **56** C2

▶**Indonesia** *country* Asia **56** D7
4th most populous country in the world and 3rd in Asia.
asia 52–53, 82
world 16–17

Indore India **74** B5
Indragiri *r.* Indon. **58** C3
Indramayu Indon. **59** E4
Indramayu, Tanjung *pt* Indon. **56** C7
Indrapura, Gunung *vol.* Indon. *see* **Kerinci, Gunung**
Indrapura, Tanjung *pt* Indon. **58** C3
Indravati *r.* India **72** D2
Indre *r.* France **38** D3
Indulkana Australia **110** C5
Indur India *see* **Nizamabad**
Indurti India **72** C2
Indus *r.* China/Pakistan **70** C7
Indus, Mouths of the Pak. **81** F5
Indus Cone *sea feature* Indian Ocean **162** L4
Indzhe Voyvoda Bulg. **46** E3
In Ebeggi *well* Alg. **91** G5
İnebolu Turkey **78** C2
I-n-Échaï *well* Mali **90** E5
İnegöl Turkey **78** B2
In Ekker Alg. **91** G4
Ineu Romania **46** B1
Inevi Turkey *see* **Cihanbeyli**
Inez U.S.A. **130** B5
In Ezzane *well* Alg. **91** H5
Infantes Spain *see* **Villanueva de los Infantes**
Infernao, Cachoeira *waterfall* Brazil **149** F2
Infiernillo, Presa *resr* Mex. **126** F8
Ing, Mae Nam *r.* Thai. **60** C3
Inga Dem. Rep. Congo **95** B6
Ingå Fin. **33** G3
Ingabu Myanmar **60** A4
Ingal Niger **93** G1
Ingallanna *watercourse* Australia **110** C4
Ingalls, Mount U.S.A. **136** B2
Inganda Dem. Rep. Congo **94** D5
Ingelstad Sweden **33** D4
Ingende Dem. Rep. Congo **94** C5
Ingeniero Guillermo Nueva Juárez Arg. **149** E5
Ingeniero Jacobacci Arg. **152** C5
Ingenika *r.* Canada **122** E3
Ingenio *r.* Peru **148** B3
Ingersoll Canada **130** C2
Ingessana Hills Sudan **96** B2
Ingezi Zimbabwe *see* **Ngezi**
Ingham Australia **111** F3
Ingichka Uzbek. **81** F2
Inglefield Land *reg.* Greenland **121** L2
Inglewood *Qld* Australia **111** G6
Inglewood *Vic.* Australia **112** B5
Inglewood U.S.A. **136** C5
Ingoka Pum *mt.* Myanmar **60** B2
Ingolstadt Germany **36** E4
Ingomar Australia **110** C6
Ingraj Bazar India **75** F4
Ingray Lake Canada **123** G1
Ingrid Christensen Coast Antarctica **167** E2
I-n-Guezzam Alg. **91** G6
I-n-Guita *well* Mali **93** F2
Ingulets Ukr. *see* **Inhulets'**
Ingulsvatn Norway **32** D2
Ingushetia *aut. rep.* Rus. Fed. *see* **Ingushetiya, Respublika**
Ingushetiya, Respublika *aut. rep.* Rus. Fed. **29** H8
Ingush Republic *aut. rep.* Rus. Fed. *see* **Ingushetiya, Respublika**
Ingwe Zambia **95** E8
Inhaca, Peninsula *pen.* Moz. **99** G5
Inhafenga Moz. **99** G4
Inhambane Moz. **99** G4
Inhambane *prov.* Moz. **99** G4
Inhambupe Brazil **150** E4
Inhamitanga Moz. **99** G3
Inhapim Brazil **151** D6
Inharrime Moz. **99** G5
Inhassoro Moz. **99** G4
Inhaúmas Brazil **150** C5
I-n-Hihaou, Adrar *hills* Alg. **91** F5
Inhulets' Ukr. **29** E7
Iniesta Spain **43** F3
Inírida *r.* Col. **146** E4
Inis Rep. of Ireland *see* **Ennis**
Inis Córthaidh Rep. of Ireland *see* **Enniscorthy**
Inishbofin *i.* Rep. of Ireland **35** A5
Inishmore *i.* Rep. of Ireland **35** B5
Inishmurray *i.* Rep. of Ireland **35** B4
Inishowen *pen.* Rep. of Ireland **34** C4
Injibara Eth. **96** C2
Injune Australia **111** G5
I-n-Kerchef *well* Mali **92** D1
Inkerman Australia **111** E3
Inklin Canada **122** C3
Inklin *r.* Canada **122** C3
Inland Kaikoura Range *mts* N.Z. **113** C3
Inland Sea Japan *see* **Seto-naikai**
Inlet U.S.A. **131** F2
I-n-Milach *well* Mali **93** E1
Inn *r.* Europe **36** E5
Innaanganeq *c.* Greenland **121** M2
Innamincka Australia **111** E5
Innamincka Regional Reserve *nature res.* Australia **111** E5
Inner Mongolia *aut. reg.* China *see* **Nei Mongol Zizhiqu**
Inner Sound *sea chan.* U.K. **34** D3
Innes National Park Australia **112** A4
Innisfail Australia **111** F3
Innisfail Canada **123** H4
Innokent'yevka Rus. Fed. **64** B2
Innsbruck Austria **36** E5
Innuksuak *r.* Canada **124** E1
Inny *r.* Rep. of Ireland **35** C5
Inocência Brazil **149** H4
Inongo Dem. Rep. Congo **94** C5
Inoni Congo **94** B5
İnönü Turkey **78** B3
Inosu Col. **146** D1
Inoucdjouac Canada *see* **Inukjuak**
Inovec *mt.* Slovakia **37** I4
Inowrocław Poland **37** I2
Inquisivi Bol. **148** D4
In Salah Alg. **91** F4

▶**Inscription, Cape** Australia **109** A6
Most westerly point of Oceania.

Insein Myanmar **60** B4
Ińsko Poland **37** G2
In Sokki, Oued *watercourse* Alg. **91** F3
Insterburg Rus. Fed. *see* **Chernyakhovsk**
Însurăţei Romania **46** E2
Insuza *r.* Zimbabwe **99** E3
Inta Rus. Fed. **28** L2
I-n-Tadéra *well* Niger **91** H5
I-n-Tadrof *well* Niger **93** H1
In Takoufi, Oued *watercourse* Alg. **91** G4
I-n-Tassit *well* Mali **93** F1
I-n-Tebezas Mali **93** F1
I-n-Téguift *well* Mali **93** F1
I-n-Telli *well* Mali **93** F1
I-n-Témegui *well* Mali **93** F1
İntepe Turkey **47** E4
Interamna Italy *see* **Teramo**
Interlaken Switz. **39** G3
International Falls U.S.A. **132** C1
Interview Island India **73** G3
Întorsura Buzăului Romania **46** E2
I-n-Touft *well* Mali **93** F1
Intracoastal Waterway *canal* U.S.A. **133** C6
Inubō-zaki *pt* Japan **65** E6
Inukjuak Canada **124** E1
Inuvik Canada **120** F3
Inuya *r.* Peru **148** B2
In'va *r.* Rus. Fed. **28** K4
Inveraray U.K. **34** D3
Invercargill N.Z. **113** B4
Inverell Australia **112** D3
Inverleigh Australia **111** E3
Inverness Canada **125** I4
Inverness U.K. **34** D3
Inverness *CA* U.S.A. **136** A2
Inverness *FL* U.S.A. **129** C6
Inverurie U.K. **34** E3
Inverway Australia **110** B3
Investigator Channel Myanmar **61** B5
Investigator Group *is* Australia **109** F8
Investigator Ridge *sea feature* Indian Ocean **162** N6
Investigator Strait Australia **109** G8
Inwood U.S.A. **130** D4
Inya Rus. Fed. **27** I4
Inyanga Zimbabwe *see* **Nyanga**
Inyanga Mountains Zimbabwe **99** G3
Inyanga National Park Zimbabwe *see* **Nyanga National Park**
Inyangani *mt.* Zimbabwe **99** G3
Inyati Zimbabwe *see* **Nyathi**
Inyazura Zimbabwe *see* **Nyazura**
Inyokern U.S.A. **136** D4
Inyo Mountains U.S.A. **136** C3
Inyonga Tanz. **97** B6
Inza Rus. Fed. **29** H5
Inzhavino Rus. Fed. **29** G5
Ioannina Greece **47** B5
Ioanninon, Limni *l.* Greece **47** B5
Iôf di Montasio *mt.* Italy **44** D1
Iokanga *r.* Rus. Fed. **28** F2
Iola U.S.A. **132** C4
Iolotan' Turkm. *see* **Yeloten**
Iona Angola **95** B9
Iona *i.* U.K. **34** C3
Iona, Parque Nacional do *nat. park* Angola **95** B9
Iona Abbey *tourist site* U.K. **34** C3
Ione U.S.A. **136** D2
Ioneşti Romania **46** D2
Ionia U.S.A. **132** E3
Ionian Islands *admin. reg.* Greece *see* **Ionioi Nisoi**
Ionian Islands *is* Greece **47** B5
Ionian Sea Greece/Italy **47** A5
Ionioi Nisoi *admin. reg.* Greece **47** A5
Iony, Ostrov *i.* Rus. Fed. **27** O4
Iori *r.* Georgia **79** F2
Ios Greece **47** D6
Ios *i.* Greece **47** D6
Iouîk Mauritania **90** A6
Iowa *r.* U.S.A. **132** D3
Iowa *state* U.S.A. **132** C3
Iowa City U.S.A. **132** D3
Iowa Falls U.S.A. **132** C3
Ipanema Brazil **151** D6
Ipanema *r.* Brazil **150** E4
Iparia Peru **148** B2
Ipatinga Brazil **151** D6
Ipatovo Rus. Fed. **29** G7
Ipeiros *admin. reg.* Greece **47** B5
Ipel' *r.* Slovakia **37** I5
Ipelegeng S. Africa **98** E5
Ipiales Col. **146** B4
Ipiaú Brazil **150** E5
Ipirá Brazil **150** E5
Ipiranga *Amazonas* Brazil **146** D5
Ipiranga *Amazonas* Brazil **147** F6
Ipiros *admin. reg.* Greece *see* **Ipeiros**
Ipixuna Brazil **148** B1
Ipixuna *r. Amazonas* Brazil **147** F6
Ipixuna *r. Amazonas* Brazil **148** B1
Ipoh Malaysia **58** C1
Ipoly *r.* Hungary/Slovakia **37** I5
Iporá Brazil **149** H4
Ippy Cent. Afr. Rep. **94** D3
İpsala Turkey **46** E4
Ipswich Australia **111** H5
Ipswich U.K. **35** G5
Ipswich U.S.A. **132** B2
Ipu Brazil **150** D3
Ipuh Indon. **58** C3
Ipupiara Brazil **150** D4

▶**Iqaluit** Canada **121** M3
Territorial capital of Nunavut.

Iquê *r.* Brazil **149** F3
Iquique Chile **148** C5
Iquiri *r.* Brazil *see* **Ituxi**
Iquitos Peru **146** C5
Ira Banda Cent. Afr. Rep. **94** D3
Iracoubo Fr. Guiana **147** H3
Irakleia Greece **46** C4
Irakleia *i.* Greece **47** D6
Irakleio Greece *see* **Iraklion**
Irakleiou, Kolpos *b.* Greece **47** D7
Iráklia *i.* Greece *see* **Irakleia**
Iraklion Greece **47** D7
Irala Para. **149** G6
Iramaia Brazil **150** D5
▶**Iran** *country* Asia **80** C4
asia 52–53, 82
Iran, Pegunungan *mts* Indon. **59** F2
Īrānshāh Iran **80** A2
Īrānshahr Iran **81** E5
Irapuato Mex. **126** F7
▶**Iraq** *country* Asia **79** E4
asia 52–53, 82
Irarrarene *reg.* Alg. **91** G4
Irataputu *r.* Brazil **147** H5
Irati Brazil **151** B8
Irati *r.* Spain **43** F1
Irayel' Rus. Fed. **28** K2
Irazu, Volcán *vol.* Costa Rica **139** H7
Irbes šaurums *sea chan.* Estonia/Latvia *see* **Irbe Strait**
Irbe Strait Estonia/Latvia **33** F4
Irbe väin *sea chan.* Estonia/Latvia *see* **Irbe Strait**
Irbid Jordan **78** C4
Irbil Iraq *see* **Arbīl**
Irbit Rus. Fed. **166** F3
Irebu Dem. Rep. Congo **94** C5
Irecê Brazil **150** D4
Iregua *r.* Spain **43** E1

▶**Ireland** *i.* Europe **35** B5
4th largest island in Europe.
europe 22–23

▶**Ireland, Republic of** *country* Europe **35** C5
europe 24–25, 48
Irene Arg. **152** E4
Ireng *r.* Guyana/Venez. **147** G4
Irgiz Kazakh. **70** B2
Irgiz *r.* Kazakh. **70** B2
Irharrhar, Oued *watercourse* Alg. **91** G3
Irharrhar, Oued *watercourse* Alg. **91** G5
Irherm Morocco **90** C3
Irhil M'Goun *mt.* Morocco **90** D3
Iri S. Korea *see* **Iksan**
Irian, Teluk *b.* Indon. *see* **Cenderawasih, Teluk**
Iriba Chad **88** D6
Iricoumé, Serra *hills* Brazil **147** G4
Īrī Dāgh *mt.* Iran **80** A2
Iringa Tanz. **97** B6
Iringa *admin. reg.* Tanz. **97** B7
Iriri *r.* Brazil **147** H5
Iriri Novo *r.* Brazil **150** A4
Irish Free State *country* Europe *see* **Ireland, Republic of**
Irish Sea Rep. of Ireland/U.K. **35** D5
Irituia Brazil **150** C2
'Irj *well* Saudi Arabia **80** B5
Irkeshtam Kyrg. *see* **Erkech-Tam**
Irkutsk Rus. Fed. **62** G1
Irkutskaya Oblast' *admin. div.* Rus. Fed. **62** G1
Irkutsk Oblast *admin. div.* Rus. Fed. *see* **Irkutskaya Oblast'**
Irmak Turkey **78** C3
Irminger Basin *sea feature* N. Atlantic Ocean **160** L2
Irminio *r. Sicily* Italy **45** E6
Irmo U.S.A. **129** C5
Irnijärvi *l.* Fin. **32** H2
Iro, Lac *l.* Chad **94** C2
Iroise, Mer d' *g.* France **38** A2
Iron Baron Australia **112** A4
Irondequoit U.S.A. **130** E2
Iron Knob Australia **112** A4
Iron Mountain U.S.A. **132** D2
Iron Mountain *mt.* U.S.A. **137** F3
Iron Range National Park Australia **111** E2
Iron River U.S.A. **132** D2
Ironton *MO* U.S.A. **132** D4
Ironton *OH* U.S.A. **130** B4
Ironwood U.S.A. **132** D2
Iroquois Canada **131** F1
Iroquois Falls Canada **124** D3
Irosin Phil. **57** F3
Irpen' Ukr. *see* **Irpin'**
Irpin' Ukr. **29** D6
'Irq al Harūrī *des.* Saudi Arabia **80** A5
Irq al Mazhūr *des.* Saudi Arabia **89** I3
'Irq Banbān *des.* Saudi Arabia **80** A5
'Irq Jahām *des.* Saudi Arabia **80** A5
Irrawaddy *admin. div.* Myanmar **60** A4
Irrawaddy *r.* Myanmar **60** A5
Irrawaddy, Mouths of the Myanmar **61** A5
Irsarybaba, Gory *hills* Turkm. **80** C1
Irshad Pass Afgh./Pak. **81** H2
Irta Rus. Fed. **28** I3

▶**Irtysh** *r.* Kazakh./Rus. Fed. **26** G3
5th longest river in Asia and 10th in the world. Part of the 2nd longest river in Asia (Ob'-Irtysh).
asia 50–51
world 6–7

Irumu Dem. Rep. Congo **94** F4
Irún Spain **43** F1
Iruña Spain *see* **Pamplona**
Irvine U.K. **34** D4
Irvine U.S.A. **130** B5
Irvine Glacier Antarctica **167** L2
Irving U.S.A. **133** B5
Irwin *r.* Australia **109** A7
Isa Nigeria **93** G2
'Isá, Ra's *pt* Yemen **89** I6
Isaac *r.* Australia **111** G4
Isaac Lake Canada **122** F4
Isabela Phil. **57** F4
Isabela, Cordillera *mts* Nicaragua **139** G6
Isabella Lake U.S.A. **136** C4
Isaccea Romania **46** F2
Isachenko, Ostrov *i.* Rus. Fed. **27** I2
Isachsen, Cape Canada **121** I2
Ísafjarðardjúp *est.* Iceland **32** [inset]
Ísafjörður Iceland **32** [inset]
Isagarh India **74** C4
Isai Kalat Pak. **81** F5
Isà Khel Pak. **81** G3
Isakogorka Rus. Fed. **28** G2
Işalniţa Romania **46** C2
Isana *r.* Col. **146** D4
Isanga Dem. Rep. Congo **94** D5
Isangano National Park Zambia **97** A7
Isaouane-n-Tifernine *des.* Alg. **91** G4
Isar *r.* Germany **37** F4
Isbister U.K. **34** F1
Iscayachi Bol. **148** D5
Ischia, Isola d' *i.* Italy **45** D4
Ise Japan **65** D6
Isefjord *b.* Denmark **33** C5
Iseke Tanz. **97** B6
Isel *r.* Austria **37** F5
Isengi Dem. Rep. Congo **94** E4
Iseo, Lago d' *l.* Italy **44** C2
Isère *r.* France **39** F4
Isère, Pointe *pt* Fr. Guiana **147** H3
Iserlohn Germany **36** C3
Isernia Italy **44** E4
Ise-shima National Park Japan **65** D6
Ise-wan *b.* Japan **65** D6
Iseyin Nigeria **93** F4
Isfahan Iran *see* **Eşfahān**
Isfana Kyrg. **81** G2
Isfandaqeh Iran *see* **Sangū'īyeh**
Isfara Tajik. **81** G1
Isherton Guyana **147** G4
Ishikari-wan *b.* Japan **64** E4
Ishim *r.* Kazakh./Rus. Fed. **26** H4
Ishim Rus. Fed. **26** G4
Ishinomaki Japan **65** E5
Ishkoshim Tajik. **81** G2
Ishkuman Jammu and Kashmir **74** B1
Ishurdi Bangl. **75** F4
Isiboro *r.* Bol. **148** D3
Isiboro Sécure, Parque Nacional *nat. park* Bol. **148** D4
Isigny-sur-Mer France **38** C2
Isil'kul' Rus. Fed. **26** H4
Isimbira Tanz. **97** B6
Isinliví Ecuador **146** B5
Isiolo Kenya **96** C4
Isiro Dem. Rep. Congo **94** E4
Isisford Australia **111** F5
Iskabad Canal Afgh. **81** F2
İskele Cyprus *see* **Trikomon**
İskenderun Turkey **78** D3
İskenderun Körfezi *b.* Turkey **78** C3
İskilip Turkey **78** C2
Iskine Kazakh. **29** J7
Iskitim Rus. Fed. **26** I4
Iskŭr *r.* Bulg. **46** D3
Iskŭr, Yazovir *resr* Bulg. **46** C3
Iskushuban Somalia **96** F2
Iskut *r.* Canada **122** D3
Isla de Salamanca, Parque Nacional *nat. park* Col. **146** C2
Isla Gorge National Park Australia **111** G5
İslahiye Turkey **78** D3
Islamabad Jammu and Kashmir *see* **Anantnag**

▶**Islamabad** Pak. **81** H3
Capital of Pakistan.

Isla Magdalena, Parque Nacional *nat. park* Chile **153** B6
Islamkot Pak. **81** G5
Islampur India **75** E4
Island *country* Europe *see* **Iceland**
Island Lagoon *salt flat* Australia **109** G7
Island Lake Canada **123** M4
Island Magee *pen.* U.K. **34** D4
Island Pond U.S.A. **131** H1
Islas Baleares *aut. comm.* Spain **43** H3
Islay *i.* U.K. **34** C4
Islaz Romania **46** D3
Isle *r.* France **38** C4

▶**Isle of Man** *i.* Irish Sea **35** D4
United Kingdom Crown Dependency.
europe 48

Isle Royale National Park U.S.A. **132** D2
Isluga, Parque Nacional *nat. park* Chile **148** C4
Ismail Ukr. *see* **Izmayil**
Ismā'īlīya Egypt *see* **Al Ismā'īlīyah**
Ismā'īlīyah *governorate* Egypt **77** A4
Ismailly Azer. *see* **İsmayıllı**
İsmayıllı Azer. **79** G2
Isnā Egypt **89** G3
Isoanala Madag. **99** [inset] J4
Isojoki Fin. **33** F3
Isoka Zambia **97** B7
Isokylä Fin. **32** G2
Isokyrö Fin. **32** F3
Isola del Liri Italy **44** D4
Isola di Capo Rizzuto Italy **45** F5
Isonzo *r.* Italy **44** D2
Isopa Tanz. **97** A7
Isorana Madag. **99** [inset] J4
Iso-Syöte *hill* Fin. **32** G2
Ispahan Iran *see* **Eşfahān**
Isparta Turkey **78** B3
Isperikh Bulg. **46** E3
Ispica *Sicily* Italy **45** E6
İspir Turkey **79** E2
Ispisar Tajik. *see* **Khŭjand**
▶**Israel** *country* Asia **77** B4
asia 52–53, 82
Israelite Bay Australia **109** C8
Isra'il *country* Asia *see* **Israel**
Issa Croatia *see* **Vis**
Issa *r.* Rus. Fed. **33** H4
Issano Guyana **147** G3
Issia Côte d'Ivoire **92** D4
Issin *tourist site* Iraq **79** F5
Issoire France **39** E4
Issoudun France **38** D3
Issuna Tanz. **97** B6
Is-sur-Tille France **39** F3
Issyk-Kul' Kyrg. *see* **Balykchy**
Issyk-Kul', Ozero *salt l.* Kyrg. *see* **Ysyk-Köl**
Iştablāt *tourist site* Iraq **79** E4

▶**İstanbul** Turkey **78** B2
2nd most populous city in Europe.

İstanbul *prov.* Turkey **46** F4
İstanbul Boğazı *strait* Turkey *see* **Bosporus**
Isten dombja *hill* Hungary **37** H5
Īstgāh-e Eznā Iran **80** B3
Isthilart Arg. **152** F2
Istiaia Greece **47** C5
Istik *r.* Tajik. **81** H2
Istmina Col. **146** B3
Istokpoga, Lake U.S.A. **129** C7
Istres France **39** F5
Istria *pen.* Croatia **44** D2
Istria Romania **46** F2
Istriţa, Dealul *hill* Romania **46** E2
Isuela *r.* Spain **43** F2
Iswaripur Bangl. **75** F5
Itabaianinha Brazil **150** E4
Itaberaba Brazil **150** D5
Itaberaí Brazil **149** H4
Itabira Brazil **151** D6
Itaboca Brazil **147** F6
Itabuna Brazil **150** E5
Itacaiuna *r.* Brazil **150** B3
Itacajá Brazil **150** C4
Itacarambi Brazil **150** C5
Itacaré Brazil **150** E5
Itacoatiara Brazil **147** G5
Itacuaí *r.* Brazil **146** D6
Itaetê Brazil **150** D5
Itagmatana Iran *see* **Hamadān**
Itaguaçu Brazil **151** D6
Itahuania Peru **148** C3
Itaí Brazil **149** H5
Itaim *r.* Brazil **150** D3
Itaiópolis Brazil **151** B8
Itaipu, Represa de *resr* Brazil **151** A8
Itäisen Suomenlahden kansallispuisto *nat. park* Fin. **33** G3
Itaituba Brazil **147** G6
Itajaí Brazil **151** B8
Itajubá Brazil **151** C7
Itaki India **75** E5
Italia *country* Europe *see* **Italy**

▶**Italy** *country* Europe **44** D3
5th most populous country in Europe.
europe 24–25, 48

Itamaracá, Ilha de *i.* Brazil **150** F3
Itamaraju Brazil **151** E6
Itamarandiba Brazil **151** D6
Itambé Brazil **150** D5
Itambé, Pico de *mt.* Brazil **151** D6
Itami *airport* Japan **65** C6
Itampolo Madag. **99** [inset] I5
Itanagar India **75** G4
Itanguari *r.* Brazil **150** C5
Itanhaém Brazil **149** I6
Itanhauã *r.* Brazil **147** F6
Itanhém *r.* Brazil **151** E6
Itany *r.* Fr. Guiana/Suriname **147** H4
Itaobim Brazil **151** D6
Itapaci Brazil **149** H3
Itapajipe Brazil **149** H4
Itaparaná *r.* Brazil **147** F6
Itaparica, Represa de *resr* Brazil **150** E4
Itapebi Brazil **151** E5
Itapebí Uruguay **152** F2
Itapemirim Brazil **151** D7
Itaperuna Brazil **151** D7
Itapetinga Brazil **150** D5
Itapetininga Brazil **149** H5
Itapeva Brazil **149** H5
Itapeva, Lago *l.* Brazil **151** B9
Itapi *r.* Brazil **147** G5
Itapicuru Brazil **150** D4
Itapicuru *r.* Brazil **150** C2
Itapicuru *r.* Brazil **150** E4
Itapicuru, Serra de *hills* Brazil **150** C3
Itapicuru Mirim Brazil **150** C2
Itapicuru Mirim *r.* Brazil **150** E4
Itapipoca Brazil **150** E2
Itapira Brazil **151** C7
Itapiranga Brazil **147** G5
Itaporanga Brazil **149** H5
Itapuranga Brazil **149** H3
Itaqui Brazil **152** F2
Itararé Brazil **149** H6
Itarsi India **74** C5
Itä-Suomi *prov.* Fin. **32** H3
Itatinga Brazil **149** H5
Itatuba Brazil **147** F6
Itatupã Brazil **147** I5
Itaueira *r.* Brazil **150** D3
Itaúna *Amazonas* Brazil **147** E5
Itaúna *Minas Gerais* Brazil **151** C7
Itbayat *i.* Phil. **57** F1
Itchen Lake Canada **123** H1
Ite Peru **148** C4
Itea Greece **47** C5
Itebero Dem. Rep. Congo **94** F5
Itende Tanz. **97** B6
Itezhi-Tezhi Dam Zambia **95** E8
Ithaca Greece *see* **Ithaki**
Ithaca *i.* Greece *see* **Ithaki**
Ithaca *MI* U.S.A. **130** A2
Ithaca *NY* U.S.A. **131** E2
Ithaki Greece **47** B5
Ithaki *i.* Greece **47** B5
Ithakis, Steno *sea chan.* Greece **47** B5
Ith Hils *ridge* Germany **36** D2
Itigi Tanz. **97** B6
Itilleq Greenland **121** N3
Itimbiri *r.* Dem. Rep. Congo **94** D4
Itinga Brazil **151** D6
Itiquira Brazil **151** A6
Itiquira *r.* Brazil **149** F4
Itiúba Brazil **150** E4
Itiúba, Serra de *hills* Brazil **150** E4
Itiyura *r.* Arg. **149** E5
Itkhari India **75** E4
Itō Japan **65** D6
Itoculo Moz. **99** I2
Itoigawa Japan **65** D5
Itoko Dem. Rep. Congo **94** D5
Iton *r.* France **38** D2
Itongafeno *mt.* Madag. **99** [inset] J4
Ittiri *Sardinia* Italy **45** B4
Ittoqqortoormiit Greenland **121** Q2
Itu Brazil **149** I5
Itu Nigeria **93** G4
Itu Abu Island *i.* S. China Sea **56** D3
Ituaçu Brazil **150** D5
Ituberá Brazil **150** E5
Ituí *r.* Brazil **146** D6
Ituiutaba Brazil **149** H4
Itula Dem. Rep. Congo **94** E5
Itumba Tanz. **97** B6
Itumbiara Brazil **149** H4
Itumbiara, Barragem *resr* Brazil **149** H4
Itungi Port Malawi **97** B7
Ituni Guyana **147** G3
Itupiranga Brazil **150** B3
Iturama Brazil **149** H4
Iturbe Para. **149** F6
Ituri *r.* Dem. Rep. Congo **94** E4
Iturup, Ostrov *i.* Rus. Fed. **54** G2
Ituverava Brazil **149** I5
Ituxi *r.* Brazil **148** D1
Ituzaingo Arg. **152** F1
Ityopia *country* Africa *see* **Ethiopia**
Itzehoe Germany **36** D2
Iuaretê Brazil **146** D4
Iuka U.S.A. **128** A5
Iul'tin Rus. Fed. **27** S3
Iuluti Moz. **99** H2
Iutica Brazil **146** D4
Ivai *r.* Brazil **149** G5
Ivakoany *mt.* Madag. **99** [inset] J4
Ivalo Fin. **32** G1
Ivalojoki *r.* Fin. **32** G1
Ivanava Belarus **29** C5
Ivanec Croatia **44** F1
Ivangorod Rus. Fed. **33** H4
Ivangrad Serb. and Mont. *see* **Berane**
Ivanhoe *N.S.W.* Australia **112** C4
Ivanhoe *W.A.* Australia **108** E3
Ivanhoe U.S.A. **132** B2
Ivanhoe Lake Canada **123** J2

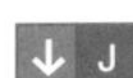

Jinping Yunnan China see Qiubei
Jinping Shan mts China 66 B3
Jinsen S. Korea see Inch'ŏn
Jinsha China 66 C3
Jinsha Jiang r. China see Yangtze
Jinsha Jiang r. China 66 C2 see Yangtze
Jinshan China see Lufeng
Jinshi Hunan China 67 D2
Jinshi Hunan China see Xinning
Jintan China 67 F2
Jintang China 66 C2
Jintur India 72 C2
Jinxi Jiangxi China 67 F3
Jinxi Liaoning China see Lianshan
Jin Xi r. China 67 F3
Jinxian China 67 F2
Jinxiang China 67 G3
Jinxiu China 67 D3
Jinyang China 66 B3
Jinyun China 67 G2
Jinz, Qā' al salt flat Jordan 77 C4
Jinzhai China 67 E2
Jinzhong China 63 I4
Jinzhou China 63 K3
Jinzhu China see Daocheng
Ji-Paraná Brazil 149 E2
Jiparaná r. Brazil 149 E2
Jipijapa Ecuador 146 A5
Jirā', Wādī watercourse Egypt 77 A5
Jirau Brazil 148 D2
Jirgatol Tajik. 81 G2
Jiri r. India 75 G4
Jirjā Egypt 89 F3
Jiroft Iran 80 D4
Jirriiban Somalia 96 F3
Jishou China 67 D2
Jishui China see Yongfeng
Jisr ash Shughūr Syria 77 C2
Jitian China see Lianshan
Jitra Malaysia 58 C1
Jiu r. Romania 46 C3
Jiuding Shan mt. China 66 B2
Jiugong Shan mt. China 67 E2
Jiujiang Jiangxi China 67 E2
Jiujiang Jiangxi China 67 F2
Jiulian China see Mojiang
Jiuling Shan mts China 67 E2
Jiulong Hong Kong China see Kowloon
Jiulong Sichuan China 66 B2
Jiuquan China 70 I4
Jiutai China 64 A3
Jiuxu China 66 C3
Jiwani Pak. 81 E5
Jixi Anhui China 67 F2
Jixi Heilong. China 64 B3
Jixian China 64 B3
Jīzah, Ahrāmāt al tourist site Egypt see Pyramids of Giza
Jīzān Saudi Arabia 89 I5
Jizera r. Czech Rep. 37 G3
Jizerské Hory mts Czech Rep. 37 G3
Jizō-zaki pt Japan 65 C6
Jizzakh Uzbek. see Dzhizak
Jizzakh Wiloyati admin. div. Uzbek. see Dzhizakskaya Oblast'
Joaçaba Brazil 151 B8
Joal-Fadiout Senegal 92 A2
Joana Peres Brazil 150 B2
João Belo Moz. see Xai-Xai
João de Almeida Angola see Chibia
João Pessoa Brazil 150 F3
João Pinheiro Brazil 151 C6
Joaquin V. González Arg. 152 D1
Job Peak U.S.A. 136 C2
Jockfall Sweden 32 F2
Jocoli Arg. 152 C3
Joda India 75 E5
Jódar Spain 42 E4
Jodhpur India 74 B4
Jodiya India 74 A5
Joensuu Fin. 32 H3
Joesjö Sweden 32 D2
Jōetsu Japan 65 D5
Jofane Moz. 99 G4
Joffre, Mount Canada 123 H5
Jogbani India 75 E4
Jogbura Nepal 74 D3
Jõgeva Estonia 33 G4
Jogighopa India 75 F4
Jogindarnagar India 74 C3
Jogjakarta Indon. see Yogyakarta
Johannesburg S. Africa 99 E5
Johan Peninsula Canada 121 L2
Johilla r. India 74 D5
John Day U.S.A. 134 C3
John Day r. U.S.A. 134 B3
John Day, Middle Fork r. U.S.A. 134 C3
John Day, North Fork r. U.S.A. 134 C3
John d'Or Prairie Canada 123 H3
John F. Kennedy airport U.S.A. 131 G3
John H. Kerr Reservoir U.S.A. 130 D5
John Jay, Mount Canada/U.S.A. 122 D3
Johnny Hoe r. Canada 122 F1
John o'Groats U.K. 34 E2
Johnson U.S.A. 131 G1
Johnsonburg U.S.A. 130 D3
Johnson City NY U.S.A. 131 F2
Johnson City TN U.S.A. 128 C4
Johnson City TX U.S.A. 133 B6
Johnston, Lake salt flat Australia 109 C8
Johnston and Sand Islands N. Pacific Ocean see Johnston Atoll

▶Johnston Atoll N. Pacific Ocean 164 G4
United States Unincorporated Territory.
oceania 104–105, 114

Johnstone Lake Canada see Old Wives Lake
Johnston Range hills Australia 109 B7
Johnstown NY U.S.A. 131 F2
Johnstown OH U.S.A. 130 B3
Johnstown PA U.S.A. 130 D3
Johor state Malaysia 58 C2
Johor, Selat strait Malaysia/Sing. 58 [inset]
Johor, Sungai Malaysia 58 [inset]
Johor Bahru Malaysia 58 C2
Jõhvi Estonia 28 C4
Joigny France 39 E3
Joinville Brazil 151 B8
Joinville France 39 F2
Joinville Island Antarctica 167 A2
Jokiperä Fin. 32 F3
Jokkmokk Sweden 32 E2
Jökulbunga hill Iceland 32 [inset]
Jökulsá á Fjöllum r. Iceland 32 [inset]
Jolarpettai India 72 C3
Joliet U.S.A. 132 D3
Joliet, Lac l. Canada 124 E3
Joliette Canada 125 F4
Jolly Lake Canada 123 H1
Jolo Phil. 57 F4
Jolo i. Phil. 57 F4
Jomard Entrance sea chan. P.N.G. 111 G1
Jombang Indon. 59 F4
Jomda China 66 A2
Jømna Norway 33 C3
Jomsom Nepal 75 D3
Jonāḩ Iran 80 C5
Jonancy U.S.A. 130 B5
Jonava Lith. 33 G5
Jondal Norway 33 B3
Jonê China 66 B1
Jonesboro AR U.S.A. 127 H4
Jonesboro LA U.S.A. 133 C5
Jones Mills U.S.A. 130 D3
Jones Sound sea chan. Canada 121 K2
Jonestown U.S.A. 131 E3
Jonesville LA U.S.A. 133 D6
Jonesville VA U.S.A. 130 B5
Jonglei Sudan 96 A3
Jonglei state Sudan 96 B3
Jonglei Canal Sudan 96 A3
Joniškis Lith. 33 F4
Jonk r. India 75 D5
Jönköping Sweden 33 D4
Jönköping county Sweden 33 D4
Jonquière Canada 125 G3
Jonzac France 38 C4
Joplin U.S.A. 132 C4
Joppa Israel see Tel Aviv-Yafo
Jora India 74 C4
▶Jordan country Asia 77 C4
asia 52–53, 82
Jordan r. Asia 78 C5
Jordan MT U.S.A. 134 F3
Jordan NY U.S.A. 131 E2
Jordan r. U.S.A. 137 F1
Jordet Norway 33 D3
Jorge Montt, Isla i. Chile 153 B7
Jorhat India 75 G4
Jorm Afgh. 81 G2
Jormvattnet Sweden 32 D2
Jörn Sweden 32 F2
Joroinen Fin. 33 G3
Jørpeland Norway 33 B4
Jos Nigeria 93 H3
José Bonifácio Brazil 149 E3
José Cardel Mex. 126 G8
José de San Martin Arg. 153 C6
José Enrique Rodó Uruguay 152 F3
Joselândia Brazil 149 F4
José Pedro Varela Uruguay 152 G3
Joseph, Lac l. Canada 125 H2
Joseph Bonaparte Gulf Australia 110 B2
Joseph City U.S.A. 137 G4
Joshimath India 74 C3
Jōshinetsu-kōgen National Park Japan 65 D5
Joshipur India 75 E5
Joshua Tree U.S.A. 137 D4
Joshua Tree National Park U.S.A. 137 E5
Jos Plateau Nigeria 93 H3
Josselin France 38 B3
Jössund Norway 32 C2
Jostedalsbreen glacier Norway 33 B3
Jostedalsbreen Nasjonalpark nat. park Norway 33 B3
Jotunheimen mts Norway 33 C3
Jotunheimen Nasjonalpark nat. park Norway 33 C3
Jouberton S. Africa 99 E5
Joué-lès-Tours France 38 D3
Joukokylä Fin. 32 G2
Joûnié Lebanon 77 B3
Joussard Canada 123 H4
Joutsa Fin. 33 G3
Joutsijärvi Fin. 32 G2
Jovellanos Cuba 129 C8
Jowai India 75 G4
Jowzjān prov. Afgh. 81 F2
Joy, Mount Canada 122 C2
Joypurhat Bangl. 75 F4
Jrayfiya well W. Sahara 90 B4
Jreïda Mauritania 92 A1
Juan Aldama Mex. 126 F7
Juan de Fuca Strait Canada/U.S.A. 120 G5
Juan de Nova i. Indian Ocean 97 D9
Juan E. Barra Arg. 152 E4
Juan Fernández Islands S. Pacific Ocean 165 M8
Juangriego Venez. 147 F2
Juanjuí Peru 148 A1
Juankoski Fin. 32 H3
Juan Mata Ortíz Mex. 135 E7
Juanshui China see Tongcheng
Juan Stuven, Isla i. Chile 153 B6
Juara Brazil 149 F2
Juaréz Mex. 133 A7
Juárez, Sierra de 135 D7
Juàzeiro Brazil 150 D4
Juàzeiro do Norte Brazil 150 E3
Juazohn Liberia 92 C4
Juba r. Somalia see Jubba
Juba Sudan 96 A3
Jubany research station Antarctica 167 A2
Jubba r. Somalia 96 D5
Jubbada Dhexe admin. reg. Somalia 96 D4
Jubbada Hoose admin. reg. Somalia 96 D4
Jubbah Saudi Arabia 89 I2
Jubbulpore India see Jabalpur
Jubilee Lake salt flat Australia 109 D7
Jubing Nepal 75 E4
Júcar r. Spain 43 F3
Juçara Brazil 149 H3
Juchitán Mex. 138 E5
Jucuruçu Brazil 151 E6
Judaidat al Hamir Iraq 79 E5
Judaydah Syria 79 D4
Judayyidat 'Ar'ar well Iraq 79 E5
Judenburg Austria 37 G5
Judian China 66 A3
Judith r. U.S.A. 134 E3
Judith Gap U.S.A. 134 E3
Juegang China see Rudong
Juego de Bolos mt. Spain 42 E3
Juelsminde Denmark 33 C5
Jufari r. Brazil 147 F5
Jugon-les-Lacs France 38 B2
Jugoslavija country Europe see Yugoslavia
Juigalpa Nicaragua 139 G6
Juillet, Lac l. Canada 125 I2
Juína Brazil 149 F2
Juina r. Brazil 149 F3
Juist i. Germany 36 C2
Juiz de Fora Brazil 151 D7
Jujuhan r. Indon. 58 C3
Jujuy prov. Arg. 148 D5
Julaca Bol. 148 D5
Julesburg U.S.A. 132 A3
Juli Peru 148 C4
Julia Brazil 146 E5
Juliaca Peru 148 C3
Julia Creek Australia 111 E4
Julian U.S.A. 137 D5
Julian, Lac l. Canada 124 E2
Julian Alps mts Slovenia see Julijske Alpe
Julianatop mt. Indon. see Mandala, Puncak
Juliana Top mt. Suriname 147 G4
Julianehåb Greenland see Qaqortoq
Julijske Alpe mts Slovenia 44 D1
Julimes Mex. 135 F7
Júlio de Castilhos Brazil 151 A9
Juliomagus France see Angers
Jullundur India see Jalandhar
Juma Uzbek. see Dzhuma
Jumba Somalia 96 D5
Jumilla Spain 43 F3
Jumla Nepal 75 D3
Jumna r. India see Yamuna
Jump r. U.S.A. 132 D2
Junagadh India 74 A5
Junagarh India 73 D2
Junaynah, Ra's al mt. Egypt 77 A5
Junction TX U.S.A. 133 B6
Junction UT U.S.A. 137 F2
Junction City KS U.S.A. 132 B4
Junction City KY U.S.A. 130 A5
Junction City OR U.S.A. 134 B3
Jundah Australia 111 E5
Jundiaí Brazil 149 I5

▶Juneau U.S.A. 120 F4
State capital of Alaska.

Junee Australia 112 C4
Jūn el Khudr b. Lebanon 77 B3
Jungfrau mt. Switz. 39 G3
Jungfrau-Aletsch-Bietschhorn tourist site Switz. 39 H3
Junggar Pendi basin China 70 G2
Jungshahi Pak. 81 F5
Junguls Sudan 96 B2
Juniata r. U.S.A. 131 E3
Junik Serb. and Mont. 46 B3
Junín Arg. 152 E3
Junín Peru 148 A2
Junín dept Peru 148 B2
Junior U.S.A. 130 D4
Juniper Mountains U.S.A. 137 F4
Junipero Serro Peak U.S.A. 136 B3
Junlian China 66 C2
Junnah, Jabal mts Egypt 77 B5
Junnar India 72 B2
Junosuando Sweden 32 F2
Junsele Sweden 32 E3
Junshan Hu l. China 67 F2
Juntura U.S.A. 134 C4
Juntusranta Fin. 32 H2
Junxi China see Datian
Junxian China see Danjiangkou
Ju'nyung China 66 A1
Ju'nyunggoin China see Ju'nyung
Juodupė Lith. 33 G4
Juoksengi Sweden 32 F2
Jupiá, Represa resr Brazil 149 H5
Juquiá Brazil 149 I6
Jur r. Sudan 94 F2
Jura mts France/Switz. 39 F4
Jura i. U.K. 34 D3
Jura, Sound of sea chan. U.K. 34 D4
Juradó Col. 146 B3
Jurbarkas Lith. 33 F5
Juremal Brazil 150 D4
Jurf ad Darāwish Jordan 77 B4
Jurgurra r. Australia 108 C4
Jurh China 64 A3
Jurhen Ul Shan mts China 75 F2
Jurien Australia 109 A7
Jurilovca Romania 46 F2
Juriti Velho Brazil 147 G5
Jūrmala Latvia 33 F4
Jurmu Fin. 32 G2
Jurong China 67 F2
Jurong Sing. 58 [inset]
Jurong, Sungai r. Sing. 58 [inset]
Jurong Island reg. Sing. 58 [inset]
Juruá r. Brazil 146 E5
Juruena Brazil 149 F3
Juruena r. Brazil 149 F1
Juruti Brazil 147 G5
Jurva Fin. 32 F3
Jusepín Venez. 147 F2
Jussey France 39 F3
Justice U.S.A. 130 C5
Justo Daract Arg. 152 D3
Jutaí Brazil 146 D6
Jutaí r. Brazil 146 E5
Jüterbog Germany 37 F3
Juti Brazil 151 A7
Jutiapa Guat. 138 G6
Juticalpa Hond. 138 G6
Jutis Sweden 32 E2
Jutland pen. Denmark 33 C4
Juuka Fin. 32 H3
Juva Fin. 33 G3
Juwain Afgh. 81 E4
Jüymand Iran 81 D3
Jüyom Iran 80 C4
Južnoukrajinsk Ukr. see Yuzhnoukrayinsk
Jyväskylä Fin. 33 G3

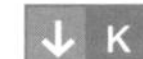

▶K2 mt. China/Jammu and Kashmir 74 C2
2nd highest mountain in the world and in Asia.
asia 50–51
world 6–7

Ka r. Nigeria 93 G3
Kaabong Uganda 96 B4
Kaa-Iya, Parque Nacional nat. park Bol. 149 E4
Kaakhka Turkm. see Kaka
Kaamanen Fin. 32 G1
Kaambooni Kenya 96 D5
Kaapstad S. Africa see Cape Town
Kaarina Fin. 33 F3
Kaarta reg. Mali 92 C2
Kaavi Fin. 32 H3
Kaba China see Habahe
Kabaena i. Indon. 57 F7
Kabakly Turkm. 81 E2
Kabala Sierra Leone 92 C3
Kabale Uganda 96 A5
Kabalega Falls National Park Uganda see Murchison Falls National Park
Kabalo Dem. Rep. Congo 95 E6
Kabambare Dem. Rep. Congo 95 E6
Kabanga Dem. Rep. Congo 95 C6
Kabangu Dem. Rep. Congo 95 D7
Kabanjahe Indon. 58 B2
Kabara i. Fiji 107 H3
Kabare Dem. Rep. Congo 94 F5
Kabarega National Park Uganda see Murchison Falls National Park
Kabaung r. Myanmar 60 B4
Kabaw Valley Myanmar 60 A3
Kabba Nigeria 93 G4
Kabbani r. India 72 C3
Kåbdalis Sweden 32 F2
Kabélawa Niger 93 I2
Kaberneeme Estonia 33 G4
Kabertene Alg. 91 F3
Kab-hegy hill Hungary 44 F1
Kabinakagami r. Canada 124 C3
Kabinda Dem. Rep. Congo 95 E6
Kabir r. Syria 77 B2
Kabīrkūh mts Iran 80 A3
Kabirwala Pak. 81 G4
Kabli Estonia 33 G4
Kabneshwar India 74 C5
Kabo Cent. Afr. Rep. 94 C3
Kābol Afgh. see Kābul
Kabompo Zambia 95 E8
Kabompo r. Zambia 95 D8
Kabondo-Dianda Dem. Rep. Congo 95 E7
Kabongo Dem. Rep. Congo 95 E6
Kabosa Island Myanmar 61 B5
Kabou Cent. Afr. Rep. 94 D3
Kabou Togo 93 F3
Kabrousse Senegal 92 A2
Kabūdeh Iran 81 E3
Kabūd Gonbad Iran 81 D2
Kabūd Rāhang Iran 80 B3

▶Kābul Afgh. 81 G3
Capital of Afghanistan.

Kābul prov. Afgh. 81 G3
Kabul r. Afgh. 81 H3
Kabunda Dem. Rep. Congo 95 F8
Kabunduk Indon. 108 B2
Kaburuang i. Indon. 57 G5
Kabushiya Sudan 89 G5
Kabwe Zambia 95 F8
Kačanik Serb. and Mont. 46 B3
Kacha Kuh mts Iran/Pak. 81 E4
Kachalinskaya Rus. Fed. 29 H6
Kachchh, Great Rann of marsh India see Kachchh, Rann of
Kachchh, Gulf of India 74 A5
Kachchh, Rann of marsh India 74 A4
Kachh Pak. 81 F4
Kachhola India 74 B4
Kachhwa India 75 D4
Kachia Nigeria 93 G3
Kachin state Myanmar 60 B2
Kachīsī Eth. 96 C2
Kacholola Zambia 97 A8
Kachug Rus. Fed. 62 H1
Kachung Uganda 96 B4
Kaçkar Dağı mt. Turkey 79 E2
Kaczawa r. Poland 37 H3
Kadaingti Myanmar 60 B4
Kadaiyanallur India 72 C4
Kadam mt. Uganda 96 B4
Kadana Chad 88 D6
Kadanai r. Afgh./Pak. 81 F4
Kadan Kyun i. Myanmar 61 B5
Kadapongan i. Indon. 59 F4
Kadarkút Hungary 44 F1
Kadaura India 74 C4
Kadavu i. Fiji 107 G3
Kadavu Passage Fiji 107 G3
Kaddam l. India 72 C2
Kade Ghana 93 E4
Kadgo, Lake salt flat Australia 109 D6
Kadhdhāb, Sinn al esc. Egypt 89 F4
Kādhimain Iraq see Al Kāẓimīyah
Kadiana Mali 92 D3
Kadijica mt. Bulg. see Kadiytsa
Kadıköy Çanakkale Turkey 46 E4
Kadıköy İstanbul Turkey 46 F4
Kadina Australia 112 A4
Kading r. Laos 60 C4
Kadınhanı Turkey 78 C3
Kadiolo Mali 92 D3
Kadiri India 72 C3
Kadirli Turkey 78 D3
Kadiyevka Ukr. see Stakhanov
Kadiytsa mt. Bulg. 46 C4
Kadmat i. India 72 B4
Kado Nigeria 93 H4
Ka-do i. N. Korea 65 A5
Kadoka U.S.A. 132 A3
Kadoma Zimbabwe 99 F3
Kadonkani Myanmar 61 A5
Kadugli Sudan 94 F2
Kaduna Nigeria 93 G3
Kaduna r. Nigeria 93 G3
Kaduna state Nigeria 93 G3
Kadur India 72 C3
Kadusam mt. China/India 66 A2
Kaduy Rus. Fed. 28 F4
Kadyy Rus. Fed. 28 G4
Kadzherom Rus. Fed. 28 J2
Kaechon N. Korea 65 A5
Kaédi Mauritania 92 B1
Kaegudeck Lake Canada 125 K3
Kaélé Cameroon 93 I3
Kaena Point U.S.A. 135 [inset] Y1
Kaeng Krachan National Park Thai. 61 B5
Kaesŏng N. Korea 65 A5
Kafa Ukr. see Feodosiya
Kafakumba Dem. Rep. Congo 95 D7
Kafan Armenia see Kapan
Kafanchan Nigeria 93 H3
Kaffin-Hausa Nigeria 93 H2
Kaffrine Senegal 92 B2
Kafia Kingi Sudan 94 E2
Kafireas, Akra pt Greece 47 D5
Kafireos, Steno sea chan. Greece 47 D6
Kafirnigan Tajik. see Kofarnihon
Kåfjordbotn Norway 32 F1
Kafolo Côte d'Ivoire 92 D3
Kafr ash Shaykh Egypt 89 F2
Kafr ash Shaykh governorate Egypt 78 B5
Kafr el Sheikh governorate Egypt see Kafr ash Shaykh
Kafret Rihama Egypt 78 A5
Kafu r. Uganda 96 B4
Kafue Zambia 95 F8
Kafue r. Zambia 95 F8
Kafue Flats marsh Zambia 95 E8
Kafue National Park Zambia 95 E8
Kaga Bandoro Cent. Afr. Rep. 94 C3
Kagan Uzbek. 81 F2
Kaganovichabad Tajik. see Kolkhozobod
Kaganovichi Pervyye Ukr. see Polis'ke
Kagarlyk Ukr. see Kaharlyk
Kåge Sweden 32 F2
Kagera admin. reg. Tanz. 96 A5
Kagera, Parc National de la nat. park Rwanda see Akagera National Park
Kağızman Turkey 79 E2
Kagmar Sudan 89 F6
Kagologolo Indon. 58 B3
Kagoshima Japan 65 B7
Kagul Moldova see Cahul
Kāhak Iran 80 D2
Kahama Tanz. 97 B5
Kaharlyk Ukr. 29 D6
Kahawero waterhole Namibia 98 B4
Kahayan r. Indon. 59 F3
Kahemba Dem. Rep. Congo 95 C6
Kahla Germany 36 E3
Kahntah Canada 122 F3
Kahnu Iran see Kahnūj
Kahnūj Iran 80 D5
Kahnwia Liberia 92 C4
Kahoka U.S.A. 132 D3
Kahoolawe i. U.S.A. 135 [inset] Z1
Kahramanmaraş Turkey 78 D3
Kahror Pak. 81 G4
Kahta Turkey 79 D3
Kahugish well Iran 80 D3
Kahuku Point U.S.A. 135 [inset] Y1
Kahul, Ozero l. Ukr. 46 F2
Kahului U.S.A. 135 [inset] Z1
Kahurangi National Park N.Z. 113 C3
Kahurangi Point N.Z. 113 C3
Kahuta Pak. 81 H3
Kahuzi-Biega, Parc National du nat. park Dem. Rep. Congo 94 E5
Kai, Kepulauan is Indon. 57 H7
Kaia r. Sudan 96 A3
Kaiama Nigeria 93 F3
Kaiapit P.N.G. 57 K7
Kaibab Plateau U.S.A. 137 F3
Kai Besar i. Indon. 57 H7
Kaib to Plateau U.S.A. 137 G3
Kaieteur Falls Guyana 147 G3
Kaifeng Henan China 67 E1
Kaifeng Henan China 67 E1
Kaihua Yunnan China see Wenshan
Kaihua Zhejiang China 67 F2
Kaijiang China 66 C2
Kai Kecil i. Indon. 57 H7
Kai Keung Leng Hong Kong China 67 [inset]
Kaikoura N.Z. 113 C3
Kailahun Sierra Leone 92 C3
Kailas mt. China see Kangrinboqê Feng
Kailas Range mts China see Gangdisê Shan
Kaili China 66 C3
Kailongong waterhole Kenya 96 B3
Kailua U.S.A. 135 [inset] Z1
Kailua Kona U.S.A. 135 [inset] Z2
Kaimana Indon. 57 H6
Kaimanawa Mountains N.Z. 113 C2
Kaimar China 75 G2
Kaimganj India 74 C4
Kaimur Range hills India 74 D4
Kainji Lake National Park Nigeria 93 G3
Kainji Reservoir Nigeria 93 G3
Kaintaragarh India 73 E1
Kaipara Harbour N.Z. 113 C2
Kaiparowits Plateau U.S.A. 137 G3
Kaiping Guangdong China 67 E4
Kaiping Yunnan China see Dêqên
Kaipokok Bay Canada 125 J2
Kaira India see Kheda
Kairala Fin. 32 G2
Kairana India 74 C3
Kairouan Tunisia 91 H2
Kaisepakte Sweden 32 E1
Kaiserslautern Germany 36 C4
Kaiser Wilhelm II Land reg. Antarctica 167 E2
Kaishantun China 64 B4
Kaišiadorys Lith. 33 G5
Kaitaia N.Z. 113 C1
Kaitangata N.Z. 113 B4
Kaitawa N.Z. 113 D2
Kaithal India 74 C3
Kaitong China see Tongyu
Kaitum Sweden 32 F2
Kaitumälven r. Sweden 32 F2
Kaiwatu Indon. 57 G7
Kaiwi Channel U.S.A. 135 [inset] Z1
Kaixian China 67 D2
Kaiyang China 66 C3
Kaiyuan Liaoning China 64 A4
Kaiyuan Yunnan China 66 B4
Kajaani Fin. 32 G2
Kajabbi Australia 111 E4
Kajaki Afgh. 81 F3
Kajang Malaysia 58 C2
Kajdar Iran 81 E5
Kajiado Kenya 96 C5
Kajo Kaji Sudan 96 A4
Kaju Iran 80 A2
Kaka Sudan 96 B2
Kaka Turkm. 81 D2
Kakaban i. Indon. 59 G2
Kakabeka Falls Canada 124 B3
Kakadu National Park Australia 110 C2
Kakagi Lake Canada 124 A3
Kakamas S. Africa 98 D6
Kakamega Kenya 96 B4
Kakana India 73 G4
Kakanj Bos.-Herz. 44 G2
Kakata Liberia 92 C4
Kakching India 75 G4
Kakenge Dem. Rep. Congo 95 D6
Kakesio Tanz. 96 B5
Kakhi Azer. see Qax
Kakhovs'ke Vodoskhovyshche resr Ukr. 29 E7
Kakhul Moldova see Cahul
Kākī Iran 80 B4
Kakinada India 73 D2
Kakinjës, Maja e mt. Albania 46 A3
Kakisa Lake Canada 123 G2
Kakogawa Japan 65 C6
Kakpin Côte d'Ivoire 92 E3
Kakrala India 74 C4
Kakrima r. Guinea 92 B3
Kakshaal-Too mts China/Kyrg. see Kokshaal-Tau
Kakuda Japan 65 E5
Kakuma Kenya 96 B4
Kakus r. Sarawak Malaysia 59 F2
Kakwa r. Canada 122 G4
Kal hill Croatia 44 E2
Kala Nigeria 93 I2
Kala Tanz. 97 A7
Kalaä Kebira Tunisia 91 H2
Kalaallit Nunaat terr. N. America see Greenland
Kalabagh Pak. 81 G3
Kalabahi Indon. 57 F7
Kalabak mt. Bulg./Greece see Radomir
Kalabáka Greece see Kalampaka
Kalabakan Sabah Malaysia 59 G1
Kalabaydh Togdheer Somalia 96 E2
Kalabaydh Woqooyi Galbeed Somalia 96 D2
Kalabo Zambia 95 D8
Kalach Rus. Fed. 29 G6
Kalacha Dida Kenya 96 C4
Kalach-na-Donu Rus. Fed. 29 G6
Kaladan r. India/Myanmar 73 G1
Kaladar Canada 131 E1
Kaladgi India 72 B2
Kalagwe Myanmar 60 B3
Kalahari Desert Africa 98 C4
Kalahari Gemsbok National Park S. Africa 98 D5
Kalaikhum Tajik. see Qal'aikhum
Kalai-Khumb Tajik. see Qal'aikhum
Kala-I-Mor Turkm. 81 E3
Kalajoki Fin. 32 F2
Kalajoki r. Fin. 32 F2
Kalak Norway 32 G1
Kalakoch hill Bulg. 46 E3
Kalalé Benin 93 F3
Kalam India 72 C1
Kalam Pak. 81 H3
Kalámai Greece see Kalamata
Kalamaria Greece 46 C4
Kalamata Greece 47 C6
Kalamazoo U.S.A. 132 E3
Kalamazoo r. U.S.A. 132 E3
Kalambau i. Indon. 59 F4
Kalamnuri India 72 C2
Kalamos i. Greece 47 B5
Kalampaka Greece 47 B5
Kalana Estonia 33 F4
Kalana Mali 92 C3
Kalanchak Ukr. 29 E7
Kalandula Angola see Calandula
Kalangala Uganda 96 B5
Kalannie Australia 109 B7
Kalanwali India 74 B3
Kalao i. Indon. 57 F7
Kalaotoa i. Indon. 57 F7
Kala Oya r. Sri Lanka 72 C4
Kalapana U.S.A. 135 [inset] Z2
Kalar watercourse Iran 81 E5
Kalār Iraq 79 F4
Kalasin Thai. 61 C4
Kalāt Balūchestān va Sīstān Iran 81 D5
Kalāt Khorāsan Iran see Kabūd Gonbad
Kalat Balochistān Pak. 81 F4
Kalat Balochistān Pak. 81 F5
Kalat, Kūh-e mt. Iran 80 D3
Kalaus r. Rus. Fed. 29 H7
Kalavad India 74 A5
Kalavryta Greece 47 C5
Kälbäcär Azer. 80 A1
Kalbarri Australia 109 A5
Kalbarri National Park Australia 109 A6
Kalbū Iran 81 D3
Kaldırım Turkey 77 B1
Kaldygayty r. Kazakh. 28 J6
Kale Turkey 47 F6
Kalecik Turkey 78 C2
Kalegauk Island Myanmar 61 B5
Kalema Dem. Rep. Congo 95 E6
Kalémié Dem. Rep. Congo 95 F6
Kalemyo Myanmar 60 A3
Kalenoye Kazakh. 29 I6
Kalesija Bos.-Herz. 44 G2
Kalevala Rus. Fed. 32 H2
Kalewa Myanmar 60 A3
Kalgan China see Zhangjiakou
Kalgoorlie Australia 109 C7
Kalguéri Niger 93 H2
Kali Croatia 44 E2
Kali r. India/Nepal 74 D3
Kaliakra, Nos pt Bulg. 46 F3
Kalianda Indon. 58 D4
Kali Gandaki r. Nepal 75 E4
Kaligiri India 72 C3
Kalima Dem. Rep. Congo 94 E5
Kalimantan reg. Indon. 59 E3
Kalimantan Barat prov. Indon. 59 E2
Kalimantan Selatan prov. Indon. 59 F3
Kalimantan Tengah prov. Indon. 59 F3
Kalimantan Timur prov. Indon. 59 G2
Kálimnos i. Greece see Kalymnos
Kalimpang India 75 F4
Kalinadi r. India 72 B3
Kali Nadi r. India 74 D4
Kalinin Rus. Fed. see Tver'
Kaliningrad Rus. Fed. 37 J1
Kaliningrad Oblast admin. div. Rus. Fed. see Kaliningradskaya Oblast'
Kaliningradskaya Oblast' admin. div. Rus. Fed. 37 J1
Kaliningradskiy Zaliv b. Rus. Fed. 37 I1
Kalinino Armenia see Tashir
Kalinino Kostromskaya Oblast' Rus. Fed. 28 G4
Kalinino Permskaya Oblast' Rus. Fed. 28 K4
Kalininsk Rus. Fed. 29 H6
Kalininskaya Rus. Fed. 29 F7
Kalininskaya Oblast' admin. div. Rus. Fed. see Tverskaya Oblast'
Kalinjara India 74 B5
Kalinkavichy Belarus 31 L2
Kalinkovichi Belarus see Kalinkavichy
Kalinovka Kazakh. 29 J6
Kaliro Uganda 96 B4
Kalis Somalia 96 F2
Kalisch Poland see Kalisz
Kalispell U.S.A. 134 D2
Kalisz Poland 37 I3
Kalisz Pomorski Poland 37 G2
Kalitva r. Rus. Fed. 29 G6
Kaliua Tanz. 97 A6
Kalix Sweden 32 F2
Kalixälven r. Sweden 32 F2
Kalkan Turkey 78 B3
Kalkaringi Australia 110 B3
Kalkaska U.S.A. 132 E2
Kalkfeld Namibia 98 C4
Kalkkuruchchi India 72 C4
Kallam India 72 C2
Kallang Sing. 58 [inset]
Kallaste Estonia 28 C4
Kallavesi l. Fin. 32 G3
Källberget Sweden 32 D3
Kallfjärden b. Sweden 32 F2
Kallifoni Greece 47 B5
Kallmet i Madh Albania 46 A4
Kallonis, Kolpos b. Greece 47 E5
Kallsjön l. Sweden 32 D3
Kallur India 72 C2
Kalmar Sweden 33 E4
Kalmar county Sweden 33 E4
Kalmarsund sea chan. Sweden 33 E4
Kalmūkh Qal'eh Iran 80 D2
Kalmunai Sri Lanka 73 D5
Kalmykia aut. rep. Rus. Fed. see Kalmykiya - Khalm'g-Tangch, Respublika
Kalmykiya - Khalm'g-Tangch, Respublika aut. rep. Rus. Fed. 29 H7
Kalmykovo Kazakh. see Taypak
Kalmytskaya Avtonomnaya Oblast' aut. rep. Rus. Fed. see Kalmykiya - Khalm'g-Tangch, Respublika
Kalnai India 75 D5
Kalni r. Bangl. 75 F4
Kalnik mts Croatia 44 F1
Kalocsa Hungary 37 I5
Kaloko Dem. Rep. Congo 95 E6
Kalol Gujarat India 74 B5
Kalol Gujarat India 74 B5
Kaloma Tanz. 97 A6
Kalomo Zambia 95 E9
Kalone Peak Canada 122 E4
Kalopanagiotis Cyprus 77 A2
Kalpa India 74 C3
Kalpeni i. India 72 B4
Kalpetta India 72 C4
Kalpi India 74 C4
Kāl-Shūr, Rūd-e r. Iran 80 D2
Kaltenkirchen Germany 36 D2
Kaltukatjara Australia 110 B5
Kaltungo Nigeria 93 H3
Kalu India 74 B3
Kalu r. India 72 B2
Kaluderica Serb. and Mont. 46 B2
Kaluga Rus. Fed. 29 F5
Kaluga Oblast admin. div. Rus. Fed. see Kaluzhskaya Oblast'
Kalukalukuang i. Indon. 59 G4
Kalulong, Bukit mt. Sarawak Malaysia 59 F2
Kalulushi Zambia 95 F8
Kalumburu Australia 110 A2
Kalundborg Denmark 33 C5
Kalupis Falls Sabah Malaysia 59 G1
Kalur Kot Pak. 81 G3
Kalush Ukr. 29 C6
Kalutara Sri Lanka 72 C5
Kaluzhskaya Oblast' admin. div. Rus. Fed. 31 M2
Kalvåg Norway 33 B3
Kalvan India 72 B1
Kalvarija Lith. 33 F5
Kalvitsa Fin. 33 G3
Kalvola Fin. 33 G3
Kalwakurti India 72 C2
Kalyan India 72 B2
Kalyandurg India 72 C3
Kalyansingapuram India 73 D2
Kalyazin Rus. Fed. 28 F4
Kalymnos Greece 47 E6
Kalymnos i. Greece 47 E6
Kama Dem. Rep. Congo 94 E5
Kama Myanmar 60 A4

▶Kama r. Rus. Fed. 28 J4
4th longest river in Europe.
europe 22–23

Kamaishi Japan 65 E5
Kamakusa Guyana 147 G3
Kamakwie Sierra Leone 92 B3
Kamal Chad 88 C4
Kamalapuram India 72 C3
Kamalia Pak. 81 H4
Kamamaung Myanmar 60 B4
Kaman India 74 C4
Kaman Turkey 78 C3
Kamanjab Namibia 98 B3
Kamaran Yemen 89 I6
Kamarān i. Yemen 76 C6

Khurayş Saudi Arabia 80 B5
Khurd, Koh-i- mt. Afgh. 81 F3
Khureit Sudan 89 E6
Khuria Tank resr India see Maniari Tank
Khurja India 74 C3
Khurmalik Afgh. 81 E3
Khurmuli Rus. Fed. 64 D2
Khurr, Wādī al watercourse Saudi Arabia 79 E5
Khushab Pak. 81 H3
Khushshah, Wādī al watercourse Jordan/Saudi Arabia 77 C5
Khust Ukr. 31 J3
Khutgaon India 72 D1
Khutmīyah, Mamarr al Egypt 77 A4
Khutse Game Reserve nature res. Botswana 98 E4
Khutu r. Rus. Fed. 64 D2
Khuwei Sudan 89 F6
Khuzdar Pak. 81 F5
Khūzestān prov. Iran 80 B4
Khvājeh Iran 80 A2
Khvalynsk Rus. Fed. 29 I5
Khvor Iran 80 C3
Khvord Nārvan Iran 80 D3
Khvormūj Iran 80 B4
Khvosh Maqām Iran 80 A2
Khvoy Iran 80 A2
Khvoynaya Rus. Fed. 28 E4
Khwae Noi r. Thai. 61 B5
Khwahan Afgh. 81 G2
Khwaja Amran mt. Pak. 81 F4
Khwaja-i-Ghar Afgh. 81 G2
Khwaja Muhammad Range mts Afgh. 81 G2
Khyber Pass Afgh./Pak. 81 G3
Kīā'ī Iran 80 D5
Kiama Australia 112 D4
Kiambi Dem. Rep. Congo 95 F6
Kiamichi r. U.S.A. 133 C5
Kiangsi prov. China see Jiangxi
Kiangsu prov. China see Jiangsu
Kiang West National Park Gambia 92 B2
Kianly Turkm. see Darta
Kiantajärvi l. Fin. 32 H2
Kiāseh Iran 80 C2
Kiato Greece 47 C5
Kibaha Tanz. 97 C6
Kibala Angola 95 B6
Kibale Uganda 96 A4
Kibale National Park Uganda 96 A4
Kibali r. Dem. Rep. Congo 94 F4
Kibangou Congo 94 B5
Kibara Tanz. 96 B5
Kibara, Monts mts Dem. Rep. Congo 95 E7
Kibaya Tanz. 97 C6
Kiberashi Tanz. 97 C6
Kiberege Tanz. 97 C6
Kiboga Uganda 96 A4
Kibombo Dem. Rep. Congo 95 E5
Kibondo Tanz. 96 A5
Kibre Mengist Eth. 96 C3
Kibris country Asia see Cyprus
Kibungo Rwanda 96 A5
Kibuye Rwanda 94 F5
Kibwesa Tanz. 97 A6
Kičevo Macedonia 46 B4
Kichi-Kichi well Chad 88 C5
Kichwamba Uganda 96 A5
Kicking Horse Pass Canada 123 G5
Kidal Mali 93 F1
Kidal admin. reg. Mali 93 F1
Kidatu Tanz. 97 C6
Kidderminster U.K. 35 E5
Kidepo Valley National Park Uganda 96 B4
Kidira Senegal 92 B2
Kidmang Jammu and Kashmir 74 C2
Kidnappers, Cape N.Z. 113 D2
Kiel Germany 36 E1
Kiel Canal Germany 36 D1
Kielce Poland 37 J3
Kielder Water resr U.K. 34 E4
Kieler Bucht b. Germany 36 E1
Kieler Förde g. Germany 36 E1
Kiembara Burkina 92 E2
Kienge Dem. Rep. Congo 95 E7

▶Kiev Ukr. 29 D6
Capital of Ukraine.

Kiffa Mauritania 92 C1
Kifisia Greece 47 C5
Kifisos r. Greece 47 C5
Kifrī Iraq 79 F4
Kifwanzondo Dem. Rep. Congo 95 C6

▶Kigali Rwanda 94 F5
Capital of Rwanda.

Kiğı Turkey 79 E3
Kiglapait Mountains Canada 125 I1
Kiglikavik Lake Canada 123 H1
Kignan Mali 92 D3
Kigoma Tanz. 97 A6
Kigoma admin. reg. Tanz. 97 A6
Kigwe Tanz. 97 B6
Kihei U.S.A. 135 [inset] Z1
Kihlanki Fin. 32 F2
Kihniö Fin. 33 F3
Kihnu i. Estonia 33 F4
Kiiminki Fin. 32 G2
Kii-sanchi mts Japan 65 C6
Kii-suidō sea chan. Japan 65 C6
Kijungu Well Tanz. 97 C6
Kikerk Lake Canada 123 H1
Kikinda Serb. and Mont. 46 B2
Kikki Pak. 81 E5
Kikládhes is Greece see Cyclades
Kiknur Rus. Fed. 28 H4
Kikondja Dem. Rep. Congo 95 E7
Kikori P.N.G. 57 J7
Kikori r. P.N.G. 57 J7
Kikwit Dem. Rep. Congo 95 C6
Kil Sweden 33 D4
Kilafors Sweden 33 E3
Kilakkarai India 72 C4
Kīlan Iran 80 C3
Kilauea U.S.A. 135 [inset] Y1
Kilauea Crater U.S.A. 135 [inset] Z2
Kilboghamn Norway 32 D2
Kilbotn Norway 32 E1
Kilchu N. Korea 65 B4
Kilcock Rep. of Ireland 35 C5
Kilcoy Australia 111 H5
Kildare Rep. of Ireland 35 C5
Kildonan Zimbabwe 99 F3
Kilekale Lake Canada 122 F1
Kilemary Rus. Fed. 28 H4
Kilembe Dem. Rep. Congo 95 C6
Kilgore U.S.A. 133 C5
Kilgour r. Australia 110 C3
Kilia Ukr. see Kiliya
Kilibo Benin 93 F3
Kilifi Kenya 96 C5
Kilik Pass China 74 B1
Kilimanjaro admin. reg. Tanz. 97 C5

▶Kilimanjaro vol. Tanz. 96 C5
Highest mountain in Africa.
africa 84–85, 86–87

Kilimanjaro National Park Tanz. 96 C5
Kilimatinde Tanz. 97 B6
Kilinailau Islands P.N.G. 107 E2
Kilindoni Tanz. 97 C6
Kilingi-Nõmme Estonia 28 C4
Kılıs Turkey 78 D3
Kilis prov. Turkey 77 C1
Kiliya Ukr. 46 F2
Kilkee Rep. of Ireland 35 B5
Kilkenny Rep. of Ireland 35 C5
Kilkis Greece 46 C4
Killala Rep. of Ireland 35 B4
Killaloe Rep. of Ireland 35 B5
Killam Canada 123 I4
Killarney Australia 111 H6
Killarney Canada 124 D4
Killarney Rep. of Ireland 35 B5
Killarney National Park Rep. of Ireland 35 B6
Killary Harbour b. Rep. of Ireland 35 B5
Killeen U.S.A. 133 B6
Killin U.K. 34 D3
Killinek Island Canada see Killiniq Island
Killini mt. Greece see Kyllini
Killiniq Canada 121 M3
Killiniq Island Canada 121 M3
Killorglin Rep. of Ireland 35 B5
Killybegs Rep. of Ireland 35 B4
Kilmarnock U.K. 34 D4
Kilmarnock U.S.A. 131 E5
Kil'mez' Rus. Fed. 28 I4
Kil'mez' r. Rus. Fed. 28 I4
Kilmore Australia 112 C5
Kilosa Tanz. 97 C6
Kilpisjärvi Fin. 32 F1
Kilpua Fin. 32 G2
Kilrush Rep. of Ireland 35 B5
Kilttan i. India 72 B4
Kilwa Dem. Rep. Congo 95 F7
Kilwa Masoko Tanz. 97 C7
Kilyazi Azer. see Giläzi
Kim Chad 94 B2
Kimambi Tanz. 97 C7
Kimanis, Teluk b. Sabah Malaysia 59 F1
Kimasozero Rus. Fed. 32 H2
Kimasozero, Ozero l. Rus. Fed. 32 H2
Kimba Australia 109 G8
Kimba Congo 94 B5
Kimball U.S.A. 132 A3
Kimbe P.N.G. 106 E2
Kimberley Canada 123 H5
Kimberley S. Africa 98 E6
Kimberley Downs Australia 108 D4
Kimberley Plateau Australia 110 A3
Kimberley Range hills Australia 109 B6
Kimbirila-Sud Côte d'Ivoire 92 D3
Kimch'aek N. Korea 65 B4
Kimch'ŏn S. Korea 65 B5
Kimhae S. Korea 65 B6
Kími Greece see Kymi
Kimito Fin. 33 F3
Kimje S. Korea 65 A6
Kimmirut Canada 121 M3
Kimolos i. Greece 47 D6
Kimolou-Sifnou, Steno sea chan. Greece 47 D6
Kimovsk Rus. Fed. 29 F5
Kimpanga Dem. Rep. Congo 95 E6
Kimpangu Dem. Rep. Congo 95 B6
Kimparana Mali 92 D2
Kimpese Dem. Rep. Congo 95 B6
Kimpoko Dem. Rep. Congo 95 B6
Kimpoku-san mt. Japan see Kinpoku-san
Kimry Rus. Fed. 31 N1
Kimsquit Canada 122 E4
Kimvula Dem. Rep. Congo 95 B6
Kinabalu, Gunung mt. Sabah Malaysia 59 G1
Kinabalu National Park Sabah Malaysia 59 G1
Kinabatangan r. Sabah Malaysia 59 G1
Kinango Kenya 97 C6
Kinaros i. Greece 47 E6
Kinaskan Lake Canada 122 D3
Kinbasket Lake Canada 122 G4
Kinbirila Côte d'Ivoire see Kimbirila-Sud
Kinbrace U.K. 34 E2
Kincaid Canada 123 J5
Kincardine Canada 130 C1
Kinchang Myanmar 60 B2
Kinchega National Park Australia 112 B4
Kincolith Canada 122 D4
Kinda Dem. Rep. Congo 95 E7
Kindamba Congo 95 B5
Kindat Myanmar 60 A3
Kinde U.S.A. 130 B2
Kindembe Dem. Rep. Congo 95 C6
Kinder U.S.A. 133 C6
Kindersley Canada 134 E2
Kindia Guinea 92 B3
Kindu Dem. Rep. Congo 94 E5
Kinel' Rus. Fed. 29 I5
Kineshma Rus. Fed. 28 G4
King r. N.T. Australia 110 C2
King r. W.A. Australia 108 E3
King and Queen Courthouse U.S.A. 131 E5
Kingaroy Australia 111 G5
King City U.S.A. 136 B3
King Edward r. Australia 108 D3
King Edward Point research station S. Georgia 153 [inset]
Kingfisher U.S.A. 133 B5
King George Bay Falkland Is 153 E7
King George Island Antarctica 167 A2
King George Islands Canada 124 E1
King George VI Falls Guyana 147 F3
Kingimbi Dem. Rep. Congo 95 B6
Kingisepp Rus. Fed. 28 D4
King Island Australia 112 B5
King Island Canada 122 E4
King Island Myanmar see Kadan Kyun
Kingisseppa Estonia see Kuressaare
Kinglake National Park Australia 112 C5
King Leopold and Queen Astrid Coast Antarctica 167 E2
King Leopold Range National Park Australia 108 D4
King Leopold Ranges hills Australia 110 A3
Kingman AZ U.S.A. 137 E4
Kingman KS U.S.A. 132 B4

▶Kingman Reef N. Pacific Ocean 165 H5
United States Unincorporated Territory.
oceania 114

King Mountain Canada 122 D3
King Mountain U.S.A. 133 A6
Kingombe Mbali Dem. Rep. Congo 94 E5
King Peak Antarctica 167 L1
King Peninsula Antarctica 167 K2
Kingri Pak. 81 G4
Kings r. U.S.A. 136 B3
Kingsburg U.S.A. 136 C3
Kings Canyon National Park U.S.A. 136 C3
Kingscote Australia 112 A4
King Sejong research station Antarctica 167 A2
Kingsland U.S.A. 129 C6
King's Lynn U.K. 35 G5
Kingsmill Group is Kiribati 107 G2
King Sound b. Australia 108 C4
Kings Peak U.S.A. 134 E4
Kingsport U.S.A. 130 B5
Kingston Australia 112 C6
Kingston Canada 131 E1

▶Kingston Jamaica 139 I5
Capital of Jamaica.

▶Kingston Norfolk I. 164 F7
Capital of Norfolk Island.

Kingston N.Z. 113 B4
Kingston MA U.S.A. 131 H3
Kingston MO U.S.A. 132 C4
Kingston NY U.S.A. 131 F3
Kingston OH U.S.A. 130 B4
Kingston PA U.S.A. 131 F3
Kingston TN U.S.A. 128 B5
Kingston South East Australia 112 A5
Kingston upon Hull U.K. 35 F5

▶Kingstown St Vincent 147 F1
Capital of St Vincent.

Kingstree U.S.A. 129 D5
Kingsville U.S.A. 133 B7
Kingswood U.K. 35 E6
Kington U.K. 35 E5
Kingungi Dem. Rep. Congo 95 C6
Kingussie U.K. 34 D3
King William Island Canada 121 J3
Kingwood TX U.S.A. 133 C6
Kingwood WV U.S.A. 130 D4
Kiniama Dem. Rep. Congo 95 F7
Kınık Turkey 47 E5
Kinkala Congo 95 B6
Kinloch N.Z. 113 B4
Kinlochleven U.K. 34 D3
Kinmen Taiwan see Chinmen
Kinmount Canada 130 D1
Kinna Sweden 33 D4
Kinnarasani r. India 72 D2
Kinnarodden pt Norway 32 G1
Kinnegad Rep. of Ireland 35 C5
Kinneret, Yam l. Israel see Galilee, Sea of
Kinniyai Sri Lanka 72 D4
Kinnula Fin. 32 G3
Kinoje r. Canada 124 D2
Kinoosao Canada 123 K3
Kinpoku-san mt. Japan 65 D5
Kinsale Rep. of Ireland 35 B6
Kinsarvik Norway 33 B3
Kinsele Dem. Rep. Congo 95 C6

▶Kinshasa Dem. Rep. Congo 95 B6
Capital of the Democratic Republic of Congo and 3rd most populous city in Africa.
world 16–17

Kinshasa municipality Dem. Rep. Congo 95 C6
Kinsley U.S.A. 132 B4
Kinston U.S.A. 128 D5
Kintai Lith. 33 F5
Kintampo Ghana 93 E3
Kintata Dem. Rep. Congo 95 B6
Kintinian Guinea 92 C3
Kintop Indon. 59 F3
Kintore Australia 110 B4
Kintore, Mount Australia 110 B5
Kintyre pen. U.K. 34 D4
Kinu Myanmar 60 A3
Kinushseo r. Canada 124 D2
Kinuso Canada 123 H4
Kinwat India 72 C2
Kinyangiri Tanz. 97 B6
Kinyeti mt. Sudan 96 B4
Kiomboi Tanz. 97 B6
Kiowa CO U.S.A. 134 F5
Kiowa KS U.S.A. 132 B4
Kipahigan Lake Canada 123 K4
Kiparissía Greece see Kyparissia
Kipawa, Lac l. Canada 124 E4
Kipelovo Rus. Fed. 28 F4
Kipengere Range mts Tanz. 97 B7
Kipili Tanz. 97 A6
Kipini Kenya 96 D5
Kipling Canada 123 K5
Kipling Station Canada see Kipling
Kiptopeke U.S.A. 131 F5
Kipungo Angola see Quipungo
Kipushi Dem. Rep. Congo 95 E7
Kipushia Dem. Rep. Congo 95 F8
Kirakat India 75 D4
Kirakira Solomon Is 107 F3
Kirandul India 72 D2
Kirané Mali 92 C2
Kiraz Turkey 47 F5
Kirbla Estonia 33 F4
Kirbyville U.S.A. 133 C6
Kirchdorf an der Krems Austria 37 G5
Kirdimi Chad 88 C5
Kirenga r. Rus. Fed. 27 K4
Kirensk Rus. Fed. 27 K4
Kirghizia country Asia see Kyrgyzstan
Kirgiz-Miyaki Rus. Fed. 29 J5
Kirgizskaya S.S.R. country Asia see Kyrgyzstan
Kirgizstan country Asia see Kyrgyzstan
Kiri Dem. Rep. Congo 94 C5
Kiriákion Greece see Kyriaki
▶Kiribati country Pacific Ocean 107 H2
oceania 104–105
Kiridh Somalia 96 E2
Kırıkhan Turkey 78 D3
Kırıkkale Turkey 78 C3
Kirillov Rus. Fed. 28 F4
Kirillovo Rus. Fed. 64 E3
Kirin China see Jilin
Kirin prov. China see Jilin
Kirinyaga mt. Kenya see Kenya, Mount
Kirishi Rus. Fed. 28 E4
Kirishima-Yaku National Park Japan 65 B7
▶Kiritimati i. Kiribati 165 H5
oceania 114
Kiriwina Islands P.N.G. see Trobriand Islands
Kırkağaç Turkey 47 E5
Kirk Bulāg Dāgh mt. Iran 80 A2
Kirkby U.K. 35 E5
Kirkby Stephen U.K. 35 E4
Kirkcaldy U.K. 34 E3
Kirkcudbright U.K. 34 D4
Kirkenær Norway 33 D3
Kirkenes Norway 32 H1
Kirkfield Canada 130 D1
Kirkkonummi Fin. 33 G3
Kirkland U.S.A. 137 F4
Kirkland Lake Canada 124 D3
Kırklareli Turkey 78 A2
Kırklareli prov. Turkey 46 E4
Kırklareli Barajı resr Turkey 46 E4
Kirkpatrick, Mount Antarctica 167 H1
Kirksville U.S.A. 132 C3
Kirkuk Iraq see Kirkūk
Kirkūk Iraq 79 F4
Kirkwall U.K. 34 E2
Kirman Iran see Kermān
Kırmır r. Turkey 78 B2
Kirobası Turkey see Mağara
Kirov Kaluzhskaya Oblast' Rus. Fed. 29 E5
Kirov Kirovskaya Oblast' Rus. Fed. 28 I4
Kirova, Zaliv b. Azer. see Qızılağac Körfäzi
Kirovabad Azer. see Gäncä
Kirovabad Tajik. see Panj
Kirovakan Armenia see Vanadzor
Kirovo Kazakh. 29 J6
Kirovo Ukr. see Kirovohrad
Kirovo Uzbek. see Besharyk
Kirov Oblast admin. div. Rus. Fed. see Kirovskaya Oblast'
Kirovo-Chepetsk Rus. Fed. 28 I4
Kirovo-Chepetskiy Rus. Fed. see Kirovo-Chepetsk
Kirovograd Ukr. see Kirovohrad
Kirovohrad Ukr. 29 E6
Kirovsk Leningradskaya Oblast' Rus. Fed. 28 D4
Kirovsk Murmanskaya Oblast' Rus. Fed. 32 I2
Kirovsk Turkm. see Babadaykhan
Kirovskaya Oblast' admin. div. Rus. Fed. 28 I4
Kirovskiy Kazakh. see Balpyk Bi
Kirovskiy Rus. Fed. 64 C3
Kırpaşa pen. Cyprus see Karpasia
Kirpili Turkm. 80 D2
Kirriemuir U.K. 34 E3
Kirs Rus. Fed. 28 J4
Kirsanov Rus. Fed. 29 G5
Kırşehir Turkey 78 C3
Kirtachi Niger 93 F2
Kirthar National Park Pak. 81 F5
Kirthar Range mts Pak. 81 F5
Kiruna Sweden 32 F2
Kirundo Burundi 94 F5
Kirundu Dem. Rep. Congo 94 E5
Kirwan Escarpment Antarctica 167 B2
Kirya Rus. Fed. 28 H5
Kiryū Japan 65 D5
Kisa Sweden 33 D4
Kisaki Tanz. 97 C6
Kisama, Parque Nacional de nat. park Angola see Quiçama, Parque Nacional do
Kisangani Dem. Rep. Congo 94 E4
Kisar i. Indon. 108 D2
Kisaran Indon. 58 B2
Kisarawe Tanz. 97 C6
Kisbér Hungary 37 I5
Kiselevsk Rus. Fed. 62 D1
Kiseljak Bos.-Herz. 44 G3
Kisel'ovka Rus. Fed. 64 D2
Kishanganj India 75 E4
Kishangarh Rajasthan India 74 A4
Kishangarh Rajasthan India 74 B4
Kishen Ganga r. India/Pak. 74 B2
Kishi Nigeria 93 F3
Kishinev Moldova see Chişinău
Kishiözen r. Kazakh./Rus. Fed. see Malyy Uzen'
Kishiwada Japan 65 C6
Kishkenekol' Kazakh. 26 H4
Kishoreganj Bangl. 75 F4
Kishtwar Jammu and Kashmir 74 B2
Kisigo r. Tanz. 97 B6
Kisii Kenya 96 B5
Kisiju Tanz. 97 C6
Kiska Island U.S.A. 120 A4
Kiskittogisu Lake Canada 123 L4
Kisko Fin. 33 F3
Kiskőrös Hungary 37 I5
Kiskunfélegyháza Hungary 37 I5
Kiskunhalas Hungary 46 A1
Kiskunmajsa Hungary 46 A1
Kiskunsági nat. park Hungary 37 I5
Kislovodsk Rus. Fed. 29 G8
Kismaayo Somalia 96 D5
Kismayu Somalia see Kismaayo
Kisoro Uganda 96 A5
Kispiox Canada 122 E4
Kispiox r. Canada 122 E4
Kisseraing Island Myanmar see Kanmaw Kyun
Kissidougou Guinea 92 C3
Kissimmee U.S.A. 129 C6
Kissimmee r. U.S.A. 129 C7
Kissimmee, Lake U.S.A. 129 C7
Kississing Lake Canada 123 K4
Kissu, Jebel mt. Sudan 88 E4
Kistanje Croatia 44 E3
Kistelek Hungary 46 A1
Kisújszállás Hungary 37 J5
Kisumu Kenya 96 B5
Kisykkamys Kazakh. see Dzhangala
Kit r. Sudan 96 A3
Kita Mali 92 C2
Kitab Uzbek. 81 F2
Kita-Daitō-jima i. Japan 63 M6
Kitaibaraki Japan 65 E5
Kitakami-gawa r. Japan 65 E5
Kita-Kyūshū Japan 65 B6
Kitale Kenya 96 B4
Kitami Japan 64 E4
Kitanda Dem. Rep. Congo 95 E6
Kitchener Canada 130 C2
Kitchigama r. Canada 124 E3
Kiteba Dem. Rep. Congo 95 E6
Kitee Fin. 32 H3
Kitendwe Dem. Rep. Congo 95 F6
Kitgum Uganda 96 B4
Kithira i. Greece see Kythira
Kithnos i. Greece see Kythnos
Kithnou, Stenón sea chan. Greece see Kythnou, Steno
Kiti, Cape Cyprus see Kition, Cape
Kitimat Canada 122 D4
Kitinen r. Fin. 32 G2
Kition, Cape Cyprus 77 A2
Kitiou, Akra c. Cyprus see Kition, Cape
Kitob Uzbek. see Kitab
Kitsa Rus. Fed. 32 I1
Kitscoty Canada 123 I4
Kittanning U.S.A. 130 D3
Kittilä Fin. 32 G2
Kittur India 72 B3
Kitty Hawk U.S.A. 128 E4
Kitui Kenya 96 C5
Kitumbini Tanz. 97 C7
Kitunda Tanz. 97 B6
Kitwanga Canada 122 D4
Kitwe Zambia 95 F8
Kitzbühel Austria 37 F5
Kitzbüheler Alpen mts Austria 37 F5
Kitzingen Germany 36 E4
Kiu Kenya 96 C5
Kiu Lom Dam Thai. 60 B4
Kiunga P.N.G. 57 J7
Kiunga Marine National Reserve nature res. Kenya 96 D5
Kiuruvesi Fin. 32 G3
Kivalo ridge Fin. 32 G2
Kivijärvi Fin. 32 G3
Kivijärvi l. Fin. 32 G3
Kivilompolo Norway 32 F1
Kiviõli Estonia 33 G4
Kivivaara Fin. 32 H3
Kivu, Lake Dem. Rep. Congo/Rwanda 94 F5
Kiwaba N'zogi Angola 95 C7
Kiwai Island P.N.G. 57 J7
Kiwawa Tanz. 97 C7
Kiyāt Saudi Arabia 89 I5
Kiyev Ukr. see Kiev
Kiyevskoye Vodokhranilishche resr Ukr. see Kyyivs'ke Vodoskhovyshche
Kıyıköy Turkey 46 F4
Kizel Rus. Fed. 28 K4
Kizema Rus. Fed. 28 H3
Kizhi, Ostrov i. Rus. Fed. 28 E3
Kızılca Dağ mt. Turkey 78 B3
Kızılcahamam Turkey 78 C2
Kızıldağ mt. Turkey 77 B1
Kızıl Dağı mt. Turkey 79 D3
Kızılırmak r. Turkey 78 C2
Kızılören Turkey 78 C3
Kızıltepe Turkey 79 E3
Kizil"yurt Rus. Fed. 79 F2
Kızkalesi Turkey 77 B1
Kizlyar Rus. Fed. 79 F2
Kizlyarskiy Zaliv b. Rus. Fed. 79 F1
Kizner Rus. Fed. 28 I4
Kizreka Rus. Fed. 32 H2
Kizyl-Arbat Turkm. see Gyzylarbat
Kizyl-Atrek Turkm. see Gyzyletrek
Kizylayak Turkm. 81 F2
Kizyl Jilga Aksai Chin 74 C2
Kizyl-Su Turkm. 80 C2
Kjøllefjord Norway 32 G1
Kladanj Bos.-Herz. 44 G2
Kladno Czech Rep. 37 G3
Kladovo Serb. and Mont. 46 C2
Klagan Sabah Malaysia 59 G1
Klagenfurt Austria 37 G5
Klagetoh U.S.A. 137 H4
Klaipėda Lith. 33 F5
Klaksvig Faroe Is see Klaksvík
Klaksvík Faroe Is 34 [inset]
Klamath r. U.S.A. 134 A4
Klamath Falls U.S.A. 134 B4
Klamath Mountains U.S.A. 134 B4
Klampo Indon. 59 G2
Klang Malaysia see Kelang
Klappan r. Canada 122 D3
Klarälven r. Sweden 31 H1
Klaten Indon. 59 E4
Klatovy Czech Rep. 37 F4
Klawer S. Africa 98 C6
Klawock U.S.A. 120 F4
Klazienaveen Neth. 36 C2
Kłecko Poland 37 H2
Kleinegga mt. Norway 33 C3
Kleinmachnow Germany 37 F2
Kleinsee S. Africa 98 C6
Kleitoria Greece 47 C6
Klekovača mt. Bos.-Herz. 44 F2
Klemtu Canada 122 D4
Kleppesto Norway 33 B3
Klerksdorp S. Africa 99 E5
Kletnya Rus. Fed. 29 E5
Kletsk Belarus see Klyetsk
Kletskaya Rus. Fed. 29 G6
Kletskiy Rus. Fed. see Kletskaya
Kleve Germany 36 C3
Kliment Bulg. 46 E3
Klimovo Rus. Fed. 31 M2
Klin Rus. Fed. 28 F4
Klina Serb. and Mont. 46 B3
Klinaklini r. Canada 122 E5
Klingkang, Banjaran mts Indon./Malaysia 59 E2
Klintsy Rus. Fed. 29 E5
Klippan Sweden 33 D4
Klis Croatia 44 F3
Klitmøller Denmark 33 C4
Klitória Greece see Kleitoria
Ključ Bos.-Herz. 44 F2
Kłobuck Poland 37 I3
Kłodawa Poland 37 I2
Kłodzko Poland 37 H3
Klondike r. Canada 122 B1
Klondike Goldrush National Historical Park nat. park U.S.A. 122 C3
Klosterneuburg Austria 37 H4
Klosters Switz. 39 H3
Klötze (Altmark) Germany 36 E2
Kluane r. Canada 122 B2
Kluane Lake Canada 122 B2
Kluane National Park Canada 122 B2
Kluang Malaysia see Keluang
Kluang, Tanjung pt Indon. 59 E3
Kluczbork Poland 37 I3
Klukhori Rus. Fed. see Karachayevsk
Klumpang, Teluk b. Indon. 59 G3
Klungkung Indon. 59 F5
Klupro Pak. 81 G5
Klyavlino Rus. Fed. 29 J5
Klyetsk Belarus 29 C5
▶Klyuchevskaya, Sopka vol. Rus. Fed. 27 Q4
world 10–11
Klyuchi Rus. Fed. 27 Q4
Knaresborough U.K. 35 F4
Knee Lake Canada 123 M4
Knetzgau Germany 36 E4
Kneževi Vinogradi Croatia 44 G2
Knezha Bulg. 46 D3
Knić Serb. and Mont. 46 B3
Knife r. U.S.A. 132 A2
Knighton U.K. 35 E5
Knights Landing U.S.A. 136 B2
Knin Croatia 44 F2
Knittelfeld Austria 37 G5
Knivsta Sweden 33 E4
Knizhovnik Bulg. 46 D4
Knjaževac Serb. and Mont. 46 C3
Knob Lake Canada see Schefferville
Knockaboy hill Rep. of Ireland 35 B6
Knockmealdown Mountains hills Rep. of Ireland 35 B5
Knokke-Heist Belgium 36 A3
Knosos tourist site Greece see Knossos
Knossós tourist site Greece see Knossos
Knossos tourist site Greece 47 D7
Knox U.S.A. 130 D3
Knox, Cape Canada 122 C4
Knox Coast Antarctica 167 F2
Knoxville GA U.S.A. 129 C5
Knoxville TN U.S.A. 128 C5
Knud Rasmussen Land reg. Greenland 121 M2
Knyazhitsy Rus. Fed. 33 H4
Knysna S. Africa 98 D7
Ko, Gora mt. Rus. Fed. 64 D3
Koani Tanz. 97 C6
Koartac Canada see Quaqtaq
Koba Indon. 59 D3
Kobayashi Japan 65 B7
Kōbe Japan 65 C6
København Denmark see Copenhagen
Kobenni Mauritania 92 C2
Koblenz Germany 36 C3
K'obo Eth. 96 C1
Koboldo Rus. Fed. 64 C1
Kobrin Belarus see Kobryn
Kobroör i. Indon. 57 H7
Kobryn Belarus 29 C5
Kobuk Valley National Park U.S.A. 120 D3
K'obulet'i Georgia 79 E2
Kobyay Rus. Fed. 27 M3
Kocaafşar r. Turkey 47 F4
Koca Dag mt. Turkey 47 F5
Kocaeli Turkey 78 B2
Kocaeli prov. Turkey 46 F4
Kočani Macedonia 46 C4
Koçarlı Turkey 47 E6
Kocasu r. Turkey 78 B2
Koceljevo Serb. and Mont. 46 A2
Kočevje Slovenia 44 E2
Koch'ang S. Korea 65 A6
Koch Bihar India 75 F4
Kocher r. Germany 36 D4
Kocherinovo Bulg. 46 C3
Kochevo Rus. Fed. 28 J4
Kochi India see Cochin
Kōchi Japan 65 C6
Koçhisar Turkey see Kızıltepe
Kochubey Rus. Fed. 29 H7
Kochylas hill Greece 47 D5
Kock Poland 37 K3
Kod India 72 B3
Kodaikanal India 72 C4
Kodari Nepal 75 E4
Kodarma India 75 E4
Kodiak U.S.A. 120 D4
Kodiak Island U.S.A. 120 D4
Kodinar India 72 A1
Kodino Rus. Fed. 28 F3
Kodiyakkarai India 72 C4
Kodok Sudan 96 B2
Kodori r. Georgia 79 E2
Kodumuru India 72 C3
Kodyma Ukr. 29 D6
Kodzhaele mt. Bulg./Greece 46 D4
Koës Namibia 98 C5
Kofa Mountains U.S.A. 137 F5
Kofarnihon Tajik. 81 G2
Kofarnihon r. Tajik. 81 G2
Koffiefontein S. Africa 98 E6
Kofinas, Oros mt. Greece 47 D7
Köflach Austria 37 G5
Koforidua Ghana 93 E4
Kōfu Japan 65 D6
Kogălniceanu airport Romania 46 F2
Kogaluc r. Canada 124 E1
Kogaluk r. Canada 125 I1
Kögart Kyrg. see Alaykuu
Køge Denmark 33 D5
Kogi state Nigeria 93 G3
Kogon Uzbek. see Kagan
Kogoni Mali 92 D2
Kohat Pak. 81 G3
Kohila Estonia 33 G4
Kohima India 75 G4
Kohkīlūyeh va Būyer Aḩmadī prov. Iran 80 B4
Kohler Range mts Antarctica 167 K2
Kohls Ranch U.S.A. 137 G4
Kohlu Pak. 81 G4
Kohouro well Chad 88 D5
Kohsan Afgh. 81 E3
Kohtla-Järve Estonia 28 C4
Koidern Canada 122 A2
Koigi Estonia 33 G4
Koihoa India 73 G4
Koilkonda India 72 C2
Koin r. Rus. Fed. 28 I3
Koi Sanjaq Iraq 79 F3
Koitere l. Fin. 32 H3
Koivu Fin. 32 G2
Kŏje-do i. S. Korea 65 B6
Kojonup Australia 109 B8
Kok r. Thai. 60 C3
Kokand Uzbek. 81 G1
Kökar Fin. 33 F4
Kok-Art Kyrg. see Alaykuu
Kokcha r. Afgh. 81 G2
Kokchetav Kazakh. see Kokshetau
Kokemäki Fin. 33 F3
Kokerboom Namibia 98 C6
Koki Senegal 92 B2
Kokkina Cyprus 77 A2
Kokkola Fin. 32 F3
Koknese Latvia 33 G4
Koko Nigeria 93 G3
Kokofata Mali 92 C2
Kokolo-Pozo Côte d'Ivoire 92 D4
Kokomo U.S.A. 132 E3
Kokong Botswana 98 D5
Kokoro Benin 93 F3
Kokou mt. Guinea 92 B3
Kokpekti Kazakh. 70 F2
Koksan N. Korea 65 A5
Kokshaal-Tau mts China/Kyrg. 70 E3
Kokshetau Kazakh. 26 G4
Koksoak r. Canada 125 G1
Kokstad S. Africa 99 F6
Koktokay China see Fuyun
Kola Rus. Fed. 32 I1
Kola r. Rus. Fed. 32 I1
Kolab r. India see Sabari
Kolabira India 73 E1
Kolachi r. Pak. 81 F5
Kolaghat India 75 E5
Kolahoi mt. Jammu and Kashmir 74 B2
Kolaka Indon. 57 F6
Kolana Indon. 108 D2
Ko Lanta Thai. 61 B7
Kola Peninsula Rus. Fed. 28 E2
Kolar Chhattisgarh India 72 D2
Kolar Karnataka India 72 C3
Kolaras India 74 C4
Kolar Gold Fields India 72 C3
Kolari Fin. 32 F2
Kolarovgrad Bulg. see Shumen
Kolašin Serb. and Mont. 46 A3
Kolayat India 74 B4
Kolberg Poland see Kołobrzeg
Kolbio Kenya 96 D5
Kolda Senegal 92 B2
Kolding Denmark 33 C5
Kole Kasai Oriental Dem. Rep. Congo 94 D5
Kole Orientale Dem. Rep. Congo 94 E4
Koléa Alg. 43 H4
Kolguyev, Ostrov i. Rus. Fed. 28 I1
Kolhan reg. India 75 E5
Kolhapur India 72 B2
Kolhumadulu Atoll Maldives 71 D11
Koliba r. Guinea/Guinea-Bissau 92 B2
Kolikata India see Kolkata
Kolima l. Fin. 32 G3
Kolín Czech Rep. 37 G3
Kolin kansallispuisto nat. park Fin. 32 H3
Kõljala Estonia 33 F4
Kolkasrags pt Latvia 33 F4

▶Kolkata India 75 F5
3rd most populous city in Asia and 7th in the world.
world 16–17

Kolkhozabad Tajik. see Kolkhozobod
Kolkhozobod Tajik. 81 G2
Kollam India see Quilon
Kollegal India 72 C3
Kolleru Lake India 72 D2
Kollo Niger 93 F2
Köln Germany see Cologne
Kolno Poland 37 J2
Koło Poland 37 I2
Kolo Tanz. 97 B6
Kołobrzeg Poland 37 G1
Kologriv Rus. Fed. 28 H4
Kolokani Mali 92 C2
Kolombangara i. Solomon Is 107 E2
Kolomea Ukr. see Kolomyya
Kolomna Rus. Fed. 29 F5
Kolomonyi Dem. Rep. Congo 95 D6
Kolomyja Ukr. see Kolomyya
Kolomyya Ukr. 29 C6
Kolondiéba Mali 92 D3
Kolonedale Indon. 57 F6
Kolonjë Albania 46 A4
Kolonkwane Botswana 98 D5
Kolozero, Ozero l. Rus. Fed. 32 I1
Kolozsvár Romania see Cluj-Napoca
Kolpashevo Rus. Fed. 26 I4
Kol'skiy Poluostrov pen. Rus. Fed. see Kola Peninsula
Kölsvallen Sweden 33 D3
Koltubanovskiy Rus. Fed. 29 I5
Kolubara r. Serb. and Mont. 46 B2
Kölük Turkey see Kahta

Koluli Eritrea 89 I6
Kolva r. Rus. Fed. 28 K2
Kolva r. Rus. Fed. 28 K3
Kolvereid Norway 32 C2
Kolvik Norway 32 G1
Kolvitsa Rus. Fed. 32 I2
Kolvitskoye, Ozero l. Rus. Fed. 28 E2
Kolwezi Dem. Rep. Congo 95 E7
Kolya r. India 72 B2
Kolyma r. Rus. Fed. 27 Q3
Kolyma Lowland Rus. Fed. see Kolymskaya Nizmennost'
Kolyma Range mts Rus. Fed. see Kolymskiy, Khrebet
Kolymskaya Nizmennost' lowland Rus. Fed. 27 P3
Kolymskiy, Khrebet mts Rus. Fed. 27 Q3
Kolymskoye Vodokhranilische resr Rus. Fed. 27 O3
Kolyshley Rus. Fed. 29 H5
Kolyuchinskaya Guba b. Rus. Fed. 120 B3
Kom mt. Bulg. 46 C3
Komadugu-gana watercourse Nigeria 93 I2
Komaga-take vol. Japan 64 E4
Komagvær Norway 32 H1
Komandnaya, Gora mt. Rus. Fed. 64 D2
Komandorskiye Ostrova is Rus. Fed. 27 Q4
Komarnica r. Serb. and Mont. 46 A3
Komárno Slovakia 37 I5
Komati r. Swaziland 99 F5
Komatipoort S. Africa 99 F5
Komatsu Japan 65 D5
Komatsushima Japan 65 C6
Komba Dem. Rep. Congo 94 E4
Komba i. Indon. 57 F7
Kombat Namibia 98 C3
Kombe Dem. Rep. Congo 95 E6
Kombe Tanz. 97 A6
Kombissiri Burkina 93 E2
Komering r. Indon. 58 D3
Komi, Respublika aut. rep. Rus. Fed. 28 I3
Komi A.S.S.R. aut. rep. Rus. Fed. see Komi, Respublika
Komintern Ukr. see Marhanets'
Komi-Permyak Autonomous Okrug admin. div. Rus. Fed. see Komi-Permyatskiy Avtonomnyy Okrug
Komi-Permyatskiy Avtonomnyy Okrug admin. div. Rus. Fed. 28 J3
Komi Republic aut. rep. Rus. Fed. see Komi, Respublika
Komiža Croatia 44 F3
Komló Hungary 44 G1
Kommunarsk Ukr. see Alchevs'k
Kommunizm, Qullai mt. Tajik. see Garmo, Qullai
Kommunizma, Pik mt. Tajik. see Garmo, Qullai
Komodo i. Indon. 108 B2
Komodo National Park Indon. 57 E7
Komodou Guinea 92 C3
Komoé r. Côte d'Ivoire 92 E4
Komono Congo 94 B5
Komoran i. Indon. 57 I7
Komotini Greece 46 D4
Kompong Cham Cambodia see Kâmpóng Cham
Kompong Chhnang Cambodia see Kâmpóng Chhnăng
Kompong Kleang Cambodia see Kâmpóng Khleăng
Kompong Som Cambodia see Sihanoukville
Kompong Som Bay Cambodia see Sihanoukville, Chhâk
Kompong Speu Cambodia see Kâmpóng Spœ
Kompong Thom Cambodia see Kâmpóng Thum
Komrat Moldova see Comrat
Komsomol Atyrauskaya Oblast' Kazakh. see Komsomol'skiy
Komsomol Kazakh. see Karabalyk
Komsomol Turkm. see Komsomol'sk
Komsomolets, Ostrov i. Rus. Fed. 27 J1
Komsomolets, Zaliv b. Kazakh. 29 J7
Komsomol'sk Turkm. 81 E2
Komsomol's'k Ukr. 29 E6
Komsomol'skiy Kazakh. 29 J7
Komsomol'skiy Rus. Fed. 27 R3
Komsomol'skiy Khanty-Mansiyskiy Avtonomnyy Okrug Rus. Fed. see Yugorsk
Komsomol'skiy Respublika Kalmykiya - Khalm'g-Tangch Rus. Fed. 29 H7
Komsomol'skiy Respublika Mordoviya Rus. Fed. 29 H5
Komsomol'sk-na-Amure Rus. Fed. 64 D2
Komuniga Bulg. 46 D4
Kon India 75 D4
Konacık Turkey 77 B1
Konada India 73 D2
Konar prov. Afgh. 81 G3
Konarak India see Konarka
Konarka India 73 E2
Konch India 74 C4
Konchezero Rus. Fed. 28 E3
Kondagaon India 73 D2
Kondapalle India 72 D2
Kondinin Australia 109 B8
Kondinskoye Rus. Fed. see Oktyabr'skoye
Kondoa Tanz. 97 B6
Kondol' Rus. Fed. 29 H5
Kondopoga Rus. Fed. 28 E3
Kondūz Afgh. 81 G2
Kondūz prov. Afgh. 81 G2
Konečka Planina mts Macedonia 46 C4
Kong Cameroon 93 I4
Kong Côte d'Ivoire 92 D3
Kông, Kaôh i. Cambodia 61 C6
Kông, Tônlé r. Cambodia 61 D5
Kong, Xé r. Laos 61 D5
Kongbo Cent. Afr. Rep. 94 D3
Kong Christian IX Land reg. Greenland 121 P3
Kong Christian X Land reg. Greenland 121 Q2
Kong Frederik VI Kyst coastal area Greenland 121 O3
Kong Frederik VIII Land reg. Greenland 121 Q2
Kong Frederik IX Land reg. Greenland 121 N3
Kong Karls Land is Svalbard 26 C2
Kongkemul mt. Indon. 59 G2
Kongola Namibia 98 D3
Kongolo Dem. Rep. Congo 95 E6
Kong Oscars Fjord inlet Greenland 121 Q2
Kongoussi Burkina 93 E2
Kongsberg Norway 33 C4
Kongsfjord Norway 32 H1
Kongsvinger Norway 33 D3
Kongur Shan mt. China 70 E4
Kongwa Tanz. 97 C6
Kong Wilhelm Land reg. Greenland 121 Q2
Konibodom Tajik. see Kanibadam
Koniecpol Poland 37 I3
Königsberg Rus. Fed. see Kaliningrad
Königsbrunn Germany 36 E4
Königs Wusterhausen Germany 37 F2
Konimekh Uzbek. see Kanimekh
Konin Poland 37 I2
Konin r. Rus. Fed. 64 D1
Konitsa Greece 47 B4
Köniz Switz. 39 G3
Konj mt. Bos.-Herz. 44 F3
Konjic Bos.-Herz. 44 F3
Konjuh mts Bos.-Herz. 44 G2
Könkämäeno r. Fin./Sweden 32 F1
Konkiep watercourse Namibia 98 C6
Konkwesso Nigeria 93 G3
Konna Mali 92 E2
Konnarock U.S.A. 130 C5
Konongo Ghana 93 E4
Konosha Rus. Fed. 28 G3
Konotop Ukr. 29 E6
Kon Plong Vietnam 61 E5
Końskie Poland 37 J3
Konso Eth. 96 C3
Konstantinograd Ukr. see Krasnohrad
Konstantinovka Rus. Fed. 64 A2
Konstantinovka Ukr. see Kostyantynivka
Konstanz Germany 36 D5
Kontagora Nigeria 93 G3
Kontcha Cameroon 93 I4
Kontiomäki Fin. 32 H2
Konttila Fin. 32 G2
Kon Tum Vietnam 61 D5
Kontum, Plateau du Vietnam 61 E5
Könugard Ukr. see Kiev
Konushin, Mys pt Rus. Fed. 28 G2
Konya Turkey 78 C3
Konz Germany 36 C4
Konzhakovskiy Kamen', Gora mt. Rus. Fed. 28 K4
Koocanusa, Lake resr Canada/U.S.A. 123 H5
Kookynie Australia 109 C7
Kooline Australia 108 B5
Koolkootinnie, Lake salt flat Australia 112 A3
Koolyanobbing Australia 109 B7
Koorawatha Australia 112 D4
Koorda Australia 109 B7
Koordarrie Australia 108 A5
Koosharem U.S.A. 137 G2
Kooskia U.S.A. 134 C3
Kootenay r. Canada 123 G5
Kootenay Lake Canada 134 C2
Kootenay National Park Canada 123 G5
Kootjieskolk S. Africa 98 D6
Kopa Zambia 97 A7
Kopaonik mts Serb. and Mont. 46 B3
Kopaonik nat. park Serb. and Mont. 46 B3
Kopargaon India 72 B2
Kópasker Iceland 32 [inset]
Koper Slovenia 44 D2
Kopet Dag mts Iran/Turkm. 80 D2
Kopet-Dag, Khrebet mts Iran/Turkm. see Kopet Dag
Köping Sweden 33 E4
Koplik Albania 46 A3
Koppa India 72 B3
Koppal India 72 C3
Koppang Norway 33 C3
Koppány r. Hungary 37 I5
Kopparberg Sweden 33 D4
Kopparberg county Sweden see Dalarna
Koppeh Dāgh mts Iran/Turkm. see Kopet Dag
Koppi r. Rus. Fed. 64 E2
Koprinka, Yazovir resr Bulg. 46 D3
Koprivnica Croatia 44 F1
Köprü r. Turkey 78 B3
Köprülü Kanyon Milli Parkı nat. park Turkey 78 B3
Kopu Estonia 33 G4
Korab mts Albania/Macedonia 46 B4
Korablino Rus. Fed. 29 G5
Koraf well Eth. 96 E3
K'orahē Eth. 96 E3
Korana r. Bos.-Herz./Croatia 44 E2
Korangal India 72 C2
Koraput India 73 D2
Korat Thai. see Nakhon Ratchasima
Koratla India 72 C2
Korba India 75 D5
Korba Tunisia 45 C6
Korbach Germany 36 D3
Korbous Tunisia 45 C6
Korbu, Gunung mt. Malaysia 58 C1
Korçë Albania 46 B4
Korčula Croatia 44 F3
Korčula i. Croatia 44 F3
Korčulanski Kanal sea chan. Croatia 44 F3
Kordestān prov. Iran 80 A3
Kord Kūy Iran 80 C2
Kordon Rus. Fed. 28 K4
▶Korea, North country Asia 65 A4
asia 52–53, 82
▶Korea, South country Asia 65 A5
asia 52–53, 82
Korea Bay g. China/N. Korea 65 A5
Koreare Indon. 108 E1
Korea Strait Japan/S. Korea 65 B6
Koregaon India 72 B2
Korem Eth. 96 C1
Korenovsk Rus. Fed. 29 F7
Korenovskaya Rus. Fed. see Korenovsk
Korets' Ukr. 29 C6
Korf Rus. Fed. 27 Q3
Körfez Turkey 78 B2
Korff Ice Rise Antarctica 167 L1
Korfovskiy Rus. Fed. 64 C2
Korgen Norway 32 D2
Korhogo Côte d'Ivoire 92 D3
Koriabo Guyana 147 G3
Kori Creek inlet India 74 A5
Korinos Greece 47 C4
Korinthos Greece see Corinth
Köris-hegy hill Hungary 37 H5
Koritsa Albania see Korçë
Kōriyama Japan 65 E5
Korkana Fin. 32 H2
Korkī Iran 80 D2
Korkodon r. Rus. Fed. 27 P3
Korkuteli Turkey 78 B3
Körkvere Estonia 33 F4
Korla China 70 G3
Kormakitis, Cape Cyprus 77 A2
Korman mt. Serb. and Mont. 46 A3
Körmend Hungary 37 H5
Kornat i. Croatia 44 E3
Kornat nat. park Croatia 44 E3
Kornsjø Norway 33 C4
Koro Côte d'Ivoire 92 D3
Koro i. Fiji 107 G3
Koro Mali 92 E2
Koroc r. Canada 125 H1
Köroğlu Dağları mts Turkey 78 C2
Köroğlu Tepesi mt. Turkey 78 C2
Korogo well Eth. 96 D3
Korogwe Tanz. 97 C6
Korom, Bahr watercourse Chad 94 C2
Koroni Greece 47 B6
Koronowo Poland 37 H2
Koropi Greece 47 C6

▶Koror Palau 57 H4
Capital of Palau.

Körös r. Romania 46 B1
Koro Sea b. Fiji 107 G3
Körösladány Hungary 37 J5
Korosten' Ukr. 29 D6
Korostyshiv Ukr. 29 D6
Korotaikha r. Rus. Fed. 28 L1
Korotnik mt. Albania 46 B3
Koro Toro Chad 88 C5
Korpilahti Fin. 33 G3
Korpilombolo Sweden 32 F2
Korpivaara Fin. 32 H3
Korpo Fin. 33 F3
Korppoo Fin. see Korpo
Korsakov Rus. Fed. 64 E3
Korskrogen Sweden 33 D3
Korsnäs Fin. 32 F3
Korsør Denmark 33 C5
Korsze Poland 37 J1
Kortala Sudan 89 F6
Kortesjärvi Fin. 32 F3
Korti Sudan 89 F5
Kortkeros Rus. Fed. 28 I3
Kortrijk Belgium 39 E1
Korucu Turkey 47 E5
Korup, Parc National de nat. park Cameroon 93 H4
Korvala Fin. 32 G2
Korwai India 74 C4
Koryakskaya, Sopka vol. Rus. Fed. 27 P4
Koryakskiy Khrebet mts Rus. Fed. 27 R3
Koryazhma Rus. Fed. 28 H3
Koryŏng S. Korea 65 B6
Korzhun Kazakh. 29 J6
Kos Greece 47 E6
Kos i. Greece 47 E6
Kosa Rus. Fed. 28 J4
Kosa r. Rus. Fed. 28 J3
Kosan N. Korea 65 A5
Koschagyl Kazakh. 29 J7
Kościan Poland 37 H2
Kościerzyna Poland 37 H1
Kosciusko U.S.A. 133 D5
Kosciusko, Mount Australia see Kosciuszko, Mount
Kosciusko Island U.S.A. 122 C3
Kosciuszko, Mount Australia 112 D5
Kosciuszko National Park Australia 112 D5
Kose Estonia 33 G4
Köseçobanlı Turkey 77 A1
Köse Dağı mt. Turkey 79 D2
Kosha Sudan 89 F4
Kosh-Agach Rus. Fed. 27 I5
Koshankol' Kazakh. 29 I6
Koshbulakskoye Vodokhranilische resr Turkm. 81 E1
Koshikijima-rettō is Japan 65 B7
Koshk Afgh. 81 E3
Koshk-e Kohneh Afgh. 81 E3
Koshki Rus. Fed. 29 I5
Kosi r. India 74 C3
Košice Slovakia 37 J4
Kosigi India 72 C3
Kosi Reservoir Nepal 75 E4
Kosjerić Serb. and Mont. 46 A3
Köşk Turkey 47 F6
Köslin Poland see Koszalin
Kosma r. Rus. Fed. 28 I2
Košnica r. Croatia 44 G2
Koson Uzbek. see Kasan
Kosŏng N. Korea 65 B5
Kosova prov. Serb. and Mont. see Kosovo
Kosovo prov. Serb. and Mont. 46 B3
Kosovo-Metohija prov. Serb. and Mont. see Kosovo
Kosovo Polje Serb. and Mont. 46 B3
Kosovo Polje plain Serb. and Mont. 46 B3
Kosovska Mitrovica Serb. and Mont. 46 B3
Kosrae atoll Micronesia 164 E5
Kossa well Mauritania 92 D2
Kossatori well Niger 93 I2
Kösseine hill Germany 36 E4
Kossol Reef Palau 57 H4
Kossou, Lac de l. Côte d'Ivoire 92 D4
Kosta-Khetagurovo Rus. Fed. see Nazran'
Kostanay Kazakh. 26 G4
Kostenets Bulg. 46 C3
Kosti Sudan 89 G6
Kostinbrod Bulg. 46 C3
Kostino Rus. Fed. 27 I3
Kostolac Serb. and Mont. 46 B2
Kostomuksha Rus. Fed. 32 H2
Kostopil' Ukr. 29 C6
Kostopol' Ukr. see Kostopil'
Kostroma Rus. Fed. 28 G4
Kostroma r. Rus. Fed. 28 G4
Kostroma Oblast admin. div. Rus. Fed. see Kostromskaya Oblast'
Kostromskaya Oblast' admin. div. Rus. Fed. 28 G4
Kostrzyn Poland 37 G2
Kostrzyń r. Poland 37 K2
Kostyantynivka Ukr. 29 F6
Kostyukovichi Belarus see Kastsyukovichy
Kosubosu Nigeria 93 F3
Kos'yu Rus. Fed. 28 K2
Kos'yu r. Rus. Fed. 28 K2
Koszalin Poland 37 H1
Kőszeg Hungary 37 H5
Kota Andhra Pradesh India 72 D3
Kota Chhattisgarh India 75 D5
Kota Rajasthan India 74 B4
Kotaagung Indon. 58 D4
Kota Baharu Malaysia see Kota Bharu
Kotabaru Kalimantan Barat Indon. 59 E3
Kotabaru Kalimantan Selatan Indon. 59 G3
Kota Belud Sabah Malaysia 59 G1
Kota Bharu Malaysia 58 C1
Kotabumi Indon. 58 D4
Kot Addu Pak. 81 G4
Kota Kinabalu Sabah Malaysia 59 G1
Kotala Fin. 32 H2
Kotapinang Indon. 58 C2
Kotari r. India 74 B4
Kota Tinggi Malaysia 58 C2
Kotawaringin Indon. 59 E3
Kotchandpur Bangl. 75 F5
Kotcho r. Canada 122 F3
Kotcho Lake Canada 122 F3
Kot Diji Pak. 81 G5
Kotdwara India 74 C3
Koteasro Afgh. 74 A2
Kotel Bulg. 46 E3
Kotel'nich Rus. Fed. 28 I4
Kotel'nikovo Rus. Fed. 29 G7
Kotel'nyy, Ostrov i. Rus. Fed. 27 N2
Kotgar India 73 D2
Kotgarh India 74 C3
Kothagudem India see Kottagudem
Köthen (Anhalt) Germany 36 E3
Kothi India 74 D4
Kotiari Naoude Senegal 92 B2
Kotido Uganda 96 B4
Kotka Fin. 33 G3
Kot Kapura India 74 B3
Kotkino Rus. Fed. 28 I2
Kotlas Rus. Fed. 28 H3
Kotli Pak. 81 H3
Kotlik U.S.A. 120 C3
Kotlina Sandomierska basin Poland 37 J3
Kötlutangi pt Iceland 32 [inset]
Kotly Rus. Fed. 28 D4
Koton-Karifi Nigeria 93 G3
Kotorkoshi Nigeria 93 G2
Kotorsko Bos.-Herz. 44 G2
Kotor Varoš Bos.-Herz. 44 F2
Kotouba Côte d'Ivoire 92 E3
Kotovo Rus. Fed. 29 H6
Kotovsk Rus. Fed. 29 G5
Kotovs'k Ukr. 41 H2
Kot Putli India 74 C4
Kotri r. India 72 D2
Kotri Pak. 81 G5
Kotronas Greece 47 C6
Kottagudem India 72 D2
Kottayam India 72 C4
Kotte Sri Lanka see Sri Jayewardenepura Kotte
Kotto r. Cent. Afr. Rep. 94 D3
Kotturu India 72 C3
Kotuy r. Rus. Fed. 27 K2
Kotwar Peak India 75 D5
Kotzebue U.S.A. 120 C3
Kotzebue Sound sea chan. U.S.A. 120 C3
Kouango Cent. Afr. Rep. 94 D3
Kouba Olanga Chad 88 C6
Koubia Guinea 92 C3
Kouchibouguac National Park Canada 125 H4
Koudougou Burkina 93 E2
Kouéré Burkina 92 E3
Koufonisi i. Kriti Greece 47 E7
Koufonisi i. Greece 47 D6
Koufos Greece 47 C5
Kougaberge mts S. Africa 98 D7
Koui Cent. Afr. Rep. 94 B3
Kouilou admin. reg. Congo 95 A6
Kouki Cent. Afr. Rep. 94 C3
Koukourou r. Cent. Afr. Rep. 94 C3
Koulamoutou Gabon 94 B5
Koulbo Chad 88 D6
Koulikoro Mali 92 D2
Koulikoro admin. reg. Mali 92 D2
Kouloudia Chad 88 B6
Koum Cameroon 93 I3
Kouma r. Cent. Afr. Rep. 94 C3
Koumac New Caledonia 107 F4
Koumala Australia 111 G4
Koumameyong Gabon 94 A4
Koumbala Cent. Afr. Rep. 94 D2
Koumbia Burkina 92 E3
Koumbia Guinea 92 B3
Koumogo Chad 94 C2
Koumra Chad 94 C2
Koundâra Guinea 92 B2
Koundian Mali 92 C2
Koundougou Burkina 92 D3
Koungheul Senegal 92 B2
Kounoupoi i. Greece 47 E6
Kounsitél Guinea 92 B3
Kountchi well Niger 93 H2
Kountze U.S.A. 133 C6
Koupéla Burkina 93 E2
Kouqian China see Yongji
Kournas Greece 47 D7
Kourou Fr. Guiana 147 H3
Kourou r. Greece 46 D4
Kouroudjél Mauritania 92 C1
Kouroussa Guinea 92 C3
Koussanar Senegal 92 B2
Koussané Mali 92 C2
Kousséri Cameroon 88 B6
Koussountou Togo 93 F3
Koutiala Mali 92 D2
Kouto Côte d'Ivoire 92 D3
Kouvola Fin. 33 G3
Kouyou r. Congo 94 C5
Kovačica Serb. and Mont. 46 B2
Kovdor Rus. Fed. 32 H2
Kovdozero Rus. Fed. 32 H2
Kovdozero, Ozero l. Rus. Fed. 32 I2
Kovel' Ukr. 29 C6
Kovernino Rus. Fed. 28 G4
Kovilpatti India 72 C4
Kovin Serb. and Mont. 46 B2
Kovno Lith. see Kaunas
Kovriga, Gora hill Rus. Fed. 28 I2
Kovrov Rus. Fed. 28 G4
Kovylkino Rus. Fed. 29 G5
Kovzhskoye, Ozero l. Rus. Fed. 28 F3
Kowanyama Australia 111 E2
Kowares waterhole Namibia 98 B3
Kowli Kosh, Gardaneh-ye pass Iran 80 C4
Kowloon Hong Kong China 67 [inset]
Kowloon Peak hill Hong Kong China 67 [inset]
Kowloon Peninsula Hong Kong China 67 [inset]
Kowr-e-Koja watercourse Iran 81 E5
Kōyama-misaki pt Japan 65 B6
Köyceğiz Turkey 78 B3
Köyceğiz Gölü l. Turkey 47 F6
Koygorodok Rus. Fed. 28 I3
Koymatdag, Gory hills Turkm. 80 C1
Koynare Bulg. 46 D3
Koyna Reservoir India 72 B2
Koyuk r. U.S.A. 120 D3
Koyulhisar Turkey 79 D2
Kozağacı Turkey see Günyüzü
Kō-zaki pt Japan 65 B6
Kozan Turkey 78 C3
Kozani Greece 47 B4
Kozara mts Bos.-Herz. 44 F2
Kozara nat. park Bos.-Herz. 44 F2
Kozarska Dubica Bos.-Herz. see Bosanska Dubica
Kozel'sk Rus. Fed. 29 E5
Kozen well Chad 88 C4
Kozhevnikovo Rus. Fed. 27 L2
Kozhikode India see Calicut
Kozhim-Iz, Gora mt. Rus. Fed. 28 K3
Kozhva Rus. Fed. 28 K2
Kozhva r. Rus. Fed. 28 K2
Kozhym r. Rus. Fed. 28 K2
Kozienice Poland 37 J3
Kozlocuy Bulg. 46 C3
Kozluk Bos.-Herz. 46 A2
Koźmin Poland 37 H3
Koz'modem'yansk Rus. Fed. 28 H4
Koznitsa mt. Bulg. 46 C3
Kożuchów Poland 37 G3
Kožuf mts Greece/Macedonia 46 C4
Kōzu-shima i. Japan 65 D6
Kozyatyn Ukr. 29 D6
Kozyörük Turkey 46 E4
Kpalimé Togo 93 F4
Kpandae Ghana 93 E3
Kpandu Ghana 93 F4
Kpungan Pass India/Myanmar 60 B2
Kra, Isthmus of Thai. 61 B6
Krabi Thai. 61 B6
Kra Buri Thai. 61 B6
Krâchéh Cambodia 61 D5
Kräckelbäcken Sweden 33 D3
Kragerø Norway 33 C4
Kragujevac Serb. and Mont. 46 B2
Krajenka Poland 37 H2
Krakatau i. Indon. 58 D4
Krakatau Volcano National Park Indon. 58 D4
Krakau Poland see Kraków
Kråkdivollen Norway 32 C3
Kraków Poland 37 I3
Kralendijk Neth. Antilles 146 D1
Kraljevica Croatia 44 E2
Kraljevo Serb. and Mont. 46 B3
Kráľova hoľa mt. Slovakia 37 J4
Kralupy nad Vltavou Czech Rep. 37 G3
Kramators'k Ukr. 29 F6
Kramfors Sweden 32 E3
Krammer est. Neth. 36 B3
Kranidi Greece 47 C6
Kranj Slovenia 44 E1
Kranji Reservoir Sing. 58 [inset]
Krapanj Croatia 44 E3
Krapkowice Poland 37 H3
Krasavino Rus. Fed. 28 H3
Krasilov Ukr. see Krasyliv
Krasino Rus. Fed. 26 F2
Kraskino Rus. Fed. 64 B4
Krāslava Latvia 33 G5
Krasnaya Polyana Rus. Fed. 29 G8
Krasnaya Zarya Rus. Fed. 29 F5
Kraśnik Poland 37 K3
Krasnoarmeysk Kazakh. see Tayynsha
Krasnoarmeysk Rus. Fed. 29 H6
Krasnoarmeysk Ukr. see Krasnoarmiys'k
Krasnoarmeyskiy Rus. Fed. 27 R3
Krasnoarmiys'k Ukr. 29 F6
Krasnoborsk Rus. Fed. 28 H3
Krasnodar Rus. Fed. 29 F7
Krasnodar Kray admin. div. Rus. Fed. see Krasnodarskiy Kray
Krasnodarskiy Kray admin. div. Rus. Fed. 29 F7
Krasnofarfornyy Rus. Fed. 31 L1
Krasnogorodskoye Rus. Fed. 33 H4
Krasnogorsk Rus. Fed. 64 E2
Krasnogorskoye Rus. Fed. 28 J4
Krasnograd Ukr. see Krasnohrad
Krasnogvardeysk Uzbek. see Bulungur
Krasnogvardeyskoye Rus. Fed. 29 G7
Krasnohrad Ukr. 29 E6
Krasnohvardiys'ke Ukr. 29 E7
Krasnokamensk Rus. Fed. 63 J2
Krasnokamsk Rus. Fed. 28 J4
Krasnokholm Rus. Fed. 29 J6
Krasnoles'ye Rus. Fed. 37 K1
Krasnoostrovskiy Rus. Fed. 33 H3
Krasnoperekops'k Ukr. 29 E7
Krasnopol'ye Rus. Fed. 64 E2
Krasnorechenskiy Rus. Fed. 64 C3
Krasnosel'kup Rus. Fed. 26 I3
Krasnoslobodsk Rus. Fed. 29 G5
Krasnotur'insk Rus. Fed. 26 G4
Krasnoufimsk Rus. Fed. 28 K4
Krasnousol'skiy Rus. Fed. 28 K5
Krasnovishersk Rus. Fed. 28 K3
Krasnovodsk Turkm. see Turkmenbashi
Krasnovodskaya Oblast' admin. div. Turkm. see Balkanskaya Oblast'
Krasnovodskiy Zaliv b. Turkm. 80 C2
Krasnovodskoye Plato plat. Turkm. 80 C1
Krasnoyar Kazakh. 29 J6
Krasnoyarovo Rus. Fed. 64 B2
Krasnoyarsk Rus. Fed. 27 J4
Krasnoyarskiy Kray admin. div. Rus. Fed. 62 E1
Krasnoyarsk Kray admin. div. Rus. Fed. see Krasnoyarskiy Kray
Krasnoye Lipetskaya Oblast' Rus. Fed. 29 F5
Krasnoye Respublika Kalmykiya - Khalm'g-Tangch Rus. Fed. see Ulan Erge
Krasnoye, Ozero l. Rus. Fed. 27 R3
Krasnozatonskiy Rus. Fed. 28 I3
Krasnoznamensk Rus. Fed. 33 F5
Krasnyye Baki Rus. Fed. 28 H4
Krasnyye Barrikady Rus. Fed. 29 H7
Krasnyye Tkachi Rus. Fed. 28 F4
Krasnyy Kamyshanik Rus. Fed. see Komsomol'skiy
Krasnyy Kholm Rus. Fed. 28 F4
Krasnyy Kut Rus. Fed. 29 H6
Krasnyy Luch Ukr. 29 F6
Krasnyy Lyman Ukr. 29 F6
Krasnyy Yar Rus. Fed. 29 I7
Krasyliv Ukr. 29 C6
Kratie Cambodia see Krâchéh
Kratovo Macedonia 46 C3
Kraulshavn Greenland see Nuussuaq
Krâvanh, Chuŏr Phnum mts Cambodia see Cardamom Range
Kraynovka Rus. Fed. 79 F2
Krechevitsy Rus. Fed. 28 D4
Krefeld Germany 36 C3
Kremaston, Techniti Limni resr Greece 47 B5
Kremenchug Ukr. see Kremenchuk
Kremenchuk Ukr. 29 E6
Kremenchuts'ka Vodoskhovyshche resr Ukr. 29 E6
Kremges Ukr. see Svitlovods'k
Kremmling U.S.A. 134 F4
Krems an der Donau Austria 37 G4
Kremsmünster Austria 37 G4
Krenitzin Islands U.S.A. 120 C4
Krepoljin Serb. and Mont. 46 B2
Kresna Bulg. 46 C4
Kresta, Zaliv g. Rus. Fed. 27 S3
Krest-Khal'dzhayy Rus. Fed. 27 N3
Krestovka Rus. Fed. 28 J2
Kresttsy Rus. Fed. 28 E4
Krestyakh Rus. Fed. 27 L3
Kretinga Lith. 33 F5
Kreuth Germany 36 E5
Kreuzeck Gruppe mts Austria 37 F5
Kreuzlingen Switz. 39 H3
Kreuztal Germany 36 C3
Kribi Cameroon 93 H5
Krichev Belarus see Krychaw
Krichim Bulg. 46 D3
Krieza Greece 47 D5
Krikellos Greece 47 B5
Krikelos, Akra pt Greece 47 E6
Kril'on, Mys c. Rus. Fed. 64 E3
Krishna r. India 72 D2
Krishna, Mouths of the India 69 G5
Krishnagiri India 72 C3
Krishnai r. India 75 F4
Krishnanagar India 75 F5
Krishnaraja Sagara l. India 72 C3
Krishnarajpet India 72 C3
Kristdala Sweden 33 E4
Kristiania Norway see Oslo
Kristiansand Norway 33 B4
Kristianstad Sweden 33 D4
Kristiansund Norway 32 B3
Kristiinankaupunki Fin. see Kristinestad
Kristinehamn Sweden 33 D4
Kristinestad Fin. 33 F3
Kristinopol' Ukr. see Chervonohrad
Kriti admin. reg. Greece 47 D7
Kriti i. Greece see Crete
Krivaja r. Bos.-Herz. 44 G2
Kriva Palanka Macedonia 46 C3
Kriva Reka r. Macedonia 46 B3
Křivoklátská Vrchovina hills Czech Rep. 37 F4
Krivoy Porog Rus. Fed. 28 E2
Krivoy Rog Ukr. see Kryvyy Rih
Križevci Croatia 44 F1
Krk mt. Bos.-Herz. 46 A2
Krk Croatia 44 E2
Krk i. Croatia 44 E2
Krka r. Croatia 44 E3
Krka r. Slovenia 44 E2
Krkonošský narodní park nat. park Czech Rep./Poland 37 G3
Krnov Czech Rep. 37 H3
Krobia Poland 37 H3
Kroknes Norway 32 H1
Krokom Sweden 32 D3
Króksfjarðarnes Iceland 32 [inset]
Krokstadøra Norway 32 C3
Krolevets' Ukr. 29 E6
Kronach Germany 36 E3
Kronfjell hill Norway 33 C4
Krŏng Kaôh Kŏng Cambodia 61 C6
Kronli India 75 G3
Kronoberg county Sweden 33 D4
Kronoby Fin. 32 F3
Kronotskiy Zaliv b. Rus. Fed. 27 Q4
Kronprins Christian Land reg. Greenland 121 Q1
Kronprins Frederik Bjerge nunataks Greenland 121 P3
Kronstadt Romania see Braşov
Kroonstad S. Africa 99 E5
Kropotkin Rus. Fed. 29 G7
Krosno Poland 37 J4
Krosno Odrzańskie Poland 37 G2
Krossen Norway 33 C4
Krotoszyn Poland 37 H3
Kroya Indon. 59 E4
Krško Slovenia 44 E2
Kruger National Park S. Africa 99 F4
Kruglyakov Rus. Fed. see Oktyabr'skiy
Krui Indon. 58 C4
Kruisfontein S. Africa 98 E7
Krujë Albania 46 A4
Krumovgrad Bulg. 46 D4
Krungkao Thai. see Ayutthaya
Krung Thep Thai. see Bangkok
Krupa Bos.-Herz. see Bosanska Krupa
Krupa na Uni Bos.-Herz. see Bosanska Krupa
Krupina Slovakia 37 I4
Krupki Belarus 29 D5
Kruševac Serb. and Mont. 46 B3
Kruševo Macedonia 46 B4
Krušné Hory mts Czech Rep. 37 F3
Kruzof Island U.S.A. 122 C3
Krychaw Belarus 29 D5
Kryezi Albania 46 B3
Krylov Seamount sea feature N. Atlantic Ocean 160 M4
Krym' pen. Ukr. see Crimea
Krymsk Rus. Fed. 29 F7
Krymskaya Rus. Fed. see Krymsk
Kryms'kyy Pivostriv pen. Ukr. see Crimea
Krynica Poland 37 J4
Krystynopol Ukr. see Chervonohrad
Krytiko Pelagos sea Greece 47 D6
Kryvyy Rih Ukr. 29 E7
Krzyż Wielkopolski Poland 37 H2
Ksabi Alg. 91 E3
Ksar el Boukhari Alg. 43 H5
Ksar el Hirane Alg. 91 F2
Ksar el Kebir Morocco 90 D2
Ksar-es-Souk Morocco see Er Rachidia
Ksenofontova Rus. Fed. 28 J3
Kskyrbulak Yuzhnyy, Gora hill Turkm. 80 C1
Ksour, Monts des mts Tunisia 91 H2
Ksour Essaf Tunisia 45 C7
Kstovo Rus. Fed. 28 H4
Ku', Jabal al hill Saudi Arabia 80 A5
Ku, Wadi el watercourse Sudan 89 E6
Kuaidamao China see Tonghua
Kuala Belait Brunei 59 F1
Kuala Dungun Malaysia see Dungun
Kualajelai Indon. 59 E3
Kuala Kangsar Malaysia 58 C1
Kualakapuas Indon. 59 F3
Kuala Kerai Malaysia 58 C1
Kuala Kinabatangan r. mouth Sabah Malaysia 59 G1
Kuala Kubu Baharu Malaysia 58 C2
Kualakurun Indon. 59 F3
Kuala Lipis Malaysia 58 C1

▶Kuala Lumpur Malaysia 58 C2
National capital of Malaysia.

Kualapembuang Indon. 59 F3
Kuala Penyu Sabah Malaysia 59 F1
Kuala Pilah Malaysia 58 C2
Kualapuu U.S.A. 135 [inset] Z1
Kualasampit Indon. 59 F3
Kualasimpang Indon. 58 B1
Kuala Terengganu Malaysia 58 C1
Kualatungal Indon. 58 C3
Kuamut Sabah Malaysia 59 G1
Kuandian China 65 A4
Kuangyuan China see Yiliang
Kuanshan Taiwan 67 G4
Kuantan Malaysia 58 C2
Kuba Azer. see Quba
Kuban' r. Rus. Fed. 29 F7
Kubār Syria 79 D4
Kubbum Sudan 94 D2
Kubenskoye, Ozero l. Rus. Fed. 28 F4
Kubnya r. Rus. Fed. 28 I5
Kubor, Mount P.N.G. 57 J7
Kubrat Bulg. 46 E3
Kubumesaäi Indon. 59 F2
Kučevo Serb. and Mont. 46 B2
Kuchaman India 74 B4
Kuchema Rus. Fed. 28 G2
Kuching Sarawak Malaysia 59 E2
Kucing Sarawak Malaysia see Kuching
Kuçovë Albania 46 A4
Küçükmenderes r. Turkey 47 E4
Küçükmenderes r. Turkey 47 E6
Kuda India 74 A5
Kudachi India 72 B2
Kudal India 72 B3
Kudirkos Naumiestis Lith. 33 F5
Kudligi India 72 C3
Kudremukh mt. India 72 B3
Kudu Nigeria 93 G3
Kudus Indon. 59 E4
Kudymkar Rus. Fed. 28 J4
Kueishan Tao i. Taiwan 67 G3
Kufstein Austria 36 F5
Kugaaruk Canada 121 K3
Kugesi Rus. Fed. 28 H4
Kugka Lhai China 75 F3
Kugluktuk Canada 120 H3
Kūh, Ra's-al- pt Iran 80 D5
Kūhak Iran 81 E5
Kūhbonān Iran 80 D4
Kūhdasht Iran 80 A3
Kūhestak Iran 80 D5
Kūhīn Iran 80 B2
Kūhīrī Iran 81 E5
Kūhistoni Badakhshon aut. rep. Tajik. 81 H2
Kuhmo Fin. 32 H2
Kuhmoinen Fin. 33 G3
Kūhpāyeh Iran 80 C3
Kūhpāyeh mt. Iran 80 D4
Kūhrān, Kūh-e mt. Iran 80 D5
Kūhrang r. Iran 80 B4
Kui Buri Thai. 61 B5
Kuimetsa Estonia 33 G4
Kuis Namibia 98 C5
Kuiseb watercourse Namibia 98 B4
Kuitan China 67 E4
Kuitin China see Kuytun
Kuito Angola 95 C8
Kuiu Island U.S.A. 122 C3
Kuivaniemi Fin. 32 G2
Kuivastu Estonia 33 F4
Kujang India 73 E1
Kujang N. Korea 65 A5
Kuji Japan 65 E4
Kujū-san vol. Japan 65 B6
Kukālār, Kūh-e hill Iran 80 B4

Kukan Rus. Fed. 64 C2
Kukawa Nigeria 93 I2
Kukerin Australia 109 B8
Kukës Albania 46 B3
Kukkola Fin. 32 G2
Kukmor Rus. Fed. 28 I4
Kukshi India 74 B5
Kukup Malaysia 58 C2
Kukurtli Turkm. 81 D2
Kukusan, Gunung hill Indon. 59 F3
Kukushtan Rus. Fed. 28 K4
Kūl r. Iran 80 C5
Kula Bulg. 46 C3
Kula Nigeria 93 G4
Kula Turkey 78 B3
Kula Serb. and Mont. 46 A2
Kulabu, Gunung mt. Indon. 58 B2
Kulachi Pak. 81 G4
Kulagino Kazakh. 29 I6
Kula Kangri mt. Bhutan 75 F3
Kulal, Mount Kenya 96 C4
Kulandy Kazakh. 70 A2
Kulao r. Pak. 81 F4
Kular Rus. Fed. 27 N2
Kulat, Gunung mt. Indon. 59 G2
Kuldiga Latvia 33 F4
Kuldja China see **Yining**
Kul'dur Rus. Fed. 64 B2
Kul'dzhuktau, Gory hills Uzbek. 81 E1
Kule Botswana 98 D4
Kulebaki Rus. Fed. 28 G5
Kulgera Australia 110 C5
Kuligi Rus. Fed. 28 J4
Kulikovo Rus. Fed. 28 H3
Kulim Malaysia 58 C1
Kulittalai India 72 C4
Kullu India 74 C3
Kulmbach Germany 36 E3
Kŭlob Tajik. 81 G2
Kulotino Rus. Fed. 28 E4
Kuloy Rus. Fed. 28 G3
Kuloy r. Rus. Fed. 28 G2
Kulp Turkey 79 E3
Kul'sary Kazakh. 26 F5
Kulshabi Sudan 94 F2
Kulu Turkey 78 C3
Kulübe Tepe mt. Turkey 78 B3
Kulunda Rus. Fed. 26 H4
Kulundinskaya Step' plain Kazakh./Rus. Fed. 62 B1
Kulundinskoye, Ozero salt l. Rus. Fed. 26 H4
Kulusuk Greenland 121 P3
Külvand Iran 80 C4
Kulwin Australia 112 B4
Kulyab Tajik. see **Kŭlob**
Kuma r. Rus. Fed. 32 H2
Kuma r. Rus. Fed. 79 F1
Kumagaya Japan 65 D5
Kumai, Teluk b. Indon. 59 E3
Kumaka Guyana 147 G4
Kumamoto Japan 65 B6
Kumano Japan 65 D6
Kumanovo Macedonia 46 B3
Kumasi Ghana 93 E4
Kumayri Armenia see **Gyumri**
Kumba Cameroon 93 H4
Kumbağ Turkey 46 E4
Kumbakonam India 72 C4
Kumbharli Ghat mt. India 72 B2
Kumbher Nepal 75 D3
Kumbo Cameroon 93 H4
Kum-Dag Turkm. see **Gumdag**
Kumel well Iran 80 C3
Kumertau Rus. Fed. 29 J5
Kumgang-san mt. N. Korea 65 B5
Kumguri India 75 F4
Kumher India 74 C4
Kŭmho-gang r. S. Korea 65 B6
Kumi S. Korea 65 B5
Kumi Uganda 96 B4
Kumla Sweden 33 D4
Kumlinge Fin. 33 F3
Kumlu Turkey 77 C1
Kummerower See l. Germany 37 F2
Kumo Nigeria 93 H3
Kŭmŏ-do i. S. Korea 65 A6
Kumon Range mts Myanmar 60 B2
Kumphawapi Thai. 60 C4
Kumputunturi hill Fin. 32 G2
Kumta India 72 B3
Kumu Dem. Rep. Congo 94 E4
Kumukahi, Cape U.S.A. 135 [inset] Z2
Kumul China see **Hami**
Kumund India 73 D1
Kumylzhenskaya Rus. Fed. see **Kumylzhenskiy**
Kumylzhenskiy Rus. Fed. 29 G6
Kun r. Myanmar 60 B4
Kunar r. Afgh. 81 G3
Kunashir, Ostrov i. Rus. Fed. 64 F3
Kunchaung Myanmar 60 B3
Kunda Dem. Rep. Congo 95 E5
Kunda Estonia 33 G4
Kunda India 75 D4
Kunda-dia-Baze Angola 95 C7
Kundapura India 72 B3
Kundar r. Afgh./Pak. 81 G3
Kundat Sabah Malaysia 59 G1
Kundelungu, Parc National de nat. park Dem. Rep. Congo 95 E7
Kundelungu Ouest, Parc National de nat. park Dem. Rep. Congo 95 E7
Kundgol India 72 B3
Kundian Pak. 81 G3
Kundur i. Indon. 58 C2
Kunduz Afgh. see **Kondūz**
Kunene admin. reg. Namibia 98 B3
Kunene r. Namibia 95 A9
Kūnes China see **Xinyuan**
Kungälv Sweden 33 C4
Kungei Alatau mts Kazakh./Kyrg. 70 E3
Kunggar China see **Maizhokunggar**
Küngöy Ala-Too mts Kazakh./Kyrg. see **Kungei Alatau**
Kungrad Uzbek. 76 F1
Kungsbacka Sweden 33 D4
Kungshamn Sweden 33 C4
Kungsör Sweden 33 E4
Kungu Dem. Rep. Congo 94 C4
Kungur mt. China see **Kongur Shan**
Kungur Rus. Fed. 28 K4
Kungyangon Myanmar 61 A4
Kunhegyes Hungary 37 J5
Kuni r. India 72 C2
Kunié i. New Caledonia see **Pins, Île des**
Kunigal India 72 C3
Kunimi-dake mt. Japan 65 B6
Kuningaküla Estonia 33 G4
Kuningan Indon. 59 E4
Kunjabar India 73 E1
Kunlavav India 74 A5
Kunlong Myanmar 60 B3
Kunlui r. India/Nepal 75 F4
Kunlun Shan mts China 70 E4
Kunlun Shankou pass China 75 G2
Kunmadaras Hungary 37 J5
Kunming China 66 B3
Kuno r. India 74 C4
Kunoy i. Faroe Is 34 [inset]
Kunsan S. Korea 65 A6
Kunshan China 67 G2
Kunszentmárton Hungary 37 J5
Kuntshankoie Dem. Rep. Congo 94 D5
Kununurra Australia 110 B2
Kunwak r. Canada 123 L2
Kunwari r. India 74 C4
Kun'ya Rus. Fed. 28 D4
Kunyang Henan China see **Yexian**
Kunyang Yunnan China see **Jinning**
Kunyang Zhejiang China see **Pingyang**
Künzelsau Germany 36 D4
Kuocang Shan mts China 67 G2
Kuolayarvi Rus. Fed. 32 H2
Kuopio Fin. 32 G3
Kupa r. Croatia/Slovenia 44 F2
Kupang Indon. 57 F8
Kupiškis Lith. 33 G5
Kuprava Latvia 33 G4
Kupreanof Island U.S.A. 120 F4
Kupreanof Point U.S.A. 120 D4
Kupwara Jammu and Kashmir 74 B2
Kup"yans'k Ukr. 29 F6
Kuqa China 70 F3
Kür r. Azer. 79 G3
Kür r. Georgia 79 F2
Kur r. Rus. Fed. 64 C2
Kura r. Azer./Georgia 79 F2
Kura r. Rus. Fed. 29 G8
Kuragwi Nigeria 93 H3
Kurakh Rus. Fed. 79 F2
Kura kurk sea chan. Estonia/Latvia see **Irbe Strait**
Kuramā, Ḩarrat lava field Saudi Arabia 89 I3
Kurashiki Japan 65 C6
Kurasia India 75 D5
Kurayn i. Saudi Arabia 80 B5
Kurayoshi Japan 65 C6
Kurban Dağı mt. Turkey 46 F4
Kurbin r. China 64 B2
Kurca r. Romania 46 B1
Kurchatov Rus. Fed. 29 E6
Kürdämir Azer. 79 G2
Kür Dili pt Azer. 79 G3
Kurduvadi India 72 B2
Kŭrdzhali Bulg. 46 D4
Kure Japan 65 C6
Küre Turkey 78 C2
Kure Atoll U.S.A. 164 G4
Kuressaare Estonia 28 B4
Kureyskoye Vodokhranilische resr Rus. Fed. 27 I3
Kurgan Rus. Fed. 26 G4
Kurganinsk Rus. Fed. 29 G7
Kurgannaya Rus. Fed. see **Kurganinsk**
Kurgantyube Tajik. see **Qŭrghonteppa**
Kuri India 74 A4
Kuria Muria Islands Oman see **Ḩalāniyāt, Juzur al**
Kuridala Australia 111 E4
Kurigram Bangl. 75 F4
Kurikka Fin. 32 F3
Kurikoma-yama vol. Japan 65 E5
Kuril Basin sea feature Sea of Okhotsk 164 D2
Kuril Islands Rus. Fed. 64 F3
Kurilovka Rus. Fed. 29 I6
Kuril'sk Rus. Fed. 54 G2
Kuril'skiye Ostrova is Rus. Fed. see **Kuril Islands**
Kuril Trench sea feature N. Pacific Ocean 164 D3
Kurkino Rus. Fed. 29 F5
Kurlovskiy Rus. Fed. 28 G5
Kurmanayevka Rus. Fed. 29 I5
Kurmuk Sudan 96 B2
Kurnool India 72 C3
Kurobe Japan 65 D5
Kuroishi Japan 64 E4
Kuroiso Japan 65 E5
Kuror, Jebel mt. Sudan 89 F4
Kuro-shima i. Japan 65 B7
Kurow N.Z. 113 B4
Kurram r. Afgh./Pak. 81 G3
Kuršėnai Lith. 33 F4
Kurshskiy Zaliv b. Lith./Rus. Fed. see **Courland Lagoon**
Kursīši Latvia 33 F4
Kuršių marios b. Lith./Rus. Fed. see **Courland Lagoon**
Kursk Rus. Fed. 29 F6
Kurskaya Rus. Fed. 29 H7
Kurskaya Oblast' admin. div. Rus. Fed. 29 F6
Kurskiy Zaliv b. Lith./Rus. Fed. see **Courland Lagoon**
Kursk Oblast admin. div. Rus. Fed. see **Kurskaya Oblast'**
Kuršumlija Serb. and Mont. 46 B3
Kurşunlu Turkey 78 C2
Kurtalan Turkey 79 E3
Kurtoğlu Burnu pt Turkey 78 B3
Kuru Fin. 33 F3
Kurū r. Greece see **Kourou**
Kuru India 75 E5
Kuru watercourse Sudan 94 E2
Kurucaşile Turkey 78 C2
Kurud India 73 D1
Kurukshetra India 74 C3
Kuruktag mts China 70 G3
Kuruman S. Africa 98 D5
Kuruman watercourse S. Africa 98 D5
Kurume Japan 65 B6
Kurumkan Rus. Fed. 63 I1
Kurun r. Sudan 96 B3
Kurunegala Sri Lanka 72 D5
Kurupam India 73 D2
Kurupukari Guyana 147 G3
Kurush, Jebel hills Sudan 89 F4
Kur'ya Rus. Fed. 28 K3
Kuryk Kazakh. 79 G2
Kuşadası Turkey 47 E6
Kuşadası Körfezi b. Turkey 78 A3
Kusary Azer. see **Qusar**
Kusawa Lake Canada 122 B2
Kuşcenneti Milli Parkı nat. park Turkey 47 E4
Kuş Gölü l. Turkey 78 A2
Kushalgarh India 74 B5
Kushalino Rus. Fed. 28 F4
Kūshank Iran 80 D3
Kushiro Japan 64 F4
Kushiro-Shitsugen National Park Japan 64 F4
Kushka Turkm. see **Gushgy**
Kushmurun Kazakh. 26 G4
Kushnarenkovo Rus. Fed. 28 J5
Kushtagi India 72 C3
Kushtia Bangl. 75 F5
Kushtih Iran 81 D4
Kushum Kazakh. 29 I6
Kushum r. Kazakh. 29 I6
Kuskokwim r. U.S.A. 120 C3
Kuskokwim Bay U.S.A. 120 C4
Kuskokwim Mountains U.S.A. 120 D3
Kuşluyan Turkey see **Gölköy**
Kusŏng N. Korea 65 A5
Kussharo-ko l. Japan 64 F4
Kustanay Kazakh. see **Kostanay**
Kustavi Fin. 33 F3
Küstence Romania see **Constanța**
Kustia Bangl. see **Kushtia**
Kut, Ko i. Thai. 61 C6
Kutacane Indon. 58 B2
Kütahya Turkey 78 B3
Kütahya prov. Turkey 47 F5
Kutai National Park Indon. 59 G2
K'ut'aisi Georgia 79 E2
Kut-al-Imara Iraq see **Al Kūt**
Kutan Rus. Fed. 79 F1
Kutaraja Indon. see **Banda Aceh**
Kutayfat Ţurayf vol. Saudi Arabia 77 D4
Kutch, Gulf of India see **Kachchh, Gulf of**
Kutch, Rann of marsh India see **Kachchh, Rann of**
Kūt-e Gapu tourist site Iran 79 G4
Kutina Croatia 44 F2
Kutkai Myanmar 60 B3
Kutná Hora Czech Rep. 37 G4
Kutno Poland 37 I2
Kuttainen Sweden 32 F1
Kutu Dem. Rep. Congo 94 C5
Kutubdia Island Bangl. 75 F5
Kutum Sudan 88 E6
Kutztown U.S.A. 131 F3
Kuujjua r. Canada 121 H2
Kuujjuaq Canada 125 G1
Kuujjuarapik Canada 124 E2
Kuuli-Mayak Turkm. 80 C1
Kuusamo Fin. 32 H2
Kuusankoski Fin. 33 G3
Kuvango Angola 95 C8
Kuvshinovo Rus. Fed. 28 E4
▶**Kuwait** country Asia 79 F5
asia 52–53, 82

▶**Kuwait** Kuwait 79 F5
Capital of Kuwait.

Kuwait Jun b. Kuwait 79 F5
Kuybyshev Kazakh. see **Kuybyshevskiy**
Kuybyshev Novosibirskaya Oblast' Rus. Fed. 26 H4
Kuybyshev Respublika Tatarstan Rus. Fed. see **Bolgar**
Kuybyshev Samarskaya Oblast' Rus. Fed. see **Samara**
Kuybysheve Ukr. 29 F7
Kuybyshevka-Vostochnaya Rus. Fed. see **Belogorsk**
Kuybyshevo Kazakh. see **Zhyngyldy**
Kuybyshevskaya Oblast' admin. div. Rus. Fed. see **Samarskaya Oblast'**
Kuybyshevskiy Kazakh. 26 G4
Kuybyshevskoye Vodokhranilishche resr Rus. Fed. 28 I5
Kuyeda Rus. Fed. 28 J4
Kuytun China 70 F3
Kuyucak Turkey 47 F6
Kuyuwini r. Guyana 147 G4
Kužiai Lith. 33 F5
Kuznetsk Rus. Fed. 29 H5
Kuznetsovs'k Ukr. 29 C6
Kuzomen' Rus. Fed. 28 F2
Kuzovatovo Rus. Fed. 29 H5
Kvænangen sea chan. Norway 32 F1
Kvaløya i. Norway 32 E1
Kvaløya i. Norway 32 F1
Kvalsund Norway 32 F1
Kvareli Georgia see **Qvareli**
Kvarnberg Sweden 33 D3
Kvarner g. Croatia 44 E2
Kvarnerić sea chan. Croatia 44 E2
Kvėdarna Lith. 33 F5
Kvenvær Norway 32 C3
Kvichak Bay U.S.A. 120 D4
Kvikkjokk Sweden 32 E2
Kvinesdal Norway 33 B4
Kvitegga mt. Norway 33 B3
Kvitøya ice feature Svalbard 26 D2
Kvitsøy Norway 33 B4
Kwa r. Dem. Rep. Congo 94 C5
Kwaga Tanz. 97 A6
Kwajalein atoll Marshall Is 164 F5
Kwakoegron Suriname 147 H3
Kwakwani Guyana 147 G3
Kwale Nigeria 93 G4
KwaMashu S. Africa 99 F6
Kwame Danso Ghana 93 E4
Kwamouth Dem. Rep. Congo 94 C5
Kwa Mtoro Tanz. 97 B6
Kwandang Indon. 57 F5
Kwangchow China see **Guangzhou**
Kwangju S. Korea 65 A6
Kwango r. Dem. Rep. Congo 95 C5
Kwangsi aut. reg. China see **Guangxi Zhuangzu Zizhiqu**
Kwangsi Chuang Autonomous Region aut. reg. China see **Guangxi Zhuangzu Zizhiqu**
Kwangtung prov. China see **Guangdong**
Kwangwazi Tanz. 97 C6
Kwania, Lake Uganda 96 B4
Kwanmo-bong mt. N. Korea 64 B4
Kwanobuhle S. Africa 98 E7
Kwanonzame S. Africa 98 E6
Kwanza r. Angola see **Cuanza**
Kwara state Nigeria 93 F3
Kwatinidubu S. Africa 99 E7
Kwazamukucinga S. Africa 98 E7
Kwazamuxolo S. Africa 98 E6
KwaZanele S. Africa 99 F5
Kwazulu-Natal prov. S. Africa 99 F6
Kweichow prov. China see **Guizhou**
Kweiyang China see **Guiyang**
Kwekwe Zimbabwe 99 F3
Kweneng admin. dist. Botswana 98 E4
Kwenge r. Dem. Rep. Congo 95 C6
Kwetabohigan r. Canada 124 D3
Kwiambana Nigeria 93 G3
Kwidzyn Poland 37 I2
Kwikila P.N.G. 106 D2
Kwilu r. Angola/Dem. Rep. Congo 95 C5
Kwisa r. Poland 37 G3
Kwitaro r. Guyana 147 G4
Kwoka mt. Indon. 57 H6
Kwoungo, Mont mt. Cent. Afr. Rep. 94 E3
Kyabé Chad 94 C2
Kyabra Australia 111 E5
Kyabra watercourse Australia 111 E5
Kyadet Myanmar 60 A3
Kyaiklat Myanmar 61 A4
Kyaikto Myanmar 60 B4
Kya-in Seikkyi Myanmar 61 B4
Kyakhta Rus. Fed. 27 K4
Kyalite Australia 112 B4
Kyancutta Australia 109 F8
Kyangin Irrawaddy Myanmar 60 A4
Kyangin Mandalay Myanmar 60 B4
Kyaukhnyat Myanmar 60 B4
Kyaukkyi Myanmar 60 B4
Kyaukme Myanmar 60 B3
Kyaukpadaung Myanmar 60 A3
Kyaukpyu Myanmar 60 A4
Kyaukse Myanmar 60 B3
Kyauktan Myanmar 61 B4
Kyauktaw Myanmar 73 G1
Kybartai Lith. 33 F5
Kybeyan Range mts Australia 112 D5
Ky Cung, Sông r. Vietnam 60 D3
Kyeintali Myanmar 60 A4
Kyela Tanz. 97 B7
Kyelang India 74 C2
Kyenjojo Uganda 96 A4
Kyeraa Ghana 93 E4
Kyidaunggan Myanmar 60 B4
Kyinderi Ghana 93 E3
Kyiv Ukr. see **Kiev**
Kyjov Czech Rep. 37 H4
Kyklades is Greece see **Cyclades**
Kyle Canada 134 E2
Kyle of Lochalsh U.K. 34 D3
Kyll r. Germany 36 C4
Kyllini mt. Greece 47 C6
Kymi Greece 47 D5
Kymis, Akra pt Greece 47 D5
Kynna r. Norway 33 D3
Kynuna Australia 111 E4
Kyoga, Lake Uganda 96 B4
Kyōga-misaki pt Japan 65 C6
Kyogle Australia 112 E3
Kyom watercourse Sudan 94 F2
Kyondo Myanmar 61 B4
Kyŏnggi-man b. S. Korea 65 A5
Kyŏngju S. Korea 65 B6
Kyongju National Park S. Korea 65 B6
Kyonpyaw Myanmar 60 A4
Kyōto Japan 65 C6
Kyparissia Greece 47 B6
Kyparissiakos Kolpos b. Greece 47 B6
Kypros country Asia see **Cyprus**
Kypshak, Ozero salt l. Kazakh. 69 E1
Kyra Panagia i. Greece 47 D5
Kyrenia Cyprus 77 A2
Kyrenia Mountains Cyprus see **Pentadaktylos Range**
▶**Kyrgyzstan** country Asia 70 D3
asia 52–53, 82
Kyrhyzh-Kytay r. Ukr. 46 F2
Kyriaki Greece 47 C5
Kyritz Germany 37 F2
Kyrnychky Ukr. 46 F2
Kytalyktakh Rus. Fed. 27 N3
Kytay, Ozero l. Ukr. 46 F2
Kythira Greece 47 C6
Kythira i. Greece 47 C6
Kythnos i. Greece 47 D6
Kythnou, Steno sea chan. Greece 47 D6
Kythrea Cyprus 77 A2
Kyunglung China 74 D3
Kyungyaung Myanmar 61 B5
Kyunhla Myanmar 60 A3
Kyuquot Canada 122 E5
Kyurdamir Azer. see **Kürdämir**
Kyūshū i. Japan 65 B7
Kyushu-Palau Ridge sea feature N. Pacific Ocean 164 D4
Kyustendil Bulg. 46 C3
Kywebwe Myanmar 60 B4
Kywong Australia 112 C4
Kyyev Ukr. see **Kiev**
Kyyiv Ukr. see **Kiev**
Kyyivs'ke Vodoskhovyshche resr Ukr. 29 D6
Kyyjärvi Fin. 32 G3
Kyyvesi l. Fin. 33 G3
Kyzan Kazakh. 29 J7
Kyzyl Moldova see **Ştefan Vodă**
Kyzyl Rus. Fed. 62 E1
Kyzyl-Art, Pereval pass Kyrg./Tajik. see **Kyzylart Pass**
Kyzylart Pass Kyrg./Tajik. 81 H2
Kyzyl-Burun Azer. see **Siyäzän**
Kyzyl-Kiya Kyrg. see **Kyzyl-Kyya**
Kyzylkoga Kazakh. 29 J6
Kyzylkum, Peski des. Kazakh./Uzbek. see **Kyzylkum Desert**
Kyzylkum Desert Kazakh./Uzbek. 70 B3
Kyzyl-Kyya Kyrg. 81 H1
Kyzyl-Mazhalyk Rus. Fed. 62 E1
Kyzylorda Kazakh. 70 C3
Kyzyl-Suu r. Kyrg. 81 G2
Kyzylzhar Kazakh. 70 C2
Kzyl-Dzhar Kazakh. see **Kyzylzhar**
Kzyl-Orda Kazakh. see **Kyzylorda**
Kzyltu Kazakh. see **Kishkenekol'**

↓ L

Laage Germany 37 F2
La Almunia de Doña Godina Spain 43 F2
La Angostura, Presa de resr Mex. 138 F5
Laanle well Somalia 96 F2
La Antigua, Salina salt pan Arg. 152 D2
La Araucania admin. reg. Chile 152 B4
Laas Aano Somalia 96 F3
Laascaanood Somalia 96 E2
La Ascensión, Bahía de b. Mex. 127 I8
Laas Dawaco Somalia 96 F2
Laasgoray Somalia 96 F2
La Asunción Venez. 147 F2

▶**Laâyoune** W. Sahara 90 B4
Capital of Western Sahara.

Lab r. Serb. and Mont. 46 B3
Laba r. Rus. Fed. 29 G7
La Babia Mex. 133 A6
La Bahía, Islas de is Hond. 138 G5
La Baie Canada 125 G3
Labala Indon. 57 F7
La Baleine, Grande Rivière de r. Canada 124 E2
La Baleine, Petite Rivière de r. Canada 124 E2
La Baleine, Rivière à r. Canada 125 H1
La Banda Arg. 152 D1
La Bañeza Spain 42 D1
Labang Sarawak Malaysia 59 F2
Labao China see **Liujiang**
La Barthe-de-Neste France 38 D5
Labasa Fiji 107 G3
La Baule-Escoublac France 38 B3
Labaz, Ozero l. Rus. Fed. 27 J2
Labazhskoye Rus. Fed. 28 J2
Labe r. Czech Rep. 37 G3
also known as Elbe (Germany)
Labé Guinea 92 B3
Labelle Canada 125 F4
La Belle U.S.A. 129 C7
La Bénoué, Parc National de nat. park Cameroon 93 I3
Laberge, Lake Canada 122 C2
La Bernarde, Sommet de mt. France 39 G5
Labi Brunei 59 F1
La Biche r. Canada 122 F3
La Biche, Lac l. Canada 123 H4
Labin Croatia 44 E2
Labinsk Rus. Fed. 29 G7
Labis Malaysia 58 C2
La Bisbal d'Empordà Spain 43 H2
La Biznaga Mex. 135 E7
La Bobia, Sierra de mts Spain 42 C1
La Bodera mt. Spain 43 E2
La Boquilla Mex. 135 F8
Labora Namibia 98 C4
La Boucle du Baoulé, Parc National de nat. park Mali 92 C2
Laboué Lebanon 77 C2
Labouheyre France 38 C4
Laboulaye Arg. 152 E3
Labrador reg. Canada 125 I2
Labrador City Canada 125 H2
Labrador Sea Canada/Greenland 121 N3
Lábrea Brazil 148 D1
La Brea Peru 146 A6
Labuan Malaysia 59 F1
Labuan i. Malaysia 59 F1
Labuhan Indon. 58 D4
Labuhanbajo Indon. 57 E7
Labuhanbilik Indon. 58 C2
Labuhanmeringgai Indon. 58 D4
Labuhanruku Indon. 58 B2
Labuk r. Sabah Malaysia 59 G1
Labuk, Telukan b. Sabah Malaysia 59 G1
Labuna Indon. 57 G6
Labutta Myanmar 61 A4
Labyrinth, Lake salt flat Australia 109 F7
Labytnangi Rus. Fed. 26 G3
Laç Albania 46 A4
Lac pref. Chad 88 B6
La Cabrera, Sierra de mts Spain 42 C1
La Calderina mt. Spain 42 E3
La Calera Chile 152 C3
Lac Allard Canada 125 I3
La Calle Alg. see **El Kala**
Lacanau, Étang de l. France 38 C4
La Capelle France 39 E2
Laćarak Serb. and Mont. 46 A2
La Carlota Arg. 152 E3
La Carlota Spain 42 D4
La Carolina Spain 42 E3
Laccadive, Minicoy and Amindivi Islands union terr. India see **Lakshadweep**
Laccadive Islands India 72 B4
Lac du Bonnet Canada 123 L5
Lacedaemon Greece see **Sparti**
La Ceiba Hond. 138 G5
Lacepede Bay Australia 112 A5
Lacepede Islands Australia 108 C4
Lacha, Ozero l. Rus. Fed. 28 F3
La Charité-sur-Loire France 39 E3
La Chartreuse, Massif de mts France 39 F4
La Châtaigneraie France 38 C3
La Châtre France 38 D3
La Chaux-de-Fonds Switz. 39 G3

▶**Lachlan** r. Australia 112 B4
5th longest river in Oceania.
oceania 102–103

La Chorrera Col. 146 C5
La Chorrera Panama 139 I7
Lachung India 75 F4
Lachute Canada 125 F4
Laçın Azer. 79 F3
La Ciotat France 39 F5
Lackawanna U.S.A. 130 D2
Lac La Biche Canada 123 I4
Lac la Martre Canada see **Wha Ti**
Lac-Mégantic Canada 125 G4
La Cogulla mt. Spain 43 G2
La Colorada Mex. 135 E7
Lacombe Canada 123 H4
La Comoé, Parc National de nat. park Côte d'Ivoire 92 E3
Lacon U.S.A. 132 D3
Laconi Sardinia Italy 45 B5
Laconia U.S.A. 131 H2
La Corey Canada 123 I4
La Coruña Spain see **A Coruña**
La Coubre, Pointe de pt France 38 C4
La Crete Canada 123 G3
La Crosse KS U.S.A. 132 B4
La Crosse VA U.S.A. 130 D5
La Crosse WI U.S.A. 132 D3
La Cruz Arg. 152 F2
La Cruz Mex. 126 F7
La Cruz Uruguay 152 F3
Lac Thiên Vietnam 61 E5
La Cuesta Mex. 126 F6
La Culebra, Sierra de mts Spain 42 C2
Lac Waswanipi l. Canada 124 E3
La Cygne U.S.A. 132 C4
Ladakh reg. Jammu and Kashmir 74 C2
Ladakh Range mts India 74 C2
L'Adamaoua, Massif de mts Cameroon 93 I4
Ladang i. Thai. 61 B7
Lądek-Zdrój Poland 37 H3
La Demanda, Sierra de mts Spain 42 E1
La Déroute, Passage de strait Channel Is/France 38 B2
Ladik Turkey 78 C2
Ladismith S. Africa 98 D7
Lādīz Iran 81 E4
Ladnun India 74 B4

▶**Ladoga, Lake** Rus. Fed. 28 D3
2nd largest lake in Europe.
europe 22–23

La Dôle mt. Switz. 39 G3
Ladon r. Greece 47 B6
Ladong China 67 D3
Ladozhskoye Ozero l. Rus. Fed. see **Ladoga, Lake**
Ladra r. Spain 42 C1
Ladrones terr. N. Pacific Ocean see **Northern Mariana Islands**
Ladu mt. India 75 G4
Ladue r. Canada/U.S.A. 122 A2
Ladushkin Rus. Fed. 37 J1
Ladva-Vetka Rus. Fed. 28 E3
Lady Barron Australia 112 D6
Ladysmith Canada 122 F5
Ladysmith S. Africa 99 F6
Ladysmith U.S.A. 132 D2
Ladzhanurges Georgia see **Lajanurpekhi**
Lae P.N.G. 57 K7
Lae Thai. 60 C4
Lærdalsøyri Norway 33 B3
La Escala Spain see **L'Escala**
La Esmeralda Arg. 152 D2
La Esmeralda Bol. 149 E5
La Esmeralda Venez. 147 E4
Læsø i. Denmark 33 C4
La Esperanza Beni Bol. 148 E3
La Esperanza Santa Cruz Bol. 149 E3
La Estrella Bol. 149 E4
Laeva Estonia 33 G4
Lævvajåk Norway 32 G1
La Falda Arg. 152 D2
La Fargeville U.S.A. 131 F1
Lafayette IN U.S.A. 132 E3
Lafayette LA U.S.A. 133 C6
Lafayette NJ U.S.A. 131 F3
Lafayette OH U.S.A. 130 B4
Lafayette TN U.S.A. 128 B4
Laferte r. Canada 123 G2
La Ferté-Bernard France 38 D2
La Ferté-Gaucher France 39 E2
La Ferté-Macé France 38 C2
Lafia Nigeria 93 H3
Lafiagi Nigeria 93 G3
Lafleche Canada 123 J5
La Flèche France 38 C3
La Follette U.S.A. 130 A5
Lafnitz r. Austria 37 H5
La Forest, Lac l. Canada 125 G2
Laforge Canada 125 F2
Laforge r. Canada 125 F2
Lafrançaise France 38 D4
La Frégate, Lac de l. Canada 125 F2
Lāft Iran 80 C5

▶**La Galite** i. Tunisia 91 H1
Most northerly point of Africa.

La Galite, Canal de sea chan. Tunisia 91 H1
La Gallareta Arg. 152 E2
Lagan' Rus. Fed. 29 H7
Lagan r. Sweden 33 D4
Lagana, Kolpos b. Greece 47 B6
Lagané well Niger 93 I2
La Garamba, Parc National de nat. park Dem. Rep. Congo 94 F3
Lagarto Brazil 150 E4
Lagbar Senegal 92 B2
Lagdo, Lac de l. Cameroon 93 I3
Lågen r. Norway 33 C3
Lågen r. Norway 33 C4
Lagh Bogal watercourse Kenya/Somalia 96 D4
Lagh Bor watercourse Kenya/Somalia 96 D4
Lagh Kutulo watercourse Kenya/Somalia 96 D4
Laghmān prov. Afgh. 81 G3
Laghouat Alg. 91 F2
La Gineta Spain 43 F3
Lagkor Co salt l. China 75 E2
La Gloria Col. 146 C2
La Gloria Mex. 133 B7
Lago prov. Moz. see **Niassa**
Lagoa Vermelha Brazil 151 B9
Lago Belgrano Arg. 153 B6
Lago Cardiel Arg. 153 C7
Lago da Pedra Brazil 150 C3
Lagodekhi Georgia 79 F2
La Gomera i. Canary Is 90 A3
La Gonâve, Île de i. Haiti 127 L8
Lagong i. Indon. 59 E2
Lago Posadas Arg. 153 C6

▶**Lagos** Nigeria 93 F4
Former capital of Nigeria. 2nd most populous city in Africa.
world 16–17

Lagos state Nigeria 93 F4
Lagos Port. 42 B4
Lagosa Tanz. 97 A6
Lagos de Moreno Mex. 126 F7
Lago Verde Brazil 149 E2
Lago Viedma Arg. 153 B7
Lagran Spain 43 E1
La Grande r. Canada 125 E2
La Grande U.S.A. 134 C3
La Grande 2, Réservoir Canada 124 E2
La Grande 3, Réservoir Canada 125 F2
La Grande 4, Réservoir Que. Canada 121 L4
La Grande 4, Réservoir Que. Canada 125 F2
La Grande Casse, Pointe de mt. France 39 G4
La Grande-Combe France 39 F4
Lagrange Australia 108 C4
La Grange CA U.S.A. 136 B3
La Grange GA U.S.A. 129 B5
La Grange TX U.S.A. 133 B6
La Gran Sabana plat. Venez. 147 F3
La Grita Venez. 146 D2
La Guajira, Península de pen. Col. 146 D2
La Guardia Arg. 152 D2
La Guardia Chile 152 C1
La Guardia Spain see **A Guardia**
Laguna Brazil 151 B9
Laguna U.S.A. 135 F6
Laguna, Ilha da i. Brazil 150 B2
Laguna Beach U.S.A. 136 D5
Laguna Dam U.S.A. 137 E5
Laguna de Laja, Parque Nacional nat. park Chile 152 C4
Laguna Mountains U.S.A. 137 D5
Lagunas Peru 146 C6
Laguna San Rafael, Parque Nacional nat. park Chile 153 B6
Laguna Yema Arg. 149 E6
Lagunillas Bol. 149 E4
Laha China 64 A2
La Habana Cuba see **Havana**
La Habra U.S.A. 136 D5
Lahad Datu Sabah Malaysia 59 G1
Lahad Datu, Telukan b. Sabah Malaysia 59 G1
La Hague, Cap de c. France 38 C2
Lahar India 74 C4
Laharpur India 74 D4
Lahat Indon. 58 C3
Lahemaa rahvuspark nat. park Estonia 33 G4
La Hève, Cap de c. France 38 D2
Lahewa Indon. 58 B2
Laḩij Yemen 76 C7
Lahn r. Germany 36 C3
Lahnstein Germany 36 C3
Laholm Sweden 33 D4
Laholmsbukten b. Sweden 33 D4
Lahontan Reservoir U.S.A. 136 C2
Lahore Pak. 74 B3
La Horqueta Venez. 147 F3
Lahr (Schwarzwald) Germany 36 C4
Lahri Pak. 81 G4
Lahti Fin. 33 G3
L'Ahzar, Vallée de watercourse Niger 93 F2
Laï Chad 94 C2
Lai'an China 67 F1
Laibach Slovenia see **Ljubljana**
Laibin China 67 D4
Laifeng China 67 D2
L'Aigle France 38 D2
Laihia Fin. 32 F3
Lai-hka Myanmar 60 B3
Lai-Hsak Myanmar 60 B3
Laingsburg S. Africa 98 D7
Lainioälven r. Sweden 32 F2
Lainsitz r. Austria 37 G4
Lair U.S.A. 130 A4
L'Aïr, Massif de mts Niger 93 H1
L'Aïr et du Ténéré, Réserve Naturelle Nationale de nature res. Niger 93 H1
Lairg U.K. 34 D2
Lais Indon. 58 C3
Laisälven r. Sweden 32 E2
Laishevo Rus. Fed. 28 I5
La Isla Col. 146 B3
La Isla, Salar de salt flat Chile 152 C1
Laitila Fin. 33 F3
Laivera well Tanz. 97 C6
Laives Italy 44 C1
Laiyang China 63 K4
Laizhou Wan b. China 63 J4
Lajamanu Australia 110 B3
Lajanurpekhi Georgia 79 E2
Lajeado Brazil 151 A9
Lajes Brazil 151 B8
Lajosmizse Hungary 37 I5
La Joya Peru 148 C4
La Joya de los Sachas Ecuador 146 B5
Lajta r. Austria/Hungary 37 H5
La Junta Bol. 149 E3
La Junta Mex. 135 F7
La Junta U.S.A. 135 G5
La Juventud, Isla de i. Cuba 127 J7
Lakadiya India 74 A5
L'Akagera, Parc National de nat. park Rwanda see **Akagera National Park**
Lakatråsk Sweden 32 F2
Lake KY U.S.A. 130 B5
Lake WY U.S.A. 134 E3
Lake Andes U.S.A. 132 B3
Lake Arthur U.S.A. 133 C6
Lake Cargelligo Australia 112 C4
Lake Chakonipau Canada 125 G1
Lake Charles U.S.A. 133 C6
Lake City CO U.S.A. 135 F5
Lake City FL U.S.A. 129 C6
Lake City MN U.S.A. 132 C2
Lake City SC U.S.A. 129 D5
Lake Clark National Park and Preserve U.S.A. 120 D3
Lake Clear U.S.A. 131 F1
Lake Cowichan Canada 122 E5
Lake District National Park U.K. 35 E4

Litoměřice Czech Rep. 37 G3
Litovel Czech Rep. 37 H4
Litovko Rus. Fed. 64 C2
Litovskaya S.S.R. country Europe see Lithuania
Little r. LA U.S.A. 133 C6
Little r. TX U.S.A. 133 B6
Little Abaco i. Bahamas 129 D7
Little Abitibi r. Canada 124 D3
Little Abitibi Lake Canada 132 F1
Little Aden Yemen see 'Adan as Sughra
Little Andaman i. India 73 G4
Little Bahama Bank sea feature Bahamas 129 D7
Little Barrier Island N.Z. 113 C2
Little Belt sea chan. Denmark 33 C5
Little Belt Mountains U.S.A. 134 E3
Little Bighorn r. U.S.A. 134 F3
Little Bitter Lake Egypt 77 A4
Little Blue r. U.S.A. 132 B4
Little Bow r. Canada 123 H5
Little Buffalo r. Canada 123 H2
Little Cayman i. Cayman Is 127 J8
Little Churchill r. Canada 123 M3
Little Coco Island Cocos Is 61 A5
Little Colorado r. U.S.A. 137 G3
Little Current Canada 124 D4
Little Current r. Canada 124 C3
Little Desert National Park Australia 112 B5
Little Egg Harbor inlet U.S.A. 131 F4
Little Exuma i. Bahamas 129 E8
Little Falls MN U.S.A. 132 C2
Little Falls NY U.S.A. 131 F2
Littlefield AZ U.S.A. 137 F3
Littlefield TX U.S.A. 133 A5
Little Fork r. U.S.A. 132 C1
Little Fort Canada 122 F5
Little Grand Rapids Canada 123 M4
Little Kanawha r. U.S.A. 130 C4
Little Karoo plat. S. Africa 98 D7
Little Lake U.S.A. 136 D4
Little Mecatina r. Canada 125 I3
Little Mecatina Island Canada see Petit Mécatina, Île du
Little Miami r. U.S.A. 130 A4
Little Minch sea chan. U.K. 34 C3
Little Missouri r. U.S.A. 134 G3
Little Muskingum r. U.S.A. 130 C4
Little Nicobar i. India 73 G5
Little Pamir mts Afgh. 81 H2
Little Powder r. U.S.A. 134 F3
Little Rann marsh India 74 A5
Little Red r. U.S.A. 133 D5
Little River U.S.A. 129 D5

▶Little Rock U.S.A. 133 C5
State capital of Arkansas.

Littlerock U.S.A. 136 D4
Little Sachigo Lake Canada 124 A2
Little Salt Lake U.S.A. 137 F3
Little Sandy Desert Australia 108 C5
Little San Salvador i. Bahamas 129 E7
Little Sioux r. U.S.A. 132 B3
Little Sitkin Island U.S.A. 120 A4
Little Smoky Canada 123 G4
Little Snake r. U.S.A. 134 E4
Littlestown U.S.A. 131 E4
Little Tibet reg. Jammu and Kashmir see Ladakh
Littleton NH U.S.A. 131 H1
Littleton WV U.S.A. 130 C4
Little Valley U.S.A. 130 D2
Little Wabash r. U.S.A. 128 A4
Little White r. U.S.A. 132 A3
Little Wind r. U.S.A. 134 E4
Little Zab r. Iraq see Zāb aş Şaghīr, Nahr az
Littoral prov. Cameroon 93 H4
Litunde Moz. 97 B3
Litvínov Czech Rep. 37 F3
Liuba China 66 C1
Liuchiu Yü i. Taiwan 67 G4
Liuchong He r. China 66 C3
Liuchow China see Liuzhou
Liuhe China 64 A4
Liuheng Dao i. China 67 G2
Liujiachang China 67 D2
Liujiang China 67 D3
Liulin China see Jonê
Liupai China see Tian'e
Liupan Shan mts China 66 C1
Liupanshui China see Lupanshui
Liupo Moz. 99 H2
Liuwa Plain Zambia 95 D8
Liuwa Plain National Park Zambia 95 D8
Liuyang China 67 E2
Liuyang He r. China 67 E2
Liuzhou China 67 D3
Līvāni Latvia 33 G4
Livanjsko Polje plain Bos.-Herz. 44 F2
Livarot France 38 D2
Livberze Latvia 33 F4
Live Oak U.S.A. 129 C6
Liveringa Australia 110 A3
Livermore U.S.A. 136 B3
Livermore, Mount U.S.A. 135 F7
Liverpool Australia 112 D4
Liverpool r. Australia 108 F3
Liverpool Canada 125 H4
Liverpool U.K. 35 E5
Liverpool Range mts Australia 112 D3
Livingston U.K. 34 E4
Livingston AL U.S.A. 129 A5
Livingston CA U.S.A. 136 B3
Livingston KY U.S.A. 130 A5
Livingston MT U.S.A. 134 E3
Livingston TN U.S.A. 129 C4
Livingston TX U.S.A. 133 C6
Livingston, Lake U.S.A. 133 C6
Livingstone Zambia 95 E9
Livingstonia Malawi 97 B7
Livingston Island Antarctica 167 L2
Livno Bos.-Herz. 44 F3
Livny Rus. Fed. 29 F5
Livo r. Rus. Fed. 32 H2
Livonia U.S.A. 130 B2
Livorno Italy 44 C3
Livradois, Monts du mts France 39 E4
Livramento do Brumado Brazil 150 D5
Livron-sur-Drôme France 39 F4
Liwā Oman 80 D5
Liwā', Wādī al watercourse Syria 77 C3
Liwale Tanz. 97 C7
Liwiec r. Poland 37 J2
Liwonde Malawi 97 B8
Liwonde National Park Malawi 97 B8
Lixian Gansu China 66 C1
Lixian Hunan China 67 D2
Lixian Sichuan China 66 B2
Lixin China 67 F1
Lixouri Greece 47 B5
Lixus Morocco see Larache
Liyang China 67 F2
Liyuan China see Sangzhi
Liz r. Port. 42 B3
Lizarda Brazil 150 C4
Lizard Point U.K. 35 D7
Lizarra Spain see Estella
Liziping China 66 B2
Lizonne r. France 38 D4
Ljig Serb. and Mont. 46 B2

▶Ljubljana Slovenia 44 E1
Capital of Slovenia.

Ljubuški Bos.-Herz. 44 F3
Ljugarn Sweden 33 E4
Ljungå Sweden 32 E3
Ljungan r. Sweden 33 E3
Ljungby Sweden 33 D4
Ljungskile Sweden 33 C4
Ljusdal Sweden 33 E3
Ljusnan r. Sweden 33 E3
Ljusne Sweden 33 E3
Ljutomer Slovenia 44 F1
Llagostera Spain 43 H2
Llaima, Volcán vol. Chile 152 C4
Llanbedr U.K. see Lampeter
Llançà Spain 43 H1
Llancanelo, Salina salt flat Arg. 152 C3
Llandeilo U.K. 35 E6
Llandovery U.K. 35 E6
Llandrindod Wells U.K. 35 E5
Llandudno U.K. 35 E5
Llanelli U.K. 35 D6
Llanes Spain 42 D1
Llangurig U.K. 35 E5
Llano U.S.A. 133 B6
Llano r. U.S.A. 133 B6
Llano Estacado plain U.S.A. 135 G6
Llanos plain Col./Venez. 146 D3
Llanquihue, Lago l. Chile 152 B5
Llansá Spain see Llançà
Llanymddyfri U.K. see Llandovery
Llata Peru 148 A2
Lleida Spain 43 G2
Llerena Spain 42 C3
Llica Bol. 148 C4
Lliria Spain 43 F3
Llobregat r. Spain 43 G2
Llodio Spain 42 E1
Lloret de Mar Spain 43 H2
Llorgara nat. park Albania 47 A4
Lloyd George, Mount Canada 122 E3
Lloyd Lake Canada 123 I3
Lloydminster Canada 123 I4
Lluchmayor Spain see Llucmajor
Llucmajor Spain 43 H3
Llullaillaco, Volcán vol. Chile 148 C6
Lô r. China/Vietnam 66 C4
Loa r. Chile 148 C5
Loa U.S.A. 137 G2
Loagan Bunut National Park Sarawak Malaysia 59 F2
Loakulu Indon. 59 G3
Loano Italy 44 B2
Loban' r. Rus. Fed. 28 I4
Lobatse Botswana 98 E5
Löbau Germany 37 G3
Lobaye pref. Cent. Afr. Rep. 94 C3
Lobaye r. Cent. Afr. Rep. 94 C4
Lobeke, Réserve du Lac res. Cameroon 94 B4
Löbenberg hill Germany 37 F3
Loberia Arg. 152 F4
Łobez Poland 37 G2
Lobito Angola 95 B8
Loboko Congo 94 C5
Lobón Spain 42 C3
Lobos Arg. 152 F3
Lobos, Cabo c. Mex. 135 D7
Lobos de Afuera, Islas is Peru 146 A6
Lobos de Tierra, Isla i. Peru 146 A6
Loburg Germany 36 F2
Locarno Switz. 39 H3
Lochaline U.K. 34 D3
Loch Baghasdail U.K. see Lochboisdale
Lochboisdale U.K. 34 C3
Lochern National Park Australia 111 E5
Loches France 38 D3
Loch Garman Rep. of Ireland see Wexford
Lochgilphead U.K. 34 D3
Lochinvar National Park Zambia 95 E8
Lochinver U.K. 34 D2
Lochmaddy U.K. 34 C3
Lochnagar mt. U.K. 34 E3
Loch nam Madadh U.K. see Lochmaddy
Łochów Poland 37 J2
Lochranza U.K. 34 D4
Lochsa r. U.S.A. 134 D3
Lochy, Loch l. U.K. 34 D3
Lock Australia 109 F8
Lockeford U.S.A. 136 B2
Lockerbie U.K. 34 E4
Lockhart Australia 112 C4
Lockhart U.S.A. 133 B6
Lockhart River Australia 111 E2
Lock Haven U.S.A. 130 E3
Löcknitz r. Germany 36 E2
Lockport U.S.A. 130 D2
Locminé France 38 B3
Lôc Ninh Vietnam 61 D6
Locorotondo Italy 45 F4
Locri Italy 45 F5
Locumba r. Peru 148 C4
Lod Israel 77 B4
Loddon r. Australia 112 B4
Lode Latvia 33 G4
Lodève France 39 E5
Lodeynoye Pole Rus. Fed. 28 E3
Lodge, Mount Canada/U.S.A. 122 B3
Lodhikheda India 74 C5
Lodhran Pak. 81 G4
Lodi Italy 44 B2
Lodi CA U.S.A. 136 B2
Lodi OH U.S.A. 130 B3
Løding Norway 32 D2
Lødingen Norway 32 D1
Lodja Dem. Rep. Congo 94 D5
Lodomeria Rus. Fed. see Vladimir
Lodosa Spain 43 E1
Lodrani India 74 A5
Lodwar Kenya 96 B4
Lodz Poland see Łódź
Łódź Poland 37 I3
Loei Thai. 60 C4
Loeriesfontein S. Africa 98 C6
Lofoten is Norway 32 D1
Lofsdalen Sweden 33 D3
Log Rus. Fed. 29 G6
Loga Niger 93 F2
Logan IA U.S.A. 132 C3
Logan NM U.S.A. 135 G6
Logan OH U.S.A. 130 B4
Logan UT U.S.A. 134 E4
Logan WV U.S.A. 130 C5

▶Logan, Mount Canada 122 A2
2nd highest mountain in North America.
northamerica 116–117

Logan, Mount U.S.A. 134 B2
Logan Creek r. Australia 111 F4
Logan Creek r. U.S.A. 132 B3
Logan Lake Canada 134 B2
Logansport IN U.S.A. 132 E3
Logansport LA U.S.A. 133 C6
Logatec Slovenia 44 E2
Lögdeälven r. Sweden 32 E3
Loge r. Angola 95 B6
Logone r. Africa 94 B1
Logone Birni Cameroon 94 B2
Logone Occidental pref. Chad 94 B2
Logone Oriental pref. Chad 94 C2
Logreşti Romania 46 C2
Logroño Spain 43 E1
Logtak Lake India 75 G4
Logudoro reg. Sardinia Italy 45 B4
Lohardaga India 75 E5
Loharu India 74 B3
Lohawat India 74 B4
Lohil r. China/India see Zayü Qu
Lohilahti Fin. 33 H3
Lohiniva Fin. 32 G2
Lohja Fin. 33 G3
Löhne Germany 36 D2
Lohne (Oldenburg) Germany 36 D2
Loi, Nam r. Myanmar 60 C3
Loikaw Myanmar 60 B4
Loi Lan mt. Myanmar/Thai. 60 B4
Loi-lem Myanmar 60 B3
Loimaa Fin. 33 F3
Loipyet Hills Myanmar 60 B2
Loir r. France 38 C3
Loir, Les Vaux du valley France 38 D3
Loire r. France 39 B3
Loi Sang mt. Myanmar 60 B3
Loi Song mt. Myanmar 60 B3
Loita Plains Kenya 96 B5
Loja Ecuador 146 B6
Loja prov. Ecuador 146 B6
Loja Spain 42 D4
Lokan r. Sabah Malaysia 59 G1
Lokandu Dem. Rep. Congo 94 E5
Lokan tekojärvi l. Fin. 32 G2
Lokeren Belgium 36 B3
Loki vol. Iceland 32 [inset]
Lokichar Kenya 96 B4
Lokichokio Kenya 96 B3
Lokka Fin. 32 G2
Løkken Denmark 33 C4
Loknya Rus. Fed. 28 D4
Lokofe Dem. Rep. Congo 94 D5
Lokoja Nigeria 93 G4
Lokolama Dem. Rep. Congo 94 C5
Lokolo r. Dem. Rep. Congo 94 C5
Lokomo Cameroon 94 B4
Lokoro r. Dem. Rep. Congo 94 C5
Lokosafa Cent. Afr. Rep. 94 C4
Lokossa Benin 93 F4
Lokot' Rus. Fed. 29 E5
Løksebotn Norway 32 E1
Lokutu Dem. Rep. Congo see Elisabetha
Lol Sudan 94 F3
Lol watercourse Sudan 94 F2
Lola Angola 95 B8
Lola Guinea 92 C4
Lola, Mount U.S.A. 136 B2
Lolland i. Denmark 33 C5
Lolle watercourse Sudan 96 A2
Lollondo Tanz. 96 B5
Lolo Dem. Rep. Congo 94 D4
Lolo U.S.A. 134 D3
Lolodorf Cameroon 93 H5
Lolo Pass U.S.A. 134 D3
Lolowau Indon. 58 B2
Lom Bulg. 46 C3
Lom r. Bulg. 46 C3
Lom Norway 33 C3
Loma U.S.A. 137 H2
Lomako r. Dem. Rep. Congo 94 D4
Lomaloma Fiji 107 H3
Lomami r. Dem. Rep. Congo 95 E4
Loma Mountains Sierra Leone 92 C3
Lomar Pass Afgh. 81 F3
Lomas Coloradas hills Arg. 153 D5
Lomas de Zamora Arg. 152 F3
Lombarda, Serra hills Brazil 147 H4
Lombardia admin. reg. Italy 44 B2
Lombardina Australia 108 C4
Lomblen i. Indon. 57 F7
Lombok Indon. 59 G5
Lombok i. Indon. 59 G5
Lombok, Selat sea chan. Indon. 59 F5

▶Lomé Togo 93 F4
Capital of Togo.

Lomela r. Dem. Rep. Congo 94 D5
Lomié Cameroon 93 I5
Lommel Belgium 36 B3
Lomond Canada 125 J3
Lomond, Loch l. U.K. 34 D3
Lomonosov Ridge sea feature Arctic Ocean 166 B1
Lomont hills France 39 G3
Lomovoye Rus. Fed. 28 G2
Lomphat Cambodia see Lumphăt
Lompoc U.S.A. 136 B4
Lom Sak Thai. 60 C4
Lomsjö Sweden 32 E2
Łomża Poland 37 K2
Lonar India 72 C2
Lonato Italy 44 C2
Lonavale India 72 B2
Loncopue Arg. 152 C4
Londa Bangl. 75 F5
Londa India 72 B3
Londinium U.K. see London
Londoko Rus. Fed. 64 C2
London Canada 130 C2

▶London U.K. 35 F6
Capital of the United Kingdom and of England. 4th most populous city in Europe.
europe 24–25
world 16–17

London KY U.S.A. 130 A5
London OH U.S.A. 130 B4
London City airport U.K. 35 G6
Londonderry U.K. 34 C4
Londonderry U.S.A. 131 G2
Londonderry, Cape Australia 110 A2
Londonderry, Isla i. Chile 153 C8
Londres Arg. 152 D1
Lone Pine U.S.A. 136 C3
Long Thai. 66 A5
Longa Angola 95 C8
Longa r. Bengo/Cuanza Sul Angola 95 B7
Longa r. Cuando Cubango Angola 95 C9
Longa, Proliv sea chan. Rus. Fed. 27 R2
Longagung Indon. 59 F2
Long Akah Sarawak Malaysia 59 F2
Long'an Guangxi China 66 C4
Long'an Sichuan China see Pingwu
Longarone Italy 44 D1
Longavi, Nevado de mt. Chile 152 C4
Long Bay U.S.A. 129 D5
Longbeach N.Z. 113 B4
Long Beach CA U.S.A. 136 C5
Long Beach WA U.S.A. 134 A3
Longbia Indon. 59 G2
Longboh Indon. 59 F2
Long Branch U.S.A. 131 G3
Longchang China 66 C2
Longcheng Anhui China see Xiaoxian
Longcheng Guangdong China see Longmen
Longcheng Jiangxi China see Pengze
Longcheng Yunnan China see Chenggong
Longchuan Guangdong China 67 E3
Longchuan Yunnan China see Nanhua
Longchuan Jiang r. China 66 A4
Long Creek r. Canada 123 K5
Long Eaton U.K. 35 F5
Longford Rep. of Ireland 35 C5
Longgang Chongqing China see Dazu
Longgang Guangdong China 67 E4
Longgi r. Indon. 59 G2
Longhope U.K. 34 E2
Longhui China 67 D3
Longhurst, Mount Antarctica 167 H1
Longibau Indon. 59 G2
Longido Tanz. 96 C5
Longikis Indon. 59 G3
Longiram Indon. 59 F3
Long Island Bahamas 129 E8
Long Island Canada 124 E2
Long Island India 73 G3
Long Island P.N.G. 57 K7
Long Island U.S.A. 131 G3
Long Island Sound sea chan. U.S.A. 131 G3
Longjiang China 63 K2
Long Jiang r. China 67 D3
Longjin Fujian China see Qingliu
Longjin Jiangxi China see Anyi
Longjuzhai China see Danfeng
Longlac Canada 124 C3
Long Lake l. Canada 124 C3
Long Lake U.S.A. 131 F2
Long Lake l. U.S.A. 131 F1
Longli China 66 C3
Longlin China 66 C3
Longmeadow U.S.A. 131 G2
Longmen China 67 E4
Longmen Shan mts China 66 C1
Longming China 66 C4
Longmont U.S.A. 134 F4
Longnan China 67 E3
Longnawan Indon. 59 F2
Longobucco Italy 45 F5
Longotoma Chile 152 C3
Longpahangai Indon. 59 F2
Long Phu Vietnam 61 D6
Longping China see Luodian
Long Point Canada 130 C2
Long Point pt Man. Canada 123 L4
Long Point pt Ont. Canada 130 C2
Long Point Bay Canada 130 C2
Long Prairie U.S.A. 132 C2
Longpujungan Indon. 59 F2
Longquan Guizhou China see Danzhai
Longquan Guizhou China see Fenggang
Longquan Zhejiang China 67 F2
Longquan Xi r. China 67 G2
Long Range Mountains Nfld. and Lab. Canada 125 J3
Long Range Mountains Nfld. and Lab. Canada 125 J4
Longreach Australia 111 F4
Longriba China 66 B1
Long Ridge U.S.A. 130 A4
Longshan Guizhou China see Longli
Longshan Hunan China 67 D2
Longsheng China 67 D3
Longs Peak U.S.A. 134 F4
Long Teru Sarawak Malaysia 59 F2
Longtian China 67 D2
Longtom Lake Canada 123 G1
Longtown U.K. 34 E4
Longué-Jumelles France 38 C3
Longue-Pointe Canada 125 H3
Longueuil Canada 125 F4
Longuyon France 39 F2
Longvale U.S.A. 136 A2
Long Valley U.S.A. 137 G4
Longview TX U.S.A. 133 C5
Longview WA U.S.A. 134 B3
Longwei Co l. China 75 F2
Longxi China 66 C1
Longxian Guangdong China see Wengyuan
Longxian Shaanxi China 66 C1
Longxi Shan mt. China 67 F3
Longxun China see Dehua
Long Xuyên Vietnam 61 D6
Longyan China 67 F3

▶Longyearbyen Svalbard 26 B2
Capital of Svalbard.

Longzhen China 64 A2
Longzhou China 66 C4
Longzhouping China see Changyang
Lonigo Italy 44 C2
Lonjsko Polje plain Croatia 44 F2
Lönsboda Sweden 33 D4
Lonsdalen valley Norway 32 D2
Lons-le-Saunier France 39 F3
Lonton Myanmar 60 B2
Lontra Brazil 147 I6
Lontra r. Brazil 150 B3
Loochoo Islands Japan see Ryukyu Islands
Looking Glass r. U.S.A. 130 A2
Lookout, Cape Canada 124 D2
Lookout, Cape U.S.A. 129 D5
Lookout, Point U.S.A. 130 B1
Lookout Point Australia 109 B8
Loolmalasin vol. crater Tanz. 96 B5
Looma Australia 108 D4
Loon r. Canada 123 H3
Loongana Australia 109 D7
Loon Lake Canada 123 I4
Loop Head Rep. of Ireland 35 B5
Lop China 74 D1
Lopary Madag. 99 [inset] J4
Lopatina, Gora mt. Rus. Fed. 64 E2
Lopatka, Cape Rus. Fed. see Lopatka, Mys
Lopatka, Mys c. Rus. Fed. 27 P4
Lopatka, Mys c. Rus. Fed. 27 P2
Lopatovo Rus. Fed. 33 H4
Lop Buri Thai. 61 C5
Lopez Phil. 57 F3
Lopez, Cap c. Gabon 94 A5
Lop Nur salt l. China 70 H3
Lopori r. Dem. Rep. Congo 94 C4
Lopphavet b. Norway 32 F1
Loppi Fin. 33 G3
Lora r. Afgh. 81 F4
Lora Norway 33 C3
Lora del Río Spain 42 D4
Lorain U.S.A. 130 B3
Loralai Pak. 81 G4
Loralai r. Pak. 81 G4
Lorca Spain 43 F4
Lord Howe Atoll Solomon Is see Ontong Java Atoll
Lord Howe Island Australia 107 E5
Lord Howe Rise sea feature S. Pacific Ocean 164 E7
Lord Loughborough Island Myanmar 61 B6
Lordsburg U.S.A. 135 E6
Lorena Brazil 151 C7
Lorengau P.N.G. 57 K6
Lorentz r. Indon. 57 I7
Lorentz National Park Indon. 57 I6
Lorenzo Geyres Uruguay 152 F3
Lorestān prov. Iran 80 B3
Loreto Brazil 150 C3
Loreto Italy 44 D3
Loreto Para. 149 F5
Loreto dept Peru 146 C5
Lorian Swamp Kenya 96 C4
Lorica Col. 146 C2
Lorient France 38 B3
Lorillard r. Canada 123 N1
Lormi India 75 D5
Lorn, Firth of est. U.K. 34 D3
Lorne Australia 111 F5
Loro r. China 75 G3
Loropéni Burkina 92 E3
Lörrach Germany 36 C5
Lorrain, Plateau France 39 G2
Lorraine Australia 111 D3
Lorraine admin. reg. France 39 G2
Lort r. Australia 109 C8
Lörudden Sweden 33 E3
Los, Îles de is Guinea 92 B3
Losai National Reserve nature res. Kenya 96 C4
Losal India 74 B4
Los Alamitos, Sierra de mt. Mex. 133 A7
Los Alamos CA U.S.A. 136 B4
Los Alamos NM U.S.A. 135 F6
Los Alerces, Parque Nacional nat. park Arg. 153 C5
Los Amores Arg. 152 F2
Los Andes Chile 152 C3
Los Angeles Chile 152 B4

▶Los Angeles U.S.A. 136 C4
3rd most populous city in North America and 6th in the world.
northamerica 118–119
world 16–17

Los Angeles Aqueduct canal U.S.A. 136 C4
Los Antiguos Arg. 153 C6
Los Argallanes, Sierra de hills Spain 42 D3
Los Banos U.S.A. 136 B3
Los Barreros mt. Spain 43 E3
Los Barrios Spain 42 D4
Los Blancos Arg. 149 E5
Los Caballos Mesteños, Llano de plain Mex. 135 F7
Los Canarreos, Archipiélago de is Cuba 127 J7
Los Chonos, Archipiélago de is Chile 153 B6
Los Choros, Islas de is Chile 152 C2
Los Cisnes, Lagunas de lakes Arg. 152 E2
Los Corales del Rosario, Parque Nacional nat. park Col. 146 C2
Los Coronados, Islas is Mex. 136 D5
Los Cusis Beni Bol. 148 D3
Los Cusis Beni Bol. 149 D3
Los Desventurados, Islas de is S. Pacific Ocean 165 M7
Los Difuntios, Lago de l. Uruguay see Negra, Lago
Los Estados, Isla de i. Arg. 153 D8
Losevo Rus. Fed. 29 G6
Loseya well Tanz. 97 C6
Los Gatos U.S.A. 136 B3
Los Glaciares, Parque Nacional nat. park Arg. 153 B7
Los Hoyos Mex. 135 E7
Los Huemules, Parque Nacional nat. park Chile 153 B6
Lošinj i. Croatia 44 E2
Los Jardines de la Reina, Archipiélago de is Cuba 127 K7
Los Juríes Arg. 152 E2
Los Lagos Chile 152 B4
Los Lagos admin. reg. Chile 152 B5
Loslau Poland see Wodzisław Śląski
Los Menucos Arg. 152 C5
Los Mexicanos, Lago de l. Mex. 135 F7
Los Mochis Mex. 126 E6
Los Mosquitos, Golfo de b. Panama 139 H7
Los Navalmorales Spain 42 D3
Los Nevados, Parque Nacional nat. park Col. 146 C3
Los Palacios y Villafranca Spain 42 D4
Lospatos East Timor 108 D2
Los Pedroches plat. Spain 42 D3
Los Picos de Europa, Parque Nacional de nat. park Spain 42 D1
Los Ríos prov. Ecuador 146 B5
Los Roques, Islas is Venez. 146 E2
Lossiemouth U.K. 34 E3
Los Taques Venez. 146 D2
Los Telares Arg. 152 E2
Los Teques Venez. 146 E2
Los Testigos is Venez. 147 F2
Lost Creek U.S.A. 130 B5
Lost Hills U.S.A. 136 C4
Lost Trail Pass U.S.A. 134 D3
Los Vientos Chile 148 C6
Los Vilos Chile 152 C2
Los Yébenes Spain 42 E3
Lot r. France 39 D4
Lota Chile 152 B4
Lotagipi Swamp Kenya 96 B3
Lote Norway 33 B3
Løten Norway 33 C3
Loth U.K. 34 E2
Lothagum Hills Sudan 96 B3
Lotikipi Plain Kenya 96 B3
Loto Dem. Rep. Congo 94 D5
Lotoi r. Dem. Rep. Congo 94 C5
Lot's Wife i. Japan see Sōfu-gan
Lotta r. Fin./Rus. Fed. 32 H1
Louang Namtha Laos 60 C3
Louangphrabang Laos 60 C4
Louang Phrabang Range mts Laos/Thai. 60 C4
Loubomo Congo 95 B6
Loučná hill Czech Rep. 37 F3
Loudéac France 38 B2
Loudi China 67 D3
Loudima Congo 95 B6
Louden U.S.A. 128 B5
Loudonville U.S.A. 130 B3
Loudun France 38 D3
Louéssé r. Congo 94 B5
L'Ouest, Pointe de pt Canada 125 H3
Louga Senegal 92 A2
Loughborough U.K. 35 F5
Lougheed Island Canada 121 I2
Loughrea Rep. of Ireland 35 B5
Louhans France 39 F3
Louisa KY U.S.A. 130 B4
Louisa VA U.S.A. 130 E4
Louisbourg Canada 125 J4
Louisburg Canada see Louisbourg
Louise Falls Canada 123 G2
Louis-Gentil Morocco see Youssoufia
Louisiade Archipelago is P.N.G. 107 E3
Louisiana U.S.A. 132 D4
Louisiana state U.S.A. 127 H5
Louis Trichardt S. Africa 99 F4
Louisville GA U.S.A. 129 C5
Louisville IL U.S.A. 128 A4
Louisville KY U.S.A. 128 B4
Louisville MS U.S.A. 129 A5
Louisville CH U.S.A. 130 C3
Louisville Ridge sea feature S. Pacific Ocean 164 G8
Louis-XIV, Pointe pt Canada 124 E2
Loukhi Rus. Fed. 28 E2
Loukoléla Congo 94 C5
Loukouo Congo 94 B5
Loulé Port. 42 B4
Loulouni Mali 92 D3
Loum Cameroon 93 H4
Louny Czech Rep. 37 F3
Loup r. U.S.A. 132 B3
Loup City U.S.A. 132 B3
Loups-Marins, Lacs des lakes Canada 125 F1
Lourdes Canada 125 J3
Lourdes France 38 C5
Lourenço Brazil 147 I4
Lourenço Marques Moz. see Maputo
Lourinhã Port. 42 B3
Lousã Port. 42 B2
Louth Australia 112 C3
Louth U.K. 35 F5
Loutra Greece 47 D6
Loutra Aidipsou Greece 47 C5
Louvain Belgium see Leuven
Louviers France 38 D2
Lövånger Sweden 32 F2
Lovasberény Hungary 37 I5
Lovat' r. Rus. Fed. 28 D4
Lövberga Sweden 32 D3
Lovćen nat. park Serb. and Mont 46 A3
Lovech Bulg. 46 D3
Loveland U.S.A. 134 F4
Lovell ME U.S.A. 131 H1
Lovell WY U.S.A. 134 E3
Lovelock U.S.A. 136 C1
Lovere Italy 44 C2
Lovers' Leap mt. U.S.A. 130 C5
Lovington U.S.A. 135 G6
Lovozero Rus. Fed. 28 E1
Lovrin Romania 46 B2
Lövstabukten b. Sweden 33 E3
Lóvua Angola 95 D6
Lóvua Angola 95 D7
Lowa Dem. Rep. Congo 94 E5
Lowa r. Dem. Rep. Congo 94 E5
Lowarai Pass Pak. 81 G3
Lowell MA U.S.A. 131 H2
Lowell OR U.S.A. 134 B4
Lowell VT U.S.A. 131 G1
Lowelli Sudan 96 B3
Lower Arrow Lake Canada 122 G5
Lower California pen. Mex. see Baja California
Lower Garry Lake Canada 123 L1
Lower Glenelg National Park Australia 112 B5
Lower Granite Gorge U.S.A. 137 F4
Lower Hutt N.Z. 113 C3
Lower Laberge Canada 122 C2
Lower Lake U.S.A. 136 A2
Lower Lough Erne l. U.K. 35 C4
Lower Peirce Reservoir Sing. 58 [inset]
Lower Red Lake U.S.A. 132 C2
Lower Saxony land Germany see Niedersachsen
Lower Tunguska r. Rus. Fed. see Nizhnyaya Tunguska
Lower Zambezi National Park Zambia 95 F8
Lowestoft U.K. 35 G5
Lowgar prov. Afgh. 81 G3
Łowicz Poland 37 I2
Lowville U.S.A. 131 F2
Loxton Australia 112 B4
Loyalsock Creek r. U.S.A. 131 E3
Loyalton U.S.A. 136 B2
Loyalty Islands New Caledonia see Loyauté, Îles
Loyang China see Luoyang
Loyauté, Îles is New Caledonia 107 F4
Loyev Belarus see Loyew
Loyew Belarus 29 D5
Loyno Rus. Fed. 28 J4
Loyola, Punta pt Arg. 153 C7
Løypskardtinden mt. Norway 32 D2
Lozère, Mont mt. France 39 E4
Loznica Serb. and Mont. 46 A2
Loznitsa Bulg. 46 E3
Lozova Ukr. 29 F6
Lozovaya Ukr. see Lozova
Loz'va r. Rus. Fed. 28 L3
Luabo Moz. 99 H3
Luacano Angola 95 D7
Luachimo r. Angola/Dem. Rep. Congo 95 D6
Lua Dekere r. Dem. Rep. Congo 94 C4
Luakila Dem. Rep. Congo 95 E6
Lualala r. Moz. 99 H3
Luambe National Park Zambia 97 B8
Luampa r. Zambia 95 E8
Lu'an China 67 F2
Luanchuan China 67 D1

▶Luanda Angola 95 B7
Capital of Angola.

Luanda prov. Angola 95 B7
Luando Angola 95 C7
Luando r. Angola 95 C7
Luang, Khao mt. Thai. 61 B6
Luanginga r. Zambia 95 D8
Luang Nam Tha Laos see Louang Namtha
Luang Prabang Laos see Louangphrabang
Luanguinga r. Angola 95 D8
Luangwa Zambia 95 F8
Luangwa r. Zambia 97 A8
Luanhaizi China 75 G2
Lua Nova Brazil 147 G6
Luanshya Zambia 95 F8
Luanza Dem. Rep. Congo 95 F7
Luao Angola see Luau
Luapula prov. Zambia 95 F7
Luar, Danau l. Indon. 59 F2
Luarca Spain 42 C1
Luashi Dem. Rep. Congo 95 D7
Luatamba Angola 95 D8
Luau Angola 95 D7
Luba Equat. Guinea 93 H5
Lubalo Angola 95 C7
Lubań Poland 37 G3
Lubāna Latvia 33 G4
Lubānas ezers l. Latvia 33 G4
Lubango Angola 95 B8
Lubao Dem. Rep. Congo 95 E6
Lubartów Poland 37 J3
Lubawa Poland 37 I2
Lübbecke Germany 36 D2
Lübben Germany 37 F3
Lübbenau Germany 37 F3
Lubbock U.S.A. 133 A5
Lübeck Germany 36 E2
Lübecker Bucht b. Germany 36 E1
Lubefu Dem. Rep. Congo 95 E6
Lubei China 63 K3
Lubelska, Wyżyna hills Poland 37 K3
Luben Poland see Lubin
Lubenka Kazakh. 29 J6
Lubéron, Montagne du ridge France 39 F5
Lubie, Jezioro l. Poland 37 G2
Lubienka r. Poland 37 I2
Lubień Kujawski Poland 37 I2
Lubin Poland 37 H3
Lublin Poland 31 J3
Lubliniec Poland 37 I3
Lubnān country Asia see Lebanon
Lubny Ukr. 29 E6
Lubok Antu Sarawak Malaysia 59 E2
Luboń Poland 37 H2
Lubraniec Poland 37 I2
Lubrin Spain 43 E4
Lübtheen Germany 36 E2
Lubudi r. Dem. Rep. Congo 95 E7
Lubuklinggau Indon. 58 C3
Lubukpakam Indon. 58 B2
Lubuksikaping Indon. 58 C2
Lubumbashi Dem. Rep. Congo 95 E7
Lubunda Dem. Rep. Congo 95 E6
Lubungu Zambia 95 E8
Lubuta Zambia 95 D9
Lubutu Dem. Rep. Congo 94 E5
Lubutu r. Dem. Rep. Congo 94 E5
Lubwe Zambia 95 F7
Lucala Angola 95 B7
Lucan Canada 130 C2
Lucanas Peru 148 B3
Lučani Serb. and Mont. 46 B3
Lucania, Mount Canada 122 A2
Lucapa Angola 95 D7
Lucas Brazil 149 G3
Lucasville U.S.A. 130 B4

Mahajan India **74** B3
Mahajanga Madag. **99** [inset] J2
Mahajanga *prov.* Madag. **99** [inset] J3
Mahakam *r.* Indon. **59** G3
Mahalapye Botswana **99** E4
Mahale Mountain National Park Tanz. **97** A6
Mahalevona Madag. **99** [inset] K2
Mahallāt Iran **80** B3
Maham India **74** C3
Māhān Iran **80** D4
Mahanadi *r.* India **73** E1
Mahanoro Madag. **99** [inset] K3
Maharajganj *Bihar* India **75** E4
Maharajganj *Uttar Pradesh* India **75** D4
Maharajpur India **74** C4
Maharashtra *state* India **72** B2
Mahārlū, Daryācheh-ye *salt l.* Iran **80** C4
Maha Sarakham Thai. **61** C4
Mahatalaky Madag. **99** [inset] J5
Mahaṭṭat Ḍab'ah Jordan **77** C4
Mahavavy *r.* Madag. **99** [inset] J2
Mahaweli Ganga *r.* Sri Lanka **72** D4
Mahazoma Madag. **99** [inset] J3
Mahbub Sudan **89** F6
Mahbubabad India **72** D2
Mahbubnagar India **72** C2
Mahd adh Dhahab Saudi Arabia **89** I4
Mahdah Oman **80** C5
Mahdia Alg. **91** F2
Mahdia Guyana **147** G3
Mahdia Tunisia **91** H2
Mahe India **72** B4
Mahé Seychelles **162** K6
Mahendragarh India **74** C3
Mahendragiri *mt.* India **73** E2
Mahenge Tanz. **97** C7
Mahesana India **74** B5
Mahgawan India **74** C4
Mahi *r.* India **74** B5
Māhī *watercourse* Iran **81** D4
Mahia Peninsula N.Z. **113** D2
Mahilyow Belarus **29** D5
Mahim India **72** B2
Mahina Mali **92** C2
Mahmudabad India **74** D4
Maḥmūd-e 'Erāqī Afgh. **81** G3
Mahmudiye Turkey **47** E5
Mahnomen U.S.A. **132** B2
Mahoba India **74** C4
Maholi India **74** D4
Mahón Spain **43** I3
Mahongo Game Park *nature res.* Namibia **98** D3
Mahony Lake Canada **122** E1
Mahou Mali **92** D2
Mahrauni India **74** C4
Mähren *reg.* Czech Rep. *see* Moravia
Mahrès Tunisia **91** H2
Māhrūd Iran **81** E3
Mahsana India *see* Mahesana
Mahur India **72** C2
Mahuva India **74** A5
Mahwa India **74** C4
Mahya Dağı *mt.* Turkey **46** E4
Mahyār Iran **80** B3
Maia American Samoa **107** I3
Maia Port. **42** B2
Maiaia Moz. *see* Nacala
Maibang India **75** G4
Maicao Col. **146** C2
Maicasagi *r.* Canada **124** E3
Maicasagi, Lac *l.* Canada **124** E3
Maîche France **39** G3
Maici *r.* Brazil **147** F6
Maicuru *r.* Brazil **147** H5
Maidstone Canada **123** I4
Maidstone U.K. **35** G6
Maiduguri Nigeria **93** I3
Maiella, Parco Nazionale della *nat. park* Italy **44** E3
Maigmó *mt.* Spain **43** F3
Mai Gudo *mt.* Eth. **96** C3
Maihar India **74** D4
Maijdi Bangl. **75** F5
Maiji Shan *mt.* China **66** C1
Maikala Range *hills* India **74** D5
Maiko *r.* Dem. Rep. Congo **94** E4
Mailan Hill *mt.* India **75** D5
Mailani India **74** D3
Maïlao Chad **94** B2
Mailsi Pak. **81** H4
Ma'in *tourist site* Yemen **76** C6
Mainaguri India **75** F4
Main Brook Canada **125** K3
Mainburg Germany **36** E4
Maindargi India **72** C2
Mai-Ndombe, Lac *l.* Dem. Rep. Congo **94** C5
Maine *state* U.S.A. **131** I1
Maine, Gulf of U.S.A. **131** I2
Mainé Hanari, Cerro *hill* Col. **146** C5
Maïné-Soroa Niger **93** I2
Maingkwan Myanmar **60** B2
Maingy Island Myanmar **61** B5
Mainkung China **66** A2
Mainland *i. Orkney, Scotland* U.K. **34** E2
Mainland *i. Shetland, Scotland* U.K. **34** F1
Mainling China **75** G3
Mainoru Australia **110** C2
Mainpat *reg.* India **75** D5
Mainpuri India **74** C4
Main Range National Park Australia **111** H6
Maintenon France **38** D2
Maintirano Madag. **99** [inset] J3
Mainua Fin. **32** G2
Mainz Germany **36** D3
Maio *i.* Cape Verde **92** [inset]
Maipó, Volcán *vol.* Chile **152** C3
Maipú *Buenos Aires* Arg. **152** F4
Maipú *Mendoza* Arg. **152** C3
Maiquetía Venez. **146** E2
Maiqu Zangbo *r.* China **75** E3
Mairi Brazil **150** D4
Maiskhal Island Bangl. **75** F5
Maitencillo Chile **152** C2
Maitengwe Botswana **99** E4
Maithon India **75** E5
Maitland *N.S.W.* Australia **112** D4
Maitland *S.A.* Australia **112** A4
Maitland, Banjaran *mts Sabah* Malaysia **59** G1
Maitri *research station* Antarctica **167** C2
Maiwo *i.* Vanuatu *see* Maéwo
Maíz, Islas del *is* Nicaragua **139** H6
Maizhokunggar China **75** F3
Maizuru Japan **65** C6
Maja Jezercë *mt.* Albania **46** A3
Majalgaon India **72** C2
Majari *r.* Brazil **147** F4
Majdanpek Serb. and Mont. **46** B2
Majene Indon. **56** E6
Majevica *mts* Bos.-Herz. **44** G2
Majhgawan India **74** D4
Majholi India **74** C5
Majiang *Guangxi* China **67** D4
Majiang *Guizhou* China **66** C3
Major, Puig *mt.* Spain **43** H3
Majorca *i.* Spain **43** H3
Majuli Island India **75** G4
Majunga Madag. *see* Mahajanga
Majuro *atoll* Marshall Is **164** F5
Majwemasweu S. Africa **99** E6
Maka Senegal **92** B2
Makabana Congo **94** B5
Makak Cameroon **93** H5
Makale Indon. **57** E6

▶**Makalu** *mt.* China/Nepal **75** E4
5th highest mountain in the world and in Asia.
asia 50–51
world 6–7

Makalu Barun National Park Nepal **75** E4
Makamba Burundi **95** F6
Makanchi Kazakh. **70** F2
Makanjila Malawi **97** B8
Makanya Tanz. **97** C6
Makanza Dem. Rep. Congo **94** C4
Makaraingo Madag. **99** [inset] J3
Makari Cameroon **93** I2
Makari Mountain National Park Tanz. *see* Mahale Mountain National Park
Makarov Rus. Fed. **64** E2
Makarov Basin *sea feature* Arctic Ocean **166** B1
Makarska Croatia **44** F3
Makar'ye Rus. Fed. **28** I4
Makassar Indon. **56** E7
Makassar, Selat Indon. *see* Macassar Strait
Makassar Strait Indon. *see* Macassar Strait
Makat Kazakh. **26** F5
Makatini Flats *lowland* S. Africa **99** G5
Makaw Myanmar **60** B2
Makay, Massif du *mts* Madag. **99** [inset] J4
Makedonija *country* Europe *see* Macedonia
Makeni Sierra Leone **92** B3
Makete Tanz. **97** B7
Makeyevka Ukr. *see* Makiyivka
Makgadikgadi *salt pan* Botswana **98** E4
Makgadikgadi Pans National Park Botswana **98** E4
Makhachkala Rus. Fed. **29** H8
Makhambet Kazakh. **29** I7
Makharadze Georgia *see* Ozurget'i
Makhfar al Ḥammām Syria **79** D4
Makhmal Turkm. **81** E2
Makhtal India **72** C2
Makian *vol.* Indon. **57** G5
Makindu Kenya **96** C5
Makinsk Kazakh. **26** H4
Makira *i.* Solomon Is *see* San Cristobal
Makiyivka Ukr. **29** F6
Makkah Saudi Arabia *see* Mecca
Makkovik, Cape Canada **125** J2
Makljen *pass* Bos.-Herz. **44** F3
Makó Hungary **46** B1
Makoa, Serra *hills* Brazil **147** G4
Makokou Gabon **94** B4
Makonde Plateau Tanz. **97** C7
Makongolosi Tanz. **97** B7
Makopong Botswana **98** D5
Makoro Dem. Rep. Congo **94** F4
Makotipoko Congo **94** C5
Makoua Congo **94** B5
Maków Mazowiecki Poland **37** J2
Makra *i.* Greece **47** D6
Makrakomi Greece **47** C5
Makran *reg.* Iran/Pak. **81** E5
Makrana India **74** B4
Makran Coast Range *mts* Pak. *see* Talar-i-Band
Makronisi *i.* Greece **47** D6
Maksatikha Rus. Fed. **31** M1
Maksi India **74** C5
Maksimovka Rus. Fed. **64** D3
Maksotag Iran **81** E4
Maksudangarh India **74** C5
Makthar Tunisia **45** B7
Mākū Iran **80** A2
Makum India **75** G4
Makumbako Tanz. **97** B7
Makunduchi Tanz. **97** C6
Makung Taiwan **67** F4
Makunguwiro Tanz. **97** C7
Makunudhoo *i.* Maldives **72** B5
Makurazaki Japan **65** B7
Makurdi Nigeria **93** H4
Makuungo Somalia **96** D4
Makuyuni Tanz. **96** C5
Mal India **75** F4
Mala Peru **148** A3
Mala Rep. of Ireland *see* Mallow
Mala *i.* Solomon Is *see* Malaita
Mala, Punta *pt* Panama **139** H7
Malabar Coast India **72** B3

▶**Malabo** Equat. Guinea **93** H5
Capital of Equatorial Guinea.

Malaca Spain *see* Málaga
Malacca Malaysia *see* Melaka
Malacca *state* Malaysia *see* Melaka
Malacca, Strait of Indon./Malaysia **58** B1
Malacky Slovakia **37** H4
Malad *r.* U.S.A. **134** D4
Malad City U.S.A. **134** D4
Maladzyechna Belarus **29** C5
Malá Fatra *nat. park* Slovakia **37** I4
Málaga Spain **42** D4
Malaga *NJ* U.S.A. **131** F4
Malaga *NM* U.S.A. **135** F6
Malaga *OH* U.S.A. **130** C4
Malagarasi *r.* Burundi/Tanz. **97** A6
Malagarasi Tanz. **97** A6
Malagón Spain **42** E3
Malagon *r.* Spain **42** C4
Malahar Indon. **108** C2
Malaimbandy Madag. **99** [inset] J4
Malaita *i.* Solomon Is **107** F2
Malaka *mt.* Indon. **59** G5
Malakal Sudan **96** A2
Malakanagiri India **73** D2
Mala Kapela *mts* Croatia **44** E2
Malakheti Nepal **74** D3
Malakula *i.* Vanuatu **107** F3
Malakwal Pak. **81** H3
Malali Guyana **147** G3
Malamala Indon. **57** F6
Malang Indon. **59** F4
Malanga Moz. **97** C8
Malangali Tanz. **97** B7
Malangana Nepal *see* Malangwa
Malange Angola *see* Malanje
Malangseidet Norway **32** E1
Malangwa Nepal **75** E4
Malanje Angola **95** C7
Malanje *prov.* Angola **95** C7
Malanville Benin **93** F3
Malanzán Arg. **152** D2
Malanzán, Sierra de *mts* Arg. **152** D2
Mälaren *l.* Sweden **33** E4
Malargüe Arg. **152** C3
Malaripo Brazil **147** H4
Malartic Canada **124** E3
Malaspina Arg. **153** D6
Malaspina Glacier U.S.A. **122** A3
Malatya Turkey **79** D3
Malaut India **74** B3
Malavate Fr. Guiana **147** H4
Malāvi Iran **80** A3
Malawali *i. Sabah* Malaysia **59** G1
▶**Malawi** *country* Africa **97** B7
africa 86–87, 100
Malawi, Lake Africa *see* Nyasa, Lake
Malawi National Park Zambia *see* Nyika National Park
Malawiya Sudan **89** H6
Malax Fin. **32** F3
Malaya *pen.* Malaysia *see* Peninsular Malaysia
Malaya Pera Rus. Fed. **28** J2
Malaya Vishera Rus. Fed. **28** E4
Malāyer Iran **80** B3
Malay Reef Australia **111** G3
▶**Malaysia** *country* Asia **59** F2
asia 52–53, 82
Malbaie *r.* Canada **125** G4
Malbaza Niger **93** G2
Malbon Australia **111** E4
Malbork Poland **37** I1
Malbrán Arg. **152** E2
Malchin Germany **37** F2
Malcolm Australia **109** C7
Malcolm, Point Australia **109** C8
Malcolm Inlet Oman *see* Ghazira, Ghubbat al
Maldegem Belgium **36** A3
Malden U.S.A. **133** D4
Malden Island Kiribati **165** H6
▶**Maldives** *country* Indian Ocean **71** D11
asia 52–53, 82
Maldonado Uruguay **152** G3

▶**Male** Maldives **69** F6
Capital of the Maldives.

Male Myanmar **60** B3
Maléa Guinea **92** C3
Maleas, Akra *pt Lesbos* Greece **47** E5
Maleas, Akra *pt* Greece **47** C6
Male Atoll Maldives **71** D11
Malebogo S. Africa **98** E6
Malegaon *Maharashtra* India **72** B1
Malegaon *Maharashtra* India **72** C2
Malei Moz. **99** H3
Malé Karpaty *hills* Slovakia **37** H4
Malek Sīāh, Kūh-e *mt.* Afgh. **81** E4
Malela Dem. Rep. Congo **95** E6
Malélé Congo **95** B6
Malele Dem. Rep. Congo **95** B6
Malema Moz. **99** H2
Malendo *watercourse* Nigeria **93** G3
Målerås Sweden **33** D4
Maler Kotla India **74** B3
Maleševske Planine *mts* Bulg./Macedonia **46** C4
Malesherbes France **38** E2
Malesina Greece **47** C5
Mālestān Afgh. **81** F3
Malestroit France **38** B3
Malgobek Rus. Fed. **29** H8
Malgomaj *l.* Sweden **32** E2
Malha Sudan **89** E6
Malhada Brazil **150** D5
Malham Saudi Arabia **80** A5
Malhargarh India **74** B4
Malheur *r.* U.S.A. **134** C3
Malheur Lake U.S.A. **134** C4
▶**Mali** *country* Africa **93** E1
africa 86–87, 100
Mali Dem. Rep. Congo **94** E5
Mali Guinea **92** B2
Malia Greece **47** D7
Maliana East Timor **57** G7
Malibu U.S.A. **136** C4
Mali Hka *r.* Myanmar **60** B2
Malikdin Afgh. **81** G3
Malik Naro *mt.* Pak. **81** E4
Mali Kyun *i.* Myanmar **61** B5
Malili Indon. **57** F6
Mali Lošinj Croatia **44** E2
Malimba, Monts *mts* Dem. Rep. Congo **95** F6
Malin Rep. of Ireland **34** C4
Malin Ukr. *see* Malyn
Malindi Kenya **96** D5
Malines Belgium *see* Mechelen
Malinga Gabon **94** B5
Malin Head Rep. of Ireland **34** C4
Malinovka *r.* Rus. Fed. **64** C3
Malinyi Tanz. **97** C7
Malipo China **66** C4
Maliq Albania **46** B4
Mali Raginac *mt.* Croatia **44** E2
Malit, Qafa e *pass* Albania **46** B3
Maliwun Myanmar **61** B6
Maliya India **74** A5
Malka *r.* Rus. Fed. **29** H8
Malka Mary Kenya **96** D3
Malkapur *Maharashtra* India **72** B2
Malkapur *Maharashtra* India **72** C1
Malkara Turkey **78** A2
Malko Tŭrnovo Bulg. **46** E4
Mallacoota Australia **112** D5
Mallaig U.K. **34** D3
Mallanga *well* Chad **88** D5
Mallawi Egypt **89** F3
Mallee Cliffs National Park Australia **112** B4
Mållejus *hill* Norway **32** F1
Mallery Lake Canada **123** L1
Mallét Brazil **151** B8
Mallia Greece *see* Malia
Mallorca *i.* Spain *see* Majorca
Mallow Rep. of Ireland **35** B5
Mallowa Well Australia **108** D5
Malm Norway **32** C2
Malmberget Sweden **32** F2
Malmédy Belgium **39** G1
Malmesbury S. Africa **98** C7
Malmesbury U.K. **35** E6
Malmköping Sweden **33** E4
Malmö Sweden **33** D5
Malmö-Sturup *airport* Sweden **33** D5
Malmslätt Sweden **33** D4
Malmyzh Rus. Fed. **28** I4
Maloca *Amazonas* Brazil **147** F5
Maloca *Pará* Brazil **147** H4
Maloca Salamaim Brazil **149** E3
Malo Crniće Serb. and Mont. **46** B2
Malombe, Lake Malawi **97** B8
Malone U.S.A. **131** F1
Malong China **66** B3
Małopolska, Wyżyna *hills* Poland **37** J3
Maloshuyka Rus. Fed. **28** F3
Malovan *pass* Bos.-Herz. **44** F3
Malovăț Romania **46** C2
Malowera Moz. **97** B8
Måløy Norway **33** B3
Maloyaroslavets Rus. Fed. **29** F5
Malozemel'skaya Tundra *lowland* Rus. Fed. **28** I2
Malpelo, Isla de *i.* N. Pacific Ocean **165** M5
Malpica Spain **42** B1
Malprabha *r.* India **72** C2
Malpura India **74** B4
Malše *r.* Czech Rep. **37** G4
Malsiras India **72** B2
▶**Malta** *country* Europe **45** E7
europe 24–25, 48
Malta Latvia **33** G4
Malta *i.* Malta **45** E7
Malta U.S.A. **134** F2
Maltahöhe Namibia **98** C5
Maltam Cameroon **88** B6
Malton U.K. **35** F4
Maluera Moz. *see* Malowera
Malukken *is* Indon. *see* Moluccas
Maluku *is* Indon. *see* Moluccas
Ma'lūlā, Jabal *mts* Syria **77** C3
Malumfashi Nigeria **93** G3
Malundano Zambia **95** E9
Malung Sweden **33** D3
Maluti Mountains Lesotho **99** F6
Malu'u Solomon Is **107** F2
Malvan India **72** B2
Malvasia Greece *see* Monemvasia
Malvern *AR* U.S.A. **133** C5
Malvern *OH* U.S.A. **130** C3
Malvérnia Moz. *see* Chicualacuala
Malvinas, Islas *terr.* S. Atlantic Ocean *see* Falkland Islands
Malwal Sudan **96** A2
Malý Dunaj *r.* Slovakia **37** I5
Malyn Ukr. **29** D6
Malyy Anyuy *r.* Rus. Fed. **27** Q3
Malyy Irgiz *r.* Rus. Fed. **29** I5
Malyy Kavkaz *mts* Asia *see* Lesser Caucasus
Malyy Lyakhovskiy, Ostrov *i.* Rus. Fed. **27** O2
Malyy Taymyr, Ostrov *i.* Rus. Fed. **27** K2
Malyy Uzen' *r.* Kazakh./Rus. Fed. **29** I6
Mama *r.* Rus. Fed. **27** O3
Mamadysh Rus. Fed. **28** I5
Mamafubedu S. Africa **99** F5
Mambahenauhan *i.* Phil. **59** G1
Mambai Brazil **150** C5
Mambal Cameroon **93** I4
Mambali Tanz. **97** B6
Mambasa Dem. Rep. Congo **94** F4
Mambéré *r.* Cent. Afr. Rep. **94** C4
Mambéré-Kadéï *pref.* Cent. Afr. Rep. **94** B3
Mambili *r.* Congo **94** C4
Mambolo Sierra Leone **92** B3
Mambrui Kenya **96** D5
Mamelodi S. Africa **99** F5
Mamers France **38** D2
Mamfé Cameroon **93** H4
Mamiá Brazil **147** F6
Mamili National Park Namibia **98** D3
Mamiña Chile **148** C5
Mamison Pass Georgia/Rus. Fed. **79** E2
Mamison Pass Rus. Fed. **29** G8
Mammoth U.S.A. **137** G5
Mammoth Cave National Park U.S.A. **128** B4
Mammoth Lakes U.S.A. **136** C3
Mamonovo Rus. Fed. **37** I1
Mamoré *r.* Bol./Brazil **148** D2
Mamori Brazil **146** E5
Mamoriá Brazil **148** D1
Mamou Guinea **92** B3
Mampikony Madag. **99** [inset] J3
Mampong Ghana **93** E4
Mamry, Jezioro *l.* Poland **37** J1
Mamuju Indon. **59** G3
Mamuno Botswana **98** D4
Mamuras Albania **46** A4
Man Côte d'Ivoire **92** D4
Man *r.* India **72** B2
Man U.S.A. **130** C5

▶**Man, Isle of** *i.* Irish Sea **35** D4
United Kingdom Crown Dependency.
europe 48

Mana Fr. Guiana **147** H3
Manabí *prov.* Ecuador **146** B5
Manacacias *r.* Col. **146** C3
Manacapuru Brazil **147** F5
Manacor Spain **43** H3
Manado Indon. **57** F5

▶**Managua** Nicaragua **138** G6
Capital of Nicaragua.

Managua, Lago de *l.* Nicaragua **138** G6
Manakara Madag. **99** [inset] J4
Manakau *mt.* N.Z. **113** C3
Manali India **74** C2

▶**Manama** Bahrain **80** B5
Capital of Bahrain.

Manamadurai India **72** C4
Manambaho *r.* Madag. **99** [inset] J3
Manambondro Madag. **99** [inset] J4
Manamelkudi India **72** C4
Manam Island P.N.G. **57** K6
Mananantañana *r.* Madag. **99** [inset] J4
Mananara *r.* Madag. **99** [inset] J4
Mananara, Parc National de *nat. park* Madag. **99** [inset] K3
Mananara Avaratra Madag. **99** [inset] K3
Manangoora Australia **110** D3
Mananjary Madag. **99** [inset] K4
Manankoliva Madag. **99** [inset] J5
Manankoro Mali **92** D3
Manantali, Lac de *l.* Mali **92** C2
Manantavadi India **72** C4
Manantenina Madag. **99** [inset] J5
Mana Pass China/India **74** C3
Mana Pools National Park Zimbabwe **99** F3

▶**Manapouri, Lake** N.Z. **113** A4
Deepest lake in Oceania.

Manapparai India **72** C4
Manarantsandry Madag. **99** [inset] J3
Manas *r.* India **75** F4
Manasa India **74** B4
Manas Hu *l.* China **70** G2

▶**Manaslu** *mt.* Nepal **75** E3
8th highest mountain in the world and in Asia.
asia 50–51
world 6–7

Manassas U.S.A. **130** E4
Manastir Macedonia *see* Bitola
Manas Wildlife Sanctuary *nature res.* Bhutan **75** F4
Manatang Indon. **108** D2
Manatí Puerto Rico **139** K5
Manatuto East Timor **57** G7
Man-aung Kyun *i.* Myanmar *see* Cheduba Island
Manaus Brazil **147** F5
Manavgat Turkey **78** B3
Manawar India **74** B5
Manawashei Sudan **88** E6
Manawatu *r.* N.Z. **113** C3
Manbazar India **75** E5
Manbij Syria **77** C1
Manchar India **72** B2
Manchester U.K. **35** E5
Manchester *CT* U.S.A. **131** G3
Manchester *IA* U.S.A. **132** D3
Manchester *KY* U.S.A. **130** B5
Manchester *MI* U.S.A. **130** A2
Manchester *NH* U.S.A. **131** H2
Manchester *OH* U.S.A. **130** B4
Manchhar Lake Pak. **81** F5
Manciano Italy **44** C3
Mancılık Turkey **78** D3
Mancınık Dağı *mts* Turkey **47** E5
Mancos *r.* U.S.A. **137** H3
Mand Pak. **81** E5
Mand, Rūd-e *r.* Iran **80** B4
Manda Bangl. **75** F4
Manda Malawi **97** B7
Manda Tanz. **97** B6
Manda, Jebel *mt.* Sudan **94** E2
Manda, Parc National de *nat. park* Chad **94** C2
Mandabe Madag. **99** [inset] J4
Mandai Sing. **58** [inset]
Mandal Afgh. **81** E3
Mandal *Gujarat* India **74** A5
Mandal *Rajasthan* India **74** B4
Mandal Norway **33** B4

▶**Mandala, Puncak** *mt.* Indon. **57** J6
3rd highest mountain in Oceania.
oceania 102–103

Mandalay Myanmar **60** B3
Mandalay *admin. div.* Myanmar **60** A3
Mandale Myanmar *see* Mandalay
Mandale *admin. div.* Myanmar *see* Mandalay
Mandalgarh India **74** B4
Mandalgovĭ Mongolia **63** H2
Mandalī Iraq **79** F4
Mandan U.S.A. **134** G3
Mandas *Sardinia* Italy **45** B5
Mandav Hills India **74** A5
Mandé, Mont de *hill* France **39** F3
Mandelieu-la-Napoule France **39** G5
Mandello del Lario Italy **44** B2
Mandera Kenya **96** D4
Manderfield U.S.A. **137** F2
Mandeville Jamaica **139** I5
Mandeville N.Z. **113** B4
Mandha India **74** A4
Mandheera Somalia **96** E2
Mandhoúdhion Greece *see* Mantoudi
Mandi India **74** C3
Mandiakui Mali **92** D2
Mandiana Guinea **92** C3
Mandi Burewala Pak. **81** H4
Mandidzuzure Zimbabwe *see* Chimanimani
Mandié Moz. **99** G3
Mandimba Moz. **97** B8
Manding, Monts *mts* Mali **92** C2
Mandji Gabon **93** H6
Mandla India **74** D5
Mandor India **74** B4
Mandoro Dem. Rep. Congo **94** F3
Mandoro Madag. **99** [inset] J3
Mandouri Togo **93** F3
Mandra Greece **47** C5
Mandraki Greece **47** E6
Mandrare *r.* Madag. **99** [inset] J5
Mandrenska *r.* Bulg. *see* Sredetska Reka
Mandritsara Madag. **99** [inset] K2
Mandsaur India **74** B4
Mandul *i.* Indon. **59** G2
Mandurah Australia **109** A8
Manduria Italy **45** F4
Mandvi *Gujarat* India **74** A5
Mandvi *Gujarat* India **74** B5
Mandya India **72** C3
Manendragarh India **75** D5
Maner India **75** E4
Maner *r.* India **72** C2
Manerbio Italy **44** C2
Manerommango Tanz. **97** C6
Manesht Kūh *mt.* Iran **80** A3
Mănești Romania **46** D2
Manfalūṭ Egypt **89** F3
Manfredonia Italy **44** E4
Manfredonia, Golfo di *g.* Italy **44** F4
Manga Brazil **150** D5
Manga Burkina **93** E3
Mangabeiras, Serra das *hills* Brazil **150** C4
Manga Grande Angola **95** B6
Mangai Dem. Rep. Congo **95** C6
Mangaia *i.* Cook Is **165** H7
Mangakino N.Z. **113** C2
Mangalagiri India **72** D2
Mangaldai India **75** G4
Mangalia Romania **46** F3
Mangalmé Chad **88** C6
Mangalore India **72** B3
Mangalvedha India **72** B2
Mangania Dem. Rep. Congo **94** D4
Mangaon India **72** B2
Mangapet India **72** D2
Mangaung S. Africa **99** E6
Mangawan India **75** D4
Mangaweka N.Z. **113** C2
Mangde Chhu *r.* Bhutan *see* Trongsa Chhu
Ma'ngê China *see* Luqu
Mangembe Dem. Rep. Congo **95** E6
Manger Norway **33** B3
Manggar Indon. **59** E3
Mangghyshlaq Kazakh. *see* Mangystau
Mangghystaū Kazakh. *see* Mangystau
Mangghystaū Oblysy *admin. div.* Kazakh. *see* Mangistauskaya Oblast'
Mangistau, Gory *hills* Kazakh. **79** G1
Mangistauskaya Oblast' *admin. div.* Kazakh. **79** H2
Manglares, Punta *pt* Col. **146** B4
Mangnai China **70** H4
Mangoaka Madag. **99** [inset] K2
Mangochi Malawi **97** B8
Mangodara Burkina **92** D3
Mangoky *r. Toliara* Madag. **99** [inset] I4
Mangoky *r. Toliara* Madag. **99** [inset] J4
Mangole *i.* Indon. **57** G6
Mangoli India **72** B2
Mangombe Dem. Rep. Congo **94** E5
Mangoro *r.* Madag. **99** [inset] K3
Mangqystaū Shyghanaghy *b.* Kazakh. *see* Mangyshlakskiy Zaliv
Mangral India **74** A5
Mangrol India **74** C4
Mangrul India **72** C1
Mangshi China *see* Luxi
Mangualde Port. **42** C2
Manguchar Pak. **81** F4
Mangueira, Lago *l.* Brazil **152** G3
Mangueirinha Brazil **151** A8
Manguéni, Plateau du Niger **91** H5
Mangui China **63** K1
Manguinha, Pontal do *pt* Brazil **150** E4
Mangula Zimbabwe *see* Mhangura
Mangum U.S.A. **133** B5
Mangunça, Ilha *i.* Brazil **150** C2
Mangyshlak Kazakh. *see* Mangystau
Mangyshlak, Poluostrov *pen.* Kazakh. **79** G1
Mangyshlak Oblast *admin. div.* Kazakh. *see* Mangistauskaya Oblast'
Mangyshlakskaya Oblast' *admin. div.* Kazakh. *see* Mangistauskaya Oblast'
Mangyshlakskiy Zaliv *b.* Kazakh. **29** I7
Mangystau Kazakh. **26** F5
Manhattan U.S.A. **132** B4
Manhuaçu Brazil **151** D7
Mani Chad **88** B6
Mani China **75** E2
Mani Col. **146** C3
Mani Nigeria **93** G2
Mania *r.* Madag. **99** [inset] J3
Maniago Italy **44** D1
Maniari Tank *resr* India **75** D5
Manica Moz. **99** G3
Manica *prov.* Moz. **99** G3
Manicaland *prov.* Zimbabwe **99** G3
Manicoré Brazil **147** F6
Manicoré *r.* Brazil **147** F6
Manicouagan Canada **125** G3
Manicouagan *r.* Canada **125** G3
Manicouagan, Réservoir Canada **125** G3
Manic Trois, Réservoir Canada **125** G3
Maniema *prov.* Dem. Rep. Congo **94** E5
Manīfah Saudi Arabia **80** B5
Maniganggo China **66** A2
Manigotagan Canada **123** L5
Manihari India **75** E4
Manihiki *atoll* Cook Is **165** H6
Maniitsoq Greenland **121** N3
Manijī *r.* Pak. **81** F5
Manikchhari Bangl. **75** G5
Manikganj Bangl. **75** F5
Manikpur India **74** D4

▶**Manila** Phil. **57** F3
Capital of the Philippines.
world 16–17

Manila U.S.A. **134** E4
Manilla Australia **112** D3
Maningrida Australia **110** C2
Maninjau, Danau *l.* Indon. **58** C3
Manipur India *see* Imphal
Manipur *state* India **75** G4
Manipur *r.* India/Myanmar **75** G5
Manisa Turkey **78** A3
Manisa *prov.* Turkey **47** F5
Manissauá Missu *r.* Brazil **150** A4
Manistee U.S.A. **132** E2
Manistee *r.* U.S.A. **132** E2
Manistique U.S.A. **132** E2
Manitoba *prov.* Canada **123** L4
Manitoba, Lake Canada **123** L5
Manito Lake Canada **123** I4
Manitou Canada **123** L5
Manitou *r.* Canada **125** H3
Manitou Falls Canada **124** A3
Manitou Islands U.S.A. **132** E2
Manitoulin Island Canada **124** D4
Manitouwadge Canada **124** C3
Manitowoc U.S.A. **132** E2
Manizales Col. **146** C3
Manja Madag. **99** [inset] J4
Manjacaze Moz. **99** G5
Manjak Madag. **99** [inset] J3
Manjeri India **72** C4
Manjhand Pak. **81** G5
Man Jiang *r.* China **64** A4
Manjil Iran **80** B2
Manjimup Australia **109** B8
Manjo Cameroon **93** H4
Manjra *r.* India **72** C2
Man Kabat Myanmar **60** B2
Mankachar India **75** F4
Mankanza Dem. Rep. Congo *see* Makanza
Mankato *KS* U.S.A. **132** B4
Mankato *MN* U.S.A. **132** C2
Mankono Côte d'Ivoire **92** D3
Mankota Canada **123** J5
Manlleu Spain **43** H2
Manmad India **72** B1
Mann *r.* Australia **110** C2
Mann, Mount Australia **110** B5
Manna Indon. **58** C4
Mannahill Australia **112** A4
Mannar Sri Lanka **72** C4
Mannar, Gulf of India/Sri Lanka **72** C4
Mannargudi India **72** C4
Manneru *r.* India **72** D3
Mannheim Germany **36** D4
Mannicolo Islands Solomon Is *see* Vanikoro Islands
Manning Canada **123** G3
Manning U.S.A. **132** A2
Mannington U.S.A. **130** C4
Männlifluh *mt.* Switz. **39** G3
Mann Ranges *mts* Australia **110** B5
Mannsville U.S.A. **131** E2
Mannu *r. Sardinia* Italy **45** B4
Mannu *r. Sardinia* Italy **45** B5
Mannu *r. Sardinia* Italy **45** B5
Mannu, Capo *c. Sardinia* Italy **45** B4
Mannville Canada **123** I4
Mano *r.* Liberia/Sierra Leone **92** C4
Manoa Bol. **148** D2
Manohar Thana India **74** C4
Manokotak U.S.A. **120** D4
Manokwari Indon. **57** H6
Manombo Atsimo Madag. **99** [inset] I4
Manompana Madag. **99** [inset] K3
Manono Dem. Rep. Congo **95** E6
Manora Head Pak. **81** F5
Mano River Liberia **92** C4
Manos, Cueva de las *tourist site* Arg. **153** C6
Manosque France **39** F5
Manouane, Lac *l.* Canada **125** G3
Man Pan Myanmar **60** B3
Manp'o N. Korea **64** A4
Manpur India **74** B5
Manra *i.* Kiribati **107** H2
Manresa Spain **43** G2
Mansa *Gujarat* India **74** B5
Mansa *Punjab* India **74** B3
Mansa Zambia **95** F7
Mansabá Guinea-Bissau **92** B2
Mansa Konko Gambia **92** B2
Man Sam Myanmar **60** B3
Mansehra Pak. **81** H3
Mansel Island Canada **121** L3
Mansel'kya *ridge* Fin./Rus. Fed. **32** H2
Mansfield Australia **112** C5
Mansfield U.K. **35** F5
Mansfield *AR* U.S.A. **133** C5
Mansfield *LA* U.S.A. **133** C5
Mansfield *OH* U.S.A. **130** B3
Mansfield *PA* U.S.A. **131** E3
Mansi Myanmar **60** A2
Mansidão Brazil **150** D4
Manso *r.* Brazil *see* Mortes, Rio das
Manso, Represa do *resr* Brazil **150** A5
Manso-Nkwanta Ghana **93** E4
Mansurlu Turkey **78** C3
Manta Ecuador **146** A5
Mantantale Dem. Rep. Congo **94** D5
Mantaro *r.* Peru **148** B3
Manteca U.S.A. **136** B3
Mantecal Venez. **146** D3
Manteigas Port. **42** C2
Mantena Brazil **151** D6
Manteo U.S.A. **128** E5
Mantes-la-Jolie France **38** D2
Manthani India **72** C2
Mantiqueira, Serra da *mts* Brazil **151** C7
Manton U.S.A. **132** E2
Mantos Blancos Chile **148** C5
Mantoudi Greece **47** C5
Mantova Italy *see* Mantua
Mäntsälä Fin. **33** G3
Mänttä Fin. **33** G3
Mantua Italy **44** C2
Mantua U.S.A. **130** C3
Mantuan Downs Australia **111** F5
Manturovo Rus. Fed. **28** H4
Mäntyharju Fin. **33** G3
Mäntyjärvi Fin. **32** G2
Manu *r.* Bol. *see* Mapiri
Manú *r.* Peru **148** C3
Manu, Parque Nacional *nat. park* Peru **148** B3
Manuae *atoll* Fr. Polynesia **165** H7
Manua Islands American Samoa **107** I3
Manuel Alves *r.* Brazil **150** B4
Manuel J. Cobo Arg. **152** F3
Manuel Rodriguez, Isla *i.* Chile **153** B8
Manuel Urbano Brazil **148** C2
Manuel Vitorino Brazil **150** D5
Manuelzinho Brazil **150** A3
Manui *i.* Indon. **57** F6
Manūjān Iran **80** D5
Manukau N.Z. **113** C2

Mauro, Monte mt. Italy 44 E4
Mauron France 38 B2
Mauros mt. Spain 42 C2
Maurs France 38 E4
Mauston U.S.A. 132 D3
Mauvezin France 38 D5
Mauzé-sur-le-Mignon France 38 C3
Mava Dem. Rep. Congo 94 E4
Mavaca r. Venez. 147 E4
Mavago Moz. 97 C8
Mavasjaure l. Sweden 32 E2
Mavengue Angola 95 C9
Mavinga Angola 95 D8
Mavrothalassa Greece 46 C4
Mavrovo nat. park Macedonia 46 B4
Mavume Moz. 99 G4
Mawa, Bukit mt. Indon. 59 F2
Ma Wan i. Hong Kong China 67 [inset]
Mawana India 74 C3
Mawanga Dem. Rep. Congo 95 C6
Mawdaung Pass Myanmar/Thai. 61 B6
Mawei China 67 F3
Mawheranui r. N.Z. see Grey
Mawjib, Wādī al r. Jordan 77 B4
Mawkhi Myanmar 61 B4
Mawkmai Myanmar 60 B3
Mawlaik Myanmar 60 A3
Mawlamyaing Myanmar see Moulmein
Mawlamyine Myanmar see Moulmein
Mawphlang India 75 F4
Mawson research station Antarctica 167 E2
Mawson Coast Antarctica 167 E2
Mawson Escarpment Antarctica 167 E2
Mawson Peninsula Antarctica 167 H2
Maw Taung mt. Myanmar 61 B6
Mawza Yemen 96 D1
Maxaas Somalia 96 E3
Maxán Arg. 152 D2
Maxhamish Lake Canada 122 F3
Maxia, Punta mt. Sardinia Italy 45 B5
Maxixe Moz. 99 G4
Maxwelton Australia 111 E4
Maya Chad 94 C3
Maya i. Indon. 59 E3
Maya r. Rus. Fed. 27 N3
Mayaguana i. Bahamas 127 L7
Mayagüez Puerto Rico 139 K5
Mayak Rus. Fed. 29 J6
Mayakovskogo mt. Tajik. 81 G2
Mayakovskogo, Pik mt. Tajik. see Mayakovskogo
Mayala Dem. Rep. Congo 95 C6
Mayama Congo 95 B5
Mayamba Dem. Rep. Congo 95 C6
Mayamey Iran 80 C2
Maya Mountains Belize/Guat. 138 G5
Mayan China see Mayanhe
Mayang China 67 D3
Mayanhe China 66 C1
Maybeury U.S.A. 130 C5
Maybole U.K. 34 D4
Maych'ew Eth. 96 C1
Maydā Shahr Afgh. 81 G3
Maydh Somalia 96 E2
Maydos Turkey see Eceabat
Mayen Germany 36 C3
Mayenne France 38 C2
Mayenne r. France 38 C3
Mayêr Kangri mt. China 75 E2
Mayerthorpe Canada 123 H4
Mayet France 38 D3
Mayfield N.Z. 113 B3
Mayi r. China 64 B3
Maykhura Tajik. 81 G2
Maykop Rus. Fed. 29 G7
Maymyo Myanmar 60 B3
Mayna Respublika Khakasiya Rus. Fed. 69 H1
Mayna Ul'yanovskaya Oblast' Rus. Fed. 29 H5
Mayna r. Rus. Fed. 62 C1
Mayne watercourse Australia 111 E4
Mayni India 72 B2
Mayo Canada 122 C2
Mayo r. Mex. 135 E8
Mayo r. Peru 146 B6
Mayo Alim Cameroon 93 I3
Mayo-Belwa Nigeria 93 I3
Mayo Darlé Cameroon 93 H4
Mayo-Kébbi pref. Chad 94 B2
Mayoko Congo 94 B5
Mayo Lake Canada 122 C2
Mayo Landing Canada see Mayo
Mayo Lara Cent. Afr. Rep. 94 B3
Mayon vol. Phil. 57 F3
Mayor, Puig mt. Spain see Major, Puig
Mayor Buratovich Arg. 152 E4
Mayor Island N.Z. 113 D2
Mayor Pablo Lagerenza Para. 149 E4

▶Mayotte terr. Africa 97 E8
French Territorial Collectivity.
africa 86–87, 100

Mayraira Point Phil. 67 G5
Maysān governorate Iraq 79 F5
Mayskiy Amurskaya Oblast' Rus. Fed. 64 B1
Mayskiy Kabardino-Balkarskaya Respublika Rus. Fed. 29 H8
Mays Landing U.S.A. 131 F4
Mayson Lake Canada 123 J3
Maysville U.S.A. 130 B4
Mayu r. Myanmar 73 G1
Mayumba Gabon 94 A5
Mayum La pass China 75 D3
Mayuram India 72 C4
Mayville MI U.S.A. 130 B2
Mayville ND U.S.A. 132 B2
Maywood U.S.A. 132 A3
Mayya Rus. Fed. 27 N3
Maza Arg. 152 E4
Mazabuka Zambia 95 E8
Mazaca Turkey see Kayseri
Mazagan Morocco see El Jadida
Mazagão Brazil 147 I5
Mazamet France 38 E5
Mazán Peru 146 C5
Māzandarān prov. Iran 80 B2
Mazao Dem. Rep. Congo 95 D7
Mazar China 70 E4
Mazar, Koh-i- mt. Afgh. 81 F3
Mazara, Val di valley Sicily Italy 45 D6
Mazara del Vallo Sicily Italy 45 D6
Mazār-e Sharīf Afgh. 81 F2
Mazarrón Spain 43 F4
Mazaruni r. Guyana 147 G3
Mazatán Mex. 135 E7
Mazatlán Mex. 126 E7
Mazatzal Peak U.S.A. 137 G4
Mazāvī watercourse Iran 80 D5
Mažeikiai Lith. 33 F4
Mazelet well Niger 93 H1
Mazı Turkey 47 E6
Mazie U.S.A. 130 B4
Mazirbe Latvia 33 F4
Mazocahui Mex. 135 E7
Mazomeno Dem. Rep. Congo 95 E6
Mazomora Tanz. 97 C6
Mazowe r. Zimbabwe 99 G3
Mazrub well Sudan 89 E6
Mazsalaca Latvia 33 G4
Māzū Iran 80 B3
Mazunga Zimbabwe 99 F4
Mazyr Belarus 29 D5
Mazzouna Tunisia 91 H2
Mba Cameroon 93 H4

▶Mbabane Swaziland 99 F5
Capital of Swaziland.

Mbacké Senegal 92 B2
Mbaéré r. Cent. Afr. Rep. 94 C4
Mbagne Mauritania 92 B1
Mbahiakro Côte d'Ivoire 92 D4
Mbaïki Cent. Afr. Rep. 94 C4
Mbakaou Cameroon 93 I4
Mbakaou, Lac de l. Cameroon 93 I4
Mbala Zambia 97 A7
Mbalabala Zimbabwe 99 F4
Mbalam Cameroon 93 I5
Mbale Uganda 96 B4
Mbalmayo Cameroon 93 H5
Mbam r. Cameroon 93 H4
Mbamba Bay Tanz. 97 B7
Mbandaka Dem. Rep. Congo 94 C5
Mbandjok Cameroon 93 H4
Mbang Cameroon 93 I5
M'banza Congo Angola 95 B6
Mbanza-Ngungu Dem. Rep. Congo 95 B6
Mbarangandu Tanz. 97 C7
Mbarara Uganda 96 A5
Mbari r. Cent. Afr. Rep. 94 D3
Mbarika Mountains Tanz. 97 C7
Mbata Cent. Afr. Rep. 94 C4
Mbati Zambia 97 A7
Mbé Cameroon 93 I4
Mbé Congo 94 B5
Mbemba Moz. 97 B8
Mbembesi Zimbabwe 99 F3
Mbemkuru r. Tanz. 97 C7
Mbéni Comoros 97 D7
Mbenqué Côte d'Ivoire 92 D3
Mberengwa Zimbabwe 99 F4
Mbereshi Zambia 95 F7
Mbeya Tanz. 97 B7
Mbeya admin. reg. Tanz. 97 B7
Mbi r. Cameroon 93 I4
Mbi r. Cent. Afr. Rep. 94 C3
Mbigou Gabon 94 A5
Mbinda Congo 94 B5
Mbinga Tanz. 97 B7
Mbini Equat. Guinea 93 H5
Mbini r. Equat. Guinea 93 H5
Mbizi Zimbabwe 99 F4
Mbizi Mountains Tanz. 97 A7
Mbo Cent. Afr. Rep. 94 C2
Mboki Cent. Afr. Rep. 94 E3
Mbomo Congo 94 B4
Mbomou pref. Cent. Afr. Rep. 94 D3
Mbomou r. Cent. Afr. Rep./Dem. Rep. Congo 94 C4
Mbon Congo 94 B5
Mbour Senegal 92 A2
Mbout Mauritania 92 B1
Mbowela Zambia 95 E8
Mbozi Tanz. 97 B7
Mbrès Cent. Afr. Rep. 94 C3
Mbrostar Albania 46 A4
Mbuji-Mayi Dem. Rep. Congo 95 D6
Mbulu Tanz. 97 B5
Mburucuyá Arg. 152 F2
Mbuyuni Tanz. 97 C6
Mbwewe Tanz. 97 C6
McAdam Canada 125 H4
McAlester U.S.A. 133 C5
McAllen U.S.A. 133 B7
McArthur r. Australia 110 D2
McArthur U.S.A. 130 B4
McBride Canada 122 F4
McCall U.S.A. 134 C3
McCamey U.S.A. 133 A6
McCammon U.S.A. 134 D4
McCarthy U.S.A. 122 A2
McCauley Island Canada 122 D4
McClintock, Mount Antarctica 167 H1
McClintock Channel Canada 121 I2
McClintock Range hills Australia 108 D4
McClure, Lake U.S.A. 136 B3
McClure Strait Canada 121 H2
McClusky U.S.A. 132 A2
McComb U.S.A. 127 H5
McConaughy, Lake U.S.A. 132 A3
McConnellsburg U.S.A. 130 E4
McConnelsville U.S.A. 130 C4
McCook U.S.A. 132 A3
McCormick U.S.A. 129 C5
McCrea r. Canada 123 H2
McCreary Canada 123 L5
McCullum, Mount Canada 122 B1
McDame Canada 122 D3
McDonald Islands Indian Ocean 163 L9
McDonald Peak U.S.A. 134 D3
McDouall Range hills Australia 110 C3
McDowell Peak U.S.A. 137 G5
McFarland U.S.A. 136 C4
McFarlane r. Canada 123 J3
McGill U.S.A. 137 E2
McGivney Canada 125 H4
McGrath AK U.S.A. 120 D3
McGrath MN U.S.A. 132 C2
McGregor r. Canada 122 F4
McGregor, Lake Canada 123 H5
McGregor Range hills Australia 111 E5
McGuire, Mount U.S.A. 134 D3
Mcherrah reg. Alg. 90 D4
Mchinga Tanz. 97 C7
Mchinji Malawi 97 B8
McIlwraith Range hills Australia 111 E2
McInnes Lake Canada 123 M4
McIntosh U.S.A. 132 A2
McKay Range hills Australia 108 C5
McKean i. Kiribati 107 H2
McKee U.S.A. 130 A5
McKeesport U.S.A. 130 D3
McKenney U.S.A. 130 E5
McKenzie U.S.A. 128 A4
McKenzie r. U.S.A. 134 B3
McKinlay Australia 111 E4
McKinlay r. Australia 111 E4

▶McKinley, Mount U.S.A. 120 D3
Highest mountain in North America.
northamerica 116–117

McKinney U.S.A. 133 B5
McKittrick U.S.A. 136 C4
McLennan Canada 123 G4
McLeod r. Canada 123 H4
McLeod Bay Canada 123 I2
McLeod Lake Canada 122 F4
McLeods Island Myanmar 61 B6
McMinnville OR U.S.A. 134 B3
McMinnville TN U.S.A. 128 B5
McMurdo research station Antarctica 167 H1
McMurdo Sound b. Antarctica 167 H1
McNary U.S.A. 137 H4
McNaughton Lake Canada see Kinbasket Lake
McPherson U.S.A. 132 B4
McQuesten r. Canada 122 B2
McRae U.S.A. 129 C5
McTavish Arm b. Canada 123 G1
McVeytown U.S.A. 130 E3
McVicar Arm b. Canada 122 F1
McWhorter U.S.A. 130 C4
Mdantsane S. Africa 99 E7
M'Daourouch Alg. 91 G1
Mead, Lake resr U.S.A. 137 E3
Meade U.S.A. 132 A4
Meade r. U.S.A. 120 D2
Meadow Australia 109 A6
Meadow U.S.A. 137 F2
Meadowbank r. Canada 123 L1
Meadow Bridge U.S.A. 130 C5
Meadow Lake Canada 123 I4
Meadow Valley Wash r. U.S.A. 137 E3
Meadowview U.S.A. 130 C5
Meadville MS U.S.A. 133 D6
Meadville PA U.S.A. 130 C3
Meaford Canada 130 C1
Meaken-dake vol. Japan 64 F4
Mealhada Port. 42 B2
Mealy Mountains Canada 125 J2
Meandarra Australia 111 G5
Meander River Canada 123 G3
Mearim r. Brazil 150 C2
Meaux France 39 E2
Mebridege r. Angola 95 B6
Mebu India 75 G3
Mebulu, Tanjung pt Indon. 59 F5
Mecanhelas Moz. 99 G2
▶Mecca Saudi Arabia 89 H4
asia 52–53
Mecca U.S.A. 135 C6
Mechanicsburg U.S.A. 130 B3
Mechanicsville IA U.S.A. 124 B5
Mechanicsville VA U.S.A. 130 E5
Mechanicville U.S.A. 131 G2
Mechelen Belgium 39 F1
Mecheria Alg. 91 E2
Mechernich Germany 36 C3
Mechiméré Chad 88 B6
Mechka r. Bulg. 46 D3
Mecidiye Turkey 46 E4
Mecitözü Turkey 78 C2
Meckenheim Germany 36 C3
Mecklenburger Bucht b. Germany 36 E1
Mecklenburg-Vorpommern land Germany 37 F2
Mecklenburg - West Pomerania land Germany see Mecklenburg-Vorpommern
Mecubúri Moz. 97 C8
Mecubúri r. Moz. 97 D8
Mecúfi Moz. 97 D8
Mecula Moz. 97 C8
Meda r. Australia 108 C4
Meda Port. 42 C2
Meda mt. Spain 42 C1
Medak India 72 C2
Medan Indon. 58 B2
Medang i. Indon. 59 G5
Médanos Buenos Aires Arg. 152 E4
Médanos Entre Ríos Arg. 152 F3
Medanosa, Punta pt Arg. 153 D7
Médanos de Coro, Parque Nacional nat. park Venez. 146 D2
Medchal India 72 C2
Médéa Alg. 91 F1
Medellín Col. 146 C3
Medenine Tunisia 91 H2
Mederdra Mauritania 92 B1
Medford NY U.S.A. 131 G3
Medford OK U.S.A. 133 B4
Medford OR U.S.A. 134 B4
Medford WI U.S.A. 132 D2
Medgidia Romania 46 F2
Mediadilet well Mali 93 E1
Media Luna Arg. 152 D3
Mediaş Romania 46 D1
Medicine Bow r. U.S.A. 134 F4
Medicine Bow Mountains U.S.A. 134 F4
Medicine Bow Peak U.S.A. 134 F4
Medicine Hat Canada 134 E2
Medicine Lodge U.S.A. 132 B4
Medina Brazil 151 D6
Medina Col. 146 C3
Medina Saudi Arabia 89 H3
Medina NY U.S.A. 130 D2
Medina OH U.S.A. 130 C3
Medina r. U.S.A. 133 B6
Medinaceli Spain 43 E2
Medina del Campo Spain 42 D2
Medina de Pomar Spain 42 E1
Medina de Rioseco Spain 42 D2
Médina Gounas Senegal 92 B2
Medina-Sidonia Spain 42 D4
Medinipur India 75 E5
Mediolanum Italy see Milan
Mediterranean Sea 41 I5
Medje Dem. Rep. Congo 94 E4
Mednogorsk Rus. Fed. 68 D1
Mednyy, Ostrov i. Rus. Fed. 164 F2
Médoc reg. France 38 C4
Mêdog China 75 G3
Medora U.S.A. 132 A2
Médouneu Gabon 94 A4
Medstead Canada 123 I4
Medu Kongkar China see Maizhokunggar
Medveđa Serb. and Mont. 46 B3
Medvedevo Rus. Fed. 28 H4
Medveditsa r. Rus. Fed. 29 G6
Medvednica mts Croatia 44 E2
Medvezh'i, Ostrova is Rus. Fed. 27 Q2
Medvezh'yegorsk Rus. Fed. 28 E3
Medzilaborce Slovakia 37 J4
Meeberrie Australia 109 A6
Meekatharra Australia 109 B6
Meeker U.S.A. 134 F4
Meeladeen Somalia 96 F2
Meelpaeg Reservoir Canada 125 J3
Meerane Germany 37 F3
Meerapalu Estonia 33 G4
Meerut India 74 C3
Mēga Eth. 96 C3
Mega i. Indon. 58 D3
Mega Escarpment Eth./Kenya 96 C3
Megalo Chorio Greece 47 E6
Megalopoli Greece 47 C6
Megalos Anthropofas i. Greece 47 E6
Meganisi i. Greece 47 B5
Mégantic, Lac l. Canada 125 G4
Megara Greece 47 C5
Megezez mt. Eth. 96 C2

▶Meghalaya state India 75 F4
Highest mean annual rainfall in the world.
world 12–13

Meghasani mt. India 75 E5
Meghna r. Bangl. 75 F5
Meghri Armenia 79 F3
Megion Rus. Fed. 26 H3
Megisti i. Greece 78 B3
Megri Armenia see Meghri
Mehadica Romania 46 C2
Mehamn Norway 32 G1
Mehar Pak. 81 F5
Meharry, Mount Australia 108 B5
Mehdia Tunisia see Mahdia
Mehedeby Sweden 33 E3
Mehekar India 72 C1
Meherpur Bangl. 75 F5
Meherrin U.S.A. 130 D5
Meherrin r. U.S.A. 130 E5
Mehidpur India 74 B5
Mehlville U.S.A. 132 D4
Mehmadabad India 74 B5
Mehndawal India 75 D4
Mehrābān Iran 80 A2
Mehrān Iran 80 C5
Mehrān watercourse Iran 80 C5
Mehrān Iraq 79 F4
Mehtar Lām Afgh. 81 G3
Mehun-sur-Yèvre France 38 E3
Meia Ponte r. Brazil 149 H4
Meicheng Anhui China see Qianshan
Meicheng Fujian China see Minqing
Meicheng Zhejiang China see Jiande
Meichengzhen China 67 D2
Meiganga Cameroon 93 I4
Meighen Island Canada 121 J2
Meigu China 66 B2
Meihekou China 64 A4
Meijiang China see Ningdu
Mei Jiang r. China 67 E3
Meikeng China 67 E3
Meiktila Myanmar 60 A3
Meilen Switz. 39 H3
Meilin China see Ganxian
Meilleur r. Canada 122 E2
Meilü China see Wuchuan
Meiningen Germany 36 E3
Meira Spain 42 C1
Meiringen Switz. 39 H3
Meishan Anhui China see Jinzhai
Meishan Sichuan China 66 B2
Meißen Germany 37 F3
Meister r. Canada 122 D2
Meitan China 66 C3
Meitingen Germany 36 E4
Meixi China 64 B3
Meixian Guangdong China see Meizhou
Meixian Shaanxi China 66 C1
Meixing China see Xiaojin
Meizhou China 67 F3
Mej r. India 74 C4
Méjan, Sommet de mt. France 39 F4
Mejaouda well Mauritania 90 D5
Mejez el Bab Tunisia 45 B6
Mejicana mt. Arg. 152 D2
Mejillones Chile 148 C5
Mejillones del Sur, Bahía de b. Chile 148 C5
Mekadio well Sudan 89 G5
Mékambo Gabon 94 B4
Mek'elē Eth. 89 H6
Mékhé Senegal 92 A2
Mekhtar Pak. 81 G4
Mekkaw Nigeria 93 F4
Meknès Morocco 90 D2
Mekong r. Xizang China 70 I6
Mekong r. Xizang/Yunnan China 70 J7
Mekong r. Laos/Thai. 60 D5
also known as Mènam Khong (Laos/Thailand)
Mekong, Mouths of the Vietnam 61 D6
Méla, Mont hill Cent. Afr. Rep. 94 D2
Melaka Malaysia 58 C2
Melaka state Malaysia 58 C2
Melalo, Tanjung pt Indon. 58 D3
Melanesia is Oceania 164 E6
Melanesian Basin sea feature Pacific Ocean 164 E5
Melawi r. Indon. 59 E2

▶Melbourne Australia 112 C5
State capital of Victoria. 2nd most populous city in Oceania
oceania 104–105
world 16–17

Melbourne U.S.A. 129 C6
Melbu Norway 32 D1
Melchor, Isla i. Chile 153 B6
Meldal Norway 32 C3
Meldorf Germany 36 D1
Meldrum U.S.A. 130 B5
Meldrum Bay Canada 124 D4
Mele, Capo c. Italy 44 B3
Melekess Rus. Fed. see Dimitrovgrad
Melenci Serb. and Mont. 46 B2
Melendiz Dağı mt. Turkey 78 C3
Melenki Rus. Fed. 28 G5
Melet Turkey see Mesudiye
Meleuz Rus. Fed. 29 J5
Mélèzes, Rivière aux r. Canada 125 G1
Melfa U.S.A. 131 F5
Mélfi Chad 94 C2
Melfi Italy 44 E4
Melfort Canada 123 J4
Melgaço Brazil 150 B2
Melgar de Fernamental Spain 42 D1
Melhus Norway 32 C3
Meliau, Gunung mt. Sabah Malaysia 59 G1
Melide Spain 42 C1
Meligalas Greece 47 B6

▶Melilla N. Africa 90 E2
Spanish Territory.
africa 100

Melilli Sicily Italy 45 E6
Melimoyu, Monte mt. Chile 153 B6
Melintang, Danau l. Indon. 59 G3
Melipilla Chile 152 C3
Melita Canada 123 K5
Melitene Turkey see Malatya
Melito di Porto Salvo Italy 45 E6
Melitopol' Ukr. 29 E7
Melk Austria 37 G4
Melka Guba Eth. 96 C3
Mellakoski Fin. 32 G2
Mellansjö Sweden 33 D3
Mellanström Sweden 32 E2
Melle Germany 36 D2
Mellègue, Barrage dam Tunisia 45 B6
Mellerud Sweden 33 D4
Mellid Spain see Melide
Mellit Sudan 89 E6
Mellizo Sur, Cerro mt. Chile 153 B7
Mellor Glacier Antarctica 167 E2
Mellrichstadt Germany 36 E3
Melmele watercourse Chad 88 C6
Melmoth S. Africa 99 F6
Mel'nichoye Rus. Fed. 64 C3
Mělník Czech Rep. 37 G3
Mel'nikovo Rus. Fed. 33 H3
Melo Uruguay 152 G3
Melolo Indon. 108 C2
Melozitna r. U.S.A. 120 D3
Melrhir, Chott salt l. Alg. 91 G2
Melrose Australia 109 C6
Melrose U.S.A. 132 C2
Melsetter Zimbabwe see Chimanimani
Melsungen Germany 36 D3
Melta, Mount Sabah Malaysia see Meliau, Gunung
Meltaus Fin. 32 G2
Melton Australia 112 C5
Melton Mowbray U.K. 35 F5
Meluan Sarawak Malaysia 59 E2
Melun France 39 E2
Melur India 72 C4
Melut Sudan 96 B2
Melville Canada 134 G2
Melville, Cape Australia 111 F2
Melville, Lake Canada 125 J2
Melville Bugt b. Greenland see Qimusseriarsuaq
Melville Island Australia 110 B1
Melville Island Canada 121 I2
Melville Peninsula Canada 121 K3
Melvin, Lough l. Rep. of Ireland/U.K. 35 B4
Mélykút Hungary 46 A1
Memaliaj Albania 47 A4
Mêmar Co salt l. China 75 D2
Memba Moz. 97 D8
Memba, Baía de b. Moz. 97 D8
Memberamo r. Indon. 57 I6
Memboro Indon. 57 E7
Memel Lith. see Klaipėda
Memel S. Africa 99 F5
Memmingen Germany 36 E5
Mempakul Sabah Malaysia 59 F1
Mempawah Indon. 55 C6
Memphis tourist site Egypt 89 F2
Memphis MI U.S.A. 130 B2
Memphis TN U.S.A. 127 H4
Memphis TX U.S.A. 133 A5
Mena Eth. 96 C3
Mena Indon. 108 D2
Mena Ukr. 29 E6
Mena U.S.A. 133 C5
Menabe mts Madag. 99 [inset] J4
Ménaka Mali 93 F2
Mènam Khong r. Laos/Thai. 61 D5 see Mekong
Menarandra r. Madag. 99 [inset] J5
Menard U.S.A. 133 B6
Mencal mt. Spain 42 E4
Mencué Arg. 152 C5
Mendanau i. Indon. 59 D3
Mendarda India 74 A5
Mendarik i. Indon. 59 D2
Mendawai Indon. 59 F3
Mendawai r. Indon. 59 F3
Mende France 39 E4
Mendebo Mountains Eth. 96 C3
Mendefera Eritrea 89 H6
Mendeleyev Ridge sea feature Arctic Ocean 166 B1
Mendeleyevsk Rus. Fed. 28 J5
Menden (Sauerland) Germany 36 C3
Mendenhall U.S.A. 133 D6
Mendenhall, Cape U.S.A. 120 C4
Mendenhall Glacier U.S.A. 122 C3
Méndez Mex. 126 G6
Mendī Eth. 68 B6
Mendi P.N.G. 57 J7
Mendip Hills U.K. 35 E6
Mendocino U.S.A. 136 A2
Mendocino, Cape U.S.A. 134 A4
Mendocino, Lake U.S.A. 136 A2
Mendota CA U.S.A. 136 B3
Mendota IL U.S.A. 132 D3
Mendoza Arg. 152 C3
Mendoza prov. Arg. 152 C3
Mene de Mauroa Venez. 146 D2
Menemen Turkey 47 E5
Menez Bré hill France 38 B2
Menfi Sicily Italy 45 D6
Menga, Puerto de pass Spain 42 D2
Mengalum i. Malaysia 59 F1
Mengcheng China 67 F1
Menggala Indon. 58 D4
Menghai China 66 B4
Mengíbar Spain 42 E4
Mengkiang r. Indon. 59 E2
Menglang China see Lancang
Menglie China see Jiangcheng
Mengmeng China see Shuangjiang
Mengong Cameroon 93 H5
Mengshan China 67 D3
Mengxian China see Mengzhou
Mengyang China see Mingshan
Mengzhou China 67 E1
Mengzi China 66 B4
Menihek Canada 125 H2
Menindee Australia 112 B4
Menindee Lake Australia 112 B4
Meningie Australia 112 A4
Menkere Rus. Fed. 27 M3
Mennecy France 39 E2
Menominee r. U.S.A. 132 E2
Menongue Angola 95 C8
Menor, Mar lag. Spain 43 F4
Menorca i. Spain see Minorca
Mensalong Indon. 59 G2
Mentakab Malaysia see Mentekab
Mentarang r. Indon. 59 G2
Mentasta Lake U.S.A. 122 A2
Mentasta Mountains U.S.A. 122 A2
Mentawai, Kepulauan is Indon. 58 B3
Mentawai, Selat sea chan. Indon. 58 C3
Mentaya r. Indon. 59 F3
Mentekab Malaysia 58 C2
Mentiras hill Port. 42 C3
Mentiras mt. Spain 43 E3
Mentok Indon. 58 D3
Menton France 39 G5
Mentone U.S.A. 133 A6
Mentuba r. Indon. 59 F3
Menufia governorate Egypt see Minūfiyah
Menukung Indon. 59 F3
Menyapa, Gunung mt. Indon. 59 G2
Menzel Bourguiba Tunisia 91 H1
Menzelet Barajı resr Turkey 78 D3
Menzelinsk Rus. Fed. 28 J5
Menzel Temime Tunisia 45 C6
Menzies Australia 109 C7
Menzies, Mount Antarctica 167 E2
Meoqui Mex. 135 F7
Mepala Angola 95 B6
Meponda Moz. 97 B8
Meppel Neth. 36 C2
Meppen Germany 36 C2
Meqheleng S. Africa 99 E6
Mequéns r. Brazil 149 E3
Mequinenza, Embalse de resr Spain 43 G2
Mer France 38 D3
Merah Indon. 59 G2
Merak Indon. 58 D4
Meråker Norway 32 C3
Meramec r. U.S.A. 132 D4
Merano Italy 44 C1
Merapi, Gunung vol. Jawa Tengah Indon. 59 E4
Merapi, Gunung vol. Jawa Timur Indon. 59 F5
Merari, Serra mt. Brazil 147 F3
Meratswe r. Botswana 98 E4
Meratus, Pegunungan mts Indon. 59 F3
Merauke Indon. 57 J7
Merawwah i. U.A.E. 80 C5
Merbein Australia 112 B4
Merca Somalia see Marka
Mercadal Spain 43 I3
Mercantour, Parc National du nat. park France 39 G4
Merced U.S.A. 136 B3
Merced r. U.S.A. 136 B3
Mercedario, Cerro mt. Arg. 152 C2
Mercedes Corrientes Arg. 152 F2
Mercedes San Luis Arg. 152 D3
Mercedes Uruguay 152 F3
Mercer ME U.S.A. 131 I1
Mercer OH U.S.A. 130 A3
Mercer PA U.S.A. 130 C3
Mercer WI U.S.A. 132 D2
Mercersburg U.S.A. 130 E4
Mercês Brazil 148 C2
Mercier Bol. 148 C2
Mercury U.S.A. 137 E3
Mercury Islands N.Z. 113 C2
Mercy, Cape Canada 166 K2
Merdenik Turkey see Göle
Meredith U.S.A. 131 H2
Meredith, Cape Falkland Is 153 E8
Meredith, Lake U.S.A. 133 A5
Meredoua Alg. 91 F4
Mereeg Somalia 96 E4
Merefa Ukr. 29 F6
Meremäe Estonia 33 G4
Merga Oasis Sudan 89 E5
Mergui Myanmar 61 B5
Mergui Archipelago is Myanmar 61 B6
Meriç r. Greece/Turkey 46 E4
Meriç r. Greece/Turkey see Evros
Merichas Greece 47 D6
Mérida Mex. 127 I7
Mérida Spain 42 C3
Mérida Venez. 146 D2
Mérida state Venez. 146 D2
Mérida, Cordillera de mts Venez. 146 D3
Meriden U.S.A. 131 G3
Meridian MS U.S.A. 129 A5
Meridian TX U.S.A. 133 B6
Mérignac France 38 C4
Merijärvi Fin. 32 G2
Merikarvia Fin. 33 F3
Merim, Laguna l. Brazil/Uruguay see Mirim, Lagoa
Merinda Australia 111 G4
Meringur Australia 112 B4
Merir i. Palau 57 H5
Merirumã Brazil 147 H4
Merkel U.S.A. 133 A5
Merkinė Lith. 33 G5
Merlimau, Pulau reg. Sing. 58 [inset]
Mermaid Reef Australia 108 B4
Merolia Australia 109 C7
Meron, Har mt. Israel 77 B3
Merošina Serb. and Mont. 46 B3
Merowe Sudan 89 F5
Merredin Australia 109 B7
Merrick hill U.K. 34 D4
Merrill MI U.S.A. 130 A2
Merrill WI U.S.A. 132 D2
Merrill, Mount Canada 122 E2
Merriman U.S.A. 132 A3
Merritt Canada 134 B2
Merritt Island U.S.A. 129 C6
Merrygoen Australia 112 D3
Mersa Fatma Eritrea 89 I6
Mersa Gulbub Eritrea 89 H5
Mersa Teklay Eritrea 89 H5
Merse r. Italy 44 C3
Merseburg (Saale) Germany 36 E3
Mersin Turkey see İçel
Mersing Malaysia 58 C2
Mersin Galgalo Eth. 96 E3
Mērsrags Latvia 33 F4
Merta India 74 B4
Merta Road India 74 B4
Merthyr Tydfil U.K. 35 E6
Merti Kenya 96 C4
Merti Plateau Kenya 96 C4
Mértola Port. 42 C4
Mertoutek Alg. 91 G4
Mertz Glacier Antarctica 167 G2
Mertz Glacier Tongue Antarctica 167 G2
Mertzon U.S.A. 133 A6
Méru France 38 E2
Meru Kenya 96 C4

▶Meru vol. Tanz. 96 C5
4th highest mountain in Africa.
africa 84–85

Meru Betiri National Park Indon. 59 F5
Merui Pak. 81 E4
Meru National Park Kenya 96 C4
Merv Turkm. see Mary
Merweville S. Africa 98 D7
Merzifon Turkey 78 C2
Merzig Germany 36 C4
Merz Peninsula Antarctica 167 L2
Mesa r. Spain 43 F2
Mesa U.S.A. 137 G5
Mesabi Range hills U.S.A. 132 C2
Mesagne Italy 45 F4
Mesara, Ormos b. Greece 47 D7
Mesa Verde National Park U.S.A. 135 E5
Meschede Germany 36 D3
Meselefors Sweden 32 E2
Mesfinto Eth. 89 H6
Mesgouez Lake Canada 125 F3
Mesha r. Rus. Fed. 28 I5
Meshed Iran see Mashhad
Meshkān Iran 80 D2
Mesimeri Greece 47 C4
Meslay-du-Maine France 38 C3
Mesola Italy 44 D2
Mesolongi Greece 47 B5
Mesolóngion Greece see Mesolongi
Mesquite U.S.A. 133 B5
Mesquite Lake U.S.A. 137 E4
Messaad Alg. 91 F2
Messak Mellet hills Libya 88 A3
Messalo r. Moz. 97 D7
Messana Sicily Italy see Messina
Messaoud, Oued watercourse Alg. 91 E4
Messier, Canal sea chan. Chile 153 B7
Messina Sicily Italy 45 E5
Messina S. Africa 99 F4
Messina, Strait of Italy 45 E5
Messini Greece 47 C6
Messiniakos Kolpos b. Greece 47 C6
Meßkirch Germany 36 D5
Messlingen Sweden 32 D3
Mesta r. Bulg. 46 D4
Mesta r. Greece see Nestos
Mestghanem Alg. see Mostaganem
Meston, Akra pt Greece 47 D5
Mesudiye Turkey 79 D2
Mesuji r. Indon. 58 D4
Meta dept Col. 146 C4
Meta r. Col./Venez. 146 E3
Métabetchouan Canada 125 G3
Meta Incognita Peninsula Canada 121 M3
Metairie U.S.A. 133 D6
Metaliferi, Munţii mts Romania 46 C1
Metallifere, Colline mts Italy 44 C3
Metán Arg. 152 D1
Metanara Eth. 96 C2
Metangula Moz. 97 B8
Metauro r. Italy 44 D3
Metema Eth. 96 C1
Meteora tourist site Greece 47 B5
Meteor Creek r. Australia 111 G5
Methoni Greece 47 B6
Methuen U.S.A. 131 H2
Metionga Lake Canada 124 B3
Metković Croatia 44 F3
Metlakatla U.S.A. 122 D4
Metlaoui Tunisia 91 H2
Metlika Slovenia 44 E2
Metoro Moz. 97 C8
Metro Indon. 58 D4
Metropolis U.S.A. 128 A4
Metsäkylä Fin. 32 H2
Metsovo Greece 47 B5
Metter U.S.A. 129 C5
Mettler U.S.A. 136 C4
Mettuppalaiyam India 72 C4
Mettur India 72 C4
Metu Eth. 96 B2
Metz France 39 G2
Metzingen Germany 36 D4
Meu r. France 38 C2
Meulaboh Indon. 58 B1
Meung-sur-Loire France 38 D3
Meurthe r. France 39 G2
Meuse r. Belgium/France 39 F1
also spelt Maas (Netherlands)
Mēwa China 66 B1
Mexia U.S.A. 133 B6
Mexiana, Ilha i. Brazil 150 B1
Mexicali Mex. 135 D6
Mexican Hat U.S.A. 137 H3
Mexican Water U.S.A. 137 H3

Mount Molloy Australia 111 F3
Mount Moresby Canada 122 C4
Mount Morgan Australia 111 G4
Mount Morris U.S.A. 130 E2
Mount Nebo U.S.A. 130 C4
Mount Olivet U.S.A. 130 A4
Mount Orab U.S.A. 130 B4
Mount Pearl Canada 125 K4
Mount Pleasant Canada 125 H4
Mount Pleasant IA U.S.A. 132 D3
Mount Pleasant MI U.S.A. 130 A2
Mount Pleasant PA U.S.A. 130 D3
Mount Pleasant TX U.S.A. 133 C5
Mount Pleasant UT U.S.A. 137 G2
Mount Rainier National Park U.S.A. 134 B3
Mount Remarkable National Park Australia 112 A4
Mount Revelstoke National Park Canada 122 G5
Mount St Helens National Volcanic Monument nat. park U.S.A. 134 B3
Mount Sanford Australia 110 B3
Mount's Bay U.K. 35 D6
Mount Shasta U.S.A. 134 B4
Mount Sterling KY U.S.A. 130 B4
Mount Sterling OH U.S.A. 130 B4
Mount Storm U.S.A. 130 D4
Mount Surprise Australia 111 F3
Mount Vernon Australia 109 B6
Mount Vernon GA U.S.A. 129 C5
Mount Vernon IL U.S.A. 128 A4
Mount Vernon KY U.S.A. 130 A5
Mount Vernon MO U.S.A. 132 C4
Mount Vernon OH U.S.A. 130 B3
Mount Vernon TX U.S.A. 133 C5
Mount Vernon WA U.S.A. 134 B2
Mount Wedge Australia 110 C4
Mount William National Park Australia 112 D6
Mount Willoughby Australia 110 C5
Moura Australia 111 G5
Moura Brazil 147 F5
Moura Port. 42 C3
Mourão Port. 42 C3
Mouraya Chad 94 D2
Mourdi, Dépression du depr. Chad 88 D5
Mourdiah Mali 92 D2
Mourenx France 38 C5
Mourne Mountains hills U.K. 35 C4
Mourre de Chanier mt. France 39 G5
Mouscron Belgium 39 E1
Mousgougou Chad 94 C2
Moussafoyo Chad 94 C2
Moussoro Chad 88 C6
Mouth of Wilson U.S.A. 130 C5
Moûtiers France 39 G4
Moutong Indon. 57 F5
Mouydir, Monts du plat. Alg. 91 F4
Mouyondzi Congo 95 B5
Mouzaki Greece 47 B5
Mouzarak Chad 88 B6
Movila Miresii Romania 46 E2
Movileni Romania 46 D2
Mowbullan, Mount Australia 111 G5
Moxahala U.S.A. 130 B4
Moxey Town Bahamas 129 D7
Moxico prov. Angola 95 C8
Moy r. Rep. of Ireland 35 B4
Moyale Eth. 96 C4
Moyamba Sierra Leone 92 B3
Moyen Atlas mts Morocco 90 D2
Moyen-Chari pref. Chad 94 C2
Moyen Congo country Africa see Congo
Moyeni Lesotho 99 E6
Moyenne-Guinée admin. reg. Guinea 92 B3
Moyen-Ogooué prov. Gabon 94 A5
Moynaq Uzbek. see Muynak
Moyo i. Indon. 59 G5
Moyo Uganda 96 A4
Moyobamba Peru 146 B6
Moyowosi r. Tanz. 97 A6
Møysalen mt. Norway 32 D1
Moyum waterhole Kenya 96 C4
Moyynty Kazakh. 70 D2
▶Mozambique country Africa 99 G4
africa 86–87, 100
Mozambique Channel Africa 99 I4
Mozambique Ridge sea feature Indian Ocean 163 J7
Mozdok Rus. Fed. 29 H8
Mozdūrān Iran 81 E2
Mozelle U.S.A. 130 B5
Mozhga Rus. Fed. 28 J4
Mozhong China 66 A1
Mozo Myanmar 60 A3
Mozyr' Belarus see Mazyr
Mpal Senegal 92 A2
Mpanda Tanz. 97 A6
Mpandamatenga Botswana 98 E3
Mpé Congo 94 B5
Mpessoba Mali 92 D2
Mpigi Uganda 96 B4
Mpika Zambia 97 A7
Mpongwe Zambia 95 F8
Mporokoso Zambia 95 F7
Mpouya Congo 94 C5
Mpui Tanz. 97 A7
Mpulungu Zambia 97 A7
Mpumalanga prov. S. Africa 99 F5
Mpwapwa Tanz. 97 C6
Mqinvartsveri mt. Georgia/Rus. Fed. see Kazbek
Mrągowo Poland 37 J2
Mrewa Zimbabwe see Murehwa
Mrežnica r. Croatia 44 E2
Mrkonjić-Grad Bos.-Herz. 44 F2
Mrocza Poland 37 H2
Mroga r. Poland 37 I2
M'Saken Tunisia 45 C7
Msambweni Kenya 97 C6
Msata Tanz. 97 C6
M'Sila Alg. 91 G2
Msta r. Rus. Fed. 28 D4
Mstislavl' Belarus see Mstsislaw
Mstsislaw Belarus 31 L2
Mszana Dolna Poland 37 J4
Mtama Tanz. 97 C7
Mtelo Kenya 96 B4
Mtera Reservoir Tanz. 97 B6
Mtoko Zimbabwe see Mutoko
Mtorashanga Zimbabwe see Mutorashanga
Mtsensk Rus. Fed. 29 F5
Mts'khet'a Georgia 79 F2
Mtukula Tanz. 97 C7
Mtwara Tanz. 97 D7
Mtwara admin. reg. Tanz. 97 C7
Mu r. Myanmar 60 A3
Mu hill Port. 42 B4
Muaguide Moz. 97 C8
Mualama Moz. 99 H3
Muana Brazil 150 B2
Muanda Dem. Rep. Congo 95 B6
Muang Khammouan Laos 60 D4
Muang Không Laos 61 D5
Muang Khôngxédôn Laos 61 D5
Muang Luang r. Thai. 61 B6
Muang Pakbeng Laos 60 C4
Muang Pakxan Laos 60 C4
Muang Phin Laos 61 D4
Muang Phôn-Hông Laos 60 C4
Muang Sam Sip Thai. 61 D5
Muang Sing Laos 60 C3
Muang Thai country Asia see Thailand
Muang Vangviang Laos 60 C4
Muang Xaignabouri Laos 60 C4
Muanza Moz. 99 G3
Muar Malaysia 58 C2
Muar r. Malaysia 58 C2
Muara Brunei 59 F1
Muaraancalong Indon. 59 G2
Muaraatap Indon. 59 G2
Muarabeliti Indon. 58 C3
Muarabungo Indon. 58 C3
Muaradua Indon. 58 D4
Muaraenim Indon. 58 C3
Muarainu Indon. 59 F3
Muarakaman Indon. 59 G3
Muaralesan Indon. 59 G2
Muararupit Indon. 58 C3
Muarasoma Indon. 58 B2
Muaras Reef Indon. 59 G2
Muaratebo Indon. 58 C3
Muaratembesi Indon. 58 C3
Muarateweh Indon. 59 F3
Muarawahau Indon. 59 G2
Muari, Ras pt Pak. 81 F5
Mubārak, Jabal mt. Jordan/Saudi Arabia 77 B5
Mubarakpur India 75 D4
Mubarek Uzbek. 81 F2
Mubarraz well Saudi Arabia 89 I2
Mubende Uganda 96 A4
Mubi Nigeria 93 I3
Muborak Uzbek. see Mubarek
Mubur i. Indon. 58 D2
Mucaba Angola 95 B6
Mucajá Brazil 147 G5
Mucajaí r. Brazil 147 F4
Mucajaí, Serra do mts Brazil 147 F4
Mučanj mt. Serb. and Mont. 46 B3
Muchinga Escarpment Zambia 95 F8
Muchiri Bol. 149 E4
Muchuan China 66 B2
Muck i. U.K. 34 C3
Muco r. Col. 146 D3
Mucojo Moz. 97 D8
Muconda Angola 95 D7
Mucubela Moz. 99 H3
Mucuim r. Brazil 147 E6
Mucumbura Moz. 99 F3
Mucundi Angola 95 C9
Mucunha Angola 95 C8
Mucupia Moz. 99 H3
Mucur Turkey 78 C3
Mucura Brazil 147 F5
Mucuri Brazil 151 E6
Mucuri r. Brazil 151 E6
Mucuripe Brazil 146 D5
Mucussueje Angola 95 D7
Muda r. Malaysia 58 C1
Mudabidri India 72 B3
Mudanjiang China 64 B3
Mudan Jiang r. China 64 B3
Mudan Ling mts China 64 A4
Mudanya Turkey 78 B2
Mudayrah Kuwait 79 F5
Mudaysīsāt, Jabal al hill Jordan 77 C4
Muddebihal India 72 C2
Muddus nationalpark nat. park Sweden 32 E2
Muddy r. U.S.A. 137 E3
Muddy Boggy Creek r. U.S.A. 133 C5
Muddy Creek r. U.S.A. 137 G2
Muddy Gap Pass U.S.A. 134 F4
Muddy Peak U.S.A. 137 E3
Mūd-e-Dahanāb Iran 81 D3
Mudgal India 72 C3
Mudgee Australia 112 D4
Mudhol India 72 B2
Mudigere India 72 B3
Mudjatik r. Canada 123 J3
Mudkhed India 72 C2
Mud Lake U.S.A. 136 D3
Mudon Myanmar 61 B4
Mudraya country Africa see Egypt
Mudug admin. reg. Somalia 96 E3
Mudukani Tanz. 97 B5
Mudumu National Park Namibia 98 D3
Mudurnu Turkey 78 B2
Mud'yuga Rus. Fed. 28 F3
Muecate Moz. 99 H2
Mueda Moz. 97 C7
Muela de Arés mt. Spain 43 F2
Mueller Range hills Australia 108 D4
Muende Moz. 97 B8
Muertos Cays is Bahamas 129 C7
Muftah well Sudan 89 G4
Muftyuga Rus. Fed. 28 H2
Mufulira Zambia 95 F8
Mufumbwe Zambia 95 E8
Mufu Shan mts China 67 E2
Muğan Düzü lowland Azer. 79 G3
Muge r. Port. 42 B3
Mugeba Moz. 99 H3
Mughalbhin Pak. see Jati
Mughal Sarai India 75 D4
Mūghār Iran 80 C3
Mughayrā' Saudi Arabia 89 H2
Mugila, Monts mts Dem. Rep. Congo 95 F6
Muğla Turkey 78 B3
Muğla prov. Turkey 47 F6
Mug Qu r. China 62 E5
Muguia Moz. 97 C8
Mugu Karnali r. Nepal 75 D3
Mugxung China 75 G1
Muḩ, Sabkhat imp. l. Syria 77 D2
Muhagiriya Sudan 94 E2
Muhala China see Yutian
Muhala Dem. Rep. Congo 95 F6
Muḩammad, Ra's pt Egypt 89 G3
Muhammadabad India 75 D4
Muhammad Qol Sudan 89 H4
Muhammarah Iran see Khorramshahr
Muhashsham, Wādī al watercourse Egypt 77 B4
Muḩaysh, Wādī al watercourse Jordan 77 C5
Mühlacker Germany 36 D4
Mühlberg Germany 37 F3
Mühldorf am Inn Germany 37 F4
Mühlhausen (Thüringen) Germany 36 E3
Mühlig-Hofmann Mountains Antarctica 167 C2
Muhos Fin. 32 G2
Muḩradah Syria 77 C2
Muhu i. Estonia 33 F4
Muhula Moz. 97 C8
Muhulu Dem. Rep. Congo 94 E5
Mui Eth. 96 B3
Mui Bai Bung c. Vietnam see Mui Ca Mau
Mui Ca Mau c. Vietnam 61 D6
Mui Dinh hd Vietnam 61 E6
Mui Đôc pt Vietnam 60 D4
Muidumbe Moz. 97 C7
Muineachán Rep. of Ireland see Monaghan
Muine Bheag Rep. of Ireland 35 C5
Muirkirk U.K. 34 D4
Mui Ron hd Vietnam 60 D4
Muisne Ecuador 146 B4
Muite Moz. 97 C8
Muju S. Korea 65 A5
Mujuí Joboti Brazil 147 H5
Mukačevo Ukr. see Mukacheve
Mukacheve Ukr. 31 J3
Mukachevo Ukr. see Mukacheve
Mukah Sarawak Malaysia 59 F2
Mukah r. Sarawak Malaysia 59 F2
Mukalla Yemen 76 D7
Mukandwara India 74 C4
Mukanga Dem. Rep. Congo 95 D6
Mukawwar, Gezirat i. Sudan 89 H4
Mukdahan Thai. 61 D4
Mukden China see Shenyang
Mukerian India 74 B3
Mukhen Rus. Fed. 64 D2
Mukhino Rus. Fed. 64 A1
Mukhtuya Rus. Fed. see Lensk
Mukinbudin Australia 109 B7
Mu Ko Chang National Park Thai. 61 C6
Mukomuko Indon. 58 C3
Mukono Uganda 96 B4
Mukoshi Zambia 95 F7
Mukry Turkm. 81 F2
Muktinath Nepal 75 D3
Muktsar India 74 B3
Mukuku Zambia 95 F8
Mukumbura Zimbabwe 99 F3
Mukunsa Zambia 95 F7
Mukur Kazakh. 29 J7
Mukutawa r. Canada 123 L4
Mul India 72 C1
Mula r. India 72 B2
Mula r. Pak. 81 F4
Mula Spain 43 F3
Mulakatholhu Atoll Maldives 71 D11
Mulaku atoll Maldives see Mulakatholhu Atoll
Mulan China 64 B3
Mulapula, Lake salt flat Australia 110 D6
Mula-tupo Panama 146 B2
Mulayh salt pan Saudi Arabia 77 D5
Mulayjah Saudi Arabia 80 B5
Mulayz, Wādī al watercourse Egypt 77 A4
Mulbagal India 72 C3
Mulbekh Jammu and Kashmir 74 C2
Mulchatna r. U.S.A. 120 D3
Mulchén Chile 152 B4
Mulde r. Germany 37 F3
Muleba Tanz. 96 A5
Mule Creek U.S.A. 134 F4
Mulegé Mex. 135 D8
Mulekatembo Zambia 97 B7
Muleshoe U.S.A. 135 G6
Mulevala Moz. 99 H3
Mulgathing Australia 109 F7
Mulhacén mt. Spain 42 E4
Mülhausen France see Mulhouse
Mulhouse France 39 G3
Muli China 66 B3
Muli Rus. Fed. see Vysokogorniy
Mulilansolo Zambia 97 B7
Muling Heilong. China 64 B3
Muling Heilong. China 64 B3
Muling r. China 64 C3
Mull i. U.K. 34 D3
Mulla Ali Iran 80 B2
Mullaaxe Beyle Somalia 96 E2
Mullaittivu Sri Lanka 72 D4
Muller, Pegunungan mts Indon. 59 F2
Mullett Lake U.S.A. 132 E2
Mullewa Australia 109 A7
Müllheim Germany 36 C5
Mullica r. U.S.A. 131 F4
Mulligan watercourse Australia 110 D5
Mullingar Rep. of Ireland 35 C5
Mull of Galloway c. U.K. 35 D4
Mull of Kintyre hd U.K. 34 D4
Mull of Oa hd U.K. 34 C4
Müllrose Germany 37 G2
Mullsjö Sweden 33 D4
Mulobezi Zambia 95 E9
Mulondo Angola 95 B8
Mulonga Plain Zambia 95 D9
Mulongo Dem. Rep. Congo 95 E6
Mulsanne France 38 D3
Mulshi Lake India 72 B2
Multai India 74 C5
Multān Iran 81 E5
Multan Pak. 81 G4
Multia Fin. 33 G3
Mulu, Gunung mt. Sarawak Malaysia 59 F1
Mulug India 72 C2
Mulumbe, Monts mts Dem. Rep. Congo 95 E7
Mulurulu Lake Australia 112 B4
Muma Dem. Rep. Congo 94 D4
Mūmān Iran 81 E5
▶Mumbai India 72 B2
2nd most populous city in Asia and 5th in the world.
world 16–17
Mumbeji Zambia 95 D8
Mumbondo Angola 95 B7
Mumbwa Zambia 95 E8
Mumbwi Tanz. 97 C6
Mume Dem. Rep. Congo 95 E7
Muminabad Tajik. see Leningrad
Mu'minobod Tajik. see Leningrad
Mumra Rus. Fed. 29 H7
Mun, Mae Nam r. Thai. 61 D5
Muna i. Indon. 57 F7
Muna Mex. 127 I7
Muna r. Rus. Fed. 27 M3
Munabao Pak. 81 G5
Munaðarnes Iceland 32 [inset]
Munagala India 72 C2
Munayshy Kazakh. 79 H2
Münchberg Germany 36 E3
München Germany see Munich
München-Gladbach Germany see Mönchengladbach
Munchique, Parque Nacional nat. park Col. 146 B4
Muncho Lake Canada 122 E3
Munch'ŏn N. Korea 65 A5
Muncie U.S.A. 132 E3
Muncoonie West, Lake salt flat Australia 110 D5
Muncy U.S.A. 131 E3
Munda Solomon Is 107 E2
Mundel Lake Sri Lanka 72 C5
Mundemba Cameroon 93 H4
Mundiwindi Australia 108 C5
Mundo r. Spain 43 F3
Mundo Novo Brazil 150 D4
Mundra India 74 A5
Mundrabilla Australia 109 D7
Munds Park U.S.A. 137 G4
Mundubbera Australia 111 G5
Mundwa India 74 B4
Muneru r. India 72 D2
Munfordville U.S.A. 128 B4
Mungallala Australia 111 F5
Mungallala Creek r. Australia 111 F6
Mungana Australia 111 F3
Mungaoli India 74 C4
Mungári Moz. 99 G3
Mungbere Dem. Rep. Congo 94 F4
Mungeli India 75 D5
Munger India 75 E4
Munger U.S.A. 130 B2
Mungeranie Australia 110 D6
Mu Nggava i. Solomon Is see Rennell
Munggresak, Tanjung pt Indon. 59 E2
Mungindi Australia 112 D3
Mungo Angola 95 C7
Mungo National Park Australia 112 B4
Mun'gyŏng S. Korea 65 A5
Munhango Angola 95 C8
Munhino Angola 95 B8
Munich Germany 36 E4
Munising U.S.A. 132 E2
Munkács Ukr. see Mukacheve
Munkedal Sweden 33 C4
Munku-Sardyk, Gora mt. Mongolia/Rus. Fed. 62 G1
Munro, Mount Australia 112 D6
Munshiganj Bangl. 75 F5
Münsingen Switz. 39 G3
Münster Niedersachsen Germany 36 E2
Münster Nordrhein-Westfalen Germany 36 C3
Munster reg. Rep. of Ireland 35 B5
Münster-Osnabrück airport Germany 36 C2
Muntadgin Australia 109 B7
Muntele Mare, Vârful mt. Romania 46 C1
Munteni Romania 46 E2
Mununga Zambia 95 F7
Munyal-Par sea feature India see Bassas de Pedro Padua Bank
Munyati r. Zimbabwe 99 F3
Munzur Vadisi Milli Parkı nat. park Turkey 79 D3
Muodoslompolo Sweden 32 F2
Muojärvi l. Fin. 32 H2
Muonio Fin. 32 F2
Muonioälven r. Fin./Sweden 32 F2
Muonionjoki r. Fin./Sweden see Muonioälven
Mupa Angola 95 B9
Mupa, Parque Nacional da nat. park Angola 95 B8
Mupfure r. Zimbabwe 99 F3
Muqaddam watercourse Sudan 89 F5
Muqdisho Somalia see Mogadishu
Muqshin, Wādī r. Oman 76 E6
Muquem Brazil 150 B5
Muqui Brazil 151 D7
Muqyr Kazakh. see Mukur
Mur r. Austria 37 H5
Muradiye Manisa Turkey 47 E5
Muradiye Turkey 79 E3
Murai, Tanjong pt Sing. 58 [inset]
Murai Reservoir Sing. 58 [inset]
Murakami Japan 65 D5
Murallón, Cerro mt. Chile 153 B7
Muramvya Burundi 94 F5
Muráň r. Slovakia 37 J4
Muranga Kenya 96 C5
Muras Spain 42 C1
Murashi Rus. Fed. 28 I4
Murat France 39 E4
Murat r. Turkey 79 D3
Muratlı Turkey 78 A2
Murayr, Jabal hill Saudi Arabia 89 I3
Muraysah, Ra's al pt Libya 88 E2
Murça Port. 42 C2
Murcheh Khvort Iran 80 B3
Murchison Australia 112 C5
Murchison watercourse Australia 109 A6
Murchison, Mount Antarctica 167 H2
Murchison Falls Uganda 96 A4
Murchison Falls National Park Uganda 96 A4
Murcia Spain 43 F4
Murcia aut. comm. Spain 43 F4
Mûr-de-Bretagne France 38 B2
Murdo U.S.A. 132 A3
Murdochville Canada 125 H3
Mürefte Turkey 46 E4
Muregi Nigeria 93 G3
Murehwa Zimbabwe 99 F3
Mureş r. Romania 46 B1
Muret France 38 D5
Murewa Zimbabwe see Murehwa
Murfjället mt. Norway 32 D2
Murfreesboro NC U.S.A. 131 E5
Murfreesboro TN U.S.A. 128 B5
Murgab Tajik. see Murghob
Murgab r. Tajik. 81 H2
Murgab Turkm. see Murgap
Murgab r. Turkm. see Murgap
Murgap Turkm. 81 E2
Murgap r. Turkm. 81 E2
Murgeni Romania 46 F1
Murge Tarantine hills Italy 45 F4
Murghab r. Afgh. 81 E3
Murgha Kibzai Pak. 81 G4
Murghob Tajik. 81 H2
Murgh Pass Afgh. 81 G3
Murgon Australia 111 G5
Murgoo Australia 109 B6
Muri India 75 E5
Mūrī Iran 80 D2
Muria, Gunung mt. Indon. 59 E4
Muriaé Brazil 151 D7
Muriege Angola 95 D7
Müritz l. Germany 37 F2
Müritz, Nationalpark nat. park Germany 37 F2
Murjek Sweden 32 F2
Murkong Selek India 75 G4
Murmansk Rus. Fed. 32 I1
Murmanskaya Oblast' admin. div. Rus. Fed. 32 I1
Murmanskiy Bereg coastal area Rus. Fed. 28 E1
Murmansk Oblast admin. div. Rus. Fed. see Murmanskaya Oblast'
Murmashi Rus. Fed. 32 I1
Muro, Capo di c. Corsica France 44 B4
Muro Lucano Italy 45 E4
Murom Rus. Fed. 28 G5
Murongo Tanz. 96 A5
Muroran Japan 64 E4
Muros Spain 42 B1
Muroto Japan 65 C6
Muroto-zaki pt Japan 65 C6
Murphy ID U.S.A. 134 C4
Murphy NC U.S.A. 128 C5
Murphys U.S.A. 136 B2
Murrah, Wādī al watercourse Egypt 77 B5
Murra Murra Australia 111 F6
▶Murray r. S.A. Australia 112 A4
3rd longest river in Oceania. Part of the longest (Murray-Darling).
oceania 102–103
Murray r. W.A. Australia 109 A8
Murray r. Canada 122 F3
Murray U.S.A. 128 A4
Murray, Lake P.N.G. 57 J7
Murray, Lake U.S.A. 129 C5
Murray, Mount Canada 122 D2
Murray Bridge Australia 112 A4
Murray City U.S.A. 130 B4
▶Murray-Darling Australia 106 B5
Longest river in Oceania.
oceania 102–103
Murray Downs Australia 110 C4
Murray Range hills Australia 109 E6
Murraysburg S. Africa 98 D6
Murray Sunset National Park Australia 112 B4
Murree Pak. 81 H3
Murroa Moz. 99 H3
▶Murrumbidgee r. Australia 112 B4
4th longest river in Oceania.
oceania 102–103
Murrupula Moz. 99 H2
Murshidabad India 75 F4
Murska Sobota Slovenia 44 F1
Murtajapur India 72 C1
Murten Switz. 39 G3
Murter Croatia 44 E3
Murter i. Croatia 44 E3
Murtoa Australia 112 B5
Murtovaara Fin. 32 H2
Muru r. Brazil 148 C2
Murua i. P.N.G. see Woodlark Island
Murud India 72 B2
Murud, Gunung mt. Indon. 59 F2
Murui r. Indon. 59 F3
Murung r. Indon. 59 F3
Murung r. Indon. 59 F3
Murupara N.Z. 113 D2
Mururoa atoll Fr. Polynesia 165 I7
Murviedro Spain see Sagunto
Murwara India 74 D5
Murygino Rus. Fed. 28 I4
Mürz r. Austria 37 G5
Murzechirla Turkm. 81 E2
Murzūq Libya 88 B3
Mürzzuschlag Austria 37 G5
Muş Turkey 79 E3
Musa Dem. Rep. Congo 94 C4
Mūša r. Latvia/Lith. 33 G4
Mūsa r. Latvia/Lith. 33 G4
Mûsa, Gebel mt. Egypt see Sinai, Mount
Mūsá, Jabal mt. Egypt see Sinai, Mount
Mūsā, Khowr-e b. Iran 80 B4
Musa Āli Terara vol. Africa 89 I6
Musabani India 75 E5
Muşabih Saudi Arabia 89 I5
Musa Khel Bazar Pak. 81 G4
Musala mt. Bulg. 46 C3
Musala i. Indon. 58 B2
Musan N. Korea 64 B4
Musandam admin. reg. Oman 80 D5
Musandam Peninsula Oman/U.A.E. 80 D5
Musa Qala, Rūd-i r. Afgh. 81 F3
Musay'īd Qatar see Umm Sa'id
Musbat well Sudan 88 E6
▶Muscat Oman 76 F5
Capital of Oman.
Muscat and Oman country Asia see Oman
Muscatine U.S.A. 132 D3
Muscongus Bay U.S.A. 131 I2
Musgrave Australia 111 E2
Musgrave Harbour Canada 125 K3
Musgrave Ranges mts Australia 110 B5
Mūshakī Afgh. 81 G3
Mushāsh al Kabid well Jordan 77 C5
Mushash Dabl well Saudi Arabia 77 C5
Mushāsh Muḍayyān well Saudi Arabia 77 D5
Mushayyish, Wādī al watercourse Jordan 77 C4
Mushenge Dem. Rep. Congo 95 D6
Mushie Dem. Rep. Congo 94 C5
Mushin Nigeria 93 F4
Musi r. India 72 C2
Musi r. Indon. 58 D3
Musica mt. Macedonia 46 B4
Music Mountain U.S.A. 137 F4
Musikot Nepal 75 D3
Musinia Peak U.S.A. 137 G2
Muskeg r. Canada 122 F2
Muskeget Channel U.S.A. 131 H3
Muskegon U.S.A. 132 E3
Muskegon r. U.S.A. 132 E3
Muskeg River Canada 122 G4
Muskingum r. U.S.A. 130 C4
Muskogee U.S.A. 133 C5
Muskoka, Lake Canada 124 E4
Muskrat Dam Lake Canada 124 B2
Muskwa r. Canada 122 F3
Muslimbagh Pak. 81 F4
Muslim-Croat Federation aut. div. Bos.-Herz. see Federacija Bosna i Hercegovina
Musoma Tanz. 96 B5
Musombe Tanz. 97 B6
Musquanousse, Lac l. Canada 125 I3
Musquaro Canada 125 I3
Musquaro, Lac l. Canada 125 I3
Mussau Island P.N.G. 106 D2
Musselburgh U.K. 34 E4
Musselshell r. U.S.A. 134 F3
Mussende Angola 95 C7
Musserra Angola 95 B6
Mussidan France 38 D4
Mussolo Angola 95 C7
Mussoorie India 74 C3
Mussuma Angola 95 D8
Mussuma r. Angola 95 D8
Mustafabad India 75 D4
Mustafakemalpaşa Turkey 78 B2
Mustahīl Eth. 96 E3
Mustang Draw watercourse U.S.A. 133 A6
Musters, Lago l. Arg. 153 C6
Mustique i. St Vincent 147 F1
Mustjala Estonia 28 B4
Mustjõgi r. Estonia 33 G4
Mustla Estonia 33 G4
Mustvee Estonia 28 C4
Musu-dan pt N. Korea 65 B4
Muswellbrook Australia 112 D4
Mūṭ Egypt 89 F3
Mut Turkey 78 C3
Mutá, Ponta do pt Brazil 150 E5
Mutanda Zambia 95 E8
Mutare Zimbabwe 99 G3
Mutina Italy see Modena
Mutis Col. 146 B3
Mutis, Gunung mt. Indon. 108 D2
Mutnyy Materik Rus. Fed. 28 J2
Mutoko Zimbabwe 99 G3
Mutombo Dem. Rep. Congo 95 D6
Mutooroo Australia 112 B4
Mutorashanga Zimbabwe 99 F3
Mutsamudu Comoros 97 E8
Mutshatsha Dem. Rep. Congo 95 E7
Mutsu Japan 64 E4
Mutsu-wan b. Japan 64 E4
Muttaburra Australia 111 F4
Muttonbird Islands N.Z. 113 A4
Mutuali Moz. 99 H2
Mutum r. Brazil 146 D6
Mutum Biyu Nigeria 93 H3
Mutungu-Tari Dem. Rep. Congo 95 C6
Mutur Sri Lanka 72 D4
Muuga Estonia 33 G4
Muurame Fin. 33 G3
Muurola Fin. 32 G2
Mu Us Shamo des. China 63 H4
Muxaluando Angola 95 B7
Muxi China see Muchuan
Muxima Angola 95 B7
Muyezerskiy Rus. Fed. 28 E3
Muyinga Burundi 96 A5
Muynak Uzbek. 76 F1
Muynoq Uzbek. see Muynak
Muyombe Zambia 97 B7
Muyuka Cameroon 93 H4
Muyumba Dem. Rep. Congo 95 E6
Muyunkum, Peski des. Kazakh. 70 C3
Muyuping China 67 D2
Muzaffarabad Pak. 81 H3
Muzaffargarh Pak. 81 G4
Muzaffarnagar India 74 C3
Muzaffarpur India 75 E4
Muzamane Moz. 99 G4
Muze Moz. 97 A8
Muzillac France 38 B3
Mūzīn Iran 81 E5
Muzon, Cape U.S.A. 122 C4
Múzquiz Mex. 133 A7
Muztag mt. Xinjiang China 70 F4
Muztag mt. Xinjiang China 70 G4
Mvadi Gabon 94 B4
Mvolo Sudan 94 F3
Mvomero Tanz. 97 C6
Mvoung r. Gabon 94 B4
Mvouti Congo 95 B6
Mvuma Zimbabwe 99 F3
Mwali i. Comoros 97 D8
Mwanisenga Tanz. 97 B6
Mwanya Zambia 97 B8
Mwanza Malawi 97 B8
Mwanza Tanz. 96 B5
Mwanza admin. reg. Tanz. 96 B5
Mwape Zambia 97 A8
Mweho Dem. Rep. Congo 95 E6
Mweka Dem. Rep. Congo 95 D6
Mwenda Zambia 95 F7
Mwene-Biji Dem. Rep. Congo 95 D7
Mwene-Ditu Dem. Rep. Congo 95 D6
Mwenezi Zimbabwe 99 F4
Mwenezi r. Zimbabwe 99 F4
Mwenga Dem. Rep. Congo 94 F5
Mwereni Kenya 97 C6
Mweru, Lake Dem. Rep. Congo/Zambia 95 F7
Mweru Plateau Tanz. 97 C7
Mweru Wantipa, Lake Zambia 95 F7
Mweru Wantipa National Park Zambia 95 F7
Mwimba Dem. Rep. Congo 95 D7
Mwingi Kenya 96 C5
Mwinilunga Zambia 95 E7
Mya, Oued watercourse Alg. 91 G3
Myaing Myanmar 60 A3
Myajlar India 74 A4
Myakit Rus. Fed. 27 P3
Myall Lakes National Park Australia 112 E4
Myanaung Myanmar 60 A4
▶Myanmar country Asia 60 A3
asia 52–53, 82
Myaundzha Rus. Fed. 27 O3
Myaungmya Myanmar 61 A4
Mycenae tourist site Greece 47 C6
Myeik Myanmar see Mergui
Myers U.S.A. 130 B4
Myingyan Myanmar 60 A3
Myinmoletkat mt. Myanmar 61 B5
Myinmu Myanmar 60 A3
Myitkyina Myanmar 60 B2
Myitson Myanmar 60 B3
Myitta Myanmar 61 B5
Myittha Myanmar 60 B3
Myittha r. Myanmar 75 G5
Myjava Slovakia 37 H4
Mykines i. Faroe Is 34 [inset]
Mykines tourist site Greece see Mycenae
Mykolayiv Ukr. 29 E7
Mykonos Greece 47 D6
Mykonos i. Greece 47 D6
Myla Rus. Fed. 28 I2
Mylae Sicily Italy see Milazzo
Mylasa Turkey see Milas
Mymensing Bangl. see Mymensingh
Mymensingh Bangl. 75 F4
Mynämäki Fin. 33 F3
Myohaung Myanmar 60 A3
Myŏnggan N. Korea 64 B4
Myory Belarus 28 C5
Myotha Myanmar 60 A3
Mýrdalsjökull ice cap Iceland 32 [inset]
Myre Norway 32 D1
Myrheden Sweden 32 F2
Myrhorod Ukr. 29 E6
Myrina Greece 47 D5
Myrnam Canada 123 I4
Myrnopillya Ukr. 46 F1
Myronivka Ukr. 29 D6
Myrtle Beach U.S.A. 129 D5
Myrtle Creek U.S.A. 134 B4
Myrtleford Australia 112 C5
Myrzakent Kazakh. 81 G1
Mysen Norway 33 C4
Mys Lazareva Rus. Fed. see Lazarev
Myślenice Poland 37 I4
Myślibórz Poland 37 G2
My Son tourist site Vietnam 61 E5
Mysore India 72 C3
Mysore state India see Karnataka
Mysovsk Rus. Fed. see Babushkin
Mys Shmidta Rus. Fed. 27 S3
Myszków Poland 37 I3
Myszyniec Poland 37 J2
Myt Rus. Fed. 28 G4
My Tho Vietnam 61 D6
Mytilene i. Greece see Lesbos
Mytilini Greece 47 E5
Mytilinioi Greece 47 E6
Mytilini Strait Greece/Turkey 47 E5
Mytishchi Rus. Fed. 28 F5
Myton U.S.A. 137 G1
Mývatn l. Iceland 32 [inset]
M'Zab Valley tourist site Alg. 91 F2
Mzamomhle S. Africa 99 E6
Mže r. Czech Rep. 37 F4
Mziha Tanz. 97 C6
Mzingwani r. Zimbabwe 99 F4
Mzuzu Malawi 97 B7

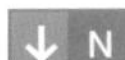

Na, Nam r. China/Vietnam 66 B4
Naab r. Germany 36 F4
Naalehu U.S.A. 135 [inset] Z2
Naam Sudan 94 F2
Naama Alg. 91 E2
Naantali Fin. 33 F3
Naas Rep. of Ireland 35 C5
Näätämö Fin. 32 H1
Naba Myanmar 60 B2
Nababdwip India see Navadwip
Nabão r. Port. 42 B3
Nabarangapur India 73 D2
Nabatiyet et Tahta Lebanon 77 B3
Nabberu, Lake salt flat Australia 109 C6
Naberera Tanz. 97 C6
Naberezhnyye Chelny Rus. Fed. 28 J5
Nabesna U.S.A. 122 A2
Nabeul Tunisia 91 H1
Nabha India 74 C3
Nabileque r. Brazil 149 F5
Nabinagar India 75 E4
Nabire Indon. 57 I6
Nabi Younés, Ras en pt Lebanon 77 B3
Nablus West Bank see Nābulus
Nabolo Ghana 93 E3
Naboomspruit S. Africa 99 F5
Nabra r. India 74 C2
Nābulus West Bank 77 B3
Nacala Moz. 99 I2
Nacaome Hond. 138 G6
Nacaroa Moz. 97 C8
Nacebe Bol. 148 D2
Nachingwea Tanz. 97 C7
Nachna India 74 A4
Náchod Czech Rep. 37 H3
Nachuge India 73 G4
Nacimiento Chile 152 B4
Nacimiento Reservoir U.S.A. 136 B4
Nacogdoches U.S.A. 133 C6
Nacozari de García Mex. 135 E7
Nada China see Danzhou

Nadaleen r. Canada 122 C2
Nådendal Fin. see Naantali
Nadi Fiji 107 G3
Nadiad India 74 B5
Nădlac Romania 46 B1
Nador Morocco 90 E2
Nădrag Romania 46 C2
Nadūshan Iran 80 C3
Nadvirna Ukr. 29 C6
Nadvornaya Ukr. see Nadvirna
Nadym Rus. Fed. 26 H3
Naenwa India 74 B4
Næstved Denmark 33 C5
Naf r. Bangl./Myanmar 75 G5
Nafas, Ra's an mt. Egypt 77 B5
Nafha, Har hill Israel 77 B4
Nafpaktos Greece 47 B5
Nafplio Greece 47 C6
Naft r. Iraq see Āb Naft
Naft-e Safīd Iran 80 B4
Naft-e Shāh Iran see Naft Shahr
Naft Shahr Iran 80 A3
Nafūd ad Daḩl des. Saudi Arabia 76 D5
Nafūd al 'Urayq des. Saudi Arabia 89 I3
Nafūd as Surrah des. Saudi Arabia 89 I4
Nafūsah, Jabal hills Libya 88 A2
Nafy Saudi Arabia 89 I3
Nag, Co l. China 75 F2
Naga Phil. 57 F3
Nagagami r. Canada 124 C3
Nagagami Lake Canada 124 C3
Naga Hills India 75 G4
Naga Hills state India see Nagaland
Nagaland state India 75 G4
Nagano Japan 65 D5
Nagaoka Japan 65 D5
Nagaon India 75 G4
Nagapatam India see Nagappattinam
Nagappattinam India 72 C4
Nagar r. Bangl./India 75 F4
Nagar Himachal Pradesh India 74 C2
Nagar Rajasthan India 74 C4
Nagaram India 72 D2
Nagarjuna Sagar Reservoir India 72 C2
Nagarzê China 75 F3
Nagasaki Japan 65 B6
Nagato Japan 65 B6
Nagaur India 74 B4
Nagavali r. India 73 D2
Nagda India 74 B5
Nagercoil India 72 C4
Nagha Kalat Pak. 81 F5
Nagina India 74 C3
Nagineh Iran 80 D3
Nagma Nepal 75 D3
Nagod India 74 D4
Nagold Germany 36 D4
Nagong Chu r. China see Parlung Zangbo
Nagorno-Karabakh aut. reg. Azer. see Dağlıq Qarabağ
Nagornyy Rus. Fed. 27 M4
Nagornyy Karabakh aut. reg. Azer. see Dağlıq Qarabağ
Nagorsk Rus. Fed. 28 I4
Nagoya Japan 65 D6
Nagpur India 74 C5
Nagqu China 75 G3
Nag Qu r. China 75 G3
Nagu Fin. 33 F3
Nagurskoye Rus. Fed. 26 E1
Nagyatád Hungary 44 F1
Nagybecskerek Serb. and Mont. see Zrenjanin
Nagyenyed Romania see Aiud
Nagyhalász Hungary 37 J4
Nagykanizsa Hungary 44 F1
Nagykáta Hungary 37 I5
Nagykőrös Hungary 37 I5
Nagyvárad Romania see Oradea
Naha Japan 63 L6
Nahan India 74 C3
Nahang r. Iran/Pak. 81 E5
Nahanni Butte Canada 122 F2
Nahanni National Park Canada 122 E2
Nahanni Range mts Canada 122 F2
Nahariyya Israel 77 B3
Nahāvand Iran 80 B3
N'Ahnet, Adrar mts Alg. 91 F4
Nahr Ouassel, Oued watercourse Alg. 43 H5
Nahuel Huapi, Parque Nacional nat. park Arg. 152 C5
Nahuel Mapá Arg. 152 D3
Nahunta U.S.A. 129 C6
Naica Mex. 135 F8
Naidor well Tanz. 97 C6
Naikliu Indon. 108 C2
Nailung China 75 G3
Na'ima Sudan 89 G6
Nain Canada 125 I1
Nā'īn Iran 80 C3
Naina India 75 D4
Naini Tal India 74 C3
Nainpur India 74 D5
Naiopué Moz. 99 H3
Nairn U.K. 34 E3

▶Nairobi Kenya 96 C5
Capital of Kenya.

Naissaar i. Estonia 33 G4
Naissus Serb. and Mont. see Niš
Naivasha Kenya 96 C5
Najafābād Iran 80 B3
Najd reg. Saudi Arabia 76 C4
Nájera Spain 43 E1
Najerilla r. Spain 43 E1
Najibabad India 74 C3
Najin N. Korea 64 B4
Najmah Saudi Arabia 80 B5
Najrān Saudi Arabia 76 C6
Nakalele Point U.S.A. 135 [inset] Z1
Nakambé watercourse Burkina/Ghana 93 E3 see White Volta
Nakamura Japan 65 C6
Nakanno Rus. Fed. 27 K3
Nakano-shima i. Japan 65 B7
Nakapanya Tanz. 97 C7
Nakasongola Uganda 96 B4
Nakatsu Japan 65 B6
Nakatsugawa Japan 65 D6
Nakfa Eritrea 89 H5
Nakhichevan' Azer. see Naxçıvan
Nakhl Egypt 89 G2
Nakhl-e Taqī Iran 80 C5
Nakhodka Rus. Fed. 64 C4
Nakhola India 75 G4
Nakhon Nayok Thai. 61 C5
Nakhon Pathom Thai. 61 C5
Nakhon Phanom Thai. 60 D4
Nakhon Ratchasima Thai. 61 C5
Nakhon Sawan Thai. 61 C5
Nakhon Si Thammarat Thai. 61 B6
Nakhtarana India 74 A5
Nakło nad Notecią Poland 37 H2
Naknek U.S.A. 120 D4
Nakodar India 74 B3
Nakonde Zambia 97 B7
Nakpanduri Ghana 93 E3
Nakskov Denmark 33 C5
Näkten l. Sweden 32 D3
Naktong-gang r. S. Korea 65 B6
Nakuru Kenya 96 C5
Nakusp Canada 134 C2
Nalázi Moz. 99 G5
Nalbari India 75 F4
Nal'chik Rus. Fed. 29 G8

Naldurg India 72 C2
Nałęczów Poland 37 K3
Nalerigu Ghana 93 E3
Nalgonda India 72 C2
Nalhati India 75 E4
Nallamala Hills India 72 C3
Nallıhan Turkey 78 B2
Nalolo Zambia 95 D8
Nalón r. Spain 38 A5
Nālūt Libya 88 A2
Namaacha Moz. 99 G5
Namacunde Angola 95 B9
Namacurra Moz. 99 H3
Namadgi National Park Australia 112 D4
Namahadi S. Africa 99 F5
Namak, Daryācheh-ye salt flat Iran 80 B3
Namak-e Mīqhān, Kavīr-e salt flat Iran 80 B3
Nāmakī watercourse Iran 80 C4
Namakkal India 72 C4
Namakzar-e Shadad salt flat Iran 80 D4
Namanga Kenya 96 C5
Namangan Uzbek. 70 D3
Namapa Moz. 97 C8
Namaponda Moz. 99 H2
Namaqua National Park S. Africa 98 C6
Namarrói Moz. 99 H2
Namasale Uganda 96 B4
Namatanai P.N.G. 107 E2
Namba Angola 95 B7
Nambour Australia 111 H5
Nambucca Heads Australia 112 E3
Nambung National Park Australia 109 A7
Năm Căn Vietnam 61 D6
Namcha Barwa mt. China see Namjagbarwa Feng
Namche Bazar Nepal 75 E4
Namch'ŏn N. Korea 65 A5
Namco China 75 F3
Nam Co salt l. China 70 H5
Namdalen valley Norway 32 D2
Namdalseid Norway 32 C2
Nam Định Vietnam 60 D3
Namen Belgium see Namur
Námestovo Slovakia 37 I4
Nametil Moz. 99 H2
Namew Lake Canada 123 K4
Nam-gang r. N. Korea 65 A5
Namhkam Myanmar 60 B3
Namhsan Myanmar 60 B3
Namialo Moz. 99 H2
▶Namib Desert Namibia 98 B5
africa 86–87
Namibe Angola 95 B8
Namibe prov. Angola 95 B8
▶Namibia country Africa 98 B4
africa 86–87, 100
Namibia Abyssal Plain sea feature N. Atlantic Ocean 161 O8
Namib-Naukluft Game Park nature res. Namibia 98 B5
Namichiga Tanz. 97 C7
Namicunde Moz. 97 C8
Namidobe Moz. 99 H3
Namīn Iran 80 B2
Namina Moz. 99 H2
Namitete Malawi 97 B8
Namjagbarwa Feng mt. China 62 E6
Namka China see Doilungdêqên
Namlan Myanmar 60 B3
Namlang r. Myanmar 60 B3
Namlea Indon. 57 G6
Namling China 75 F3
Nam Nao National Park Thai. 60 C4
Nam Ngum Reservoir Laos 60 C4
Namoi r. Australia 112 D3
Nampa Canada 123 G3
Nampa mt. Nepal 74 D3
Nampa U.S.A. 134 C4
Nampala Mali 92 D2
Namp'o N. Korea 65 A5
Nampuecha Moz. 97 D8
Nampula Moz. 99 H2
Nampula prov. Moz. 99 H2
Nam Pung Reservoir Thai. 60 C4
Namrup India 75 G4
Namsai Myanmar 60 B2
Namsang Myanmar 60 B3
Namsos Norway 32 C2
Namsskogan Norway 32 D2
Namtari Nigeria 93 I3
Namtok Myanmar 60 B4
Nam Tok Thai. 61 B5
Namtok Chattakan National Park Thai. 60 C4
Namtok Mae Surin National Park Thai. 60 B4
Namton Myanmar 60 B3
Namtsy Rus. Fed. 27 M3
Namtu Myanmar 60 B3
Namu Canada 122 E5
Namuli, Monte mt. Moz. 99 H2
Namuno Moz. 97 C8
Namur Belgium 39 F1
Namutoni Namibia 98 C3
Namwala Zambia 95 E8
Namwera Malawi 97 B8
Namwŏn S. Korea 65 A6
Namya Ra Myanmar 60 B2
Namyit Island S. China Sea 56 D3
Namysłów Poland 37 H3
Nan Thai. 60 C4
Nan, Mae Nam r. Thai. 60 C5
Nana r. Cent. Afr. Rep. 94 B3
Nana Bakassa Cent. Afr. Rep. 94 C3
Nana Barya r. Cent. Afr. Rep./Chad 94 C3
Nana-Grébizi pref. Cent. Afr. Rep. 94 C3
Nanaimo Canada 134 B2
Nana-Mambéré pref. Cent. Afr. Rep. 94 B3
Nan'an China 67 F3
Nanango Australia 111 H5
Nananib Plateau Namibia 98 C5
Nan'ao China see Dayu
Nanao Japan 65 D5
Nanatsu-shima i. Japan 65 D5
Nanay r. Peru 146 C5
Nanbai China see Zunyi
Nanbin China see Shizhu
Nanbu China 66 C2
Nancha China 64 B3
Nanchang Jiangxi China 67 E2
Nanchang Jiangxi China 67 E2
Nancheng China 67 F3
Nanchong China 66 C2
Nanchuan China 66 C2
Ñancorainza Bol. 149 E5
Nancowry i. India 73 G5
Nancut Canada 122 E4
Nancy France 39 G2
Nanda Devi mt. India 74 D3
Nanda Kot mt. India 74 D3
Nandan China 66 C3
Nanded India 72 C2
Nander India see Nanded
Nandewar Range mts Australia 112 D3
Nandgaon India 72 B1
Nandi Zimbabwe 99 F4
Nandikotkur India 72 C3
Nanding He r. China 66 A4
Nandod India 74 B5
Nandu Jiang r. China 67 D4
Nandura India 72 C1
Nandurbar India 74 B5
Nandyal India 72 C3
Nanfeng Guangdong China 67 D4
Nanfeng Jiangxi China 67 F3

Nang China 75 G3
Nangade Moz. 97 C7
Nanga Eboko Cameroon 93 I4
Nangah Dedai Indon. 59 E3
Nangahembaloh Indon. 59 F2
Nangahkemangai Indon. 59 F3
Nangahpinoh Indon. 59 E3
Nangahtempuai Indon. 59 F2
Nangalala Australia 110 C2
Nanganga Tanz. 97 C7
Nangang Shan mts China 64 B4

▶Nanga Parbat mt. Jammu and Kashmir 74 B2
9th highest mountain in the world and in Asia.
asia 50–51
world 6–7

Nangarhār prov. Afgh. 81 G3
Nangatayap Indon. 59 E3
Nangbéto, Retenue de resr Togo 93 F4
Nangin Myanmar 61 B6
Nangis France 39 E2
Nangnim-sanmaek mts N. Korea 65 A4
Nangqên China 66 A1
Nangulangwa Tanz. 97 C7
Nanguneri India 72 C4
Nanhua China 66 B3
Nanhui China 67 G2
Nani Afgh. 81 G3
Nanisivik Canada 121 K2
Nanjangud India 72 C3
Nanjian China 66 B3
Nanjiang China 66 C1
Nanjie China see Guangning
Nanjing China 67 F1
Nanji Shan i. China 67 G3
Nanka Jiang r. China 66 A4
Nankang Jiangxi China 67 E3
Nankang Jiangxi China see Xingzi
Nanking China see Nanjing
Nankoku Japan 65 C6
Nankova Angola 95 C9
Nanlan He r. China 66 A4
Nanling China 67 F2
Nan Ling mts China 67 D3
Nanliu Jiang r. China 67 D4
Nanlong China see Nanbu
Nanmulingzue China see Namling
Nannine Australia 109 B6
Nanning China 67 D4
Nannup Australia 109 A8
Na Noi Thai. 60 C4
Nanortalik Greenland 121 O3
Nanpan Jiang r. China 66 C3
Nanpara India 75 D4
Nanping Fujian China 67 F3
Nanping Sichuan China 66 C1
Nanpu China see Pucheng
Nanpu Xi r. China 67 F3
Nanqiao China see Fengxian
Nanri Dao i. China 67 F3
Nansa r. Spain 42 D1
Nansebo Eth. 96 C3
Nansei-shotō Japan see Ryukyu Islands
Nansen Basin sea feature Arctic Ocean 166 H1
Nansenga Zambia 95 E8
Nansen Land reg. Greenland 121 O1
Nansen Sound sea chan. Canada 121 J1
Nanshan Island S. China Sea 56 E3
Nansha Qundao is S. China Sea see Spratly Islands
Nansio Tanz. 96 B5
Nantes France 38 C3
Nantes à Brest, Canal de France 38 B3
Nanthi Kadal lag. Sri Lanka 72 D4
Nantiat France 38 D3
Nanticoke Canada 130 C2
Nanticoke MD U.S.A. 131 F4
Nanticoke PA U.S.A. 131 E3
Nanticoke r. U.S.A. 131 F4
Nanton Canada 123 H5
Nantong China 67 G2
Nantou China 67 [inset]
Nant'ou Taiwan 67 G4
Nantucket U.S.A. 131 H3
Nantucket Island U.S.A. 131 I3
Nantucket Sound g. U.S.A. 131 H3
Nantulo Moz. 97 C8
Nanumaga i. Tuvalu see Nanumanga
Nanumanga i. Tuvalu 107 G2
Nanumea i. Tuvalu 107 G2
Nanuque Brazil 151 D6
Nanusa, Kepulauan is Indon. 57 G5
Nanutarra Roadhouse Australia 108 A5
Nanxi China 66 C2
Nanxian China 67 E2
Nanxiong China 67 E3
Nanyandang Shan mt. China 67 G3
Nanyang China 67 E1
Nanyuki Kenya 96 C5
Nanzamu China 64 A4
Nanzhang China 67 D2
Nanzhao China see Zhao'an
Nanzhou China see Nanxian
Naogaon Bangl. 75 F4
Naokot Pak. 81 G5
Naoli r. China 64 C3
Naomid, Dasht-e des. Afgh./Iran 81 E3
Naousa Greece 46 C4
Napa U.S.A. 136 A2
Napaktulik Lake Canada 123 H1
Napanee Canada 131 E1
Napasar India 74 B4
Napasoq Greenland 121 N3
Naperville U.S.A. 132 D3
Napier N.Z. 113 D2
Napier Peninsula Australia 110 C2
Napier Range hills Australia 108 D4
Naples Italy 45 E4
Naples FL U.S.A. 129 C7
Naples ME U.S.A. 131 H2
Naples NY U.S.A. 131 E2
Naples UT U.S.A. 137 H1
Napo prov. Ecuador 146 B5
Napo r. Ecuador 146 C5
Napoleon ND U.S.A. 132 B2
Napoleon OH U.S.A. 130 A3
Napoli Italy see Naples
Napoli, Golfo di b. Italy 45 E4
Naposta Arg. 152 E4
Naqb Mālihah mt. Egypt 77 A5
Nara Japan 65 C6
Nara Mali 92 D2
Narach Belarus 33 G5
Narach, Vozyera l. Belarus 33 G5
Naracoorte Australia 112 B5
Naradhan Australia 112 C4
Narail Bangl. 75 F5
Naraina India 74 B4
Narang Afgh. 74 A2
Naranjal Ecuador 146 B5
Naranjal Peru 146 C6
Naraq Iran 80 B3
Narasannapeta India 73 E2
Narasapatnam, Point India 73 D2
Narasapur India 73 D2
Narasaraopet India 72 D2
Narathiwat Thai. 61 C7
Nara Visa U.S.A. 133 A5
Narayanganj Bangl. 75 F5
Narayanganj India 74 D5
Narayangaon India 72 B2
Narayanpet India 72 C2
Naray Kelay Afgh. 81 G3

Narbada r. India see Narmada
Narbo France see Narbonne
Narbonne France 39 E5
Narbuvoll Norway 33 C3
Narcea r. Spain 42 C1
Narcondam Island India 73 G3
Nardin Iran 80 C2
Nardò Italy 45 G4
Narechi r. Pak. 81 G4
Narembeen Australia 109 B8
Nares Abyssal Plain sea feature S. Atlantic Ocean 160 J4
Nares Deep sea feature N. Atlantic Ocean 160 J4
Nares Strait Canada/Greenland 121 L2
Naretha Australia 109 D7
Narew r. Poland 37 J2
Nari r. Pak. 81 F4
Naria Bangl. 75 F5
Narib Namibia 98 C5
Narie, Jezioro l. Poland 37 J2
Narimanov Rus. Fed. 29 H7
Narimskiy Khrebet mts Kazakh. 70 F2
Narin Afgh. 81 G2
Narince Turkey 79 D3
Narin Gol watercourse China 75 G1
Nariño dept Col. 146 B4
Narizon, Punta pt Mex. 135 E8
Narken Sweden 32 F2
Narmada r. India 74 B5
Narnaul India 74 C3
Narni Italy 44 D3
Narnia Italy see Narni
Narodnaya, Gora mt. Rus. Fed. 28 L2
Naro-Fominsk Rus. Fed. 28 F5
Narok Kenya 96 B5
Narooma Australia 112 D5
Narowlya Belarus 29 D6
Narrabri Australia 112 D3
Narragansett Bay U.S.A. 131 H3
Narrandera Australia 112 C4
Narran Lake Australia 112 C3
Narrogin Australia 109 B8
Narromine Australia 112 D4
Narrows U.S.A. 130 C5
Narrowsburg U.S.A. 131 F3
Narsalik Greenland 121 O3
Narsaq Greenland 121 O3
Narsarsuaq Greenland 121 O3
Narsimhapur India 74 C5
Narsingdi Bangl. 75 F5
Narsinghgarh India 74 C5
Narsipatnam India 73 D2
Nartë Albania 46 A4
Nartkala Rus. Fed. 79 E2
Naruto Japan 65 C6
Narva Estonia 28 D4
Narva r. Estonia/Rus. Fed. 33 H4
Narva Bay Estonia/Rus. Fed. 28 C4
Narva-Jõesuu Estonia 33 H4
Narva laht b. Estonia/Rus. Fed. see Narva Bay
Narva Reservoir Estonia/Rus. Fed. see Narvskoye Vodokhranilishche
Narvik Norway 32 E1
Narvskiy Zaliv b. Estonia/Rus. Fed. see Narva Bay
Narvskoye Vodokhranilishche resr Estonia/Rus. Fed. 33 H4
Narwana India 74 C3
Narwar India 74 C4
Nar'yan-Mar Rus. Fed. 28 J2
Naryn Kyrg. 62 B3
Naryn r. Kyrg./Uzbek. 70 D3
Naryn Rus. Fed. 62 F1
Näsby Sweden 33 E4
Naseby N.Z. 113 B4
Nashik India 72 B1
Nashua U.S.A. 131 H2
Nashville AR U.S.A. 133 C5

▶Nashville TN U.S.A. 128 B4
State capital of Tennessee.

Našice Croatia 44 G2
Nasielsk Poland 37 J2
Näsijärvi l. Fin. 33 F3
Nasik India see Nashik
Nasir Sudan 96 B2
Nasirabad Bangl. see Mymensingh
Nasirabad India 74 B4
Nasirabad Pak. 81 G4
Naskaupi r. Canada 125 I2
Nasmganj India 75 E4
Nasondoye Dem. Rep. Congo 95 E7
Nasosnyy Azer. see Hacı Zeynalabdin
Naşr Egypt 78 B5
Naşrābād Eşfahān Iran 80 B3
Naşrābād Khorāsan Iran 81 D3
Naşrānī, Jabal an mts Syria 77 C3
Nasratabad Iran see Zābol
Naşrīan-e-Pā'īn Iran 80 A3
Nass r. Canada 122 D4
Nassarawa Nigeria 93 G3
Nassarawa state Nigeria 93 H3
Nassau r. Australia 111 E2

▶Nassau Bahamas 129 D7
Capital of The Bahamas.

Nassau i. Cook Is 165 G6
Nassau U.S.A. 131 G2
Nassawadox U.S.A. 131 F5
Nasser, Lake resr Egypt 89 G4
Nassian Côte d'Ivoire 92 E3
Nässjö Sweden 33 D4
Nastapoca r. Canada 124 E1
Nastapoka Islands Canada 124 E1
Nasu-dake vol. Japan 65 D5
Nasva Rus. Fed. 28 D4
Nata Botswana 99 E4
Nata watercourse Botswana/Zimbabwe 99 E4
Natal Brazil 150 F3
Natal Indon. 58 B2
Natal prov. S. Africa see Kwazulu-Natal
Natal Basin sea feature Indian Ocean 163 J8
Natal Drakensberg National Park S. Africa 99 F6
Naṭanz Iran 80 B3
Natashquan Canada 125 I3
Natashquan r. Canada 125 I3
Natchez U.S.A. 127 H5
Natchitoches U.S.A. 133 C6
Nathalia Australia 112 C5
Nathana India 74 B3
Nathdwara India 74 B4
Natiaboani Burkina 93 F3
National City U.S.A. 136 D5
Natitingou Benin 93 F3
Natividade Brazil 150 C4
Natla r. Canada 122 D2
Natmauk Myanmar 60 A3
Natogyi Myanmar 60 A3
Nátora Mex. 135 E7
Natore Bangl. 75 F4
Natori Japan 65 E5
Natron, Lake salt l. Tanz. 96 C5
Nattai National Park Australia 112 D4
Nattaung mt. Myanmar 60 B4
Nattavaara Sweden 32 F2
Na'tū Iran 81 E3
Natuna, Kepulauan is Indon. 59 D1
Natuna Besar i. Indon. 59 E1
Natural Bridge U.S.A. 130 D5

Natural Bridges National Monument nat. park U.S.A. 137 G3
Naturaliste, Cape Australia 109 A8
Naturaliste Channel Australia 109 A5
Naturaliste Plateau sea feature Indian Ocean 163 O8
Nau Tajik. see Nov
Naucelle France 38 E4
Nauchas Namibia 98 C4
Nau Co l. China 75 D2
Nauen Germany 37 F2
Naugatuck U.S.A. 131 G3
Nau Hissar Pak. 81 F4
Naujoji Akmenė Lith. 33 F4
Naukh India 74 B4
Naulila Angola 95 B9
Naumburg (Saale) Germany 36 E3
Naungpale Myanmar 60 B4
Na'ūr Jordan 78 C5
Naurskaya Rus. Fed. 79 F2
Nauru i. Nauru 107 F2
▶Nauru country S. Pacific Ocean 107 F2
oceania 104–105, 114
Naushahro Firoz Pak. 81 G5
Naushara Pak. 81 G5
Naustdal Norway 33 B3
Nautaca Uzbek. see Karshi
Nautonwa India 75 D4
Nautsi Rus. Fed. 32 H1
Nava r. Dem. Rep. Congo 94 E4
Navabad Tajik. see Novobod
Navacerrada, Puerto de pass Spain 42 E2
Navachica mt. Spain 42 E4
Navadwip India 75 F5
Navahermosa Spain 42 D3
Navajo r. U.S.A. 135 F5
Navajo Mountain U.S.A. 137 G3
Navalmoral de la Mata Spain 42 D3
Navalvillar de Pela Spain 42 D3
Navan Rep. of Ireland 35 C5
Navangar India see Jamnagar
Navapolatsk Belarus 31 L2
Navarin, Mys c. Rus. Fed. 27 R3
Navarino, Isla i. Chile 153 D8
Navarra aut. comm. Spain 43 F1
Navarre aut. comm. Spain see Navarra
Navarrenx France 38 C5
Navarro Peru 146 C6
Navarro r. U.S.A. 136 A2
Navashino Rus. Fed. 28 G5
Navasota U.S.A. 133 B6
Navasota r. U.S.A. 133 B6

▶Navassa Island terr. West Indies 139 I5
United States Unincorporated Territory.
northamerica 118–119, 140

Naver r. U.K. 34 D2
Navia Spain 42 C1
Navia r. Spain 42 C1
Navidad Chile 152 C3
Navidad r. U.S.A. 133 B6
Navirai Brazil 151 A7
Navlakhi India 74 A5
Navlya Rus. Fed. 29 E5
Năvodari Romania 46 F2
Navoi Uzbek. 81 F1
Navoiyskaya Oblast' admin. div. Uzbek. 81 E1
Navojoa Mex. 135 E8
Navoy Oblast admin. div. Uzbek. see Navoiyskaya Oblast'
Návpaktos Greece see Nafpaktos
Návplion Greece see Nafplio
Navrongo Ghana 93 E3
Navşar Turkey see Şemdinli
Navsari India 72 B1
Nawa India 74 B4
Nawá Syria 78 D4
Nawabganj Bangl. 75 F4
Nawabganj India 75 D4
Nawabshah Pak. 81 G5
Nawada India 75 E4
Nāwah Afgh. 81 F3
Nawakot Nepal 75 E4
Nawalgarh India 74 B4
Nawar, Dasht-i imp. l. Afgh. 81 F3
Nawāşif, Ḩarrāt lava field Saudi Arabia 89 I4
Nawnghkio Myanmar 60 B3
Nawngleng Myanmar 60 B3
Nawoiy Uzbek. see Navoi
Nawoiy Wiloyati admin. div. Uzbek. see Navoiyskaya Oblast'
Naxçıvan Azer. 79 F3
Naxi China 66 C2
Naxos Greece 47 D6
Naxos i. Greece 47 D6
Naya Col. 146 B4
Nayagarh India 73 E1
Nayak Afgh. 81 F3
Nāy Band, Kūh-e mt. Iran 80 D3
Nayong China 66 C3
Nayoro Japan 64 E3
Nayuchi Malawi 97 B8
Nayudupeta India 72 C3
Nayyāl, Wādī watercourse Saudi Arabia 79 D5
Nazare Brazil 146 E4
Nazaré Brazil 147 H6
Nazareth Israel 77 B3
Nazareth U.S.A. 131 F3
Nazário Brazil 149 H4
Nazas Mex. 126 F6
Nazas r. Mex. 126 F6
Nazca Peru 148 B3
Nazca Ridge sea feature S. Pacific Ocean 165 M7
Nāzīk Iran 80 A2
Nazilli Turkey 78 B3
Nazımiye Turkey 79 D3
Nazinon r. Burkina/Ghana 93 E3 see Red Volta
Nazira India 75 G4
Nazir Hat Bangl. 75 F5
Nazko Canada 122 F4
Nazko r. Canada 122 F4
Nazran' Rus. Fed. 29 H8
Nazrēt Eth. 96 C2
Nazwá Oman 76 F5
Nazyvayevsk Rus. Fed. 26 H4
Nbâk Mauritania 92 B2
Ncheu Malawi see Ntcheu
Ncue Equat. Guinea 93 H5
Ndala Tanz. 97 B6
N'dalatando Angola 95 B7
Ndali Benin 93 F3
Ndanda Cent. Afr. Rep. 94 D3
Ndareda Tanz. 97 B6
Ndélé Cent. Afr. Rep. 94 D2
Ndélélé Cameroon 94 B3
Ndendé Gabon 94 A5
Ndende i. Solomon Is see Ndeni
Ndeni i. Solomon Is 107 F3
Ndikiniméki Cameroon 93 H4
Ndim Cent. Afr. Rep. 94 B3
N'Djamena Chad see Ndjamena

▶Ndjamena Chad 88 B6
Capital of Chad.

Ndji r. Cent. Afr. Rep. 94 D3
Ndjim r. Cameroon 93 H4
Ndjolé Gabon 94 A5
Ndjouani i. Comoros see Nzwani
Ndjounou Gabon 94 B5

Ndogo, Lagune lag. Gabon 94 A5
Ndoi i. Fiji see Doi
Ndok Cameroon 94 B3
Ndola Zambia 95 F8
Ndoto mt. Kenya 96 B4
Ndougou Gabon 94 A5
Nduke i. Solomon Is see Kolombangara
Ndumbwe Tanz. 97 C7
Nduye Dem. Rep. Congo 94 F4
Nea Anchialos Greece 47 C5
Nea Apollonia Greece 46 C4
Neagh, Lough l. U.K. 35 C4
Neah Bay U.S.A. 134 A2
Neajlov r. Romania 46 D2
Nea Karvali Greece 46 D4
Neale, Lake salt flat Australia 110 B5
Neales watercourse Australia 110 D5
Nea Liosia Greece 47 C5
Nea Makri Greece 47 C5
Nea Moudania Greece 47 C4
Nea Peramos Greece 46 D4
Neapoli Kriti Greece 47 D7
Neapoli Peloponnisos Greece 47 C6
Neapolis Italy see Naples
Nea Roda Greece 47 C4
Nea Santa Greece 46 C4
Neath U.K. 35 E6
Nea Zichni Greece 46 C4
Nebbi Uganda 96 A4
Nebbou Burkina 93 E3
Nebine Creek r. Australia 111 F6
Nebitdag Turkm. 80 C2
Nebo Australia 111 G4
Nebolchi Rus. Fed. 28 E4
Nebraska state U.S.A. 134 G4
Nebraska City U.S.A. 132 C3
Nebrodi, Monti mts Sicily Italy 45 E6
Neches r. U.S.A. 133 C6
Nechí r. Col. 146 C2
Nechisar National Park Eth. 96 C3
Neckarsulm Germany 36 D4
Necker Island U.S.A. 165 H4
Necochea Arg. 152 F4
Necocli Col. 146 B2
Nedelišće Croatia 44 F1
Nederland country Europe see Netherlands
Nederlandse Antillen terr. West Indies see Netherlands Antilles
Neder Rijn r. Neth. 36 B3
Nedlouc, Lac l. Canada 125 F1
Nedluk Lake Canada see Nedlouc, Lac
Nêdong China 75 F3
Nedre Soppero Sweden 32 F1
Nedstrand Norway 33 B4
Needham U.S.A. 131 H2
Needles U.S.A. 137 E4
Needmore U.S.A. 130 D4
Neemuch India see Nimach
Neepawa Canada 123 L5
Nefta Tunisia 91 G2
Neftçala Azer. 79 G3
Neftechala Azer. see Neftçala
Neftechala Azer. see 26 Bakı Komissarı
Neftegorsk Rus. Fed. 29 I5
Neftekamsk Rus. Fed. 28 J4
Neftekumsk Rus. Fed. 29 H7
Nefteyugansk Rus. Fed. 26 H3
Neftezavodsk Turkm. see Seydi
Nefza Tunisia 45 B6
Negada Weyn well Eth. 96 E3
Negage Angola 95 B6
Négala Mali 92 C2
Negār Iran 80 D4
Negara Bali Indon. 59 F5
Negara Kalimantan Selatan Indon. 59 F3
Negara r. Indon. 59 F3
Negēlē Oromia Eth. 96 C3
Negēlē Oromia Eth. 96 C3
Negeri Sembilan state Malaysia 58 C2
Negev des. Israel 77 B4
Negomane Moz. 97 C7
Negombo Sri Lanka 72 C5
Negotin Serb. and Mont. 46 C2
Negotino Macedonia 46 C4
Negra, Cordillera mts Peru 148 A2
Negra, Lago l. Uruguay 152 G3
Negra, Serranía de mts Bol. 149 E3
Negrais, Cape Myanmar 61 A5
Negratín, Embalse de resr Spain 43 E4
Nègrepelisse France 38 D4
Negri r. Australia 110 B3
Negri Romania 46 E1
Négrine Alg. 91 G2
Negri Sembilan state Malaysia see Negeri Sembilan
Negritos Peru 146 A6
Negro r. Arg. 152 E5
Negro r. Brazil 149 F4
Negro r. Para. 149 F6
Negro r. S. America 147 G5
Negro r. Uruguay 152 F3
Negro, Cabo c. Morocco 42 D5
Negroponte i. Greece see Evvoia
Negros i. Phil. 57 F4
Negru Vodă Romania 46 F3
Nehalem r. U.S.A. 134 B3
Nehavand Iran 80 B3
Nehbandān Iran 81 E4
Nehe China 63 K2
Nehoiu Romania 46 E2
Nehone Angola 95 C9
Neiafu Tonga 107 H3
Neijiang China 66 C2
Neill Island India 73 G4
Nei Mongol Zizhiqu aut. reg. China 64 A4
Neiße r. Germany/Poland 37 G2
Neiva Col. 146 C4
Neixiang China 67 D1
Nejanilini Lake Canada 123 L3
Nejd reg. Saudi Arabia see Najd
Neka Iran 80 C2
Neka r. Iran 80 C2
Nek'emtē Eth. 96 C2
Neksø Denmark 33 D5
Nela r. Spain 42 E1
Nelamangala India 72 C3
Nelas Port. 42 C2
Nelia Australia 111 E4
Nelidovo Rus. Fed. 28 E4
Neligh U.S.A. 132 B3
Nel'kan Khabarovskiy Kray Rus. Fed. 27 N4
Nel'kan Rus. Fed. 27 O3
Nellore India 72 C3
Nelson Arg. 152 E2
Nelson Canada 134 C2
Nelson r. Canada 123 M3
Nelson N.Z. 113 C3
Nelson AZ U.S.A. 137 F4
Nelson NE U.S.A. 132 B3
Nelson NV U.S.A. 137 E4
Nelson, Cape Australia 112 B5
Nelson, Estrecho strait Chile 153 B7
Nelson Bay Australia 112 E4
Nelson Forks Canada 122 F3
Nelson House Canada 123 L4
Nelson Lakes National Park N.Z. 113 C3
Nelspruit S. Africa 99 F5
Nem r. Rus. Fed. 28 J3
Néma Mauritania 92 D1
Nema Rus. Fed. 28 I4
Neman Rus. Fed. 33 F5
Neman r. Rus. Fed. 33 F5
Ne'matābād Iran 81 D4
Nemausus France see Nîmes
Nembe Nigeria 93 G4
Nemda r. Rus. Fed. 28 G4

Orientale *prov.* Dem. Rep. Congo **94** E4
Oriente Brazil **149** D2
Orihuela Spain **43** F3
Orikhiv Ukr. **29** E7
Orikum Albania **47** A4
Orillia Canada **130** D1
Orimattila Fin. **33** G3
Orin U.S.A. **134** F4
▶**Orinoco** *r.* Col./Venez. **147** F2
southamerica **154**
Orinoco Delta Venez. **147** F2
Oripää Fin. **33** F3
Oriskany U.S.A. **131** F2
Orissa *state* India **73** E1
Orissaare Estonia **31** C1
Oristano *Sardinia* Italy **45** B5
Oristano, Golfo di *b. Sardinia* Italy **45** B5
Orivesi Fin. **33** G3
Orivesi *l.* Fin. **32** H3
Oriximiná Brazil **147** H5
Orizaba Mex. **126** G8

▶**Orizaba, Pico de** *vol.* Mex. **126** G5
3rd highest mountain in North America.
northamerica **116–117**

Orjonikidzeobod Tajik. *see* **Kofarnihon**
Örkelljunga Sweden **33** D4
Orkhomenós Greece *see* **Orchomenos**
Orkney *is* U.K. **34** E2
Orla *r.* Poland **37** H2
Orla *r.* Poland **37** H3
Orland U.S.A. **136** A2
Orlando U.S.A. **129** C6
Orleaes Brazil **151** E9
Orléans France **38** D3
Orleans U.S.A. **131** I3
Orléans, Île d' *i.* Canada **125** G4
Orléansville Alg. *see* **Ech Chélif**
Orlické Hory *mts* Czech Rep. **37** H3
Orlik Rus. Fed. **62** F1
Orlik, Vodní nádrž *resr* Czech Rep. **37** G4
Orlov Rus. Fed. **28** I4
Orlov Gay Rus. Fed. **29** I6
Orlovo Rus. Fed. **29** F6
Orlovskaya Oblast' *admin. div.* Rus. Fed. **29** F5
Orlovskiy Rus. Fed. **29** G7
Orly *airport* France **38** E2
Ormara Pak. **81** F5
Ormara, Ras *hd* Pak. **81** F5
Ormília Greece *see* **Ormylia**
Ormoc Phil. **57** F3
Ormond Beach U.S.A. **129** C6
Ormskirk U.K. **35** E5
Ormylia Greece **47** C4
Orne *r.* France **38** C2
Orne *r.* France **38** D2
Orneta Poland **37** J1
Ornö *i.* Sweden **33** E4
Örnsköldsvik Sweden **32** E3
Oro, Lac *l.* Mali **92** E1
Orobayaya Bol. **149** E3
Orobie, Alpi *mts* Italy **44** B1
Orocó Brazil **150** E4
Orocué Col. **146** D3
Orodara Burkina **92** D3
Orofino U.S.A. **134** C3
Oro Grande U.S.A. **136** D4
Orol Dengizi *salt l.* Kazakh./Uzbek. *see* Aral Sea
Oromia *admin. reg.* Eth. **96** C2
Oromocto Canada **125** H4
Oron Israel **77** B4
Oron Nigeria **93** H4
Orona *i.* Kiribati **107** H2
Orono U.S.A. **128** F2
Oronoque Guyana **147** G4
Oronoque *r.* Guyana **147** G4
Orontes *r.* Lebanon/Syria **77** C2
Oroqen Zizhiqi China *see* **Alihe**
Ororbia Spain **43** F1
Orós Brazil **150** E3
Orós, Açude *resr* Brazil **150** E3
Orosei *Sardinia* Italy **45** B4
Orosei, Golfo di *b. Sardinia* Italy **45** B4
Orosháza Hungary **37** J5
Oroszlány Hungary **37** I5
Oro Valley U.S.A. **137** G5
Oroville *CA* U.S.A. **136** B2
Oroville *WA* U.S.A. **134** C2
Oroville, Lake *resr* U.S.A. **136** B2
Orrkjølen *hill* Norway **33** C3
Orsa Sweden **33** D3
Orsha Belarus **29** D5
Orsjön *l.* Sweden **33** E3
Orsk Rus. Fed. **26** F4
Orșova Romania **46** C2
Ørsta Norway **33** B3
Ortaca Turkey **47** F6
Orta Nova Italy **44** E4
Orta Toroslar *plat.* Turkey **77** A1
Orte Italy **44** D3
Ortegal, Cabo *c.* Spain **42** C1
Orteguaza *r.* Col. **146** C4
Orthez France **38** C5
Ortigueira Spain **42** C1
Ortiz Mex. **135** E7
Ortíz Venez. **146** E2
Ortles *mt.* Italy **44** C1
Ortona Italy **44** E3
Ortonville *MI* U.S.A. **130** B2
Ortonville *MN* U.S.A. **132** B2
Ortospana Afgh. *see* **Kābul**
Örtülü Turkey *see* **Şenkaya**
Orulgan, Khrebet *mts* Rus. Fed. **27** M3
Orumbo Boka *hill* Côte d'Ivoire **92** D4
Orūmīyeh Iran *see* **Urmia**
Orūmīyeh, Daryācheh-ye *salt l.* Iran *see* Urmia, Lake
Oruro Bol. **148** D4
Oruro *dept* Bol. **148** D4
Orūzgān *prov.* Afgh. **81** F3
Orvault France **38** C3
Orvieto Italy **44** D3
Orville Coast Antarctica **167** L1
Orwell *OH* U.S.A. **130** C3
Orwell *VT* U.S.A. **131** G2
Oryakhovo Bulg. **46** C3
Oryol Rus. Fed. *see* **Orel**
Orzyc *r.* Poland **37** J2
Orzysz Poland **37** J2
Os Norway **33** C3
Osa *r.* Poland **37** I2
Osa Rus. Fed. **28** J4
Osa, Península de *pen.* Costa Rica **139** H7
Osage U.S.A. **130** C4
Osage *r.* U.S.A. **132** C4
▶**Ōsaka** Japan **65** C6
world **16–17**
Osborne U.S.A. **132** B4
Oscar Fr. Guiana **147** H4
Oscar Range *hills* Australia **108** D4
Osceola *AR* U.S.A. **133** D5
Osceola *IA* U.S.A. **132** C3
Osceola *MO* U.S.A. **132** C4
Osceola *NE* U.S.A. **132** B3
Oschersleben (Bode) Germany **36** E2
Oschiri *Sardinia* Italy **45** B4
Oscoda U.S.A. **130** B1
Osečina Serb. and Mont. **46** A2
Ösel *i.* Estonia *see* **Hiiumaa**
Osensjøen *l.* Norway **33** C3
Osetr *r.* Rus. Fed. **29** F5
Osgoode Canada **124** F4
Osgood Mountains U.S.A. **134** C4
Osh Kyrg. **70** D3
Osh *admin. div.* Kyrg. **81** H1
Oshakati Namibia **98** B3
Oshana *admin. reg.* Namibia **98** B3
Oshawa Canada **130** D2
Oshika-hantō *pen.* Japan **65** E5
Oshikango Namibia **98** B3
Oshikoto *admin. reg.* Namibia **98** C3
Oshikuku Namibia **98** B3
Ō-shima *i.* Japan **64** D4
Ō-shima *i.* Japan **65** D6
Oshin *r.* Nigeria **93** G3
Oshivelo Namibia **98** C3
Oshkosh *NE* U.S.A. **132** A3
Oshkosh *WI* U.S.A. **132** D2
Oshmyany Belarus *see* **Ashmyany**
Oshnovīyeh Iran **80** A2
Osh Oblast *admin. div.* Kyrg. *see* **Osh**
Oshogbo Nigeria **93** G4
Oshper Rus. Fed. **28** L2
Oshskaya Oblast' *admin. div.* Kyrg. *see* **Osh**
Oshtorān Kūh *mt.* Iran **80** B3
Oshun *state* Nigeria **93** G4
Oshwe Dem. Rep. Congo **94** C5
Osica de Sus Romania **46** D2
Osijek Croatia **44** G2
Osikovitsa Bulg. **46** D3
Osilinka *r.* Canada **122** E3
Osimo Italy **44** D3
Osipaonica Serb. and Mont. **46** B2
Osipenko Ukr. *see* **Berdyans'k**
Osipovichi Belarus *see* **Asipovichy**
Osire Namibia **98** C4
Osiyan India **74** B4
Osizweni S. Africa **99** F5
Osječenica *mts* Bos.-Herz. **44** F2
Oskaloosa U.S.A. **132** C3
Oskarshamn Sweden **33** E4
Oskarström Sweden **33** D4
Öskemen Kazakh. *see* **Ust'-Kamenogorsk**
Oskol *r.* Rus. Fed. **29** F6
Oslava *r.* Czech Rep. **37** H4

▶**Oslo** Norway **33** C4
Capital of Norway.

Oslo *airport* Norway *see* **Gardermoen**
Oslofjorden *sea chan.* Norway **33** C4
Osmanabad India **72** C2
Osmancık Turkey **78** C2
Osmaniye Turkey **78** D3
Os'mino Rus. Fed. **28** D4
Osmussaar *i.* Estonia **33** F4
Osnabrück Germany **36** D2
Osno Lubuskie Poland **37** G2
Oso *r.* Dem. Rep. Congo **94** E5
Osogbo Nigeria *see* **Oshogbo**
Osogovske Planine *mts* Bulg./Macedonia **46** C3
Osor *hill* Croatia **44** E2
Osório Brazil **151** B9
Osorno Chile **152** B5
Osorno Spain **42** D1
Osoyoos Canada **134** C2
Osøyri Norway **30** F1
Ospino Venez. **146** D2
Osprey Reef Australia **111** F2
Oss Neth. **36** B3
Ossa *hill* Port. **42** C3
Ossa, Mount Australia **112** C6
Osse *r.* Nigeria **93** G4
Osseo U.S.A. **132** D2
Ossining U.S.A. **131** G3
Ossokmanuan Lake Canada **125** H2
Ossora Rus. Fed. **27** Q4
Ostashkov Rus. Fed. **28** E4
Oste *r.* Germany **36** D2
Ostend Belgium **36** A3
Ostende Belgium *see* **Ostend**
Osterburg (Altmark) Germany **36** E2
Österbybruk Sweden **33** E3
Österbymo Sweden **33** D4
Österdalälven *l.* Sweden **33** D3
Österfärnebo Sweden **33** E3
Östergotland *county* Sweden **33** D4
Osterholz-Scharmbeck Germany **36** D2
Ostermundigen Switz. **39** G3
Österreich *country* Europe *see* **Austria**
Östersund Sweden **32** D3
Östervåla Sweden **33** E3
Østfold *county* Norway **33** C4
Östhammar Sweden **33** E3
Östra Kvarken *strait* Fin./Sweden **32** F3
Ostrava Czech Rep. **37** I4
Ostróda Poland **37** I2
Ostrogozhsk Rus. Fed. **29** F6
Oštro Koplje *mt.* Serb. and Mont. **46** B3
Ostrołęka Poland **37** J2
Ostrov Czech Rep. **37** F3
Ostrov Romania **46** E2
Ostrov Romania **46** F2
Ostrov Rus. Fed. **28** D4
Ostrovets Poland *see* Ostrowiec Świętokrzyski
Ostrovskoye Rus. Fed. **28** G4
Ostrow Poland *see* **Ostrów Wielkopolski**
Ostrowiec Poland *see* Ostrowiec Świętokrzyski
Ostrowiec Świętokrzyski Poland **37** J3
Ostrów Mazowiecka Poland **37** J2
Ostrowo Poland *see* **Ostrów Wielkopolski**
Ostrów Wielkopolski Poland **37** H3
Ostrzeszów Poland **37** H3
Ostseebad Binz Germany **37** F1
Ostuni Italy **45** F4
Osum *r.* Albania **47** A4
Osŭm *r.* Bulg. **46** D3
Ōsumi-kaikyō *sea chan.* Japan **65** B7
Ōsumi-shotō *is* Japan **65** B7
Osun *state* Nigeria *see* **Oshun**
Osuna Spain **42** D4
Oswego *KS* U.S.A. **132** C4
Oswego *NY* U.S.A. **131** E2
Oswego *r.* U.S.A. **131** E2
Oswestry U.K. **35** E5
Oświęcim Poland **37** I3
Ōta Japan **65** D5
Otago Peninsula N.Z. **113** B4
Otaki N.Z. **113** C3
Otaru Japan **64** E4
Otava Fin. **33** G3
Otavalo Ecuador **146** B4
Otavi Namibia **98** C3
Ōtawara Japan **65** E5
Otchinjau Angola **95** B9
Otelnuc, Lac *l.* Canada **125** H2
Oțelu Roșu Romania **46** C2
Otematata N.Z. **113** B4
Otepää Estonia **33** G4
Otepää kõrgustik *hills* Estonia **33** G4
Oteren Norway **32** E1
Oteros *r.* Mex. **135** E8
Otgon Tenger Uul *mt.* Mongolia **70** I2
Othe, Forêt d' *for.* France **39** E2
Othello U.S.A. **134** C3
Othonoi *i.* Greece **47** A5
Oti *r.* Ghana/Togo **93** F3
Otira N.Z. **113** B3
Otish, Monts *hills* Canada **125** G3
Otjinene Namibia **98** C4
Otjitambi Namibia **98** B3
Otjiwarongo Namibia **98** C4
Otjovasandu *waterhole* Namibia **98** B3
Otjozondjupa *admin. reg.* Namibia **98** C4
Otočac Croatia **44** E2
Otok Croatia **44** G2
Otoka Bos.-Herz. **44** F2
Otoro, Jebel *mt.* Sudan **96** A2
Otorohanga N.Z. **113** C2
Otpor Rus. Fed. *see* **Zabaykal'sk**
Otradnoye Rus. Fed. *see* **Otradnyy**
Otradnyy Rus. Fed. **29** I5
Otranto Italy **45** G4
Otranto, Strait of Albania/Italy **31** I5
Otrogovo Rus. Fed. *see* **Stepnoye**
Otrokovice Czech Rep. **37** H4
Otrozhnyy Rus. Fed. **27** R3
Otsego Lake U.S.A. **131** F2
Ōtsu Japan **65** C6
Otta Norway **33** C3

▶**Ottawa** Canada **124** F4
Capital of Canada.

Ottawa *r.* Canada **124** F4
Ottawa *IL* U.S.A. **132** D3
Ottawa *KS* U.S.A. **132** C4
Ottawa *OH* U.S.A. **130** A3
Ottawa Islands Canada **124** D1
Otter *r.* U.K. **35** E6
Otterburn U.K. **34** E4
Otterstad Sweden **33** D4
Ottignies Belgium **36** B3
Ottumwa U.S.A. **132** C3
Otukpa Nigeria **93** G4
Otukpo Nigeria **93** H4
Otway U.S.A. **130** B4
Otway, Bahía *b.* Chile **153** B8
Otway, Cape Australia **112** B5
Otway, Seno *b.* Chile **153** C8
Otway National Park Australia **112** B5
Otwock Poland **37** J2
Ötztaler Alpen *mts* Austria **36** E5
Ou, Nam *r.* Laos **60** C3
Ouacha Niger **93** H2
Ouachita *r.* U.S.A. **133** D6
Ouachita, Lake U.S.A. **133** C5
Ouachita Mountains *AR/OK* U.S.A. **127** H5
Ouachita Mountains *AR/OK* U.S.A. **133** C5
Ouadâne Mauritania **90** C5
Ouadda Cent. Afr. Rep. **94** D2
Ouaddaï *pref.* Chad **88** D6
Ouadjinkarem *well* Niger **91** G5
Ouâd Nâga Mauritania **92** B1

▶**Ouagadougou** Burkina **93** E2
Capital of Burkina.

Ouahigouya Burkina **93** E2
Ouahran Alg. *see* **Oran**
Ouaka *pref.* Cent. Afr. Rep. **94** D3
Ouaka *r.* Cent. Afr. Rep. **94** C3
Oualâta Mauritania **92** D1
Oualé *r.* Burkina **93** F3
Oualia Mali **92** C2
Ouallam Niger **93** F2
Ouallene Alg. **91** F4
Ouanary Fr. Guiana **147** I3
Ouanazein *well* Chad **88** C5
Ouanda-Djailé Cent. Afr. Rep. **94** D2
Ouandago Cent. Afr. Rep. **94** C3
Ouandja *Haute-Kotto* Cent. Afr. Rep. **94** D2
Ouandja *Vakaga* Cent. Afr. Rep. **94** D2
Ouango Cent. Afr. Rep. **94** D3
Ouangolodougou Côte d'Ivoire **92** D3
Ouani Kalaoua *well* Niger **93** G2
Ouanne *r.* France **39** E3
Ouaqui Fr. Guiana **147** H4
Ouara *r.* Cent. Afr. Rep. **94** E3
Ouargaye Burkina **93** F3
Ouargla Alg. **91** G3
Ouarissibitil *well* Mali **93** F1
Ouaritoufoulout *well* Mali **93** F1
Ouarkziz, Jbel *ridge* Alg./Morocco **90** C3
Ouarogou Burkina *see* **Ouargaye**
Ouarzazate Morocco **90** D3
Ouatagouna Mali **93** F2
Oubangui *r.* Cent. Afr. Rep./Dem. Rep. Congo *see* **Ubangi**
Oubergpas *pass* S. Africa **98** E7
Oudenaarde Belgium **39** E1
Oudon *r.* France **38** C3
Oudtshoorn S. Africa **98** D7
Oued Zem Morocco **90** D2
Ouéléssébougou Mali **92** D3
Ouémé *r.* Benin **93** F4
Ouessa Burkina **92** E3
Ouessant, Île d' *i.* France **38** A2
Ouésso Congo **94** C4
Ouest *prov.* Cameroon **93** H4
Ouezzane Morocco **90** D2
Oughterard Rep. of Ireland **35** B5
Ouham *pref.* Cent. Afr. Rep. **94** C3
Ouham *r.* Cent. Afr. Rep./Chad **94** C2
Ouham Pendé *pref.* Cent. Afr. Rep. **94** C3
Ouidah Benin **93** F4
Ouinardene Mali **93** E1
Ouiriego Mex. **135** E8
Ouistreham France **38** C2
Oujâf *well* Mauritania **92** D1
Oujda Morocco **91** E2
Oujeft Mauritania **92** B1
Oulad Teïma Morocco **90** C3
Oulainen Fin. **32** G2
Oulangan kansallispuisto *nat. park* Fin. **32** H2
Ould Yenjé Mauritania **92** C2
Ouled Djellal Alg. **91** G2
Ouled Farès Alg. **43** G4
Ouled Naïl, Monts des *mts* Alg. **91** F2
Ouled Saïd *well* Alg. **91** F3
Ouli Cameroon **94** B3
Oullins France **39** F4
Oulu Fin. **32** G2
Oulu *prov.* Fin. **32** G2
Oulujärvi *l.* Fin. **32** G2
Oulujoki *r.* Fin. **32** G2
Oulx Italy **44** A2
Oum-Chalouba Chad **88** D6
Oumé Côte d'Ivoire **92** D4
Oum el Bouaghi Alg. **91** G2
Oum-Hadjer Chad **88** C6
Oumm ed Droûs Guebli, Sebkhet *salt flat* Mauritania **90** C5
Oumm ed Droûs Telli, Sebkha *salt flat* Mauritania **90** C4
Oumm el A'sel *well* Mali **90** D5
Ounara Morocco **90** C3
Oungre Canada **123** K5
Ounianga Kébir Chad **88** D5
Ounianga Sérir Chad **88** D5
Ounissoui *well* Niger **93** I1
Our *r.* Lux. **39** G2
Ourcq *r.* France **39** E2
Ouré Kaba Guinea **92** C3
Ourense Spain **42** C1
Ouricurí Brazil **150** D3
Ourinhos Brazil **149** H5
Ourini Chad **88** D5
Ourique Port. **42** B4
Ouro Brazil **150** C4
Ouro Preto Brazil **151** D7
Ourthe *r.* Belgium **39** F1
Ouse *r.* U.K. **35** F5
Oust *r.* France **38** B3
Outamba Kilimi National Park Sierra Leone **92** B3
Outaouais, Rivière des *r.* Canada *see* Ottawa
Outardes *r.* Canada **125** G3
Outardes Quatre, Réservoir Canada **125** G3
Outat Oulad el Haj Morocco **90** E2
Outer Hebrides *is* U.K. **34** C3
Outer Mongolia *country* Asia *see* Mongolia
Outer Santa Barbara Channel U.S.A. **136** C5
Outjo Namibia **98** C4
Outlook Canada **123** J5
Outoul Alg. **91** G5
Out Skerries *is* U.K. **34** F1
Ouvéa *i.* New Caledonia **107** F4
Ouyanghai Shuiku *resr* China **67** E3
Ouyen Australia **112** B4
Ova *r.* Turkey **46** E4
Ovace, Punta d' *mt. Corsica* France **44** B4
Ovacık Turkey **79** D3
Ovada Italy **44** B2
Ovaeymiri Turkey **47** E6
Ovalle Chile **152** C2
Ovamboland *reg.* Namibia **98** B3
Ovan Gabon **94** B4
Ovar Port. **42** B2
Oveng Cameroon **93** I5
Ovens *r.* Australia **112** C5
Overhalla Norway **32** C2
Överkalix Sweden **32** F2
Overlander Roadhouse Australia **109** A6
Overland Park U.S.A. **132** C4
Övermark Fin. **33** F3
Overo, Volcán *vol.* Arg. **152** C3
Overton U.S.A. **137** E3
Övertorneå Sweden **32** F2
Överum Sweden **33** E4
Överuman *l.* Sweden **32** D2
Ovid *MI* U.S.A. **130** A2
Ovid *NY* U.S.A. **131** E2
Ovidiu Romania **46** F2
Oviedo Spain **42** D1
Ovišrags *hd* Latvia **33** F4
Øvre Anarjokka Nasjonalpark *nat. park* Norway **32** G1
Øvre Dividal Nasjonalpark *nat. park* Norway **32** E1
Øvre Pasvik Nasjonalpark *nat. park* Norway **32** H1
Övre Soppero Sweden **32** F1
Ovruch Ukr. **29** D6
Owaka N.Z. **113** B4
Owando Congo **94** B5
Owase Japan **65** D6
Owasso U.S.A. **133** C4
Owatonna U.S.A. **132** C2
Owbeh Afgh. **81** E3
Owego U.S.A. **131** E2
Owen Falls Dam Uganda **96** B4
Owen Island Myanmar **61** B6
Owen River N.Z. **113** C3
Owens *r.* U.S.A. **136** D3
Owensboro U.S.A. **128** B4
Owens Lake U.S.A. **136** D3
Owen Sound Canada **130** C1
Owen Springs Australia **110** C4
Owen Stanley Range *mts* P.N.G. **106** D2
Owensville U.S.A. **132** D4
Owenton U.S.A. **130** A4
Owerri Nigeria **93** G4
Owikeno Lake Canada **122** E5
Owingsville U.S.A. **130** E4
Owl *r.* Canada **123** M3
Owl Creek *r.* U.S.A. **134** E4
Owo Nigeria **93** G4
Owosso U.S.A. **130** A2
Owyhee *r.* U.S.A. **134** C4
Owyhee Mountains U.S.A. **134** C4
Owyhee North Fork *r.* U.S.A. **134** C4
Owyhee South Fork *r.* U.S.A. **134** C4
Oxapampa Peru **148** B2
Öxarfjörður *b.* Iceland **32** [inset]
Oxbow Canada **123** K5
Ox Creek *r.* U.S.A. **132** A1
Oxelösund Sweden **33** E4
Oxford N.Z. **113** C3
Oxford U.K. **35** F6
Oxford *MA* U.S.A. **131** H2
Oxford *ME* U.S.A. **131** H1
Oxford *MS* U.S.A. **127** I5
Oxford *NC* U.S.A. **128** D4
Oxford *NY* U.S.A. **131** F2
Oxford *OH* U.S.A. **130** A4
Oxford *PA* U.S.A. **131** F4
Oxford House Canada **123** M4
Oxford Lake Canada **123** M4
Oxley Australia **112** C4
Oxleys Peak Australia **112** D3
Oxley Wild Rivers National Park Australia **112** E3
Ox Mountains *hills* Rep. of Ireland *see* Slieve Gamph
Oxnard U.S.A. **136** C4
Oxus *r.* Asia *see* **Amudar'ya**
Oxylithos Greece **47** D5
Oya *r. Sarawak* Malaysia **59** E2
Oyama Japan **65** D5
Ō-yama *vol.* Japan **65** D6
Oyapock *r.* Brazil/Fr. Guiana **147** I3
Oyem Gabon **94** A4
Oyen Canada **123** I5
Øyeren *l.* Norway **33** C4
Oykel *r.* U.K. **34** D3
Oymyakon Rus. Fed. **27** O3
Oyo Congo **94** B5
Oyo Nigeria **93** F4
Oyo *state* Nigeria **93** F3
Oyo Sudan **89** H4
Oyón Peru **148** A2
Oyonnax France **39** F3
Oy-Tal Kyrg. **81** H1
Oytograk China **75** D1
Oyukludağı *mt.* Turkey **77** A1
Oyyl Kazakh. *see* **Uil**
Özalp Turkey **79** F3
Ozamiz Phil. **57** F4
Ozark *AL* U.S.A. **129** B6
Ozark *AR* U.S.A. **133** C5
Ozark *MO* U.S.A. **132** C4
Ozark Plateau U.S.A. **132** C4
Ozarks, Lake of the U.S.A. **132** C4
Ożarów Poland **37** J3
Özbaşı Turkey **47** E6
Ozbekiston *country* Asia *see* **Uzbekistan**
Ózd Hungary **37** J4
Özdere Turkey **47** E6
Ozerne Ukr. **46** F2
Ozernovskiy Rus. Fed. **27** P4
Ozernoye Rus. Fed. **29** I6
Ozernyy Rus. Fed. **31** M2
Ozery Rus. Fed. **29** F5
Ozeryane Rus. Fed. **64** B2
Ozhogina *r.* Rus. Fed. **27** P3
Ozieri *Sardinia* Italy **45** B4
Ozimek Poland **37** I3
Ozinki Rus. Fed. **29** I6
Ozona U.S.A. **133** A6
Ozorków Poland **37** I3
Ozurget'i Georgia **79** E2

↓ P

Pâ Burkina **92** E3
Paakkola Fin. **32** G2
Paamiut Greenland **121** O3
Pa-an Myanmar **60** B4
Paarl S. Africa **98** C7
Paatsjoki *r.* Europe *see* **Patsoyoki**
P'abal-li N. Korea **65** B4
Pabianice Poland **37** I3
Pabianitz Poland *see* **Pabianice**
Pabna Bangl. **75** F4
Pabradė Lith. **33** G5
Pab Range *mts* Pak. **81** F5
Pacaás, Serra dos *hills* Brazil **149** D2
Pacaás Novos, Parque Nacional *nat. park* Brazil **149** E2
Pacahuaras *r.* Bol. **148** D2
Pacajus Brazil **150** E3
Pacaraimã, Serra *mts* S. America *see* Pakaraima Mountains
Pacaraima Mountains S. America *see* Pakaraima Mountains
Pacarán Peru **148** B3
Pacasmayo Peru **148** A1
Pacatuba Brazil **150** E2
Pacaya Samiria, Reserva Nacional *nature res.* Peru **146** C6
Paceco *Sicily* Italy **45** D6
Pacheco Mex. **135** E7
Pachia *i.* Greece **47** D6
Pachía Peru **148** C4
Pachino *Sicily* Italy **45** E6
Pachitea *r.* Peru **148** B2
Pachmarhi India **74** C5
Pachor India **74** C5
Pachora India **72** B1
Pachpadra India **74** B4
Pachuca Mex. **126** G7
Pacific-Antarctic Ridge *sea feature* S. Pacific Ocean **165** H9
Pacific Grove U.S.A. **136** B3

▶**Pacific Ocean** **165** G5
Largest ocean in the world.
oceans **156–157,168**

Pacific Rim National Park Canada **122** E5
Pacinan, Tanjung *pt* Indon. **59** F4
Pačir Serb. and Mont. **46** A2
Pacitan Indon. **59** E5
Packsattel *pass* Austria **37** G5
Pacov Czech Rep. **37** G4
Pacoval Brazil **147** H5
Paczków Poland **37** H3
Padali Rus. Fed. *see* **Amursk**
Padampur India **74** B3
Padang *Kalimantan Barat* Indon. **59** E3
Padang *Sumatera Barat, Sumatra* Indon. **58** C3
Padang *i.* Indon. **58** C2
Padangpanjang Indon. **58** C3
Padangsidimpuan Indon. **58** B2
Padangtikar Indon. **59** E3
Padangtikar *i.* Indon. **59** E3
Padas *r. Sabah* Malaysia **59** F1
Padasjoki Fin. **33** G3
Padatha, Kūh-e *mt.* Iran **80** B3
Padauiri *r.* Brazil **147** E5
Padaung Myanmar **60** A4
Padcaya Bol. **148** D5
Paddington Australia **112** C4
Paderborn Germany **36** D3
Padeșu, Vârful *mt.* Romania **46** C2
Padilla Bol. **149** D4
Padina Romania **46** E2
Padina Serb. and Mont. **46** B2
Padinska Skela Serb. and Mont. **46** B2
Padjelanta nationalpark *nat. park* Sweden **32** E2
Padmanabhapuram India **72** C4
Padmapur India **74** D5
Padova Italy *see* **Padua**
Padra India **74** B5
Padrão, Ponta *pt* Angola **95** B6
Padrauna India **75** E4
Padre Caro *hill* Spain **42** C4
Padre Island U.S.A. **133** B7
Padrón Spain **42** B1
Padua India **73** D2
Padua Italy **44** C2
Paducah *KY* U.S.A. **128** A4
Paducah *TX* U.S.A. **133** A5
Padum Jammu and Kashmir **74** C2
Pădurea Craiului, Munții *mts* Romania **46** C1
Paekdu-san *mt.* China/N. Korea **64** B4
Paengnyŏng-do *i.* S. Korea **65** A5
Paeroa N.Z. **113** C2
Paestum *tourist site* Italy **45** E4
Pafos Cyprus *see* **Paphos**
Pafúri Moz. **99** F4
Pag Croatia **44** E2
Pag *i.* Croatia **44** E2
Paga Conta Brazil **147** H6
Pagadian Phil. **57** F4
Pagai Selatan *i.* Indon. **58** C3
Pagai Utara *i.* Indon. **58** C3
Pagalu *i.* Equat. Guinea *see* **Annobón**
Pagan *i.* N. Mariana Is **57** K2
Pagaralam Indon. **58** C3
Pagasitikos Kolpos *b.* Greece **47** C5
Pagatan *Kalimantan Selatan* Indon. **59** F3
Pagatan *Kalimantan Tengah* Indon. **59** F3
Page U.S.A. **137** G3
Pagerdewa Indon. **58** D3
Paget, Mount S. Georgia **153** [inset]
Paget Cay *reef* Australia **111** H3
Paghman *mt.* Afgh. **81** G3
Pagiriai Lith. **33** G5
Pagon *i.* N. Mariana Is *see* **Pagan**
Pagosa Springs U.S.A. **135** F5
Pagouda Togo **93** F3
Pagqên China *see* **Gadê**
Pagri China **75** F4
Pagwi P.N.G. **57** J6
Pahala U.S.A. **135** [inset] Z2
Pahang *r.* Malaysia **58** C2
Pahang *state* Malaysia **58** C2
Paharpur *tourist site* Bangl. **75** F4
Paharpur Pak. **81** G3
Pahauman Indon. **59** E2
Pahlavī Dezh Iran *see* **Āq Qal'eh**
Pahlgam Jammu and Kashmir **74** B2
Pahra Kariz Afgh. **81** E3
Pahranagat Range *mts* U.S.A. **137** E3
Pahrump U.S.A. **137** E3
Pahuj *r.* India **74** C4
Pahute Mesa *plat.* U.S.A. **137** D3
Paiaguás Brazil **149** F4
Paicines U.S.A. **136** B3
Paide Estonia **28** C4
Paiján Peru **148** A1
Päijänne *l.* Fin. **33** G3
Paikü Co *l.* China **70** G6
Paila *r.* Bol. **149** D4
Pailing China *see* **Chun'an**
Paillaco Chile **152** B5
Paimio Fin. **33** F3
Paimpol France **38** B2
Painan Indon. **58** C3
Paine Chile **152** C3
Paine, Cerro *mt.* Chile **153** B7
Painesville U.S.A. **130** C3
Painted Desert U.S.A. **137** G3
Painted Rock Dam U.S.A. **137** F5
Paint Hills Canada *see* **Wemindji**
Paint Lake Canada **123** L4
Paint Rock U.S.A. **133** B6
Paintsville U.S.A. **130** B5
Pairi *r.* India **73** D1
Paisley Canada **130** C1
Paisley U.K. **34** D4
País Vasco *aut. comm.* Spain **43** E1
Paita Peru **146** A6
Paitan, Teluk *b. Sabah* Malaysia **59** G1
Paithan India **72** B2
Paitou China **67** G2
Paiva *r.* Port. **42** B2
Paiva Couceiro Angola *see* **Quipungo**
Paizhou China **67** E2
Pajala Sweden **32** F2
Pajan Ecuador **146** A5
Pajęczno Poland **37** I3
Pakala India **72** C3
Pakanbaru Indon. *see* **Pekanbaru**
Pakaraima Mountains S. America **147** F4
Pakaur India **75** E4
Pakch'ŏn N. Korea **65** A5
Pakesley Canada **124** D4
Pakhachi Rus. Fed. **27** Q3
Pakhiá *i.* Greece *see* **Pachia**
Pakhoi China *see* **Beihai**

▶**Pakistan** *country* Asia **81** F4
4th most populous country in Asia and 6th in the world.
asia **52–53, 82**
world **16–17**

Pakkat Indon. **58** B2
Paklenica *nat. park* Croatia **44** E2
Paknampho Thai. *see* **Nakhon Sawan**
Pakokku Myanmar **60** A3
Pakowki Lake *imp. l.* Canada **123** I5
Pakpattan Pak. **81** H4
Pak Phanang Thai. **61** C6
Pak Phayun Thai. **61** C7
Pakrac Croatia **44** F2
Pakruojis Lith. **33** F5
Paks Hungary **37** I5
Pakse Laos *see* **Pakxé**
Pak Tam Chung *Hong Kong* China **67** [inset]
Pak Thong Chai Thai. **61** C5
Paktīā *prov.* Afgh. **81** G3
Paktīkā *prov.* Afgh. **81** G3
Pakwash Lake Canada **123** M5
Pakxé Laos **61** D5
Pal Senegal *see* **Mpal**
Pala Chad **94** B2
Pala Myanmar **61** B5
Palabuhanratu Indon. **59** D4
Palabuhanratu, Teluk *b.* Indon. **58** D4
Palacios Bol. **148** D3
Palaestinia *reg.* Asia *see* **Palestine**
Palafrugell Spain **43** H2
Palagiano Italy **45** F4
Palagruža *i.* Croatia **44** F3
Palaia Fokaia Greece **47** C6
Palaikastro Greece **47** E7
Palaiochora Greece **47** C7
Palaiókastron Greece *see* **Palaikastro**
Palairos Greece **47** B5
Palaiseau France **38** E2
Palakkat India *see* **Palghat**
Palamakoloi Botswana **98** D4
Palam Pur India **74** C2
Palana India **74** B4
Palana Rus. Fed. **27** P4
Palancia *r.* Spain **43** F3
Palandur India **72** D1
Palanga Lith. **33** F5
Palangān, Kūh-e *mts* Iran **81** E4
Palangkaraya Indon. **59** F3
Palani India **72** C4
Palanpur India **74** B4
Palantak Pak. **81** F5
Palapye Botswana **99** E4
Palar *r.* India **72** D3
Palasbari India **75** F4
Palas de Rei Spain **42** C1
Palatka Rus. Fed. **27** P3
Palatka U.S.A. **129** C6
Palau *Sardinia* Italy **44** B4
▶**Palau** *country* N. Pacific Ocean **57** H4
asia **52–53, 82**
Palau Islands Palau **57** H4
Palauk Myanmar **61** B5
Palaw Myanmar **61** B5
Palawan *i.* Phil. **56** E4
Palawan Trough *sea feature* N. Pacific Ocean **164** B5
Palayankottai India **72** C4
Palazzo, Punta *pt Corsica* France **44** B3
Paldiski Estonia **33** G4
Pale Bos.-Herz. **44** G3
Palembang Indon. **58** D3
Palena *Aisén* Chile **153** B5
Palena *Los Lagos* Chile **153** C5
Palencia Spain **42** D1
Palermo Arg. **149** D6
Palermo *Sicily* Italy **45** D5
Palermo Punta Raisi *airport Sicily* Italy **45** D5
Palestine *reg.* Asia **77** B3
Palestine U.S.A. **133** C6
Paletwa Myanmar **60** A3
Palghar India **72** B2
Palghat India **72** C4
Palgrave, Mount Australia **108** A5
Palhoca Brazil **151** B8
Pali *Madhya Pradesh* India **74** D5
Pali *Maharashtra* India **72** B2
Pali *Rajasthan* India **74** B4

▶**Palikir** Micronesia **164** E5
Capital of Micronesia.

Palinuro, Capo *c.* Italy **45** E4
Paliouri Greece **47** C5
Paliouri, Akra *pt* Greece **47** C5
Palisade U.S.A. **134** E5
Palitana India **74** A5
Palja *hill* Sweden **32** E2
Paljakka *hill* Fin. **32** H2
Pälkäne Fin. **33** G3
Palk Bay Sri Lanka **72** C4
Palkohda India **73** D2
Palkonda Range *mts* India **72** C3
Palkot India **75** E5
Palk Strait India/Sri Lanka **72** C4
Palladani India **72** C4
Pallapalla *mt.* Peru **148** B3
Pallas ja Ounastunturin kansallispuisto *nat. park* Fin. **32** F1
Pallasovka Rus. Fed. **29** H6
Pallavaram India **72** D3
Palleru *r.* India **72** D2
Pallinup *r.* Australia **109** B8
Pallisa Uganda **96** B4
Palliser, Cape N.Z. **113** C3
Palliser, Îles *is* Fr. Polynesia **165** I7
Palliser Bay N.Z. **113** C3

Peipus, Lake Estonia/Rus. Fed. 28 C4
Peiraias Greece see Piraeus
Peitz Germany 37 G3
Peixe Brazil 150 B5
Peixe r. Brazil 149 H3
Peixian Jiangsu China 67 F1
Peixian Jiangsu China see Pizhou
Peixoto de Azevedo Brazil 150 A4
Peixoto de Azevedo r. Brazil 149 G2
Pejantan i. Indon. 59 D2
Peje Serb. and Mont. see Peć
Pek r. Serb. and Mont. 46 B2
Pekalongan Indon. 59 E4
Pekan Malaysia 58 C2
Pekanbaru Indon. 58 C2
Pékans, Rivière aux r. Canada 125 H2
Peki Ghana 93 F4
Pekin U.S.A. 132 D3
Peking China see Beijing
Pelabuhan Kelang Malaysia 58 C2
Pelabuhan Sandakan inlet Sabah Malaysia 59 G1
Pelada, Pampa hills Arg. 153 C6
Pelado mt. Spain 43 F3
Pelagie, Isole is Sicily Italy 45 D7
Pelagonija plain Macedonia 46 B4
Pelagonisou, Diavlos sea chan. Greece 47 D5
Pelaihari Indon. 59 F3
Pelalawan Indon. 58 C2
Pelapis i. Indon. 59 E3
Pelasgia Greece 47 C5
Pelasyía Greece see Pelasgia
Pelat, Mont mt. France 39 G4
Pelawanbesar Indon. 59 G2
Peleaga, Vârful mt. Romania 46 C2
Pelechuco Bol. 148 C3
Pelee Island Canada 130 B3
Pelee Point Canada 130 B3
Peleliu i. Palau 57 H4
Peleng i. Indon. 57 F6
Peles Rus. Fed. 28 I3
Pelhřimov Czech Rep. 37 G4
Pelican Lake Canada 123 K4
Pelican Narrows Canada 123 K4
Pelister mt. Macedonia 46 B4
Pelister nat. park Macedonia 46 B4
Pelješac pen. Croatia 44 F3
Pelkosenniemi Fin. 32 G2
Pellatt Lake Canada 123 I1
Pellegrue France 38 D4
Pelleluhu Islands P.N.G. 57 J6
Pello Fin. 32 F2
Pellworm i. Germany 36 D1
Pelly r. Canada 122 B2
Pelly Crossing Canada 122 B2
Pelly Lake Canada 123 K1
Pelly Mountains Canada 122 C2
Pelokang is Indon. 59 G4
▶Peloponnese reg. Greece 47 C6
europe 24–25
Peloponnisos admin. reg. Greece 47 C6
Peloritani, Monti mts Sicily Italy 45 E6
Pelotas Brazil 152 G2
Pelotas, Rio das r. Brazil 151 B8
Pelovo Bulg. 46 D3
Pelplin Poland 37 I2
Peltovuoma Fin. 32 G1
Pelusium tourist site Egypt 77 A4
Pelusium, Bay of Egypt see Tînah, Khalîj at
Pelvoux, Massif du mts France 39 G4
Pemalang Indon. 59 E4
Pemangkat Indon. 59 E2
Pemarung, Pulau i. Indon. 59 G3
Pematangsiantar Indon. 58 B2
Pemba Moz. 97 D8
Pemba Zambia 95 E9
Pemba, Baía de b. Moz. 97 D8
Pemba Channel Tanz. 97 C6
Pemba Island Tanz. 97 C6
Pemba North admin. reg. Tanz. 97 C6
Pemba South admin. reg. Tanz. 97 C6
Pemberton Canada 122 F5
Pembina r. Canada 123 H4
Pembina r. U.S.A. 132 B1
Pembroke Canada 124 E4
Pembroke U.K. 35 D6
Pembroke U.S.A. 129 C5
Pembroke, Cape Falkland Is 153 F7
Pembroke Pines U.S.A. 129 C7
Pembrokeshire Coast National Park U.K. 35 D6
Pembuanghulu Indon. 59 F3
Pen India 72 B2
Pen r. Myanmar 60 A3
Pena Barrosa Bol. 148 D5
Peña Cabollera mt. Spain 42 E2
Peña de Francia mt. Spain 42 C2
Peña de Izaga mt. Spain 43 F1
Peña de Oroel mt. Spain 43 F1
Peñafiel Spain 42 D2
Peñagolosa mt. Spain 43 F2
Peñalara mt. Spain 42 E2
Peñalba de Santiago tourist site Spain 42 C1
Peñalsordo Spain 42 D3
Penamacor Port. 42 C2
Penambo Range mts Sarawak Malaysia see Tama Abu, Banjaran
Peña Mira mt. Spain 42 C2
Peña Nevada, Cerro mt. Mex. 126 G7
Penang state Malaysia see Pinang
Peñaranda de Bracamonte Spain 42 D2
Penarie Australia 112 B4
Peñarroya mt. Spain 43 F2
Peñarroya-Pueblonuevo Spain 42 D3
Peñas, Cabo de c. Spain 42 D1
Penas, Golfo de g. Chile 153 B6
Peñasco watercourse U.S.A. 135 F6
Peña Ubiña mt. Spain 42 D1
Peña Utrera hill Spain 42 C3
Pench r. India 74 C5
Pencheng China see Ruichang
Pench National Park India 74 C5
Pendé r. Cent. Afr. Rep. 94 C3
Pendik Turkey 46 F4
Pendleton U.S.A. 134 C3
Pendleton Bay Canada 122 E4
Pendopo Indon. 58 C3
Pend Oreille r. U.S.A. 134 C2
Pend Oreille Lake U.S.A. 134 C2
Pendra India 75 D5
Pendzhikent Tajik. see Panjakent
Penebangan i. Indon. 59 E3
Peneda Gerês, Parque Nacional da nat. park Port. 42 B2
Pene-Mende Dem. Rep. Congo 95 F6
Penetanguishene Canada 130 D1
Penfield U.S.A. 130 D3
Penfro U.K. see Pembroke
Peng'an China 66 C2
Penganga r. India 72 C2
Peng Chau i. Hong Kong China 67 [inset]
P'engchia Yü i. Taiwan 67 G3
Penge Dem. Rep. Congo 95 E6
P'enghu Ch'üntao is Taiwan 67 F4
P'enghu Liehtao is Taiwan see P'enghu Ch'üntao
P'enghu Tao i. Taiwan 67 F4
Pengiki i. Indon. 59 E2
Pengshan China 66 B2
Pengshui China 66 D2
Peng Siang, Sungai r. Sing. 58 [inset]
Pengwa Myanmar 60 A3
Pengxi China 66 C2
Pengze China 67 F2
Penhalonga Zimbabwe 99 G3
Penhook U.S.A. 130 D5
Peniche Port. 42 B3
Penicuik U.K. 34 E4
Penida i. Indon. 59 F5
Peninga Rus. Fed. 28 E3
Peninsular Malaysia Malaysia 58 D1
Penitente, Serra do hills Brazil 150 C4
Pênjwin Iraq 79 F4
Penmarch France 38 A3
Penmarch, Pointe de pt France 38 A3
Penn U.S.A. see Penn Hills
Penna, Punta della pt Italy 44 E3
Penne Italy 44 D3
Pennell Coast Antarctica 167 H2
Penner r. India 72 D3
Penneshaw Australia 109 G8
Penn Hills U.S.A. 130 D3
Pennine, Alpi mts Italy/Switz. 44 A2
Pennine Alps mts Italy/Switz. see Pennine, Alpi
Pennines hills U.K. 35 E4
Pennington Gap U.S.A. 130 B5
Pennsboro U.S.A. 130 C4
Pennsville U.S.A. 131 F4
Pennsylvania state U.S.A. 130 D3
Penny Icecap Canada 121 M3
Penny Point Antarctica 167 H1
Penobscot Bay U.S.A. 131 I1
Penola Australia 112 B5
Penong Australia 109 F7
Penonomé Panama 139 H7
Penrhyn atoll Cook Is 165 H6
Penrhyn Basin sea feature S. Pacific Ocean 165 H6
Penrith U.K. 35 E4
Pensacola U.S.A. 129 B6
Pensacola Bay i. U.S.A. 129 B6
Pensacola Mountains Antarctica 167 L1
Pensamiento Bol. 149 E3
Pentadaktylos Range mts Cyprus 77 A2
Pentakota India 73 D2
Pentecost Island Vanuatu 107 F3
Pentecôte r. Canada 125 H3
Pentecôte, Île i. Vanuatu see Pentecost Island
Penteleu, Vârful mt. Romania 46 E2
Penticton Canada 134 C2
Pentland Australia 111 F4
Pentland Firth sea chan. U.K. 34 E2
Penukonda India 72 C3
Penunjok, Tanjong pt Malaysia 58 C1
Penwegon Myanmar 60 B4
Penygadair hill U.K. 35 E5
Penylan Lake Canada 123 J2
Penza Rus. Fed. 29 H5
Penzance U.K. 35 D6
Penza Oblast admin. div. Rus. Fed. see Penzenskaya Oblast'
Penzenskaya Oblast' admin. div. Rus. Fed. 29 H5
Penzhinskaya Guba b. Rus. Fed. 27 Q3
Peoples Creek r. U.S.A. 134 E2
Peoria AZ U.S.A. 137 F5
Peoria IL U.S.A. 132 D3
Pepel Sierra Leone 92 B3
Peper Sudan 96 B3
Pëqin Albania 46 A4
Pequop Mountains U.S.A. 137 E1
Pera Head Australia 111 E2
Peraitepuy Venez. 147 F3
Perak i. Malaysia 58 B1
Perak r. Malaysia 58 C1
Perak state Malaysia 58 C1
Perama Greece 47 D7
Perambalur India 72 C4
Perämeren kansallispuisto nat. park Fin. 32 G2
Perä-Posio Fin. 32 G2
Perche, Collines du hills France 38 D2
Percival Lakes salt flat Australia 108 D5
Percy France 38 C2
Percy Isles Australia 111 G4
Perdida r. Brazil 150 C4
Perdido r. Brazil 149 F5
Perdido, Monte mt. Spain 43 G1
Perdiguère, Pic mt. France/Spain 43 G1
Perdika Greece 47 B5
Perdizes Brazil 149 I4
Perdu, Lac l. Canada 125 G3
Peregrebnoye Rus. Fed. 26 G3
Pereira Col. 146 C3
Pereira Barreto Brazil 149 H5
Pereira de Eça Angola see Ondjiva
Pereiro Brazil 150 E3
Perelyub Rus. Fed. 29 I6
Peremetnoye Kazakh. 29 I6
Peremul Par reef India 72 B4
Peremyshlyany Ukr. 29 C6
Perené r. Peru 148 B2
Perenjori Australia 109 B7
Pereslavl'-Zalesskiy Rus. Fed. 28 F4
Peretu Romania 46 D2
Perevolotskiy Rus. Fed. 29 J6
Pereyaslavka Rus. Fed. 64 C3
Pereyaslav-Khmel'nitskiy Ukr. see Pereyaslav-Khmel'nyts'kyy
Pereyaslav-Khmel'nyts'kyy Ukr. 29 D6
Pérez Chile 152 C1
Perg Austria 37 G4
Pergamino Arg. 152 E3
Pergola Italy 44 D3
Perhentian Besar i. Malaysia 58 C1
Perho Fin. 32 G3
Periam Romania 46 B1
Péribonca r. Canada 125 F3
Pericos Mex. 126 E6
Peridot U.S.A. 137 G5
Périers France 38 C2
Périgueux France 38 D4
Perijá, Parque Nacional nat. park Venez. 146 C2
Perija, Sierra de mts Venez. 146 C2
Peringat Malaysia 58 C1
Periprava Romania 46 F2
Perişoru Romania 46 E2
Peristera i. Greece 47 C5
Peristerio Greece 47 C5
Perito Moreno Arg. 153 C6
Perito Moreno, Parque Nacional nat. park Arg. 153 B6
Perivar r. India 72 C4
Perlas, Punta de pt Nicaragua 139 H6
Perleberg Germany 36 E2
Perlis state Malaysia 58 C1
Permas Rus. Fed. 28 H4
Përmet Albania 47 B4
Perm Oblast admin. div. Rus. Fed. see Permskaya Oblast'
Permskaya Oblast' admin. div. Rus. Fed. 28 K4
Permuda i. Croatia 44 E2
Pernambuco Brazil see Recife
Pernambuco state Brazil 150 E4
Pernambuco Plain sea feature S. Atlantic Ocean 160 M6
Pernatty Lagoon salt flat Australia 112 A3
Pernik Bulg. 46 C3
Perniö Fin. 33 F3
Pernov Estonia see Pärnu
Peron Islands Australia 110 B2
Péronnas France 39 F3
Péronne France 39 E2
Perote Mex. 126 G8
Perpignan France 39 E5
Perrégaux Alg. see Mohammadia
Perris U.S.A. 136 D5
Perros-Guirec France 38 B2
Perry r. Canada 123 K1
Perry FL U.S.A. 129 C6
Perry MI U.S.A. 130 A2
Perry OK U.S.A. 133 B4
Perry Hall U.S.A. 131 E4
Perrysburg U.S.A. 130 B3
Perryton U.S.A. 133 A4
Perryville AR U.S.A. 133 C5
Perryville KY U.S.A. 130 A5
Persepolis tourist site Iran 80 C4
Persia country Asia see Iran
Persian Gulf Asia see The Gulf
Persis prov. Iran see Fārs
Pertek Turkey 79 D3
Perth Tas. Australia 112 C6

▶Perth W.A. Australia 109 A7
State capital of Western Australia. 4th most populous city in Oceania.

Perth Canada 131 E1
Perth U.K. 34 E3
Perth-Andover Canada 125 H4
Perth Basin sea feature Indian Ocean 163 O7
Pertominsk Rus. Fed. 28 F2
Pertuis France 39 F5
Pertuis Breton sea chan. France 38 C3
Pertuis d'Antioche sea chan. France 38 C3
Pertunmaa Fin. 33 G3
Pertusato, Capo c. Corsica France 44 B4
Perú Bol. 148 D3
Peru atoll Kiribati see Beru

▶Peru country S. America 148 B2
3rd largest and 4th most populous country in South America.
southamerica 144–145, 154

Peru U.S.A. 132 E3
Peru-Chile Trench sea feature S. Pacific Ocean 165 M6
Perugia Italy 44 D3
Peruíbe Brazil 149 I6
Perusia Italy see Perugia
Pervomaysk Rus. Fed. 29 G5
Pervomays'k Ukr. 29 D6
Pervomayskiy Arkhangel'skaya Oblast' Rus. Fed. see Novodvinsk
Pervomayskiy Orenburgskaya Oblast' Rus. Fed. 29 J6
Pervomayskiy Tambovskaya Oblast' Rus. Fed. 29 G5
Pervomays'kyy Ukr. 29 F6
Pervorechenskiy Rus. Fed. 27 Q3
Pesaguan r. Indon. 59 E3
Pesaro Italy 44 D3
Pescadores is Taiwan see P'enghu Ch'üntao
Pescadores, Punta pt Peru 148 B4
Pescara Italy 44 E3
Pescara r. Italy 44 E3
Pescari Romania 46 B2
Peschanokopskoye Rus. Fed. 29 G7
Peschanoye Rus. Fed. see Yashkul'
Peschanyy, Mys pt Kazakh. 79 G2
Peschici Italy 44 F4
Pescia Italy 44 C3
Pesha r. Rus. Fed. 28 H2
Peshanjan Afgh. 81 E3
Peshawar Pak. 81 G3
Peshkopi Albania 46 B4
Peshnyye, Ostrova is Kazakh. see Bol'shiye Peshnyye, Ostrova
Peshtera Bulg. 46 D3
Peshtigo r. U.S.A. 128 B2
Peski Turkm. 81 E2
Peski Karakumy des. Turkm. see Karakum Desert
Peskovka Rus. Fed. 28 J4
Pesnica Slovenia 44 E1
Peso da Régua Port. 42 C2
Pesqueira Brazil 150 E4
Pesqueira Mex. 135 E7
Pessac France 38 C4
Pestovo Rus. Fed. 28 E4
Pestravka Rus. Fed. 29 I5
Petah Tiqwa Israel 77 B3
Petäjävesi Fin. 33 G3
Petalidi Greece 47 B6
Petalioi i. Greece 47 D5
Petaluma U.S.A. 136 A2
Pétange Lux. 39 F2
Petangis Indon. 59 F3
Petare Venez. 146 E2
Petas Greece 47 B5
Petatlán Mex. 138 D5
Petauke Zambia 97 A8
Petenwell Lake U.S.A. 132 D2
Peterbell Canada 124 D3
Peterborough Australia 112 A4
Peterborough Canada 130 D1
Peterborough U.K. 35 F5
Peterborough U.S.A. 131 H2
Peterhead U.K. 34 F3
Peter I Island Antarctica 167 K2
Petermann Bjerg nunatak Greenland 121 Q2
Petermann Ranges mts Australia 110 B5
Peter Pond Lake Canada 123 I4
Petersburg AK U.S.A. 122 C3
Petersburg IL U.S.A. 132 D4
Petersburg NY U.S.A. 131 G2
Petersburg OH U.S.A. 130 C3
Petersburg VA U.S.A. 130 E5
Petersburg WV U.S.A. 130 D4
Petershagen Germany 36 D2
Peters Mine Guyana 147 G3
Peterstown U.S.A. 130 C5
Petersville U.S.A. 120 D3
Peter the Great Bay Rus. Fed. see Petra Velikogo, Zaliv
Petervárad Serb. and Mont. see Petrovaradin
Peterwardein Serb. and Mont. see Petrovaradin
Peth India 72 B2
Petilia Policastro Italy 45 F5
Petit Atlas mts Morocco see Anti Atlas
Petite Creuse r. France 38 D3
Petitjean Morocco see Sidi Kacem
Petit Lac Manicouagan l. Canada 125 H2
Petit Maine r. France 38 C3
Petit Mécatina r. Nfld. and Lab./Que. Canada see Little Mecatina
Petit Mécatina r. Nfld. and Lab./Que. Canada 125 J3
Petit Mécatina, Île du i. Canada 125 J3
Petit Morin r. France 39 E2
Petitot r. Canada 122 F2
Petit St-Bernard, Col du pass France 39 G4
Petkula Fin. 32 G2
Petlad India 74 B5
Peto Mex. 138 G4
Petoskey U.S.A. 132 E2
Petra tourist site Jordan 78 C5
Petra tou Romiou tourist site Cyprus see Aphrodite's Birthplace
Petra Velikogo, Zaliv b. Rus. Fed. 64 B4
Petre, Point Canada 131 E2
Petrich Bulg. 46 C4
Petrified Forest National Park U.S.A. 137 H4
Petrikau Poland see Piotrków Trybunalski
Petrikov Belarus see Pyetrykaw
Petrinja Croatia 44 F2
Petro, Cerro de mt. Chile 152 C2
Petroaleksandrovsk Uzbek. see Turtkul'
Petrograd Rus. Fed. see St Petersburg
Petrokov Poland see Piotrków Trybunalski
Petrolândia Brazil 150 E4
Petrolia Canada 130 B2
Petrolina Amazonas Brazil 146 E5
Petrolina Pernambuco Brazil 150 D4
Petron, Limni l. Greece 46 B4
Petropavl Kazakh. see Petropavlovsk
Petropavlovsk Kazakh. 26 G4
Petropavlovsk Rus. Fed. see Petropavlovsk-Kamchatskiy
Petropavlovsk-Kamchatskiy Rus. Fed. 27 P4
Petroşani Romania 46 C2
Petrovac Bos.-Herz. see Bosanski Petrovac
Petrovac Serb. and Mont. 46 B2
Petrovaradin Serb. and Mont. 46 A2
Petrovsk Rus. Fed. 29 H5
Petrovskoye Rus. Fed. see Svetlograd
Petrovsk-Zabaykal'skiy Rus. Fed. 27 K4
Petrov Val Rus. Fed. 29 H6
Petrozavodsk Rus. Fed. 28 E3
Petsamo Rus. Fed. see Pechenga
Pettau Slovenia see Ptuj
Petukhovo Rus. Fed. 26 G4
Petushki Rus. Fed. 28 F5
Peuetsagu, Gunung vol. Indon. 58 B1
Peurasuvanto Fin. 32 G2
Peureula Indon. 58 B1
Pevek Rus. Fed. 27 R3
Pêxung China 75 G2
Peza r. Rus. Fed. 28 H2
Pézenas France 39 E5
Pezinok Slovakia 37 H4
Pfaffenhofen an der Ilm Germany 36 E4
Pfälzer Wald hills Germany 36 C4
Pfarrkirchen Germany 37 F4
Pforzheim Germany 36 D4
Pfullendorf Germany 36 D5
Pfungstadt Germany 36 D4
Phagwara India 74 B3
Phahameng S. Africa 99 E6
Phalaborwa S. Africa 99 F4
Phalia Pak. 81 H3
Phalodi India 74 B4
Phalsbourg France 39 G2
Phalsund India 74 A4
Phaltan India 72 B2
Phalut Peak India/Nepal 75 F4
Phangan, Ko i. Thai. 61 C6
Phangnga Thai. 61 B6
Phan Rang Vietnam 61 E6
Phan Ri Vietnam 61 E6
Phan Thiêt Vietnam 61 E6
Phan Thiêt, Vinh b. Vietnam 61 E6
Phaplu Nepal 75 E4
Phat Diêm Vietnam 60 D3
Phatthalung Thai. 61 C7
Phayao Thai. 60 B4
Phek India 75 G4
Phelp r. Australia 110 C2
Phenix U.S.A. 130 D5
Phenix City U.S.A. 129 B5
Phet Buri Thai. 61 B5
Phetchabun Thai. 61 C4
Phichit Thai. 61 C4
Philadelphia Jordan see 'Ammān
Philadelphia Turkey see Alaşehir
Philadelphia MS U.S.A. 129 A5
Philadelphia NY U.S.A. 131 F1
Philadelphia PA U.S.A. 131 F4
Philae tourist site Egypt 89 G4
Philip U.S.A. 132 A2
Philip Atoll Micronesia see Sorol
Philippeville Alg. see Skikda
Philippeville Belgium 39 F1
Philippi U.S.A. 130 C4
Philippi, Lake salt flat Australia 110 D5
Philippine Basin sea feature N. Pacific Ocean 164 C4
▶Philippines country Asia 57 F3
asia 52–53, 82
Philippine Sea N. Pacific Ocean 164 C4

▶Philippine Trench sea feature N. Pacific Ocean 164 C4
3rd deepest trench in the world.

Philippopolis Bulg. see Plovdiv
Philip Smith Mountains U.S.A. 120 E3
Phillips U.S.A. 132 D2
Phillips Arm Canada 122 E5
Phillipsburg U.S.A. 132 B4
Phillipson, Lake salt flat Australia 110 C6
Phillips Range hills Australia 108 D4
Philomelium Turkey see Akşehir
Philpott Reservoir U.S.A. 130 C5
Phimun Mangsahan Thai. 61 D5
Phiritona S. Africa 99 E5
Phitsanulok Thai. 60 C4

▶Phnom Penh Cambodia 61 D6
Capital of Cambodia.

Pho, Laem pt Thai. 61 C7

▶Phoenix U.S.A. 137 F5
State capital of Arizona.

Phoenix Island Kiribati see Rawaki
Phoenix Islands Kiribati 107 H2
Phoenixville U.S.A. 131 F3
Phon Thai. 61 C5
Phong Nha Vietnam 60 D4
Phôngsali Laos 60 C3
Phong Saly Laos see Phôngsali
Phong Thô Vietnam 60 C3
Phosphate Hill Australia 111 E4
Phrae Thai. 60 C4
Phra Nakhon Si Ayutthaya Thai. see Ayutthaya
Phra Saeng Thai. 61 B6
Phra Thong, Ko i. Thai. 61 B6
Phuchong-Nayoi National Park Thai. 61 D5
Phu Cuong Vietnam see Thu Dâu Môt
Phuduhudu Botswana 98 E4
Phuentsholing Bhutan 75 F4
Phuket Thai. 61 B7
Phuket, Ko i. Thai. 61 B7
Phulabani India 73 E1
Phulpur India 75 D4
Phu Luang Wildlife Reserve Thai. 60 C4
Phu Ly Vietnam 60 D3
Phumĭ Chhuk Cambodia 61 D6
Phumĭ Kâmpóng Trâlach Cambodia 61 D5
Phumĭ Mlu Prey Cambodia 61 D5
Phumĭ Prâmaôy Cambodia 61 C5
Phumĭ Sâmraông Cambodia 61 C5
Phuntsholing Bhutan see Phuentsholing
Phu Phac Mo mt. Vietnam 60 C3
Phu Phan National Park Thai. 60 C4
Phu Quôc, Đao i. Vietnam 61 C6
Phu Tho Vietnam 60 D3
Phu Vinh Vietnam see Tra Vinh
Piabung, Gunung mt. Indon. 59 F2
Piaca Brazil 150 C3
Piacenza Italy 44 B2
Piacouadie, Lac l. Canada 125 G3
Piadena Italy 44 C2
Piagochioui r. Canada 124 E2
Piana di Catania plain Sicily Italy 45 E6
Piangil Australia 112 B4
Pianoro Italy 44 C2
Pianosa, Isola i. Italy 44 C3
Piaseczno Poland 37 J2
Piatã Brazil 150 D5
Piatra Romania 46 D3
Piatra Neamț Romania 31 K4
Piatra Olt Romania 46 D2
Piauí r. Brazil 150 D3
Piauí state Brazil 150 D3
Piauí, Serra de hills Brazil 150 D4
Piave r. Italy 44 D2
Piazza Armerina Sicily Italy 45 E6
Piazzi, Isla i. Chile 153 B7
Pibor r. Sudan 96 B2
Pibor Post Sudan 96 B3
Pic r. Canada 124 C3
Pica Chile 148 C5
Picacho U.S.A. 137 G5
Picachos, Cerro dos mt. Mex. 135 D7
Picardie admin. reg. France 39 E2
Picardie reg. France 38 D2
Picassent Spain 43 F3
Picayune U.S.A. 127 I5
Picháchic Mex. 135 F7
Pichanal Arg. 149 D5
Pichilemu Chile 152 B3
Pichilingue Mex. 126 D7
Pichi Mahuida Arg. 152 D4
Pichincha prov. Ecuador 146 B5
Pichor India 74 C4
Pickens U.S.A. 130 C4
Pickering U.K. 35 F4
Pickle Lake Canada 124 B3
Pico da Neblina, Parque Nacional do nat. park Brazil 147 E4
Picos Brazil 150 D3
Picos, Punta dos pt Spain 42 B2
Picota Peru 146 B6
Pico Truncado Arg. 153 D6
Picton Australia 112 D4
Picton Canada 131 E2
Picton N.Z. 113 C3
Picton, Mount Australia 112 C6
Picuí Brazil 150 E3
Picún Leufú Arg. 152 C4
Pidarak Pak. 81 E5
Pidurutalagala mt. Sri Lanka 72 D5
Pie de Palo, Sierra mts Arg. 152 C2
Piedimonte Matese Italy 44 E4
Piedmont admin. reg. Italy see Piemonte
Piedmont MO U.S.A. 132 D4
Piedmont OH U.S.A. 130 C3
Piedra r. Spain 43 F2
Piedrabuena Spain 42 D3
Piedra de Aguila Arg. 152 C5
Piedrafita Spain see Pedrafita do Cebreiro
Piedrahita Spain 42 D2
Piedralaves Spain 42 D2
Piedras, Punta pt Arg. 152 F3
Piedras Blancas Point U.S.A. 136 B4
Piedras Negras Guat. 138 F5
Piedras Negras Mex. 126 F6
Pieksämäki Fin. 33 G3
Pielavesi Fin. 32 G3
Pielavesi l. Fin. 32 G3
Pielinen l. Fin. 32 H3
Pieljekaise nationalpark nat. park Sweden 32 E2
Piemonte admin. reg. Italy 44 A2
Pieniężno Poland 37 J1
Pieniński Park Narodowy nat. park Poland 37 J4
Pieninský nat. park Slovakia 37 J4
Pieńsk Poland 37 G3
Pierce U.S.A. 132 B3
Pierce Lake Canada 123 M4
Pierceland Canada 123 I4
Pieria mts Greece 47 C4

▶Pierre U.S.A. 132 A2
State capital of South Dakota.

Pierre, Bayou r. U.S.A. 133 D6
Pierrelatte France 39 F4
Pieskehaure l. Sweden 32 E2
Piešťany Slovakia 37 H4
Pietermaritzburg S. Africa 99 F6
Pietersaari Fin. see Jakobstad
Pietersburg S. Africa 99 F4
Pietraperzia Sicily Italy 45 E6
Pietrasanta Italy 44 C3
Pietra Spada, Passo di pass Italy 45 F5
Pietrosa mt. Romania 31 K4
Pietrosu, Vârful mt. Romania 29 C7
Pieve di Cadore Italy 44 D1
Pievepelago Italy 44 C2
Pigeon r. Canada/U.S.A. 132 D1
Pigeon Bay Canada 130 B3
Pigeon Lake Canada 123 H4
Pigg r. U.S.A. 130 D5
Piggott U.S.A. 133 D4
Pigg's Peak Swaziland 99 F5
Pigon, Limni l. Greece 47 B5
Pigüé Arg. 152 E4
Pi He r. China 67 F1
Pihkva järv l. Estonia/Rus. Fed. see Pskov, Lake
Pihlajavesi l. Fin. 33 H3
Pihtipudas Fin. 32 G3
Piispajärvi Fin. 32 H2
Piji China see Puge
Pikalevo Rus. Fed. 28 E4
Pikelot i. Micronesia 164 D5
Pikes Peak U.S.A. 134 F5
Piketberg S. Africa 98 C7
Piketon U.S.A. 130 B4
Pikeville U.S.A. 130 B5
Pikounda Congo 94 C4
Pila Arg. 152 F4
Piła Poland 37 H2
Pilanesberg National Park S. Africa 99 E5
Pilani India 74 B3
Pilar Buenos Aires Arg. 152 F3
Pilar Córdoba Arg. 152 E2
Pilar Para. 149 F6
Pilas Spain 42 C4
Pilat, Mont mt. France 39 F4
Pilaya r. Bol. 149 D5
Pilcaniyeu Arg. 152 C5
Pilcomayo r. Bol./Para. 149 F6
Pilenkovo Georgia see Gantiadi
Piler India 72 C3
Pili Greece see Pyli
Pili, Cerro mt. Chile 148 D5
Pilibhit India 74 C3
Pilica r. Poland 37 J3
Pilipinas country Asia see Philippines
Pillau Rus. Fed. see Baltiysk
Pillcopata Peru 148 C3
Pilliga Australia 112 D3
Pillsbury, Lake U.S.A. 136 A2
Pil'na Rus. Fed. 28 H5
Pil'nya, Ozero l. Rus. Fed. 28 K1
Pilões, Serra dos mts Brazil 151 C6
Pilón r. Mex. 133 B7
Pilos Greece see Pylos
Pilot Peak U.S.A. 136 D2
Pilot Point U.S.A. 120 D4
Pilot Rock U.S.A. 134 C3
Pilot Station U.S.A. 120 C3
Pilsen Czech Rep. see Plzeň
Pilu, Nam r. Myanmar 60 B4
Pima U.S.A. 137 H5
Pimenta Bueno Brazil 149 E2
Pimpalner India 72 B1
Pimpri India 72 B1
Pimu Dem. Rep. Congo 94 D4
Pin r. Myanmar 60 A3
Pinahat India 74 C4
Pinaleno Mountains U.S.A. 137 G5
Pinang Malaysia see George Town
Pinang i. Malaysia 58 C1
Pinang state Malaysia 58 C1
Pinar mt. Spain 42 D4
Pinar, Puerto del pass Spain 43 E3
Pınarbaşı Turkey 78 D3
Pinar del Río Cuba 127 J7
Pinarhisar Turkey 46 E4
Piñas Ecuador 146 B5
Pinatubo, Mt vol. Phil. 57 F2
Pincher Creek Canada 123 H5
Pinconning U.S.A. 130 B2
Pińczów Poland 37 J3
Pindaíba Brazil 149 G3
Pindar Australia 109 A7
Pindar r. India 74 C3
Pindaré r. Brazil 150 C2
Pindhos Óros mts Greece see Pindus Mountains
Pindi Batiau Pak. 81 H4
Pindi Gheb Pak. 81 H3
Pindobal Brazil 150 B2
Pindos mts Greece see Pindus Mountains
Pindos nat. park Greece 47 B5
Pindus Mountains Greece 47 B5
Pindwara India 74 B4
Pine watercourse Australia 112 B4
Pine r. U.S.A. 130 A2
Pine, Cape Canada 125 K4
Pine Bluff U.S.A. 127 H5
Pine Bluffs U.S.A. 134 F4
Pine City U.S.A. 132 C2
Pine Creek Australia 110 B2
Pine Creek r. U.S.A. 130 E3
Pine Creek watercourse U.S.A. 137 D1
Pinecrest U.S.A. 136 B2
Pinedale U.S.A. 134 E4
Pine Dock Canada 123 L5
Pine Falls Canada 123 L5
Pinega Rus. Fed. 28 G2
Pinega r. Rus. Fed. 28 G2
Pinegrove Australia 109 A6
Pine Hills CA U.S.A. 136 D4
Pine Hills FL U.S.A. 129 C6
Pinehouse Lake Canada 123 J4
Pinehouse Lake l. Canada 123 J4
Pineimuta r. Canada 124 B2
Pineios r. Greece 47 C5
Pineiou, Techniti Limni resr Greece 47 B6
Pine Island Bay Antarctica 163 A10
Pine Island Glacier Antarctica 167 K1
Pine Islands FL U.S.A. 129 C7
Pine Islands FL U.S.A. 129 C7
Pine Knot U.S.A. 130 A5
Pine Peak U.S.A. 137 F4
Pine Point Canada 123 H2
Pineridge U.S.A. 136 C3
Pine Ridge U.S.A. 134 G4
Pinerolo Italy 44 A2
Pines, Isle of i. Cuba see La Juventud, Isla de
Pines, Isle of i. New Caledonia see Pins, Île des
Pineto Italy 44 E3
Pinetop U.S.A. 137 H4
Pine Valley U.S.A. 131 E2
Pineville KY U.S.A. 130 B5
Pineville LA U.S.A. 133 C6
Pineville WV U.S.A. 130 C5
Ping, Mae Nam r. Thai. 61 C5
Pingal Jammu and Kashmir 74 B1
Pingba China 66 C3
Pingbian China 66 B4
Pingchang China 66 C2
Pingdingshan China 67 E1
Pingdong Taiwan see P'ingtung
Pingdu China see Anfu
Pingguo China 66 C4
Pinghai China 67 E4
Pinghe China 67 F3
Pinghu China 67 G2
Pingjiang China 67 E2
Pingle China 67 D3
Pingli China 67 D1
Pingliang China 63 H4
Pinglu China 67 D1
Pingma China see Tiandong
Pingnan China 67 D4
Pingshan Guangdong China see Huidong
Pingshan Sichuan China 66 C2
Pingshan Yunnan China see Luquan
Pingshi China 67 E3
Pingtan China 67 F3
Pingtan Dao i. China see Haitan Dao
P'ingtung Taiwan 67 G4
Pingwu China 66 C1
Pingxi China see Yuping
Pingxiang Guangxi China 66 C4
Pingxiang Jiangxi China 67 E3
Pingyang Heilong. China 64 A2
Pingyang Zhejiang China 67 G3
Pingyu China 67 E1
Pingyuan China 67 E3
Pingyuanjie China 66 B4
Pingzhai China 66 D3
Pinhal Novo Port. 42 B3
Pinheiro Brazil 150 C2
Pinheiro Machado Brazil 152 G2
Pinhel Port. 42 C2
Pini i. Indon. 58 B2
Pinilla r. Spain 43 E3
Piniós r. Greece see Pineios
Pinjarra Australia 109 A8
Pinkafeld Austria 37 H5
Pink Mountain Canada 122 F3
Pinlaung Myanmar 60 B3
Pinlebu Myanmar 60 A2
Pinnacle hill U.S.A. 130 D4
Pinnacles National Monument nat. park U.S.A. 136 B3
Pinnaroo Australia 112 B4
Pinneberg Germany 36 D2
Pinnes, Akra pt Greece 47 D4
Pinofranqueado Spain 42 C2
Pinoh r. Indon. 59 E3
Pinos, Isla de i. Cuba see La Juventud, Isla de
Pinos, Mount U.S.A. 136 C4
Pinoso Spain 43 F3
Pinoso mt. Spain 43 E2
Pinotepa Nacional Mex. 138 E5
Pins, Île des i. New Caledonia 107 F4
Pins, Pointe aux pt Canada 130 C2
Pinsk Belarus 29 C5
Pintados Chile 148 C5
Pintasan Sabah Malaysia 59 G1
Pinto Spain 42 E2
Pintura U.S.A. 137 F3

Port St-Louis Madag. *see* Antsohimbondrona
Port Saint Lucie City U.S.A. **129** C7
Port Salvador Falkland Is **153** F7
Ports de Beseit *mts* Spain **43** G2
Port Shelter *b.* Hong Kong China **67** [inset]
Port Shepstone S. Africa **99** F6
Port Simpson Canada *see* Lax Kw'alaams
Portsmouth U.K. **35** F6
Portsmouth *NH* U.S.A. **131** H2
Portsmouth *OH* U.S.A. **130** B4
Portsmouth *VA* U.S.A. **131** E5
Port Stanley Falkland Is *see* **Stanley**
Port Stephens Falkland Is **153** E8
Port Sudan Sudan **89** H5
Port Sulphur U.S.A. **133** D6
Port-sur-Saône France **39** G3
Port Swettenham Malaysia *see* Pelabuhan Kelang
Port Talbot U.K. **35** E6
Porttipahdan tekojärvi *l.* Fin. **32** G1
Port Townsend U.S.A. **134** B2
▶**Portugal** *country* Europe **42** C3
europe 24–25, 48
Portugalete Spain **42** E1
Portugália Angola *see* **Chitato**
Portuguesa *state* Venez. **146** D2
Portuguese East Africa *country* Africa *see* **Mozambique**
Portuguese Guinea *country* Africa *see* **Guinea-Bissau**
Portuguese Timor *country* Asia *see* **East Timor**
Portuguese West Africa *country* Africa *see* **Angola**
Portumna Rep. of Ireland **35** B5
Portus Herculis Monoeci *country* Europe *see* **Monaco**
Port-Vendres France **39** E5
Port Victoria Australia **112** A4

▶**Port Vila** Vanuatu **107** F3
Capital of Vanuatu.

Portville U.S.A. **130** D2
Port Vladimir Rus. Fed. **32** I1
Port Waikato N.Z. **113** C2
Port Wakefield Australia **112** A4
Port Warrender Australia **110** A2
Port Washington U.S.A. **132** E3
Porumamilla India **72** C3
Porvenir *Pando* Bol. **148** C2
Porvenir *Santa Cruz* Bol. **149** E3
Porvenir Chile **153** C8
Porvoo Fin. **33** G3
Poryŏng S. Korea **65** A5
Porzuna Spain **42** D3
Posada *Sardinia* Italy **45** B4
Posada *r. Sardinia* Italy **45** B4
Posada Spain **42** D1
Posadas Arg. **152** G1
Posadas Spain **42** D4
Poschiavo Switz. **39** I3
Poseidonia Greece **47** D6
Poseidonia *tourist site* Italy *see* **Paestum**
Posen Poland *see* **Poznań**
Poshekhon'ye Rus. Fed. **28** F4
Poshekon'ye-Volodarsk Rus. Fed. *see* Poshekhon'ye
Posht *watercourse* Iran **81** D4
Posht-e Badam Iran **80** C3
Poshteh-ye Chaqvir *hill* Iran **81** D4
Posht-e Küh *mts* Iran **80** A3
Posht Küh *hill* Iran **80** B2
Posio Fin. **32** H2
Poso Indon. **57** F6
Posorja Ecuador **146** A5
Posse Brazil **150** C5
Pößneck Germany **36** E3
Post U.S.A. **133** A5
Poşta Călnău Romania **46** E2
Poşta Cîlnău Romania *see* **Poşta Călnău**
Postavy Belarus *see* **Pastavy**
Poste-de-la-Baleine Canada *see* Kuujjuarapik
Postmasburg S. Africa **98** D6
Postojna Slovenia **44** E2
Poston U.S.A. **137** E4
Postville Canada **125** J2
Postville U.S.A. **132** D3
Post Weygand Alg. **91** F4
Postysheve Ukr. *see* **Krasnoarmiys'k**
Posušje Bos.-Herz. **44** F3
Pota Indon. **108** C2
Potamia Greece **46** D4
Potamos Greece **47** C6
Potamos Greece **46** D2
Poté Brazil **151** D6
Poteau U.S.A. **133** C5
Potegaon India **72** D2
Potentia Italy *see* **Potenza**
Potenza Italy **45** E4
Potenza *r.* Italy **44** D3
Potgietersrus S. Africa **99** F5
Poti *r.* Brazil **150** D3
P'ot'i Georgia **79** E2
Potiraguá Brazil **150** E5
Potiskum Nigeria **93** H3
Potnarvin Vanuatu **107** F3
Poto Peru **148** C3
Po Toi *i.* Hong Kong China **67** [inset]
Potomac *r.* U.S.A. **131** E4
Potomac, South Branch *r.* U.S.A. **130** D4
Potomana, Gunung *mt.* Indon. **108** D2
Potoru Sierra Leone **92** C4
Potosí Bol. **148** D4
Potosí *dept* Bol. **148** D5
Potosi Mountain U.S.A. **137** E4
Potrerillos Chile **152** C1
Potrero del Llano Mex. **135** F7
Potro *r.* Peru **146** B6
Potsdam Germany **37** F2
Potsdam U.S.A. **131** F1
Pottangi India **73** D2
Pottendorf Austria **37** H5
Potter Valley U.S.A. **136** A2
Potterville U.S.A. **130** A2
Pottsville U.S.A. **131** E3
Pouce Coupe Canada **122** F4
Pouch Cove Canada **125** K4
Poughkeepsie U.S.A. **131** G3
Poultney U.S.A. **131** G2
Pouma Cameroon **93** H5
Pouso Alegre Brazil **151** C7
Poutasi Samoa **107** H3
Poŭthĭsăt Cambodia **61** C5
Považská Bystrica Slovakia **37** I4
Povenets Rus. Fed. **28** E3
Poverty Bay N.Z. **113** D2
Povlen *mt.* Serb. and Mont. **46** A2
Póvoa de Varzim Port. **42** B2
Povorino Rus. Fed. **29** G6
Povorotnyy, Mys *hd* Rus. Fed. **64** C4
Powder *r. MT* U.S.A. **134** F3
Powder *r. OR* U.S.A. **134** C3
Powder, South Fork *r.* U.S.A. **134** F4
Powder River U.S.A. **134** F4
Powell U.S.A. **134** E3
Powell *r.* U.S.A. **130** B5
Powell, Lake *resr* U.S.A. **137** G3
Powell Creek *watercourse* Australia **111** E5
Powell River Canada **134** A2
Powhatan U.S.A. **130** E5
Powhatan Point U.S.A. **130** C4
Powidzkie, Jezioro *l.* Poland **37** H2
Powo China **66** A1
Poxoréu Brazil **150** A5
Poyang China *see* **Boyang**
Poyang Hu *l.* China **67** F2
Poyan Reservoir Sing. **58** [inset]
Poyarkovo Rus. Fed. **64** B2
Poyo, Cerro *mt.* Spain **43** E4
Poysdorf Austria **37** H4
Pozantı Turkey **78** C3
Požarevac Serb. and Mont. **46** B2
Poza Rica Mex. **126** G7
Požega Croatia **44** F2
Požega Serb. and Mont. **46** B3
Pozhva Rus. Fed. **28** K4
Poznań Poland **37** H2
Pozo Alcón Spain **42** E4
Pozo Betbeder Arg. **152** D1
Pozoblanco Spain **42** D3
Pozo Colorado Para. **149** F5
Pozo del Tigre Arg. **149** E6
Pozo Hondo Arg. **152** D1
Pozohondo Spain **43** F3
Pozo Nuevo Mex. **135** E7
Pozos, Punta *pt* Arg. **153** D6
Pozsony Slovakia *see* **Bratislava**
Pozuzo Peru **148** B2
Pozzallo *Sicily* Italy **45** E6
Pozzuoli Italy **45** E4
Pra *r.* Ghana **93** E4
Prabumulih Indon. **58** D3
Prabuty Poland **37** I2
Prachatice Czech Rep. **37** G4
Prachi *r.* India **73** E2
Prachin Buri Thai. **61** C5
Prachuap Khiri Khan Thai. **61** B6
Pradairo *mt.* Spain **42** C1
Praděd *mt.* Czech Rep. **37** H3
Prades France **38** E5
Prado Brazil **151** E6

▶**Prague** Czech Rep. **37** G3
Capital of the Czech Republic.

Praha Czech Rep. *see* **Prague**
Prahova *r.* Romania **46** E2

▶**Praia** Cape Verde **92** [inset]
Capital of Cape Verde.

Praia do Bilene Moz. **99** G5
Praia Rica Brazil **149** G3
Prainha *Amazonas* Brazil **149** E1
Prainha *Pará* Brazil **147** H5
Prairie Australia **111** F4
Prairie City U.S.A. **134** C3
Prairie Dog Town Fork *r.* U.S.A. **133** A5
Prairie du Chien U.S.A. **132** D3
Prakhon Chai Thai. **61** C5
Pram *r.* Austria **37** F4
Pramanta Greece **47** B5
Pran *r.* Thai. **61** C5
Pran Buri Thai. **61** B5
Pranhita *r.* India **72** C2
Prapat Indon. **58** B2
Prasonisi, Akra *pt* Greece **47** E7
Praszka Poland **37** I3
Prat *i.* Chile **153** B7
Prata Brazil **149** H4
Prata *r.* Brazil **149** H4
Pratapgarh India **74** B4
Pratas Islands China *see* Dongsha Qundao
Prat de Llobregat Spain *see* El Prat de Llobregat
Prathes Thai *country* Asia *see* **Thailand**
Prato Italy **44** C3
Pratt U.S.A. **132** B4
Prattville U.S.A. **129** B5
Pravara *r.* India **72** B2
Pravdinsk Rus. Fed. **37** J1
Pravia Spain **42** C1
Praya Indon. **59** G5
Preah, Prêk *r.* Cambodia **61** D5
Preăh Vihear Cambodia **61** D5
Prechistoye Rus. Fed. **28** G4
Precipice National Park Australia **111** G5
Predazzo Italy **44** C1
Predeal Romania **46** D2
Preeceville Canada **134** G2
Pré-en-Pail France **38** C2
Preetz Germany **36** E1
Pregolya *r.* Rus. Fed. **37** J1
Preiļi Latvia **33** G4
Prekornica *mts* Serb. and Mont. **46** A3
Prémery France **39** E3
Premnitz Germany **37** F2
Prenj *mts* Bos.-Herz. **44** F3
Prentiss U.S.A. **133** D6
Prenzlau Germany **37** F2
Preobrazheniye Rus. Fed. **64** C4
Preparis Island Cocos Is **61** A5
Preparis North Channel Cocos Is **61** A5
Preparis South Channel Cocos Is **61** A5
Přerov Czech Rep. **37** H4
Presanella, Cima *mt.* Italy **44** C1
Prescott *AR* U.S.A. **133** C5
Prescott *AZ* U.S.A. **137** F4
Prescott Valley U.S.A. **137** F4
Preševo Serb. and Mont. **46** B3
Presidencia Roca Arg. **152** F1
Presidencia Roque Sáenz Peña Arg. **152** E1
Presidente Dutra Brazil **150** C3
Presidente Eduardo Frei *research station* Antarctica **167** A2
Presidente Epitácio Brazil **149** G5
Presidente Hermes Brazil **149** E2
Presidente Juan Perón *prov.* Arg. *see* Chaco
Presidente Olegário Brazil **151** C6
Presidente Prudente Brazil **149** H5
Presidio U.S.A. **135** F7
Preslav Bulg. *see* **Veliki Preslav**
Prešov Slovakia **37** J4
Prespa, Lake Europe **46** B4
Prespansko Ezero *l.* Europe *see* Prespa, Lake
Prespes *nat. park* Greece **46** B4
Prespës, Liqeni i *l.* Europe *see* Prespa, Lake
Presque Isle U.S.A. **128** F2
Pressbaum Austria **37** H4
Pressburg Slovakia *see* **Bratislava**
Prestea Ghana **93** E4
Přeštice Czech Rep. **37** F4
Preston U.K. **35** E5
Preston *ID* U.S.A. **134** E4
Preston *MD* U.S.A. **131** F4
Preston *MN* U.S.A. **132** C3
Preston, Cape Australia **108** B5
Prestonsburg U.S.A. **130** E5
Prestwick U.K. **34** D4
Preto *r. Bahia* Brazil **150** D4
Preto *r. Minas Gerais* Brazil **151** C6
Preto *r. Rondônia* Brazil **149** E2

▶**Pretoria** S. Africa **99** F5
Official capital of South Africa.
world 8–9

Pretoria-Witwatersrand-Vereeniging *prov.* S. Africa *see* **Gauteng**
Preussisch-Eylau Rus. Fed. *see* Bagrationovsk
Preußisch Stargard Poland *see* Starogard Gdański
Preveza Greece **47** B5
Prey Vêng Cambodia **61** D6
Priamurskiy Rus. Fed. **64** C2
Priaral'skiye Karakumy, Peski *des.* Kazakh. **70** B2
Priargunsk Rus. Fed. **63** J1
Pribilof Islands U.S.A. **120** B4
Pribinić Bos.-Herz. **44** F2
Priboj Serb. and Mont. **46** A3
Příbram Czech Rep. **37** G4
Price *r.* Australia **110** B2
Price Canada **125** G3
Price *NC* U.S.A. **130** D5
Price *UT* U.S.A. **137** G2
Price *r.* U.S.A. **137** G2
Prichard *AL* U.S.A. **129** A6
Prichard *WV* U.S.A. **130** B4
Priego de Córdoba Spain **42** D4
Priekule Latvia **33** F4
Priekulė Lith. **33** F5
Prienai Lith. **33** F5
Prieska S. Africa **98** D6
Prieto *hill* Spain **42** E3
Prievidza Slovakia **37** I4
Prijedor Bos.-Herz. **44** F2
Prijepolje Serb. and Mont. **46** A3
Prikaspiyskaya Nizmennost' *lowland* Kazakh./Rus. Fed. *see* **Caspian Lowland**
Prilep Macedonia **46** B4
Priluki Ukr. *see* **Pryluky**
Primavera Bol. **148** D2
Primavera do Leste Brazil **150** A5
Primeira Cruz Brazil **150** D2
Primorsk Rus. Fed. **29** H6
Primorsk Ukr. *see* **Prymors'k**
Primorskiy Kray *admin. div.* Rus. Fed. **64** C3
Primorsko-Akhtarsk Rus. Fed. **29** F7
Primrose Lake Canada **123** I4
Prince Albert Canada **123** J4
Prince Albert Mountains Antarctica **167** H1
Prince Albert National Park Canada **123** J4
Prince Albert Peninsula Canada **121** H2
Prince Albert Road S. Africa **98** D7
Prince Albert Sound *sea chan.* Canada **121** H2
Prince Alfred, Cape Canada **120** G2
Prince Charles Island Canada **121** L3
Prince Charles Mountains Antarctica **167** E2
Prince Edward Island *prov.* Canada **125** I4

▶**Prince Edward Islands** Indian Ocean **163** J9
Part of South Africa.

Prince Edward Point Canada **131** E2
Prince Frederick U.S.A. **131** E4
Prince George Canada **122** F4
Prince Harald Coast Antarctica **167** D2
Prince Karl Foreland *i.* Svalbard *see* Prins Karls Forland
Prince of Wales, Cape U.S.A. **120** C3
Prince of Wales Island Australia **111** E1
Prince of Wales Island Canada **121** J2
Prince of Wales Island U.S.A. **120** F4
Prince of Wales Strait Canada **121** H2
Prince Patrick Island Canada **121** H2
Prince Regent *r.* Australia **108** D3
Prince Regent Inlet *sea chan.* Canada **121** J2
Prince Rupert Canada **122** D4
Princess Anne U.S.A. **131** F4
Princess Astrid Coast Antarctica **167** C2
Princess Charlotte Bay Australia **111** E2
Princess Elizabeth Land *reg.* Antarctica **167** E2
Princess Mary Lake Canada **123** L1
Princess May Range *hills* Australia **108** D3
Princess Ragnhild Coast Antarctica **167** C2
Princess Royal Island Canada **122** D4
Princeton Canada **134** B2
Princeton *CA* U.S.A. **136** A2
Princeton *IL* U.S.A. **132** D3
Princeton *IN* U.S.A. **128** B4
Princeton *KY* U.S.A. **128** B4
Princeton *MO* U.S.A. **132** C3
Princeton *NJ* U.S.A. **131** F3
Prince William Sound *b.* U.S.A. **120** E3
Príncipe *i.* São Tomé and Príncipe **93** G5
Prineville U.S.A. **134** B3
Prinos Greece **46** D4
Prins Karls Forland *i.* Svalbard **26** B2
Prinzapolca Nicaragua **139** H6
Prior, Cabo *c.* Spain **42** B1
Priozersk Rus. Fed. **28** D3
Priozyorsk Rus. Fed. *see* **Priozersk**
Pripet *r.* Belarus/Ukr. **29** C5
also spelt Pryp"yat' (Ukraine) *or* Prypyats' (Belarus)
Pripet Marshes Belarus/Ukr. **29** C6
Pripolyarnyy Ural *mts* Rus. Fed. **28** K2
Prirechnyy Rus. Fed. **32** H1
Priseka *hill* Croatia **44** F2
Priština Serb. and Mont. **46** B3
Prithvipur India **74** C4
Pritzwalk Germany **37** F2
Privas France **39** F4
Privlaka Croatia **44** E2
Privolzhsk Rus. Fed. **28** G4
Privolzhskaya Vozvyshennost' *hills* Rus. Fed. **29** H6
Privolzhskiy Rus. Fed. **29** H6
Privolzh'ye Rus. Fed. **29** I5
Priyutnoye Rus. Fed. **29** G7
Prizren Serb. and Mont. **46** B3
Prizzi *Sicily* Italy **45** D6
Prnjavor Bos.-Herz. **44** F2
Probištip Macedonia **46** C3
Probolinggo Indon. **59** F4
Prochowice Poland **37** H3
Proctorville U.S.A. **130** B4
Proddatur India **72** C3
Proença-a-Nova Port. **42** C3
Professor van Blommestein Meer *resr* Suriname **147** H3
Progreso Hond. **138** G5
Progreso *Coahuila* Mex. **133** A7
Progreso Mex. **127** I7
Progress Rus. Fed. **64** B2
Progresso Brazil **148** C2
Prokhladnyy Rus. Fed. **29** H8
Prokletije *mts* Albania/Serb. and Mont. **46** A3
Prokop'yevsk Rus. Fed. **62** D1
Prokuplje Serb. and Mont. **46** B3
Proletarsk Rus. Fed. **29** G7
Proletarskaya Rus. Fed. *see* **Proletarsk**
Prome Myanmar *see* **Pyè**
Promissão Brazil **149** G4
Promontorio del Gargano *plat.* Italy **44** E4
Pronino Rus. Fed. **28** G4
Prophet *r.* Canada **122** F3
Prophet River Canada **122** F3
Propriá Brazil **150** E4
Proserpine Australia **111** G4
Proskurov Ukr. *see* **Khmel'nyts'kyy**
Prosna *r.* Poland **37** H2
Prosotsani Greece **46** C4
Prospect *NY* U.S.A. **131** F2
Prospect *OH* U.S.A. **130** B3
Prospect *OR* U.S.A. **134** B4
Prospect *PA* U.S.A. **130** C3
Prostějov Czech Rep. **37** H4
Proston Australia **111** G5
Proszowice Poland **37** J3
Proti *i.* Greece **47** B6
Provadiya Bulg. **46** E3
Prøven Greenland *see* **Kangersuatsiaq**
Provence-Alpes-Côte-d'Azur *admin. reg.* France **39** G5
Providence *MD* U.S.A. *see* **Annapolis**

▶**Providence** *RI* U.S.A. **131** H3
State capital of Rhode Island.

Providence, Cape N.Z. **113** A4
Providence Atoll *i.* Seychelles **97** F7
Providencia Ecuador **146** B5
Providencia, Isla de *i.* Caribbean Sea **139** H6
Providência, Serra de *hills* Brazil **149** E2
Provideniya Rus. Fed. **27** S3
Providential Channel Australia **111** E2
Provincetown U.S.A. **131** H2
Provincia Col. **146** C3
Provins France **39** E2
Provo U.S.A. **137** G1
Provost Canada **123** I4
Prrenjas Albania **46** B4
Pru *r.* Ghana **93** E3
Prub *r.* Rus. Fed. **28** J3
Prudentópolis Brazil **151** B8
Prudhoe Bay U.S.A. **120** E2
Prudhoe Island Australia **111** G4
Prudnik Poland **37** H3
Prüm Germany **36** C3
Prundeni Romania **46** D2
Prundu Romania **46** E2
Pruntytown U.S.A. **130** C4
Prusa Turkey *see* **Bursa**
Prushkov Poland *see* **Pruszków**
Pruszcz Gdański Poland **37** I1
Pruszków Poland **37** J2
Prut *r.* Europe **46** F2
Prydz Bay Antarctica **167** E2
Pryelbrusskiy Natsional'nyy Park *nat. park* Rus. Fed. **79** E2
Pryluky Ukr. **29** E6
Prymors'k Ukr. **29** F7
Prymors'ke Ukr. **46** F2
Pryp"yat' *r.* Ukr. *see* **Pripet**
Prypyats' *r.* Belarus **29** C5 *see* **Pripet**
Przasnysz Poland **37** J2
Przedbórz Poland **37** I3
Przemyśl Poland **31** J3
Przheval'sk Kyrg. *see* **Karakol**
Przysucha Poland **37** J3
Psachna Greece **47** C5
Psakhná Greece *see* **Psachna**
Psara Greece **47** D5
Psara *i.* Greece **47** D5
Psathoura *i.* Greece **47** D5
Psebay Rus. Fed. **79** E1
Pserimos *i.* Greece **47** E6
Pskov Rus. Fed. **28** D4
Pskov, Lake Estonia/Rus. Fed. **28** C4
Pskov Oblast *admin. div.* Rus. Fed. *see* Pskovskaya Oblast'
Pskovskaya Oblast' *admin. div.* Rus. Fed. **28** D4
Pskovskoye Ozero *l.* Estonia/Rus. Fed. *see* **Pskov, Lake**
Psunj *mts* Croatia **44** F2
Ptolemaida Greece **46** B4
Ptolemais Israel *see* **'Akko**
Ptuj Slovenia **44** E1
Pu *r.* Indon. **58** C3
Puaka *hill* Sing. **58** [inset]
Pu'an *Guizhou* China **66** C3
Pu'an *Sichuan* China *see* **Jiange**
Pucacuro Peru **146** C5
Pucacuro *r.* Peru **146** C5
Pucalá Peru **146** B6
Pucallpa Peru **148** B2
Pucará Bol. **149** D4
Pucarani Bol. **148** C4
Puca Urco Peru **146** D5
Pucheng *Fujian* China **67** F3
Pucheng *Shaanxi* China **67** D1
Puchezh Rus. Fed. **28** G4
Puch'ŏn S. Korea **65** A5
Pucioasa Romania **46** D2
Puck Poland **37** I1
Pucka, Zatoka *b.* Poland **37** I1
Puçol Spain **43** F3
Pucón Chile **152** C4
Pudai *watercourse* Afgh. *see* **Dor**
Pūdanū Iran **80** C3
Pudasjärvi Fin. **32** G2
Puding China **66** C3
Pudozh Rus. Fed. **28** F3
Puducheri *Pondicherry* India *see* **Pondicherry**
Puduchcheri India *see* **Pondicherry**
Pudukkottai India **72** C4
Puebla *Baja California* Mex. **137** E5
Puebla Mex. **126** G8
Puebla de Don Fadrique Spain **43** E4
Puebla de Obando Spain **42** C3
Puebla de Zaragoza Mex. *see* **Puebla**
Pueblo U.S.A. **135** F5
Pueblo Hundido Chile **152** C1
Pueblo Viejo Col. **146** E4
Pueblo Yaqui Mex. **135** E8
Puech de Rouet *hill* France **38** E4
Puelches Arg. **152** D4
Puelén Arg. **152** D4
Puenteareas Spain *see* **Ponteareas**
Puente del Inca Arg. **152** C3
Puente-Genil Spain **42** D4
Puente la Reina Spain **43** F1
Puentes de García Rodríguez Spain *see* As Pontes de García Rodríguez
Puente Torres Venez. **146** D2
Pu'er China **66** B4
Puerco *watercourse AZ* U.S.A. **137** G4
Puerco *watercourse NM* U.S.A. **135** F6
Puerto Aisén Chile **153** B6
Puerto Alejandría Bol. **148** D3
Puerto Alfonso Col. **146** D5
Puerto America Peru **146** B6
Puerto Ángel Mex. **138** E5
Puerto Antequera Para. **149** F6
Puerto Armuelles Panama **139** H7
Puerto Asís Col. **146** B4
Puerto Ayacucho Venez. **146** E3
Puerto Bajo Pisagua Chile **153** B6
Puerto Barrios Guat. **138** G5
Puerto Berrío Col. **146** C3
Puerto Boyaca Col. **146** C3
Puerto Cabello Venez. **146** D2
Puerto Cabezas Nicaragua **139** H6
Puerto Carreño Col. **146** E3
Puerto Casado Para. **149** F5
Puerto Cavinas Bol. **148** D3
Puerto Cerpera Peru **146** C5
Puerto Ceticayo Peru **148** C2
Puerto Chacabuco Chile **153** B6
Puerto Chicama Peru **148** A1
Puerto Cisnes Chile **153** B6
Puerto Coig Arg. **153** C7
Puerto Córdoba Col. **146** D5
Puerto Cortés Costa Rica **139** H7
Puerto Cortés Mex. **126** D7
Puerto Cumarebo Venez. **146** D2
Puerto de Cabras Canary Is *see* Puerto del Rosario
Puerto Definitivo Peru **148** C3
Puerto del Rosario Canary Is **90** B3
Puerto del Son Spain *see* **Porto do Son**
Puerto de Nutrias Venez. **146** D2
Puerto de Pollensa Spain *see* Port de Pollença
Puerto Escondido Mex. **138** E5
Puerto Estrella Col. **146** D1
Puerto Flamenco Chile **152** C1
Puerto Francisco de Orellana Ecuador **146** B5
Puerto Génova Bol. **148** D3
Puerto Grether Bol. **149** D4
Puerto Guarani Para. **149** F5
Puerto Harberton Arg. **153** D8
Puerto Heath Bol. **148** C3
Puerto Huitoto Col. **146** C4
Puerto Ingeniero Ibáñez Chile **153** B6
Puerto Inírida Col. **146** E4
Puerto Isabel Bol. **149** F4
Puerto La Paz Arg. **149** E5
Puerto Leguízamo Col. **146** C5
Puerto Lempira Hond. **139** H5
Puerto Libertad Mex. **135** D7
Puertollano Spain **42** D3
Puerto Lobos Arg. **153** D5
Puerto Lopez Col. **146** D2
Puerto Lopéz Col. **146** C3
Puerto López Ecuador **146** A5
Puerto Lumbreras Spain **43** F4
Puerto Madryn Arg. **153** D5
Puerto Maldonado Peru **148** C3
Puerto Mamoré Bol. **148** D4
Puerto Máncora Peru **146** A6
Puerto María Auxiliadora Para. **149** F5
Puerto Marquez Bol. **148** D3
Puerto Melinka Chile **153** B5
Puerto México Mex. *see* **Coatzacoalcos**
Puerto Miranda Venez. **146** E3
Puerto Montt Chile **153** B5
Puerto Natales Chile **153** B7
Puerto Nuevo Col. **146** D3
Puerto Ordaz Venez. **147** F2
Puerto Ospina Col. **146** C4
Puerto Páez Venez. **146** E3
Puerto Pando Bol. **148** D3
Puerto Pardo Peru **146** B5
Puerto Peñasco Mex. **135** D7
Puerto Pirámides Arg. **153** D5
Puerto Píritu Venez. **147** E2
Puerto Pizarro Col. **146** C5
Puerto Plata Dom. Rep. **127** L8
Puerto Portillo Peru **148** B2
Puerto Prado Peru **148** B2
Puerto Presidente Stroessner Para. *see* **Ciudad del Este**
Puerto Princesa Phil. **56** E4
Puerto Quepos Costa Rica **139** H7
Puerto Real Spain **42** C4
Puerto Rico Arg. **152** G1
Puerto Rico Bol. **148** D2
Puerto Rico Col. **146** C4

▶**Puerto Rico** *terr.* West Indies **139** K5
United States Commonwealth.
northamerica 118–119, 140

▶**Puerto Rico Trench** *sea feature* Caribbean Sea **160** J4
Deepest trench in the Atlantic Ocean.

Puerto Saavedra Chile **152** B4
Puerto Salgar Col. **146** C3
Puerto San Agustin Peru **146** D5
Puerto San Carlos Chile **153** B6
Puerto San José Guat. **138** F6
Puerto Santa Cruz Arg. **153** C7
Puerto Sastre Para. **149** F5
Puerto Saucedo Bol. **149** E3
Puertos de Beceite *mts* Spain *see* Ports de Beseit
Puerto Siles Bol. **148** D3
Puerto Socorro Peru **146** D5
Puerto Suárez Bol. **149** F4
Puerto Tahuantisuyo Peru **148** C3
Puerto Tejado Col. **146** B4
Puerto Tunigrama Peru **146** B5
Puerto Vallarta Mex. **126** E7
Puerto Varas Chile **153** B5
Puerto Victoria Peru **148** B2
Puerto Villazon Bol. **149** E3
Puerto Visser Arg. **153** D6
Puerto Wilches Col. **146** C3
Puerto Yartou Chile **153** C8
Pugachev Rus. Fed. **29** I5
Pugachevo Rus. Fed. **28** J4
Pugal India **74** B3
Puga Puga, Ilha *i.* Moz. **99** H3
Puge China **66** B3
Puglia *admin. reg.* Italy **44** E4
Pugwash Canada **125** I4
Pūhāl-e Khamīr, Kūh-e *mts* Iran **80** C5
Puhiwaero *c.* N.Z. *see* **South West Cape**
Puhja Estonia **33** G4
Pui Romania **46** C2
Puigmal *mt.* France/Spain **43** H1
Pui O Wan *b.* Hong Kong China **67** [inset]
Puiseaux France **39** E2
Puits 29 *well* Chad **88** C6
Puits 30 *well* Chad **88** C6
Puji China *see* **Wugong**
Pujiang China **67** F2
Pukaki, Lake N.Z. **113** B4
Puk'an-san National Park S. Korea **65** A5
Pukapuka *atoll* Cook Is **165** G6
Pukaskwa National Park Canada **124** C3
Pukatawagan Canada **123** K4
Pukch'ŏng N. Korea **65** B4
Pukë Albania **46** A3
Pukekohe N.Z. **113** C2
Puketeraki Range *mts* N.Z. **113** C3
Pukeuri Junction N.Z. **113** B4
Puksoozero Rus. Fed. **28** G3
Puksubaek-san *mt.* N. Korea **65** A4
Pula China *see* **Nyingchi**
Pula Croatia **44** D2
Pula *Sardinia* Italy **45** B5
Pulangpisau Indon. **59** F3
Pular, Cerro *mt.* Chile **148** C6
Pulaski *NY* U.S.A. **131** E2
Pulaski *TN* U.S.A. **128** B5
Pulaski *VA* U.S.A. **130** C5
Pulau *r.* Indon. **57** I7
Pulau Pinang *state* Malaysia *see* **Pinang**
Puławy Poland **37** J3
Pulheim Germany **36** C3
Pulicat India **72** D3
Pulicat Lake *inlet* India **72** D3
Pulivendla India **72** C3
Pulkau *r.* Austria **37** H4
Pulkkila Fin. **32** G2
Pulo Anna *i.* Palau **57** H5
Pulog, Mount Phil. **57** F2
Pułtusk Poland **37** J2
Pulu China **75** D1
Pülümür Turkey **79** D3
Puma Yumco *l.* China **75** F3
Pumiao China *see* **Yongning**
Pumpkin Creek *r.* U.S.A. **134** F3
Puná, Isla *i.* Ecuador **146** A5
Puna de Atacama *plat.* Arg. **152** D1
Punakha Bhutan **75** F4
Punata Bol. **148** D4
Punch Pak. **74** B2
Punchaw Canada **122** F4
Punda Maria S. Africa **99** F4
Pundri India **74** C3
Pune India **72** B2
Punganuru India **72** C3
Punggol Sing. **58** [inset]
Punggol, Sungai *r.* Sing. **58** [inset]
Púnguè *r.* Moz. **99** G3
Punia Dem. Rep. Congo **94** E5
Puning China **67** F4
Punitaqui Chile **152** C2
Punjab *state* India **74** B3
Punjab *prov.* Pak. **81** G4
Punmah Glacier China/Jammu and Kashmir **74** C2
Puno Peru **148** C3
Puno *dept* Peru **148** C3
Punpun *r.* India **75** E4
Punta, Cerro de *mt.* Puerto Rico **139** K5
Punta Alta Arg. **152** E4
Punta Arenas Chile **153** C8
Punta Balestrieri *mt. Sardinia* Italy **45** B4
Punta de Bombón Peru **148** C4
Punta de Díaz Chile **152** C2
Punta Delgada Arg. **153** E5
Punta de los Llanos Arg. **152** D2
Punta Gorda Belize **138** G5
Punta Negra, Salar *salt flat* Chile **148** C6
Punta Prieta Mex. **135** D7
Puntarenas Costa Rica **139** H6
Punta Umbría Spain **42** C4
Punto Fijo Venez. **146** D2
Puntón de Guara *mt.* Spain **43** F1
Punxsutawney U.S.A. **130** D3
Puolanka Fin. **32** G2
Puquio Peru **148** B3
Pur *r.* Rus. Fed. **26** H3
Puracé, Parque Nacional *nat. park* Col. **146** B4
Puranpur India **74** D3
Purari *r.* P.N.G. **57** J7
Purbalingga Indon. **59** E4
Purcell U.S.A. **133** B5
Purcell Mountains Canada **134** C2
Purcellville U.S.A. **130** E4
Purén Chile **152** B4
Purgatoire *r.* U.S.A. **132** A4
Puri India **73** E2
Purmerend Neth. **36** B2
Purna India **72** C2
Purna *r. Maharashtra* India **72** C2
Purna *r. Maharashtra* India **74** C5
Purnabhaba *r.* India **75** F4
Purnea India *see* **Purnia**
Purnia India **75** E4
Purnululu National Park Australia **108** E4
Purranque Chile **152** B5
Pursat Cambodia *see* **Poŭthĭsăt**
Puruê *r.* Brazil **146** D5
Purukcahu Indon. **59** F3
Puruliya India **75** E5

▶**Purus** *r.* Peru **147** F5
3rd longest river in South America.
southamerica 142–143

Puruvesi *l.* Fin. **33** H3
Purvomay Bulg. **46** D3
Purwakarta Indon. **59** D4
Purwareja Indon. **59** E4
Purwodadi Indon. **59** E4
Purwokerto Indon. **59** E4
Puryŏng N. Korea **64** B4
Pus *r.* India **72** C2
Pusa *r.* Spain **42** D3
Pusad India **72** C2
Pusan S. Korea **65** B5
Pusatdamai Indon. **59** E2
Pusatlı Dağı *mt.* Turkey **77** A1
Pushemskiy Rus. Fed. **28** H3
Pushkar India **74** B4
Pushkin Rus. Fed. **28** D4
Pushkino Azer. *see* **Biläsuvar**
Pushkino Rus. Fed. **29** H6
Pushkinskaya, Gora *mt.* Rus. Fed. **64** E3
Pusht-i Āsmān *spring* Iran **80** D3
Püspökladány Hungary **37** J5
Pusti Lisac *mt.* Serb. and Mont. **46** A3
Pustoshka Rus. Fed. **31** L1
Pusur *r.* Bangl. **75** F5
Puszcza Natecka *for.* Poland **37** G2
Putahow Lake Canada **123** K3
Putao Myanmar **60** B2
Putbus Germany **37** F1
Puteoli Italy *see* **Pozzuoli**
Puthein Myanmar *see* **Bassein**
Putian China **67** F3
Putignano Italy **45** F4
Putina Peru **148** C3
Puting China *see* **De'an**
Puting, Tanjung *pt* Indon. **59** E3
Putlitz Germany **36** F2
Putna *r.* Romania **46** E2
Putnam U.S.A. **131** H3
Putney U.S.A. **131** G2
Putoi *i.* Hong Kong China *see* **Po Toi**
Putorana, Gory *mts* Rus. Fed. **27** J3

▶**Putrajaya** Malaysia **58** C2
Administrative capital of Malaysia.

Putre Chile **148** C4
Putsonderwater S. Africa **98** D6
Puttalam Sri Lanka **72** C4
Puttalam Lagoon Sri Lanka **72** C4
Puttgarden Germany **36** E1
Puttur India **72** B3
Putubumba Dem. Rep. Congo **95** C6
Putumayo *dept* Col. **146** C4
Putumayo *r.* Col. **146** D5
Pütürge Turkey **79** D3
Putusibau Indon. **59** F2
Puula *l.* Fin. **33** G3
Puumala Fin. **33** H3
Puuwai U.S.A. **135** [inset] Y1
Puvurnituq Canada **121** L3
Puyallup U.S.A. **134** B3
Puyang *Henan* China **63** J4
Puyang *Zhejiang* China *see* **Pujiang**
Puy de Dôme *mt.* France **39** E4
Puy de Montoncel *mt.* France **39** E4
Puy de Sancy *mt.* France **39** E4
Puyehue, Parque Nacional *nat. park* Chile **152** C5
Puy Gris *mt.* France **39** G4
Puyo Ecuador **146** B5
Puysegur Point N.Z. **113** A4
Puzol Spain *see* **Puçol**
Pwani *admin. reg.* Tanz. **97** C6
Pweto Dem. Rep. Congo **95** F7
Pwllheli U.K. **35** D5
Pyalitsa Rus. Fed. **28** F2
Pyal'ma Rus. Fed. **28** E3
Pyamalaw *r.* Myanmar **61** A5
Pyandzh *r.* Afgh./Tajik. **81** G2
Pyandzh *Khatlon* Tajik. *see* **Dusti**
Pyandzh *Khatlon* Tajik. *see* **Panj**
Pyaozero, Ozero *l.* Rus. Fed. **32** H2
Pyaozerskiy Rus. Fed. **32** H2
Pyapon Myanmar **61** A4

Pyasina r. Rus. Fed. 27 I2
Pyasino, Ozero l. Rus. Fed. 27 I3
Pyasinskiy Zaliv b. Rus. Fed. 27 I2
Pyatigorsk Rus. Fed. 29 G7
Pyatikhatki Ukr. see P"yatykhatky
Pyatimar Kazakh. see Pyatimarskoye
Pyatimarskoye Kazakh. 29 I6
P"yatykhatky Ukr. 29 E6
Pyaunglaung r. Myanmar 60 B4
Pyawbwe Myanmar 60 B3
Pyè Myanmar 60 A4
Pye, Mount N.Z. 113 B4
Pyetrykaw Belarus 29 D5
Pygmalion Point India 73 G5
Pyhäjärvi l. Fin. 32 G3
Pyhäjärvi l. Fin. 32 G3
Pyhäjärvi l. Fin. 33 F3
Pyhäjärvi l. Fin. 33 H3
Pyhäjoki Fin. 32 G2
Pyhäjoki r. Fin. 32 G2
Pyhäntä Fin. 32 G2
Pyhäranta Fin. 33 F3
Pyhäsalmi Fin. 32 G3
Pyhäselkä Fin. 32 H3
Pyhäselkä l. Fin. 32 H3
Pyhätunturin kansallispuisto nat. park Fin. 32 G2
Pyhtää Fin. 33 G3
Pyin Myanmar see Pyè
Pyingaing Myanmar 60 A3
Pyinmana Myanmar 60 B4
Pyli Greece 47 E6
Pyl'karamo Rus. Fed. 26 I3
Pylos Greece 47 B6
Pymatuning Reservoir U.S.A. 130 C3
Pyŏksŏng N. Korea 65 A5
Pyŏktong N. Korea 65 A4
P'yŏnggang N. Korea 65 A5
P'yŏngsong N. Korea 65 A5
P'yŏngt'aek S. Korea 65 A5

▶P'yŏngyang N. Korea 65 A5
Capital of North Korea.

Pyŏnsan Bando National Park S. Korea 65 A6
Pyramid Lake U.S.A. 136 C1
Pyramid Range mts U.S.A. 136 C2
▶Pyramids of Giza tourist site Egypt 89 F2 africa 86–87
Pyrenees mts Europe 43 H1
Pyrénées mts Europe see Pyrenees
Pyrénées Occidentales, Parc National des nat. park France/Spain 43 F1
Pyrgetos Greece 47 C5
Pyrgi Greece 47 D5
Pyrgos Greece 47 B6
Pyryatyn Ukr. 29 E6
Pyrzyce Poland 37 G2
Pyshchug Rus. Fed. 28 H4
Pyszna r. Poland 37 I3
Pytalovo Rus. Fed. 28 C4
Pyu Myanmar 60 B4
Pyxaria mt. Greece 47 C5

Q

Qā', Wādī al watercourse Saudi Arabia 89 I3
Qaa Lebanon 77 C2
Qaanaaq Greenland see Thule
Qābil Oman 76 F5
Qabka China see Xaitongmoin
Qabnag China 75 G3
Qabqa China see Gonghe
Qabr Bandar tourist site Iraq 79 E5
Qacentina Alg. see Constantine
Qacha's Nek Lesotho 99 F6
Qadamgāl Iran 81 D2
Qādes Afgh. 81 E3
Qaḍimah Saudi Arabia 89 H4
Qādir Karam Iraq 79 F4
Qādisīyah, Sadd dam Iraq 79 E4
Qadisiyah Dam Iraq see Qādisīyah, Sadd
Qā'emiyeh Iran 80 B4
Qagan Nur China 63 I3
Qagan Nur l. China 64 A3
Qagan Tohoi China 75 G2
Qagan Us China see Dulan
Qagca China 66 A1
Qagchêng China see Xiangcheng
Qā' Ḩaẕawẕā' depr. Saudi Arabia 89 H2
Qahd, Wādī watercourse Saudi Arabia 89 I3
Qahremānshahr Iran see Kermānshāh
Qaidam He r. China 75 G1
Qaidam Pendi basin China 70 H4
Qainaqangma China 75 F2
Qaisar Afgh. 81 F3
Qaisar r. Afgh. 81 F2
Qaisar, Koh-i- mt. Afgh. 81 F3
Qalā Diza Iraq 79 F3
Qala'en Nahl Sudan 89 G6
Qala-i-Fateh Afgh. 81 E4
Qala-i-Kang Afgh. 81 E4
Qal'aikhum Tajik. 81 G2
Qalamat ar Rakabah oasis Saudi Arabia 76 E5
Qalamat Fāris oasis Saudi Arabia 76 E6
Qalansīyah Yemen 76 E7
Qala Shinia Takht Afgh. 81 F3
Qalāt Afgh. 81 F3
Qal'at al Azlam Saudi Arabia 89 G3
Qal'at al Ḩiṣn tourist site Syria 77 C2
Qal'at al Marqab tourist site Syria 77 B2
Qal'at al Mu'aẓẓam Saudi Arabia 89 H3
Qal'at Bīshah Saudi Arabia 89 I4
Qal'at Muqaybirah, Jabal mt. Syria 77 D2
Qal'at Ṣāliḩ Iraq 79 F5
Qala Vali Afgh. 81 E3
Qal'eh Iran 80 C2
Qal'eh Dāgh mt. Iran 80 A2
Qal 'eh-ye Bost Afgh. 81 F4
Qal 'eh-ye Now Afgh. 81 E3
Qalīb Bāqūr well Iraq 79 F5
Qalqīlya West Bank 77 B3
Qalti el Adusa well Sudan 89 E5
Qalyūb Egypt 78 B5
Qalyūbīyah governorate Egypt 78 B5
Qamalung China 66 A1
Qamanirjuaq Lake Canada 123 M2
Qamanittuaq Canada see Baker Lake
Qamar, Ghubbat al b. Yemen 76 E6
Qamar Bay Yemen see Qamar, Ghubbat al
Qamashi Uzbek. see Kamashi
Qamdo China 66 A2
Qam Hadīl Saudi Arabia 89 I5
Qamīnis Libya 88 C2
Qamruddin Karez Pak. 81 G4
Qamṣar Iran 80 B3
Qandahar Afgh. see Kandahār
Qandala Somalia 96 F2
Qandaranbashi mt. Iran 80 A2
Qandyaghash Kazakh. see Kandyagash
Qangzê China 74 C3
Qapshagay Kazakh. see Kapchagay
Qapshagay Bögeni resr Kazakh. see Kapchagayskoye Vodokhranilishche
Qaqortoq Greenland 121 O3
Qara Āghach r. Iran see Mand, Rūd-e
Qarabutaq Kazakh. see Karabutak
Qaraçala Azer. 80 B2
Qarachōq, Jabal mts Iraq 79 E4
Qara Ertis r. China/Kazakh. see Ertix He
Qaraghandy Kazakh. see Karaganda
Qaraghayly Kazakh. see Karagayly
Qārah Egypt 78 A5
Qārah Saudi Arabia 89 I2
Qārah, Jabal al hill Saudi Arabia 76 C6
Qarah Bāgh Ghaznī Afgh. 81 G3
Qarah Bāgh Kābul Afgh. 81 G3
Qaraköl Kazakh. see Karakol'
Qaranqu r. Iran 80 A2
Qaraqum des. Kazakh. see Karakum Desert
Qaraqum des. Turkm. see Karakum Desert
Qara Şū Chāy r. Syria/Turkey see Karasu
Qara Tarai mt. Afgh. 81 F3
Qarataū Kazakh. see Karatau
Qarataū Zhotasy mts Kazakh. see Karatau, Khrebet
Qaratöbe Kazakh. see Karatobe
Qaraton Kazakh. see Karaton
Qardho Somalia 96 F2
Qardud Sudan 94 F2
Qareh Chāy r. Iran 80 B3
Qareh Dāgh mts Iran 80 A2
Qareh Qāch, Kūh-e mts Iran 80 C3
Qareh Sū r. Iran 80 A2
Qarhan China 75 G1
Qarkilik China see Ruoqiang
Qarn al Kabsh, Jabal mt. Egypt 89 G2
Qarnayṭ, Jabal hill Saudi Arabia 89 I4
Qarokŭl l. Tajik. 81 H2
Qarqan China see Qiemo
Qarqan He r. China 70 G4
Qarqaraly Kazakh. see Karkaralinsk
Qarqīn Afgh. 81 F2
Qarrit, Qafa e pass Albania 46 B4
Qarshi Uzbek. see Karshi
Qarshi Chŭli plain Uzbek. see Karshinskaya Step'
Qartaba Lebanon 77 B2
Qārūh, Jazīrat i. Kuwait 79 G5
Qārūn, Birkat l. Egypt 89 F2
Qaryat al Ulyā Saudi Arabia 80 A5
Qasamī Iran 80 D3
Qasa Murg mts Afgh. 81 E3
Qasba India 75 E4
Qāsemābād Khorāsan Iran 80 D3
Qāsemābād Khorāsan Iran 81 D2
Qashqadaryo r. Uzbek. see Kashkadar'ya
Qashqadaryo Wiloyati admin. div. Uzbek. see Kashkadar'inskaya Oblast'
Qasigiannguit Greenland 121 N3
Qaşr al Azraq Jordan 77 C4
Qaşr al Farāfirah Egypt 89 E3
Qasr al Ḩayr tourist site Syria 77 C2
Qasr al Khubbāz Iraq 79 E4
Qaşr 'Amrah tourist site Jordan 77 C4
Qaşr aş Şabīyah Kuwait 79 G5
Qaşr Burqu' tourist site Jordan 77 C3
Qaşr-e-Qand Iran 81 E5
Qaşr-e Shīrīn Iran 79 F4
Qaşr Larocu Libya 88 B3
Qaşr Shaqrah tourist site Iraq 79 F5
Qaţanā Syria 77 C3
▶Qatar country Asia 80 B5 asia 52–53, 82
Qatlish Iran 80 D2
Qaţrānī, Jabal esc. Egypt 89 F2
Qaţrūyeh Iran 80 C4
Qattara Depression Egypt 89 E2
Qaţţārah, Munkhafaḑ al Egypt see Qattara Depression
Qaţţārah, Ra's esc. Egypt 89 E2
Qaţţinah, Buḩayrat resr Syria 77 C2
Qavāmābād Iran 80 D4
Qax Azer. 79 F2
Qāyen Iran 81 D3
Qaynar Kazakh. see Kaynar
Qayroqqum Tajik. 81 G1
Qaysīyah, Qa' al imp. l. Jordan 77 C4
Qayyārah Iraq 79 E4
Qazaq Shyghanaghy b. Kazakh. see Kazakhskiy Zaliv
Qazaqstan country Asia see Kazakhstan
Qazax Azer. 79 F2
Qazımämmäd Azer. 79 G2
Qazvīn Iran 80 B2
Qazvin prov. Iran 80 B2
Qelelevu i. Fiji 107 H3
Qena Egypt see Qinā
Qeqertarsuaq Greenland 121 N3
Qeqertarsuaq i. Greenland 121 N3
Qeqertarsuatsiaat Greenland 121 N3
Qeqertarsuup Tunua b. Greenland 121 N3
Qeshlāq Iran 80 A3
Qeshm Iran 80 D5
Qeshm i. Iran 80 D5
Qeydār Iran 80 B2
Qeys i. Iran 80 C5
Qezel Owzan, Rūdkhāneh-ye r. Iran 80 B2
Qeẕi'ot Israel 77 B4
Qian r. China 66 C1
Qiancheng China 67 D3
Qiang r. China 67 F1
Qian Gorlos China see Qianguozhen
Qianguozhen China 64 A3
Qianjiang Chongqing China 67 D2
Qianjiang Hubei China 67 E2
Qianjin China 64 C3
Qianjin China 66 B2
Qianshan China 67 F2
Qianwei China 66 B2
Qianxi China 66 C3
Qianxian China 66 D1
Qianyang Hunan China 67 D3
Qianyang Shaanxi China 66 C1
Qianyang Zhejiang China 67 F2
Qianyou China see Zhashui
Qiaojia China 66 B3
Qiaotou China 66 B3
Qiaowa China see Muli
Qibā' Saudi Arabia 89 J3
Qibing S. Africa 99 E6
Qichun China 67 E2
Qidong Hunan China 67 E3
Qidong Jiangsu China 67 G2
Qiemo China 70 G4
Qijiang China 66 C2
Qijiaojing China 70 H3
Qikiqtarjuaq Canada 121 M3
Qila Ladgasht Pak. 81 E5
Qila Safed Pak. 81 E4
Qila Saifullah Pak. 81 G4
Qili China see Shitai
Qilian Shan mts China 70 I4
Qillak i. Greenland 121 P3
Qimantag mts China 75 F1
Qimen China 67 F2
Qimusseriarsuaq b. Greenland 121 M2
Qinā Egypt 89 G3
Qinā, Wādī watercourse Egypt 89 G3
Qin'an China 66 C1
Qincheng China see Nanfeng
Qing r. China 64 A4
Qing'an China 64 A3
Qingdao China 63 K4
Qinggang China 64 A3
Qingguandu China 67 D2
Qinghai prov. China 70 I4
Qinghai Hu salt l. China 70 J4
Qinghai Nanshan mts China 70 I4
Qingjiang Jiangsu China see Huaiyin
Qingjiang Jiangxi China see Zhangshu
Qing Jiang r. China 67 D2
Qingliu China 67 F3
Qingpu China 67 G2
Qingquan China see Xishui
Qingshan China see Dedu
Qingshuihe China 66 A1
Qingshuilang Shan mts China 66 A3
Qingtian China 67 G2
Qingyang Anhui China 67 F2
Qingyang Jiangsu China see Sihong
Qingyuan Gansu China see Weiyuan
Qingyuan Guangdong China 67 E4
Qingyuan Guangxi China see Yizhou
Qingyuan Liaoning China 64 A4
Qingyuan Zhejiang China 67 F3
Qingzang Gaoyuan plat. China see Tibet, Plateau of
Qingzhen China 66 C3
Qingzhou China 67 D2
Qinhuangdao China 63 J4
Qinjiang China see Shicheng
Qin Ling mts China 67 C1
Qinting China see Lianhua
Qinzhou China 67 D4
Qinzhou Wan b. China 67 D4
Qionghai China 67 D5
Qiongjiexue China see Qonggyai
Qionglai China 66 B2
Qionglai Shan mts China 66 B2
Qiongshan China 67 D5
Qiongxi China see Hongyuan
Qiongzhou Haixia strait China see Hainan Strait
Qiqihar China 63 K2
Qīr Iran 80 C4
Qira China 74 D1
Qiryat Gat Israel 77 B4
Qiryat Shemona Israel 77 B3
Qishan China see Qimen
Qishn Yemen 76 E6
Qishon r. Israel 77 B3
Qishrān Island Saudi Arabia 89 I4
Qitab ash Shāmah vol. crater Saudi Arabia 89 H2
Qitaihe China 64 B3
Qiubei China 66 C3
Qiujin China 67 E2
Qixian China 67 E1
Qixing r. China 64 C3
Qiyang China 67 D3
Qizhou Liedao i. China 67 D5
Qızılağac Körfäzi b. Azer. 80 B2
Qizil-Art, Aghbai pass Kyrg./Tajik. see Kyzylart Pass
Qogir Feng mt. China/Jammu and Kashmir see K2
Qojūr Iran 80 A2
Qom Iran 80 B3
Qom prov. Iran 80 B3
Qomdo China see Qumdo
Qomisheh Iran 80 B3
Qomolangma Feng mt. China/Nepal see Everest, Mount
Qonaqkänd Azer. 79 G2
Qonggyai China 75 F3
Qongrat Uzbek. see Kungrad
Qooriga Neegro b. Somalia 96 F3
Qoornoq Greenland 121 N3
Qoqek China see Tacheng
Qornet es Saouda mt. Lebanon 77 C2
Qorowulbozor Uzbek. see Karaulbazar
Qoroy, Gardaneh-ye pass Iran 80 B2
Qorveh Iran 80 A3
Qosh Tepe Iraq 79 E3
Qosshaghyl Kazakh. see Koschagyl
Qostanay Kazakh. see Kostanay
Qoţbābād Iran 80 D5
Qoţūr Iran 79 F3
Quabbin Reservoir U.S.A. 131 G2
Quadra Island Canada 122 E5
Quadros, Lago dos l. Brazil 151 B9
Quail Mountains U.S.A. 137 D4
Quairading Australia 109 B8
Quakenbrück Germany 36 C2
Quamby Australia 111 E4
Quanah U.S.A. 133 B5
Quanbao Shan mt. China 67 D1
Quân Đao Cô Tô is Vietnam 60 D3
Quan Dao Hoang Sa is S. China Sea see Paracel Islands
Quân Đao Nam Du i. Vietnam 61 D6
Quan Dao Truong Sa is S. China Sea see Spratly Islands
Quang Ngai Vietnam 61 E5
Quang Tri Vietnam 60 D4
Quan He r. China 67 E1
Quanjiang China see Suichuan
Quan Long Vietnam see Ca Mau
Quannan China 67 E3
Quan Phu Quoc i. Vietnam see Phu Quốc, Đao
Quanshang China 67 F3
Quanwan Hong Kong China see Tsuen Wan
Quanzhou Fujian China 67 F3
Quanzhou Guangxi China 67 D3
Qu'Appelle r. Canada 134 G2
Quaqtaq Canada 121 M3
Quaraí Brazil 152 F2
Quarry Bay Hong Kong China 67 [inset]
Quarryville U.S.A. 131 E4
Quarteira Port. 42 B4
Quartu Sant'Elena Sardinia Italy 45 B5
Quartzite Mountain U.S.A. 137 D3
Quartzsite U.S.A. 137 E5
Quaryat al Faw tourist site Saudi Arabia 76 D6
Quba Azer. 79 G2
Quchan Iran 81 D2
Queanbeyan Australia 112 D4

▶Québec Canada 125 G4
Provincial capital of Québec.

Québec prov. Canada 125 F2
Quedas Moz. 99 G3
Quedlinburg Germany 36 E3
Queen Adelaide Islands Chile see La Reina Adelaida, Archipiélago de
Queen Alia airport Jordan 77 B4
Queen Charlotte Canada 122 C4
Queen Charlotte Bay Falkland Is 153 E7
Queen Charlotte Islands Canada 122 C4
Queen Charlotte Sound sea chan. Canada 122 D5
Queen Charlotte Strait Canada 122 E5
Queen Elizabeth Islands Canada 121 I2
Queen Elizabeth National Park Uganda 96 A5
Queen Mary Land reg. Antarctica 167 F2
Queen Maud Gulf Canada 121 I3
Queen Maud Land reg. Antarctica 167 B2
Queen Maud Land reg. Antarctica 167 O10
Queen Maud Mountains Antarctica 167 J1
Queenscliff Australia 112 C5
Queensland state Australia 111 F4
Queenstown Australia 112 C6
Queenstown N.Z. 113 B4
Queenstown Rep. of Ireland see Cóbh
Queenstown S. Africa 99 E6
Queenstown Sing. 58 [inset]
Queenstown U.S.A. 131 E4
Quehua Bol. 148 D4
Queiba well Chad 88 D5
Queimada Brazil 149 E2
Queimada, Ilha i. Brazil 150 B2
Queimadas Brazil 150 E4
Quela Angola 95 C7
Quelimane Moz. 99 H3
Quellón Chile 153 B5
Quelpart Island S. Korea see Cheju-do
Quemado U.S.A. 135 E6
Quembo r. Angola 95 D8
Quemoy i. Taiwan see Chinmen Tao
Quemú-Quemú Arg. 152 E4
Quepem India 72 B3
Que Que Zimbabwe see Kwekwe
Querência Brazil 150 A5
Querétaro Mex. 126 F7
Querfurt Germany 36 E3
Querobabi Mex. 135 E7
Querpon Peru 146 B6
Quesada Spain 42 E4
Quesat watercourse W. Sahara 90 C4
Queshan China 67 E1
Quesnel Canada 122 F4
Quesnel r. Canada 122 F4
Quesnel Lake Canada 122 F4
Quetena de Lipez r. Bol. 148 D5
Quetta Pak. 81 F4
Quetzaltenango Guat. 138 F6
Queuco Chile 152 C4
Queulat, Parque Nacional nat. park Chile 153 B6
Queupán Arg. 152 D5

▶Quezon City Phil. 57 F3
Former capital of the Philippines.

Qugayatang China 75 F3
Quibala Angola 95 B7
Quibaxe Angola 95 B7
Quibdó Col. 146 B3
Quiberon France 38 B3
Quíbor Venez. 146 D2
Quicama, Parque Nacional do nat. park Angola 95 B7
Quiet Lake Canada 122 C2
Quilán, Cabo c. Chile 153 B5
Quilandi India 72 B4
Quilca Peru 148 B4
Quilenda Angola 95 B7
Quilengues Angola 95 B8
Quillacollo Bol. 148 D4
Quillan France 38 E5
Quill Lakes Canada 134 F2
Quillota Chile 152 C3
Quilmes Arg. 152 F3
Quilon India 72 C4
Quilpie Australia 111 F5
Quilpué Chile 152 C3
Quimbele Angola 95 C6
Quimilí Arg. 152 E1
Quimper France 38 A3
Quimperlé France 38 B3
Quinault r. U.S.A. 134 A3
Quince Mil Peru 148 C3
Quincinetto Italy 44 A2
Quincy CA U.S.A. 136 B2
Quincy FL U.S.A. 129 B6
Quincy IL U.S.A. 132 D4
Quincy MI U.S.A. 130 A3
Quincy OH U.S.A. 130 B3
Quines Arg. 152 D3
Quinga Moz. 99 I2
Quinhagak U.S.A. 120 C4
Quinhámel Guinea-Bissau 92 B3
Qui Nhon Vietnam 61 E5
Quinn r. U.S.A. 134 C4
Quinn Canyon Range mts U.S.A. 137 E3
Quinnimont U.S.A. 130 C5
Quiñones Bol. 148 D2
Quintanar de la Orden Spain 42 E3
Quintin France 38 B2
Quinto r. Arg. 152 D3
Quinto Spain 43 F2
Quinzau Angola 95 B6
Quipapá Brazil 150 F4
Quipungo Angola 95 B8
Quiquive r. Bol. 148 D3
Quirihue Chile 152 B4
Quirima Angola 95 C7
Quirindi Australia 112 D3
Quirinópolis Brazil 149 H4
Quiroga Bol. 148 D4
Quiroga Spain 42 C1
Quisiro Venez. 146 D2
Quissac France 39 F5
Quitapa Angola 95 C7
Quiterajo Moz. 97 D7
Quitexe Angola see Dange
Quitilipi Arg. 152 E1
Quitman GA U.S.A. 129 C6
Quitman MS U.S.A. 129 A5

▶Quito Ecuador 146 B5
Capital of Ecuador.

Quitovac Mex. 135 D7
Quitralco, Parque Nacional nat. park Chile 153 B6
Quixadá Brazil 150 E3
Quixeramobim Brazil 150 E3
Qujiang China see Quxian
Qu Jiang r. China 66 C2
Qujing China 66 B3
Qulandy Kazakh. see Kulandy
Quljuqtow Toghi hills Uzbek. see Kul'dzhuktau, Gory
Qulsary Kazakh. see Kul'sary
Qumar He r. China 70 H5
Qumarheyan China 75 G2
Qumarlêb China 75 G2
Qumdo China 75 G3
Qunayyin, Sabkhat al salt marsh Libya 88 D2
Qŭnghirot Uzbek. see Kungrad
Qu'nyido China 66 A2
Quoich r. Canada 123 M1
Quoin Island Australia 110 B2
Quong Muztag mt. China 75 D2
Quorn Australia 112 A4
Quoxo r. Botswana 98 E4
Qupen China see Jinchuan
Qŭqon Uzbek. see Kokand
Quraymah tourist site Saudi Arabia 77 C5
Qurayyah, Wādī watercourse Egypt 77 B4
Qurayyat al Milḩ l. Jordan 77 C4
Qŭrghonteppa Tajik. 81 G2
Qusar Azer. 79 G2
Qushan China see Beichuan
Qūshchī Iran 80 A2
Qūsheh Dāgh mts Iran 80 A2
Qusmuryn Kazakh. see Kushmurun
Qusum China 75 G3
Quthing Lesotho see Moyeni
Quttinirpaaq National Park Canada 121 L1
Qutū' Island Saudi Arabia 89 I5
Quwayq, Nahr r. Syria/Turkey 77 C2
Quxar China see Lhazê
Quxian China 66 C2
Qüxü China 75 F3
Quyang China see Jingzhou
Quyūn Eshek i. Iran 80 A2
Quzhou China 67 F2
Qvareli Georgia 79 F2
Qypshaq Kōli salt l. Kazakh. see Kypshak, Ozero
Qyteti Stalin Albania see Kuçovë
Qyzan Kazakh. see Kyzan
Qyzylorda Kazakh. see Kyzylorda
Qyzyltū Kazakh. see Kishkenekol'
Qyzylzhar Kazakh. see Kyzylzhar

Raab r. Austria 37 H5
Raab Hungary see Győr
Raahe Fin. 32 G2
Rääkkylä Fin. 32 H3
Raalte Neth. 36 C2
Ra'an, Khashm ar hill Saudi Arabia 89 I3
Raanujärvi Fin. 32 G2
Raas i. Indon. 59 F4
Raasay i. U.K. 34 C3
Rab i. Croatia 44 E2
Rába r. Hungary 37 H5
Raba Indon. 59 G5
Raba r. Poland 37 J3
Rabaale Somalia 96 F2
Rabak Sudan 89 G6
Rabang China 74 D2
Rabat Gozo Malta see Victoria
Rabat Malta 45 E7

▶Rabat Morocco 90 D2
Capital of Morocco.

Rabatakbaytal Tajik. see Akbaytal
Rabāt-e Kamah Iran 81 D3
Rabaul P.N.G. 107 E2
Rabbath Ammon Jordan see 'Ammān
Rabbi r. Italy 44 D2
Rabbit r. Canada 122 E3
Rabbit Flat Australia 110 B4
Rabbitskin r. Canada 122 F2
Rábca r. Hungary 37 H5
Rabidine well Niger 93 G2
Rābigh Saudi Arabia 89 H4
Rabka Poland 37 I4
Rabkob India see Dharmjaygarh
Rabnabad Islands Bangl. 75 F5
Râbniţa Moldova see Rîbniţa
Rābor Iran 80 D4
Rabotoqbaytal Tajik. see Akbaytal
Rabt Sbayta des. W. Sahara 90 B5
Rabyānah oasis Libya 88 D3
Racaka China see Riwoqê
Racalmuto Sicily Italy 45 D6
Racconigi Italy 44 A2
Raccoon Creek r. U.S.A. 130 B4
Race, Cape Canada 160 K2
Raceland U.S.A. 133 D6
Race Point U.S.A. 131 H2
Rachaïya Lebanon 77 B3
Rachel U.S.A. 137 E3
Rach Gia Vietnam 61 D6
Rach Gia, Vinh b. Vietnam 61 D6
Raciąż Poland 37 J2
Racibórz Poland 37 I3
Racine WI U.S.A. 132 E3
Racine WV U.S.A. 130 C4
Răciu Romania 46 D1
Racoș Romania 46 D1
Radashkovichy Belarus 33 G5
Rădăuţi Romania 31 K4
Radbuza r. Czech Rep. 37 F4
Radcliff U.S.A. 128 B4
Radde Rus. Fed. 64 B2
Rade Norway 33 C4
Radebeul Germany 37 F3
Radew r. Poland 37 G1
Radford U.S.A. 130 C5
Radhanpur India 74 A5
Radisson Que. Canada 124 E2
Radisson Sask. Canada 123 J4
Radium Hot Springs Canada 123 G5
Radlinski, Mount Antarctica 167 K1
Radnevo Bulg. 46 D3
Rado de Tumaco inlet Col. 146 B4
Radom Poland 37 J3
Radom Sudan 94 E2
Radomir Bulg. 46 C3
Radomir mt. Bulg./Greece 46 C4
Radomka r. Poland 37 J3
Radom National Park Sudan 94 D2
Radomsko Poland 37 I3
Radoshkovichi Belarus see Radashkovichy
Radovets Bulg. 46 E4
Radoviš Macedonia 46 C4
Radovljica Slovenia 44 E1
Radstock, Cape Australia 109 F8
Radunia r. Poland 37 I1
Radviliškis Lith. 33 F5
Raḑwá, Jabal mt. Saudi Arabia 89 H3
Rae Bareli India 74 D4
Raecreek r. Canada 122 B1
Rae-Edzo Canada 123 G2
Raeford U.S.A. 128 D5
Rae Lakes Canada 123 G1
Raeside, Lake salt flat Australia 109 C7
Raetihi N.Z. 113 C2
Rāf hill Saudi Arabia 89 H2
Rafaela Arg. 152 E2
Rafaḩ Gaza see Rafiah
Rafaï Cent. Afr. Rep. 94 D3
Raffadali Sicily Italy 45 D6
Rafḩā' Saudi Arabia 89 I2
Rafiah Gaza 77 B4
Rafina Greece 47 D5
Rafsanjān Iran 80 C4
Raga Sudan 94 E2
Ragag Sudan 94 E2
Ragana Latvia 33 G4
Ragged, Mount Australia 109 C8
Raghogarh India 74 C4
Rago Nasjonalpark nat. park Norway 32 E2
Ragueneau Canada 125 G3
Ragusa Croatia see Dubrovnik
Ragusa Sicily Italy 45 E6
Raha India 75 G4
Raha Indon. 57 F6
Rahachow Belarus 29 D5
Rahad r. Sudan 89 G6
Rahad Canal Sudan 89 G6
Rahad el Berdi Sudan 94 D2
Rahad Wahal well Sudan 88 E6
Rahaeng Thai. see Tak
Rahaţ, Ḩarrat lava field Saudi Arabia 89 I4
Rahatgaon India 74 C5
Rahimatpur India 72 B2
Rahimyar Khan Pak. 81 G4
Rāhjerd Iran 80 B3
Rahuri India 72 B2
Rahzanak Afgh. 81 E3
Raiatea i. Fr. Polynesia 165 H7
Raibu i. Indon. see Air
Raichur India 72 C2
Raiganj India 75 F4
Raigarh Chhattisgarh India 75 D5
Raigarh Orissa India 73 D2
Raijua i. Indon. 108 C2
Railroad Valley U.S.A. 137 E2
Raimangal r. Bangl. 75 F5
Raimbault, Lac l. Canada 125 G2
Rainbow Lake Canada 122 G3
Raine Island Australia 111 F1
Rainelle U.S.A. 130 C5
Raini r. Pak. 81 G4
Rainier, Mount vol. U.S.A. 134 B3
Rainy r. U.S.A. 132 C1
Rainy Lake Canada 124 A3
Raippaluoto i. Fin. 32 F3
Raipur Bangl. 75 F5
Raipur Chhattisgarh India 75 D5
Raipur Rajasthan India 74 B4
Raipur W. Bengal India 75 E5
Rairangpur India 75 E5
Raisen India 74 C5
Raisinghnagar India 74 B3
Raisio Fin. 33 F3
Raistakka Fin. 32 H2
Raitalai India 74 C5
Raivavae i. Fr. Polynesia 165 I7
Raiwind Pak. 74 B3
Raja Estonia 33 G4
Raja, Ujung pt Indon. 58 B2
Rajabasa, Gunung vol. Indon. 58 D4
Rajagangapur India 75 E5
Rajahmundry India 73 D2
Raja-Jooseppi Fin. 32 H1
Rajaldesar India 74 B3
Rajampet India 72 C3
Rajang r. Sarawak Malaysia 59 E2
Rajanpur Pak. 81 G4
Rajapalaiyam India 72 C4
Rajapur India 72 B2
Rajasthan state India 74 B4
Rajasthan Canal India 74 B3
Rajauli India 75 E4
Rajbari Bangl. 75 F5
Rajgarh Madhya Pradesh India 74 C4
Rajgarh Rajasthan India 74 B3
Rajgarh Rajasthan India 74 C4
Rajgród Poland 37 K2
Räjijovsset Fin. see Raja-Jooseppi
Rajim India 73 D1
Rajkot India 74 A5
Rajmahal Hills India 75 E4
Raj Nandgaon India 74 D5
Rajpipla India 74 B5
Rajpur India 74 B5
Rajpura India 74 C3
Rajputana Agency state India see Rajasthan
Rajsamand India 74 B4
Rajshahi Bangl. 75 F4
Rajshahi admin. div. Bangl. 75 F4
Rājū Syria 77 C1
Rajula India 74 B5
Rajur India 72 C1
Rajura India see Ahmadpur
Raka China 75 E3
Rakai Uganda 96 A5
Rakaia r. N.Z. 113 C3
Rakan, Ra's pt Qatar 80 B5
Rakaposhi mt. Jammu and Kashmir 74 B1
Raka Zangbo r. China see Dongxuung Zangbo
Rakhaing state Myanmar see Arakan
Rakhine state Myanmar see Arakan
Rakhiv Ukr. 41 G2
Rakhshan r. Pak. 81 E5
Rakiraki Fiji 107 G3
Rakit i. Indon. 59 E4
Rakitnitsa r. Bulg. 46 D3
Rakitnoye Rus. Fed. 64 C3
Rakiura i. N.Z. see Stewart Island
Rakke Estonia 28 C4
Rakkestad Norway 33 C4
Rakni r. Pak. 81 G4
Rakops Botswana 98 E4
Rakovník Czech Rep. 37 F3
Rakovski Bulg. 46 D3
Rakushechnyy, Mys pt Kazakh. 79 G2
Rakvere Estonia 28 C4
Raleigh MS U.S.A. 133 D5

▶Raleigh NC U.S.A. 128 D5
State capital of North Carolina.

Ralston Canada 123 I5
Ralston U.S.A. 131 E3
Ram r. Canada 122 F2
Ramacca Sicily Italy 45 E6
Ramaditas Chile 148 C5
Ramah Canada 125 I1
Ramalho, Serra do hills Brazil 150 C5
Ramallah West Bank 77 B4
Ramallo Arg. 152 E3
Ramanagaram India 72 C3
Ramanathapuram India 72 C4
Ramanuj Ganj India 75 D5
Ramas, Cape India 72 B3
Ramatlabama S. Africa 98 E5
Ramayampet India 72 C2
Ramberg Norway 32 D1
Rambervillers France 39 G2
Rambouillet France 38 D2
Ramdurg India 72 B3
Ramechhap Nepal 75 E4
Rame Head U.K. 35 D6
Rameshki Rus. Fed. 31 N1
Rameswaram India 72 C4
Ramezān Kalak Iran 81 E5
Ramgarh Bangl. 75 F5
Ramgarh Jharkhand India 75 E5
Ramgarh Rajasthan India 74 A4
Rāmhormoz Iran 80 B4
Ramingining Australia 110 C2
Ramit Tajik. see Romit
Ramla Israel 77 B4
Ramlat al Ghāfah des. Saudi Arabia 76 E5
Ramlat Dahm des. Saudi Arabia/Yemen 76 D6
Ramlat Rabyānah des. Libya see Rebiana Sand Sea
Ramm, Jabal mts Jordan 78 C5
Ramnad India see Ramanathapuram
Ramnagar Madhya Pradesh India 74 D4
Ramnagar Uttaranchal India 74 C3
Ramnagar Jammu and Kashmir 74 B2
Ramnäs Sweden 33 E4
Râmnicul Sărat r. Romania 46 E2
Râmnicu Sărat Romania 46 E2
Râmnicu Vâlcea Romania 46 D2
Ramokgwebane Botswana 99 E4
Ramona U.S.A. 136 D5
Ramonville-St-Agne France 38 D5
Ramos Arizpe Mex. 133 A7
Ramotswa Botswana 98 E5
Rampart of Genghis Khan tourist site Asia 63 I2
Ramparts r. Canada 122 D1
Rampur Uttar Pradesh India 74 C3
Rampur Uttar Pradesh India 74 C3
Rampura India 74 B4
Rampur Boalia Bangl. see Rajshahi
Rampur Hat India 75 E4
Ramree Myanmar 60 A4
Ramree Island Myanmar 60 A4
Ramsele Sweden 32 E3
Ramsey Isle of Man 35 D4
Ramsey Lake Canada 124 D4
Ramsgate U.K. 35 G6
Ramshai Hat India 75 G4
Rāmshir Iran 80 B4
Ramsing mt. India 75 G3
Ramsjö Sweden 33 D3
Ramtek India 74 C5
Ramu Bangl. 75 G5
Ramu r. P.N.G. 57 J6
Ramundberget Sweden 32 D3
Ramusio, Lac l. Canada 125 I2

Ramvik Sweden 32 E3
Ramygala Lith. 33 G5
Rana, Cerro hill Col. 146 D4
Rañadoiro, Puerto de pass Spain 42 C1
Rañadoiro, Sierra de mts Spain 42 C1
Ranaghat India 75 F5
Ranai i. U.S.A. see Lanai
Rana Pratap Sagar resr India 74 B4
Ranapur India 74 B5
Rånåsfoss Norway 33 C3
Ranau Sabah Malaysia 59 G1
Ranau, Danau l. Indon. 58 C4
Rancagua Chile 152 C3
Rance r. France 38 B2
Rancharia Brazil 149 H5
Rancheria Canada 122 D2
Ranchester U.S.A. 134 F3
Ranchi India 75 E5
Rancho Cordova U.S.A. 136 B2
Rancho de Caçados Tapiúnas Brazil 149 F2
Ranco, Lago l. Chile 152 B5
Randallstown U.S.A. 131 E4
Randazzo Sicily Italy 45 E6
Randers Denmark 33 C4
Randijaure l. Sweden 32 E2
Randolph MA U.S.A. 131 H2
Randolph NY U.S.A. 130 D2
Randolph UT U.S.A. 134 E4
Randolph VT U.S.A. 131 G2
Randow r. Germany 37 G2
Randsburg U.S.A. 136 D4
Randsfjorden l. Norway 33 C3
Randsjö Sweden 33 D3
Randsverk Norway 33 C3
Råneå Sweden 32 F2
Ranfurly N.Z. 113 B4
Ranga r. India 60 A2
Rangae Thai. 61 C7
Rangamati Bangl. 75 G5
Rangapara North India 75 G4
Rangas, Tanjung pt Indon. 59 G3
Rangasa, Tanjung pt Indon. 59 G3
Rangaunu Bay N.Z. 113 C1
Rangeley Lake U.S.A. 128 F2
Rangely U.S.A. 137 H1
Ranger Lake Canada 124 D4
Rangi India 72 D1
Rangia Patharughat India 75 F4
Rangiauria i. S. Pacific Ocean see Pitt Island
Rangiora N.Z. 113 C3
Rangitata r. N.Z. 113 B4
Rangitikei r. N.Z. 113 C3
Rangkasbitung Indon. 58 D4
Rangke China see Zamtang
Rangkŭl Tajik. 81 H2
Rangôn Myanmar see Rangoon
Rangôn admin. div. Myanmar see Yangôn

▶Rangoon Myanmar 60 B4
Capital of Myanmar.

Rangoon admin. div. Myanmar see Yangôn
Rangoon r. Myanmar 61 B4
Rangpur Bangl. 75 F4
Rangsang i. Indon. 58 C2
Rangse Myanmar 60 A2
Rani India 74 B4
Rania India 74 B3
Ranibennur India 72 B3
Raniganj India 75 E5
Ranijula Peak India 75 D5
Ranikhet India 74 C3
Ranipur Pak. 81 G5
Raniwara India 74 B4
Ranken watercourse Australia 110 D4
Rankin U.S.A. 133 A6
Rankin Inlet Canada 123 M2
Rankin Inlet inlet Canada 123 M2
Rankin's Springs Australia 112 C4
Rankovićevo Serb. and Mont. see Kraljevo
Rannes Australia 111 G5
Ranneye Rus. Fed. 29 J6
Rannoch, Loch l. U.K. 34 D3
Ranobe r. Madag. 99 [inset] J3
Ranohira Madag. 99 [inset] J4
Ranomafana Madag. 99 [inset] K3
Ranomatana Madag. 99 [inset] J5
Ranong Thai. 61 B6
Ranotsara Avaratra Madag. 99 [inset] J4
Ranpur India 74 A5
Ransiki Indon. 57 H6
Rantasalmi Fin. 33 H3
Rantau Indon. 59 F3
Rantau i. Indon. 58 C2
Rantaukampar Indon. 58 C2
Rantaupanjang Kalimantan Tengah Indon. 59 F3
Rantaupanjang Kalimantan Timur Indon. 59 G2
Rantauprapat Indon. 58 B2
Rantaupulut Indon. 59 F3
Rantoul U.S.A. 132 D3
Rantsila Fin. 32 G2
Ranua Fin. 32 G2
Ranxë Albania 46 A4
Rānya Iraq 79 F3
Ranyah, Wādī watercourse Saudi Arabia 89 I4
Rao Go mt. Laos/Vietnam 60 D4
Raohe China 64 C3
Raoul Island N.Z. 107 H4
Rapa i. Fr. Polynesia 165 I7
Rapallo Italy 44 B2
Rapar Gujarat India 74 A5
Rapar Punjab India 74 C3
Rapch watercourse Iran 81 D5
Rapidan r. U.S.A. 130 E4
Rapid Bay Australia 112 A4
Rapid City U.S.A. 134 G3
Rāpina Estonia 33 G4
Rapirrān r. Brazil 148 D2
Rapla Estonia 28 C4
Rappahannock r. U.S.A. 131 E5
Rapti r. India 75 D4
Rapulo r. Bol. 148 D3
Rapur Andhra Pradesh India 72 C3
Rapur Gujarat India 74 A5
Raqqa Syria see Ar Raqqah
Raquette r. U.S.A. 131 F1
Raquette Lake U.S.A. 131 F2
Rara National Park Nepal 75 D3
Raritan Bay U.S.A. 131 F3
Raroia atoll Fr. Polynesia 165 I7
Rarotonga i. Cook Is 165 H7
Ras India 74 B4
Raša r. Croatia 44 E2
Rasa, Punta pt Arg. 152 E5
Ra's ad Daqm Oman 76 F6
Ra's al Ḥikmah Egypt 89 E2
Ras al Khaimah U.A.E. see Ra's al Khaymah
Ra's al Khaymah U.A.E. 80 C5
Ra's al Mish'āb Saudi Arabia 79 G5
Ra's an Naqb Jordan 78 C5
Ra's ash Shaykh Humayd Saudi Arabia 78 C5

▶Ras Dashen mt. Eth. 96 C1
5th highest mountain in Africa.
africa 84–85

Raseiniai Lith. 33 F5
Ras el Ma Alg. 91 E2
Râs el Mâ Mali 92 D1
Ra's Ghārib Egypt 89 G2
Rashad Sudan 96 A2
Rashid Egypt 89 F2
Rashid Qala Afgh. 81 F4
Rasht Iran 80 B2
Rasina Estonia 33 G4
Rasina r. Serb. and Mont. 46 B3
Råsjö Sweden 33 D3
Raška Serb. and Mont. 46 B3
Raskam mts China 74 B1
Ras Koh mt. Pak. 81 F4
Raskoh mts Pak. 81 F4
Ras Maskan pt Somalia 96 D2
Râşnov Romania 46 D2
Raso da Catarina hills Brazil 150 E4
Rason Lake salt flat Australia 110 A6
Rasova Romania 46 E2
Rasovo Bulg. 46 C3
Rasra India 75 D4
Rass Jebel Tunisia 45 C6
Rasskazovo Rus. Fed. 29 G5
Rast Romania 46 C3
Ras Tannūrah Saudi Arabia 76 E4
Rastatt Germany 36 D4
Rastede Germany 36 D2
Råstojaure l. Sweden 32 F1
Ratae U.K. see Leicester
Ratai, Gunung mt. Indon. 58 D4
Ratangarh Madhya Pradesh India 74 B4
Ratangarh Rajasthan India 74 B3
Ratanpur Chhattisgarh India 75 D5
Ratanpur Gujarat India 74 B5
Rätansbyn Sweden 33 D3
Rat Buri Thai. 61 B5
Rath India 74 C4
Rathbun Lake U.S.A. 132 C3
Rathedaung Myanmar 73 G1
Rathenow Germany 37 F2
Rathlin Island U.K. 34 C4
Rathluirc Rep. of Ireland 35 B5
Ratibor Poland see Racibórz
Ratisbon Germany see Regensburg
Ratiya India 74 B3
Rat Lake Canada 123 L3
Ratlam India 74 B5
Ratnagiri India 72 B2
Ratnapura Sri Lanka 72 D5
Ratne Ukr. 29 C6
Ratno Ukr. see Ratne
Rato Dero Pak. 81 G5
Raton U.S.A. 135 F5
Rattray Head U.K. 34 F3
Rättvik Sweden 33 D3
Ratz, Mount Canada 122 C3
Ratzeburg Germany 36 E2
Raub Malaysia 58 C2
Rauch Arg. 152 F4
Rauðamýri Iceland 32 [inset]
Raudanjoki r. Fin. 32 G2
Râu de Mori Romania 46 C2
Raudhatain Kuwait 79 F5
Raudna r. Estonia 33 G4
Raudondvaris Lith. 33 F5
Raufarhöfn Iceland 32 [inset]
Raukumara Range mts N.Z. 113 D2
Raul r. India 73 D1
Rauma Fin. 33 F3
Raurkela India 75 E5
Rauschen Rus. Fed. see Svetlogorsk
Rautalampi Fin. 32 G3
Rautavaara Fin. 32 H3
Rautjärvi Fin. 33 H3
Rauza India see Khuldabad
Ravalli U.S.A. 134 D3
Ravānsar Iran 80 A3
Ravanusa Sicily Italy 45 D6
Rāvar Iran 80 D4
Ravena U.S.A. 131 G2
Ravenna Italy 44 D2
Ravenna NE U.S.A. 132 B3
Ravenna OH U.S.A. 130 C3
Ravenshoe Australia 111 F3
Ravensthorpe Australia 109 C8
Ravenswood Australia 111 F4
Ravenswood U.S.A. 130 C4
Raver India 74 C5
Ravi r. Pak. 81 G4
Ravna Gora hill Croatia 44 F2
Ravnina Turkm. 81 E2
Rāwah Iraq 79 E4
Rawaki i. Kiribati 107 H2
Rawala Kot Pak. 81 H3
Rawalpindi Pak. 81 H3
Rawalpindi Lake Canada 123 H1
Rawa Mazowiecka Poland 37 J3
Rawāndiz Iraq 79 F3
Rawas r. Indon. 58 C3
Rawatsar India 74 B3
Rawghah watercourse Saudi Arabia 77 C5
Rawi i. Thai. 61 B7
Rawicz Poland 37 H3
Rawka r. Poland 37 J2
Rawlinna Australia 109 D7
Rawlins U.S.A. 134 F4
Rawlinson, Mount Australia 109 D6
Rawlinson Range hills Australia 109 E6
Rawnina Turkm. see Ravnina
Rawson Arg. 153 D5
Rawu China 66 A2
Raxaul India 75 E4
Ray, Cape Canada 125 J4
Raya, Bukit mt. Kalimantan Barat/Kalimantan Tengah Indon. 59 E3
Raya, Bukit mt. Kalimantan Barat Indon. 59 F3
Rayachoti India 72 C3
Rayadurg India 72 C3
Rayagarha India 73 D2
Rayak Lebanon 77 C3
Raychikhinsk Rus. Fed. 64 B2
Rāyen Iran 80 D4
Rayes Peak U.S.A. 136 C4
Rayevskiy Rus. Fed. 28 J5
Raymond Canada 123 H5
Raymond U.S.A. 131 H2
Raymondville U.S.A. 133 B7
Raymore Canada 123 J5
Rayna India 75 E5
Rayner Glacier Antarctica 167 D2
Rayones Mex. 133 A7
Rayong Thai. 61 C5
Raystown Lake U.S.A. 130 D3
Rayth al Khayl watercourse Saudi Arabia 77 C5
Rayville U.S.A. 133 D5
Raz, Pointe du pt France 38 A2
Razan Iran 80 B3
Razan India 73 D2
Razan Iran 80 B3
Razāzah, Buḥayrat ar l. Iraq 79 E4
Razdan Armenia see Hrazdan
Razdel'naya Ukr. see Rozdil'na
Razdol'noye Rus. Fed. 64 B4
Razeh Iran 80 B3
Razgrad Bulg. 46 E3
Razhêng Zangbo r. China 75 F3
Razim, Lacul lag. Romania 46 F2
Razlog Bulg. 46 C4
Raz"yezd 3km Rus. Fed. see Novyy Urgal
R. D. Bailey Lake U.S.A. 130 C5
Ré, Île de i. France 38 C3
Reading U.K. 35 F6
Reading MI U.S.A. 130 A3
Reading OH U.S.A. 130 A4
Reading PA U.S.A. 131 F3
Reagile S. Africa 99 E5
Real r. Brazil 150 E4
Reales mt. Spain 42 D4
Realicó Arg. 152 D3
Réalmont France 38 E5
Reăng Kesei Cambodia 61 C5
Reata Mex. 133 A7
Reate Italy see Rieti
Rebaa Alg. 91 H3
Rebbenesøy i. Norway 32 E1
Rebecca, Lake salt flat Australia 109 C7
Rebiana Sand Sea des. Libya 88 D3
Rebollera mt. Spain 42 D3
Reboly Rus. Fed. 32 H3
Rebrebti Dhubo well Eth. 96 E3
Rebun-tō i. Japan 64 E3
Recaş Romania 46 B2
Recherche, Archipelago of the is Australia 109 C8
Rechitsa Belarus see Rechytsa
Rechna Doab lowland Pak. 81 H4
Rechytsa Belarus 29 D5
Recife Brazil 150 F4
Recife, Cape S. Africa 98 E7
Recinto Chile 152 C4
Recklinghausen Germany 36 C3
Recknitz r. Germany 37 F1
Reconquista Arg. 152 F2
Recreio Brazil 149 F2
Recreo Arg. 152 D2
Rectorville U.S.A. 130 B4
Recz Poland 37 G2
Red r. Australia 111 E3
Red r. Canada 122 E3
Red r. Canada/U.S.A. 123 L5
Red r. U.S.A. 133 D6
Red, North Fork r. U.S.A. 133 B5
Redang i. Malaysia 58 C1
Red Bank U.S.A. 131 F3
Red Basin China see Sichuan Pendi
Red Bay Canada 125 J3
Redberry Lake Canada 123 J4
Red Bluff hill Australia 109 B6
Red Bluff U.S.A. 136 A1
Red Butte mt. U.S.A. 137 F4
Redcar U.K. 35 F4
Redcliff Canada 134 E2
Redcliff Zimbabwe 99 F3
Redcliffe, Mount Australia 109 C7
Red Cliffs Australia 112 B4
Red Cloud U.S.A. 132 B3
Red Deer Canada 123 H4
Red Deer r. Canada 123 I5
Red Deer Lake Canada 123 K4
Redding U.S.A. 136 A1
Redditch U.K. 35 F5
Red Earth Creek Canada 123 H3
Redenção Pará Brazil 150 B3
Redenção Piauí Brazil 150 C4
Redeyef Tunisia 91 H2
Redfield U.S.A. 132 B2
Red Granite Mountain Canada 122 B2
Red Hills U.S.A. 132 B4
Red Hook U.S.A. 131 G3
Red Idol Gorge China 75 F3
Red Indian Lake Canada 125 J3
Redkino Rus. Fed. 28 F4
Redknife r. Canada 122 G2
Red Lake Canada 123 M5
Red Lake U.S.A. 137 F4
Red Lake r. U.S.A. 132 B2
Red Lakes U.S.A. 132 C1
Redlands U.S.A. 136 D4
Red Lion NJ U.S.A. 131 F4
Red Lion PA U.S.A. 131 E4
Red Lodge U.S.A. 134 E3
Redmesa U.S.A. 137 H3
Redmond OR U.S.A. 134 B3
Redmond UT U.S.A. 137 G2
Red Oak U.S.A. 132 C3
Redojari waterhole Kenya 96 C5
Redon France 38 B3
Redondela Spain 42 B1
Redondo Port. 42 C3
Redondo Beach U.S.A. 136 C5
Red Peak U.S.A. 134 D3
Red River r. Vietnam 60 D3
Red Rock Canada 124 B3
Red Rock AZ U.S.A. 137 G5
Red Rock PA U.S.A. 131 E3
Red Rock r. U.S.A. 134 D3
Red Sea Africa/Asia 76 A4
Red Sea state Sudan 89 G5
Redstone Canada 122 F4
Red Volta r. Burkina/Ghana 93 E3
also known as Nazinon (Burkina)
Redwater r. U.S.A. 134 F2
Red Willow Creek r. U.S.A. 132 A3
Red Wing U.S.A. 132 C2
Redwood City U.S.A. 136 A3
Redwood Falls U.S.A. 132 C2
Redwood National Park U.S.A. 134 A4
Redwood Valley U.S.A. 136 A2
Ree, Lough l. Rep. of Ireland 35 C5
Reed City U.S.A. 132 E3
Reed Lake Canada 123 K4
Reedley U.S.A. 136 C3
Reedsport U.S.A. 134 A4
Reedsville OH U.S.A. 130 C4
Reedsville PA U.S.A. 130 E3
Reedville U.S.A. 131 E5
Reedy Creek watercourse Australia 111 F4
Reedy Glacier Antarctica 167 J1
Reefton N.Z. 113 B3
Reese U.S.A. 130 B2
Reese r. U.S.A. 136 D1
Refahiye Turkey 79 D3
Reform U.S.A. 129 A5
Refugio U.S.A. 133 B6
Rega r. Poland 37 G1
Regen Germany 37 F4
Regensburg Germany 36 F4
Reggane Alg. 91 F4
Reggio Calabria Italy see Reggio di Calabria
Reggio Emilia-Romagna Italy see Reggio nell'Emilia
Reggio di Calabria Italy 45 E5
Reggio Emilia Italy see Reggio nell'Emilia
Reggio nell'Emilia Italy 44 C2
Reghin Romania 46 D1
Regi Afgh. 81 F3

▶Regina Canada 134 F2
Provincial capital of Saskatchewan.

Régina Fr. Guiana 147 H3
Registro Brazil 149 I6
Regium Lepidum Italy see Reggio nell'Emilia
Regozero Rus. Fed. 32 H2
Rehli India 74 C5
Rehoboth Namibia 98 C4
Rehoboth Bay U.S.A. 131 F4
Rehovot Israel 77 B4
Reichenbach Germany 37 F3
Reichshoffen France 39 G2
Reid Australia 109 E7
Reidsville U.S.A. 128 D4
Reiley Peak U.S.A. 137 G5
Reims France 39 F2
Reinach Switz. 39 G3
Reinbek Germany 36 E2
Reindeer r. Canada 123 K4
Reindeer Island Canada 123 L4
Reindeer Lake Canada 123 K3
Reinosa Spain 42 D1
Reiphólsfjöll hill Iceland 32 [inset]
Reisa Nasjonalpark nat. park Norway 32 F1
Reisjärvi Fin. 32 G3
Reisterstown U.S.A. 131 E4
Reitz S. Africa 99 F5
Reivilo S. Africa 98 E5
Rekapalle India 72 D2
Rekohua i. S. Pacific Ocean see Chatham Island
Reliance Canada 123 I2
Relizane Alg. 91 F2
Remada Tunisia 91 H2
Remarkable, Mount Australia 112 A4
Rembang Indon. 59 E4
Remel el Abiod des. Tunisia 91 H3
Remeshk Iran 81 D5
Remeskylä Fin. 32 G3
Remi France see Reims
Remington U.S.A. 130 E4
Remiremont France 39 G2
Remmel Mountain U.S.A. 134 B2
Remo Glacier Jammu and Kashmir 74 C2
Rempang i. Indon. 58 D2
Remscheid Germany 36 C3
Rena Norway 33 C3
Rena r. Norway 33 C3
Renaix Belgium see Ronse
Renapur India 72 C2
Renard Islands P.N.G. 111 H1
Rende China see Xundian
Rend Lake U.S.A. 128 A4
Rendsburg Germany 36 D1
Renedo Spain 42 E1
René-Levasseur, Île i. Canada 125 G3
Renens Switz. 39 G3
Renfrew Canada 124 E4
Rengat Indon. 58 C3
Rengo Chile 152 C3
Ren He r. China 67 D1
Renheji China 67 E2
Renhua China 67 E3
Renhuai China 66 C3
Reni Ukr. 29 D7
Renick U.S.A. 130 C5
Renigunta India 72 C3
Renmark Australia 112 B4
Rennell i. Solomon Is 107 F3
Rennell, Islas is Chile 153 B7
Rennerod Germany 36 D3
Renner Springs Australia 110 C3
Rennes France 38 C2
Rennes, Bassin de basin France 38 C2
Rennick Glacier Antarctica 167 H2
Rennie Canada 123 M5
Reno r. Italy 44 D2
Reno U.S.A. 136 C2
Renovo U.S.A. 130 E3
Renshou China 66 C2
Rentjärn Sweden 32 E2
Renton U.S.A. 134 B3
Renukut India 75 D4
Renwick N.Z. 113 C3
Réo Burkina 93 E2
Reo Indon. 57 F7
Repembe r. Moz. 99 G4
Repetek Turkm. 81 E2
Repokaira reg. Fin. 32 G1
Reposaari Fin. 33 F3
Republic U.S.A. 134 C2
Republican r. U.S.A. 132 B4
Republican, South Fork r. U.S.A. 132 A3
Republika Srpska aut. div. Bos.-Herz. 44 F2
Repulse Bay b. Australia 111 G4
Repulse Bay Canada 121 K3
Repvåg Norway 32 G1
Requena Peru 146 C6
Requena Spain 43 F3
Réquista France 39 E4
Reşadiye Turkey 79 E3
Reşadiye Turkey 78 D2
Reşadiye Yarımadası pen. Turkey 47 E6
Resag, Gunung mt. Indon. 58 D4
Resava r. Serb. and Mont. 46 B2
Resen Macedonia 46 B4
Reserva Brazil 151 B8
Reserve U.S.A. 135 E6
Reshi China 67 D2
Resia, Passo di pass Austria/Italy 36 E5
Resistencia Arg. 152 F1
Reşiţa Romania 46 B2
Reško Poland 37 G2
Resolute Bay Canada 121 J2
Resolution Island Canada 121 M3
Resolution Island N.Z. 113 A4
Restefond, Col de pass France 39 G4
Restelica Serb. and Mont. 46 B4
Restinga Seca Brazil 151 A9
Resülayn Turkey see Ceylanpınar
Retalhuleu Guat. 138 F6
Retem, Oued er watercourse Alg. 91 G2
Retén Llico Chile 152 B3
Retezat, Parcul Naţional nat. park Romania 46 C2
Retford U.K. 35 F5
Rethel France 39 F2
Réthimnon Greece see Rethymno
Rethymno Greece 47 D7
Retiers France 38 C3
Retortillo tourist site Spain 42 D1
Retuerta mt. Spain 43 F2

▶Réunion terr. Indian Ocean 162 K7
French Overseas Department.
africa 86–87, 100

Reus Spain 43 G2
Reusam, Pulau i. Indon. 58 B2
Reutlingen Germany 36 D4
Reval Estonia see Tallinn
Revda Rus. Fed. 28 E2
Revel Estonia see Tallinn
Revel France 38 E5
Revelganj India 75 E4
Revelstoke Canada 134 C2
Reventazón Peru 146 A6
Revermont reg. France 39 F4
Reviga Romania 46 E2
Reviga r. Romania 46 E2
Revigny-sur-Ornain France 39 F2
Revillagigedo, Islas is Mex. 126 D8
Revillagigedo Island U.S.A. 120 F4
Revolyutsii, Pik mt. Tajik. see Revolyutsiya, Qullai
Revolyutsiya, Qullai mt. Tajik. 81 H2
Revúca Slovakia 37 J4
Revuè r. Moz. 99 G3
Rewa India 75 D4
Rewari India 74 C3
Rexburg U.S.A. 134 E4
Rey, Isla del i. Panama 146 B2
Reyes Bol. 148 D3
Reyes, Point U.S.A. 136 A2
Reyes, Punta pt Col. 146 B4
Reyhanlı Turkey 77 C1
Reykjanes Ridge sea feature N. Atlantic Ocean 160 L2
Reykjanestá pt Iceland 32 [inset]

▶Reykjavík Iceland 32 [inset]
Capital of Iceland.

Reykjavik Iceland see Reykjavík
Reynolds Range mts Australia 110 C4
Reynosa Mex. 126 G6
Reyssouze r. France 39 F3
Rezā, Kūh-e hill Iran 80 B3
Reẓā'īyeh Iran see Urmia
Reẓā'īyeh, Daryācheh-ye salt l. Iran see Urmia, Lake
Rēzekne Latvia 33 G4
Rezovska Reka r. Bulg./Turkey 46 F4
Rezvāndeh Iran see Reẕvānshahr
Reẕvānshahr Iran 80 B2
R. F. Magón Mex. see Ricardo Flores Magón
Rgotina Serb. and Mont. 46 C2
Rharbi, Oued el watercourse Alg. 91 F3
Rhegium Italy see Reggio di Calabria
Rheims France see Reims
Rhein r. Germany 36 C4 see Rhine
Rheine Germany 36 C2
Rheinland-Pfalz land Germany 36 C4
Rheinsberg Germany 37 F2
Rheinwaldhorn mt. Switz. 39 H3
Rhemilès well Alg. 90 D3
Rheris, Oued watercourse Morocco 90 D3
Rhin r. France 36 C4 see Rhine
Rhine r. Europe 36 C4
also spelt Rhein (Germany) or Rhin (France)
Rhinelander U.S.A. 132 D2
Rhineland-Palatinate land Germany see Rheinland-Pfalz
Rhinluch marsh Germany 37 F2
Rhino Camp Uganda 96 A4
Rhinow Germany 37 F2
Rhir, Cap c. Morocco 90 C3
Rho Italy 44 B2
Rhode Island state U.S.A. 131 H3
Rhodes Greece 47 F6
Rhodes i. Greece 47 F6
Rhodesia country Africa see Zimbabwe
Rhodes Inyanga National Park Zimbabwe see Nyanga National Park
Rhodes Matopos National Park Zimbabwe see Matobo National Park
Rhodope Mountains Bulg./Greece 46 C4
Rhodus i. Greece see Rhodes
Rhône r. France/Switz. 39 F5
Rhône-Alpes admin. reg. France 39 F4
Rhube, Oasis of Syria see Ruḥbah
Rhum i. U.K. see Rum
Rhuthun U.K. see Ruthin
Rhyl U.K. 35 E5
Riachão Brazil 150 C3
Riacho de Santana Brazil 150 D5
Rialma Brazil 149 H3
Rialp, Pantà de resr Spain 43 G2
Rialto U.S.A. 136 D4
Riangnom Sudan 94 F2
Riaño, Embalse de resr Spain 42 D1
Riansáres r. Spain 42 E3
Riasi Jammu and Kashmir 74 B2
Riau prov. Indon. 58 C2
Riau, Kepulauan is Indon. 58 D2
Riaza r. Spain 42 E2
Ribadavia Spain 42 B1
Ribadeo Spain 42 C1
Ribadesella Spain 42 D1
Ribas do Rio Pardo Brazil 151 A7
Ribat-i-Shur waterhole Iran 80 D3
Ribáuè Moz. 99 H2
Ribble r. U.K. 35 E5
Ribe Denmark 33 C5
Ribeirão Preto Brazil 149 I5
Ribera Sicily Italy 45 D6
Ribérac France 38 D4
Riberalta Bol. 148 D2
Ribnica Slovenia 44 E2
Rîbniţa Moldova 31 L4
Ribnitz-Damgarten Germany 37 F1
Rica Aventura Chile 148 C5
Říčany Czech Rep. 37 G4
Ricardo Flores Magón Mex. 135 F7
Riccione Italy 44 D2
Rice CA U.S.A. 137 E4
Rice VA U.S.A. 130 D5
Rice Lake l. Canada 130 D1
Rice Lake U.S.A. 132 D2
Richards Bay S. Africa 99 G6
Richards Inlet Antarctica 167 H1
Richards Island Canada 120 F3
Richardson r. Canada 123 I3
Richardson Island Canada 123 G1
Richardson Mountains Canada 120 F3
Richardson Mountains N.Z. 113 B4
Richard Toll Senegal 92 B1
Richelieu France 38 D3
Richfield U.S.A. 137 F2
Richfield Springs U.S.A. 131 F2
Richford NY U.S.A. 131 E2
Richford VT U.S.A. 128 E2
Richgrove U.S.A. 136 C4
Richibucto Canada 125 H4
Rich Lake Canada 123 I4
Richland U.S.A. 134 C3
Richland Center U.S.A. 132 D3
Richlands U.S.A. 130 C5
Richmond N.S.W. Australia 112 D4
Richmond Qld Australia 111 E4
Richmond Canada 125 F4
Richmond N.Z. 113 C3
Richmond KwaZulu-Natal S. Africa 99 F6
Richmond N. Cape S. Africa 98 D6
Richmond CA U.S.A. 136 A3
Richmond IN U.S.A. 130 A4
Richmond KY U.S.A. 130 A5
Richmond MI U.S.A. 130 B2

▶Richmond VA U.S.A. 130 E5
State capital of Virginia.

Richmond Dale U.S.A. 130 B4
Richmond Hill U.S.A. 129 C6
Richtersveld National Park S. Africa 98 C6
Richvale U.S.A. 136 B2
Richwood U.S.A. 130 C4
Rickleån r. Sweden 32 F2
Ricobayo, Embalse de resr Spain 42 D2
Ricomagus France see Riom
Riddell Nunataks nunataks Antarctica 167 E2
Ridder Kazakh. see Leninogorsk
Riddlesburg U.S.A. 130 D3
Rideau Lakes Canada 131 E1
Ridge r. Canada 124 C3
Ridgecrest U.S.A. 136 D4
Ridgefield U.S.A. 131 G3
Ridgeland MS U.S.A. 133 D5
Ridgeland SC U.S.A. 129 C5
Ridgetown Canada 130 C2
Ridgeway U.S.A. 130 D5
Ridgway U.S.A. 130 D3
Riding Mountain National Park Canada 123 K5
Ridley r. Australia 108 B5
Riecito Venez. 146 D2
Ried im Innkreis Austria 37 F4
Riedlingen Germany 36 D4
Rieppesgai'sa mt. Norway 32 F1
Riesa Germany 37 F3
Riesco, Isla i. Chile 153 B8
Riesi Sicily Italy 45 E6
Riet r. S. Africa 98 D6
Riet watercourse S. Africa 98 D6
Rietavas Lith. 33 F5
Rietfontein S. Africa 98 D5
Rieti Italy 44 D3
Rietschen Germany 37 G3
Rifā'ī, Tall mt. Jordan/Syria 77 C3
Rifeng China see Lichuan
Rifle U.S.A. 134 F5
Rift Valley prov. Kenya 96 B4
Rift Valley Lakes National Park Eth. see Abijatta-Shalla National Park
Riga Latvia see Rīga

▶Rīga Latvia 33 G4
Capital of Latvia.

Riga, Gulf of Estonia/Latvia 33 F4
Rigacikun Nigeria 93 G3
Rigān Iran 81 D4
Rīgas jūras līcis b. Estonia/Latvia see Riga, Gulf of
Rig-Rig Chad 88 B6
Rigsel r. Spain 43 F1
Riia laht b. Estonia/Latvia see Riga, Gulf of
Riihimäki Fin. 33 G3
Riiser-Larsen Ice Shelf Antarctica 167 B2
Riisipere Estonia 33 G4
Riisitunturin kansallispuisto nat. park Fin. 32 H2
Riito Mex. 135 D6
Rijau Nigeria 93 G3
Riječki Zaliv b. Croatia 44 E2
Rijeka Croatia 44 E2
Rikuchū-kaigan National Park Japan 65 E5
Rila mts Bulg. 46 C3
Rila China 75 E3
Riley U.S.A. 134 C4
Rillieux-la-Pape France 39 F4
Rillito U.S.A. 137 G5
Rima watercourse Niger/Nigeria 93 G2
Rimah, Wādī al watercourse Saudi Arabia 89 I3
Rimau, Pulau i. Indon. 58 D3
Rimava r. Slovakia 37 J4
Rimavská Sobota Slovakia 37 J4
Rimbey Canada 123 H4
Rimbo Sweden 33 E4
Rimersburg U.S.A. 130 D3
Rimforsa Sweden 33 D4
Rimini Italy 44 D2
Râmnicu Sărat Romania see Râmnicu Sărat
Râmnicu Vâlcea Romania see Râmnicu Vâlcea
Rimouski Canada 125 G3
Rinbung China 75 F3
Rincón, Cerro del mt. Chile 148 D6
Rinconada Arg. 148 D6
Rincón del Bonete, Lago Artificial de resr Uruguay 152 F3
Rincón de los Sauces Arg. 152 C4
Rincón de Romos Mex. 126 F7
Rind r. India 74 D4
Rindal Norway 32 C3
Rineia i. Greece 47 D6
Ringas India 74 B4
Ringebu Norway 33 C3
Ringim Nigeria 93 H2
Ringkøbing Denmark 33 C4
Ringkøbing Fjord lag. Denmark 33 C5
Ringsted Denmark 33 C5
Ringvassøy i. Norway 32 E1
Ringwood U.K. 35 F6
Ringwood U.S.A. 131 F3
Rinia i. Greece see Rineia
Rinteln Germany 36 D2
Rinya r. Hungary 44 F2
Rio Alegre Brazil 149 F4
Riobamba Ecuador 146 B5
Rio Blanco U.S.A. 134 F5
Rio Branco Brazil 148 D2
Rio Branco state Brazil see Roraima
Rio Branco, Parque Nacional do nat. park Brazil 147 F4
Río Bravo, Parque Internacional del nat. park Mex. 133 A6
Rio Brilhante Brazil 151 A7
Río Bueno Chile 152 B5
Río Caribe Venez. 147 F2
Rio Casca Brazil 151 D7
Rio Chico Arg. 153 C7
Río Chico Venez. 147 E2
Rio Claro Brazil 149 I5
Rio Claro Trin. and Tob. 147 F2
Río Colorado Arg. 152 D4
Río Corrientes Ecuador 146 B5
Río Cuarto Arg. 152 D3
Rio das Almas r. Brazil 149 H3

▶Rio de Janeiro Brazil 151 D7
3rd most populous city in South America. Former capital of Brazil.
southamerica 144–145
world 16–17

Rio de Janeiro state Brazil 151 D7

▶Río de la Plata-Paraná S. America 152 F4
2nd longest river in South America and 9th in the world.
southamerica 142–143
world 6–7

Rio Dell U.S.A. 134 A4
Rio do Sul Brazil 151 B8
Río Formoso Brazil 150 F4
Río Gallegos Arg. 153 C7
Río Grande Arg. 153 C8
Río Grande Bol. 148 C5
Rio Grande Brazil 152 G3
Río Grande Mex. 126 F7
Rio Grande r. Mex./U.S.A. 135 H8
Rio Grande City U.S.A. 133 B7
Rio Grande do Norte state Brazil 150 E3
Rio Grande do Sul state Brazil 151 A9
Rio Grande Rise sea feature S. Atlantic Ocean 161 L8
Riohacha Col. 146 C2
Río Hondo, Embalse resr Arg. 152 D1
Rioja Peru 146 B6
Rio Largo Brazil 150 F4
Riom France 39 E4
Rio Maior Port. 42 B3
Riom-ès-Montagnes France 39 E4
Río Muerto Arg. 152 E1
Río Mulatos Bol. 148 D4
Río Muni reg. Equat. Guinea 93 H5
Río Negro prov. Arg. 152 D4
Rionero in Vulture Italy 44 E4
Rioni r. Georgia 79 E2
Rio Pardo de Minas Brazil 150 D5
Rio Rancho U.S.A. 135 F6
Ríos Spain 42 C2
Riosucio Col. 146 E3
Río Tercero Arg. 152 D3
Río Tigre Ecuador 146 B5
Rio Tinto Brazil 150 F3
Riou, Oued watercourse Alg. 43 G5
Riou Lake Canada 123 J3
Rio Verde Brazil 149 H4
Río Verde Chile 153 C8
Rioverde Ecuador 146 B4

Río Verde Mex. 126 G7
Rio Verde de Mato Grosso Brazil 151 A6
Rio Vista U.S.A. 136 B2
Riozinho Brazil 148 D2
Riozinho r. Brazil 146 E5
Ripanj Serb. and Mont. 46 B2
Ripky Ukr. 29 D6
Ripley MS U.S.A. 128 A5
Ripley NY U.S.A. 130 D2
Ripley OH U.S.A. 130 B4
Ripley TN U.S.A. 133 D5
Ripley WV U.S.A. 130 C4
Ripoll Spain 43 H1
Ripon U.K. 35 F4
Ripon U.S.A. 136 B3
Riposto Sicily Italy 45 E6
Risān 'Unayzah hill Egypt 77 A4
Risasi Dem. Rep. Congo 94 E5
Risbäck Sweden 32 D2
Risco Plateado mt. Arg. 152 C3
Rishiri-tō i. Japan 64 E3
Rishon Le Ẓiyyon Israel 77 B4
Rising Sun IN U.S.A. 130 A4
Rising Sun MD U.S.A. 131 E4
Risle r. France 38 D2
Risnjak nat. park Croatia 44 E2
Rîşnov Romania see Râşnov
Rison U.S.A. 133 C5
Rissa Norway 32 C3
Ristiina Fin. 33 G3
Ristijärvi Fin. 32 H2
Ristikent Rus. Fed. 32 H1
Risum China 74 C2
Ritan r. Indon. 59 F2
Ritchie S. Africa 98 E6
Ritchie's Archipelago is India 73 G3
Ritch Island Canada 123 G1
Ritscher Upland mts Antarctica 167 B2
Ritsem Sweden 32 E2
Ritzville U.S.A. 134 C3
Riu, Mount P.N.G. 111 H1
Rivadavia Buenos Aires Arg. 152 E3
Rivadavia Mendoza Arg. 152 C3
Rivadavia Salta Arg. 149 E6
Rivadavia Chile 152 C2
Riva del Garda Italy 44 C2
Riva Palacio Mex. 135 F7
Rivarolo Canavese Italy 44 A2
Rivas Nicaragua 139 G6
Rīvash Iran 80 D3
Rive-de-Gier France 39 F4
Rivera Arg. 152 E4
Rivera Uruguay 152 G2
River Cess Liberia 92 C4
Riverhead U.S.A. 131 G3
Riverina Australia 109 C7
Riverina reg. Australia 112 C4
Rivero, Isla i. Chile 153 B6
Rivers state Nigeria 93 G4
Riversdale S. Africa 98 D7
Riverside U.S.A. 136 D5
Riversleigh Australia 110 D3
Riverton N.Z. 113 B4
Riverton UT U.S.A. 137 G1
Riverton WY U.S.A. 134 E4
Riverview Canada 125 H4
River View S. Africa 99 G6
Rives France 39 F4
Rivesaltes France 39 E5
Rivesville U.S.A. 130 C4
Rivière-au-Renard Canada 125 H3
Rivière Bleue Canada 125 G4
Rivière-du-Loup Canada 125 G4
Riviere-Pentecote Canada 125 H3
Riviere-Pigou Canada 125 H3
Rivne Ukr. 29 C6
Rivoli Italy 44 A2
Riwaka N.Z. 113 C3
Riwoqê China 66 A2

▶Riyadh Saudi Arabia 76 D5
Capital of Saudi Arabia.

Riza well Iran 80 C3
Rize Turkey 79 E2
Rizhao China 63 J4
Rizokarpaso Cyprus see Rizokarpason
Rizokarpason Cyprus 77 B2
Rīzū well Iran 80 D3
Rīzū'īyeh Iran 80 D4
Rjukan Norway 33 C4
Rkîz, Lac l. Mauritania 92 B1
Roa Norway 33 C3
Roa Spain 42 E2
Roach Lake U.S.A. 137 E4
Roads U.S.A. 130 B4

▶Road Town Virgin Is (U.K.) 139 L5
Capital of the British Virgin Islands.

Roan Fell hill U.K. 34 E4
Roanne France 39 F3
Roanoke AL U.S.A. 129 B5
Roanoke VA U.S.A. 130 D5
Roanoke r. U.S.A. 130 E5
Roanoke Rapids U.S.A. 130 E5
Roan Plateau U.S.A. 137 H2
Roaringwater Bay Rep. of Ireland 35 B6
Roatán Hond. 138 G5
Robat r. Afgh. 81 E4
Robāţ Iran 80 D4
Robāţ-e Khān Iran 80 D3
Robāţ-e Shahr-e Bābak Iran 80 C4
Robāţe Tork Iran 80 B3
Robāţ-e Ţoroq Iran 81 D2
Robāţ Karīm Iran 80 C3
Robāţ-Sang Iran 81 D3
Robat Thana Pak. 81 E4
Robb Canada 123 G4
Robbins Island Australia 112 C6
Robe r. Australia 108 A5
Robe, Mount Australia 112 B3
Röbel Germany 37 F2
Robert Glacier Antarctica 167 D2
Robert Lee U.S.A. 133 A6
Roberts U.S.A. 134 D4
Roberts, Mount Australia 111 H6
Robertsburg U.S.A. 130 C4
Roberts Butte mt. Antarctica 167 H2
Roberts Creek Mountain U.S.A. 137 D2
Robertsfors Sweden 32 F2
Robertsganj India 75 D4
Robert S. Kerr Reservoir U.S.A. 133 C5
Robertson, Lac l. Canada 125 J3
Robertson Bay Antarctica 167 H2
Robertson Island Antarctica 167 A2
Robertson Range hills Australia 108 C5
Robertsport Liberia 92 C4
Robert Williams Angola see Caála
Roberval Canada 125 F3
Robeson Channel Canada/Greenland 121 M1
Robhanais, Rubha hd U.K. see Butt of Lewis
Robinson r. Australia 110 D3
Robinson Canada 122 C2
Robinson U.S.A. 130 A4
Robinson Mountains U.S.A. 122 A2
Robinson Range hills Australia 109 B6
Robinvale Australia 112 B4
Roblin Canada 134 G2
Robore Bol. 149 F4
Robsart Canada 123 I5
Robson, Mount Canada 122 G4
Robstown U.S.A. 133 B7
Roby U.S.A. 133 A5
Roçadas Angola see Xangongo
Roca Partida, Isla i. Mex. 126 D8
Rocas, Atol das atoll Brazil 150 F2
Rocca Busambra mt. Sicily Italy 45 D6
Rocca Imperiale Italy 45 F4
Roccastrada Italy 44 C3
Roc de Montalet mt. France 39 E5
Roc d'Enfer mt. France 39 G3
Rocha Uruguay 152 G3
Rochdale U.K. 35 E5
Rochechouart France 38 D4
Roche de Vic hill France 38 D4
Rochedo Brazil 151 A6
Rochefort Belgium 39 F1
Rochefort France 38 C4
Rochefort, Lac l. Canada 125 F1
Rochegda Rus. Fed. 28 G3
Rochester IN U.S.A. 132 E3
Rochester MN U.S.A. 132 C2
Rochester NH U.S.A. 131 H2
Rochester NY U.S.A. 130 E2
Roc'h Trévezel hill France 38 B2
Rocina r. Spain 42 C4
Rock r. Canada 122 E2
Rock r. IA U.S.A. 132 B3
Rock r. IL U.S.A. 132 D3
Rockall i. N. Atlantic Ocean 30 A1
Rockall Bank sea feature N. Atlantic Ocean 30 A1
Rock Bay Canada 122 E5
Rock Creek Canada 122 B1
Rock Creek r. U.S.A. 134 F2
Rockdale U.S.A. 133 B6
Rockefeller Plateau Antarctica 167 J1
Rockford AL U.S.A. 129 B5
Rockford IL U.S.A. 132 D3
Rockford OH U.S.A. 130 A3
Rockglen Canada 123 J5
Rock Hall U.S.A. 131 E4
Rockhampton Australia 111 G4
Rockhampton Downs Australia 110 C3
Rock Hill U.S.A. 129 C5
Rockingham Australia 109 A8
Rockingham U.S.A. 128 D5
Rockingham Bay Australia 111 F3
Rockinghorse Lake Canada 123 H1
Rockland U.S.A. 131 I1
Rocklands Reservoir Australia 112 B5
Rocklea Australia 108 B5
Rocknest Lake Canada 123 H1
Rock Point U.S.A. 137 H3
Rockport U.S.A. 130 C4
Rock Rapids U.S.A. 132 B3
Rock River U.S.A. 134 F4
Rock Sound Bahamas 129 D7
Rock Springs MT U.S.A. 134 F3
Rocksprings U.S.A. 133 A6
Rock Springs WY U.S.A. 134 E4
Rockstone Guyana 147 G3
Rockville IN U.S.A. 128 B4
Rockville MD U.S.A. 131 E4
Rockwell City U.S.A. 132 C3
Rockwood U.S.A. 130 B2
Rocky Ford U.S.A. 132 A4
Rocky Fork Lake U.S.A. 130 B4
Rocky Harbour Canada 125 J3
Rocky Lane Canada 123 G3
Rocky Mount NC U.S.A. 128 D5
Rocky Mount VA U.S.A. 130 D5
Rocky Mountain House Canada 123 H4
Rocky Mountain National Park U.S.A. 134 F4
Rocky Mountains U.S.A. 134 F4
Rocroi France 39 F2
Rodberg Norway 33 C3
Rødbyhavn Denmark 33 C5
Roddickton Canada 125 K3
Rödeby Sweden 33 D4
Rodez France 39 E4
Rodholívos Greece see Rodolivos
Rodhópolis Greece see Rodopoli
Ródhos i. Greece see Rhodes
Rodi i. Greece see Rhodes
Roding Germany 37 F4
Rødlia Norway 32 D2
Rodnichek Rus. Fed. see Rodnichok
Rodnichok Rus. Fed. 29 G6
Rodolfo Sanchez Toboada Mex. 135 C7
Rodolivos Greece 46 C4
Rodonit, Kepi i pt Albania 46 A4
Rodopi Planina mts Bulg./Greece see Rhodope Mountains
Rodopoli Greece 46 C4
Rodos Greece see Rhodes
Rodos i. Greece see Rhodes
Rodosto Turkey see Tekirdağ
Rodoya i. Norway 32 D2
Rodrigues Peru 146 C6
Rodrigues Island Mauritius 162 L7
Rødsand Norway 32 H1
Roebourne Australia 108 B5
Roebuck Bay Australia 108 C4
Roedtan S. Africa 99 F5
Roe Plains Australia 109 D7
Roermond Neth. 36 B3
Roeselare Belgium 39 E1
Roes Welcome Sound sea chan. Canada 123 O1
Rogachev Belarus see Rahachow
Rogagua, Laguna l. Bol. 148 D3
Rogaland county Norway 33 B4
Rogatica Bos.-Herz. 46 A3
Rogers Canada 134 C2
Rogers U.S.A. 133 C4
Rogers, Mount U.S.A. 130 C5
Rogers City U.S.A. 132 F2
Rogers Lake U.S.A. 136 D4
Roggan, Lac l. Canada 124 E2
Roggeveen Basin sea feature S. Pacific Ocean 165 M8
Roggeveld plat. S. Africa 98 D7
Roggeveldberge esc. S. Africa 98 D7
Rogliano Italy 45 F5
Rognan Norway 32 D2
Rögnitz r. Germany 36 E2
Rogoźno Poland 37 H2
Rogue r. U.S.A. 134 A4
Roha India 72 B2
Rohnert Park U.S.A. 136 A2
Rohrbach in Oberösterreich Austria 37 F4
Rohri Pak. 74 A4
Rohtak India 74 C3
Rohuküla Estonia 33 F4
Roi Et Thai. 61 C4
Roi Georges, Îles du is Fr. Polynesia 165 I6
Roine l. Fin. 33 G3
Roja Latvia 33 F4
Rojas Arg. 152 E3
Röjdåfors Sweden 33 D3
Rojhan Pak. 81 G4
Rojo Aguado, Laguna l. Bol. 148 D3
Rokan r. Indon. 58 C2
Rokeby Australia 111 E2
Rokeby National Park Australia 111 E2
Rokiškis Lith. 33 G5
Roknäs Sweden 32 F2
Rokycany Czech Rep. 37 F4
Rokytne Ukr. 29 C6
Rola Kangri mt. China 75 F2
Rolas, Ilha das i. São Tomé and Príncipe 93 G6
Rolim de Moura Brazil 149 E2
Roll U.S.A. 137 F5
Rolla MO U.S.A. 133 D4
Rolla ND U.S.A. 132 B1
Rollag Norway 33 C3
Rolleston Australia 111 G5
Rolleston N.Z. 113 C3
Rolleville Bahamas 129 E8
Rolling Fork U.S.A. 133 D5
Rolvsøya i. Norway 32 G1
Rom mt. Uganda 96 B4
Roma Australia 111 G5
Roma i. Indon. 57 G7
Roma Italy see Rome
Romaine r. Canada 125 I3
Roman Romania 31 K4
Romanâ, Câmpia plain Romania 46 C2
Romanaţilor, Câmpia plain Romania 46 C2
Romanche Gap sea feature S. Atlantic Ocean 160 M6
Romanet, Lac l. Canada 125 H1
▶Romania country Europe 46 D1
europe 24–25, 48
Roman-Kosh mt. Ukr. 78 C1
Romanovka Moldova see Basarabeasca
Romanovka Rus. Fed. 63 I1
Romans-sur-Isère France 39 F4
Romanzof, Cape U.S.A. 120 C3
Romão Brazil 147 F5
Rombas France 39 G2

▶Rome Italy 44 D4
Capital of Italy.

Rome GA U.S.A. 129 B5
Rome NY U.S.A. 131 F2
Romeo U.S.A. 130 B2
Romford U.K. 35 G6
Romilly-sur-Seine France 39 E2
Romit Tajik. 81 G2
Romney U.S.A. 130 D4
Romny Ukr. 29 E6
Rømø i. Denmark 33 C5
Romorantin-Lanthenay France 38 D3
Rompin r. Malaysia 58 C2
Romu mt. Indon. 59 G5
Romulus U.S.A. 130 B2
Ron India 72 B3
Rona i. U.K. 34 D2
Ronas Hill U.K. 34 F1
Roncador, Serra do hills Brazil 150 A5
Roncador Reef Solomon Is 107 E2
Ronceverte U.S.A. 130 C5
Ronda Spain 42 D4
Ronda, Serranía de mts Spain 42 D4
Ronda das Salinas Brazil 149 E3
Rondane Nasjonalpark nat. park Norway 33 C3
Ronde i. Grenada 147 F1
Rondon Brazil 149 G5
Rondón Col. 146 D3
▶Rondônia state Brazil 149 E2
southamerica 144–145
Rondonópolis Brazil 151 A6
Rong'an China 67 D3
Rongbaca China 66 A2
Rongcheng Anhui China see Qingyang
Rongcheng Guangxi China see Rongxian
Rongcheng Hubei China see Jianli
Rong Chu r. China 75 F3
Rongelap atoll Marshall Is 164 F6
Rongjiang Guizhou China 67 D3
Rongjiang Jiangxi China see Nankang
Rong Jiang r. China 67 D4
Rongjiawan China see Yueyang
Rongklang Range mts Myanmar 60 A3
Rongmei China see Hefeng
Rongxian Guangxi China 67 D4
Rongxian Sichuan China 66 C2
Rongzhag China see Danba
Rønne Denmark 33 D5
Ronneby Sweden 33 D4
Ronne Entrance strait Antarctica 167 L2
Ronne Ice Shelf Antarctica 167 L1
Ronnenberg Germany 36 D2
Ronse Belgium 39 E1
Ronuro r. Brazil 150 A5
Rooke Island P.N.G. see Umboi
Roorkee India 74 C3
Roosendaal Neth. 36 B3
Roosevelt AZ U.S.A. 137 G5
Roosevelt UT U.S.A. 137 H1
Roosevelt, Mount Canada 122 E3
Roosevelt Island Antarctica 167 I1
Roosna-Alliku Estonia 33 G4
Root r. Canada 122 F2
Root r. U.S.A. 132 D3
Ropa r. Poland 37 J4
Ropczyce Poland 37 J3
Roper r. Australia 110 C2
Roper Bar Australia 110 C2
Roquebrune-sur-Argens France 39 G5
Roquefort France 38 C4
Roquetas de Mar Spain 43 E4
Roraima state Brazil 147 F4
Roraima, Mount Guyana 147 F3
Rori India 74 B3
Røros Norway 33 C3
Rorschach Switz. 39 H3
Rørvik Norway 32 C2
Roś, Jezioro l. Poland 37 J2
Rosal de la Frontera Spain 42 C4
Rosalia U.S.A. 134 C3
Rosamond U.S.A. 136 C4
Rosamond Lake U.S.A. 136 C4
Rosario Jujuy Arg. 148 D5
Rosario Santa Fé Arg. 152 E3
Rosário Brazil 150 C2
Rosario Baja California Mex. 135 D7
Rosario Coahuila Mex. 133 A7
Rosario Mex. 126 E7
Rosario Sonora Mex. 135 E8
Rosario Para. 149 F6
Rosario Venez. 146 C2
Rosario de la Frontera Arg. 152 D1
Rosario de Lerma Arg. 148 D6
Rosário do Sul Brazil 151 A9
Rosário Oeste Brazil 149 F3
Rosarito Baja California Mex. 135 D7
Rosarito Baja California Mex. 136 D5
Rosarno Italy 45 E5
Rosas Spain see Roses
Rosas, Golfo de b. Spain see Roses, Golf de
Rosa Zárate Ecuador 146 B4
Roscoff France 38 B2
Roscommon Rep. of Ireland 35 B5
Roscommon U.S.A. 130 A1
Roscrea Rep. of Ireland 35 C5
Rose r. Australia 110 C2
Rose, Mount U.S.A. 136 C2

▶Roseau Dominica 139 L5
Capital of Dominica.

Roseau U.S.A. 132 C1
Roseau r. U.S.A. 132 B1
Roseberth Australia 111 D5
Rosebery Australia 112 C6
Rose Blanche Canada 125 J4
Rosebud r. Canada 123 H5
Rosebud Creek r. U.S.A. 134 F3
Roseburg U.S.A. 134 B4
Rose City U.S.A. 130 A1
Rosedale U.S.A. 133 D5
Roseires Reservoir Sudan 96 B2
Rosenberg U.S.A. 133 C6
Rosendal Norway 33 B4
Rosengarten Germany 36 D2
Rosenheim Germany 36 F5
Rose Peak U.S.A. 137 H5
Rose Point Canada 122 D4
Roses Spain 43 H1
Roses, Golf de b. Spain 43 H1
Roseto degli Abruzzi Italy 44 E3
Rosetown Canada 134 F2
Rosetta Egypt see Rashīd
Rose Valley Canada 123 K4
Roseville U.S.A. 136 B2
Roshkhvār Iran 81 D3
Rosh Pinah Namibia 98 C5
Rosignano Marittimo Italy 44 C3
Roşiori de Vede Romania 46 D2
Rositsa Bulg. 46 E3
Rositsa r. Bulg. 46 D3
Roskilde Denmark 33 D5
Roslavl' Rus. Fed. 29 E5
Roslyakovo Rus. Fed. 32 I1
Roslyatino Rus. Fed. 28 H4
Rosolina Italy 44 D2
Rosporden France 38 B3
Ross Australia 112 C6
Ross r. Canada 122 C2
Ross N.Z. 113 B3
Ross, Mount N.Z. 113 C3
Rossano Italy 45 F5
Rossan Point Rep. of Ireland 34 B4
Ross Barnett Reservoir U.S.A. 133 D5
Ross Bay Junction Canada 125 H2
Ross Dependency Antarctica 167 I2
Rossel Island P.N.G. 111 H1
Ross Ice Shelf Antarctica 167 I1
Rössing Namibia 98 B4
Ross Island Antarctica 167 H1
Ross Island Myanmar see Daung Kyun
Rossiyskaya Sovetskaya Federativnaya Sotsialisticheskaya Respublika country Asia/Europe see Russian Federation
Rossland Canada 122 G5
Rosslare Rep. of Ireland 35 C5
Rosslare Harbour Rep. of Ireland 35 C5
Rosso Mauritania 92 B3
Rossön Sweden 32 D3
Ross-on-Wye U.K. 35 E6
Rossosh' Rus. Fed. 29 F6
Ross River Australia 110 C4
Ross River Canada 122 C2
Ross Sea Antarctica 167 H1
Røssvatnet l. Norway 32 D2
Rosswood Canada 122 D4
Rōst Iraq 79 F3
Røst Norway 32 D2
Rostāq Afgh. 81 G2
Rostāq Fārs Iran 80 C4
Rostāq Hormozgan Iran 80 C5
Røsthavet sea chan. Norway 32 D2
Rosthern Canada 123 J4
Rostock Germany 36 F1
Rostonsölkä ridge Sweden 32 F1
Rostov Rus. Fed. 28 F4
Rostov-na-Donu Rus. Fed. 29 F7
Rostov Oblast admin. div. Rus. Fed. see Rostovskaya Oblast'
Rostov-on-Don Rus. Fed. see Rostov-na-Donu
Rostovskaya Oblast' admin. div. Rus. Fed. 29 G7
Rostrenen France 38 B2
Røsvik Norway 32 D2
Roswell U.S.A. 135 F6
Rota i. N. Mariana Is 57 K3
Rotch Island Kiribati see Tamana
Rote i. Indon. 57 F8
Rotenburg (Wümme) Germany 36 D2
Rote Wand mt. Austria 36 D5
Roth Germany 36 E4
Rothenburg ob der Tauber Germany 36 E4
Rothera research station Antarctica 167 L2
Rotherham N.Z. 113 C3
Rotherham U.K. 35 F5
Rothesay U.K. 34 D4
Rothschild Island Antarctica 163 C10
Roti Indon. 108 C2
Roti i. Indon. see Rote
Roto Australia 112 C4
Rotomagus France see Rouen
Rotomanu N.Z. 113 B3
Rotorua N.Z. 113 D2
Rotorua, Lake N.Z. 113 D2
Rott r. Germany 37 F4
Rottenmann Austria 37 G5
Rotterdam Neth. 36 B3
Rotterdam U.S.A. 131 G2
Rottnest Island Australia 109 A8
Rottweil Germany 36 D4
Rotuma i. Fiji 107 G3
Rötviken Sweden 32 D3
Rötz Germany 37 F4
Roubaix France 39 E1
Roudnice nad Labem Czech Rep. 37 G3
Rouen France 38 D2
Rouhia Tunisia 45 B7
Roui, Oued er watercourse Niger 88 A4
Roulers Belgium see Roeselare
Roumania country Europe see Romania
Roundeyed Lake Canada 125 G2
Roundhead U.S.A. 130 B3
Round Mountain mt. Australia 112 E3
Round Mountain U.S.A. 136 D2
Round Rock AZ U.S.A. 137 H3
Round Rock TX U.S.A. 133 B6
Roundup U.S.A. 134 E3
Roura Fr. Guiana 147 H3
Rousay i. U.K. 34 E2
Roussillon France 39 F4
Rouyn Canada 124 E3
Rovaniemi Fin. 32 G2
Rovato Italy 44 C2
Roven'ki Rus. Fed. 29 F6
Rovereto Italy 44 C2
Roversi Arg. 152 E1
Rovigo Italy 44 C2
Rovinari Romania 46 C2
Rovinj Croatia 44 D2
Rovkul'skoye, Ozero l. Rus. Fed. 32 H3
Rovno Ukr. see Rivne
Rovnoye Rus. Fed. 29 H6
Rowlesburg U.S.A. 130 D4
Rowley Island Canada 121 L3
Rowley Shoals sea feature Australia 108 B4
Równe Ukr. see Rivne
Rów Polski r. Poland 37 H3
Roxas Mindoro Phil. 57 F3
Roxas Palawan Phil. 56 E3
Roxas Panay Phil. 57 F3
Roxboro U.S.A. 128 D4
Roxborough Downs Australia 110 D4
Roxburgh N.Z. 113 B4
Roxby Downs Australia 109 G7
Roxen l. Sweden 33 D4
Roxo r. Port. 42 B4
Roxo, Barragem do resr Port. 42 B4
Royal Canal Rep. of Ireland 35 C5
Royal Chitwan National Park Nepal 75 E4
Royale, Île i. Canada see Cape Breton Island
Royale, Isle i. U.S.A. 132 D1
Royal Oak U.S.A. 130 B2
Royan France 38 C4
Roye France 39 E2
Roy Hill Australia 108 B5
Royston U.K. 35 F5
Röyttä Fin. 32 G2
Rožaje Serb. and Mont. 46 B3
Różan Poland 37 J2
Rožanj hill Serb. and Mont. 46 A2
Rozdil'na Ukr. 29 D7
Rozhdestvenskoye Rus. Fed. 28 H4
Rozino Bulg. 46 D3
Rozivka Ukr. 29 F7
Rožňava Slovakia 37 J4
Rozveh Iran 80 B3
Rrëshen Albania 46 A4
Rrogozhinë Albania 46 A4
Rtishchevo Rus. Fed. 29 G5
Ruacana Namibia 98 B3
Ruaha National Park Tanz. 97 B6
Ruahine Range mts N.Z. 113 D3
Ruanda country Africa see Rwanda
Ruapehu, Mount vol. N.Z. 113 C2
Ruapuke Island N.Z. 113 B4
Ruarwe Malawi 97 B7
Ruatoria N.Z. 113 D2

▶Rub' al Khālī des. Saudi Arabia 76 D6
Largest uninterrupted stretch of sand in the world.

Rubaydā reg. Saudi Arabia 80 B5
Rubeho Mountains Tanz. 97 C6
Rubi r. Dem. Rep. Congo 94 E4
Rubicon r. U.S.A. 136 B2
Rubondo National Park Tanz. 96 A5
Rubtsovsk Rus. Fed. 26 I4
Rubuga Tanz. 97 B6
Rubūţ, Jabal ar hill Saudi Arabia 89 I5
Ruby U.S.A. 120 D3
Ruby Dome mt. U.S.A. 137 E1
Ruby Lake U.S.A. 137 E1
Ruby Mountains U.S.A. 137 E1
Rubys Inn U.S.A. 137 F3
Rucăr Romania 46 D2
Ruchay Belarus 33 G5
Rucheng Guangdong China see Ruyuan
Rucheng Hunan China 67 E3
Ruciane-Nida Poland 37 J2
Ruckersville U.S.A. 130 D4
Rudall River National Park Australia 108 C5
Rudalls watercourse Australia 110 C4
Rudarpur India 75 D4
Rudauli India 75 D4
Rudbar Afgh. 81 E4
Rūdbār Iran 80 B2
Rūd-e Kor watercourse Iran 80 C4
Rudina pass Serb. and Mont. 46 A3
Rūd-i-Shur watercourse Iran 80 D4
Rūdiškės Lith. 33 G5
Rudkøbing Denmark 33 C5
Rudna Glava Serb. and Mont. 46 C2
Rudnaya Pristan' Primorskiy Kray Rus. Fed. 64 C3
Rudnaya Pristan' Primorskiy Kray Rus. Fed. 64 C4
Rudnichnyy Rus. Fed. 28 J4
Rudnik Poland 37 K3
Rudnik Ingichka Uzbek. see Ingichka
Rudnya Smolenskaya Oblast' Rus. Fed. 29 D5
Rudnya Volgogradskaya Oblast' Rus. Fed. 29 H6
Rudnyy Kazakh. 26 G4
Rudnyy Rus. Fed. 64 C3
Rudolf, Lake salt l. Eth./Kenya see Turkana, Lake

▶Rudol'fa, Ostrov i. Rus. Fed. 26 F1
Most northerly point of Europe.

Rudolph Island Rus. Fed. see Rudol'fa, Ostrov
Rudolstadt Germany 36 E3
Rudong China 67 G1
Rudozem Bulg. 46 D4
Rūdsar Iran 80 B2
Rue France 38 D1
Ruen mt. Macedonia see Rujen
Ruenya r. Zimbabwe 99 G3
Rufa'a Sudan 89 G6
Ruffec France 38 D3
Rufiji r. Tanz. 97 C7
Rufino Arg. 152 E3
Rufisque Senegal 92 A2
Rufunsa Zambia 95 F8
Rugāji Latvia 33 G4
Rugao China 67 G1
Rugby U.K. 35 F5
Rugby U.S.A. 134 G2
Rügen i. Germany 37 F1
Rugged Mountain Canada 122 E5
Rugheiwa well Sudan 89 F6
Ruhangino Tanz. 97 C7
Ruḥayyat al Ḥamr'ā' waterhole Saudi Arabia 80 A5
Ruḥbah oasis Syria 77 C3
Ruhengeri Rwanda 94 F5
Ruhnu i. Estonia 33 F4
Ruhr r. Germany 36 C3
Ruhudji r. Tanz. 97 B7
Ruhuna National Park Sri Lanka 72 D5
Rui'an China 67 G3
Ruichang China 67 E2
Ruidoso U.S.A. 135 F6
Ruijin China 67 E3
Ruiz Mex. 126 E7
Ruiz, Nevado del vol. Col. 146 C3
Ruj mt. Bulg. 46 C3
Rujaylah, Ḥarrat ar lava field Jordan 77 C3
Rujen mt. Macedonia 46 C3
Rūjiena Latvia 33 G4
Ruki r. Dem. Rep. Congo 94 C4
Rukumkot Nepal 75 D3
Rukungiri Uganda 96 A5
Rukwa admin. reg. Tanz. 97 A6
Rukwa, Lake Tanz. 97 B7
Rūl Ḍadnah U.A.E. 80 D5
Ruleville U.S.A. 133 D5
Rulin China see Chengbu
Rulong China see Xinlong
Rūm Iran 81 D3
Rum i. U.K. 34 C3
Rum r. U.S.A. 132 C2
Rum, Jebel mts Jordan see Ramm, Jabal
Ruma Serb. and Mont. 46 A2
Rumāh Saudi Arabia 80 A5
Ruma National Park Kenya 96 B5
Rumania country Europe see Romania
Rumbek Sudan 94 F3
Rumblar r. Spain 42 E3
Rumburk Czech Rep. 37 G3
Rum Cay i. Bahamas 129 E8
Rumford U.S.A. 131 H1
Rumia Poland 37 I1
Rumilly France 39 F4
Rummānā hill Syria 77 D3
Rumoi Japan 64 E4
Rumphi Malawi 97 B7
Runan China 67 E1
Runaway, Cape N.Z. 113 D2
Runcorn U.K. 35 E5
Runcu Romania 46 C2
Runde r. Zimbabwe 99 G4
Rundu Namibia 98 C3
Rundvik Sweden 32 E3
Rüng, Kaôh i. Cambodia 61 C6
Rungan r. Indon. 59 F3
Rungu Dem. Rep. Congo 94 E4
Rungwa Rukwa Tanz. 97 A6
Rungwa Singida Tanz. 97 B6
Rungwa r. Tanz. 97 A6
Runing China see Runan
Rūniz-e Bālā Iran 80 C4
Runn l. Sweden 33 D3
Running Springs U.S.A. 136 D4
Running Water watercourse U.S.A. 133 A5
Runton Range hills Australia 108 C5
Ruokolahti Fin. 33 H3
Ruoqiang China 70 G4
Ruovesi Fin. 33 G3
Rupa India 75 G4
Rupat i. Indon. 58 C2
Rupea Romania 46 D1
Rupert r. Canada 124 E3
Rupert U.S.A. 130 C5
Rupert Bay Canada 124 E3
Rupert Coast Antarctica 167 J1
Rupert Creek r. Australia 111 E4
Rupnagar India 74 B4
Rupshu reg. Jammu and Kashmir 74 C2
Ruqqād, Wādī ar watercourse Israel 77 B3
Rural Retreat U.S.A. 130 C5
Rurrenabaque Bol. 148 D3
Rusaddir N. Africa see Melilla
Rusape Zimbabwe 99 G3
Ruschuk Bulg. see Ruse
Ruse Bulg. 46 D3
Rusenski Lom nat. park Bulg. 46 E3
Rusera India 75 E4
Ruşeţu Romania 46 E2
Rushan Tajik. see Rushon
Rushanskiy Khrebet mts Tajik. see Rushon, Qatorkŭhi
Rush Creek r. U.S.A. 132 A4
Rushford U.S.A. 132 D3
Rushmere U.S.A. 131 E5
Rushon Tajik. 81 G2
Rushon, Qatorkŭhi mts Tajik. 81 G2
Rushville IN U.S.A. 128 B4
Rushville OH U.S.A. 130 B4
Rushworth Australia 112 C5
Rusk U.S.A. 133 C6
Ruskele Sweden 32 E2
Ruskin U.S.A. 129 C7
Rusokastro Bulg. 46 E3
Rušona Latvia 33 G4
Russas Brazil 150 E3
Russell Canada 134 G2
Russell N.Z. 113 C1
Russell U.S.A. 132 B4
Russell Bay Antarctica 167 J2
Russell Lake Man. Canada 123 K3
Russell Lake N.W.T. Canada 123 H2
Russellville AL U.S.A. 129 B5
Russellville AR U.S.A. 133 C5
Russellville KY U.S.A. 128 B4
Russellville OH U.S.A. 130 B4
Rüsselsheim Germany 36 D3
Russi Italy 44 D2
Russia country Asia/Europe see Russian Federation

▶Russian Federation country Asia/Europe 27 F3
Largest country in the world, Europe and Asia. Most populous country in Europe, 5th in Asia and 7th in the world.
europe 24–25, 48
asia 52–53, 82
world 8–9, 16–17

Russian Soviet Federal Socialist Republic country Asia/Europe see Russian Federation
Russkiy Kameshkir Rus. Fed. 29 H5
Russkiy Zavorot, Poluostrov pen. Rus. Fed. 28 J1
Russkoye Ust'ye Rus. Fed. 27 O2
Rust'avi Georgia 79 F2
Rustburg U.S.A. 130 D5
Rustenburg S. Africa 99 E5
Ruston U.S.A. 133 C5
Rutana Burundi 95 F5
Rutanzige, Lake Dem. Rep. Congo/Uganda see Edward, Lake
Rute Spain 42 D4
Ruteng Indon. 57 F7
Rutenga Zimbabwe 99 F4
Rutherfordton U.S.A. 128 C5
Ruther Glen U.S.A. 130 E5
Ruthin U.K. 35 E5
Rutland U.S.A. 131 G2
Rutland Island India 73 G4
Rutland Plains Australia 111 E2
Rutledge Lake Canada 123 I2
Rutög China 70 E5
Rutog Xizang China 75 E3
Rutog Xizang China 75 G3
Rutshuru Dem. Rep. Congo 94 F5
Rutul Rus. Fed. 79 F2
Ruukki Fin. 32 G2
Ruvaslahti Fin. 32 H3
Ruvo di Puglia Italy 44 F4
Ruvozero Rus. Fed. 32 H2
Ruvu Tanz. see Pangani
Ruvuma r. Moz./Tanz. 97 D7
Ruvuma admin. reg. Tanz. 97 C7
Ruwayshid, Wādī watercourse Jordan 79 D4
Ruwayṭah, Wādī watercourse Jordan 77 C5
Ruweijil pt Saudi Arabia 77 B5
Ruweis U.A.E. 80 C5
Ruwenzori mts Dem. Rep. Congo/Uganda 94 F5
Ruwenzori National Park Uganda see Queen Elizabeth National Park
Ruya r. Zimbabwe 99 G3
Ruyuan China 67 E3
Ruza Rus. Fed. 28 F5
Ruzayevka Kazakh. 26 G4
Ruzayevka Rus. Fed. 29 H5
Ruzhou China 67 E1
Ružomberok Slovakia 37 I4
▶Rwanda country Africa 94 F5
africa 86–87, 100
Ryābād Iran 80 C2
Ryazan' Rus. Fed. 29 F5
Ryazan Oblast admin. div. Rus. Fed. see Ryazanskaya Oblast'
Ryazanskaya Oblast' admin. div. Rus. Fed. 29 G5
Ryazhsk Rus. Fed. 29 G5
Rybachiy, Poluostrov pen. Rus. Fed. 32 I1
Rybach'ye Kyrg. see Balykchy
Rybinsk Rus. Fed. 28 F4
Rybinskoye Vodokhranilishche resr Rus. Fed. 28 F4
Rybnik Poland 37 I3
Rybnitsa Moldova see Rîbniţa
Rybreka Rus. Fed. 28 E3
Rychnov nad Kněžnou Czech Rep. 37 H3
Rycroft Canada 122 G4
Ryd Sweden 33 D4
Rydberg Peninsula Antarctica 167 L2
Ryde U.K. 35 F6
Ryegate U.S.A. 134 E3
Rye Patch Reservoir U.S.A. 136 C1
Ryki Poland 37 J3
Rykovo Ukr. see Yenakiyeve
Ryl'sk Rus. Fed. 29 E6

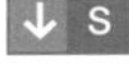

Salt watercourse S. Africa 98 D7
Salt Spain 43 H2
Salt r. AZ U.S.A. 137 F5
Salt r. MO U.S.A. 132 D4
Salt r. WY U.S.A. 134 E4
Salta Arg. 148 D6
Salta prov. Arg. 152 D1
Saltaire U.K. 35 F5
Saltash U.K. 35 D6
Salt Creek r. U.S.A. 130 B4
Saltee Islands Rep. of Ireland 35 C5
Saltery Bay Canada 134 A2
Saltfjellet Svartisen Nasjonalpark nat. park Norway 32 D2
Salt Fork Arkansas r. U.S.A. 133 B4
Salt Fork Lake U.S.A. 130 C3
Salt Fork Red r. U.S.A. 133 B5
Saltillo Mex. 126 F6

▶Salt Lake City U.S.A. 134 E4
State capital of Utah.

Salt Lick U.S.A. 130 B4
Salto Arg. 152 E3
Salto Brazil 149 I5
Salto r. Italy 44 D3
Salto Uruguay 152 F2
Salto da Divisa Brazil 151 E6
Salto del Guairá Para. 149 G6
Salto Grande, Embalse de resr Uruguay 152 F2
Salton City U.S.A. 137 D5
Salton Sea salt l. U.S.A. 137 E5
Saltpond Ghana 93 E4
Salt River Canada 123 H2
Saltville U.S.A. 130 C5
Saluda SC U.S.A. 129 C5
Saluda VA U.S.A. 131 E5
Saluda r. U.S.A. 129 C5
Salumbar India 74 B4
Saluq, Kūh-e mt. Iran 80 D2
Salur India 73 D2
Saluzzo Italy 44 A2
Salvador Brazil 150 E5
Salvador country Central America see El Salvador
Salvador, Lake U.S.A. 133 D6
Salvador Mazza Arg. 149 E5
Salvaterra Brazil 150 B2
Salviac France 38 D4
Salwah Saudi Arabia 80 B5
Salwah, Dawḥat b. Qatar/Saudi Arabia 80 B5
Salween r. China 70 I7
Salween r. China/Myanmar 60 B4
also known as Mae Nam Khong or Thanlwin (Myanmar) or Nu Jiang (China)
Salyan Azer. 79 G3
Sal'yany Azer. see Salyan
Salyersville U.S.A. 130 B5
Salza r. Austria 37 G5
Salzach r. Austria/Germany 37 F4
Salzburg Austria 37 F5
Salzgitter Germany 36 E2
Salzkotten Germany 36 D3
Salzwedel Germany 36 E2
Sam Gabon 94 A4
Sam India 74 A4
Sam, Nam r. Laos/Vietnam 60 D4
Šamac Bos.-Herz. see Bosanski Šamac
Samae San, Laem pt Thai. 61 C5
Samāh well Saudi Arabia 80 A4
Samaida Iran see Someydeh
Samaipata Bol. 149 E4
Samak, Tanjung pt Indon. 58 D3
Samakoulou Mali 92 C2
Samalayuca Mex. 135 F7
Samālūṭ Egypt 89 F2
Samana India 74 C3
Samana Cay i. Bahamas 129 E8
Samanala mt. Sri Lanka see Adam's Peak
Samandağı Turkey 78 C3
Samangān prov. Afgh. 81 F2
Samangān Iran 81 E3
Samani Japan 64 E4
Samaniego Col. 146 B4
Samanlı Dağları mts Turkey 46 F4
Samannūd Egypt 78 B5
Samar i. Phil. 57 G3
Samara Rus. Fed. 29 I5
Samara r. Rus. Fed. 29 I5
Samarahan Sarawak Malaysia see Sri Aman
Samarai P.N.G. 107 E3
Samara Oblast admin. div. Rus. Fed. see Samarskaya Oblast'
Samarga Rus. Fed. 64 D3
Samaria nat. park Greece 47 C7
Samariapo Venez. 146 E3
Samarinda Indon. 59 G3
Samarka Rus. Fed. 64 C3
Samarkand Uzbek. 81 F2
Samarkand, Pik mt. Tajik. 81 G2
Samarkand Oblast admin. div. Uzbek. see Samarkandskaya Oblast'
Samarkandskaya Oblast' admin. div. Uzbek. 81 F2
Samarobriva France see Amiens
Samarqand Uzbek. see Samarkand
Samarqand, Qullai mt. Tajik. see Samarkand, Pik
Samarqand Wiloyati admin. div. Uzbek. see Samarkandskaya Oblast'
Sāmarrā' Iraq 79 E4
Samarskaya Oblast' admin. div. Rus. Fed. 29 I5
Samasata Pak. 81 G4
Samassi Sardinia Italy 45 B5
Samastipur India 75 E4
Samaúma Brazil 147 F6
Şamaxı Azer. 79 G2
Samba Dem. Rep. Congo 95 E6
Samba r. Indon. 59 F3
Samba Jammu and Kashmir 74 B2
Samba Cajú Angola 95 B7
Sambaliung mts Indon. 59 G2
Sambalpur India 75 D5
Sambar, Tanjung pt Indon. 59 E3
Sambas Indon. 59 E2
Sambat Ukr. see Kiev
Sambava Madag. 99 [inset] K2
Sambhal India 74 C3
Sambhar India 74 B4
Sambhar Lake India 74 B4
Sambir Ukr. 31 J3
Sambo Angola 95 C8
Sambo Indon. 59 G3
Samboja Indon. 59 G3
Sambor Ukr. see Sambir
Sâmbor Dam Cambodia 61 D5
Samborombón, Bahía b. Arg. 152 F3
Samch'ŏnp'o S. Korea see Sach'on
Sameikkon Myanmar 60 A3
Samer France 38 D1
Samet, Ko i. Thai. 61 C5
Samfya Zambia 95 F7
Samḥah i. Yemen 76 E7
Sami India 74 A5
Sami Pak. 81 E5
Samiria r. Peru 146 C6
Samirum Iran see Yazd-e Khvāst
Samka Myanmar 60 B3
Şämkir Azer. 79 F2
Sam Neua Laos see Xam Hua
Samnū Libya 88 B3
▶Samoa country S. Pacific Ocean 107 H3
oceania 104–105, 114
Samoa Basin sea feature S. Pacific Ocean 165 G7
Samoa i Sisifo country S. Pacific Ocean see Samoa
Samobor Croatia 44 E2
Samoded Rus. Fed. 28 G3
Samokov Bulg. 46 C3
Šamorín Slovakia 37 H4
Samos Greece 47 E6
Samos i. Greece 47 E6
Samosir i. Indon. 58 B2
Samothrace i. Greece see Samothraki
Samothraki Greece 46 D4
Samothraki i. Greece 47 D4
Samovodene Bulg. 46 D3
Samoylovka Rus. Fed. 29 G6
Sampa Côte d'Ivoire 92 E4
Sampacho Arg. 152 D3
Sampit Indon. 59 F3
Sampit r. Indon. 59 F3
Sampit, Teluk b. Indon. 59 F3
Sampwe Dem. Rep. Congo 95 E7
Sam Rayburn Reservoir U.S.A. 133 C6
Samreboe Ghana 93 E4
Samrong Cambodia see Phumĭ Sâmraông
Samsang China 75 D3
Sam Sao, Phou mts Laos/Vietnam 60 C3
Samsø i. Denmark 33 C5
Samsø Bælt sea chan. Denmark 33 C5
Sâm Sơn Vietnam 60 D4
Samsun Turkey 78 D2
Samtens Germany 37 F1
Samthar India 74 C4
Samtredia Georgia 79 E2
Samui, Ko i. Thai. 61 C6
Samundri Pak. 81 H4
Samur r. Azer./Rus. Fed. 79 G2
Samut Prakan Thai. 61 C5
Samut Sakhon Thai. 61 C5
Samut Songkhram Thai. 61 C5
San Mali 92 D2
San r. Poland 37 J3
San, Phou mt. Laos 60 C4
San, Tônlé r. Cambodia 61 D5
Sana r. Bos.-Herz. 44 F2

▶Ṣan'ā' Yemen 76 C6
Capital of Yemen.

Sanaag admin. reg. Somalia 96 E2
San Adrián, Cabo de c. Spain 42 B1
Sanae research station Antarctica 167 B2
Sanaga r. Cameroon 93 H5
San Agostín U.S.A. see St Augustine
San Agustín Col. 146 B4
Sanak Island U.S.A. 120 C4
Sanandaj Iran 80 A3
Sanando Mali 92 D2
San Andreas U.S.A. 136 B2
San Andrés Bol. 149 D3
San Andrés Col. 146 C3
San Andrés, Isla de i. Caribbean Sea 139 H6
San Andrés del Rabanedo Spain 42 D1
San Andres Mountains U.S.A. 135 F6
San Andrés Tuxtla Mex. 138 E5
San Angelo U.S.A. 133 A6
Sanankoroba Mali 92 D2
San Antolín de Ibias Spain 42 C1
San Antonio Chile 152 C1
San Antonio Peru 146 C5
San Antonio NM U.S.A. 135 F6
San Antonio TX U.S.A. 133 B6
San Antonio r. CA U.S.A. 136 B4
San Antonio r. TX U.S.A. 133 B6
San Antonio, Cabo c. Arg. 152 F4
San Antonio, Cabo c. Cuba 127 J7
San Antonio Abad Spain 43 G3
San Antonio de los Cobres Arg. 148 D6
San Antonio de Palé Equat. Guinea 93 G6
San Antonio de Tamanaco Venez. 147 E2
San Antonio Este Arg. 152 D5
San Antonio Oeste Arg. 152 D5
San Antonio Reservoir U.S.A. 136 B4
San Augustín Arg. 152 F4
San Augustín de Valle Fértil Arg. 152 D2
San Augustine U.S.A. 133 C6
Sanawad India 74 C5
San Bartolomeo in Galdo Italy 44 E4
San Benedetto del Tronto Italy 44 D3
San Benedicto, Isla i. Mex. 126 D8
San Benito r. U.S.A. 136 B3
San Benito Mountain U.S.A. 136 B3
San Bernardino U.S.A. 136 D4
San Bernardino, Passo di pass Switz. 39 H3
San Bernardino Mountains U.S.A. 137 D4
San Bernardo Chile 152 C3
San Blas Arg. 152 D2
San Blas, Archipiélago de is Panama 146 B2
San Blas, Cape U.S.A. 129 B6
San Blas, Cordillera de mts Panama 146 B2
San Borja Bol. 148 D3
Sanborn U.S.A. 132 C3
Sanbornville U.S.A. 131 H2
San Buenaventura Mex. 133 A7
Sança Moz. 99 G3
San Candido Italy 44 D1
San Caprasio hill Spain 43 F2
San Carlos Mendoza Arg. 152 C3
San Carlos Salta Arg. 152 D1
San Carlos Chile 152 C4
San Carlos Equat. Guinea see Luba
San Carlos Mex. 133 A6
San Carlos Para. 149 F5
San Carlos Uruguay 152 G3
San Carlos U.S.A. 137 G5
San Carlos Amazonas Venez. 146 E4
San Carlos Apure Venez. 146 E3
San Carlos Cojedes Venez. 146 D2
San Carlos de Bariloche Arg. 152 C5
San Carlos de Bolívar Arg. 152 E4
San Carlos de la Ràpita Spain see Sant Carles de la Ràpita
San Carlos del Zulia Venez. 146 D2
San Carlos Lake U.S.A. 137 G5
San Cayetano Arg. 152 F4
San Celoni Spain see Sant Celoni
Sancerre France 39 E3
Sancerrois, Collines du hills France 39 E3
Sancha China 66 C1
Sanchahe China see Fuyu
Sancha He r. China 66 C3
Sanchi India 74 C5
San Chien Pau mt. Laos 60 C3
Sanchor India 74 A4
San Clemente Chile 152 C3
San Clemente U.S.A. 136 D5
San Clemente del Tuyú Arg. 152 F4
San Clemente Island U.S.A. 136 C5
Sancoins France 39 E3
San Cristóbal Arg. 152 E2
San Cristóbal Potosí Bol. 148 D5
San Cristóbal Santa Cruz Bol. 149 E3
San Cristóbal Col. 146 C5
San Cristobal i. Solomon Is 107 F3
San Cristóbal Venez. 146 C3
San Cristóbal de las Casas Mex. 138 F5
San Cristobal Wash watercourse U.S.A. 137 F5
Sancti Spíritus Cuba 127 K7
Sand r. S. Africa 99 F4
Sandakan Sabah Malaysia 59 G1
Sandakphu Peak India 75 F4
Sandanski Bulg. 46 C4
Sandaré Mali 92 C2
Sanday i. U.K. 34 E2
Sandbukt Norway 32 F1
Sand Cay reef India 72 B4
Sande Sogn og Fjordane Norway 33 B3
Sande Vestfold Norway 33 C4
Sandefjord Norway 33 C4
Sandefjord airport Norway 33 C4
Sandercock Nunataks nunataks Antarctica 167 D2
Sanders U.S.A. 137 H4
Sanderson U.S.A. 133 A6
Sandersville U.S.A. 129 C5
Sandfire Roadhouse Australia 108 C4
Sandfloeggi mt. Norway 33 B4
Sand Hill r. U.S.A. 132 B2
Sand Hills U.S.A. 132 A3
Sandhornøy i. Norway 32 D2
Sandi India 74 D4
Sandia Peru 148 C3
San Diego U.S.A. 136 D5
San Diego, Cabo c. Arg. 153 D8
San Diego, Sierra mts Mex. 135 E7
Sandıklı Turkey 78 B3
Sandila India 74 D4
Sanding i. Indon. 58 C3
Sand Lake Canada 123 M5
Sandnes Norway 33 B4
Sandø i. Faroe Is see Sandoy
Sandoa Dem. Rep. Congo 95 D7
Sandomierz Poland 37 J3
Sândominic Romania 46 D1
San Donà di Piave Italy 44 D2
Sandover watercourse Australia 110 D4
Sandovo Rus. Fed. 28 F4
Sandoway Myanmar 60 A4
Sandoy i. Faroe Is 34 [inset]
Sandpoint U.S.A. 134 C2
Sandray i. U.K. 34 C3
Sandringham Australia 110 D5
Sandsele Sweden 32 E2
Sandspit Canada 122 D4
Sand Springs U.S.A. 133 B4
Sand Springs Salt Flat U.S.A. 136 C2
Sandstone Australia 109 B6
Sandstone U.S.A. 132 C2
Sandu Guizhou China 66 C3
Sandu Hunan China 67 E3
Sandur India 72 C3
Sandusky MI U.S.A. 130 B2
Sandusky OH U.S.A. 130 B3
Sandusky Bay U.S.A. 130 B3
Sandveld mts S. Africa 98 C6
Sandvika Akershus Norway 33 C4
Sandvika Nord-Trøndelag Norway 32 D3
Sandviken Sweden 33 E3
Sandwich U.S.A. 131 H3
Sandwich Bay Canada 125 J2
Sandwich Island Vanuatu see Éfaté
Sandwip Bangl. 75 F5
Sandwip Channel Bangl. 75 F5
Sandy U.S.A. 137 G1
Sandy r. U.S.A. 131 I1
Sandy Bay Canada 123 K4
Sandy Cape Qld Australia 111 H5
Sandy Cape Tas. Australia 112 C6
Sandy Creek r. Australia 111 D3
Sandy Island Australia 108 C3
Sandykachi Turkm. 81 E2
Sandykly Gumy des. Turkm. see Sundukli, Peski
Sandy Lake Canada 123 M4
Sandy Lake l. Canada 123 M4
Sandy Springs U.S.A. 129 B5
Sandyville U.S.A. 130 C4
San Estanislao Para. 149 F6
San Fabián de Alico Chile 152 C4
San Felipe Chile 152 C3
San Felipe Baja California Mex. 135 D7
San Felipe Chihuahua Mex. 135 F8
San Felipe Venez. 146 D2
San Feliú de Guíxols Spain see Sant Feliu de Guíxols
San Fernando Arg. 152 F3
San Fernando Chile 152 C3
San Fernando Baja California Mex. 135 D7
San Fernando Tamaulipas Mex. 126 G7
San Fernando Phil. 57 F2
San Fernando Spain 42 C4
San Fernando Trin. and Tob. 147 F2
San Fernando U.S.A. 136 C4
San Fernando de Apure Venez. 146 E3
San Fernando de Atabapo Venez. 146 E3
San Filipe Creek watercourse U.S.A. 137 E5
Sånfjället nationalpark nat. park Sweden 33 D3
Sanford r. Australia 109 A6
Sanford FL U.S.A. 129 C6
Sanford ME U.S.A. 131 H2
Sanford MI U.S.A. 130 A2
Sanford NC U.S.A. 128 D5
San Francisco Arg. 152 E2
San Francisco Mex. 135 D7
▶San Francisco U.S.A. 136 A3
world 16–17
San Francisco r. U.S.A. 135 E6
San Francisco, Paso de pass Arg. 152 C1
San Francisco Bay inlet U.S.A. 136 A3
San Francisco del Oro Mex. 135 F8
San Francisco de Macorís Dom. Rep. 139 J5
San Francisco de Paula, Cabo c. Arg. 153 D7
San Francisco Javier Spain 43 G3
Sanga Dem. Rep. Congo 95 F6
San Gabriel Ecuador 146 B4
San Gabriel, Punta pt Mex. 135 D7
San Gabriel Mountains U.S.A. 136 C4
Sangai, Parque Nacional nat. park Ecuador 146 B5
Sangaigerong Indon. 58 D3
Sa'ngain China 66 A2
Sangam India 72 C3
Sangameshwar India 72 B2
Sangamner India 72 B2
Sangamon r. U.S.A. 132 D3
Sangān Iran 81 D3
Sangan, Koh-i- mt. Afgh. 81 F3
Sangar r. Pak. 81 G4
Sangaréa Guinea 92 B3
Sangareddi India 72 C2
Sangarédi Guinea 92 B3
Sangaria India 74 B3
Sangasanga Indon. 59 G3
Sangasso Mali see Zangasso
Sangaste Estonia 33 G4
San Gavino Monreale Sardinia Italy 45 B5
Sangay, Volcán vol. Ecuador 146 B5
Sang Bast Iran 81 D3
Sangbé Cameroon 93 I4
Sangbur Afgh. 81 E3
Sangeang i. Indon. 108 B2
Sanger U.S.A. 136 C3
Sangerfield U.S.A. 131 F2
Sangerhausen Germany 36 E3
Sanggar, Teluk b. Indon. 59 G5
Sanggarmai China 66 B1
Sanggau Indon. 59 E2
Sangha admin. reg. Congo 94 B4
Sangha r. Congo 94 C5
Sangha-Mbaéré pref. Cent. Afr. Rep. 94 C4
Sanghar Pak. 81 G5
San Gil Col. 146 C3
San Giovanni in Fiore Italy 45 F5
Sangir India 74 B5
Sangir i. Indon. 57 G5
Sangir, Kepulauan is Indon. 57 F5
Sangju S. Korea 65 B5
Sangkapura Indon. 59 F4
Sângke, Stœng r. Cambodia 61 C5
Sangkulirang Indon. 59 G2
Sangkulirang, Teluk b. Indon. 59 G2
Sangla Pak. 81 H4
Sangli India 72 B2
San Glorio, Puerto de pass Spain 42 D1
Sangmélima Cameroon 93 H5
Sango Zimbabwe 99 F4
Sangod India 74 C4
Sangole India 72 B2
Sangpi China see Xiangcheng
Sang Qu r. China 66 A2
Sangre de Cristo Range mts U.S.A. 135 F5
Sangre Grande Trin. and Tob. 147 F2
Sangri China 75 G3
Sangro r. Italy 44 E3
Sangrur India 74 B3
Sangsang China 75 E3
Sangu r. Bangl. 75 F5
Sangue r. Brazil 149 F2
Sangüesa Spain 43 F1
San Guiliano Milanese Italy 44 B2
Sangū'īyeh Iran 80 D4
Sangzhi China 67 D2
Sanhe China see Sandu
San Hipólito, Punta pt Mex. 135 D8
Sanhūr Egypt 89 F2
San Ignacio Beni Bol. 148 D3
San Ignacio Santa Cruz Bol. 149 E4
San Ignacio Santa Cruz Bol. 149 E4
San Ignacio Mex. 135 D8
San Ignacio Para. 149 F6
San Ignacio Peru 146 B6
San Ignacio, Laguna l. Mex. 135 D8
Sanikiluaq Canada 124 E1
Sanin-kaigan National Park Japan 65 C6
Sanitz Germany 37 F1
Sāniyat al Fawākhir well Libya 88 C3
San Jacinto Peak U.S.A. 137 D5
Sanjai r. India 75 E5
San Jaime Arg. 152 F2
San Javier Arg. 152 F2
San Javier Beni Bol. 148 D3
San Javier Santa Cruz Bol. 149 E4
Sanjawi Pak. 81 G4
Sanjbod Iran 80 B2
Sanjiang Guangxi China 67 D3
Sanjiang Guizhou China see Jinping
Sanjō Japan 65 D5
San Joaquín Bol. 148 D3
San Joaquín Para. 149 F6
San Joaquin U.S.A. 136 B3
San Joaquin r. U.S.A. 136 B2
San Joaquin Valley U.S.A. 136 B3
San Jon U.S.A. 135 G6
San Jorge Arg. 152 E2
San Jorge, Golfo de g. Arg. 153 D6
San Jorge, Golfo de g. Spain see Sant Jordi, Golf de

▶San José Costa Rica 139 H7
Capital of Costa Rica.

San Jose Phil. 57 F2
San Jose CA U.S.A. 136 B3
San Jose NM U.S.A. 135 F6
San Jose watercourse U.S.A. 135 F6
San José Venez. 146 E2
San José, Cabo c. Arg. 153 D6
San José, Cuchilla de hills Uruguay 152 F3
San José, Golfo g. Arg. 153 D5
San José, Isla i. Mex. 126 D7
San José, Volcán vol. Chile 152 C3
San José de Amacuro Venez. 147 F2
San Jose de Buenavista Phil. 57 F3
San José de Chiquitos Bol. 149 E4
San José de Comondú Mex. 126 D6
San José de Gracia Mex. 135 E7
San José de Jáchal Arg. 152 C2
San José de la Dormida Arg. 152 E2
San José del Boquerón Arg. 152 E1
San José del Cabo Mex. 126 E7
San José del Guaviare Col. 146 C4
San José de Mayo Uruguay 152 F3
San José de Ocuné Col. 146 D3
San Juan Arg. 152 C2
San Juan prov. Arg. 152 C2
San Juan Bol. 149 E4
San Juan Col. 146 B2
San Juan r. Col. 146 B3
San Juan r. Costa Rica/Nicaragua 139 H6
San Juan Mex. 135 F8
San Juan Peru 148 B3

▶San Juan Puerto Rico 139 K5
Capital of Puerto Rico.

San Juan r. CA U.S.A. 136 B4
San Juan r. UT U.S.A. 137 G3
San Juan Venez. 147 E3
San Juan, Cabo c. Equat. Guinea 93 H5
San Juan Bautista Para. 149 F6
San Juan Bautista Spain 43 G3
San Juan Bautista Tuxtepec Mex. 138 E5
San Juan Capistrano U.S.A. 136 D5
San Juan de César Col. 146 C2
San Juan dela Costa Chile 152 B5
San Juan de la Peña, Sierra de mts Spain 43 F1
San Juan de los Cayos Venez. 146 D2
San Juan de los Morros Venez. 146 E2
San Juan del Río Mex. 126 G7
San Juan de Salvamento Arg. 153 E8
San Juan Islands U.S.A. 134 B2
San Juanito Mex. 135 F8
San Juan Mountains U.S.A. 135 F5
San Julián Arg. 153 D7
San Just mt. Spain 43 F2
San Justo Arg. 152 E2
Sankarani r. Côte d'Ivoire/Guinea 92 C3
Sankarankovil India 72 C4
Sankeshwar India 72 B2
Sankh r. India 75 E5
Sankosh r. Bhutan see Sunkosh
Sankra Chhattisgarh India 73 D1
Sankra Rajasthan India 74 A4
Sankt Andrä Austria 37 G5
Sankt Gallen Switz. 39 H3
Sankt Gotthard Hungary see Szentgotthárd
Sankt Moritz Switz. 39 H3
Sankt-Peterburg Rus. Fed. see St Petersburg
Sankt Peter-Ording Germany 36 D1
Sankt Pölten Austria 37 G4
Sankt Veit an der Glan Austria 37 G5
Sankt Wendel Germany 36 C4
Sankuru r. Dem. Rep. Congo 95 D6
San Leandro U.S.A. 136 A3
San Leonardo in Passiria Italy 44 C1
Şanlıurfa Turkey 79 D3
San Lorenzo Arg. 152 E3
San Lorenzo Beni Bol. 148 D3
San Lorenzo Pando Bol. 148 D2
San Lorenzo Tarija Bol. 148 D5
San Lorenzo Ecuador 146 B4
San Lorenzo Mex. 135 F7
San Lorenzo Peru 148 C2
San Lorenzo mt. Spain 42 E1
San Lorenzo, Cabo c. Ecuador 146 A5
San Lorenzo, Cerro mt. Arg./Chile 153 B6
Sanlúcar de Barrameda Spain 42 C4
San Lucas Bol. 148 D5
San Lucas Baja California Sur Mex. 126 E7
San Lucas Baja California Sur Mex. 135 D8
San Lucas, Serranía de mts Col. 146 C3
San Luis Arg. 152 D3
San Luis prov. Arg. 152 D3
San Luis Peru 146 C5
San Luis AZ U.S.A. 137 E5
San Luis CO U.S.A. 135 F5
San Luis, Sierra de mts Arg. 152 D3
San Luisito Mex. 135 D7
San Luis Obispo U.S.A. 136 B4
San Luis Obispo Bay U.S.A. 136 B4
San Luis Potosí Mex. 126 F7
San Luis Reservoir U.S.A. 136 B3
San Luis Río Colorado Mex. 135 D6
Sanluri Sardinia Italy 45 B5
San Manuel U.S.A. 137 G5
San Marcello Pistoiese Italy 44 C2
San Marcos Col. 146 C2
San Marcos U.S.A. 133 B6
▶San Marino country Europe 44 D3
europe 24–25, 48

▶San Marino San Marino 44 D3
Capital of San Marino.

San Martín research station Antarctica 167 L2
San Martín Catamarca Arg. 152 D2
San Martín Mendoza Arg. 152 C3
San Martín r. Bol. 149 E3
San Martín dept Peru 148 A1
San Martín, Lago l. Arg./Chile 153 B7
San Martín de los Andes Arg. 152 C5
San Martín de Valdeiglesias Spain 42 D2
San-Martino-di-Lota Corsica France 39 H5
San Mateo Peru 146 D5
San Mateo U.S.A. 136 A3
San Mateo Venez. 147 E2
San Matías Bol. 149 F4
San Matías, Golfo g. Arg. 152 D5
San Mauricio Venez. 146 E2
Sanmen China 67 G2
Sanmen Wan b. China 67 G2
Sanmenxia China 67 D1
San Miguel Bol. 149 E4
San Miguel r. Bol. 149 E3
San Miguel r. Col. 146 C4
San Miguel El Salvador 138 G6
San Miguel Panama 146 B2
San Miguel U.S.A. 136 B4
San Miguel de Horcasitas r. Mex. 135 E7
San Miguel de Huachi Bol. 148 D3
San Miguel de Tucumán Arg. 152 D1
San Miguel do Araguaia Brazil 150 B5
San Miguel Island U.S.A. 136 B4
San Miguel Islands Phil. 59 G1
San Miguelito Panama 146 B2
Sanming China 67 F3
San Miniato Italy 44 C3
Sanndatti India 72 B3
Sanndraigh i. U.K. see Sandray
Sannicandro Garganico Italy 44 E4
San Nicolás de los Arroyos Arg. 152 E3
San Nicolas Island U.S.A. 136 C5
Sânnicolau Mare Romania 46 B1
Sanniquellie Liberia 92 C4
Sanok Poland 31 J3
San Onofre Col. 146 C2
San Pablo Arg. 153 D8
San Pablo Bol. 148 D5
San Pablo r. Bol. 149 E3
San Pablo Col. 146 D3
San Pablo Phil. 57 F3
San Pablo de Manta Ecuador see Manta
San Pedro Buenos Aires Arg. 152 F3
San Pedro Catamarca Arg. 152 D1
San Pedro Jujuy Arg. 148 D6
San Pedro Misiones Arg. 152 G1
San Pedro Bol. 149 E4
San-Pédro Côte d'Ivoire 92 D4
San Pedro Mex. 126 D7
San Pedro r. Mex. 135 F7
San Pedro watercourse U.S.A. 137 G5
San Pedro, Sierra de mts Spain 42 C3
San Pedro Channel U.S.A. 136 C5
San Pedro de Atacama Chile 148 C5
San Pedro de las Colonias Mex. 126 F6
San Pedro del Pinatar Spain 43 F4
San Pedro de Macorís Dom. Rep. 139 K5
San Pedro de Ycuamandyyú Para. 149 F6
San Pedro el Saucito Mex. 135 E7
San Pedro Martir, Parque Nacional nat. park Mex. 135 D7
San Pedro Sula Hond. 138 G5
San Pietro, Isola di i. Sardinia Italy 45 B5
San Pietro in Cariano Italy 44 C2
San Pitch r. U.S.A. 137 G2
Sanquhar U.K. 34 E4
Sanquianga, Parque Nacional nat. park Col. 146 B4
San Quintín, Cabo c. Mex. 135 C7
San Rafael Arg. 152 C3
San Rafael Bol. 149 E4
San Rafael U.S.A. 136 A3
San Rafael r. U.S.A. 137 G2
San Rafael Venez. 146 D2
San Rafael del Moján Venez. see San Rafael
San Rafael Knob mt. U.S.A. 137 G2
San Rafael Mountains U.S.A. 136 B4
San Ramón Beni Bol. 148 D3
San Ramón Santa Cruz Bol. 149 E4
San Remo Italy 44 A3
San Rodrigo watercourse Mex. 133 A6
San Roque Andalucía Spain 42 D4
San Roque Galicia Spain 42 B1
San Roque Galicia Spain 42 B1
San Saba U.S.A. 133 B6
San Saba r. U.S.A. 133 B6
Sansalé Guinea 92 B3
San Salvador Arg. 152 F2
San Salvador i. Bahamas 129 E7

▶San Salvador El Salvador 138 G6
Capital of El Salvador.

San Salvador de Jujuy Arg. 148 D6
San Salvo Italy 44 E3
Sansané Haoussa Niger 93 F2
Sansanné-Mango Togo 93 F3
San Sebastián Arg. 153 C8
San Sebastián hill Spain 42 B1
San Sebastián, Bahía de b. Arg. 153 C8
San Sebastián de los Reyes Spain 42 E2
Sansepolcro Italy 44 D3
San Severino Marche Italy 44 D3
San Severo Italy 44 E4
San Silvestre Bol. 148 C2
Sanski Most Bos.-Herz. 44 F2
Sansoral Islands Palau see Sonsorol Islands
Sansui China 67 D3
Santa Peru 148 A2
Santa r. Peru 148 A2
Santa Ana Arg. 152 D1
Santa Ana La Paz Bol. 148 D3
Santa Ana Santa Cruz Bol. 149 F4
Santa Ana El Salvador 138 G6
Santa Ana Mex. 135 E7
Santa Ana U.S.A. 136 D5
Santa Ana de Yacuma Bol. 148 D3
Santa Anna U.S.A. 133 B6
Santa Bárbara Brazil 149 F3
Santa Bárbara Mex. 126 E6
Santa Bárbara mt. Spain 43 E4
Santa Barbara U.S.A. 136 C4
Santa Bárbara Venez. 146 D3
Santa Bárbara, Serra de hills Brazil 151 A7
Santa Barbara Channel U.S.A. 136 B4
Santa Bárbara d'Oeste Brazil 149 I5
Santa Barbara do Sul Brazil 151 A9
Santa Barbara Island U.S.A. 136 C5
Santa Catalina Chile 152 C1
Santa Catalina Venez. 147 F2
Santa Catalina, Gulf of U.S.A. 136 D5
Santa Catalina de Armada Spain 42 B1
Santa Catalina Island U.S.A. 136 C5
Santa Catarina state Brazil 151 B8
Santa Catarina Baja California Mex. 135 D7
Santa Catarina Nuevo León Mex. 133 A7
Santa Catarina, Ilha de i. Brazil 151 B8
Santa Clara Cuba 127 K7
Santa Clara r. Mex. 135 F7
Santa Clara r. U.S.A. 136 C4
Santa Clara, Barragem de resr Port. 42 B4
Santa Clarita U.S.A. 136 C4
Santa Clotilde Peru 146 C5
Santa Coloma de Gramanet Spain 43 H2
Santa Comba Angola see Waku-Kungo
Santa Comba Dão Port. 42 B2
Santa Croce Camerina Sicily Italy 45 E6
Santa Cruz prov. Arg. 153 C7
Santa Cruz r. Arg. 153 C7
Santa Cruz Bol. 149 E4
Santa Cruz dept Bol. 149 E4
Santa Cruz Pará Brazil 147 H5
Santa Cruz Pará Brazil 150 B2
Santa Cruz mt. Spain 43 F2
Santa Cruz U.S.A. 136 A3
Santa Cruz watercourse U.S.A. 137 G5
Santa Cruz Cabrália Brazil 151 E6
Santa Cruz de la Palma Canary Is 90 A3
Santa Cruz del Sur Cuba 127 K7
Santa Cruz de Mudela Spain 42 E3

▶Santa Cruz de Tenerife Canary Is 90 A3
Joint capital of the Canary Islands.

Santa Cruz do Sul Brazil 151 A9
Santa Cruz Island U.S.A. 136 C4
Santa Cruz Islands Solomon Is 107 F3
Santa Elena Arg. 152 F2
Santa Elena Bol. 148 D5
Santa Elena Venez. 147 F3
Santa Elena, Cabo c. Costa Rica 138 G6
Santa Elena, Punta pt Ecuador 146 A5
Santa Eufemia, Golfo di g. Italy 45 F5
Santa Eugenia Spain 42 B1
Santa Eulalia del Río Spain 43 G3
Santa Fé Arg. 152 E2
Santa Fé prov. Arg. 152 E2
Santa Fe Spain 42 E4

▶Santa Fe U.S.A. 135 F6
State capital of New Mexico.

Santa Fé de Bogotá Col. see Bogotá
Santafé de Bogotá municipality Col. 146 C4
Santa Fé do Sul Brazil 149 H5
Sant'Agata di Militello Sicily Italy 45 E5
Santa Helena Brazil 150 C2
Santa Helena de Goiás Brazil 149 H4
Santai China 66 C2
Santa Inês Bahia Brazil 150 E5
Santa Inês Maranhão Brazil 150 C2
Santa Inés, Isla i. Chile 153 B8
Santa Isabel Arg. 152 D4
Santa Isabel Brazil 149 E3
Santa Isabel Equat. Guinea see Malabo
Santa Isabel i. Solomon Is 107 E2
Santa Isabel, Ilha Grande de i. Brazil 150 D2
Santa Isabel, Sierra mts Mex. 135 D7
Santa Isabel do Araguaia Brazil 150 B3
Santalpur India 74 A5
Santa Lucia Chile 148 C5
Santa Lucía Ecuador 146 B5
Santa Lucía, Cerro de mt. Spain 42 D4
Santa Lucia Range mts U.S.A. 136 B3
Santa Luzia Maranhão Brazil 150 C3
Santa Luzia Paraíba Brazil 150 E3
Santa Luzia i. Cape Verde 92 [inset]
Santa Magdalena Arg. 152 E3
Santa Margarita Arg. 152 E2
Santa Margarita U.S.A. 136 B4
Santa Margarita, Isla i. Mex. 126 D7
Santa María Arg. 152 D1
Santa Maria Bol. 149 E3
Santa Maria Amazonas Brazil 147 G5
Santa Maria Pará Brazil 147 H5
Santa Maria Rio Grande do Sul Brazil 151 A9
Santa Maria Cape Verde 92 [inset]
Santa María r. Mex. 135 F7
Santa Maria U.S.A. 136 B4
Santa Maria r. U.S.A. 137 F4
Santa María Venez. 146 E3
Santa Maria, Cabo de c. Moz. 99 G5
Santa Maria, Cabo de c. Port. 42 C4
Santa Maria, Chapadão de hills Brazil 150 C5
Santa María, Punta pt Peru 148 B3
Santa Maria, Serra de hills Brazil 150 C5
Santa Maria das Barreiras Brazil 150 B4
Santa Maria da Vitória Brazil 150 C5
Santa María de Ipire Venez. 147 E2
Santa Maria di Leuca, Capo c. Italy 45 G5
Santa Maria do Suaçuí Brazil 151 D6
Santa Maria Island Vanuatu 107 F3
Santa Maria Mountains U.S.A. 137 F4
Santa Marina Salina Isole Lipari Italy 45 E5
Santa Marta Col. 146 C2
Santa Marta, Cabo de c. Angola 95 B8
Santa Maura i. Greece see Lefkada

Sipura, Selat sea chan. Indon. 58 B3
Siq, Wādī as watercourse Egypt 77 A5
Siquisique Venez. 146 D2
Sir r. Pak. 81 G5
Sira India 72 C3
Sira Norway 33 B4
Şīr Abū Nu'āyr i. U.A.E. 80 C5
Si Racha Thai. 61 C5
Siracusa Sicily Italy see Syracuse
Siraha Nepal see Sirha
Sirajganj Bangl. 75 F4
Sir Alexander, Mount Canada 122 F4
Şiran Turkey 79 D2
Sirathu India 75 D4
Sirba r. Burkina/Niger 93 F2
Sirbāl, Jabal mt. Egypt 77 A5
Şīr Banī Yās i. U.A.E. 80 C5
Sircilla India see Sirsilla
Sirdaryo r. Asia see Syrdar'ya
Sirdaryo Uzbek. see Syrdar'ya
Sirdaryo Wiloyati admin. div. Uzbek. see Syrdar'inskaya Oblast'
Sirdingka China see Lhari
Sire Tanz. 97 A6
Sir Edward Pellew Group is Australia 110 D2
Siret r. Romania 46 F2
Sir Graham Moore Islands Australia 108 D3
Sirha Nepal 75 E4
Sirḥān, Wādī as watercourse Jordan/Saudi Arabia 77 C4
Şiria Romania 46 B1
Šīrīk Iran 80 D5
Sirik, Tanjong pt Sarawak Malaysia 59 E2
Siri Kit Dam Thai. 60 C4
Sirikit Reservoir Thai. 60 C4
Sirina i. Greece see Syrna
Siritoi r. Pak. 81 G4
Sirjā Iran 81 E5
Sir James MacBrien, Mount Canada 122 E2
Sīrjān Iran 80 C4
Sirjan salt flat Iran 80 C4
Sirkka Fin. 32 G2
Sirmaur India 74 C3
Sirmilik National Park Canada 121 L2
Sirmium Serb. and Mont. see Sremska Mitrovica
Sirmour India 75 D4
Sirmur India see Sirmaur
Şırnak Turkey 79 E3
Sirniö Fin. 32 H2
Sirohi India 74 B4
Sironcha India 72 D2
Sironj India 74 C4
Síros i. Greece see Syros
Siroua, Jbel mt. Morocco 90 D3
Sirpur India 72 C2
Sirrei Eth. 96 D3
Sirretta Peak U.S.A. 136 C4
Sīrrī, Jazīreh-ye i. Iran 80 C5
Sirsa India 74 B3
Sir Sandford, Mount Canada 122 G5
Sirsi Karnataka India 72 B3
Sirsi Uttar Pradesh India 74 C3
Sirsilla India 72 C2
Sirte Libya 88 C2
Sirte, Gulf of Libya 88 C2
Sir Thomas, Mount Australia 110 B5
Siruguppa India 72 C3
Sirupa r. Mex. 135 E7
Sirur India 72 B2
Širvintos Lith. 33 G5
Sīrwān r. Iraq 79 F4
Sir Wilfrid Laurier, Mount Canada 122 G4
Sir William Thompson Range hills Australia 111 E2
Sis Turkey see Kozan
Sisak Croatia 44 F2
Sisaket Thai. 61 D5
Sisante Spain 43 E3
Siscia Croatia see Sisak
Sishen S. Africa 98 D5
Sisian Armenia 79 F3
Sisimiut Greenland 121 N3
Sisipuk Lake Canada 123 K4
Sisogúichic Mex. 135 F8
Sisŏphŏn Cambodia 61 C5
Sisquoc r. U.S.A. 136 B4
Sisseton U.S.A. 132 B2
Sissili r. Burkina 93 E3
Sissonville U.S.A. 130 C4
Sistan, Daryācheh-ye marsh Afgh. 81 E4
Sisteron France 39 F4
Sisters U.S.A. 134 B3
Sistersville U.S.A. 130 C4
Sisto r. Italy 44 D4
Sitalike Tanz. 97 A6
Sitamarhi India 75 E4
Sitamau India 74 B5
Sitampiky Madag. 99 [inset] J3
Sitang China see Sinan
Sitapur India 74 D4
Siteia Greece 47 E7
Siteki Swaziland 99 F5
Sithonia pen. Greece 47 C4
Sitia Greece see Siteia
Sitila Moz. 99 G4
Siting China 66 C3
Sítio da Abadia Brazil 150 C5
Sítio do Mato Brazil 150 D5
Sitka U.S.A. 120 F4
Sitnica r. Serb. and Mont. 46 B3
Sitno mt. Slovakia 37 I4
Sitrah oasis Egypt 89 E2
Sittang r. Myanmar 60 B4
Sittard Neth. 36 B3
Sittaung Myanmar 60 A2
Sittaung r. Myanmar see Sittang
Sittoung r. Myanmar see Sittang
Sittwe Myanmar 62 E7
Situbondo Indon. 59 F4
Siumpain, Rubha an t- hd U.K. see Tiumpan Head
Siuri India 75 E5
Sivaganga India 72 C4
Sivakasi India 72 C4
Sivaki Rus. Fed. 64 A1
Sivand Iran 80 C4
Sivas Turkey 78 D3
Sivaslı Turkey 78 B3
Siverek Turkey 79 D3
Siverskiy Rus. Fed. 28 D4
Sivers'kyy Donets' r. Rus. Fed./Ukr. see Severskiy Donets
Sivomaskinskiy Rus. Fed. 28 L2
Sivrice Turkey 79 D3
Sivrihisar Turkey 78 B3
Sīwah Egypt 89 E2
Sīwah, Wāḥāt oasis Egypt 89 E2
Siwalik Range mts India/Nepal 74 C3
Siwan India 75 E4
Siwana India 74 B4
Six Cross Roads Barbados 147 G1
Six-Fours-les-Plages France 39 F5
Sixian China 67 F1
Sixtymile Canada 122 A1
Siyabuswa S. Africa 99 F5
Siyang Guangxi China see Shangsi
Siyang Jiangsu China 67 F1
Siyäzän Azer. 79 G2
Siyuni Iran 80 C3
Sjenica Serb. and Mont. 46 B3
Sjoa Norway 33 C3
Sjöbo Sweden 33 D5
Sjøholt Norway 32 B3
Sjona sea chan. Norway 32 D2
Sjoutnäset Sweden 32 D2
Sjøvegan Norway 32 E1
Skäckerfjällen mts Sweden 32 D3
Skadarsko Jezero nat. park Serb. and Mont. 46 A3
Skadovs'k Ukr. 29 E7
Skærbæk Denmark 33 C5
Skaftafell nat. park Iceland 32 [inset] C2
Skagafjörður inlet Iceland 32 [inset]
Skagen Denmark 33 C4
Skagern l. Sweden 33 D4
Skagerrak strait Denmark/Norway 33 C4
Skagit r. U.S.A. 134 B2
Skagway U.S.A. 120 F4
Skaidi Norway 32 G1
Skala Notio Aigaio Greece 47 E6
Skala Peloponnisos Greece 47 C6
Skala Kallonis Greece 47 E5
Skaland Norway 28 A1
Skallelv Norway 32 H1
Skalmodal Sweden 32 D2
Skanderborg Denmark 33 C4
Skåne county Sweden 33 D5
Skaneateles U.S.A. 131 E2
Skaneateles Lake U.S.A. 131 E2
Skånevik Norway 33 B4
Skantzoura i. Greece 47 D5
Skara Sweden 33 D4
Skara Brae tourist site U.K. 34 E2
Skarberget Norway 32 E1
Skardarsko Jezero l. Albania/Serb. and Mont. see Scutari, Lake
Skardu Jammu and Kashmir 74 B2
Skare Norway 33 B4
Skärgårdshavets Nationalpark nat. park Fin. 33 F4
Skarnes Norway 33 C3
Skärplinge Sweden 33 E3
Skärsjövålen Sweden 33 D3
Skarszewy Poland 37 I1
Skarvedalseggen mt. Norway 33 C3
Skarvsjöby Sweden 32 E2
Skaryszew Poland 37 J3
Skarżysko-Kamienna Poland 37 J3
Skaudvilė Lith. 33 F5
Skaulo Sweden 32 F2
Skawa r. Poland 37 I3
Skawina Poland 37 I4
Skaymat W. Sahara 90 B4
Skeena r. Canada 122 D4
Skeena Mountains Canada 122 D3
Skegness U.K. 35 G5
Skeiðarársandur sand area Iceland 32 [inset]
Skeleton Coast Game Park nature res. Namibia 98 B3
Skellefteå Sweden 32 F2
Skellefteälven r. Sweden 32 F2
Skeppshamn Sweden 33 E3
Skerries Rep. of Ireland 35 C5
Skhimatárion Greece see Schimatari
Skhira Tunisia 40 E5
Skhiza i. Greece see Schiza
Ski Norway 33 C4
Skiathos Greece 47 C5
Skiathos i. Greece 47 C5
Skibbereen Rep. of Ireland 35 B6
Skibotn Norway 32 F1
Skiddaw hill U.K. 35 E4
Skien Norway 33 C4
Skierniewice Poland 37 J3
Skikda Alg. 91 G1
Skinari, Akra pt Greece 47 B6
Skio Jammu and Kashmir 74 C2
Skipton Australia 112 B5
Skipton U.K. 35 E5
Skiropoúla i. Greece see Skyropoula
Skíros i. Greece see Skyros
Skive Denmark 33 C4
Skjálfandafljót r. Iceland 32 [inset]
Skjerkeknuten hill Norway 33 B4
Skjern Denmark 33 C5
Skjern Norway 32 C2
Skobelev Uzbek. see Fergana
Skobeleva, Pik mt. Kyrg. 81 H2
Skocjanske Jame tourist site Slovenia 44 D2
Škofja Loka Slovenia 44 E1
Skog Sweden 33 E3
Skoganvarre Norway 32 G1
Skogfoss Norway 32 H1
Skoki Poland 37 H2
Sköllersta Sweden 33 D4
Skomvær is Norway 32 C2
Skopelos i. Greece 47 C5
Skopia hill Greece 47 D5
Skopin Rus. Fed. 29 F5

▶Skopje Macedonia 46 B4
Capital of Macedonia.

Skoplje Macedonia see Skopje
Skopunarfjørður sea chan. Faroe Is 34 [inset]
Skórcz Poland 37 I2
Skorodnoye Rus. Fed. 29 F6
Skørping Denmark 33 C4
Skotoussa Greece 46 C4
Skotterud Norway 33 D4
Skoutari Greece 46 C4
Skoutaros Greece 47 E5
Skövde Sweden 33 D4
Skovorodino Rus. Fed. 27 M4
Skowhegan U.S.A. 128 F2
Skrīveri Latvia 33 G4
Skröven Sweden 32 F2
Skrunda Latvia 33 F4
Skrwa r. Poland 37 I2
Skúgvoy i. Faroe Is 34 [inset]
Skukum, Mount Canada 122 C2
Skukuza S. Africa 99 F5
Skuleskogens nationalpark nat. park Sweden 32 E3
Skull Valley U.S.A. 137 F4
Skultuna Sweden 33 E4
Skunk r. U.S.A. 132 D3
Skuodas Lith. 33 F4
Skurup Sweden 33 D5
Skŭt r. Bulg. 46 C3
Skutskär Sweden 33 E3
Skvyra Ukr. 29 D6
Skwierzyna Poland 37 G2
Skye i. U.K. 34 C3
Skykula hill Norway 33 B4
Skyring, Seno b. Chile 153 B8
Skyropoula i. Greece 47 D5
Skyros Greece 47 D5
Skyros i. Greece 47 D5
Skytrain Ice Rise Antarctica 167 L1
Slættaratindur hill Faroe Is 34 [inset]
Slagelse Denmark 33 C5
Slagnäs Sweden 32 E2
Slamet, Gunung vol. Indon. 59 E4
Slana U.S.A. 122 A2
Slaney r. Rep. of Ireland 35 C5
Slănic r. Romania 46 E2
Slănic Moldova Romania 46 E1
Slanské Vrchy mts Slovakia 37 J4
Slantsy Rus. Fed. 28 D4
Slaný Czech Rep. 37 G3
Slapovi Krke nat. park Croatia 44 E3
Slashers Reefs Australia 111 F3
Śląska, Wyżyna hills Poland 37 I3
Slatina Croatia 44 F2
Slatina Romania 46 D2
Slatina-Timiş Romania 46 C2
Slaty Fork U.S.A. 130 C4
Slautnoye Rus. Fed. 27 Q3
Slave r. Canada 123 H2
Slave Coast Africa 93 F4
Slave Lake Canada 123 H4
Slave Point Canada 123 H2
Slavgorod Belarus see Slawharad
Slavgorod Rus. Fed. 62 B1
Slavonska Požega Croatia see Požega
Slavonski Brod Croatia 44 G2
Slavutych Ukr. 29 D6
Slavyanka Kazakh. see Myrzakent
Slavyanka Rus. Fed. 64 B4
Slavyansk Ukr. see Slov"yans'k
Slavyanskaya Rus. Fed. see Slavyansk-na-Kubani
Slavyansk-na-Kubani Rus. Fed. 29 F7
Sława Poland 37 H3
Slawharad Belarus 29 D5
Sławno Poland 37 H1
Slayton U.S.A. 132 C3
Sleaford U.K. 35 F5
Sleat, Sound of sea chan. U.K. 34 D3
Sled Lake Canada 123 J4
Sleeper Islands Canada 124 E1
Sleptsovskaya Rus. Fed. 29 H8
Slessor Glacier Antarctica 167 B1
Ślęża hill Poland 37 H3
Slick Rock U.S.A. 137 H2
Slidell U.S.A. 133 D6
Slide Mountain U.S.A. 131 F3
Slidre Norway 33 C3
Slieve Car hill Rep. of Ireland 35 B4
Slieve Donard hill U.K. 35 D4
Slieve Gamph hills Rep. of Ireland 35 B5
Slieve Mish Mountains hills Rep. of Ireland 35 A5
Sligachan U.K. 34 C3
Sligeach Rep. of Ireland see Sligo
Sligo Rep. of Ireland 35 B4
Sligo U.S.A. 130 D3
Sligo Bay Rep. of Ireland 35 B4
Slippery Rock U.S.A. 130 C3
Sliven Bulg. 46 E3
Slivnitsa Bulg. 46 D3
Slivo Pole Bulg. 46 E3
Sljeme mt. Croatia 44 E2
Sloan r. Canada 123 G1
Sloan U.S.A. 137 E4
Sloat U.S.A. 136 B2
Sloboda Rus. Fed. see Ezhva
Slobodchikovo Rus. Fed. 28 I3
Slobodskoy Rus. Fed. 28 I4
Slobozia Romania 46 E2
Slobozia Bradului Romania 46 E2
Słomniki Poland 37 J3
Slonim Belarus 29 C5
Slough U.K. 35 F6
▶Slovakia country Europe 37 I4
europe 24–25, 48
▶Slovenia country Europe 44 E1
europe 24–25, 48
Slovenija country Europe see Slovenia
Slovenj Gradec Slovenia 44 E1
Slovenska Bistrica Slovenia 44 E1
Slovenske Gorice hills Slovenia 44 E1
Slovenské Rudohorie mts Slovakia 37 I4
Slovensko country Europe see Slovakia
Slovenský kras mts Slovakia 37 J4
Slovenský raj nat. park Slovakia 37 J4
Slov"yans'k Ukr. 29 F6
Słowiński Park Narodowy nat. park Poland 37 H1
Słubice Poland 37 G2
Slunj Croatia 44 E2
Słupca Poland 37 H2
Słupia r. Poland 37 H1
Słupsk Poland 37 H1
Slussfors Sweden 32 E2
Slutsk Belarus 29 C5
Slyne Head Rep. of Ireland 35 A5
Slyudyanka Rus. Fed. 27 K4
Smackover U.S.A. 133 C5
Smålandsstenar Sweden 33 D4
Small Point U.S.A. 131 I2
Smallwood Reservoir Canada 125 H2
Smalyavichy Belarus 29 D5
Smarhon' Belarus 29 C5
Smeaton Canada 123 J4
Smederevo Serb. and Mont. 46 B2
Smederevska Palanka Serb. and Mont. 46 B2
Smeeni Romania 46 E2
Smela Ukr. see Smila
Smethport U.S.A. 130 D3
Smila Ukr. 29 D6
Smiltene Latvia 33 G4
Smirnykh Rus. Fed. 64 E2
Smith Canada 123 H4
Smith r. MT U.S.A. 134 E3
Smith r. VA U.S.A. 130 D5
Smith Arm b. Canada 122 F1
Smith Center U.S.A. 132 B4
Smithers Canada 122 E4
Smithers Landing Canada 122 E4
Smithfield UT U.S.A. 134 E4
Smithfield VA U.S.A. 131 E5
Smith Glacier Antarctica 167 K1
Smith Island India 73 G3
Smith Island U.S.A. 131 E4
Smith Mountain Lake U.S.A. 130 D5
Smith River Canada 122 E3
Smithsburg U.S.A. 130 E4
Smiths Falls Canada 131 E1
Smithton Australia 112 C6
Smithville TN U.S.A. 128 B5
Smithville WV U.S.A. 130 C4
Smjörfjöll mts Iceland 32 [inset]
Smoke Creek Desert U.S.A. 136 C1
Smoky r. Canada 122 G3
Smoky Bay Australia 109 F8
Smoky Cape Australia 112 E3
Smoky Falls Canada 124 D3
Smoky Hill r. U.S.A. 132 A4
Smoky Hill, North Fork r. U.S.A. 134 G5
Smoky Hills KS U.S.A. 126 G4
Smoky Hills KS U.S.A. 132 B4
Smoky Lake Canada 123 H4
Smoky Mountains U.S.A. 134 D4
Smøla i. Norway 32 B3
Smolensk Rus. Fed. 29 E5
Smolenskaya Oblast' admin. div. Rus. Fed. 29 E5
Smolensk Oblast admin. div. Rus. Fed. see Smolenskaya Oblast'
Smolensko-Moskovskaya Vozvyshennost' hills Rus. Fed. 31 M2
Smolevichi Belarus see Smalyavichy
Smolikas mt. Greece 47 B4
Smolyan Bulg. 46 D4
Smolyoninovo Rus. Fed. 64 C4
Smooth Rock Falls Canada 124 D3
Smoothrock Lake Canada 124 B3
Smoothstone Lake Canada 123 J4
Smørfjord Norway 32 G1
Smorgon' Belarus see Smarhon'
Smyadovo Bulg. 46 E3
Smyley Island Antarctica 167 L2
Smyrna Turkey see İzmir
Smyrna DE U.S.A. 131 F4
Smyrna GA U.S.A. 129 B5
Smyrna TN U.S.A. 128 B5
Snæfell mt. Iceland 32 [inset]
Snaefell hill Isle of Man 35 D4
Snæfellsnes pen. Iceland 32 [inset]
Snake r. Canada 122 C1
Snake r. U.S.A. 134 C3
Snake Range mts U.S.A. 137 E2
Snake River Canada 122 F3
Snake River Plain U.S.A. 134 D4
Snare r. Canada 123 G2
Snare Lake Canada 123 J3
Snare Lakes Canada see Wekweti
Snares Islands N.Z. 107 F6
Snåsa Norway 32 D2
Snåsvatn l. Norway 32 D2
Sneedville U.S.A. 130 B5
Sneek Neth. 36 B2
Sneem Rep. of Ireland 35 B6
Sneeuberge mts S. Africa 98 E6
Snegamook Lake Canada 125 I2
Sněžka mt. Czech Rep. 37 G3
Snežnik mt. Slovenia 44 E2
Śniardwy, Jezioro l. Poland 37 J2
Sniečkus Lith. see Visaginas
Śnieżka mt. Czech Rep. see Sněžka
Śnieżnik mt. Poland 37 H3
Snihurivka Ukr. 29 E7
Snøhetta mt. Norway 33 C3
Snønuten mt. Norway 33 B4
Snovsk Ukr. see Shchors
Snowbird Lake Canada 123 K2
Snowdon mt. U.K. 35 D5
Snowdonia National Park U.K. 35 E5
Snowdrift Canada see Łutselk'e
Snowdrift r. Canada 123 I2
Snowflake U.S.A. 137 G4
Snow Hill MD U.S.A. 131 F4
Snow Hill NC U.S.A. 128 D5
Snow Lake Canada 123 K4
Snowtown Australia 112 A4
Snowy r. Australia 112 D5
Snowy Mountain U.S.A. 131 F2
Snowy Mountains Australia 112 C5
Snug Harbour Canada 125 K2
Snyder OK U.S.A. 133 B5
Snyder TX U.S.A. 133 A5
Soahany Madag. 99 [inset] J3
Soaigh i. U.K. see Soay
Soalala Madag. 99 [inset] J3
Soanierana-Ivongo Madag. 99 [inset] K3
Soan-kundo is S. Korea 65 A6
Soata Col. 146 C3
Soay i. U.K. 34 B3
Sobaek-sanmaek mts S. Korea 65 A6
Sobaek-san National Park S. Korea 65 B5
Sobat r. Sudan 96 A2
Soběslav Czech Rep. 37 G4
Sobger r. Indon. 57 J6
Sobinka Rus. Fed. 28 G5
Sobradinho, Barragem de resr Brazil 150 D4
Sobrado Brazil 150 D4
Sobral Brazil 150 D2
Soča r. Italy see Isonzo
Sochaczew Poland 37 J2
Sochi Rus. Fed. 29 F8
Sochos Greece 46 C4
Society Islands Fr. Polynesia 165 H7
Socol Romania 46 B2
Socompa Chile 148 C6
Socorro Col. 146 C3
Socorro U.S.A. 135 F6
Socorro, Isla i. Mex. 126 D8
Socotra i. Yemen 76 E7
Socovos Spain 43 F3
Soc Trăng Vietnam 61 D6
Socuéllamos Spain 42 E3
Soda Lake CA U.S.A. 136 C4
Soda Lake CA U.S.A. 137 D4
Sodankylä Fin. 32 G2
Soda Plains Aksai Chin 74 C2
Soda Springs U.S.A. 134 E4
Söderhamn Sweden 33 E3
Söderköping Sweden 33 E4
Södermanland county Sweden 33 E4
Södertälje Sweden 33 E4
Sodiri Sudan 89 F6
Sodo Eth. 96 C3
Södra Kvarken strait Fin./Sweden 33 E3
Soë Indon. 57 F7
Soekmekaar S. Africa 99 F4
Soerabaia Indon. see Surabaya
Soest Germany 36 D3
Sofades Greece 47 C5
Sofala Moz. 99 G4
Sofala prov. Moz. 99 G3
Sofala, Baía de b. Moz. 99 G4

▶Sofia Bulg. 46 C3
Capital of Bulgaria.

Sofia r. Madag. 99 [inset] J2
Sofiko Greece 47 C6
Sofiya Bulg. see Sofia
Sofiyevka Ukr. see Vil'nyans'k
Sofiysk Khabarovskiy Kray Rus. Fed. 64 C1
Sofiysk Khabarovskiy Kray Rus. Fed. 64 D2
Sofporog Rus. Fed. 32 H2
Softa Kalesi tourist site Turkey 77 A1
Sōfu-gan i. Japan 65 E7
Sog China 70 H5
Sogamoso Col. 146 C3
Sogda Rus. Fed. 64 C2
Sogma China 74 D2
Søgne Norway 33 B4
Sognefjorden inlet Norway 33 B3
Sogn og Fjordane county Norway 33 B3
Sogo Hills Kenya 96 C4
Sogolle well Chad 88 B6
Sog Qu r. China 75 G2
Söğüt Turkey 78 B2
Söğüt Dağı mts Turkey 78 B3
Soḥâg Egypt see Sawhāj
Sohagpur India 74 C5
Sohan r. Pak. 81 G3
Sohano P.N.G. 107 E2
Sohar Oman see Şuḥār
Sohela India 75 D5
Sohna India 74 C3
Sohng Gwe, Khao hill Myanmar/Thai. 61 B5
Soignies Belgium 39 F1
Soila China 66 A2
Soini Fin. 32 G3
Soissons France 39 E2
Sojat India 74 B4
Sojat Road India 74 B4
Sok r. Rus. Fed. 29 I5
Sokch'o S. Korea 65 B5
Söke Turkey 78 A3
Sokele Dem. Rep. Congo 95 E7
Sokhós Greece see Sochos
Sokhumi Georgia 79 E2
Sokiryany Ukr. see Sokyryany
Sokobanja Serb. and Mont. 46 B3
Sokodé Togo 93 F3
Soko Islands Hong Kong China 67 [inset]
Sokol Rus. Fed. 28 G4
Sokolac Bos.-Herz. 44 G3
Sokolo Mali 92 D2
Sokolov Czech Rep. 37 F3
Sokołów Podlaski Poland 37 K2
Sokolozero, Ozero l. Rus. Fed. 32 H2
Sokosti hill Fin. 32 H1
Sokoto Nigeria 93 G2
Sokoto r. Nigeria 93 G3
Sokoto state Nigeria 93 G2
Sokourala Guinea 92 C3
Sokyryany Ukr. 29 C6
Sola r. Poland 37 I4
Sola i. Tonga see Ata
Solan India 74 C3
Solander Island N.Z. 113 A4
Solapur India 72 B2
Soldado Bartra Peru 146 C5
Soldotna U.S.A. 120 D3
Solec Kujawski Poland 37 I2
Soledad Arg. 152 E2
Soledad U.S.A. 136 B3
Soledad Venez. 147 F2
Soledade Brazil 146 D6
Sølen mt. Norway 33 C3
Solenzo Burkina 92 D2
Solfjellsjøen Norway 32 D2
Solginskiy Rus. Fed. 28 G3
Solhan Turkey 79 E3
Soligalich Rus. Fed. 28 G4
Soligorsk Belarus see Salihorsk
Solihull U.K. 35 F5
Solikamsk Rus. Fed. 28 K4
Sol'-Iletsk Rus. Fed. 29 J6
Soliman Tunisia 45 C6
Solingen Germany 36 C3
Solita Col. 146 C4
Sol-Karmala Rus. Fed. see Severnoye
Sollefteå Sweden 32 E3
Sollentuna Sweden 33 E4
Sóller Spain 43 H3
Solling hills Germany 36 D3
Solnechnyy Khabarovskiy Kray Rus. Fed. 64 D2
Solnechnyy Khabarovskiy Kray Rus. Fed. see Gornyy
Solo r. Indon. 59 F4
Solofra Italy 45 E4
Solok Indon. 58 C3
Solomon U.S.A. 137 H5
Solomon r. U.S.A. 132 B4
Solomon, North Fork r. U.S.A. 132 B4
Solomon, South Fork r. U.S.A. 132 B4

▶Solomon Islands country S. Pacific Ocean 107 F2
4th largest and 5th most populous country in Oceania.
oceania 104–105, 114

Solomon Sea P.N.G./Solomon Is 107 E2
Solor i. Indon. 108 C2
Solor, Kepulauan is Indon. 57 F7
Solotcha Rus. Fed. 29 F5
Solothurn Switz. 39 G3
Solovetskiye Ostrova is Rus. Fed. 28 E2
Solsona Spain 43 G2
Solt Hungary 37 I5
Šolta i. Croatia 44 F3
Soltānābād Khorāsan Iran 80 D2
Soltānābād Khorāsan Iran 81 D3
Soltānābād Tehrān Iran 80 B3
Soltān-e Bakva Afgh. 81 E3
Soltānī, Khowr-e b. Iran 80 B4
Soltanqolī Iran 80 A3
Soltau Germany 36 D2
Sol'tsy Rus. Fed. 28 D4
Soltvadkert Hungary 37 I5
Solunska Glava mt. Macedonia 46 B4
Solvay U.S.A. 131 E2
Sölvesborg Sweden 33 D4
Solway Firth est. U.K. 34 E4
Solwezi Zambia 95 E8
Sōma Japan 65 E5
Soma Turkey 78 A3
Somabhula Zimbabwe 99 F3
Somabula Zimbabwe see Somabhula
Somali admin. reg. Eth. 96 D3
▶Somalia country Africa 96 E4
africa 86–87, 100
Somali Basin sea feature Indian Ocean 162 K6
Somali Republic country Africa see Somalia
Somanga Tanz. 97 C7
Somanya Ghana 93 E4
Sombo Angola 95 D7
Sombor Serb. and Mont. 46 A2
Sombrerete Mex. 126 F7
Sombrero Chile 153 C8
Sombrero Channel India 73 G5
Somdari India 74 B4
Somero Fin. 33 F3
Somerset KY U.S.A. 130 A5
Somerset MI U.S.A. 130 A2
Somerset OH U.S.A. 130 B4
Somerset PA U.S.A. 130 D4
Somerset East S. Africa 98 E7
Somerset Island Canada 121 J2
Somerset West S. Africa 98 C7
Somersworth U.S.A. 131 H2
Somerton U.S.A. 137 E5
Somerville U.S.A. 131 F3
Someşu Cald r. Romania 46 C1
Someydeh Iran 80 A3
Sommarøy Norway 32 E1
Somme r. France 38 D1
Sommen l. Sweden 33 D4
Sömmerda Germany 36 E3
Somnath India 72 A1
Somosomo Fiji 107 H3
Sompolno Poland 37 I2
Somport, Col du pass France/Spain 43 F1
Šomrda hill Serb. and Mont. 46 B2
Somuncurá, Mesa Volcánica de plat. Arg. 152 D5
Somvarpet India 72 B3
Son r. India 74 E4
Sonag China see Zêkog
Sonai r. India 75 G4
Sonai r. India 75 G4
Sonakhan India 75 D5
Sonamukhi India 75 E5
Sonapur India 73 D1
Sonari India 75 G4
Sondalo Italy 44 C1
Sønderborg Denmark 33 C5
Sondershausen Germany 36 E3
Sønderup Denmark 33 C4
Søndre Strømfjord Greenland see Kangerlussuaq
Søndre Strømfjord inlet Greenland see Kangerlussuaq
Sondrio Italy 44 B1
Song Nigeria 93 I3
Songad India 74 A5
Songbai China see Shennongjia
Songbu China 67 E2
Sông Cau Vietnam 61 E5
Songcheng China see Xiapu
Sông Đa, Hô resr Vietnam 60 D3
Songea Tanz. 97 B7
Songgan N. Korea 65 A4
Sông Hông r. Vietnam see Red River
Songhua Hu resr China 64 A4
Songhua Jiang r. China 64 C3
Songjiang Jilin China 64 B4
Songjiang Shanghai China 67 G2
Songjianghe China 64 A4
Sŏngjin N. Korea see Kimch'aek
Songkan China 66 C2
Songkhla Thai. 61 C7
Song Khram, Mae Nam r. Thai. 60 D4
Songmai China see Dêrong
Songming China 66 B3
Songnam S. Korea 65 A5
Songnim N. Korea 65 A5
Songnim-san National Park S. Korea 65 A5
Songo Angola 95 B6
Songo Moz. 99 G2
Songololo Bas-Congo Dem. Rep. Congo 95 B6
Songololo Bas-Congo Dem. Rep. Congo see Mbanza-Ngungu
Songpan China 66 B1
Songsak India 75 F4
Sŏngsan S. Korea 65 A6
Songshan China see Ziyun
Song Shan mt. China 67 E1
Songtao China 67 D2
Songxi China 67 F3
Songxian China 67 E1
Songyang China see Songming
Songyuan Fujian China see Songxi
Songyuan Jilin China 64 A3
Songzi China 67 D2
Sonhat India 75 D5
Sonid Youqi China see Saihan Tal
Sonipat India 74 C3
Sonkach India 74 C5
Sonkajärvi Fin. 28 C3
Sonkovo Rus. Fed. 28 F4
Son La Vietnam 60 C3
Sonmiani Bay Pak. 81 F5
Sonneberg Germany 36 E3
Sonnenjoch mt. Austria 36 F5
Sono r. Minas Gerais Brazil 151 C6
Sono r. Tocantins Brazil 150 B4
Sonoita watercourse Mex. 135 D7
Sonoma U.S.A. 136 A2
Sonora r. Mex. 135 E7
Sonora state Mex. 137 E5
Sonora CA U.S.A. 136 B3
Sonora TX U.S.A. 133 A6
Sonoran Desert National Monument nat. park U.S.A. 137 F5
Sonqor Iran 80 A3
Sonseca Spain 42 E3
Son Servera Spain 43 H3
Sonsón Col. 146 C3
Sonsonate El Salvador 138 G6
Sonsorol Islands Palau 57 H4
Sơn Tây Vietnam 60 D3
Sonthofen Germany 36 E5
Soochow China see Suzhou
Soomaaliya country Africa see Somalia
Sopo watercourse Sudan 94 E2
Sopot Bulg. 46 D3
Sopot Poland 37 I1
Sopron Hungary 37 H5
Sopu-Korgon Kyrg. 81 H1
Sopur Jammu and Kashmir 74 B2
Sôr r. Port. 42 B3
Sor r. Spain 42 C1
Sora Italy 44 D4
Sorab India 72 B3
Soråker Sweden 33 E3
Sŏrak-san mt. S. Korea 65 B5
Sorak-san National Park S. Korea 65 B5
Sorata Bol. 148 C3
Sorbas Spain 43 E4
Sorbe r. Spain 42 E2
Sor Donyztau dry lake Kazakh. 70 A2
Soreq r. Israel 77 B4
Sorgono Sardinia Italy 45 B4
Sorgues France 39 F4
Sorgues r. France 39 E5
Sorgun Turkey 78 C3
Sorgun r. Turkey 77 B1
Soria Spain 43 E2
Sorikmarapi vol. Indon. 58 B2
Sørkappøya i. Svalbard 26 B2
Sor Kaydak dry lake Kazakh. 79 H1
Sorkh, Kūh-e mts Iran 80 C3
Sorkheh Iran 80 C3
Sørland Norway 32 D2
Sørli Norway 32 D2
Sor Mertvyy Kultuk dry lake Kazakh. 29 J7
Sorø Denmark 33 C5
Soro India 75 E5
Soro, Monte mt. Sicily Italy 45 E6
Soroca Moldova 29 D6
Sorocaba Brazil 149 I5
Sorochinsk Rus. Fed. 29 J5
Soroki Moldova see Soroca
Sorol atoll Micronesia 57 J4
Sorong Indon. 57 H6
Sororó r. Brazil 150 B3
Soroti Uganda 96 B4
Sørøya i. Norway 32 F1
Sorp Turkey see Reşadiye
Sorraia r. Port. 42 B3
Sorrento Italy 45 E4
Sorsatunturi hill Fin. 32 H2
Sorsele Sweden 32 E2
Sorso Sardinia Italy 45 B4
Sorsogon Phil. 57 F3
Sortavala Rus. Fed. 28 D3
Sortland Norway 32 D1
Sortot Sudan 89 F5
Sør-Trøndelag county Norway 32 C3
Sørvær Norway 32 F1
Sørvågen Norway 32 D2
Sõrve väin sea chan. Estonia/Latvia see Irbe Strait
Soshanguve S. Africa 99 F5
Sosna r. Rus. Fed. 29 F5
Sosnogorsk Rus. Fed. 28 J3
Sosnovka Arkhangel'skaya Oblast' Rus. Fed. 28 H3
Sosnovka Murmanskaya Oblast' Rus. Fed. 28 G2
Sosnovka Tambovskaya Oblast' Rus. Fed. 29 G5
Sosnovo Rus. Fed. 28 D3
Sosnovo-Ozerskoye Rus. Fed. 63 I1
Sosnovyy Rus. Fed. 32 I2
Sosnovyy Bor Rus. Fed. 28 D4
Sosnowiec Poland 37 I3
Sosnowitz Poland see Sosnowiec
Sosso Cent. Afr. Rep. 94 B4
Sota r. Benin 93 F3
Sotang China 75 G3
Sotério r. Brazil 149 D2
Sotillo r. Spain 42 D3
Sotkamo Fin. 32 H2
Soto Arg. 152 D2
Sotouboua Togo 93 F3
Sotteville-lès-Rouen France 38 D2
Souanké Congo 94 B4
Soubré Côte d'Ivoire 92 D4
Souda Greece 47 D7
Soudan Australia 110 D4
Soúdha Greece see Souda
Soufli Greece 46 E4
Soufrière St Lucia 139 L6
Soufrière vol. St Vincent 139 L6
Souguéta Guinea 92 B3
Souillac France 38 D4
Souk Ahras Alg. 91 G1
Souk el Arbaâ du Rharb Morocco 90 D2
Soukoukoutane Niger 93 F2
Souk Tleta Taghramet Morocco 42 D5
Sŏul S. Korea see Seoul
Soulac-sur-Mer France 38 C4
Sounding Creek r. Canada 123 I4
Sounfat well Mali see Tessoûnfat
Sounio nat. park Greece 47 D6
Soûr Lebanon see Tyre
Soure Brazil 150 B2
Sour el Ghozlane Alg. 43 H4
Souris Man. Canada 134 G2
Souris P.E.I. Canada 125 I4
Souris r. Canada 134 H2

Suata Venez. 147 E2
Suau P.N.G. 111 G1
Subang Indon. 59 D4
Subansiri r. India 60 A2
Subarnarekha r. India 75 E5
Sübāshī Iran 80 B3
Subaşı Turkey 46 F4
Subcetate Romania 46 D1
Subeita tourist site Israel see Shivta
Subiaco Italy 44 E4
Subi Besar i. Indon. 59 E2
Subi Kecil i. Indon. 59 E2
Sublette U.S.A. 132 A4
Subotica Serb. and Mont. 46 A1
Success, Lake U.S.A. 136 C3
Suceava Romania 31 K4
Sucha Beskidzka Poland 37 I4
Suchan Rus. Fed. see Partizansk
Suchan r. Col. 146 B3
Suchedniów Poland 37 J3
Sucio r. Col. 146 B2
Suck r. Rep. of Ireland 35 B5

▶Sucre Bol. 148 D4
Legislative capital of Bolivia.
world 8–9

Sucre dept Col. 146 C3
Sucre state Venez. 147 F2
Sucuaro Col. 146 D3
Sucumbíos prov. Ecuador 146 B5
Sucunduri r. Brazil 147 G6
Sucuriú r. Brazil 150 H5
Suczawa Romania see Suceava
Sud prov. Cameroon 93 H5
Suda Rus. Fed. 28 F4
Sudak Ukr. 78 C1

▶Sudan country Africa 89 F5
Largest country in Africa and 10th
largest in the world.
africa 86–87, 100
world 8–9

Suday Rus. Fed. 28 G4
Sudayr, Sha'īb watercourse Iraq 79 F5
Sudbury Canada 124 D4
Sudbury U.K. 35 G6
Sudd swamp Sudan 96 A3
Sudest Island P.N.G. see Tagula Island
Sudetenland mts Czech Rep./Poland 37 G3
Sudety mts Czech Rep./Poland 37 G3
Sudislavl' Rus. Fed. 28 G4
Sud-Kivu prov. Dem. Rep. Congo 94 F5
Sudlersville U.S.A. 131 F4
Sudoeste Alentejanoe Costa
  Vicentina, Parque Natural do
  nature res. Port. 42 B4
Sudogda Rus. Fed. 28 G4
Sud-Ouest prov. Cameroon 93 H4
Sudr Egypt 89 G2
Suđuroy i. Faroe Is 34 [inset]
Suđuroyarfjørður sea chan. Faroe Is 34 [inset]
Sue watercourse Sudan 94 F3
Sueca Spain 43 F3
Süedinenie Bulg. 46 D3
Suez Egypt 89 G2
Suez, Gulf of Egypt 89 G2
▶Suez Canal Egypt 89 G2
africa 86–87
Şufaynah Saudi Arabia 89 I4
Suffolk U.S.A. 131 E5
Sūfīān Iran 80 A2
Sufi-Kurgan Kyrg. see Sopu-Korgon
Sugarbush Hill U.S.A. 132 D2
Sugarloaf Mountain U.S.A. 128 F2
Sugarloaf Point Australia 112 E4
Sugut r. Sabah Malaysia 59 G1
Sugut, Tanjong pt Sabah Malaysia 59 G1
Suhaia Romania 46 D3
Sühāj Egypt see Sawhāj
Şuḩār Oman 76 F5
Şuḩaymī, Wādī as watercourse Egypt 77 A4
Sühbaatar Mongolia 62 H1
Suheli Par i. India 72 B4
Suhl Germany 36 E3
Suhopolje Croatia 44 F2
Suhum Ghana 93 D4
Şuḩut Turkey 78 B3
Šuiá Missur r. Brazil 150 A4
Sui'an China see Zhangpu
Suibin China 64 B3
Suichang China 67 F2
Suicheng Fujian China see Jianning
Suicheng Guangdong China see Suixi
Suichuan China 67 G3
Suid-Afrika country Africa see
  South Africa, Republic of
Suidzhikurmsy Turkm. see Madau
Suifen r. China 64 C4
Suifenhe China 64 C3
Suigam India 74 A4
Suihua China 64 A3
Suijiang China 66 D2
Suileng China 64 A3
Suining Hunan China 67 F3
Suining Jiangsu China 67 F1
Suining Sichuan China 66 C2
Suiping China 67 E1
Suippes France 39 E2
Suir r. Rep. of Ireland 35 C5
Suisse country Europe see Switzerland
Suixi Anhui China 67 F1
Suixi Guangdong China 67 D4
Suixian Henan China 67 E1
Suixian Hubei China see Suizhou
Suiyang China 66 C3
Suizhai China see Xiancheng
Suizhong China 65 A2
Suizhou China 67 E1
Sujangarh India 74 B4
Sujawal Pak. 81 G5
Sukabumi Indon. 59 D4
Sukadana Kalimantan Barat Indon. 59 E3
Sukadana Lampung, Sumatra Indon. 58 D4
Sukadana, Teluk b. Indon. 59 E3
Sukagawa Japan 65 E5
Sukaramai Indon. 59 E3
Sukarnapura Indon. see Jayapura
Sukarno, Puntjak mt. Indon. see Jaya, Puncak
Suket India 74 C4
Sukeva Fin. 32 O4
Sukhinichi Rus. Fed. 29 E5
Sukhona r. Rus. Fed. 28 H3
Sukhothai Thai. 60 B4
Sukhumi Georgia see Sokhumi
Sukhum-Kale Georgia see Sokhumi
Sukkertoppen Greenland see Maniitsoq
Sukkozero Rus. Fed. 28 E3
Sukkur Pak. 81 G5
Sukkur Barrage Pak. 81 G5
Sukma India 73 D2
Sukpay Rus. Fed. 64 D3
Sukpay r. Rus. Fed. 64 D3
Sukri r. India 74 B4
Sukses Namibia see ...
Suktel r. India 73 D1
Sukumo Japan 65 C6
Sukun i. Indon. 108 C2
Sula r. Rus. Fed. 28 I2

Sula, Kepulauan is Indon. 57 G6
Sula, Ozero l. Rus. Fed. 32 H3
Sulabesi i. Indon. 57 G6
Sulaiman Ranges mts Pak. 81 G4
Sulak Rus. Fed. 79 F2
Sulak r. Rus. Fed. 79 F2
Sülär Iran 80 B4
Sula Sgeir i. U.K. 34 C2
Sulawesi i. Indon. see Celebes
Sulaymān Beg Iraq 79 F4
Sulci Sardinia Italy see Sant'Antioco
Sulcis Sardinia Italy see Sant'Antioco
Sulechów Poland 37 G2
Suledeh Iran 80 I3
Sulejów Poland 37 I3
Sulejowskie, Jezioro l. Poland 37 I3
Sule Skerry i. U.K. 34 D2
Sule Stack i. U.K. 34 D2
Sulima Sierra Leone 92 C4
Sulina Romania 46 F2
Sulina, Brațul watercourse Romania 46 F2
Suliskongen mt. Norway 32 I3
Sulitjelma Norway 32 I3
Sullana Peru 146 A6
Sullivan IN U.S.A. 126 B4
Sullivan Bay Canada 122 E5
Sullivan Island Myanmar see Lanbi Kyun
Sullivan Lake Canada 123 I5
Sully-sur-Loire France 38 F3
Sulmo Italy see Sulmona
Sulmona Italy 44 E4
Süloğlu Turkey 46 F4
Sulphur LA U.S.A. 133 C6
Sulphur OK U.S.A. 133 C5
Sulphur r. U.S.A. 133 C5
Sulphur Springs U.S.A. 133 C5
Sulphur Springs Draw watercourse
  U.S.A. 133 A5
Sultan Canada 124 D4
Sultan, Koh-i- mts Pak. 81 E4
Sultanabad Iran see Arāk
Sultanbeyli Turkey 46 F4
Sultanhanı Turkey 78 C3
Sultaniça Turkey 46 F4
Sultaniye Turkey see Karapınar
Sultanpur India 75 E4
Sultansandzharskoye
  Vodokhranilishche resr Turkm. 81 E1
Sulu Dem. Rep. Congo 94 D5
Sulu Archipelago is Phil. 57 F4
Sulu Basin sea feature N. Pacific Ocean
  164 C5
Sülüklü Turkey 78 C3
Sülüktü Kyrg. 81 G2
Suluntah Libya 88 D1
Sülüq Libya 88 D2
Suluru India 72 D3
Sulu Sea N. Pacific Ocean 164 B5
Sulyukta Kyrg. see Sülüktü
Sulzbach-Rosenberg Germany 36 F4
Sulzberger Bay Antarctica 167 I1
Sumampa Arg. 152 E2
Sumapaz, Parque Nacional nat. park
  Col. 146 C4
Sumatera i. Indon. see Sumatra
Sumatera Barat prov. Indon. 58 C3
Sumatera Selatan prov. Indon. 58 C3
Sumatera Utara prov. Indon. 58 B2

▶Sumatra i. Indon. 58 B2
2nd largest island in Asia and 6th in the
world.
asia 50–51
world 6–7

Sumaúma Brazil 149 E1
Šumava mts Czech Rep. 37 F4
Šumava r. part Czech Rep. 37 F4
Sumba i. Indon. 57 F7
Sumba, Île i. Dem. Rep. Congo 94 C4
Sumba, Selat sea chan. Indon. 57 F7
Sumbar r. Turkm. 80 C2
Sumbawa i. Indon. 59 G5
Sumbawabesar Indon. 59 G5
Sumbawanga Tanz. 97 A6
Sumbay Peru 148 C3
Sumbe Angola 95 B7
Sumbing, Gunung vol. Indon. 58 C3
Sumbu Zambia 97 A7
Sumbu National Park Zambia 95 F7
Sumburgh U.K. 34 F2
Sumburgh Head U.K. 34 F2
Sumbuya Sierra Leone 92 C4
Sumdo Aksai Chin 74 C2
Sumdo China 66 B2
Sumdum, Mount U.S.A. 122 C3
Sumé Brazil 147 K5
Sume'eh Sarā Iran 80 B2
Sümeg Hungary 37 H5
Sumeih Sudan 94 C2
Sumenep Indon. 59 F4
Sumerpur India 74 B4
Sumgait Azer. see Sumqayıt
Sumisu-jima i. Japan 65 F7
Summel Iraq 79 E3
Summer Beaver Canada 124 B2
Summerford Canada 125 K3
Summerland Canada 123 I5
Summerside Canada 125 I4
Summersville U.S.A. 130 C4
Summersville Lake U.S.A. 130 C4
Summerville GA U.S.A. 129 B5
Summerville SC U.S.A. 129 C5
Summit Lake B.C. Canada 122 F3
Summit Lake B.C. Canada 122 F4
Summit Mountain U.S.A. 137 D2
Summit Peak U.S.A. 135 F5
Sumnal Aksai Chin 74 C2
Sumner N.Z. 113 C4
Sumner U.S.A. 133 D5
Sumner Strait U.S.A. 122 C3
Šumperk Czech Rep. 37 H4
Sumprabum Myanmar 60 B2
Sumpu Japan see Shizuoka
Sumqayıt Azer. 79 G2
Sumqayıt r. Azer. 79 G2
Sumskiy Posad Rus. Fed. 28 F2
Sumter U.S.A. 129 C5
Sumur Jammu and Kashmir 74 C2
Sumy Ukr. 29 E6
Sun r. U.S.A. 134 I3
Sunam India 74 B3
Sunamganj Bangl. 75 F4
Sunan N. Korea 65 A5
Sunbula Kuh mts Iran 80 A3
Sunbury Australia 112 B6
Sunbury NC U.S.A. 131 E5
Sunbury OH U.S.A. 130 D3
Sunbury PA U.S.A. 131 E3
Sunchales Arg. 152 D2
Suncho Corral Arg. 152 E1
Sunch'ŏn N. Korea 65 A5
Sunch'ŏn S. Korea 65 A6
Sun City S. Africa 99 G5
Sun City U.S.A. 137 F5
Suncook U.S.A. 131 H2
Sunda, Selat strait Indon. 58 D4
Sundance U.S.A. 134 F3
Sundarbans r. Bangl./India 75 F5
Sundarbans National Park Bangl./India
  75 F5

Sundargarh India 75 E5
Sundarnagar India 74 C3
Sunda Shelf sea feature Indian Ocean
  162 O5
Sunda Strait Indon. see Sunda, Selat
Sunda Trench sea feature Indian Ocean
  see Java Trench
Sunday Strait Australia 108 C4
Sunderland U.K. 34 F4
Sündiken Dağları mts Turkey 78 B3
Sundre Canada 123 H5
Sundridge Canada 124 E4
Sundsvall Sweden 33 J3
Sundukli, Peski des. Turkm. 81 E2
Sunga Tanz. 97 C6
Sungaiapit Indon. 58 C2
Sungaiguntung Indon. 58 C2
Sungailiat Indon. 58 D3
Sungaipenuh Indon. 59 E2
Sungari r. China see Songhua Jiang
Sungei Petani Malaysia 58 C1
Sungei Seletar Reservoir Sing. 58 [inset]
Sungikai Sudan 89 F6
Sungkiang China see Songjiang
Sungo Moz. 99 G3
Sungqu China see Songpan
Sungurlare Bulg. 46 E3
Sungurlu Turkey 78 C2
Sunkosh r. Bhutan 75 F4
Sun Kosi r. Nepal 75 F4
Sunndal Norway 32 C3
Sunndalsøra Norway 32 C3
Sunne Sweden 33 H4
Sunnyside UT U.S.A. 137 G2
Sunnyside WA U.S.A. 134 C3
Sunnyvale U.S.A. 136 A3
Sunset House Canada 123 G4
Sunset Peak hill Hong Kong China
  67 [inset]
Suntar Rus. Fed. 27 L3
Suntsar Pak. 81 E5
Sunwi-do i. N. Korea 65 A5
Sunwu China 64 B2
Sunyani Ghana 92 C4
Suojanperä Fin. 32 H1
Suolahti Fin. 32 O3
Suoločielgi Fin. see Saariselkä
Suoluvuobmi Norway 32 M1
Suomenniemi Fin. 33 O3
Suomi country Europe see Finland
Suŏ-nada b. Japan 65 B6
Suonenjoki Fin. 32 O3
Suong r. Laos 60 C4
Suong Cambodia 61 D6
Suontee Fin. 32 O3
Suontienselkä l. Fin. 32 O3
Suoyarvi Rus. Fed. 28 E3
Supa India 72 B3
Supai U.S.A. 137 F3
Supaul India 75 F4
Superfosfatnyy Uzbek. 81 F2
Superior AZ U.S.A. 137 G5
Superior MT U.S.A. 134 D3
Superior WI U.S.A. 132 A2

▶Superior, Lake Canada/U.S.A. 132 E2
Largest lake in North America and 2nd
in the world.
northamerica 116–117
world 6–7

Supetar Croatia 44 F3
Suphan Buri Thai. 61 C5
Süphan Dağı mt. Turkey 79 E3
Supiori i. Indon. 57 I6
Support Force Glacier Antarctica 167 A1
Sup'sa r. Georgia 79 F2
Supung N. Korea 65 A4
Süq ar Rubū' Saudi Arabia 89 I4
Süq ash Shuyūkh Iraq 79 G5
Suqian China 67 F1
Süq Suwayq Saudi Arabia 89 H3
Suquţrá i. Yemen see Socotra
Sur r. Ghana 89 I3
Şūr Hungary 37 I5
Sur, Point U.S.A. 136 B3
Sur, Punta pt Arg. 152 E3
Sura r. Rus. Fed. 29 H4
Surab Pak. 81 F4
Surabaya Indon. 59 F4
Surajpur India 75 D5
Sūrak Iran 81 E5
Surakarta Indon. 59 E4
Sura Mare Romania 46 D2
Şūran Iran 81 E5
Şūrān Syria 77 C2
Surára Brazil 147 F6
Surat Australia 111 G5
Surat India 74 B5
Suratgarh India 74 B3
Surat Thani Thai. 61 B6
Surazh Rus. Fed. 29 E5
Surbiton Australia 111 F4
Sürdäsh Iraq 79 F3
Surdila-Greci Romania 46 E2
Surdulica Serb. and Mont. 46 C3
Süre r. Germany/Lux. 39 G2
Surendranagar India 74 B5
Surf U.S.A. 136 B4
Surgères France 38 D3
Surgut Rus. Fed. 26 H3
Suri India see Siuri
Suriapet India 72 C2
Surigao Phil. 57 G4
Surimena Col. 146 C4
Surin Thai. 61 C5

▶Suriname country S. America 147 G3
southamerica 144–145, 154
Suriname r. Suriname 147 H3
Suripá Venez. 146 D3
Suriyān Iran 80 C4
Surkhāb, Daryā-ye r. Afgh. 81 G3
Surkhandar'ya r. Uzbek. see
  Surkhondaryo
Surkhandar'ya Oblast' admin. div. Uzbek.
  see Surkhandar'inskaya Oblast'
Surkhandar'inskaya Oblast' admin. div.
  Uzbek. 81 G2
Surkhet Nepal 75 D3
Surkhob r. Tajik. 81 H2
Surkhondaryo r. Uzbek. see
  Surkhandar'ya
Surkhondaryo Wiloyati admin. div.
  Uzbek. see Surkhandar'inskaya Oblast'
Surmāq Iran 80 C3
Sürmene Turkey 79 E2
Surnadalsøra Norway 32 C3
Surnevo Bulg. 46 D3
Surovikino Rus. Fed. 29 G6
Surprise Canada 122 C3
Surrey Canada 122 F5
Surskoye Rus. Fed. 29 H5
Surt Libya see Sirte
Surt, Khalīj g. Libya see Sirte, Gulf of
Surtsey i. Iceland 32 [inset]
Sürü Iran 80 D5
Suru r. Romania 46 D2
Surubiú r. Brazil 150 B2
Sürüç Turkey 79 D3
Suruga-wan b. Japan 65 D6

Surulangun Indon. 58 C3
Surumu r. Brazil 147 F4
Surupet India see Suriapet
Susa Italy 44 A2
Suša r. Croatia 44 F3
Sušac i. Croatia 44 F3
Susah Tunisia see Sousse
Susaki Japan 65 C6
Susan U.S.A. 131 E5
Süsangerd Iran 80 B4
Susanville U.S.A. 136 B1
Suşehri Turkey 79 D2
Susner India 74 C5
Susong China 67 F2
Susquehanna U.S.A. 131 F3
Susquehanna, West Branch r. U.S.A.
  130 E3
Susques Arg. 148 D5
Sussex Canada 125 I4
Sussex U.S.A. 131 F3
Susuman Rus. Fed. 27 O3
Susurluk Turkey 78 B3
Suswa, Mount Kenya 96 B5
Susz Poland 37 I2
Sutak Jammu and Kashmir 74 C2
Sutherland Australia 112 D4
Sutherland S. Africa 98 D7
Sutherland NE U.S.A. 132 A3
Sutherland r. U.S.A. 128 D5
Sutherland Range hills Australia 109 D6
Sutjeska nat. park Bos.-Herz. 44 G3
Sutlej r. India/Pak. 74 A3
Sutter U.S.A. 136 B2
Sutton r. Canada 124 D2
Sutton U.S.A. 130 C4
Sutton Coldfield U.K. 35 F5
Sutton Lake Canada 124 C2
Suttor r. Australia 111 F4
Sutwik Island U.S.A. 120 D4
Sutyr' r. Rus. Fed. 64 C2
Suure-Jaani Estonia 33 G4
Suurpea Estonia 33 G4

▶Suva Fiji 107 G3
Capital of Fiji.

Suvalki Poland see Suwałki
Suvorov Ukr. 46 F2
Suvorove Ukr. 46 F2
Suvorovo Moldova see Ştefan Vodă
Suwakong Indon. 59 F3
Suwałki Poland 37 K1
Suwannaphum Thai. 61 C5
Suwannee r. U.S.A. 129 C6
Suwanose-jima i. Japan 65 B7
Suwaran, Gunung mt. Indon. 59 G2
Suwarrow atoll Cook Is 165 H6
Suwayqīyah, Hawr as imp. l. Iraq 79 G4
Suwayr well Saudi Arabia 89 I2
Suways, Khalīj as g. Egypt see
  Suez, Gulf of
Suways, Qanāt as canal Egypt see
  Suez Canal
Suweilih Jordan see Suwaylih
Suweis, Khalīg el g. Egypt see
  Suez, Gulf of
Suweis, Qanâ el canal Egypt see
  Suez Canal
Suwŏn S. Korea 65 A5
Suz, Mys pt Kazakh. 79 H2
Sūzā Iran 80 D5
Suzaka Japan 65 E5
Suzdal' Rus. Fed. 28 G4
Suzhou Anhui China 67 F1
Suzhou Jiangsu China see Jiuquan
Suzhou Jiangsu China 67 G2
Suzi r. China 64 A4
Suzu Japan 65 D5
Suzuka Japan 65 D6
Suzu-misaki pt Japan 65 D5
Suzzara Italy 44 C2

▶Svalbard terr. Arctic Ocean 26 B2
Part of Norway.

Svalenik Bulg. 46 E3
Svanstein Sweden 32 F2
Svappavaara Sweden 32 F2
Svärdsjö Sweden 33 J3
Svärtlän r. Sweden 33 J4
Svartenhuk Halvø pen. Greenland see
  Sigguup Nunaa
Svatove Ukr. 29 F6
Svay Riĕng Cambodia 61 D6
Svecha Rus. Fed. 28 H4
Svédasai Lith. 33 N9
Sveg Sweden 33 I3
Svegsjön l. Sweden 33 I3
Sveio Norway 33 B4
Svelgen Norway 32 B3
Svellingen Norway 32 C3
Švenčionėliai Lith. 33 O9
Švenčionys Lith. 33 O9
Svendborg Denmark 33 G5
Svenljunga Sweden 33 H4
Svenstavik Sweden 32 I3
Sverdlovs'k Ukr. 29 F6
Sverdlovsk Rus. Fed. see Yekaterinburg
Sverdlovs'k Ukr. 29 F6
Sverdlovskaya Oblast' admin. div.
  Rus. Fed. see Sverdlovskaya Oblast'
Sverdlovsk Oblast admin. div. Rus. Fed.
  see Sverdlovskaya Oblast'
Sverdrup Channel Canada 121 J2
Sverdrup Islands Canada 121 J2
Sverige country Europe see Sweden
Sveta Andrija i. Croatia 44 E3
Sveti Jure mt. Croatia 44 F3
Sveti Nikole Macedonia 46 B4
Svetlaya Rus. Fed. 64 D3
Svetlodarskoye Rus. Fed. 64 E2
Svetlograd Rus. Fed. 29 G7
Svetlopolyansk Rus. Fed. 28 J4
Svetlogorsk Belarus see Svyetlahorsk
Svetlogorsk Kaliningradskoy Oblast'
  Rus. Fed. 33 T5
Svetlogorsk Krasnoyarskiy Kray Rus. Fed.
  27 J3
Svetlyy Rus. Fed. 29 G7
Svetlyy Rus. Fed. 29 H6
Svetogorsk Rus. Fed. 28 D3
Svetozarevo Serb. and Mont. see Jagodina
Svíahnúkar vol. Iceland 32 [inset]
Svidník Slovakia 37 J4
Svilaja mts Croatia 44 F3
Svilajnac Serb. and Mont. 46 B2
Svilengrad Bulg. 46 E4
Svinecea Mare, Vârful mt. Romania
  31 J4
Svínoy i. Faroe Is see Svínoy
Svínoy i. Faroe Is 34 [inset]
Svir Belarus 33 O9
Svir' r. Rus. Fed. 28 F3
Svishtov Bulg. 46 D3
Svitavy Czech Rep. 37 H4
Svitlovods'k Ukr. 29 F6
Svitlovods'k Ukr. see Svitlovods'k
Svoboda r. Romania 46 D2

Svobodnyy Rus. Fed. 64 B2
Svoge Bulg. 46 C3
Svolvær Norway 32 I1
Svrljig Serb. and Mont. 46 C3
Svrljiške Planine mts Serb. and Mont.
  46 C3
Svyatoy Nos, Mys c. Rus. Fed. 28 I2
Svyetlahorsk Belarus 31 L2
Swabi Pak. 81 H3
Swain Reefs Australia 111 H4
Swainsboro U.S.A. 129 C5
Swains Island American Samoa 107 H3
Swakop watercourse Namibia 98 B4
Swakopmund Namibia 98 B4
Swale r. U.K. 35 F4
Swallow Islands Solomon Is 107 F3
Swampy r. Canada 125 F3
Swan r. Australia 109 A7
Swan r. Man./Sask. Canada 123 K4
Swan r. Ont. Canada 124 C2
Swanage U.K. 35 F6
Swana-Mume Dem. Rep. Congo 95 E7
Swandale U.S.A. 130 C4
Swan Hill Australia 112 B4
Swan Hills Canada 123 H4
Swan Islands Caribbean Sea 139 H5
Swan Lake Canada 123 K4
Swan Lake U.S.A. 128 E3
Swanquarter U.S.A. 129 E5
Swan River Canada 134 G1
Swansea Australia 112 B6
Swansea U.K. 35 E6
Swansea Bay U.K. 35 E6
Swanton U.S.A. 136 A3
Swart Nossob watercourse Namibia see
  Black Nossob
Swartruggens S. Africa 99 G5
Swartz Creek U.S.A. 130 E2
Swarzędz Poland 37 H2
Swasey Peak U.S.A. 137 F2
Swat r. Pak. 81 G3
Swatow China see Shantou

▶Swaziland country Africa 99 F5
africa 86–87, 100

▶Sweden country Europe 33 D3
5th largest country in Europe.
europe 24–25, 48

Sweet Home U.S.A. 134 B3
Sweet Springs U.S.A. 130 C5
Sweetwater U.S.A. 133 A5
Sweetwater r. U.S.A. 134 F4
Swellendam S. Africa 98 D7
Świder r. Poland 37 J2
Świdnica Poland 37 H3
Świdwin Poland 37 G2
Świebodzice Poland 37 H3
Świebodzin Poland 37 G2
Świecie Poland 37 H2
Świętokrzyskie, Góry hills Poland 37 J3
Świętokrzyski Park Narodowy nat. park
  Poland 37 J3
Swift r. U.S.A. 131 H1
Swift Current Canada 134 F2
Swilly, Lough inlet Rep. of Ireland 34 C4
Swindon U.K. 35 F6
Świnoujście Poland 37 G2
Swiss Confederation country Europe see
  Switzerland
Swiss National Park Switz. 39 I3

▶Switzerland country Europe 39 H3
europe 24–25, 48

Swords Rep. of Ireland 35 C5
Swords Range hills Australia 111 E4
Syamozero, Ozero l. Rus. Fed. 28 E3
Syamzha Rus. Fed. 28 G3
Syang Nepal 75 D3
Syas'troy Rus. Fed. 28 F3
Sychevka Rus. Fed. 28 E5
Syców Poland 37 H3

▶Sydney Australia 112 D4
State capital of New South Wales. Most
populous city in Oceania.
oceania 104–105
world 16–17

Sydney Canada 125 I4
Sydney Island Kiribati see Manra
Sydney Lake Canada 123 M5
Syeverodonets'k Ukr. 29 F6
Sykesville U.S.A. 130 E3
Sykkylven Norway 32 B3
Syktyvkar Rus. Fed. 28 I3
Sylacauga U.S.A. 129 B5
Sylhet Bangl. 75 F4
Sylhet admin. div. Bangl. 75 F4
Sylt i. Germany 36 D1
Sylva r. Rus. Fed. 28 I4
Sylva U.S.A. 128 C5
Sylvania GA U.S.A. 129 C5
Sylvania OH U.S.A. 130 D3
Sylvan Lake Canada 123 H4
Sylvester, Lake salt flat Australia 110 C3
Sylvia, Mount Canada 122 E3
Symi Greece 47 E6
Symi i. Greece 47 E6
Syracuse Sicily Italy see Syracuse
Syracuse KS U.S.A. 132 A4
Syracuse NY U.S.A. 131 E2
Syrdar'inskaya Oblast' admin. div.
  Uzbek. 81 G1
Syr Darya r. Asia 70 C3
Syrdar'ya Uzbek. 81 G1
Syrdar'ya r. Asia see Syr Darya
Syrdaryinskiy Uzbek. see Syrdar'ya

▶Syria country Asia 79 D4
asia 52–53, 82

Syrian Desert Asia 79 D4
Syriam Myanmar 60 B3
Syrna i. Greece 47 E6
Syros i. Greece 47 D6
Syrskiy Rus. Fed. 29 F5
Sysmä Fin. 33 G3
Sysola r. Rus. Fed. 28 I3
Syumsi Rus. Fed. 28 J4
Syun' r. Rus. Fed. 28 J5
Syurkum Rus. Fed. 64 E2
Syurkum, Mys pt Rus. Fed. 64 E2
Syzran' Rus. Fed. 29 H5
Szabadka Serb. and Mont. see Subotica
Szadek Poland 37 I3
Szamocin Poland 37 H2
Szamotuły Poland 37 H2
Szarvas Hungary 37 J5
Szazhalombatta Hungary 37 I5
Szczecin Poland 37 G2
Szczecinek Poland 37 H2
Szczeciński, Zalew b. Poland 37 G2
Szczekociny Poland 37 I3
Szczytna Poland 37 H3
Szczytno Poland 37 K2
Szechwan prov. China see Sichuan
Szeged Hungary 46 B1
Szeghalom Hungary 37 J5

Székesfehérvár Hungary 37 I5
Szekszárd Hungary 37 J5
Szentes Hungary 37 J5
Szentgotthárd Hungary 37 H5
Szentlőrinc Hungary 44 F1
Szerencs Hungary 37 J4
Szeska Góra hill Poland 37 K1
Szigetszentmiklós Hungary 37 I5
Szigetvár Hungary 44 F1
Szkwa r. Poland 37 K2
Szolnok Hungary 37 J5
Szombathely Hungary 37 H5
Sztálinváros Hungary see Dunaújváros
Sztum Poland 37 I2
Szydłowiec Poland 37 J3
Szypliszki Poland 33 T5

Taabo, Lac de l. Côte d'Ivoire 92 C4
Taagga Duudka reg. Somalia 96 D2
Tab Hungary 37 I5
Tābah Saudi Arabia 89 I3
Tabajara Brazil 149 G3
Tabakat well Mali 92 E1
Tabanan Indon. 59 F5
Tabang Indon. 59 G2
Tabang r. Indon. 59 G2
Ţabaqah Syria 77 D2
Tabar Islands P.N.G. 107 E2
Tabarka Tunisia 45 B6
Tabas Iran 80 D3
Tābāsīn Iran 80 D4
Tābask, Kūh-e mt. Iran 80 B4
Tabatinga Brazil 146 D6
Tabatinga, Serra da hills Brazil 150 C4
Tabédé well Chad 88 D6
Tabelbala Alg. 90 D3
Taber Canada 123 H5
Tabernas Spain 43 E5
Tabernes de Valldigna Spain see
  Tavernes de la Valldigna
Tabet, Nam r. Myanmar 60 B2
Tabia Tsaka salt l. China 75 E3
Tabir r. Indon. 58 C3
Tabiteuea atoll Kiribati 164 C6
Table Cape N.Z. 113 F4
Table Island India 61 A4
Table Rock Reservoir U.S.A. 133 C4
Tabligbo Togo 92 E4
Taboca Brazil 147 F5
Tabocal r. Brazil 147 F5
Tabong Myanmar 60 B2
Tábor Czech Rep. 37 G4
Tabora Tanz. 97 B6
Tabora admin. reg. Tanz. 97 B6
Taboshar Tajik. 81 G2
Tabou Côte d'Ivoire 92 C4
Tabrīchat well Mali 93 F1
Tabrīz Iran 80 A2
Tabuaeran i. Kiribati 165 H5
Tabūk Saudi Arabia 89 H3
Tabūk prov. Saudi Arabia 77 B5
Tabulam Australia 112 E3
Tabuyung Indon. 58 B2
Täby Sweden 33 J4
Tacaimbó Brazil 147 K5
Tacana, Serra hills Venez. 147 H5
Tacheng China 70 F2
Tachie Canada 122 E4
Táchira state Venez. 146 C2
Tachiumet well Libya 88 A3
Tachov Czech Rep. 37 F4
Tacina r. Italy 45 F5
Taciuã, Lago l. Brazil 147 F6
Tacloban Phil. 57 G3
Tacna Col. 146 C4
Tacna Peru 148 C4
Tacna dept Peru 148 C4
Tacoma U.S.A. 134 C3
Taco Pozo Arg. 152 E1
Tacuarembó Uruguay 152 G2
Tadelaka well Niger 93 F3
Tademaït, Plateau du Alg. 91 F3
Tadine New Caledonia 107 F4
Tadjentourt hill Alg. 91 F4
Tadjikistan country Asia see Tajikistan
Tadjoura Djibouti 96 D2
Tadjoura, Golfe de g. Djibouti 96 D2
Tadjrouna Alg. 91 F2
Tadmur Syria 79 D4
Tadó Col. 146 B3
Tadohae Haesang National Park
  S. Korea 65 A6
Tadoule Lake Canada 123 L3
Tadpatri India 72 C3
Tadrart Acacus tourist site Libya 88 A3
Tadwale India 72 C2
Tadzhikabad Tajik. see Tojikobod
Tadzhikskaya S.S.R. country Asia see
  Tajikistan
T'aean Haean National Park S. Korea
  65 A5
T'aebaek-sanmaek mts
  N. Korea/S. Korea 65 A5
Taebla Estonia 33 F4
Taech'ŏn S. Korea see Poryŏng
Taech'ŏng-do i. S. Korea 65 A5
Taedong-man b. N. Korea 65 A5
Taegu S. Korea 65 B5
Taehüksan-kundo is S. Korea 65 A6
Taejŏn S. Korea 65 A5
Taejŏng S. Korea 65 A6
T'aepaek S. Korea 65 B5
Ta'erqi China 63 K2
Tafahi i. Tonga 107 I3
Tafalla Spain 43 F2
Tafassasset, Oued watercourse
  Alg./Niger 91 H5
Tafelberg mt. Suriname 147 G4
Tafila Jordan see At Tafilah
Tafiré Côte d'Ivoire 92 C4
Tafí Viejo Arg. 152 D1
Tafresh Iran 80 B3
Taft Iran 80 D4
Taft U.S.A. 135 C5
Taftān, Kūh-e mt. Iran 81 E4
Taftanāz Syria 77 C2
Tagab Sudan 89 F5
Taganet Keyna well Mali 92 E1
Taganrog Rus. Fed. 29 F7
Taganrog, Gulf of Rus. Fed./Ukr. 29 F7
Taganrogskiy Zaliv b. Rus. Fed./Ukr. see
  Taganrog, Gulf of
Tagant admin. reg. Mauritania 92 C1
Tagarev, Gora mt. Iran/Turkm. 80 D2
Tagay Rus. Fed. 29 H5
Tagaza well Mali 93 E2
Tagbilaran Phil. 57 G4
Tagchagpu Ri mt. China 75 D3
Tagdempt Alg. see Tiaret
Tagerhanmt well Mali 90 D4
Tagish Canada 122 C2
Tagish Lake Canada 122 C3
Tagliamento r. Italy 44 E2
Tagnout Chaggueret well Mali 91 F3
Tagôuraret well Mauritania 92 D1
Tagtabazar Turkm. 81 E3

Taguatinga Brazil 150 C5
Taguenout Haggueret *well* Mali *see* Tagnout Chagguerет
Tagula P.N.G. 111 H1
Tagula Island P.N.G. 107 E3
Tagus *r.* Port./Spain 42 C3
also known as Tajo (Portugal) *or* Tejo (Spain)
Tah, Sabkhat *salt pan* Morocco 90 B4
Taha China 64 A3
Tahan, Gunung *mt.* Malaysia 58 C1
Tahanroz'ka Zatoka *b.* Rus. Fed./Ukr. *see* Taganrog, Gulf of
Tahat, Mont *mt.* Alg. 91 G5
Tahaurawe *i.* U.S.A. *see* Kahoolawe
Tahe China 64 A1
Taheke N.Z. 113 C1
Tahifet Alg. 91 G5
Tahiti *i.* Fr. Polynesia 165 I7
Tahlab *r.* Iran/Pak. 81 E4
Tahlab, Dasht-i *plain* Pak. 81 E4
Tahlequah U.S.A. 133 C5
Tahltan Canada 122 D3
Tahoe, Lake U.S.A. 136 B2
Tahoe City U.S.A. 136 B2
Tahoe Vista U.S.A. 136 B2
Tahoka U.S.A. 133 A5
Tahoua Niger 93 G2
Tahoua *dept* Niger 93 G2
Tahrūd Iran 80 D4
Tahrūd *r.* Iran 80 D4
Ţahţā Egypt 89 F3
Tahtsa Peak Canada 122 E4
Tahua Bol. 148 D4
Tahuamanú Peru 148 C2
Tahulandang *i.* Indon. 57 G5
Taï Côte d'Ivoire 92 D4
Taï, Parc National de *nat. park* Côte d'Ivoire 92 D4
Tai'an China 63 J4
Taibai China 66 C1
Taibai Shan *mt.* China 66 C1
Taibei Taiwan *see* T'aipei
Taibilla *r.* Spain 43 E3
Taibilla, Sierra de *mts* Spain 43 E3
Taibus Qi China *see* Baochang
T'aichung Taiwan 67 G3
Taidong Taiwan *see* T'aitung
Taieri *r.* N.Z. 113 B4
Taihape N.Z. 113 C2
Taihe *Anhui* China 67 E1
Taihe *Jiangxi* China 67 E3
Taihe *Sichuan* China *see* Shehong
Taihezhen China *see* Shehong
Tai Ho Wan *Hong Kong* China 67 [inset]
Taihu China 67 E2
Tai Hu *l.* China 67 G2
Taikang *Heilong.* China 64 A3
Taikang *Henan* China 67 E1
Taikkyi Myanmar 60 A4
Tailako East Timor 108 D2
Tai Lam Chung Reservoir *Hong Kong* China 67 [inset]
Taileleo Indon. 58 B3
Tailem Bend Australia 112 A4
Tai Long Wan *b.* *Hong Kong* China 67 [inset]
Tailuge Taiwan *see* T'ailuko
T'ailuko Taiwan 67 G3
Taim Brazil 152 G3
Tai Mo Shan *hill* *Hong Kong* China 67 [inset]
Tain *r.* Ghana 93 E3
Tain U.K. 34 D3
T'ainan Taiwan 67 G4
Tainaro, Akra *pt* Greece 47 C6
Tai O *Hong Kong* China 67 [inset]
Taiobeiras Brazil 150 D5
Taipalsaari Fin. 33 H3
Tai Pang Wan *b.* *Hong Kong* China *see* Mirs Bay

▶T'aipei Taiwan 67 G3
Capital of Taiwan.

Taipei Taiwan *see* T'aipei
Taiping *Guangdong* China *see* Shixing
Taiping *Guangdong* China 67 E4
Taiping *Guangxi* China *see* Chongzuo
Taiping *Guangxi* China 67 D4
Taiping Malaysia 58 C1
Tai Po *Hong Kong* China 67 [inset]
Tai Poutini National Park N.Z. *see* Westland National Park
Taipu Brazil 150 F3
Taipudia India 75 G4
Tairbeart U.K. *see* Tarbert
Tai Rom Yen National Park Thai. 61 B6
Tairuq Iran 80 A3
Tais Indon. 58 C4
Taishan China 67 E4
Tai Shek Mo *hill* *Hong Kong* China *see* Crest Hill
Taishun China 67 F3
Taita Hills Kenya 96 C5
Taitaitanopo *i.* Indon. 58 C3
Taitanu N.Z. 113 C3
Taitao, Península de *pen.* Chile 153 B6
Taitao, Punta *pt* Chile 153 B6
Taiti *mt.* Kenya 96 B4
Tai To Yan *mt.* *Hong Kong* China 67 [inset]
T'aitung Taiwan 67 G4
Taivalkoski Fin. 32 H2
Taivaskero *hill* Fin. 32 G1
▶Taiwan *country* Asia 67 G4
asia 52–53, 82
Taiwan Haixia *strait* China/Taiwan *see* Taiwan Strait
Taiwan Shan *mts* Taiwan *see* Chungyang Shanmo
Taiwan Strait China/Taiwan 67 F4
Taixian China *see* Jiangyan
Taixing China 67 G1
Taïyetos Óros *mts* Greece *see* Tavgetos
Taiyuan China 63 I4
Tai Yue Shan *i.* *Hong Kong* China *see* Lantau Island
Taizhong Taiwan *see* T'aichung
Taizhou *Jiangsu* China 67 F1
Taizhou *Zhejiang* China 67 G2
Taizhou Liedao *i.* China 67 G2
Ta'izz Yemen 76 C7
Tajam, Tanjong *pt* Sing. 58 [inset]
Tajamulco, Volcán de *vol.* Guat. 138 F5
Tajarḥī Libya 88 B3
Tajem, Gunung *hill* Indon. 59 D3
Tāj-e Malekī Iran 80 B4
Tajerouine Tunisia 45 B7
▶Tajikistan *country* Asia 81 G2
asia 52–53, 82
Tajitos Mex. 135 D7
Taj Mahal *tourist site* India 74 C4
Tajo *r.* Spain 42 E2 *see* Tagus
Tajsara, Cordillera de *mts* Bol. 148 D5
Tajuña *r.* Spain 43 E2
Tak Thai. 60 B4
Takāb Iran 80 A2
Takabba Kenya 96 D4
Takadja Cent. Afr. Rep. 94 D2
Takaka N.Z. 113 C3
Takalaou Chad 94 C2
Takalous, Oued *watercourse* Alg. 91 G5
Takama Guyana 147 G3
Takamatsu Japan 65 C6
Takaoka Japan 65 D5
Takapau N.Z. 113 D3
Takapuna N.Z. 113 C2
Takasaki Japan 65 D5
Takatokwane Botswana 98 E5
Takatshwaane Botswana 98 D4
Takatu *r.* Brazil/Guyana 147 G4
Ta-Kaw Myanmar 60 B3
Takayama Japan 65 D5
Tak Bai Thai. 61 C7
Takefu Japan 65 D6
Takengon Indon. 58 B1
Takeo Cambodia *see* Takêv
Takeo Japan 65 B6
Take-shima *i.* N. Pacific Ocean *see* Liancourt Rocks
Takestān Iran 80 B2
Taketa Japan 65 B6
Takêv Cambodia 61 D6
Takfon Tajik. 81 G2
Takhādīd *well* Iraq 79 F5
Takhar *prov.* Afgh. 81 G2
Takhatpur India 75 D5
Takhiatash Uzbek. *see* Gulabie
Takhini *r.* Canada 122 C2
Takhini Hotspring Canada 122 C2
Ta Khli Thai. 61 C5
Ta Khmau Cambodia 61 D6
Takhta-Bazar Turkm. *see* Tagtabazar
Takhteh Iran 80 C4
Takht-i-Sulaiman *mt.* Pak. 81 G4
Takht-i-Suleiman *mt.* Iran 80 B2
Takiéta Niger 93 H2
Takijuq Lake Canada *see* Napaktulik Lake
Takikawa Japan 64 E4
Takisung Indon. 59 F3
Takla Lake Canada 122 E4
Takla Landing Canada 122 E4
Takla Makan *des.* China *see* Taklimakan Desert
▶Taklimakan Desert China 70 F4
asia 50–51
Taklimakan Shamo *des.* China *see* Taklimakan Desert
Takoradi Ghana 93 E4
Takpa Shiri *mt.* China 75 G3
Taku Canada 122 C3
Taku *r.* Canada/U.S.A. 120 F4
Takua Pa Thai. 61 B6
Takum Nigeria 93 H4
Takundi Dem. Rep. Congo 95 C6
Tala Uruguay 152 G3
Talachyn Belarus 29 D5
Talagang Pak. 81 H3
Talaiassa, Serra *hill* Spain 43 G3
Talaja India 74 B5
Talakan *Amurskaya Oblast'* Rus. Fed. 64 B2
Talakan *Khabarovskiy Kray* Rus. Fed. 64 C2
Talala India 72 A1
Talandzha Rus. Fed. 64 B2
Talangbatu Indon. 58 D3
Talara Peru 146 A6
Talar-i-Band *mts* Pak. 81 E5
Talas Kyrg. 70 D3
Tal'at al Jamā'ah, Rujm *mt.* Jordan 77 B4
Talata-Mafara Nigeria 93 G2
Ţal 'at Mūsá *mt.* Lebanon/Syria 77 C2
Talaud, Kepulauan *is* Indon. 57 G5
Talavera de la Reina Spain 42 D3
Talawanta Australia 111 E3
Talawgyi Myanmar 60 B2
Talaya Rus. Fed. 27 P3
Talayuelo *mt.* Spain 43 E3
Talbehat India 74 C4
Talbotton U.S.A. 129 B5
Talbragar *r.* Australia 112 D4
Talca Chile 152 C3
Talca, Punta *pt* Chile 152 C3
Talcahuano Chile 152 B4
Talcher India 73 E1
Taldan Rus. Fed. 64 A1
Taldom Rus. Fed. 28 F4
Taldyk, Pereval *pass* Kyrg. 81 H2
Taldykorgan Kazakh. 70 E3
Taldy-Kurgan Kazakh. *see* Taldykorgan
Taldyqorghan Kazakh. *see* Taldykorgan
Talen India 74 C5
Tālesh Iran *see* Hashtpar
Talguharai Sudan 89 G5
Talhah Saudi Arabia 89 I5
Taliabu *i.* Indon. 57 F6
Talikota India 72 C2
Talimardzhan Uzbek. 81 F2
Taliouine Morocco 90 D3
Taliparamba India 72 B3
Tali Post Sudan 96 A3
Talisay Phil. 57 F3
Talisayan Indon. 59 G2
Taliş Dağları *mts* Azer./Iran 79 G3
Talitsa Rus. Fed. 28 H4
Taliwang Indon. 59 G4
Tallacootra, Lake *salt flat* Australia 109 F7
Talladega U.S.A. 129 B5
Tall 'Afar Iraq 79 E3

▶Tallahassee U.S.A. 129 B6
State capital of Florida.

Tallangatta Australia 112 C5
Tallapoosa *r.* U.S.A. 129 B5
Tall Baydar Syria 79 E3

▶Tallinn Estonia 28 C4
Capital of Estonia.

Tall Kalakh Syria 78 D4
Tall Kayf Iraq 79 E3
Tall Kūjik Syria 79 E3
Tallmadge U.S.A. 130 C3
Tallulah U.S.A. 127 H5
Tall 'Uwaynāt Iraq 79 E3
Tallymerjen Uzbek. *see* Talimardzhan
Talmiā Brazil 147 H4
Talmont-St-Hilaire France 38 C3
Tal'ne Ukr. 29 D6
Tal'noye Ukr. *see* Tal'ne
Talod India 74 B5
Taloda India 74 B5
Talodi Sudan 96 A2
Taloga U.S.A. 133 B4
Talon, Lac *l.* Canada 125 H2
Tāloqān Afgh. 81 G2
Talos Dome *ice feature* Antarctica 167 H2
Ta Loung San *mt.* Laos 60 C3
Talovaya Rus. Fed. 29 G6
Taloyoak Canada 121 J3
Tal Pass Pak. 81 H3
Talras *well* Niger 93 H2
Talsi Latvia 33 F4
Tal Siyāh Iran 81 E4
Taltal Chile 152 C1
Taltson *r.* Canada 123 H2
Talu China 75 G3
Talu Indon. 58 B2
Talvik Norway 32 F1
Talwood Australia 111 G6
Taly Rus. Fed. 29 G6
Talyawalka *r.* Australia 112 B4
Talyshskiye Gory *mts* Azer./Iran *see* Taliş Dağları
Talyy Rus. Fed. 28 J2
Tama Abu, Banjaran *mts* *Sarawak* Malaysia 59 F2
Tamabo Range *mts* *Sarawak* Malaysia *see* Tama Abu, Banjaran
Tamai, Nam *r.* Myanmar 60 B2
Tamala Australia 109 A6
Tamale Ghana 93 E3
Tamalelt *well* Mali 93 F2
Tamalung Indon. 59 F3
Tamana *i.* Kiribati 107 G2
Tamanar Morocco 90 C3
Tamanco Peru 146 C6
Tamanhint Libya 88 B3
Tamani Mali 92 D2
Taman Negara National Park Malaysia 58 C1
Tamano Japan 65 C6
Tamanrasset Alg. 91 G5
Tamanrasset, Oued *watercourse* Alg. 91 F5
Tamanthi Myanmar 60 A2
Tamaqua U.S.A. 131 F3
Tamar India 75 E5
Tamar Syria *see* Tadmur
Tamar *r.* U.K. 35 D6
Tamaradant *well* Mali 93 F1
Tamarugal, Pampa de *plain* Chile 148 C4
Tamási Hungary 37 I5
Tamatave Madag. *see* Toamasina
Tamaulipas *state* Mex. 133 B7
Tambach Kenya 96 B4
Tambacounda Senegal 92 B2
Tambangsawah Indon. 58 C3
Tambaoura, Falaise de *esc.* Mali 92 C2
Tambaqui Brazil 147 F6
Tambelan, Kepulauan *is* Indon. 59 D2
Tambelan Besar *i.* Indon. 59 D2
Tambellup Australia 109 B8
Tamberu Indon. 59 F4
Tambo Australia 111 F5
Tambo *r.* Australia 112 C5
Tambo *r.* Peru 148 C4
Tambobamba Peru 148 B3
Tambo Grande Peru 146 A6
Tambohorano Madag. 99 [inset] I3
Tambopata *r.* Peru 148 C3
Tambor Angola 95 B9
Tambora, Gunung *vol.* Indon. 59 G5
Tamboril Brazil 150 D3
Tamboryacu *r.* Peru 146 C5
Tamboura Cent. Afr. Rep. 94 E3
Tambov Rus. Fed. 29 G5
Tambovka Rus. Fed. 64 B2
Tambov Oblast *admin. div.* Rus. Fed. *see* Tambovskaya Oblast'
Tambovskaya Oblast' *admin. div.* Rus. Fed. 29 G5
Tambre *r.* Spain 42 B1
Tambunan *Sabah* Malaysia 59 G1
Tambunan, Bukit *hill* *Sabah* Malaysia 59 G1
Tambura Sudan 94 E3
Tâmchekkeţ Mauritania 92 C1
Tame Col. 146 D3
Tâmega *r.* Port. 42 B2
Tamel Aike Arg. 153 C7
Tamelos, Akra *pt* Greece 47 D6
Tamenghest Alg. *see* Tamanrasset
Tamenglong India 75 G4
Tamesna *reg.* Niger 93 G1
Tamgak, Adrar *mt.* Niger 93 H1
Tamgout de Lalla Khedidja *mt.* Alg. 43 I4
Tamgué, Massif du *mt.* Guinea 92 B2
Tamia India 74 C5
Tamiahua, Laguna de *lag.* Mex. 126 G7
Tamiami Canal U.S.A. 129 C7
Tamiang *r.* Indon. 58 B1
Tamiang, Ujung *pt* Indon. 58 B1
Tamil Nadu *state* India 72 C4
Tamiš *r.* Serb. and Mont. 46 B2
Ţāmīyah Egypt 89 F2
Tamīyah, Jabal *hill* Saudi Arabia 89 I3
Tamjit *well* Niger 93 H1
Tamlelt, Plaine de *plain* Morocco 90 E2
Tamluk India 75 E5
Tammaro *r.* Italy 44 E4
Tammarvi *r.* Canada 123 K1
Tammela Fin. 32 H2
Tammerfors Fin. *see* Tampere
Tammisaaren Saariston Kansallispuisto *nat. park* Fin. *see* Ekenäs skärgårds Nationalpark
Tammisaari Fin. *see* Ekenäs
Tamnava *r.* Serb. and Mont. 46 B2
Tamou Niger 93 F2
Tampa U.S.A. 129 C7
Tampa Bay U.S.A. 129 C7
Tampang Indon. 58 D4
Tampere Fin. 33 F3
Tampico Mex. 126 G7
Tampines Sing. 58 [inset]
Tampines, Sungai *r.* Sing. 58 [inset]
Tamsagbulag Mongolia 63 J2
Tamshiyacu Peru 146 C6
Tamsweg Austria 37 F5
Tamu Myanmar 60 A2
Tamur *r.* Nepal 75 E4
Tamworth Australia 112 D3
Tamworth U.K. 35 F5
Tana *r.* Fin./Norway *see* Tenojoki
Tana *r.* Kenya 96 D5
Tana Madag. *see* Antananarivo
Tana *r.* U.S.A. 122 A2
Tana *i.* Vanuatu *see* Tanna
Tana, Lake Eth. 96 C2
Tanabe Japan 65 C6
Tana Bru Norway 32 H1
Tanacross U.S.A. 122 A2
Tanafjorden *inlet* Norway 32 H1
Tanaga Island U.S.A. 120 B4
Tanagro *r.* Italy 45 E4
Tanah, Tanjung *pt* Indon. 59 E4
Tanahbala *i.* Indon. 58 B3
Tanahgrogot Indon. 59 G3
Tanahjampea *i.* Indon. 57 F7
Tanahmasa *i.* Indon. 58 B3
Tanahmerah Indon. 59 G2
Tanahputih Indon. 58 C2
Tanakpur India 74 D3
Tanami Australia 110 B3
Tanami Desert Australia 110 B3
Tân An Vietnam 61 D6
Tanana *r.* U.S.A. 122 A2
Tananarive Madag. *see* Antananarivo
Tanāqīb, Ra's *pt* Saudi Arabia 80 B5
Tanaro *r.* Italy 44 B2
Tanbar Australia 111 E5
Tancheng *Fujian* China *see* Pingtan
Tancheng *Shandong* China 67 F1
Tanch'ŏn N. Korea 65 B4
Tanda Côte d'Ivoire 92 E4
Tanda *Uttar Pradesh* India 74 C3
Tanda *Uttar Pradesh* India 75 D4
Ţăndărei Romania 46 E2
Tandaué Angola 95 C9
Tandek *Sabah* Malaysia 59 G1
Tandi India 74 C2
Tandil Arg. 152 F4
Tandjilé *pref.* Chad 94 C2
Tando Adam Pak. 81 G5
Tando Alahyar Pak. 81 G5
Tando Bago Pak. 81 G5
Tando Muhammad Khan Pak. 81 G5
Tandou Lake *imp. l.* Australia 112 B4
Tandula *r.* India 74 D5
Tandur *Andhra Pradesh* India 72 C2
Tandur *Andhra Pradesh* India 72 C2
Tanega-shima *i.* Japan 65 B7
Tanen Taunggyi *mts* Thai. 60 B4
Taneytown U.S.A. 131 E4
Tanezrouft *reg.* Alg./Mali 91 E5
Tanezrouft Tan-Ahenet *reg.* Alg. 91 E5
Ţanf, Jabal aţ *hill* Syria 77 D3
Tanga Tanz. 97 C6
Tanga *admin. reg.* Tanz. 97 C6
Tangahe N.Z. 113 C2
Tangail Bangl. 75 F4
Tanga Islands P.N.G. 107 E2
Tangalla Sri Lanka 72 D5
Tanganyika *country* Africa *see* Tanzania

▶Tanganyika, Lake Africa 95 F6
Deepest and 2nd largest lake in Africa and 7th largest in the world.
africa 84–85
world 6–7

Tangar Iran 80 C2
Tangasseri India 72 C4
Tangdan China 66 B3
Tangeli Iran 80 C2
Tange Promontory *hd* Antarctica 163 K10
Tanger Morocco *see* Tangier
Tangerang Indon. 59 D4
Tangermünde Germany 36 E2
Tang-e Sarkheh Iran 81 D5
Tanggor China 66 B1
Tanggulashan China *see* Tuotuoheyan
Tanggula Shan *mt.* China 70 H5
Tanggula Shan *mts* China 70 G5
Tanggula Shankou *pass* China 70 H5
Tangguo China 75 E3
Tanghe China 67 E1
Tang He *r.* China 67 E1
Tangi Pak. 81 G3
Tangier Morocco 90 D2
Tangkittebak, Gunung *mt.* Indon. 58 D4
Tang La *pass* China 75 F4
Tanglag China 66 A1
Tanglin Sing. 58 [inset]
Tangmai China 75 G3
Tangorin Australia 111 F4
Tangra Yumco *salt l.* China 70 G5
Tangse Indon. 58 A1
Tangshan China 63 J4
Tangte *mt.* Myanmar 60 B3
Tanguieta Benin 93 F3
Tangwang *r.* China 64 B3
Tangxianzhen China 67 E2
Tang-yan Myanmar 60 B3
Tangyan He *r.* China 67 D2
Tangyuan China 64 B3
Tanhaçu Brazil 150 D5
Tanhua Fin. 32 G2
Taniantaweng Shan *mts* China 66 A2
Tanimbar, Kepulauan *is* Indon. 57 H7
Tanintharī Myanmar *see* Tenasserim
Tanintharyi Myanmar *see* Tenasserim
Tanintharyi *admin. div.* Myanmar *see* Tenasserim
Taninthayi Myanmar *see* Tenasserim
Tanjah Morocco *see* Tangier
Tanjay Phil. 57 F4
Tanjore India *see* Thanjavur
Tanjung *Kalimantan Selatan* Indon. 59 F3
Tanjung *Jambi, Sumatra* Indon. 58 D3
Tanjungbalai *Sumatera Utara, Sumatra* Indon. 58 B2
Tanjungbalai *Sumatera Utara, Sumatra* Indon. 58 C2
Tanjungbatu *Kalimantan Timur* Indon. 59 G2
Tanjungbatu *Riau, Sumatra* Indon. 58 C2
Tanjungbuayabuaya, Pulau *i.* Indon. 59 G2
Tanjunggaru Indon. 59 G3
Tanjungkarang-Telukbetung Indon. *see* Bandar Lampung
Tanjungpandan Indon. 59 D3
Tanjungpinang Indon. 58 D2
Tanjungpura Indon. 58 B2
Tanjung Puting National Park Indon. 59 F3
Tanjungraja Indon. 58 C3
Tanjungredeb Indon. 59 G2
Tanjungsaleh *i.* Indon. 59 E3
Tanjungsatai Indon. 59 E3
Tanjungselor Indon. 59 G2
Tank Pak. 81 G3
Tankara India 74 A5
Tankhala India 74 B5
Tankse Jammu and Kashmir 74 C2
Tankuhi India 75 E4
Tankwa-Karoo National Park S. Africa 98 C7
Tanlwe *r.* Myanmar 60 A4
Tanna *i.* Vanuatu 107 F3
Tännäs Sweden 33 D3
Tanner, Mount Canada 122 G5
Tannila Fin. 32 G2
Tannu-Ola, Khrebet *mts* Rus. Fed. 62 E1
Tannu Tuva *aut. rep.* Rus. Fed. *see* Tyva, Respublika
Tanot India 74 A4
Tanout Niger 93 H2
Tansen Nepal 75 D4
Tanshui Taiwan 67 G3
Tansila Burkina 92 D2
Ţanţā Egypt 89 F2
Tantabin Myanmar 60 A3
Tan-Tan Morocco 90 C3
Tantoyuca Mex. 126 G7
Tantpur India 74 C4
Tantura Israel 77 B3
Tanuku India 73 D2
Tanumshede Sweden 33 C4
Tanwakka, Sabkhat *well* W. Sahara 90 B5
▶Tanzania *country* Africa 97 B6
africa 86–87, 100
Tanzilla *r.* Canada 122 D3
Tao, Ko *i.* Thai. 61 B5
Tao'an China *see* Taonan
Taocheng *Fujian* China *see* Yongchun
Taocheng *Guangdong* China *see* Daxin
Taodeni Mali *see* Taoudenni
Tao He *r.* China 66 B1
Taohong China *see* Longhui
Taohuaping China *see* Longhui
Taojiang China 67 E2
Taolanaro Madag. *see* Tôlañaro
Taonan China 63 K2
Taongi *atoll* Marshall Is 164 F5
Taormina *Sicily* Italy 45 E6
Taos U.S.A. 135 F5
Taouardeï *well* Mali 93 F1
Taoudenni Mali 90 E5
Taounate Morocco 90 D2
Taounnant *well* Mali 91 E5
Taourirt Morocco 90 E2
Taoxi China 67 F3
Taoyuan China 67 D2
T'aoyüan Taiwan 67 G3
Taozhou China *see* Guangde
Tapa Estonia 28 C4
Tapachula Mex. 138 F6
Tapajós *r.* Brazil 147 H5
Tapaktuan Indon. 58 B2
Tapalqué Arg. 152 E4
Tapan Indon. 58 C3
Tapan Turkey *see* Mansurlu
Tapanahoni *r.* Suriname 147 H3
Tapanuli, Teluk *b.* Indon. 58 B2
Tapara, Serra do *hills* Brazil 147 H5
Tapauá Brazil 147 E6
Tapauá *r.* Brazil 147 E6
Tapera *Rio Grande do Sul* Brazil 151 A9
Tapera *Roraima* Brazil 147 F5
Tapera Chile 153 C6
Tapes Brazil 152 H2
Tapeta Liberia 92 C4
Tapi *r.* India 74 B5
Tapia, Sierra de *hills* Bol. 149 F4
Tapi Aike Arg. 153 C7
Tapiau Rus. Fed. *see* Gvardeysk
Tapiche *r.* Peru 146 C6
Tápió *r.* Hungary 37 J5
Tápiószecső Hungary 37 I5
Tapiracanga Brazil 150 C5
Tapirapé *r.* Brazil 150 B4
Tapirapuã Brazil 149 F3
Tapis *mt.* Malaysia 58 C1
Taplejung Nepal 75 E4
Tap Mun Chau *i.* *Hong Kong* China 67 [inset]
Tapoa *watercourse* Burkina 93 F2
Tapol Chad 94 B2
Tapolca Hungary 37 H5
Ta-pom Myanmar 60 B3
Tappahannock U.S.A. 131 E5
Tappal India 74 C3
Tappeh, Kūh-e *hill* Iran 80 B3
Taprobane *country* Asia *see* Sri Lanka
Tapuaenuku *mt.* N.Z. 113 C3
Tapulonanjing *mt.* Indon. 58 B2
Tapung *r.* Indon. 58 C2
Tapurucuara Brazil 147 E5
Taquara Brazil 151 B9
Taquari Brazil 151 A6
Taquari *r.* Brazil 149 F4
Taquaritinga Brazil 149 H5
Tara Australia 111 G5
Tara *r.* Bos.-Herz./Serb. and Mont. 46 A3
Tara *nat. park* Serb. and Mont. 46 A3
Taraba *r.* Nigeria 93 H3
Taraba *state* Nigeria 93 H3
Tarabuco Bol. 148 D4
Tarābulus Libya *see* Tripoli
Taraclia Moldova 46 F2
Taracua Brazil 146 D4
Tarāghin Libya 88 B3
Tarairá *r.* Brazil *see* Traíra
Tarakan Indon. 59 G2
Tarakan *i.* Indon. 59 G2
Taraklı Turkey 78 B2
Tarakliya Moldova *see* Taraclia
Taran, Mys *pt* Rus. Fed. 31 I2
Tarana India 74 C5
Taranagar India 74 B3
Taranaki, Mount *vol.* N.Z. 113 C2
Tarancón Spain 42 E2
Tarangambadi India 72 C4
Tarangara Chad 94 C2
Tarangire National Park Tanz. 97 C6
Taranto Italy 45 F4
Taranto, Golfo di *g.* Italy 45 F4
Tarapacá *admin. reg.* Chile 148 C4
Tarapacá Col. 146 D5
Tarapoto Peru 146 B6
Tarare France 39 F4
Tararua Range *mts* N.Z. 113 C3
Tarascon-sur-Ariège France 38 D5
Tarasovskiy Rus. Fed. 29 G6
Tarat Alg. 91 H4
Tarata Peru 148 C4
Tarauacá Brazil 148 C2
Tarauacá *r.* Brazil 148 C1
Taravo *r.* *Corsica* France 44 B4
Tarawera N.Z. 113 D2
Tarawera, Mount N.Z. 113 D2
Taraz Kazakh. 70 D3
Tarazona Spain 43 F2
Tarazona de la Mancha Spain 43 F3
Tarbagatay, Khrebet *mts* Kazakh. 70 F2
Tarbat Ness *pt* U.K. 34 E3
Tarbert Rep. of Ireland 35 B5
Tarbert *Argyll and Bute, Scotland* U.K. 34 D4
Tarbert *Western Isles, Scotland* U.K. 34 C3
Tarbes France 38 D5
Tarbet U.K. 34 D3
Tarboro U.S.A. 128 D5
Tarcoola Australia 109 F7
Ţarcului, Munţii *mts* Romania 46 C2
Tardes *r.* France 38 E3
Tardoire *r.* France 38 D4
Tardoki-Yani, Gora *mt.* Rus. Fed. 64 D2
Taree Australia 112 E3
Tareifing Sudan 96 B2
Tärendö Sweden 32 F2
Tarentum Italy *see* Taranto
Tareya Rus. Fed. 27 J2
Ţarfā, Ra's aţ *pt* Saudi Arabia 89 I5
Tarfaya Morocco 90 B4
Targa *well* Niger 93 G1
Targhee Pass U.S.A. 134 E3
Târgovişte Romania 46 D2
Târgu Bujor Romania 46 E2
Târgu Cărbuneşti Romania 46 C2
Targuist Morocco 90 D2
Târgu Jiu Romania 46 C2
Târgu Mureş Romania 46 D1
Târgu Ocna Romania 46 E1
Târgu Secuiesc Romania 46 E1
Targyailing China 75 E3
Tarhān Iran 80 A3
Tarhmanant *well* Mali *see* Taghmanant
Tarhūnah Libya 88 B1
Tari P.N.G. 57 J7
Tarif U.A.E. 80 C5
Tarifa Spain 42 D4
Tarifa, Punta de *pt* Spain 42 D4
Tarija Bol. 149 D5
Tarija *dept* Bol. 149 D5
Tarikere India 72 B3
Tariku *r.* Indon. 57 I6
Tarim Yemen 76 D6
Tarim Basin China 70 F4
Tarime Tanz. 96 B5
Tarim He *r.* China 70 G3
Tarim Pendi *basin* China *see* Tarim Basin
Taringuiti Bol. 149 E5
Tarin Kowt Afgh. 81 F3
Taritatu *r.* Indon. 57 I6
Taritipan *Sabah* Malaysia *see* Tandek
Tarka, Vallée de *watercourse* Niger 93 G2
Tarkio U.S.A. 132 C3
Tarko-Sale Rus. Fed. 26 H3
Tarkwa Ghana 93 E4
Tarlac Phil. 57 F2
Tarlo River National Park Australia 112 D4
Tarlton U.S.A. 130 B4
Tarma Peru 148 B2
Tarn *r.* France 39 D4
Tarna *r.* Hungary 37 I5
Tärnaby Sweden 32 D2
Tarnak *r.* Afgh. 81 F4
Târnava Mare *r.* Romania 46 C1
Târnava Mică *r.* Romania 46 C1
Târnăveni Romania 46 D1
Tarnobrzeg Poland 37 J3
Tarnogskiy Gorodok Rus. Fed. 28 G3
Tarnopol Ukr. *see* Ternopil'
Tarnos France 38 C5
Tarnów Poland 37 J3
Tarnowitz Poland *see* Tarnowskie Góry
Tarnowskie Góry Poland 37 I3
Taro *r.* Italy 44 C2
Taro Co *salt l.* China 75 D3
Ţārom Iran 80 C4
Taroom Australia 111 G5
Taroudannt Morocco 90 C3
Tarpaulin Swamp Australia 110 D3
Tarpon Springs U.S.A. 129 C6
Tarq Iran 80 B3
Tarquinia Italy 44 C3
Tarquinii Italy *see* Tarquinia
Tarracina Italy *see* Terracina
Tarraco Spain *see* Tarragona
Tarragona Spain 43 G2
Tårrajaur Sweden 32 E2
Tarraleah Australia 112 C6
Tarrant Point Australia 111 D3
Tarras N.Z. 113 B4
Tarrasa Spain *see* Terrassa
Tàrrega Spain 43 G2
Tarrong China *see* Nyêmo
Tarso Ahon *mt.* Chad 88 C4
Tarso Emissi *mt.* Chad 88 C4
Tarso Kobour *mt.* Chad 88 C4
Tarsus Turkey 78 C3
Tarta Turkm. *see* Darta
Tartagal *Salta* Arg. 149 E5
Tartagal *Santa Fé* Arg. 152 F2
Tärtär *r.* Azer. 80 A1
Tartas France 38 C5
Tartu Estonia 28 C4
Ţarţūs Syria 78 C4
Ţarţūs *governorate* Syria 77 C2
Tarumovka Rus. Fed. 79 F1
Tarung Hka *r.* Myanmar 60 B2
Tarūt Saudi Arabia 80 B5
Tarutung Indon. 58 B2
Tarutyne Ukr. 46 F1
Tarvisio Italy 44 D1
Tarvisium Italy *see* Treviso
Tarvo Bol. 149 E3
Tarz Iran 80 D4
Taseko Mountain Canada 122 F5
Tasendjanet, Oued *watercourse* Alg. 91 F4
Tasgaon India 72 B2
Tashauz Turkm. *see* Dashkhovuz
Tashauzskaya Oblast' *admin. div.* Turkm. *see* Dashkhovuzskaya Oblast'
Tashbunar *r.* Ukr. 46 F2
Tashi Chho Bhutan *see* Thimphu
Tashigang Bhutan *see* Trashigang
Tashino Rus. Fed. *see* Pervomaysk
Tashir Armenia 79 F2
Tashk, Daryācheh-ye *l.* Iran 80 C4

▶Tashkent Uzbek. 70 C3
Capital of Uzbekistan.

Tashkent Oblast *admin. div.* Uzbek. *see* Tashkentskaya Oblast'
Tashkentskaya Oblast' *admin. div.* Uzbek. 81 G1
Tashkepri Turkm. 81 E2
Tash-Kömür Kyrg. 70 D3
Tash-Kumyr Kyrg. *see* Tash-Kömür
Tashla Rus. Fed. 29 J6
Tāshqurghān Afgh. *see* Kholm
Tasialujjuaq, Lac *l.* Canada 125 F1
Tasiat, Lac *l.* Canada 125 F1
Tasiilaq Greenland *see* Ammassalik
Tasikmalaya Indon. 59 E4
Tasiujaq Canada 125 G1
Task *well* Niger 93 H2
Tasker Niger 93 H2
Taskesken Kazakh. 70 F2
Taşköprü Turkey 78 C2
Tasman Abyssal Plain *sea feature* Tasman Sea 163 R8
Tasman Basin *sea feature* Tasman Sea 163 R8
Tasman Bay N.Z. 113 C3

▶Tasmania *state* Australia 106 D6
4th largest island in Oceania.
oceania 102–103, 114

Tasman Mountains N.Z. 113 C3
Tasman Peninsula Australia 112 D6
Tasman Sea S. Pacific Ocean 107 G6
Taşova Turkey 78 D2
Tassara Niger 93 G1
Tassi Gabon 94 A5
Tassialouc, Lac *l.* Canada 125 F1
Tassili du Hoggar *plat.* Alg. 91 G5
Tassili n'Ajjer *plat.* Alg. 91 G4
Tas-Tumus Rus. Fed. 27 M3
Tasty Kazakh. 70 C3
Tasu Canada 122 C4
Taşucu Turkey 77 A1
Tas-Yuryakh Rus. Fed. 27 L3
Tata Hungary 37 I5
Tata Morocco 90 D3
Tataba Indon. 57 F6
Tatabánya Hungary 37 I5
Tatamagouche Canada 125 I4
Tata Mailau, Gunung *mt.* East Timor 57 G7
Tatanagar India 75 E5
Tataouine Tunisia 91 H2
Tatarbunary Ukr. 29 D7
Tatarpur India 74 C4
Tatarsk Rus. Fed. 26 I4
Tatarskaya A.S.S.R. *aut. rep.* Rus. Fed. *see* Tatarstan, Respublika
Tatarskiy Proliv *strait* Rus. Fed. 64 E2
Tatarstan, Respublika *aut. rep.* Rus. Fed. 28 I5
Tatar Strait Rus. Fed. *see* Tatarskiy Proliv
Tatau *Sarawak* Malaysia 59 F2
Tatavi *r.* Iran 80 A2
Tate *r.* Australia 111 E3
Tateyama Japan 65 D6
Tathlina Lake Canada 123 G2
Tathlith Saudi Arabia 89 I5
Tathlīth, Wādī *watercourse* Saudi Arabia 68 C4
Tathra Australia 112 D5
Tati Botswana 99 E4
Tâtîlt *well* Mauritania 92 B1
Tatishchevo Rus. Fed. 29 H6
Tatkon Myanmar 60 B3
Tatla Lake Canada 122 E5
Tatlayoko Lake Canada 122 E5
Tatnam, Cape Canada 123 N3
Tatra Mountains Poland/Slovakia 37 I4
Tatranský *nat. park* Slovakia 37 J4
Tatry Poland/Slovakia *see* Tatra Mountains
Tatrzański Park Narodowy *nat. park* Poland 37 I4
Tatshenshini *r.* Canada 122 B3
Tatta Pak. 81 F5
Tatuí Brazil 149 I5
Tatuk Mountain Canada 122 E4
Tatum U.S.A. 135 G6
Tatvan Turkey 79 E3
Tau *i.* American Samoa 107 I3
Taua Brazil 150 D3
Tauapeçaçu Brazil 147 F5
Tauariã Brazil 147 F6
Taubaté Brazil 151 C7
Tauber *r.* Germany 36 D4
Tauberbischofsheim Germany 36 D4
Tauchik Kazakh. 79 G1
Taufkirchen (Vils) Germany 36 F4
Tauini *r.* Brazil 147 G4
Taukum, Peski *des.* Kazakh. 70 D3
Taumarunui N.Z. 113 C2
Taumaturgo Brazil 148 B2
Taunay Brazil 149 G5
Taung S. Africa 98 E5

Taungdwingyi Myanmar 60 A3
Taunggyi Myanmar 60 B3
Taunglau Myanmar 60 B3
Taungnyo Range mts Myanmar 61 B4
Taungtha Myanmar 60 A3
Taunqup Myanmar 60 A4
Taunsa Pak. 81 G4
Taunton U.K. 35 E6
Taunton U.S.A. 131 H3
Taunus hills Germany 36 C3
Taupo N.Z. 113 D2
Taupo, Lake N.Z. 113 C2
Tauragė Lith. 33 F5
Tauramena Col. 146 C3
Tauranga N.Z. 113 D2
Taurasia Italy see Turin
Taurianova Italy 45 F5
Taurion r. France 38 D4
Tauroa Point N.Z. 113 C1
Taurus Mountains Turkey 78 C3
Taŭshyq Kazakh. see Tauchik
Tauste Spain 43 F2
Tauu Islands P.N.G. 107 E2
Tauz Azer. see Tovuz
Tavagnacco Italy 44 D1
Tavas Turkey 78 B3
Tavastehus Fin. see Hämeenlinna
Tavda Rus. Fed. 26 G4
Tavelsjö Sweden 32 F2
Tavernes de la Valldigna Spain 43 F3
Taveuni i. Fiji 107 H3
Tavgetos mts Greece 47 C6
Taviano Italy 45 G5
Tavignano r. Corsica France 44 B3
Tavil'dara Tajik. 81 G2
Tavira Port. 42 C4
Tavistock Canada 130 C2
Tavistock U.K. 35 D6
Tavoy Myanmar 61 B5
Tavoy b. Myanmar 61 B5
Tavoy Island Myanmar see Mali Kyun
Tavoy Point Myanmar 61 B5
Tavşanlı Turkey 78 B3
Taw r. U.K. 35 D6
Tawakoni, Lake U.S.A. 133 C5
Tawallah Range hills Australia 110 C2
Tawang India 75 F4
Tawas Bay U.S.A. 130 B1
Tawas City U.S.A. 130 B1
Tawau Sabah Malaysia 59 G1
Tawau, Telukan b. Sabah Malaysia 59 G1
Tawè Myanmar see Tavoy
Taweisha Sudan 88 E6
Tawi r. India 74 B2
Ṭawī Ḥafir well U.A.E. 80 C5
Tawila Sudan 88 E6
Ṭawīl Murra well U.A.E. 80 C5
Tawitawi i. Phil. 57 E4
Tawmaw Myanmar 60 B2
Tawu Taiwan 67 G4
Taxkorgan China 70 E4
Tay r. Canada 122 C2
Tay r. U.K. 34 E3
Tay, Firth of est. U.K. 34 E3
Tay, Lake salt flat Australia 109 C8
Tay, Loch l. U.K. 34 D3
Tayan Indon. 59 E2
Tayeeglow Somalia 96 E3
Tayga Rus. Fed. 27 I4
Taylor Canada 122 F3
Taylor NE U.S.A. 132 B3
Taylor TX U.S.A. 133 B6
Taylor, Mount U.S.A. 135 F6
Taylorsville U.S.A. 128 B4
Taylorville U.S.A. 128 A4
Taymā' Saudi Arabia 89 H3
Taymura r. Rus. Fed. 27 J3
Taymyr, Ozero l. Rus. Fed. 27 K2
Taymyr, Poluostrov pen. Rus. Fed. see Taymyr Peninsula
Taymyr Peninsula Rus. Fed. 27 I2
Tây Ninh Vietnam 61 D6
Taypak Kazakh. 29 I6
Taypaq Kazakh. see Taypak
Tayshet Rus. Fed. 27 J4
Taysoygan, Peski des. Kazakh. 29 J6
Tayspun tourist site Iraq see Ctesiphon
Taytay Phil. 56 E3
Tayu Indon. 59 E4
Tayuan China 64 A2
Tayyebād Iran 81 E3
Tayynsha Kazakh. 26 G4
Taz r. Rus. Fed. 26 H3
Taza Morocco 90 E2
Tāza Khurmātū Iraq 79 F4
Taze Myanmar 60 A3
Tazeh Kand Azer. 80 A2
Tazenakht Morocco 90 D3
Tazewell TN U.S.A. 130 B5
Tazewell VA U.S.A. 130 C5
Tazin r. Canada 123 I2
Tāzirbū Libya 88 D3
Tazirbu Water Wells Field Libya 88 D3
Tazizilet well Niger 93 H1
Tazlău Romania 46 E1
Tazlău r. Romania 46 E1
Tazmalt Alg. 43 I4
Tazoghrane Tunisia 45 C6
Tazouikert hill Mali 91 E5
Tazovskaya Guba sea chan. Rus. Fed. 26 H3
Tazovskiy Rus. Fed. 26 H3
Tazrouk Alg. 91 G5
Tazzarine Morocco 90 D3
Tazzouguert Morocco 90 E2
Tbessa Alg. see Tébessa
Tbilisi Georgia see T'bilisi

▶T'bilisi Georgia 79 F2
Capital of Georgia.

Tchabal Mbabo mt. Cameroon 93 I4
Tchad country Africa see Chad
Tchamba Togo 93 F3
Tchaourou Benin 93 F3
Tchetti Benin 93 F4
Tchibanga Gabon 94 A5
Tchidoutene watercourse Niger 93 G1
Tchié well Chad 88 C5
Tchigaï, Plateau du Niger 91 I5
Tchin-Tabaradene Niger 93 G2
Tcholliré Cameroon 93 I3
Tczew Poland 37 I1
Te, Prêk r. Cambodia 61 D5
Tea r. Brazil 146 E5
Te Anau N.Z. 113 A4
Te Anau, Lake N.Z. 113 A4
Teano Italy 44 E4
Teanum Sidicinum Italy see Teano
Teapa Mex. 138 F5
Te Araroa N.Z. 113 D2
Te Aroha N.Z. 113 C2
Teate Italy see Chieti
Te Awamutu N.Z. 113 C2
Tébarat Niger 93 G2
Tebedu Sarawak Malaysia 59 E2
Teberda Rus. Fed. 29 G8
Tebesjuak Lake Canada 123 L2
Tébessa Alg. 91 H2
Tébessa, Monts de mts Alg. 91 H2
Tebicuary Para. 149 F6
Tebicuary r. Para. 149 F6
Tebingtinggi Sumatera Utara, Sumatra Indon. 58 B2
Tebingtinggi Sumatera Selatan, Sumatra Indon. 58 C3
Tebo r. Indon. 58 C3
Tébourba Tunisia 45 B6
Téboursouk Tunisia 45 B6
Tebulos Mt'a Georgia/Rus. Fed. 29 H8
Tecate Mex. 137 D5
Tece Turkey 77 B1
Tech r. France 39 E5
Techiman Ghana 93 E4
Tecka Arg. 153 C5
Tecka r. Arg. 153 C5
Tecoripa Mex. 135 E7
Técpan Mex. 138 D5
Tecuci Romania 46 E2
Tecumseh U.S.A. 132 B3
Ted Somalia 96 D3
Tedzhen Turkm. 81 E2
Tedzhen r. Turkm. 81 E2
Tedzhenstroy Turkm. 81 E2
Teec Nos Pos U.S.A. 137 H3
Teeli Rus. Fed. 27 J4
Tees r. U.K. 35 F4
Teeswater Canada 130 C1
Tefé Brazil 147 E5
Tefé r. Brazil 147 E5
Tefé, Lago l. Brazil 147 E5
Tefedest mts Alg. 91 G4
Téfoûlet well Mali 93 F1
Tegal Indon. 59 E4
Tegel airport Germany 37 F2
Tegina Nigeria 93 G3

▶Tegucigalpa Hond. 138 G6
Capital of Honduras.

Teguidda-n-Tessoumt Niger 93 G1
Tehachapi U.S.A. 136 C4
Tehachapi Mountains U.S.A. 136 C4
Tehachapi Pass U.S.A. 136 C4
Tehek Lake Canada 123 M1
Teheran Iran see Tehrān
Tehery Lake Canada 123 M1
Téhini Côte d'Ivoire 92 E3
Tehran Iran see Tehrān

▶Tehrān Iran 80 B3
Capital of Iran.

Tehrān prov. Iran 80 B3
Tehri Madhya Pradesh India see Tikamgarh
Tehri Uttaranchal India 74 C3
Tehuacán Mex. 138 E5
Tehuantepec, Gulf of Mex. 138 F5
Tehuantepec, Istmo de isthmus Mex. 138 F5
Teide, Pico del vol. Canary Is 90 A3
Teifi r. U.K. 35 D5
Teïkoumit well Mali 93 F1
Teiu Romania 46 D2
Teiuş Romania 46 C1
Teixeira Brazil 150 E3
Teixeira de Sousa Angola see Luau
Tejakula Indon. 108 A2
Tejen Turkm. see Tedzhen
Tejgaon Bangl. 75 F5
Tejira well Niger 93 H2
Tejo r. Port. 42 E2 see Tagus
Tekapo, Lake N.Z. 113 B3
Tekari India 75 E4
Tekezē Wenz r. Eritrea/Eth. 89 H6
Tekiliktag mt. China 74 D1
Tekin Rus. Fed. 64 C2
Tekirdağ Turkey 78 A2
Tekirdağ prov. Turkey 46 E4
Tekkali India 73 E2
Tekman Turkey 79 E3
Teknaf Bangl. 75 G5
Tekong Kechil, Pulau i. Sing. 58 [inset]
Tekouiat, Oued watercourse Alg. 91 F5
Tékro well Chad 88 D5
Te Kuiti N.Z. 113 C2
Tel r. India 73 D1
Tela Dem. Rep. Congo 95 F8
Telanaipura Indon. see Jambi
Télataï Mali 93 F1
T'elavi Georgia 79 F2
Tel Aviv-Yafo Israel 77 B3
Telč Czech Rep. 37 G4
Telchac Puerto Mex. 127 I7
Tele r. Dem. Rep. Congo 94 D4
Télé, Lac l. Mali 92 E1
Teleajen r. Romania 46 D2
Telegapulang Indon. 59 F3
Telegraph Creek Canada 122 D3
Telêmaco Borba Brazil 151 B8
Telemark county Norway 33 C4
Telén Arg. 152 D4
Telen r. Indon. 59 G2
Teleorman r. Romania 46 D3
Telertheba, Djebel mt. Alg. 91 G4
Telescope Peak U.S.A. 136 D3
Teles Pires r. Brazil 149 F1
Telfer Mining Centre Australia 108 C5
Telford U.K. 35 E5
Telfs Austria 36 E5
Telīg well Mali 90 E5
Télimélé Guinea 92 B3
Télissour well Chad 88 D5
Teljo, Jebel mt. Sudan 89 E6
Tell Atlas mts Alg. see Atlas Tellien
Teller U.S.A. 120 C3
Tell es-Sultan West Bank see Jericho
Tellicherry India 72 B4
Telluride U.S.A. 135 F5
Tel Megiddo tourist site Israel 77 B3
Telo Indon. 58 B3
Telo Martius France see Toulon
Tel'pos-Iz, Gora mt. Rus. Fed. 28 K3
Telsen Arg. 153 D5
Telšiai Lith. 33 F5
Teluk Anson Malaysia 58 C1
Telukbajur Indon. see Telukbayur
Telukbatang Indon. 59 E3
Telukbayur Indon. 58 C3
Telukbetung Indon. see Bandar Lampung
Telukdalam Indon. 58 B2
Teluk Intan Malaysia see Teluk Anson
Telukkuantan Indon. 58 C3
Teluknaga Indon. 59 D4
Telukpakedai Indon. 59 E3
Tema Ghana 93 F4
Temagami Lake Canada 124 E4
Temaju i. Indon. 59 E2
Temanggung Indon. 59 E4
Temba S. Africa 99 F5
Tembagapura Indon. 57 I6
Tembenchi r. Rus. Fed. 27 J3
Tembesi r. Indon. 58 C3
Tembilahan Indon. 58 C3
Tembisa S. Africa 99 F5
Tembo Aluma Angola 95 C6
Tembwe Zambia 97 B7
Teme r. U.K. 35 E5
Temecula U.S.A. 136 D5
Temengor, Tasik resr Malaysia 58 C1
Téméra Mali 93 E1
Temerin Serb. and Mont. 46 A2
Temerluh Malaysia 58 C2
Teminabuan Indon. 57 H6
Temirtau Kazakh. 70 D1
Témiscamie r. Canada 125 F3
Témiscaming Canada 124 E4
Témiscouata, Lac l. Canada 125 G4
Temiyang i. Indon. 58 D2
Temmes Fin. 32 G2
Temnikov Rus. Fed. 29 G5
Temo r. Sardinia Italy 45 B4
Temora Australia 112 C4
Temósachic Mex. 135 F7
Tempe U.S.A. 137 G5
Tempe Downs Australia 110 C5
Tempelhof airport Germany 37 F2
Tempio Pausania Sardinia Italy 44 B4
Temple U.S.A. 133 B6
Temple Bay Australia 111 E2
Templemore Rep. of Ireland 35 C5
Templeton watercourse Australia 110 D4
Templin Germany 37 F2
Tempué Angola 95 C8
Temryuk Rus. Fed. 29 F7
Temryukskiy Zaliv b. Rus. Fed. 29 F7
Temuco Chile 152 B4
Temuka N.Z. 113 B4
Tena Ecuador 146 B5
Tenabo Mex. 127 H7
Tenabo, Mount U.S.A. 137 D1
Tenali India 72 D2
Tenasserim Myanmar 61 B5
Tenasserim admin. div. Myanmar 61 B5
Tenasserim r. Myanmar 61 B5
Tenby U.K. 35 D6
Tence France 39 F4
Tendaho Eth. 96 D2
Tende France 39 G4
Tende, Col de pass France/Italy 44 A2
Ten Degree Channel India 73 G4
Tendelti Sudan 89 F6
Te-n-Dghâmcha, Sebkhet salt marsh Mauritania 92 B1
Tendō Japan 65 E5
Tendrara Morocco 90 E2
Tendre, Mont mt. Switz. 39 G3
Tendukheda India 74 C5
Téné r. Guinea 92 C3
Tenedos i. Turkey see Bozcaada
Ténenkou Mali 92 D2
Ténéré du Tafassâsset des. Niger 88 A4
Tenerife i. Canary Is 90 A3
Ténès Alg. 91 F1
Ténès, Cap c. Alg. 43 G4
Tenevo Bulg. 46 E3
Teng, Nam r. Myanmar 60 B4
Tengah, Kepulauan is Indon. 59 G4
Tengah, Sungai r. Sing. 58 [inset]
Tengcheng China see Tengxian
Tengchong China 66 A3
Tenge Kazakh. 79 H2
Tengeh Reservoir Sing. 58 [inset]
Tenggarong Indon. 59 G3
Tengger Shamo des. China 62 G4
Tengiz, Ozero salt l. Kazakh. 70 C1
Tengréla Côte d'Ivoire 92 D3
Ten'gushevo Rus. Fed. 29 G5
Tengxian China 67 D4
Teniente Enciso, Parque Nacional nat. park Para. 149 E5
Te-n-Ioubrar, Sebkhet salt marsh Mauritania 92 A1
Tenkasi India 72 C4
Tenke Dem. Rep. Congo 95 E7
Tenkeli Rus. Fed. 27 O2
Tenkodogo Burkina 93 E3
Ten Mile Lake salt flat Australia 109 C6
Tenna r. Italy 44 D3
Tennant Creek Australia 110 C3
Tennessee r. U.S.A. 128 A4
Tennessee state U.S.A. 130 A5
Tennessee Pass U.S.A. 134 F5
Tennholmfjorden sea chan. Norway 32 D2
Tenniöjoki r. Fin./Rus. Fed. 32 H2
Teno Chile 152 C3
Tenojoki r. Fin./Norway 32 H1
Tenom Sabah Malaysia 59 F1
Tenosique Mex. 138 F5
Tenteno Indon. 57 F6
Tenterfield Australia 112 E3
Ten Thousand Islands U.S.A. 129 C7
Tentudia mt. Spain 42 C3
Tenu r. France 38 C3
Teodoro Sampaio Brazil 149 G5
Teófilo Otôni Brazil 151 D6
Teonthar India 75 D4
Teopisca Mex. 138 F5
Tepa Indon. 57 G7
Tepache Mex. 135 E7
Te Paki N.Z. 113 C1
Tepasto Fin. 32 G2
Tepehuanes Mex. 126 E6
Tepeköy Turkey see Karakoçan
Tepelenë Albania 47 B4
Teplá Vrchovina hills Czech Rep. 37 F4
Tepequem, Serra mts Brazil 147 F4
Tepic Mex. 126 F7
Teplá r. Czech Rep. 37 F3
Teplaya Gora Rus. Fed. 28 K4
Teplice Czech Rep. 37 F3
Teploye Rus. Fed. 29 F5
Tepopa, Punta pt Mex. 135 D7
Tequila Mex. 126 F7
Ter r. Spain 43 H1
Téra Niger 93 F2
Tera r. Port. 42 B3
Tera r. Spain 42 D2
Terakeka Sudan 96 A3
Teram Kangri mt. China/Jammu and Kashmir 74 C2
Teramo Italy 44 D3
Terang Australia 112 B5
Teratani r. Pak. 81 G4
Tercan Turkey 79 E3
Terebovlya Ukr. 29 C6
Teregova Romania 46 C2
Terek Rus. Fed. 79 F2
Terek r. Rus. Fed. 29 H8
Teren'ga Rus. Fed. 29 I5
Terengganu state Malaysia 58 C1
Terenos Brazil 151 A7
Terentang Indon. 59 E3
Terentang, Pulau i. Indon. 59 G3
Tereshka r. Rus. Fed. 29 H6
Teresina Brazil 150 D3
Teresina de Goias Brazil 150 C5
Teresita Col. 146 D4
Teressa Island India 73 G4
Terges r. Port. 42 C4
Tergeste Italy see Trieste
Tergnier France 39 E2
Teriberka r. Rus. Fed. 32 I1
Terka Reba Eth. 96 D3
Terkezi well Chad 88 D5
Terlingua Creek r. U.S.A. 133 A6
Termas de Socos Chile 152 C2
Terme Turkey 78 D2
Termez Uzbek. 81 F2
Termination Island Australia 109 C8
Termini Imerese Sicily Italy 45 D6
Termini Imerese, Golfo di b. Sicily Italy 45 D5
Términos, Laguna de lag. Mex. 138 F5
Termit well Niger 88 A5
Termit, Massif de hill Niger 93 H1
Termit-Kaoboul Niger 93 H2
Termiz Uzbek. see Termez
Termoli Italy 44 E4
Termonde Belgium see Dendermonde
Tern r. U.K. 35 E5
Ternate Indon. 57 G5
Terneuzen Neth. 36 A3
Terney Rus. Fed. 64 D3
Terni Italy 44 D3
Ternitz Austria 37 H5
Ternopil' Ukr. 29 C6
Ternopol' Ukr. see Ternopil'
Terpeniya, Mys c. Rus. Fed. 64 F2
Terpeniya, Zaliv g. Rus. Fed. 64 E2
Terra Alta U.S.A. 130 D4
Terra Bella U.S.A. 136 C4
Terrace Canada 122 D4
Terracina Italy 44 D4
Terralba Sardinia Italy 45 B5
Terra Nova Bay Antarctica 167 H1
Terra Nova National Park Canada 125 K3
Terranuova Bracciolini Italy 44 C3
Terra Preta Brazil 147 G6
Terrasini Sicily Italy 45 D5
Terrassa Spain 43 H2
Terrasson-la-Villedieu France 38 D4
Terrazas Mex. 135 F7
Terrebonne Bay U.S.A. 133 D6
Terre Haute U.S.A. 128 B4
Terrell U.S.A. 133 B5
Terre Plaine plain France 39 F3
Terril mt. Spain 42 D4
Terry U.S.A. 134 F3
Terschelling i. Neth. 36 B2
Terskey Alatau, Khrebet mts Kyrg. see Terskey Ala-Too
Terskey Ala-Too mts Kyrg. 70 E3
Terskiy Bereg coastal area Rus. Fed. 28 F2
Tersko-Kumskiy Kanal canal Rus. Fed. 79 F1
Tertenia Sardinia Italy 45 B5
Teruel Spain 43 F2
Terutao i. Thai. 61 B7
Terutao National Park Thai. 61 B7
Tervel Bulg. 46 E3
Tervola Fin. 32 G2
Tešanj Bos.-Herz. 44 F2
Teseney Eritrea 89 H6
Tesha r. Rus. Fed. 28 G5
Teshekpuk Lake U.S.A. 120 D2
Teshio-dake mt. Japan 64 E4
Teshio-gawa r. Japan 64 E3
Tešica Serb. and Mont. 46 B3
Teslin Canada 122 C2
Teslin r. Canada 122 C2
Teslin Lake Canada 122 C2
Tesluí r. Romania 46 D2
Teso Santo hill Spain 42 D2
Tesovo-Netyl'skiy Rus. Fed. 28 D4
Tessalit Mali 91 F5
Tessaoua Niger 93 G2
Tesséroukane well Niger 93 G1
Tessolo Moz. 99 G4
Tessoûnfat well Mali 91 F5
Test r. U.K. 35 F6
Testour Tunisia 45 B6
Têt r. France 39 E5
Tete Moz. 99 G3
Tete prov. Moz. 99 G2
Tetehosi Indon. 58 B2
Tête Jaune Cache Canada 122 G4
Te Teko N.Z. 113 D2
Teteriv r. Ukr. 29 D6
Teterow Germany 37 F2
Teteven Bulg. 46 D3
Tetlin U.S.A. 122 A2
Tetlin Junction U.S.A. 122 A2
Tetlin Lake U.S.A. 122 A2
Teton r. U.S.A. 134 E3
Tétouan Morocco 90 D2
Tetovo Macedonia 46 B3
Tetuán Morocco see Tétouan
Tetulia sea chan. Bangl. 75 F5
Tetyukhe Rus. Fed. see Dal'negorsk
Tetyukhe-Pristan' Rus. Fed. see Rudnaya Pristan'
Tetyushi Rus. Fed. 28 I5
Teuchezhsk Rus. Fed. see Adygeysk
Teuco r. Arg. 149 E6
Teulada Sardinia Italy 45 B5
Teulada, Capo c. Sardinia Italy 45 B5
Teunom Indon. 58 A1
Teunom r. Indon. 58 A1
Teutoburger Wald hills Germany 36 D2
Teuva Fin. 33 F3
Tevere r. Italy see Tiber
Teverya Israel see Tiberias
Teviot r. U.K. 34 E4
Teviothead U.K. 34 E4
Te Waewae Bay N.Z. 113 A4
Te Waiponamu i. N.Z. see South Island
Tewane Botswana 99 E4
Tewantin Australia 111 H5
Teweh r. Indon. 59 F3
Te Wharau N.Z. 113 C3
Têwo China 66 B1
Texarkana AR U.S.A. 133 C5
Texarkana TX U.S.A. 133 C5
Texas Australia 111 G6
Texas state U.S.A. 135 H7
Texel i. Neth. 36 B2
Texoma, Lake U.S.A. 133 B5
Teyateyaneng Lesotho 99 E6
Teykovo Rus. Fed. 28 G4
Teyvareh Afgh. 81 F3
Teza r. Rus. Fed. 28 G4
Tezpur India 75 G4
Tezu India 60 B2
Tfaritiy W. Sahara 90 C4
Tha, Nam r. Laos 60 C3
Tha-anne r. Canada 123 M2
Thabana-Ntlenyana mt. Lesotho 99 F6
Thaba Putsoa mt. Lesotho 99 E6
Thaba-Tseka Lesotho 99 F6
Thabazimbi S. Africa 99 E5
Thabeikkyin Myanmar 60 B3
Thab Lan National Park Thai. 61 C5
Tha Bo Laos 60 C4
Thabong S. Africa 99 E5
Thabyedaung Myanmar 60 B3
Thac Ba, Hồ l. Vietnam 60 D3
Thade r. Myanmar 60 A4
Thagyettaw Myanmar 61 B5
Tha Hin Thai. see Lop Buri
Thai Binh Vietnam 60 D3

▶Thailand country Asia 61 C4
asia 52–53, 82

Thailand, Gulf of Asia 61 C6
Thai Muang Thai. 61 B6
Thai Nguyên Vietnam 60 D3
Thaj Saudi Arabia 80 B5
Thakurgaon Bangl. 75 F4
Thakurtola India 74 D5
Thal Pak. 81 G3
Thala Tunisia 91 H2
Thalang Thai. 61 B6
Thalassery India see Tellicherry
Thal Desert Pak. 81 G4
Thale (Harz) Germany 36 E3
Thale Luang lag. Thai. 61 C7
Thalgau Austria 37 F5
Tha Li Thai. 60 C4
Thaliparamba India see Taliparamba
Thallon Australia 111 G6
Thamad Bū Hashīshah well Libya 88 C3
Thamaga Botswana 98 E5
Thamar, Jabal mt. Yemen 76 D7
Thamarīt Oman 76 E6
Thames r. Canada 130 B2
Thames N.Z. 113 C2
Thames est. U.K. 35 G6
Thames r. U.K. 35 G6
Thamesford Canada 130 C2
Thamesville Canada 130 C2
Thamūd Yemen 76 D6
Thamugadi tourist site Alg. see Timgad
Thana India see Thane
Thana Ghazi India 74 C4
Thanatpin Myanmar 60 B4
Thanbyuzayat Myanmar 61 B5
Thandla India 74 B5
Thandwè Myanmar see Sandoway
Thane India 72 B2
Thangadh India 74 A5
Thangoo Australia 108 C4
Thanh Hoa Vietnam 60 D4
Thanjavur India 72 C4
Than Kyun i. Myanmar 61 B6
Thanlwin r. Myanmar see Salween
Thano Bula Khan Pak. 81 F5
Thaoge r. Botswana 98 D3
Thaolintoa Lake Canada 123 L2
Thap Put Thai. 61 B6
Thap Sakae Thai. 61 B6
Thara India 74 A5
Tharad India 74 A4
Tharaka Kenya 96 C5
Thar Desert India/Pak. 74 A4
Thargomindah Australia 111 E5
Tharrawaddy Myanmar 60 A4
Tharrawaw Myanmar 60 A4
Tharthār, Buḥayrat ath l. Iraq 79 E4
Thasos Greece 46 D4
Thasos i. Greece 46 D4
Thatë, Mali i mt. Albania 46 B4
Thât Khê Vietnam 60 D3
Thaton Myanmar 60 B4
Thau, Bassin de lag. France 39 E5
Thaungdut Myanmar 60 A2
Thaungyin r. Myanmar/Thai. 60 B4
Tha Uthen Thai. 60 D4
Thawr, Jabal mt. Jordan 77 B5
Thayawthadangyi Kyun i. Myanmar 61 B5
Thayetmyo Myanmar 60 A4
Thazi Myanmar 60 B3
The Aldermen Islands N.Z. 113 D2
Theba U.S.A. 137 F5
Thebae tourist site Egypt see Thebes

▶The Bahamas country West Indies 129 E7
northamerica 118–119, 140

Thebes tourist site Egypt 89 G3
Thebes Greece see Thiva
The Broads nat. park U.K. 35 G5
The Brothers is Hong Kong China 67 [inset]
The Brothers is Yemen see Al Ikhwān
The Calvados Chain is P.N.G. 111 H1
The Cheviot hill U.K. 34 E4
The Coorong inlet Australia 112 A4
The Dalles U.S.A. 134 B3
Thedford U.S.A. 132 A3
The English Company's Islands Australia 110 D1
The Entrance Australia 112 D4
The Fens reg. U.K. 35 F5

▶The Gambia country Africa 92 A2
africa 86–87, 100

The Grenadines is St Vincent 147 F1
The Gulf Asia 80 B4

▶The Hague Neth. 36 B2
Seat of government of the Netherlands.
world 8–9

The Hunters Hills N.Z. 113 B4
Theinkun Myanmar 61 B6
Theinzeik Myanmar 60 B4
The Key N.Z. 113 A4
Thekulthili Lake Canada 123 I2
The Lakes National Park Australia 112 C5
Thelon r. Canada 123 L1
The Lynd Junction Australia 111 F3
Themar Germany 36 E3
Thembalihle S. Africa 99 F5
The Minch sea chan. U.K. 34 C2
The Mullet b. Rep. of Ireland 35 A4
Theni India 74 C5
Thenia Alg. 43 H4
Theniet El Had Alg. 43 H5
Thenon France 38 D4
Theodore Australia 111 G5
Theodore Canada 123 K5
Theodore Roosevelt r. Brazil 149 E1
Theodore Roosevelt Lake U.S.A. 137 G5
Theodore Roosevelt National Park U.S.A. 132 A2
Theodosia Ukr. see Feodosiya
The Officer Creek watercourse Australia 110 C5
The Paps hill Rep. of Ireland 35 B5
The Pas Canada 123 K4
Thera i. Greece see Thira
Thérain r. France 38 E2
Theresa U.S.A. 131 F1
Theresa Creek r. Australia 111 G4
Thermaïkos Kolpos g. Greece 47 C4
Thermo Greece 47 B5
Thérmon Greece see Thermo
Thermopolis U.S.A. 134 E4
The Salt Lake salt flat Australia 112 B3

▶The Settlement Christmas I. 164 B6
Capital of Christmas Island.

The Skaw spit Denmark see Grenen
The Slot sea chan. Solomon Is see New Georgia Sound
The Solent strait U.K. 35 F6
Thessalia admin. reg. Greece 47 B5
Thessalon Canada 124 D4
Thessalonica Greece see Thessaloniki
Thessaloniki Greece 46 C4
Thessaly admin. reg. Greece see Thessalia
The Terraces hills Australia 109 C7
Thetford U.K. 35 G5
Thetford Mines Canada 125 G4
Thetkethaung r. Myanmar 61 A5
The Triangle mts Myanmar 60 B2
The Twins Australia 110 C6
Theun r. Laos 60 D4
Theva-i-Ra reef Fiji see Ceva-i-Ra

▶The Valley Anguilla 139 L5
Capital of Anguilla.

Thevenard Island Australia 108 A5
Theveste Alg. see Tébessa
The Wash b. U.K. 35 G5
The Woodlands U.S.A. 133 C6
Thiamis r. Greece see Thyamis
Thibodaux U.S.A. 133 D6
Thief River Falls U.S.A. 132 B1
Thiel Neth. see Tiel
Thiel Mountains Antarctica 167 K1
Thielsen, Mount U.S.A. 134 B4
Thielt Belgium see Tielt
Thiers France 39 E4
Thiès Senegal 92 A2
Thika Kenya 96 C5
Thikombia i. Fiji see Cikobia
Thiladhunmathee Atoll Maldives 72 B5
Thilogne Senegal 92 B2
Thimbu Bhutan see Thimphu

▶Thimphu Bhutan 75 F4
Capital of Bhutan.

Thingvallavatn (Þingvallavatn) l. Iceland 32 [inset]
Thingvellir (Þingvellir) Iceland 32 [inset]
Thionville France 39 G2
Thira Greece 47 D6
Thira i. Greece 47 D6
Thirasia i. Greece 47 D6
Thirsk U.K. 35 F4
Thirty Mile Lake Canada 123 L2
Thiruvananthapuram India see Trivandrum
Thiruvarur India 72 C4
Thiruvattiyur India see Tiruvottiyur
Thissavros, Techniti Limni resr Greece 46 D4
Thisted Denmark 33 C4
Thistilfjörður (Þistilfjörður) b. Iceland 32 [inset]
Thistle Creek Canada 122 B2
Thityabin Myanmar 60 A3
Thiva Greece 47 C5
Thivai Greece see Thiva
Thiviers France 38 D4
Thjórsá (Þjórsá) r. Iceland 32 [inset]
Thlewiaza r. Canada 123 M2
Thoa r. Canada 123 I2
Thô Chu, Đao i. Vietnam 61 C6
Thoen Thai. 60 B4
Thoeng Thai. 60 C4
Thohoyandou S. Africa 99 F4
Tholen i. Neth. 36 B3
Thomas Hubbard, Cape Canada 121 J1
Thomaston CT U.S.A. 131 G3
Thomaston GA U.S.A. 129 B5
Thomaston ME U.S.A. 131 I1
Thomastown Rep. of Ireland 35 C5
Thomasville AL U.S.A. 129 B6
Thomasville GA U.S.A. 129 C6
Thomasville NC U.S.A. 128 C5
Thompson Canada 123 L4
Thompson r. Canada 122 F5
Thompson U.S.A. 137 H2
Thompson r. U.S.A. 132 C4
Thompson Falls U.S.A. 134 D3
Thompson Peak U.S.A. 135 F6
Thompson's Falls Kenya see Nyahururu
Thompson Sound Canada 122 E5
Thomson watercourse Australia 111 E5
Thomson U.S.A. 129 C5
Thon Buri Thai. 61 C5
Thongwa Myanmar 60 B4
Thonon-les-Bains France 39 G3
Thoreau U.S.A. 135 E6
Thorhild Canada 123 H4
Thórisvatn (Þórisvatn) l. Iceland 32 [inset]
Thorn Poland see Toruń
Thorne U.K. 35 F5
Thorne U.S.A. 136 C2
Thornhill U.K. 34 E4
Thornton r. Australia 110 D3
Thorsby Canada 123 H4
Thorshavn Faroe Is see Tórshavn
Thorshavnheiane reg. Antarctica 167 C2
Thórshöfn (Þórshöfn) Iceland 32 [inset]
Thorvaldsfell (Þorvaldsfell) vol. Iceland 32 [inset]
Thouars France 38 C3
Thouet r. France 38 C3
Thourout Belgium see Torhout
Thousand Islands Canada/U.S.A. 131 E1
Thousand Lake Mountain U.S.A. 137 G2
Thousand Oaks U.S.A. 136 C4
Thousandsticks U.S.A. 130 B5
Thrace reg. Turkey 78 A2
Thraki reg. Turkey see Thrace
Thrakiko Pelagos sea Greece 47 D4
Three Forks U.S.A. 134 E3
Three Gorges Project resr China 67 D2
Three Hummock Island Australia 112 C6
Three Kings Islands N.Z. 113 C1
Three Pagodas Pass Myanmar/Thai. 61 B5
Three Points, Cape Ghana 93 E4
Three Rivers CA U.S.A. 136 C3
Three Rivers TX U.S.A. 133 B6
Three Sisters mt. U.S.A. 134 B3
Three Springs Australia 109 A7
Thrissur India see Trichur
Throckmorton U.S.A. 133 B5
Throssell, Lake salt flat Australia 109 D6
Throssel Range hills Australia 108 C5
Thrushton National Park Australia 111 F5
Thubun Lakes Canada 123 I2
Thu Dâu Môt Vietnam 61 D6
Thuin Belgium 39 F1
Thul Sudan 96 B2
Thul watercourse Sudan 96 A2
Thule Greenland 121 M2
Thuli Zimbabwe 99 F4
Thuli r. Zimbabwe 99 F4
Thun Switz. 39 G3
Thunda Australia 111 E5
Thundelarra Australia 109 B7
Thunder Bay Canada 124 B3
Thunder Creek r. Canada 123 J5
Thuner See l. Switz. 39 G3
Thung Salaeng Luang National Park Thai. 60 C4
Thung Song Thai. 61 B6
Thung Wa Thai. 61 B7
Thur r. Switz. 39 H3
Thüringen land Germany 36 E3
Thüringer Becken reg. Germany 36 E3
Thüringer Wald mts Germany 36 E3
Thuringia land Germany see Thüringen
Thuringian Forest mts Germany see Thüringer Wald
Thurles Rep. of Ireland 35 C5
Thursby U.K. 34 E4
Thursday Island Australia 111 E1
Thurso U.K. 34 E2
Thurso r. U.K. 34 E2
Thurston Island Antarctica 167 K2
Thusis Switz. 39 H3
Thwaites Glacier Tongue Antarctica 167 K1
Thyamis r. Greece 47 B5
Thyatira Turkey see Akhisar
Thyborøn Denmark 33 C4
Thylungra Australia 111 E5
Thyolo Malawi 97 B9
Thyou Burkina 93 E3
Thyou Burkina see Tiou
Thysville Dem. Rep. Congo see Mbanza-Ngungu
Tiāb Iran 80 D5
Tiahuanaco Bol. 148 C4
Tiancang China 70 I3
Tianchang China 67 F1
Tiancheng China see Chongyang
Tianchi China see Lezhi
Tiandeng China 66 C4
Tiandiba China see Jinyang
Tiandong China 66 C4
Tian'e China 66 C3
Tianfanjie China 67 F2

White Sands National Monument nat. park U.S.A. 135 F6
Whitesburg U.S.A. 130 B5
White Sea Rus. Fed. 28 F2
White Stone U.S.A. 131 E5
White Sulphur Springs MT U.S.A. 134 E3
White Sulphur Springs WV U.S.A. 130 C5
Whitesville U.S.A. 130 C5
Whiteville U.S.A. 129 D5
White Volta r. Burkina/Ghana 93 E3
White Volta watercourse Burkina/Ghana 93 E3
White Water U.S.A. 137 D5
Whitewater CO U.S.A. 134 E5
Whitewater WI U.S.A. 132 D3
Whitewater Baldy mt. U.S.A. 135 E6
White Well Australia 109 E7
White Woman Creek r. U.S.A. 132 A4
Whitewood Australia 111 E4
Whitewood Canada 123 K5
Whithorn U.K. 35 D4
Whitianga N.Z. 113 C2
Whitley City U.S.A. 130 A5
Whitmire U.S.A. 129 C5
Whitmore Mountains Antarctica 167 K1
Whitney, Lake U.S.A. 133 B6
Whitney, Mount U.S.A. 136 C3
Whitstable U.K. 35 G6
Whitsunday Group is Australia 111 G4
Whitsunday Island National Park Australia 111 G4
Whitsun Island Vanuatu see Pentecost Island
Whittemore U.S.A. 130 B1
Whittier U.S.A. 136 C5
Whittlesey U.K. 35 F5
Whitton Australia 112 C4
Whitula watercourse Australia 111 E5
Wholdaia Lake Canada 123 J2
Whyalla Australia 112 A4
Whydah Benin see Ouidah
Wiang Kosai National Park Thai. 60 B4
Wiang Pa Pao Thai. 60 B4
Wiang Phran Thai. 56 A1
Wiang Sa Thai. 60 C4
Wiarton Canada 130 C1
Wibaux U.S.A. 134 F3
Wichelen Belgium 36 A3
Wichita U.S.A. 132 B4
Wichita r. U.S.A. 133 B5
Wichita Falls U.S.A. 133 B5
Wichita Mountains U.S.A. 133 B5
Wick U.K. 34 E2
Wickenburg U.S.A. 135 D6
Wickepin Australia 109 B8
Wickham r. Australia 110 B3
Wickham, Cape Australia 112 B5
Wicklow Rep. of Ireland 35 C5
Wicklow Head Rep. of Ireland 35 D5
Wicklow Mountains Rep. of Ireland 35 C5
Wicklow Mountains National Park Rep. of Ireland 35 C5
Widawa r. Poland 37 H3
Widawka r. Poland 37 I3
Widerøe, Mount Antarctica 167 C2
Widgiemooltha Australia 109 C7
Wi-do i. S. Korea 65 A6
Wied r. Germany 36 C3
Wiehengebirge hills Germany 36 D2
Wieleń Poland 37 H2
Wielka Sowa mt. Poland 37 H3
Wielkopolskie, Pojezierze reg. Poland 37 H2
Wielkopolski Park Narodowy nat. park Poland 37 H2
Wieluń Poland 37 I3
Wien Austria see Vienna
Wiener Neustadt Austria 37 H5
Wiensberg mt. Austria 37 G4
Wieprz r. Poland 37 J3
Wieprza r. Poland 37 H1
Wieringerwerf Neth. 36 B2
Wieruszów Poland 37 I3
Wierzyca r. Poland 37 I2
Wiesbaden Germany 36 D3
Wiesloch Germany 36 D4
Wiesmoor Germany 36 C2
Wieżyca hill Poland 37 I1
Wigan U.K. 35 E5
Wiggins U.S.A. 129 A6
Wight, Isle of i. U.K. 35 F6
Wigierski Park Narodowy nat. park Poland 37 K1
Wignes Lake Canada 123 J2
Wigtown U.K. 34 D4
Wigtown Bay U.K. 35 D4
Wikieup U.S.A. 137 F4
Wik'ro Eth. 89 H6
Wil Switz. 39 H3
Wilberforce, Cape Australia 110 D1
Wilbur U.S.A. 134 C3
Wilburton U.S.A. 133 C5
Wilcannia Australia 112 B3
Wilcox U.S.A. 130 D3
Wilczek Land i. Rus. Fed. see Vil'cheka, Zemlya
Wildcat Peak U.S.A. 137 D2
Wild Coast S. Africa 99 F6
Wilderness U.S.A. 130 E4
Wildeshausen Germany 36 D2
Wildhay r. Canada 122 G4
Wildhorn mt. Switz. 39 G3
Wild Horse Draw r. U.S.A. 135 F7
Wild Horse Hill mt. U.S.A. 132 A3
Wildon Austria 37 G5
Wild Rice r. MN U.S.A. 132 B2
Wild Rice r. ND U.S.A. 132 B2
Wildwood FL U.S.A. 129 C6
Wildwood NJ U.S.A. 131 F4
Wiley Ford U.S.A. 130 D4
Wilga r. Poland 37 J3
Wilge r. S. Africa 99 F5
Wilgena Australia 109 F7

▶Wilhelm, Mount P.N.G. 57 J7
5th highest mountain in Oceania.
oceania 102–103

Wilhelmina Gebergte mts Suriname 147 G4
Wilhelm-Pieck-Stadt Germany see Guben
Wilhelmsburg Austria 37 G4
Wilhelmshaven Germany 36 D2
Wilhelmstal Namibia 98 C4
Wilkes-Barre U.S.A. 131 F3
Wilkesboro U.S.A. 128 C4
Wilkes Coast Antarctica 167 G2
Wilkes Land reg. Antarctica 167 G2
Wilkie Canada 134 E1
Wilkins Coast Antarctica 167 L2
Wilkins Ice Shelf Antarctica 167 L2
Wilkinson Lakes salt flat Australia 110 C6
Will, Mount Canada 122 D3
Willamette r. U.S.A. 134 B3
Willandra Billabong watercourse Australia 112 C4
Willandra National Park Australia 112 C4
Willapa Bay U.S.A. 134 A3
Willard Mex. 135 E7
Willard NM U.S.A. 135 F6
Willard OH U.S.A. 130 B3
Willards U.S.A. 131 F4
Willcox U.S.A. 135 E6

▶Willemstad Neth. Antilles 146 D1
Capital of the Netherlands Antilles.

Willeroo Australia 110 B2
William r. Canada 123 I3
William, Mount Australia 112 B5
William Creek Australia 110 D6
William Lake Canada 123 L4
Williams Australia 109 B8
Williams r. Australia 111 E4
Williams AZ U.S.A. 137 F4
Williams CA U.S.A. 136 A2
Williamsburg IA U.S.A. 132 C3
Williamsburg KY U.S.A. 130 A5
Williamsburg OH U.S.A. 130 A4
Williamsburg VA U.S.A. 131 E5
Williams Lake Canada 122 F4
Williamson NY U.S.A. 131 E2
Williamson WV U.S.A. 130 B5
Williamsport IN U.S.A. 128 B3
Williamsport OH U.S.A. 130 B4
Williamsport PA U.S.A. 131 E3
Williamston U.S.A. 128 D5
Williamstown KY U.S.A. 130 A4
Williamstown MA U.S.A. 131 G2
Williamstown NY U.S.A. 131 F2
Willimantic U.S.A. 131 G3
Willis Group atolls Australia 111 G3
Willis Islands S. Georgia 153 [inset]
Williston S. Africa 98 D6
Williston FL U.S.A. 129 C6
Williston ND U.S.A. 134 G2
Williston SC U.S.A. 129 C5
Williston Lake Canada 122 F4
Willits U.S.A. 136 A2
Willmar U.S.A. 132 C2
Willoughby U.S.A. 130 C3
Willow r. Canada 122 F4
Willow Bunch Canada 134 F2
Willow Creek r. Canada 123 H5
Willow Creek U.S.A. 134 B4
Willow Hill U.S.A. 130 E3
Willow Lake Canada 122 G2
Willowlake r. Canada 122 F2
Willowmore S. Africa 98 D7
Willows U.S.A. 136 A2
Willow Springs U.S.A. 132 D4
Willowvale S. Africa 99 F7
Wills, Lake salt flat Australia 110 B4
Wills Creek watercourse Australia 111 E4
Wilmington Australia 112 A4
Wilmington DE U.S.A. 131 F4
Wilmington NC U.S.A. 129 D5
Wilmington OH U.S.A. 130 B4
Wilmington VT U.S.A. 131 G2
Wilmington Island U.S.A. 129 C5
Wilmore U.S.A. 130 A5
Wilno Lith. see Vilnius
Wilpattu National Park Sri Lanka 72 D4
Wilpena watercourse Australia 112 A3
Wilson watercourse Australia 111 E5
Wilson atoll Micronesia see Ifalik
Wilson NC U.S.A. 128 D5
Wilson NY U.S.A. 130 D2
Wilson, Mount CO U.S.A. 135 F5
Wilson, Mount NV U.S.A. 137 E2
Wilsonia U.S.A. 136 C3
Wilson Lake resr U.S.A. 128 B5
Wilsons U.S.A. 130 E5
Wilson's Promontory pen. Australia 112 C5
Wilson's Promontory National Park Australia 112 C5
Wilton r. Australia 110 C2
Wilton ME U.S.A. 131 H1
Wilton NH U.S.A. 131 H2
Wiltz Lux. 39 F2
Wiluna Australia 109 C6
Wimmera r. Australia 112 B5
Wina r. Cameroon see Vina
Winamac U.S.A. 132 E3
Winam Gulf Kenya 96 B5
Winbin watercourse Australia 111 F5
Winburg S. Africa 99 E6
Wincanton U.K. 35 E6
Winchester U.K. 35 F6
Winchester IN U.S.A. 130 A3
Winchester KY U.S.A. 130 A5
Winchester NH U.S.A. 131 G2
Winchester TN U.S.A. 128 B5
Winchester VA U.S.A. 130 D4
Wind r. Canada 122 C1
Wind r. U.S.A. 134 E4
Windau Latvia see Ventspils
Windber U.S.A. 130 D3
Wind Cave National Park U.S.A. 132 A3
Windermere U.K. 35 E4
Windham U.S.A. 130 C3

▶Windhoek Namibia 98 C4
Capital of Namibia.

Windigo r. Canada 121 J4
Windigo Lake Canada 124 B2
Windischgarsten Austria 37 G5
Wind Mountain U.S.A. 135 F6
Windom U.S.A. 132 C3
Windorah Australia 111 E5
Window Rock U.S.A. 137 H4
Wind Ridge U.S.A. 130 C4
Wind River Range mts U.S.A. 134 E4
Winds, Bay of Antarctica 167 F2
Windsor Nfld. and Lab. Canada 125 K3
Windsor N.S. Canada 125 H4
Windsor Ont. Canada 130 B2
Windsor U.K. 35 F6
Windsor NC U.S.A. 128 D4
Windsor NY U.S.A. 131 F2
Windsor VA U.S.A. 131 E5
Windsor VT U.S.A. 131 G2
Windsor Locks U.S.A. 131 G3
Windward Islands Caribbean Sea 139 L5
Windward Passage Cuba/Haiti 127 L8
Winefred Lake Canada 123 I4
Winfield AL U.S.A. 129 B5
Winfield KS U.S.A. 132 B4
Winfield WV U.S.A. 130 C4
Wingate Mountains hills Australia 110 B2
Wingham Canada 130 C2
Winifreda Arg. 152 D4
Winisk Canada 124 C2
Winisk r. Canada 124 C2
Winisk Lake Canada 124 C2
Winkana Myanmar 61 B5
Winkelman U.S.A. 137 G5
Winkler Canada 123 L5
Winlock U.S.A. 134 B3
Winneba Ghana 93 E4
Winnebago U.S.A. 132 C3
Winnebago, Lake U.S.A. 132 D2
Winnecke Creek watercourse Australia 110 B3
Winnemucca U.S.A. 134 C4
Winnemucca Lake U.S.A. 136 C1
Winner U.S.A. 132 A3
Winnett U.S.A. 134 E3
Winnfield U.S.A. 133 C6
Winnibigoshish, Lake U.S.A. 132 C2
Winning Australia 108 A5

▶Winnipeg Canada 123 L5
Provincial capital of Manitoba.

Winnipeg r. Canada 123 L5
Winnipeg, Lake Canada 123 L5
Winnipegosis Canada 123 L5
Winnipegosis, Lake Canada 134 G1
Winnipesaukee, Lake U.S.A. 131 H2
Winnsboro U.S.A. 129 C5
Winona AZ U.S.A. 137 G4
Winona MN U.S.A. 132 D2
Winona MO U.S.A. 132 D4
Winona MS U.S.A. 127 I5
Winooski r. U.S.A. 131 G1
Winschoten Neth. 36 C2
Winsen (Aller) Germany 36 D2
Winsen (Luhe) Germany 36 E2
Winslow U.S.A. 137 G4
Winsted U.S.A. 131 G3
Winston-Salem U.S.A. 128 C4
Winterberg Germany 36 D3
Winter Haven U.S.A. 129 C6
Winterport U.S.A. 131 I1
Winters CA U.S.A. 136 B2
Winters TX U.S.A. 133 B6
Winterset U.S.A. 132 C3
Winterswijk Neth. 36 C3
Winterthur Switz. 39 H3
Winthrop U.S.A. 131 I1
Winton Australia 111 E4
Winton N.Z. 113 B4
Winton U.S.A. 128 D4
Wirrabara Australia 112 A4
Wirraminna Australia 109 G7
Wirrulla Australia 109 F8
Wisbech U.K. 35 G5
Wiscasset U.S.A. 131 I1
Wisconsin r. U.S.A. 132 D3
Wisconsin state U.S.A. 132 D2
Wisconsin Rapids U.S.A. 132 D2
Wise U.S.A. 130 B5
Wisil Dabarow Somalia 96 F3
Wisła r. Poland see Vistula
Wisłok r. Poland 37 K3
Wisłoka r. Poland 37 J3
Wismar Germany 36 E2
Wisner U.S.A. 133 D6
Wistaria Canada 122 E4
Witbooisvlei Namibia 98 C5
Witham r. U.K. 35 G5
Withernsea U.K. 35 G5
Withlacoochee r. FL U.S.A. 129 C6
Withlacoochee r. FL U.S.A. 129 C6
Witjira National Park Australia 110 C5
Witkowo Poland 37 H2
Witney U.K. 35 F6
Witnica Poland 37 G2
Wittenberg Germany see Lutherstadt Wittenberg
Wittenberg U.S.A. 128 A2
Wittenberge Germany 36 E2
Wittenburg Germany 36 E2
Wittenheim France 39 G3
Wittenoom Australia 108 B5
Wittenoom Gorge Australia see Wittenoom
Witti, Banjaran mts Sabah Malaysia 59 G1
Wittingen Germany 36 E2
Wittlich Germany 36 C4
Wittmund Germany 36 C2
Wittow pen. Germany 37 F1
Wittstock Germany 37 F2
Witu Kenya 96 D5
Witu Islands P.N.G. 106 D2
Witvlei Namibia 98 C4
Witzenhausen Germany 36 D3
Wivenhoe, Lake Australia 111 H5
Wkra r. Poland 37 J2
Władysławowo Poland 37 I1
Włocławek Poland 37 I2
Włoszczowa Poland 37 I3
Wobkent Uzbek. see Vabkent
Wodonga Australia 112 C5
Wodzisław Śląski Poland 37 I3
Wohko watercourse Sudan 94 F3
Wohlthat Mountains Antarctica 167 C2
Wokam i. Indon. 57 H7
Woken r. China 64 B3
Wokha India 75 G4
Woking U.K. 35 F6
Wokingham watercourse Australia 111 E4
Woko National Park Australia 112 D3
Wolcott U.S.A. 131 E2
Wołczyn Poland 37 I3
Woldegk Germany 37 F2
Wolea atoll Micronesia see Woleai
Woleai atoll Micronesia 57 J4
Woleu-Ntem prov. Gabon 94 A4
Wolf r. Canada 122 C2
Wolf r. U.S.A. 132 D2
Wolf Creek MT U.S.A. 134 D3
Wolf Creek OR U.S.A. 134 B4
Wolf Creek r. U.S.A. 133 B4
Wolf Creek Pass U.S.A. 135 F5
Wolfeboro U.S.A. 131 H2
Wolfen Germany 37 F3
Wolfenbüttel Germany 36 E2
Wolfhagen Germany 36 D3
Wolf Lake Canada 122 D2
Wolf Point U.S.A. 134 F2
Wolfsberg Austria 37 G5
Wolfsburg Germany 36 E2
Wolfville Canada 125 H4
Wolgast Germany 37 F1
Wolin Poland 37 G2
Wolin i. Poland 37 G2
Woliński Park Narodowy nat. park Poland 37 G2
Wollaston, Islas is Chile 153 D8
Wollaston Lake Canada 123 K3
Wollaston Lake l. Canada 123 K3
Wollaston Peninsula Canada 121 H3
Wollemi National Park Australia 112 D4
Wollerau Switz. 39 H3
Wollongong Australia 112 D4
Wolmirstedt Germany 36 E2
Wołomin Poland 37 J2
Wołów Poland 37 H3
Wolowaru Indon. 108 C2
Wolseley Australia 112 B5
Wolsztyn Poland 37 H2
Wolvega Neth. 36 C2
Wolverhampton U.K. 35 E5
Wolya r. Indon. 58 A1
Wonarah Australia 110 D3
Wondai Australia 111 G5
Wong Chhu r. Bhutan 75 F4
Wong Chuk Hang Hong Kong China 67 [inset]
Wong Leng hill Hong Kong China 67 [inset]
Wŏnju S. Korea 65 A5
Wonogiri Indon. 59 E4
Wonowon Canada 122 F3
Wonreli Indon. 108 D2
Wŏnsan N. Korea 65 A5
Wonthaggi Australia 112 C5
Woocalla Australia 112 A3
Wood, Mount Canada 122 A2
Woodbourne U.S.A. 131 F3
Woodbridge NJ U.S.A. 131 F3
Woodbridge VA U.S.A. 131 E4
Wood Buffalo National Park Canada 123 H3
Woodburn IN U.S.A. 130 A3
Woodburn OR U.S.A. 134 B3
Woodbury U.S.A. 131 F4
Woodend Australia 112 C5
Woodfords U.S.A. 136 C2
Woodhall Spa U.K. 35 F5
Wood Lake Canada 123 K4
Woodlake U.S.A. 136 C3
Woodland CA U.S.A. 136 B2
Woodland WA U.S.A. 134 B3
Woodlands Sing. 58 [inset]
Woodlark Island P.N.G. 107 E2
Woodridge Canada 123 L5
Woodroffe watercourse Australia 110 D4
Woodroffe, Mount Australia 110 B5
Woods, Lake salt flat Australia 110 C3
Woods, Lake of the Canada/U.S.A. 121 J5
Woodsfield U.S.A. 130 C4
Woods Hole U.S.A. 131 H3
Woodstock Australia 111 F3
Woodstock N.B. Canada 125 H4
Woodstock Ont. Canada 130 C2
Woodstock IL U.S.A. 132 D3
Woodstock VA U.S.A. 130 D4
Woodstock VT U.S.A. 131 G2
Woodstown U.S.A. 131 F4
Woodsville U.S.A. 131 G1
Woodville N.Z. 113 C3
Woodville MS U.S.A. 133 D6
Woodville OH U.S.A. 130 B3
Woodville TX U.S.A. 133 C6
Woodward U.S.A. 133 B4
Woody U.S.A. 136 C4
Wooi Indon. 57 I6
Wooler U.K. 34 E4
Woolgoolga Australia 112 E3
Woolla Downs Australia 110 C4
Woollard, Mount Antarctica 167 K1
Woolwine U.S.A. 130 C5
Woomera Australia 109 G7
Woomera Prohibited Area Australia 110 C6
Woonsocket U.S.A. 132 B2
Wooramel r. Australia 109 A6
Wooster U.S.A. 130 C3
Woqooyi Galbeed admin. reg. Somalia 96 D2
Worak-san National Park S. Korea 65 B5
Worbody Point Australia 111 E2
Worcester S. Africa 98 C7
Worcester U.K. 35 E5
Worcester MA U.S.A. 131 H2
Worcester NY U.S.A. 131 F2
Wörgl Austria 36 F5
Workai i. Indon. 57 H7
Workington U.K. 35 E4
Worland U.S.A. 134 F3
Worms Germany 36 D4
Worofla Côte d'Ivoire 92 D3
Wörth am Rhein Germany 36 D4
Worthing U.K. 35 F6
Worthington MN U.S.A. 132 C3
Worthington OH U.S.A. 130 B3
Wotje atoll Marshall Is 164 F6
Wotu Indon. 57 F6
Wour Chad 88 B4
Wouri r. Cameroon 93 H4
Wowoni i. Indon. 57 F6
Wozrojdeniye Oroli i. Uzbek. see Vozrozhdeniya, Ostrov
Wrangel Island Rus. Fed. 27 S2
Wrangell U.S.A. 122 C3
Wrangell Island U.S.A. 122 C3
Wrangell Mountains U.S.A. 122 A2
Wrangell-St Elias National Park and Preserve AK U.S.A. 122 A2
Wrath, Cape U.K. 34 D2
Wray U.S.A. 134 G4
Wreck Reef Australia 111 H4
Wrecsam U.K. see Wrexham
Wrens U.S.A. 129 C5
Wrexham U.K. 35 E5
Wriezen Germany 37 G2
Wrightmyo India 73 G4
Wright Patman Lake U.S.A. 133 C5
Wrightson, Mount U.S.A. 135 E7
Wrightsville U.S.A. 129 C5
Wrightwood U.S.A. 136 D4
Wrigley Canada 122 F2
Wrigley U.S.A. 130 B4
Wrigley Gulf Antarctica 167 J2
Wrocław Poland 37 H3
Wronki Poland 37 H2
Września Poland 37 H2
Wschowa Poland 37 H3
Wu'an China see Changtai
Wubin Australia 106 A5
Wuchang Heilong. China 64 A3
Wuchang Hubei China 67 E2
Wuchow China see Wuzhou
Wuchuan China 67 D4
Wudang Shan mts China 67 D1
Wuday'ah well Saudi Arabia 76 D6
Wudil Nigeria 93 H3
Wudinna Australia 109 F8
Wudu China 66 C1
Wufeng Hubei China 67 D2
Wufeng Yunnan China see Zhenxiong
Wugang China 67 D3
Wugong China 66 D1
Wuhai China 63 H4
Wuhan China 67 E2
Wuhe China 67 F1
Wuhu Anhui China 67 F2
Wuhu Anhui China 67 F2
Wuhua China 67 E4
Wujang China 74 C2
Wujiang China 67 G2
Wu Jiang r. China 66 C2
Wujin Jiangsu China see Changzhou
Wujin Sichuan China see Xinjin
Wukang China see Deqing
Wukari Nigeria 93 H4
Wulian Feng mts China 66 B2
Wuliang Shan mts China 66 B3
Wuliaru i. Indon. 57 H7
Wuling Shan mts China 67 D2
Wulong China 66 C2
Wulongji China see Huaibin
Wum Cameroon 93 H4
Wumeng Shan mts China 66 B3
Wuming China 67 D4
Wümme r. Germany 36 D2
Wungda China 66 B2
Wuning China 67 E2
Wunnummin Lake Canada 124 B2
Wun Rog Sudan 94 F2
Wun Shwai Sudan 94 F2
Wunstorf Germany 36 D2
Wuntho Myanmar 60 A3
Wupatki National Monument nat. park U.S.A. 137 G4
Wuping China 67 F3
Wuppertal Germany 36 C3
Wuppertal S. Africa 98 C7
Wuqia China 81 H2
Wuquan China see Wuyang
Wuranga Australia 109 B7
Würm r. Germany 36 E4
Wurno Nigeria 93 G2
Wurzbach Germany 36 E3
Würzburg Germany 36 D4
Wurzen Germany 37 F3
Wushan Chongqing China 67 D2
Wushan Gansu China 66 C1
Wu Shan mts China 67 D2
Wusheng China 66 C2
Wüstegarten hill Germany 36 D3
Wusuli Jiang r. Rus. Fed. see Ussuri
Wutong r. China 64 B3
Wuvulu Island P.N.G. 57 J6
Wuwei Anhui China 67 F2
Wuwei Gansu China 62 G4
Wuxi Chongqing China 67 D2
Wuxi Hunan China see Luxi
Wuxi Jiangsu China 67 G2
Wuxia China see Wushan
Wuxing China see Huzhou
Wuxu China 67 D4
Wuxuan China 67 D4
Wuxue China 67 E2
Wuyang Guizhou China see Zhenyuan
Wuyang Henan China 67 E1
Wuyi China 67 F2
Wuyiling China 64 B2
Wuyishan China 67 F3
Wuyi Shan mts China 67 F3
Wuyi Shan tourist site China 67 F3
Wuyuan Jiangxi China 67 F2
Wuyuan Nei Mongol China 63 H3
Wuyuan Zhejiang China see Haiyan
Wuyun China see Jinyun
Wuzhen China 67 D2
Wuzhi Shan mts China 67 D5
Wuzhong China 63 H4
Wuzhou China 67 D4
Wyalkatchem Australia 109 B7
Wyalusing U.S.A. 131 E3
Wyandra Australia 111 F5
Wye r. U.K. 35 E6
Wye Mills U.S.A. 131 E4
Wylliesburg U.S.A. 130 D5
Wyloo Australia 108 B5
Wymondham U.K. 35 G5
Wynbring Australia 109 F7
Wyndham Australia 110 B2
Wyndham-Werribee Australia 112 C5
Wynne U.S.A. 133 D5
Wynyard Canada 134 F2
Wyola Lake salt flat Australia 110 B6
Wyoming DE U.S.A. 131 F4
Wyoming MI U.S.A. 132 E3
Wyoming state U.S.A. 134 F4
Wyoming Range mts U.S.A. 134 E4
Wyong Australia 112 D4
Wyperfeld National Park Australia 112 B4
Wysoka Poland 37 H2
Wyszków Poland 37 J2
Wytheville U.S.A. 130 C5
Wyżnica r. Poland 37 J3

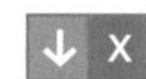

X

Xaafuun Somalia 96 F2

▶Xaafuun, Raas pt Somalia 96 F2
Most easterly point of Africa.

Xaçmaz Azer. 79 G2
Xade Botswana 98 D4
Xagnay China 75 D2
Xago China 75 F3
Xagquka China 75 G3
Xaidulla China 74 C1
Xainza China 75 F3
Xaitongmoin China 75 F3
Xai-Xai Moz. 99 G5
Xalin Somalia 96 F2
Xamba China 63 H3
Xambioá Brazil 150 B3
Xam Hua Laos 60 D3
Xá-Muteba Angola 95 C7
Xan r. Laos 60 C4
Xan, Xé r. Vietnam 61 D5
Xangda China see Nangqên
Xangdoring China see Xungba
Xangongo Angola 95 B9
Xankändi Azer. 79 F3
Xanlar Azer. 79 F2
Xanthi Greece 46 D4
Xanxerê Brazil 151 A8
Xapuri Brazil 148 C2
Xarardheere Somalia 96 E3
Xarba La pass China 75 E3
Xarrama r. Port. 42 B3
Xarrë Albania 47 B5
Xarsingma China see Yadong
Xassengue Angola 95 C7
Xátiva Spain 43 F3
Xau, Lake Botswana 98 E4
Xaudum watercourse Botswana/Namibia 98 D3
Xavantes, Serra dos hills Brazil 150 B5
Xa Vo Đat Vietnam 61 D6
Xenia U.S.A. 130 B4
Xeriuini r. Brazil 147 F5
Xero Potamos r. Cyprus see Xeros
Xeros r. Cyprus 77 A2
Xiabole Shan mt. China 64 A2
Xiachengzi China 64 B3
Xiachuan Dao i. China 67 E4
Xiaguan China see Dali
Xiajiang Jiangxi China 67 E3
Xiajiang Xizang China see Qusum
Xiamen China 67 F3
Xi'an China 67 D1
Xiancheng China 67 E1
Xianfeng China 67 D2
Xiangcheng Henan China 67 E1
Xiangcheng Sichuan China 66 A2
Xiangcheng Yunnan China see Xiangyun
Xiangfan China 67 E1
Xiangfeng China see Laifeng
Xianggang Hong Kong China see Hong Kong
Xianggang Tebie Xingzhengqu special admin. reg. China see Hong Kong
Xianghuang Qi China see Xin Bulag
Xiangjiang China see Huichang
Xiang Jiang r. China 67 E2
Xiangkhoang Laos 60 C4
Xiangkhoang Plateau Laos 60 C4
Xiangkou China see Wulong
Xiangquan He r. China 74 C3
Xiangshan Yunnan China see Menghai
Xiangshan Zhejiang China 67 G2
Xiangshan Gang b. China 67 G2
Xiangshui China 67 F1
Xiangshuiba China 67 D3
Xiangtan China 67 E3
Xiangxiang China 67 E3
Xiangyang China see Xiangfan
Xiangyang Hu l. China 75 F2
Xiangyin China 67 E2
Xiangyun China 66 B3
Xianju China 67 G2
Xianning China 67 E2
Xiannümiao China see Jiangdu
Xianshui China see Dawu
Xianshui He r. China 66 B2
Xiantao China 67 E2
Xianxia Ling mts China 67 F3
Xianyang China 67 D1
Xianyou China 67 F3
Xiaochang China 67 E2
Xiaodong China 67 C4
Xiaogan China 67 E2
Xiao Hinggan Ling mts China 64 A2
Xiaojin China 66 B2
Xiaomei China 67 F3
Xiaonanchuan China 75 G2
Xiaosanjiang China 67 E3
Xiaoshan China 67 G2
Xiao Surmang China 66 A1
Xiaotao China 67 F3
Xiaoxi China see Pinghe
Xiaoxian China 67 F1
Xiaoxiang Ling mts China 66 B2
Xiaoyi China see Gongyi
Xiapu China 67 G3
Xiaqiong China see Batang
Xiayanjing China see Yanjing
Xiayingpan Guizhou China see Lupanshui
Xiayingpan Guizhou China see Luzhi
Xibdê China 66 A2
Xibing China 67 F3
Xibu China see Dongshan
Xichang China 66 B3
Xichou China 66 C4
Xichuan China 67 D1
Xide China 66 B2
Xidu China see Hengyang
Xié r. Brazil 146 E4
Xiemahe' China 67 D2
Xieng Khouang Laos see Xiangkhoang
Xieyang Dao i. China 67 D4
Xifei He r. China 67 F1
Xifeng Guizhou China 66 C3
Xifeng Liaoning China 64 A4
Xigazê China 70 G6
Xihan Shui r. China 66 C1
Xihe China 66 C1
Xi He r. China 66 C2
Xi Jiang r. China 67 E4
Xijir Ulan Hu salt l. China 75 F2
Xilagani Greece see Xylagani
Xiligou China see Ulan
Xilin China 66 C3
Xilinhot China 63 J3
Xilókastron Greece see Xylokastro
Xilópolis Greece see Xylopoli
Ximiao China 70 J3
Xin'an Anhui China see Lai'an
Xin'an Henan China 67 E1
Xin'anjiang Shuiku resr China 67 F2
Xin Bulag China 27 L5
Xincai China 67 E1
Xinchang China see Yifeng
Xincheng Fujian China see Gutian
Xincheng Guangdong China see Xinxing
Xincheng Guangxi China 67 D3
Xincheng Sichuan China see Zhaojue
Xincun China see Dongchuan
Xindi Guangxi China 67 D4
Xindi Hubei China see Honghu
Xindu Guangxi China 67 D4
Xindu Sichuan China see Luhuo
Xindu Sichuan China 66 C2
Xinduqiao China 66 B2
Xinfeng Guangdong China 67 E3
Xinfeng Jiangxi China 67 E3
Xinfengjiang Shuiku resr China 67 E4
Xing'an China 67 D3
Xingan China 67 E3
Xingba China see Lhünzê
Xinge Angola 95 C7
Xingguo Gansu China see Qin'an
Xingguo Jiangxi China 67 E3
Xinghai China 70 I4
Xinghua China 67 F1
Xinghua Wan b. China 67 F3
Xingkai China 64 C3
Xingkai Hu l. China/Rus. Fed. see Khanka, Lake
Xinglong China 64 A2
Xinglongzhen China 64 A3
Xingning China 67 E3
Xingou China 67 E2
Xingping China 67 D1
Xingren China 66 C3
Xingsagoinba China 66 B1
Xingshan Guizhou China see Majiang
Xingshan Hubei China 67 D2
Xingtai China 63 I4
Xingu r. Brazil 147 H5
Xinguara Brazil 150 B3
Xingyang China 67 E1
Xingyi China 66 C3
Xingzi China 67 F2
Xinhua Guangdong China see Huadu
Xinhua Hunan China 67 D3
Xinhua Yunnan China see Qiaojia
Xinhua Yunnan China see Funing
Xinhuang China 67 D3
Xining China 70 J4
Xinji China see Xinxian
Xinjian China 67 E2
Xinjiang aut. reg. China see Xinjiang Uygur Zizhiqu
Xin Jiang r. China 67 F2
Xinjiangkou China see Songzi
Xinjiang Uygur Autonomous Region aut. reg. China see Xinjiang Uygur Zizhiqu
Xinjiang Uygur Zizhiqu aut. reg. China 70 E3
Xinjie China see Yuanyang
Xinjin China 66 B2
Xinjing China see Jingxi
Xinling China see Badong
Xinlong China 66 B2
Xinmi China 67 E1
Xinmian China see Shimian
Xinning Guangxi China see Fusui
Xinning Hunan China 67 D3
Xinning Jiangxi China see Wuning
Xinning Sichuan China see Kaijiang
Xinqing China 64 B2
Xinquan China 67 F3
Xinshi China see Jingshan
Xinshiba China see Ganluo
Xintai China 63 J4
Xintian China 67 E3
Xinxian China 67 E2
Xinxiang China 63 I4
Xinxing China 67 E4
Xinyang China 67 E1
Xinyang Gang r. China 67 G1
Xinye r. China 67 F1
Xinyi Guangdong China 67 D4
Xinyi Jiangsu China 67 F1
Xinying China 67 D5
Xinying Taiwan see Hsinying
Xinyu China 67 E3
Xinyuan Qinghai China see Tianjun
Xinyuan Xinjiang China 70 F3
Xinzheng China 67 E1
Xinzhou Guangxi China see Longlin
Xinzhou Guizhou China see Huangping
Xinzhou Hubei China 67 E2
Xinzhou Shanxi China 63 I4
Xinzhu Taiwan see Hsinchu
Xinzo de Limia Spain 42 C1
Xiongshan China see Zhenghe
Xiongzhou China see Nanxiong
Xipamanu r. Bol./Brazil 148 D2
Xiping Henan China 67 D1
Xiping Henan China 67 E1
Xiqing Shan mts China 66 B1
Xique Xique Brazil 150 D4

▶Yukon r. Canada/U.S.A. 120 C3
5th longest river in North America.
northamerica 116–117

↓ Z

▶Zagreb Croatia 44 E2
Capital of Croatia.

▶Zambezi r. Africa 95 F8
4th longest river in Africa.
africa 84–85

▶Zomba Malawi 97 B8
Former capital of Malawi.

acknowledgements

maps and data

General

Maps designed and created by HarperCollins Reference, Glasgow, UK
Design: One O'Clock Gun Design Consultants Ltd, Edinburgh, UK
Perspective views and cross-sections (pp22–23, 50–51, 84–85, 102–103, 116–117, 142–143, 156–157) and globes (pp10–11, 156–157): Alan Collinson Design, Llandudno, UK

The publishers would like to thank all national survey departments, road, rail and national park authorities, statistical offices and national place name committees throughout the world for their valuable assistance, and in particular the following:
British Antarctic Survey, Cambridge, UK
Tony Champion, Professor of Population Geography, University of Newcastle upon Tyne, UK
Mr P J M Geelan, London, UK

International Boundary Research Unit, University of Durham, UK
The Meteorological Office, Bracknell, Berkshire, UK
Permanent Committee on Geographical Names for British Official Use, London, UK

Data

Antarctica (p167): Antarctic Digital Database (versions 1 and 2), © Scientific Committee on Antarctic Research (SCAR), Cambridge, UK (1993, 1998)
Bathymetric data: The GEBCO Digital Atlas published by the British Oceanographic Data Centre on behalf of IOC and IHO, 1994
Earthquakes data (pp10–11): United States Geological Survey (USGS) National Earthquakes Information Center, Denver, USA

photographs and images

page	image	satellite/sensor	credit
1	Namib Desert		John Beatty/Getty Images/Stone
5	Wasatch Mountains	Space Shuttle	NASA
6–7	Mount Everest	Space Shuttle	NASA
	Nile Valley	MODIS	MODIS/NASA
	Caspian Sea	MODIS	MODIS/NASA
	Greenland	MODIS	MODIS/NASA
8–9	Washington D.C.		US Geological Society/ Science Photo Library
	La Paz	SPOT	CNES, 1991 Distribution Spot Image/Science Photo Library
	Cape Town	Landsat	NRSC LTD/ Science Photo Library
10–11	San Andreas Fault		Georg Gerster/ Science Photo Library
	Klyuchevskaya Volcano	Space Shuttle	Digital Image © CORBIS, Original image courtesy of NASA/CORBIS
	Mount St Helens		Roger Ressmeyer/CORBIS
12–13	Hurricane Floyd	NOAA GOES	NASA/Goddard Space Flight Center/Science Photo Library
	El Niño	TOPEX/ Poseidon	NASA/Science Photo Library
	Annual precipitation map	Microwave infrared Sensor	NASA/Goddard Space Flight Centre
	Climate change maps		Met. Office, Hadley Centre for Climate Prediction and Research
14–15	La Paz		Ron Giling/Still Pictures
	Death Valley		Simon Fraser/ Science Photo Library
	Amazon		Pictor ImageState
	Spitsbergen		Klaus Andrews/Still Pictures
	Everglades	Landsat	Earth Satellite Corporation/ Science Photo Library
	Lake Chad	Landsat	Landsat image courtesy of USGS Eros Data Center
	Bolivia	Landsat	NASA/Goddard Space Flight Center/Science Photo Library
16–17	Côte d'Ivoire		Mark Edwards/Still pictures
	Tōkyō		Cities Revealed aerial photography © The GeoInformation Group, 1998
18–19	Geostationary Satellites map		Telegeography, Inc., Washington D.C., USA
	San Francisco Airport		NRSC-Still Pictures
	International telecommunications traffic map		Telegeography, Inc., Washington D.C., USA
20	European Central Bank		Wim Van Cappellen /Still Pictures
	World Bank Headquarters		The World Bank, PIC Europe
	UN Headquarters		Ron Gilling/Still Pictures
	European Parliament		Martin Specht/Still Pictures
21	Croatia	Space Shuttle	NASA
22–23	Caucasus	MODIS	MODIS/NASA
	Finland		Geoslides Photography
	Iceland	MODIS	MODIS/NASA
24–25	Alps	Space Shuttle	NASA
	Venice	IKONOS	IKONOS satellite imagery provided by Space Imaging, Thornton, Colorado, www.spaceimaging.com
	London		Cities Revealed aerial photography © The GeoInformation Group, 1999
	Peloponnese Peninsula	Space Shuttle	NASA
	Gibraltar		D. Tatlow/Panos Pictures
	Bosporus	SPOT	CNES, 1991 Distribution Spot Image/Science Photo Library
48	Italy	AVHRR	Earth Satellite Corporation/ Science Photo Library
	Paris	IKONOS	Space Imaging Europe/ Science Photo Library
	Amsterdam	IKONOS	Space Imaging Europe/ Science Photo Library
	Brussels		Wim Van Cappellon/Still Pictures
49	Tigris	Space Shuttle	NASA
50–51	Yangtze	MODIS	MODIS/NASA
	Taklimakan Desert	SIR-C/X-SAR	NASA/JPL
	Aral Sea	MODIS	MODIS/NASA
	Kamchatka Peninsula	MODIS	MODIS/NASA
52–53	Bali		Yann Arthus-Bertrand/CORBIS
	Hong Kong	IKONOS	IKONOS satellite imagery provided by Space Imaging, Thornton, Colorado, www.spaceimaging.com
	Great Wall		Georg Gerster/ NGS Image Collection
	Mecca	IKONOS	IKONOS satellite imagery provided by Space Imaging, Thornton, Colorado, www.spaceimaging.com
	Tōkyō	Terra/ ASTER	NASA
	Himalaya	Space Shuttle	NASA/Science Photo Library
82	Indian subcontinent	AVHRR	Earth Satellite Corporation/ Science Photo Library
	Ganges Delta	SPOT	CNES, 1987 Distribution Spot Image/Science Photo Library
	Beijing	IKONOS	IKONOS satellite imagery provided by Space Imaging, Thornton, Colorado, www.spaceimaging.com
	Cyprus	MODIS	MODIS/NASA
83	Bazaruto Island	Space Shuttle	NASA
84–85	Lake Victoria	MODIS	MODIS/NASA
	Congo	Space Shuttle	NASA
	Sahara	SPOT	CNES, 1988 Distribution Spot Image/Science Photo Library
	Okavango Delta	Space Shuttle	NASA
86–87	Namib Desert	Space Shuttle	NASA
	Mt Kilimanjaro	Landsat	Nigel Press Association/ Science Photo Library
	Aldabra Islands	Space Shuttle	NASA
	Pyramids	IKONOS	IKONOS satellite imagery provided by Space Imaging, Thornton, Colorado, www.spaceimaging.com
	Suez Canal	SPOT	CNES, 1991 Distribution Spot Image/Science Photo Library
	Abidjan	SPOT	CNES, 1988 Distribution Spot Image/Science Photo Library
100	Sinai	Space Shuttle	NASA
	Madagascar	MODIS	MODIS/NASA
	Niger Delta	Space Shuttle	NASA
	Victoria Falls		Roger De La Harpe, Gallo Images/CORBIS
101	Banks Peninsula	Space Shuttle	NASA
102–103	Banks Peninsula		Lloyd Homer © Institute of Geological and Nuclear Sciences Ltd
	Heron Island	IKONOS	IKONOS satellite imagery provided by Space Imaging, Thornton, Colorado, www.spaceimaging.com
	Lake Eyre	Space Shuttle	NASA
104–105	Great Barrier Reef	Space Shuttle	NASA
	Nikumaroro	IKONOS	IKONOS satellite imagery provided by Space Imaging, Thornton, Colorado, www.spaceimaging.com
	Sydney	IKONOS	IKONOS satellite imagery provided by Space Imaging, Thornton, Colorado, www.spaceimaging.com
	Canterbury Plains	Space Shuttle	NASA
	Alofi		NZ Aerial Mapping Ltd www.nzam.com
	Melbourne	SPOT	CNES, 1990 Distribution Spot Image/Science Photo Library
114	New Zealand	Landsat	M-SAT Ltd/ Science Photo Library
	Tahiti and Moorea	SPOT	CNES, Distribution Spot Image/Science Photo Library
	Wellington		NZ Aerial Mapping Ltd www.nzam.com
	Uluru (Ayers Rock)		ImageState
	Tasmania	SeaWiFS	Image provided by ORBIMAGE. © Orbital Imaging Corporation and processing by NASA Goddard Space Flight Center.
	Kiritimati Island	Space Shuttle	NASA
	Mount Cook		Mike Schroder/Still Pictures
	Canberra		The aerial photograph on page 114 courtesy Geoscience Australia, Canberra. Crown Copyright ©. All rights reserved. www.ga.gov.au/nmd
115	Grand Canyon	Space Shuttle	NASA
116–117	Great Salt Lake	Space Shuttle	NASA
	Mississippi	Terra/MISR	MISR/NASA
	Baffin Island	MODIS	MODIS/NASA
	Popocatepetl	SPOT	CNES, 1996 Distribution Spot Image/Science Photo Library
118–119	Alaska	MODIS	MODIS/NASA
	Grand Canyon	SPOT	CNES, 1996 Distribution Spot Image/Science Photo Library
	New York		NRSC/Still Pictures
	Panama Canal	Landsat	Clifton-Campbell Imaging Inc. www.tmarchive.com
	Los Angeles	Landsat	Infoterra
	Florida	MODIS	MODIS/NASA
140	Cuba	MODIS	MODIS/NASA
	Montreal	Space Shuttle	NASA
	The Pentagon	IKONOS	IKONOS satellite imagery provided by Space Imaging, Thornton, Colorado, www.spaceimaging.com
	Mexicali	Terra/ ASTER	NASA
141	Andes	Space Shuttle	NASA
142–143	Altiplano	Space Shuttle	NASA
	Manaus	Terra/MISR	NASA
	Tierra del Fuego	MODIS	MODIS/NASA
	Lake Viedma	Space Shuttle	NASA
144–145	Andes/Chile	Space Shuttle	NASA/Science Photo Library
	Galapagos Islands	SPOT	CNES, 1988 Distribution Spot Image/Science Photo Library
	Santiago	Landsat	Earth Satellite Corporation/ Science Photo Library
	Rio de Janeiro	SPOT	Earth Satellite Corporation/ Science Photo Library
	Rondônia	MODIS	MODIS/NASA
	Atacama Desert	SPOT	CNES, 1986 Distribution Spot Image/Science Photo Library
154	Falkland Islands	MODIS	MODIS/NASA
	Lake Titicaca	Space Shuttle	NASA
	Amazon rainforest		Dr Morley Read/ Science Photo Library
	Buenos Aires	Landsat	Earth Satellite Corporation/ Science Photo Library
	Orinoco River	Space Shuttle	NASA
	Angel Falls		Jay Dickman/CORBIS
	Machupicchu		David Nunuk/ Science Photo Library
	Brasilia	SPOT	CNES, 1995 Distribution Spot Image/Science Photo Library
155	Larsen B ice shelf	Space Shuttle	NASA
156–157	Surface winds	QuikSCAT/ SeaWinds	NASA/JPL/Caltech
	Intertropical Convergence Zone	GOES	GOES Project Science Office/NASA
	Tropical cyclone Dina	MODIS	MODIS/NASA/GSFC
158–159	Antarctica	AVHRR	NRSC Ltd/ Science Photo Library
	Ozone Hole	TOMS	NASA/Goddard Space Flight Center
	Arctic Ocean		B&C Alexander
	Nentsy herders		B&C Alexander
168	Alaska		Chris Madeley/ Science Photo Library
	Isla Socorro	Terra/MISR	NASA/GSFC/JPL, MISR Team
	Larsen Ice Shelf	Landsat	NASA
	Hurricane Elena	Space Shuttle	NASA

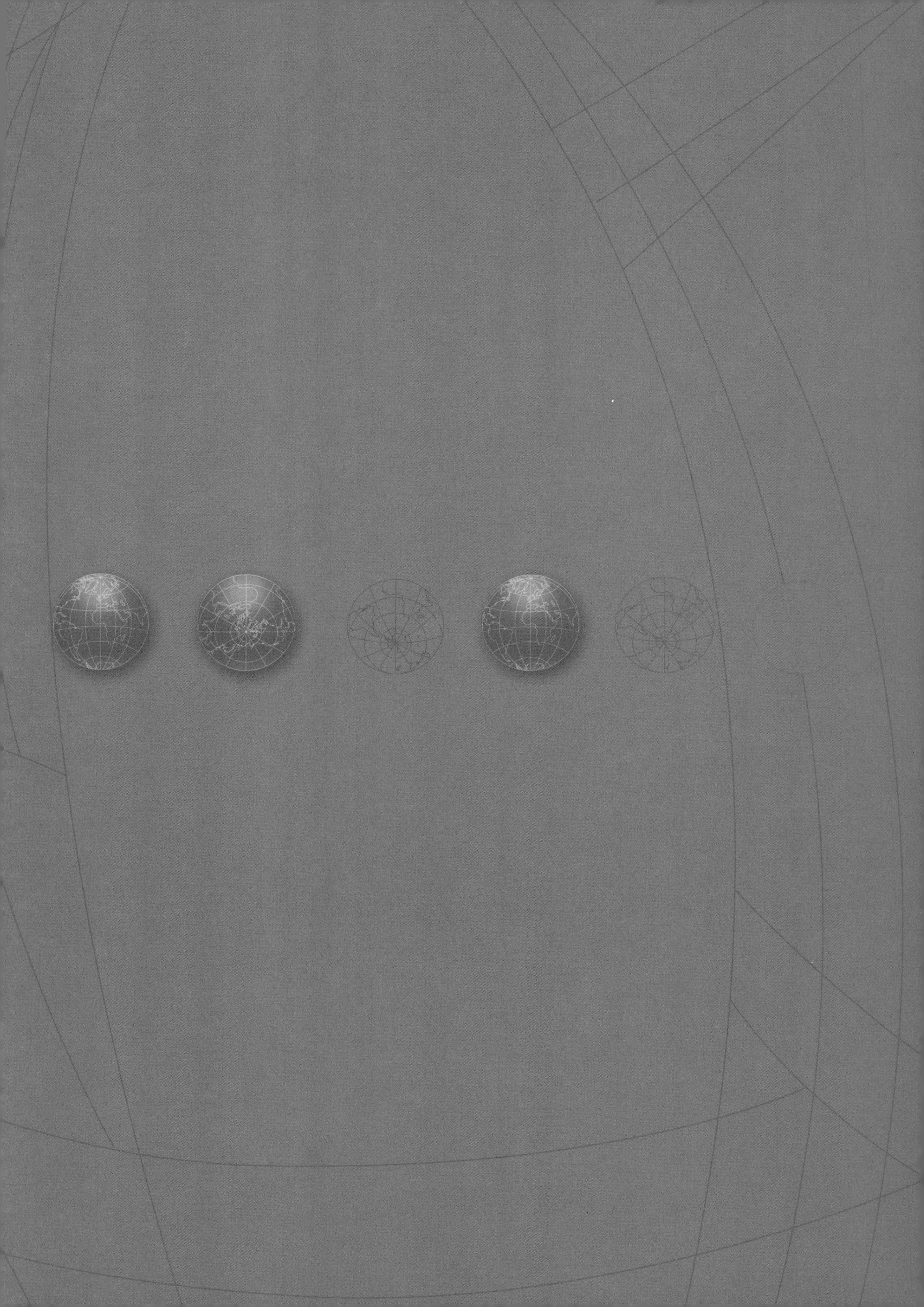